QUANTITATIVE ANALYSIS FOR MANAGEMENT

QUANTITATIVE METHODS AND APPLIED STATISTICS SERIES

ALLYN AND BACON

Barry Render, Consulting Editor
Roy E. Crummer Graduate School of Business, Rollins College

QUANTITATIVE ANALYSIS FOR MANAGEMENT

FOURTH EDITION

BARRY RENDER

Charles Harwood Professor of Management Science
Roy E. Crummer Graduate School of Business, Rollins College

RALPH M. STAIR, Jr.

Professor of Information and Management Sciences
Florida State University

Allyn and Bacon
BOSTON   LONDON   TORONTO   SYDNEY   TOKYO   SINGAPORE

Series Editor: Rich Wohl
Series Editorial Assistant: Cheryl Ten Eick
Cover Administrator: Linda Dickinson
Composition and Manufacturing Buyer: Louise Richardson
Editorial-Production Service: York Production Services
Text Designer: Deborah Schneck
Editorial-Production Administrator: Mary Beth Finch
Index: Kathy Kemp, Assimilate, Inc.

Library of Congress Cataloging-in-Publication Data

Render, Barry.
    Quantitative analysis for management/Barry Render, Ralph M.
Stair, Jr.—4th ed.
      p.   cm.
    Includes bibliographical references (p.   ) and index.
    ISBN 0-206-12669-3
    1. Management science.   2. Operations research.   I. Stair, Ralph
M.   II. Title.
    T56.R544   1990
    858.4′03—dc20   90–1224
                                                                               CIP

ISBN: 0-205-12669-3
        0-205-12673-1   (5¼″ disks)
        0-205-12675-8   (3½″ disks)

Printed in the United States of America

10   9   8   7   6   5   4   95   94   93   92

*To our past, present
and future students.*

Brief Contents

Modules

Contents

ix

Preface

Overview

This fourth edition of *Quantitative Analysis for Management* continues to provide the reader with the skills to apply the techniques of quantitative analysis in all kinds of organizational decision-making situations. The chapters cover every major topic in the quantitative analysis/management science field. There is probably more material included than most instructors can cover in a typical first course, but we have found that the resulting flexibility of topic selection is appreciated by instructors who need to tailor their courses to different audiences and curricula.

We show how each technique works, discuss the assumptions and limitations of the models, and illustrate the real-world usefulness of each technique with many applications in both profit-making and nonprofit organizations. We have kept the notation, terminology, and equations standard with other books. As in the first three editions, we have tried to write a text that is easy to understand and use. Algebra is the only mathematics prerequisite.

Features Retained from the Previous Edition

This book is student oriented; the following features have proved to be effective aids to the learning process.

- Key idea markers are placed in the margin to highlight especially important concepts.

- Margin notes highlight other important points.

- QA Application boxes summarize published articles illustrating how real organizations have used quantitative analysis to solve problems.

- History boxes briefly describe how a technique was discovered.

- Glossaries at the end of each chapter define important terms.

- Key equations are listed at the end of each chapter, which summarize the mathematical material.

- Discussion questions at the end of each chapter test the student's understanding of concepts.

- Problems in every chapter are applications oriented and test the student's ability to solve exam-type problems. They are graded by three levels: introductory (1 dot), moderate (2 dots), and challenging (three dots).

- Case studies at the ends of most chapters provide challenging managerial applications.

- End-of-chapter bibliographies provide a selection of more advanced books and interesting, practical articles.

KEY CHANGES IN THE FOURTH EDITION

Content

- *Expanded coverage of forecasting:* As forecasting remains one of the most important functions of any organization, and as accurate forecasts can make the difference between profitability and loss, we have greatly expanded our coverage of these techniques in Chapter 4. We have added new material on trend adjustments in exponential smoothing, seasonality, standard errors of the estimate, and monitoring and controlling the forecast.

- *Added coverage of the Karmarkar method in linear programming:* The Karmarkar method has received considerable interest as a possible alternative to the simplex method. Therefore, we have now included a discussion of its overall approach and impact. However, we do not discuss its specific solution techniques, as they are beyond the scope of this book.

- *Combined transportation and assignment chapters:* In order to streamline the book, the chapters on the transportation method and the assignment technique have been combined into one chapter. The basic coverage and step-by-step approach for these techniques remain.

- *Expanded coverage of expert systems and artificial intelligence:* New information on the concepts of expert systems, artificial intelligence, and decision support systems has been added to Chapter 1.

- *Added printouts to illustrate computer solutions:* The role of computer software for solving quantitative problems is discussed and contrasted throughout the book. We have included sample printouts from a variety of popular commercial programs, including Lindo, Storm, Supertree, and Expert Choice.

Pedagogy

- *New and enhanced end-of-chapter problems:* Additional problems have been added. Many of these new problems stress problem formulation and interpretation, in addition to those which focus on calculation.

- *Solved problems:* Brand new in this edition, and included at the end of appropriate chapters, they serve as a model for students in solving their own homework problems.

- *AB:QM Software:* This new and upgraded software package (for DOS machines) now accompanies the text. AB:QM (Allyn & Bacon: Quantitative Methods) covers more topics, and is both faster and easier to use. Instructions and examples for using this program are located in Chapter 1 and in optional sections throughout the text. The software closely matches the approach and terminology of the text itself.

• *Data set problems:* Because real world problems involve large data sets, and because more students are using the computer in solving problems, we have added a set of problems specifically for analyzing larger amounts of data with the computer. These data sets are also available to instructors on disk.

In addition, the Applications of QA boxes and chapter references have been updated to reflect the most current information.

SUPPLEMENTS

We have greatly expanded our supplement package. Details of the package can be found in the Annotated Instructor's Edition. It includes:

• An Annotated Instructor's Edition (new for this edition)

• An Instructor's Solutions Manual

• A Study Guide by John Harpell at West Virginia University

• A Testbank prepared by Michael Hanna at the University of Houston. This testbank is also available on our computerized testing software, the *A&B Test Manager*.

• 200 Transparency Masters (new for this edition)

• Two video tapes; one from The Institute of Management Sciences (The Edelman Award Winners) and the other from The Consortium for Mathematics and Its Applications ("For All Practical Purposes") developed with major funding by the Annenberg/CPB Project (new for this edition)

• AB:QM Software in either a $5\frac{1}{4}$" or $3\frac{1}{2}$" format (new for this edition)

• Data Disk for marked problems (new for this edition)

ACKNOWLEDGMENTS

We gratefully thank the many users of the previous editions who provided many important suggestions and ideas for this edition. The Roy E. Crummer School of Business at Rollins College and the Department of Information and Management Science at The Florida State University provided support and a conducive environment for development of this text. Professor Jerry Kinard (Dean at Francis Marion College) and the late Professor Joe C. Iverstine contributed several fine cases. Professor Michael Hanna at the University of Houston prepared the test bank. Professor John Harpell at West Virginia University prepared the Study Guide. Thanks to all.

We would also like to express our appreciation to the reviewers of the past and present editions:

Past Editions:
Stephen Achtenhagen, San Jose University
Robert Fiore, Springfield College
Irwin Greenberg, George Mason University
Gordon Jacox, Weber State College
Douglas Lonnstrom, Siena College
Ralph Miller, California State Polytechnic University

David Murphy, Boston College
Robert Myers, University of Louisville
Alan D. Olinsky, Bryant College
Savas Ozatalay, Widener University
William Rife, West Virginia University
John Swearingen, Bryant College
Grover Rodich, Portland State University
F. S. Tanaka, Slippery Rock State University
Jack Taylor, Portland State University
M. Keith Thomas, Olivet College
James Vigen, California State College, Bakersfield
William Webster, The University of Texas at San Antonio

Present Edition:
Edward Chu, California State University, Dominguez Hills
L.W. Shell, Nicholls State University
M. Jill Austin, Middle Tennessee State University
Frank G. Forst, Loyola University of Chicago
Michael E. Hanna, University of Houston–Clear Lake
Darlene R. Lanier, Louisiana State University
Jooh Lee, Glassboro State College
Harvey Nye, Central State University
Ed Gillenwater, University of Mississippi
Robert R. Hill, University of Houston–Clear Lake

QUANTITATIVE ANALYSIS FOR MANAGEMENT

1

Introduction to Quantitative Analysis

1.1
INTRODUCTION

People have been using mathematical tools to help solve problems for thousands of years; however, the formal study and application of quantitative techniques to practical decision making is largely a product of the twentieth century. The techniques we will study in this book have been successfully applied to an increasingly wide variety of complex problems in business, government, health care, education, and many other areas. Many such successful uses will be discussed throughout this book.

It isn't enough though just to know the mathematics of how a particular quantitative technique works; you must also be familiar with the limitations, assumptions, and specific applicability of the technique. The successful use of quantitative techniques usually results in a solution that is timely, accurate, flexible, economical, reliable, and easy to understand and use.

1.2
WHAT IS QUANTITATIVE ANALYSIS?

quantitative analysis defined

Quantitative analysis is the scientific approach to managerial decision making. Whim, emotions, and guesswork are not part of the quantitative analysis approach. This approach starts with data. Like raw material for a factory, these data are manipulated or processed into information that is valuable to people making decisions. This processing and manipulating of raw data into meaningful information is the heart of quantitative analysis. Computers have been instrumental in the increasing use of quantitative analysis.

In solving a problem, managers must consider both qualitative and quantitative factors. For example, we might consider several different investment alternatives, including certificates of deposit at a bank, investments in the stock market, and an investment in real estate. We can use quantitative analysis to determine how much our investment will be worth in the future when deposited at a bank at a given interest rate for a certain number of years. Quantitative analysis can also be used in computing financial ratios from the balance sheets for several companies whose stock we are considering. Some real estate companies have developed computer programs that use quantitative analysis to analyze cash flows and rates of return for investment property.

quantitative analysis, qualitative factors

In addition to quantitative analysis, *qualitative* factors should also be considered. The weather, state and federal legislation, new technological breakthroughs, the outcome of an election, and so on may all be factors that are difficult to quantify.

Because of the importance of qualitative factors, the role of quantitative analysis in the decision-making process can vary. When there is a lack of qualitative factors and when the problem, model, and input data remain the same, the results of quantitative analysis can *automate* the decision-making process. For example, some companies use quantitative inventory models to determine automatically *when* to order additional new materials.

In most cases, however, quantitative analysis will be an *aid* to the decision-making process. The results of quantitative analysis will be combined with other (qualitative) information in making decisions.

1.3
AN APPLICATION: POLISHING THE BIG APPLE OR CLEANING UP NEW YORK CITY[1]

Perhaps a real-life case will give you an appreciation of the usefulness of the quantitative analysis (QA) approach. Let's consider how QA was used to make New York City a cleaner place to live.

The Problem

The Department of Sanitation of New York City faced a number of difficult problems. With about 12,000 employees and a half billion dollar annual budget, the department has the responsibility of keeping New York clean. But New York City had a reputation of not being an overly clean city. During the mid-1970s, a cleanliness rating system revealed that the city went from a 72% rating concerning its city streets to a very low 56%. In 1980, the department dipped even further to a 53% overall rating, and it continued to drop in the 1980s. Many workers at the Department of Sanitation believed that street cleaning was low on the city's priority list compared, for example, to refuse collection. In general, staff and employee morale were low. Furthermore, there appeared to be little or no coordination with other agencies when it came to making the city a cleaner place to live. These problems prompted the department to take a closer look at some of the problems and to consider the use of quantitative analysis.

Tackling the Problems

The first step in attacking the problems of dirt, low morale, and a lack of coordination was to build a knowledge base. The QA teams did this with the monthly rating system established from the city's 59 community districts. Furthermore, the Department of Sanitation had collected detailed information about the use of personnel, weather conditions, the status of various pieces of cleaning equipment, and the number and percentage of collection loads not picked up. If anything, the analysis group had more data than it knew what to do with. These input data, however, were critical in developing and testing a series of models.

dirt, low morale, and a lack of coordination

The QA models that were developed clearly showed a strong relationship between personnel levels and overall cleanliness. They also revealed that some districts in New York City had a much better payoff or a better utilization of personnel than others. Some areas, such as Wall Street, required about five times more cleaners than other districts. Some models

[1] Adopted from Lucius J. Riccio, Joseph Miller, and Ann Litke, "Polishing the Big Apple: How Management Science Has Helped Make New York Streets Cleaner," *Interfaces*, Vol. 16, No. 1, January–February 1986, pp. 83–88.

revealed that illegally parked cars caused problems with keeping the streets clean. Just one less car in some circumstances could mean a substantial improvement in the ability to keep streets or certain areas clean. Thus, one proposed solution called for cooperation between the Department of Sanitation and New York's Department of Transportation to coordinate a ticketing program to reduce the number of illegally parked cars.

Part of the overall solution was to develop a plan to improve worker morale. Programs were developed to give recognition to individuals in areas that were able to increase their overall cleanliness rating. Zone or "conference" winners were selected and announced. The street cleaners in the winning area received a ticket to a local sporting event. Winning workers also had their names thrown in a hat for a drawing to receive an all-expenses-paid trip to the Super Bowl.

the results of quantitative analysis

The results of the quantitative analysis approach were remarkable. After being fully implemented, the QA techniques led to near record levels of overall cleanliness and to great improvement in the productivity of the work force. It was also estimated that the techniques saved the city of New York about $12 million annually. In a speech, then Mayor Edward I. Koch stated, "The Department of Sanitation, through a variety of programs, has produced absolutely phenomenal productivity savings and is deserving of a reinvestment of some of those funds."

1.4
THE QUANTITATIVE ANALYSIS APPROACH

How did New York City's quantitative analysis group approach the problem that was to be analyzed? In general terms, the analysis followed seven steps, as outlined in Figure 1.1.

The quantitative analysis approach consists of defining the problem, developing a model, acquiring input data, developing a solution, testing the solution, analyzing the results, and implementing the results. One step

---

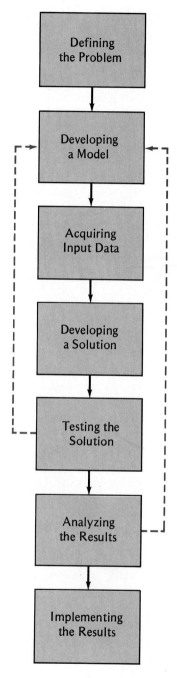

FIGURE 1.1
The Quantitative Analysis Approach

does not have to be completely finished before the next is started; in most cases one or more of these steps will be modified to some extent before the final results are implemented. This would cause all of the subsequent steps to be changed. In some cases, testing the solution might reveal that the model or the input data are not correct. This would mean that all steps that follow defining the problem would need to be modified.

Defining the Problem

The first step in the quantitative approach is to develop a clear, concise statement of the problem. This statement will give direction and meaning to the following steps.

KEY IDEA

In many cases, defining the problem is the most important and the most difficult step. It is essential to go beyond the symptoms of the problem and identify the true causes. One problem may be related to other problems; solving one problem without regard to other related problems can make the entire situation worse. Thus, it is important to analyze how the solution to one problem impacts on other problems or the situation in general.

concentrate on only a few problems

It is likely that an organization will have *several* problems. However, a quantitative analysis group usually cannot deal with all of an organization's problems at one time. Thus, it is usually necessary to concentrate on only a few problems. For most companies, this means selecting those problems whose solutions will result in the greatest increase in profits or reduction in costs to the company. The importance of selecting the right problems to solve cannot be overemphasized. Experience has shown that bad problem definition is a major reason for failure of management science or operations research groups to serve their organizations well.

When the problem is difficult to quantify, it may be necessary to develop *specific, measurable* objectives. A problem might be inadequate health care delivery in a hospital. The objectives might be to increase the number of beds, reduce the average number of days a patient spends in the hospital, increase the doctor-to-patient ratio, and so on. When objectives are used, however, the real problem should be kept in mind. It is important to avoid obtaining specific and measurable objectives that may not solve the real problem.

Developing a Model

Once we select the problem to be analyzed, the next step is to develop a *model*. Simply stated, a model is a representation (usually mathematical) of a situation.

Even though you might not have been aware of it, you have been using models most of your life. You may have developed models about people's behavior. Your model might be that friendship is based on reciprocity, an exchange of favors. If you need a favor like a small loan, your model would suggest that you ask a good friend.

types of models

Of course, there are many other types of models. Architects sometimes make a *physical model* of a building that they will construct. Engineers develop *scale models* of chemical plants, called pilot plants. A *schematic model* is a picture, drawing, or chart of reality. Automobiles, lawn mowers, gears, fans, typewriters, and numerous other devices have schematic models (drawings and pictures) that reveal how these devices work. What sets quantitative analysis apart from other techniques is that the models that are used are mathematical. A *mathematical model* is a set of mathematical relationships. In most cases, these relationships are expressed in equations and inequalities.

While there is considerable flexibility in the development of models, most of the models presented in this book will contain one or more variables and parameters. A *variable*, as the name implies, is a measurable quantity that may vary or is subject to change. Variables can be *controllable* or *uncontrollable*. A controllable variable is also called a *decision variable*. An example would be how many new street cleaners to order. A *parameter* is a measurable quantity that is inherent in the problem. The cost of placing an order for more street cleaners is an example of a parameter. In most cases, variables are unknown quantities, while parameters are known quantities. The model should be carefully developed. It should be solvable, realistic, and easy to understand and modify, and the required input data should be obtainable. The model developer has to be careful to include the appropriate amount of detail to be solvable yet realistic.

variables and parameters

Acquiring Input Data

Once we have developed a model, we must obtain the data that are used in the model (input data). Obtaining accurate data for the model is essential, since even if the model is a perfect representation of reality, improper data will result in misleading results. This situation is called garbage in, garbage out (GIGO). For a larger problem, collecting accurate data can be one of the most difficult steps in performing quantitative analysis.

garbage in, garbage out

There are a number of sources that can be used in collecting data. In some cases, company reports and documents can be used to obtain the necessary data. Another source is interviews with employees or other persons related to the firm. These individuals can sometimes provide excellent information, and their experience and judgments can be invaluable. A production foreman, for example, might be able to tell you with a great degree of accuracy the amount of time that it takes to produce a particular product. Sampling and direct measurement provide other sources of data for the model. You may need to know how many pounds of a raw material are used in producing a new photochemical product. This information can be obtained by going to the plant and actually measuring with scales the amount of raw material that is being used. In other cases, statistical sampling procedures can be used to obtain data.

Developing a Solution

Developing a solution involves manipulating the model to arrive at the best (optimal) solution to the problem. In some cases, this requires that an equation be solved for the best decision. In other cases, you can use a *trial and error* method, trying various approaches and picking the one that results in the best decision. For some problems, you may wish to try all possible values for the variables in the model to arrive at the best decision. This is called *complete enumeration*. This book will also show you how to solve very difficult and complex problems by repeating a few simple steps until you find the best solution. A series of steps or procedures that are repeated is called an *algorithm*, named after Algorismus, an Arab mathematician of the ninth century.

The accuracy of the results depends on the accuracy of the input data and the model. If the input data are accurate to only two significant digits, then the results can be accurate to only two significant digits. For example, the results of dividing 2.6 by 1.4 should be 1.9 and not 1.857142857.

Testing the Solution

Before a solution can be analyzed and implemented, it needs to be completely tested. Because the solution depends on the input data and the model, both require testing.

testing the data and model

Testing the input data and the model includes determining the accuracy and completeness of the data used by the model. Inaccurate data will lead to an inaccurate solution. There are several ways to test input data. One method of testing the data is to collect additional data from a different source. If the original data were collected using interviews, perhaps some additional data can be collected by direct measurement or sampling. These additional data can then be compared to the original data, and statistical tests can be employed to determine whether or not there are differences between the original data and the additional data. If there are significant differences, more effort is required to obtain accurate input data. If the data are accurate but the results are inconsistent with the problem, the model may not be appropriate. The model can be checked to make sure it is logical and represents the real situation.

While most of the quantitative techniques discussed in this book have been computerized, you will most likely be required to solve a number of problems by hand. To help detect both logical and computational mistakes, you should check the results to make sure they are consistent with the structure of the problem. For example, (1.96)(301.7) is close to (2)(300), which is equal to 600. If your computations are significantly different from 600, you know you have made a mistake.

Analyzing the Results

Analyzing the results starts with determining the implications of the solution. In most cases, a solution to a problem will result in some kind of action or change in the way an organization is operating. The implications of these actions or changes must be determined and analyzed before the results are implemented.

the use of sensitivity analysis

Because a model is only an approximation of reality, the sensitivity of the solution to changes in the model and input data is a very important part of analyzing the results. This type of analysis is called *sensitivity analysis* or *postoptimality analysis*. It determines how much the solution will change if there were changes in the model or the input data. When the solution is sensitive to changes in the input data and the model specification, additional testing should be performed to make sure that the model and input data are accurate and valid. If the model or data are wrong, the solution could be wrong, resulting in financial losses or reduced profits.

Implementing the Results

The final step is to *implement* the results. This is the process of incorporating the solution into the company. This can be much more difficult than you would imagine. Even if the solution is optimal and will result in thousands of dollars in additional profits, if managers resist the new solution, all of the efforts of the analysis are of no value. Experience has shown that a large number of quantitative analysis teams have failed in their efforts because they have failed to implement a good, workable solution properly.

After the solution has been implemented, it should be closely monitored. Over time, there may be numerous changes that call for modifications of the original solution. A changing economy, fluctuating demand, and model enhancements requested by managers and decision makers are only a few examples of changes that might require the analysis to be modified.

1.5
AN OVERVIEW OF THIS BOOK

Probability Theory and Forecasting

Probability theory is the first topic covered in this book (Chapters 2 and 3). Since most decision making involves an uncertain future, you will find probability included in many of the techniques discussed; thus, a knowledge of probability theory is essential. This book covers what a probability distribution or function is, how to determine probabilities, and how probability theory can be used.

Forecasting is the process of making projections into the future. You will learn about several forecasting techniques in Chapter 4 and the ways they can be applied to predict such quantities as future sales, housing starts, the future cost of lumber and other materials, unemployment, the crime rate, the number of students attending a certain university, and so on.

Decision Theory

Since better decision making is at the heart of quantitative analysis, the next topic to be discussed is decision theory. In Chapters 5–7, three different types of decision-making models are covered; these are models under certainty, under risk, and under uncertainty. Also illustrated are decision tables and decision trees, which can be used to graphically represent and solve decision-making problems. In Chapter 6, the topics of multifactor decision making and the analytic hierarchy process (AHP) are covered.

Inventory Control

One of the most important aspects of managing a company is controlling inventory. Inventory can represent as much as 40% of a company's total assets. In Chapters 8 and 9, we present a number of different inventory models and decision-making approaches to handle unique situations and assumptions. Any inventory model, regardless of its complexity or sophistication, only answers two basic questions: "How much inventory should be ordered?" and "When should orders for additional inventory be placed?" For most inventory control models, the goal is to minimize total inventory costs. In the two inventory chapters, quantity discounts, planned shortages, stockout policies, material requirements planning, Kanban, and the production of inventory will be explored.

Linear Programming

Linear programming is one of the most popular and widely used quantitative techniques. Four chapters are devoted to this topic. In Chapter 10, a graphical method is presented. In Chapter 11, an algebraic solution technique called the simplex method, which is used for larger and more complex linear programming problems, is explored. In Chapter 12, we show how the solution to a linear programming problem may be interpreted and modified if there are changes in the original problem. Finally, Chapter 13 provides examples of many applications of linear programming, not only in manufacturing, but in hospitals, banks, stock brokerage firms, law firms, and in marketing research.

Regardless of size or complexity, all linear programming problems take the same form: they allocate scarce resources among competing alternatives. The resources may be time, product availability, labor force limitations, and so on. The alternatives may be the production of different products, the selection of different investment strategies, production plans, ingredients in cattle feed, and so on. In most cases, linear programming either maximizes profits or minimizes costs without using more scarce resources than are available.

Other Mathematical Programming Topics

A large number of mathematical programming techniques are extensions or modifications of linear programming. We devote two chapters to these other techniques.

The transportation problem, a special case of linear programming, is discussed in Chapter 14. Although linear programming can be used to solve this type of problem, the transportation method is much more efficient. All transportation problems are concerned with transporting products or services from given sources to specified locations or destinations at the least cost. The assignment problem, another special case of linear programming, is also discussed in Chapter 14. Its objective is to assign workers to jobs, machines to tasks, teachers to classes, managers to projects, and so on, while minimizing total assignment costs. While this type of problem can be solved using either linear programming or the transportation method, the assignment method is faster and more efficient.

Goal and integer programming are two final mathematical programming techniques and are the topic of Chapter 15. Goal programming allows us to build models that have more than one objective. A firm may, for example, not only want to maximize profit in its production facility, but also maximize market share and maintain full employment. Like linear programming problems, goal programming problems can be solved graphically or by a modified simplex method.

Integer programming is a category of linear programming models that recognizes that some business problems must have integer solutions. You cannot manufacture 1.38 submarines, for example. In Chapter 15 we illustrate how to solve such a problem with a procedure known as the branch and bound method.

Queuing Theory and Simulation

In many problems, we are concerned with how many people to place at service locations: for example, how many people should a service station hire; how many nurses should a hospital have on duty; how many tellers should be at bank service windows. As the number of people placed at service locations increases, the number of people waiting for service decreases. Queuing theory (Chapter 16) helps us determine the average number of people that would have to wait in line for service given the number of people that are performing the service. In addition, queuing theory can tell us the average time that a person will have to wait in line, the average time that a person will have to wait until the service has been completed, and more. If we know the cost of delay and the cost of hiring additional service personnel, it is possible to determine the number of service personnel that will minimize total waiting and service cost.

Simulation, discussed in Chapter 17, is a general technique that allows us to develop a dynamic model that acts like a real process. The simulation model is run many times, and the results are used to make better decisions. Developing a good simulation model can be difficult, but simulation allows us to solve problems that are difficult or impossible to solve otherwise.

Network Models and Markov Analysis

Network models are a popular and widely used quantitative technique. They are covered in Chapter 18. These models help managers plan, schedule, monitor, and control large projects, such as the construction of a building, building a ship, or planning for a spaceflight. Network models break large, complex projects down into tasks or subprojects that require a certain amount of time and resources to complete. Then network analysis helps managers determine: (1) total project completion time, (2) activities that, if delayed, would delay the entire project, (3) probability that a project will be completed by a certain date, (4) least-cost ways of shortening total project completion time, and (5) amount of time that the activities or subprojects can be delayed without delaying the entire project. There are several network techniques available. This book investigates both program evaluation and review technique (PERT) and critical path method (CPM).

In addition to PERT and CPM, several other network techniques are covered. The minimal-spanning tree technique determines the path through the network that connects all of the nodes while minimizing total distance. The maximal-flow technique finds the maximum flow of any quantity or substance through a network. Finally, the shortest-route technique can find the shortest path through a network.

Markov analysis (Chapter 19), which is based on probability theory, allows a manager to determine such information as future market shares both in the short and long run. This technique is excellent not only for predicting future market shares, but also for determining the probability that a machine will be functioning properly in the future, the probability that adverse traffic conditions will exist in a few hours, the number of people who will never pay their debts in the long run, and so on. If the current situation is known, along with the propensity of the system to change over time, it is possible to use Markov analysis to predict future conditions.

Mathematical Tools, Game Theory, and Dynamic Programming

There are three learning modules at the end of this book: mathematical tools, game theory, and dynamic programming. The first module allows

---

APPLICATIONS OF QA

Apollo 11 Launch Owes Success to Quantitative Analysis

Back in 1969, Robert F. Freitag headed the NASA team responsible for landing the Apollo 11 safely on the moon. The success of the lunar mission can be traced to quantitative analysis techniques that ensured that thousands of small tasks would come together to meet a single giant objective. Freitag shares his observations about that historic event:

I think the feeling most of us in NASA shared was, "My gosh, now we really have to do it." When you think that the enterprise we were about to undertake was ten times larger than any that had ever been undertaken, including the Manhattan Project, it was a pretty awesome event.

What you do is break it down into pieces: the launch site, the launch vehicles, the space craft, the lunar module, and worldwide tracking networks, for example. Then, once these pieces are broken down, you assign them to one organization or another. They, in turn, take those small pieces, like the rocket, and break it down into engines or structures or guidance equipment. And this breakdown, or "tree," is the really tough part about managing.

In the Apollo program, it was decided that three NASA centers would do the work. One was Huntsville, where Dr. Von Braun and his team built the rocket. The other was Houston, where Dr. Gerous and his team built the space craft and controlled the flight operations. The third was Cape Canaveral, where Dr. Debries and his team did the launching and the preparation of the rocket.

Those three centers were pieces, and they could break their pieces down into about 10 or 20 major industrial contractors who would build pieces of the rocket. And then each of those industrial contractors would break them down into maybe 20 to 30 or 50 subcontractors—and they, in turn, would break them down into perhaps 300,000 or 400,000 pieces, each of which would end up being the job of one person. But you need to be sure that the pieces come together at the right time, and that they work when put together. Management science helps with that. The total number of people who worked on the Apollo was about 400,000 to 500,000, all working toward a single objective. But that objective was clear when President Kennedy said, "I want to land a man on the moon and have him safely returned to the earth, and to do so within the decade." Of course, Congress set aside $20 billion. So you had cost, performance, and schedule, and you knew what the job was in one simple sentence. It took a lot of effort to make that happen.

Source: Introduction to Contemporary Mathematics New York: W. H. Freeman and Co., 1988, pp. 2–3.

you to brush up on matrix manipulation and determinants. The module on game theory deals with determining the best strategy in limited competitive situations. The module on dynamic programming investigates dynamic and sequential decisions.

1.6
POSSIBLE PROBLEMS IN THE QA APPROACH

We have presented the quantitative analysis approach as a logical, systematic means of tackling decision-making problems. Even when these steps are carefully followed, there are many difficulties that can hurt the chances of implementing solutions to real-world problems. We now take a look at what can happen during each of the steps.

Defining the Problem

One view of decision makers is that they sit at a desk all day long waiting until a problem arises and then stand up and attack the problem until it is solved. Once it is solved, they sit down, relax, and wait for the next big problem. In the worlds of business, government, and education, problems are, unfortunately, not easily identified. There are four roadblocks that quantitative analysts face in defining a problem. We use an application, inventory analysis, throughout this section as an example.

◀ KEY IDEA

Conflicting Viewpoints. The first difficulty is that quantitative analysts must often consider conflicting viewpoints in defining the problem. For example, there are at least two views that managers take when dealing with inventory problems. Financial managers usually feel that inventory is too high, as inventory represents cash not available for other investments. Sales managers, on the other hand, often feel that inventory is too low, as high levels of inventory may be needed to fill an unexpected order. If analysts assume either one of these statements as the problem definition, they have essentially accepted one manager's perception and can expect resistance from the other manager when the "solution" emerges. So it's important to consider both points of view before stating the problem.

Impact on Other Departments. The next difficulty is that problems do not exist in isolation and are not owned by just one department of a firm. Inventory is closely tied with cash flows and various production problems. A change in ordering policy can seriously hurt cash flows and upset production schedules to the point that savings on inventory are more than offset by increased costs for finance and production. The problem statement should thus be as broad as possible and include the input from all departments that have a stake in the solution.

Beginning Assumptions. The third difficulty is that people have a tendency to state problems in terms of solutions. The statement that inventory is too low implies a solution that inventory levels should be raised. The quantitative analyst who starts off with this assumption will probably indeed find that inventory should be raised. From an implementation standpoint, a "good" solution to the *right* problem is much better than an "optimal" solution to the *wrong* problem.

Solution Outdated. Even with the best of problem statements, however, there is a fourth danger. The problem can change as the model is being developed. In our rapidly changing business environment, it is not unusual for problems to appear or disappear virtually overnight. The analyst who presents a solution to a problem that no longer exists can't expect credit for providing timely help.

Developing a Model

Fitting the Textbook Models. One problem in developing quantitative models is that a manager's perception of a problem won't always match the textbook approach. Most inventory models involve minimizing the total of holding and ordering costs. Some managers view these costs as unimportant; instead, they see the problem in terms of cash flow, turnover, and levels of customer satisfaction. Results of a model based on holding and ordering costs are probably not acceptable to such managers.

Understanding the Model. A second major concern involves the trade-off between complexity of the model and ease of understanding. Managers simply will not use the results of a model they do not understand. Complex problems, though, require complex models. One trade-off is to simplify assumptions in order to make the model easier to understand. The model loses some of its reality but gains some acceptance by management.

One simplifying assumption in inventory modeling is that demand is known and constant. This means probability distributions are not needed and it allows us to build simple, easy-to-understand models. Demand, however, is rarely known and constant, so the model we build lacks some reality. Introducing probability distributions provides more realism but may put comprehension beyond all but the most mathematically sophisticated managers. One approach is for the quantitative analyst to start with the simple model and make sure it is completely understood. Later, more complex models can be slowly introduced as managers gain more confidence in using the new approach.

KEY IDEA

Acquiring Input Data

Gathering the data to be used in the quantitative approach to problem solving is often no simple task. One-fifth of all firms in a recent study had difficulty with data access.

Using Accounting Data. One problem is that most data generated in a firm come from basic accounting reports. The accounting department collects its inventory data, for example, in terms of cash flows and turnover. But quantitative analysts tackling an inventory problem need to collect data on holding costs and ordering costs. If they ask for such data, they may be shocked to find it was just never collected for those specified costs.

Gene Woolsey, former editor of the journal *Interfaces*, tells a story of a young quantitative analyst sent down to accounting to get "the inventory holding cost per item per day for part 23456/AZ." The accountant asked the young man if he wanted the first-in, first-out figure, the last-in, first-out figure, the lower of cost or market figure, or the "how-we-do-it" figure. The young man replied that the inventory model only required one number. The accountant at the next desk said "Hell, Joe, give the kid a number." The kid was given a number and departed.[2]

Validity of Data. This lack of "good, clean data" means that whatever data are available must often be distilled and manipulated (we call it "fudging") before being used in a model. Unfortunately, the validity of the results of a model is no better than the validity of the data that go into the model. You cannot blame a manager for resisting a model's "scientific" results when he or she knows questionable data were used as input.

Developing a Solution

Hard-to-Understand Mathematics. The first concern in developing solutions is that although the mathematical models we use may be complex and powerful, they may not be completely understood. Fancy solutions to problems may have faulty logic or data. The aura of mathematics often causes managers to remain silent when they should be critical. The well-known operations researcher C. W. Churchman cautions that "because mathematics has been so reversed a discipline in recent years, it tends to lull the unsuspecting into believing that he who thinks elaborately thinks well."[3]

Only One Answer Is Limiting. The second problem is that quantitative models usually give just one answer to a problem. Most managers would like to have a *range* of options and not be put in a take-it-or-leave-it position.

We recall the story of the analyst whose job was to find the best location in the city for a new garbage incinerator plant. Her extensive mathematical calculations revealed one best spot: it was centrally located, on the necessary truck lines, and so on. What she neglected to note was that it was also across the street from the home of a city council member—and hence what you might call a less than optimal solution!

A more appropriate strategy is for an analyst to present a range of options, indicating the effect each solution has on the objective function. This gives managers a choice as well as information on how much it will cost to deviate from the optimal solution. It also allows problems to be

[2] R. E. D. Woolsey, "The Measure of MS/OR Application or Let's Hear It for the Bean Counters," *Interfaces*, Vol. 5, No. 2, February 1975.

[3] C. W. Churchman, "Relativity Models in the Social Sciences," *Interfaces*, Vol. 4, No. 1, November 1973.

viewed from a broader perspective since nonquantitative factors can be considered.

Testing the Solution

The results of QA often take the form of predictions of how things will work in the future if certain changes are made now. To get a preview of how well solutions will really work, managers are often asked how good the solution looks to them. The problem is that complex models tend to give solutions that are not intuitively obvious. And such solutions tend to be rejected by managers. The quantitative analyst now has the chance to work through the model and the assumptions with the manager in an effort to convince the manager of the validity of the results. In the process of convincing the manager, the analyst will have to review each and every assumption that went into the model. If there are errors, they may be revealed during this review. In addition, the manager will be casting a critical eye on everything that went into the model and, if he or she can be convinced that the model is valid, there is a good chance that the solution results are also valid.

Analyzing the Results

Once the solution has been tested, the results must be analyzed in terms of how they will affect the total organization. You should be aware that even small changes in organizations are often difficult to bring about. If the results indicate large changes in organization policy, the quantitative analyst can expect resistance. In analyzing the results the analyst should ascertain who must change and by how much, if the people who must change will be better or worse off, and who has the power to direct the change.

1.7
IMPLEMENTATION—NOT JUST THE FINAL STEP

We have just presented some of the many problems that can affect the ultimate acceptance of the QA approach and use of its models. It should be clear now that implementation isn't just another step that takes place after the modeling process is over. Each one of these steps greatly affects the chances of implementing the results of a quantitative study.

Lack of Commitment and Resistance to Change

Even though many business decisions can be made intuitively, based on hunches and experience, there are more and more situations in which quantitative models can assist. Some managers, however, fear that the use of a formal analysis process will reduce their decision-making power. Others fear it may expose some previous intuitive decisions as inadequate. Still others just feel uncomfortable having to reverse their thinking patterns

---

APPLICATIONS OF QA

Implementing Study Results at the Texas Department of Human Resources

One of the last steps of any quantitative analysis or management science problem is to implement the results of the analysis. Without proper implementation, a lot of time and money expended in the analysis can be wasted. This was the case with the Texas Department of Human Resources (TDHR). The TDHR spent approximately $1 million on a study. This study, the Biennial Survey, was not used to the extent originally hoped for. It was to be used by various decision makers in determining client needs, program requirements, resource demands, and looking at future conditions in general.

The Texas Department of Human Resources serves approximately 1.2 million clients with a budget that is over $3 billion. The fact that the $1 million survey was virtually unused by agency decision makers was a big disappointment to the TDHR. As a result, it commissioned a second study to investigate why the survey was not used to a greater extent.

The second study uncovered many potential problems and revealing attitudes about the survey. To begin with, the second study did confirm that the report was not used to a great extent. It also uncovered that there was no general agreement about the overall purpose of the report and how it could be used to help in the decision-making process. Because the report was difficult to use and poorly organized, many decision makers believed that the price of the report and time needed to use it were too high. Furthermore, there was no agreement as to which level of decision maker or staff should use the data.

As a result of these problems, a marketing strategy was suggested for implementation in future reports. This strategy included a number of important points. To begin with, a better conceptualization of the survey and its purpose would be required. Secondly, it would be better to create a number of different reports that are specifically oriented toward various agencies and decision makers instead of one overall report that attempts to satisfy everyone. Futhermore, the reports should clearly establish how the data were collected, the limitations of the data, and how a decision maker might use the data. It was also concluded that an easy-to-use reference system was needed to help decision makers quickly and efficiently find the information that they needed. In addition, the reports should be visually attractive and stimulating. The old adage, one picture is worth a thousand words, should have been used when developing reports for managers. Samples of how the data can be analyzed and used should also have been included. Finally, a systematic approach to actually distributing the reports needed to be developed. Follow-up meetings and programs to help decision makers use the reports once they are distributed were also deemed to be important factors.

As a result of the second study, a marketing approach was used in a new survey. Many of the recommendations of the marketing strategy for implementation were used. For example, two smaller reports were developed and distributed to specific types of decision makers. The overall result of this marketing approach was greater and better use of the data. If a considerable amount of money is to be spent on developing surveys and making analysis, a marketing strategy is critical in order for the results to be implemented and used correctly. With the new approach, the Associate Commissioner for the Texas Department of Human Resources, Thomas Suehs, stated that "the marketing approach used by our staff in the second Biennial Survey resulted in substantial use of their analysis by agency decision makers."

Source: Adapted from Reuben McDaniel and Donde Ashmos, "Marketing The Results Of Analysis," *Interfaces,* Vol. 15, No. 4, July–August 1985, pp. 70–76.

---

with formal decision making. These managers often argue against the use of quantitative methods.

Gene Woolsey suggests that action-oriented managers do not like the lengthy formal decision-making process, but prefer to get things done quickly. He advocates the use of "quick and dirty" techniques that can yield immediate results and thus slowly indoctrinate the manager to the use of quantitative methods.[4] Once managers see some quick results that have a substantial payoff, the stage is set for convincing them that quantitative analysis is a beneficial tool.

We have known for some time that management support and user involvement are critical to the successful implementation of quantitative analysis projects. A Swedish study found that only 40% of projects suggested by quantitative analysts were ever implemented.[5] But 70% of the quantitative projects initiated by users, and fully 98% of projects suggested by top managers, *were* implemented.

Lack of Commitment
by Quantitative Analysts

Just as manager attitudes are to blame for some implementation problems, analysts' attitudes are to blame for others. When the quantitative analyst is not an integral part of the department facing the problem, he or she sometimes tends to treat the modeling activity as an end in itself. That is, the analyst accepts the problem as stated by the manager and builds a model to solve only that problem. When the results are computed, he or she hands them back to the manager and considers the job done. The analyst who does not care whether or not these results help make the final decision is not concerned with implementation.

Successful implementation requires that the analyst not *tell* the users what to do, but work with them and take their feelings into account. An article in *Operations Research* describes an inventory control system that calculated reorder points and order quantities.[6] But instead of insisting that computer-calculated quantities be ordered, a manual override feature was installed. This allowed users to disregard the calculated figures and substitute their own. The override was used quite often when the system was first installed. Gradually, however, as users came to realize that the calculated figures were right more often than not, they allowed the system's figures to stand. Eventually the override feature was used only in special circumstances. This is a good example of how good relationships can aid in model implementation.

1.8
DEVELOPMENT OF QA WITHIN
AN ORGANIZATION

One of the important factors in the acceptance and implementation of an innovation such as quantitative analysis is its "age" in the organization.

---

[4] R. E. D. Woolsey and H. Swanson, *Operations Research for Immediate Application: A Quick and Dirty Manual* (New York: Harper and Row, 1975).

[5] Lars Lannstedt, "Factors Related to the Implementation of Operations Research Solution," *Interfaces*, Vol. 5, No. 2, February 1975.

[6] J. Bishop, "Experience with a Successful System for Forecasting and Inventory Control," *Operations Research*, Vol. 3, No. 2, 1972.

The longer an innovation has been around in an organization, the more acceptance you would expect to find. In the book, *Implementing Operations Research/Management Science*, six phases in the development of a QA activity are put forth.[7]

I. *Prebirth.* During this phase, someone in the organization "gets religion" about quantitative analysis techniques and attempts to convince colleagues of the potential benefits of using such techniques. It is important to have the support of top management in order to proceed any further in the quantitative activity development.

II. *Missionary.* For this phase, a quantitative analyst or two is brought in to attempt to "convert the natives" and to explain more thoroughly the benefits of using the new techniques. Just as many religious missionaries have found themselves unwelcome, so many a quantitative activity has died during this phase. Again, top management's support is essential in order to proceed to the next phase.

III. *Organization Development.* This phase involves active bargaining with the user departments in order to gain a few small projects to work on. Several features are important during this phase:

A. The location of the activity in the organization should be centralized and fairly well established at this point.

B. The projects selected should be ones that are fairly standard and will yield significant results in a short period of time using common models such as inventory control.

C. Dependence of top management should be decreased during this phase.

IV. *Sophisticated Projects.* During this phase, the QA effort has achieved some status by solving some standard projects with significant results. The members of the group can now turn their attention to more sophisticated applications.

V. *Maturity.* By the time this phase is reached, the use of mathematical models has gained routine acceptance in the organization.

VI. *Diffusion.* Finally, the quantitative analysis function consists of small groups spread out among various departments of the organization. At this phase, the support of top management is not necessary in order to ensure implementation. One survey indicated that, contrary to previous studies and trends, less than half (48%) of the companies that used QA techniques had specialized quantitative departments. This indicates that the function of quantitative analysis in organizations is beginning to mature to the point where the activities are dispersed throughout the organization. This dispersal should help solve some of the communications problems we noted that are typical in the analyst-manager interface. An increase in implementation will most likely result.

[7] A. S. Bean et al., "Structural and Behavioral Correlates of Implementation in U.S. Business Organizations," *Implementing Operations Research/Management Science*, Schultz and Slevin, eds. (New York: American Elsevier, 1975).

1.9
QUANTITATIVE ANALYSIS, DECISION SUPPORT SYSTEMS, AND ARTIFICIAL INTELLIGENCE

Management Information Systems

Quantitative models have become an integral part of computer-based *management information systems.* A management information system (MIS) is an important tool in business. It is simply an organized way of getting the right information to the right people in the right place at the right time. Getting the right information to the right manager can often involve using quantitative models. After all, if a manager needs help in ordering and stocking decisions, *forecasting models* to project demand and *inventory models* to compute optimal order policies can be vital.

Figure 1.2 illustrates how a management information system can be used to support decision making. Note that the comprehensive database has all sorts of files and records—from sales, inventory, and financial data to subjective management inputs and sales/financial forecasts.

The MIS also contains a comprehensive set of QA models to help produce ordering, scheduling, product mix, machine utilization, and personnel reports. Trend analysis, forecasting models, linear programming, production scheduling and product mix models, PERT control models, simulation planning models, and decision theory models to evaluate alternative investment strategies can all be part of the system.

In order to be able to extract information in the right place at the right time, direct manager-computer interface is becoming popular. This means that computer programs are needed to allow the decision maker to "speak" online to the MIS, usually through terminals or microcomputers. If an application is more complex, the quantitative analyst may act as the interface and handle the data request by writing programs to extract the information.

Decision Support Systems

DSS

Along with today's advances in computer technology, we are also seeing the development of decision support systems, expert systems, and artificial intelligence. In a *decision support system (DSS)*, a system is developed to support rather than replace managerial decision making. Typically, decision support systems are oriented toward poorly structured problems. DSS is interactive and allows the use of "what-if" questions. Managers can try out different decisions, alter input data, and quickly see the results of these changes in the solutions to problems. In developing the software that accompanies this book, we have attempted to use the notions of DSS in providing flexible yet powerful decision-making tools.

Artificial Intelligence

The field of artificial intelligence (AI) began in the mid-1950s at a conference at Dartmouth College. During this conference, concepts and theories related

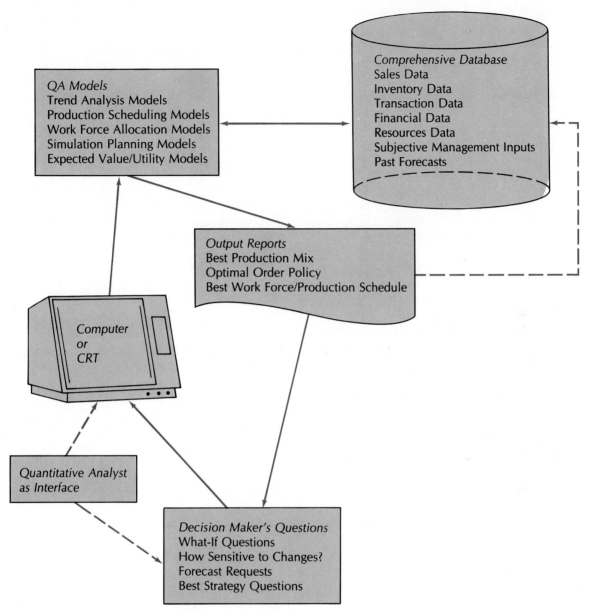

FIGURE 1.2
Decision Support System

to the use of computer systems and technology to act like or simulate human intelligence were explored. These concepts were called *artificial intelligence*. Since this early beginning, many strides have been made. Artificial intelligence has grown into a number of important and practical subfields with broad implications for quantitative analysis and society in general. Artificial intelligence attempts to develop systems and procedures that mimic or act like intelligent and rational decision makers. These systems

beginning of artificial intelligence and expert systems

may contain components or aspects that are difficult to quantify. Furthermore, large databases or knowledge bases containing expert opinions are captured. An overview of the artificial intelligence field is shown in Figure 1.3.

KEY IDEA →

overview of artificial intelligence

The three primary components or practical applications of artificial intelligence are expert systems, robotics, and natural languages. *Expert systems* allow us to develop technology that acts and responds like experts in a particular field. Expert systems have been developed to diagnose medical problems, explore for oil, and make good decisions based on available information. The field of *robotics* is concerned with developing devices that have movement and response capabilities far beyond traditional mechanical equipment. With robotics, we can develop mechanical systems to accurately spray paint cars and other products, handle hazardous and dangerous materials, and perform delicate manipulations that only human beings could perform in the past. *Natural languages* attempt to understand and process statements and commands using language that you would find in normal, everyday conversations. Although these three categories of artificial intelligence are still at the beginning stages of development, positive results have already been achieved.

Applications of Artificial Intelligence. There are numerous examples of developed and installed systems that use the notions of artificial intelligence and expert systems. For example, MYCIN is an expert system started at Stanford University to analyze and propose treatments for various blood infections. AT&T has developed a system that helps to analyze the maintenance of telephone networks and cables. ACE.DELTA, developed by General Electric Corporation, can be used to help analyze repair problems for various types of engines. Atlantic Richfield, a major oil company, uses supercomputers and expert systems to help in oil exploration. Other applications include financial investment planning, external auditing, com-

use of expert systems

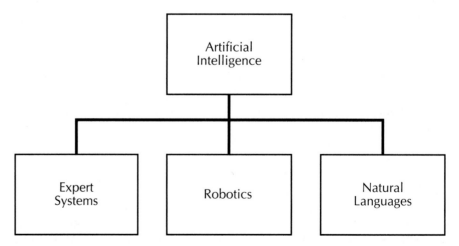

FIGURE 1.3
Overview of Artificial Intelligence

mercial loan approval, advertising and media selection strategies, inventory control and planning, design and configuration of computer systems, career planning, and a system for developing strategic objectives.

Many strides have been made in the area of robotics. Artificial intelligence has been used to assist in making machines traverse rough and uneven terrain. While everyday activities such as walking or running seem commonplace, developing computer programs and systems to allow machines to perform these functions is difficult and complex. Another area receiving considerable attention in the area of robotics is <u>vision sciences</u>. Although most people can look at various objects and quickly determine what is in a room, this process is very difficult for a computer system. Seeing various light and dark shades through lenses and interpreting these patterns as specific objects requires advanced artificial intelligence skills.

Natural language systems are also being developed and used. Such systems have the ability to understand common English sentences or commands. Instead of developing detailed programs in a language such as COBOL, natural language processors have the ability to understand and then act upon ordinary English sentences.

new developments in artificial intelligence

Benefits of Artificial Intelligence. The potential benefits of artificial intelligence and expert systems are many and varied. While benefits are not guaranteed, these systems can be used as competitive weapons in the marketplace. Some of the potential benefits are:

1. Superior decision making.

2. Better quality.

3. Lowered cost.

4. Greater reliability.

5. Effective utilization of scarce resources.

6. Performing dangerous or hazardous operations without endangering human life.

7. Enhanced problem solving.

8. Greater flexibility in the utilization of scarce resources.

Use of Expert Systems. One of the most promising applications of artificial intelligence is the use of expert systems on complex or difficult to solve problems. An expert system includes all equipment, devices, procedures, and software used to capture the essence of a human expert in a particular field. In order to effectively use an expert system, it must be carefully developed. This development process is shown in Figure 1.4. An expert system is built by one or more individuals called *knowledge engineers*. Knowledge engineers have the expertise and the skill to convert information given to them by experts in a field into computerized systems that act as experts. There are numerous advantages of capturing expertise. For example, use of experience and good judgment can be lost when valued

development of expert systems

FIGURE 1.4
Expert System Development

employees retire. With an expert system, their knowledge and experience can be captured and used for generations to come. In addition, the knowledge and experience of valued experts can be used by many individuals in a variety of settings to solve specific problems.

After the expert system has been developed, an effective delivery system must be employed to allow users to gain the benefits of the expert system. The use of an expert system is shown in Figure 1.5. The user goes through an interface system to activate the expert system. As can be seen, the expert system consists of a rule base, a knowledge base, and an inference engine. The rule base contains important rules about the particular field that is captured in the expert system. These rules are typically expressed as IF-THEN statements. In general, IF-THEN constructs allow the expert system to capture important rules and judgments. The knowledge base consists of data and experience that are captured and placed into the expert system. Finally, the expert system has an inference engine that allows the manipulation of the rule base and knowledge base to get meaningful results for the user. The interface consists of people, equipment, procedures, and

KEY IDEA

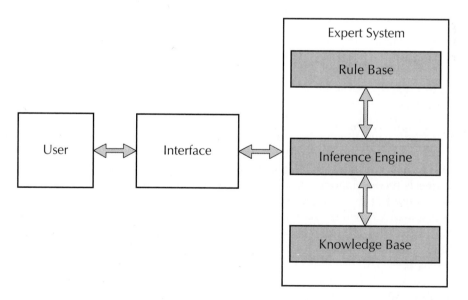

FIGURE 1.5
Use of an Expert System

systems that allow the effective use of the expert system. In most cases, a manager or other decision maker does not have the skills needed to directly access and manipulate the expert system. The interface allows managers and decision makers to gain the benefits of an expert system without spending time becoming technical experts in the use of the system. With proper development and careful use, artificial intelligence and expert systems can yield substantial benefits.

1.10
USE OF MICROCOMPUTERS
IN QUANTITATIVE ANALYSIS

Two software packages will be featured throughout this book. AB:QM is a comprehensive software package that accompanies this book. STORM is a popular package that many schools make available to students. In the appropriate chapters, we will illustrate the use of these two packages. In addition, we will show how other software packages such as Lindo, Super Tree, and Expert Choice can be used with a specific quantitative analysis technique. In the rest of this section, we will give you an overview of AB:QM and STORM.

using AB:QM, STORM, and other programs

Use of AB:QM in Quantitative Analysis

AB:QM (short for Allyn & Bacon:Quantitative Methods) is a software package that allows you to solve many of the quantitative problems discussed in this book. In all, this software package includes 44 programs in 17 categories or menu selections, including linear programming, integer programming, zero-one programming, goal programming, the transportation method, the assignment technique, break-even analysis, decision theory, network models, CPM/PERT techniques, inventory control, queuing theory, dynamic programming, simulation, forecasting, Markov analysis, and game theory. The package is easy to use and does not require previous coursework in computers.

overview of AB:QM

Basic Requirements and Capabilities. AB:QM runs on IBM and IBM-compatible computer systems (including many IBM PS/2 models). It requires 256K of RAM (random access memory). An EPSON or compatible printer is recommended. A color monitor or monochrome monitor may be used. One floppy disk drive is acceptable, although two disk drives or a hard disk are recommended.

The program comes on two 5-1/4-inch floppy disks or one 3-1/2-inch floppy disk. The software can be run from either a floppy disk drive or from a hard disk.

Getting started. How you start AB:QM depends on whether you are part of a network, have a hard disk system, or have a floppy disk system. Here are the appropriate steps for each type of system.

STARTING AB:QM WITH A FLOPPY DISK SYSTEM

Step 1: Boot the computer system by putting DOS (disk operating system) in the A drive and turning on the computer. If the computer is already on, you can hold down the control (Ctrl) and alternate (Alt) keys and press the delete (Del) key. Once this is done, you will get the A prompt, which looks like A>. You have now booted the computer system.

Step 2: Insert the AB:QM floppy disk into the A drive. If you have a 5-1/4-inch drive, there will be two disks. Insert disk 1. If you have a 3-1/2-inch drive, there is only one disk, which you insert.

Step 3: Type QM and press the return (or enter) key. This will start program execution. Typing qm in lower case letters will also work.

STARTING AB:QM WITH A HARD DISK SYSTEM

Step 1: Boot the computer system by turning on the computer without any floppy disk in the A drive. You can also hold down Ctrl and Alt and press Del. If your computer is already on, it is not necessary to boot the computer.

Step 2: Make sure the AB:QM programs are transferred to a directory on the hard disk. This may already be done for you. If not, you can use the COPY *.* command to copy all of the files from the floppy disks to the hard disk. If you are not sure how to copy the programs, you may need to ask your instructor or a lab assistant.

Step 3: Get into the directory that contains the AB:QM programs. This can be done with the Change Directory (CD) command. For example, if you type CD QM at the C prompt, you'll be in the QM subdirectory instead of the root directory (assuming that the QM directory exists and contains the AB:QM programs).

Step 4: Type QM. This will start the execution of the programs.

Note that hard disk systems can be configured in a number of different ways. If you are having trouble, you may have to get assistance from your instructor or a lab assistant.

STARTING AB:QM FROM A NETWORK

Step 1: Log onto the network. This step will vary according to the network at your school. In most cases, you will need an identification number and password.

Step 2: Go to the AB:QM directory or menu. This step will vary according to how the network is set up. In many cases, you will see AB:QM as a menu selection after you log on. In other cases, you will have to give several commands to get to the AB:QM menu.

Step 3: Type QM. This will start the programs.

Note that today, many schools use a network to tie personal computers together. Networks are different, and each school will have policies concerning the use of its network. Make sure you understand the operation of the network and the policies or rules that exist at your school. After you are finished with AB:QM, it is important to properly log off the network. If you are having any problems, you may have to get assistance from your instructor or a lab assistant.

Menu Selections. Once you have typed QM at the A or C prompt, the menu is displayed. See Program 1.1.

PROGRAM 1.1
Main Menu of AB:QM

```
───────────────────────── Menu 1 ─────────────────────────

  A    Linear Programming            J     CPM/PERT
  B    All Integer Programming       K     Inventory Models
  C    Zero One Programming          L     Queuing Theory
  D    Goal Programming              M     Dynamic Programming
  E    Transportation                N     Simulation
  F    Assignment                    O     Forecasting
  G    Break-Even Analysis           P     Markov Analysis
  H    Decision Theory               Q     Game Theory
  I    Network Models              Esc     Exit AB:QM
```

Running One of the Programs. Once in the menu, you can type the appropriate letter or move the cursor to highlight the application you wish to run and then press the return key. This will start the execution of the desired program.

Every program in AB:QM has the same type of screen layout or appearance. Three areas appear on the screen. The upper area or upper window contains initial data for the particular application. Included are the problem title and other model parameters that set the overall structure for the application. The middle window is where detailed data entry occurs. Specific values for the model are entered in the middle window. Both the upper and the middle windows act like a spreadsheet. The cursor can be used to highlight the appropriate area, and data can be entered by pressing the correct keys. Changes can be made easily. Simply move the cursor to the place the change is to occur and type in the new or corrected value. The lower window contains the commands that are used for all applications of AB:QM. Here are some of the most useful commands:

screen layout for AB:QM

← KEY IDEA

COMMAND	EXPLANATION
Help	Help is used to get on-screen assistance for an application.
New	New is used to enter new data into an application.
Load	Load is used to retrieve data that have been previously saved using the Save command.
Save	Save is used to save data onto a floppy disk or a hard disk. It is recommended that data *not* be saved onto one of the program disks.
Edit	Edit is used to alter or change any of the values of the particular model. In some cases, the Edit command cannot be used; for example, it cannot be used to change the overall structure of a problem, such as the number of alternatives, or the overall size of the problem. In these cases, new data must be entered from scratch.
Run	Run is used to execute the program. This command will first display the data entered and then the actual program output.
Print	Print can be used to print results on the printer, a disk file, or both. You may print results only *after* the Run command has been given.
Install	Install is used to set various parameters for the AB:QM program.
Directory	Directory is used to get a listing of files for a particular floppy disk or a subdirectory on a hard disk.
Esc	The escape (Esc) key is used to back out of any application. Pressing the Esc key will exit what you are doing and bring you to the next highest level. Pressing the Esc key repeatedly will eventually cause the computer to exit from AB:QM and return you to the DOS level. (Note that this is similar to the use of the Esc key in Lotus and other spreadsheet software.)

The commands in AB:QM are executed by typing the first letter of the command. For example, the Edit command is invoked by typing the letter E.

Use of a Data and Backup Disk. Although there is a limited amount of free space on the program disks, it is recommended that you keep a separate data disk to store the results of AB:QM. In addition, you should also keep a backup copy of all files on your data disk in case of unexpected problems.

Getting Results from AB:QM. Once you have run a program using AB:QM, you can send the results to a printer, a disk drive, or both from the Print command. By typing the letter P you will start the Print command. The computer will then ask you if you want your output sent to the printer, a disk device, or both. Of course, if you send output to a printer, make sure that the printer is on and loaded with paper. If you tell the computer to send the output to a disk device, the computer will ask you for a file specification. For example, B:LP1 could be used to save the results on a floppy disk in the B drive with a file name of LP1.

using the Print command

If you are using a word processor, saving the output to a disk file is a good choice. Most word processors allow you to upload or insert other disk files into a document. Thus, you will be able to include output from AB:QM directly into a professionally executed report using a word processor.

Potential Problems. When you first start to run AB:QM, you may encounter problems. Typical problems and their solutions are briefly outlined here:

PROBLEM	SOLUTION
Program title not on the screen	Check to make sure that you have the correct program disk in the disk drive and that the disk is not damaged.
Red disk light stays on	This means that the disk drive is still spinning. Do not take out the disk while the red disk light is on because this could damage the disk. Instead, reboot the computer by holding the Ctrl and Alt keys and pressing the Del key.
Messages saying invalid command or file not found	If you type QM to start the program and get either one of these messages, the computer cannot find the QM file. You may not have the correct disk in a floppy drive. If you are using a hard disk system, you may be in the wrong subdirectory.

Exiting from AB:QM. The best way to exit from AB:QM and get back to the DOS level is to first get to the menu of AB:QM. If you are in a subdirectory, press the Esc key to get back to the main menu. Then, press the Esc key to exit AB:QM and get back to DOS. In general, you can keep pressing the Esc key to get back to DOS. You will see the current disk drive prompt displayed, for example, A> for the A disk drive or C> for the hard disk. At this point, you can run another program or turn off the computer.

using the Esc key

A Forecasting Example of AB:QM. To give you a better example of how to use AB:QM, we will go through a forecasting example. (Forecasting is covered in Chapter 4.) In this example, we will have the computer determine the best equation for future sales given the following data:

Vacuum Cleaner Data

SALES (Y)	ADVERTISING BUDGET (X)
23	$1,000
25	2,000
30	3,000
31	4,000
35	5,000
36	6,000

Our equation will be Sales = Intercept + (Slope) (Ad budget). Given the data for sales and ad budget, the computer will determine the best values for the intercept and slope. The forecasting submenu is letter F. Thus, we press the F key to get into the forecasting program. See Program 1.2. Next we press the D key to get into the regression program. The computer will display a blank data entry screen. As discussed previously, the same type of blank screen is displayed for every application. The screen is divided into three areas. The top area is for general problem data. The

the basic equation

PROGRAM 1.2
Forecasting Submenu

```
┌──────────────────── Menu ────────────────────┐
│   A      Simple & Weighted Moving Averages    │
│   B      Exponential Smoothing                │
│   C      Least Squares Method                 │
│   D      Simple Regression                    │
│   E      Multiple Regression                  │
│  Esc     Back to Main Menu                    │
│                                               │
└───────────────────────────────────────────────┘
```

middle and largest area is for detailed data entry, and the bottom area shows the commands that we can give.

Because this is the first time we have run the forecasting program, we might want to get information about the program. When we press the H key (for help), we will get the first help screen. In most cases, there is more help information than can fit on a single screen. By pressing the down arrow or the page down (PgDn) key, additional information will appear. In general, we can use the up or down arrow or page up (PgUp) and page down (PgDn) keys to obtain the information or help we want. The help screens for our initial request are shown in Program 1.3.

getting help

When you are finished with the help menu, press the Esc key to get back to the data entry screen. Again, you will see the blank data entry screen. At this stage, we want to enter data for our problem, so we press the N key for the New command to enter data. In the top window, the computer will ask us to enter the problem title. We type VACUUM CLEANER SALES DATA and press the return key. Next, the computer will ask us to enter the number of observations. We type 6 and press the return key. Next, the computer will go to the middle window and ask us to enter the values for the six observations. When we have entered all values, the computer will beep to indicate that all values have been entered. The completed data entry screen is shown in Program 1.4.

entering new data

Let's say we made an error in the third observation. Instead of entering 30 sales we entered 300. To correct this problem, we press the E key for the Edit command and the computer places us in the edit mode. We move the cursor to the mistake by using the arrow keys. The computer will highlight the value to be corrected. Then we type in the correct value and press the return key. Again, we will be put into the data entry screen with the correct value in place.

Edit command— correcting errors

With the data correct, we would like to execute the program and see the results. We do this by pressing the R key for the Run command. The computer will first display the input data. By using the arrow keys or page up and page down keys, we will be able to see all of the output as shown in Program 1.5.

Run command

Look carefully at the output. As you can see, the coefficient for the intercept is 20.4. The coefficient for the slope (called b 1 here) is 0.0027. Thus our equation for sales is: Sales = 20.4 + 0.0027 (Ad budget). If we

PROGRAM 1.3
Help Screens

```
***** Program Description *****

Purpose
-------


The Simple Regression Model consists of one dependent variable and one independent
variable, which are assumed to be linearly related. The dependent variable is the
variable to be forecast, and the independent variable is an explanatory variable.
This model uses the Least Squares Method to estimate the values of slope and
intercept.


Limitation of System
--------------------
1. Maximum number of observations : 50


Explanation of Key Words and How to Input Data
----------------------------------------------

<< Upper Window >>

1. Type the problem title or your comment for later reference purposes.
2. Enter the number of observations.

<< Middle Window >>

1. Input the value of the dependent variable in column Y for each observation.
2. Input the value of the independent variable in column X for each observation.
```

want to predict sales for the budget of 3,750, the equation would be Sales = 20.4 + 0.0027 (3,750) = 30.5. Thus, sales would be about 30 units. At this point, don't be concerned with the output from this program; it will be explained in Chapter 4.

Now, let's say we would like to save the data on a floppy disk in the A drive. We do this by pressing the S key for the Save command. The computer will ask us to enter the file specification without an extension. We enter a:sales and press the return key.

Save command

If we want to retrieve data previously saved, we press the L key for the Load command. The computer will ask us to enter a file specification (without extension). For example, we can enter a:sales to have the computer retrieve the sales data.

Load command

If we are completing a homework problem, we will want to get a printed copy of the results. We press the P key for the Print command. The computer will ask us if we want the results on the *Printer*, *Disk* file, or *Both*. Type

Print command

PROGRAM 1.4
Data Entry Screen

Forecasting / Simple Regression

Problem Title:	VACUUM CLEANER SALES DATA	
Number of Observations	6	

	Y	X
Observation 1	23	1000
Observation 2	25	2000
Observation 3	30	3000
Observation 4	31	4000
Observation 5	35	5000
Observation 6	36	6000

Help New Load Save Edit Run Print Install Directory Esc

P for the printer, D for the disk, or B for both. If you are using a word processing program, you may want to print to a disk file and then retrieve the results from the disk file into your word processing program.

Install command

AB:QM allows us to specify a default disk drive where our data will be stored. The default disk is called the *working directory*. If you have a hard disk, you may want your data stored on floppy disks in the A drive instead of on the hard disk (C drive). This can be accomplished by pressing the letter I key for Install and typing the drive specification, A:, and then pressing the return key.

Directory command

The final command we will investigate is the Directory command, which gives us a list of all AB:QM files that we have saved on the working directory. At this time, our working directory is the A drive; of course, we can always change the working directory with the Install command. We press the D key for the Directory command, and the computer will display all of the AB:QM files on the A drive. As seen in Program 1.6, the only file that is on the floppy disk in the A drive is SALES.FCT.—the data for the sales example. The letters FCT, which stand for forecasting are the file extension. AB:QM automatically placed this extension on the file name.

PROGRAM 1.5
Running the Program

```
Program: Forecasting / Simple Regression

Problem Title: VACUUM CLEANER SALES DATA

***** Input Data *****

Obs.          Y              X

  1        23.000        1000.000
  2        25.000        2000.000
  3        30.000        3000.000
  4        31.000        4000.000
  5        35.000        5000.000
  6        36.000        6000.000


***** Program Output *****

Parameter       Coefficient        SE B           t

Intercept         20.4000         0.9700       21.0303
   b 1             0.0027         0.0002       11.0120

Coefficient of determination   :      0.9681
Correlation coefficient        :      0.9839
Standard Error                 :      1.0420

Prediction Error

             Observed        Predicted
Obs.          Value           Value         Residual

  1          23.000          23.143         -0.143
  2          25.000          25.886         -0.886
  3          30.000          28.629          1.371
  4          31.000          31.371         -0.371
  5          35.000          34.114          0.886
  6          36.000          36.857         -0.857

Mean Absolute Deviation (MAD) :              0.9029

ANOVA Table

Source of
Variation              SS           df           MS

Regression          131.657         1         131.657
Residual              4.343         4           1.086

Total               136.000         5
F*  =     121.263

***** End of Output *****
```

PROGRAM 1.6
Directory Command

Forecasting / Simple Regression

```
*** Working Directory: a

SALES.FCT

*** Disk status ***

 78.26% used.
 158720 total bytes available on disk.




ESC
```

Use of STORM

STORM is an integrated package of programs used to perform a variety of
applications in quantitative analysis. This package is relatively easy to use
and is popular at many colleges and universities. The complete software
main menu package consists of 16 programs or modules. The main menu for STORM
displays the 16 programs or modules shown in Program 1.7.

Although there are a few programs contained in the main menu for
STORM that are not appropriate for this book, the following programs in
STORM can be used: linear and integer programming, the assignment
technique, transportation, distance networks, flow networks, project management, queuing analysis, inventory management, forecasting, and material requirements planning. The use of STORM will be described in the
appropriate chapters throughout this book.

STORM programs are screen or menu oriented, which means that the
user is presented with a series of screens and asked to enter values at the
appropriate location. An editor provided with STORM allows the user to
screen oriented efficiently enter the appropriate data. The editor is screen oriented and the
user is presented with similar screens for each application. The actual
display screen on the computer is divided into the problem description
area and the problem data area. In addition, STORM shows the current
location of the cursor or pointer and provides a convenient entry box, a

PROGRAM 1.7
Main Menu for STORM

```
    1)   Linear & Integer Programming
    2)   Assignment
    3)   Transportation
    4)   Distance Networks (Paths, Tours, Trees)
    5)   Flow Networks (Max Flow, Transshipment)
    6)   Project Management (PERT/CPM)
    7)   Queueing Analysis
    8)   Inventory Management
    9)   Facility Layout
   10)   Assembly Line Balancing
   11)   Investment Analysis
   12)   Forecasting
   13)   Production Scheduling
   14)   Material Requirements Planning
   15)   Statistical Process Control
   16)   Statistics
```

```
           : Select option   1 :
```

prompt line that will assist the user in making the correct entry, and a help line that provides additional information.

STORM has the flexibility to allow the complete package of programs **flexibility** to be configured for a particular system or desired setup. Parameters for default disk drives and output formats are possible. Page lengths, margins, offsets, and much more can be specified. How values are displayed can also be set by configuring the STORM package. Getting a directory of existing data files, saving current data on disk, editing previously stored data, and printing the results of a STORM program are all possible. If your school is using the STORM package, refer to the program manual for details about how to use all of its features.

GLOSSARY

Artificial Intelligence. The ability of a computer system to act like an expert or intelligent individual.

Quantitative Analysis or **Management Science.** A scientific approach using quantitative techniques as a tool in decision making.

Problem. A statement, which should come from a manager, that indicates a problem to be solved or an objective or goal to be reached.

Decision Support System. A computer system that supports rather than replaces a decision maker.

Model. A representation of reality or of a real-life situation.

Mathematical Model. A model that uses mathematical equations and statements to represent the relationships within the model.

Input Data. Data that are used in the model in arriving at the final solution.

Sensitivity Analysis. Determining how sensitive the solution is to changes in the formulation of the problem.

Algorithm. A set of logical and mathematical operations performed in a specific sequence.

DISCUSSION QUESTIONS AND PROBLEMS

1–1 What is the difference between quantitative and qualitative analysis? Give several examples.

1–2 Define quantitative analysis. What are some of the organizations that support the use of the scientific approach?

1–3 What is the quantitative analysis process? Give several examples of this process.

1–4 Briefly trace the history of quantitative analysis. What happened to the development of quantitative analysis during World War II?

1–5 Give some examples of the different types of models. What is a mathematical model? Develop two examples of mathematical models.

1–6 What are some of the sources of input data?

1–7 What is implementation, and why is it important?

1–8 Describe the use of sensitivity analysis and postoptimality analysis in analyzing the results.

1–9 Briefly describe some of the quantitative analysis techniques covered in this book.

1–10 Managers are quick to claim that quantitative analysts talk to them in a jargon that doesn't sound like English. List four terms that might not be understood by a manager. Then explain in nontechnical terms what each term means.

1–11 Why do you think many quantitative analysts don't like to participate in the implementation process? What could be done to change this attitude?

1–12 Should people who will be using the results of a new quantitative model such as linear programming become involved in the technical aspects of the problem-solving procedure?

1–13 Do you think that business majors with a specialization in QA would make better analysts than mathematics majors who have strong statistics, calculus, algebra, and math skills? Why?

1–14 C. W. Churchman once said "mathematics . . . tends to lull the unsuspecting into believing that he who thinks elaborately thinks well." Do you think that the best QA models are the ones that are most elaborate and complex mathematically? Why?

1–15 Visit a large business or organization in your area that claims it uses QA techniques. In what phase of development is the QA activity?

1–16 What are the advantages and disadvantages of having QA staffers spread out (diffused) throughout an organization, as opposed to located in one office?

1–17 How is the implementation of QA models tied to a management information system?

BIBLIOGRAPHY

Ackoff, R. L. *Scientific Method: Optimizing Applied Research Decisions.* New York: John Wiley & Sons, Inc., 1962.

Anderson, J. C., and Hoffman, T. R. "A Perspective on the Implementation of Management Science." *Academy of Management Review* Vol. 3, No. 3, July 1978.

Anderson, J. C., and Janson, M. A. "Methods for Managerial Problem Cause Analysis." *Interfaces* Vol. 9, No. 5, November 1979.

Bean, A. S., Neal, R. D., Radnor, M., and Tansik, D. A. "Structural and Behavioral Correlates of Implementation in U.S. Business Organizations," in *Implementing Operations Research/Management Science,* Schultz and Slevin, eds. New York: American Elsevier, 1975.

Bishop, Jack, Jr. "Experience with a Successful System for Forecasting and Inventory Control." *Operations Research* Vol. 3, No. 3, 1972.

Blaylock, Bruce K., and Rees, Loren P. "Cognitive Style and Usefulness of Information." *Decision Sciences* Vol. 15, No. 1, Winter 1984.

Bonczek, R. H., Holsapple, R. H., Whinston, C. W., and Whinston, A. B. "Future Directions for Developing Decision Support Systems." *Decision Sciences* Vol. 11, No. 4, October 1980.

Churchman, C. W. "Relativity Models in the Social Sciences." *Interfaces* Vol. 4, No. 1, November 1973.

Churchman, C. West. *The Systems Approach.* New York: Delacort Press, 1968.

Davis, K. R. "The Process of Problem Finding: A Production-Marketing Example." *Interfaces* Vol. 8, No. 1, November 1977.

Engemann, K. J., Singh, B. J., and Vesoniarakis, M. D. "A Study of Errors, Fines and Losses Related to Money Transfer in a Major Bank." *Interfaces* Vol. 9, No. 4, August 1979.

Fordyce, Kenneth, and others. "Artificial Intelligence and the Management Science Practitioner: One Definition of Knowledge-Based Expert Systems." *Interfaces* Vol. 19, No. 5, September–October 1989.

Fries, B. E. "Bibliography of Operations Research in Health-Care Systems." *Operations Research* Vol. 24, 1976.

Ginzberg, M. J. "Steps Towards Effective Implementation of MS and MIS." *Interfaces* Vol. 8, No. 3, May 1978.

Ginzberg, M. J. "Finding an Adequate Measure of OR/MS Effectiveness." *Interfaces,* Vol. 8, No. 4, August 1978.

Grayson, C. J. "Management Science and Business Practice." *Harvard Business Review* Vol. 51, 1973.

Gupta, J. N. D. "Management Science Implementation: Experiences of a Practicing O. R. Manager." *Interfaces* Vol. 7, No. 3, May 1977.

Hilton, Ronald W. "Determinants of Information Value." *Management Science,* January 1981.

Keeney, Ralph L. "Potential Research Topics in Decision Analysis." *Decision Sciences* Vol. 13, No. 4, October 1982.

Lannstedt, Lars. "Factors Related to the Implementation of Operations Research Solutions." *Interfaces* Vol. 5, No. 2, February 1975.

Liberatore, Matthew J., and Titus, George J. "The Practice of Management Science in R & D Project Management." *Management Sciences* Vol. 29, No. 8, August 1983.

Schultz, R., and Slevin, D. (eds.). *Implementing Operations/Management Science.* New York: American Elsevier, 1975.

Schwenk, Charles R., and Thomas, Howard. "Effects of Conflicting Analysis of Managerial Decision Making: A Laboratory Experiment." *Decision Sciences* Vol. 14, No. 4, Fall 1983.

Shyevor, H. N. "All Around the Model-Perspectives on MS Applications." *Interfaces* Vol. 9, No. 4, August 1979.

Thomas, G., and DaCosta, J. "A Sample Survey of Corporate Operation Research." *Interfaces* Vol. 9, No. 4, August 1979.

Watkins, Paul R. "Perceived Information Structure: Implications for Decision Support System Design." *Decision Sciences* Vol. 13, No. 1, January 1982.

Watson, H. J., and Marett, P. G. "A Survey of Management Science Implementation Problems." *Interfaces* Vol. 9, No. 4, August 1979.

Wolak, F. W., "Implementation and the Process of Adopting Managerial Technology." *Interfaces* Vol. 5, No. 3, May 1975.

Woolsey, R. E. D. "The Measure of MS/OR Application or Let's Hear It for the Bean Counters." *Interfaces* Vol. 5, No. 2, February 1975.

Wysocki, R. K., "OR/MS Implementation Research: A Bibliography." *Interfaces* Vol. 9, No. 2, February 1979.

Zeleny, M. "Managers Without Management Science." *Interfaces* Vol. 5, No. 4, August 1975.

2

Probability Concepts

2.1
INTRODUCTION

Life would be simpler if we knew without doubt what was going to happen in the future. The outcome of any decision would depend only on how logical and rational the decision was. If you lost money in the stock market, it would be because you failed to consider all of the information or to make a logical decision. If you got caught in the rain, it would be because you simply forgot your umbrella. You could always avoid building a plant that was too large, investing in a company that would lose money, running out of supplies, or losing crops because of bad weather. There would be no such thing as a risky investment. Life would be simpler, but boring.

quantifying risks

It wasn't until the sixteenth century that people started to quantify risks and to apply this concept to everyday situations. Today, the idea of risk or probability is a part of our lives. "There is a 40 percent chance of rain in Omaha today." "The Florida State University Seminoles are favored 2 to 1 over the Louisiana State University Tigers this Saturday." "There is a 50-50 chance that the stock market will reach an all-time high next month."

 KEY IDEA

A probability is a numerical statement about the likelihood that an event will occur. In this and the next chapter on probability we shall examine the basic concepts, terms, and relationships of probability that are useful in solving many quantitative analysis problems. Table 2.1 lists some of the topics covered in this book that rely on probability theory. You can see that the study of quantitative analysis would be quite difficult without it.

2.2
FUNDAMENTAL CONCEPTS

There are two basic statements about the mathematics of probability.

KEY IDEA

1. The probability, P, of any event or state of nature occurring is greater than or equal to 0 and less than or equal to 1. That is,

TABLE 2.1 Chapters in This Book That Use Probability

CHAPTER	TITLE
2	Probability Concepts
3	Probability Distributions
4	Forecasting
5	Fundamentals of Decision Theory
6	Decision Trees and Utility Theory
7	Marginal Analysis and the Normal Distribution
9	Inventory Control Models: II
16	Waiting Lines: Queuing Theory
17	Simulation
18	Network Models
19	Markov Analysis
Module B	Game Theory

$$0 \leqslant P(\text{Event}) \leqslant 1 \qquad (2\text{-}1)$$

A probability of 0 indicates that an event is never expected to occur. A probability of 1 means an event is always expected to occur.

2. The sum of the simple probabilities for all possible outcomes of an activity must equal 1.

Both of these concepts are illustrated in Example 1.

Example 1: Two Laws of Probability

Demand for white latex paint at Diversey Paint and Supply has always been 0, 1, 2, 3, or 4 gallons per day. (There are no other possible outcomes and when one occurs, no other can.) Over the past 200 working days, the owner notes the following frequencies of demand.

QUANTITY DEMANDED (IN GALLONS)	NUMBER OF DAYS
0	40
1	80
2	50
3	20
4	10
Total	200

If this past distribution is a good indicator of future sales, we can find the probability of each possible outcome occurring in the future by converting the data into percentages of the total.

QUANTITY DEMANDED	PROBABILITY	
0	.20	$(= {}^{40}\!/_{200})$
1	.40	$(= {}^{80}\!/_{200})$
2	.25	$(= {}^{50}\!/_{200})$
3	.10	$(= {}^{20}\!/_{200})$
4	.05	$(= {}^{10}\!/_{200})$
Total	1.00	$(= {}^{200}\!/_{200})$

past data converted to probabilities

Thus the probability that sales are 2 gallons of paint on any given day is $P(2 \text{ gallons}) = .25 = 25\%$. The probability of any level of sales must be greater than or equal to 0 and less than or equal to 1. Since 0, 1, 2, 3, and 4 gallons exhaust all possible events or outcomes, the sum of their probability values must equal 1.

Types of Probability

There are two different ways to determine probability: the *objective approach* and the *subjective approach*.

objective probability:
relative frequency and
logical approaches

Objective Probability. Example 1 provided us with an illustration of objective probability assessment. The probability of any paint demand level was the *relative frequency* of occurrence of that demand in a large number of trial observations (200 days in this case). In general,

$$P(\text{Event}) = \frac{\text{Number of occurrences of the event}}{\text{Total number of trials or outcomes}}$$

Objective probability can also be set using what is called the *classical* or *logical method.* Without performing a series of trials, we can often logically determine what the probabilities of various events should be. For example, the probability of tossing a fair coin once and getting a head is:

$$P(\text{Head}) = \frac{1}{2} \quad \begin{array}{l} \text{— number of ways of getting a head} \\ \text{— number of possible outcomes (head or tail)} \end{array}$$

Likewise, the probability of drawing a spade out of a deck of 52 playing cards can be logically set as:

$$P(\text{Spade}) = \frac{13}{52} \quad \begin{array}{l} \text{— number of chances of drawing a spade} \\ \text{— number of total possible outcomes} \end{array}$$

$$= \frac{1}{4} = .25 = 25\%$$

subjective probability

Subjective Probability. When logic and past history are not appropriate, probability values can be assessed *subjectively.* The accuracy of subjective probabilities depends on the experience and judgment of the person making the estimates.

A number of probability values cannot be determined unless the subjective approach is used. What is the probability that the price of gasoline will be over four dollars in the next few years? What is the probability that our economy will be in a severe depression in 1998? What is the probability that you will be president of a major corporation within 20 years?

There are several methods for making subjective probability assessments. Opinion polls can be used to help in determining subjective probabilities for possible election returns and potential political candidates. In some cases, experience and judgment must be used in making subjective assessments of probability values. A production manager, for example, might believe that the probability of manufacturing a new product without a single defect is .85. In the Delphi method, a panel of experts is assembled to make their predictions of the future. This approach will be discussed in Chapter 4.

2.3
MUTUALLY EXCLUSIVE AND COLLECTIVELY EXHAUSTIVE EVENTS

KEY IDEA

Events are said to be *mutually exclusive* if only one of the events can occur on any one trial. They are called *collectively exhaustive* if the list of outcomes includes every possible outcome. Many common experiences involve events that have both of these properties. In tossing a coin, for example, the possible outcomes are a head or a tail. Since both of them cannot occur on any one toss, the outcomes head and tail are mutually exclusive. Since obtaining a head and a tail represent every possible outcome, they are also collectively exhaustive.

toss of a coin has
mutually exclusive and
collectively exhaustive
events

Example 2: Rolling a Die

Rolling a die is a simple experiment that has six possible outcomes, each listed in the following table with its corresponding probability.

OUTCOME OF ROLL	PROBABILITY
1	$\frac{1}{6}$
2	$\frac{1}{6}$
3	$\frac{1}{6}$
4	$\frac{1}{6}$
5	$\frac{1}{6}$
6	$\frac{1}{6}$
Total	1

These events are both mutually exclusive (on any roll, only one of the six events can occur) and are also collectively exhaustive (one of them must occur and hence they total in probability to 1).

Example 3: Drawing a Card

You are asked to draw one card from a deck of 52 playing cards. Using a logical probability assessment, it is easy to set some of the relationships such as:

$$P(\text{Drawing a 7}) = \frac{4}{52} = \frac{1}{13}$$

$$P(\text{Drawing a heart}) = \frac{13}{52} = \frac{1}{4}$$

We also see that these events (drawing a 7 and drawing a heart) are *not* mutually exclusive since a 7 of hearts can be drawn. They are also *not* collectively exhaustive since there are other cards in the deck besides 7s and hearts.

You can test your understanding of these concepts by going through the following cases.

DRAWS	MUTUALLY EXCLUSIVE?	COLLECTIVELY EXHAUSTIVE?
1. Draw a spade and a club	Yes	No
2. Draw a face card and a number card	Yes	Yes
3. Draw an ace and a 3	Yes	No
4. Draw a club and a nonclub	Yes	Yes
5. Draw a 5 and a diamond	No	No
6. Draw a red card and a diamond	No	No

Adding Mutually Exclusive Events

Often we are interested in whether one event *or* a second event will occur. When these two events are mutually exclusive, the law of addition is simply as follows:

law of addition for
mutually exclusive events

$$P(\text{Event } A \text{ or Event } B) = P(\text{Event } A) + P(\text{Event } B)$$

or more briefly,

$$P(A \text{ or } B) = P(A) + P(B) \tag{2-2}$$

For example, we just saw that the events drawing a spade or drawing a club out of a deck of cards are mutually exclusive. Since $P(\text{Spade}) = {}^{13}/_{52}$, and $P(\text{Club}) = {}^{13}/_{52}$, the probability of drawing either a spade or a club is:

$$
\begin{aligned}
P(\text{Spade or Club}) &= P(\text{Spade}) + P(\text{Club}) \\
&= {}^{13}/_{52} + {}^{13}/_{52} \\
&= {}^{26}/_{52} = {}^{1}/_{2} = .50 = 50\%
\end{aligned}
$$

The *Venn diagram* in Figure 2.1 depicts the probability of the occurrence of mutually exclusive events.

Law of Addition for Events That Are Not Mutually Exclusive

When two events are not mutually exclusive, Equation 2-2 must be modified to account for double counting. The correct equation reduces the probability by subtracting the chance of both events occurring together.

$$
\begin{aligned}
P(\text{Event } A \text{ or Event } B) = {} & P(\text{Event } A) + P(\text{Event } B) \\
& - P(\text{Event } A \text{ and Event } B \text{ both occurring})
\end{aligned}
$$

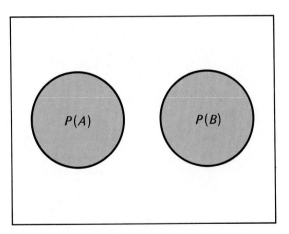

$$P(A \text{ or } B) = P(A) + P(B)$$

FIGURE 2.1
Addition Law for Events That Are Mutually Exclusive

This can be expressed in shorter form as:

$$P(A \text{ or } B) = P(A) + P(B) - P(A \text{ and } B) \qquad (2\text{-}3)$$

Figure 2.2 illustrates this concept of subtracting the probability of outcomes that are common to both events. When events are mutually exclusive, the area of overlap, called the *intersection,* is 0, as shown in Figure 2.1.

Let us consider the events drawing a 5 and drawing a diamond out of the card deck. These events are not mutually exclusive, so Equation 2-3 must be applied to compute the probability of either a 5 or a diamond being drawn.

$$
\begin{aligned}
P(\text{Five } or \text{ Diamond}) &= P(\text{Five}) + P(\text{Diamond}) - P(\text{Five } and \text{ Diamond}) \\
&= \tfrac{4}{52} + \tfrac{13}{52} - \tfrac{1}{52} \\
&= \tfrac{16}{52} = \tfrac{4}{13}
\end{aligned}
$$

2.4
STATISTICALLY INDEPENDENT EVENTS

Events may be either independent or dependent. When they are *independent,* the occurrence of one event has no effect on the probability of occurrence of the second event. Let us examine four sets of events and determine which are independent.

KEY IDEA

1. **(a)** Your education
   (b) Your income level ⎰ *Dependent events.* Can you explain why?

2. **(a)** Draw a jack of hearts from a full 52-card deck
   (b) Draw a jack of clubs from a full 52-card deck ⎱ *Independent events*

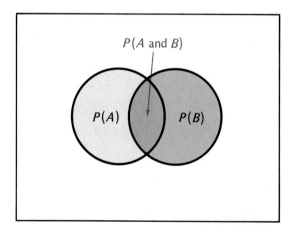

$$P(A \text{ or } B) = P(A) + P(B) - P(A \text{ and } B)$$

Venn diagram shows intersection of events *A* and *B*

FIGURE 2.2

Addition Law for Events That Are Not Mutually Exclusive

3. (a) Chicago Cubs win the
       National League pennant   } *Dependent Events*
   (b) Chicago Cubs win the World Series

4. (a) Snow in Santiago, Chile   } *Independent Events*
   (b) Rain in Tel Aviv, Israel

The three types of probability under both statistical independence and statistical dependence are (1) marginal, (2) joint, and (3) conditional. When events are independent, these three are very easy to compute, as we shall see.

marginal or simple probability

A *marginal* (or a *simple*) *probability* is just the probability of an event occurring. For example, if we toss a fair die, the marginal probability of a 2 landing face up is $P(\text{die is a 2}) = \frac{1}{6} = .166$. Because each separate toss is an independent event (that is, what we get on the first toss has absolutely no effect on any later tosses) the marginal probability for each possible outcome is $\frac{1}{6}$.

joint probability for independent events

The *joint* *probability* of two or more *independent* events occurring is the product of their marginal or simple probabilities. This may be written as:

$$P(AB) = P(A) \times P(B) \tag{2-4}$$

where

$P(AB) =$ joint probability of events A and B occurring together, or one after the other,

$P(A) =$ marginal probability of event A, and

$P(B) =$ marginal probability of event B.

The probability, for example, of tossing a 6 on the first roll of a die and a 2 on the second roll is:

$$P(\text{6 on first and 2 on second roll}) = P(\text{tossing a 6}) \times P(\text{tossing a 2})$$
$$= (\tfrac{1}{6}) \times (\tfrac{1}{6}) = \tfrac{1}{36}$$
$$= .028$$

conditional probability

The third type, *conditional probability*, is expressed as $P(B|A)$, or "the probability of event B, given that event A has occurred." Likewise, $P(A|B)$ would mean the conditional probability of event A, given that event B has taken place. Since when events are independent the occurrence of one *in no way* affects the outcome of another, $P(A|B) = P(A)$ and $P(B|A) = P(B)$.

Example 4: Probabilities When Events Are Independent

A bucket contains 3 black balls and 7 green balls. We draw a ball from the bucket, replace it, and draw a second ball. We can determine the probability of each of the following events occurring:

1. A black ball is drawn on the first draw.

$$P(B) = .30 \quad \textit{(This is a marginal probability.)}$$

2. Two green balls are drawn.

$$P(GG) = P(G) \times P(G) = (.7)(.7) = .49$$

(This is a joint probability for two independent events.)

3. A black ball is drawn on the second draw if the first draw is green.

$$P(B|G) = P(B) = .30 \quad \textit{(This is a conditional probability, but equal to the marginal because the two draws are independent events.)}$$

4. A green ball is drawn on the second draw if the first draw was green.

$$P(G|G) = P(G) = .70 \quad \textit{(This is a conditional probability as above.)}$$

2.5
STATISTICALLY DEPENDENT EVENTS

When events are statistically dependent, the occurrence of one event affects the probability of occurrence of some other event. Marginal, conditional, and joint probabilities exist under dependence as they did under independence, but the form of the latter two are changed.

one event affects the chance of another occurring

A *marginal probability* is computed exactly as it was for independent events. Again, the marginal probability of the event A occurring is denoted $P(A)$.

Calculating a *conditional probability* under dependence is somewhat more involved than it is under independence. The formula for the conditional probability of A, given that event B has taken place, is now stated as:

$$P(A|B) = \frac{P(AB)}{P(B)} \qquad (2\text{-}5)$$

KEY IDEA

The use of this important formula, often referred to as *Bayes's law* or *Bayes's theorem,* is best defined by an example.

Example 5: Probabilities When Events Are Dependent

Assume we have an urn containing 10 balls of the following descriptions:

> 4 are white (W) and lettered (L)
> 2 are white (W) and numbered (N)
> 3 are yellow (Y) and lettered (L)
> 1 is yellow (Y) and numbered (N)

You randomly draw a ball from the urn and see that it is yellow. What then, we may ask, is the probability that the ball is lettered? (See Figure 2.3.)

Since there are 10 balls, it is a simple matter to tabulate a series of useful probabilities.

$$P(WL) = {}^4\!/_{10} = .4 \qquad P(YL) = {}^3\!/_{10} = .3$$

$$P(WN) = {}^2\!/_{10} = .2 \qquad P(YN) = {}^1\!/_{10} = .1$$

$$P(W) = {}^6\!/_{10} = .6, \text{ or } P(W) = P(WL) + P(WN) = .4 + .2 = .6$$

$$P(L) = {}^7\!/_{10} = .7, \text{ or } P(L) = P(WL) + P(YL) = .4 + .3 = .7$$

$$P(Y) = {}^4\!/_{10} = .4, \text{ or } P(Y) = P(YL) + P(YN) = .3 + .1 = .4$$

$$P(N) = {}^3\!/_{10} = .3, \text{ or } P(N) = P(WN) + P(YN) = .2 + .1 = .3$$

We may now apply Bayes's law to calculate the conditional probability that the ball drawn is lettered, given that it is yellow.

$$P(L|Y) = \frac{P(YL)}{P(Y)} = \frac{0.3}{0.4} = .75$$

This equation shows that we divided the probability of *yellow* and *lettered* balls (3 out of 10) by the probability of yellow balls (*4 out of 10*). There is a 0.75 probability that the yellow ball that you drew is lettered.

You may recall that the formula for a joint probability under statistical independence was simply $P(AB) = P(A) \times P(B)$. When events are *dependent*, however, the *joint probability* is derived from Bayes's conditional formula. Equation 2-6 reads as "the joint probability of events A and B occurring is equal to the conditional probability of event A, given that B occurred, multiplied by the probability of event B."

joint probability for dependent events

$$P(AB) = P(A|B) \times P(B) \tag{2-6}$$

We can use this formula to verify the joint probability that $P(YL) = 0.3$, which was obtained by inspection in Example 5, by multiplying $P(L|Y)$ times $P(Y)$.

$$P(YL) = P(L|Y) \times P(Y) = (.75)(.4) = .3$$

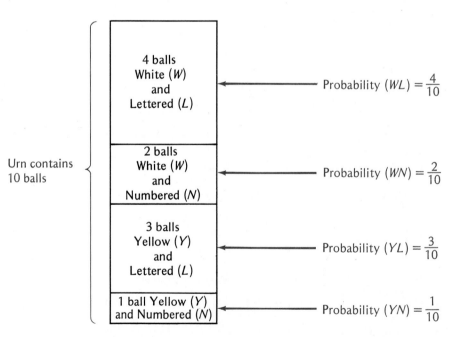

FIGURE 2.3
Example 5's Dependent Events

APPLICATIONS OF QA

Qantas Airways

Qantas Airways Limited, the Australian national airline, faced a major cost problem regarding the number of reserve crews needed for aircraft delays. When a plane was delayed, the working hours of the onboard cabin crew sometimes exceeded contract limits and a fresh (reserve) crew was called in as a replacement.

Prior to this study, which used *conditional probabilities,* setting the number of reserve crews was based on experience and guesswork. The objective of the quantitative analysis was to minimize the total costs of both the reserve crews and overnight delays. Since the study, management can estimate the expected number of aircraft overnight delays (and costs) for each of any number of reserve crews.

The probability study of Qantas cost only $3,000 (Australian dollars). The benefits were as follows (all figures are in Australian dollars):

Reduction of 27 cabin crews	$532,000
Training cost savings for 27 flight attendants	84,700
Opportunity cost for return on capital investment (at 10% annually)	61,760
	$678,460

In addition, resulting nonfinancial gains included reduction in reserve duties and management's acceptance of dealing with the risk of overnight delays.

Source: A. Gaballa, "Planning Callout Reserves for Aircraft Delays," *Interfaces,* Vol. 9, No. 2, Part 2, February 1979, pp. 78–86.

Example 6: Joint Probabilities When Events Are Dependent

Your stockbroker informs you that if the stock market reaches the 3,600 point level by January, there is a 70% probability that Tubeless Electronics will go up in value. Your own feeling is that there is only a 40% chance of the market average reaching 3,600 points by January.

Can you calculate the probability that *both* the stock market will reach 3,600 points *and* the price of Tubeless Electronics will go up?

Let M represent the event of the stock market reaching the 3,600 level, and let T be the event that Tubeless goes up in value. Then,

$$P(MT) = P(T|M) \times P(M) = (.70)(.40) = .28$$

Thus, there is only a 28% chance that *both* events will occur.

2.6
REVISING PROBABILITIES WITH BAYES'S THEOREM

Bayes's theorem can also be used to incorporate additional information as it is made available and help create *revised* or *posterior probabilities.* This means that we can take new or recent data, then revise and improve upon our old probability estimates for an event (see Figure 2.4). Let us consider the following example.

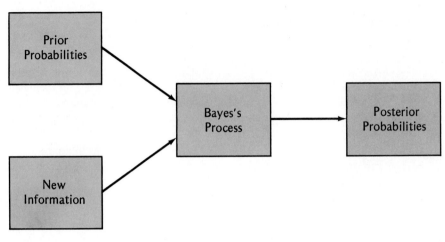

FIGURE 2.4
Using Bayes's Process

Example 7: Posterior Probabilities

A cup contains two dice identical in appearance. One, however, is fair (unbiased) and the other is loaded (biased). The probability of rolling a 3 on the fair die is $\frac{1}{6}$ or .166. The probability of tossing the same number on the loaded die is .60.

We have no idea which die is which, but select one by chance and toss it. The result is a 3. Given this additional piece of information, can we find the (revised) probability that the die rolled was fair? Can we determine the probability it was the loaded die that was rolled?

The answer to these questions is *yes*, and we do so by using the formula for joint probability under statistical dependence and Bayes's theorem.

First, we take stock of the information and probabilities available. We know, for example, that since we randomly selected the die to roll, the probability of it being fair or loaded is .50.

$$P(\text{Fair}) = .50 \qquad P(\text{Loaded}) = .50$$

computing posterior probabilities

We also know that

$$P(3|\text{Fair}) = .166 \qquad P(3|\text{Loaded}) = .60$$

Next, we compute joint probabilities $P(3 \text{ and Fair})$ and $P(3 \text{ and Loaded})$, using the formula $P(AB) = P(A|B) \times P(B)$.

$$P(3 \text{ and Fair}) = P(3|\text{Fair}) \times P(\text{Fair}) = (.166)(.50) = .083$$
$$P(3 \text{ and Loaded}) = P(3|\text{Loaded}) \times P(\text{Loaded}) = (.60)(.50) = .300$$

A 3 can occur in combination with the state "fair die" or in combination with the state "loaded die." The sum of their probabilities gives the unconditional or marginal probability of a 3 on the toss, namely, $P(3) = .083 + .300 = .383$.

If a 3 does occur, and if we do not know which die it came from, the probability that the die rolled was the fair one is:

$$P(\text{Fair}|3) = \frac{P(\text{Fair and } 3)}{P(3)} = \frac{.083}{.383} = .22$$

The probability that the die rolled was loaded is:

$$P(\text{Loaded}|3) = \frac{P(\text{Loaded and } 3)}{P(3)} = \frac{.300}{.383} = .78$$

These two conditional probabilities are called the revised or posterior probabilities for the next roll of the die.

Before the die was rolled in the preceding example, the best we could say was that there was a 50-50 chance that it was fair (.50 probability) and a 50-50 chance it was loaded. After one roll of the die, however, we are able to revise our *prior probability* estimates. The new posterior estimate is that there is a .78 probability that the die rolled was loaded and only a .22 probability that it was not.

revising prior probability by adding new information

A General Form of Bayes's Theorem

Revised probabilities can also be computed in a more direct way using a *general* form for Bayes's theorem. We originally saw in Equation 2-5 that Bayes's law for the conditional probability of event *A*, given event *B*, is:

$$P(A|B) = \frac{P(AB)}{P(B)}$$

However, in the appendix to this chapter we have gone through the mathematical steps to show that:

$$P(A|B) = \frac{P(B|A)P(A)}{P(B|A)P(A) + P(B|\overline{A})P(\overline{A})} \tag{2-7}$$

where

$\overline{A}$ = the complement of the event *A*; for example if *A* is the event "fair die," then $\overline{A}$ is "unfair" or "loaded die."

Now let's return to Example 7.

Although it may not be obvious to you at first glance, we used this basic equation to compute the revised probabilities. For example, if we want the probability that the fair die was rolled given the first toss was a 3, namely, *P*(Fair die|3 rolled), we can let:

Event "Fair die" replace *A* in Equation 2-7

Event "Loaded die" replace $\overline{A}$ in Equation 2-7

Event "3 rolled" replace *B* in Equation 2-7

We can then rewrite Equation 2-7 and solve as follows:

$$P(\text{Fair die}|3 \text{ rolled}) = \frac{P(3|\text{Fair})P(\text{Fair})}{P(3|\text{Fair})P(\text{Fair}) + P(3|\text{Loaded})P(\text{Loaded})}$$

$$= \frac{(.166)(.50)}{(.166)(.50) + (.60)(.50)}$$

$$= \frac{.083}{.383} = .22$$

This is the same answer we computed in Example 7. Can you use this alternative approach to show that P(Loaded die|3 rolled) = .78? Either method is perfectly acceptable, but when we deal with probability revisions again in Chapter 6, we may find that Equation 2-7 is easier to apply.

2.7
FURTHER PROBABILITY REVISIONS

Although one revision of prior probabilities can provide useful posterior probability estimates, additional information can be gained from performing the experiment a second time. If it is financially worthwhile, a decision maker may even decide to make several more revisions.

Example 8: A Second Probability Revision

Returning to Example 7 we now attempt to obtain further information about the posterior probabilities as to whether the die just rolled is fair or loaded. To do so, let us toss the die a second time. Again, we roll a 3. What are the further revised probabilities?

To answer this question, we proceed as before, with only one exception. The probabilities P(Fair) = .50 and P(Loaded) = .50 remain the same, but now we must compute $P(3,3|$Fair$)$ = (.166)(.166) = .027 and $P(3,3|$Loaded$)$ = (.6)(.6) = .36. With these joint probabilities of two 3s on successive rolls, given the two types of dice, we may revise the probabilities.

$$P(3,3 \text{ and Fair}) = P(3,3|\text{Fair}) \times P(\text{Fair}) = (.027)(.5) = .013$$

$$P(3,3 \text{ and Loaded}) = P(3,3|\text{Loaded}) \times P(\text{Loaded}) = (.36)(.5) = .18$$

Thus, the probability of rolling two 3s, a marginal probability, is .013 + .18 = .193, the sum of the two joint probabilities.

$$P(\text{Fair}|3,3) = \frac{P(3,3 \text{ and Fair})}{P(3,3)} = \frac{.013}{.193} = .067$$

$$P(\text{Loaded}|3,3) = \frac{P(3,3 \text{ and Loaded})}{P(3,3)} = \frac{.18}{.193} = .933$$

What has this second roll accomplished? Before we rolled the die the first time, we knew only that there was a .50 probability that it was either fair or loaded. When the first die was rolled in Example 7, we were able to revise these probabilities to be:

Probability the die is fair = .22

Probability the die is loaded = .78

Now, after the second roll in Example 8, our refined revisions tell us that:

new posterior probabilities

Probability the die is fair = .067

Probability the die is loaded = .933

This type of information can be extremely valuable in business decision making.

2.8
SUMMARY

This chapter presented the fundamental concepts of probability. Probability values can be obtained objectively or subjectively. A single probability value must be between 0 and 1, and the sum of all probability values for all possible outcomes must sum to 1. In addition, probability values and events can have a number of properties. These properties include mutually exclusive, collectively exhaustive, statistically independent, and statistically dependent events. Rules for computing probability values depend on these fundamental properties. It is also possible to revise probability values when new information becomes available. This can be done using Bayes's theorem.

The topics presented in this chapter and Chapter 3 will be very important in many of the chapters to come. Basic probability concepts and distributions are used for decision theory, inventory control, Markov analysis, program evaluation and review technique, and simulation.

GLOSSARY

Probability. A statement about the likelihood of an event occurring. It is expressed as a numerical value between 0 and 1, inclusive.

Relative Frequency Approach. An objective way of determining probabilities based on observing frequencies over a number of trials.

Classical or Logical Approach. An objective way of assessing probabilities based on logic.

Subjective Approach. A method of determining probability values based on experience or judgment.

Mutually Exclusive Events. A situation in which only one event can occur on any given trial or experiment.

Collectively Exhaustive Events. A collection of all possible outcomes of an experiment.

Marginal Probability. The simple probability of an event occurring.

Joint Probability. The probability of events occurring together (or one after the other).

Conditional Probability. The probability of one event occurring given that another has taken place.

Independent Events. The situation in which the occurrence of one event has no effect on the probability of occurrence of a second event.

Dependent Events. The situation in which the occurrence of one event affects the probability of occurrence of some other event.

Revised or Posterior Probability. A probability value that results from new or revised information and prior probabilities.

Prior Probability. A probability value determined before new or additional information is obtained. It is sometimes called an *a priori* probability estimate.

Bayes's Theorem. A formula that allows us to compute conditional probabilities when dealing with statistically dependent events.

KEY EQUATIONS

(2-1) $0 \leq P(\text{Event}) \leq 1$
A basic statement of probability.

(2-2) $P(A \text{ or } B) = P(A) + P(B)$
Law of addition for mutually exclusive events.

(2-3) $P(A \text{ or } B) = P(A) + P(B) - P(A \text{ and } B)$
Law of addition for events that are *not* mutually exclusive.

(2-4) $P(AB) = P(A) \times P(B)$
Joint probability for independent events.

(2-5) $P(A|B) = \dfrac{P(AB)}{P(B)}$
Bayes's law for conditional probabilities.

(2-6) $P(AB) = P(A|B) \times P(B)$
Joint probability for dependent events: a restatement of Bayes's law.

(2-7) $P(A|B) = \dfrac{P(B|A)P(A)}{P(B|A)P(A) + P(B|\bar{A})P(\bar{A})}$
A restatement of Bayes's law in general form.

DISCUSSION QUESTIONS AND PROBLEMS

Discussion Questions

2-1 What are the two basic laws of probability?

2-2 What is the meaning of mutually exclusive events; what is meant by collectively exhaustive? Given an example of each.

2-3 Describe the different approaches used in determining probability values.

2-4 Why is the probability of the intersection of two events subtracted in the sum of the probability of two events?

2-5 What is the difference between events that are dependent and events that are independent?

2-6 What is Bayes's theorem and when can it be used?

2-7 How can probability revisions assist in managerial decision making?

Problems

· **2-8** A student taking Management Science 301 at East Haven University will receive one of five possible grades for the course: A, B, C, D, or F. The distribution of grades over the past two years is as follows:

GRADE	NUMBER OF STUDENTS
A	80
B	75
C	90
D	30
F	25
Total	300

If this past distribution is a good indicator of future grades, what is the probability of a student receiving a C in the course?

· **2-9** A silver dollar is flipped twice. Calculate the probability of each of the following occurring.
  (a) A head on the first flip.
  (b) A tail on the second flip given that the first toss was a head.
  (c) Two tails.
  (d) A tail on the first and a head on the second.
  (e) A tail on the first and a head on the second *or* a head on the first and a tail on the second.
  (f) At least one head on the two flips.

· **2-10** An urn contains 8 red chips, 10 green chips, and 2 white chips. A chip is drawn and replaced, and then a second chip drawn. What is the probability of:
  (a) A white chip on the first draw?
  (b) A white chip on the first draw and a red on the second?
  (c) Two green chips being drawn?
  (d) A red chip on the second, given that a white chip was drawn on the first?

· **2-11** Evertight, a leading manufacturer of quality nails, produces 1-, 2-, 3-, 4-, and 5-inch nails for various uses. In the production process, if there is an overrun or if the nails are slightly defective, they are placed in a common bin. Yesterday, 651 of the 1-inch nails, 243 of the 2-inch nails, 41 of the 3-inch nails, 451 of the 4-inch nails, and 333 of the 5-inch nails were placed in the bin.
  (a) What is the probability of reaching into the bin and getting a 4-inch nail?
  (b) What is the probability of getting a 5-inch nail?
  (c) If a particular application requires a nail that is 3 inches or shorter, what is the probability of getting a nail that will satisfy the requirements of the application?

: **2-12** Last year, at Northern Manufacturing Company, 200 people had colds during the year. One hundred fifty-five people who did no exercising had colds, while the remainder of the people with colds were involved in a weekly exercise program. Half of the one thousand employees were involved in some type of exercise.
  (a) What is the probability that an employee will have a cold next year?
  (b) Given that an employee is involved in an exercise program, what is the probability that he or she will get a cold?
  (c) What is the probability that an employee that is not involved in an exercise program will get a cold next year?
  (d) Are exercising and getting a cold independent events? Explain your answer.

: **2-13** The Springfield Kings, a professional basketball team, has won 12 out of its last 20 games and is expected to continue winning at the same percentage rate. The team's ticket manager is anxious to attract a large crowd to tomorrow's game, but believes that depends on how well the Kings perform tonight against the Galveston Comets. He assesses the probability of drawing a large crowd to be .90, should the team win tonight. What is the probability that the team wins tonight and that there will be a large crowd at tomorrow's game?

: **2-14** Professor David Mashley teaches two undergraduate statistics courses at Kansas College. The class for Statistics 201 consists of 7 sophomores and 3 juniors. The more advanced course, Statistics 301, has 2 sophomores and 8 juniors enrolled. As an example of a business sampling technique, Professor Mashley randomly selects, from the stack of Statistics 201 registration cards, the class card of one student and then places that card back in the stack. If that student was a sophomore, Mashley draws another card from the Statistics 201 stack; if not, he randomly draws a card from the Statistics 301 group. Are these two draws independent events?
What is the probability of:
(a) A junior's name on the first draw?
(b) A junior's name on the second draw, given that a sophomore's name was drawn first?
(c) A junior's name on the second draw, given that a junior's name was drawn first?
(d) A sophomore's name on both draws?
(e) A junior's name on both draws?
(f) One sophomore's name and one junior's name on the two draws, regardless of order drawn?

: **2-15** The oasis outpost of Abu Ilan, in the heart of the Negev desert, has a population of 20 Bedouin tribesmen and 20 Farima tribesmen. El Kamin, a nearby oasis, has a population of 32 Bedouins and 8 Farima.

A lost Israeli soldier, accidentally separated from his army unit, is wandering through the desert and arrives at the edge of one of the oases. The soldier has no idea which oasis he has found, but the first person he spots at a distance is a Bedouin. What is the probability that he wandered into Abu Ilan? What is the probability that he is in El Kamin?

: **2-16** The lost Israeli soldier mentioned in Problem 2-15 decides to rest for a few minutes before entering the desert oasis he has just found. (He reasons that he may need his strength should the oasis tribesmen be hostile.) Closing his eyes, he dozes off for 15 minutes, wakes, and walks toward the center of the oasis. The first person he spots this time he again recognizes as a Bedouin. What is the posterior probability that he is in El Kamin?

: **2-17** Ace Machine Works estimates that the probability their lathe tool is properly adjusted is .8. When the lathe is properly adjusted, there is a .9 probability that the parts produced pass inspection. If the lathe is out of adjustment, however, the probability of a good part being produced is only .2. A part randomly chosen is inspected and found to be acceptable. At this point, what is the posterior probability that the lathe tool is properly adjusted?

: **2-18** The Boston South Fifth Street Softball League consists of three teams: Mama's Boys, team 1; The Killers, team 2; and The Machos, team 3. Each team plays the other teams just once during the season. The win-loss record for the past five years is below:

WINNERS	(1)	(2)	(3)
Mama's Boys (1)	X	3	4
The Killers (2)	2	X	1
The Machos (3)	1	4	X

Each row represents the number of wins over the past five years. Mama's Boys beat The Killers 3 times, and beat The Machos 4 times, and so on.
(a) What is the probability that The Killers will win every game next year?
(b) What is the probability that The Machos will win at least one game next year?
(c) What is the probability that Mama's Boys will win exactly one game next year?
(d) What is the probability that The Killers will win less than two games next year?

: **2-19** The schedule for The Killers next year is as follows (refer to Problem 2-18):

Game 1   The Machos
Game 2   Mama's Boys

(a) What is the probability that The Killers will win their first game?
(b) What is the probability that The Killers will win their last game?
(c) What is the probability that The Killers will break even—win exactly one game?
(d) What is the probability that The Killers will win every game?
(e) What is the probability that The Killers will lose every game?
(f) Would you want to be the coach of The Killers?

: **2-20** The Northside Rifle team has two markspersons, Dick and Sally. Dick hits a bull's-eye 90% of the time, and Sally hits a bull's-eye 95% of the time.
(a) What is the probability that either Dick or Sally or both will hit the bull's-eye if each takes one shot?
(b) What is the probability that Dick and Sally will both hit the bull's-eye?
(c) Did you make any assumptions in answering the preceding questions? If you answered yes, do you think that you are justified in making the assumption(s)?

: **2-21** In a sample of 1,000 representing a survey from the entire population, 650 people were from Laketown, and the rest of the people were from River City. Out of the sample, 19 people had some form of cancer. Thirteen of these people were from Laketown.
(a) Are the events of living in Laketown and having some sort of cancer independent?
(b) Which city would you prefer to live in, assuming your main objective was to avoid having cancer?

: **2-22** Compute the probability of "loaded die, given that a 3 was rolled," as shown in Example 7, this time using the general form of Bayes's theorem from Equation 2-7.

BIBLIOGRAPHY

Campbell, S. *Flaws and Fallacies in Statistical Thinking*. Englewood Cliffs, N.J.: Prentice-Hall, Inc., 1974.

Feller, W. *An Introduction to Probability Theory and Its Applications* Vols. 1 and 2, New York: John Wiley & Sons, Inc., 1957 and 1968.

Hamburg, Morris. *Statistical Analysis for Decision Making*, 4th ed. San Diego: Harcourt Brace Jovanovich, 1987.

Huff, D. *How to Lie with Statistics*. New York: W. W. Norton & Company, Inc., 1954.

Lapin, Lawrence L. *Statistics for Modern Business Decision*, 4 ed. San Diego: Harcourt Brace Jovanovich, 1987.

McClave, James T., and Bensen, P. George. *Statistics for Business and Economics*, 3rd ed. San Francisco: Dellon Publishing, 1985.

APPENDIX
DERIVATION OF BAYES'S THEOREM

Derivation of Bayes's Theorem in the General Form

We know that the following three formulas are correct:

$$P(A|B) = \frac{P(AB)}{P(B)} \tag{1}$$

$$P(B|A) = \frac{P(AB)}{P(A)}$$

which can be rewritten as $P(AB) = P(B|A)P(A)$ (2)

$$P(B|\overline{A}) = \frac{P(\overline{A}B)}{P(\overline{A})}$$

which can be rewritten as $P(\overline{A}B) = P(B|\overline{A})P(\overline{A})$ (3)

Furthermore, by definition, we note that:

$$\begin{aligned} P(B) &= P(AB) + P(\overline{A}B) \\ &= P(B|A)P(A) + P(B|\overline{A})P(\overline{A}) \end{aligned} \tag{4}$$

$\underset{\text{from (2)}}{} \qquad \underset{\text{from (3)}}{}$

Substituting Equations 2 and 4 into Equation 1, we have

$$\begin{aligned} P(A|B) &= \frac{P(AB)}{P(B)} \qquad \text{from (2)} \\ &= \frac{P(B|A)P(A)}{P(B|A)P(A) + P(B|\overline{A})P(\overline{A})} \end{aligned} \tag{5}$$

from (4)

This is the general form of Bayes's theorem shown as Equation 2-7 in this chapter.

3

Probability Distributions

CHAPTER OUTLINE

3.1
INTRODUCTION

The purpose of this chapter is to bridge the gap between the fundamentals of probability covered in the last chapter and the use of probability in future chapters. For example, in the next several chapters we will need to determine the expected value of a probability distribution to help select the best decision among a number of alternatives. In other chapters, we will need to compute the standard deviation and variance of a probability distribution. An understanding of probability distributions and their use is a prerequisite for about half of the chapters in this book.

The objective of this chapter is to cover the following topics:

1. Random variables.

2. Types of probability distributions.

3. Binomial and Poisson distributions.

4. Normal and exponential distributions.

3.2
RANDOM VARIABLES

In Chapter 2 we discussed various ways of assigning probability values to the outcomes of an experiment. In this chapter, we use this probability information to compute the expected outcome, variance, and standard deviation of the experiment.

outcome numbers can be the random variable

A *random variable* assigns a real number to every possible outcome or event in an experiment. It is normally represented by a letter such as X or Y. When the outcome itself is numerical or quantitative, the outcome numbers can be the random variable. For example, consider refrigerator sales at an appliance store. The number of refrigerators sold during a given day can be the random variable. Using X to represent this random variable, we can express this relationship as follows:

$$X = \text{number of refrigerators sold during the day}$$

In general, whenever the experiment has quantifiable outcomes, it is beneficial to define these quantitative outcomes as the random variable. Examples are given in Table 3.1.

When the outcome itself is not numerical or quantitative, it is necessary to define a random variable that associates each outcome with a unique real number. Several examples are given in Table 3.2.

types of random variables

There are two types of random variables: *discrete random variables* and *continuous random variables*. Developing probability distributions and making computations based on these distributions depends on the type of random variable.

A random variable is a *discrete random variable* if it can assume only a finite or limited set of values. Which of the random variables in Table 3.1

TABLE 3.1 Examples of Random Variables

EXPERIMENT	OUTCOME	RANDOM VARIABLES	RANGE OF RANDOM VARIABLES
Stock 50 Christmas trees	Number of Christmas trees sold	X = number of Christmas trees sold	0, 1, 2, . . . ,50
Inspect 600 items	Number of acceptable items	Y = number of acceptable items	0, 1, 2, . . . ,600
Send out 5,000 sales letters	Number of people responding to the letters	Z = number of people responding to the letters	0, 1, 2, . . . ,5,000
Build an apartment building	Percent of building completed after 4 months	R = percent of building completed after 4 months	$0 \leqslant R \leqslant 100$
Test the lifetime of a light bulb (minutes)	Length of time the bulb lasts up to 80,000 minutes	S = time the bulb burns	$0 \leqslant S \leqslant 80,000$

are discrete random variables? Looking at Table 3.1, we can see that stocking 50 Christmas trees, inspecting 600 items, and sending out 5,000 letters are all examples of discrete random variables. Each of these random variables can only assume a finite or limited set of values. The number of Christmas trees sold, for example, can only be integer numbers from 0 to 50. There are 51 values that the random variable X can assume in this example.

A *continuous random variable* is a random variable that has an infinite or an unlimited set of values. Are there any examples of continuous random variables in Table 3.1 or Table 3.2? Looking at Table 3.1, we can see that testing the lifetime of a light bulb is an experiment that can be described

← KEY IDEA

TABLE 3.2 Random Variables for Outcomes That Are Not Numbers

EXPERIMENT	OUTCOMES	RANDOM VARIABLES	RANGE OF RANDOM VARIABLES
Students respond to a questionnaire	Strongly agree (SA) Agree (A) Neutral (N) Disagree (D) Strongly disagree (SD)	$X = \begin{cases} 5 \text{ if SA} \\ 4 \text{ if A} \\ 3 \text{ if N} \\ 2 \text{ if D} \\ 1 \text{ if SD} \end{cases}$	1, 2, 3, 4, 5
One machine is inspected	Defective Not defective	$Y = \begin{cases} 0 \text{ if defective} \\ 1 \text{ if not defective} \end{cases}$	0, 1
Consumers respond to how they like a product	Good Average Poor	$Z = \begin{cases} 3 \text{ if good} \\ 2 \text{ if average} \\ 1 \text{ if poor} \end{cases}$	1, 2, 3

with a continuous random variable. In this case, the random variable, S, is the time the bulb burns. It can last for 3,206 minutes, 6,500.7 minutes, 251.726 minutes, or any other value between 0 and 80,000 minutes. In most cases, the range of continuous random variable is stated as: Lower value $\leq S \leq$ Upper value, such as $0 \leq S \leq 80,000$. The random variable R in Table 3.1 is also continuous. Can you explain why?

3.3
PROBABILITY DISTRIBUTIONS

In the last chapter, we discussed probability values of an event. In this chapter, we explore the properties of *probability distributions*. We see how popular distributions, such as the uniform, normal, Poisson, binomial, and exponential probability distributions can save us time and effort. Since selection of the appropriate probability distribution depends partially on whether or not the random variable is *discrete* or *continuous*, we consider each of these types separately.

Probability Distribution of a Discrete Random Variable

When we have a *discrete random variable*, there is a probability value assigned to each event. These values must be between 0 and 1, and they must sum to 1. Let's look at an example.

The 100 students in Dr. Pat Shannon's statistics class have just completed the instructor evaluations at the end of the course. Dr. Shannon is particularly interested in student response to the textbook because he is in the process of writing a competing statistics book. One of the questions on the evaluation survey was:

"The textbook was well written and helped me acquire the necessary information."

5. Strongly Agree

4. Agree

3. Neutral

2. Disagree

1. Strongly Disagree

assigning a random variable

characteristics of all probability distributions

The students' response to this question in the survey is summarized in Table 3.3. Also shown is the random variable X and the corresponding probability for each possible outcome. This discrete probability distribution was computed using the relative frequency approach presented in Chapter 2.

The distribution follows the three rules required of all probability distributions: (1) the events are mutually exclusive and collectively exhaustive, (2) the individual probability values are between 0 and 1 inclusive, and (3) the total of the probability values sum to 1.

TABLE 3.3 Probability Distribution for Textbook Question

OUTCOME	RANDOM VARIABLE (X)	NUMBER RESPONDING	PROBABILITY $P(X)$
Strongly agree	5	10	$.1 = {}^{10}\!/_{100}$
Agree	4	20	$.2 = {}^{20}\!/_{100}$
Neutral	3	30	$.3 = {}^{30}\!/_{100}$
Disagree	2	30	$.3 = {}^{30}\!/_{100}$
Strongly disagree	1	10	$.1 = {}^{10}\!/_{100}$
		Total 100	$1.0 = {}^{100}\!/_{100}$

While listing the probability distribution as we did in Table 3.3 is adequate, it can be difficult to get an idea about the characteristics of the distribution. To overcome this problem, the probability values are often presented in a graph form. The graph of the distribution in Table 3.3 is shown in Figure 3.1.

The graph of this probability distribution gives us a picture of its shape. It helps us identify the central tendency of the distribution, called the *expected value*, and the amount of variability or spread of the distribution, called the *variance*.

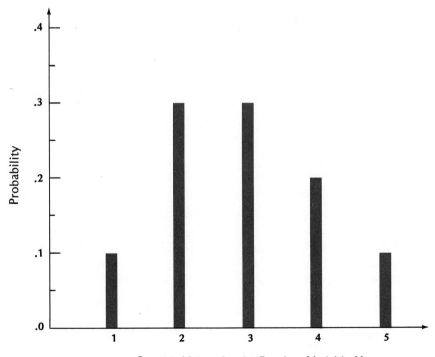

Possible Values for the Random Variable X

FIGURE 3.1
Probability Function for Dr. Shannon's Class

Expected Value of a Discrete Probability Distribution

central tendency or the average

Once we have established a probability distribution, the first characteristic that is usually of interest is the "central tendency," or average of the distribution. The expected value, a measure of central tendency, is computed as a weighted average of the values of the random variable:

$$E(X) = \sum_{i=1}^{n} X_i P(X_i) = X_1 P(X_1) + X_2 P(X_2) + \cdots + X_n P(X_n) \tag{3-1}$$

where

X_i = the random variable's possible values,

$P(X_i)$ = the probability of each of the random variable's possible values,

$\sum_{i=1}^{n}$ = the summation sign indicating we are adding all n possible values, and

$E(X)$ = the expected value of the random variable.

$E(X)$ for Shannon's class

The expected value of any discrete probability distribution can be computed by multiplying each possible value of the random variable, X_i, times the probability, $P(X_i)$, that outcome will occur, and summing the results, Σ. Here is how the expected value can be computed for the textbook question:

$$E(X) = \sum_{i=1}^{5} X_i P(X_i) = X_1 P(X_1) + X_2 P(X_2) + X_3 P(X_3) + X_4 P(X_4) + X_5 P(X_5)$$

$$= (5)(.1) + (4)(.2) + (3)(.3) + (2)(.3) + (1)(.1)$$

$$= 2.9$$

The expected value of 2.9 implies that the mean response is between Disagree (2) and Neutral (3), and that the average response is closer to Neutral, which is 3. Looking at Figure 3.1, this is consistent with the shape of the probability function.

Variance of a Discrete Probability Distribution

In addition to the central tendency of a probability distribution, most people are interested in the variability or the spread of the distribution. If the variability is low, it is much more likely that the outcome of an experiment will be close to the average or expected value. On the other hand, if the variability of the distribution is high, which means that the probability is spread out over the various random variable values, then there is less chance that the outcome of an experiment will be close to the expected value.

The *variance* of a probability distribution is a number that reveals the overall spread or dispersion of the distribution. For a discrete probability distribution, it can be computed using the following equation:

$$\text{Variance} = \sum_{i=1}^{n} (X_i - E(X))^2 P(X_i) \tag{3-2}$$

where

X_i = the random variable's possible values,

$E(X)$ = the expected value of the random variable,

$(X_i - E(X))$ = the difference between each value of the random variable and the expected value, and

$P(X_i)$ = probability of each possible value of the random variable.

To compute the variance, each value of the random variable is subtracted from the expected value, squared, and multiplied times the probability of occurrence of that value. The results are then summed to obtain the variance. Here is how this procedure is done for Dr. Shannon's textbook question:

computing variance for Shannon's class

$$\text{Variance} = \sum_{i=1}^{5} (X_i - E(X))^2 P(X_i)$$

$$\text{Variance} = (5 - 2.9)^2(.1) + (4 - 2.9)^2(.2) + (3 - 2.9)^2(.3)$$
$$+ (2 - 2.9)^2(.3) + (1 - 2.9)^2(.1)$$
$$= (2.1)^2(.1) + (1.1)^2(.2) + (.1)^2(.3) + (-.9)^2(.3) + (-1.9)^2(.1)$$
$$= .441 + .242 + .003 + .243 + .361$$
$$= 1.29$$

standard deviation

A related measure of dispersion or spread is the *standard deviation*. This quantity is also used in many computations involved with probability distributions. The standard deviation is just the square root of the variance.

$$\sigma = \sqrt{\text{Variance}} \qquad (3\text{-}3)$$

where

$$\sqrt{} = \text{square root, and}$$

$$\sigma = \text{standard deviation.}$$

The standard deviation for the textbook question is:

$$\sigma = \sqrt{\text{Variance}}$$
$$= \sqrt{1.29} = 1.14$$

Probability Distribution of a Continuous Random Variable

There are many examples of *continuous random variables*. The time it takes to finish a project, the number of ounces in a barrel of butter, the high temperature during a given day, the exact length of a given type of lumber, and the weight of a railroad car of coal are all examples of continuous random variables. Since random variables can take on an infinite number of values, the fundamental probability rules for continuous random variables must be modified.

As with discrete probability distributions, the sum of the probability values must equal 1. Because there are an infinite number of values of the random variables, however, the probability of each value of the random

probability rules for continuous distributions

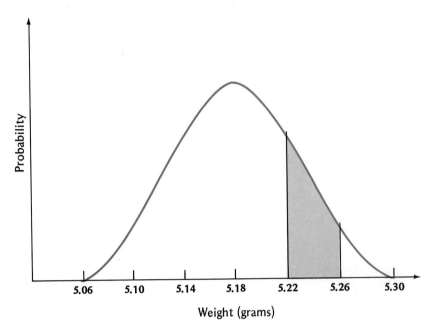

FIGURE 3.2
Sample Density Function

variable must be 0. If the probability values for the random variable values were greater than 0, then the sum would be infinitely large.

With a continuous probability distribution, there is a continuous mathematical function that describes the probability distribution. This function is called the *probability density function* or simply the *probability function*. It is usually represented by $f(X)$.

We now look at the sketch of a sample density function in Figure 3.2. This curve represents the probability density function for the weight of a particular machined part. The weight could vary from 5.06 to 5.30 grams, with weights around 5.18 grams being the most likely. The shaded area represents the probability the weight is between 5.22 and 5.26 grams.

If we wanted to know the probability of a part weighing exactly 5.1300000 grams, for example, we would have to compute the area of a slice of width 0. Of course, this would be 0. This result may seem strange, but if we insist on enough decimal places of accuracy, we are bound to find that the weight differs from 5.1300000 grams *exactly*, be the difference ever so slight.

Uniform Distributions

uniform distribution

The *uniform probability density function* is used to describe a continuous probability distribution that has a range of continuous values from point a to point b, inclusive. It is described by the following equation:

$$f(X) = \begin{cases} \dfrac{1}{b-a} & \text{for } a \leq X \leq b \\[2mm] 0 & \text{otherwise} \end{cases}$$

(3-4)

probability density function

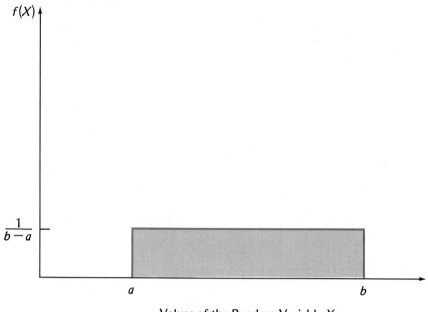

FIGURE 3.3
Uniform Probability Density Function

This distribution assumes that there is an equally likely chance that any point along this range will occur. Thus, the probability looks like a box, as in Figure 3.3.

In order to find the probability that a value will fall within a range or interval inside of a and b, we locate the range and find the area between the range and the top of the probability distribution. Since the area is always a rectangle, this is done by multiplying the base of the rectangle which is the range or interval, times the height, which is always $1/(b - a)$. Let's look at an example.

A project manager would like to determine the probability that a project will be between 70% and 80% complete in six months. At the present time, the project is 50% complete, and the manager believes that project completion follows a uniform probability density function that ranges from 50% complete, which is the current state, to 100% complete. Figure 3.4 graphically represents this situation.

In order to get the desired probability, we need to find the shaded area— a rectangle that represents the probability that the project will be between 70% and 80% complete at the end of six months. This area is computed as follows:

$$\text{Probability} = (\text{base}) \cdot (\text{height})$$
$$= (80 - 70)\left(\frac{1}{100 - 50}\right)$$
$$= (10)\left(\frac{1}{50}\right) = 0.20$$

area as a measure of probability

a uniform distribution example

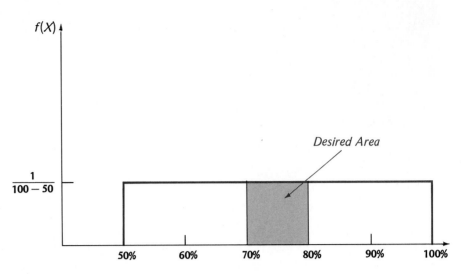

FIGURE 3.4
Uniform Distribution for a Project Manager

the use of calculus

Finding the area under the curve for a uniform probability density function is fairly easy because the area is always a rectangle. Other continuous probability density functions are not so simple, and finding the area under the curve, the expected value, and the variance may require the use of calculus. Fortunately, the work for some of the popular continuous distributions has already been done for us in tables, as we will see shortly.

In this section, we have investigated the fundamental characteristics and properties of probability distributions in general. In the next four sections, we will introduce two important discrete probability distributions—the binomial distribution and the Poisson distribution—and two useful continuous distributions—the normal distribution and the exponential distribution.

3.4
THE BINOMIAL DISTRIBUTION

Many business experiments can be characterized by the *Bernoulli process*, which follows the *binomial probability distribution*. In order to be a Bernoulli process, an experiment must have the following characteristics:

characteristics of Bernoulli process

1. Each trial in a Bernoulli process has only two possible outcomes—either yes or no, success or failure, heads or tails, pass or fail, and so on.

2. Regardless of how many times the experiment is performed, the probability of the outcome stays the same.

3. The trials are statistically independent.

4. The number of trials is known and is either 1, 2, 3, 4, 5, and so on.

To analyze a Bernoulli process, we need to know the values of: (1) the probability of success on a single trial, p, and the probability of a failure on a single trial, q (which equals $1 - p$); (2) the number of successes desired, r; and (3) the number of trials performed, n.

A common example of a Bernoulli process is flipping a coin. If we wish to compute the probability of getting exactly 4 heads on 5 tosses of a fair coin, the Bernoulli process parameters are:

p = probability of heads = .5

q = probability of tails (nonheads) = $1 - p$ = .5

r = number of successes desired = 4

n = number of trials performed = 5

There are two ways of solving these Bernoulli problems to find the desired probabilities. The first is to apply the formula, called the *binomial probability formula*, given in Equation 3-5.

binomial formula

$$\text{Probability of } r \text{ successes in } n \text{ trials} = \frac{n!}{r!(n - r)!} p^r q^{n-r} \qquad \text{(3-5)}$$

The symbol ! means *factorial*. To compute 5!, for example, we just multiply $5 \times 4 \times 3 \times 2 \times 1 = 120$. Likewise, $4! = 4 \times 3 \times 2 \times 1 = 24$, $1! = 1$, and $0! = 1$.

Although Equation 3-5 works well in small problems, it can become cumbersome when large values of n and r are inserted. The second method is to make use of *binomial distribution tables*. Both approaches are illustrated in the following sections.

Solving Problems with the Binomial Formula

Using the binomial probability formula, we can solve for the probability of getting exactly four heads in five tosses of a coin.

formula approach to solving binomial problems

$$p = .5 \qquad q = .5 \qquad r = 4 \qquad n = 5$$

$$\begin{aligned}\text{Probability of } r \text{ successes in } n \text{ trials} &= \frac{n!}{r!(n - r)!} p^r q^{n-r} = \frac{5!}{4!(5 - 4)!}(.5)^4(.5)^1 \\ &= \frac{5 \times 4 \times 3 \times 2 \times 1}{(4 \times 3 \times 2 \times 1)(1)}(.5)^4(.5)^1\end{aligned}$$

or

$$\text{Probability} = \frac{120}{(24)(1)}(.0625)(.5) = .15625$$

Thus, the probability that 4 tosses out of 5 will land heads up is .15625 or 16 percent.

Using Equation 3-5, it is also possible to determine the entire probability distribution for a binomial experiment. The probability distribution of flipping a fair coin 5 times is shown in Table 3.4 and then graphed in Figure 3.5.

TABLE 3.4. Binomial Probability Distribution

(NUMBER OF HEADS) (r)	PROBABILITY $= \dfrac{5!}{r!(5-r)!}(.5)^r(.5)^{5-r}$
0	$.03125 = \dfrac{5!}{0!(5-0)!}(.5)^0(.5)^{5-0}$
1	$.15625 = \dfrac{5!}{1!(5-1)!}(.5)^1(.5)^{5-1}$
2	$.3125 = \dfrac{5!}{2!(5-2)!}(.5)^2(.5)^{5-2}$
3	$.3125 = \dfrac{5!}{3!(5-3)!}(.5)^3(.5)^{5-3}$
4	$.15625 = \dfrac{5!}{4!(5-4)!}(.5)^4(.5)^{5-4}$
5	$.03125 = \dfrac{5!}{5!(5-5)!}(.5)^5(.5)^{5-5}$

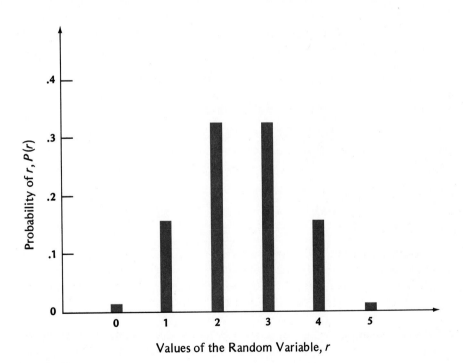

FIGURE 3.5
Binomial Probability Distribution When $n = 5$,
$p = 0.50$

Solving Problems with Binomial Tables

MSA Electronics is experimenting with the manufacture of a new type of transistor that is very difficult to mass-produce at an acceptable quality level. Every hour a supervisor takes a random sample of 6 transistors produced on the assembly line. The probability that any one transistor is defective is considered to be .13. MSA wants to know the probability of finding 4 or more defects in the lot sampled.

The elements in this problem would be:

$$p = .13 \qquad r = 4 \text{ defects} \qquad n = 6 \text{ trials}$$

The question posed may be easily answered by using a *cumulative* binomial distribution table. Such tables can be very lengthy. For the sake of brevity, we present in Table 3.5 only that portion of a binomial table corresponding to $n = 6$. Appendix C contains a complete binomial table for a broad range of n, r, and p values.

Since the probability of MSA finding any one defect is .13, we look through the $n = 6$ table until we find the column where $p = .13$. We then move down that column until we are opposite the $r = 4$ row. The answer there is found to be 0034, which is interpreted to be a probability of .0034 that there are 4 or more defects in the sample. This value has been shaded in Table 3.5.

There is an easy way to compute the expected value and variance of the binomial distribution. The appropriate equations are:

expected value and variance

$$\text{Expected value} = np \qquad\qquad\qquad \textbf{(3-6)}$$

$$\text{Variance} = np(1 - p) \qquad\qquad \textbf{(3-7)}$$

The expected value and variance for MSA Electronics can be computed as follows:

$$\text{Expected value} = np$$
$$= (6)(.13) = .78$$
$$\text{Variance} = np(1 - p)$$
$$= (6)(.13)(1 - .13) = .6786$$

3.5
THE POISSON DISTRIBUTION

Our second important discrete probability distribution is the *Poisson distribution*.[1] We examine it because of its key role in queuing theory, the topic of Chapter 16. The distribution describes situations in which customers arrive independently during a certain time interval, and the number of arrivals depends on the length of the time interval. Examples are patients arriving at a health clinic, customers arriving at a bank window, passengers arriving at an airport, and telephone calls going through a central exchange.

---

[1] This distribution, derived by Simeon Poisson in 1837, is pronounced ''pwah-sahn.''

The formula for the Poisson distribution is:

$$P(X) = \frac{\lambda^x e^{-\lambda}}{X!} \tag{3-8}$$

TABLE 3.5. A Sample Table for the Cumulative Binomial Distribution

$P(R \geq r | n, p)$

$n = 6$

P / R	01	02	03	04	05	06	07	08	09	10
1	0585	1142	1670	2172	2649	3101	3530	3936	4321	4686
2	0015	0057	0125	0216	0328	0459	0608	0773	0952	1143
3		0002	0005	0012	0022	0038	0058	0085	0118	0159
4					0001	0002	0003	0005	0008	0013
5										0001

P / R	11	12	13	14	15	16	17	18	19	20
1	5030	5356	5664	5954	6229	6487	6731	6960	7176	7397
2	1345	1556	1776	2003	2235	2472	2713	2956	3201	3446
3	0206	0261	0324	0395	0473	0560	0655	0759	0870	0989
4	0018	0025	0034	0045	0059	0075	0094	0116	0141	0170
5	0001	0001	0002	0003	0004	0005	0007	0010	0013	0016
6										0001

P / R	21	22	23	24	25	26	27	28	29	30
1	7569	7748	7916	8073	8220	8358	8487	8607	8719	8824
2	3692	3937	4180	4422	4661	4896	5128	5356	5580	5798
3	1115	1250	1391	1539	1694	1856	2023	2196	2374	2557
4	0202	0239	0280	0326	0376	0431	0492	0557	0628	0705
5	0020	0025	0031	0038	0046	0056	0067	0079	0093	0109
6	0001	0001	0001	0002	0002	0003	0004	0005	0006	0007

P / R	31	32	33	34	35	36	37	38	39	40
1	8921	9011	9095	9173	9246	9313	9375	9432	9485	9533
2	6012	6220	6422	6619	6809	6994	7172	7343	7508	7667
3	2744	2936	3130	3328	3529	3732	3937	4143	4350	4557
4	0787	0875	0969	1069	1174	1286	1404	1527	1657	1792
5	0127	0148	0170	0195	0223	0254	0288	0325	0365	0410
6	0009	0011	0013	0015	0018	0022	0026	0030	0035	0041

P / R	41	42	43	44	45	46	47	48	49	50
1	9578	9619	9657	9692	9723	9752	9778	9802	9824	9844
2	7819	7965	8105	8238	8364	8485	8599	8707	8810	8906
3	4764	4971	5177	5382	5585	5786	5985	6180	6373	6563
4	1933	2080	2232	2390	2553	2721	2893	3070	3252	3438
5	0458	0510	0566	0627	0692	0762	0837	0917	1003	1094
6	0048	0055	0063	0073	0083	0095	0108	0122	0138	0156

Source: Reprinted from Robert O. Schlaifer, *Introduction to Statistics for Business Decisions,* published by McGraw-Hill Book Company, 1961, by permission of the copyright holder, the President and Fellows of Harvard College.

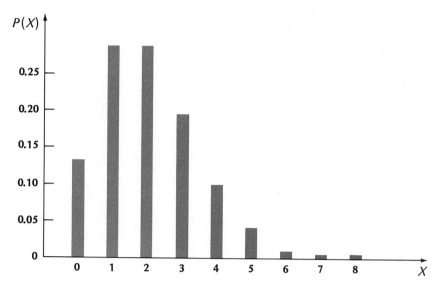

FIGURE 3.6
Sample Poisson Distribution with λ = 2

where

P(X) = the probability of exactly X arrivals or occurrences,

λ = the average number of arrivals per unit of time (the mean arrival rate), pronounced "lambda,"

e = 2.718, the base of the natural logarithms, and

X = the specific value (0, 1, 2, 3, and so on) of the random variable.

The mean and variance of the Poisson distribution are equal and are simply computed as:

$$\text{Expected value} = \lambda \qquad (3\text{-}9)$$

$$\text{Variance} = \lambda \qquad (3\text{-}10)$$

A sample distribution for λ = 2 arrivals is shown in Figure 3.6 (the values plotted are derived from tables in Appendix D). Further examples and details are discussed in Chapter 16.

3.6
THE NORMAL DISTRIBUTION

One of the most popular and useful continuous probability distributions is the *normal distribution*. The probability density function of this distribution is given by the rather complex formula:

$$f(X) = \frac{1}{\sigma\sqrt{2\pi}} e^{\frac{-\frac{1}{2}(X - \mu)^2}{\sigma^2}} \qquad (3\text{-}11)$$

The normal distribution is completely specified when values for the mean, μ, and the standard deviation, σ, are known. Figure 3.7 shows several

mean and standard deviation

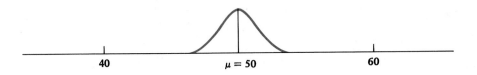

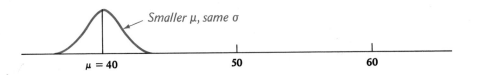

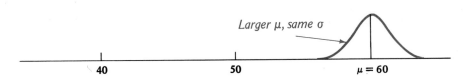

FIGURE 3.7
Normal Distribution with Different Values for μ

different normal distributions with the same standard deviation and different means.

changes in the mean

As shown in Figure 3.7, differing values of μ will shift the average or center of the normal distribution. The overall shape of the distribution remains the same. On the other hand, when the standard deviation is varied, the normal curve either flattens out or becomes steeper. This is shown in Figure 3.8.

changes in the standard deviation

As the standard deviation, σ, becomes smaller, the normal distribution becomes steeper. When the standard deviation becomes larger, the normal distribution has a tendency to flatten out or become broader.

The Area under the Normal Curve

Because the normal distribution is symmetrical, its midpoint (and highest point) is at the mean. Values on the X axis are then measured in terms of how many standard deviations they lie from the mean.

As you may recall from our earlier discussion of the uniform distribution, the area under the curve (in a continuous distribution) describes the probability that a random variable has a value in a specified interval. When dealing with the uniform distribution, it was easy to compute the area

commonly used relationships

between any points *a* and *b*. The normal distribution requires mathematical calculations beyond the scope of this text, but tables that provide areas or probabilities are readily available. For example, Figure 3.9 illustrates three commonly used relationships that have been derived from standard normal

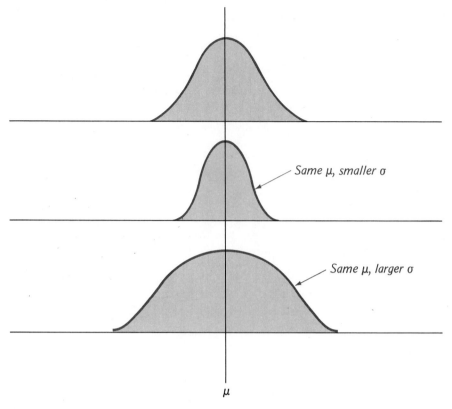

FIGURE 3.8
Normal Distribution with Different Values for σ

tables (to be discussed shortly). The area from point *a* to point *b* in the first drawing represents the probability, 68%, that the random variable will be within 1 standard deviation of the mean. In the middle graph, we see that about 95.4% of the area lies within plus or minus 2 standard deviations of the mean. The third figure shows that 99.7% lies between ± 3σ.

Translating Figure 3.9 into an application implies that if the mean I.Q. in the United States is μ = 100 points, and if the standard deviation is σ = 15 points, we can make the following statements:

1. 68% of the population have I.Q.s between 85 and 115 points (namely, ±1σ).

2. 95.4% of the people have I.Q.s between 70 and 130 points (±2σ).

3. 99.7% of the population have I.Q.s in the range from 55 to 145 points (±3σ).

4. Only 16% of the people have I.Q.s greater than 115 points (from first graph, the area to the right of +1σ).

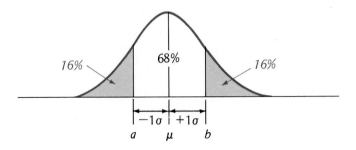

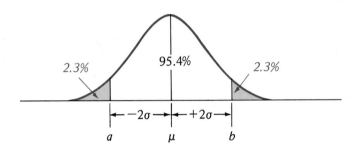

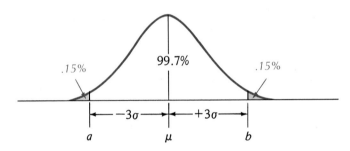

FIGURE 3.9
Three Common Areas under Normal Curves

Many more interesting remarks could likewise be drawn from these data. Can you tell the probability a person selected at random has an I.Q. less than 70? Greater than 145? Less than 145?

Using the Standard Normal Table

To use a table to find normal probability values, we follow two steps.

use of the standard normal distribution

  Step 1: Convert the normal distribution to what we call a *standard normal distribution*. A standard normal distribution is one that has a mean of 0 and a standard deviation of 1. All normal tables are set up to handle random variables with $\mu = 0$ and $\sigma = 1$. Without a standard normal distribution, a different table would be needed for each pair of μ and σ values. We call

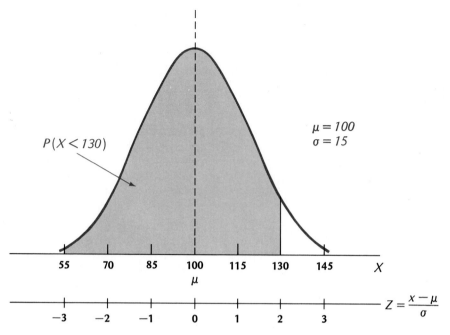

FIGURE 3.10
Normal Distribution Showing the Relationship
Between Z Values and X Values

the new standard random variable Z. The value for Z for any normal distribution is computed from this equation:

$$Z = \frac{X - \mu}{\sigma} \qquad (3\text{-}12)$$

where

X = the value of the random variable we want to measure,

μ = the mean of the distribution,

σ = the standard deviation of the distribution, and

Z = the number of standard deviations from X to the mean, μ.

For example, if $\mu = 100$, $\sigma = 15$, and we are interested in finding the probability that the random variable X is less than 130, then we want $P(X < 130)$.

$$Z = \frac{X - \mu}{\sigma} = \frac{130 - 100}{15} = \frac{30}{15} = 2 \text{ standard deviations}$$

This means that the point X is 2.0 standard deviations to the right of the mean. This is shown in Figure 3.10.

Step 2: Look up the probability from a table of normal curve areas. Table 3.6, which also appears as Appendix A, is such a table of areas for the standard normal distribution. It is set up to provide the area under the curve to the left of any specified value of Z.

use of normal curves

TABLE 3.6. The Standardized Normal Distribution Function

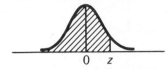

Z					Area: Under the Normal Curve					
	00	.01	.02	.03	.04	.05	.06	.07	.08	.09
0.0	.50000	.50399	.50798	.51197	.51595	.51994	.52392	.52790	.53188	.53586
0.1	.53983	.54380	.54776	.55172	.55567	.55962	.56356	.56749	.57142	.57535
0.2	.57926	.58317	.58706	.59095	.59483	.59871	.60257	.60642	.61026	.61409
0.3	.61791	.62172	.62552	.62930	.63307	.63683	.64058	.64431	.64803	.65173
0.4	.65542	.65910	.66276	.66640	.67003	.67364	.67724	.68082	.68439	.68793
0.5	.69146	.69497	.69847	.70194	.70540	.70884	.71226	.71566	.71904	.72240
0.6	.72575	.72907	.73237	.73536	.73891	.74215	.74537	.74857	.75175	.75490
0.7	.75804	.76115	.76424	.76730	.77035	.77337	.77637	.77935	.78230	.78524
0.8	.78814	.79103	.79389	.79673	.79955	.80234	.80511	.80785	.81057	.81327
0.9	.81594	.81859	.82121	.82381	.82639	.82894	.83147	.83398	.83646	.83891
1.0	.84134	.84375	.84614	.84849	.85083	.85314	.85543	.85769	.85993	.86214
1.1	.86433	.86650	.86864	.87076	.87286	.87493	.87698	.87900	.88100	.88298
1.2	.88493	.88686	.88877	.89065	.89251	.89435	.89617	.89796	.89973	.90147
1.3	.90320	.90490	.90658	.90824	.90988	.91149	.91309	.91466	.91621	.91774
1.4	.91924	.92073	.92220	.92364	.92507	.92647	.92785	.92922	.93056	.93189
1.5	.93319	.93448	.93574	.93699	.93822	.93943	.94062	.94179	.94295	.94408
1.6	.94520	.94630	.94738	.94845	.94950	.95053	.95154	.95254	.95352	.95449
1.7	.95543	.95637	.95728	.95818	.95907	.95994	.96080	.96164	.96246	.96327
1.8	.96407	.96485	.96562	.96638	.96712	.96784	.96856	.96926	.96995	.97062
1.9	.97128	.97193	.97257	.97320	.97381	.97441	.97500	.97558	.97615	.97670
2.0	.97725	.97784	.97831	.97882	.97932	.97982	.98030	.98077	.98124	.98169
2.1	.98214	.98257	.98300	.98341	.98382	.98422	.98461	.98500	.98537	.98574
2.2	.98610	.98645	.98679	.98713	.98745	.98778	.98809	.98840	.98870	.98899
2.3	.98928	.98956	.98983	.99010	.99036	.99061	.99086	.99111	.99134	.99158
2.4	.99180	.99202	.99224	.99245	.99266	.99286	.99305	.99324	.99343	.99361
2.5	.99379	.99396	.99413	.99430	.99446	.99461	.99477	.99492	.99506	.99520
2.6	.99534	.99547	.99560	.99573	.99585	.99598	.99609	.99621	.99632	.99643
2.7	.99653	.99664	.99674	.99683	.99693	.99702	.99711	.99720	.99728	.99736
2.8	.99744	.99752	.99760	.99767	.99774	.99781	.99788	.99795	.99801	.99807
2.9	.99813	.99819	.99825	.99831	.99836	.99841	.99846	.99851	.99856	.99861
3.0	.99865	.99869	.99874	.99878	.99882	.99886	.99899	.99893	.99896	.99900
3.1	.99903	.99906	.99910	.99913	.99916	.99918	.99921	.99924	.99926	.99929
3.2	.99931	.99934	.99936	.99938	.99940	.99942	.99944	.99946	.99948	.99950
3.3	.99952	.99953	.99955	.99957	.99958	.99960	.99961	.99962	.99964	.99965
3.4	.99966	.99968	.99969	.99970	.99971	.99972	.99973	.99974	.99975	.99976
3.5	.99977	.99978	.99978	.99979	.99980	.99981	.99981	.99982	.99983	.99983
3.6	.99984	.99985	.99985	.99986	.99986	.99987	.99987	.99988	.99988	.99989
3.7	.99989	.99990	.99990	.99990	.99991	.99991	.99992	.99992	.99992	.99992
3.8	.99993	.99993	.99993	.99994	.99994	.99994	.99994	.99995	.99995	.99995
3.9	.99995	.99995	.99996	.99996	.99996	.99996	.99996	.99996	.99997	.99997

Source: From *Quantitative Approaches to Management,* Fourth Edition, by Richard I. Levin and Charles A. Kirkpatrick. Copyright © 1978, 1975, 1971, 1965 by McGraw-Hill, Inc. Used with the permission of McGraw-Hill Book Company.

Let's see how Table 3.6 can be used. The column on the left lists values of Z, with the second decimal place of Z appearing in the top row. For example, for a value of $Z = 2.00$ as just computed, find 2.0 in the left-hand column and .00 in the top row. In the body of the table, we find that the area sought is .97725, or 97.7%. Thus,

$$P(X < 130) = P(Z < 2.00) = 97.7\%$$

This suggests that if the mean I.Q. score is 100 with a standard deviation of 15 points, the probability that a randomly selected person's I.Q. is less than 130 is 97.7%. By referring back to Figure 3.9, we see that this probability could also have been derived from the middle graph. (Note that $1.0 - .977 = .023 = 2.3\%$, which is the area in the right-hand tail of the curve.)

To feel comfortable with the use of the standard normal probability table, we need to work a few more examples. We now use the Haynes Construction Company as a case in point.

Haynes Construction Company Example

Haynes Construction Company builds primarily three- and four-unit apartment buildings (called triplexes and quadraplexes) for investors, and it is believed that the total construction time in days follows a normal distribution. The mean time to construct a triplex is 100 days, and the standard deviation is 20 days. Recently, the president of Haynes Construction signed a contract to complete a triplex in 125 days. Failure to complete the triplex in 125 days would result in severe penalty fees. What is the probability that Haynes Construction will not be in violation of their construction contract? The normal distribution for the construction of triplexes is shown in Figure 3.11.

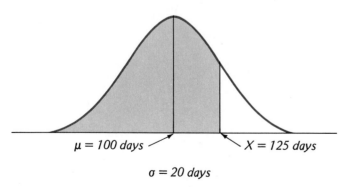

$\mu = 100\ days$ $X = 125\ days$

$\sigma = 20\ days$

FIGURE 3.11
Normal Distribution for Haynes Construction

In order to compute this probability, we need to find the shaded area under the curve. We begin by computing Z for this problem:

$$Z = \frac{X - \mu}{\sigma}$$

$$= \frac{125 - 100}{20}$$

$$= \frac{25}{20} = 1.25$$

Looking in Table 3.6 for a Z value of 1.25, we find an area under the curve of .89435. (We do this by looking up 1.2 in the left-hand column of the table, and then moving to the .05 column to find the values for Z = 1.25.) Therefore, the probability of not violating the contract is .89435, or about an 89% chance.

Now let us look at the Haynes problem from another perspective. If the firm finishes this triplex in 75 days or less, it will be awarded a bonus payment of $5,000. What is the probability Haynes will receive the bonus?

Figure 3.12 illustrates the probability we are looking for in the shaded area. The first step is again to compute the Z value:

$$Z = \frac{X - \mu}{\sigma} = \frac{75 - 100}{20} = \frac{-25}{20} - -1.25$$

This Z value indicates that 75 days is −1.25 standard deviations to the left of the mean. But the standard normal table is structured to handle only positive Z values. To solve this problem, we observe that the curve is symmetric. The probability Haynes will finish in *less than 75 days is equivalent* to the probability it will finish in *more than 125 days*. A moment ago (in Figure 3.11), we found the probability Haynes will finish in less than 125 days. That value was .89435. So the probability it takes more than 125 days is:

$$P(X > 125) = 1.0 - P(X < 125) = 1.0 - .89435 = .10565$$

Thus, the probability of completing the triplex in 75 days is .10565, or about 10%.

One final example: What is the probability the triplex will take between 110 and 125 days? We see in Figure 3.13 that:

$$P(110 < X < 125) = P(X < 125) - P(X < 110)$$

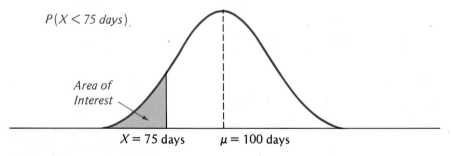

FIGURE 3.12
Probability Haynes Will Receive the Bonus by Finishing in 75 Days

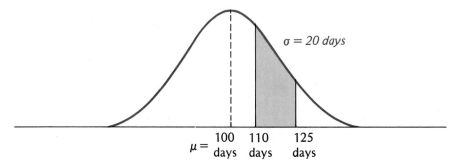

FIGURE 3.13
Probability of Haynes' Completion between 110 and 125 Days

That is, the shaded area in the graph can be computed by finding the probability of completing the building in 125 days or less *minus* the probability of completing it in 110 days or less.

Recall that $P(X < 125$ days$)$ is equal to .89435. To find $P(X < 110$ days$)$, we follow the two steps developed earlier.

1. $Z = \dfrac{X - \mu}{\sigma} = \dfrac{110 - 100}{20} = \dfrac{10}{20} = .50$ standard deviations

2. From Table 3.6, the area for $Z = .50$ is .69146. So the probability the triplex can be completed in less than 110 days is .69146. Finally,

$$P(110 < X < 125) = .89435 - .69146 = .20289$$

The probability that it will take between 110 and 125 days is about 20%.

3.7
THE EXPONENTIAL DISTRIBUTION

The *exponential distribution*, also called the *negative exponential distribution*, is used along with the Poisson distribution in dealing with queuing problems. While the discrete Poisson distribution describes the number of arrivals in a time interval, the exponential distribution describes the service times. The exponential distribution is a continuous distribution. Its probability function is given by:

$$f(X) = \mu e^{-\mu x} \qquad (3\text{-}13)$$

exponential distribution and queuing theory

where

> X = random variable (service times),
>
> μ = average number of units the service facility can handle in a specific period of time
>
> e = 2.718 (the base of natural logarithms).

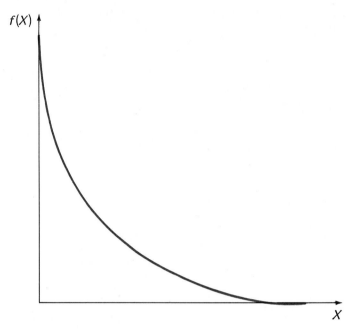

FIGURE 3.14
Negative Exponential Distribution

The general shape of the exponential distribution is shown in Figure 3.14. Its expected value and variance can be shown to be:

$$\text{Expected value} = \frac{1}{\mu} \qquad \text{(3-14)}$$

$$\text{Variance} = \frac{1}{\mu^2} \qquad \text{(3-15)}$$

The exponential distribution will be illustrated again in Chapter 16.

3.8
SUMMARY

The purpose of this chapter is to bridge the gap between probability theory and the application of probability distributions in future chapters. In this chapter, we covered the topics of random variables, discrete probability distributions (such as binomial and Poisson), and continuous probability distributions (such as uniform, normal, and exponential).

A probability distribution is any statement of a probability function having a set of collectively exhaustive and mutually exclusive events. All probability distributions follow the probability rules discussed in Chapter 2, namely, that any probability value must be between 0 and 1 and that the sum of the probability values for the events in the probability distribution must sum to 1.

The normal distribution is the most popular and widely used *continuous* probability distribution. Three other chapters will involve normal distribution applications: decision theory (Chapter 7), inventory (Chapter 9), and PERT (Chapter 18).

GLOSSARY

Random Variable. A variable that assigns a number to every possible outcome of an experiment.

Discrete Random Variable. A random variable that can only assume a finite or limited set of values.

Continuous Random Variable. A random variable that can assume an infinite or unlimited set of values.

Probability Distribution. The set of all possible values of a random variable and their associated probabilities.

Discrete Probability Distribution. A probability distribution with a discrete random variable.

Continuous Probability Distribution. A probability distribution with a continuous random variable.

Expected Value. The (weighted) average of a probability distribution.

Variance. A measure of dispersion or spread of the probability distribution.

Standard Deviation. The square root of the variance.

Probability Density Function. The mathematical function that describes a continuous probability distribution. It is represented by $f(X)$.

Uniform Probability Distribution. A continuous probability function that has a uniform or a flat probability density function.

Binomial Distribution. The distribution of a discrete random variable that describes the number of successes in independent trials.

Poisson Distribution. A discrete probability distribution used in queuing theory.

Normal Distribution. A continuous bell-shaped distribution that is a function of two parameters, the mean and standard deviation of the distribution.

Negative Exponential Distribution. A continuous probability distribution that describes the time between customer arrivals in a queuing situation.

KEY EQUATIONS

(3-1) $\quad E(X) = \sum_{i=1}^{n} X_i P(X_i)$

This equation computes the expected value of a discrete probability distribution.

(3-2) $\quad \text{Variance} = \sum_{i=1}^{n} (X_i - E(X))^2 P(X_i)$

This equation computes the variance of a discrete probability distribution.

(3-3) $\quad \sigma = \sqrt{\text{Variance}}$

This equation computes the standard deviation from the variance.

(3-4) $f(X) = \begin{cases} \dfrac{1}{b-a} & \text{for } a \leqslant X \leqslant b \\ 0 & \text{otherwise} \end{cases}$

This is the density function of the uniform probability distribution.

(3-5) $\text{Probability} = \dfrac{n!}{r!(n-r)!} p^r q^{n-r}$

This is the binomial probability distribution.

(3-6) $\text{Expected value} = np$

This equation computes the expected value of the binomial probability distribution.

(3-7) $\text{Variance} = np(1-p)$

This equation computes the variance of the binomial probability distribution.

(3-8) $P(X) = \dfrac{\lambda^x e^{-\lambda}}{X!}$

The Poisson distribution.

(3-9) $\text{Expected value} = \lambda$

The mean of a Poisson distribution.

(3-10) $\text{Variance} = \lambda$

The variance of a Poisson distribution.

(3-11) $f(X) = \dfrac{1}{\sigma\sqrt{2\pi}} e^{\dfrac{-\frac{1}{2}(X-\mu)^2}{\sigma^2}}$

This is the density function for the normal probability distribution.

(3-12) $Z = \dfrac{X-\mu}{\sigma}$

This equation computes the number of standard deviations, Z, the point X is from the mean μ.

(3-13) $f(X) = \mu e^{-\mu X}$

The exponential distribution.

(3-14) $\text{Expected value} = \dfrac{1}{\mu}$

The expected value of an exponential distribution.

(3-15) $\text{Variance} = \dfrac{1}{\mu^2}$

The variance of an exponential distribution.

DISCUSSION QUESTIONS AND PROBLEMS

Discussion Questions

3-1 What is a random variable? What are the different types of random variables?

3-2 What is the difference between a discrete probability distribution and a continuous probability distribution? Give your own example of each.

3-3 What is the expected value, and what does it measure? How is it computed for a discrete probability distribution?

3-4 What is the variance, and what does it measure? How is it computed for a discrete probability distribution?

3-5 What is the Bernoulli process? What probability distribution describes the Bernoulli process, and what conditions must be satisfied before this distribution can be used?

3-6 What type of distribution is the binomial distribution? What type of distribution is the normal distribution?

3-7 Name three business processes that can be described by the normal distribution.

3-8 After evaluating student response to a question about a case used in class, the instructor constructed the following probability distribution. What kind of probability distribution is it?

Response	Random Variable, X	Probability
Excellent	5	.05
Good	4	.25
Average	3	.40
Fair	2	.15
Poor	1	.15

Problems

· **3-9** Which of the following are probability distributions? Why?

(a)

Random Variable X	Probability
−2	.1
−1	.2
0	.3
1	.25
2	.15

(b)

Random Variable Y	Probability
1	1.1
1.5	.2
2	.3
2.5	.25
3	− 1.25

(c)

Random Variable Z	Probability
1	.1
2	.2
3	.3
4	.4
5	.0

· **3-10.** Harrington Health Food stocks 5 loaves of Neutro-Bread. The probability distribution for the sales of Neutro-Bread is listed in the following table. How many loaves will Harrington sell on the average?

Number of Loaves Sold	Probability
0	.05
1	.15
2	.2
3	.25
4	.20
5	.15

· **3-11** What is the expected value and variance of the following probability distribution?

Random Variable, X	Probability
1	.05
2	.05
3	.10
4	.10
5	.15
6	.15
7	.25
8	.15

· **3-12** This year, Jan Rich, who is ranked number one in women's singles in tennis, and Marie Wacker, who is ranked number three, will play 4 times. If Marie can beat Jan 3 times, she will be ranked number one. The two players have played 20 times before, and Jan has won 15 games. It is expected that this pattern will continue in the future. What is the probability that Marie will be ranked number one after this year? What is the probability that Marie will win all 4 games this year against Jan?

: 3-13 It was stated in this chapter that the probability values for any probability distribution must sum to 1. Prove that this is the case for the uniform probability distribution.

· 3-14 Over the last two months, the Wilmington Phantoms have been encountering trouble with one of their star basketball players. During the last 30 games, he has fouled out 15 times. The owner of the basketball team has stated that if this player fouls out 2 times in their next 5 games, the player will be fined $200. What is the probability that the player will be fined? What is the probability that the player will foul out of all 5 games? What is the probability that the player will not foul out of any of the next 5 games?

· 3-15 Best of the Sea Tuna processes and packages tuna in a plant located in the state of Washington. Their most popular size is the 12-ounce can. In the past, the processing equipment has placed anywhere from 11 to 15 ounces of tuna in a can. The president of Best of the Sea Tuna believes that this process follows a uniform distribution. What is the probability that a can will contain from 11.5 to 12.5 ounces of tuna? What is the probability that a can will contain exactly 12 ounces of tuna?

· 3-16 Sales for Fast Kat, a 16-foot catamaran sailboat, have averaged 250 boats per month over the last five years with a standard deviation of 25 boats. Assuming that the demand is about the same as past years and follows a normal curve, what is the probability sales will be less than 280 boats?

: 3-17 Refer to Problem 3-16. What is the probability that sales will be over 265 boats during the next month? What is the probability that sales will be under 250 boats next month?

· 3-18 Precision Parts is a job shop that specializes in producing electric motor shafts. The average shaft size for the E300 electric motor is 0.55 inches, with a standard deviation of 0.10 inches. It is normally distributed. What is the probability that a shaft selected at random will be between 0.55 and 0.65 inches?

: 3-19 Refer to Problem 3-18. What is the probability that a shaft size will be greater than 0.65 inches? What is the probability that a shaft size will be between 0.53 and 0.59 inches? What is the probability that a shaft size will be under 0.45 inches?

: 3-20 An industrial oven used to cure sand cores for a factory manufacturing engine blocks for small cars is able to maintain fairly constant temperatures. The temperature range of the oven follows a normal distribution with a mean of 450°F and a standard deviation of 25°F. Leslie Larsen, president of the factory, is concerned about the large number of defective cores that have been produced in the last several months. If the oven gets hotter than 475°F, the core is defective. What is the probability that the oven will cause a core to be defective? What is the probability that the temperature of the oven will range from 460 to 470°F?

· 3-21 Wisconsin Cheese Processor, Inc., produces equipment that processes cheese products. Ken Newgren is particularly concerned about a new cheese processor that has been producing defective cheese crocks. The piece of equipment produces 5 cheese crocks during every cycle of the equipment.

The probability that any one of the cheese crocks is defective is .2. Ken would like to determine the probability distribution of defective cheese crocks from this new piece of equipment. There can be 0, 1, 2, 3, 4, or 5 defective cheese crocks for any cycle of the equipment.

: **3-22** Refer to Problem 3-21.
  (a) Determine the expected value and variance of the distribution described in Problem 3-21, using Equations 3-1 and 3-2.
  (b) Determine the expected value and variance of the distribution described in Problem 3-21, using Equations 3-6 and 3-7.
  (c) Compare your answers in (a) and (b) above. Will these equations always be consistent for this type of distribution?

: **3-23** Natway, a national distribution company of home vacuum cleaners, recommends that its salespersons make only two calls per day, one in the morning and one in the afternoon. Twenty-five percent of the time a sales call will result in a sale, and the profit from each sale is $125.
  (a) Develop the probability distribution for sales during a five-day week.
  (b) Determine the mean and variance of this distribution.
  (c) What is the expected weekly profit for a salesperson?

· **3-24** The weight in ounces of cans of pears follows a uniform distribution. The range has been from 9.6 to 13.2 ounces.
  (a) What is the probability that the weight will be between 10 and 11 ounces?
  (b) What is the probability that the weight will be between 9.6 and 9.8 ounces?
  (c) What is the expected value of this distribution?

: **3-25** Steve Goodman, production foreman for the Florida Gold Fruit Company, estimates that the average sale of oranges is 4,700 and the standard deviation is 500 oranges. Sales follow a normal distribution.
  (a) What is the probability that sales will be greater than 5,500 oranges?
  (b) What is the probability that sales will be greater than 4,500 oranges?
  (c) What is the probability that sales will be less than 4,900 oranges?
  (d) What is the probability that sales will be less than 4,300 oranges?

: **3-26** Susan Williams has been the production manager of Medical Suppliers, Inc., for the past 17 years. Medical Suppliers, Inc., is a producer of bandages and arm slings. During the past 5 years, the demand for No-Stick bandages has been fairly constant. On the average, sales have been about 87,000 packages of No-Stick. Susan has reason to believe that the distribution of No-Stick follows a normal curve, with a standard deviation of 4,000 packages. What is the probability that sales will be less than 81,000 packages?

: **3-27** Armstrong Faber produces a standard number two pencil called Ultra-Lite. Since Chuck Armstrong started Armstrong Faber, sales have grown steadily. With the increase in the price of wood products, however, Chuck has been forced to increase the price of the Ultra-Lite pencils. As a result, the demand for Ultra-Lite has been fairly stable over the past six years. On the average, Armstrong Faber has sold 457,000 pencils each year. Furthermore, 90% of the time sales have been between 460,000 and 454,000 pencils. It is expected that the sales follow a normal distribution with a mean of 457,000 pencils. Estimate the standard deviation of this distribution. (*Hint:* Work backward from the normal table to find Z. Then apply Equation 3-12.)

: **3-28** Patients arrive at the emergency room of Costa Valley Hospital at an average of 5 per day. The demand for emergency room treatment at Costa Valley follows a Poisson distribution.

    (a) Using Appendix D, compute the probability of exactly 0, 1, 2, 3, 4, and 5 arrivals per day.

    (b) What is the sum of these probabilities, and why is the number less than 1?

: **3-29** Using the data in Problem 3-28, determine the probability of more than 3 visits for emergency room service on any given day.

: **3-30** Cars arrive at Carla's Muffler shop for repair work at an average of 3 per hour, following an exponential distribution.

    (a) What is the expected time between arrivals?

    (b) What is the variance of the time between arrivals?

    (c) What is the probability there are *no* arrivals for a full hour after a random customer has just entered the shop.

CASE STUDY

WTVX

WTVX, Channel 6, is located in Eugene, Oregon, home of the University of Oregon's football team. The station was owned and operated by George Wilcox, a former Duck (University of Oregon football player). Although there were other television stations in Eugene, WTVX was the only station that had a weatherperson who was a member of the American Meteorological Society (AMS). Every night, Joe Hummel would be introduced as the only weatherperson in Eugene who was a member of the AMS. This was George's idea, and he believed that this gave his station the mark of quality and helped with market share.

In addition to being a member of AMS, Joe was also the most popular person on any of the local news programs. Joe was always trying to find innovative ways to make the weather interesting, and this was especially difficult during the winter months when the weather seemed to remain the same over long periods of time. Joe's forecast for next month, for example, was that there would be a 70% chance of rain *every* day, and that what happens on one day (rain or shine) was not in any way dependent on what happened the day before.

One of Joe's most popular features of the weather report was to invite questions during the actual broadcast. Questions would be phoned in, and they were answered on the spot by Joe. Once

a ten-year-old boy asked what caused fog, and Joe did an excellent job of describing some of the various causes.

Occasionally, Joe would make a mistake. For example, a high school senior asked Joe what the chances were of getting 15 days of rain in the next month (30 days). Joe made a quick calculation: $(70\%) \times (15\ \text{days}/30\ \text{days}) = (70\%)\ (\frac{1}{2}) = 35\%$. Joe quickly found out what it is like being wrong in a university town. He had over 50 phone calls from scientists, mathematicians, and other university professors, telling him that he had made a big mistake in computing the chances of getting 15 days of rain during the next 30 days. Although Joe didn't understand all of the formulas the professors mentioned, he was determined to find the correct answer and make a correction during a future broadcast.

Discussion Questions

1. What are the chances of getting 15 days of rain during the next 30 days?

2. What do you think about Joe's assumptions concerning the weather for the next 30 days?

Source: Barry Render and Ralph M. Stair, *Cases and Readings in Quantitative Analysis for Management,* Boston: Allyn and Bacon, Inc., 1982.

Century Chemical Company

Century Chemical Company, formed in 1955 as a result of the merger of three smaller firms, produces chlorine and caustic soda through the electrolysis of brine. Century's largest plant, located in St. Gabriel, Louisiana, produces approximately 1,500 tons of chlorine and 1,700 tons of caustic soda daily. The St. Gabriel plant operates at capacity; its entire output is sold.

A major problem confronting Century Chemical Corporation is associated with its chlorine collection and handling system. The system incorporates headers that collect chlorine gas from the electrolytic cells. The gas then passes through heat exchangers for cooling and condensation of water entrapped in the chlorine. Residual water in the chlorine gas is removed by "scrubbing" with concentrated sulfuric acid. Thereafter, the dry chlorine gas is chilled by being bubbled through liquid chlorine before being fed to the chlorine compressor. The chlorine compressor is the "heart" of the handling system. It pulls the gas from the cells through the cooling and drying system. Then it compresses the gas for liquefaction and storage as liquid chlorine.

A major problem for the production manager of Century Chemical is the gradual deterioration of the plant's compressor capacity because of the fouling of component parts. The reliability of Century's centrifugal compressor at its St. Gabriel complex is .92. The 8% downtime includes cleaning and restoration of capacity as well as other mechanical/electrical failures. Heretofore, management at Century has chosen to incur the downtime and lost sales associated with compressor failures. However, from time to time, management considers the installation of a spare compressor. Currently, the cost of such an installation is estimated to total $800,000. The spare compressor is also projected to have a .92 reliability factor.

Approximately 12 hours of downtime are required to change over to an installed spare compressor. Profit and overhead contribution for chlorine is estimated at $50 per ton; the profit and overhead contribution for caustic soda is $40 per ton. Century's cost of capital or opportunity cost is estimated to equal 20%. Useful life of the compressor installation is estimated to be 10 years. Salvage is assumed to be zero. The effective tax rate is 40%.

Discussion Question

Should management of Century Chemical install the spare compressor? Why or why not? (*Hint:* The present value factor of 20% over 10 years is 4.192.)

Source: Professor Jerry Kinard of Francis Marion College and the late Joe Iverstine, formerly of Southeastern Louisiana State University. Reprinted with permission.

BIBLIOGRAPHY

Refer to references at end of Chapter 2.

4

Forecasting

CHAPTER OUTLINE

4.1
INTRODUCTION

Every day managers make decisions without knowing what will happen in the future. Inventory is ordered though no one knows what sales will be, new equipment is purchased though no one knows the demand for products, and investments are made though no one knows what profits will be. Managers are always trying to reduce this uncertainty and to make better estimates of what will happen in the future. Accomplishing this is the main purpose of forecasting.

KEY IDEA

There are many ways to forecast the future. In numerous firms (especially smaller ones), the entire process is subjective, involving seat-of-the-pants methods, intuition, and years of experience. There are also many *quantitative* forecasting models such as moving averages, exponential smoothing, trend projections, and least squares regression analysis.

Regardless of the method that is used to make the forecast, the same eight overall procedures are used:

forecasting system steps

1. Determine the use of the forecast—what objective are we trying to obtain?

2. Select the items or quantities that are to be forecasted.

3. Determine the time horizon of the forecast—is it one to thirty days (short term), one month to one year (medium term), or more than one year (long term)?

4. Select the forecasting model or models.

5. Gather the data needed to make the forecast.

6. Validate the forecasting model.

7. Make the forecast.

8. Implement the results.

These steps present a systematic way of initiating, designing, and implementing a forecasting system. When the forecasting system is to be used to generate forecasts regularly over time, data must be collected routinely, and the actual computations or procedures used to make the forecast can be done automatically. When a computer system is used, computer forecasting files and programs are needed.

no single method is best

There is seldom one single superior forecasting method. One organization may find regression effective, another firm may use several approaches, and a third may combine both quantitative and subjective techniques. Whatever tool works best for a firm is the one that should be used.

4.2
TYPES OF FORECASTS

In this chapter, we consider forecasting models that can be classified into one of three categories. These categories, shown in Figure 4.1, are time series models, causal models, and judgmental models.

Time Series Models

Time series models attempt to predict the future by using historical data. These models make the assumption that what happens in the future is a function of what has happened in the past. In other words, time series models look at what has happened over a period of time and use a series of past data to make a forecast. Thus, if we are forecasting weekly sales for lawn mowers, we use the past weekly sales for lawn mowers in making the forecast. The time series models we examine in this chapter are moving average, exponential smoothing, and trend projections.

Causal Models

Causal models incorporate the variables or factors that might influence the quantity being forecasted into the forecasting model. For example, daily sales of a cola drink might depend on the season, the average temperature, the average humidity, whether it is a weekend or a weekday, and so on. Thus, a causal model would attempt to include factors for temperature, humidity, season, day of the week, and so on. Causal models may also include past sales data as time series models do.

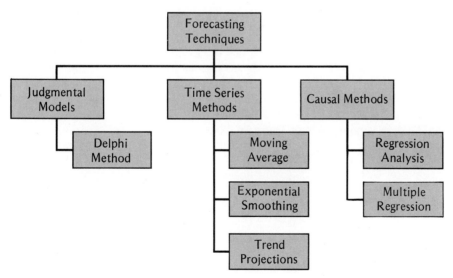

FIGURE 4.1
Forecasting Models Discussed

Judgmental Models

While time series and causal models rely on quantitative data, *judgmental models* attempt to incorporate qualitative or subjective factors into the forecasting model. Opinions by experts, individual experiences and judgments, and other subjective factors may be considered. Judgmental models are especially useful when subjective factors are expected to be very important or when accurate quantitative data is difficult to obtain.

4.3
SCATTER DIAGRAMS

obtaining ideas about a relationship

To get a quick idea if any relationship exists between two variables, a *scatter diagram* may be plotted on a two-dimensional graph. The values of the independent variable (such as time) may be measured on the horizontal (X) axis and the proposed dependent variables (such as sales) placed on the vertical (Y) axis. Let us consider the example of a firm that needs to forecast sales for three different products.

Wacker Distributors notes that annual sales for three of its products—televisions, radios, and stereos—over the past ten years are as shown in Table 4.1.

One simple way to examine these historical data, and perhaps use them to establish a forecast, is to draw a scatter diagram for each product. (See Figure 4.2.) This picture, showing the relationship between sales of a product and time, is useful in spotting trends or cycles. An exact mathematical model that describes the situation can then be developed if it appears reasonable to do so.

4.4
TIME SERIES FORECASTING MODELS

A time series is based on a sequence of evenly spaced (weekly, monthly, quarterly, and so on) data points. Examples include weekly sales of IBM PS/2s, quarterly earnings reports of AT&T stock, daily shipments of Ev-

TABLE 4.1 Annual Sales of Three Products

YEAR	TELEVISIONS	RADIOS	STEREOS
1	250	300	110
2	250	310	100
3	250	320	120
4	250	330	140
5	250	340	170
6	250	350	150
7	250	360	160
8	250	370	190
9	250	380	200
10	250	390	190

(a)

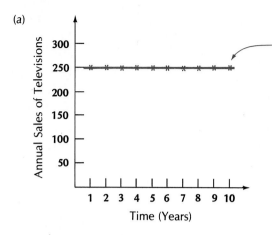

Sales appear to be constant over time. This horizontal line could be described by the equation:

$$Sales = 250$$

That is, no matter what year (1, 2, 3, and so on) we insert into the equation, sales will not change. A good estimate of future sales (in year 11) is 250 televisions!

(b)

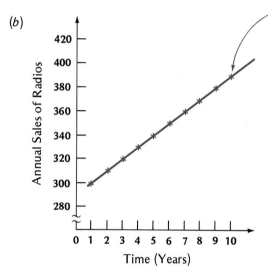

Sales appear to be increasing at a constant rate of ten radios each year. If the line is extended left to the vertical axis, we see that sales would be 290 in year 0. The equation

$$Sales = 290 + 10(Year)$$

best describes this relationship between sales and time. A reasonable estimate of radio sales in year 11 is 400, in year 12, 410 radios.

(c)

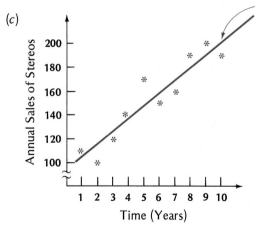

This trend line may not be perfectly accurate because of variation each year. But stereo sales do appear to have been increasing over the past ten years. If we had to forecast future sales, we would probably pick a larger figure each year.

FIGURE 4.2
Scatter Diagram for Sales

eready batteries, and annual U.S. consumer price indices. Forecasting time series data implies that future values are predicted *only* from past values (such as we saw in Table 4.1) and that other variables, no matter how potentially valuable, are ignored.

Decomposition of a Time Series

Analyzing time series means breaking down past data into components and then projecting them forward. A time series typically has four components: trend, seasonality, cycles, and random variation.

four components of a time series

1. *Trend* (*T*) is the gradual upward or downward movement of the data over time.

2. *Seasonality* (*S*) is a pattern of the demand fluctuation above or below the trend line that occurs every year.

3. *Cycles* (*C*) are patterns in the data that occur every several years. They are usually tied into the business cycle.

4. *Random variations* (*R*) are "blips" in the data caused by chance and unusual situations; they follow no discernible pattern.

Figure 4.3 shows a time series and its components.

There are two general forms of time series models in statistics. The most widely used is a multiplicative model, which assumes that demand is the product of the four components:

$$\text{Demand} = T \times S \times C \times R$$

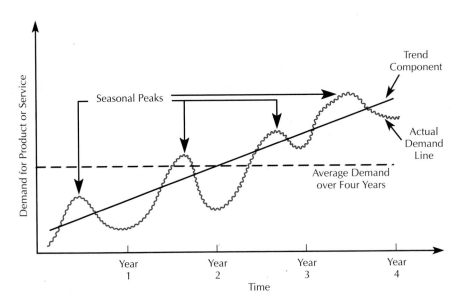

FIGURE 4.3
Product Demand Charted over Four Years with Trend and Seasonality Indicated

An additive model adds the components together to provide an estimate. It is stated as:

$$\text{Demand} = T + S + C + R$$

In most real-world models, forecasters assume that the random variations are averaged out over time. They then concentrate on only the seasonal component and a component that is a combination of trend and cyclical factors.

Moving Averages

Moving averages are useful if we can assume that market demands will stay fairly steady over time. A four-month moving average is found by simply summing the demand during the past four months and dividing by four. With each passing month, the most recent month's data are added to the sum of the previous three months' data, and the earliest month is dropped. This tends to smooth out short-term irregularities in the data series.

meaning of moving averages

Mathematically, the moving average, which serves as an estimate of the next period's demand, is expressed as:

$$\text{Moving average} = \frac{\Sigma \text{ Demand in previous } n \text{ periods}}{n} \quad \text{(4-1)}$$

where n is the number of periods in the moving average—for example, four, five, or six months, respectively, for a four-, five-, or six-period moving average.

Storage shed sales at Wallace Garden Supply are shown in the middle column of Table 4.2. A three-month moving average is indicated on the right.

When there is a trend or pattern, weights can be used to place more emphasis on recent values. This makes the techniques more responsive to changes since latter periods may be more heavily weighted. Deciding which weights to use requires some experience and a bit of luck. Choice of weights

using weights

TABLE 4.2 Wallace Garden Supply Shed Sales

MONTH	ACTUAL SHED SALES	THREE-MONTH MOVING AVERAGE
January	10	
February	12	
March	13	
April	16	$(10 + 12 + 13)/3 = 11\frac{2}{3}$
May	19	$(12 + 13 + 16)/3 = 13\frac{2}{3}$
June	23	$(13 + 16 + 19)/3 = 16$
July	26	$(16 + 19 + 23)/3 = 19\frac{1}{3}$
August	30	$(19 + 23 + 26)/3 = 22\frac{2}{3}$
September	28	$(23 + 26 + 30)/3 = 26\frac{1}{3}$
October	18	$(26 + 30 + 28)/3 = 28$
November	16	$(30 + 28 + 18)/3 = 25\frac{1}{3}$
December	14	$(28 + 18 + 16)/3 = 20\frac{2}{3}$

is somewhat arbitrary since there is no set formula to determine them. If the latest month or period is weighted too heavily, the forecast might reflect a large unusual change in the demand or sales pattern too quickly.

A *weighted moving average* may be expressed mathematically as:

$$\frac{\text{Weighted}}{\text{moving average}} = \frac{\Sigma\ (\text{Weight for period } n)(\text{Demand in period } n)}{\Sigma\ \text{Weights}} \qquad (4\text{-}2)$$

Wallace Garden Supply decides to forecast storage shed sales by weighting the past three months as follows:

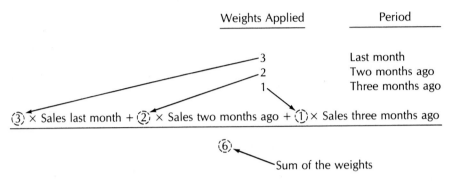

The results of this weighted average forecast are shown in Table 4.3. In this particular forecasting situation, you can see that weighting the latest month more heavily provides a much more accurate projection.

problems with moving averages

Both simple and weighted moving averages are effective in smoothing out sudden fluctuations in the demand pattern in order to provide stable estimates. Moving averages do, however, have three problems. First, increasing the size of n (the number of periods averaged) does smooth out fluctuations better, but it makes the method less sensitive to *real* changes in the data. Second, moving averages cannot pick up trends very well.

TABLE 4.3 Weighted Moving Average Forecast for Wallace Garden Supply

MONTH	ACTUAL SHED SALES	THREE-MONTH WEIGHTED MOVING AVERAGE
January	10	
February	12	
March	13	
April	16	$[(3 \times 13) + (2 \times 12) + (10)]/6 = 12\frac{1}{6}$
May	19	$[(3 \times 16) + (2 \times 13) + (12)]/6 = 14\frac{1}{3}$
June	23	$[(3 \times 19) + (2 \times 16) + (13)]/6 = 17$
July	26	$[(3 \times 23) + (2 \times 19) + (16)]/6 = 20\frac{1}{2}$
August	30	$[(3 \times 26) + (2 \times 23) + (19)]/6 = 23\frac{5}{6}$
September	28	$[(3 \times 30) + (2 \times 26) + (23)]/6 = 27\frac{1}{2}$
October	18	$[(3 \times 28) + (2 \times 30) + (26)]/6 = 28\frac{1}{3}$
November	16	$[(3 \times 18) + (2 \times 28) + (30)]/6 = 23\frac{1}{3}$
December	14	$[(3 \times 16) + (2 \times 18) + (28)]/6 = 18\frac{2}{3}$

Since they are averages, they will always stay within past levels and will not predict a change to either a higher or lower level. The third problem is that moving averages require extensive record keeping of past data.

Exponential Smoothing

Exponential smoothing is a forecasting method that is easy to use and efficiently handled by computers. Although it is a type of moving average technique, it involves little record keeping of past data. The basic exponential smoothing formula can be shown as follows:

New forecast = Last period's forecast
            $+ \alpha$ (Last period's actual demand $-$ Last period's forecast)　　**(4-3)**

where α is a weight (or *smoothing constant*) that has a value between 0 and 1, inclusive. Equation 4-3 can also be written mathematically as:

$$F_t = F_{t-1} + \alpha(A_{t-1} - F_{t-1}) \qquad\qquad (4\text{-}4)$$

where

$$F_t = \text{the new forecast,}$$

$$F_{t-1} = \text{the previous forecast,}$$

$$\alpha = \text{smoothing constant } (0 \leq \alpha \leq 1), \text{ and}$$

$$A_{t-1} = \text{previous period's actual demand.}$$

The concept here is not complex. The latest estimate of demand is equal to our old estimate adjusted by a fraction of the difference between the last period's actual demand and the old estimate.

The *smoothing constant*, α, can be changed to give more weight to recent data, when it is high, or more weight to past data, when it is low. For example, when $\alpha = .5$, it can be shown mathematically that the new forecast is based almost entirely on demand in the last three periods. When $\alpha = .1$, the forecast places little weight on recent demand and takes *many* periods (about 19) of historic values into account.[1]

smoothing constant

In January, a demand for 142 of a certain car model for February was predicted by a dealer. Actual February demand was 153 autos. Using a smoothing constant of $\alpha = .20$, we can forecast the March demand using the exponential smoothing model. Substituting into the formula, we obtain:

New forecast (for March demand) = 142 + .2(153 − 142)
                              = 144.2

Thus, the demand forecast for the cars in March is 144.

Suppose actual demand for the cars in March was 136. A forecast for the demand in April, using the exponential smoothing model with a constant of $\alpha = .20$, can be made.

New forecast (for April demand) = 144.2 + .2(136 − 144.2)
                              = 142.6, or 143 autos

[1] The term *exponential smoothing* is used because the weight that any one period's demand makes in a forecast demand decreases exponentially over time. See an advanced forecasting book for an algebraic proof.

forecast error

Selecting the Smoothing Constant. The exponential smoothing approach is easy to use, and it has been successfully applied by banks, manufacturing companies, wholesalers, and other organizations. The appropriate value of the smoothing constant, α, however, can make the difference between an accurate forecast and an inaccurate forecast. In picking a value for the smoothing constant, the objective is to obtain the most accurate forecast. The overall accuracy of a forecasting model can be determined by comparing the forecasted values with the actual or observed values.

The forecast error is defined as:

$$\text{Forecast error} = \text{Demand} - \text{Forecast}$$

One measure of the overall forecast error for a model is the *mean absolute deviation* (MAD). This is computed by taking the sum of the absolute values of the individual forecast errors and dividing by the number of periods of data (n):

$$\text{MAD} = \frac{\Sigma|\text{Forecast errors}|}{n} \tag{4-5}$$

MAD example

Let us apply this concept with a trial-and-error testing of two values of α in the following example. The Port of Baltimore has unloaded large quantities of grain from ships during the past eight quarters. The port's operations manager wants to test the use of exponential smoothing to see how well the technique works in predicting tonnage unloaded. He assumes that the forecast of grain unloaded in the first quarter was 175 tons. Two values of α are examined, $\alpha = .10$ and $\alpha = .50$. Table 4.4 shows the *detailed* calculations for $\alpha = .10$ only.

To evaluate the accuracy of each smoothing constant we can compute the absolute deviations and MADs (see Table 4.5). Based on this analysis, a smoothing constant of $\alpha = .10$ is preferred to $\alpha = .50$ because its MAD is smaller.

Besides the mean absolute deviations, there are three other measures of the accuracy of historical errors in forecasting that are sometimes used.

TABLE 4.4 Port of Baltimore Exponential Smoothing Forecasts for $\alpha = .10$ and $\alpha = .50$

QUARTER	ACTUAL TONNAGE UNLOADED	ROUNDED FORECAST USING $\alpha = .10$*	ROUNDED FORECAST USING $\alpha = .50$*
1	180	175	175
2	168	$176 = 175.00 + .10(180 - 175)$	178
3	159	$175 = 175.50 + .10(168 - 175.50)$	173
4	175	$173 = 174.75 + .10(159 - 174.75)$	166
5	190	$173 = 173.18 + .10(175 - 173.18)$	170
6	205	$175 = 173.36 + .10(190 - 173.36)$	180
7	180	$178 = 175.02 + .10(205 - 175.02)$	193
8	182	$178 = 178.02 + .10(180 - 178.02)$	186
9	?	$179 = 178.22 + .10(182 - 178.22)$	184

* Forecasts rounded to the nearest ton.

TABLE 4.5 Absolute Deviations and MADs for Port of Baltimore Example

QUARTER	ACTUAL TONNAGE UNLOADED	ROUNDED FORECAST WITH $\alpha = .10$	ABSOLUTE DEVIATIONS FOR $\alpha = .10$	ROUNDED FORECAST WITH $\alpha = .50$	ABSOLUTE DEVIATION FOR $\alpha = .50$
1	180	175	5	175	5
2	168	176	8	178	10
3	159	175	16	173	14
4	175	173	2	166	9
5	190	173	17	170	20
6	205	175	30	180	25
7	180	178	2	193	13
8	182	178	4	186	4
		Sum of absolute deviations	84		100
		$\text{MAD} = \dfrac{\Sigma\lvert\text{deviations}\rvert}{n} = 10.50$			MAD = 12.50

Mean squared error (MSE) is the average of the squared differences between the forecasted and observed values. *Mean absolute percent error* (MAPE) is the absolute difference between the forecasted and observed values expressed as a percentage of the observed values. *Bias* tells whether the forecast is too high or too low, and by how much. In effect, bias provides the average total error and its direction.

MSE and MAPE error measures

Exponential Smoothing with Trend Adjustment. As with any moving average technique, simple exponential smoothing fails to respond to trends. To illustrate a more complex exponential smoothing model, let us consider one that adjusts for trend. The idea is to compute a simple exponential smoothing forecast as illustrated and then adjust for positive or negative lag in trend. The formula is:

Forecast including trend (FIT_t) = New forecast (F_t) + Trend correction (T_t)

To smooth out the trend, the equation for the trend correction uses a smoothing constant, β, in the same way the simple exponential model uses α. T_t is computed by

$$T_t = T_{t-1} + \beta(F_t - F_{t-1}) \qquad (4\text{-}6)$$

where

T_t = smoothed trend for period t,

T_{t-1} = smoothed trend for previous period,

β = trend smoothing constant that we select,

F_t = simple exponential smoothed forecast for period t, and

F_{t-1} = forecast for previous period.

There are three steps to compute a trend-adjusted forecast.

Step 1: Compute a simple exponential forecast for time period t (F_t).

Step 2: Compute the trend by using the equation:

$$T_t = T_{t-1} + \beta(F_t - F_{t-1})$$

To start step 2 for the first time, an initial trend value must be inserted (either by a good guess or by observed past data). After that, the trend is computed.

Step 3: Calculate the trend adjusted exponential smoothing forecast (FIT_t) by this formula:

$$FIT_t = F_t + T_t$$

As an example, we consider a large Portland manufacturer that uses exponential smoothing to forecast demand for a pollution control equipment product. It appears that a trend is present.

MONTH	DEMAND		MONTH	DEMAND
1	12		6	26
2	17		7	31
3	20		8	32
4	19		9	36
5	24			

Smoothing constants are assigned the values of $\alpha = .2$ and $\beta = .4$. Assume the initial forecast for month 1 was 11 units.

Step 1: Forecast for month 2 (F_2) = Forecast for month 1 (F_1) + α (Month 1 demand − Forecast for month 1):

$$F_2 = 11 + .2 (12 - 11) = 11.0 + .2 = 11.2 \text{ units}$$

Step 2: Compute the trend present. Assume an initial trend adjustment of zero, that is, $T_1 = 0$.

$$T_2 = T_1 + \beta(F_2 - F_1)$$
$$= 0 + .4(11.2 - 11.0)$$
$$= .08$$

Step 3: Compute the forecast including trend (FIT):

$$FIT_2 = F_2 + T_2$$
$$= 11.2 + .08$$
$$= 11.28 \text{ units}$$

We will do the same calculations for the third month also.

Step 1: $F_3 = F_2 + \alpha$ (Demand in month 2 − F_2)
$$= 11.2 + .2(17 - 11.2) = 12.36$$

Step 2: $T_3 = T_2 + \beta(F_3 - F_2) = .08 + .4(12.36 - 11.2) = .54$

Step 3: $FIT_3 = F_3 + T_3 = 12.36 + .54 = 12.90$

TABLE 4.6 Portland Manufacturer's Data for Trend-Adjusted Exponential Smoothing

MONTH	ACTUAL DEMAND	FORECAST, F_t (WITHOUT TREND)	TREND	ADJUSTED FIT_t
1	12	11.00	0	—
2	17	11.20	.08	11.28
3	20	12.36	.54	12.90
4	19	13.89	1.15	15.04
5	24	14.91	1.56	16.47
6	26	16.73	2.29	19.02
7	31	18.58	3.03	21.61
8	32	21.07	4.03	25.09
9	36	23.25	4.90	28.15

So the simple exponential forecast (without trend) for month 2 was 11.2 units, and the trend-adjusted forecast was 11.28 units. In month 3, the simple forecast (without trend) was 12.36 units, and the trend-adjusted forecast was 12.90 units. Naturally, different values of T_1 and β can produce even better estimates.

Table 4.6 completes the forecasts for the nine-month period. Figure 4.4 compares actual demand, forecast without trend (F_t) and forecast with trend (FIT_t).

The value of the trend smoothing constant, β, resembles the α constant in that a high β is more responsive to recent changes in trend. A low β gives less weight to the most recent trends to smooth out the trend present.

β's responsiveness

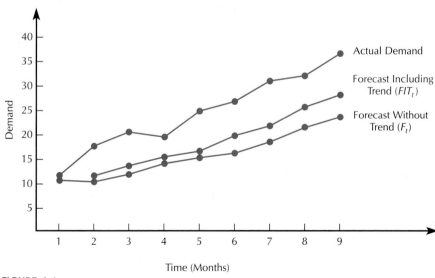

FIGURE 4.4

Comparison of Portland Manufacturer's Actual Demand, Forecast with Trend (*FIT_t*), and Forecast without Trend (*F_t*)

Values of β can be found by the trial-and-error approach, with the MAD used as a measure of comparison.

Simple exponential smoothing is often referred to as first-order smoothing, and trend-adjusted smoothing is called second-order, or double smoothing. Other advanced exponential smoothing models are also in use; they include seasonal-adjusted and triple smoothing, but these are beyond the scope of this book.[2]

Trend Projections

The last time series forecasting method we discuss in this section is *trend projection*. This technique fits a trend line to a series of historical data points, and then projects the line into the future for medium- to long-range forecasts. There are several mathematical trend equations that can be developed (for example, exponential and quadratic), but in this section we look at linear (straight line) trends only.

Let us consider the case of Midwestern Manufacturing Company; that firm's demand for electrical generators over the period 1984–1990 is shown in Table 4.7.

least squares method

If we decide to develop a linear trend line by a precise statistical method, as opposed to "eyeballing" the line as we did in Figure 4.2(c), the *least squares method* may be applied. This approach results in a straight line that minimizes the sum of the squares of the vertical differences from the line to each of the actual observations. Figure 4.5 illustrates the least squares approach.

A least squares line is described in terms of its Y-intercept (the height at which it intercepts the Y-axis) and its slope (the angle of the line). If we can compute the Y-intercept and slope, the line can be expressed by the following equation:

need to solve for Y-intercept and slope

$$\hat{Y} = a + bX \tag{4-7}$$

TABLE 4.7 Midwestern Manufacturing's Demand

YEAR	ELECTRICAL GENERATORS SOLD
1984	74
1985	79
1986	80
1987	90
1988	105
1989	142
1990	122

[2] For more details, see E. S. Gardner, "Exponential Smoothing: The State of the Art," *Journal of Forecasting* Vol. 4, No. 1, March 1985, or R. Brown, *Smoothing, Forecasting and Prediction*, Englewood Cliffs, N.J.: Prentice-Hall, 1973.

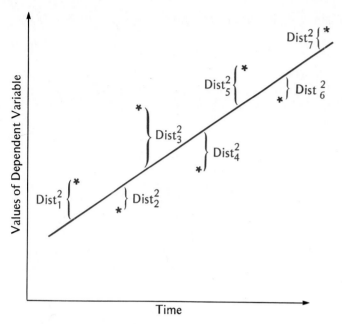

FIGURE 4.5
**Least Squares Method for Finding the Best Fitting
Straight Line**

where

$\hat{Y}$ (pronounced Y-hat) = computed value of the variable
to be predicted (called the
dependent variable),

a = Y-axis intercept,

b = slope of the least squares line (or
the rate of change in Y for given
changes in X), and

X = the independent variable.

Statisticians have developed equations that we can use to find the values
of a and b for any straight line. The slope, b, is found by:

$$b = \frac{\Sigma XY - n\overline{X}\,\overline{Y}}{\Sigma X^2 - n\overline{X}^2}$$ (4-8) **the slope equation b**

where

b = slope of the straight line,

Σ = summation sign for n data points,

X = values of the independent variable, time here,

Y = values of the dependent variable, generator sales,

$\overline{X}$ = the average of the values of the Xs,

$\overline{Y}$ = the average of the values of the Ys, and

n = the number of data points or observations, 7 in this case.

The Y-intercept, a, is then computed as follows:

the intercept equation a

$$a = \overline{Y} - b\overline{X} \qquad (4\text{-}9)$$

Transforming Time Variables. With a series of data over time, we can minimize the computations by transforming the values of X (time) to simpler numbers. Thus, in the case of Midwestern Manufacturing's data, we can designate 1984 as year 1, 1985 as year 2, and so on. This is shown in Table 4.8.

$$\overline{X} = \frac{\Sigma X}{n} = \frac{28}{7} = 4 \qquad \overline{Y} = \frac{\Sigma Y}{n} = \frac{692}{7} = 98.86$$

$$b = \frac{\Sigma XY - n\overline{X}\,\overline{Y}}{\Sigma X^2 - n\overline{X}^2} = \frac{3{,}063 - (7)(4)(98.86)}{140 - (7)(4^2)} = \frac{295}{28} = 10.54$$

$$a = \overline{Y} - b\overline{X} = 98.86 - 10.54(4) = 56.70$$

Hence, the least squares trend equation is $\hat{Y} = 56.70 + 10.54X$. To project demand in 1991, we first denote the year 1991 in our new coding system as $X = 8$:

$$\text{(Sales in 1991)} = 56.70 + 10.54(8)$$
$$= 141.02, \text{ or } 141 \text{ generators}$$

We can estimate demand for 1992 by inserting $X = 9$ in the same equation:

$$\text{(Sales in 1992)} = 56.70 + 10.54(9)$$
$$= 151.56, \text{ or } 152 \text{ generators}$$

To check the validity of the model, we plot historical demand and the trend line in Figure 4.6. In this case, we may wish to be cautious and try to understand the 1989–1990 swings in demand.

Seasonal Variations. Time series forecasting such as that in the example of Midwestern Manufacturing involves looking at the *trend* of data over a series of time observations. Sometimes, however, recurring variations at certain seasons of the year make a *seasonal* adjustment in the trend line forecast necessary. Demand for coal and fuel oil, for example, usually peaks during cold winter months. Demand for golf clubs or suntan lotion may be highest in summer. Analyzing data in monthly or quarterly terms usually makes it easy to spot seasonal patterns. Seasonal indices can then be de-

TABLE 4.8 Midwestern Manufacturing's Trend Calculations

YEAR	TIME PERIOD	GENERATOR DEMAND	X^2	XY
1984	1	74	1	74
1985	2	79	4	158
1986	3	80	9	240
1987	4	90	16	360
1988	5	105	25	525
1989	6	142	36	852
1990	7	122	49	854
	$\Sigma X = 28$	$\Sigma Y = 692$	$\Sigma X^2 = 140$	$\Sigma XY = 3{,}063$

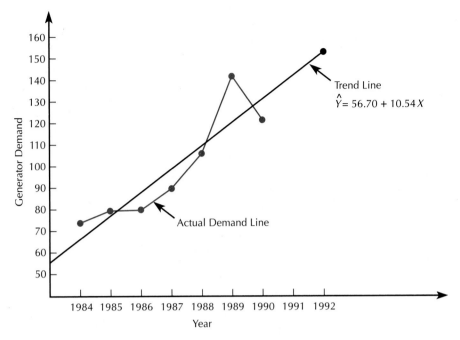

FIGURE 4.6
Electrical Generators and the Computed Trend Line

veloped by several common methods. The next example illustrates one way to compute seasonal factors from historical data.

Monthly sales of one brand of telephone answering machine at Eichler Supplies are shown in Table 4.9 for the two most recent years.

TABLE 4.9 Answering Machine Sales and Seasonal Indices

MONTH	SALES DEMAND YEAR 1	SALES DEMAND YEAR 2	AVERAGE TWO-YEAR DEMAND	AVERAGE MONTHLY DEMAND*	SEASONAL INDEX†
January	80	100	90	94	.957
February	75	85	80	94	.851
March	80	90	85	94	.904
April	90	110	100	94	1.064
May	115	131	123	94	1.309
June	110	120	115	94	1.223
July	100	110	105	94	1.117
August	90	110	100	94	1.064
September	85	95	90	94	.957
October	75	85	80	94	.851
November	75	85	80	94	.851
December	80	80	80	94	.851

Total average demand = 1,128

* Average monthly demand $= \dfrac{1,128}{12 \text{ months}} = 94$

† Seasonal index $= \dfrac{\text{Average two-year demand}}{\text{Average monthly demand}}$

APPLICATIONS OF QA

Personnel Forecasting in New York's Sanitation Department

In 1978 Norman Steisel was appointed the commissioner of New York City's Department of Sanitation by then Mayor Edward Koch. Prior to that time, many people felt that the city's Department of Sanitation was a municipal embarrassment. The generally used measures of performance for the department were way down from previous years, and there was general dissatisfaction with the overall operation of the department. In a few short years, Commissioner Steisel was able to make great strides and significant improvements.

One of the major problems facing the Department of Sanitation was an inadequate personnel forecasting model that could be used for planning purposes. Commissioner Steisel assigned Deputy Commissioner Christopher Beemer the responsibility for developing a new personnel forecasting model. This was a fairly difficult task because of the seasonal nature of the workload of the department. Depending on the weather and the time of the year, personnel needs could vary substantially. There were a number of important factors to be considered in the forecast. Some of these factors included the tons of garbage to be collected, the availability of disposal sites, truck capacities,

the number of litter baskets, special events and parade cleanup, clerical support, the availability of mechanical broom cleaning equipment, and other related factors.

The overall objective of the model was to predict personnel needs. In addition, personnel shortages and surpluses were to be determined. During a period of personnel shortages, overtime was to be used to meet the necessary requirements. Because of the expense of overtime work, the forecasting model was to be used to minimize overtime whenever possible.

Using a regression forecasting technique, a computerized personnel forecasting model was developed. As a result of the model's development and other steps taken, the department was able to increase its performance rating and to provide better service to the city of New York. In 1983, then Mayor Koch stated: "I am quite proud of the remarkable record of accomplishment of New York City's Department of Sanitation."

Source: Adapted from Lucius Riccio, "Management Science in New York's Department of Sanitation," *Interfaces* Vol. 14, No. 2, March–April 1984, pp. 1–13.

Using the seasonal indices from Table 4.9, if we expected the third year's annual demand for answering machines to be 1,200 units, we would forecast the monthly demand as follows:

Jan. $\dfrac{1,200}{12} \times .957 = 96$ July $\dfrac{1,200}{12} \times 1.117 = 112$

Feb. $\dfrac{1,200}{12} \times .851 = 85$ Aug. $\dfrac{1,200}{12} \times 1.064 = 106$

Mar. $\dfrac{1,200}{12} \times .904 = 90$ Sept. $\dfrac{1,200}{12} \times .957 = 96$

Apr. $\dfrac{1,200}{12} \times 1.064 = 106$ Oct. $\dfrac{1,200}{12} \times .851 = 85$

May $\dfrac{1,200}{12} \times 1.309 = 131$ Nov. $\dfrac{1,200}{12} \times .851 = 85$

June $\dfrac{1,200}{12} \times 1.223 = 122$ Dec. $\dfrac{1,200}{12} \times .851 = 85$

For simplicity, trend calculations were ignored in the previous example. The following example illustrates how indices that have already been prepared can be applied to adjust trend line forecasts and seasonal adjustments.

A San Diego hospital used 66 months of adult inpatient hospital days to reach the following equation:

$$\hat{Y} = 8{,}091 + 21.5X$$

where

$$\hat{Y} = \text{patient days, and}$$
$$X = \text{time, in months.}$$

Based on this model, the hospital forecasts patient days for the next month (period 67) to be:

$$\text{Patient days} = 8{,}091 + 21.5(67) = 9{,}530 \qquad \text{(trend only)}$$

As well as this model recognized the slight upward trend line in the demand for inpatient services, it ignored the seasonality that the administration knew to be present. Table 4.10 provides seasonal indices based on the same 66 months. Such seasonal data, by the way, were found to be typical of hospitals nationwide. Note that January, March, July, and August seem to exhibit significantly higher patient days on average, while February, September, November, and December experience lower patient days.

To correct the time series extrapolation for seasonality, the hospital multiplied the monthly forecast by the appropriate seasonality index. Thus, for period 67, which was a January,

TABLE 4.10 Seasonality Indices for Adult Inpatient Days at San Diego Hospital

MONTH	SEASONALITY INDEX
January	1.0436
February	0.9669
March	1.0203
April	1.0087
May	0.9935
June	0.9906
July	1.0302
August	1.0405
September	0.9653
October	1.0048
November	0.9598
December	0.9805

Source: W. E. Sterk and E. G. Shryock, ''Modern Methods Improve Hospital Forecasting,'' *Healthcare Financial Management* March 1987, p. 97.

Patient days = (9,530)(1.0436) = 9,946 (trend and seasonal)

Using this method, patient days were forecasted for January through June (periods 67 through 72) as 9,946, 9,236, 9,768, 9,678, 9,554, and 9,547. This study led to better forecasts as well as to more accurate forecast budgets.

4.5
CAUSAL FORECASTING METHODS

Causal forecasting models usually consider several variables that are related to the variable being predicted. Once these related variables have been found, a statistical model is built and used to forecast the variable of interest. This approach is more powerful than the time series methods that use only the historic values of the forecasted variable.

dependent and independent variables

Many factors can be considered in a causal analysis. For example, the sales of a product might be related to the firm's advertising budget, the price charged, competitors' prices, promotional strategies, and even the economy and unemployment rates. In this case, sales would be called the *dependent variable*, while the other variables would be called *independent variables*. Our job as quantitative analysts is to develop the best statistical relationship between sales and the set of independent variables. The most common quantitative causal forecasting model is *regression analysis*.

Using Regression Analysis to Forecast

Triple A Construction Company renovates old homes in Albany. Over time, the company has found that its dollar volume of renovation work is dependent on the Albany area payroll. The figures for Triple A's revenues and the amount of money earned by wage earners in Albany for the past six years are presented in Table 4.11.

Triple A wants to establish a mathematical relationship that will help predict sales. Just as we did with the least squares method of trend projection, we can let Y represent the dependent variable that we want to forecast, sales in this case. But now the independent variable, X, is not time; it is the Albany area payroll.

TABLE 4.11 Triple A Construction Company Sales

Y TRIPLE A'S SALES ($100,000's)	X LOCAL PAYROLL ($100,000,000's)
2.0	1
3.0	3
2.5	4
2.0	2
2.0	1
3.5	7

Least squares regression analysis may now be used to establish the statistical model. The same basic model applies:

$$\hat{Y} = a + bX$$

where

$\hat{Y}$ = value of the dependent variable, sales here,

a = Y-axis intercept,

b = slope of the regression line, and

X = the independent variable, payroll.

The calculations for a and b follow:

SALES Y	PAYROLL X	X^2	XY
2.0	1	1	2.0
3.0	3	9	9.0
2.5	4	16	10.0
2.0	2	4	4.0
2.0	1	1	2.0
3.5	7	49	24.5
$\Sigma Y = 15.0$	$\Sigma X = 18$	$\Sigma X^2 = 80$	$\Sigma XY = 51.5$

determining *a* and *b*

$$\overline{X} = \frac{\Sigma X}{6} = \frac{18}{6} = 3$$

$$\overline{Y} = \frac{\Sigma Y}{6} = \frac{15}{6} = 2.5$$

$$b = \frac{\Sigma XY - n\overline{X}\,\overline{Y}}{\Sigma X^2 - n\overline{X}^2} = \frac{51.5 - (6)(3)(2.5)}{80 - (6)(3^2)} = .25$$

$$a = \overline{Y} - b\overline{X} = 2.5 - (.25)(3) = 1.75$$

The estimated regression equation therefore is:

$$\hat{Y} = 1.75 + .25X$$

or

$$\text{Sales} = 1.75 + .25 \text{ (payroll)}$$

If the local Chamber of Commerce predicts that the Albany area payroll will be six hundred million dollars next year, an estimate of sales for Triple A is found with the regression equation.

making the forecast

$$\text{Sales (\$100,000's)} = 1.75 + .25(6) = 1.75 + 1.50 = 3.25$$

or

$$\text{Sales} = \$325,000$$

The final part of Triple A's problem illustrates a central weakness of causal forecasting methods such as regression. We see that even once a regression equation is computed, it is necessary to provide a forecast of the independent variable, payroll, before estimating the dependent variable (Y) for the next time period. Although not a problem in the case of all

weakness of regression

forecasts, you can imagine the difficulty of determining future values of *some* common independent variables (such as unemployment rates, gross national product, price indices, and so on).

Standard Error of the Estimate

The forecast of $325,000 for Triple A's sales in the preceding example is called a *point estimate* of Y. The point estimate is really the mean, or expected value, of a distribution of possible values of sales. Figure 4.7 illustrates this concept.

To measure the accuracy of the regression estimates we need to compute the *standard error of the estimate*, $S_{Y,X}$. This is called the *standard deviation of the regression*. Equation 4-10 is the same expression found in most statistics books for computing the standard deviation of an arithmetic mean:

$$S_{Y,X} = \sqrt{\frac{\Sigma(Y - Y_c)^2}{n - 2}} \qquad \text{(4-10)}$$

where

Y = the Y-value of each data point,

Y_c = the computed value of the dependent variable, from the regression equation,

n = the number of data points.

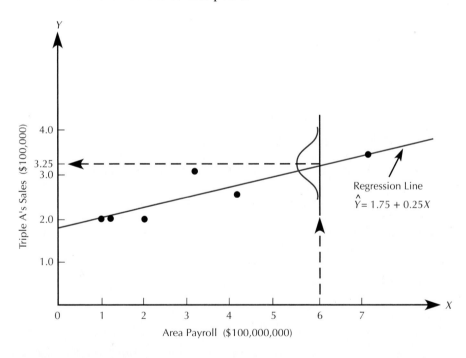

FIGURE 4.7
Distribution about the Point Estimate of $6 Hundred Million Payroll

TABLE 4.12 Triple A's Calculations Including New Column for Y^2

Y	X	X^2	XY	Y^2	
2.0	1	1	2.0	4.0	←
3.0	3	9	9.0	9.0	
2.5	4	16	10.0	6.25	New
2.0	2	4	4.0	4.0	column
2.0	1	1	2.0	4.0	
3.5	7	49	24.5	12.25	
$\Sigma Y = 15.0$	$\Sigma X = 18$	$\Sigma X^2 = 80$	$\Sigma XY = 51.5$	$\Sigma Y^2 = 39.5$	

Equation 4-11 may look more complex, but it is actually an easier-to-use version of Equation 4-10. Either formula provides the same answer and can be used in setting up prediction intervals around the point estimate.[3]

$$S_{Y,X} = \sqrt{\frac{\Sigma Y^2 - a\Sigma Y - b\Sigma XY}{n-2}} \qquad (4\text{-}11)$$

Let us compute the standard error of the estimate for Triple A's data in the previous section. The only number we will need that is not available to solve for $S_{Y,X}$ is ΣY^2. Some quick addition in Table 4.12 reveals $\Sigma Y^2 = 39.5$. Therefore,

$$S_{Y,X} = \sqrt{\frac{\Sigma Y^2 - a\Sigma Y - b\Sigma XY}{n-2}}$$

$$= \sqrt{\frac{39.5 - 1.75\,(15.0) - 0.25\,(51.5)}{6-2}}$$

$$= \sqrt{0.09375} = 0.306 \text{ (in \$ hundred thousands)}$$

The standard error of the estimate is then \$30,600 in sales.

Correlation Coefficients for Regression Lines

The regression equation is one way of expressing the nature of the relationship between two variables.[4] The equation shows how one variable relates to the value and changes in another variable.

Another way to evaluate the relationship between two variables is to compute the *coefficient of correlation*. This measure expresses the degree or strength of the linear relationship. It is usually identified as *r* and can be any number between and including +1 and −1. Figure 4.8 illustrates what different values of *r* might look like.

measuring the strength of the linear relationship

---

[3] When the sample size is large (*n* > 30), the prediction interval for an individual value of *Y* can be computed using normal tables. When the number of observations is small, the *t*-distribution is appropriate. See any good statistics textbook for details, such as Neter, Wasserman, and Whitmore's *Applied Statistics*, 3rd ed., Newton, Mass.: Allyn and Bacon, 1988.

[4] Regression lines are not always cause-and-effect relationships. In general, they describe the relationship between the movement of variables.

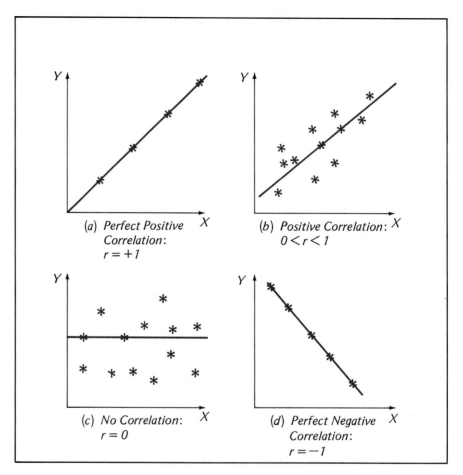

FIGURE 4.8
Four Values of the Correlation Coefficient

To compute r we use much of the same data needed earlier to calculate a and b for the regression line. The rather lengthy equation for r is:

$$r = \frac{n\Sigma XY - \Sigma X \Sigma Y}{\sqrt{[n\Sigma X^2 - (\Sigma X)^2][n\Sigma Y^2 - (\Sigma Y)^2]}}$$ (4-12)

Using the data in Table 4.12 we can compute the coefficient of correlation for Triple A Construction Company.

$$r = \frac{(6)(51.5) - (18)(15.0)}{\sqrt{[(6)(80) - (18)^2][(6)(39.5) - (15.0)^2]}} = \frac{309 - 270}{\sqrt{(156)(12)}} = \frac{39}{\sqrt{1872}}$$

$$= \frac{39}{43.3} = .901$$

This r of .901 appears to be a significant correlation and helps to confirm the closeness of the relationship of the two variables.

Although the coefficient of correlation is the most commonly used measure to describe the relationship between two variables, another measure does exist—the *coefficient of determination*. This is simply the square of the coefficient of correlation, namely, r^2. The value of r^2 will always be a positive number in the range of $0 \leq r^2 \leq 1$. The coefficient of determination is the percent of variation in the dependent variable (Y) that is explained by the regression equation. In Triple A's case, the value of r^2 is .81, indicating that 81% of the total variation is explained by the regression equation.

Multiple Regression Analysis

Multiple regression is a practical extension of the model we just observed. It allows us to build a model with several independent variables. For example, if Triple A Construction wanted to include average annual interest rates in its model to forecast renovation sales, the proper equation would be:

adding another independent variable

$$\hat{Y} = a + b_1 X_1 + b_2 X_2 \qquad (4\text{-}13)$$

where

$$\hat{Y} = \text{the dependent variable, sales,}$$
$$a = Y\text{-intercept,}$$
$$X_1 \text{ and } X_2 = \text{values of the two independent variables, area}$$
$$\text{payroll and interest rates, respectively, and}$$
$$b_1 \text{ and } b_2 = \text{slopes for } X_1 \text{ and } X_2\text{, respectively.}$$

The mathematics of multiple regression becomes quite complex, especially when more than two independent variables are considered, so we leave formulas for a, b_1, and b_2 to more advanced texts. For now, let's assume that the new regression line, calculated by a computer, is:

$$\hat{Y} = a + b_1 X_1 + b_2 X_2$$
$$= 1.80 + .30X_1 - 5.0X_2$$

Further, we find the new coefficient of correlation is .96, implying the inclusion of the variable X_2, interest rates, adds even more strength to the linear relationship.

We can now estimate Triple A's sales from Equation 4-13 if we substitute in values for next year's payroll and interest rates. If Albany's payroll will be six hundred million dollars and interest rates will be .12 (12%), sales will be forecast as:

$$\text{Sales (\$100,000's)} = 1.80 + .30(6) - 5.0(.12)$$
$$= 1.80 + 1.80 - .60$$
$$= 3.00$$
$$\text{Sales} = \$300,000$$

the new forecast

Should interest rates drop to only .08, or 8%, can you see that the sales forecast would increase to $320,000?

APPLICATIONS OF QA

ARTS PLAN: IMPLEMENTATION, EVOLUTION, AND USE

ARTS PLAN is a user-oriented, decision support system designed to aid a performing arts manager in planning a schedule of performing arts events. First implemented in 1976 by management of the Lively Arts at Stanford (LAS) program, the model consists of two major components: (1) a forecasting system to predict attendance at a scheduled event and (2) an interactive planning model by which the manager can test the impact of scheduling different performing arts events on total attendance for the year. For five years, management's use of the model was monitored in order to examine the evolution of this marketing tool. While there are a number of articles reporting the successful implementation of marketing models, relatively few examine the nature of model development and use after the introductory period.

The original ARTS PLAN forecasting model was constructed and estimated using data from 90 performances given over a three-year period ending in spring 1976. Based on the type of performing arts event (for example, dance, jazz, chamber music), the quarter in which it was presented (fall, winter, spring), and other factors, a dummy-variable multiple linear regression with an R^2 of .79 (see Equation 4-12) was developed. Most important, and somewhat surprising, was the finding that, in general, the name of the individual performer was not needed (after controlling the other variables) to forecast attendance accurately. This meant that a forecasting system could be built for performers who had not previously been on campus.

The ARTS PLAN system allows the manager to revise the regression forecasts based on additional information or plans, such as special promotions, that the manager may have. The model initially yielded highly accurate forecasts, but it became less accurate over time, which suggested a need for revision. However, too frequent revisions of any modeling system may erode management confidence in that system. Furthermore, methods that automatically revise forecasts to take account of the most recent data may sometimes produce decreased accuracy due to incorporation of random error in the prediction and other factors. Consequently, a major issue from the standpoint of model accuracy and management confidence concerns when and how the model should be revised.

Annual updating of the regression coefficients was rejected for three main reasons. First, management considered the ARTS PLAN system to be highly accurate; thus there was no managerial impetus to change. Second, frequent revision of the model, for example, by adding the most recent year's data to the database, would likely have had only a small effect on predicted attendance. Third, highly sophisticated forecasting methods do not necessarily produce more accurate forecasts than simpler approaches.

Over time, management began to use the ARTS PLAN system in new ways. For instance, when management actively developed the sale of series (subscription) tickets for the first time in 1978–1979, the ARTS PLAN forecasts were used as the base case for estimating sales. In general, it appears likely that models originally developed for one purpose may be successfully adapted for other uses as management's needs evolve and familiarity with a model increases.

One of the reasons that managers employ decision aids is to reduce uncertainty in a problem situation, not to acknowledge and quantify it. Use of the ARTS PLAN system appears to have accomplished a reduction in uncertainty.

Source: Charles B. Weinberg. *Marketing Science* Vol. 5, No. 2, Spring 1986, pp. 143–158.

4.6
MONITORING AND CONTROLLING FORECASTS

Once a forecast has been completed, it is important that it not be forgotten. No manager wants to be reminded when his or her forecast is horribly inaccurate, but a firm needs to determine why the actual demand (or whatever variable is being examined) differed significantly from that projected.[5]

One way to monitor forecasts to ensure they are performing well is to employ a tracking signal. A *tracking signal* is a measurement of how well the forecast is predicting actual values. As forecasts are updated every week, month, or quarter, the newly available demand data are compared to the forecast values.

tracking signal

The tracking signal is computed as the *running sum of the forecast errors* (RSFE) divided by the mean absolute deviation.

$$
\begin{aligned}
\text{Tracking signal} &= \frac{\text{RSFE}}{\text{MAD}} \\
&= \frac{\Sigma(\text{Actual demand in period } i - \text{Forecast demand in period } i)}{\text{MAD}}
\end{aligned}
$$

(4-14)

where

$$
\text{MAD} = \frac{\Sigma|\text{Forecast errors}|}{}
$$

as seen earlier in Equation 4-5.

Positive tracking signals indicate that demand is greater than the forecast. Negative signals mean that demand is less than forecast. A good tracking signal, that is, one with a low RSFE, has about as much positive error as it has negative error. In other words, small deviations are okay, but the positive and negative ones should balance one another so the tracking signal centers closely around zero.

Once tracking signals are calculated, they are compared to predetermined control limits. When a tracking signal exceeds an upper or lower limit, a signal is tripped. This means there is a problem with the forecasting method, and management may want to reevaluate the way it forecasts demand. Figure 4.9 shows the graph of a tracking signal that is exceeding the range of acceptable variation. If the model being used is exponential smoothing, perhaps the smoothing constant needs to be readjusted.

How do firms decide what the upper and lower tracking limits should be? There is no single answer, but they try to find reasonable values—in other words, limits not so low as to be triggered with every small forecast error and not so high as to allow bad forecasts to be regularly overlooked. George Plossl and Oliver Wight, two inventory control experts, suggested using maximums of ±4 MADs (for high-volume stock items) and ±8 MADs (for lower-volume items).[6] Other forecasters suggest slightly lower ranges. One MAD is equivalent to approximately .8 standard deviations, so that ±2 MADs = ±1.6 standard deviations, ±3 MADs = ±2.4 standard deviations, and ±4 MADs = ±3.2 standard deviations. This suggests that

setting tracking limits

[5] If the forecaster *is* accurate, that individual usually makes sure that everyone is aware of his or her talents. Very seldom does one read articles in *Fortune, Forbes,* or *The Wall Street Journal,* however, about money managers who are consistently off by 25% in their stock market forecasts.

[6] See G. W. Plossl and O. W. Wight, *Production and Inventory Control,* Englewood Cliffs, N.J.: Prentice-Hall, 1967.

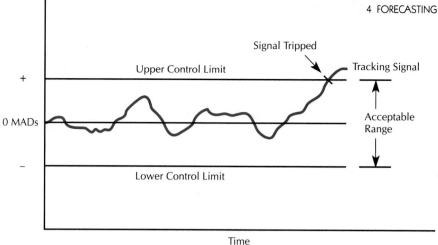

FIGURE 4.9
Plot of Tracking Signals

for a forecast to be "in control," 89% of the errors are expected to fall within ±2 MADs, 98% within ±3 MADs, or 99.9% within ±4 MADs.[7]

The following example shows how the tracking signal and RSFE can be computed. Kimball's Bakery's quarterly sales of croissants (in thousands), as well as forecast demand and error computations, are shown below. The objective is to compute the tracking signal and determine whether forecasts are performing adequately.

QUARTER	FORECAST DEMAND	ACTUAL DEMAND	ERROR	RSFE	FORECAST ERROR	CUMULATIVE ERROR	MAD	TRACKING SIGNAL
1	100	90	−10	−10	10	10	10.0	−1
2	100	95	−5	−15	5	15	7.5	−2
3	100	115	+15	0	15	30	10.0	0
4	110	100	−10	−10	10	40	10.0	−1
5	110	125	+15	+5	15	55	11.0	+0.5
6	110	140	+30	+35	30	85	14.2	+2.5

$$\text{MAD} = \frac{\Sigma \text{ Forecast errors}}{n} = \frac{85}{6}$$

$$= 14.2$$

$$\text{Tracking signal} = \frac{\text{RSFE}}{\text{MAD}} = \frac{35}{14.2}$$

$$= 2.5 \text{ MADs}$$

This tracking signal is within acceptable limits. We see that it drifted from −2.0 MADs to +2.5 MADs.

---

[7] To prove these three percentages to yourself, just set up a normal curve for ±1.6 standard deviations (Z values). Using the Normal Table in Appendix A you find that the area under that curve is 0.89. This represents ±2 MADs. Likewise, ±3 MADs = ±2.4 standard deviations, encompasses 98% of the area, and so on for ±4 MADs.

Adaptive Smoothing

A lot of research has been published on the subject of adaptive forecasting. This refers to computer monitoring of tracking signals and self-adjustment if a signal passes its preset limit. In exponential smoothing, the α and β coefficients are first selected based on values that minimize error forecasts and then adjusted accordingly whenever the computer notes an errant tracking signal. This is called *adaptive smoothing*.

4.7
THE DELPHI TECHNIQUE

Any discussion of forecasting would be incomplete without an example of a judgmental forecasting method. One of the most popular is the Delphi technique.

The *Delphi technique* is a group process that allows experts who may be located in different geographical areas to make forecasts. There are three different types of participants in the Delphi process: (1) decision makers, (2) staff personnel, and (3) respondents. The *decision makers* consist of a group of experts who will be making the actual forecast. To be manageable, this group usually consists of five to ten members. The *staff personnel* assist the decision makers in the Delphi process. This includes the preparation, distribution, collection, and summarization of questionnaires and survey results. This group is responsible for all clerical tasks as well. The *respondents* are a group of people whose judgments are valued and are being sought. This group provides valuable inputs to the decision makers before the forecast is made.

Delphi technique

The actual forecasting procedure is:

1. Select decision maker, staff, and respondent groups.

2. Develop and administer first questionnaire.

3. Analyze first questionnaire.

4. Develop and administer second questionnaire.

5. Analyze second questionnaire.

6. Do final analysis and present results.

7. Develop the forecast.

The main idea behind the Delphi technique is a feedback process. The results of the first questionnaire are tabulated and sent back to the respondents along with a second questionnaire that is based on the insights and results from the first questionnaire. The respondents answer the second

feedback process

APPLICATIONS OF QA

Flood Forecasting at NOAA

One of the major components of the National Oceanic and Atmospheric Administration (NOAA) is the national weather service (NWS). Saving lives and reducing property damage is one of the major objectives of the NWS. To accomplish this mission, an effective flood forecasting-response system is needed. The importance of an accurate and fast flood forecast cannot be over emphasized. Hundreds of lives and millions of dollars are at stake. In the United States, there are approximately 20,000 flood-prone areas. The NWS, at this time, develops approximately 3,000 flood warnings for specific areas or forecast points.

The flood forecast-response (FFR) system involves a number of steps. The first step is data collection. In this step, data from the field regarding potential floods are collected and sent to river forecast centers. The second step is the actual forecasting procedure. This includes a number of important mathematical models that transform rainfall, runoff, and a number of other factors into the actual flood forecasts. A flood forecast indicates the magnitude of the flood crest and the time of

Source: Adapted from Roman Krzysztofowizz and Donald R. Davis, "Toward Improving Flood Forecast-Response Systems," *Interfaces* Vol. 14, No. 3, May–June 1984, pp. 1–14.

arrival of the flood crest at specific points along rivers. The third step is the dissemination of the information to the appropriate points. Radio, telephone, and television coverage are all used to inform both public and private organizations and individuals of the potential of floods as a result of the forecast. The fourth step is the decision procedure step. Formal decision models are used to help formulate responses to various flood conditions. This includes the specific type of protective action to be taken. The fifth step is the actual implementation of the specific actions to be taken to both prevent and to cope with flood type conditions.

In many forecasting situations, like the flood forecast-response system described here, a lot more is involved than simply making the forecast. The appropriate data must be systematically collected, and the results must be carefully analyzed and disseminated so the appropriate decisions can be made. Robert Clark, director of the Office of Hydrology of the National Weather Service stated that: "The work reported on has been a great value in examining the response of the entire flood forecast system including data collection, forecasting, dissemination, decisions by floodplain dwellers, and protective actions."

questionnaire, the final results are tabulated, and the decision makers, using their judgment, experience, and the results of the two questionnaires, make the forecast.

The Delphi technique can be modified to satisfy the needs of a particular forecast. In some cases, three or four questionnaires can be used. While the Delphi technique has been used successfully, it usually takes several time-consuming iterations and requires the involvement of a large number of people.

A Delphi Forecast for Alaska

Alaska is an interesting, dynamic, and diverse state. In 1982, the Alaska Department of Commerce and Economic Development sought to obtain expert opinion concerning important matters about the future. Alaska has always been and still is highly dependent upon a single industry—oil. It has been estimated that over 90% of its state government budget derives from approximately 1.5 million barrels of oil per day that pass from Prudhoe Bay to destinations all over the United States.

To become less dependent on oil, Alaska looked at other resources and industries that could become an important part of its economy. To do this, a forecast of future trends, policies, and possible courses of action was needed.

Out of all the different types of forecasting methods available, the Delphi technique was selected. The Delphi technique is an excellent process when a number of expert opinions are to be combined into a meaningful forecast of the future. In addition, the Delphi technique can be used to assist group decision making.

The participants that were identified included current and former legislators, government agency heads, former governors, corporate presidents, national leaders, geologists, political scientists, econ-omists, and environmentalists. Sixty percent of the individuals extended invitations to participate accepted. This yielded an initial panel of 91 members.

The actual Delphi technique started with the first two rounds, which were done independently. In the final round, participants considered interactions, concentrated on the most significant events and policies, and developed individual scenarios. The Delphi panel predicted that Alaska's population will reach 633,000 by the year 2000. The study also looked at other key variables and factors for the state of Alaska. Furthermore, the study helped establish a division of mining within state government. A number of requests for copies of the Delphi survey by both the public and the private sector have been made, and other Delphi forecasts are currently underway. The year after the initial survey was done, a short follow-up was sent to the participants. Almost all people who participated in the initial study continued with their participation, and the predictions a year later were very stable.

Source: Adapted from Ted Eschenbach and George Geistauts, "A Delphi Forecast for Alaska," *Interfaces*, Vol. 15, No. 6, November–December 1985, pp. 100–109.

4.8
USING THE COMPUTER TO FORECAST

Forecast calculations are seldom performed by hand in this day of computers. Numerous university and commercial packaged programs (such as SAS, SPSS, BIOMED, SYSTAB and Minitab) are readily available to handle time series and causal projections. Even spreadsheet software, such as Lotus 1-2-3, can effectively manage small-to-medium forecasting problems.

Several mainframe-oriented packages, such as General Electric's Time Series Forecasting (called FCST1 and FCST2), are oriented toward organizations that need to perform large-scale regression and exponential smoothing projections. A large number of corporations use forecasting programs that also incorporate inventory control routines. Examples are IBM's IMPACT (Inventory Management Program and Control Technique) and COGS (Consumer Goods Program).

AB:QM Sample Computer Runs

In this section we'll look at the microcomputer forecasting software package AB:QM. AB:QM can project moving averages (both simple and weighted), do simple exponential smoothing, handle least squares trend projection, and solve linear regression (causal) problems.

To illustrate AB:QM, let's use the data in Table 4.13. We will forecast generator sales by moving averages, exponential smoothing, and then trend projection. Finally, linear regression will be used to attempt to establish a causal relationship between advertising budget and sales.

TABLE 4.13 Midwestern Manufacturing Data

YEAR	GENERATORS SOLD	ADVERTISING BUDGET ($)
1984	74	1,200
1985	79	1,500
1986	80	2,200
1987	90	2,000
1988	105	2,000
1989	142	2,500
1990	122	2,450

Programs 4.1 through 4.4 show AB:QM's four microcomputer forecasting options, with a sample run for each.

Program 4.1 is a simple moving average model using a three-year moving period. Its forecast for 1991 (period 8) is 123, with a MAD of 23.58.

Program 4.2 uses an alpha weight of .30 in an exponential smoothing model, where we select an initial forecast of 74, equal to 1984's actual sales figure. The result for 1991 (period 8) is a forecast of 110 (rounding upward) with a MAD of 16.94.

PROGRAM 4.1
Midwestern Manufacturing (Simple Moving Average)

```
Forecasting / Simple & Weighted Moving Average

Problem Title :  PROGRAM 4.1 MIDWESTERN MANUFACTURING
Number of Moving Periods      3          Weighted? (1=no/2=yes)   1
Number of Periods             7
```

```
             Data
Period  1     74
Period  2     79
Period  3     80
Period  4     90
Period  5    105
Period  6    142
Period  7    122
```

```
Help  New  Load  Save  Edit  Run  Print  Install  Directory  Esc
```

Program: Forecasting / Simple & Weighted Moving Average
Problem Title : PROGRAM 4.1 MIDWESTERN MANUFACTURING

***** Input Data *****

Number of Moving Periods :   3
Number of Periods   :   7
Weighted?   :   No

Input data are shown below.

***** Program Output *****

Period	Data	Forecast	Forecast Error
1	74.000		
2	79.000		
3	80.000		
4	90.000	77.667	-12.333
5	105.000	83.000	-22.000
6	142.000	91.667	-50.333
7	122.000	112.333	-9.667
8		123.000	

```
Mean Absolute Deviation        :     23.5833
Mean Square Error              :    554.4082
Mean Forecast Error            :    -23.5833
Running Sum of Forecast Error  :     94.3333
Tracking Signal                :      4.0000
```

***** End of Output *****

127

Forecasting / Exponential Smoothing

Problem Title : PROGRAM 4.2 MIDWESTERN MANUFACTURING
Alpha   .30   Initial Estimated Forecast 74
Number of Periods   7

Data
Period 1   74
Period 2   79
Period 3   80
Period 4   90
Period 5   105
Period 6   142
Period 7   122

Help   New   Load   Save   Edit   Run   Print   Install   Directory   Esc

Program: Forecasting / Exponential Smoothing

Problem Title : PROGRAM 4.2 MIDWESTERN MANUFACTURING

***** Input Data *****

Alpha   :   0.300
Initial Estimated Forecast :   74.000
Number of Periods   :   7

Input data are shown below.

***** Program Output *****

Period	Data	Forecast	Forecast Error
1	74.000	74.000	0.000
2	79.000	74.000	−5.000
3	80.000	75.500	−4.500
4	90.000	76.850	−13.150
5	105.000	80.795	−24.205
6	142.000	88.056	−53.944
7	122.000	104.240	−17.760
8		109.568	

Mean Absolute Deviation   :   16.9370
Mean Square Error   :   554.4082
Mean Forecast Error   :   −16.9370
Running Sum of Forecast Error :   118.5590
Tracking Signal   :   7.0000

***** End of Output *****

128

Program 4.3 employs least squares trend projection, and produces the model:

$$\text{Sales} = 56.71 + 10.54 \ (\text{Year})$$

If Year = 8, then the sales forecast will be 141 generators. The MAD is only 10.01.

PROGRAM 4.3
Midwestern Manufacturing (Least Squares Method)

```
Forecasting / Least Squares Method

 Problem Title :  PROGRAM 4.3 MIDWESTERN MANUFACTURING

 Number of Observations        7


                    Data
 Observation  1      74
 Observation  2      79
 Observation  3      80
 Observation  4      90
 Observation  5     105
 Observation  6     142
 Observation  7     122




 Help  New  Load  Save  Edit  Run  Print  Install  Directory  Esc
```

(continued)

PROGRAM 4.3
Midwestern Manufacturing (Least Squares Method) (Continued)

```
Program: Forecasting / Least Squares Method
Problem Title :   PROGRAM 4.3 MIDWESTERN MANUFACTURING
***** Input Data *****
```

Obs.	Data(Y)
1	74.000
2	79.000
3	80.000
4	90.000
5	105.000
6	142.000
7	122.000

```
***** Program Output *****
```

Parameter	Coefficient	SE B	t
Intercept	56.7143	10.5073	5.3976
b 1	10.5357	2.3495	4.4842

```
Coefficient of determination    :      0.8009
Correlation coefficient         :      0.8949
Standard Error                  :     12.4324
Mean Absolute Deviation (MAD)   :     10.0119
```

ANOVA Table

Source of Variation	SS	df	MS
Regression	3108.036	1	3108.036
Residual	772.821	5	154.564
Total	3880.857	6	

```
F*   =      20.108

***** End of Output *****
```

Finally, Program 4.4 uses regression to examine the relationship between generator sales (Y) and advertising budget (X). The least squares model that results is:

$$\text{Sales} = 15.62 + .0421 \text{ (Ad budget)}$$

R^2 is .6291 and MAD is 12.64.

PROGRAM 4.4
Midwestern Manufacturing (Simple Regression)

```
Forecasting / Simple Regression

Problem Title :  PROGRAM 4.4 MIDWESTERN MANUFACTURING

Number of Observations          7


                        Y           X
Observation  1          74        1200
Observation  2          79        1500
Observation  3          80        2200
Observation  4          90        2000
Observation  5         105        2000
Observation  6         142        2500
Observation  7         122        2450




Help  New  Load  Save  Edit  Run  Print  Install  Directory  Esc
```

(continued)

Program: Forecasting / Simple Regression

Problem Title :   PROGRAM 4.4 MIDWESTERN MANUFACTURING

***** Input Data *****

Obs.	Y	X
1	74.000	1200.000
2	79.000	1500.000
3	80.000	2200.000
4	90.000	2000.000
5	105.000	2000.000
6	142.000	2500.000
7	122.000	2450.000

***** Program Output *****

Parameter	Coefficient	SE B	t
Intercept	15.6157	29.2961	0.5330
b 1	0.0421	0.0144	2.9120

Coefficient of determination	:	0.6291
Correlation coefficient	:	0.7931
Standard Error	:	16.9677

Prediction Error

Obs.	Observed Value	Predicted Value	Residual
1	74.000	66.102	7.898
2	79.000	78.723	0.277
3	80.000	108.173	-28.173
4	90.000	99.759	-9.759
5	105.000	99.759	5.241
6	142.000	120.794	21.206
7	122.000	118.691	3.309

Mean Absolute Deviation (MAD) :   12.6439

ANOVA Table

Source of Variation	SS	df	MS
Regression	2441.347	1	2441.347
Residual	1439.510	5	287.902
Total	3880.857	6	

F* =   8.480

***** End of Output *****

4.9
SUMMARY

Forecasts are a critical part of a manager's function. Demand forecasts drive the production, capacity, and scheduling systems in a firm and affect the financial, marketing, and personnel planning functions.

This chapter introduced you to three types of forecasting models—time series, causal, and judgmental. Moving averages, exponential smoothing, and trend projection time series models were developed; a popular causal model, regression analysis, was illustrated; and a judgmental model called the Delphi technique was explored. In addition, we explained the use of scatter diagrams, correlation coefficients, and the analysis of forecasting accuracy. In future chapters, you will see the usefulness of these techniques in determining values for the various decision-making models.

Table 4.14 compares seven forecasting approaches on a variety of scales, including time span, sophistication, computer needs, financial needs, inputs, and accuracy. It is excerpted from one of several excellent articles on forecasting in the *Harvard Business Review* that we recommend you read.[8]

No forecasting method, as you can see in Table 4.14 and as we learned in this chapter, is perfect under all conditions. And even once management has found a satisfactory approach, it must still monitor and control its forecasts to make sure errors do not get out of hand. Forecasting can often be a very challenging, but rewarding, part of managing.

[8] The articles are by J. C. Chambers and others, "How to Choose the Right Forecasting Technique," *Harvard Business Review* Vol. 49, No. 1, July–August 1971, pp. 45–74, and D. M. Georgoff and R. G. Murdick, "Manager's Guide to Forecasting," *Harvard Business Review* Vol. 64, No. 1, January–February 1986, pp. 110–120.

TABLE 4.14 A Comparison of Forecasting Methods

		NAIVE EXTRAPOLATION	DELPHI TECHNIQUE	MOVING AVERAGES	EXPONENTIAL SMOOTHING	TIME SERIES EXTRAPOLATION	REGRESSION MODELS
Time	Span — Is the forecast period a: Present need, or Short-, Medium-, or Long-term projection?	Present need to Medium	Medium or Long	Short, Medium, or Long	Present need to Short or Medium	Short, Medium, or Long	Short, Medium, or Long
	Urgency — Is the forecast needed immediately?	Rapid results are a strong advantage of this technique. Devel. time Short Execution time Short	Urgency seriously compromises quality. Dev Moderate Ex Moderate to Long	Rapid results are a strong advantage of this technique. Dev Short Ex Short		Computation is quick if data are available; data gathering can cause delays. Dev Short to Moderate Ex Short	Model formulation takes time, but forecast computation is quick. Dev Moderate to Long Ex Short to Moderate
	Frequency — Are frequent forecast updates needed?	Can easily accommodate frequent updates.	Usually used for one-time forecasts, but they can be revised as new information becomes available.	Forecast can be systematically updated easily.	↑	↑	Forecast can be updated quickly if data are available.
Resource requirements	Mathematical sophistication — Are quantitative skills limited?	Minimal quantitative capabilities are required.					A fundamental competency level is required.
	Computer — Are computer capabilities limited?	Computer capabilities are not essential.		A computer is helpful for repetitive updating.	↑	A computer is helpful for repetitive updating.	A computer is essential for most cases.
	Financial — Are only limited resources available?	Very inexpensive to implement and maintain.	Expense depends on makeup and affiliation of participants.	If data are readily available, out-of-pocket costs are minimal.	↑	If data are readily available, out-of-pocket costs are minimal.	If data are on hand, development costs are moderate.
Input	Antecedent — Are only limited past data available?	Some past data are required, but extended history is not essential.	↑	Past history is essential.	Only recent forecasts and current data are required once alpha is determined.	↑	Past history is essential with detail required.
Output	Accuracy — Is a high level of accuracy critical?	Often provides a limited practical level of accuracy.	Not particularly accurate, but usually most accurate when horizons are extended and conditions are dynamic.	Accurate under stable conditions.	Generally rates high in accuracy for short-term forecasts.	Normally accurate for trends and stationary series.	Can be accurate if variable relationships are stable and the proportion of explained variance is high.

Source: D. M. Georgoff and R. G. Murdick, "Manager's Guide to Forecasting," *Harvard Business Review* Vol. 64, No. 1, January–February, 1986, pp. 110–120.

GLOSSARY

Time Series Models. Models that forecast using only historical data.

Causal Models. Models that forecast using variables and factors in addition to time.

Judgmental Models. Models that forecast using judgments, experience, and qualitative and subjective data.

Scatter Diagrams. Diagrams of the variable to be forecasted, plotted against another variable, such as time.

Moving Average. A forecasting technique that averages past values in computing the forecast.

Weighted Moving Average. A moving average forecasting method that places different weights on past values.

Exponential Smoothing. A forecasting method that is a combination of the last forecast and the last observed value.

Smoothing Constant. A value between 0 and 1 that is used in an exponential smoothing forecast. It is generally in the range from 0.1 to 0.3.

Mean Absolute Deviation (MAD). A technique for determining the accuracy of a forecasting model by taking the average of the absolute deviations.

Mean Squared Error (MSE). A technique for determining the accuracy of a forecasting model by taking the average of the squared error terms for a forecasting model.

Mean Absolute Percent Error (MAPE). A technique for determining the accuracy of a forecasting model by taking the average of the absolute errors as a percentage of the observed values.

Bias. A technique for determining the accuracy of a forecasting model by measuring the average total error and its direction.

Least Squares. A procedure used in trend projection and regression analysis to minimize the squared distances between the estimated straight line and the observed values.

Regression Analysis. A forecasting procedure that uses the least squares approach on one or more independent variables to develop a forecasting model.

Standard Error of the Estimate. A measure of the accuracy of regression estimates.

Correlation Coefficient. A measure of the strength of relationship between two variables.

Tracking signal. A measure of how well the forecast is predicting actual values.

Delphi. A judgmental forecasting technique that uses decision makers, staff personnel, and respondents to determine a forecast.

Decision-Making Group. A group of experts in a Delphi technique that has the responsibility of making the forecast.

KEY EQUATIONS

(4-1) Moving average $= \dfrac{\sum\limits_{i=1}^{n} \text{Demand in previous } n \text{ periods}}{n}$

An equation for computing a moving average forecast.

(4-2) Weighted moving average $= \dfrac{\Sigma \left(\begin{array}{c}\text{Weight for} \\ \text{period } n\end{array}\right)\left(\begin{array}{c}\text{Demand in} \\ \text{period } n\end{array}\right)}{\Sigma \text{ Weights}}$

An equation for computing a weighted moving average forecast.

(4-3) New forecast = Last period's forecast + α (Last period's actual demand − Last period's forecast)

An equation for computing an exponential smoothing forecast.

(4-4) $F_t = F_{t-1} + \alpha(A_{t-1} - F_{t-1})$

Equation 4-3 rewritten mathematically.

(4-5) $\text{MAD} = \dfrac{\Sigma \, |\text{Forecast errors}|}{n}$

A measure of overall forecast error called mean absolute deviation.

(4-6) $T_t = T_{t-1} + \beta(F_t - F_{t-1})$

Trend component of an exponential smoothing model.

(4-7) $\hat{Y} = a + bX$

A least squares straight line used in trend projection and regression analysis forecasting.

(4-8) $b = \dfrac{\Sigma XY - n\overline{X}\,\overline{Y}}{\Sigma X^2 - n\overline{X}^2}$

An equation used to compute the slope, b, of a regression line.

(4-9) $a = \overline{Y} - b\overline{X}$

An equation used to compute the Y-intercept, a, of a regression line.

(4-10) $S_{Y,X} = \sqrt{\dfrac{\Sigma(Y - Y_c)^2}{n - 2}}$

Standard error of the estimate.

(4-11) $S_{Y,X} = \sqrt{\dfrac{\Sigma Y^2 - a\Sigma Y - b\Sigma XY}{n - 2}}$

Another way to express Equation 4-10.

(4-12) $r = \dfrac{n\Sigma XY - \Sigma X\Sigma Y}{\sqrt{[n\Sigma X^2 - (\Sigma X)^2][n\Sigma Y^2 - (\Sigma Y)^2]}}$

Correlation coefficient.

(4-13) $\hat{Y} = a + b_1X_1 + b_2X_2$

The least squares line used in multiple regression.

(4-14) Tracking signal $= \dfrac{\text{RSFE}}{\text{MAD}} = \dfrac{\Sigma \left(\begin{array}{c}\text{Actual demand} \\ \text{in period } i\end{array} - \begin{array}{c}\text{Forecast demand} \\ \text{in period } i\end{array}\right)}{\text{MAD}}$

An equation for monitoring forecasts.

SOLVED PROBLEMS

Solved Problem 4-1

Demand for patient surgery at Washington General Hospital has increased steadily in the past few years, as seen in the following table.

YEAR	OUTPATIENT SURGERIES PERFORMED
1	45
2	50
3	52
4	56
5	58
6	

The director of medical services predicted six years ago that demand in year 1 would be 42 surgeries.

Using exponential smoothing with a weight of $\alpha = 0.20$, develop forecasts for years 2 through 6. What is the MAD?

Solution

YEAR	ACTUAL	FORECAST (SMOOTHED)	ERROR	|ERROR|
1	45	42	-3	3
2	50	$42.6 = 42 + .2(45-42)$	-7.4	7.4
3	52	$44.1 = 42.6 + .2(50-42.6)$	-7.9	7.9
4	56	$45.7 = 44.1 + .2(52-44.1)$	-10.3	10.3
5	58	$47.7 = 45.7 + .2(56-45.7)$	-10.3	10.3
6	—	$49.8 = 47.7 + .2(58-47.7)$		38.9

$$\text{MAD} = \frac{\Sigma|\text{Errors}|}{n} = \frac{38.9}{5} = 7.78$$

Solved Problem 4-2

Room registrations in the Toronto Towers Plaza Hotel have been recorded for the past nine years. Management would like to determine the mathematical trend of guest registration in order to project future occupancy. This estimate would help the hotel determine whether a future expansion will be needed. Given the following time series data, develop a regression equation relating registrations to time. Then forecast 1992 registrations. Room registrations are in thousands:

1982: 17   1983: 16   1984: 16   1985: 21   1986: 20

1987: 20   1988: 23   1989: 25   1990: 24

Solution

YEAR	TRANSFORMED YEAR X	REGISTRANTS Y (1,000's)	X^2	XY
1982	1	17	1	17
1983	2	16	4	32
1984	3	16	9	48
1985	4	21	16	84
1986	5	20	25	100
1987	6	20	36	120
1988	7	23	49	161
1989	8	25	64	200
1990	9	24	81	216
	$\Sigma X = 45$	$\Sigma Y = 182$	$\Sigma X^2 = 285$	$\Sigma XY = 978$

$$\overline{X} = \frac{45}{9} = 5, \qquad \overline{Y} = \frac{182}{9} = 20.22$$

$$b = \frac{\Sigma XY - n\overline{X}\,\overline{Y}}{\Sigma X^2 - n\overline{X}^2} = \frac{978 - (9)(5)(20.22)}{285 - (9)(25)} = \frac{978 - 909.9}{285 - 225} = \frac{68.1}{60} = 1.135$$

$$a = \overline{Y} - b\overline{X} = 20.22 - (1.135)(5) = 20.22 - 5.675 = 14.545$$

$$\hat{Y}\text{ (registrations)} = 14.545 + 1.135X$$

The projection of registrations in 1992 (which is $X = 11$ in the coding system used) is

$$\hat{Y} = 14.545 + (1.135)(11) = 27.03$$

or 27,030 guests in 1992.

Solved Problem 4-3

Quarterly demand for Jaguar XJ6s at a New York auto dealer are forecast with the equation:

$$\hat{Y} = 10 + 3X$$

where

X = quarters: quarter I of 1989 = 0,
    quarter II of 1989 = 1,
    quarter III of 1989 = 2,
    quarter IV of 1989 = 3,
    quarter I of 1990 = 4,
    and so on,

and

$$\hat{Y} = \text{quarterly demand.}$$

The demand for sports sedans is seasonal and the indices for quarters I, II, III, and IV are .80, 1.00, 1.30, and .90, respectively. Forecast demand for each quarter of 1991. Then seasonalize each forecast to adjust for quarterly variations.

Solution

Quarter II of 1990 is coded $X = 5$; quarter III of 1990, $X = 6$; and quarter IV of 1990, $X = 7$. Hence, quarter I of 1991 is coded $X = 8$; quarter II, $X = 9$; and so on.

$\hat{Y}(1991 \text{ quarter I}) = 10 + 3(8) = 34$	Adjusted forecast $= (0.80)(34) = 27.2$
$\hat{Y}(1991 \text{ quarter II}) = 10 + 3(9) = 37$	Adjusted forecast $= (1.00)(37) = 37$
$\hat{Y}(1991 \text{ quarter III}) = 10 + 3(10) = 40$	Adjusted forecast $= (1.30)(40) = 52$
$\hat{Y}(1991 \text{ quarter IV}) = 10 + 3(11) = 43$	Adjusted forecast $= (0.90)(43) = 38.7$

DISCUSSION QUESTIONS AND PROBLEMS

Discussion Questions

4-1 Briefly describe the steps that are used to develop a forecasting system.

4-2 What is a time series forecasting model?

4-3 What is the difference between a causal model and a time series model?

4-4 What is a judgmental forecasting model, and when is it appropriate?

4-5 What is the meaning of least squares in a regression model?

4-6 What are some of the problems and drawbacks of the moving average forecasting model?

4-7 What effect does the value of the smoothing constant have on the weight given to the past forecast and the past observed value?

4-8 Briefly describe the Delphi technique.

4-9 What is MAD, and why is it important in the selection and use of forecasting models?

Problems

4-10 John Smith has developed the following forecasting model:

$$\hat{Y} = 36 + 4.3 X1$$

where

$\hat{Y} =$ demand for K10 air conditioners, and

$X1 =$ the outside temperature (°F).

(a) Forecast demand for K10 when the temperature is 70°F.

(b) What is the demand for a temperature of 80°F?

(c) What is demand for a temperature of 90°F?

· 4-11 Develop a four-month moving average forecast for Wallace Garden Supply. A three-month moving average forecast was developed in the section on moving averages.

· 4-12 Using MAD, determine whether the forecast in Problem 4-11 or the forecast in the section concerning Wallace Garden Supply is more accurate.

: 4-13 Data collected on the yearly demand for 50-lb. bags of fertilizer at Wallace Garden Supply are shown in the following table. Develop a three-year moving average to forecast sales. Then estimate demand again with a weighted moving average in which sales in the most recent year are given a weight of 2 and sales in the other two years are each given a weight of 1. Which method do you think is best?

YEAR	DEMAND FOR FERTILIZER (1,000'S OF BAGS)
1	4
2	6
3	4
4	5
5	10
6	8
7	7
8	9
9	12
10	14
11	15

· 4-14 Develop a two- and a four-year moving average for the demand for fertilizer in Problem 4-13.

: 4-15 In Problems 4-13 and 4-14, four different forecasts were developed for the demand for fertilizer. These four forecasts are a two-year moving average, a three-year moving average, a weighted moving average, and a four-year moving average. Which one would you use? Explain your answer.

: 4-16 Use exponential smoothing with a smoothing constant of .3 to forecast the demand for fertilizer given in Problem 4-13. Assume that last period's forecast for year 1 is 5,000 bags to begin the procedure. Would you prefer to use the exponential smoothing model or the weighted average model developed in Problem 4-13? Explain your answer.

· 4-17 Sales of Cool-Man air conditioners have grown steadily during the past five years.

YEAR	SALES
1985	450
1986	495
1987	518
1988	563
1989	584
1990	?

The sales manager had predicted in 1984 that 1985 sales would be 410 air conditioners. Using exponential smoothing with an alpha weight of $\alpha = .30$, develop forecasts for 1986 through 1990.

4-18 Using smoothing constants of .6 and .9, develop a forecast for the sales of Cool-Man air conditioners. See Problem 4-17.

4-19 What effect did the smoothing constant have on the forecast for Cool-Man air conditioners? See Problems 4-17 and 4-18. Which smoothing constant gives the most accurate forecast?

4-20 Use a three-year moving average forecasting model to forecast the sales of Cool-Man air conditioners. See Problem 4-17.

4-21 Using the trend projection method, develop a forecasting model for the sales of Cool-Man air conditioners. See Problem 4-17.

4-22 Would you use exponential smoothing with a smoothing constant of .3, a three-year moving average, or trend to predict the sales of Cool-Man air conditioners? Refer to Problems 4-17, 4-20, and 4-21.

4-23 The operations manager of a musical instrument distributor feels that demand for bass drums may be related to the number of television appearances by the popular rock group Green Shades during the previous month. The manager has collected the data shown in the following table.

DEMAND FOR BASS DRUMS	GREEN SHADES TV APPEARANCES
3	3
6	4
7	7
5	6
10	8
8	5

(a) Graph these data to see whether a linear equation might describe the relationship between the group's television shows and bass drum sales.

(b) Use the least squares regression method to derive a forecasting equation.

(c) What is your estimate for bass drum sales if the Green Shades performed on TV nine times last month?

4-24 Sales of industrial vacuum cleaners at R. Lowenthal Supply Co. over the past 13 months are shown on the following page.

SALES (THOUSANDS)	MONTH
11	January
14	February
16	March
10	April
15	May
17	June
11	July
14	August
17	September
12	October
14	November
16	December
11	January

(a) Using a moving average with three periods, determine the demand for vacuum cleaners for next February.

(b) Using a weighted moving average with three periods, determine the demand for vacuum cleaners for February. Use 3, 2, and 1 for the weights of the most recent, second most recent, and third most recent periods, respectively. For example, if you were forecasting the demand for February, November would have a weight of 1, December would have a weight of 2, and January would have a weight of 3.

(c) Evaluate the accuracy of each of these methods.

(d) What other factors might R. Lowenthal consider in forecasting sales?

: 4-25 Passenger miles flown on Northeast Airlines, a commuter firm serving the Boston hub, are shown below for the past 12 weeks.

WEEK	ACTUAL PASSENGER MILES (1,000'S)
1	17
2	21
3	19
4	23
5	18
6	16
7	20
8	18
9	22
10	20
11	15
12	22

(a) Assuming an initial forecast for week 1 of 17,000 miles, use exponential smoothing to compute miles for weeks 2 through 12. Use $\alpha = .2$.

(b) What is the MAD for this model?

: **4-26** Emergency calls to Winter Park, Florida's 911 system for the past 24 weeks are shown below.

WEEK	CALLS	WEEK	CALLS
1	50	13	55
2	35	14	35
3	25	15	25
4	40	16	55
5	45	17	55
6	35	18	40
7	20	19	35
8	30	20	60
9	35	21	75
10	20	22	50
11	15	23	40
12	40	24	65

(a) Compute the exponentially smoothed forecast of calls for each week. Assume an initial forecast of 50 calls in the first week and use $\alpha = .1$. What is the forecast for the 25th week?

(b) Reforecast each period using $\alpha = .6$.

(c) Actual calls during the 25th week were 85. Which smoothing constant provides a superior forecast? Explain and justify the measure of error used.

: **4-27** Using the 911 call data in Problem 4-26, forecast calls for weeks 2 through 25 with a trend-adjusted exponential smoothing model. Assume an initial forecast for 50 calls again for week 1 and an initial trend of 0. Use smoothing constants of $\alpha = .3$ and $\beta = .1$. Is this model better than that of Problem 4-26? What adjustment might be useful for further improvement? (Again, assume actual calls in week 25 were 85.)

: **4-28** Consulting income at Kate Walsh Associates for the period February–July has been as follows:

MONTH	INCOME ($1,000'S)
February	70.0
March	68.5
April	64.8
May	71.7
June	71.3
July	72.8

Use trend-adjusted exponential smoothing to forecast August's income. Assume that the initial forecast for February is $65,000 and the initial trend adjustment is 0. The smoothing constants selected are $\alpha = .1$ and $\beta = .2$.

: **4-29** Resolve Problem 4-28 with $\alpha = .1$ and $\beta = .8$. Using MAD, which smoothing constants provide a better forecast?

· **4-30** A study to determine the correlation between bank deposits and consumer price indices in Birmingham, Alabama, revealed the following (which was based on $n = 5$ years of data):

$$\Sigma X = 15$$
$$\Sigma X^2 = 55$$
$$\Sigma XY = 70$$
$$\Sigma Y = 20$$
$$\Sigma Y^2 = 130$$

Find the coefficient of correlation. What does it imply to you?

: **4-31** The accountant at O. H. Hall Coal Distributors, Inc., notes that the demand for coal seems to be tied to an index of weather severity developed by the U.S. Weather Bureau. That is, when weather was extremely cold in the United States over the past five years (and hence the index was high), coal sales were high. The accountant proposes that one good forecast of next year's coal demand could be made by developing a regression equation and then consulting the *Farmer's Almanac* to see how severe next year's winter will be.

(a) Derive a least squares regression and compute the coefficient of correlation for the data in the following table.

(b) Also compute the standard error of the estimate.

COAL SALES (IN MILLIONS OF TONS) Y	WEATHER INDEX X
4	2
1	1
4	4
6	5
5	3

: **4-32** Bus and subway ridership in Washington, D.C., during the summer months is believed to be heavily tied to the number of tourists visiting the city. During the past 12 years, the following data have been obtained.

YEAR	NO. OF TOURISTS (MILLIONS)	RIDERSHIP (100,000'S)
1979	7	15
1980	2	10
1981	6	13
1982	4	15
1983	14	25
1984	15	27
1985	16	24
1986	12	20
1987	14	27
1988	20	44
1989	15	34
1990	7	17

(a) Plot these data and decide if a linear model is reasonable.

(b) Develop a regression relationship.

(c) What is expected ridership if 10 million tourists visit the city?

(d) If there are no tourists at all, explain the predicted ridership.

: **4-33** Accountants at the firm Walker and Walker believed that several traveling executives submit unusually high travel vouchers when they return from business trips. The accountants took a sample of 200 vouchers submitted from the past year; they then developed the following multiple regression equation relating expected travel cost ($\hat{Y}$) to number of days on the road (X_1) and distance travelled (X_2) in miles:

$$\hat{Y} = \$90.00 + \$48.50X_1 + \$0.40X_2$$

The coefficient of correlation computed was .68.
(a) If Thomas Williams returns from a 300-mile trip that took him out of town for five days, what is the expected amount he should claim as expenses?
(b) Williams submitted a reimbursement request for $685; what should the accountant do?
(c) Comment on the validity of this model. Should any other variables be included? Which ones? Why?

: **4-34** Dr. Jerilyn Ross, a New York City psychologist, specializes in treating patients who are phobic and afraid to leave their homes. The following table indicates how many patients Dr. Ross has seen each year for the past ten years. It also indicates what the robbery rate was in New York City during the same year.

YEAR	NUMBER OF PATIENTS	CRIME RATE (ROBBERIES PER 1,000 POPULATION)
1981	36	58.3
1982	33	61.6
1983	40	73.4
1984	41	75.7
1985	40	81.1
1986	55	89.0
1987	60	101.1
1988	54	94.8
1989	58	103.3
1990	61	116.2

Using trend analysis, how many patients do you think Dr. Ross will see in 1991, 1992, and 1993? How well does the model fit the data?

: **4-35** Using the data in Problem 4-34, apply linear regression to study the relationship between the crime rate and Dr. Ross's patient load. If the robbery rate increases to 131.2 in 1991, how many phobic patients will Dr. Ross treat? If the crime rate drops to 90.6, what is the patient projection?

· **4-36** Management of Davis's Department Store has used time series extrapolation to forecast retail sales for the next four quarters. The sales estimates are $100,000, $120,000, $140,000, and $160,000 for the respective quarters. Seasonal indices for the four quarters have been found to be 1.30, .90, .70, and 1.15, respectively. Compute a seasonalized or adjusted sales forecast.

· **4-37** In the past, Judy Holmes's tire dealership sold an average of 1,000 radials each year. In the past two years 200 and 250, respectively, were sold in fall, 300 and 350 in winter, 150 and 165 in spring, and 300 and 285 in summer. With a major expansion planned, Ms. Holmes projects sales next year to increase to 1,200 radials. What will the demand be each season?

: **4-38** Thirteen students entered the undergraduate business program at Rollins College two years ago. The following table indicates what their grade point averages (GPAs) were after being in the program for two years and what each student scored on the SAT exam when he or she was in high school. Is there a meaningful relationship between grades and SAT scores? If a student scores a 350 on the SAT, what do you think his or her GPA will be? What about a student who scores 800?

STUDENT	SAT SCORE	GPA
A	421	2.90
B	377	2.93
C	585	3.00
D	690	3.45
E	608	3.66
F	390	2.88
G	415	2.15
H	481	2.53
I	729	3.22
J	501	1.99
K	613	2.75
L	709	3.90
M	366	1.60

Data Set Problem

4-39 Aronson Savings and Loan is proud of its long tradition in Altamonte Springs, Florida. Begun by Eileen Aronson two years after World War II, the S&L has bucked the trend of financial and liquidity problems that have plagued the industry since 1985. Deposits have increased slowly but surely over the years, despite recessions in 1954, 1969, and 1981. Ms. Aronson believes it necessary to have a long-range strategic plan for her firm, including a five-year forecast of deposits. She examines the past deposit data and also peruses Florida's Gross State Product (GSP) over the same 44 years. (GSP is analogous to Gross National Product, GNP, but on the state level.)

(a) Using exponential smoothing, with $\alpha = .6$, then trend analysis, and finally, linear regression, discuss which forecasting model fits best for Aronson's strategic plan. Justify why one model should be selected over another.

(b) Carefully examine the data. Can you make a case for excluding a portion of the information. Why? Would that change your choice of model?

YEAR	DEPOSITS[1]	GSP[2]	YEAR	DEPOSITS[1]	GSP[2]	YEAR	DEPOSITS[1]	GSP[2]
1947	.25	.4	1962	2.3	1.6	1977	24.1	3.9
1948	.24	.4	1963	2.8	1.5	1978	25.6	3.8
1949	.24	.5	1964	2.8	1.6	1979	30.3	3.8
1950	.26	.7	1965	2.7	1.7	1980	36.0	3.7
1951	.25	.9	1966	3.9	1.9	1981	31.1	4.1
1952	.30	1.0	1967	4.9	1.9	1982	31.7	4.1
1953	.31	1.4	1968	5.3	2.3	1983	38.5	4.0
1954	.32	1.7	1969	6.2	2.5	1984	47.9	4.5
1955	.24	1.3	1970	4.1	2.8	1985	49.1	4.6
1956	.26	1.2	1971	4.5	2.9	1986	55.8	4.5
1957	.25	1.1	1972	6.1	3.4	1987	70.1	4.6
1958	.33	.9	1973	7.7	3.8	1988	70.9	4.6
1959	.50	1.2	1974	10.1	4.1	1989	79.1	4.7
1960	.95	1.2	1975	15.2	4.0	1990	94.0	5.0
1961	1.7	1.2	1976	18.1	4.0			

[1] In $ millions.
[2] In $ billions.

The North-South Airline*

In January 1988, Northern Airlines merged with Southeast Airlines to create the fourth largest U.S. carrier. The new North-South Airline inherited both an aging fleet of Boeing 727-200 aircraft and Stephen Ruth. Ruth was a tough former secretary of the navy who stepped in as new president and chairman of the board.

Ruth's first concern in creating a financially solid company was maintenance costs. It was commonly surmised in the airline industry that maintenance costs rise with the age of the aircraft. He quickly noticed that historically there had been a significant difference in the reported B727-200 maintenance costs (from ATA Form 41's) both in the airframe and engine areas between Northern Airlines and Southeast Airlines, with Southeast having the newer fleet.

On February 12, 1988, Peg Young, vice president for operations and maintenance, was called into Ruth's office and asked to study the issue. Specifically, Ruth wanted to know whether the average fleet age was correlated to direct airframe maintenance costs, and whether there was a relationship between average fleet age and direct engine maintenance costs. Young was to report back by February 26 with the answer, along with quantitative and graphical descriptions of the relationship.

Young's first step was to have her staff construct the average age of Northern and Southeastern B727-200 fleets, by quarter, since the introduction of that aircraft to service by each airline in late 1977 and early 1978. The average age of each fleet was calculated by first multiplying the total number of calendar days each aircraft had been in service at the pertinent point in time by the average daily utilization of the respective fleet to total fleet hours flown. The total fleet hours flown was then divided by the number of aircraft in service at that time, giving the age of the "average" aircraft in the fleet.

The average utilization was found by taking the actual total fleet hours flown at September 30, 1987, from Northern and Southeastern data, and dividing by the total days in service for all aircraft at that time. The average utilization for Southeast was 8.3 hours per day, and the average utilization for Northern was 8.7 hours per day. Since the available cost data were calculated for each yearly period ending at the end of the first quarter, average fleet age was calculated at the same points in time.

The fleet data are shown in the following table. Airframe cost data and engine cost data are both shown paired with fleet average age in that table.

Prepare Peg Young's response to Stephen Ruth.

* Dates and names of airlines and individuals have been changed in this case to maintain confidentiality. The data and issues described here are actual.

(cont'd)

North-South Airline Data for Boeing 727-200 Jets

	NORTHERN AIRLINE DATA			SOUTHEAST AIRLINE DATA		
YEAR	AIRFRAME COST PER AIRCRAFT	ENGINE COST PER AIRCRAFT	AVERAGE AGE (HOURS)	AIRFRAME COST PER AIRCRAFT	ENGINE COST PER AIRCRAFT	AVERAGE AGE (HOURS)
1981	$51.80	$43.49	6,512	$13.29	$18.86	5107
1982	54.92	38.58	8,404	25.15	31.55	8145
1983	69.70	51.48	11,077	32.18	40.43	7360
1984	68.90	58.72	11,717	31.78	22.10	5773
1985	63.72	45.47	13,275	25.34	19.69	7150
1986	84.73	50.26	15,215	32.78	32.58	9364
1987	78.74	79.60	18,390	35.56	38.07	8259

CASE STUDY

Kwik Lube

Dick Johnson received his Ph.D. in the early 1960s from the University of Southern California when he was 25 years old. He accepted a teaching position as an assistant professor of English with the University of Washington, and in 1972 wrote one of the leading textbooks in basic English principles. At the age of 45, Dick retired from the University of Washington with a net worth of approximately a half-million dollars.

Although Dick enjoyed traveling, he found retirement somewhat boring, and in 1979, during one of his trips to Los Angeles, he came across a very interesting type of new business. It was a small gas station that specialized only in oil changes and lubrication jobs. The old gas station had been remodeled, the gas pumps had been removed, and the large sign above the small building read "OIL AND LUBE—$10 and 10 MINUTES." For two hours, Dick observed the converted gas station from a restaurant across the street, and although the mechanics were never able to do a complete oil and lubrication job in ten minutes, they were fast and had plenty of business.

The next day, Dick talked with one of the mechanics and found that the owner, George Day, at one time ran the old gas station. During the next month, Dick made three trips to Los Angeles to talk to George about how he got into the business and how the business worked. Dick paid George $1,000 for his advice and information and promised never to compete directly with George or ever to open or operate a similar type of business in the Los Angeles area.

After talking to his lawyer and accountant, Dick started to organize a new business—Kwik Lube. The first Kwik Lube station was designed to be similar to the small converted gas station in Los Angeles. The building was new and attractive, and the equipment was of the best quality and very expensive. In March 1980, Dick had built his first Kwik Lube, and he purchased options to buy two other commercial lots for two additional Kwik Lube stations. In May 1980, Dick decided to exercise his options, and by the end of 1980, he had completed two additional Kwik Lubes in the Seattle area. The total gross revenues in 1980 from all three stations was $26,000.

Between 1980 and 1984, business picked up rapidly. Total gross sales in 1981 and 1982 were $68,000 and $75,000, respectively. In 1983, total gross sales for the three Kwik Lube stations was $75,000, and in 1984, total gross sales were $78,000. Dick was convinced that this sales increase was due to his not significantly increasing the price of his basic service, which was to change the oil, change the filter, and do a lube job. In 1980, the total price was $9.95. In 1983, the total price per job was $10.50, and by 1984, the total price was only $10.95. Dick was pleased with the operation of Kwik Lube, especially when he considered the consequences of the recession in 1983, which in his opinion reduced his potential sales for 1983 and

1984. But Dick was still not satisfied with this success.

A number of franchised service stations, transmission shops, brake and shock stores, and muffler shops were doing extremely well. The type of products and services offered by Kwik Lube were similar to these franchise operations. In addition to running his three Kwik Lube stations in Seattle, Dick desired to franchise his idea in other cities in Washington and in other states such as Oregon, Idaho, and Montana. During the last three years, Dick had acquired considerable knowledge about this type of business. He was able to obtain the best possible prices for oil, lubricants, and filters. If he franchised Kwik Lube, he would even be able able to make a profit from selling oil, filters, and lubricants.

Dick invested over $5,000 in lawyers' fees and another $2,000 in talking to other companies in the franchise business. He decided to set his franchise fee at $8,000, plus 6% of the gross sales of the stations. In addition, each new Kwik Lube station had to conform to exacting standards for the building and all of the equipment. Depending on the location, Dick could build and equip a Kwik Lube station for under $100,000. Like his own Kwik Lube stations, these new stations would have two-car or vehicle bays. In 1985, Dick sold his first franchise to T. A. Williams and another franchise to an investor in Eugene, Oregon. By 1988, Dick had sold a total of 11 franchises in Spokane, Washington; Eugene, Oregon; Portland, Oregon; Butte, Montana; and Boise, Idaho. In addition, Dick experienced a substantial growth rate for total gross sales for his three Kwik Lube stations in Seattle. In 1985, total gross sales were $99,000. In 1986, total gross sales were $104,000; in 1987, $120,000; and in 1988, $133,000.

Dick knew that it would only be a matter of time before someone else would start to compete directly with his Kwik Lube stations, but he never believed that the first competition would be in Seattle. Construction on the first two Speedy Lube stations started in 1988, and both stations were in operation in early 1989. The two stores were almost identical to the Kwik Lube stations, but Speedy Lube was priced two dollars less than Kwik Lube's current price, which was now $14.95. Dick never dreamed that this new competition would cut so deeply into his total gross sales. Total gross sales for the three Kwik Lube stations in Seattle dropped to $111,000 for 1989, and the situation did not look

any better for 1990. (Indeed, when 1990 figures became available, sales were again only $111,000.)

Soon after the total gross sales figures came in for 1989, Dick got some startling information from one of his friends in Spokane. Over 50% of the stock in Speedy Lube, Inc. was owned by Richland, Inc., a holding company owned by T. A. Williams. Dick was outraged that one of the people who purchased a franchise from him was directly competing with his Kwik Lube stores and in direct violation of the franchise contract, which contained a noncompetition clause in fine print.

Dick had only two goals for the coming year: (1) to shut down the two Speedy Lube stations and (2) to regain his lost sales for the two years from T. A. Williams. Both objectives were to be accomplished with a lawsuit. Dick Johnson's lawyer strongly suggested that Dick employ an expert witness to testify on his behalf against Speedy Lube. While there seemed to be no question about who would win the case, Dick's lawyer believed that an expert witness could more accurately determine the damages. In addition, most juries place more importance on expert testimony. As a result, Dick decided to employ the services of Dr. Warren Gunn.

Dr. Gunn was a professor of marketing at Eastern Washington University, which was very close to Spokane. He had more than ten years experience as an expert witness, and his specialty was determining damages for antitrust and franchise cases. His basic strategy was to find data about the same industry or a similar one in a location resembling the area in which the original problem occurred. In this case, Dr. Gunn needed data about the fast oil and lubrication business in a location similar to Seattle. Because Dick originally obtained his idea from a small station in Los Angeles and because Los Angeles had hundreds of these types of businesses by 1989, Dr. Gunn decided to collect data in the Los Angeles area. This would require the development and pilot testing of a questionnaire that could determine the total gross number of cars serviced for fast oil and lubrication businesses in the Los Angeles area between 1980 and 1990.

Although the questionnaire study would cost $2,000 to perform, Dr. Gunn and Dick both believed that it was the best approach. The data were collected in two weeks, and are summarized in the table. Both Dr. Gunn and Dick knew that if the results of the questionnaire were not favorable, they would not use it during the case.

(cont'd)

Analysis of Average Fast Oil and Lubrication. Total Gross Sales of Cars Serviced at Los Angeles Stations (Using Two Bays as a Basis for Comparison)

YEAR	AVERAGE TOTAL SALES $
1980	19,000
1981	22,000
1982	25,000
1983	24,000
1984	26,000
1985	33,000
1986	35,000
1987	39,000
1988	44,000
1989	47,000
1990	52,000

Discussion Questions

1. Using the data in the table, compute the loss for Kwik Lube stations during the last two years using regression.

2. Was it worth $2,000 to perform the marketing research?

3. Estimate the total loss in gross sales for Dick's Kwik Lube stations over the two-year period. How accurate can the results claim to be?

4. What other factors might be introduced into the lawsuit?

Source: B. Render, R. M. Stair, and I. Greenberg, *Cases and Readings in Management Science*, 2nd ed., Boston: Allyn and Bacon, Inc., 1990. This case was prepared by Professor R. M. Stair, Florida State University and Professor I. Greenberg, George Mason University.

BIBLIOGRAPHY

Ashley, R., and Guerard, J. "Applications of Time Series Analysis to Texas Financial Forecasting." *Interfaces* Vol. 13, No. 4, August 1983, pp. 46–55.

Ashton, A. H., and Ashton, R. H. "Aggregating Subjective Forecasts." *Management Science* Vol. 31, No. 12, December 1985, pp. 1499–1508.

Becker, B. C., and Sapienza, A. "Forecasting Hospital Reimbursement." *Hospital and Health Services Administration* Vol. 32, November 1987, pp. 521–530.

Box, G. E. P., and Jenkins, G. *Time Series Analysis: Forecasting and Control.* San Francisco: Holden Day, 1970.

Brazziel, William F. "Forecasting Older Student Enrollment: A Cohort and Participation Rate Model." *Journal of Higher Education* Vol. 58, No. 2, March–April 1987, pp. 222–231.

Brown, R. G. *Statistical Forecasting for Inventory Control.* New York: McGraw-Hill, 1959.

Bunn, D. W., and Seigal, J. P. "Forecasting the Effects of Television Programming upon Electricity Loads." *Journal of the Operational Research Society* Vol. 34, January 1983, pp. 17–25.

Chambers, J. C., Satinder, C., Mullick, S. K., and Smith, D. D. "How to Choose the Right Forecasting Technique." *Harvard Business Review* Vol. 49, No. 4, July–August 1971, pp. 45–74.

Claycombe, W. W., and Sullivan, W. G. "Current Forecasting Techniques." *Journal of System Management* September 1978, pp. 18–20.

Gardner, E. S. "Exponential Smoothing: The State of the Art." *Journal of Forecasting* Vol. 4, No. 1, March 1985.

Georgoff, D. M., and Murdick, R. G. "Managers Guide to Forecasting." *Harvard Business Review* Vol. 64, No. 1, January–February 1986, pp. 110–120.

Gips, J., and Sullivan, B. "Sales Forecasting—Replacing Magic with Logic." *Production and Inventory Management Review* Vol. 2, No. 2, February 1982.

Guerard, John B., Jr., and Beidleman, Carl R. "Composite Earnings Forecasting Efficiency." *Interfaces* Vol. 17, No. 5, September–October 1987, pp. 103–113.

Heizer, J., and Render, B. *Production and Operations Management.* 2nd edition. Boston: Allyn and Bacon, 1991.

Holz, B. W., and Wroth, J. M. "Improving Strength Forecasts: Support for Army Manpower Management." *Interfaces* Vol. 10, No. 6, December 1980, pp. 31–52.

Lane, D., et al. "Forecasting Demand for Long Term Care Services." *Health Services Research* Vol. 20, No. 4, October 1985, pp. 435–459.

Lee, D. R. "A Forecast of Lodging Supply and Demand." *The Cornell HRA Quarterly* August 1984, pp. 27–40.

Mabert, V. A., and Stocco, R. L. "Managing and Monitoring a Forecasting System: The Chemical Bank Experience." *Journal of Bank Research* Autumn 1982, pp. 195–201.

MacStravic, R. S. "An Early Warning Technique." *Hospital and Health Services Administration* Vol. 31, No. 1, January–February 1986, pp. 86–98.

Mahmoud, E. "Accuracy in Forecasting: A Summary." *Journal of Forecasting* April–June 1984.

Makridakis, S., Wheelright, S. C., and McGee, V. E., *Forecasting Methods and Applications.* 2nd edition. New York: John Wiley and Sons, 1983.

Parker, G. C., and Segura, E. L., "How to Get a Better Forecast." *Harvard Business Review* March–April 1971, pp. 99–109.

Plossl, G. W., and Wight, O. W. *Production and Inventory Control.* Englewood Cliffs, N.J.: Prentice-Hall, 1967.

Render, B., Stair, R. M., and Greenberg, I. *Cases and Readings in Management Science*, 2nd edition. Boston: Allyn and Bacon, Inc., 1990.

Schnaars, S. P., and Bavuso, R. J. "Extrapolation Models on Very Short-term Forecasts." *Journal of Business Research* Vol. 14, 1986, pp. 27–36.

Van Dyke, D. T. "Why Economists Make Mistakes." *The Bankers Magazine* May–June 1986, pp. 69–75.

Weinberg, Charles B. "Arts Plan: Implementation, Evolution, and Usage." *Marketing Science* Vol. 5, No. 2, Spring 1986.

5

Fundamentals of Decision Theory

5.1
INTRODUCTION

To a great extent, the successes or failures that a person experiences in life depend on the decisions he or she makes. The individual who managed the ill-fated space shuttle *Challenger* is no longer working for NASA. The person who designed the top-selling Mustang became president of Ford. Why and how did these people make their respective decisions? In general, what is involved in making good decisions? One decision may make the difference between a successful and an unsuccessful career.

Decision theory is an analytic and systematic approach to studying decision making. In this and the next two chapters, we present the mathematical models useful in helping managers make the best possible decisions.

good versus bad decisions

What makes the difference between good and bad decisions? A good decision is one that is based on logic, considers all available data and possible alternatives, and applies the quantitative approach we are about to describe. Occasionally, a good decision results in an unexpected or unfavorable outcome. But if it is made properly, it is *still* a good decision. A bad decision is one that is not based on logic, does not use all available information, does not consider all alternatives, and does not employ appropriate quantitative techniques. If you make a bad decision, but are lucky and a favorable outcome occurs, you have *still* made a bad decision. Managers make many decisions. Although occasionally good decisions yield bad results, in the long run, using decision theory will result in successful outcomes.

5.2
THE SIX STEPS IN DECISION THEORY

Whether you are deciding about getting a haircut today, building a multimillion dollar plant, or buying a new camera, the steps in making a good decision are basically the same. These six steps are:

1. Clearly define the problem at hand.

2. List the possible alternatives.

3. Identify the possible outcomes.

4. List the payoff or profit of each combination of alternatives and outcomes.

5. Select one of the mathematical decision theory models.

6. Apply the model and make your decision.

We use the Thompson Lumber Company case as an example to illustrate these decision theory steps. John Thompson is the founder and president of Thompson Lumber Company, a profitable firm located in Portland, Oregon.

154

Step 1: The problem that John Thompson identifies is whether to expand his product line by manufacturing and marketing a new product—backyard storage sheds.

Step 2: Thompson's second step is to generate the alternatives that are available to him. In decision theory, an *alternative* is defined as a course of action or a strategy that may be chosen by the decision maker. John decides that his alternatives are to construct: (1) a large new plant to manufacture the storage sheds, (2) a small plant, or (3) no plant at all (that is, he has the option of not developing the new product line.)

One of the biggest mistakes that decision makers make is to leave out some important alternatives. Although a particular alternative may seem to be inappropriate or of little value, it might turn out to be the best choice.

Step 3: The third step involves identifying the possible outcomes of the various alternatives. The criteria for action are established at this time. Thompson determines that there are only two possible outcomes: the market for the storage sheds could be favorable, meaning there is a high demand for the product, or it could be unfavorable, meaning there is a low demand for the sheds.

A common mistake is to forget about some of the possible outcomes. Optimistic decision makers tend to ignore bad outcomes, while pessimistic managers may discount a favorable outcome. If you don't consider all possibilities, you will not be making a logical decision and the results may be undesirable. If you do not think the worst can happen, you may design another Edsel automobile. In decision theory, those outcomes over which the decision maker has little or no control are called *states of nature*.

Step 4: Thompson's next step is to express the payoff resulting from each possible combination of alternatives and outcomes. Since in this case he wants to maximize his profits, he can use *profit* to evaluate each consequence. Not every decision, of course, can be based on money alone—any appropriate means of measuring benefit is acceptable. In decision theory, we call such payoffs or profits *conditional values*.

John Thompson has already evaluated the potential profits associated with the various outcomes. With a favorable market, he thinks a large facility would result in a net profit of $200,000 to his firm. This $200,000 is a *conditional value* because Thompson's receiving the money is conditional upon both his building a large factory and having a good market. The conditional value if the market is unfavorable would be a $180,000 net loss. A small plant would result in a net profit of $100,000 in a favorable market, but a net loss of $20,000 would occur if the market was unfavorable. Finally, doing nothing would result in a $0 profit in either market.

The easiest way to present these values is by constructing a *decision table*, sometimes called a *payoff table*. A decision table for Thompson's conditional values is shown in Table 5.1. All of the alternatives are listed down the left side of the table and all of the possible outcomes or states of nature are listed across the top. The body of the table contains the actual payoffs.

TABLE 5.1 Decision Table with Conditional Values for Thompson Lumber

	STATES OF NATURE	
ALTERNATIVES	FAVORABLE MARKET ($)	UNFAVORABLE MARKET ($)
Construct large plant	200,000	−180,000
Construct small plant	100,000	−20,000
Do nothing	0	0

Note: It is important to include all alternatives, including "Do nothing."

select and apply decision theory model

Steps 5 and 6: The last two steps are to select a decision theory model and apply it to the data to help make the decision. Selecting the model depends on the environment in which you're operating and the amount of risk and uncertainty involved.

5.3
TYPES OF DECISION-MAKING ENVIRONMENTS

The types of decisions people make depend on how much knowledge or information they have about the situation. Three decision-making environments are defined and explained as follows.

Type 1. Decision Making under Certainty. In this environment, decision makers know with certainty the consequence of every alternative or decision choice. Naturally, they will choose the alternative that will maximize their well-being or will result in the best outcome. For example, let's say you have $1,000 to invest for a one-year period. One alternative is to open a savings account paying 6% interest and another is to invest in a government treasury bond paying 10% interest. If both investments are secure and guaranteed, then there is a certainty that the treasury bond will be the better investment. The return after one year will be $100 in interest.

Type 2. Decision Making under Risk. Here the decision maker knows the probability of occurrence of each outcome. We know, for example, that the probability of being dealt a club is .25. The probability of rolling a 5 on a die is $\frac{1}{6}$.

In decision making under risk, the decision maker attempts to maximize his or her expected well-being. Decision theory models for business problems in this environment typically employ two equivalent criteria—maximization of expected monetary value and minimization of expected loss.

Type 3. Decision Making under Uncertainty. In this category, the decision maker does not even know the probabilities of the various outcomes. As an example, the probability that a Democrat will be president of the United States 25 years from now is not known. Sometimes it is impossible to assess the probability of success of a new undertaking or product. The criteria for decision making under uncertainty is explained in Section 5.5 of this chapter.

Let's see how decision making under certainty (the type 1 environment) could affect John Thompson. Here we assume that John knows exactly what will happen in the future. If it turns out he knows with certainty that the market for storage sheds will be favorable, what should he do? Look again at Thompson Lumber's conditional values in Table 5.1. Because the market is favorable, he should build the large plant, which has the highest profit of $200,000.

Few managers would be fortunate enough to have complete information and knowledge about the states of nature under consideration. Decision making under risk, discussed next, is a more realistic situation—and slightly more complicated.

5.4
DECISION MAKING UNDER RISK

Decision making under risk is a probabilistic decision situation. Several possible states of nature may occur, each with a given probability. In this section, we consider one of the most popular methods of making decisions under risk, namely, selecting that alternative with the highest expected monetary value. We also look at the concepts of perfect information and opportunity loss.

probabilities are known

Expected Monetary Value (EMV)

Given a decision table with conditional values (payoffs) and probability assessments for all states of nature, it is possible to determine the *expected monetary value* (EMV) for each alternative if the decision could be repeated a large number of times. The EMV for an alternative is just the sum of possible payoffs of the alternative, each weighted by the probability of that payoff occurring.

EMV

$$
\begin{aligned}
\text{EMV (Alternative } i) = \ &(\text{Payoff of first state of nature}) \\
&\times (\text{Probability of first state of nature}) \\
&+ (\text{Payoff of second state of nature}) \quad \text{(5-1)} \\
&\times (\text{Probability of second state of nature}) \\
&+ \cdots + (\text{Payoff of last state of nature}) \\
&\times (\text{Probability of last state of nature})
\end{aligned}
$$

Suppose John Thompson now believes that the probability of a favorable market is exactly the same as the probability of an unfavorable market; that is, each state of nature has a .50 probability. Which alternative would give the greatest expected monetary value? To determine this, John has expanded the decision table, as shown in Table 5.2. His calculations are:

EMV(Large facility) = (.50)($200,000) + (.50)(−$180,000) = $10,000

EMV(Small facility) = (.50)($100,000) + (.50)(−$20,000) = $40,000

EMV(Do nothing) = (.50)($0) + (.50)($0) = $0

TABLE 5.2 Decision Table with Probabilities and EMVs for Thompson Lumber

| | STATES OF NATURE | | |
ALTERNATIVES	FAVORABLE MARKET ($)	UNFAVORABLE MARKET ($)	EMV COMPUTED ($)
Large facility	200,000	−180,000	10,000
Small facility	100,000	−20,000	40,000
Do nothing	0	0	0
Probabilities	.50	.50	

The largest expected value results from the second alternative, building a small factory. Thus, Thompson should proceed with the project and put up a small plant to manufacture storage sheds. The EMVs for the large plant and for doing nothing are $10,000 and $0, respectively.

Expected Value of Perfect Information

John Thompson has been approached by Scientific Marketing, Inc., a firm that proposes to help John make the decision about whether or not to build the plant to produce storage sheds. Scientific Marketing claims that its technical analysis will tell John with certainty whether or not the market is favorable for his proposed product. In other words, it will change his environment from one of decision making under risk to one of decision making under certainty. This information could prevent John from making a very expensive mistake. Scientific Marketing would charge Thompson $65,000 for the information. What would you recommend to John? Should he hire the firm to make the marketing study? Even if the information from the study is perfectly accurate, is it worth $65,000? What would it be worth? Although some of these questions are difficult to answer, determining the value of such *perfect information* can be very useful. It places an upper bound

⊏KEY IDEA▶

on what you would be willing to spend on information such as that being sold by Scientific Marketing. In this section, two related terms are investigated: the *expected value of perfect information* (EVPI) and the *expected value with perfect information.* These techniques can help John make his decision about hiring the marketing firm.

The expected value *with* perfect information is the expected or average return, in the long run, if we have perfect information before a decision has to be made. In order to calculate this value, we choose the best alternative for each state of nature and multiply its payoff times the probability of occurrence of that state of nature.

Expected value *with* perfect information

$$
\begin{aligned}
&= \text{(Best outcome or consequence for first state of nature)} \\
&\quad \times \text{(Probability of first state of nature)} \\
&\quad + \text{(Best outcome for second state of nature)} \\
&\quad \times \text{(Probability of second state of nature)} \\
&\quad + \cdots + \text{(Best outcome for last state of nature)} \\
&\quad \times \text{(Probability of last state of nature)}
\end{aligned}
\tag{5-2}
$$

The expected value of perfect information, EVPI, is the expected outcome *with* perfect information minus the expected outcome *without* perfect information, namely, the maximum EMV.

computing EVPI

$$\begin{aligned} \text{EVPI} = \;& \text{Expected value with perfect information} \qquad (5\text{-}3) \\ & - \text{Maximum EMV} \end{aligned}$$

By referring back to Table 5.2, Thompson can calculate the maximum that he would pay for information, that is, the expected value of perfect information, or EVPI. He follows a two-stage process. First of all, the expected value *with* perfect information is computed. Then, using this result, EVPI is calculated. The procedure is outlined as follows.

1. The best outcome for the state of nature "favorable market" is "build a large facility" with a payoff of $200,000. The best outcome for the state of nature "unfavorable market" is "do nothing" with a payoff of $0. Expected value with perfect information = ($200,000)(.50) + ($0)(.50) = $100,000. Thus, if we had perfect information, we would expect, on the average, $100,000 if the decision could be repeated many times.

2. The maximum EMV is $40,000, which is the expected outcome without perfect information.

$$\begin{aligned} \text{EVPI} = \;& \text{Expected value } \textit{with} \text{ perfect information} \\ & - \text{Maximum EMV} \\ = \;& \$100{,}000 - \$40{,}000 = \$60{,}000 \end{aligned}$$

Thus, the *most* Thompson would be willing to pay for perfect information is $60,000. This, of course, is again based on the assumption that the probability of each state of nature is .50.

Opportunity Loss

An alternative approach to maximizing expected monetary value (EMV) is to minimize *expected opportunity loss* (EOL). Opportunity loss, sometimes called regret, refers to the difference between the optimal profit or payoff and the actual payoff received. In other words, it's the amount lost by not picking the best alternative.

cost of not picking best solution

The minimum expected opportunity loss is found by constructing an opportunity loss table and computing EOL for each alternative. Let's see how the procedure works for the Thompson Lumber case.

Step 1: The first step is to create the opportunity loss table. This is done by determining the opportunity loss for not choosing the best alternative for each state of nature. Opportunity loss for any state of nature, or any column, is calculated by subtracting each outcome in the column from the *best* outcome in the same column. For a favorable market, the best outcome is $200,000 as a result of the first alternative, building a large facility. For

opportunity loss table

TABLE 5.3 Determining Opportunity Losses for Thompson Lumber

STATES OF NATURE	
FAVORABLE MARKET ($)	UNFAVORABLE MARKET ($)
200,000 − 200,000	0 − (−180,000)
200,000 − 100,000	0 − (−20,000)
200,000 − 0	0 − 0

an unfavorable market, the best outcome is $0 as a result of the third alternative, doing nothing. Table 5.3 illustrates these comparisons.

Using Table 5.3, an opportunity loss table can be constructed. The values in Table 5.4 represent the opportunity loss for each state of nature for not choosing the best alternative.

TABLE 5.4 Opportunity Loss Table for Thompson Lumber

	STATES OF NATURE	
ALTERNATIVES	FAVORABLE MARKET ($)	UNFAVORABLE MARKET ($)
Large facility	0	180,000
Small facility	100,000	20,000
Do nothing	200,000	0
Probabilities	.50	.50

Step 2: EOL is computed by multiplying the probability of each state of nature times the appropriate opportunity loss value.

$$\text{EOL (Building large facility)} = (.5)(\$0) + (.5)(\$180,000)$$
$$= \$90,000$$

$$\text{EOL (Building small facility)} = (.5)(\$100,000) + (.5)(\$20,000)$$
$$= \$60,000$$

computing EOL

$$\text{EOL (Do nothing)} = (.5)(\$200,000) + (.5)(\$0)$$
$$= \$100,000$$

Using minimum EOL as the decision criterion, the best decision would be the second alternative, build a small facility.

It is important to note that minimum EOL will *always* result in the same decision as maximum EMV, and that the following relationship always holds: EVPI = minimum EOL. Referring to the Thompson case, EVPI = $60,000 = minimum EOL.

5.5
DECISION MAKING UNDER UNCERTAINTY

When the probability of occurrence of each state of nature can be assessed, the EMV or EOL decision criteria are usually appropriate. When a manager *cannot* assess the outcome probability with confidence or when virtually no probability data are available, other decision criteria are required. This type of problem has been referred to as decision making under uncertainty. The criteria that we will cover in this section include:

1. Maximax.

2. Maximin.

3. Equally likely.

4. Criterion of realism.

5. Minimax.

The first four criteria can be computed directly from the decision table, while the minimax criterion normally requires the use of the opportunity loss table. Let's take a look at each of the five models and apply them to Thompson Lumber. It is now assumed that no probability information about the two outcomes is available to Thompson.

Maximax

The maximax criterion finds the alternative that *max*imizes the *max*imum outcome or consequence for every alternative. You first locate the maximum outcome within every alternative, and then pick that alternative with the maximum number. Since this decision criterion locates the alternative with the *highest* possible gain, it has been called an *optimistic decision criterion.*

maximax is an optimistic approach

In Table 5.5, we see that Thompson's maximax choice is the first alternative, to build a large facility. This is the maximum of the maximum number within each row or alternative.

TABLE 5.5 Thompson's Maximax Decision

	STATES OF NATURE		
ALTERNATIVES	FAVORABLE MARKET ($)	UNFAVORABLE MARKET ($)	MAXIMUM IN ROW ($)
Construct large plant	200,000	−180,000	(200,000) Maximax
Construct small plant	100,000	−20,000	100,000
Do nothing	0	0	0

Maximin

This criterion finds the alternative that *max*imizes the *min*imum outcome or consequence for every alternative. You first locate the minimum outcome within every alternative and then pick that alternative with the maximum number. Since this decision criterion locates the alternative that has the least possible *loss*, it has been called a *pessimistic decision criterion.*

maximin is a pessimistic approach

APPLICATIONS OF QA

Using EOL in the National Weather Service

The National Weather Service (NWS), a major part of the National Oceanic and Atmospheric Administration (NOAA), has reducing property damage and saving lives as its major objectives. One of NWS's responsibilities is to handle the flood forecast-response system that collects data, analyzes data, and forecasts potential flood points at various rivers and water ways throughout the United States. An effective flood forecast-response system is essential. A better system could mean lives and millions of dollars saved.

Any type of forecasting methodology is inherently inaccurate to some extent. In trying to improve or refine an existing forecasting technique, the potential benefits of the improvements must be compared and contrasted with the cost associated with the improvements. The expected opportunity loss (EOL), which is the same numerically as the expected value of perfect information (EVPI), places an upper bound on how much one would be expected to pay if perfect information were available. Making expected opportunity loss calculations, it was determined that the expected opportunity loss for the forecast system itself was $1,453,000 annually. The expected opportunity loss for the response system was $248,000. The total was approximately $1.7 million. These values were determined for a particular area. The expected opportunity loss concept was also used to look at the notion of shortening the processing time by two hours and relaxing or releasing various decision constraints. The total opportunity loss for both the forecast and the response system for shortening the processing time by two hours was $1.617 million, and the expected opportunity loss for the total system for relaxing or releasing decision constraints was estimated to be $538,000.

Using expected opportunity loss in this case allowed decision makers to place economic values on the various forecasts and help determine potential benefits to the public for improvements in the forecasting system. Robert Clark, director of the Office of Hydrology of the National Weather Service stated,

> [This] work was of great value in preparing the NWS program development plan for improving Hydrologic Services as it allowed us to identify benefits from improved flood forecasting much more explicitly than would have been possible otherwise. We have every intention of making continued use of this model to identify potential improvements in the nation's flood forecasting system and provide estimates of the value of these improvements.

Source: Roman Krzysztofozwizz and D. R. Davis, "Toward Improving Flood Forecast-Response System," *Interfaces* Vol. 14, No. 3, May–June 1984.

Thompson's maximin choice, to do nothing, is shown in Table 5.6. This is the maximum of the minimum number within each row or alternative.

TABLE 5.6 Thompson's Maximin Decision

	STATES OF NATURE		
ALTERNATIVES	FAVORABLE MARKET ($)	UNFAVORABLE MARKET ($)	MINIMUM IN ROW ($)
Construct large plant	200,000	−180,000	−180,000
Construct small plant	100,000	−20,000	−20,000
Do nothing	0	0	0 Maximin

Equally Likely (Laplace)

The equally likely, also called Laplace, decision criterion finds that alternative with the highest average outcome. You first calculate the average outcome for every alternative, which is the sum of all outcomes divided by the number of outcomes. Then pick that alternative with the maximum number. The equally likely approach assumes that all probabilities of occurrence for the states of nature are equal, and thus each state of nature is equally likely.

highest average outcome

The equally likely choice for Thompson Lumber is the second alternative, to build a small plant. This strategy, shown in Table 5.7, is the maximum of the average outcome of each alternative.

TABLE 5.7 Thompson's Equally Likely Decision

| | STATES OF NATURE | | |
| | FAVORABLE MARKET ($) | UNFAVORABLE MARKET ($) | ROW AVERAGE ($) |
ALTERNATIVES			
Construct large plant	200,000	−180,000	10,000
Construct small plant	100,000	−20,000	40,000
			Equally likely
Do nothing	0	0	0

Criterion of Realism (Hurwicz Criterion)

Often called the weighted average, this criterion is a compromise between an optimistic and a pessimistic decision. To begin with, a coefficient of realism, α, is selected. This coefficient is between 0 and 1. When α is close to 1, the decision maker is optimistic about the future. When α is close to 0, the decision maker is pessimistic about the future. The advantage of this approach is that it allows the decision maker to build in personal feelings about relative optimism and pessimism. The formula is as follows:

weighted average approach

Criterion of realism = α(Maximum in row) + $(1 - \alpha)$(Minimum in row)

If we assume that John Thompson sets his coefficient of realism, α, to be .80, the best decision would be to build a large plant. As seen in Table 5.8, this alternative has the highest weighted average: $124,000 = (.80)(\$200,000) + (.20)(-\$180,000)$.

Minimax

The last decision criterion we discuss is based on opportunity loss. Minimax finds the alternative that *min*imizes the *max*imum opportunity loss within each alternative. You first find the maximum opportunity loss within each alternative. Then pick that alternative with the minimum number.

minimax based on opportunity loss

APPLICATIONS OF QA

Using Decision Theory in Forest Management

Prescribed fire is a modern forest management technique used to obtain a long-term healthy forest system. Although this technique is effective, there are many uncertainties involved with prescribed fire procedures. Heat and humidity factors, precipitation, and uncertainties about fire behavior can cause this forest management technique to be problematic. While prescribed fire can assist in eliminating forest residues and can enhance wildlife habitats, it also has the potential of destroying habitats due to uncontrolled or out-of-hand burning.

There are three major decision types or categories that must be carefully considered in the effective planning and execution of this policy. The first set of decisions deals with treatment selection—those areas that are to be treated with prescribed fire. These decisions can be made several months or even years before the actual burning process. Secondly, various planning decisions are made several weeks or months before the actual burn. These planning decisions consider the overall objectives of the burn, fuel and residue conditions, fire-fighting techniques to be employed, scheduling, and deployment of equipment.

Thirdly, execution decisions are made a few days prior to the burn and during the burning process itself. Execution decisions look at daily and hourly weather conditions and forecasts. In addition, the decision to initiate or delay the burn is made. Should the burn continue, be modified, or shut down? Is there a need for additional fire suppressing and retarding forces? These and related concerns are important execution decisions.

Decision tree analysis coupled with decision making under uncertainty have been used to assist in making effective prescribed fire decisions in areas of the Tahoe National Forest, the Prescott National Forest, and the Gifford Pinchot National Forest. Decision alternatives and possible states of nature were compared so total cost and potential losses could be reviewed. The result of decision analysis was a successful burning program for areas within these national forests.

Source: David Conch, Stephen Hass, David Radloff, and Richard Yanchik, "Using Fire in Forest Management: Decision Making Under Uncertainty," *Interfaces* Vol. 14, No. 5, September–October 1984, pp. 8–19.

TABLE 5.8 Thompson's Criterion of Realism Decision (also called Hurwicz Criterion)

ALTERNATIVES	STATES OF NATURE		CRITERION OF REALISM OR WEIGHTED AVERAGE ($\alpha = .8$) ($)
	FAVORABLE MARKET ($)	UNFAVORABLE MARKET ($)	
Construct large plant	200,000	−180,000	124,000 *Realism*
Construct small plant	100,000	−20,000	76,000
Do nothing	0	0	0

Thompson's opportunity loss table is shown as Table 5.9. We can see that the minimax choice is the second alternative, build a small facility. Doing so minimizes the maximum opportunity loss.

TABLE 5.9 Thompson's MINIMAX Decision Using Opportunity Loss

| ALTERNATIVES | STATES OF NATURE | | MAXIMUM IN ROW ($) |
	FAVORABLE MARKET ($)	UNFAVORABLE MARKET ($)	
Construct large plant	0	180,000	180,000
Construct small plant	100,000	20,000	100,000 ← Minimax
Do nothing	200,000	0	200,000

5.6
USING THE COMPUTER TO SOLVE DECISION THEORY PROBLEMS

Both AB:QM and STORM can be used to solve decision theory problems. These software packages will be fully explored in Chapter 6. In this chapter, we will give you an overview of AB:QM so you can solve simple EMV and decision making under uncertainty problems.

Like other AB:QM programs, we begin with the main menu. We then access a submenu with the following choices:

A   Decision Making Under Risk
B   Decision Making Under Uncertainty
C   Decision Tree Analysis
D   Bayes' Decision Rule

We can use both decision making under risk (menu selection A) and decision making under uncertainty (menu selection B) to solve some of the problems discussed in this chapter. Programs 5-1 and 5-2 show data input and output for typical problems. Refer to Chapter 6 for a complete discussion of how to use AB:QM and STORM in solving a wider variety of decision-making problems.

5.7
SUMMARY

The basics of decision theory discussed in this chapter will be expanded upon in the next two chapters. In Chapter 6, we present decision trees and utility theory. Decision trees are particularly useful when there are sequential decisions to be made. Utility theory assists the decision maker in incorporating factors other than monetary values into the decision process. Then in Chapter 7, we discuss marginal analysis and the normal curve. You will see that marginal analysis can be used to simplify otherwise

PROGRAM 5.1
Decision Making under Risk Using AB:QM

```
Program: Decision Theory / Decision Making Under Risk

Problem Title : Thompson

***** Input Data *****

Type of Problem : Profit Problem

                         Event  1      Event  2

Probability              0.500        0.500

Alternative  1  200000.000 -180000.000
Alternative  2  100000.000  -20000.000
Alternative  3       0.000       0.000

***** Program Output*****

Expected Profit Table

Alternative              Expected Profit

      1                     10000.000
      2                     40000.000 <=
      3                         0.000

  <= indicate(s) the best alternative(s)

***** End of Output*****
```

PROGRAM 5.2
Decision Making under Uncertainty Using AB:QM

```
Program: Decision Theory / Decision Making Under Uncertainty

Problem Title : Thompson

***** Input Data *****

Type of Problem : Profit Problem

Hurwicz Alpha Coefficient:        0.800
```

(continued)

	Event 1	Event 2
Alternative 1	200000.000	-180000.000
Alternative 2	100000.000	-20000.000
Alternative 3	0.000	0.000

***** Program Output*****

Laplace

Alternative	Expected Value
1	10000.000
2	40000.000 <=
3	0.000

Maximin

Alternative	Expected Value
1	-180000.000
2	-20000.000
3	0.000 <=

Maximax

Alternative	Maximax Payoff
1	200000.000 <=
2	100000.000
3	0.000

Hurwicz

Alternative	Hurwicz Payoff
1	124000.000 <=
2	76000.000
3	0.000

Minimax

Alternative	Maximum Regret
1	180000.000
2	100000.000 <=
3	200000.000

<= indicate(s) the best alternative(s)

***** End of Output*****

complex decision-making problems. The normal curve will be introduced to handle decision-making problems that involve continuous probability distributions for the states of nature.

GLOSSARY

Alternative. A course of action or a strategy that may be chosen by a decision maker.

State of Nature. An outcome or occurrence over which the decision maker has little or no control.

Conditional Value or Payoff. A consequence or outcome, normally expressed in a monetary value, that occurs as a result of a particular alternative and state of nature.

Decision Making under Certainty. A decision-making environment in which the future outcomes or states of nature are known.

Decision Making under Risk. A decision-making environment in which several outcomes or states of nature may occur as a result of a decision or alternative. The probabilities of the outcomes or states of nature are known.

Decision Making under Uncertainty. A decision-making environment in which several outcomes or states of nature may occur. The probabilities of these outcomes, however, are not known.

Expected Monetary Value (EMV). The average or expected monetary outcome of a decision if it can be repeated many times. This is determined by multiplying the monetary outcomes by their respective probabilities. The results are then added to arrive at EMV.

Expected Value with Perfect Information. The average or expected value of the decision if you knew what would happen ahead of time. You have perfect knowledge.

Expected Value of Perfect Information (EVPI). The average or expected value of information if it were completely accurate. The information is perfect.

Expected Opportunity Loss. The amount you would lose by not picking the best alternative. For any state of nature, this is the difference between the consequences of any alternative and the best possible alternative.

Maximax. An optimistic decision-making criterion. This is the alternative with the highest possible return.

Maximin. A pessimistic decision-making criterion. This alternative maximizes the minimum outcome. It is the best of the worst possible outcomes.

Equally Likely. A decision criterion that places an equal weight on all states of nature.

Coefficient of Realism (α). A number from 0 to 1. When the coefficient is close to one, the decision criterion is optimistic. When the coefficient is close to zero, the decision criterion is pessimistic.

Minimax. A criterion that minimizes the maximum opportunity loss.

KEY EQUATIONS

(5-1) EMV (Alternative i) = (payoff of first state of nature) × (its probability) + (payoff of second state of nature) × (its probability) + $\cdots$ + (payoff of last state of nature) × (its probability)

This equation computes expected monetary values.

(5-2) Expected value *with* perfect information = (best outcome for first state of nature) × (its probability) + (best outcome for second state of nature) × (its probability) + $\cdots$ + (best outcome for last state of nature) × (its probability)

(5-3) EVPI = Expected value *with* perfect information − maximum EMV

This equation calculates the expected value of perfect information.

SOLVED PROBLEMS

Solved Problem 5-1

Maria Rojas is considering the possibility of opening a small dress shop on Fairbanks Avenue, a few blocks from the university. She has located a good mall that attracts students. Her options are to open a small shop, a medium-sized shop, or no shop at all. The market for a dress shop can be good, average, or bad. The probabilities for these three possibilities are .2 for a good market, .5 for an average market, and .3 for a bad market. The net profit or loss for the medium-sized or small shops for the various market conditions are given below. Building no shop at all yields no loss and no gain. What do you recommend?

ALTERNATIVES	GOOD MARKET ($)	AVERAGE MARKET ($)	BAD MARKET ($)
Small shop	75,000	25,000	−40,000
Medium-sized shop	100,000	35,000	−60,000
No shop	0	0	0

Solution

The problem can be solved by developing a payoff table that contains all alternatives, states of nature, and probability values. The expected monetary value (EMV) for each alternative is also computed. See the following table.

Payoff Table

ALTERNATIVES	STATE OF NATURE			EMV ($)
	GOOD MARKET ($)	AVERAGE MARKET ($)	BAD MARKET ($)	
Small shop	75,000	25,000	−40,000	15,500
Medium-sized shop	100,000	35,000	−60,000	19,500
No shop	0	0	0	0
Probabilities	.20	.50	.30	

$$\text{EMV (small shop)} = (.2)(\$75,000) + (.5)(\$25,000) + (.3)(-\$40,000)$$
$$= \$15,500$$

$$\text{EMV (medium-sized shop)} = (.2)(\$100,000) + (.5)(\$35,000) + (.3)(-\$60,000)$$
$$= \$19,500$$

$$\text{EMV (no shop)} = (.2)(\$0) + (.5)(\$0) + (.3)(\$0) = \$0$$

As can be seen, the best decision is to build the medium-sized shop. The EMV for this alternative is $19,500.

Solved Problem 5-2

Cal Bender and Becky Addison have known each other since high school. Two years ago, they entered the same university and today they are taking undergraduate courses in the business school. Both hope to graduate with degrees in finance. In an attempt to make extra money and to use some of the knowledge gained from their business courses, Cal and Becky have decided to look into the possibility of starting a small company that would provide typing services to students who needed term papers or other reports typed in a professional manner. Using a systems approach, Cal and Becky have identified three strategies. Strategy 1 is to invest in a fairly expensive microcomputer system with a high-quality laser printer. In a favorable market, they should be able to obtain a net profit of $10,000 over the next two years. If the market is unfavorable, they can lose $8,000. Strategy 2 is to purchase a less expensive system. With a favorable market, they could get a return during the next two years of $8,000. With an unfavorable market, they would incur a loss of $4,000. Their final strategy, strategy 3, is to do nothing. Cal is basically a risk taker, while Becky tries to avoid risk.

(a) What type of decision procedure should Cal use? What would Cal's decision be?

(b) What type of decision maker is Becky? What decision would Becky make?

(c) If Cal and Becky were indifferent to risk, what type of decision approach should they use? What would you recommend if this were the case?

Solution

The problem is one of decision making under uncertainty. Before answering the specific questions, a decision table should be developed showing the alternatives, states of nature, and related consequences.

ALTERNATIVES	FAVORABLE MARKET ($)	UNFAVORABLE MARKET ($)
Strategy 1	10,000	−8,000
Strategy 2	8,000	−4,000
Strategy 3	0	0

(a) Since Cal is a risk taker, he should use the maximax decision criteria. This approach selects the row that has the highest or maximum value. The $10,000 value, which is the maximum value from the table, is in row 1. Thus Cal's decision is to select strategy 1, which is an optimistic decision approach.

(b) Becky should use the maximin decision criteria. The minimum or worst outcome for each row, or strategy, is identified. These outcomes are $-$8,000 for strategy 1, $-$4,000 for strategy 2, and $0 for strategy 3. The maximum of these values is selected. Thus, Becky would select strategy 3, which reflects a pessimistic decision approach.

(c) If Cal and Becky are indifferent to risk, they should use the equally likely approach. This approach selects the alternative that maximizes the row averages. The row average for strategy 1 is $1,000 [$1,000 = ($10,000 $-$ $8,000)/2]. The row average for strategy 2 is $2,000, and the row average for strategy 3 is $0. Thus, using the equally likely approach, the decision is to select strategy 2, which maximizes the row averages.

DISCUSSION QUESTIONS AND PROBLEMS

Discussion Questions

5-1 Give an example of a good decision you made that resulted in a bad outcome. Also give an example of a bad decision you made that had a good outcome. Why was each decision good or bad?

5-2 Describe what is involved in the decision process.

5-3 What is an alternative? What is a state of nature?

5-4 Discuss the differences between decision making under certainty, decision making under risk, and decision making under uncertainty.

5-5 Mary Lillich is trying to decide whether to invest in real estate, stocks, or certificates of deposit. How well she does depends on whether the economy enters a period of recession or inflation. Develop a decision table (excluding the conditional values) to describe this situation.

5-6 Describe the meaning of EMV and EVPI. Provide an example in which EVPI can help a manager.

5-7 What techniques are used to solve decision-making problems under uncertainty? Which technique results in an optimistic decision? Which technique results in a pessimistic decision?

Problems

 · **5-8** Dr. Kenneth Brown is the principal owner of Brown Oil, Inc. After quitting his university teaching job, Ken has been able to increase his annual salary by a factor of over 100. At the present time, Ken is considering the possibility of purchasing some more equipment for Brown Oil. His alternatives are shown in the following table.

EQUIPMENT	FAVORABLE MARKET ($)	UNFAVORABLE MARKET ($)
SUB 100	300,000	– 200,000
OILER J	250,000	– 100,000
TEXAN	75,000	– 18,000

For example, if Ken purchases a SUB 100, and if there is a favorable market, he will realize a profit of $300,000. On the other hand, if the market is unfavorable, Ken will suffer a loss of $200,000. But Ken has always been a very optimistic decision maker.

(a) What type of decision is Ken facing?

(b) What decision criterion should he use?

(c) What alternative is best?

· 5-9 Although Ken Brown (discussed in Problem 5-8) is the principal owner of Brown Oil, his brother Bob is credited with making the company a financial success. Bob is vice president of finance. Bob attributes his success to his pessimistic attitude about business and the oil industry. Given the same information from Problem 5-8, it is likely that Bob will arrive at a different decision. What decision criterion should Bob use, and what alternative will he select?

· 5-10 The *Lubricant* is an expensive oil newsletter that many oil giants subscribe to, including Ken Brown. In the last issue, the letter described how the demand for oil products would be extremely high. Apparently, the American consumer will continue to use oil products even if the price of these products doubles. Indeed, one of the articles in the *Lubricant* stated that the chances of a favorable market for oil products was 70%, while the chance of an unfavorable market was only 30%. Ken would like to use these probabilities in determining the best decision. (See Problem 5-8 for details.)

(a) What decision model should be used?

(b) What is the optimal decision?

(c) Ken believes that the $300,000 figure for the SUB 100 with a favorable market is too high. How much lower would this figure have to be for Ken to change his decision made in part (b) of this problem?

· 5-11 Allen Young has always been proud of his personal investment strategies and has done very well over the last several years. He invests primarily in the stock market. Over the last several months, however, Allen has become very concerned about the stock market as a good investment. In some cases, it would have been better for Allen to have his money in a bank than in the market. During the next six months, Allen must decide whether to invest $10,000 in the stock market or in a six-month certificate of deposit (CD) at an interest rate of 9%. If the market is good, Allen believes that he could get a 14% return on his money. With a fair market, he expects to get an 8% return. If the market is bad, he will most likely get no return at all—in other words, the return would be 0%. Allen estimates that the probability of a good market is .4, the probability of a fair market is .4, and the probability of a bad market is .2.

(a) Develop a decision table for this problem.

(b) What is the best decision?

: 5-12 Janet Kim, president of Kim Manufacturing, Inc., is considering whether or not to build more manufacturing plants in Wisconsin. Her decision is summarized in the following table.

ALTERNATIVES	FAVORABLE MARKET ($)	UNFAVORABLE MARKET ($)
Build large plant	400,000	$-300,000$
Build small plant	80,000	$-10,000$
Don't build	0	0
Market probabilities	.4	.6

(a) Construct an opportunity loss table.
(b) Determine EOL and the best strategy.
(c) What is the expected value of perfect information?

 : 5-13 Helen Murvis, hospital administrator for Portland General Hospital, is trying to determine whether to build a large wing on to the existing hospital, build a small wing, or no wing at all. If the population of Portland continues to grow, a wing could return $150,000 to the hospital each year. If the small wing were built, it would return $60,000 to the hospital each year if the population continues to grow. If the population of Portland remains the same, the hospital would encounter a loss of $85,000 if the large wing were built. Furthermore, a loss of $45,000 would be realized if the small wing were constructed and the population remains the same. Unfortunately, Helen does not have any information about the future population of Portland.

(a) What type of decision problem is this?
(b) Construct a decision table.
(c) Using the equally likely criterion, determine the best alternative.

· **5-14** In Problem 5-11, you helped Allen Young determine the best investment strategy. Now, Young is thinking about paying for a stock market newsletter. A friend of Young said that these types of letters could predict very accurately whether the market would be good, fair, or poor. Then, based on these predictions, Young could make better investment decisions.

(a) What is the most that Young would be willing to pay for a newsletter?
(b) Young now believes that a good market will only give a return of 11% instead of 14%. Will this information change the amount that Young would be willing to pay for the newsletter? If your answer is yes, determine the most that Young would be willing to pay, given this new information.

 : 5-15 Hardie Lord, Helen Murvis's boss, is not convinced that Helen used the correct decision technique (refer to Problem 5-13). Hardie believes that Helen should use a coefficient of realism of .75 in determining the best alternative. Hardie thinks of himself as a realist.

(a) Develop a decision table for this problem.
(b) Using the criterion of realism, what is the best decision?
(c) Did Hardie's decision technique result in a decision that was different from Helen's?

: **5-16** Brilliant Color is a small supplier of chemicals and equipment that is used by some photographic stores to process 35-mm film. One product that Brilliant Color supplies is BC-6. John Kubick, president of Brilliant Color, normally stocks 11, 12, or 13 cases of BC-6 each week. For each case that John sells he receives a profit of $35. Because BC-6, like many photographic chemicals, has a very short shelf life, if a case is not sold by the end of the week John must discard it. Since each case costs John $56, he loses $56 for every case that is not sold by the end of the week. There is a probability of .45 of selling 11 cases, a probability of .35 of selling 12 cases, and a probability of .2 of selling 13 cases.

   (a) Construct a decision table for this problem. Include all conditional values and probabilities in the table.
   (b) What is your recommended course of action?
   (c) If John is able to develop BC-6 with an ingredient that stabilizes it so it no longer has to be discarded, how would this change your recommended course of action?

: **5-17** Today's Electronics specializes in manufacturing modern electronic components. It also builds the equipment that produces the components. Phyllis Weinberger, who is responsible for advising the president of Today's Electronics on electronic manufacturing equipment, has developed the following table concerning a proposed facility.

	PROFITS ($)		
	STRONG MARKET	FAIR MARKET	POOR MARKET
Large-sized facility	550,000	110,000	−310,000
Medium-sized facility	300,000	129,000	−100,000
Small-sized facility	200,000	100,000	−32,000
No facility	0	0	0

   (a) Develop an opportunity loss table.
   (b) What is the minimax decision?

: **5-18** Megley Cheese Company is a small manufacturer of several different cheese products. One of the products is a cheese spread that is sold to retail outlets. Jason Megley must decide how many cases of cheese spread to manufacture each month. The probability that the demand will be six cases is .1, for 7 cases is .3, for 8 cases is .5, and for 9 cases is .1. The cost of every case is $45, and the price that Jason gets for each case is $95. Unfortunately, any cases not sold by the end of the month are of no value due to spoilage. How many cases of cheese should Jason manufacture each month?

: **5-19** Even though independent gasoline stations have been having a difficult time, Susan Solomon has been thinking about starting her own independent gasoline station. Susan's problem is to decide how large her station should be. The annual returns will depend on both the size of her station and a number of marketing factors related to the oil industry and demand for gasoline. After a careful analysis, Susan developed the following table.

SIZE OF FIRST STATION	GOOD MARKET ($)	FAIR MARKET ($)	POOR MARKET ($)
Small	50,000	20,000	−10,000
Medium	80,000	30,000	−20,000
Large	100,000	30,000	−40,000
Very large	300,000	25,000	−160,000

For example, if Susan constructs a small station and the market is good, she will realize a profit of $50,000.

(a) Develop a decision table for this decision.
(b) What is the maximax decision?
(c) What is the maximin decision?
(d) What is the equally likely decision?
(e) What is the criterion of realism decision? Use an α value of .8.
(f) Develop an opportunity loss table.
(g) What is the minimax decision?

5-20 Dorothy Stanyard has three major routes to take to work. She can take Tennessee Street the entire way, she can take several back streets to work, or she can use the expressway. The traffic patterns are very complex, however. Under good conditions, Tennessee Street is the fastest route. When Tennessee is congested, then one of the other routes is usually preferable. Over the last two months, Dorothy has tried each route several times under different traffic conditions. This information is summarized in minutes of travel time to work in the following table.

	NO TRAFFIC CONGESTION	MILD TRAFFIC CONGESTION	SEVERE TRAFFIC CONGESTION
Tennessee Street	15	30	45
Back roads	20	25	35
Expressway	30	30	30

In the past 60 days, Dorothy encountered severe traffic congestion 10 days and mild traffic congestion 20 days. Assume that the last 60 days are typical of traffic conditions.

(a) Develop a decision table for this decision.
(b) What route should Dorothy take?
(c) Dorothy is about to buy a radio for her car that would tell her the exact traffic conditions before she started to work each morning. How much time in minutes on the average would Dorothy save by buying the radio?

5-21 Farm Grown, Inc., produces cases of perishable food products. Each case contains an assortment of vegetables and other farm products. Each case costs $5 and sells for $15. If there are any cases not sold by the end of the day, they are sold to a large food processing company for $3 a case. The probability that daily demand will be 100 cases is .3, the probability that daily demand will be 200 cases is .4, and the probability that daily demand will be 300 cases is .3. Farm Grown has a policy of always satisfying customer demands. If its own supply of cases is less than the demand, then they buy the necessary vegetables from a competitor. The estimated cost of doing this is $16 per case.

(a) Draw a decision table for this problem.

(b) What do you recommend?

Data Set Problem

5-22 Chris Dunphy, executive vice president for marketing and sales of Sumu Electronics, is considering the possibility of introducing a new line of inexpensive wristwatches, which would be oriented primarily toward young adults. The watch would have a plastic faceplate and wristband and a variety of features, including an alarm, a chronograph, and the ability to store and retrieve various split times. The watch has been designed to come in a variety of colors and styles. The retail price of the watch is expected to be $19. At this price, Chris feels that there is a substantial market for the watch. To help gain further information, Chris has hired a marketing research firm to study the market potential for this new venture.

The marketing research team conducted a survey and a pilot study to determine the potential market for the new watch being considered by Sumu. The team, realizing that there is market risk associated with any new product, looked at the potential market on a five-point scale. The number 1 represents the poorest or weakest market for the new product, while the number 5 represents the most optimistic market for the new watches. Using the five-point scale, the marketing research team looked at a variety of production, or stocking, policies related to each of the marketing segments. The stocking policies involve producing 100,000 to 500,000 watches.

The worst market scenario for Sumu was still expected to bring profitability through all stocking ranges. (Remember, the worst case marketing scenario was assigned a value of 1 on the five-point scale.) The probability of having a 1-type market was estimated to be .10. A stocking policy of 100,000 units was expected to return a net profit of $100,000 for Sumu. A stocking policy of 150,000 units was expected to return only $90,000. Likewise, higher stocking policies for a market potential of 1 were expected to yield lower profits. A stocking policy of 200,000 was expected to return $85,000 in net profits. The stocking policies of 250,000, 300,000, 350,000, 400,000, 450,000, and 500,000 were expected to yield net profits of $80,000, $65,000, $50,000, $45,000, $30,000, and $20,000, respectively.

The next-best market scenario was categorized by the number 2. This market potential was categorized as below average, and the marketing research team estimated that the chance of getting a below average market was 20%. The net profit for the beginning stocking policy of 100,000 units was estimated to be $110,000. The net profit for stocking 150,000 units was $120,000. If Sumu stocked 200,000 units, the net profit would be $110,000. A net profit of $120,000 would be realized if the stocking policy was 250,000 units. Stocking policies of 300,000, 350,000, 400,000, 450,000, and 500,000 would result in net profits of $100,000, $100,000, $95,000, $90,000, and $85,000, respectively.

The marketing research team estimated that the probability of an average market was 50%. This average market was coded with a 3 on the five-point scale. In general, profits were significantly higher for all stocking policies with this average market scenario. As before, profitability figures were estimated for all of the stocking policies ranging from 100,000 to 500,000 units.

The net profitabilities for this range are $120,000, $140,000, $135,000, $155,000, $155,000, $160,000, $170,000, $165,000, and $160,000.

A good market potential for the watches was given a 4 on the five-point scale. The probability, however, of a good market was relatively low. It was estimated to be .1. Net profitability factors for stocking policies that range from 100,000 to 500,000 units were estimated to be $135,000, $155,000, $160,000, $170,000, $180,000, $190,000, $200,000, $230,000, and $270,000.

The probability of a very good market was estimated to be .1. This market received a 5 on the scale. Profitability factors for this market, in general, were higher. The profitability factors for stocking policies that range from 100,000 to 500,000 were $140,000, $170,000, $175,000, $180,000, $195,000, $210,000, $230,000, $245,000, and $295,000.

(a) Determine the expected monetary values for each of the stocking policy alternatives. Which stocking policy do you recommend?

(b) What is the expected value of perfect information for this situation?

(c) Chris has just received information that the original probability estimations were not accurate. Market 2 has a probability of .28, while market 5 has a probability of .02. Does this new information change any decisions?

(d) Chris has also received new information about stocking 500,000 watches. The return given a very good market is now estimated to be $340,000. What is the impact of the new probability values (given in c) and the new return for a very good market for stocking 500,000 units?

BIBLIOGRAPHY

Azoury, Katy S., and Miller, Bruce L. "A Comparison of the Optimal Ordering Levels of Bayesion and Non-Bayesion Inventory Models." *Management Science* Vol. 30, No. 8, August 1984, pp. 993–1003.

Brown, R. "Do Managers Find Decision Theory Useful?" *Harvard Business Review,* May–June 1970, pp. 78–89.

Clarke, John R. "The Application of Decision Analysis to Clinical Medicine." *Interfaces* Vol. 17, No. 2, March–April 1987, pp. 27–34.

Cohan, David, Hass, Stephen M., Radloff, David L., and Yancik, Richard F. "Using Fire in Forest Management: Decision Making Under Uncertainty." *Interfaces* Vol. 14, No. 5, September–October 1984, pp. 8–19.

Fishburn, Peter C. "Multiattribute Nonlinear Utility Theory." *Management Science* Vol. 30, No. 11, November 1984, pp. 1301–1310.

Flinn, R., and Turban, E. "Decision Tree Analysis for Industrial Research." *Research Management* Vol. 13, No. 1, January 1970, pp. 27–34.

Harvey, Charles M. "Decision Analysis Models for Social Attitudes Towards Inequity." *Management Science* Vol. 31, No. 10, October 1985, pp. 1199–1213.

Hilton, Ronald W., and Swieringa, Robert J. "Decision Flexibility and Perceived Information Value." *Decision Sciences* Vol. 13, No. 3, July 1982, pp. 357–379.

Hosseini, Jinoos. "Decision Analysis and Its Application in the Choice between Two Wildcat Oil Ventures." *Interfaces* Vol. 16, No. 2, March–April 1986, pp. 75–85.

Janssen, C. T. L., and Daniel, T. E. "A Decision Theory Example in Football." *Decision Sciences* Vol. 15, 1984, pp. 253–259.

Luce, R., and Raiffa, H. *Games and Decisions.* New York: John Wiley & Sons, Inc., 1957.

Luna, Robert E., and Reid, Richard A. "Mortgage Selection Using a Decision Tree Approach." *Interfaces* Vol. 16, No. 3, May–June 1986, pp. 73–81.

Maier, Steven F., Peterson, D. W., and Vander Weide, J. H. "An Empirical Bayes Estimate of Market Risk." *Management Science* Vol. 28, No. 7, July 1982, pp. 728–737.

Meador, C., and Ness, D. "Decision Support Systems: An Application to Corporate Planning." *Sloan Management Review* Vol. 15, No. 2, Winter 1974, pp. 51–68.

Minch, Robert P., and Saunders, G. Lawrence. "Computerized Information Systems Supporting Multicriterial Decision Making." *Decision Sciences* Vol. 17, No. 3, Summer 1987, pp. 395–413.

Mosler, K. C. "Stochastic Dominance Decision Rules When the Attributes are Utility Dependent." *Management Science* Vol. 30, No. 11, November 1984, pp. 1311–1322.

Pratt, J. W., Raiffa, H., and Schlaifer, R. *Introduction to Statistical Decision Theory.* New York: McGraw-Hill, 1965.

Raiffa, H. *Decision Analysis.* Reading, Mass.: Addison-Wesley Publishing Co., Inc., 1968.

Render, B., and Stair, R. M. *Cases and Readings in Quantitative Analysis.* Boston: Allyn and Bacon, Inc., 1982.

Rose, Gerald L. "Organizational Behavior and Decision Making in the 1980's: A Critique." *Decision Sciences* Vol. 12, No. 3, July 1981, pp. 380–383.

Schlaifer, R. *Analysis of Decisions Under Uncertainty.* New York: McGraw-Hill Book Company, 1969.

Spronk, Jaap, & Zionts, Stanley. "A Special Issue on Multiple

Criteria Decision Making." *Management Science* Vol. 30, No. 11, November 1984, pp. 1265–1267.

Trader, Ramona L. "A Bayesian Technique for Selecting a Linear Forecasting Model." *Management Science* Vol. 29, No. 5, May 1983, pp. 622–632.

Ulvila, Jacob W. "Postal Automation (ZIP + 4) Technology: A Decision Analysis." *Interfaces* Vol. 17, No. 2, March–April 1987, pp. 1–12.

Weber, M. "A Method of Multiattribute Decision Making with Incomplete Information." *Management Science* Vol. 31, No. 11, November 1985, pp. 1365–1371.

Winkler, R. *Introduction to Bayesian Inference and Decision.* New York: Holt, Rinehart and Winston, 1972.

Winkler, Robert L. "Research Decisions in Decision Making Under Uncertainty." *Decision Sciences* Vol. 14, No. 4, October 1982, pp. 517–533.

Winter, Frederick W. "An Application of Computerized Decision Tree Models in Management-Union Bargaining." *Interfaces* Vol. 15, No. 2, March–April 1985, pp. 74–80.

6

Decision Trees and Utility Theory

CHAPTER OUTLINE

6.1
INTRODUCTION

In the last chapter we saw that problems with just a few alternatives and states of nature could be analyzed by using decision tables. This chapter moves us a step further in exploring decision theory by introducing the topics of decision trees, probability assessment, utility theory, and multifactor decision making.

6.2
DECISION TREES

Any problem that can be presented in a decision table can also be graphically illustrated in a *decision tree*. Let's take another look at the Thompson Lumber Company case first presented in Chapter 5. You may recall that John Thompson was trying to decide whether to expand his operation by building a new plant to produce storage sheds. A simple decision tree to represent John's decision is shown in Figure 6.1. Note that the tree presents the decision and outcomes in a sequential order. First, John decides whether to build a large plant, small plant, or no plant. Then, once that decision is made, the possible states of nature or outcomes (favorable or unfavorable market) will occur.

All decision trees are similar in that they contain *decision points* or *nodes* and *state of nature points* or *nodes*. These symbols are:

symbols used in decision trees

☐   A decision node from which one of several alternatives may be chosen.

◯   A state of nature node out of which one state of nature will occur.

Analyzing problems with decision trees involves five steps:

1. Define the problem.

2. Structure or draw the decision tree.

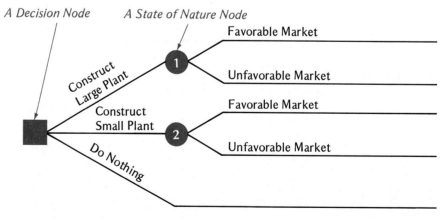

FIGURE 6.1
Thompson's Decision Tree

180

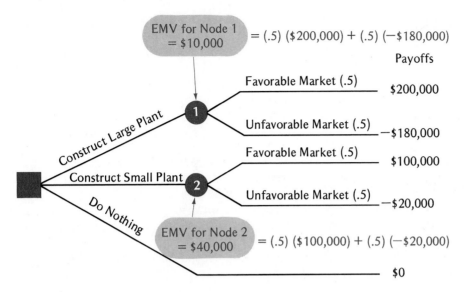

FIGURE 6.2
Completed and Solved Decision Tree for Thompson Lumber

3. Assign probabilities to the states of nature.

4. Estimate payoffs for each possible combination of alternatives and states of nature.

5. Solve the problem by computing expected monetary values (EMVs) for each state of nature node. This is done by working backward, that is, starting at the right of the tree and working back to decision nodes on the left.

A completed and solved decision tree for Thompson Lumber is presented in Figure 6.2. Note that the payoffs are placed at the right side of each of the tree's branches. The probabilities (first used by Thompson in Chapter 5) are placed in parentheses next to each state of nature. The expected monetary values for each state of nature node are then calculated and placed by their respective nodes. The EMV of the first node is $10,000. This represents the branch from the decision node to construct a large plant. The EMV for node 2, to construct a small plant, is $40,000. Building no plant or doing nothing has, of course, a payoff of $0. The branch leaving the decision node leading to the state of nature node with the highest EMV should be chosen. In Thompson's case, a small plant should be built.

A More Complex Decision for Thompson Lumber

When a *sequence* of decisions needs to be made, decision trees are much more powerful tools than decision tables. Let's say that John Thompson has two decisions to make, with the second decision dependent on the outcome of the first. Before deciding about building a new plant, John has the option of conducting his own marketing research survey, at a cost of $10,000. The information from his survey could help him decide whether to build a large plant, a small plant, or not to build at all. John recognizes that such a market survey will not provide him with *perfect* information, but it may help quite a bit nevertheless.

all outcomes and alternatives must be considered

John's new decision tree is represented in Figure 6.3. Let's take a careful look at this more complex tree. Note that *all possible outcomes and alternatives* are included in their logical sequence. This is one of the strengths of using decision trees in making decisions. The user is forced to examine all possible outcomes, including unfavorable ones. He or she is also forced to make decisions in a logical, sequential manner.

first and second decision points

Examining the tree, we see that Thompson's first decision point is whether or not to conduct the $10,000 market survey. If he chooses not to do the study (the lower part of the tree), he can either build a large plant, a small plant, or no plant. This is John's second decision point. The market will either be favorable (.50 probability) or unfavorable (also .50 probability) if he builds. The payoffs for each of the possible consequences are listed along the right side. As a matter of fact, the lower portion of John's tree is *identical* to the simpler decision tree shown in Figure 6.2. Why is this so?

The upper part of Figure 6.3 reflects the decision to conduct the market survey. State of nature node number 1 has two branches coming out of it. There is a 45% chance that the survey results will indicate a favorable market for storage sheds. We also note that the probability is .55 that the survey results will be negative.[1]

conditional probabilities

The rest of the probabilities shown in parenthesis in Figure 6.3 are all *conditional probabilities*.[2] For example, .78 is the probability of a favorable market for the sheds given a favorable result from the market survey. Of course, you would expect to find a high probability of a favorable market given that the research indicated that the market was good. Don't forget, though, there is a chance that John's $10,000 market survey didn't result in perfect or even reliable information. Any market research study is subject to error. In this case, there's a 22% chance that the market for sheds will be unfavorable given that the survey results are positive.

We note that there is a 27% chance that the market for sheds will be favorable given that John's survey results are negative. The probability is much higher, .73, that the market will actually be unfavorable given that the survey was negative.

Finally, when we look to the payoff column in Figure 6.3, we see that $10,000, the cost of the marketing study, had to be subtracted from each of the top ten tree branches. Thus, a large plant with a favorable market would normally net a $200,000 profit. But because the market study was conducted, this figure is reduced by $10,000 to $190,000. In the unfavorable

---

[1] An explanation of how these two probabilities can be obtained is the topic of Section 6.3 of this chapter. For now, let's assume that Thompson's experience provides them and accept them as reasonable.

[2] The derivation of these probabilities (.78, .22, .27, and .73) is also discussed in the next section.

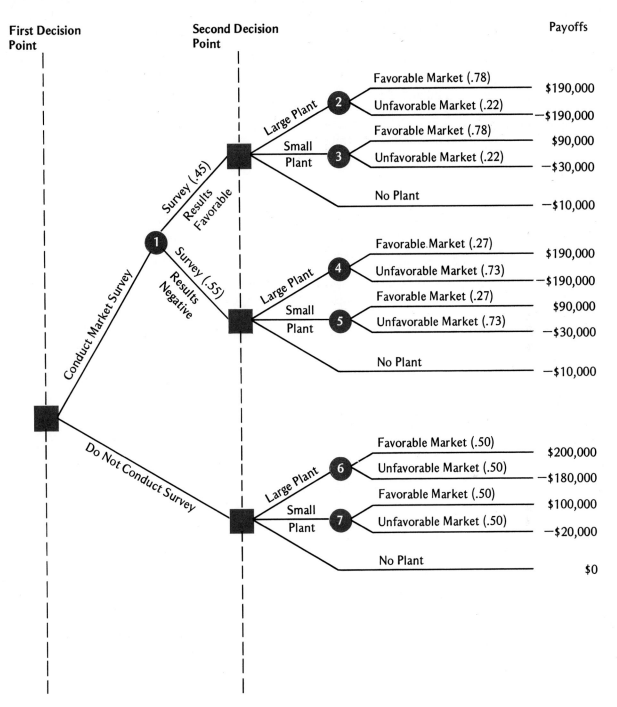

FIGURE 6.3
Larger Decision Tree with Payoffs and Probabilities
for Thompson Lumber

case, the loss of $180,000 would increase to $190,000. Similarly, conducting the survey and building no plant now results in a −$10,000 payoff.

With all probabilities and payoffs specified, we can start calculating the expected monetary value of each of the branches. We begin at the end, or right side of the decision tree and work back toward the origin. When we finish, the best decision will be known.

computing the EMV of each branch

1. Given favorable survey results,

favorable survey results

$$\text{EMV(node 2)} = \text{EMV (Large plant|Positive survey)}$$
$$= (.78)(\$190,000) + (.22)(-\$190,000) = \$106,400$$
$$\text{EMV(node 3)} = \text{EMV (Small plant|Positive survey)}$$
$$= (.78)(\$90,000) + (.22)(-\$30,000) = \$63,500$$

The EMV of no plant in this case is −$10,000. Thus, if the survey results are favorable, a large plant should be built.

2. Given negative survey results,

unfavorable survey results

$$\text{EMV(node 4)} = \text{EMV (Large plant|Negative survey)}$$
$$= (.27)(\$190,000) + (.73)(-\$190,000) = -\$87,400$$
$$\text{EMV(node 5)} = \text{EMV (Small plant|Negative survey)}$$
$$= (.27)(\$90,000) + (.73)(-\$30,000) = \$2,400$$

The EMV of no plant is again −$10,000 for this branch. Thus, given a negative survey result, John should build a small plant with an expected value of $2,400.

3. Continuing on the upper part of the tree and moving backward, we compute the expected value of conducting the market survey.

$$\text{EMV(node 1)} = \text{EMV (Conduct survey)}$$
$$= (.45)(\$106,400) + (.55)(\$2,400)$$
$$= \$47,880 + \$1,320 = \$49,200$$

4. If the market survey is *not* conducted,

$$\text{EMV(node 6)} = \text{EMV (Large plant)}$$
$$= (.50)(\$200,000) + (.50)(-\$180,000)$$
$$= \$10,000$$
$$\text{EMV(node 7)} = \text{EMV (Small plant)}$$
$$= (.50)(\$100,000) + (.50)(-\$20,000)$$
$$= \$40,000$$

The EMV of no plant is $0.

Thus, building a small plant is the best choice, given the marketing research is not performed.

5. Since the expected monetary value of conducting the survey is $49,200, versus an EMV of $40,000 for not conducting the study, the best choice is to *seek* marketing information. If the survey results are favorable, John should build the large plant; but if the research is negative, John should build the small plant.

In Figure 6.4, these expected values are placed on the decision

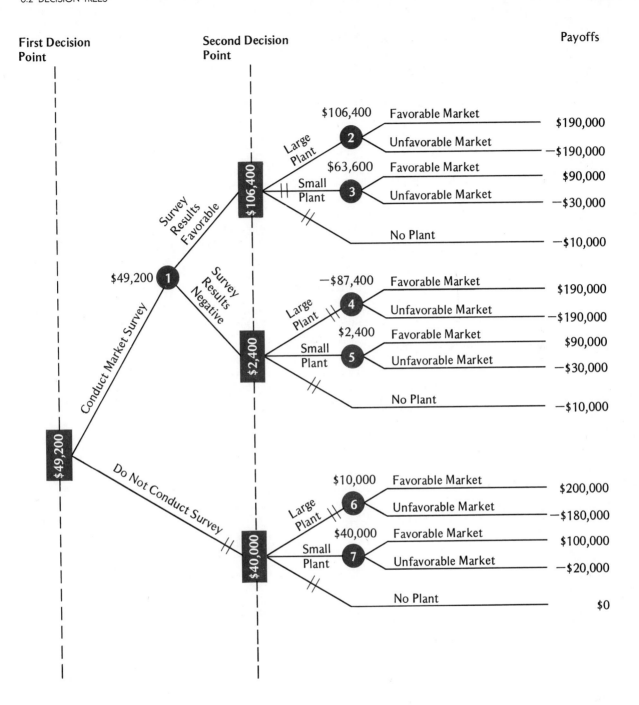

FIGURE 6.4
Thompson's Decision Tree with EMVs Shown

eliminating alternatives

tree. Notice on the tree that a pair of slash lines // through a decision branch indicates that a particular alternative is dropped from further consideration. This is because its EMV is lower than the best alternative. Once you have solved several decision tree problems, you may find it easier to do all of your computations on the tree diagram.

Expected Value of Sample Information

EVSI measures value of sample information

With the market survey he intends to conduct, John Thompson knows that his best decision will be to build a large plant if the survey is favorable or a small plant if the survey results are negative. But John also realizes that conducting the market research is not free. He would like to know what the actual value of doing a survey is. One way of measuring the value of market information is to compute the *expected value of sample information* (EVSI).

$$\text{EVSI} = \begin{pmatrix} \text{Expected value of best} \\ \text{decision } with \text{ sample} \\ \text{information, assuming} \\ \text{no cost to gather it} \end{pmatrix} - \begin{pmatrix} \text{Expected value} \\ \text{of best decision} \\ without \text{ sample} \\ \text{information} \end{pmatrix} \qquad (6\text{-}1)$$

In John's case, his EMV would be $59,200 *if* he hadn't already subtracted the $10,000 study cost from each payoff. (Do you see why this is so? If not, add $10,000 back into each payoff, as in the original Thompson problem, and recompute the EMV of conducting the market study.) From the lower branch of Figure 6.4, we see that the EMV of *not* gathering the sample information is $40,000. Thus,

$$\text{EVSI} = \$59,200 - \$40,000 = \$19,200$$

This means that John could have paid up to $19,200 for a market study and still come out ahead. Since it costs only $10,000, the survey is indeed worthwhile.

6.3
HOW PROBABILITY VALUES ARE ESTIMATED BY BAYESIAN ANALYSIS

There are many ways of getting probability data for a problem such as Thompson's. The numbers (such as .78, .22, .27, .73 in Figure 6.3) can be assessed by a manager based on experience and intuition. They can be derived from historical data, or they can be computed from other available data using Bayes's theorem. We discuss this last option in this section.

The Bayes's theorem approach recognizes that a decision maker does not know with certainty what state of nature will occur. It allows the manager to revise his or her initial or prior probability assessments. The revised probabilities are called *posterior probabilities*. (Before continuing, you may wish to review Bayes's theorem in Chapter 2.)

Using Decision Trees for the *S.S. Kuniang*

The following decision theory problem started on April 9, 1981, when the *S. S. Kuniang* ran aground on the Florida coast. The British-built ship was declared a total loss, and the owners decided to sell the salvage rights to the ship at a sealed bid auction.

The New England Electric System (NEES) was interested in the possibility of making a bid on the ship. The NEES is a publicly owned utility holding company serving approximately 1 million customers in New Hampshire, Rhode Island, and Massachusetts.

The decision of the New England Electric System was a complicated one. One of the difficulties related to the Jones Act that regulates shipping. In part, this act gives priorities to certain ships built, owned, and operated by Americans. This could mean that, if restored, the *Kuniang* might not be considered American built, owned, and operated and thus would have to wait long periods of time at certain port facilities to be unloaded. Another generally overlooked U.S. law offered a potential solution. If it could be proven that the previous owners declared the ship a total loss and if the cost of repairs was at least three times the salvage value of the ship, the ship would be considered American built and therefore would be given priority at certain U.S. ports.

A major problem was to determine the salvage value of the ship. This salvage value was assigned by the U.S. Coast Guard. An unanswered question that the Coast Guard was unwilling to resolve before the auction was whether or not the auction price would become the new salvage value or if an original Coast Guard salvage value could be used. NEES estimated that repairs would cost around $15 million. In addition, the ship could be fitted with self-unloading equipment that would cost an additional $21 million. This extra expense could be incurred to help make the ship become a "Jones Act" ship. Would the cost be worthwhile or would it be more practical to buy an American-built ship?

This complicated decision was solved by using a decision tree and decision tree analysis. If NEES decided to place a bid, they could either win or lose the bid. If they lost the bid, they had several other options in terms of buying ships. Of course, there were shipping business risks regardless of which ship they would acquire if they lost the bid. If they won the bid, they wouldn't know whether the bid price or the scrap value price would be used by the Coast Guard when determining the salvage value of the ship. This represented a very important state of nature. At the end of each of these branches, NEES could either put on the self-loader or not. In both cases, the risks of the shipping business had to be taken into account. The shipping business could either be favorable or not favorable. With this information, the decision tree shown on the next page was constructed.

The first decision was whether or not to place a bid. Following this, the win or loss of the bid became the first states of nature from the decision tree. If NEES won the bid, the Coast Guard could either use the bid price or the scrap value for the salvage value. At the end of this branch, the decision to build or not to build the self-loader had to be made. In either case, the market could be either favorable or unfavorable for the shipping business. If NEES lost the bid, they had to make the decision of what type of ship to acquire. For each type of ship, the potential payoff for either a favorable or unfavorable shipping business had to be determined.

Using decision theory, the net present return or value of each of the decision branches was determined. The final decision reached was to place a bid for the *Kuniang* of $6,700,000.

As it turned out, NEES came in second. The winning bid was $10,000,000. The U.S. Coast Guard placed a value on the *Kuniang* as the scrap value and not the bid price in determining the salvage value of the ship. They further issued a ruling that future valuations would take into account the wrecked ship's worth as a function of the auction. Ed Brown, the chairman and CEO of the New England Electric System, stated that the analysis was useful and an excellent learning experience.

Source: Adapted from David Bell, "Bidding for *S. S. Kuniang,*" *Interfaces* Vol. 14, No. 2, March–April 1984, pp. 17–23.

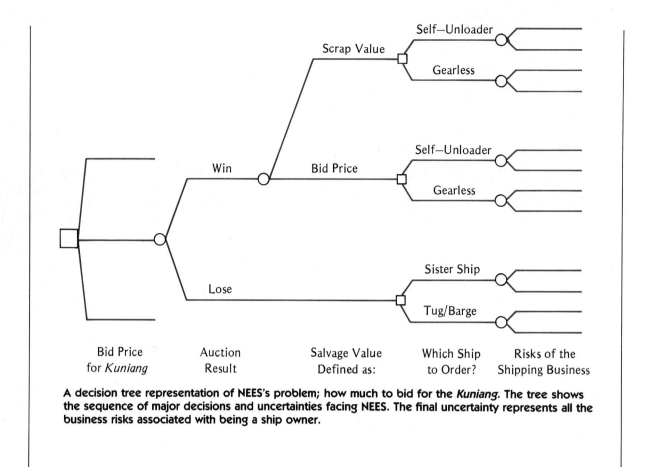

A decision tree representation of NEES's problem; how much to bid for the *Kuniang*. The tree shows the sequence of major decisions and uncertainties facing NEES. The final uncertainty represents all the business risks associated with being a ship owner.

Calculating Revised Probabilities

In the Thompson Lumber case solved in Section 6.2, we made the assumptions that the following four conditional probabilities were known:

$$P(\text{Favorable market(FM)}|\text{Survey results positive}) = .78$$
$$P(\text{Unfavorable market(UM)}|\text{Survey results positive}) = .22$$
$$P(\text{Favorable market(FM)}|\text{Survey results negative}) = .27$$
$$P(\text{Unfavorable market(UM)}|\text{Survey results negative}) = .73$$

We now show how John Thompson was able to derive these values with Bayes's theorem.

From discussions with market research specialists at the local university, John knows that special surveys such as his can either be positive (that is, predict a favorable market) or be negative (predict an unfavorable market). The experts have told John that, statistically, of all new *favorable market* (FM) products, market surveys were positive and correctly predicted success 70% of the time. Thirty percent of the time the surveys falsely predicted negative results or an *unfavorable market* (UM). On the other hand, when

deriving conditional probabilities

there was actually an unfavorable market for a new product, 80% of the surveys correctly predicted negative results. The surveys incorrectly predicted positive results the remaining 20% of the time. These conditional probabilities are summarized in Table 6.1. They are an indication of the accuracy of the survey that John is thinking of undertaking.

TABLE 6.1 Market Survey Reliability in Predicting Actual States of Nature

| | ACTUAL STATES OF NATURE | |
RESULTS OF SURVEY	FAVORABLE MARKET (FM)	UNFAVORABLE MARKET (UM)
Positive (predicts favorable market for product)	$P(\text{Survey positive}|FM) = .70$	$P(\text{Survey positive}|UM) = .20$
Negative (predicts unfavorable market for product)	$P(\text{Survey negative}|FM) = .30$	$P(\text{Survey negative}|UM) = .80$

Recall that without any market survey information, John's best estimates of a favorable and unfavorable market were:

$$P(FM) = .50$$
$$P(UM) = .50$$

These are referred to as the prior probabilities.

We are now ready to compute Thompson's revised or posterior probabilities. These desired probabilities are the reverse of the probabilities in Table 6.1. We need the probability of a favorable or unfavorable market given a positive or negative result from the market study. The general form of Bayes's theorem presented in Chapter 2 was:

$$P(A|B) = \frac{P(B|A) \cdot P(A)}{P(B|A) \cdot P(A) + P(B|\overline{A}) \cdot P(\overline{A})} \tag{6-2}$$

where

$$A, B = \text{any two events, and}$$
$$\overline{A} = \text{the complement of } A.$$

Substituting the appropriate numbers into this equation, we obtain the conditional probabilities, given that the market survey is positive:

$$P(FM|\text{Survey positive}) = \frac{P(\text{Survey positive}|FM) \cdot P(FM)}{P(\text{Survey positive}|FM) \cdot P(FM) + P(\text{Survey positive}|UM) \cdot P(UM)}$$

$$= \frac{(.70)(.50)}{(.70)(.50) + (.20)(.50)} = \frac{.35}{.45} = .78$$

$$P(UM|\text{Survey positive}) = \frac{P(\text{Survey positive}|UM) \cdot P(UM)}{P(\text{Survey positive}|UM) \cdot P(UM) + P(\text{Survey positive}|FM) \cdot P(FM)}$$

$$= \frac{(.20)(.50)}{(.20)(.50) + (.70)(.50)} = \frac{.10}{.45} = .22$$

An alternative method for these calculations is to use a probability table as shown in Table 6.2.

TABLE 6.2 Probability Revisions Given a Positive Survey

STATE OF NATURE	CONDITIONAL PROBABILITIES P(SURVEY POSITIVE|STATE OF NATURE)		PRIOR PROBABILITIES		JOINT PROBABILITIES	POSTERIOR PROBABILITIES $P\left(\dfrac{\text{STATE OF}}{\text{NATURE}} \middle\| \dfrac{\text{SURVEY}}{\text{POSITIVE}}\right)$		
FM	.70	$\times$	.50	$=$	.35	$\dfrac{.35}{.45}$	$=$	.78
UM	.20	$\times$	.50	$=$	.10	$\dfrac{.10}{.45}$	$=$	.22
		P(Survey results positive) $=$			$\overline{.45}$			$\overline{1.00}$

The conditional probabilities, given the market survey is negative, are:

$$P(\text{FM}|\text{Survey negative}) = \frac{P(\text{Survey negative}|\text{FM}) \cdot P(\text{FM})}{P(\text{Survey negative}|\text{FM}) \cdot P(\text{FM}) + P(\text{Survey negative}|\text{UM}) \cdot P(\text{UM})}$$

$$= \frac{(.30)(.50)}{(.30)(.50) + (.80)(.50)} = \frac{.15}{.55} = .27$$

$$P(\text{UM}|\text{Survey negative}) = \frac{P(\text{Survey negative}|\text{UM}) \cdot P(\text{UM})}{P(\text{Survey negative}|\text{UM}) \cdot P(\text{UM}) + P(\text{Survey negative}|\text{FM}) \cdot P(\text{FM})}$$

$$= \frac{(.80)(.50)}{(.80)(.50) + (.30)(.50)} = \frac{.40}{.55} = .73$$

These computations could have been performed in a table instead, as in Table 6.3.

TABLE 6.3 Probability Revisions Given a Negative Survey

STATE OF NATURE	CONDITIONAL PROBABILITIES P(SURVEY NEGATIVE|STATE OF NATURE)		PRIOR PROBABILITIES		JOINT PROBABILITIES	POSTERIOR PROBABILITIES $P\left(\dfrac{\text{STATE OF}}{\text{NATURE}} \middle\| \dfrac{\text{SURVEY}}{\text{NEGATIVE}}\right)$		
FM	.30	$\times$	.50	$=$	.15	$\dfrac{.15}{.55}$	$=$	.27
UM	.80	$\times$	.50	$=$	.40	$\dfrac{.40}{.55}$	$=$	.73
		P(Survey results negative) $=$			$\overline{.55}$			$\overline{1.00}$

The posterior probabilities now provide John Thompson with estimates of each state of nature if the survey results are positive or negative. As you know, John's *prior probability* of success without a market survey was only .50. Now he is aware that the probability of successfully marketing storage

---

APPLICATIONS OF QA

Decision Trees in Selecting Drilling Sites

Where to drill for oil can make the difference between a successful wildcatter and one that goes into bankruptcy. This type of decision can be classified as a decision under uncertainty. In drilling cases, there can be a large number of alternatives and a large number of possible consequences.

In order to be a successful wildcatter, a tremendous amount of investigation, detailed research, and paperwork has to be done. And perhaps a bit of luck is also needed. After the wildcatter first investigates the potential for oil, he or she must obtain an agreement from the landowner for drilling rights. Then the necessary steps required to place and operate a drilling rig on the land must be taken.

A number of variables must be considered in order to make a good decision. Both seismic and magnetic approaches are used to obtain important geographical information. The location of other oil wells or oil-producing areas is another important factor that must be taken into account. There are important economic and political factors as well—for example, oil prices, tax treatment for drilling for oil, potential inflation, competition, and operating costs.

Two lease areas in Kentucky—Blair East and Blair West—were investigated. Decision tree analysis was used to structure the possible decision alternatives as well as the states of nature that could result. In this case, the decision was whether or not to drill exploratory wells in either Blair East or Blair West. The decision included the analysis of 74 different possibilities or states of nature. The net present value of the various monetary contributions for the alternatives and possible states of nature were used in picking the best alternative. A contribution was defined as the net cash inflow minus operation expenses.

The decision analysis for this oil exploration decision provided the operator with a valuable decision tool. It allowed the quantification of important variables and a systematic approach to making the best decision. While no monetary savings were reported, the president of the oil company indicated that the use of decision tree analysis was a useful aid in the selection of drilling sites. The president further commented that decision tree analysis provided a systematic way of planning oil exploration decisions and clearer insight into the numerous and varied financial outcomes that are possible for any given alternative.

Source: Jinoos Hosseini, "Decision Analysis and Its Application in the Choice Between Two Wildcat Oil Ventures," *Interfaces,* Vol. 16, No. 2, March–April 1986, pp. 75–85.

---

sheds will be .78 if his survey shows positive results. His chances of success drop to 27% if the survey report is negative. This is valuable management information, as we saw in the earlier decision tree analysis.

new probabilities provide valuable information

A Potential Problem in Using Survey Results

In many decision-making problems, survey results or pilot studies are done before an actual decision (such as building a new plant or taking a particular course of action) is made. As discussed earlier in this section, Bayes's analysis is used to help determine the correct conditional probabilities that are needed to solve these types of decision theory problems. In computing these conditional probabilities, we need to have data about the surveys and their accuracies. If a decision to build a plant or to take another course of action is actually made, then we can determine the accuracy of our surveys. Unfortunately, we cannot get data about those situations where the decision was not to build a plant or not to take some course of action.

Thus, when we use survey results, we are basing our probabilities only on those cases where a decision to build a plant or take some course of action is actually made. This means that conditional probability information is not quite as accurate as we would like. Even so, calculating conditional probabilities helps to refine the decision-making process and, in general, to make better decisions.

6.4
UTILITY THEORY

EMV not always the best approach

So far we have used EMV to make decisions. In practice, however, using EMV could lead to bad decisions in many cases. For example, suppose you are the lucky holder of a lottery ticket. Five minutes from now a fair coin could be flipped, and if it comes up tails, you would win $5 million. If it comes up heads, you would win nothing.

Just a moment ago a wealthy individual offered you $2 million for your ticket. Let's assume you have no doubts about the validity of the offer. The person will give you a certified check for the full amount, and you are absolutely sure the check would be good.

A decision tree is shown in Figure 6.5. EMV indicates you should hold on to your ticket, but what would you do? Just think, $2 million for *sure* instead of a 50% chance at nothing. Suppose you were greedy enough to hold on to the ticket, and then lost. How would you explain that to your friends? Wouldn't $2 million be enough to be comfortable for a while?

Most people would sell for $2 million. Most of us, in fact, would probably be willing to settle for a lot less. Just how low we would go is, of course,

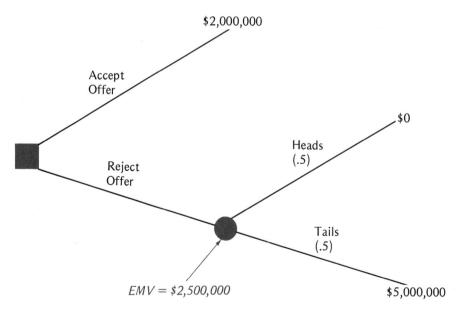

FIGURE 6.5
Your Decision Tree for the Lottery Ticket

a matter of personal preference. People have different feelings about seeking or avoiding risk. EMV is not a good way to make these types of decisions.

One way to incorporate your own attitudes toward risk is through *utility theory*. The next section explores first how to measure utility and then how to use utility measures in decision making.

Measuring Utility and Constructing a Utility Curve

Utility assessment begins by assigning the worst outcome a utility of 0 and the best outcome a utility of 1. All other outcomes will have a utility value between 0 and 1. In determining the utilities of all outcomes, other than the best or worst outcome, a *standard gamble* is considered. This gamble is shown in Figure 6.6.

determining utility using a standard gamble

In Figure 6.6, p is the probability of obtaining the best outcome, and $(1 - p)$ is the probability of obtaining the worst outcome. Assessing the utility of any other outcome involves determining the probability, p, that makes you indifferent between alternative 1, which is the gamble between the best and worst outcome, and alternative 2, which is obtaining the other outcome for sure. When you are indifferent between alternative 1 and alternative 2, then the expected utilities for these two alternatives must be equal. This relationship is shown in Equation 6-3:

determining the probability, p, that makes you indifferent

Expected utility of alternative 2 = Expected utility of alternative 1

Utility of other outcome = (p)(Utility of *best* outcome, which is 1) + $(1 - p)$(Utility of the *worst* outcome, which is 0)

Utility of other outcome = $(p)(1) + (1 - p)(0) = p$ (6-3)

Now, all you have to do is to determine the value of the probability (p) that makes you indifferent between alternatives 1 and 2. In setting the probability, you should be aware that utility assessment is completely sub-

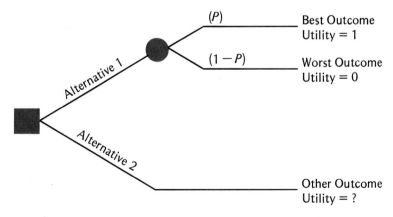

FIGURE 6.6
Standard Gamble for Utility Assessment

jective. It's a value set by the decision maker that can't be measured on an objective scale. Let's take a look at an example.

Jane Dickson would like to construct a utility curve revealing her preference for money between $0 and $10,000. A *utility curve* is a graph that plots utility value versus monetary value. She can either invest her money in a bank savings account or she can invest the same money in a real estate deal.

If the money is invested in the bank, in three years Jane would have $5,000. If she invested in the real estate, after three years she could either have nothing or $10,000. Jane, however, is very conservative. Unless there is an 80% chance of getting $10,000 from the real estate deal, Jane would prefer to have her money in the bank where it is safe. What Jane has done here is to assess her utility for $5,000. When there is an 80% chance (this means that p is .8) of getting $10,000, Jane is indifferent between putting her money in real estate or putting it in the bank. Jane's utility for $5,000 is thus equal to .8, which is the same as the value for p. This utility assessment is shown in Figure 6.7.

determining other utility values

Other utility values can be assessed in the same way. For example, what is Jane's utility for $7,000? What value of p would make Jane indifferent between $7,000 and the gamble that would result in either $10,000 or $0? For Jane, there must be a 90% chance of getting the $10,000. Otherwise, she would prefer the $7,000 for sure. Thus, her utility for $7,000 is .90. Jane's utility for $3,000 can be determined in the same way. If there were a 50% chance of obtaining the $10,000, Jane would be indifferent between having $3,000 for sure and taking the gamble of either winning the $10,000 or getting nothing. Thus, the utility of $3,000 for Jane is .5. Of course, this process can be continued until Jane has assessed her utility for as many monetary values as she wants. These assessments, however, are enough to get an idea of Jane's feelings toward risk. In fact, we can plot these

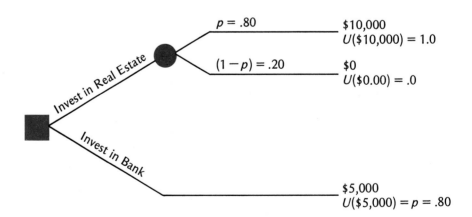

Utility for $5,000 = $U(\$5,000) = pU(\$10,000) + (1-p)\,U(\$0) = (.8)(1) + (.2)(0) = .8$

FIGURE 6.7
Utility of $5,000

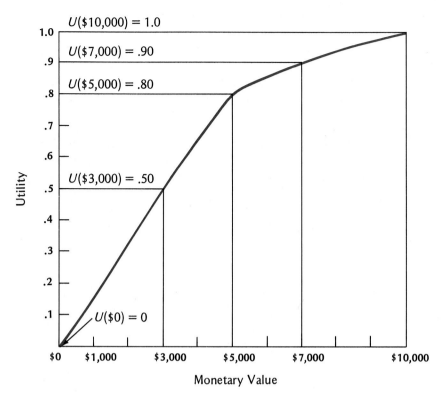

FIGURE 6.8
Utility Curves for Jane Dickson

points in a so-called *utility curve,* as was done in Figure 6.8. In the figure, the assessed utility points of $3,000, $5,000, and $7,000 are shown by dots, and the rest of the curve is eyeballed in.

constructing a utility curve

Jane's utility curve is typical of a *risk avoider.* A risk avoider is a decision maker who gets less utility or pleasure from a greater risk and tends to avoid situations in which high losses might occur. As monetary value increases on her utility curve, the utility increases at a slower rate.

Figure 6.9 illustrates that an individual who is a *risk seeker* has an opposite shaped utility curve. This decision maker gets more utility from a greater risk and higher potential payoff. As monetary value increases on his or her utility curve, the utility increases at an increasing rate. A person who is *indifferent* to risk has a utility curve that is a straight line.

The shape of a person's utility curve depends on the specific decision being considered, the person's psychological frame of mind, and how the person feels about the future. It may well be that you have one utility curve for some situations you face and completely different curves for others.

Utility as a Decision-Making Criterion

After a utility curve has been determined, the utility values from the curve are used in making decisions. Monetary outcomes or values are replaced

utility values replacing monetary values

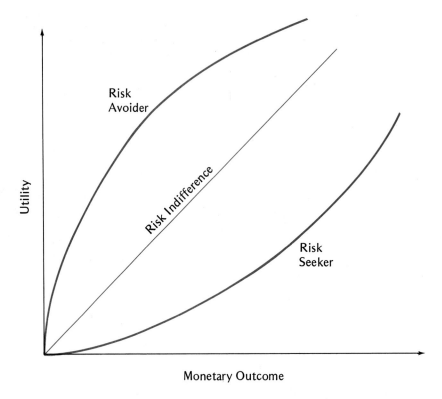

FIGURE 6.9
Preferences for Risk

with the appropriate utility values and then the decision analysis is performed as usual. Let's take a look at an example in which a decision tree is used and expected utility values are computed in selecting the best alternative.

Mark Simkin loves to gamble. He decides to play a game that involves tossing thumbtacks in the air. If the point on the thumbtack is facing up

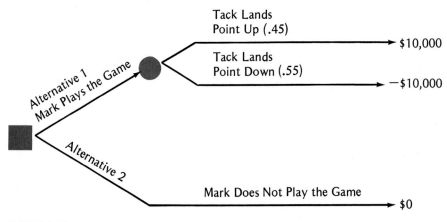

FIGURE 6.10
Decision Facing Mark Simkin

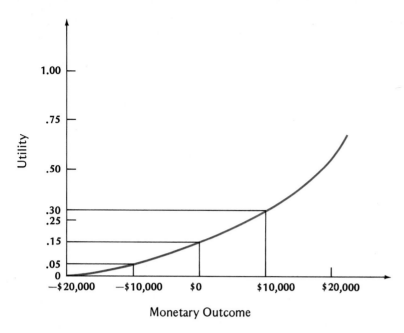

FIGURE 6.11
Utility Curve for Mark Simkin

after it lands, Mark wins $10,000. If the point on the thumbtack is down, Mark loses $10,000. Should Mark play the game (alternative 1) or should he not play the game (alternative 2)?

Alternatives 1 and 2 are displayed in the tree in Figure 6.10. As can be seen, alternative 1 is to play the game. Mark believes that there is a 45% chance of winning $10,000 and a 55% chance of suffering the $10,000 loss. Alternative 2 is not to gamble. What should Mark do? Of course, this depends on Mark's utility for money. As previously stated, he likes to gamble. Using the procedure just outlined, Mark was able to construct a utility curve showing his preference for money. This curve appears in Figure 6.11.

We see that Mark's utility for −$10,000 is .05, his utility for not playing ($0) is .15, and his utility for $10,000 is .30. These values can now be used in the decision tree. Mark's objective is to maximize his expected utility, which can be done as follows:

Step 1:
$$U(-\$10,000) = .05$$
$$U(\$0) = .15$$
$$U(\$10,000) = .30$$

Step 2: Replace monetary values with utility values. Refer to Figure 6.12.

Here are the utilities for alternatives 1 and 2.

E(Alternative 1: Play the game) $= (.45)(.30) + (.55)(.05)$
$\qquad\qquad\qquad\qquad\qquad\qquad = .135 + .027 = .1625$

determining expected utility

E(Alternative 2: Don't play the game) $= .15$

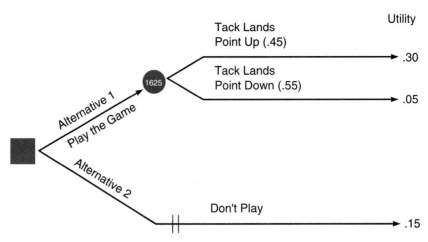

FIGURE 6.12
Using Expected Utilities in Decision Making

Therefore, alternative 1 is the best strategy using utility as the decision criterion. If EMV had been used, alternative 2 would have been the best strategy. The utility curve is a risk-seeker utility curve, and the choice of playing the game certainly reflects this preference for risk.

6.5
MULTIFACTOR DECISION MAKING

Many decision-making problems involve a number of factors. For example, if you are considering a new job, factors might include starting salary, career advancement opportunities, work location, the people you'll be working with on the job, the type of work you will be doing, and assorted fringe benefits. If you are considering the purchase of a personal computer, there are a number of important factors to consider as well: price, memory capacity, compatibility with other computers, flexibility, brand name, software availability, the existence of any user groups or clubs, and the support of the computer manufacturer and the local computer store. In buying a new or used car, such factors as color, style, make and model, year, number of miles (if it's a used car), price, dealership or individual you are purchasing the car from, warranties, and cost of insurance may be important factors to consider.

multifactor evaluation process

In *multifactor decision making*, individuals subjectively and intuitively consider the various factors in making their selection. For difficult decisions, a quantitative approach is recommended. All of the important factors can then be given appropriate weights and each alternative, such as a car, a computer, or a new job prospect, can be evaluated in terms of these factors. This approach is called the *multifactor evaluation process* (MFEP).

analytic hierarchy process

In other cases, we may not be able to quantify our preferences for various factors and alternatives. We then use the analytic hierarchy process. This process uses pairwise comparisons and then computes the weighting factors and evaluations for us. We begin with a discussion of the multifactor evaluation process.

The Multifactor Evaluation Process

With the multifactor evaluation process, we start by listing the factors and their relative importance on a scale from 0 to 1.

Let's consider an example. Steve Markel, an undergraduate business major, is looking at several job opportunities. After discussing the employment situation with his academic advisor and the director of the placement center, Steve has determined that the only three factors really important to him are salary, career advancement opportunities, and location of the new job. Furthermore, Steve has decided that career advancement opportunities are the most important to him. He has given this a weight of .6. Steve has placed salary next, with a weight of .3. Finally, Steve has given location an importance weight of .1. As with any MFEP problem, the importance weights for factors must sum to 1. See Table 6.4.

TABLE 6.4 Factor Weights

FACTOR	IMPORTANCE (WEIGHT)
Salary	.3
Career advancement	.6
Location	.1

At this time, Steve feels confident that he will get offers from AA Company, EDS, Ltd., and PW, Inc. For each of these jobs, Steve evaluated, or rated, the various factors on a 0 to 1 scale. For AA Company, Steve gave salary an evaluation of .7, career advancement an evaluation of .9, and location an evaluation of .6. For EDS, Steve evaluated salary as .8, career advancement as .7, and location as .8. For PW, Inc., Steve gave salary a weight of .9, career advancement an evaluation of .6, and location an evaluation of .9. The results are shown in Table 6.5.

Given this information, Steve can determine a total weighted evaluation for each of the alternatives or job possibilities. Each company is given a factor evaluation for the three factors, and then the factor weights are multiplied times the factor evaluation and summed to get a total weighted evaluation for each company. As you can see in Table 6.6, AA Company has received a total weighted evaluation of .81. The same type of analysis

TABLE 6.5 Factor Evaluations

FACTOR	AA CO.	EDS, LTD.	PW, INC.
Salary	.7	.8	.9
Career advancement	.9	.7	.6
Location	.6	.8	.9

TABLE 6.6 Evaluation of AA Co.

FACTOR NAME	FACTOR WEIGHTS		FACTOR EVALUATION		WEIGHTED EVALUATION
Salary	.3	×	.7	=	.21
Career	.6	×	.9	=	.54
Location	.1	×	.6	=	.06
Total	1				.81

TABLE 6.7 Evaluation of EDS, Ltd.

FACTOR NAME	FACTOR WEIGHTS		FACTOR EVALUATION		WEIGHTED EVALUATION
Salary	.3	×	.8	=	.24
Career	.6	×	.7	=	.42
Location	.1	×	.8	=	.08
Total	1				.74

TABLE 6.8 Evaluation of PW, Inc.

FACTOR NAME	FACTOR WEIGHTS		FACTOR EVALUATION		WEIGHTED EVALUATION
Salary	.3	×	.9	=	.27
Career	.6	×	.6	=	.36
Location	.1	×	.9	=	.09
Total	1				.72

is done for EDS, Ltd. and PW, Inc., in Tables 6.7 and 6.8. As you can see from the analysis, AA Company received the highest total weighted evaluation. EDS, Ltd. was next with a total weighted evaluation of .74, and PW, Inc. was last with a total weighted evaluation of .72. Using the multifactor evaluation process, Steve's decision was to go with AA Company because it had the highest total weighted evaluation.

The Analytic Hierarchy Process

In situations where we can assign evaluations and weights to the various decision factors, the multifactor evaluation process described in the previous section works fine. In other cases, decision makers may have difficulties in accurately determining the various factor weights and evaluations. In this case, the *analytic hierarchy process* (AHP) can be used. AHP was developed by Thomas L. Saaty, and published in his 1980 book, *The Analytic Hierarchy Process.*

using pairwise comparisons

This process involves pairwise comparisons. The decision maker starts by laying out the overall hierarchy of the decision. This hierarchy reveals the factors to be considered as well as the various alternatives in the decision. Then, a number of pairwise comparisons are done, which result in the determination of *factor weights* and *factor evaluations.* They are the same types of weights and evaluations discussed in the previous section and shown in Tables 6.4 through 6.8. As before, the alternative with the highest total weighted score is selected as the best alternative.

As an example of this process, we take the case of Judy Grim, who is looking for a new computer system for her small business. She has determined that the most important overall factors are hardware, software, and vendor support. Furthermore, Judy has narrowed down her alternatives to three possible computer systems. She has labeled these SYSTEM-1, SYSTEM-2, and SYSTEM-3. To begin, Judy has placed these factors and alternatives into a decision hierarchy. See Figure 6.13.

three factors and three alternatives identified

The decision hierarchy for the computer selection has three different levels. The top level describes the overall decision. As you can see in Figure 6.13, this overall decision is to select the best computer system. The middle level in the hierarchy describes the factors that are to be considered— hardware, software, and vendor support. Judy could decide to use a number of additional alternatives. But for this example, we keep our alternatives to only three to show you the types of calculations that are to be performed using AHP. The lower level of the decision hierarchy reveals the alternatives. (Alternatives have also been called items or systems.) As you can see, the alternatives include the three different computer systems.

The key to using AHP is pairwise comparisons. The decision maker, Judy Grim, needs to compare two different alternatives using a scale that

first step: pairwise comparisons

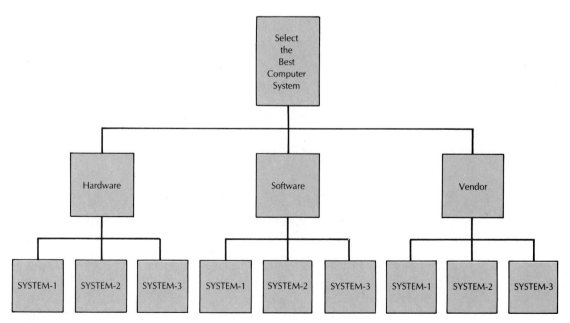

FIGURE 6.13
Decision Hierarchy for Computer System Selection

Use the Following Scale for Pairwise Comparison:
  1—Equally Preferred
  2—Equally to Moderately Preferred
  3—Moderately Preferred
  4—Moderately to Strongly Preferred
  5—Strongly Preferred
  6—Strongly to Very Strongly Preferred
  7—Very Strongly Preferred
  8—Very to Extremely Strongly Preferred
  9—Extremely Preferred

FIGURE 6.14
Scale for Pairwise Comparison

ranges from equally preferred to extremely preferred. This is shown in Figure 6.14.

Judy begins by looking at the hardware factor and by comparing computer SYSTEM-1 to computer SYSTEM-2. Using the scale in Figure 6.14, Judy determines that the hardware for computer SYSTEM-1 is moderately preferred to computer SYSTEM-2. Thus, Judy uses the number 3, representing moderately preferred. Next, Judy compares the hardware for SYSTEM-1 to SYSTEM-3. She believes that the hardware for computer SYSTEM-1 is extremely preferred to computer SYSTEM-3. This is a numerical score of 9. Finally, Judy considers the only other pairwise comparison, which is the hardware for computer SYSTEM-2 compared to the hardware for computer SYSTEM-3. She believes that the hardware for computer SYSTEM-2 is strongly to very strongly preferred to the hardware for computer SYSTEM-3, a score of 6. With these pairwise comparisons, Judy constructs a pairwise comparison matrix for hardware. This is shown below.

HARDWARE	SYSTEM-1	SYSTEM-2	SYSTEM-3
SYSTEM-1		3	9
SYSTEM-2			6
SYSTEM-3			

The pairwise comparison matrix just shown reveals Judy's preferences for hardware concerning the three computer systems. From this information, using AHP, we can determine the evaluation factors for hardware for the three computer systems.

Look at the upper left corner of the pairwise comparison matrix. This upper left corner compares computer SYSTEM-1 to itself for hardware. When comparing anything to itself, the evaluation scale must be 1, representing equally preferred. Thus, we can place the number 1 in the upper left corner, which compares SYSTEM-1 to itself. The same can be said for comparing SYSTEM-2 to itself and comparing SYSTEM-3 to itself. Each of these must also get a score of 1, which represents equally preferred. In general, for any pairwise comparison matrix, we will place 1s down the diagonal from the upper left corner to the lower right corner. To finish

1s on the diagonal

such a table, we make the observation that if alternative A is twice as preferred to alternative B, we can conclude that alternative B is preferred only one half as much as alternative A. Thus, if alternative A receives a score of 2 relative to alternative B, then alternative B should receive a score of $\frac{1}{2}$ when compared to alternative A. We can use this same logic to complete the lower left side of the matrix of pairwise comparisons:

HARDWARE	SYSTEM-1	SYSTEM-2	SYSTEM-3
SYSTEM-1	1	3	9
SYSTEM-2	$\frac{1}{3}$	1	6
SYSTEM-3	$\frac{1}{9}$	$\frac{1}{6}$	1

Look at this newest matrix of pairwise comparisons. You will see that there are 1s down the diagonal from the upper left to the lower right corner. Then, look at the lower left part of the table. In the second row and first column of this table, you can see that SYSTEM-2 received a score of $\frac{1}{3}$ compared to SYSTEM-1. This is because SYSTEM-1 received a score of 3 over SYSTEM-2 from the original assessment. Now, look at the third row. The same has been done. SYSTEM-3 compared to SYSTEM-1, in row 3 column 1 of the table, received a score of $\frac{1}{9}$. This is because SYSTEM-1 compared to SYSTEM-3 received a score of 9 in the original pairwise comparison. In a likewise fashion, SYSTEM-3 compared to SYSTEM-2 received a score of $\frac{1}{6}$ in the third row and second column of the table. This is because when comparing SYSTEM-2 to SYSTEM-3 in the original pairwise comparison, the score of 6 was given.

completing the lower left portion of the matrix

Now that we have the completed matrix of pairwise comparisons, we can start to compute the evaluations for hardware. We start by converting the numbers in the matrix of pairwise comparisons to decimals to make them easier to work with and getting column totals:

second step: converting matrix to decimals

HARDWARE	SYSTEM-1	SYSTEM-2	SYSTEM-3
SYSTEM-1	1	3	9
SYSTEM-2	.3333	1	6
SYSTEM-3	.1111	.1677	1
Column Totals	1.444	4.1667	16.0

third step: column totals

Once the column totals have been determined, the numbers in the matrix are divided by their respective column totals as follows:

HARDWARE	SYSTEM-1	SYSTEM-2	SYSTEM-3
SYSTEM-1	.6923	.7200	.5625
SYSTEM-2	.2300	.2400	.3750
SYSTEM-3	.0769	.0400	.0625

To determine the priorities for hardware for the three computer systems, we simply find the average of the various rows from the matrix of numbers as follows:

fourth step: computing hardware priorities by averaging rows

HARDWARE		
Row Averages	$\begin{bmatrix} .6583 \\ .2819 \\ .0598 \end{bmatrix}$	$\begin{array}{l} = (.6923 + .7200 + .5625)/3 \\ = (.2300 + .2400 + .3750)/3 \\ = (.0769 + .0400 + .0625)/3 \end{array}$

The results are displayed in Table 6.9. As you can see, the factor evaluation for SYSTEM-1 is .6583. For SYSTEM-2 and SYSTEM-3, the factor evaluations are .2819 and .0598. The same procedure is used to get the factor evaluations for all the other factors, which are software and vendor support in this case. But before we do this, we need to determine if our responses are consistent by determining a *consistency ratio*.

fifth step: consistency ratio

TABLE 6.9 Factor Evaluation for Hardware

FACTOR	SYSTEM-1	SYSTEM-2	SYSTEM-3
Hardware	.6583	.2819	.0598

To arrive at the consistency ratio, we begin by determining the weighted sum vector. This is done by multiplying the factor evaluation number for the first system or alternative times the first column of the original pairwise comparison matrix. We multiply the second factor evaluation times the second column, and the third factor times the third column of the original matrix of pairwise comparisons. Then, we sum these values over the rows.

$$\text{Weighted sum vector} = \begin{bmatrix} (.6583)(1) & + & (.2819)(3) & + & (.0598)(9) \\ (.6583)(.3333) & + & (.2819)(1) & + & (.0598)(6) \\ (.6583)(.1111) & + & (.2819)(.1677) & + & (.0598)(1) \end{bmatrix} = \begin{bmatrix} 2.0423 \\ .8602 \\ .1799 \end{bmatrix}$$

sixth step: consistency vector

The next step is to determine the consistency vector. This is done by dividing the weighted sum vector by the factor evaluation values determined previously.

$$\text{Consistency vector} = \begin{bmatrix} 2.0423/.6583 \\ .8602/.2819 \\ .1799/.0598 \end{bmatrix} = \begin{bmatrix} 3.1025 \\ 3.0512 \\ 3.0086 \end{bmatrix}$$

seventh step: lambda and the consistency index

Now that we have found the consistency vector, we need to compute values for two more terms, lambda (λ) and the consistency index (CI), before the final consistency ratio can be computed. The value for lambda is simply the average value of the consistency vector. The formula for CI is:

$$CI = \frac{\lambda - n}{n - 1} \tag{6-4}$$

where

n is the number of items or systems being compared.

In this case, $n = 3$ for three different computer systems being compared. The results of the calculations are as follows:

$$\lambda = (3.1025 + 3.0512 + 3.0086)/3$$
$$\lambda = 3.0541$$
$$CI = (\lambda - n)/(n - 1)$$
$$= (3.0541 - 3)/(3 - 1) = .0270$$

Finally, we are now in a position to compute the consistency ratio. The consistency ratio (CR) is equal to the consistency index divided by the random index (RI), which is determined from a table. The random index is a direct function of the number of alternatives or systems being considered. This table is shown, followed by the final calculation of the consistency ratio.

n	RI
2	.00
3	.58
4	.90
5	1.12
6	1.24
7	1.32
8	1.41

$n \rightarrow 3 \rightarrow .58$

In general,
$$CR = \frac{CI}{RI} \qquad (6\text{-}5)$$

In this case,
$$CR = \frac{CI}{RI} = \frac{.0270}{.58} = .0466$$

The consistency ratio tells us how consistent we are with our answers. A higher number means we are less consistent, while a lower number means that we are more consistent. In general, if the consistency ratio is .10 or less, the decision maker's answers are relatively consistent. For a consistency ratio that is greater than .10, the decision maker should seriously consider reevaluating his or her responses during the pairwise comparisons that were used to obtain the original matrix of pairwise comparisons.

As you can see from the analysis, we are relatively consistent with our responses, so there is no need to reevaluate the pairwise comparison responses. If you look at the original pairwise comparison matrix, this makes sense. The hardware for SYSTEM-1 was moderately preferred to the hardware for SYSTEM-2. The hardware for SYSTEM-1 was extremely preferred to the hardware for SYSTEM-3. This implies that the hardware for SYSTEM-2 should be preferred over the hardware for SYSTEM-3. From our responses, the hardware for SYSTEM-2 was strongly to very strongly preferred over the hardware for SYSTEM-3, as indicated by the number 6. Thus, our original assessments of the pairwise comparison matrix seem to be consistent, and the consistency ratio that we computed supports our observations.

Although the calculations to compute the consistency ratio are fairly involved, they are an important step in using the analytical hierarchy process. So far, we have determined the factor evaluations for hardware for

factor evaluations for software and vendor support

the three different computer systems along with a consistency ratio for these evaluations. Now, we can make the same calculations for the other factors, namely software and vendor support. As before, we start with the matrix of pairwise comparisons. We perform the same calculations and end up with the various factor evaluations for both software and vendor support. We begin by presenting the matrix of pairwise comparisons for both software and vendor support.

SOFTWARE	SYSTEM-1	SYSTEM-2	SYSTEM-3
SYSTEM-1			
SYSTEM-2	2		
SYSTEM-3	8	5	

VENDOR SUPPORT	SYSTEM-1	SYSTEM-2	SYSTEM-3
SYSTEM-1		1	6
SYSTEM-2			3
SYSTEM-3			

With the matrices shown, we can perform the same types of calculations to determine the factor evaluations for both software and vendor support for the three computer systems. The data, for the three different systems, are summarized in Table 6.10. We also need to determine the consistency ratios for both software and support. As it turns out, both consistency ratios are under .10, meaning that the responses to the pairwise comparison are acceptably consistent.

You should note that the factor evaluations for the three factors and three different computer systems shown in Table 6.10 are similar to the factor evaluations in Table 6.5 for the job selection problem. The major difference is that we had to use the analytic hierarchy process to determine these factor evaluations using pairwise comparisons, because we were not comfortable in our abilities to subjectively assess these factors without some assistance.

why we used pairwise comparisons

Next, we need to determine the various factor weights. When we used the multifactor evaluation process, it was assumed that we could simply determine these values subjectively. Another approach is to use the analytic hierarchy process and pairwise comparisons to determine the factor weights for hardware, software, and vendor support. In comparing the three dif-

TABLE 6.10 Factor Evaluations

FACTOR	SYSTEM-1	SYSTEM-2	SYSTEM-3
Hardware	.6583	.2819	.0598
Software	.0874	.1622	.7504
Vendor	.4967	.3967	.1066

| APPLICATIONS OF QA |

Applications of the Analytic Hierachy Process

From the time the analytic hierarchy process (AHP) was introduced, the technique has enjoyed wide application and popularity. The overall approach is appropriate when a decision can be decomposed into a hierarchy of interrelated decision criteria. It is also appropriate in situations where subjective assessments of various decision components are relevant and can be made. In most cases, a number from -9 to 9 reflects the comparison, or judgment, between two factors in the hierarchical decision problem.

Because of its flexible structure, AHP has been used in almost every type of decision problem. Recently, more than 130 published papers on the application of AHP have been identified, and the applications have been categorized into 29 application areas.

APPLICATION	NUMBER OF PAPERS
Accounting and finance	5
Architecture and design	2
Capital investment	2
Computers and information systems	8
Conflict analysis	12
Decision support	4
Economics	8
Energy	15
Futures research	3
Decision making	9
Health care	5
Higher education	6
Long-range planning	7
Manufacturing and production	7

Marketing	5
Military	9
Optimization	10
Politics	6
Portfolio selection	2
Public sector and legal planning	3
Regional and urban planning	3
R & D management	7
Resource allocation	6
Risk analysis	4
Sociology	2
Space exploration	2
Sports and games	6
Surveys of applications	5
Transportation	4

In addition to being used by itself, AHP has been combined with a number of traditional quantitative analysis techniques. In many applications, AHP is used to determine the parameters or input for other quantitative analysis approaches. Some of the techniques supported by AHP include probability theory, dynamic programming, game theory, goal programming, integer programming, linear programming, multiple-objective optimization, network analysis, nonlinear programming, quadratic programming, time series analysis, and utility theory.

Source: Bruce Golden, Edward Wasil, and Douglas Levey, "Applications of the Analytic Hierarchy Process: A Categorized, Annotated Bibliography," Working Paper Series MS/S 88-007, College of Business and Management, University of Maryland at College Park.

ferent factors, we determine that software is the most important. Software is very to extremely strongly preferred over hardware (number 8). Software is moderately preferred over vendor support (number 3). In comparing vendor support to hardware, we decide that vendor support is more important. Vendor support is moderately preferred to hardware (number 3). With these values, we can construct the pairwise comparison matrix and then compute the weights for hardware, software, and support. We also need to compute a consistency ratio to make sure that our responses are consistent. As with software and vendor support, the actual calculations for determining the factor weights are left for you to make on your own. After making the appropriate calculations, the factor weights for hardware, software, and vendor support are shown in Table 6.11.

TABLE 6.11 Factor Weights

FACTOR	FACTOR WEIGHT
Hardware	.0820
Software	.6816
Vendor	.2364

ranking the three computer systems

Once the factor weights have been determined, we can multiply the factor evaluations in Table 6.10 times the factor weights in Table 6.11. This is the same procedure we used for the job selection decision in the previous section on the multifactor evaluation process. It will give us the overall ranking for the three different computer systems, which is shown in Table 6.12. As you can see, SYSTEM-3 received the highest final ranking and is selected as the best computer system.

TABLE 6.12 Total Weighted Evaluations

SYSTEM OR ALTERNATIVE	TOTAL WEIGHTED EVALUATION
SYSTEM-1	.2310
SYSTEM-2	.2275
SYSTEM-3*	.5416

* System-3 is selected.

A Comparison of MFEP and AHP

Multifactor decision making has a number of useful and important applications. If you know or can determine with confidence and accuracy the factor weights and factor evaluations, MFEP is preferred. If not, you should use AHP. As it turns out, AHP also gives the factor weights and factor evaluations from which the final selection can be made. The only difference is that with AHP we compute the factor weights and factor evaluations from a number of pairwise comparison matrices. We also compute a consistency ratio to make sure that our responses to the original pairwise comparison matrix are consistent and acceptable. If they are not, we should **importance of consistency** go back and perform the pairwise comparison again. Although AHP involves a larger number of calculations, it is preferred to MFEP in cases where we do not feel confident or comfortable in determining factor weights or factor evaluations without making pairwise comparisons. Fortunately, computer programs can perform all of the necessary calculations.

6.6
USE OF MICROCOMPUTERS IN DECISION THEORY

In this section we will investigate three software packages that can be used in decision theory. First, we will illustrate a number of programs that can be run with the AB:QM package. Second, we will explore Expert Choice, which can be used to solve AHP problems; and third, we'll look at Super Tree, which has been designed for decision tree analysis.

Use of AB:QM in Decision Theory

When the AB:QM decision theory programs start, a submenu will appear on the screen as shown in Program 6.1.

PROGRAM 6.1 Decision Theory Submenu for AB:QM

```
                    Decision Theory
┌──────────────────── Menu ────────────────────┐
│                                               │
│    A    Decision Making Under Risk            │
│    B    Decision Making Under Uncertainty     │
│    C    Decision Tree                         │
│    D    Bayes' Decision Rule                  │
│  Esc  Back to Main Menu                       │
│                                               │
└───────────────────────────────────────────────┘
```

As you can see, we can perform decision making under risk, decision making under uncertainty, decision tree analysis, or analysis using Bayes's decision rule. We will start with decision making under risk. For this application, we can have up to 20 alternatives and 20 states of nature. The basic data entered for the Thompson Lumber Company problem are shown in Program 6.2. Notice that at the top of the screen there are three areas where overall problem data are added. Detailed data are added in the middle area of the screen. The commands discussed in Chapter 1 are listed at the bottom.

Once the data have been correctly entered, we can execute, or run, the program and obtain the desired output. Program output for Thompson Lumber is also shown in Program 6.2.

Decision making under uncertainty problems can also be solved using AB:QM. For this decision model, there can be between 2 and 20 alternatives and events, or states of nature. The main difference between the input screen for decision making under risk and decision making under uncertainty is the lack of probability values for the decision making under uncertainty model. The output for the decision making under uncertainty model includes Laplace, maximin, maximax, and Hurwicz solutions. The Laplace solution is the equally likely solution that we discussed in this chapter. The Hurwicz solution is equivalent to the coefficient of realism, where a coefficient for α is entered. The input screen and the output for the decision making under uncertainty model are shown in Program 6.3.

The decision tree program of AB:QM can be used to solve a sequential decision problem. The program can handle between 2 and 50 different branches. In the Thompson Lumber decision problem, we considered a decision to conduct a survey followed by a decision to build or not to build a plant. The upper branch of the decision problem was to build a large plant, a small plant, or no plant at all (given a favorable result from the

basic capabilities

decision making under risk

decision making under uncertainty

decision tree problems

PROGRAM 6.2 Decision Making Under Risk Thompson Lumber on AB:QM

Decision Theory / Decision Making Under Risk

```
┌─────────────────────────────────────────────────────────────────────┐
│  Problem Title :  Thompson Problem                                    │
│  Profit=1 / Cost=2                  1                                 │
│  Number of Alternatives             3          Number of Events    2  │
│ ───────────────────────────────────────────────────────────────────  │
│                                                                       │
│                     Event 1     Event 2                               │
│  Probability            .5          .5                                │
│  Alternative 1      200000     -180000                                │
│  Alternative 2      100000      -20000                                │
│  Alternative 3           0           0                                │
│                                                                       │
│                                                                       │
│                                                                       │
│                                                                       │
│                                                                       │
│                                                                       │
│ ───────────────────────────────────────────────────────────────────  │
│  Help   New   Load   Save   Edit   Run   Print   Install   Directory   Esc │
└─────────────────────────────────────────────────────────────────────┘
```

PROGRAM 6.2 output (continued)

Decision Theory / Decision Making Under Risk

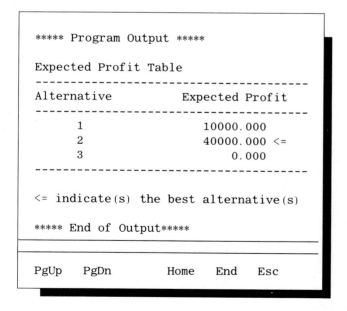

```
┌──────────────────────────────────────────────┐
│  ***** Program Output *****                   │
│                                               │
│  Expected Profit Table                        │
│  ------------------------------------------   │
│  Alternative          Expected Profit         │
│  ------------------------------------------   │
│       1                  10000.000            │
│       2                  40000.000 <=         │
│       3                      0.000            │
│  ------------------------------------------   │
│                                               │
│  <= indicate(s) the best alternative(s)       │
│                                               │
│  ***** End of Output*****                     │
│ ───────────────────────────────────────────  │
│  PgUp    PgDn       Home   End   Esc          │
└──────────────────────────────────────────────┘
```

market survey). The expected monetary value for this situation, given a positive survey result, was $106,400. In this section we solve the same decision problem using AB:QM. The input screen for the upper branch of the decision tree and the output from the program are shown in Program 6.4.

PROGRAM 6.3 Decision Making Under Uncertainty Example Using AB:QM

Decision Theory / Decision Making Under Uncertainty

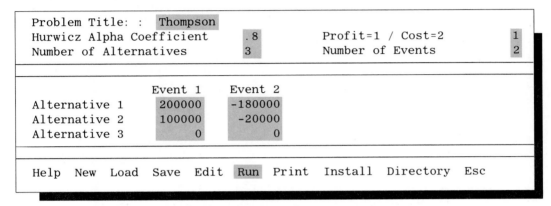

	Event 1	Event 2
Alternative 1	200000	-180000
Alternative 2	100000	-20000
Alternative 3	0	0

Help   New   Load   Save   Edit   Run   Print   Install   Directory   Esc

PROGRAM 6.3 output (continued)

```
***** Program Output *****

Laplace                                    Hurwicz
-----------------------------------        -----------------------------------
Alternative      Expected Value            Alternative      Hurwicz Payoff
-----------------------------------        -----------------------------------
    1               10000.000                  1              124000.000 <=
    2               40000.000 <=               2               76000.000
    3                   0.000                  3                   0.000
-----------------------------------        -----------------------------------


Maximin                                    Minimax
-----------------------------------        -----------------------------------
Alternative      Expected Value            Alternative      Maximum Regret
-----------------------------------        -----------------------------------
    1             -180000.000                  1              180000.000
    2              -20000.000                  2              100000.000 <=
    3                   0.000 <=               3              200000.000
-----------------------------------        -----------------------------------


Maximax                                      <=  indicate(s) the best alternative(s)
-----------------------------------        ***** End of Output *****
Alternative      Maximax Payoff
-----------------------------------
    1              200000.000 <=
    2              100000.000
    3                   0.000
-----------------------------------
```

PROGRAM 6.4 Decision Tree Analysis Using AB:QM; SN = Starting
Node; EN = Ending Node; d = Decision Branch; e = Event, or State-of-
Nature Branch

```
Decision Theory / Decision Tree
```

```
Problem Title :  Thompson Tree Upper Branch
Profit=1 / Cost=2                   1
Number of Branches                  7


                    SN EN T Probability Profit/Cost
     Branch  1       1   2 d
     Branch  2       1   3 d
     Branch  3       1   8 d                        -10000
     Branch  4       2   4 e        .78             190000
     Branch  5       2   5 e        .22            -190000
     Branch  6       3   6 e        .78              90000
     Branch  7       3   7 e        .22             -30000
```

PROGRAM 6.4 output (continued)

```
***** Program Output *****

----------------------------------------------------------------
    Nodes        Type      Probability   Payoff   Decision
----------------------------------------------------------------
   1 ->  2     Decision      None      106400.000 <=   choice
   1 ->  3     Decision      None       63600.000
   1 ->  8     Decision      None      -10000.000
   2 ->  4     Event        0.780      148200.000
   2 ->  5     Event        0.220      -41800.000
   3 ->  6     Event        0.780       70200.000
   3 ->  7     Event        0.220       -6600.000
----------------------------------------------------------------

The conditional payoff of solution :  106400.000

***** End of Output *****
```

Bayes's analysis

Bayes's analysis can also be performed from the AB:QM decision theory
submenu. In the Thompson Lumber decision problem, we computed conditional probabilities using Bayes's theorem. Now we make the same calculations using AB:QM, which can handle between 2 and 20 alternatives
and events. The data input screen and output for Bayes's program are
shown in Program 6.5.

PROGRAM 6.5 The Use of Bayes's Theorem: AB:QM Software

Decision Theory / Bayes' Decision Rule

```
Problem Title :   Thompson - Probability Revision

Number of Alternatives        2        Number of Events        2

              Prior    Event 1    Event 2
Alternative 1    .5       .70        .30
Alternative 2    .5       .20        .80




Help   New   Load   Save   Edit   Run   Print   Install   Directory   Esc
```

PROGRAM 6.5 output (continued)

```
***** Program Output *****

Bayes' Decision Rule
---------------------------------------
             Posterior Probability
---------------------------------------
Alternative       Event 1    Event 2
---------------------------------------
     1            0.778      0.273
     2            0.222      0.727
---------------------------------------


***** End of Output *****
```

Use of Expert Choice for AHP

Commercial and student software packages that handle AHP are available. Expert Choice, by R. F. Dyer, E. A. Forman, E. H. Forman, and G. Jouflas, is an example. This software package allows the decision maker to structure

PROGRAM 6.6 Starting Screens for Expert Choice

```
                        Expert Choice Textbook Version
                 THIS PROGRAM LICENSED FOR TEXTBOOK USE ONLY

This textbook version of Expert Choice is designed to introduce you to the
concepts of making complex, rational decisions using straightforward yet
powerful methods such as:
        o pairwise relative judgments
        o redundancy to reduce error
        o consistency measures
        o verbal, numerical or graphical input
        o an algorithm that produces ratio scale priorities
        o what if analysis
        o easy model construction and alteration

While the textbook version is limited to small problems, the commercial
version of Expert Choice is designed for real world problems that typically
involve dozens or hundreds of criteria. The commercial version provides:
        o hierarchical structuring of criteria, subcriteria, scenarios, players
        o a more comprehensive sensitivity analysis module
        o a 'ratings' module for hundreds of alternatives
        o structural adjust, product adjust and geometric mean features
        o additional reporting options, and more.

Press P to print an order form or <Space> to continue:
EXPERT CHOICE is based on the theory called the ANALYTIC HIERARCHY
PROCESS(AHP). The AHP was developed by the well-known mathematician
Thomas L. Saaty. There are three books available on the subject
from Expert Choice, Inc.


DECISION MAKING FOR LEADERS, Saaty, Thomas L., RWS Publications,
paperback edition, 1988, 291 pp., is a 'how-to' book showing problems
structured with the AHP and giving numerous applications. $20.00.

MULTI-CRITERIA DECISION MAKING: THE ANALYTIC HIERARCHY PROCESS,
Saaty, Thomas L., RWS Publications paperback edition, 1988, 468 pp.,
gives the mathematical foundations of the AHP. $25.00.

MARKETING DECISIONS USING EXPERT CHOICE, R.F. Dyer, E.A. Forman,
E.H. Forman, G. Jouflas, published by DSS, Inc., 1988, 201 pp., is a
workbook of applications and case studies in marketing using the
AHP and the Expert Choice software. $25.00.
```

the decision in a hierarchy for solution. The starting menu for the student version of Expert Choice is shown in Program 6.6.

The opening screens shown in Program 6.6 reveal the capabilities of Expert Choice and list several reference books for students and instructors. Once the opening screens are displayed, the user can go into the edit mode to enter the actual structure of the decision. We will use the overall structure of the computer selection model discussed in this chapter, which is shown graphically in Program 6.7. At this stage, the user can enter more elements to the decision or perform other functions; the functions are shown on the bottom of the screen (see Program 6.7). Additional aspects or levels of the decision structure can be added by using the Edit function. At this time, we would like to compare hardware, software, and vendor support, so we use the Compare function.

One of the advantages of Expert Choice is the ease of making comparisons. Instead of entering numeric values, the user is presented with a graphic scale on the screen with choices ranging from equally preferred to extremely preferred. After answering a few simple questions, the user simply moves the cursor up toward extremely preferred or down toward equally preferred. By pressing the return key, the user locks in the preference for any comparison. Some decision makers are more comfortable using graphic scales than entering numbers, and this approach may also be more accurate. Once all of the comparisons have been made, the com-

making comparisons

PROGRAM 6.7 Problem Structure of Computer Selection Model

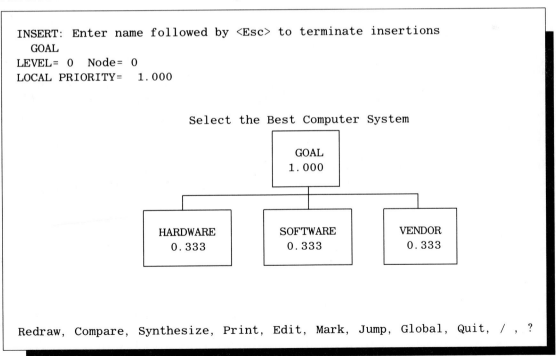

PROGRAM 6.8 System Priorities With Expert Choice

```
          JUDGMENTS AND PRIORITIES WITH RESPECT TO
          GOAL TO Select the Best Computer System

                HARDWARE   SOFTWARE   VENDOR
HARDWARE                    (9.0)     (4.0)
SOFTWARE                               4.0
```

puter displays the numeric values of the choices. The results for the computer selection decision are shown in Program 6-8.

As you can see in Program 6.8, the actual comparisons are slightly different compared to the problem as solved earlier in this chapter. Software is extremely preferred to hardware (number 9), software is moderately to strongly preferred to vendor support (number 4), and vendor support is moderately to strongly preferred to hardware (number 4). Thus, software is most important, vendor support is next, and hardware is least important.

Once the preferences have been entered graphically, the actual numeric importance factors are determined and the consistency ratio is computed. These results are graphically displayed on the screen along with the numeric values. Because the comparisons are slightly different from those presented earlier in this chapter, the overall importance factors are also slightly different. See Program 6.9.

Programs like Expert Choice can simplify decision making. Expert Choice also has the ability to print results, edit decision structures, and set global parameters.

Use of Super Tree for Decision Tree Analysis

Super Tree is a flexible and comprehensive package that allows a decision maker to analyze a variety of decision problems. The decision maker enters

PROGRAM 6.9 Factor Evaluation Using Expert Choice

```
0.066
HARDWARE XXXXXX

0.717
SOFTWARE XXXXXXXXXXXXXXXXXXXXXXXXXXXXXXXXXXXXXXXXXXXXXXXXXXXXXXXXXXXXXXXXXXXXXXXXXXXX

0.217
VENDOR   XXXXXXXXXXXXXXXXXXXXX

                INCONSISTENCY RATIO = 0.032
```

PROGRAM 6.10 Structure of Super Tree

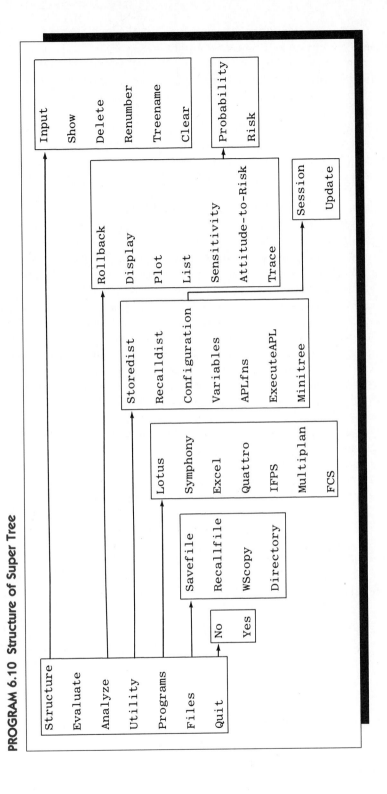

the problem structure, evaluates the situation, analyzes the problem, and saves the results on disk. In addition, Super Tree has a number of useful utilities and the ability to interface with other programs including Lotus, Excel, and Multiplan. The overall structure of the Super Tree software package is shown in Program 6.10.

functions of Super Tree

The functions of Super Tree, which are shown in the left portion of Program 6.10, include structure, evaluate, analyze, utility, programs, files, and quit. The opening or beginning menu for Super Tree is shown in Program 6-11. The structure function allows the decision maker to input the values and structure of the decision tree. This function also allows the decision maker to see the structure on the screen, to delete various nodes, to renumber nodes, to provide a name for the decision tree, and to clear previously stored structures.

The evaluate and analyze functions are used to perform a variety of tasks in investigating the decision tree. They allow the decision maker to plot probability distributions, compute expected values, determine the impact of changes on various aspects of the decision tree, and compute such quantities as the expected value of perfect information (EVPI). The utility and programs functions allow the decision maker to tailor-make various attributes of Super Tree. As mentioned previously and as seen in Program 6-10, Super Tree can interact with numerous software packages produced by other companies. In addition, the utility function allows the decision maker to store probability distributions in a DOS file, plot distributions that have been saved previously, configure Super Tree using parameters, select various decision criteria, specify the format of various data values and points, specify disk drives, and much more.

Thompson decision problem

In order to see the usefulness of Super Tree, we will go through part of the Thompson Lumber decision tree problem—the upper portion of the decision tree shown in Figure 6.4. Upon entering Super Tree, we request

PROGRAM 6.11 Main Menu of Super Tree

```
Structure Evaluate Analyze Utility Programs Files Quit
Input, Show, Delete, Renumber, Treename, Clear
───────────────────── STUDENT VERSION ─────────────────────




                SUPERTREE, VERSION 5.37
            © STRATEGIC DECISIONS GROUP, 1988


Esc to discard input or move to higher menu
PgUp to view previous screens
Ctrl PrtSc to use printer
```

PROGRAM 6.12 Decision Node Using Super Tree

```
                 DECISION/CHANCE NODE ENTRY
        Use F1 to input screen data; Esc to discard screen data.

                        NODE NUMBER:  1

        TYPE:  DECISION              OUTCOMES  DEPEND  ON  NODES:

        NUMBER  OF  BRANCHES:  3

        NODE  NAME:  SURVEY

                                                SUCCESSOR
                OUTCOME          REWARD          NODE

                LARGE              0              2

                SMALL              0              3

                NOPLANT            0              8
```

the structure function. Once we have done this, we are able to key in the various nodes and decision points for the upper branch of the Thompson Lumber decision tree problem. Program 6.12 shows the overall decision. As you can see, our alternatives are to build a large plant, a small plant, or no plant. The successor nodes, which indicate favorable or unfavorable markets related to building the large or small plant, are entered into Super Tree in the same way. Finally, we have to key in ending node numbers for the decision tree; an example is shown in Program 6.13. Note that node 7 indicates the situation of building a small plant and realizing an unfavorable market. The economic consequence for this particular situation is −$30,000.

Once we have entered all the node values and numbers, we can display

PROGRAM 6.13 Entering an Endpoint in Super Tree

```
                        NODE  NUMBER:  7

        Type:  ENDPOINT

        Name/value of endpoint:

           −30000

        No further information is needed for endpoints specified as numerical values.
```

PROGRAM 6.14 Decision Tree Structure Using Super Tree

```
Tree name:  THOMPSON

STRUCTURE        NAMES        OUTCOMES                   PROBABILITIES

1 D  2  3  8     SURVEY       LARGE  SMALL  NOPLANT
2 C  4  5        LARGE        FAVORABLE  UNFAVORABLE     .78  .22
3 C  6  7        SMALL        FAVORABLE  UNFAVORABLE     .78  .22
4 E              190000
5 E             -190000
6 E              90000
7 E             -30000
8 E             -10000
```

the overall structure of the decision tree as shown in Program 6.14. The column on the far left shows the node numbers for the decision structure. Node 1 indicates the decision of building a large, small, or no plant after survey results have been received. Node 2 looks at favorable or unfavorable markets given a large facility is to be built. As you can see, the appropriate probability values have been entered. Node 3 is the option of building a small plant and realizing either a favorable or an unfavorable market; again, probability values have been entered. For nodes 2 and 3, you can see the letter C after the node number; this indicates that the node type is *chance*. The chance node types represent states of nature. Now refer to node 1. The decision type here is represented by the letter D next to the 1; this indicates a *decision* node. Now, refer to nodes 4, 5, 6, and 7, all of which have the letter E after the node number; this indicates that these are *ending* node numbers. Node 4 indicates the ending position of building a large plant and having a favorable market. As you can see in Program 6-14, 190,000 has been entered; $190,000 is the economic consequence of building a large plant and having a favorable market. Node 5 represents building a large plant and having an unfavorable market. The economic consequence is −$190,000. Node 6 represents building a small plant with a favorable market, and node 7 is building a small plant with an unfavorable market. Finally, node 8 represents the decision to build no plant at all. All of these nodes are based upon performing a survey and receiving survey results.

performing decision analysis

Once the structure of the decision tree has been entered into Super Tree, the next step is to perform decision analysis. The results are shown in Program 6.15. As you can see, the Super Tree program correctly computes the expected value of the upper branch of the decision tree as $106,400. (Refer to Figure 6.4.)

The same type of analysis can be done for the other nodes of the Thompson Lumber problem. Once a problem has been entered, a variety of graphs

PROGRAM 6.15 Output for Decision Tree Analysis Using Super Tree

```
Rollback Display Plot List Sensitivity Trace Attitude-to-Risk
Obtain expected value/certain equivalent for tree·
───────────────── STUDENT VERSION ─────────────────
   SURVEY        EXP VAL   PROBS LARGE            EXP VAL
   LARGE        106400.00  0.780 FAVORABLE       190000.00
                           0.220 UNFAVORABLE    −190000.00
   SMALL         63600.00
   NOPLANT      −10000.00
>> Tree Drawn        11/2/89   2:59:19   THOMPSON
>> Expected Value: 106400.00
```

and output can be generated. For example, Program 6-16 is a histogram plot of probability values for the upper branch or node of the problem. The probability values range from .05 to .85 in increments of .05. You can see that the probability of −$190,000 is approximately .22, which represents

PROGRAM 6.16 Histogram Plot of Probability Values Using Super Tree

```
Rollback Display Plot List Sensitivity Trace Attitude-to-Risk
Obtain expected value/certain equivalent for tree
───────────────── STUDENT VERSION ─────────────────



  P    .85
  R    .80                            **** (about 78% probability)
  O    .75                            ****
  B    .70                            ****
  A    .65                            ****
  B    .60                            ****
  I    .55                            ****
  L    .50                            ****
  I    .45                            ****
  T    .40                            ****
  Y    .35                            ****
       .30                            ****
       .25                            ****
       .20 **** (about 22% probability) ****
       .15 ****                        ****
       .10 ****                        ****
       .05 ****                        ****

 −190000.00                        190000.00
```

a probability of 22% for the unfavorable market given that a large plant has been constructed. In a like fashion, the histogram reveals that the probability of $190,000 is .78; this represents the probability of receiving a favorable market given that a large plant was constructed. Other graphs can be developed to show both histograms and cumulative probability distributions.

other features of Super Tree

In addition to performing basic decision tree analysis, Super Tree can perform many other useful and interesting functions. For example, utility values can be used instead of economic monetary values in analyzing the decision tree. The value of imperfect and perfect information can be computed. Sensitivity analysis can be performed to reveal the impact of a change in the problem structure on the resulting solution to the decision problem. It is also possible to use more complex payoff or outcome values, including the use of relationships and formulas. This type of decision tree analysis can even perform net present value computations to include the time value of money and the impact of various interest rates. These and similar features make Super Tree an interesting and useful product for analyzing sequential or complex decisions.

6.7
SUMMARY

This chapter described the use of decision trees and utility theory. It also introduced the concept of multifactor decision making. When it is possible to accurately determine factor evaluations and factor weights, the multifactor evaluation process can be used to make the best selection. When it is not possible to make accurate estimations, the analytic hierarchy process can be used. This process uses pairwise comparisons to determine the factor evaluations and factor weights. The technique also includes the calculation of a consistency ratio to make sure that pairwise judgments are internally consistent and accurate enough for use.

In both Chapters 5 and 6, we have assumed that the states of nature are discrete. Under many decision-making environments, however, states of nature may follow a continuous probability distribution such as the normal curve. Furthermore, certain types of decision-making problems can be solved in a more efficient way without using either decision tables or decision trees. One example of this is the use of marginal analysis. In the next chapter, marginal analysis and the use of the normal curve in decision making will be explored.

GLOSSARY

Sequential Decisions. Decisions where the outcome of one decision influences other decisions.

Utility Theory. A theory that allows decision makers to incorporate their risk preference and other factors into the decision-making process.

Utility Assessment. The process of determining the utility of various outcomes. This is normally done using a standard gamble between any outcome for sure and a gamble between the worst and best outcome.

Utility Curve. A graph or curve that reveals the relationship between utility and monetary values. Once this curve has been constructed, utility values from the curve can be used in the decision-making process.

Risk Avoider. An individual who avoids risk. On the utility curve, as the monetary value increases, the utility increases at a decreasing rate. This decision maker gets less utility for a greater risk and higher potential returns.

Risk Seeker. An individual who seeks risk. On the utility curve, as the monetary value increases, the utility increases at an increasing rate. This decision maker gets more pleasure for a greater risk and higher potential returns.

Multifactor Decision Making. A decision-making environment where multiple factors are to be considered in making the final selection.

Multifactor Evaluation Process (MFEP). A multifactor decision-making approach where the factor weights and factor evaluations can be accurately determined and used in the decision-making process.

Analytic Hierarchy Process (AHP). A process that uses pairwise comparisons to determine factor evaluations and factor weights in a multifactor decision-making environment.

Factor Evaluations. These are evaluations on a scale from 0 to 1 that indicate our preference on a particular factor on a particular alternative or item.

Factor Weights. These are weights that range from 0 to 1 that give the relative importance of one factor to another. The factor weights for all factors in a multifactor decision-making environment must sum to 1.

KEY EQUATIONS

(6-1) Expected value of sample information (EVSI) =

$$\begin{pmatrix} \text{Expected value of best} \\ \text{decision } \textit{with} \text{ sample} \\ \text{information} \end{pmatrix} - \begin{pmatrix} \text{Expected value of best} \\ \text{decision } \textit{without} \\ \text{sample information} \end{pmatrix}$$

(6-2) $P(A|B) = \dfrac{P(B|A) \cdot P(A)}{P(B|A) \cdot P(A) + P(B|\overline{A}) \cdot P(\overline{A})}$

Bayes's theorem—it yields the conditional value of event A given that event B has occurred.

(6-3) Utility of other outcome $= (p)(1) + (1 - p)(0) = p$
The equation determining the utility of an intermediate outcome.

(6-4) $CI = (\lambda - n)/(n - 1)$
Consistency index.

(6-5) $CR = CI/RI$
Consistency ratio

where   RI = the random index,

λ = average of the weighted sum vector divided by the factor evaluations, and

n = the number of alternatives or items.

SOLVED PROBLEMS

Solved Problem 6-1

Monica Britt has enjoyed sailing small boats since she was seven years old when her mother first started sailing with her. Today, Monica is considering the possibility of starting a company to produce small sailboats for the recreational market. Unlike other mass-produced sailboats, however, these boats will be made specifically for children between the ages of 10 and 15. The boats will be of the highest quality, and extremely stable, and the sail size will be reduced to prevent problems of capsizing.

Because of the expense involved in developing the initial molds and acquiring the necessary equipment to produce fiberglass sailboats for young children, Monica has decided to conduct a pilot study to make sure that the market for the sailboats will be adequate. She estimates that the pilot study will cost her $10,000. Furthermore, the pilot study can either be successful or not successful. Her basic decisions are to build a large manufacturing facility, a small manufacturing facility, or no facility at all. With a favorable market, Monica can expect to make $90,000 from the large facility or $60,000 from the smaller facility. If the market is unfavorable, however, Monica estimates that she would lose $30,000 with a large facility, while she would only lose $20,000 with the small facility. Monica estimates that the probability of a favorable market given a successful pilot study is .8. The probability of an unfavorable market given an unsuccessful pilot study result is estimated to be .9. Monica feels that there is a 50-50 chance that the pilot study will be successful. Of course, Monica could bypass the pilot study and simply make the decision as to whether to build a large plant, small plant, or no facility at all. Without doing any testing in a pilot study, she estimates that the probability of a successful market is .6. What do you recommend?

Solution

Before Monica starts to solve this problem, she should develop a decision tree that shows all alternatives, states of nature, probability values, and economic consequences. This decision tree follows:

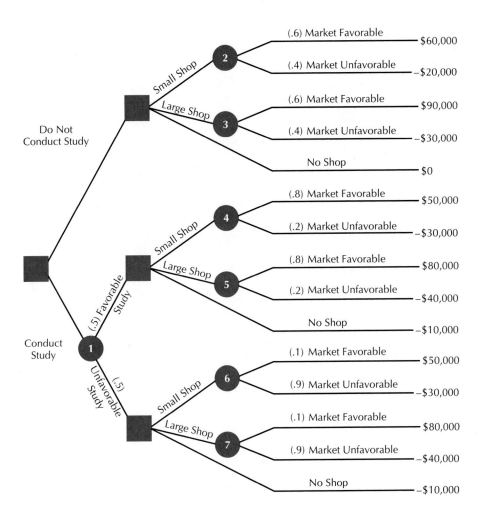

Once the decision tree has been developed, Monica can solve the problem by computing expected monetary values starting at the end points of the decision tree. The final solution is shown on the revised decision tree, which follows. The optimal solution is to *not* conduct the study but to construct the large plant directly. The expected monetary value is $42,000.

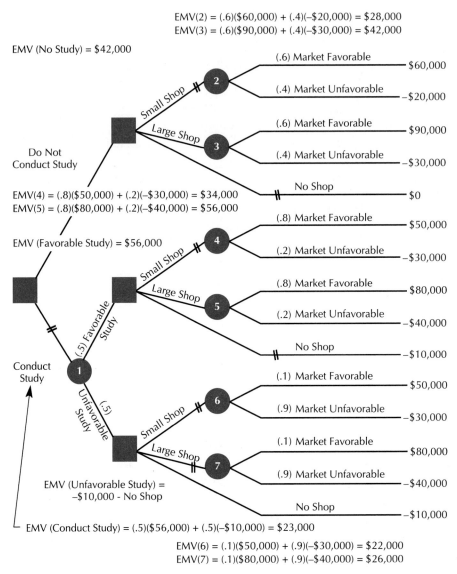

EMV(2) = (.6)($60,000) + (.4)(–$20,000) = $28,000
EMV(3) = (.6)($90,000) + (.4)(–$30,000) = $42,000

EMV (No Study) = $42,000

(.6) Market Favorable — $60,000
(.4) Market Unfavorable — –$20,000

(.6) Market Favorable — $90,000
(.4) Market Unfavorable — –$30,000

No Shop — $0

EMV(4) = (.8)($50,000) + (.2)(–$30,000) = $34,000
EMV(5) = (.8)($80,000) + (.2)(–$40,000) = $56,000

EMV (Favorable Study) = $56,000

(.8) Market Favorable — $50,000
(.2) Market Unfavorable — –$30,000

(.8) Market Favorable — $80,000
(.2) Market Unfavorable — –$40,000

No Shop — –$10,000

Conduct Study

(.5) Favorable Study

(.5) Unfavorable Study

(.1) Market Favorable — $50,000
(.9) Market Unfavorable — –$30,000

(.1) Market Favorable — $80,000
(.9) Market Unfavorable — –$40,000

No Shop — –$10,000

EMV (Unfavorable Study) = –$10,000 - No Shop

EMV (Conduct Study) = (.5)($56,000) + (.5)(–$10,000) = $23,000

EMV(6) = (.1)($50,000) + (.9)(–$30,000) = $22,000
EMV(7) = (.1)($80,000) + (.9)(–$40,000) = $26,000

Best Decision is No Study and Build the Large Plant. The EMV is $42,000

Solved Problem 6-2

Developing a small driving range for golfers of all abilities has long been a desire of John Jenkins. John, however, believes that the chance of a successful driving range is only about 40%. A friend of John's has suggested that he conduct a survey in the community to get a better feeling of the demand for such a facility. There is a .9 probability that the research will be favorable if the driving range facility will be successful. Furthermore, it is estimated that there is a .8 probability that the marketing research will be unfavorable if indeed the facility will be unsuccessful.

John would like to determine the chances of a successful driving range given a favorable result from the marketing survey.

Solution

This problem requires the use of Bayes's theorem. Before we start to solve the problem, we will define the following terms:

$P(SF)$ = Probability of successful driving range facility

$P(UF)$ = Probability of unsuccessful driving range facility

$P(RF|SF)$ = Probability that the research will be favorable given a successful driving range facility

$P(RU|SF)$ = Probability that the research will be unfavorable given a successful driving range facility

$P(RU|UF)$ = Probability that the research will be unfavorable given an unsuccessful driving range facility

$P(RF|UF)$ = Probability that the research will be favorable given an unsuccessful driving range facility

Now, we can summarize what we know:

$$P(SF) = .4$$
$$P(RF|SF) = .9$$
$$P(RU|UF) = .8$$

From this information, we can compute three additional probabilities that we need to solve the problem:

$$P(UF) = 1 - P(SF) = 1 - .4 = .6$$
$$P(RU|SF) = 1 - P(RF|SF) = 1 - .9 = .1$$
$$P(RF|UF) = 1 - P(RU|UF) = 1 - .8 = .2$$

Now we can put these values into Bayes's theorem to compute the desired probability:

$$P(SF|RF) = \frac{P(RF|SF)P(SF)}{P(RF|SF)P(SF) + P(RF|UF)P(UF)}$$

$$= \frac{(.9)(.4)}{(.9)(.4) + (.2)(.6)}$$

$$= .36/(.36 + .12) = .36/.48 = .75$$

In addition to using formulas to solve John's problem, it is possible to perform all calculations in a table:

Revised Probabilities Given a Favorable Research Result

STATE OF NATURE	CONDITIONAL PROBABILITY	PRIOR PROBABILITY	JOINT PROBABILITY	POSTERIOR PROBABILITY
Favorable market	.9	.4	.36	.36/.48 = .75
Unfavorable market	.2	.6	.12	.12/.48 = .25
			.48	

As you can see from the table, the results are the same. The probability of a successful driving range given a favorable research result is .36/.48 or .75.

Solved Problem 6-3

Like many students before her, Anne Martin is facing a difficult and important career decision. While at school, Anne worked for a local accounting firm. She did a good job and the firm has given her a standing offer to work for them for $20,000. She can take as much time as she wants to make her decision. There are, however, two other companies that are interested in her. Barnes Accounting has given her an offer of $22,000. Unfortunately, Barnes has given her only two weeks to make a decision. The company that Anne would really like to work for is Ketchum Accounting Services. This company, she feels, may make her an offer of $28,000. Unfortunately, Anne is quite uncertain about whether Ketchum will offer her the position. Thus, Anne has to make a difficult decision. Should she accept the offer from Barnes for $22,000, or should she wait and hope to get the offer from Ketchum? If she waits and doesn't get the offer from Ketchum, she can always go back to her old job for $20,000. The worst situation would be her old job, while the best situation would be the job with Ketchum. For Anne to be indifferent between taking the job with Barnes and the gamble of waiting and trying to get the job with Ketchum, the probability of landing the job at Ketchum would have to be .6. Given this information, what utility should Anne place on the three jobs?

Solution

The problem facing Anne Martin is one of determining utility values. We begin by assigning a utility value of 1 to the best situation, which is obtaining a job from Ketchum. We also assign a utility value of 0 to the worst outcome in this situation, which is keeping the old job. Furthermore, the problem states that the probability for Anne to be indifferent between taking the job with Barnes and taking the gamble of waiting and trying to get the job with Ketchum is .6. This indifference situation can be shown in the following diagram:

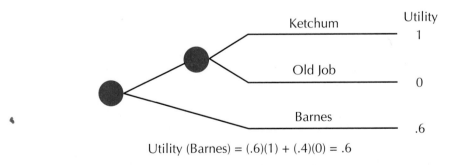

Utility (Barnes) = (.6)(1) + (.4)(0) = .6

Given the information and diagram, Anne can proceed to determine her indifference point. This point is where the utility (U) for getting the job with Barnes is equal to the gamble of getting the job with Ketchum, with a .6 probability, and her old job, with a .4 probability. The appropriate calculations are:

$$U \text{ (Ketchum)} = 1.0$$
$$U \text{ (Old Job)} = 0$$
$$U \text{ (Barnes)} = (.6)U(\text{Ketchum}) + (.4)U(\text{Old Job})$$
$$= (.6)(1) + (.4)(0) = .6$$

DISCUSSION QUESTIONS AND PROBLEMS

Discussion Questions

6-1 Under what conditions is a decision tree preferable to a decision table?

6-2 What information should be placed on a decision tree?

6-3 Describe how you would determine the best decision using the EMV criterion with a decision tree.

6-4 What is the difference between prior and posterior probabilities?

6-5 What is the purpose of Bayesian analysis? Describe how you would use Bayesian analysis in the decision-making process.

6-6 Discuss some of the problems with using the EMV criterion. Give an example of a situation in which it would be inappropriate.

6-7 What is the overall purpose of utility theory?

6-8 Briefly discuss how a utility function can be assessed. What is a standard gamble, and how is it used in determining utility values?

6-9 How is a utility curve used in selecting the best decision for a particular problem?

6-10 What is a risk seeker? What is a risk avoider? How does the utility curve for these types of decision makers differ?

6-11 Draw a utility curve for a decision maker that is indifferent to risk. If a decision maker is indifferent to risk, will using utility values give a different decision than using EMV?

Problems

· **6-12** A group of medical professionals is considering the construction of a private clinic. If the medical demand is high (that is, there is a favorable market for the clinic), the doctors could realize a net profit of $100,000. If the market is not favorable, they could lose $40,000. Of course, they don't have to proceed at all, in which case there is no cost. In the absence of any market data, the best the doctors can guess is that there is a 50-50 chance the clinic will be successful.

Construct a decision tree to help analyze this problem. What should the medical professionals do?

 : **6-13** The doctors in Problem 6-12 have been approached by a market research firm that offers to perform a study of the market, at a fee of $5,000. The market researchers claim their experience enables them to use Bayes's theorem to make the following statements of probability:

Probability of a favorable market given a favorable study = .82

Probability of an unfavorable market given a favorable study = .18

Probability of a favorable market given an unfavorable study = .11

Probability of an unfavorable market given an unfavorable study = .89

Probability of a favorable research study = .55

Probability of an unfavorable research study = .45

(a) Develop a new decision tree for the medical professionals to reflect the options now open with the market study.
(b) Use the EMV approach to recommend a strategy.
(c) What is the expected value of sample information? How much might the doctors be willing to pay for a market study?

: 6-14 Jerry Young is thinking about opening a bicycle shop in his hometown. Jerry loves to take his own bike on 50-mile trips with his friends, but he believes that any small business should only be started if there is a good chance of making a profit. Jerry can open a small shop, a large shop, or no shop at all. Because there will be a five-year lease on the building that Jerry is thinking about using, he wants to make sure that he makes the correct decision. Jerry is also thinking about hiring his old marketing professor to conduct a marketing research study. If the study is conducted, the results could be either favorable or unfavorable. Develop a decision tree for Jerry.

: 6-15 Jerry Young (of Problem 6-14) has done some analysis about the profitability of the bicycle shop. If Jerry builds the large bicycle shop, he will earn $60,000 if the market is favorable, but he will lose $40,000 if the market is unfavorable. The small shop will return a $30,000 profit in a favorable market and a $10,000 loss in an unfavorable market. At the present time, he believes that there is a 50-50 chance that the market will be favorable. His old marketing professor will charge him $5,000 for the marketing research. It is estimated that there is a .6 probability that the survey will be favorable. Furthermore, there is a .9 probability that the market will be favorable given a favorable outcome from the study. However, the marketing professor has warned Jerry that there is only a probability of .12 of a favorable market if the marketing research results are not favorable. Jerry is confused. What should he do?

: 6-16 In Problem 6-15, Jerry Young determined whether or not he should seek marketing information from his marketing professor and whether or not he should open a bicycle shop. In this problem, Jerry's marketing professor estimated that there was a .6 probability that the marketing research would be favorable. Jerry, however, is not sure that this probability is correct. How sensitive is Jerry's decision, made in Problem 6-15, to this probability value? How far can this probability value deviate from .6 without causing Jerry to change his decision?

: 6-17 Karen Kimp would like to start a small dress shop, but she has decided that it would not work unless the probability of a successful shop (SS) is .6 or greater, or the probability of an unsuccessful shop (US) is .4 or less. At the present time, she believes that the chances of a successful or unsuccessful dress shop are about the same (50%). In today's local paper, there was an article that described a study done on the potential of retail stores, which Karen believed applied to her. She found out that the probability of a favorable study given a successful shop (Favorable study|SS) was .9, and the probability of an unfavorable study given a successful shop (Unfavorable study|SS) was .1. Furthermore, the probability of an unfavorable study given an unsuccessful shop (Unfavorable study|US) was .7, and the probability of a favorable study given an unsuccessful shop (Favorable study|US) was .3. Help Karen by revising the probability that the dress shop will be successful.

: **6-18** Bill Holliday is not sure what he should do. He can either build a quadplex (that is, a building with four apartments), a duplex, gather additional information, or simply do nothing. If he gathers additional information, the results could be either favorable or unfavorable, but it would cost him $3,000 to gather the information. Bill believes that there is a 50-50 chance that the information will be favorable. If the rental market is favorable, Bill will earn $15,000 with the quadplex or $5,000 with the duplex. Bill doesn't have the financial resources to do both. With an unfavorable rental market, however, Bill could lose $20,000 with the quadplex or $10,000 with the duplex. Without gathering additional information, Bill estimates that the probability of a favorable rental market is .7. A favorable report from the study would increase the probability of a favorable rental market to .9. Furthermore, an unfavorable report from the additional information would decrease the probability of a favorable rental market to .4. Of course, Bill could forget all of these numbers and do nothing. What is your advice to Bill?

: **6-19** Before the marketing research was done, Peter Martin believed that there was a 50-50 chance that his brother's food store would be a success. The research team determined that there is a .8 probability that the marketing research will be favorable given a successful food store. Moreover, there is a .7 probability that the marketing research will be unfavorable given an unsuccessful food store. This information is based on past experience.

(a) If the marketing research is favorable, what is Peter's revised probability of a successful food store for his brother?

(b) If the marketing research is unfavorable, what is Peter's revised probability of a successful food store for his brother?

: **6-20** Mark Martinko has been a class A racquetball player for the last five years, and one of his biggest goals is to own and operate a racquetball facility. Unfortunately, Mark thinks that the chance of a successful racquetball facility is only 30%. Mark's lawyer has recommended that he employ one of the local marketing research groups to conduct a survey concerning the success or failure of a racquetball facility. There is a .8 probability that the research will be favorable given a successful racquetball facility. In addition, there is a .7 probability that the research will be unfavorable given an unsuccessful facility.

(a) Compute revised probabilities of a successful racquetball facility given a favorable and an unfavorable survey using the equations presented in this chapter.

(b) Compute revised probabilities of a successful racquetball facility given a favorable and an unfavorable survey using tables to make your computations.

: **6-21** Kuality Komponents buys on-off switches from two suppliers. The quality of the switches from the suppliers is indicated below:

PERCENT DEFECTIVE	PROBABILITY FOR SUPPLIER A	PROBABILITY FOR SUPPLIER B
1	.70	.30
3	.20	.40
5	.10	.30

For example, the probability of getting a batch of switches that are 1% defective from supplier A is .70. Since Kuality Komponents orders 10,000 switches per order, this would mean that there is a .7 probability of getting 100 defective switches out of the 10,000 switches if supplier A is used to fill the order. A defective switch can be repaired for 50¢. Although the quality of supplier B is lower, it will sell an order of 10,000 switches for $37 less than supplier A.

(a) Develop a decision tree.
(b) Which supplier should Kuality Komponents use?
(c) For how much less would supplier B have to sell an order of 10,000 switches than supplier A for Kuality Komponents to be indifferent between the two suppliers?

: **6-22** Jim Sellers is thinking about producing a new type of electric razor for men. If the market were favorable, he would get a return of $100,000, but if the market for this new type of razor were unfavorable, he would lose $60,000. Since Ron Bush is a good friend of Jim Sellers, Jim is considering the possibility of using Bush Marketing Research to gather additional information about the market for the razor. Bush has suggested that Jim either use a survey or a pilot study to test the market. The survey would be a sophisticated questionnaire administered to a test market. It will cost $5,000. Another alternative is to actually run a pilot study. This would involve producing a limited number of the new razors and actually trying to sell them in two cities that are typical of American cities. The pilot study is more accurate, but is also more expensive. It will cost $20,000. Ron Bush has suggested that it would be a good idea for Jim to conduct either the survey or the pilot before Jim makes the decision concerning whether or not to produce the new razor. But Jim is not sure if the value of the survey or the pilot is worth the cost.

Jim estimates that the probability of a successful market without performing a survey or pilot study is .5. Furthermore, the probability of a favorable survey result given a favorable market for razors is .7, and the probability of a favorable survey result given an unsuccessful market for razors is .2. In addition, the probability of an unfavorable pilot study given an unfavorable market is .9, and the probability of an unsuccessful pilot study result given a favorable market for razors is .2.

(a) Draw the decision tree for this problem without the probability values.
(b) Compute the revised probabilities needed to complete the decision, and place these values in the decision tree.
(c) What is the best decision for Jim? Use expected monetary value as the decision criterion.

: **6-23** Jim Sellers has been able to estimate his utility for a number of different values. He would like to use these utility values in making the decision in Problem 6-22. The utility values are: $U(-\$80,000) = 0$, $U(-\$65,000) = .5$, $U(-\$60,000) = .55$, $U(-\$20,000) = .7$, $U(-\$5,000) = .8$, $U(\$0) = .81$, $U(\$80,000) = .9$, $U(\$95,000) = .95$, and $U(\$100,000) = 1$. Resolve Problem 6-22 using utility values. Is Jim a risk avoider?

: **6-24** In Problem 6-13, you helped the medical professionals analyze their decision using expected monetary value as the decision criterion. This group has also assessed their utility for money: $U(-\$45,000) = 0$, $U(-\$40,000) = .1$, $U(-\$5,000) = .7$, $U(\$0) = .9$, $U(\$95,000) = .99$, and $U(\$100,000) = 1$. Use expected utility as the decision criterion, and determine the best decision for the medical professionals. Are the medical professionals risk seekers or risk avoiders?

· **6-25** Rhonda Radner has just been approached by her investment counselor, Charlie Armstrong. Charlie has an investment that would cost Rhonda $500. If the investment is a success, Rhonda could double her money, but if it is a failure, she could lose the initial investment. Charlie believes that there is a .6 probability that Rhonda will double her investment and get $1,000. Charlie reasons that the expected return of this investment is $600 ($600 = $0 × .4 + $1,000 × .6). Since the cost is only $500, Charlie has urged Rhonda to make the investment. Rhonda, however, does not agree with Charlie. She would only consider investing the $500 if the probability of getting $1,000 is .8. Rhonda believes that the investment with a .6 probability of getting $1,000 is only worth $300. Plot a utility curve for Rhonda. What is Rhonda's preference for risk?

· **6-26** Charlie Armstrong cannot understand why Rhonda is not willing to make the investment. (See Problem 6-25.) Charlie believes that the investment is worth $600 with a probability of .6. Furthermore, Charlie believes that the investment is worth $800 if the probability of getting $1,000 is .8. Plot the utility curve for Charlie Armstrong. What is his preference for risk?

: **6-27** In this chapter, a decision tree was developed for John Thompson. (See Figure 6.3 for the complete decision tree analysis.) After completing the analysis, John was not completely sure that he is indifferent to risk. After going through a number of standard gambles, John was able to assess his utility for money. Here are some of the utility assessments: $U(-\$190,000) = 0$, $U(-\$180,000) = .05$, $U(-\$30,000) = .15$, $U(-\$20,000) = .1$, $U(-\$10,000) = .2$, $U(\$0) = .3$, $U(\$90,000) = .5$, $U(\$100,000) = .6$, $U(\$190,000) = .95$, and $U(\$200,000) = 1.0$. If John maximizes his expected utility, does his decision change?

: **6-28** In the past few years, the traffic problems in Lynn McKell's hometown have gotten worse. Now, Broad Street is congested about half the time. The normal travel time to work for Lynn is only 15 minutes when Broad Street is used and there is no congestion. With congestion, however, it takes Lynn 40 minutes to get to work. If Lynn decides to take the expressway, it will take 30 minutes regardless of the traffic conditions. Lynn's utility for waiting is: $U(15 \text{ minutes}) = .9$, $U(30 \text{ minutes}) = .7$, and $U(40 \text{ minutes}) = .2$.

(a) Which route will minimize Lynn's expected travel time?
(b) Which route will maximize Lynn's utility?
(c) When it comes to travel time, is Lynn a risk seeker or a risk avoider?

: **6-29** Jack Belkin considers himself an expert when it comes to fine food and beverage, and Jack is proud to tell his out-of-town friends that the best restaurant that he has encountered, Old Tavern, is located in his hometown. Big Burger, a national franchise, is the worst restaurant he has ever been to. Unfortunately, Jack's kids love the french fries at Big Burger, and when his family is deciding where to eat, his kids always say "Let's flip a coin to see if we go to Big Burger or Old Tavern." Jack hates Big Burger, but his kids hate Old Tavern. Jack's wife always has a compromise. She wants to go to Ralph's Diner instead of flipping a coin. But Jack is totally indifferent to these two alternatives. Once when Jack and his wife were alone, his wife suggested that they flip a coin to see if they would go to Old Tavern or Ralph's Diner. (Jack's wife did not like the rich food at Old Tavern.) When Jack demurred at this gamble, his wife proposed that they simply go to the Vacation Inn Restaurant, which was slightly more expensive than Ralph's Diner. Again, Jack was totally indifferent to this choice. Determine Jack's utility for restaurants.

: **6-30** Jack Belkin's kids love to play games while riding in the car, and this outing was no exception. (See Problem 6-29 for some additional details.) The entire family was about 50 miles from home, and Jack was looking forward to eating at the Vacation Inn Restaurant, which was a compromise restaurant choice. His oldest kid said, "Let's make a bet. If we see three red Volkswagens between here and home, we will eat at Big Burger. Otherwise, we will go to Old Tavern." Jack believes that the probability of seeing three red Volkswagens is very low—about .20. Should Jack take his kids' bet, or should he tell them that they are eating at Vacation Inn Restaurant and that is final?

: **6-31** After driving down the road and seeing one red Volkswagen, Jack Belkin had second thoughts abut his probability assessment. (Refer to Problem 6-30.) In Problem 6-30, Jack estimated that the probability of seeing three red Volkswagens before the family got home was .20. How sensitive is Jack's decision in Problem 6-30 to his probability assessment? What probability would make him indifferent between the bet his kid proposed and eating at Vacation Inn Restaurant?

: **6-32** Coren Chemical Inc. develops industrial chemicals that are used by other manufacturers to produce photographic chemicals, preservatives, and lubricants. One of their products, K-1000, is used by several photographic companies to make a chemical that is used in the film developing process. To efficiently produce K-1000, Coren Chemical uses the batch approach, where a certain number of gallons is produced at one time. This reduces setup costs and allows Coren Chemical to produce K-1000 at a competitive price. Unfortunately, K-1000 has a very short shelf life of about one month.

Coren Chemical produces K-1000 in batches of 500 gallons, 1,000 gallons, 1,500 gallons and 2,000 gallons. Using historical data, David Coren was able to determine that the probability of selling 500 gallons of K-1000 is .2. The probabilities of selling 1,000, 1,500, and 2,000 gallons are .3, .4, and .1 respectively. The question facing David is how many gallons to produce of K-1000 in the next batch run. K-1000 sells for $20 per gallon. Manufacturing cost is $12 per gallon, and handling costs and warehousing costs are estimated to be $1 per gallon. In the past, David has allocated advertising costs to K-1000 at $3 per gallon. If K-1000 is not sold after the batch run, the chemical loses much of its important properties as a developer. It can, however, be sold at a salvage value of $13 per gallon. Furthermore, David has guaranteed to his suppliers that there will always be adequate supply of K-1000. If David does run out, he has agreed to purchase a comparable chemical from a competitor at $25 per gallon. Since David sells all of the chemical at $20 per gallon, his shortage means that David loses the $5 to buy the more expensive chemical in addition to the handling and advertising costs.

(a) Develop a decision tree for this problem.
(b) What is the best solution?
(c) Determine the expected value of perfect information.

: **6-33** The Jamis Corporation is involved with waste management. During the last ten years, it has become one of the largest waste disposal companies in the midwest, serving primarily Wisconsin, Illinois, and Michigan. Bob Jamis, president of the company, is considering the possibility of establishing a waste treatment plant in Mississippi. From past experience, Bob believes that a small plant in upper Mississippi would yield a $500,000 profit regardless of the market for the facility. The success of a medium-sized waste treatment plant would depend on the market. With a low demand for waste treatment, Bob expects a $200,000 return. A medium demand would yield a $700,000 return in Bob's estimation, and a high demand would return $800,000. While a large facility is much riskier, the potential return is much greater. With a high demand for waste treatment in Mississippi, the large facility should return a million dollars. With a medium demand, the large facility will only return $400,000. Bob estimates that the large facility would be a big loser if there is a low demand for waste treatment. He estimates that he would lose approximately $200,000 with a large treatment facility if demand was indeed low. Looking at the economic conditions for the upper part of the state of Mississippi and using his experience in the field, Bob estimates that the probability of a low demand for treatment plants is .15. The probability for a medium-sized facility is approximately .40, and the probability of a high demand for a waste treatment facility is .45.

Because of the large potential investment and the possibility of a loss, Bob has decided to hire a market research team that is based in Jackson, Mississippi. This team will perform a survey to get a better feeling for the probability of a low, medium, or high demand for a waste treatment facility. The cost of the survey is $50,000. To help Bob determine whether or not to go ahead with the survey, the marketing research firm has provided Bob with the following information:

P(Survey results|Possible outcomes)

		SURVEY RESULTS		
		LOW SURVEY RESULTS	MEDIUM SURVEY RESULTS	HIGH SURVEY RESULTS
Possible Outcomes	Low demand	.7	.2	.1
	Medium demand	.4	.5	.1
	High demand	.1	.3	.6

As you see, the survey could result in three possible outcomes. Low survey results mean that a low demand is likely. In a likewise fashion medium survey results or high survey results would mean a medium or a high demand, respectively. What should Bob do?

: **6-34** Monetary values are sometimes inappropriate in decision theory. In such cases, the concepts of utility theory can be used. Locate a friend or someone you know who has not worked Problem 6-33. Using a standard gamble for utility assessment, determine the utility values for all of the monetary outcomes for Problem 6-33. Then, construct a utility curve. In some cases, this may require several rounds of utility assessment to get an accurate and consistent utility curve. Then, using the utility values and the utility curve, resolve Problem 6-33. Is the friend or individual you know a risk taker or a risk avoider? Did you have any difficulties in assessing a utility curve? If so, explain. Discuss the usefulness as well as the potential problems in the use of utility theory in making decisions.

: **6-35** George Lyon is about to buy a compact stereo cassette player. He is currently considering three brands—Sun, Hitek, and Surgo. The important factors to George are the price, color, warranty, size of the unit, and brand name. George has determined factor weights of .4, .1, .1, .1, and .3 respectively. Furthermore, George has determined factor evaluations for all of the factors for the three different manufacturers of the unit he is considering. The Sun unit has factor evaluations of .7, .9, .8, .8, and .9 for the price, color, warranty, size, and brand-name factors. The Hitek unit has factor evaluations of .6, .9, .9, .8, and .9 for these factors. Finally, Surgo has factor evaluations of .8, .4, .4, .2, and .6 for the same factors of price, color, warranty, size, and brand name. Determine the total weighted evaluation for the three manufacturers. Which one should George select?

: **6-36** Linda Frieden is thinking about buying a new car. There are three different car models she is considering—car 1, car 2, and car 3. An important factor for Linda is the price. She has determined that car 1 is equally to moderately preferred to car 2. Car 1 is very strongly preferred to car 3, and car 2 is moderately to strongly preferred to car 3. Determine the priorities or factor evaluations for the three cars for price. What is the consistency ratio?

: **6-37** Linda Frieden (Problem 6-36) is also concerned about the warranty for the three cars she is considering. The second car is moderately preferred to the first car in terms of warranty. The third car is very to extremely strongly preferred over the first car, and the third car is strongly preferred over the second car. Determine the factor evaluations or priorities for the three cars for car warranty. Compute the consistency ratio.

: **6-38** Linda Frieden (Problems 6-36 and 6-37) would like to consider style as an important factor in making a decision to purchase a new car. Car 2 is moderately preferred to car 1 in terms of style, but car 1 is moderately preferred to car 3 in terms of style. Furthermore, car 2 is very to extremely strongly preferred over car 3. Determine the factor evaluations for style concerning the three cars and compute the consistency ratio.

: **6-39** Linda Frieden (Problems 6-36–6-38) now must determine the relative weights for the three factors of price, warranty, and style. She believes that the price is equally to moderately preferred over warranty, and that price is extremely preferred to style. She also believes that the car warranty is strongly to very strongly preferred over the style. Using this information, determine the weights for these three factors. Also determine the consistency ratio to make sure that the above values are consistent enough to use in the analysis. In Problems 6-36–6-38, Linda has determined factor evaluations for price, warranty, and style for the three cars. Using the information you determined in this problem along with the solutions to the above three problems, determine the final rankings for each car. Which car should be selected?

: **6-40** Jim Locke, an undergraduate student in the E.S.U. College of Business, is trying to decide which microcomputer to purchase with the money his parents gave him for Christmas. He has reduced the number of computers he has been considering to three, calling them system 1 (S1), system 2 (S2), and system 3 (S3). For each computer, he would like to consider the price, the brand name, the memory capacity, speed, flexibility, and compatibility with IBM PCs.

In order to make the correct decision, he has decided to make pairwise comparisons for all the factors. For price, the first computer system is equally to moderately preferred over the second computer system and very to extremely strongly preferred over the third computer system. The second computer system is strongly preferred over the third computer system.

For brand name, the first computer system is equally preferred to the second computer system, while the first computer system is strongly to very strongly preferred over the third computer system. The second computer system is moderately to strongly preferred over the third computer system.

When it comes to memory, the second computer is equally to moderately preferred over the first computer system, and the third computer system is very strongly preferred over the first computer system. Furthermore, the third computer system is strongly to very strongly preferred over the second computer system.

For speed, the second computer system is moderately preferred to the first computer system, but the first computer system is equally to moderately preferred over the third computer system. Furthermore, the second computer system is strongly preferred over the third computer system.

For the flexibility factor, the third computer system is very to extremely strongly preferred over the first computer system, and the second computer system is equally to moderately preferred over the first computer system. The third computer system is also moderately to strongly preferred over the second computer system.

Finally, Jim has used pairwise comparisons to look at how compatible each computer system is with the IBM PC. Using this analysis, he has determined that the first computer system is very to extremely strongly preferred over the second computer system when it comes to compatibility. The first computer system is moderately to strongly preferred over the third computer system, and the third computer system is moderately preferred over the second computer system.

When it comes to comparing the factors, Jim has used pairwise comparisons to look at price, brand name, memory, speed, flexibility, and compatibility. Here are the results of the analysis. Price is extremely preferred to brand name, moderately to strongly preferred to memory, strongly preferred to speed, moderately preferred to flexibility, and equally to moderately preferred to PC compatibility. In other words, price is a very important factor. The computer's memory is equally to moderately preferred to brand name, speed is equally preferred to brand name, flexibility is moderately to strongly preferred to brand name, and PC compatibility is strongly preferred to brand name. In looking at memory, Jim has determined that memory is equally to moderately preferred to speed. PC compatibility, however, is strongly to very strongly preferred to memory, and overall flexibility is equally to moderately preferred to the computer's memory. PC compatibility is strongly to very strongly preferred to speed, and flexibility is moderately preferred to speed. Finally, Jim has determined that PC compatibility is equally to moderately preferred to flexibility.

Using all of these preferences for pairwise comparisons, determine the priorities or factor evaluations, along with the appropriate consistency ratios for price, brand name, memory, speed, flexibility, and PC compatibility for the three different computer systems. In addition, determine the overall weights for each of the factors. Which computer system should be selected?

: **6-41** Maria Mooney is responsible for selecting 25 personal computer systems for a middle-level manager support center. She has narrowed down her choices to three possibilities. In her deliberations, she has referred to these computers as system-1, system-2, and system-3. In order to help her make the proper selection, Maria has gathered together a group of five middle-level managers who are knowledgeable about personal computer systems. This group has identified eight factors that are to be considered: processor speed, processor type, memory size, the type and speed of the hard disk, the floppy disk system, the keyboard facility, the warranty offered by the manufacturer, and service provided by the local dealer. Using the analytic hierarchy process in a group setting, Maria has determined the preference of the three potential personal computer systems for all of the eight factors. The results are summarized below.

The first factor to consider was processor speed. This was measured primarily using clock speed. For this factor, system-2 was strongly to very strongly preferred to system-1. System-3 was moderately preferred to system-1, and system-3 was moderately preferred to system-2.

The second factor was processor type. Popular types include the 286 chip as well as the 386 chip. For this factor, there was no difference between systems. In other words, all personal computer systems were equally preferred.

The third factor was memory size. For this factor, system-1 was moderately preferred to system-2. System-1 was very to extremely strongly preferred to system-3, and system-2 was strongly preferred to system-3.

The fourth factor was the availability and type of the hard disk system. A number of considerations were explored for this factor, including disk size, cost, and disk retrieval speed. For this factor, system-2 was strongly to very strongly preferred to system-1. System-3 was equally to moderately preferred to system-1, and it was strongly preferred to system-2.

The fifth factor was the floppy disk system. Considerations included the cost, access speed, and storage capacities. For this factor, all systems were equally preferred.

The keyboard layout and functioning, was the sixth factor to be considered. The overall layout of the keyboard, its feel, and the number and types of keys were all important characteristics that were explored. The group decided that system-1 was moderately to strongly preferred to system-2 and very to extremely strongly preferred to system-3. In addition, system-2 was strongly to very strongly preferred to system-3.

The seventh factor was the warranty offered by the manufacturer. The length of the warranty and the basic coverage were the two primary considerations for this factor. System-2 was very to extremely strongly preferred to system-1. System-3 was equally to moderately preferred to system-1 and moderately preferred to system-2.

The final factor was service, which incorporated numerous considerations in dealing with the local computer store. Important considerations included store policies, the size and competency of the repair shop, turnaround time for repairs, procedures for emergency problems, and the availability of backup machines and equipment in case of system failure. For this factor, the group determined that system-1 was equally to moderately preferred to system-2 and very to extremely strongly preferred to system-3. System-2 was moderately to strongly preferred to system-3.

The final deliberation of the committee was to determine the relative weights, or importance ratings, for the various factors. The committee compared all eight factors together. The factors in order of priority included processor speed, processor type, memory size, hard disk facilities, the floppy disk system, the keyboard, the warranty from the manufacturer, and service from the local dealer or computer store. Each factor was then compared to all other factors using the analytic hierarchy process. Here are the results: (1) Processor speed was equally to moderately preferred to processor type, equally to moderately preferred to memory size, moderately preferred to the hard disk, strongly preferred to the floppy disk system, strongly to very strongly preferred to the keyboard, very strongly preferred to the warranty, and very to extremely strongly preferred to service. (2) The next most important factor was processor type. Processor type was equally preferred to memory size, moderately preferred to the hard disk system, moderately to strongly preferred to the floppy disk system, strongly preferred to the keyboard, strongly to very strongly preferred to the warranty, and strongly to very strongly preferred to local service. (3) The third most important factor was memory size. It was equally to moderately preferred to the hard drive system, strongly preferred to the floppy drive system, very strongly preferred to the keyboard, very to extremely strongly preferred to the warranty, and extremely preferred to local service. (4) Next was the hard disk system. This factor was equally to moderately preferred to the floppy disk system, moderately preferred to the keyboard, moderately to strongly preferred to the warranty, and strongly preferred to local service. (5) Next in order of importance was the floppy disk system. It was strongly to very strongly preferred to the keyboard, very strongly preferred to the warranty, and very to extremely strongly preferred to local service. (6) The keyboard was next. It was strongly to very strongly preferred to the warranty, and very strongly preferred to local service. (7) Finally, the warranty was strongly to very strongly preferred to the local service. Using these data, determine the weights for each of the eight factors, the ranking score for each system, and that system which has the highest overall weighted average.

Data Set Problem

6-42 Lane Bailey must decide how many large Christmas trees to stock. To simplify the problem, he is looking at the possibility of stocking 100, 200, 300, 400, or 500 trees. These stocking options are summarized in the following table:

Basic Decisions

NODES	DECISION NUMBER	STOCKING POLICY (NUMBER OF TREES)
$1 \rightarrow 2$	1	100
$1 \rightarrow 3$	2	200
$1 \rightarrow 4$	3	300
$1 \rightarrow 5$	4	400
$1 \rightarrow 6$	5	500

For each decision alternative, there are five possible states of nature representing possible demand values. These values, along with their probabilities and expected profits, are summarized in the following tables:

Stocking 100 Trees

NODES	DEMAND	PROBABILITY	PROFITS ($)
2 → 7	100	.10	1,000,000
2 → 8	200	.30	1,000,000
2 → 9	300	.40	1,000,000
2 → 10	400	.10	1,000,000
2 → 11	500	.10	1,000,000

Stocking 200 Trees

NODES	DEMAND	PROBABILITY	PROFITS ($)
3 → 12	100	.10	800,000
3 → 13	200	.30	900,000
3 → 14	300	.40	1,000,000
3 → 15	400	.10	1,100,000
3 → 16	500	.10	1,200,000

Stocking 300 Trees

NODES	DEMAND	PROBABILITY	PROFITS ($)
4 → 17	100	.10	700,000
4 → 18	200	.30	800,000
4 → 19	300	.40	1,000,000
4 → 20	400	.10	1,200,000
4 → 21	500	.10	1,300,000

Stocking 400 Trees

NODES	DEMAND	PROBABILITY	PROFITS ($)
5 → 22	100	.10	600,000
5 → 23	200	.30	800,000
5 → 24	300	.40	1,000,000
5 → 25	400	.10	1,100,000
5 → 26	500	.10	1,300,000

Stocking 500 Trees

NODES	DEMAND	PROBABILITY	PROFITS ($)
6 → 27	100	.10	500,000
6 → 28	200	.30	600,000
6 → 29	300	.40	1,000,000
6 → 30	400	.10	1,200,000
6 → 31	500	.10	1,300,000

(a) What is the best stocking policy given the information available?

(b) Lane believes that he may be able to get a quantity discount for stocking 500 trees. This would increase his profits. He believes he may be able to make $100 more for each level of demand. Does this change the stocking decision?

(c) What if Lane receives $200 more for each level of demand for stocking 500 trees?

(d) What if Lane receives $400 more for each level of demand for stocking 500 trees?

The Executive Fisherman

Lee Stepina, a successful middle-level manager for Toykin, Inc., could never recall why he had such a passion for fishing. Perhaps it was because, as a young boy, he spent many hours by a small pond only two blocks from his house fishing for the big one. More likely, however, his great passion for fishing was a direct result of his family's way of life. When Lee was growing up, his parents owned and operated a small bakery. The family lived on the top floor, while the bakery was located on the first floor and the basement. The bakery business was tough, and it required that the family stay up late at night preparing fresh baked goods for the next day. As a result, Lee's family would work hard at night but sleep late in the morning. When Lee came home after school, his parents were well rested and ready for recreation. This recreation was almost always fishing on the local pond. While the family business changed over the years, from out of the bakery business into the vending business, Lee kept his late night work habits and his love for fishing.

His love for fishing, however, gave him a guilt complex. While he was a successful executive for Toykin, his true interest remained fishing. Lee would often come to work and carefully hide his best fishing tackle in the back seat or the trunk of his car. Unfortunately, executives at Toykin were expected to give 110% every day. Any hint of outside interests or activities that could take time away from the pursuit of higher profits for Toykin could spell disaster for an executive's career.

These were very difficult times for Lee. He much preferred fishing and tinkering in his basement with fishing poles and other gear to reading profit and loss statements or trying to come up with newer advertising campaigns for Toykin. It was during these hard times that Lee finally decided to make a very risky move. He would give up excellent fringe benefits, a relatively high salary, and the comfort of corporate perks—including country clubs and spas—to be on his own and doing what he liked to do.

With enough money to feed the family for a year and a half and with venture capital from friends of the family, Lee decided to quit the corporate world and start out on his own. During the first three months, Lee scrambled to get additional funding for his small company while he finalized plans for the new product he would develop. After three months, Lee had both the necessary financing and an idea that he felt would be a winner. Lee had also found the perfect name for his new company—Executive Fisherman.

The main product that Executive Fisherman would make for the first year or so was the best-quality fishing rod, reel, and other tackle available on the market. In addition, the fishing gear would be oriented toward the executive or higher-class market. The Executive Fisherman would be a complete fishing package. Furthermore, all of the gear could be broken down and efficiently placed in a beautifully styled executive-type briefcase. The briefcase would be customized with foam rubber padding and ingenious compartments within the padding that would hold the rod, reel, fishing line, hooks, lures, and all of the other paraphernalia expected by the diehard fisherman. As an added benefit, the foam rubber and compartments could easily be removed as one unit to make the briefcase suitable for carrying reports, papers, pens and pencils, and other executive necessities.

The dual-purpose briefcase was the pride of Lee Stepina's design. No longer would executives have to feel guilty about their passion for fishing. On most days, executives could use the briefcase for its normal business purpose. Then, on other days, the executive could insert the foam rubber padding, the containers, and all of the fishing gear for a quick getaway to the local fishing hole. Furthermore, the Executive Fisherman could easily be taken on an airplane, in a car, or on a train. It was excellent for travel, and the equipment itself was of the highest quality.

The price of the briefcase with all of the compartments and foam rubber padding would be $75 if purchased alone. The fishing equipment would have a price of $50 if purchased alone. Therefore, the total price was $125. When purchased together, the Executive Fisherman would have a retail price of $99.

Lee was convinced that the Executive Fisherman would be a smashing success. However, years on the corporate ladder had taught him important lessons. He knew that before he could sink a lot of money into the Executive Fisherman, he would have to do his homework. He decided that it would be best to hire a research team to help him determine if the project would be successful or not before he spent all of the venture capital. Lee estimated that it would cost approximately $50,000 to develop the equipment necessary to produce the Executive Fisherman. He estimated that if the venture were successful, it would gross $200,000. In Lee's opinion, there was a 60% chance of a successful venture. Lee realized that, if the venture was successful, the profit, after deducting the equipment cost, would be $150,000. On the other hand, a failure would cost $50,000.

Lee and his backers decided to contact several marketing firms who would make their own estimates. Two firms looked particularly interesting. Crittenden Marketing Incorporated (CMI) would charge $10,000 to conduct a survey. This was an experienced research team that had a proven track record. The track record for CMI is shown in the following table, which shows the results of the last 100 marketing surveys performed by CMI.

As seen in the table, 55 of the firms that CMI helped actually had a successful venture or project. Thirty-five of these firms had favorable survey results, while only 20 had unfavorable survey results. The remaining 45 companies assisted by CMI had unsuccessful ventures. Fifteen of these 45 firms had survey results that were favorable, while 30 of these firms had unfavorable survey results.

Master Marketers Incorporated (MMI) was another firm that specialized in performing marketing research. Its cost of performing the research would be $30,000. This firm also has an interesting track record. The chance of getting a favorable survey result, given a successful venture, was 90%. On the other hand, the likelihood of getting an unfavorable survey result given an unsuccessful venture was 80%.

For the first time, Lee was uncertain and confused. He didn't know whether to blindly go ahead with Executive Fisherman, to stop all development and seek employment, to hire CMI, or to hire MMI for additional information.

Discussion Questions

1. Should Lee hire either CMI or MMI to perform marketing research to give him additional information about the likelihood of success for Executive Fisherman?
2. If you were in Lee's position, what would you do?

Success Figures for CMI

OUTCOME	SURVEY RESULTS		
	FAVORABLE	UNFAVORABLE	TOTALS
Successful Venture	35	20	55
Unsuccessful Venture	15	30	45

Sixty-Six-Year-Old Patient with a Hernia

A 66-year-old man has an inguinal hernia which he has asked a surgeon on your staff to repair by surgery.

Two years ago the patient had a heart attack which makes him face a higher-than-average risk of dying during surgery. He has had his hernia for a year. His internist said he should wear a truss which will hold the hernia in and thereby avoid the risk of operation. The patient has been wearing the truss. It is not uncomfortable or painful, but when he goes to his friend's swimming pool he is embarrassed by it. To avoid this embarrassment, he decided to be admitted for surgery.

The anesthesiologist explained the risks to him as follows: If he wears a truss, there is a 97% chance of living out the rest of his life without having the hernia strangulate (the intestinal bulge is pinched off, meaning loss of blood supply and emergency surgery). There is a 3% chance of strangulation. If strangulation occurs, there will be an emergency operation that has a 15% operative mortality. This

patient is expected to live eight years. The emergency operative mortality would on the average be expected to shorten his life to four years. (This is because strangulation is assumed to occur halfway through his expected lifetime.)

If the patient chooses the elective surgery today, he faces a 5% operative mortality and a loss of eight years of life, and a 95% chance of surviving the operation and living out his remaining eight years. The elective surgery will cost about $1,500. Aware of these risks, he has chosen elective surgery now.

Discussion Questions

1. Do you think the patient *should* have the surgery now?

2. What other factors might be considered?

Source: Copyright © 1977 by the President and Fellows of Harvard College. Reproduced by permission. This case was prepared by Duncan Neuhauser.

BIBLIOGRAPHY

Chatterjee, R. "A Practical Bayesian Approach to Selection of Optimal Market Testing Strategies." *Journal of Marketing Research* Vol. 25, November 1988, pp. 363–375.

Currim, I. S. "Disaggregate Tree-Structured Modeling of Consumer Choice Data." *Journal of Marketing Research* Vol. 25, August 1988, pp. 253–265.

Dubois, R. W., and Brook, R. H. "Assessing Clinical Decision Making: Is the Ideal System Feasible?" *Inquiry* Vol. 25, Spring 1988, pp. 59–64.

Epley, D. R. "A Beginner's Decision-Tree for Understanding the 1986 Tax Reform Act." *The Real Estate Appraiser and Analyst* Vol. 54, Winter 1988, pp. 45–50.

Freedman, J. S. "Decision-Tree Analysis: A Valuable Real Estate Investment Tool." *Pension World* Vol. 24, November 1988, pp. 20–22.

Fryar, E. O., and others. "Bayesian Evaluation of a Specific Hypothesis." *American Journal of Agricultural Economics* Vol. 70, August 1988, pp. 685–692.

Greer, O. L. "A Decision-Tree Approach to the Design and Implementation of Accounting and Information Systems for Small Businesses." *Journal of Small Business Management* Vol. 27, January 1989, pp. 8–16.

Heian, B. C., and Gale, J. R. "Mortgage Selection Using a Decision-Tree Approach: An Extension." *Interfaces* Vol. 18, July–August 1988, pp. 72–83.

Hughes, Warren. "Decision Making Using the Analytic Hierarchy Process: The Falklands Crisis." *Proceedings of the 1986 Annual Meeting of the Decision Sciences Institute* Vol. 2, 1986, pp. 768–770.

Saaty, Thomas. "A Scaling Method for Priorities in Hierarchical Structures." *Journal of Mathematical Psychology* Vol. 15, No. 3, 1977, pp. 234–281.

Saaty, Thomas. *The Analytic Hierarchy Process.* New York: McGraw-Hill, 1980.

Saaty, Thomas, and Kearn, K. *Analytical Planning—The Organization of Systems.* Oxford: Pergamon Press, 1985.

Schoner, B., and Wedley, W. C. "Ambiguous Criteria Weights in AHP: Consequences and Solutions." *Decision Sciences* Vol. 20, Summer 1989, pp. 462–475.

Shyy, G. "Bullish or Bearish: A Bayesian Dichotomous Model to Forecast Turning Points in the Foreign Exchange Market." *Journal of Economics and Business* Vol. 41, February 1989, pp. 49–60.

Wind, Yoram, and Saaty, Thomas. "Marketing Applications of the Analytic Hierarchy Process." *Management Science* Vol. 26, No. 7, July 1980, pp. 641–658.

Zahedi, F. "The Analytic Hierarchy Process—A Survey of the Method and its Applications." *Interfaces* Vol. 16, No. 4, 1986, pp. 96–108.

7

Marginal Analysis and the Normal Distribution

7.1
INTRODUCTION

In Chapters 5 and 6, we assumed that Thompson Lumber Company faced only a small number of states of nature and decision alternatives. But what if there were fifty, a hundred, or even thousands of states and/or alternatives? If you used a decision tree or decision table, solving the problem would be virtually impossible. This chapter shows how decision theory can be extended to handle problems of such a magnitude.

many states of nature and alternatives

We begin with the case of a firm facing two decision alternatives under conditions of numerous states of nature. The normal probability distribution, which is widely applicable in business decision making, is first used to describe the states of nature. Later in this chapter, it is also used to represent many decision alternatives that are possible when a firm is selecting an inventory ordering policy.

7.2
BREAK-EVEN ANALYSIS AND THE NORMAL DISTRIBUTION

Break-even analysis, often called *cost-volume analysis*, answers several common management questions relating the effect of a decision to overall revenues or costs. At what point will we break even, or when will revenues equal costs? At a certain sales volume or demand level, what revenues will be generated? If we add a new product line, will this action increase revenues? In this section we look at the basic concepts of break-even analysis and explore how the normal probability distribution can be used in the decision-making process.

cost-volume analysis

Barclay Brothers New Product Decision

The Barclay Brothers Company is a large manufacturer of adult parlor games. Its marketing vice president, Rudy Barclay, must make the decision whether or not to introduce a new game called *Strategy* into the competitive market. Naturally, the company is concerned with costs, potential demand, and profit it can expect to make if it markets *Strategy*.

Rudy identifies the following relevant costs:

Fixed cost = $36,000   (*Costs that do not vary with volume produced, such as new equipment, insurance, rent, and so on*)

Variable cost per game produced = $4   (*Costs that are proportional to the number of games produced, such as materials, and labor*)

The selling price per unit is set at $10.

The *break-even point* is that number of games at which total revenues are equal to total costs. It can be expressed by Equation 7-1.[1]

$$\text{Break-even point (in units)} = \frac{\text{Fixed cost}}{\text{Price/unit} - \text{Variable cost/unit}} \quad \text{(7-1)}$$

computing the break-even point

So in Barclay's case,

$$\text{Break-even point (in games)} = \frac{\$36,000}{\$10 - \$4} = \frac{\$36,000}{\$6}$$
$$= 6,000 \text{ games of } Strategy$$

Any demand for the new game that exceeds 6,000 units will result in a profit, while a demand less than 6,000 units will cause a loss. For example, if it turns out that demand is 11,000 games of *Strategy*, Barclay's profit would be $30,000 as seen in the following equation.

Revenue (11,000 games × $10/game)		$110,000
Less expenses		
Fixed cost	$36,000	
Variable cost (11,000 games × $4/game)	44,000	
Total expense		80,000
Profit		$30,000

If demand is exactly 6,000 games (the break-even point), you should be able to compute for yourself that profit equals $0.

Rudy Barclay now has one useful piece of information that will help him make the decision about introducing the new product. If demand is less than 6,000 units, a loss will be incurred. But actual demand is not known. Rudy decides to turn to the use of a probability distribution to estimate demand.

Probability Distribution of Demand

Actual demand for the new game can be at any level—0 units, 1 unit, 2 units, 3 units, up to many thousands of units. Rudy needs to establish the probability of various levels of demand in order to proceed.

In many business situations the normal probability distribution is used to estimate the demand for a new product. It is appropriate when sales are symmetric around the mean expected demand and follow a bell-shaped distribution. Figure 7.1 illustrates a typical normal curve that we discussed at length in Chapter 3. Each curve has a unique shape that depends upon two factors: the mean of the distribution (μ) and the standard deviation of the distribution (σ).

In order for Rudy Barclay to use the normal distribution in decision making, he must be able to specify values for μ and σ. This isn't always easy for a manager to do directly, but if he has some idea of the spread, an analyst can determine the appropriate values. In the Barclay example, Rudy might think that the most likely sales figure is 8,000, but that demand might go as low as 5,000 or as high as 11,000. Sales could conceivably go

finding the mean and standard deviation

---

[1] For a detailed explanation of the break-even equation, see the appendix to this chapter.

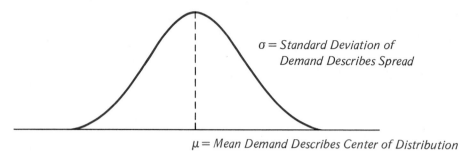

FIGURE 7.1
Shape of a Typical Normal Distribution

even beyond those limits; say there is a 15% chance of being below 5,000 and another 15% chance of being above 11,000.

Since this is a symmetric distribution, Rudy decides that a normal curve is appropriate. In Chapter 3, we saw how to take the data in a normal curve such as Figure 7.2 and compute the value of the standard deviation. The formula for calculating the number of standard deviations that any value of demand is away from the mean is:

$$Z = \frac{\text{Demand} - \mu}{\sigma} \qquad (7\text{-}2)$$

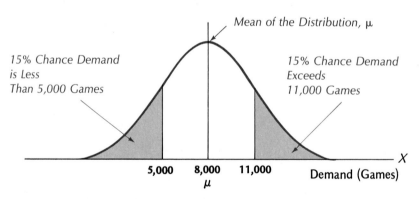

FIGURE 7.2
Normal Distribution for Barclay's Demand

where Z is the number of standard deviations above or below the mean, μ. It is provided in the table in Appendix A.

We see that the area under the curve to the left of 11,000 units demanded is 85% of the total area, or .85. From Appendix A, the Z value for .85 is approximately 1.04. This means that a demand of 11,000 units is 1.04 standard deviations to the right of the mean, μ.

With $\mu = 8,000$, $Z = 1.04$, and a demand of 11,000, we can easily compute σ.

$$Z = \frac{\text{Demand} - \mu}{\sigma}$$

or

$$1.04 = \frac{11,000 - 8,000}{\sigma}$$

or

$$1.04\sigma = 3,000$$

or

$$\sigma = \frac{3,000}{1.04} = 2,885 \text{ units}$$

At last, we can state that Barclay's demand appears to be normally distributed, with a mean of 8,000 games and a standard deviation of 2,885 games. This allows us to answer some questions of great financial interest to management—such as what is the probability of breaking even? Recalling that the break-even point is 6,000 games of *Strategy*, we must find the number of standard deviations from 6,000 to the mean.

probability of breaking even

$$Z = \frac{\text{Break-even point} - \mu}{\sigma}$$

$$= \frac{6,000 - 8,000}{2,885} = \frac{-2000}{2885} = -0.69$$

This is represented in Figure 7.3. Since Appendix A is set up to handle only positive Z values, we can find the Z value for +.69, which is .7549 or 75.49% of the area under the curve. The area under the curve for −.69 is just 1 minus the area computed for +.69, or 1 − .7549. Thus, 24.51% of the area under the curve is to the left of the break-even point of 6,000 units. Hence,

$$P(\text{Loss}) = P(\text{Demand} < \text{Break-even}) = .2451 = 24.51\%$$
$$P(\text{Profit}) = P(\text{Demand} > \text{Break-even}) = .7549 = 75.49\%$$

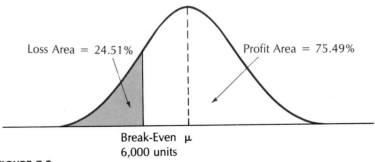

Loss Area = 24.51%   Profit Area = 75.49%

Break-Even μ
6,000 units

FIGURE 7.3
Probability of Breaking Even for Barclay's New Game

The fact that there is a 75% chance of making a profit is useful management information for Rudy to consider.

Before leaving the topic of break-even analysis, we should point out two caveats:

assumptions used

1. We have assumed that demand is normally distributed. If we should find that this is not reasonable, other distributions may be applied. These are beyond the scope of this text.

2. We have assumed that demand was the only random variable. If one of the other variables (price, variable cost, or fixed costs) were a random variable, a similar procedure could be followed. If two or more variables are both random, the mathematics becomes very complex. This is also beyond our level of treatment.

Using EMV to Make a Decision

In addition to knowing the probability of suffering a loss with *Strategy*, Barclay is concerned about the expected monetary value (EMV) of producing the new game. He knows, of course, that the option of not developing *Strategy* has an expected monetary value of $0. That is, if the game is not produced and marketed, his profit will be $0. If, however, the EMV of producing the game is greater than $0, he will recommend that more profitable strategy.

To compute the EMV for this strategy, Barclay uses the expected demand, μ, in the following linear profit function.

computing EMV

$$
\begin{aligned}
\text{EMV} &= (\text{Price/unit} - \text{Variable cost/unit})(\text{Mean demand}) \qquad (7\text{-}3) \\
&\quad - \text{Fixed costs} \\
&= (\$10 - \$4)(8{,}000 \text{ units}) - \$36{,}000 \\
&= \$48{,}000 - \$36{,}000 \\
&= \$12{,}000
\end{aligned}
$$

Rudy has two choices at this point. He can recommend that the firm proceed with the new game: if so, he estimates there is a 75% chance of at least breaking even and an expected monetary value of $12,000. *Or*, he might prefer to do further marketing research before making a decision. This brings up the subject of the expected value of perfect information.

7.3
EVPI AND THE NORMAL DISTRIBUTION

In Chapter 5, you saw that the expected value of perfect information (EVPI) and the expected opportunity loss (EOL) were equal. The EVPI places an upper limit on the amount someone such as Rudy Barclay would be willing to spend on marketing information. The expected opportunity loss is that loss a manager would incur by not choosing the best alternative.

Let's return to the Barclay Brothers problem to see how to compute EVPI and EOL associated with introducing the new game. Two steps are involved:

1. Determine the opportunity loss function.

2. Use the opportunity loss function and the unit normal loss integral (found in Appendix B) to find EOL, which is the same as EVPI.

Opportunity Loss Function

The *opportunity loss function* describes the loss that would be suffered by making the wrong decision. We saw earlier that Rudy's break-even point is 6,000 sets of the game *Strategy*. If Rudy produces and markets the new game and sales are greater than 6,000 units, he has made the right decision; in this case there is no opportunity loss ($0). If, however, he introduces *Strategy* and sales are *less* than 6,000 games, he has selected the wrong alternative. The opportunity loss is just the money lost if demand is less than the break-even point; for example, if demand is 5,999 games, Barclay loses $6 (= $10 Price/unit − $4 Cost/unit). With a $6 loss for each unit of sales less than the break-even point, the total opportunity loss is $6 multiplied times the number of units under 6,000. If only 5,000 games are sold, the opportunity loss will be 1,000 units less than the break-even point times $6 per unit = $6,000. For any level of sales, *X*, Barclay's opportunity loss function can be expressed as follows:

loss from making wrong decision

$$\text{Opportunity loss} = \begin{cases} \$6(6{,}000 - X) & \textit{for } X \leq 6{,}000 \textit{ games} \\ \$0 & \textit{for } X > 6{,}000 \textit{ games} \end{cases}$$

In *general*, the opportunity loss function can be computed by:

$$\text{Opportu-} \atop \text{nity loss} = \begin{cases} K(\textit{Break-even point} - X) & \textit{for } X \leq \textit{Break-even point} \\ \$0 & \textit{for } X > \textit{Break-even point} \end{cases} \quad (7\text{-}4)$$

loss function

where

K = the loss per unit when sales are below the break-even point, and

X = sales in units.

Expected Opportunity Loss

The second step is to find the expected opportunity loss. This is the sum of the opportunity losses multiplied by the appropriate probability values. But in Barclay's case there are a very large number of possible sales values. If the break-even point is 6,000 games, there will be 6,000 possible sales values, from 0, 1, 2, 3, up to 6,000 units. Thus, determining the EOL would require setting 6,000 probability values that correspond to the 6,000 possible sales values. These numbers would be multiplied and added together—a very lengthy and tedious task.

When we assume that there are an infinite (or very large) number of possible sales values that follow a normal distribution, the calculations are much easier. Indeed, when the *unit normal loss integral* is used, EOL can be computed as follows:

unit normal loss integral

$$\text{EOL} = K\sigma N(D) \quad (7\text{-}5)$$

where

EOL = expected opportunity loss,

K = loss per unit when sales are below the break-even point,

σ = standard deviation of the distribution.

$$D = \left| \frac{\mu - \text{Break-even point}}{\sigma} \right| \quad (7\text{-}6)$$

where

$$| \; | = \text{absolute value sign,}$$
$$\mu = \text{mean sales, and}$$

$N(D)$ = the value for the unit normal loss integral in Appendix B for a given value of D.

Here is how Rudy can compute EOL for his situation.

$$K = \$6$$
$$\sigma = 2{,}885$$
$$D = \left| \frac{8{,}000 - 6{,}000}{2{,}885} \right| = .69 = .60 + .09$$

using the unit normal loss integral table

Now refer to the unit normal loss integral table. Look in the ".6" row and read over to the ".09" column. This is $N(.69)$, which is .1453.

$$N(.69) = .1453$$

Therefore,

$$\text{EOL} = K\sigma N(.69)$$
$$= (6)(2885)(.1453) = \$2{,}515.14$$

Since EVPI and EOL are equivalent, the expected value of perfect information is also $2,515.14. This is the maximum amount that Rudy should be willing to spend on additional marketing information.

The relationship between the opportunity loss function and the normal distribution is shown in Figure 7.4. This graph shows both the opportunity

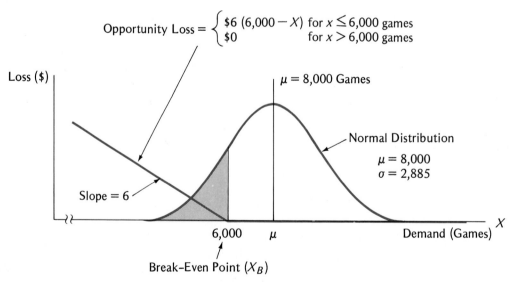

FIGURE 7.4
Barclay's Opportunity Loss Function

loss and the normal distribution with a mean of 8,000 games and a standard deviation of 2,885. To the right of the break-even point we note that the loss function is 0. To the left of the break-even point, the opportunity loss function increases at a rate of $6 per unit, hence the slope of -6. The use of Appendix B and Equation 7-5 allows us to multiply the $6 unit loss times each of the probabilities between 6,000 units and 0 units and to sum these multiplications.

7.4
MARGINAL ANALYSIS

So far, we have considered cases where there were many states of nature but only two decision alternatives. What happens when the number of alternatives is also very large?

For certain types of problems, an approach called *marginal analysis* can be used. Marginal analysis is a decision-making approach that can help select the optimal inventory level. It involves two new terms—marginal profit and marginal loss. Let's say you are a newspaper distributor; each daily paper costs you 19¢ and can be sold for 35¢. But if a paper is not sold at the end of the day, it is completely worthless (a 0¢ salvage value). In this case, the *marginal profit* (MP) is the profit made by selling each additional paper, namely, 16¢ (= 35¢ − 19¢). The *marginal loss* (ML) is the loss caused by stocking, but not selling, each additional newspaper—it would be 19¢ for every paper remaining at the end of the day.

marginal profit

marginal loss

When there are a manageable number of alternatives and states of nature, and we know the probabilities for each state of nature, then *marginal analysis with discrete distributions* can be used. When there are a very large number of possible alternatives and states of nature, and the probability distribution of the states of nature can be described with a normal distribution, then *marginal analysis with the normal distribution* is appropriate. Both of these techniques are discussed in the following sections.

Marginal Analysis with Discrete Distributions

Finding the best inventory level to stock is not difficult when we follow the marginal analysis procedure. Given any inventory level, we would only add an additional unit to our inventory level if its expected marginal profit equals or exceeds its expected marginal loss. This relationship is expressed symbolically below. First, we let

KEY IDEA

P = Probability that demand will be greater than or equal to a given supply (or the probability of selling at *least* one additional unit)

$1 - P$ = Probability that demand will be less than supply

The expected marginal profit is then found by multiplying the probability that a given unit will be sold by the marginal profit, P(MP). Likewise, the expected marginal loss is the probability of not selling the unit multiplied by the marginal loss, or $(1 - P)$(ML).

expected marginal profit and loss

The optimal decision rule is:

$$P(MP) \geqslant (1 - P)(ML)$$

With some basic mathematic manipulations, we can determine the level of P that will help solve marginal analysis problems:

finding the optimal probability level

$$P(MP) \geqslant ML - P(ML)$$

or

$$P(MP) + P(ML) \geqslant ML$$

or

$$P(MP + ML) \geqslant ML$$

or

$$P \geqslant \frac{ML}{MP + ML} \qquad (7\text{-}7)$$

In other words, as long as the probability of selling one more unit (P) is greater than or equal to ML/(MP + ML), we would stock the additional unit. An inventory example will illustrate the concept.

Café du Donut is a popular New Orleans dining spot on the edge of the French Quarter. Its specialty is coffee and donuts; it buys the donuts fresh daily from a large industrial bakery. The café pays $4 for each carton (containing two dozen donuts) delivered each morning. Any cartons not sold at the end of the day are thrown away, for they would not be fresh enough to meet the café's standards. If a carton of donuts is sold, the total revenue is $6. Hence the marginal profit per carton of donuts is:

$$MP = \text{marginal profit} = \$6 - \$4 = \$2$$

The marginal loss is ML = $4, since the donuts cannot be returned or salvaged at day's end.

From past sales, the café's manager estimates that the daily sales will follow the probability distribution shown in Table 7.1. Management then follows three steps to find the optimal number of cartons of donuts to order each day.

TABLE 7.1 Café du Donut's Probability Distribution

DAILY SALES (CARTONS OF DONUTS)	PROBABILITY SALES WILL BE AT THIS LEVEL
4	.05
5	.15
6	.15
7	.20
8	.25
9	.10
10	.10
Total	1.00

Step 1: Determine the value of P for the decision rule.

$$P \geqslant \frac{ML}{ML + MP} = \frac{\$4}{\$4 + \$2} = \frac{4}{6} = .66$$

$$P \geqslant .66$$

Step 2: Add a new column to the table to reflect the probability that donut sales will be at each level *or greater*. This is shown in the right column of Table 7.2.

TABLE 7.2 Marginal Analysis for Café du Donut

DAILY SALES (CARTONS OF DONUTS)	PROBABILITY SALES WILL BE AT THIS LEVEL	PROBABILITY SALES WILL BE AT THIS LEVEL OR GREATER
4	.05	$1.00 \geqslant .66$
5	.15	$.95 \geqslant .66$
6	.15	$.80 \geqslant .66$
7	.20	.65
8	.25	.45
9	.10	.20
10	.10	.10
Total	1.00	

For example, the probability sales will be four cartons or greater is 1.00 ($= .05 + .15 + .15 + .20 + .25 + .10 + .10$) since sales have always been between four and ten cartons per day. Likewise the probability sales will be eight cartons or greater is .45 ($= .25 + .10 + .10$), namely, the sum of probabilities for sales of eight, or nine, or ten cartons.

Step 3: Keep ordering additional cartons as long as the probability of selling at least one additional carton is greater than P, which is the indifference or break-even probability. If Café du Donut orders six cartons, marginal profits will still be greater than marginal loss.

$$P \text{ at 6 cartons} \geqslant \frac{ML}{ML + MP}$$

since $.80 \geqslant .66$.

If seven cartons are ordered, however, the probability of selling seven or more cartons (.65) is *not* greater than .66. Thus, the expected marginal loss will be greater than the expected marginal profit if seven cartons are ordered. In other words, the café can expect to lose money on the seventh carton if it is purchased. The optimal decision is to order six cartons each day.

This problem *could* have been placed in a decision table and solved, but the table would require seven rows and seven columns (one for each sales level). Although marginal analysis with discrete distributions is very efficient compared to decision tables, where there are over 15 or 20 different alternatives and states of nature, marginal analysis with the normal distribution may be more appropriate.

Marginal Analysis with the Normal Distribution

When product demand or sales follow a normal distribution, which is a common business situation, marginal analysis with the normal distribution can be applied. First we need to find four values:

1. The average or mean sales for the product, μ.

2. The standard deviation of sales, σ.

3. The marginal profit for the product, MP.

4. The marginal loss for the product, ML.

Once these quantities are known, the process of finding the best stocking policy is somewhat similar to marginal analysis with discrete distributions.

Step 1: Determine the value of *P*. With the normal distribution, *P* is equal to ML/(ML + MP).

$$P = \frac{ML}{ML + MP}$$

Step 2: Locate *P* on the normal distribution. For a given area under the curve, we can find *Z* from the standard normal table (Appendix A). Then, using the relationship

$$Z = \frac{X^* - \mu}{\sigma} \qquad (7\text{-}8)$$

we can solve for X^*, the optimal stocking policy.

An illustration will help explain. Demand for copies of the *Chicago Tribune* newspaper at Joe's Newsstand is normally distributed and has averaged 50 papers per day, with a standard deviation of 10 papers. With a marginal loss of 4¢ and a marginal profit of 6¢, what daily stocking policy should Joe follow?

Step 1: Joe should stock *Tribunes* until the probability of having a demand at a given level or greater is at least ML/(ML + MP).

$$P = \frac{ML}{ML + MP} = \frac{4¢}{4¢ + 6¢} = \frac{4}{10} = .40$$

Step 2: Figure 7.5 shows the normal distribution. Since the normal table has cumulative areas under the curve between the left side and any point, we look for .60 (= 1.0 − .40) in order to get the corresponding *Z* value.

$$Z = .25 \qquad \text{standard deviations from the mean}$$

In this problem, $\mu = 50$ and $\sigma = 10$, so

$$.25 = \frac{X^* - 50}{10}$$

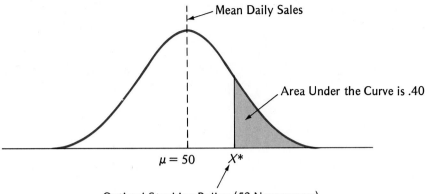

FIGURE 7.5
Joe's Stocking Decision for *Chicago Tribunes*

or

$$X^* = 10(.25) + 50 = 52.5, \text{ or } 53 \text{ newspapers}$$

Thus, Joe should order 53 *Chicago Tribunes* daily.

This same procedure can be used when P is greater than .50. Let's say Joe's Newsstand also stocks the *Chicago Sun-Times* and its marginal loss is 8¢ and marginal profit is 2¢. The daily sales have averaged 100 *Sun-Times* with a standard deviation of 10 papers. The optimal stocking policy is as follows:

Step 1: $P = \dfrac{ML}{ML + MP} = \dfrac{8¢}{8¢ + 2¢} = \dfrac{8}{10} = .80$

Step 2: The normal curve is shown in Figure 7.6. Since the normal curve is symmetrical, we find Z for an area under the curve of .80 and multiply this number by -1.

$Z = -.84$ standard deviations from the mean for an area of .80

With $\mu = 100$ and $\sigma = 10$,

$$-.84 = \frac{X^* - 100}{10}$$

or

$$X^* = -8.4 + 100 = 91.6, \text{ or } 92 \text{ papers}$$

So Joe should order 92 *Sun-Times* every day.

The optimal stocking policies in these two examples are intuitively consistent. When marginal profit is *greater* than marginal loss, we would expect X^* to be *greater than* the average demand, μ, and when marginal profit is *less* than marginal loss, we would expect the optimal stocking policy, X^*, to be *less than* μ.

optimal stocking policies should be intuitively consistent

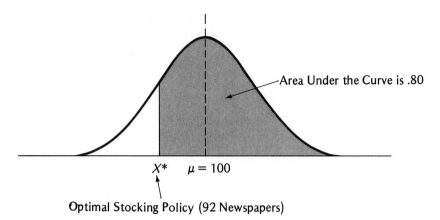

FIGURE 7.6
Joe's Stocking Decision for *Chicago Sun-Times*

7.5
SUMMARY

In this chapter, we looked at decision theory problems that involved many states of nature and alternatives. As an alternative to decision tables and decision trees, we learned to use the normal distribution to solve break-even problems, find the expected monetary value and EVPI, and determine the optimal stocking policy with marginal analysis. We need to know the mean and standard deviation of the normal distribution and to be certain it is the appropriate probability distribution to apply. Other continuous distributions can also be used, but they are beyond the level of this text.

GLOSSARY

Break-Even Analysis. The analysis of relationships between profit, costs, and demand level.

Opportunity Loss Function. A function that relates opportunity loss in dollars to sales in units.

Unit Normal Loss Integral. A table that is used in the determination of EOL and EVPI.

Marginal Analysis. A decision-making technique that uses marginal profit and marginal loss in determining optimal decision policies. Marginal analysis is used when the number of alternatives and states of nature is large.

Marginal Profit. The additional profit that would be realized by stocking and selling one more unit.

Marginal Loss. The loss that would be incurred by stocking and not selling an additional unit.

KEY EQUATIONS

(7-1) Break-even point (in units) $= \dfrac{\text{Fixed cost}}{\text{Price/unit } - \text{ Variable cost/unit}}$

The formula that provides the volume at which total revenue equals total costs.

(7-2) $Z = \dfrac{\text{Demand} - \mu}{\sigma}$

The number of standard deviations that demand is from the mean, μ.

(7-3) EMV = (Price/unit $-$ Variable cost/unit)(Mean demand) $-$ Fixed costs

The expected monetary value.

(7-4) Opportunity loss $= \begin{cases} K(\text{Break-even point } - X) & \textit{for } X \leq \textit{Break-even point} \\ \$0 & \textit{for } X > \textit{Break-even point} \end{cases}$

The opportunity loss function.

(7-5) EOL $= K\sigma N(D)$

The expected opportunity loss.

(7-6) $D = \left| \dfrac{\mu - \text{Break-even point}}{\sigma} \right|$

An intermediate value used to compute EOL.

(7-7) $P \geq \dfrac{ML}{ML + MP}$

Equation used in marginal analysis to compute stocking policies.

(7-8) $Z = \dfrac{X^* - \mu}{\sigma}$

Equation used in marginal analysis to compute the optimal stocking policy, X^*, when demand follows a normal distribution.

SOLVED PROBLEMS

Solved Problem 7-1

Advanced Software is considering a modification of its personal computer graphics program. The firm estimates that sales for the new product, if developed, will be approximately 80,000. Sales are expected to be normally distributed. The standard deviation is estimated to be 8,000. The software will cost $120 to produce, including development, documentation, and the cost of disks and distribution; it will sell for $250. Fixed costs are estimated to be $7,800,000. What is the company's break-even point? Determine EMV. Compute EVPI.

Solution

The data for Advanced Software are summarized below:

$$\mu = 80{,}000$$
$$\sigma = 8{,}000$$
$$\text{Price/unit} = \$250$$
$$\text{Variable cost/unit} = \$120$$
$$\text{Fixed cost} = \$7{,}800{,}000$$

The first step for Advanced Software is to determine the company's break-even point. The break-even point is equal to the fixed cost divided by the price per unit minus the variable cost per unit:

$$\text{Break-even point} = \frac{\$7{,}800{,}000}{\$250 - \$120} = 60{,}000 \text{ units}$$

The next step is to compute the expected monetary value (EMV). This is equal to the unit price minus the variable cost per unit times the mean or average sales, minus fixed costs:

$$
\begin{aligned}
\text{EMV} &= (\text{Price/unit} - \text{Variable cost/unit})(\text{Mean sales}) \text{ fixed costs} \\
&= (\$250 - \$120\ 80{,}000) - 7{,}800{,}000 \\
&= (\$130\ 80{,}000) - 7{,}800{,}000 = \$2{,}600{,}000
\end{aligned}
$$

The final step is to compute the expected value of perfect information (EVPI). This is done using the unit normal loss integral table in Appendix B:

$$
\begin{aligned}
D &= \left| \frac{(\mu - \text{Break-even point})}{\sigma} \right| \\
&= \frac{80{,}000 - 60{,}000}{8{,}000} = \frac{20{,}000}{8{,}000} = 2.5 \\
N(D) &= .002004 \\
K &= 250 - 120 = 130 \\
\text{EVPI} = \text{EOL} &= (K)(\sigma)(N(D)) \\
&= (130)(8{,}000)(.002004) \\
&= \$2{,}084
\end{aligned}
$$

Solved Problem 7-2

Rick Miller has just opened a new bakery in Frisco, Colorado, called Morning Fresh. In performing an economic analysis, Rick has determined that the marginal cost or loss for each dozen doughnuts sold is $4. The marginal profit is estimated to be $2.75 per dozen doughnuts. At this time, Rick is considering stocking 10, 15, 20, 25, or 30 dozen doughnuts. The probability of selling 10 dozen doughnuts is 10%. The chance of selling 15 dozen doughnuts is 20%. There is a 30% chance that Morning Fresh will sell either 20 or 25 dozen doughnuts. Finally, there is a 10% chance of selling 30 dozen doughnuts, which is considered by Rick to be the most that Morning Fresh would be able to accommodate. What is your recommendation to Rick?

Solution

The problem facing Rick Miller involves the use of marginal analysis. First, we need to know the marginal loss and the marginal profit. This information was given in the problem: the marginal loss is $4, while the marginal profit is $2.75. Now we can compute the probability of selling one more unit (P):

$$P \geq \frac{\text{ML}}{\text{ML} + \text{MP}} = \frac{\$4}{\$4 + \$2.75} = .59$$

The probability of selling one more unit, which in this case is a dozen doughnuts, is .59. The next step is to develop a table showing the probability of selling doughnuts at a particular level or greater. The solution is to stock additional doughnuts as long as P is greater than or equal to .59. As seen in the table, the solution is to stock 20 dozen doughnuts.

DEMAND	PROBABILITY AT THIS LEVEL	PROBABILITY AT THIS LEVEL OR GREATER
10	.1	1.00
15	.2	.90
20	.3	.70 ←
25	.3	.40
30	.1	.10
Total	1.0	

DISCUSSION QUESTIONS AND PROBLEMS

Discussion Questions

7-1 What is the purpose of conducting break-even analysis?

7-2 Under what circumstances can the normal distribution be used in break-even analysis? What does it usually represent?

7-3 What assumption do you have to make about the relationship between EMV and a state of nature when you are using the mean to determine the value of EMV?

7-4 Describe how EVPI can be determined when the distribution of the states of nature follows a normal distribution.

7-5 Under what circumstances is marginal analysis appropriate?

7-6 What information is necessary in determining the optimal stocking policy using marginal analysis when the state of nature is discrete?

7-7 What information is necessary in determining the optimal stocking policy using marginal analysis when the state of nature follows a normal distribution?

Problems

· **7-8** A publishing company is planning on developing an advanced quantitative analysis book for graduate students in doctoral programs. The company estimates that sales will be normally distributed, with mean sales of 60,000 copies and a standard deviation of 10,000 books. The book will cost $16 to produce and will sell for $24; fixed costs will be $160,000.

    (a) What is the company's break-even point?

    (b) What is the EMV?

: **7-9** Refer to Problem 7-8.

    (a) What is the opportunity loss function?

    (b) Compute the expected opportunity loss.

    (c) What is the EVPI?

    (d) What is the probability the new book will be profitable?

    (e) What do you recommend that the firm do?

: **7-10** Barclay Brothers Company, the firm discussed in this chapter, thinks it underestimated the mean for its game *Strategy*. Rudy Barclay thinks expected sales may be 9,000 games. He also thinks there is a 20% chance sales will be less than 6,000 games and a 20% chance he can sell more than 12,000 games.

    (a) What is the new standard deviation of demand?

    (b) What is the probability the firm will incur a loss?

    (c) What is the EMV?

    (d) How much should Rudy be willing to pay now for a marketing research study?

· **7-11** True-Lens, Inc. is considering producing the popular long-wearing contact lenses. Fixed costs will be $24,000 with a variable cost per set of lenses of $8. The lenses will sell for $24 per set to optometrists.

    (a) What is the firm's break-even point?

    (b) If expected sales are 2,000 sets, what should True-Lens do and what are the expected profits?

· **7-12** Leisure Supplies produces sinks and ranges for travel trailers and recreational vehicles. The unit price on their double sink is $28 and the unit cost is $20. The fixed cost in producing the double sink is $16,000. Mean sales for double sinks have been 35,000 units, and the standard deviation has been estimated to be 8,000 sinks. Determine the expected monetary value for these sinks. If the standard deviation were actually 16,000 units instead of 8,000 units, what effect would this have on the expected monetary value?

: **7-13** Belt Office Supplies sells desks, lamps, chairs, and other related supplies. The company's executive lamp sells for $45, and Elizabeth Belt has determined that the break-even point for executive lamps is 30 lamps per year. If Elizabeth does not make the break-even point, she loses $10 per lamp. The mean sales for executive lamps have been 45, and the standard deviation is 30.

    (a) Determine the opportunity loss function.

    (b) Determine the expected opportunity loss.

    (c) What is the EVPI?

: **7-14** Elizabeth Belt is not completely certain that the loss per lamp is $10 if sales are below the break-even point. (Refer to Problem 7-13.) The loss per lamp could be as low as $8 or as high as $15. What effect would these two values have on the expected opportunity loss?

· **7-15** Leisure Supplies is considering the possibility of using a new process for producing sinks. This new process would increase the fixed cost by $16,000. In other words, the fixed cost would double (see Problem 7-12). This new process will improve the quality of the sinks and reduce the cost it takes to produce each sink. It will only cost $19 to produce the sinks using the new process.

(a) What do you recommend?

(b) Leisure Supplies is considering the possibility of increasing the purchase price to $32 using the old process given in Problem 7-12. It is expected that this will lower the mean sales to 26,000 units. Should Leisure Supplies increase the selling price?

: **7-16** Quality Cleaners specializes in cleaning apartment units and office buildings. While the work is not too enjoyable, Joe Boyett has been able to realize a considerable profit in the Chicago area. Joe is now thinking about opening another Quality Cleaners in Milwaukee. In order to break even, Joe would need to get 200 cleaning jobs per year. For every job under 200, Joe will lose $80. Joe estimates that the average sales in Milwaukee are 350 jobs per year with a standard deviation of 150 jobs. A marketing research team has approached Joe with a proposition to perform a marketing study on the potential for his cleaning business in Milwaukee. What is the most that Joe would be willing to pay for the marketing research?

: **7-17** Teresa Granger is the manager of Chicago Cheese, which produces cheese spreads and other cheese-related products. E-Z Spread Cheese is a product that has always been popular. The probability of sales, in cases, is presented below:

DEMAND IN CASES	PROBABILITY
10	.2
11	.3
12	.2
13	.2
14	.1

A case of E-Z Spread Cheese sells for $100 and has a cost of $75. Any cheese that is not sold by the end of the week is sold to a local food processor for $50. Teresa never sells cheese that is more than a week old. How many cases of E-Z Spread Cheese should Teresa produce each week?

: **7-18** Harry's Hardware does a brisk business during the year, but during Christmas, Harry's Hardware sells Christmas trees for a substantial profit. Unfortunately, any trees not sold at the end of the season are totally worthless. Thus, the number of trees that are stocked for a given season is a very important decision. The following table reveals the demand for Christmas trees.

DEMAND FOR CHRISTMAS TREES	PROBABILITY
50	.05
75	.1
100	.2
125	.3
150	.2
175	.1
200	.05

Harry sells trees for $15 each, but his cost is only $6.

(a) How many trees should Harry stock at his hardware store?

(b) If the cost increased to $12 per tree, how many trees should Harry stock?

(c) Harry is thinking about increasing the price to $18 per tree. Assume the cost per tree is $6. It is expected that the probability of selling 50, 75, 100, or 125 trees will be .25 each. Harry does not expect to sell more than 125 trees with this price increase. What do you recommend?

7-19 In addition to selling Christmas trees during the Christmas holidays, Harry's Hardware sells all of the ordinary hardware items. One of the most popular items is Great Glue HH, a glue that is made just for Harry's Hardware. The selling price is $2 per bottle, but unfortunately, the glue gets hard and unusable after one month. The cost of the glue is 75¢. During the past several months, the mean sales of glue have been 60 units, and the standard deviation is 7. How many bottles of glue should Harry's Hardware stock? Assume sales follow a normal distribution.

7-20 Diane Kennedy is contemplating the possibility of going into competition with Primary Pumps, a manufacturer of industrial water pumps. Diane has gathered some interesting information from a friend of hers who works for Primary. Diane has been told that the mean sales for Primary are 5,000 units and the standard deviation is 50 units. The opportunity loss per pump is $100. Furthermore, Diane has been told that the most that Primary is willing to spend for marketing research for the demand potential for pumps is $500. Diane is interested in knowing the break-even point for Primary Pumps. Given this information, compute the break-even point.

7-21 The marginal loss on Washington Reds, a brand of apples from the state of Washington, is $35 per case. The marginal profit is $15 per case. During the past year, the mean sales of Washington Reds in cases was 45,000 cases, and the standard deviation was 4,450. How many cases of Washington Reds should be brought to market? Assume sales follow a normal distribution.

7-22 Linda Stanyon has been the production manager for Plano Produce for over eight years. Plano Produce is a small company located near Plano, Illinois. On the average, 400 cases of tomatoes are sold each day. In addition, 85% of the time the sales are between 350 and 450 cases. Each case sells for $3. All cases that are not sold must be discarded. A case costs approximately $2. How many cases of tomatoes should Linda stock?

7-23 Jack Fuller estimates that the break-even point for EM 5, a standard electrical motor, is 500 motors. For any motor that is not sold, there is an opportunity loss of $15. The average sales have been 700 motors, and 20% of the time sales have been between 650 and 750 motors. Jack has just been approached by Radner Research, a firm that specializes in performing marketing studies for industrial products, to perform a standard marketing study. What is the most that Jack would be willing to pay for the marketing research?

: **7-24** Jack Fuller believes that he has made a mistake in his sales figures for EM 5. (See Problem 7-23 for details.) He believes that the average sales are 750 instead of 700 units. Furthermore, he estimates that 20% of the time, sales will be between 700 and 800 units. What effect will these changes have on your estimate of the amount that Jack should be willing to pay for the marketing research?

: **7-25** Paula Shoemaker produces a weekly stock market report for an exclusive readership. She normally sells 3,000 reports per week, and 70% of the time her sales range from 2,990 to 3,010. The report costs Paula $15 to produce, but Paula is able to sell reports for $350 each. Of course, any reports not sold by the end of the week have no value. How many reports should Paula produce each week?

BIBLIOGRAPHY

Refer to references at end of Chapters 5 and 6.

Appendix: Derivation of Break-Even Point

1. Total costs = Fixed cost + (Variable cost/unit)(Number of units)

2. Total revenues = (Price/unit)(Number of units)

3. At break-even point, Total costs = Total revenues

4. Or, Fixed cost + (Variable cost/unit)(Number of units) = (Price/unit)(Number of units)

5. Solving for the number of units at the break-even point, we get:

$$\text{Break-even point (in units)} = \frac{\text{Fixed cost}}{\text{Price/unit} = \text{Variable cost/unit}}$$

This equation is the same as Equation 7-1 in this chapter.

8

Inventory Control Models: I

8.1
INTRODUCTION

Inventory is one of the most expensive and important assets to many companies, representing as much as 40% of total invested capital. Managers have long recognized that good inventory control is crucial. On one hand, a firm can try to reduce costs by reducing on-hand inventory levels. On the other hand, customers become dissatisfied when frequent inventory outages, called stockouts, occur. Thus, companies must make the balance between low and high inventory levels. As you would expect, cost minimization is the major factor in obtaining this delicate balance.

inventory

Inventory is any stored resource that is used to satisfy a current or a future need. Raw materials, work-in-process, and finished goods are examples of inventory. Inventory levels for finished goods are a direct function of demand. Once we determine the demand for completed clothes dryers, for example, it is possible to use this information to determine how much sheet metal, paint, electric motors, switches, and other raw materials and work-in-process are needed to produce the finished product.

All organizations have some type of inventory planning and control system. A bank has methods to control its inventory of cash. A hospital has methods used to control blood supplies and other important items. State and federal governments, schools, and, of course, virtually every manufacturing and production organization, are concerned with inventory planning and control.

Studying how organizations control their inventory is equivalent to studying how they achieve their objectives by supplying goods and services to their customers. Inventory is the common thread that ties all of the functions and departments of the organization together.

inventory planning

Figure 8.1 illustrates the basic components of an inventory planning and control system. The *planning* phase is primarily concerned with what inventory is to be stocked and how it is to be acquired (whether it is to be manufactured or purchased). This information is then used in *forecasting* demand for the inventory and in *controlling* inventory levels. The feedback

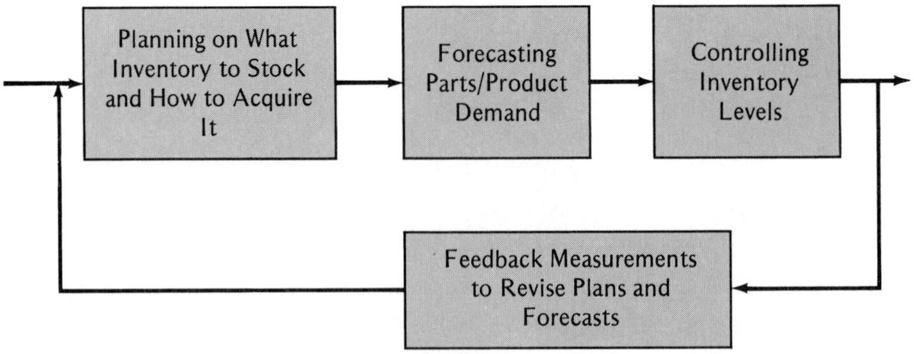

FIGURE 8.1
Inventory Planning and Control

loop in Figure 8.1 provides a way of revising the plan and forecast based on experiences and observation.

Through inventory planning, an organization determines what goods and/or services are to be produced. In cases of physical products, the organization must also determine whether or not to produce these goods, or purchase them from another manufacturer. Once this has been determined, the next step is to forecast the demand. As discussed in Chapter 4, there are many mathematical techniques that can be used in forecasting demand for a particular product. The emphasis in this chapter is on inventory control, that is, how to maintain adequate inventory levels within an organization.

use of forecasting

8.2
IMPORTANCE OF INVENTORY CONTROL

Inventory control serves several important functions and adds a great deal of flexibility to the operation of the firm. Six uses of inventory are:

1. The decoupling function.
2. Storing resources.
3. A hedge against inflation.
4. Irregular supply and demand.
5. Quantity discounts.
6. Avoiding stockouts and shortages.

The Decoupling Function

One of the major functions of inventory is to *decouple* manufacturing processes within the organization. If you did not store inventory, there could be many delays and inefficiencies. For example, when one manufacturing activity has to be completed before a second activity can be started, it could stop the entire process. If, however, you have some stored inventory between each process, it could act as a buffer.

inventory can act as a buffer

Storing Resources

Agricultural and seafood products often have definite seasons over which they can be harvested or caught, but the demand for these products is somewhat constant during the year. In these and similar cases, inventory can be used to store these resources.

In a manufacturing process, raw materials can be stored by themselves or in work-in-process or in the finished product. Thus, if your company makes lawn mowers, you might obtain lawn mower tires from another manufacturer. If you have 400 finished lawn mowers and 300 tires in inventory, you actually have 1,900 tires stored in inventory. Three hundred tires are stored by themselves, and 1,600 (1,600 = 4 tires per lawn mower

resources can be stored in work-in-process

× 400 lawn mowers) tires are stored in the finished lawn mowers. In the same sense, *labor* can be stored in inventory. If you have 500 subassemblies, and it takes 50 hours of labor to produce each assembly, you actually have 25,000 labor hours stored in inventory in the subassemblies. In general, any resource, physical or otherwise, can be stored in inventory.

A Hedge against Inflation

increasing cost of inventory

Storing an organization's resources in inventory can be a hedge against inflation. If you place cash reserves in the bank, you might be able to get a 10% return. On the other hand, some materials have increased in price by over 15% per year. Thus, it may be a better investment to keep your financial reserves in inventory. Of course, you will have to consider the cost of holding or carrying the inventory.

Irregular Supply and Demand

When the supply or demand for an inventory item is irregular, storing certain amounts in inventory is absolutely necessary. If the greatest demand for Diet-Delight beverage is during the summer, you will have to make sure that there is enough supply to meet this irregular demand. This might require that you produce more of the soft drink in the winter than is actually needed to meet the winter demand. The inventory levels of Diet-Delight will gradually build up over the winter, but this inventory will be needed in the summer. The same is true for irregular *supplies*.

Quantity Discounts

Another use of inventory is to take advantage of quantity discounts. Many suppliers offer discounts for large orders. For example, an electric jigsaw might normally cost $10 per unit. If you order 300 or more saws in one order, your supplier may lower the cost to only $8.75. Purchasing in larger quantities can substantially reduce the cost of products. There are, however, some disadvantages of buying in larger quantities. You will have higher storage costs and higher costs due to spoilage, damaged stock, theft, insurance, and so on. Furthermore, by investing in more inventory, you will have less cash to invest elsewhere.

Avoiding Stockouts and Shortages

Another important function of inventory is to avoid shortages or stockouts. If you are repeatedly out of stock, customers are likely to go elsewhere to satisfy their needs. Lost goodwill can be an expensive price to pay for not having the right item at the right time.

8.3
THE INVENTORY DECISION

Even though there are literally millions of different types of products produced in our society, there are only two decisions that you have to make when controlling inventory:

1. How much to order.

2. When to order.

The purpose of all inventory models and techniques is to determine rationally how much to order and when to order. As you know, inventory fulfills many important functions within the organization. But as the inventory levels go up to provide these functions, the cost of storing and holding inventory also increases. Thus, you must reach a fine balance in establishing inventory levels. A major objective in controlling inventory is to minimize total inventory costs. Some of the most significant inventory costs are:

minimizing inventory costs

1. Cost of the items.

2. Cost of ordering.

3. Cost of carrying, or holding, inventory.

4. Cost of safety stock.

5. Cost of stockouts.

The inventory models discussed in *this* chapter assume that demand and the time it takes to receive an order are known and constant and that no quantity discounts are given. When this is the case, the most significant costs are the cost of placing an order and the cost of holding inventory

ordering costs and carrying costs

TABLE 8.1 Inventory Cost Factors

ORDERING COST FACTORS	CARRYING COST FACTORS
1. Developing and sending purchase orders	**1.** Cost of capital
2. Processing and inspecting incoming inventory	**2.** Taxes
	3. Insurance
3. Bill paying	**4.** Spoilage
4. Inventory inquiries	**5.** Theft
5. Utilities, phone bills, and so forth, for the purchasing department	**6.** Obsolescence
	7. Salaries and wages for warehouse employees
6. Salaries and wages for purchasing department employees	**8.** Utilities and building costs for the warehouse
7. Supplies such as forms and paper for the purchasing department	**9.** Supplies such as forms and paper for the warehouse

items over a period of time (see Table 8.1 for a list of important factors making up these costs). Hence, in making inventory decisions, the overall objective is to minimize the sum of the carrying costs and the ordering costs. In Chapter 9 we will discuss several more sophisticated inventory models.

8.4
ECONOMIC ORDER QUANTITY (EOQ): DETERMINING HOW MUCH TO ORDER

The *economic order quantity* (EOQ) is one of the oldest and most commonly known inventory control techniques. Research on its use dates back to a 1915 publication by Ford W. Harris. EOQ is still used by a large number of organizations today. This technique is relatively easy to use, but it does make a number of assumptions. Some of the more important assumptions are:

assumptions of the EOQ model

1. Demand is known and constant.

2. The lead time, that is, the time between the placement of the order and the receipt of the order, is known and constant.

3. The receipt of inventory is instantaneous. In other words, the inventory from an order arrives in one batch, at one point in time.

4. Quantity discounts are not possible.

5. The only variable costs are the cost of placing an order, *ordering cost*, and the cost of holding or storing inventory over time, *holding* or *carrying cost.*

6. If orders are placed at the right time, stockouts or shortages can be completely avoided.

With these assumptions, inventory usage has a sawtooth shape as in Figure 8.2. In Figure 8.2, Q represents the amount that is ordered. If this amount is 500 dresses, all 500 dresses arrive at one time when an order is received. Thus, the inventory level jumps from 0 to 500 dresses. In general, an inventory level increases from 0 to Q units when an order arrives.

Because demand is constant over time, inventory drops at a uniform rate over time. (Refer to the sloped line in Figure 8.2.) Another order is placed such that when the inventory level reaches 0, the new order is received and the inventory level again jumps to Q units, represented by the vertical lines. This process continues indefinitely over time.

inventory usage curve

Inventory Costs

The objective of most inventory models is to minimize the total costs. With the assumptions just given, the significant costs are the ordering cost and the carrying, or holding, cost. All other costs, such as the cost of the inventory itself, are constant. Thus, if we minimize the sum of the ordering

minimizing ordering and carrying cost

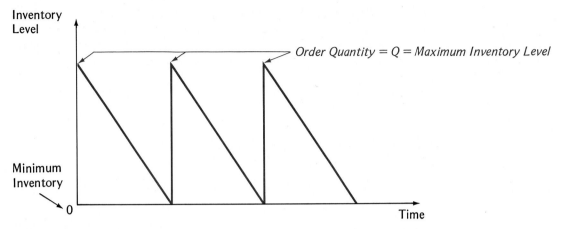

FIGURE 8.2
Inventory Usage over Time

and carrying costs, we are also minimizing the total costs. To help visualize this, Figure 8.3 graphs total costs as a function of the order quantity, Q. The optimal order size, Q^*, is the quantity that minimizes the total costs. As the quantity ordered increases, the total number of orders placed per year decreases. Thus, as the quantity ordered increases, the annual ordering cost decreases. But as the order quantity increases, the carrying cost increases due to larger average inventories that the firm has to maintain.

total cost as a function of the order quantity

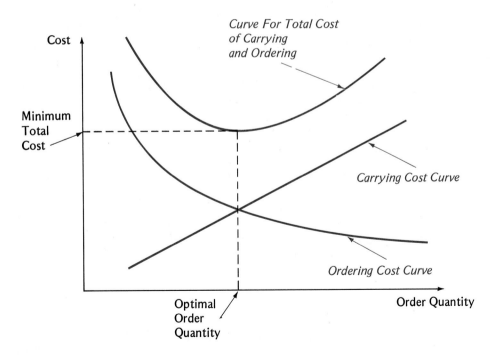

FIGURE 8.3
Total Cost as a Function of Order Quantity

TABLE 8.2 Computing Average Inventory

| | INVENTORY LEVEL | | |
DAY	BEGINNING	ENDING	AVERAGE
April 1 (order received)	10	8	9
April 2	8	6	7
April 3	6	4	5
April 4	4	2	3
April 5	2	0	1

Maximum level April 1 = 10 units
Total of daily averages = 9 + 7 + 5 + 3 + 1 = 25
Number of days = 5
Average inventory level = $^{25}/_5$ = 5 units

Note in Figure 8.3 that the optimal order quantity occurred at the point where the ordering cost curve and the carrying cost curve intersected. This was not by chance. With the type of cost functions that we investigate in this chapter, the optimal quantity occurs at a point where the ordering cost is equal to the carrying cost. This is an important fact to remember.

Now that you have a better understanding of inventory costs, let's see how we can determine the optimal order quantity that minimizes these costs. In determining the *annual* carrying cost, it is convenient to use the average on-hand inventory level. We then multiply the average inventory level times a factor called *inventory carrying cost per unit per year* to determine the annual inventory cost. Table 8.2 illustrates how *average inventory* can be calculated. It is important to note that the average inventory level for this problem is equal to one-half of the maximum level of 10. (This is due to a constant demand, coupled with the fact that ending inventory is 0.) This maximum level is equal to the order quantity. Thus, the average inventory in units is simply calculated as one-half of the order quantity.

determining annual carrying cost

$$\text{Average inventory level} = Q/2 \qquad \textbf{(8-1)}$$

Finding the Economic Order Quantity

We pointed out that the optimal order quantity is the point that minimizes the total cost, where total cost is the sum of ordering cost and carrying cost. We also indicated graphically that the optimal order quantity was at the point where the ordering cost was equal to the carrying cost. Now, let's develop equations that directly solve for the optimum. To accomplish this, the following steps need to be performed.[1]

determining Q* by setting ordering cost equal to carrying cost

1. Develop an expression for ordering cost.

2. Develop an expression for carrying cost.

---

[1] The use of calculus in determining Q* is shown in the appendix to this chapter.

3. Set ordering cost equal to carrying cost.

4. Solve this equation for the desired optimum.

Using the following variables, we can determine ordering cost, carrying cost, and Q^*, the economic order quantity:

Q = Number of pieces per order

Q^* = Optimal number of pieces per order

D = Annual demand in units, for the inventory item

C_o = Ordering cost for each order

C_h = Holding or carrying cost per unit per year

Here is the step-by-step procedure:

1. Annual ordering cost = (No. of orders placed per year)
   × (Order cost per order)

$$= \frac{\text{Annual demand}}{\text{No. of units in each order}} \times (\text{Order cost per order})$$

$$= \left(\frac{D}{Q}\right) \times (C_o) = \frac{D}{Q}(C_o)$$

2. Annual holding or carrying cost = (Average inventory level)
   × (Carrying cost per unit per year)

$$= \left(\frac{\text{Order quantity}}{2}\right) \times (\text{Carrying cost per unit per year})$$

$$= \left(\frac{Q}{2}\right) \times (C_h) = \frac{Q}{2} C_h$$

3. Optimal order quantity is found when ordering cost = carrying cost, namely:

$$\frac{D}{Q} C_o = \frac{Q}{2} C_h$$

4. To solve for Q^*, simply cross-multiply terms and isolate Q on the left of the equal sign:

$$Q = Q^* = \sqrt{\frac{2DC_o}{C_h}} \qquad (8\text{-}2)$$

Now that the equation for the optimal order quantity, Q^*, has been derived, it is possible to solve inventory problems directly.

KEY IDEA

Sumco, a company that sells pump housings to other manufacturers, would like to reduce its inventory cost by determining the optimal number of pump housings to obtain per order. The annual demand is 1,000 units, the ordering cost is $10 per order, and the average carrying cost per unit per year is $.50. Using these figures, we can calculate the optimal number of units per order.

determining optimal number of units per order

$$Q^* = \sqrt{\frac{2DC_o}{C_h}}$$

$$Q^* = \sqrt{\frac{2(1,000)(10)}{.50}}$$

$$Q^* = \sqrt{40,000}$$

$$Q^* = 200 \text{ units}$$

The total annual inventory cost is the sum of the ordering costs and the carrying costs.

determining the total annual inventory cost

Total annual cost = Order cost + Holding cost

In terms of the variables in the model, total cost (TC) can now be expressed as:

$$TC = \frac{D}{Q} C_o + \frac{Q}{2} C_h \qquad \text{(8-3)}$$

The total annual inventory cost for Sumco is computed as follows:

$$TC = \frac{D}{Q} C_o + \frac{Q}{2} C_h$$

$$= \frac{1000}{200}(10) + \frac{200}{2}(.5)$$

$$= \$50 + \$50 = \$100$$

As you might expect, the ordering cost is equal to the carrying cost. You may wish to try different values for Q, such as 100 or 300 pumps. You will find that the minimum total cost occurs when Q is 200 units. The economic order quantity, Q^*, is 200 pumps.

Purchase Cost of Inventory Items

Sometimes the total inventory cost expression is written to include the actual cost of the material purchased. Purchase cost does not depend on the particular order policy found to be optimal, since regardless of how many orders are placed each year, we still incur the same annual purchase cost of $D \times P$, where P is the price per unit and D is the annual demand in units.[2]

It is useful to know how to calculate the average inventory level in dollar terms when the price per unit is given. This can be done as follows.

With the variable Q representing the quantity of units ordered, and assuming a unit price of P, we can determine the average dollar value of inventory.

$$\text{Average dollar level} = \frac{(PQ)}{2} \qquad \text{(8-4)}$$

This formula is analogous to Equation 8-1.

---

[2] In Chapter 9 we will discuss the case in which price can affect order policy, that is, when quantity discounts are offered.

Inventory carrying costs for many businesses and industries are also often expressed as an annual percentage of the unit cost or price. When this is the case, a new variable is introduced.

Let I = annual inventory holding charge as a percent of cost. Then the cost of storing one unit of inventory for the year, C_h, is given by $C_h = IP$, where P is the unit price or cost of an inventory item. Q^* can be expressed, in this case, as:

$$Q^* = \sqrt{\frac{2DC_o}{IP}} \qquad (8\text{-}5)$$

annual carrying cost as a percentage of the cost per unit

8.5
REORDER POINT (ROP): DETERMINING WHEN TO ORDER

Now that we have decided how much to order, we look at the second inventory question, when to order. In most simple inventory models, it is assumed that receipt of an order is instantaneous. That is, we assume that a firm waits until its inventory level for a particular item reaches 0, places an order, and receives the items in stock immediately.

As we all know, however, the time between the placing and receipt of an order, called lead time or delivery time, is often a few days or even a few weeks. Thus, the *when to order* decision is usually expressed in terms of a *reorder point*, the inventory level at which an order should be placed.

The reorder point, ROP, is given as:

ROP = (Demand per day) × (Lead time for a new order in days)   (8-6)
= $d \times L$

 KEY IDEA

Figure 8.4 shows the reorder point graphically. The slope of the graph is the daily inventory usage. This is expressed in units demanded per day, d. The *lead time, L,* is the time that it takes to receive an order. Thus, if an order is placed when the inventory level reaches the ROP, the new inventory arrives at the same instant the inventory is reaching 0. Let's take a look at an example.

Procomp's demand for computer chips is 8,000 per year. The firm has a daily demand of 40 units. On the average, delivery of an order takes three working days. The reorder point for chips is calculated as follows:

determining the reorder point (ROP)

ROP = Reorder point = $d \times L$ = 40 units per day × 3 days
ROP = 120 units

Hence, when the inventory stock of chips drops to 120, an order should be placed. The order will arrive three days later, just as the firm's stock is depleted to 0. It should be mentioned that this calculation assumes that all of the assumptions listed previously are correct. When demand is not known with complete certainty, then these calculations have to be modified. This is discussed further in Chapter 9.

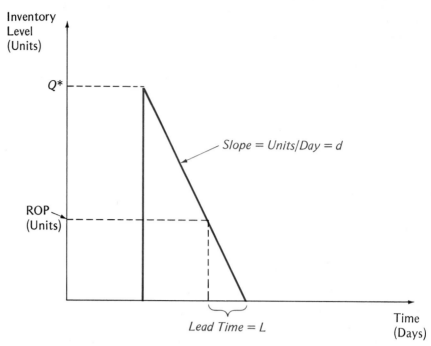

FIGURE 8.4
Reorder Point (ROP) Curve

8.6
FIXED PERIOD INVENTORY CONTROL SYSTEM

The previous sections have discussed the derivation and use of the economic order quantity. This quantity determines *how much* is to be ordered. Since the approach results in a fixed number for the order quantity, it has been called the *fixed order system*. Another approach is to determine a fixed number that answers the *when to order* question. This is called the *fixed period inventory control system*. Although there are several quantities that can be computed with this type of system, the most commonly computed quantities are the optimal number of order per year, Y^*, and the optimal number of days between orders, N^*. The optimal number of days between orders has also been called the optimal number of days' supply per order. As will be seen, these quantities result in an identical solution to the inventory control problem. They are simply looking at the same problem from a different point of view. We begin by investigating the optimal number of orders per year, Y^*.

optimal number of orders per year and optimal number of days between orders

Determining the Optimal Number of Orders per Year, Y^*

computing Y^* when Q^* is known

Determining Y^* tells us how many times per year an order should be placed. If annual demand is 100 and the economic order quantity is 50 units per

Inland Steel Uses Systems Contracts to Control Inventory Costs

Sound inventory control involves much more than computing the economic order quantity. In most cases, other practical and financial considerations must be taken into account to minimize total inventory costs and to provide tighter control on inventory levels. Both practical and financial considerations led Inland Steel to consider several inventory policies, including systems contracts.

Inland Steel produces approximately 5.5 million tons of steel each year. The steel mill has two blast furnaces that supply steel to four casting operations. Yet, steel inventory is not the company's only inventory concern. For many large corporations, office equipment such as typewriters, printers, and fax machines can represent a substantial investment. Furthermore, all steel-processing facilities are controlled through computers, which are considered office equipment by Inland Steel.

Tricia Wynn, a project buyer for Inland Steel, was concerned about high costs and a lack of stan-

dardization for office equipment. To overcome these problems, she developed a comprehensive inventory ordering system that took advantage of standardization and contract buying. The result was a contract ordering system that provided superior equipment at substantial savings. Most of the equipment was leased or rented. The new system provided low monthly rates for office equipment, free installation, and a 30-day free trial. Another advantage was a floating system contract. With this type of contract, there is no termination date, which helps reduce the time and costs of maintaining leasing agreements. The bottom line is that a systems contract approach allowed Inland Steel to order quality office equipment for fewer dollars.

Source: K. Evans-Correia, "All Systems Go," *Purchasing,* March 23, 1989, pp. 106–107.

---

order, how many orders must be placed every year? In order to meet demand, two orders of 50 units each must be placed to satisfy the annual demand of 100 units. This relationship is shown in Equation 8-7.

$$Y^* = \frac{D}{Q^*} \tag{8-7}$$

Sumco, in a previous example, determined that its economic order quantity was 200 pump housings and its annual demand was 1,000 pump housings. The optimal number of orders per year, Y^*, can be computed as follows:

$$Y^* = \frac{1,000}{200} = 5 \text{ orders per year}$$

In order to use this equation, it is necessary to determine the economic order quantity, Q^*, first. When you do not want to calculate the economic order quantity first, there is a way of directly solving for the optimal number of orders per year. This can be done as follows:

computing Y^* when Q^* is unknown

$$Y^* = \frac{D}{Q^*}$$

But we know that

$$Q^* = \sqrt{\frac{2DC_o}{C_h}}$$

Thus,

$$Y^* = \frac{D}{\sqrt{\dfrac{2DC_o}{C_h}}}$$

Rearranging terms and solving, we get:

$$Y^* = \sqrt{\frac{DC_h}{2C_o}} \qquad \text{(8-8)}$$

Now, using Equation 8-8, we can solve for Y^* directly. Let's use Sumco to test the validity of Equation 8-8. As you recall, Sumco sells pump housings to other manufacturers. The annual demand, D, is 1,000 units; the ordering cost, C_o, is \$10; and the carrying cost, C_h, is \$.50. These numbers are placed in Equation 8-8 to solve for Y^*.

$$Y^* = \sqrt{\frac{DC_h}{2C_o}}$$

$$= \sqrt{\frac{(1,000)(.5)}{(2)(10)}} = \sqrt{\frac{500}{20}}$$

$$= \sqrt{25} = 5 \text{ orders per year}$$

Determining the Optimal Number of Days between Orders, N^*

Another approach is to determine the number of days between orders, N^*. This tells you how many days you will be able to operate after receiving an order without running out of inventory. In the case of Sumco, the optimal number of orders per year was 5. What is the number of days between any two orders? In other words, what is the number of days' supply per order? With 365 days in a year and 5 orders per year, each order will last 73 days (73 days = 365 days per year divided by 5 orders per year).[3]

This relationship is shown in Equation 8-9:

$$N^* = \frac{365}{Y^*} \qquad \text{(8-9)}$$

But we know that

$$Y^* = \sqrt{\frac{DC_h}{2C_o}}$$

computing N^* when Y^* is unknown

It is also possible to solve for N^* directly when we have not previously determined Y^*. This can be done as follows:

$$N^* = \frac{365}{Y^*}$$

---

[3] If you use the number of working days in a year, such as 200 working days, then this number replaces 365 in the following equations.

Thus,

$$N^* = \frac{365}{\sqrt{\dfrac{DC_h}{2C_o}}}$$

Rearranging terms, we get,

$$N^* = \sqrt{\frac{266{,}450C_o}{DC_h}} \qquad (8\text{-}10)$$

Using the data for Sumco, we can solve for N^* directly without knowing either Y^* or Q^*. With a demand of 1,000 units, a carrying cost of $.50, and an ordering cost of $10, we get the following:

$$N^* = \sqrt{\frac{266{,}450C_o}{DC_h}}$$

$$= \sqrt{\frac{(266{,}450)(10)}{(1000)(.5)}} = \sqrt{\frac{2{,}664{,}500}{500}} = \sqrt{5329} = 73 \text{ days}$$

In this section, we have investigated the fixed period inventory control system. Once you determine when to order, you then order enough to satisfy demand until the next order. This is usually Q^*. For Sumco, this would still be 200 units. In addition, we have shown a simple way of determining Y^* if you already know Q^*, and we have shown a simple way of determining N^* if you already know Y^*. Furthermore, we have shown how these quantities can be determined directly from the annual demand, ordering cost, and carrying cost. These equations were derived by using straightforward algebraic manipulations. They could also be developed by setting ordering cost equal to carrying costs or by developing the total cost equations and using calculus. These approaches are explored further in the problems at the end of this chapter.

Y^* and N^* can also be determined by setting ordering cost equal to carrying cost or by using calculus

8.7 SENSITIVITY ANALYSIS

In the preceding examples we developed formulas that can be used to solve directly for Q^*, N^*, and Y^*. These formulas assume that all input values are known with certainty. What would happen, though, if one of the input values changed—for example, the cost of placing an order rises by $5?

The answer is that if any of the values used in one of the formulas changes, the optimal value changes also. Determining the effect of these changes is called *sensitivity analysis*. One approach to sensitivity analysis is to recalculate the optimal quantity when one of the inputs changes.

How would the order quantity be affected if Sumco's cost of placing an order were actually $40 instead of $10? Assume the annual demand for Sumco pump housings is still the same, namely, $D = 1,000$ units and that carrying cost is $.50 per unit per year.

$$Q^* = \sqrt{\frac{2DC_o}{C_h}} = \sqrt{\frac{2(1000)(40)}{.50}} = \sqrt{160{,}000}$$

$$Q^* = 400 \text{ units}$$

Thus, when the ordering cost *increases* by a *multiple of 4*, the optimal order quantity *doubles*.

KEY IDEA →

In order to determine how sensitive the optimal solution is to a change in one of the variables in an equation, it is not always necessary to completely recalculate the order quantity Q^*. Usually, it is possible to determine the effect of a change in the optimal quantity by inspecting the basic EOQ formula.

Let us look at the formula for the optimal number of units to order equation derived previously. What effect would the following individual changes have on the value of Q^*?

1. Ordering cost increases by a factor of 4.

2. Carrying cost increases by a factor of 4.

3. The total number of pieces of inventory sold per year (or the annual demand) *decreases* by a factor of 9.

The EOQ formula is given as $Q^* = \sqrt{\dfrac{2DC_o}{C_h}}$

The following shortcuts can be used to test the effect of the changes listed.

determining the new optimal order quantity

1. The optimal order quantity will increase by a factor of 2 when C_o increases by a factor of 4. To see this we simply replace C_o in the formula by an ordering cost of 4 times that number, namely $(4)(C_o)$.

$$Q^* = \sqrt{\frac{2D(4)(C_o)}{C_h}}$$

Bringing the number 4 outside the square root sign yields:

$$Q^* = 2\sqrt{\frac{2DC_o}{C_h}} = 2 \times \text{(Previous optimal order quantity)}$$

2. The optimal order quantity will decrease by a factor of $\frac{1}{2}$ when C_h increases by a factor of 4.

$$Q^* = \sqrt{\frac{2DC_o}{(4)(C_h)}}$$

$$Q^* = \frac{1}{2}\sqrt{\frac{2DC_o}{C_h}} = \frac{1}{2} \times \text{(Previous optimal order quantity)}$$

3. The optimal order size will decrease by a factor of $\frac{1}{3}$ (or become $\frac{1}{3}$ of what it was before) when D decreases by a factor of 9.

$$Q^* = \sqrt{\frac{2(\frac{1}{9})(D)C_o}{C_h}}$$

$$Q^* = \frac{1}{3}\sqrt{\frac{2DC_o}{C_h}} = \frac{1}{3} \times \text{(Previous optimal order quantity)}$$

Blue Bell Trims Its Inventory

Blue Bell is one of the world's largest apparel manufacturers, with annual sales totaling over one billion dollars. Headquartered in Greensboro, North Carolina, it employs over 27,000 people worldwide. Blue Bell has three major businesses, the largest of which is the Wrangler Group. Wrangler manufactures denim and corduroy jeans and several other product lines in sports and casual apparel. In basic styles of men's jeans, Wrangler makes 35 million pairs of jeans a year in 37 plants. There are over 10,000 individual stock keeping units (called SKUs) manufactured and stocked.

One task Blue Bell faced was to find a better balance of the cost of carrying inventory against the risk of shortages. Data analysis showed that inventory had not been well balanced at the SKU level. Some SKUs showed months of supply whereas others were out-of-stock. Thus, unless a systematic approach could be developed to con-

sistently achieve a "balanced" inventory at the SKU level, it would be difficult for Blue Bell to attain a dramatic reduction in inventory.

When this effort began, the economic and competitive pressures that Blue Bell faced were severe. The high cost of carrying inventory had become particularly acute. Short-term interest rates were hovering at 20 percent, and as a result, net interest expenses for Blue Bell had ballooned. Financing inventory had dramatically pushed up Blue Bell's cost of doing business.

Management science provided the means for senior executives and other managers to swiftly take effective action to turn the situation around. A new production planning process was designed, tested, and implemented that reduced inventories more than 31 percent (from $371 million to $256 million) without a decrease in sales or customer service. The new process also reduced manufacturing costs by approximately $1 million. The strong support of top management was a major factor in this achievement, and that support was communicated down the line so that employees at every level became enthusiastically involved.

Source: J. R. Edwards, H. M. Wagner, and W. P. Wood, *Interfaces* Vol. 15, No. 1, January–February 1985, pp. 34-52.

In each of these, we note that the optimal value of Q^* changes by the square root of the change in a variable used in the formula.

8.8
SUMMARY

In this chapter, we introduced the fundamentals of inventory control theory. We showed that the two most important questions are: (1) how much to order, and (2) when to order.

We investigated the economic order quantity, which determines how much to order, and the reorder point, which determines when to order. In addition, we discussed the fixed period inventory control system. Finally, we explored the use of sensitivity analysis. We use this analysis when we want to determine what happens to computations when one or more of the values used in one of the equations changes.

The inventory models presented in this chapter make a number of assumptions: (1) known and constant demand and lead times, (2) instantaneous receipt of inventory, (3) no quantity discounts, (4) no stockouts or shortages, and (5) the only variable costs are ordering costs and carrying costs. If these assumptions are valid, then the inventory models and techniques discussed in this chapter provide optimal solutions. On the other hand, if these assumptions do not hold, the analysis presented in this chapter may lead you to the wrong conclusions and decisions. In the next chapter, we relax and eliminate some of these assumptions. Although the inventory models in the next chapter are slightly more complex, they are preferable when the assumptions of this chapter do not apply.

GLOSSARY

EOQ. Economic order quantity. The amount of inventory ordered that will minimize the total inventory cost. It is also called the optimal order quantity, or Q^*.

Average Inventory. The average inventory on hand. In this chapter, the average inventory is $Q/2$.

Reorder Point (ROP). The number of units on hand when an order for more inventory is placed.

Lead Time. The time it takes to receive an order after it is placed (called L in the chapter).

Sensitivity Analysis. The process of determining how sensitive the optimal solution is to changes in the values used in the equations.

KEY EQUATIONS

(8-1) Average inventory level $= Q/2$

(8-2) $Q^* = \sqrt{\dfrac{2DC_o}{C_h}}$

The economic order quantity.

(8-3) $TC = \dfrac{D}{Q}C_o + \dfrac{Q}{2}C_h$

Total inventory cost.

(8-4) Average dollar level $= \dfrac{(PQ)}{2}$

(8-5) $Q^* = \sqrt{\dfrac{2DC_o}{IP}}$

The economic order quantity using the carrying cost, I, as a percentage of price, P.

(8-6) $ROP = d \times L$

The reorder point, where $d =$ daily demand and $L =$ lead time in days.

(8-7) $Y^* = \dfrac{D}{Q^*}$

Optimal number of orders per year.

(8-8) $\quad Y^* = \sqrt{\dfrac{DC_h}{2C_o}}$

Optimal number of orders per year.

(8-9) $\quad N^* = \dfrac{365}{Y^*}$

Optimal number of days between orders.

(8-10) $\quad N^* = \sqrt{\dfrac{266{,}450C_o}{DC_h}}$

Optimal number of days between orders.

SOLVED PROBLEMS

Solved Problem 8-1

Patterson Electronics supplies microcomputer circuitry to a company that incorporates microprocessors into refrigerators and other home appliances. Currently, Patterson orders components from various suppliers. One of the components is ordered in batches of 150 units. It has been estimated that annual demand for these components is 250. Furthermore, carrying cost is estimated to be $1 per unit per year. For the order policy to be optimal, determine what the ordering cost would have to be.

Solution

The data for Patterson Electronics can be summarized as follows:

$$Q = 150 \text{ units}$$
$$D = 250 \text{ units}$$
$$C_h = \$1$$

Given an annual demand of 250, a carrying cost of $1, and an order quantity of 150, Patterson Electronics must determine what the ordering cost would have to be for the order policy of 150 units to be optimal. To find the answer to this problem, we must solve the traditional economic order quantity equation for the ordering cost. As you can see in the calculations that follow, an ordering cost of $45 is needed for the order quantity of 150 units to be optimal.

$$Q = \sqrt{\dfrac{2DC_o}{C_h}}$$

$$C_o = (Q^2)\left(\dfrac{C_h}{2D}\right)$$

$$= \dfrac{(150)^2(1)}{2(250)}$$

$$= \dfrac{22{,}500}{500} = \$45$$

Solved Problem 8-2

Annual demand for a popular speaker component for small stereo systems is 40,000. Dan Thesing estimates that the ordering cost is $15 per order. Furthermore, carrying cost is estimated to be $3 per unit per year. At this time, it takes 30 days between the time that Dan places an order and the time when the order is received. During this time, daily demand is 250 units. What is the optimal number of days between orders?

Solution

The data for the problem that Dan Thesing is facing is summarized as follows:

$$D = 40{,}000 \text{ units}$$
$$C_o = \$15$$
$$C_h = \$3$$
$$\text{Lead time} = 30 \text{ days}$$
$$\text{Daily demand} = 250 \text{ units}$$

In order to determine the optimal number of days between orders, we will determine the economic order quantity, Q^*, and the optimal number of orders per year, Y^*. As you can see from the calculations that follow, the optimal number of days between orders is approximately 6 days.

$$Q^* = \sqrt{\frac{2DC_o}{C_h}} = \sqrt{\frac{(2)(40{,}000)(15)}{3}}$$
$$= 632$$

$$Y^* = \frac{D}{Q^*} = 63.3$$

$$N^* = \frac{365}{Y^*} = \frac{365}{63.3} = 5.77$$

DISCUSSION QUESTIONS AND PROBLEMS

Discussion Questions

8-1 Why is inventory an important consideration for managers?

8-2 What is the purpose of inventory control?

8-3 Under what circumstances can inventory be used as a hedge against inflation?

8-4 Why wouldn't a company always store large quantities of inventory to eliminate shortages and stockouts?

8-5 Describe the major decisions that must be made in inventory control.

8-6 What are some of the assumptions made in using the economic order quantity?

8-7 Discuss the major inventory costs that are used in determining the economic order quantity.

8-8 What are some of the methods that are used in actually determining the equation for the economic order quantity?

8-9 What is the reorder point? How is it determined?

8-10 Describe some of the optimal quantities in fixed period inventory control systems.

8-11 What is the purpose of sensitivity analysis?

Problems

: 8-12 Develop the equation for the optimal number of orders per year. Use the symbols developed in this chapter. You should use the following steps:

(a) Determine the annual carrying cost.
(b) Determine the annual ordering cost.
(c) Set the annual ordering cost equal to the annual carrying cost.
(d) Solve for the optimal number of orders per year.

: 8-13 Develop the equation for the optimal number of days between orders. Use the same variables that are used in this chapter and the following steps:

(a) Determine the annual carrying cost.
(b) Determine the annual ordering cost.
(c) Set the annual carrying cost equal to the annual ordering cost.
(d) Solve for the optimal number of days between orders.

: 8–14 Using the variables presented in this chapter, develop the equations for the optimal number of orders per month and the optimal number of weeks between orders. Use the following procedure in obtaining both equations:

(a) Determine the annual ordering cost.
(b) Determine the annual carrying cost.
(c) Set the annual ordering cost equal to the annual carrying cost.
(d) Solve for the optimal quantity.

· 8-15 Lila Battle has determined that the annual demand for number 6 screws is 100,000 screws. Lila, who works in her brother's hardware store, is in charge of purchasing. She estimates that it costs $10 every time an order is placed. This cost includes her wages, the cost of the forms used in placing the order, and so on. Furthermore, she estimates that the cost of carrying one screw in inventory for a year is one-half of one cent. How many number 6 screws should Lila order at a time?

· 8-16 It takes approximately two weeks for an order of number 6 screws to arrive once the order has been placed. (Refer to Problem 8-15.) The demand for number 6 screws is fairly constant, and on the average, Lila has observed that her brother's hardware store sells 500 of these screws each day. The store is open four days per week, and closed for two weeks in summer. Since the demand is fairly constant, Lila believes that she can avoid stockouts completely if she only orders the number 6 screws at the correct time. What is the reorder point?

: 8-17 Lila's brother believes that she places too many orders for screws per year. He believes that an order should be placed only twice per year. If Lila follows her brother's policy, how much more would this cost every year over the ordering policy that she developed in Problem 8-15? If only two orders were placed each year, what effect would this have on the reorder point (ROP)?

: **8-18** Barbara Bright is the purchasing agent for West Valve Co. West Valve sells industrial valves and fluid control devices. One of the most popular valves is the Western, which has an annual demand of 4,000 units. The cost of each valve is $90 and the inventory carrying cost is estimated to be 10% of the cost of each valve. Barbara has made a study of the costs involved in placing an order for any of the valves that West Valve stocks, and she has concluded that the average ordering cost is $25 per order. Furthermore, it takes about two weeks for an order to arrive from the supplier, and during this time the demand per week for West valves is approximately 80.

(a) What is the economic order quantity?
(b) What is the reorder point?
(c) What is the total annual inventory cost (carrying cost + ordering cost)?
(d) What is the optimal number of orders per year?
(e) What is the optimal number of days between any two orders?

· **8-19** Ken Ramsing has been in the lumber business for most of his life. Ken's biggest competitor is Pacific Woods. Through many years of experience, Ken knows that the ordering cost for an order of plywood is $25 and that the carrying cost is 25% of the unit cost. Both Ken and Pacific Woods receive plywood in loads that cost $100 per load. Furthermore, Ken and Pacific Woods use the same supplier of plywood, and Ken was able to find out that Pacific Woods orders in quantities of 4,000 loads at a time. Ken also knows that 4,000 loads is the economic order quantity for Pacific Woods. What is the annual demand in loads of plywood for Pacific Woods?

· **8-20** Shoe Shine is a local retail shoe store located on the north side of Centerville. Annual demand for a popular sandal is 500 sandals, and John Dirk, the owner of Shoe Shine, has been in the habit of ordering 100 sandals at a time. John estimates that the ordering cost is $10 per order. The cost of the sandal is $5. For John's ordering policy to be correct, what would the carrying cost as a percentage of the unit cost have to be? If the carrying cost were 10% of the cost, what would the optimal order quantity be?

: **8-21** In Problem 8-15 you helped Lila Battle determine the optimal order quantity for number 6 screws. She had estimated that the ordering cost was $10 per order. At this time, though, she believes that this estimate was too low. Although she does not know the exact ordering cost, she believes that it could be as high as $40 per order. How would the optimal order quantity change if the ordering cost were $20, $30, and $40?

: **8-22** Annual demand for the Doll two-drawer filing cabinet is 50,000 units. Bill Doll, president of Doll Office Suppliers, controls one of the largest office supply stores in Nevada. He estimates that the ordering cost is $10 per order. The carrying cost is $4 per unit per year. It takes 25 days between the time that Bill places an order for the two-drawer filing cabinets and the time when they are received at his warehouse. During this time, the daily demand is estimated to be 250 units.

(a) What is the economic order quantity?
(b) What is the reorder point?
(c) What is the optimal number of orders per year?
(d) What is the optimal number of days between orders?
(e) What is the optimal number of orders per month?
(f) What is the optimal number of weeks between orders?

: **8-23** Pampered Pet, Inc., is a large pet store located in Eastwood Mall. Although the store specializes in dogs, it also sells fish, turtle, and bird supplies.

Everlast Leader, which is a leather lead for dogs, costs Pampered Pet $7 each. There is an annual demand for 6,000 Everlast Leaders. The manager of Pampered Pet has determined that the ordering cost is $10 per order, and the carrying cost as a percent of the unit cost is 15%. Pampered Pet is now considering a new supplier of Everlast Leaders. Each lead would cost only $6.65, but in order to get this discount, Pampered Pet would have to buy shipments of 3,000 Everlast Leaders at a time. Should Pampered Pet use the new supplier and take this discount for quantity buying?

: **8-24** Douglas Boats is a supplier of boating equipment for the states of Oregon and Washington. It sells 5,000 White Marine WM-4 diesel engines every year. These engines are shipped to Douglas in a shipping container that is 100 cubic feet, and Douglas Boats keeps the warehouse full of these WM-4 motors. The warehouse can hold 5,000 cubic feet of boating supplies. Douglas estimates that the ordering cost is $10 per order, and the carrying cost is estimated to be $10 per motor per year. Douglas Boats is considering the possibility of expanding the warehouse for the WM-4 motors. How much should Douglas Boats expand, and how much would it be worth for the company to make the expansion?

: **8-25** Bill Doll (see Problem 8-22) now believes that the carrying cost may be as high as $16 per unit per year. Furthermore, Bill estimates that the lead time is 35 days instead of 25 days. Resolve Problem 8-22 using $16 for the carrying cost with a lead time of 35 days.

: **8-26** Northern Distributors is a wholesale organization that supplies retail stores with lawn care and household products. One building is used to store Neverfail lawn mowers. The building is 25 feet wide by 40 feet deep by 8 feet high. Anna Young, manager of the warehouse, estimates that about 60% of the warehouse can be used to store the Neverfail lawn mowers. The remaining 40% is used for walkways and a small office. Each Neverfail lawn mower comes in a box that is 5 feet by 4 feet by 2 feet high. The annual demand for these lawn mowers is 12,000, and the ordering cost for Northern Distributors is $30 per order. It is estimated that it costs Northern $2 per lawn mower per year for storage. Northern Distributors is thinking about increasing the size of the warehouse. The company can only do this by making the warehouse deeper. At the present time, the warehouse is 40 feet deep. How many feet of depth should be added on to the warehouse to minimize the annual inventory costs? How much should the company be willing to pay for this addition? Remember that only 60% of the total area can be used to store Neverfail lawn mowers.

Sturdivant Sound Systems

Sturdivant Sound Systems manufactures and sells stereo and CD sound systems in both console and component styles. All parts of the sound systems, with the exception of turntables, are produced in the Rochester, New York, plant. Turntables used in the assembly of Sturdivant's systems are purchased from Morris Electronics of Concord, New Hampshire.

Jason Pierce, purchasing agent for Sturdivant Sound Systems, submits a purchase requisition for the multispeed turntables once every four weeks. The company's annual requirements total 5,000 units (20 per working day), and the cost per unit is $60. (Sturdivant does not purchase in greater quantities because Morris Electronics, the supplier, does not offer quantity discounts.) Rarely does a shortage of turntables occur because Morris promises delivery within one week following receipt of a purchase requisition. (Total time between date of order and date of receipt is ten days.)

Associated with the purchase of each shipment are procurement costs. These costs, which amount

Source: Professor Jerry Kinard (Francis Marion College) and the late Professor Joe C. Iverstine. Used with permission of author.

to $20 per order, include the costs of preparing the requisition, inspecting and storing the delivered goods, updating inventory records, and issuing a voucher and a check for payment. In addition to procurement costs, Sturdivant Sound Systems incurs inventory carrying costs which include insurance, storage, handling, taxes, and so forth. These costs equal $6 per unit per year.

Beginning in August of this year, management of Sturdivant Sound Systems will embark on a company-wide cost control program in an attempt to improve its profits. One of the areas to be closely scrutinized for possible cost savings is inventory procurement.

Discussion Questions

1. Compute the optimal order quantity.

2. Determine the appropriate reorder point (in units).

3. Compute the cost savings which the company will realize if it implements the optimal inventory procurement decision.

4. Should procurement costs be considered a linear function of the number of orders?

Western Ranchman Outfitters

Western Ranchman Outfitters (WRO) is a family-owned and -operated mail order and retail store business in Cheyenne, Wyoming. It bills itself as "The Nation's Finest Western Store" and carries high-quality western apparel and riding supplies. Its catalog is mailed all over the world; the store and its president, John Veta, have appeared in a short article in *Fortune* magazine; and clothes from WRO were featured in an issue of *Mademoiselle*.

One of WRO's most staple items is the button front, shrink-to-fit blue jean made by Levi Strauss (model no. 501). This is the original riveted denim pant that cowboys shrunk by sitting in a tub of hot

water. It is the epitome of durability and fit and is still a popular jean. When Veta was asked his stock-out philosophy for this item, he answered, "Would you expect a drugstore to have aspirin?" Furthermore, Veta has had a pleasant relationship with Levi Strauss for all the years of his business career.

Don Randell, director of merchandising, takes a physical inventory of this item once a month. His records show annual usage, amount on hand, quantity ordered, and quantity received (which has been averaging 185 pairs per month, except in January–March when it averages 150 pairs per month), all dated by the month. The store attempts to keep a safety stock adequate for 60 days for two reasons: production problems of the supplier and a hedge against unusually large orders.

Randell described the problems of ordering: "The rag business," as it is known, "is made up of the most disorganized group of people I've ever had the opportunity to be associated with." The problems he cited include not specifying a delivery date, unexplained late deliveries, a general lack of productivity, and lead times of up to six months.

Randell contrasted this situation with his experience in the flexible packaging industry, where reliability was a hallmark and a delay of a single day warranted notification of the customer.

The most recent eight-month period is used to illustrate WRO's ordering difficulties. While the sample figures in the accompanying table may seem peculiar, they reflect WRO's philosophy of offering a full range of sizes and Randell's attempts to predict Levi Strauss' delivery pattern so that the store is close to obtaining the stock it needs. For example, in the last eight months, no one bought a pair sized 27 × 36. Nevertheless, six were ordered and received so that should such a customer ap-

Source: Barry Render, and others, *Cases and Readings in Management Science*, 2nd ed., Boston: Allyn and Bacon, Inc., 1990.

pear, he would be able to satisfy his needs. For size 27 × 34, 33 were ordered, but only 21 were received, which is very close to the 18 sold in the eight months of the previous year. The 27-inch and 28-inch waist sizes shown in the table are but two of the many available waist sizes, of course—waist sizes up to 60 inches are produced and sold.

Randell places an order for Levi blue jeans every month, doing his best to ensure an adequate supply for the business. Normally, WRO customers are not disappointed when requesting the Levi 501. However, in the past two months, the Wyoming Game and Fish Department has been requiring extra pairs of this jean, and WRO has not always had this exact jean in stock. Since there are at least four styles that satisfy the state requirements, the problem is usually overcome with other styles or brands.

Annual demand at WRO for the Levi 501 is 2,000 pair. The cost of placing an order is about $10, the carrying cost is 12%, and the cost of the Levi to WRO is $10.05 per pair.

Discussion Question

Evaluate Randell's ordering policy. How does it compare with formal mathematical approaches?

Usage and Ordering of the Levi 501 for Selected Sizes

SIZE (IN INCHES) WAIST × LENGTH	USAGE	NUMBER ORDERED	NUMBER RECEIVED
27 × 28	11	—	—
27 × 29	1	—	—
27 × 30	6	—	—
27 × 31	0	—	—
27 × 32	4	—	—
27 × 33	—	—	—
27 × 34	18	33	21
27 × 36	—	6	6
28 × 28	—	—	—
28 × 29	—	—	—
28 × 30	—	—	—
28 × 31	—	3	3
28 × 32	4	—	—
28 × 33	7	—	—
28 × 34	8	21	12
28 × 36	27	30	18
	86	93	60*

* Approximately 65% of the number ordered were received.

BIBLIOGRAPHY

Badinetti, Ralph D. "Optimal Safety Stock Investment Through Subjective Evaluation of Stockout Costs." *Management Science* Vol. 17, No. 3, 1986, pp. 312–328.

Banerjee, V. "Joint Economic Lot Size for Purchaser and Vendor." *Decision Sciences* Vol. 17, No. 3, Summer 1986, pp. 292–311.

Chakravarty, Amiya K. "Joint Inventory Replenishment with Group Discounts Based on Invoice Value." *Management Science* Vol. 30, No. 9, September 1984, pp. 1105–1112.

Das, Chandrasekhar. "A Unified Approach to the Price Break Economic Order Quantity (EOQ) Problem." *Decision Sciences* Vol. 15, No. 3, pp. 350–358.

Davis, Robert A., and Gaither, Norman. "Optimal Ordering Policies Under Conditions of Extended Payment Privileges." *Management Science* Vol. 30, No. 9, pp. 499–509.

Mamer, John W. and Smith, Stephen H. "Job Completion Based Inventory Systems: Optimal Policies for Repair Kits and Spare Machines." *Management Science* Vol. 31, No. 6, June 1985, pp. 703–718.

Minch, Robert P., and Sanders, G. Lawrence. "Computer-ized Information Systems Supporting Multicriteria Decision Making." *Decision Sciences* Vol. 17, No. 3, pp. 395–413.

Mitra, A. & Cox, J. F. "EOQ Formula: Is It Valid Under Inflationary Conditions?" *Decision Sciences* Vol. 14, No. 4, 1983, pp. 360–374.

Noori, A. Hamid, and Keller, Gerald. "Lot Size Reorder Point." *Decision Sciences* Vol. 17, No. 3, Summer 1986, pp. 285–291.

Orlicky, J. *Material Requirements Planning.* New York: Mc-Graw-Hill Book Co., 1975.

Roundy, Robin. "98% Effective Inter-Ratio Lot-Sizing for One-Warehouse Multi-Retailer Systems." *Management Science* Vol. 31, No. 11, November 1985, pp. 1416–1430.

Van Ness, Paul D. and Stevenson, William J. "Reorder Point Models with Discrete Probability Distributions." *Decision Sciences* Vol. 14, No. 3, 1983, pp. 363–369.

Veral, Emre A., and LaForge, R. Lawrence. "The Performance of a Simple Incremental Lot Sizing Rule in a Multilevel Inventory Environment." *Decision Sciences* Vol. 16, No. 1, Winter 1985, pp. 57–72.

Appendix: Determining EOQ with Calculus

In this appendix we investigate how the economic order quantity, Q^*, can be determined using calculus. Although the other optimal quantities are not determined, the procedure is the same. The first step is to develop a total cost equation that is a function of the optimal quantity, in this case, Q. Then the first derivative is computed and set equal to 0. Finally, we solve for the optimal quantity. Here is how this is done with the economic order quantity.

1. Develop the equation for the total cost.

$$\text{Total cost} = \text{Ordering cost} + \text{Carrying cost} \qquad TC = \frac{DC_o}{Q} + \frac{QC_h}{2}$$

2. Take the first derivative and set it equal to 0.

$$\frac{dTC}{dQ} = 0 = \frac{dTC}{dQ} = -\frac{DC_o}{Q^2} + \frac{C_h}{2} = 0$$

3. Solve for the optimal quantity.

$$-\frac{DC_o}{Q^2} + \frac{C_h}{2} = 0 \qquad \frac{C_h}{2} = \frac{DC_o}{Q^2} \qquad \frac{Q^3 C_h}{2} = DC_o \qquad Q^2 = \frac{2DC_o}{C_h} \qquad Q = \sqrt{\frac{2DC_o}{C_h}}$$

In more complex inventory problems, setting ordering cost equal to carrying cost does not give the optimal solution. In these cases, it is necessary to use calculus to determine the best inventory policy.

9

Inventory Control Models: II

9.1
INTRODUCTION

The fundamentals of inventory control were presented in Chapter 8. By making a number of assumptions, it was possible to develop some straightforward and easy-to-use inventory techniques that determine when to order and how much to order. However, the assumptions of Chapter 8 often do not apply. For example, in some production processes, inventory gradually builds up over time instead of being instantaneously received. In addition, discounts are often available when supplies are purchased in large quantities. Sometimes, shortages and stockouts cannot be avoided because demand is not known or constant.

Although the inventory models we look at in this chapter are more complex than the economic order quantity (EOQ) model seen earlier, the fundamental objectives are still the same. We are still trying to minimize total inventory cost. We begin this chapter by investigating how EOQ can be used in the production process.

9.2
EOQ WITHOUT THE INSTANTANEOUS RECEIPT ASSUMPTION

When a firm receives its inventory over a period of time, a new model is needed that does not require the *instantaneous inventory receipt* assumption of Chapter 8. This new model is applicable when inventory continuously flows or builds up over a period of time after an order has been placed or when units are produced and sold simultaneously. Under these circumstances, the daily demand rate must be taken into account. Figure 9.1 shows inventory levels as a function of time. Because this model is especially **production run model** suited to the production environment, it is commonly called the *production run model*.

In the production process, instead of having an ordering cost, there will be a *setup cost*. This is the cost of setting up the production facility to manufacture the desired product. It normally includes the salaries and wages of employees who are responsible for setting up the equipment, engineering and design costs of making the setup, paperwork, supplies, utilities, and so on. The carrying cost per unit is composed of the same factors as the traditional EOQ model presented in the previous chapter, although the annual carrying cost equation changes.

solving the production run model The production run model can be derived by setting setup costs equal to holding or carrying costs and solving for the order quantity. Let's start by developing the expression for carrying cost. You should note, however, that making setup cost equal to carrying cost does not always guarantee optimal solutions for models more complex than the production run model.

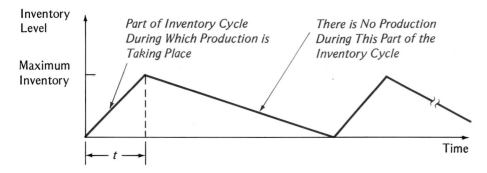

FIGURE 9.1
Inventory Control and the Production Process

Determining the Annual Carrying Cost

Using the following variables, we can determine the expression for annual inventory carrying cost for the production run model:

Q = Number of pieces per order

C_h = Holding or carrying cost per unit per year

p = Daily product rate

d = Daily demand rate

t = Length of the production run in days

1. Annual inventory holding or carrying cost

    = (Average inventory level) × (Carrying cost per unit per year)

    = (Average inventory level) × C_h

2. Average inventory level = $\frac{1}{2}$ (Maximum inventory level)

3. Maximum inventory level

    $$= \begin{array}{c}\text{(Total produced during} \\ \text{the production run)}\end{array} - \begin{array}{c}\text{(Total used during} \\ \text{the production run)}\end{array}$$

    But Q = Total produced = pt, and thus $t = Q/p$. Therefore maximum inventory level = $p(Q/p) - d(Q/p) = Q - (d/p)Q = Q(1 - d/p)$.

4. Annual inventory carrying cost (or simply carrying cost)

    $$= \frac{1}{2}(\text{Maximum inventory level}) \times C_h \qquad \textbf{(9-1)}$$

    $$= \frac{1}{2} \times Q(1 - d/p) \times C_h$$

(*Note:* This is the same as the carrying cost developed in the EOQ model in the last chapter except that the factor $(1 - d/p)$ appears in the expression for carrying cost.)

Finding the Annual Setup Cost or the Annual Ordering Cost

When a product is being produced over time, setup cost replaces the ordering cost. Here is how *annual setup cost* and *annual ordering cost* can be determined.

1. Annual setup cost $= \left(\begin{array}{c}\text{Number of setups} \\ \text{per year}\end{array}\right)\left(\begin{array}{c}\text{Setup cost} \\ \text{per setup}\end{array}\right)$ (9-2)

$$= \frac{D}{Q_p} C_s$$

where

D = annual demand in units,

Q_p = quantity produced in one batch, and

C_s = setup cost per setup.

2. Annual ordering cost $= \dfrac{D}{Q} C_0$ (9-3)

(See Chapter 8.)

As you can see, the form of the equation for the annual setup cost is identical to the form of the equation for the annual ordering cost. In determining the optimal order quantity, we will use the variables presented in Equation 9-3 for the case where the inventory is ordered instead of produced. It should be noted, however, that the same optimal equation can be used in determining the optimal production quantity, Q_p^*, as well. Q_p and C_s would replace Q and C_o in the equation.

Determining the Optimal Order Quantity and Production Quantity

With this model, it is possible to determine the optimal quantity by setting the ordering cost equal to the carrying cost and solving for the desired quantity. Here is how this can be accomplished when the inventory is ordered.

1. Ordering cost $= \dfrac{D}{Q} C_o.$

2. Carrying cost $= \frac{1}{2} C_h Q \left(1 - \dfrac{d}{p}\right).$

3. Set ordering cost equal to carrying cost.

$$\frac{D}{Q} C_o = \frac{1}{2} C_h Q \left(1 - \frac{d}{p}\right)$$

4. Solve for Q^*.

$$Q^2 = \frac{2DC_o}{C_h\left(1 - \dfrac{d}{p}\right)}$$

$$Q^* = \sqrt{\frac{2DC_o}{C_h\left(1 - \dfrac{d}{p}\right)}} \qquad (9\text{-}4) \qquad \textbf{optimal order quantity}$$

The same calculations can be made to determine the optimal production quantity, Q_p^*. The results of these calculations appear in Equation 9-5.

$$Q_p^* = \sqrt{\frac{2DC_s}{C_h\left(1 - \dfrac{d}{p}\right)}} \qquad (9\text{-}5) \qquad \textbf{optimal production quantity}$$

Brown Manufacturing Example

Brown Manufacturing produces commercial refrigeration units in batches. The firm's estimated demand for the year is 10,000 units. It costs about $100 to set up the manufacturing process, and the carrying cost is about 50¢ per unit per year. Once the production process has been set up, 80 refrigeration units can be manufactured daily. The demand during the production period has traditionally been 60 units each day. How many refrigeration units should Brown Manufacturing produce in each batch? How long should the production part of the cycle shown in Figure 9.1 last? Here is the solution:

$$\text{Annual demand} = D = 10{,}000 \text{ units}$$
$$\text{Setup cost} = C_s = \$100$$
$$\text{Carrying cost} = C_h = \$.50 \text{ per unit per year}$$
$$\text{Daily production rate} = p = 80 \text{ units daily}$$
$$\text{Daily demand rate} = d = 60 \text{ units daily}$$

1. $Q_p^* = \sqrt{\dfrac{2DC_s}{C_h\left(1 - \dfrac{d}{p}\right)}}$

2. $Q_p^* = \sqrt{\dfrac{2 \times 10{,}000 \times 100}{.5\left(1 - \dfrac{60}{80}\right)}}$

$$Q_p^* = \sqrt{\frac{2{,}000{,}000}{.5(\frac{1}{4})}} = \sqrt{16{,}000{,}000}$$

$$Q_p^* = 4{,}000 \text{ units}$$

If $Q_p^* = 4{,}000$ units and we know that 80 units can be produced daily, the length of each production cycle will be $Q/p = 4{,}000/80 = 50$ days. Thus, when Brown decides to produce refrigeration units, the equipment will be set up to manufacture the units for a 50-day time span.

We now turn to a model with different assumptions, the quantity discount model.

9.3
QUANTITY DISCOUNT MODELS

To increase sales, many companies offer quantity discounts to their customers. A *quantity discount* is simply a reduced cost (C) for the item when it is purchased in larger quantities. It is not uncommon to have a discount schedule with several discounts for large orders. A typical quantity discount schedule appears in Table 9.1.

As can be seen in the table, the normal cost for the item is $5. When 1,000 to 1,999 units are ordered at one time, then the cost per unit drops to $4.80, and when the quantity ordered at one time is 2,000 units or more, the cost is $4.75 per unit. As always, management must decide when and how much to order. But with quantity discounts, how does the manager make these decisions?

As with other inventory models discussed so far, the overall objective will be to minimize the total cost. Since the unit cost for the third discount in Table 9.1 is lowest, you might be tempted to order 2,000 units or more to take advantage of the lower material cost. Placing an order for that quantity with the greatest discount cost, however, might not minimize the total inventory cost. As the discount quantity goes up, the material cost goes down, but the carrying cost increases because the orders are large. Thus, the major trade-off when considering quantity discounts is between the reduced material cost and the increased carrying cost. When we include the cost of the material, the equation for the total annual inventory cost becomes:

minimizing total cost

$$\text{Total cost} = \text{Material cost} + \text{Ordering cost} + \text{Carrying cost}$$

$$\text{Total cost} = DC + \frac{D}{Q} C_o + \frac{Q}{2} C_h \qquad \text{(9-6)}$$

where

$$D = \text{annual demand in units,}$$
$$C_o = \text{ordering cost per order,}$$
$$C = \text{cost per unit, and}$$
$$C_h = \text{holding cost per unit per year.}$$

TABLE 9.1 A Quantity Discount Schedule

DISCOUNT NUMBER	DISCOUNT QUANTITY	DISCOUNT (%)	DISCOUNT COST ($)
1	0 to 999	0	5.00
2	1,000 to 1,999	4	4.80
3	2,000 and over	5	4.75

Now, we have to determine the quantity that minimizes the total annual inventory cost. This process involves four steps:

1. For each discount, calculate a Q^* value using the following equation:

$$Q^* = \sqrt{\frac{2DC_o}{IC}}$$

calculate Q^* values

Note that the carrying cost is IC instead of C_h. Because the cost of the item is a factor in annual carrying cost, we cannot assume that the carrying cost is a constant when the cost per unit changes for each quantity discount. Thus, it is common to express the carrying cost (I) as a percentage of unit cost (C) instead of as a constant cost per unit per year, C_h.

I is used instead of C_h

2. For any discount, if the order quantity is too low to qualify for the discount, adjust the order quantity upward to the lowest quantity that qualifies for the discount. For example, if Q^* for discount 2 in Table 9.1 were 500 units, you would adjust this value up to 1,000 units. Look at the second discount in Table 9.1. Order quantities between 1,000 and 1,999 qualify for the 4% discount. Thus, we adjust the order quantity up to be 1,000 units if Q^* is below 1,000 units.

adjust the Q^* values

The reasoning for step 2 may not be obvious. If the order quantity is below the quantity range that qualifies for a discount, a quantity within this range may still result in the lowest total cost.

As seen in Figure 9.2, the total cost curve is broken into three different total cost curves. There is a total cost curve for the first ($0 \le Q \le 999$), second ($1,000 \le Q \le 1,999$), and third ($Q \ge 2,000$) discount. Look at the total cost (TC) curve for discount 2. Q^* for discount 2 is less than the allowable discount range, which is from 1,000 to 1,999 units. As seen in the figure, the lowest allowable quantity in this range, which is 1,000 units, is the quantity that minimizes the total cost. Thus, the second step is needed to ensure that we do not discard an order quantity that may indeed produce the minimum cost. It should be noted that an order quantity computed in step 1 that is greater than the range that would qualify it for a discount may be discarded.

total cost curve is broken into parts

3. Using the total cost Equation 9-6, compute a total cost for every Q^* determined in steps 1 and 2. If you had to adjust Q^* upward because it was below the allowable quantity range, make sure to use the adjusted value for Q^*.

compute total cost

4. Select that Q^* that has the lowest total cost as computed in step 3. It will be the quantity that minimizes the total inventory cost.

select Q^* with lowest total cost

Let's see how this procedure can be applied by showing an example. Brass Department Store stocks toy race cars. Recently, the store was given a quantity discount schedule for the cars; this quantity schedule was shown in Table 9.1. Thus, the normal cost for the toy race cars is $5. For orders between 1,000 and 1,999 units, the unit cost is $4.80, and for orders of

Brass Department store example

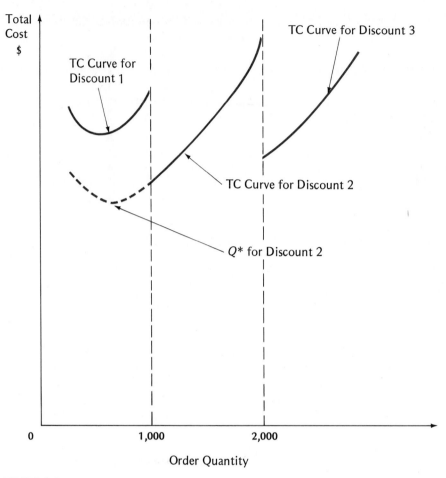

FIGURE 9.2
Total Cost Curve for the Quantity Discount Model

2,000 or more units, the unit cost is $4.75. Furthermore, the ordering cost is $49 per order, the annual demand is 5,000 race cars, and the inventory carrying charge as a percentage of cost, I, is 20% or .2. What order quantity will minimize the total inventory cost?

The first step is to compute Q^* for every discount in Table 9.1. This is done as follows:

Q^* values are computed

$$Q_1^* = \sqrt{\frac{(2)(5,000)(49)}{(.2)(5.00)}} = 700 \text{ cars per order}$$

$$Q_2^* = \sqrt{\frac{(2)(5,000)(49)}{(.2)(4.80)}} = 714 \text{ cars per order}$$

$$Q_3^* = \sqrt{\frac{(2)(5,000)(49)}{(.2)(4.75)}} = 718 \text{ cars per order}$$

The second step is to adjust those values of Q^* that are below the allowable discount range. Since Q_1^* is between 0 and 999, it does not have to be adjusted. Q_2^* is below the allowable range of 1,000 to 1,999, and therefore, it must be adjusted to 1,000 units. The same is true for Q_3^*; it must be adjusted to 2,000 units. After this step, the following order quantities must be tested in the total cost equation:

$$Q_1^* = 700$$

$$Q_2^* = 1,000\text{—adjusted}$$

$$Q_3^* = 2,000\text{—adjusted}$$

Q* values are adjusted

The third step is to use the total cost Equation 9-6 and compute a total cost for each of the order quantities. This is accomplished with the aid of Table 9.2.

total cost is computed

TABLE 9.2 Total Cost Computations for Brass Department Store

DISCOUNT NUMBER	UNIT PRICE	ORDER QUANTITY	ANNUAL MATERIAL COST ($)	ANNUAL ORDERING COST ($)	ANNUAL CARRYING COST ($)	TOTAL ($)
1	$5.00	700	25,000	350	350	25,700
2	$4.80	1,000	24,000	245	480	24,725
3	$4.75	2,000	23,750	122.5	950	24,822.5

The fourth step is to select that order quantity with the lowest total cost. Looking at Table 9.2, you can see that an order quantity of 1,000 toy race cars minimizes the total cost. It should be recognized, however, that the total cost for ordering 2,000 cars is only slightly greater than the total cost for ordering 1,000 cars. Thus, if the third discount cost is lowered to $4.65, for example, then this order quantity might be the one that minimizes the total inventory cost.

Q* is selected

9.4
PLANNED SHORTAGES

In previous inventory models, we have not allowed inventory shortages where there was not sufficient stock to meet current demand. There are many situations, however, that suggest that *planned shortages* or *stockouts* may be advisable. This is especially true with high inventory carrying costs for expensive items. Car dealerships and appliance stores rarely stock every model for this reason.

In the following model, we assume that stockouts and back ordering are allowed. This model is called the *back order* or *planned shortages inventory model*. A back order is the situation in which a customer places an order, finds that the supplier is out of stock, and waits for the next shipment (the back order) to arrive. The model assumes that the customer's sale will not be lost due to the stockout. It also assumes that back orders will be satisfied before any new demand for the product. We use the following variables in the back order model:

assumptions of the model

Q = Number of pieces per order

D = Annual demand in units

$$C_h = \text{Carrying cost per unit per year}$$
$$C_o = \text{Ordering cost for each order}$$
$$C_b = \text{Back ordering cost per unit per year}$$
$$Q - S = \text{Remaining units after back order is satisfied}$$
$$S = \text{Amount back ordered}$$

back ordering cost

Two variables you have not seen before have been used. The first, C_b, is the *back ordering cost per unit per year*. As with regular orders, a back order is placed when a shortage occurs for the desired units or products. Thus, all of the costs of placing an ordinary order are involved in placing a back order. In addition, there is a cost that is due to customer dissatisfaction, or the loss of goodwill. For example, customers are not likely to keep buying from a supplier who is regularly out of stock and who regularly has to back order. Therefore, the back order cost includes a cost factor to account for the inconvenience of the back order to the customer. Since the back order cost depends upon how long a customer waits to receive an order, it is similar to the inventory carrying cost and is expressed in dollars per unit per year.

customer dissatisfaction cost

amount back ordered is S

The other new variable is S, which is the amount back ordered. $Q - S$ is the number of units remaining after the back order has been satisfied. Allowing back orders changes the inventory usage curve. When back orders are allowed, this curve has the appearance shown in Figure 9.3.

Finding Optimal Order and Back Order Levels

Given data for the preceding variables, we would like to determine optimal values for the order quantity, Q^*, and the optimal number of units that are actually back ordered, S^*. The previously used technique of setting ordering cost equal to carrying cost does not work because of the back ordering cost. Thus, it is necessary to develop a total cost equation. Then, calculus can be used to solve for the optimal quantities.

The total annual cost will be:

$$TC = \text{Ordering cost} + \text{Carrying cost} + \text{Back ordering cost}$$

ordering cost

The ordering cost is identical to the ordering cost developed for the traditional EOQ model. (See Chapter 8.)

$$\text{Ordering cost} = \frac{D}{Q} C_o$$

carrying cost

The carrying cost is the average inventory level times the holding or carrying cost per unit per year, C_h.

$$\text{Carrying cost} = (\text{Average inventory level})(C_h)$$

Now, the problem is to compute the average inventory level. In the past, this has been the maximum inventory level divided by 2. In this case, this would be $(Q - S)/2$. But this is the average inventory level during the period when we still have inventory, t, and not over the total time, T. Note

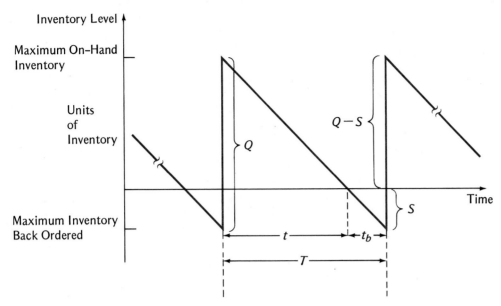

FIGURE 9.3
Inventory Usage with Back Ordering

that in Figure 9.3, important variables are:

t = Time between the receipt of an order and
　　 when the inventory level drops to 0

t_b = Time during which back order or stockouts will occur

T = Total time: $T = t + t_b$

The average inventory level over the total time period is a weighted average.

$$\text{Average inventory level} = \frac{\left(\begin{array}{c}\text{Average level}\\ \text{over } t\end{array}\right) t + \left(\begin{array}{c}\text{Average level}\\ \text{over } t_b\end{array}\right) t_b}{T}$$

$$= \frac{\left(\dfrac{Q - S}{2}\right) t + 0 t_b}{T}$$

$$= \frac{\left(\dfrac{Q - S}{2}\right) t}{T}$$

Since there is no inventory during t_b, the average is 0.

Because we want to calculate optimal values for Q and S, we need to express t and T in terms of Q and S. In general,

$$\text{Time period in days} = \frac{\text{Total units over time period}}{\text{Demand in units per day } (d)}$$

$$t = \frac{Q - S}{d}$$

and

$$T = \frac{Q}{d}$$

Using these values, we can express the average inventory level in terms of Q and S alone.

$$\text{Average inventory level} = \frac{\left(\dfrac{Q-S}{2}\right)t}{T}$$

$$= \frac{\left(\dfrac{Q-S}{2}\right)\left(\dfrac{Q-S}{d}\right)}{\dfrac{Q}{d}}$$

$$= \frac{(Q-S)^2}{2Q}$$

$$\text{Carrying cost} = \left(\begin{array}{c}\text{Average}\\\text{inventory}\\\text{level}\end{array}\right)C_h$$

$$= \frac{(Q-S)^2}{2Q}C_h$$

Back ordering cost must be computed in the same way. The average number of units on back order is:

$$\begin{array}{c}\text{Average number of}\\\text{units on back order}\end{array} = \frac{0t + \left(\dfrac{S}{2}\right)t_b}{T}$$

$$= \frac{\left(\dfrac{S}{2}\right)t_b}{T}$$

Again, we must express t_b and T as a function of Q and S.

$$t_b = \frac{S}{d}$$

$$T = \frac{Q}{d}$$

Thus,

$$\begin{array}{c}\text{Average number of}\\\text{units on back order}\end{array} = \frac{\left(\dfrac{S}{2}\right)\left(\dfrac{S}{d}\right)}{\dfrac{Q}{d}} = \frac{S^2}{2Q}$$

$$\begin{array}{c}\text{Back ordering}\\\text{cost}\end{array} = \left(\begin{array}{c}\text{Average number of}\\\text{units on back order}\end{array}\right)C_b$$

$$= \frac{S^2}{2Q}C_b$$

Now we can write the expression for total annual cost.

total cost

$$TC = \frac{\text{Ordering}}{\text{cost}} + \frac{\text{Carrying}}{\text{cost}} + \frac{\text{Back ordering}}{\text{cost}} \quad (9\text{-}7)$$

$$= \frac{D}{Q} C_o + \frac{(Q - S)^2}{2Q} C_h + \frac{S^2}{2Q} C_b$$

The optimal values for the order quantity, Q^*, and units back ordered, S^*, are found by using calculus. This is shown in the appendix to this chapter. The results are as follows:

$$Q^* = \sqrt{\frac{2DC_o}{C_h} \left(\frac{C_h + C_b}{C_b} \right)} \quad (9\text{-}8)$$

optimal values for Q^* and S^*

$$S^* = Q^* \left(\frac{C_h}{C_h + C_b} \right) \quad (9\text{-}9)$$

Butch Radner's Planned Shortages

Butch Radner, a supplier of ladies' garments, is trying to determine how many dresses to order for his fall collection. Because the number of different styles and sizes is extremely large, he has decided to have planned shortages. While customers are not happy with these shortages, back orders are very common because Butch is a charming man and his styles are beautiful. So far, no one has canceled an order because of the delay. The demand for a particular dress is 10,000 units. The carrying cost is $2 per dress per year, and the ordering cost is $7.50 per order. Butch estimates that his back ordering cost is $10 per dress per year. How many dresses should Butch order? How many garments will be back ordered each inventory cycle? The calculations are:

$$D = 10,000 \text{ dresses}$$
$$C_h = \$2$$
$$C_o = \$7.50$$
$$C_b = \$10$$

$$Q^* = \sqrt{\frac{(2)(10,000)(7.5)}{2} \left(\frac{2 + 10}{10} \right)}$$

$$= \sqrt{75,000 \left(\frac{12}{10} \right)} = 300 \text{ dresses per order}$$

$$S^* = Q^* \left(\frac{C_h}{C_h + C_b} \right)$$

$$= 300 \left(\frac{2}{2 + 10} \right) = 50 \text{ dresses per back order}$$

9.5
USE OF SAFETY STOCK

Use of the back order inventory model assumes that a customer patiently waits until his or her order can be filled and that demand is certain. When

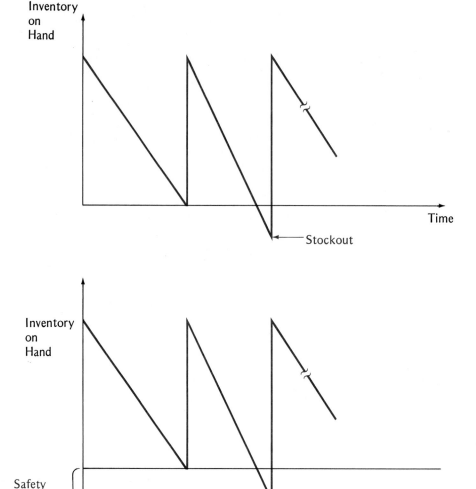

FIGURE 9.4
Use of Safety Stock

management believes that these assumptions are not valid, it may turn to
the use of *safety stock.*[1]

Safety stock is additional stock that is kept on hand. If, for example,
safety stock for an item is 50 units, you are carrying an average of 50 units
more of inventory during the year. When demand is unusually high, you
avoiding stockouts   dip into the safety stock instead of encountering a *stockout*. Thus, the main
purpose of safety stock is to avoid stockouts when the demand is higher
than expected. Its use is shown in Figure 9.4. Note that although stockouts
can often be avoided by using safety stock there is still a chance that they

[1] Safety stock is used only when demand is uncertain, and models under uncertainty are
generally much harder to deal with than models under certainty.

may occur. The demand may be so high that all of the safety stock is used up, and thus there is still a stockout.

One of the best ways of maintaining a safety stock level is to use the reorder point, ROP. This can be accomplished by adding the number of units of safety stock as a buffer to the reorder point. As you recall,

safety stock and the reorder point

$$\text{Reorder point} = \text{ROP} = d \times L$$

$$d = \text{Daily demand}$$

$$L = \text{Order lead time or the number of working days it takes to deliver an order}$$

With the inclusion of safety stock, the reorder point becomes

$$\text{ROP} = d \times L + \text{SS} \qquad (9\text{-}10)$$
$$\text{SS} = \text{Safety stock}$$

 KEY IDEA

How to determine the correct amount of safety stock is the only remaining question. If cost data are available, the objective is to minimize total cost. If cost data are not available, then it is necessary to establish a service level or policy.

Safety Stock with Known Stockout Costs

When the economic order quantity is fixed, and the reorder point is used to place orders, the only time that a stockout can occur is during the lead time. As you recall, the lead time is the time between when the order is placed and when it is received. In the techniques discussed here, it is necessary to know the probability of demand during the lead time and the cost of a stockout. In this section we use a discrete probability distribution to describe the probability of demand over the lead time. This approach, however, could also be modified when the demand follows a continuous probability distribution.

probability of demand

In this section, we use a stockout cost per unit. But what should be included in this cost? We make the assumption that if a stockout occurs we lose forever that particular sale. Thus, if there is a profit margin of $.10 per unit, we should include this as part of the stockout cost. Furthermore, we lose some customers because of stockouts and therefore lose their business for their lifetime. These costs must also be included in the stockout cost. In general, stockout costs should include all costs that are a direct or indirect result of a stockout. Once we know the probability of demand over the lead time and the cost of a stockout, it is possible to determine the best safety stock level. The best safety stock level is the one that minimizes the total cost. Here is an example.

stockout cost

minimizing total cost

ABCO, Inc., has determined that its reorder point is 50($d \times L$) units. Its carrying cost per unit per year is $5 and stockout cost is $40 per unit. ABCO has experienced the probability distribution for inventory demand during the reorder period shown in Table 9.3. The optimal number of orders per year is 6.[2]

[2] We have assumed that we already know Q^* and ROP. If this assumption is not made, then Q^*, ROP, and safety stock would have to be determined simultaneously. This requires a more complex solution.

TABLE 9.3 Probability of Demand for ABCO, Inc.

NUMBER OF UNITS		PROBABILITY
	30	.2
	40	.2
ROP ⟶	50	.3
	60	.2
	70	.1
		1.0

minimizing additional carrying cost plus stockout cost

ABCO's overall objective is to find the safety stock that minimizes the total additional inventory carrying costs and stockout costs on an annual basis. The annual carrying cost is simply the carrying costs times the additional units over the ROP. For example, if the safety stock is 20 units, which implies that the new ROP with safety stock is 70 = (50 + 20), then the additional annual carrying cost is $5 × 20 = $100.

The stockout cost is more difficult to compute. For any safety stock level, it is the expected cost of stocking out. This is computed by multiplying *the number of units short* times *the probability* times *the stockout cost* times *the number of times per year the stockout can occur* (or the number of orders per year). Stockout costs are then added for each possible stockout level for a given ROP. For 0 safety stock, a shortage of 10 units occurs if demand is 60, and a shortage of 20 units occurs if demand is 70. Thus the stockout costs for 0 safety stock is (10 units short) × (.2 probability) × ($40 per stockout) × (6 possible stockouts per year) + (20 units short) × (.1 probability) × ($40) × (6). Table 9.4 summarizes the total costs for each alternative. The safety stock with the lowest total cost is 20 units. With this safety stock, the reorder point becomes 50 + 20 = 70 units.

TABLE 9.4 Total Cost for ABCO, Inc.

SAFETY STOCK	ADDITIONAL CARRYING COST	STOCKOUT COSTS	TOTAL COSTS ($)
20	20 × $5 = $100	$0	100
10	10 × $5 = $50	10 × .1 × $40 × 6 = $240	290
0	$0	10 × .2 × $40 × 6 + 20 × .1 × $40 × 6 = $960	960

Safety Stock with Unknown Stockout Costs

When stockout costs are not available or if they do not apply, then the preceding type of analysis cannot be used. Actually, there are many situations when stockout costs are unknown or extremely difficult to determine. For example, let's assume that you run a small bicycle shop that sells mopeds and bicycles with a one-year service warranty. Any adjustments made within the year are done at no charge to the customer. If the customer comes in for maintenance under the warranty, and you do not have the necessary part, what is the stockout cost? It cannot be lost profit because the maintenance is done free of charge. Thus, the major stockout cost is the loss of goodwill. The customer may not buy another bicycle from your shop if you have a poor service record. In this situation, it could be very difficult to determine the stockout cost. In other cases, a stockout cost may simply not apply. What is the stockout cost for life-saving drugs in a hospital? The drug may only cost $10 per bottle. Is the stockout cost $10? Is it $100 or $10,000? Perhaps the stockout cost should be $1 million. What is the cost when a life may be lost as a result of not having the drug?

determining stockout costs may be difficult or impossible

An alternate approach to determining safety stock levels is to use a *service level*. In general, a service level is the percent of the time that you will *not* be out of stock of a particular item. Stated in other terms, the chance or probability of having a stockout is one minus the service level. This relationship is expressed as:

$$\text{Service level} = 1 - \text{Probability of a stockout}$$

or

$$\text{Probability of a stockout} = 1 - \text{Service level}$$

In order to determine the safety stock level, it is only necessary to know the probability of demand during the lead time and the desired service level. Here is an example of how the safety stock level can be determined when the probability of demand over the lead time follows a normal curve.

service level and the normal distribution

The Hinsdale Company carries an inventory item that has a normally distributed demand during the reorder period. The mean (average) demand is 350 units and the standard deviation is 10. Hinsdale wants to follow a policy that results in stockouts occurring only 5% of the time. How much safety stock should be maintained? Figure 9.5 may help you to visualize the example.

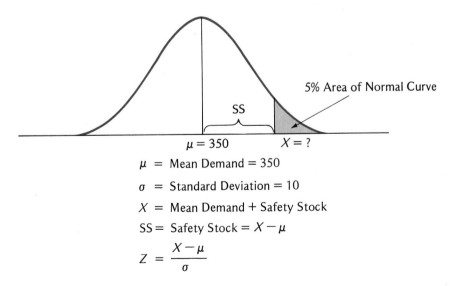

FIGURE 9.5
Safety Stock and the Normal Distribution

We use the properties of a standardized normal curve to get a Z value for an area under the normal curve of $.95 = (1 - .05)$. Using a normal table (see Appendix A), we find a Z value of 1.65.

$$Z = 1.65$$

$$Z \text{ is also equal to } \frac{X - \mu}{\sigma} = \frac{SS}{\sigma}$$

$$Z = 1.65 = \frac{SS}{\sigma}$$

Solving for safety stock gives the following (since stock is usually in integer amounts):

$$SS = (1.65)(10) = 16.5 \text{ units, or 17 units}$$

service levels, safety stock, and carrying costs

Different safety stock levels will be generated for different service levels. The relationship between service levels and safety stock, however, is not linear. As the service level increases, the safety stock increases at increasing rate. Indeed, at service levels greater than 97%, the safety stock becomes very large. Of course, high levels of safety stock mean higher carrying costs. If you are using a service level, you should be aware of how much your service level is costing you in terms of carrying the safety stock in inventory. Let's assume that Hinsdale has a carrying cost of $1 per unit per year. What is the carrying cost for service levels that range from 90% to 99.99%? This cost information is summarized in Table 9.5.

Table 9.5 is developed by looking in the normal curve table for every service level. Finding the service level in the body of the table, we can obtain the Z value from the table in the standard way. Next, the Z values must be converted into the safety stock in units. As you recall, the standard deviation of sales during lead time for Hinsdale is 10. Therefore, the relationship between Z and the safety stock can be developed as follows:

1. We know that $Z = \dfrac{X - \mu}{\sigma}$

2. And that $SS = X - \mu$

TABLE 9.5 Cost of Different Service Levels

SERVICE LEVEL (%)	Z VALUE FROM NORMAL CURVE TABLE	SAFETY STOCK (UNITS)	CARRYING COST ($)
90	1.28	12.8	12.80
91	1.34	13.4	13.40
92	1.41	14.1	14.10
93	1.48	14.8	14.80
94	1.55	15.5	15.50
95	1.65	16.5	16.50
96	1.75	17.5	17.50
97	1.88	18.8	18.80
98	2.05	20.5	20.50
99	2.32	23.2	23.20
99.99	3.72	37.2	37.20

3. Thus we can rewrite Z as $Z = \dfrac{SS}{\sigma}$

4. Or by transposing terms

$$SS = Z\sigma = (Z)(10) \qquad (9\text{--}11)$$

Thus, the safety stock can be determined by multiplying the Z values by 10. Since the carrying cost is \$1 per unit per year, the carrying cost is the same numerically as the safety stock. A graph of the carrying cost as a function of service level is given in Figure 9.6.

As you can see from Figure 9.6, the carrying cost is increasing at an increasing rate. Moreover, the carrying cost gets extremely large when the service level is greater than 98%. Therefore, as you are setting service levels,

carrying cost increases at an increasing rate

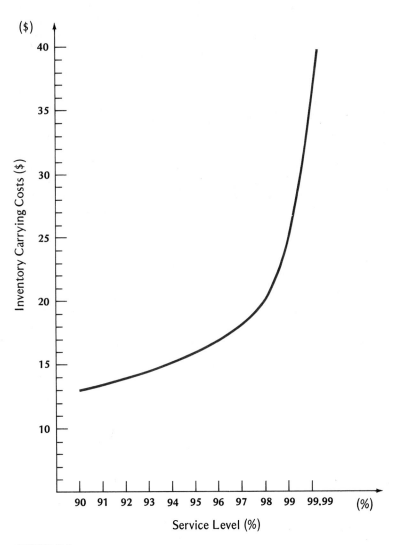

FIGURE 9.6
Service Level versus Annual Carrying Costs

you should be aware of the additional carrying cost that you will encounter. Although Figure 9.6 was developed for a specific case, the general shape of the curve is the same for all service level problems.

9.6
ABC ANALYSIS AND JOINT ORDERING

In the previous sections, we showed how to develop inventory policies using quantitative techniques. There are also some very *practical* considerations that should be incorporated into inventory decisions. Let's explore some of them.

ABC Analysis

The purpose of *ABC analysis* is to divide all of a company's inventory items into three groups, the A group, the B group, and the C group. Then, depending on the group, it is necessary to decide how the inventory levels should be controlled in general. ABC analysis recognizes the fact that some inventory items are more important than others. A brief description of each group follows, with general guidelines as to which items are A, B, C.

the A group

The inventory items in the A group are critical to the functioning and operation of the organization. As a result, their inventory levels must be carefully monitored. These items typically make up over 70% of the company's *business in dollars*. Usually, they are only 10% of all inventory items. In other words, a *few inventory items are very important to the company*. As a result, the inventory control techniques discussed in Chapter 8 and in this chapter should be used where appropriate for every item in the A group. (Refer to Table 9.6.)

the B group

The items in the B group are important to the organization, but they are not critical. Thus, it may not be necessary to constantly monitor the levels of all of these items. B group items typically represent about 20% of the company's business and comprise about 20% of the items in inventory. The use of the quantitative inventory models should be used on only some of the items. The cost of implementing and using a quantitative inventory control technique must be carefully balanced with the benefits of better inventory control. Usually, less than half of B group items are carefully controlled through the use of quantitative inventory control techniques.

the C group

The items in the C group are not that important to the operation of the organization. These items represent perhaps only 10% of the company's

TABLE 9.6 Summary of ABC Analysis

INVENTORY GROUP	DOLLAR USAGE (%)	INVENTORY ITEMS (%)	ARE COMPLEX QUANTITATIVE CONTROL TECHNIQUES USED?
A	70	10	Yes
B	20	20	In some cases
C	10	70	No

APPLICATIONS OF QA

Using the ABC Control Method in Hospital Inventory

In order to help control inventory, a hospital used ABC analysis to classify a group of 47 disposable stock keeping units (SKUs). The following ten-step procedure was used to place ABC analysis into effect:

1. Select those SKUs to undergo analysis.

2. Determine the number of SKUs utilized during the past year.

3. Compute the average unit cost for each SKU.

4. Compute the total annual dollar usage cost for all SKUs.

5. Sort, or order, SKUs in descending order on the basis of total annual usage values.

6. Identify and label each SKU descriptively.

7. Compute the cumulative percentage associated with each SKU.

8. Determine the cumulative total dollar usage for each SKU.

9. Calculate the percentage of final cumulative total dollar usage for each SKU.

10. Determine the appropriate categories or divisions for all units using SKU analysis.

Of the 47 SKUs, the first ten were identified as being in category A. These ten units represented approximately 74% of the annual usage. Category B items represented approximately 18% of the annual usage, while category C items represented only 8%. Using this type of analysis, priority could be given to the class A items so that inventory costs could be controlled more effectively. SKUs placed in category A were monitored very closely. Forecasts were updated monthly. Stock reordering and replenishment occurred weekly or more frequently for these items. For the 13 items in category B, ordering took place biweekly, and some emphasis was placed on negotiating price discounts through blanket order commitments. The 24 items in category C were ordered automatically. The items were counted and reordered on a preestablished basis every two or three months, as time permitted. In many cases, a trigger concept was employed to initiate the purchase of the items when needed.

Although the ABC approach is fairly simple, it is powerful and allows effective inventory management. In the hospital setting described, the ABC approach was used to tightly control category A items, which represented the highest percentage of cumulative annual usage.

Source: Richard Reid, "The ABC Method in Hospital Inventory Management: A Practical Approach," *Production and Inventory Management*, fourth quarter, 1987.

---

business in dollars. They might, however, comprise 70% of the items in inventory. In other words, there are a large number of inventory items that represent a small amount of business. Group C could include inexpensive items such as bolts, washers, screws, and so forth. They are not controlled using quantitative inventory techniques, for the cost of implementing and using these techniques would exceed the value gained. Although complex quantitative models are not applied, group C items must be checked and ordered. One approach is to use joint ordering.

Joint Ordering

Joint ordering is the process of ordering two or more different inventory items on the same purchase order from the same supplier. When an order is placed for an item in the A or B group, the items in the C group can be checked and ordered if their quantities are low. Furthermore, it may be

KEY IDEA

desirable to order some of the items in the A or B group even though they have not reached their reorder point.

As with other inventory strategies, joint ordering is done to lower total inventory cost. It can save a firm money by lowering ordering costs in several ways:

cost savings of joint ordering

1. It is much less expensive to add another inventory item to the same order than place a second order by itself.

2. There may be savings in transportation costs by shipping several items together.

3. Unloading and receiving costs may be less.

4. There may be inspection-related cost savings, especially if a company has a rigorous quality control system that monitors incoming parts.

Joint ordering can reduce total inventory cost, but how can it be carried out? When should items be joint ordered? How many units should be ordered using joint ordering?

Going back to the basics of inventory control, the only two decisions that can be made are when to order and how much to order. Since all of

ordering decisions

cost savings can be reflected in the annual ordering cost, the only quantity that is directly affected is order quantity. The reorder point, which answers the *when to order* question, is not a function of the ordering cost. Thus, joint ordering has a tendency to reduce the ordering cost, which changes the optimal order quantity. So we can actually have two optimal order quantities. Without joint ordering, we have the traditional order quantity. With joint ordering, we have the optimal order quantity for joint orders.

In a Chapter 8 example, we determined that the optimal order quantity for Sumco was 200 pump housings. The annual demand was 1,000 units, the ordering cost was $10 per order, and the carrying cost was $.50 per unit per year. The total inventory cost (ordering + carrying cost) was $100. With joint ordering, it is expected that the ordering cost will be reduced to $7.50. Sumco believes that it can joint order pump housings with other items and thus reduce total inventory cost. If these items are joint ordered, what will be the optimal order quantity? What is the total cost with joint ordering?

$$Q^* \text{ Joint ordering} = \sqrt{\frac{2(1,000)(7.5)}{.50}}$$
$$= \sqrt{30000}$$

$$Q^* \text{ Joint ordering} = 173 \text{ units}$$

$$\text{TC with joint ordering} = \frac{1,000}{173} \times 7.5 + \frac{173}{2} \times .5$$
$$= \$43.30 + \$43.30$$
$$= \$86.60$$

Joint ordering has reduced the optimal order quantity from 200 to 173 units ordered. Moreover, it has resulted in a reduction of the total inventory cost from $100 per year to $86.60 per year, which is over a 15% cost savings.

In this example, we assumed that Sumco's pump housings are joint ordered all of the time. The total cost was reduced, the order quantity was reduced, and the number of orders per year was increased to meet the same annual demand. In most cases, though, you will not be able to place joint orders all of the time. Thus, the cost savings will not be quite as great as those just described. It might also be desirable to modify the reorder point from time to time. Let's say that you have two different types of electric drills, $\frac{1}{4}$-inch standard drills and $\frac{1}{4}$-inch reversible drills. Let's further assume that you have to order the standard drills because you have reached the reorder point. For the reversible drill, you may be only a few drills away from the reorder point as well. You now have a choice. Do you place a joint order for the reversible drills even though you have not reached the reorder point and will therefore incur an increased carrying cost? Or should you wait a few days or weeks until you have reached the reorder point for reversible drills and place an order for them alone? If you place a joint order, you will save on ordering cost, but you will have a higher carrying cost because you will have to hold larger inventories for a longer period of time. Thus, you have the same type of trade-off between ordering cost and carrying cost. As usual, you should make the decision on a total cost basis.

joint order decision is based on total cost

9.7
DEPENDENT DEMAND: THE CASE FOR
MATERIAL REQUIREMENTS PLANNING (MRP)

In all of the inventory models we've discussed in Chapters 8 and 9, we assumed that the demand for one item was independent of the demand for other items. For example, the demand for refrigerators is usually independent of the demand for toaster ovens. Many inventory problems, however, are interrelated; the demand for one item is dependent on the demand for another item. Consider a manufacturer of small power lawn mowers. The demand for lawn mower wheels and spark plugs is dependent on the demand for lawn mowers. Four wheels and one spark plug are needed for each finished lawn mower. Usually when the demand for different items is dependent, the relationship between the items is known and constant. Thus, you should forecast the demand for the final products and compute the requirements for component parts.

KEY IDEA

As with the previously discussed inventory models, the major questions that must be answered are *how much to order* and *when to order*. But with dependent demand, inventory scheduling and planning can be very complex indeed. In these situations, *material requirements planning* (MRP) can be effectively employed. Some of the benefits of MRP are:

benefits of MRP

1. Increased customer service and satisfaction.

2. Reduced inventory costs.

3. Better inventory planning and scheduling.

4. Higher total sales.

Computerized Inventory Control at General Motors

In a recent report by the Business-Higher Education Forum, a strategy for American industry was outlined. One of the important aspects of the strategy was the notion of an industry-university partnership. Such a partnership was undertaken by General Motors, United Auto Workers personnel, and students and faculty at the University of Alabama. The overall purpose of this partnership was to attempt to develop cost savings techniques for a GM carburetor assembly plant. The carburetor assembly plant, located in Tuscaloosa, needed to cut costs by approximately $2 million annually or face being shut down. One joint project was to investigate the automated inventory analysis system at the Rochester Products Division. The inventory system consisted of about 8,000 end products, or items, and approximately 20,000 component parts used to make the end products. Like most classic inventory problems, the objective was to try to determine inventory stock levels in such a way that future demand could be satisfied while

eliminating excess inventory and reducing total costs.

Three overall components make up the computerized inventory system: a forecasting module, a parts explosion model that uses MRP, and an economic analysis module to look at various costing decisions. Total cost for inventory management consisted of carrying cost, procurement or ordering cost for future demand, the cost of delayed tax write-off, various tax savings on salvaged items, and any cost inflow from the salvaged items. The overall objective of the inventory analysis was to minimize total cost. The result was a one-time $420,000 cost savings plus an expected $135,000 per year additional savings.

Source: Adapted from Gary Mason, Joseph Mellichamp, David Miller, Thomas Gilligan, and Grady Cook, "A Joint Industry-Labor-University Cost Saving Venture," *Interfaces* Vol. 14, No. 6, November–December 1984, pp. 70–79.

---

5. Faster response to market changes and shifts.

6. Reduced inventory levels without reduced customer service.

Although most MRP systems are computerized, the analysis is straightforward and similar from one computerized system to the next. Here is the typical procedure.

The Material Structure Tree

material structure tree

Step one is to develop a material structure tree. Let's say that demand for product A is 50 units. Each unit of A requires 2 units of B and 3 units of C. Now, each unit of B requires 2 units of D and 3 units of E. Furthermore, each unit of C requires 1 unit of E and 2 units of F. Thus, the demand for B, C, D, E, and F is completely dependent on the demand for A. Given this information, a material structure tree can be developed for the related inventory items. See Figure 9.7.

The structure tree has three levels—0, 1, and 2. Items above any level are called *parents*, and items below any level are called *components*. There are three parents—A, B, and C. Each parent item has at least one level below it. Items B, C, D, E, and F are components because each item has at least one level above it. In this structure tree, B and C are both parents and components.

parents and components

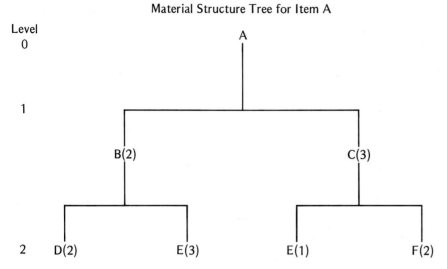

FIGURE 9.7
Material Structure Tree for Item A

Note that the number in the parentheses in Figure 9.7 indicates how many units of that particular item are needed to make the item immediately above it. Thus B(2) means that it takes 2 units of B for every unit of A, and F(2) means that it takes 2 units of F for every unit of C.

Once the material structure tree has been developed, the number of units of each item required to satisfy demand can be determined. This information can be displayed as follows:

determining gross requirements

$$
\begin{aligned}
\text{Part B:} & \quad 2 \times \text{number of As} = 2 \times \ 50 = 100 \\
\text{Part C:} & \quad 3 \times \text{number of As} = 3 \times \ 50 = 150 \\
\text{Part D:} & \quad 2 \times \text{number of Bs} = 2 \times 100 = 200 \\
\text{Part E:} & \quad 3 \times \text{number of Bs} + \\
& \quad 1 \times \text{number of Cs} = 3 \times 100 + \\
& \quad \qquad\qquad\qquad\quad 1 \times 150 = 450 \\
\text{Part F:} & \quad 2 \times \text{number of Cs} = 2 \times 150 = 300
\end{aligned}
$$

Thus, for 50 units of A we need 100 units of B, 150 units of C, 200 units of D, 450 units of E, and 300 units of F. Of course, the numbers in this table could have been determined directly from the material structure tree by multiplying the numbers along the branches times the demand for A, which is 50 units for this problem. For example, the number of units of D needed is simply $2 \times 2 \times 50 = 200$ units.

Gross and Net Material Requirements Plan

The next step is to construct a gross material requirements plan. This is a time schedule that shows when an item must be ordered from suppliers when there is no inventory on hand, or when the production of an item must be started in order to satisfy the demand for the finished product at

gross material requirements plan

a particular date. Let's assume that all of the items are produced or manufactured by the same company. It takes one week to make A; two weeks to make B; one week to make C; one week to make D; two weeks to make E; and three weeks to make F. With this information, the gross material requirements plan can be constructed to reveal the production schedule needed to satisfy the demand of 50 units of A at a future date. Refer to Figure 9.8.

The interpretation of the material in Figure 9.8 is as follows: If you want 50 units of A at week 6, you must start the manufacturing process in week 5. Thus, in week 5 you need 100 units of B and 150 units of C. These two items take 2 weeks and 1 week to produce. (See the lead times.) Production of B should be started in week 3, and C should be started in week 4. (See the order release for these items.) Working backwards, the same computations can be made for all the other items. The material requirements plan graphically reveals when each item should be started and completed in order to have 50 units of A at week 6. Now, a net requirement plan can be developed given the on-hand inventory in Table 9.7; here is how it is done.

Week

		1	2	3	4	5	6	
A	Required Date						50	Lead Time = 1 Week
	Order Release					50		
B	Required Date					100		Lead Time = 2 Weeks
	Order Release			100				
C	Required Date					150		Lead Time = 1 Week
	Order Release				150			
D	Required Date			200				Lead Time = 1 Week
	Order Release		200					
E	Required Date			300	150			Lead Time = 2 Weeks
	Order Release	300	150					
F	Required Date				300			Lead Time = 3 Weeks
	Order Release	300						

FIGURE 9.8
Gross Material Requirements Plan for 50 Units of A

TABLE 9.7 On-Hand Inventory

ITEM	ON-HAND INVENTORY
A	10
B	15
C	20
D	10
E	10
F	5

Using these data, we can develop a net material requirements plan that includes gross requirements, on-hand inventory, net requirements, planned-order receipts, and planned-order releases for each item. It is developed by beginning with A and working backwards through the other items. Figure 9.9 shows a net material requirements plan for product A.

net material requirements plan

The net requirements plan is constructed like the gross requirements plan. Starting with item A, we work backwards determining net requirements for all items. These computations are done by constantly referring to the structure tree and lead times. The gross requirements for A are 50 units in week 6. Ten items are on hand, and thus, the net requirements and planned-order receipt are both 40 items in week 6. Because of the one-week lead time, the planned-order release is 40 items in week 5. (See the arrow connecting the order receipt and order release.) Look down column 5 and refer to the structure tree in Figure 9.7. Eighty (2 × 40) items of B and 120 = 3 × 40 items of C are required in week 5 in order to have a total of 50 items of A in week 6. The letter A in the upper-right corner for items B and C means that this demand for B and C was generated as a result of the demand for the parent, A. Now the same type of analysis is done for B and C to determine the net requirements for D, E, and F.

Two or More End Products

So far, we have only considered one end product. For most manufacturing companies, there are normally two or more end products that use some of the same parts or components. All of the end products must be incorporated into a single net material requirements plan.

In the MRP example just discussed, we developed a net material requirements plan for product A. Now, we'll show how to modify the net material requirements plan when a second end product is introduced. The second end product will be called AA. The material structure tree for product AA is shown below:

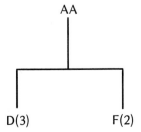

Item		Week 1	2	3	4	5	6	Lead Time
A	Gross						50	1
	On-Hand 10						10	
	Net						40	
	Order Receipt						40	
	Order Release					40		
B	Gross					80[A]		2
	On-Hand 15					15		
	Net					65		
	Order Receipt					65		
	Order Release			65				
C	Gross					120[A]		1
	On-Hand 20					20		
	Net					100		
	Order Receipt					100		
	Order Release				100			
D	Gross			130[B]				1
	On-Hand 10			10				
	Net			120				
	Order Receipt			120				
	Order Release		120					
E	Gross			195[B]	100[C]			2
	On-Hand 10			10	0			
	Net			185	100			
	Order Receipt			185	100			
	Order Release	185	100					
F	Gross				200[C]			3
	On-Hand 5				5			
	Net				195			
	Order Receipt				195			
	Order Release	195						

FIGURE 9.9
Net Material Requirements Plan

Let's assume that we need 10 units of AA. With this information, we can compute the gross requirements for AA:

Part D: $3 \times$ number of AAs $= 3 \times 10 = 30$

Part F: $2 \times$ number of AAs $= 2 \times 10 = 20$

In order to develop a net material requirements plan, we need to know the lead time for AA. Let's assume that it is one week. We also assume that we need 10 units of AA in week 6, and that we have no units of AA on hand. Now, we are in a position to modify the net material requirements plan for product A to include AA. This is done in Figure 9.10.

Look at the top row of Figure 9.10. As you can see, we have a gross requirement of 10 units of AA in week 6. Since we don't have any units of AA on hand, the net requirement is also 10 units of AA. Because it takes

Item	Inventory	Week 1	2	3	4	5	6	Lead Time
AA	Gross On-Hand: 0 Net Order Receipt Order Release					 10	10 0 10 10 	1 Week
A	Gross On Hand: 10 Net Order Receipt Order Release					 40	50 10 40 40 	1 Week
B	Gross On Hand: 15 Net Order Receipt Order Release			 65		80^A 15 65 65 		2 Weeks
C	Gross On Hand: 20 Net Order Receipt Order Release				 100	120^A 20 100 100 		1 Week
D	Gross On Hand: 10 Net Order Receipt Order Release		 120	130^B 10 120 120 	 30	30^{AA} 0 30 30 		1 Week
E	Gross On Hand: 10 Net Order Receipt Order Release	185	100	195^B 10 185 185 	100^C 0 100 100 			2 Weeks
F	Gross On Hand: 5 Net Order Receipt Order Release	195	20		200^C 5 195 195 	20^{AA} 0 20 20 		3 Weeks

FIGURE 9.10
Net Material Requirements Plan, Including AA

one week to make AA, the order release of 10 units of AA is in week 5. This means that we start making AA in week 5 and have the finished units in week 6.

Because we start making AA in week 5, we must have 30 units of D and 20 units of F in week 5. See the rows for D and F in Figure 9.10. The lead time for D is one week. Thus, we must give the order release in week 4 to have the finished units of D in week 5. Note that there was no inventory on hand for D in week 5. The original 10 units of inventory of D were used in week 5 to make B, which was subsequently used to make A. We also need to have 20 units of F in week 5 in order to produce 10 units of AA by week 6. Again, we have no on-hand inventory of F in week 5. The original 5 units were used in week 4 to make C, which was subsequently used to make A. The lead time for F is three weeks. Thus, the order release for 20 units of F must be in week 2. See the F row in Figure 9.10.

This example shows how the inventory requirements of two products can be reflected in the same net material requirements plan. Some manufacturing companies can have over 100 end products that must be coordinated in the same net material requirements plan. Although such a situation can be very complicated, the same principles we used in this example are employed. And remember that computer programs have been developed to handle large and complex manufacturing operations.

In addition to using MRP to handle end products and finished goods, MRP can also be used to handle spare parts and components. This is important because most manufacturing companies sell spare parts and components for maintenance. A net material requirements plan should also reflect these spare parts and components.

9.8
THE KANBAN SYSTEM

During the past decade, there has been a trend to make the manufacturing process more efficient. One objective is to have less in-process inventory on hand. This is known as *just-in-time* (JIT) inventory. With this approach, inventory arrives just in time to be used during the manufacturing process to product subparts, assemblies, or finished goods. One technique of implementing JIT is a manual procedure called *Kanban*. Kanban in Japanese means *card*. With a dual-card Kanban system, there is a conveyance Kanban, or C-Kanban, and a production Kanban, or P-Kanban. The Kanban system is very simple. Here is how it works.

Just-in-time (JIT) inventory

1. A user takes a container of parts or inventory along with its accompanying C-Kanban to his or her work area. When there are no more parts or the container is empty, the user returns the empty container along with the C-Kanban to the producer area.

2. At the producer area, there is a full container of parts along with a P-Kanban. The user detaches the P-Kanban from the full container of parts. Then, the user takes the full container of parts along with the original C-Kanban back to his or her area for immediate use.

APPLICATIONS OF QA

Using Just-in-Time (JIT) Principles to Improve Ecuador's Health Care Delivery System

The just-in-time control technique has helped reduce inventory levels and costs. The technique is especially appropriate when inventory systems are given a high priority, which was the situation in this case of the health care delivery in Ecuador.

Ecuador's medical supply system was experiencing poor planning and inadequate replenishment policies. The Ecuadorian Ministry of Public Health (MOH), along with several related organizations, considered several approaches to solving the problem of medical supply shortages. Like many other developing countries, Ecuador has a greater demand for health services than it can supply. In the past, the solution has been to develop highly visible facilities like hospitals. This approach, however, tends to centralize facilities and health care delivery, and the result is inferior health care delivery in rural or remote areas.

The medical delivery system is key to many health care systems. Unfortunately, the existing delivery system in Ecuador was inadequate and unable to meet health care demands for the most fundamental items (for example, aspirin, gauze, cotton, eye ointment, and cough syrup). To help

resolve the problem, six provinces representing diverse geographical areas were selected for study. Twenty-five percent of Ecuador's community health workers were within these provinces.

As a result of the study, procedures were initiated that allowed medical supplies to be received in one day in most cases. The major trade-off was between distance and number of supply sites. An algorithm was employed to minimize the number of facilities or sets of facilities needed to meet basic health supply needs. The new procedures called for community health workers to travel directly to the nearest MOH office and to personally place and receive orders for needed supplies. This approach mimics a JIT concept and has helped to improve the delivery of important medical supplies.

The implementation of the JIT concept in Ecuador helped provide an efficient, service-oriented health care delivery system.

Source: H. L. Smith, K. R. Mangelsdorf, J. C. Luna, and R. A. Reid, "Supplying Ecuador's Health Workers Just in Time," *Interfaces* Vol. 19, No. 3, May–June 1989, pp. 1–12.

3. The detached P-Kanban goes back into the producer area along with the empty container. The P-Kanban is a signal that new parts are to be manufactured or that new parts are to be placed into the container. When the container is filled, the P-Kanban is attached to the container.

4. This process repeats itself during the typical work day. The dual-card Kanban system is shown in Figure 9.11.

As seen in Figure 9.11, full containers along with their C-Kanban go from the storage area to a user area, typically on a manufacturing line. During the production process, parts in the container are used up. When the container is empty, the empty container along with the same C-Kanban goes back to the storage area. Here, the user picks up a new full container. The P-Kanban from the full container is removed and sent back to the production area along with the empty container to be refilled.

At a minimum, two containers are required using the Kanban system. One container is used at the user area, while another container is being refilled for future use. In reality, there are usually more than two containers. This is how inventory control is accomplished. Inventory managers can

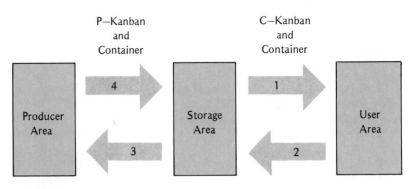

FIGURE 9.11
The Kanban System

introduce additional containers and their associated P-Kanbans into the system. In a likewise fashion, the inventory manager can remove containers and the P-Kanbans to have tighter control over inventory buildups.

controlling inventory costs and uncovering production bottlenecks

In addition to being a simple and easy to implement system, the Kanban system can also be very effective in controlling inventory costs and even in uncovering production bottlenecks. Inventory arrives at the user area or on the manufacturing line just when it is needed. Inventory does not build up unnecessarily, cluttering the production line or adding to unnecessary inventory expense. The Kanban system reduces inventory levels and makes for a more effective operation. It is like putting the production line on an inventory diet. Like any diet, the inventory diet imposed by the Kanban system makes the production operation more streamlined. Furthermore, production bottlenecks and problems can be uncovered. Many production managers remove containers and their associated P-Kanban from the Kanban system in order to starve the production line to uncover bottlenecks and potential problems.

Kanban rules

In implementing a Kanban system, a number of work rules or Kanban rules are normally implemented. One typical Kanban rule is that no containers are filled without the appropriate P-Kanban. Another rule is that each container must hold exactly the specified number of parts or inventory items. These and similar rules make the production process more efficient. Only those parts that are actually needed are produced. The production department does not produce inventory just to keep busy. It only produces inventory or parts when they are needed in the user area or on an actual manufacturing line.

9.9
USING THE COMPUTER TO SOLVE INVENTORY CONTROL PROBLEMS

Two software packages, AB:QM and STORM, will be highlighted in this chapter. AB:QM can solve most of the inventory problems presented in the chapter, and it is easy to use. STORM can also be used to solve many inventory control problems. In addition, STORM has a powerful program for MRP problems.

The Use of AB:QM in Inventory Control

Once the inventory models are selected from the Main Menu of AB:QM, an inventory submenu consisting of five separate programs is shown (Program 9.1): ABC analysis, EOQ, economic lot size, planned shortages, and quantity discounts.

The first inventory model we will demonstrate is basic economic order quantity (EOQ). For our example we entered an annual demand of 1,000 units, a lead time of 3 days, an ordering cost of $10 per order, and a holding cost of $.50 per unit per year. We also entered the number of business days per year as 365. The data input screen along with the output for this example are shown in Program 9.2.

The second problem we will investigate is the production run model, which is called the economic lot size model in AB:QM. For this example, annual demand is 10,000 units. The daily demand rate is 60 units per day, and the daily production rate is 80 units. The lead time for the problem is 3 days, the setup cost is $100 per setup, and the holding cost is $.50 per unit per year. With these data, we can solve the production run model. The input screen and the results from running the program are shown in Program 9.3.

AB:QM inventory models

economic order quantity model

production run model

PROGRAM 9.1 Inventory Submenu for AB:QM

```
───────────── Menu ─────────────

  A    ABC Analysis
  B    EOQ
  C    Economic Lot Size  (Production Run)
  D    Planned Shortage  (Back Order)
  E    Quantity Discount

Esc Back to Main Menu
```

PROGRAM 9.2 Basic EOQ Model Using AB:QM

```
Inventory Models / EOQ

  Problem Title :   Economic Order Quantity



    Annual demand    (units/year)               1000
    Business days    (days/year)                 365
    Lead time        (days)                        3
    Ordering cost    ($/order)                    10
    Holding cost     ($/unit/year)               .5









  Help   New   Load   Save   Edit   Run   Print   Install   Directory   Esc


***** Program Output *****

  Optimal order quantity    (units/order)   :   200.000
  Number of orders          (orders/year)   :     5.000
  Inventory cycle           (days)          :    73.000
  Maximum inventory level   (units)         :   200.000
  Average inventory level   (units)         :   100.000
  Reorder point             (units)         :     8.219
  Demand rate               (units/day)     :     2.740
  Total holding cost        ($/year)        :    50.000
  Total ordering cost       ($/year)        :    50.000
  Total inventory cost      ($/year)        :   100.000

  ***** End of Output *****
```

PROGRAM 9.3 The Production Run Model Using AB:QM

```
Inventory Models / Economic Lot Size

Problem Title :  Production Run Model



    Annual demand     (units/year)        10000
    Demand rate       (units/day)            60
    Lead time         (days)                  3
    Setup cost        ($/setup)             100
    Holding cost      ($/unit/year)          .5
    Production rate   (units/day)            80








  Help  New  Load  Save  Edit  Run  Print  Install  Directory  Esc


***** Program Output *****

Optimal order quantity    (units/order)    :    4000.000
Number of orders          (orders/year)    :       2.500
Production cycle          (days)           :      50.000
Maximum inventory level   (units)          :    1000.000
Average inventory level   (units)          :     500.000
Reorder point             (units)          :     180.000
Demand rate               (units/day)      :      60.000
Total holding cost        ($/year)         :     250.000
Total setup cost          ($/setup)        :     250.000
Total inventory cost      ($/year)         :     500.000

***** End of Output *****
```

quantity discount model   A quantity discount problem in AB:QM can handle up to 50 price breaks. We will demonstrate the program with the model discussed in this chapter: it uses three price breaks. For quantities ranging from 0 units to 999 units—the first price break—the price per unit is $5. The second price break ranges from 1,000 to 1,999 units; unit price for this quantity is $4.80. Finally, the third price break starts at 2,000 units and is unlimited on the upper end; the unit price for this model is $4.75. The data input screen and program output are shown in Program 9.4.

PROGRAM 9.4 Quantity Discount Model Using AB:QM

```
Inventory Models / Quantity Discount

Problem Title :  Quantity Discount
Method type(1:All/2:Increment)1
Number of price breaks        3

                                         Lower       Upper
                                         Quantity    Quantity Unit Price
Annual demand (units/year)     5000      XXX      XXXXXXXXXX XXXXXXXXXX
Business days (days/year)      365       XXX      XXXXXXXXXX XXXXXXXXXX
Lead time      (days)          3         XXX      XXXXXXXXXX XXXXXXXXXX
Ordering cost ($/order)        49        XXX      XXXXXXXXXX XXXXXXXXXX
Holding cost as a fraction     2         XXX      XXXXXXXXXX XXXXXXXXXX
Price break  1                                0         999           5
Price break  2                             1000        1999        4.80
Price break  3                             2000     1000000        4.75




Help  New  Load  Save  Edit  Run  Print  Install  Directory  Esc
```

PROGRAM 9.4 Continued

```
***** Program Output *****

ALL UNIT DISCOUNT


Optimal order price     :         4.800
Optimal order quantity  :      1000.000
Total inventory cost    :     24725.000
Reorder point           :        41.096

***** End of Output *****
```

The ABC analysis model in AB:QM will handle up to a maximum of 50   **ABC analysis**
items. For every item, we enter the total demand and unit price. The output
from the program includes the annual dollar volume, percentage of items,
and percentage of cost. Sample input data screen and program output are
shown in Program 9.5.

PROGRAM 9.5 ABC Analysis Using AB:QM

```
Inventory Models / ABC Analysis

Problem Title :  ABC Analysis Sample Problem

Number of Items            3


              Demand        Price
Item 1         7000          10
Item 2         2000          10
Item 3         1000          10









Help   New   Load   Save   Edit   Run   Print   Install   Directory   Esc
```

PROGRAM 9.5 Continued

```
Program: Inventory Models / ABC Analysis

Problem Title : ABC Analysis

***** Input Data *****


                    Demand          Price

Item 1              7000.00         10.00
Item 2              2000.00         10.00
Item 3              1000.00         10.00


***** Program Output *****

Item      Annual        Unit       Annual $     Percentage    Percentage
Number    demand        cost       volume       of items      of cost

  1       7000.000      10.000     70000.000     70.000        70.000
  2       2000.000      10.000     20000.000     90.000        90.000
  3       1000.000      10.000     10000.000    100.000       100.000

Total                              100000.000

***** End of Output *****
```

planned shortage model

The final AB:QM inventory program we will consider is the planned shortage model. This model requires values for the annual demand, the number of business days, lead time, ordering cost, holding cost, and stockout (or back order) cost. A sample input screen and output are shown in Program 9.6.

PROGRAM 9.6 Planned Shortage Model Using AB:QM

```
Inventory Models / Planned Shortage

Problem Title :  Planned Shortage Sample Problem


    Annual demand  (units/year)        10000
    Business days  (days/year)           365
    Lead time      (days)                  3
    Ordering cost  ($/order)             7.5
    Holding cost   ($/unit/year)           2
    Stockout cost  ($/unit/year)          10


    Help   New   Load   Save   Edit   Run   Print   Install   Directory   Esc
```

PROGRAM 9.6 Continued

```
***** Program Output *****

Optimal order quantity    (units/order)    :    300.000
Number of orders          (orders/year)    :     33.333
Inventory cycle           (days)           :     10.950
Maximum inventory level   (units)          :    250.000
Average inventory level   (units)          :    125.000
Reorder point             (units)          :     82.192
Demand rate               (units/day)      :     27.397
Total holding cost        ($/year)         :    208.333
Total ordering cost       ($/year)         :    250.000
Total inventory cost      ($/year)         :    500.000
Total shortage cost       ($/year)         :     41.667
Shortage backordered       (units)         :     50.000

***** End of Output *****
```

Use of STORM in Inventory Control

STORM programs for inventory management allow you to determine optimal order quantities and total inventory cost and to perform ABC and MRP analysis. The specific inventory functions supported by STORM include finding the standard economic order quantity as well as determination of order quantities for the production run model in which items are received or produced over time. STORM does not, however, have the ability to perform quantity discount analysis or to perform back order calculations. As with other STORM programs, the inventory control programs are menu driven. We will begin with a simple economic order quantity problem.

After you select inventory management from the main menu, STORM shows you an opening screen that allows you to read an existing data file or to create a new data set. The opening screen and other screens needed to perform the Sumco problem, which was discussed in Chapter 8, are shown in Program 9.7.

economic order quantity

```
                         INVENTORY MANAGEMENT : INPUT

                    ┌─────────────────────────────────────┐
                    │  1)   Read an existing data file     │
                    │  2)   Create a new data set          │
                    └─────────────────────────────────────┘

                    ┌─────────────────────────────────────┐
                    │       Select option    2             │
                    └─────────────────────────────────────┘
```

```
                      Press any key when ready
         ──── STORM EDITOR : Inventory Management Module ────

    Title : SUMCO
    Number of items           :          1 : Default order/setup cost :    10.
    Default carrying rate, %  :        10. : Time periods per year     :     1.
    Default service level, %  :    99.999 :
                                           :
```

```
    R1  : C2    DEMAND/PD UNIT VALUE ORDR/SETUP CARRY RATE  SIGMA(PD)  LEAD TIME
    ITEM   1      1000.         5.        .          .          0.         0.
```

```
                       INVENTORY MANAGEMENT : OUTPUT

            ┌────────────────────────────────────────────────────┐
            │  1)   Aggregate inventory values                   │
            │  2)   Working stock exchange table                 │
            │  3)   ABC classification of items                  │
            │  4)   Order quantity for all items                 │
            │  5)   Cost report for all items                    │
            │  6)   Projected inventory status for all items     │
            │  7)   Detailed report for selected items           │
            └────────────────────────────────────────────────────┘

                    ┌─────────────────────────────────────┐
                    │       Select option    4             │
                    └─────────────────────────────────────┘
```

```
                                 SUMCO
                          ORDERING INFORMATION
```

Item Name		Item ID	Orders / Setups	Order Size	Reorder Point	Max Orders Outstanding
ITEM	1	1	5.0	200	0	1

```
                                 SUMCO
                         ANNUAL COST INFORMATION
```

Item Name		Item ID	Order Cost	Working Stock Cost	Safety Stock Cost	Total Cost
ITEM	1	1	50.00	50.00	0.00	100.00

As you can see, we first selected number 2—create a new data set—from the main input menu. Once this is done, the STORM editor produces a screen that is used to enter the appropriate values. After entering the title SUMCO, we entered the other values. Because STORM does not have the ability to input carry cost in dollars per unit per year, it is necessary to enter the carrying cost rate as a percentage. As you can see, we entered 10%. We also entered a unit value of $5 to give us an equivalent carrying cost of $.50 per unit per year. Once the appropriate data have been entered, STORM produces the output menu, which gives us seven choices. We selected option 4 to display the order quantity for all items. The results are also shown in Program 9.7. As you can see, we obtained the same results we calculated in Chapter 8. The economic order quantity, or order size, is 200. The total cost is $100.

Another inventory problem that can be solved by STORM is the pro- **production run model** duction run model. As in the previous problem, we start from the STORM editor where we are asked to enter the problem title along with other important information. The problem title we entered was BROWN (for the Brown Manufacturing example that was discussed earlier in this chapter). See Program 9.8, screen *a*. The carrying rate as a percentage of the inventory price is 10%. In addition, the time periods per year are 167, which we chose to make the problem characteristics similar to the problem discussed earlier. On occasion, it is necessary to enter values in such a way to make the problem characteristics reflective of the true situation or problem at hand. Next, we are presented with another screen (*b*) where the production rate per day or per period is entered. As you can see, we entered 80.

Once the basic data have been entered, the user is given a variety of process options (*c*): edit the current data set, save the current data set, print the current data set, and execute the module with the current data set. We selected option 4, which executes the module with the current data set. As a result, the computer displayed the beginning ordering information, all cost factors, and the economic order quantity (*d*).

The final application of STORM for this chapter is material requirements planning (MRP). Unlike the other modules or programs, the MRP system **MRP** requires that five data files be created before the program is run. Sample screens from the MRP problem discussed in this chapter are shown in Program 9.9, *a* through *d*.

PROGRAM 9.8 Production Run Inventory Model Using STORM

(*a*)

```
──────────────── STORM EDITOR : Inventory Management Module ────────────────

   Title : BROWN
   Number of items               1 : Default order/setup cost    100.
   Default carrying rate, %     10. : Time periods per year       167.
   Default service level, %   99.999 :
```

(*b*)

```
   R1   : C10  CARRY RATE  SIGMA(PD)  LEAD TIME  SERV LEVEL  PACKAGING   PRODN/PD
   ITEM    1         .        0.         0.          .           1        80.
```

(*c*)

```
                     INVENTORY MANAGEMENT : PROCESS

           1)   Edit the current data set
           2)   Save the current data set
           3)   Print the current data set
           4)   Execute the module with the current data set

                     Select option    4
```

(*d*)

```
                            BROWN
                     ORDERING INFORMATION
   Item          Item   Orders /   Order    Reorder  Max Orders
   Name           ID     Setups     Size     Point   Outstanding
   ITEM    1       1       2.5       4004       0         1

                            BROWN
                     ANNUAL COST INFORMATION
   Item          Item    Order    Working    Safety      Total
   Name           ID     Cost   Stock Cost  Stock Cost    Cost
   ITEM    1       1     250.25    250.25      0.00      500.50
```

PROGRAM 9.9 STORM's MRP Program

(*a*) Main Storm MRP Screen

```
              MATERIAL REQUIREMENTS PLANNING : FILE SELECTION

          1)    Execute the module (if all files ready)
          2)    Bill of Material file
          3)    Master Schedule file
          4)    Inventory Status file
          5)    Item Master file
          6)    Resource Capacity file
          7)    Create new data files from BOM file

                      Select option    2
```

(*b*) On-hand: Inventory for all items, from Figure 9.9

```
──────────── STORM EDITOR : Inventory Status File — MRP Module ────────────

  Title : INVENTORY STATUS FILE
  Total number of material items                     :    6
  Maximal lead time in time buckets                  :    3
  Maximal number of periods for firm planned orders  :    6
  Annual carrying charge rate, per cent              :    0.
```

R1 : C1	ITEM ID	SAFE STOCK	ON HAND	PAST DUE	RECEIPT 1	RECEIPT 2
ITEM 1	1	0	10	0	0	0
ITEM 2	2	0	15	0	0	0
ITEM 3	3	0	20	0	0	0
ITEM 4	4	0	10	0	0	0
ITEM 5	5	0	10	0	0	0
ITEM 6	6	0	5	0	0	0

PROGRAM 9.9 Continued

(c) Storm's Main Output Menu

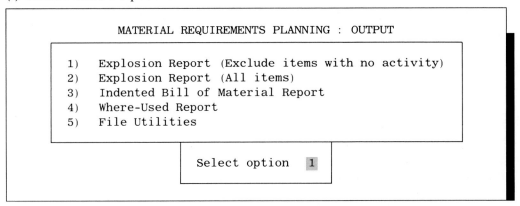

(d) This output table corresponds to Item A in Figure 9.9.

```
                      MASTER SCHEDULE FILE
                      EXPLOSION REPORT
    Planning     Gross    Sched'd   Projected   – Planned Orders –
    Period       Reqts    Receipts   On hand    Lot for Lot   Lot sized

    ITEM   1        1              Level 0    LT = 1     Lot size LFL
    Annual demand = 0             Scrap %  = 0.00
    Order/Setup Cost = 0.00       Total order/setup cost = 0.00
    Unit Value = 0.00             Total carrying cost    = 0.00
    Safety stock = 0
```

	GR	SR	OH	LFL	PO
PAST DUE	0		10		
PERIOD 1	0	0	10	0	0
PERIOD 2	0	0	10	0	0
PERIOD 3	0	0	10	0	0
PERIOD 4	0	0	10	0	0
PERIOD 5	0	0	10	40	40
PERIOD 6	50	0	0	0	0

9.10
SUMMARY

You have been exposed to a number of different inventory control techniques in Chapters 8 and 9. We saw that there are many factors to consider: there may be quantity discounts, back orders may be allowed, inventory may not arrive in one large batch, or a firm may decide to employ the safety stock concept. There is also the possibility of joint ordering. In addition, demand may follow a complex probability distribution instead of being constant. In some cases, demand is *dependent* and a technique such as material requirements planning (MRP) is needed. The Kanban system can be used to make inventory control more efficient. Although it is beyond the scope of this book to develop one model to handle all of these factors, even the most sophisticated inventory model would make the same types of decisions we made. That is, the two major questions that all inventory models attempt to answer are *how much to order* and *when to order* in such a way that the total inventory cost is at a minimum. Knowing this makes it much easier to understand inventory models in general.

GLOSSARY

Instantaneous Inventory Receipt. A system in which inventory is received or obtained at one point in time and not over a period of time.

Production Run Model. An inventory model in which inventory is produced or manufactured instead of being ordered or purchased. This model eliminates the instantaneous receipt assumption.

Annual Setup Cost. The cost to set up the manufacturing or production process for the production run model.

Quantity Discount. The cost per unit when large orders of an inventory item are placed.

Planned Shortages. A situation where stockouts are planned.

Back Ordering Cost per Unit per Year (C_b). The cost of placing back orders for items that are not in stock.

Safety Stock. Extra inventory that is used to help avoid stockouts.

Stockout. A situation that occurs when there is no inventory on hand.

Safety Stock with Known Stockout Costs. An inventory model in which the probability of demand during lead time and the stockout cost per unit are known.

Safety Stock with Unknown Stockout Costs. An inventory model in which the probability of demand during lead time is known. The stockout cost is not known.

Service Level. The chance expressed as a percent, that there will not be a stockout. Service level = 1 − probability of a stockout.

ABC Analysis. An analysis that divides inventory into three groups. Group A is more important than group B, which is more important than group C.

Joint Ordering. Ordering two or more inventory items on the same order from the same supplier.

Material Requirements Planning. An inventory model that can handle dependent demand.

Just-in-Time (JIT) Inventory. An approach whereby inventory arrives just in time to be used in the manufacturing process.

Kanban. A manual JIT system developed by the Japanese. Kanban means *card* in Japanese.

KEY EQUATIONS

(9-4) $\quad Q^* = \sqrt{\dfrac{2DC_o}{C_h \left(1 - \dfrac{d}{p}\right)}}$

Order quantity when inventory is received over time.

(9-5) $Q_p^* = \sqrt{\dfrac{2DC_s}{C_h\left(1 - \dfrac{d}{p}\right)}}$

Optimal production quantity.

(9-6) $TC = DC + \dfrac{D}{Q}C_o + \dfrac{Q}{2}C_h$

Total inventory cost with quantity discounts.

(9-7) $TC = \dfrac{D}{Q}C_o + \dfrac{(Q - S)^2}{2Q}C_h + \dfrac{S^2}{2Q}C_b$

Total inventory cost with planned shortages.

(9-8) $Q^* = \sqrt{\dfrac{2DC_o}{C_h}\left(\dfrac{C_h + C_b}{C_b}\right)}$

Order quantity with planned shortages.

(9-9) $S^* = Q^*\left(\dfrac{C_h}{C_h + C_b}\right)$

Amount back ordered.

(9-10) $ROP = d \times L + SS$

Reorder point with safety stock.

(9-11) $SS = Z\sigma$

Safety stock using the normal curve.

SOLVED PROBLEMS

Solved Problem 9-1

Flemming Accessories produces paper slicers used in offices and in art stores. The minislicer has been one of its most popular items: annual demand is 6,750 units. Kristen Flemming, owner of the firm, produces the minislicers in batches. On average, Kristen can manufacture 125 minislicers per day. Demand for these slicers during the production process is 30 per day. The setup cost for the equipment necessary to produce the minislicers is $150. Carrying costs are $1 per minislicer per year. How many minislicers should Kristen manufacturer in each batch?

Solution

The data for Flemming Accessories is summarized as follows:

$$D = 6{,}750 \text{ units}$$
$$C_s = \$150$$
$$C_h = \$1$$

$$d = 30 \text{ units}$$
$$p = 125 \text{ units}$$

This particular problem is a production run problem that involves a daily production rate and a daily demand rate. The appropriate calculations are shown here:

$$Q^* = \sqrt{\frac{2DC_s}{C_h(1 - d/p)}}$$

$$Q^* = \sqrt{\frac{(2)(6,750)(150)}{1(1 - 30/125)}}$$

$$= 1,632$$

Solved Problem 9-2

Dorsey Distributors has an annual demand for a metal detector of 1,400. The cost of a typical detector to Dorsey is $400. Carrying cost is estimated to be 20% of the unit cost, and ordering cost is $25 per order. If Dorsey orders in quantities of 300 or more, it can get a 5% discount on the cost of the detectors. Should Dorsey take the quantity discount?

Solution

The solution to any quantity discount model involves determining the total cost of each alternative after order quantities have been computed and adjusted for the original problem and every discount. We will start the analysis with no discount:

$$\text{EOQ(no discount)} = \sqrt{\frac{(2)(1,400)(25)}{(.2)(400)}}$$

$$= 29.6 \text{ units}$$

Total cost(no discount) = Material cost + Ordering cost + Carrying cost
$$= (\$400)(1,400) + (1,400)(25)/(29.6) + (29.6)(\$400)(.2)/2$$
$$= \$560,000 + \$1,182 + \$1,182 = \$562,400$$

The next step is to compute total cost for the discount:

$$\text{EOQ(with discount)} = \sqrt{\frac{(2)(1,400)(25)}{(.2)(\$380)}}$$

$$= 30.3 \text{ units}$$

$$\text{EOQ(Adjusted)} = 300 \text{ units}$$

Because this last economic order quantity is below the discounted price, we must adjust the order quantity to 300 units. The next step is to compute total cost.

Total cost(with discount) = Material cost + Ordering cost + Carrying cost
$$= (\$380)(1,400) + (1,400)(25)/(300) + (300)(\$400)(.2)/2$$
$$= \$532,000 + \$117 + \$12,000 = \$544,117$$

The optimal strategy is to order 300 units at a total cost of $544,117.

Solved Problem 9-3

Mary Berger realizes that it is simply impossible to keep a supply of all types of fabric and sewing materials in her fabric store. The annual demand for one type of fabric Mary occasionally stocks is 4,000. The ordering cost is $40 per order, and the carrying cost is $3 per bundle of fabric per year. Further, Mary estimates that the total cost of using a back ordering policy is $100 per unit per year. If she uses the back ordering policy, how many bundles or units of this particular fabric should Mary order at one time? How many bundles of the fabric will be back ordered?

Solution

Berger's situation is a back ordering economic order quantity problem. The data for this problem are summarized as follows:

$$D = 4,000 \text{ units}$$
$$C_o = \$40$$
$$C_h = \$3$$
$$C_b = \$100$$

For Mary to solve this problem, she must use the appropriate back ordering equations for the economic order quantity and the number of bundles that will be back ordered. The calculations shown indicate that the optimal number of bundles to order at one time is 331 and that the number of bundles that will be back ordered is 9.65.

$$Q^* = \sqrt{\frac{2DC_o}{C_h}\left(\frac{C_h + C_b}{C_b}\right)}$$

$$= \sqrt{\frac{(2)\,(4,000)\,(40)}{3}\left(\frac{3 + 100}{100}\right)}$$

$$= 331 \text{ units}$$

$$S^* = Q^*\left(\frac{C_h}{C_h + C_b}\right)$$

$$= 331\left(\frac{3}{3 + 100}\right)$$

$$= 9.65 \text{ units per back order}$$

DISCUSSION QUESTIONS AND PROBLEMS

Discussion Questions

9-1 What assumptions are made in the production run model?

9-2 What happens to the production run model when the daily production rate becomes very large?

9-3 In the quantity discount model, why is the carrying cost expressed as a percentage of the unit cost, I, instead of the cost per unit per year, C_h?

9-4 Briefly describe what is involved in solving a quantity discount model.

9-5 What assumptions are made in the planned shortages model?

9-6 Discuss the methods that are used in determining safety stock when the stockout cost is known and when the stockout cost is unknown.

9-7 Briefly describe what is meant by joint ordering and ABC analysis. What is the purpose of these inventory techniques?

PROBLEMS

· **9-8** Jan Gentry is the owner of a small company that produces electric scissors used to cut fabric. The annual demand is for 8,000 scissors, and Jan produces the scissors in batches. On the average, Jan can produce 150 scissors per day, and during the production process, demand for scissors has been about 40 scissors per day. The cost to set up the production process is $100, and it costs Jan 30¢ to carry one pair of scissors for one year. How many scissors should Jan produce in each batch?

· **9-9** Jim Overstreet, inventory control manager for Itex, receives wheel bearings from Wheel-Rite, a small producer of metal parts. Unfortunately, Wheel-Rite can only produce 500 wheel bearings per day. Itex receives 10,000 wheel bearings from Wheel-Rite each year. Since Itex operates 200 working days each year, the average daily demand of wheel bearings by Itex is 50. The ordering cost for Itex is $40 per order, and the carrying cost is 60¢ per wheel bearing per year. How many wheel bearings should Itex order from Wheel-Rite at one time? Wheel-Rite has agreed to ship the maximum number of wheel bearings that it produces each day to Itex once an order has been received.

: **9-10** North Manufacturing has a demand for 1,000 pumps each year. The cost of a pump is $50. It costs North Manufacturing $40 to place an order, and the carrying cost is 25% of the unit cost. If pumps are ordered in quantities of 200, North Manufacturing can get a 3% discount on the cost of the pumps. Should North Manufacturing order 200 pumps at a time and take the 3% discount?

· **9-11** Although Mary Henry never wants to be out of stock, it is simply impossible for her to keep a supply of every kitchen appliance from every manufacturer. Mary has an annual demand for Good Point, a popular range, of approximately 3,000 units. The ordering cost is $25, and the carrying cost is $4 per unit per year. Because Good Point is such a popular range, when customers ask for this range and Mary is out of stock, the customers always place a back order. Although Mary doesn't like disappointing customers, she knows that she will not lose sales when she doesn't have any Good Point ranges in stock. Mary estimates that the total cost of back ordering is $75 per unit per year. How many Good Point ranges should Mary order at one time? How many ranges will be back ordered?

: **9-12** Mr. Beautiful, an organization that sells weight training sets, has an ordering cost of $40 for the BB-1 set. (BB-1 stands for Body Beautiful Number 1.) The carrying cost for BB-1 is $5 per set per year. In order to meet demand, Mr. Beautiful orders large quantities of BB-1 seven times a year. The stockout cost for BB-1 is estimated to be $50 per set. Over the last several years, Mr. Beautiful has observed the following demand during the lead time for BB-1.

DEMAND DURING LEAD TIME	PROBABILITY
40	.1
50	.2
60	.2
70	.2
80	.2
90	.1

The reorder point for BB-1 is 60 units. What level of safety stock should be maintained for BB-1?

: **9-13** Linda Lechner is in charge of maintaining hospital supplies at General Hospital. During the past year, the mean lead time demand for bandage BX-5 was 60. Furthermore, the standard deviation for BX-5 was 7. Ms. Lechner would like to maintain a 90% service level. What safety stock level do you recommend for BX-5?

: **9-14** Ralph Janaro simply does not have time to analyze all of the items in his company's inventory. As a young manager, he has more important things to do. Below is a table of six items in inventory along with the unit cost and the demand in units.

IDENTIFICATION CODE	UNIT COST	DEMAND IN UNITS
XX1	$ 5.84	1,200
B66	$ 5.40	1,110
3CPO	$ 1.12	896
33CP	$74.54	1,104
R2D2	$ 2.00	1,110
RMS	$ 2.08	961

Which item(s) should be carefully controlled using a quantitative inventory technique, and what item(s) should not be closely controlled?

: **9-15** In the past, George Wright always placed orders for wooden spice racks separately. The annual demand for spice racks is 3,000 units. The ordering cost is $35 per order, and the carrying cost is $1 per unit per year. George is now ordering several other products from the same supplier. If George orders the spice racks along with other products from the same supplier, he will be able to reduce the ordering cost to $25 per order.

(a) What is the order quantity without joint ordering?
(b) What is the order quantity with joint ordering?
(c) What is the cost savings of using joint ordering?

: **9-16** Dick Vidamann cannot believe the number of health food products available on the market. Dick's store, Do It Natural, is known for stocking many healthful food products. Dick's customers are also very loyal, and if Dick doesn't have a particular health food product, they will place an order and be content to wait until a new shipment arrives. Vitayum is not one of Dick's most popular food supplements, but Dick does order Vitayum on a regular basis. The annual demand for Vitayum is 500 bottles. The ordering cost is

(a) How many bottles of Vitayum should Dick order if he doesn't allow back ordering?

(b) How many bottles of Vitayum should he order with back ordering?

(c) If the lead time is 10 days and the daily demand is 3 bottles per day, what is the reorder point when back ordering is allowed?

(d) What is the amount back ordered?

: 9-17 The demand for barbeque grills has been fairly large in the past several years, and Home Supplies, Inc., usually orders new barbeque grills five times a year. It is estimated that the ordering cost is $60 per order. The carrying cost is $10 per grill per year. Furthermore, Home Supplies, Inc., has estimated that the stockout cost is $50 per unit. The reorder point is 650 units. Although the demand each year is high, it varies considerably. The demand during the lead time appears in the following table.

DEMAND DURING LEAD TIME	PROBABILITY
600	.3
650	.2
700	.1
750	.1
800	.05
850	.05
900	.05
950	.05
1000	.05
1050	.03
1100	.02
	1.00

The lead time is 12 working days. How much safety stock should Home Supplies, Inc., maintain?

: 9-18 Dillard Travey receives 5,000 tripods annually from Quality Suppliers to meet his annual demand. Dillard runs a large photographic outlet, and the tripods are used primarily with 35-mm cameras. The ordering cost is $15 per order, and the carrying cost is 50¢ per unit per year. Quality is starting a new option for its customers. When an order is placed, Quality will ship one-third of the order every week for three weeks instead of shipping the entire order at one time. Weekly demand over the lead time is 100 tripods.

(a) What is the order quantity if Dillard has the entire order shipped at one time?

(b) What is the order quantity if Dillard has the order shipped over three weeks using the new option from Quality Suppliers, Inc.?

(c) Calculate the total cost for each option. What do you recommend?

: 9-19 Linda Lechner has just been severely chastised for her inventory policy. See Problem 9-13. Sue Surowski, her boss, believes that the service level should be either 95% or 98%. Compute the safety stock levels for a 95% and a 98% service level. Linda knows that the carrying cost of BX-5 is 50¢ per unit per year. Compute the carrying cost that is associated with a 90%, 95%, and a 98% service level.

: 9-20 Quality Suppliers, Inc., has decided to extend its shipping option. Refer to Problem 9-18 for details. Now, Quality Suppliers is offering to ship the amount ordered in five equal shipments once each week. It will take five weeks for this entire order to be received. What is the order quantity and total cost for this new shipping option?

: 9-21 Xemex has collected the following inventory data for the six items that it stocks:

ITEM CODE	UNIT COST ($)	ANNUAL DEMAND IN UNITS	ORDERING COST ($)	CARRYING COST AS A PERCENTAGE OF UNIT COST (%)
1	10.60	600	40	20
2	11.00	450	30	25
3	2.25	500	50	15
4	150.00	560	40	15
5	4.00	540	35	16
6	4.10	490	40	17

Lynn Robinson, Xemex's inventory manager, does not feel that all of the items can be controlled.

What order quantities do you recommend for which inventory product(s)?

: 9-22 The demand for Rocky Flier football dolls is 10,000 dolls per year. The ordering cost is $20 per order, and the carrying cost is $2 per doll per year.

(a) Compute the order quantity.

(b) Compute the order quantity when back ordering is allowed and the back ordering cost is $40 per doll per year.

(c) Compute the order quantity when back ordering is allowed and the back ordering cost is $100 per doll per year.

(d) Compute the order quantity when back ordering is allowed and the back ordering cost is $500 per doll per year.

(e) Compute the order quantity when back ordering is allowed and the back ordering cost is $1,000 per doll per year.

(f) What happens to the order quantity as the back ordering cost increases?

(g) What assumptions are made with the back ordering model?

: 9-23 Georgia Products offers the following discount schedule for its four-by-eight-foot sheets of quality plywood:

ORDER	UNIT COST ($)
9 sheets or less	18.00
10 to 50 sheets	17.50
More than 50 sheets	17.25

Home Sweet Home Company orders plywood from Georgia Products. Home Sweet Home has an ordering cost of $45. The carrying cost is 20%, and the annual demand is 100 sheets. What do you recommend?

: **9-24** The demand for product S is 100 units. Each unit of S requires 1 unit of T and $\frac{1}{2}$ unit of U. Each unit of T requires 1 unit of V, 2 units of W, and 1 unit of X. Finally, each unit of U requires $\frac{1}{2}$ unit of Y and 3 units of Z. All items are manufactured by the same firm. It takes two weeks to make S; one week to make T; two weeks to make U; two weeks to make V; three weeks to make W; one week to make X; two weeks to make Y; and one week to make Z.

(a) Construct a material structure tree and a gross material requirements plan for the dependent inventory items.

(b) Identify all levels, parents, and components.

(c) Construct a net material requirements plan from the data and the following on-hand inventory:

ITEM	ON-HAND INVENTORY
S	20
T	20
U	10
V	30
W	30
X	25
Y	15
Z	10

: **9-25** Sunbright Citrus Products produces orange juice, grapefruit juice, and other citrus-related items. Sunbright obtains fruit concentrate from a cooperative in Orlando consisting of approximately 50 citrus growers. The cooperative will sell a minimum of 100 cans of fruit concentrate to citrus processors, such as Sunbright. The cost per can is $9.90.

Last year, a cooperative developed the Incentive Bonus Program (IBP) to give an incentive to their large customers to buy in quantity. Here is how the incentive bonus program works. If 200 cans of concentrate are purchased, 10 cans of free concentrate are included in the deal. In addition, the names of the companies purchasing the concentrate are added to a drawing for a new personal computer. The personal computer has a value of about $3,000, and currently there are about 1,000 companies that are eligible for this drawing. At 300 cans of concentrate, the cooperative will give away 30 free cans and will also place the company name in the drawing for the personal computer. When the quantity goes up to 400 cans of concentrate, 40 cans of concentrate will be given away free with the order. In addition, the company is also placed in a drawing for the personal computer and a free trip for two. The value of the trip for two is approximately $5,000. About 800 companies are expected to qualify and to be in the running for this trip. If the order quantity is 500 cans or greater, the cooperative will offer 50 cans of free concentrate. In addition, the company will be placed in a drawing for the computer, the trip, and a new car. The car has an estimated value of $10,000, and it is estimated that there are approximately 600 companies that will qualify to be in this particular drawing.

Sunbright estimates that its annual demand for fruit concentrate is 1,000 cans. In addition, the ordering cost is estimated to be $10.00, while the carrying cost is estimated to be 10%. The purchasing manager, Larry Giunipero, is intrigued with the incentive bonus system. He would sure like a new car. Unfortunately, Larry doesn't know if the company will let him keep the new car if he gets it. If Sunbright lets Larry keep the car, the trip, or the computer if he wins it, what should Larry do? If the company decides that it will keep the car, the trip, or the computer if they are won, would this change Larry's decision? What should Larry do?

9-26 Conradi Pest Control is in the business of producing quality pesticides for commercial applications. Conradi is known for the free red hats that it gives out with Conradi's slogan on it, "Something bugging you—get Conradi Pest Control." Conradi develops the "bug be gone" formula and sells it in 5-gallon containers. These 5-gallon containers contain secret ingredients developed by the chemical engineers of Conradi Pest Control, in addition to 2 quarts of chemicals obtained from an outside supplier. Normally, Conradi sells 2,000 gallons of its pest control products every year. Billy Conradi, the fourth generation of Conradis to run the company, is very cost conscious. His great grandfather developed a successful company by watching his pennies, and the young Conradi is inclined to do the same. He estimates administrative costs to be approximately $1.00 per gallon of pesticide. Furthermore, overhead and advertising allocations are estimated to be $.50 and $.30 per gallon, respectively.

Sue Simon orders most of the products, including the 2 quarts that are needed from the outside company to produce the 5-gallon containers of pesticide. Ten dollars is allocated for Sue's work as a clerk for placing routine orders. If a special order is required because Conradi runs out of pesticides, a $15.00 charge is allocated. Furthermore, spoilage is estimated to be $1.00 per quart and shelving costs are estimated to be $1.50 per quart. Because of the outstanding job that "bug be gone" does, the younger Conradi knows that if he is temporarily out of stock, customers will come back another day to pick up their orders. Conradi keeps an adequate supply of the in-house chemicals to produce the pesticide. How many orders of the 2-quart material required from the outside supplier should Conradi make every year?

9-27 George Grim used to be an accounting professor at a state university. Several years ago, he started to develop seminars and programs for the CPA review course. The CPA review course is a course to help accounting students and others interested in passing the CPA exam. In order to develop an effective seminar, George developed a number of books and other related materials to help. The main product was the CPA review manual developed by George. The manual was an instant success for his seminars and other seminars and courses across the country. Today, George spends most of his time refining and distributing this CPA review manual. The price of the manual is $45.95. George's total cost to manufacture and produce the manual is $32.90.

George wants to avoid stockouts or to develop a stockout policy that would be cost-effective. If there is a stockout on the CPA review manual, George loses the profit from the sale of the manual.

George has determined from past experience that the reorder point from his printer is 400 units, assuming no safety stock. The question that George must answer is how much safety stock he should have as a buffer. On the average, George places one order per year for the CPA review manual. The frequency of demand for the CPA review manuals during lead time is given below:

DEMAND	FREQUENCY
300	1
350	2
400	2
450	3
500	4
550	5
600	4
650	4
700	3
750	2
800	2

George estimates that his carrying cost per unit per year is $7. What level of safety stock should George carry to minimize total inventory costs?

Data Set Problem

9-28 Rob Roller has been in charge of inventory policy at Cyclorama, a large retail bicycle shop in Orlando, Florida. He now orders Chrome-Moly frames from Frameco, a local frame supplier. Cyclorama builds each bike by adding different Shamino component groups to each frame. Currently, Cyclorama's annual demand for frames is 2,000 per year. The lead time is ten days, and the ordering cost per order is $50. Holding cost is estimated to be 25% of unit cost. Frameco offers the following discounts:

PRICE BREAK	LOWER QUANTITY UNITS	UPPER QUANTITY UNITS	UNIT PRICE ($)
1	0	10	220.00
2	11	20	219.99
3	21	30	219.98
4	31	40	219.97
5	41	50	219.96
6	51	60	219.95
7	61	70	219.94
8	71	80	219.93
9	81	90	219.92
10	91	100	219.91
11	101	110	219.90
12	111	120	219.89
13	121	130	219.88
14	131	140	219.87
15	141		219.86

(a) What is the optimal order quantity and the total inventory cost for Cyclorama given the data?
(b) Rob is optimistic about future demand. If annual demand becomes 3,000 frames, what is the impact on the optimal order quantity?
(c) What is the impact if annual demand is 4,000 frames?
(d) In general, what happens to the order quantity, total inventory cost, and inventory cost per unit as demand increases?

Professional Video Management

Ever since the introduction of the first home video systems for television, Steve Goodman has dreamed about manufacturing his own video system for professionals. During the early years of home video, Steve watched a lot of his favorite old movies on his home video and planned the eventual development of his own video system. He intended it to be used primarily by television stations, advertising agencies, and other individuals and groups that wanted the best in video systems. The overall configuration of this system is shown in the illustration.

The basic system includes a comprehensive control box, two separate video tape systems, a video disk, and a professional-quality television set. All these devices are fully integrated. In addition, the basic system comes with an elaborate remote control device. This device can operate both video systems, the video disk, and the TV system with ease. The remote control device works by sending in-

frared signals to the control box, which in turn controls the other devices in the system.

Steve's unique contribution to video systems is the control box. The control box is an advanced microprocessor with the ability to coordinate the use and function of the other devices attached to it.

Steve's professional video system has numerous advantages over similar systems. To begin with, special effects can be introduced easily. Images from the video disk, one of the video systems, and the television system can easily be placed on the other video system. In addition, it is possible to connect the control box to several popular microcomputers, including the MacIntosh, the IBM Personal System/2, the Radio Shack Model 2000, and advanced Atari and Coleco computer systems. This makes it possible to develop attractive graphics on the microcomputer and to transfer them directly to the video system. It is also possible to hook a

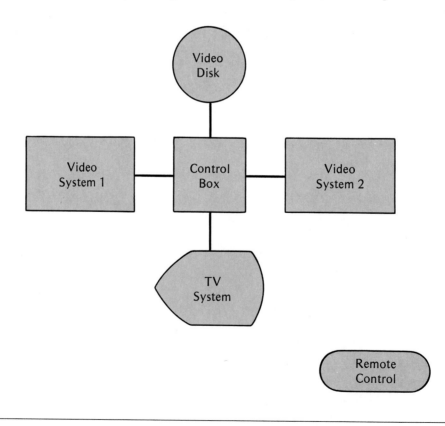

stereo system to the control box to integrate the highest quality stereo sound into the system and record it on one of the video systems.

The two video systems also offer remarkable flexibility in editing. Several special editing buttons were placed on the remote control station. It is possible to first record a program on one video system and then to edit it by using the other video tape system to add and delete sections.

One of the best features of Steve's professional video system is the price. The basic system, including the control box, both video systems, the video disk, and the television system, has a retail price of $1,995.

Steve found manufacturers for the television system, the control box, and the video disk system in the United States. Because video tape systems are more popular, Steve had more choices. After extensive research, he was able to eliminate all of the potential suppliers but two. Both of these suppliers are Japanese companies. Toshiki is a new company located outside of Tokyo, Japan. Like other suppliers, Toshiki offers quantity discounts. For quantities ranging from 0 to 2,000 units, Toshiki would charge Steve a price of $250 per video system. For quantities that ranged between 2,000 and 8,000 units, the per unit cost would be $230. For quantities ranging from 8,000 to 20,000 units, the unit price drops to $220. For more than 20,000 units, the per unit price of the video systems would be only $210.

The other Japanese supplier is Kony. Although Kony originally started in Japan, also outside of Tokyo, it now has offices and manufacturing facilities around the world. One of these manufacturing facilities is located less than 100 miles north of Atlanta, Georgia. Like Toshiki, Kony offers quantity discounts for its video tape systems. For quantities ranging from 0 to 1,000, Kony's per unit cost is $250. For quantities that range from 1,000 to 5,000 units, the unit cost is $240; and for over 5,000 units, the unit cost drops to $220.

Because Kony has manufacturing facilities located in the United States, the cost to place an order and the delivery time are much more favorable than they are with Toshiki. The estimated per order cost from Kony is $40, and the expected delivery time is two weeks. On the other hand, the ordering cost is higher and delivery time is longer for Toshiki. The additional paper work and problems associated with ordering directly from Japan would increase Steve's cost to $90 per order. Furthermore, the delivery time for Toshiki is three months. Steve estimates that his carrying cost would be 30%. This is due primarily to storage and handling cost as well as the potential for technological obsolescence.

For the first year or so of operations, Steve decided to sell only the basic unit: the control box, the television set, the video disk, and the two video tape systems. The demand for the complete system was fairly constant during the past six months. For example, June sales were 7,970; July sales were 8,070; August sales were 7,950; and September sales were 8,010. This demand pattern is expected to continue for the next several months.

Discussion Questions:

1. What are the reorder points for Kony and Toshiki?

2. If you were Steve, which company would you choose to supply the video tape systems for your professional video system?

3. Steve is considering several alternative strategies. The first would be to sell all of the components separately. The second strategy would be to modify the control box to allow other video tape systems to be used as well as the video tape systems supplied by Steve. In general, what impact would the adoption of these strategies have on the reorder point and inventory control for Steve?

CASE STUDY

Touro Infirmary

Touro Infirmary is a medium-sized teaching hospital located in New Orleans. The department of dietetics must meet varying needs for feeding of patients, staff, and visitors. The nutritional requirements of the patients are diverse, which necessitates a complex menu structure. Diet options include sodium-restricted, bland, calorie-restricted, and numerous other regimes.

The bed capacity for the institution is 500; approximately 1,500 meals are needed daily for patients. Since Touro has a large number of Jewish patients, a unique demand is the frequent serving of kosher food. Kosher food must be prepared and served in accordance with strict religious rules. For example, the food must be blessed by a rabbi and prepared with equipment that is used exclusively for kosher products. Additionally, there are restrictions placed upon the food combinations that can be offered in a kosher meal and certain types of meats and fishes may not be served.

Approximately 1,825 kosher meals are served to Touro patients over a one-year period. The number per day appears to follow a Poisson distribution. Because the hospital cannot prepare these meals in its kitchens, all kosher meals are ordered from Schreiber Foods in New York, and are shipped by air mail. The cost per dinner is $3.50. If more than 150 dinners are ordered at once, the price is reduced to $3.25 per dinner. The order is placed by telephone and shipment can be expected to be received in three working days. The cost of placing an order is $10. It is estimated that carrying costs are 25% of the meal cost; the many additional requirements of religious laws, including special silverware, are part of the reason for this high cost.

A problem arises when a patient orders a kosher meal and the hospital has run out of stock. An alternative source is available in New Orleans but at a premium of $10. Another unusual problem is storage. A separate freezer must be used to store the kosher food. The present freezer has a capacity of 75 dinners. Patton Industries offers a commercial freezer that has a capacity of 225 dinners. The cost of the freezer is $1,800 and it has a useful life of ten years.

The head of the dietary department, Mrs. Kathy Fedorko, has requested an inventory analysis to determine a method for inventory control that will minimize costs.

Discussion Questions

1. What is the optimal amount to be ordered and how often? At what point should the hospital reorder?

2. Besides quantitative methods to determine proper inventory control, what other considerations should be taken into account? Is there an alternative method that will minimize costs?

3. Should the hospital purchase the larger freezer?

Source; Barry Render, and others, *Cases and Readings in Management Science,* 2nd edition, Boston: Allyn and Bacon, Inc., 1990.

BIBLIOGRAPHY

In addition to references at the end of Chapter 8, see:

Clifton, R. G. "JIT: Fad or Future Fact?" *Industrial Distribution* Vol. 78, June 1989, p. 60.

Dowst, S. "Beware the Seven Deadly Sins of Just-in-Time." *Purchasing* Vol. 106, March 23, 1989, pp. 127+.

LaForge, R. L., and McNichols, C. W. "An Integrative, Experiential Approach to Production Management Education." *Decision Sciences* Vol. 20, Winter 1989, pp. 198–207.

Mandel, M. J., and others. "Are Inventories Really Under Control?" *Business Week* July 31, 1989, p. 71.

McClelland, M. K., and Wagner, H. M. "Location of Inventories in an MRP Environment." *Decision Sciences* Vol. 19, Summer 1988, pp. 858–879.

Muller, E. J. "Harley's Got the Handle on Inbound." *Distribution* Vol. 88, March 1989, pp. 70+.

Mullins, P. J. "B-Line to Efficiency." *Automotive Industries* Vol. 169, May 1989, pp. 68–69.

Penlesky, R. J., and others. "Open Order Due Date Maintainance in MRP Systems." *Management Science* Vol. 35, May 1989, pp. 571–584.

Raturi, A. S., and Hill, A. V. "An Experimental Analysis of Capacity-Sensitive Setup Parameters for MRP Lot Sizing." *Decision Sciences* Vol. 19, Fall 1988, pp. 782–800.

Stokes, C. R. "JIT: Will Suppliers Embrace Their New Roles?" *Business* Vol. 39, April–June 1989, pp. 37–43.

Tatikonda, L. U., and Tatikonda, R. J. "What Are the Critical

Success Factors of MRP?" *Management Accounting* Vol. 70, May 1989, p. 34.

Teresko, J. "Decentralization Yields Solutions." *Industry Week* Vol. 238, March 20, 1989, pp. 51–53.

Vollmann, T. E., Berry, W. L., and Whybark, D. C. *Manufacturing Planning and Control Systems*. Homewood, Ill.: Irwin, Inc., 1988.

Wacker, J. G., "Effective Planning and Cost Control for Restaurants: Making Resource Requirements Planning Work." *Production and Inventory Management* First Quarter 1985, pp. 55–69.

Wallace, T. V., ed. *APICS Dictionary*. 5th edition, 1986.

Appendix: Solving the Planned Shortages (Back Order) Model with Calculus

To solve for the optimal values of Q (order quantity) and S (units back ordered), we take partial derivatives of the total cost function with respect to each of the two variables, Q and S. Each partial derivative is set equal to 0, and the two resulting equations are solved simultaneously. The total cost, from Equation 9–7, was seen to be:

$$TC = \frac{D}{Q}C_o + \frac{(Q - S)^2}{2Q}C_h + \frac{S^2}{2Q}C_b \tag{1}$$

This can be rewritten as:

$$TC = \frac{D}{Q}C_o + \frac{Q^2 - 2QS + S^2}{2Q}C_h + \frac{S^2}{2Q}C_b \tag{2}$$

$$= \frac{D}{Q}C_o + \frac{Q}{2}C_h - SC_h + \frac{S^2}{2Q}(C_h + C_b)$$

The partial derivative with respect to Q is:

$$\frac{\partial TC}{\partial Q} = -\frac{D}{Q^2}C_o + \frac{C_h}{2} - \frac{S^2(C_h + C_b)}{2Q^2} = 0 \tag{3}$$

The partial derivative with respect to S is:

$$\frac{\partial TC}{\partial S} = \frac{C_h + C_b}{Q}S - C_h = 0 \tag{4}$$

Equation 4 can be solved for S:

$$S = Q\left[\frac{C_h}{C_h + C_b}\right] \tag{5}$$

Substituting this value for S into Equation 3 and solving for Q^* yields:

$$Q^* = \sqrt{\frac{2DC_o}{C_h}\left(\frac{C_h + C_b}{C_b}\right)} \tag{6}$$

10

Linear Programming: Graphical Methods

10.1
INTRODUCTION

linear programming
defined

Many management decisions involve trying to make the most effective use of an organization's resources. Resources typically include machinery, labor, money, time, warehouse space, or raw materials. These resources may be used to produce products (such as machinery, furniture, food, or clothing) or services (such as schedules for shipping and production, advertising policies, or investment decisions). *Linear programming* (LP) is a widely used mathematical technique designed to help managers in planning and decision making relative to resource allocation. We shall devote this and the next three chapters to illustrating how and why linear programming works.

Despite its name, linear programming, and the more general category of techniques called *"mathematical" programming*, has very little to do with computer programming. In the world of quantitative analysis, programming refers to modeling and solving a problem mathematically. Computer programming has, however, played an important role in the advancement and use of LP. Many real-life LP problems are too cumbersome to solve by hand or even with a calculator. In Chapter 12, we give examples of how valuable a computer program can be in solving a linear programming problem.

10.2
REQUIREMENTS OF A LINEAR PROGRAMMING PROBLEM

properties of LP
problems

LP has been applied extensively in the past 30 years to military, industrial, financial, marketing, accounting, and agricultural problems. Even though these applications are diverse, all LP problems have four properties in common.

1. First, all problems seek to *maximize* or *minimize* some quantity, usually profit or cost. We refer to this property as the *objective function* of an LP problem. The major objective of a typical manufacturer is to maximize dollar profits. In the case of a trucking or railroad distribution system, the objective might be to minimize shipping costs. In any event, this objective must be clearly stated and mathematically defined. It does not matter, by the way, whether profits or costs are measured in cents, dollars, or millions of dollars.

2. The second property that LP problems have in common is the presence of restrictions, or *constraints*, that limit the degree to which we can pursue our objective. For example, deciding how many units of each product in a firm's product line to manufacture is restricted by available personnel and machinery. Selection of an advertising policy or a financial portfolio is limited by the amount of money available to be spent or invested. We want, therefore, to maximize or minimize a quantity (the objective function) subject to limited resources (the constraints).

3. Third, there must be alternative courses of action to choose from. For example, if a company produces three different products, management may use LP to decide how to allocate among them its limited production resources (of personnel, machinery, and so on). Should it devote all manufacturing capacity to make only the first product; should it produce equal amounts of each product; or should it allocate the resources in some other ratio? If there were no alternatives to select from, we would not need LP.

4. Finally, the objective and constraints in linear programming problems must be expressed in terms of *linear* equations or inequalities. Linear mathematical relationships just mean that all terms used in the objective function and constraints are of the first degree (that is, not squared, or to the third or higher power, or appearing more than once). Hence, the equation $2A + 5B = 10$ *is* an acceptable linear function. But an equation of the sort $2A^2 + 5B^3 + 3AB = 10$ is *not* linear because the variable A is squared, the variable B is cubed, and the two variables appear again as a product of each other.

You will see the term *inequality* quite often when we discuss linear programming problems. By inequalities we mean that not all LP constraints need be of the form $A + B = C$. This particular relationship, called *an equation*, implies that the term A plus the term B are together exactly equal to the term C. In most LP problems, we see inequalities of the form $A + B \leq C$ or $A + B \geq C$. The first of these means that A plus B is less than or equal to C. The second means that A plus B is greater than or equal to C. This concept provides a lot of flexibility in defining problem limitations.

inequality

Basic Assumptions of LP

Technically, there are five additional requirements of an LP problem that you should be aware of:

1. We assume that conditions of *certainty* exist; that is, numbers in the objective and constraints are known with certainty and do not change during the period being studied.

certainty

2. We also assume that *proportionality* exists in the objective and constraints. This means that if production of 1 unit of a product uses 3 hours of a particular scarce resource, then making 10 units of that product uses 30 hours of the resource.

proportionality

3. The third technical assumption deals with *additivity*, meaning that the total of all activities equals the sum of each individual activity. For example, if an objective is to maximize profit = $8 per unit of first product made plus $3 per unit of second product made, and if one unit of each product is actually produced, then the profit contributions of $8 and $3 must add up to produce a sum of $11.

additivity

HISTORY

How Linear Programming Started

Linear programming was conceptually developed before World War II by the outstanding Soviet mathematician, A. N. Kolmogorov. An early application of linear programming, by Stigler in 1945, was in the area we today call "diet problems."

The major advances in the field, however, took place in 1947 and later when George D. Dantzig developed the solution procedure known as the simplex algorithm. Dantzig, then an Air Force mathematician, was assigned to work on logistics problems. He noticed that many problems involving limited resources and more than one demand could be set up in terms of a series of equations and inequalities. Although early LP applications were military in nature, industrial applications rapidly became apparent with the spread of business computers. In 1984, N. Karmarkar developed an algorithm which appears to be superior to the simplex method for many very large applications.

---

divisibility

4. We make the *divisibility* assumption that solutions need not be in whole numbers (integers). Instead, they are divisible and may take any fractional value. If a fraction of a product cannot be produced (like one-third of a submarine), an *integer programming problem* exists. Integer programming is discussed in more detail in Chapter 15.

nonnegativity

5. Finally, we assume that all answers or variables are *nonnegative*. Negative values of physical quantities are an impossible situation: you simply cannot produce a negative number of chairs, shirts, lamps, or computers.

10.3
FORMULATING LINEAR PROGRAMMING PROBLEMS

product mix problem

One of the most common linear programming applications is the *product mix problem*. Two or more products are usually produced using limited resources such as personnel, machines, raw materials, and so forth. The profit that the firm seeks to maximize is based on the profit contribution per unit of each product. (Profit contribution, you may recall, is just the selling price per unit minus the variable cost per unit.) The company would like to determine how many units of each product it should produce so as to maximize overall profit given its limited resources.

The Flair Furniture Company

The Flair Furniture Company produces inexpensive tables and chairs. The production process for each is similar in that both require a certain number of hours of carpentry work and a certain number of labor hours in the painting and varnishing department. Each table takes 4 hours of carpentry and 2 hours in the painting and varnishing shop. Each chair requires 3 hours in carpentry and 1 hour in painting and varnishing. During the current production period, 240 hours of carpentry time are available and

100 hours in painting and varnishing time are available. Each table sold yields a profit of $7; each chair produced is sold for a $5 profit.

Flair Furniture's problem is to determine the best possible combination of tables and chairs to manufacture in order to reach the maximum profit. The firm would like this production mix situation formulated as a linear programming problem.

We begin by summarizing the information needed to formulate and solve this problem (see Table 10.1). Further, let us introduce some simple notation for use in the objective function and constraints:

$$X_1 = \text{number of tables to be produced}$$

$$X_2 = \text{number of chairs to be produced}$$

Table 10.1 Flair Furniture Company Problem Data

	HOURS REQUIRED TO PRODUCE 1 UNIT		AVAILABLE HOURS
DEPARTMENT	(X_1) TABLES	(X_2) CHAIRS	THIS WEEK
Carpentry	4	3	240
Painting and varnishing	2	1	100
Profit per unit	$7	$5	

Now we can create the LP objective function in terms of X_1 and X_2. The objective function is:

$$\text{Maximize profit} = \$7X_1 + \$5X_2$$

objective of the problem

Our next step is to develop mathematical relationships to describe the two constraints in this problem. One general relationship is that the amount of a resource *used* is to be less than or equal to ($\leq$) the amount of resource *available*.

In the case of the carpentry department, the total time used is:

(4 hours per table)(Number of tables produced)

+ (3 hours per chair)(Number of chairs produced)

So the first constraint may be stated as follows: Carpentry time used is $\leq$ carpentry time available.

resource constraints

$$4X_1 + 3X_2 \leq 240 \text{ (hours of carpentry time)}$$

Similarly, the second constraint is: Painting and varnishing time used is $\leq$ painting and varnishing time available.

② $X_1 + 1X_2 \leq 100$ *(hours of painting and varnishing time)*

(This means that each table produced takes two hours of the painting and varnishing resource.)

Both of these constraints represent production capacity restrictions and, of course, affect the total profit. For example, Flair Furniture cannot produce 70 tables during the production period because if $X_1 = 70$, both constraints will be violated. It also cannot make $X_1 = 50$ tables and $X_2 = 10$ chairs.

Why? Because this would violate the second constraint that no more than 100 hours of painting and varnishing time be allocated. Hence, we note one more important aspect of linear programming; that is, certain interactions will exist between variables. The more units of one product that a firm produces, the less it can make of other products. How this concept of interaction affects the optimal solution is seen as we now tackle the graphical solution approach.

10.4
GRAPHICAL SOLUTION TO A LINEAR PROGRAMMING PROBLEM

graphical method

The easiest way to solve a small LP problem such as that of the Flair Furniture Company is with the graphical solution approach. The graphical procedure is useful only when there are two decision variables (such as number of tables to produce, X_1, and number of chairs to produce, X_2) in the problem. When there are more than two variables, it is *not* possible to plot the solution on a two-dimensional graph and we must turn to more complex approaches—the topic of Chapter 11. But the graphical method is invaluable in providing us with insights into how other approaches work. For that reason alone, it is worthwhile to spend the rest of this chapter exploring graphical solutions as an intuitive basis for the chapters on mathematical programming that follow.

Graphical Representation of Constraints

In order to find the optimal solution to a linear programming problem, we must first identify a set, or region, of feasible solutions. The first step in doing so is to plot each of the problem's constraints on a graph.

The variable X_1 (tables, in our example) is usually plotted as the horizontal axis of the graph and the variable X_2 (chairs) is plotted as the vertical axis. In order to obtain meaningful solutions, the values for X_1 and X_2 must be nonnegative numbers. That is, all potential solutions must represent real tables and real chairs. Mathematically, this means that:

nonnegativity constraints

$$X_1 \geq 0 \quad \textit{(number of tables produced is greater than or equal to 0)}$$

$$X_2 \geq 0 \quad \textit{(number of chairs produced is greater than or equal to 0)}$$

Adding these *nonnegativity constraints* means that we are always working in the first (or northeast) quadrant of a graph. See Figure 10.1.

The complete problem may now be restated mathematically as:

mathematical statement of the LP problem

$$\text{Maximize profit} = \$7X_1 + \$5X_2$$

subject to the constraints:

$$4X_1 + 3X_2 \leq 240 \quad \textit{(carpentry constraint)}$$

$$2X_1 + 1X_2 \leq 100 \quad \textit{(painting and varnishing constraint)}$$

$$X_1 \geq 0 \quad \textit{(first nonnegativity constraint)}$$

$$X_2 \geq 0 \quad \textit{(second nonnegativity constraint)}$$

APPLICATIONS OF QA

Linear Programming at New England Apple Products

Clothing fashions change every year. And so do food habits. As we shop our supermarket, new products are found and old ones disappear. A decade ago, for example, fruit juices were drunk mostly at breakfast time or when one was sick. Now we drink them anytime. One consequence is that juice companies have created new blends to meet demand.

New England Apple Products, the manufacturer of the *Very Fine* beverage line, now has sixteen different juice beverages, ranging from apple-

cherry to cranapple to grapefruit. There are a large number of combinations of fruit juice possibilities, but New England Apple only has limited supplies of each as ingredients. The firm uses linear programming to decide which combinations to market and how much of each to make. The bottom line question is: "What product mix will yield the best profit?" Although there are many listed ingredients on the side of a bottle of fruit juice blend, LP is one *hidden* ingredient.

To represent the first constraint graphically, $4X_1 + 3X_2 \leq 240$, we convert the inequality into an equality, more commonly called an equation, as follows:

$$4X_1 + 3X_2 = 240$$

As you may recall from elementary algebra, a linear equation in two variables is a straight line. The easiest way to plot the line is to find any two points that satisfy the equation, then draw the straight line through them. The two easiest points to find are generally the points at which the line intersects the X_1 and X_2 axes.

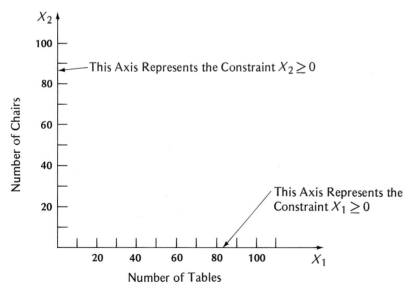

FIGURE 10.1
Quadrant Containing All Positive Values

**plotting the first
constraint**

When Flair Furniture produces no tables, namely $X_1 = 0$, it implies that:

$$4(0) + 3X_2 = 240$$

or

$$3X_2 = 240$$

or

$$X_2 = 80$$

In other words, if *all* of the carpentry time available is used to produce chairs, then 80 chairs *could* be made. Thus, this constraint equation crosses the vertical axis at 80.

To find the point at which the line crosses the horizontal axis, we assume the firm makes no chairs, that is, $X_2 = 0$. Then,

$$4X_1 + 3(0) = 240$$

or

$$4X_1 = 240$$

or

$$X_1 = 60$$

Hence, when $X_2 = 0$, we see that $4X_1 = 240$, and that $X_1 = 60$.

The carpentry constraint is illustrated in Figure 10.2. It is bounded by the line running from point $A(X_1 = 0, X_2 = 80)$ to point $B(X_1 = 60, X_2 = 0)$.

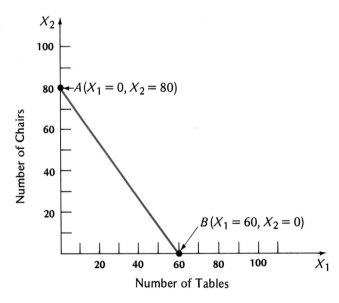

FIGURE 10.2
Graph of Carpentry Constraint Equation $4X_1 + 3X_2 = 240$

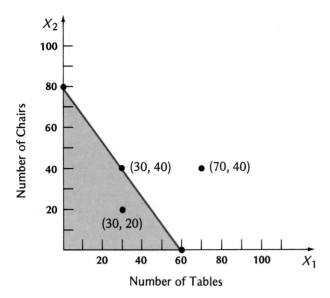

FIGURE 10.3
Region That Satisfies the Carpentry Constraint

Recall, however, that the actual carpentry constraint was the *inequality* $4X_1 + 3X_2 \leq 240$. How can we identify all of the solution points that satisfy this constraint? It turns out that there are three possibilities. First, we know that any point that lies *on* the line $4X_1 + 3X_2 = 240$ satisfies the constraint. Any combination of tables and chairs on the line will use up all 240 hours of carpentry time.[1] We see this by picking a point such as $X_1 = 30$ tables and $X_2 = 40$ chairs (see Figure 10.3). You should be able to see how exactly 240 hours of the carpentry resource are used.

The real question is, where are the problem points satisfying $4X_1 + 3X_2 < 240$? We can answer this question by checking two possible solution points, let's say ($X_1 = 30$, $X_2 = 20$) and ($X_1 = 70$, $X_2 = 40$). You see in Figure 10.3 that the first point is below the constraint line and that the second point lies above it. Let us examine the first solution more carefully. If we substitute the (X_1, X_2) values into the carpentry constraint, the result is:

$$4(X_1 = 30) + 3(X_2 = 20) = 4(30) + 3(20) = 120 + 60 = 180$$

Since 180 is less than the 240 hours available, the point (30, 20) satisfies the constraint. For the second solution point, we follow the same procedure.

$$4(X_1 = 70) + 3(X_2 = 40) = 4(70) + 3(40) = 280 + 120 = 400$$

Four hundred exceeds the carpentry time available and hence violates the constraint. So we now know that the point (70, 40) is an unacceptable production level. As a matter of fact, any point *above* the constraint line violates that restriction. (This is something you may wish to test for yourself

graphical representation of an inequality

---
[1] Thus, what we have done is to plot the constraint equation in its most binding position, that is, using all of the carpentry resource.

plotting the second constraint

with a few other points.) And any points *below* the line do not violate the constraint. In Figure 10.3 the shaded region represents all points that satisfy the original inequality constraint.

Next, let us identify the solution corresponding to the second constraint, which limits the time available in the painting and varnishing department. That constraint was given as $2X_1 + 1X_2 \le 100$. As before, we start by changing the inequality to an equation:

$$2X_1 + 1X_2 = 100$$

Line *CD* in Figure 10.4 represents all combinations of tables and chairs that use exactly 100 hours of painting and varnishing department time. It is constructed in a fashion similar to the first constraint. When $X_1 = 0$, then,

$$2(0) + 1X_2 = 100$$

or

$$X_2 = 100$$

When $X_2 = 0$, then,

$$2X_1 + 1(0) = 100$$

or

$$2X_1 = 100$$

or

$$X_1 = 50$$

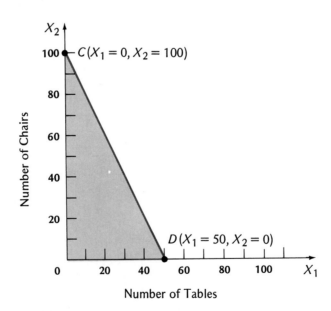

FIGURE 10.4
Region That Satisfies the Painting and Varnishing Constraint

The constraint is bounded by the line between $C(X_1 = 0, X_2 = 100)$ to $D(X_1 = 50, X_2 = 0)$ and the shaded area again contains all possible combinations that do not exceed 100 hours. Thus, the shaded area represents the original inequality $2X_1 + 1X_2 \leq 100$.

Now that each individual constraint has been plotted on a graph, it is time to move on to the next step. We recognize that in order to produce a chair or a table both the carpentry and painting and varnishing departments must be used. In an LP problem we need to find that set of solution points that satisfies *all* of the constraints *simultaneously*. Hence, the constraints should be redrawn on one graph (or superimposed one upon the other). This is shown in Figure 10.5.

satisfying both inequalities

The shaded region now represents the area of solutions that does not exceed either of the two Flair Furniture constraints. It is known by the term *area of feasible solutions* or, more simply, the *feasible region*. The feasible region in a linear programming problem must satisfy *all* conditions specified by the problem's constraints, and is thus the region where all constraints overlap. Any point in the region would be a *feasible solution* to the Flair Furniture problem; any point outside the shaded area would represent an *infeasible solution*. Hence, it would be feasible to manufacture 30 tables and 20 chairs ($X_1 = 30$, $X_2 = 20$) during a production period because both constraints are observed.

feasible region

Carpentry constraint	$4X_1 + 3X_2 \leq 240$ hours available
	$4(30) + 3(20) = 180$ hours used $\checkmark$
Painting constraint	$2X_1 + 1X_2 \leq 100$ hours available
	$2(30) + 1(20) = 80$ hours used $\checkmark$

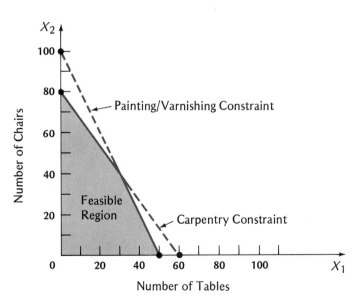

FIGURE 10.5
**Feasible Solution Region for the Flair Furniture
Company Problem**

APPLICATIONS OF QA

Selecting Tenants in a Shopping Mall

Homart Development Company is one of the largest commercial land developers in the United States. The firm currently owns or is developing 31 regional shopping centers and 18 major office buildings and is involved in land development of properties that total over 1,000 acres.

Homart's shopping center development business involves identifying opportunities for development, conducting feasibility analyses, obtaining the necessary governmental approvals, overseeing design and construction, leasing, and then managing the properties as long-term investments. Regional shopping centers contain approximately 1 million square feet of selling area and represent investments of $60 million and more. Profits from shopping center development are a major component of Homart's total profits.

In developing a new center, Homart's first step is to evaluate feasibility considering factors such as marketing demographics, building costs, and expected revenues. Next, Homart produces a tentative floor plan, or footprint, for the mall, which outlines sizes, shapes, and spaces for large department stores. Leasing agreements are reached with the two or three major department stores that will act as anchor stores for the mall. The anchor stores largely determine the character of the center and provide the visibility needed to attract customers. These stores are able to negotiate highly favorable occupancy agreements; typically they either pay low rent or receive other concessions. Homart's profits are made primarily from the rent paid by the nonanchor tenants—the smaller stores that lease space along the aisles of the mall. Since the durations of the original lease agreements are typically 5 to 15 years, the initial decisions allocating space to potential tenants and establishing the tenant mix are crucial to the success of the investment.

Source: J. Bean, and others, *Interfaces* Vol. 18, No. 2, March–April 1988, pp. 1–9.

The tenant mix describes the desired stores in the mall by their size, general location, and type of merchandise or service provided. For example, the tenant mix might specify two small jewelry stores in a central section of the mall and a medium-sized shoe store and a large restaurant in one of the side aisles. In the past, Homart developed a plan for tenant mix using rules of thumb developed over years of experience in mall development. The leasing agents would use this plan as a basis for negotiation with potential tenants.

Now Homart treats the tenant-mix problem, including interaction effects, as a type of *linear program* model. First, the model assumes that tenants can be classified into categories according to the type of merchandise or service they provide. Second, it assumes that for each store type, store sizes can be made into distinct categories. For example, a small jewelry store is said to contain about 700 square feet and a large one about 2,200 square feet. To provide a third descriptor of potential tenants, the mall is divided into areas according to differences in the value of the space. A central walkway between two major stores sees more traffic than does a side aisle leading to the parking lot. For this reason, the walkway's tenants can expect more sales, and space there commands higher rent than space along the side aisle.

The tenant mix model is a powerful tool for enhancing Homart's mall planning and leasing activities. Determining and implementing the ideal mall mix obviously consists of more than calculating the mathematically optimal allocation of space among store categories. It entails building a mix in which each tenant provides a unique service or product. The model is not intended to substitute for decision making in the field or at the executive level of Homart. Rather, it is a tool for generating and updating merchandise plans throughout the leasing process and for establishing financial standards against which the performance of shopping centers can be measured.

But it would violate both of the constraints to produce 70 tables and 40 chairs, as we see here mathematically:

Carpentry constraint $4X_1 + 3X_2 \leq 240$ hours available
$4(70) + 3(40) = 400$ hours used $\otimes$

Painting constraint $2X_1 + 1X_2 \leqslant 100$ hours available
                          $2(70) + 1(40) = 180$ hours used $\otimes$

Furthermore, it would also be infeasible to manufacture 50 tables and 5 chairs ($X_1 = 50$, $X_2 = 5$). Can you see why?

Carpentry constraint $4X_1 + 3X_2 \leqslant 240$ hours available
                          $4(50) + 3(5) = 215$ hours used $\oslash$

Painting constraint $2X_1 + 1X_2 \leqslant 100$ hours available
                          $2(50) + 1(5) = 105$ hours used $\otimes$

This possible solution falls within the time available in carpentry but exceeds the time available in painting and varnishing and thus falls outside the feasible region.

Iso-Profit Line Solution Method

Now that the feasible region has been graphed, we may proceed to find the optimal solution to the problem. The optimal solution is the point lying in the feasible region that produces the highest profit. Yet there are many, many possible solution points in the region. How do we go about selecting the best one, the one yielding the highest profit?

There are a few different approaches that can be taken in solving for the optimal solution once the feasible region has been established graphically. The speediest one to apply is called the *iso-profit line method*.

iso-profit method

We start the technique by letting profits equal some arbitrary, but small, dollar amount. For the Flair Furniture problem we may choose a profit of $210. This is a profit level that can easily be obtained without violating either of the two constraints. The objective function can be written as $210 = 7X_1 + 5X_2$.

This expression is just the equation of a line; we call it an *iso-profit line*. It represents all combinations of (X_1, X_2) that would yield a total profit of $210. To plot the profit line, we proceed exactly as we did to plot a constraint line. First, let $X_1 = 0$ and solve for the point at which the line crosses the X_2 axis.

$$\$210 = \$7(0) + \$5X_2$$

$$X_2 = 42 \text{ chairs}$$

Then, let $X_2 = 0$ and solve for X_1.

$$\$210 = \$7X_1 + \$5(0)$$

$$X_1 = 30 \text{ tables}$$

We can now connect these two points with a straight line. This profit line is illustrated in Figure 10.6. All points on the line represent feasible solutions that produce a profit of $210.[2]

Now, obviously, the iso-profit line for $210 does not produce the highest possible profit to the firm. In Figure 10.7, we try graphing two more lines,

graphing parallel profit lines

[2] *Iso* means equal or similar. Thus an iso-profit line represents a line with all profits the same, in this case $210.

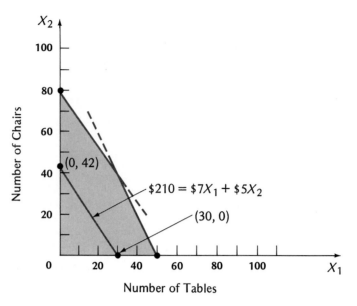

FIGURE 10.6
A Profit Line of \$210 Plotted for the Flair Furniture Company

each yielding a higher profit. The middle equation, $\$280 = \$7X_1 + \$5X_2$, was plotted in the same fashion as the lower line. When $X_1 = 0$,

$$\$280 = \$7(0) + \$5X_2$$

$$X_2 = 56$$

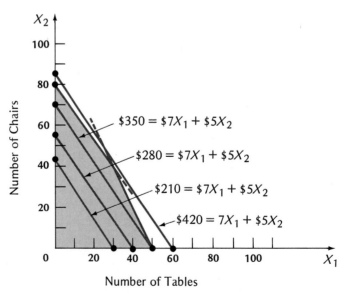

FIGURE 10.7
Four Iso-Profit Lines Plotted for the Flair Furniture Company

When $X_2 = 0$,

$$\$280 = \$7X_1 + \$5(0)$$

$$X_1 = 40$$

Again, any combination of tables (X_1) and chairs (X_2) on this iso-profit line produces a total profit of $280.

Note that the third line generates a profit of $350, even more of an improvement. The further we move from the 0 origin, the higher our profit will be. Another important point to note is that these iso-profit lines are parallel. We now have two clues as to how to find the optimal solution to the original problem. We can draw a series of parallel profit lines (by carefully moving our ruler in a plane parallel to the first profit line). The highest profit line that still touches some point of the feasible region pinpoints the optimal solution. Notice that the fourth line ($420) is too high to be considered.

The highest possible iso-profit line is illustrated in Figure 10.8. It touches the tip of the feasible region at the corner point ($X_1 = 30$, $X_2 = 40$) and yields a profit of $410.

highest iso-profit line

The Corner Point Solution Method

A second approach to solving linear programming problems employs the *corner point method*. This technique is simpler, conceptually, than the iso-profit line approach, but it involves looking at the profit at every corner point of the feasible region.

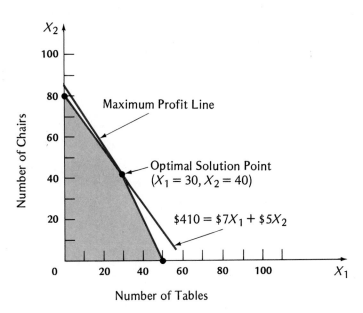

FIGURE 10.8
Optimal Solution to the Flair Furniture Problem

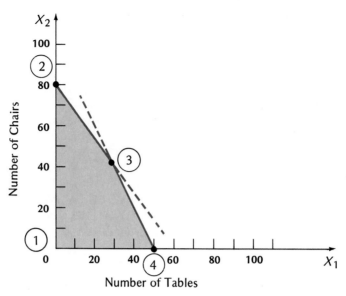

FIGURE 10.9
Four Corner Points of the Feasible Region

optimal solution at corner point

The mathematical theory behind linear programming states that an optimal solution to any problem (that is, the values of X_1, X_2 that yield the maximum profit) will lie at a *corner point*, or *extreme point*, of the feasible region. Hence, it is only necessary to find the values of the variables at each corner; the maximum profit or optimal solution will lie at one (or more) of them.

testing corner points ① ② and ④

Once again we can see (in Figure 10.9) that the feasible region for the Flair Furniture Company problem is a four-sided polygon with four corner, or extreme, points. These points are labeled ①, ②, ③, and ④ on the graph. To find the (X_1, X_2) values producing the maximum profit, we find out what the coordinates of each corner point are and test their profit levels.

> Point ①: ($X_1 = 0$, $X_2 = 0$)   Profit = $7(0) + $5(0) = $0
>
> Point ②: ($X_1 = 0$, $X_2 = 80$)   Profit = $7(0) + $5(80) = $400
>
> Point ④: ($X_1 = 50$, $X_2 = 0$)   Profit = $7(50) + $5(0) = $350

solving for corner point

We skipped corner point ③ momentarily because, in order to find its coordinates *accurately*, we have to solve for the intersection of the two constraint lines.[3] As you may recall from your last course in algebra, we can apply the method of *simultaneous equations* to the two constraint equations:

$$4X_1 + 3X_2 = 240 \quad \text{(\textit{carpentry line})}$$

$$2X_1 + 1X_2 = 100 \quad \text{(\textit{painting line})}$$

---

[3] Of course, if a graph is perfectly drawn, you can always find point ③ by a careful examination of the intersection's coordinates. Otherwise, the algebraic method shown here provides more precision.

To solve these equations simultaneously, we multiply the second equation by -2.

$$-2(2X_1 + 1X_2 = 100) = -4X_1 - 2X_2 = -200$$

and then add it to the first equation:

$$\frac{+4X_1 + 3X_2 = 240}{+ 1X_2 = 40}$$

or

$$X_2 = 40$$

Doing this has enabled us to eliminate one variable, X_1, and to solve for X_2. We can now substitute 40 for X_2 in either of the original equations and solve for X_1. Let's use the first equation. When $X_2 = 40$, then,

$$4X_1 + 3(40) = 240$$
$$4X_1 + 120 = 240$$

or

$$4X_1 = 120$$
$$X_1 = 30$$

Thus point ③ has the coordinates ($X_1 = 30$, $X_2 = 40$); we can compute its profit level to complete the analysis.

Point ③: ($X_1 = 30$, $X_2 = 40$)   Profit $= \$7(30) + \$5(40) = \$410$

Because point ③ produces the highest profit of any corner point, the product mix of $X_1 = 30$ tables and $X_2 = 40$ chairs is the optimal solution to Flair Furniture's problem. This solution yields a profit of \$410 per production period, which is the same figure we obtained using the iso-profit line method.

10.5
SOLVING MINIMIZATION PROBLEMS

Many linear programming problems involve minimizing an objective such as cost instead of maximizing a profit function. A restaurant, for example, may wish to develop a work schedule to meet staffing needs while minimizing the total number of employees. A manufacturer may seek to distribute its products from several factories to its many regional warehouses in such a way as to minimize total shipping costs. A hospital may want to provide a daily meal plan for its patients that meets certain nutritional standards while at the same time minimizing food purchase costs.

Minimization problems can be solved graphically by first setting up the feasible solution region and then using either the corner point method or an iso-cost line approach (which is analogous to the iso-profit approach in maximization problems) to find the values of X_1 and X_2 that yield the minimum cost. Let's take a look at a common LP problem referred to as

---

APPLICATIONS OF QA

Manpower Planning at United Airlines with LP

In 1984, United Airlines started air service to cities in all of the 50 states, the only airline at that time to do so. The expansion required to achieve this growth created personnel scheduling problems but provided the potential for great cost savings. That year, United dramatically increased its operating profit to over $500 million from an operating profit of $160 million the year before. One major contributor to this increased profit was the ability to tightly control costs. In the past, United was not completely satisfied with the way it scheduled personnel. For example, 11 United reservation offices employed over 4,000 full-time or part-time sales representatives. Approximately 1,000 full-time or part-time customer service agents worked at the 10 largest airports United serviced.

As a result of the expansion, United Airlines had as a major objective—the efficient and effective scheduling of personnel. In 1982, the Station Manpower Planning Project had been initiated. Its objectives were to determine the needs for personnel

Source: Thomas Hollorann and Judson Byrn, "United Airlines Stationed Manpower Planning System," *Interfaces* Vol. 16, No. 1, January–February 1986, pp. 39–50.

as a result of the expansion, to identify any excess personnel capacity, to produce a more timely and accurate schedule, and to reduce total scheduling costs while maintaining adequate customer service.

Before the personnel planning project, schedules were typically done by hand at the various reservation offices. Clearly, with the expansion, new and better planning approaches were needed.

The Station Manpower Planning System employs both linear and integer programming along with other techniques to perform the forecasting of personnel requirements as well as the actual scheduling of people. Used since 1983, it currently schedules work for approximately 4,000 employees on a regular basis, with plans to schedule 10,000 employees in the near future. In addition to having the potential of being more timely, the integer and linear programming approaches also resulted in cost savings. It has been estimated that over $6 million has been saved annually by using the new system. In addition, the scheduled employees, the operating managers, and upper-level managers are very pleased with the overall performance of their new personnel planning system.

---

the diet problem. This situation is similar to the one that the hospital faces in feeding its patients at the least cost.

The Holiday Meal Turkey Ranch

The Holiday Meal Turkey Ranch is considering buying two different brands of turkey feed and blending them to provide a good, low-cost diet for its turkeys. Each feed contains, in varying proportions, some or all of the three nutritional ingredients essential for fattening turkeys. Each pound of brand 1 purchased, for example, contains 5 ounces of ingredient A, 4 ounces of ingredient B, and $\frac{1}{2}$ ounce of ingredient C. Each pound of brand 2 contains 10 ounces of ingredient A, 3 ounces of ingredient B, but no ingredient C. The brand 1 feed costs the ranch 2¢ a pound, while the brand 2 feed costs 3¢ a pound. The owner of the ranch would like to use LP to determine the lowest-cost diet that meets the minimum monthly intake requirement for each nutritional ingredient.

Table 10.2 summarizes the relevant information. If we let

$$X_1 = \text{Number of pounds of brand 1 feed purchased}$$

$$X_2 = \text{Number of pounds of brand 2 feed purchased}$$

Table 10.2 Holiday Meal Turkey Ranch Data

INGREDIENT	COMPOSITION OF EACH POUND OF FEED (OZ.)		MINIMUM MONTHLY REQUIREMENT PER TURKEY (OZ.)
	BRAND 1 FEED	BRAND 2 FEED	
A	5	10	90
B	4	3	48
C	½	0	1½
Cost per pound	2¢	3¢	

then we may proceed to formulate this linear programming problem as follows:

$$\text{Minimize cost (in cents)} = 2X_1 + 3X_2$$

subject to these constraints:

$$5X_1 + 10X_2 \geq 90 \text{ ounces} \quad \textit{(ingredient A constraint)}$$

$$4X_1 + 3X_2 \geq 48 \text{ ounces} \quad \textit{(ingredient B constraint)}$$

$$\tfrac{1}{2}X_1 \geq 1\tfrac{1}{2} \text{ ounces} \quad \textit{(ingredient C constraint)}$$

$$X_1 \geq 0 \quad \textit{(nonnegativity constraint)}$$

$$X_2 \geq 0 \quad \textit{(nonnegativity constraint)}$$

Before solving this problem, we want to be sure to note three features that affect its solution. First, you should be aware that the third constraint implies that the farmer *must* purchase enough brand 1 feed to meet the minimum standards for the C nutritional ingredient. Buying only brand 2 would not be feasible because it lacks C. Second, as the problem is formulated, we will be solving for the best blend of brands 1 and 2 to buy per turkey per month. If the ranch houses 5,000 turkeys in a given month, it need simply multiply the X_1 and X_2 quantities by 5,000 in order to decide how much feed to order overall. And third, we are now dealing with a series of greater-than-or-equal-to constraints. These cause the feasible solution area to be above the constraint lines, a common situation when handling minimization LP problems.

Using the Corner Point Method on a Minimization Problem

To solve the Holiday Meal Turkey Ranch problem, we first construct the feasible solution region. This is done by plotting each of the three constraint equations as in Figure 10.10. You may note that the third constraint, $\frac{1}{2}X_1 \geq 1\frac{1}{2}$, may be rewritten and plotted as $X_1 \geq 3$. (This involves multiplying both sides of the inequality by 2, but does not change the position of the constraint line in any way.) Minimization problems are often unbounded outward (that is, on the right side and on top), but this causes no difficulty in solving them. As long as they are bounded inward (on the left side and the bottom), corner points may be established. The optimal solution will lie at one of the corners as it would in a maximization problem.

feasible solution region for minimization problem

KEY IDEA

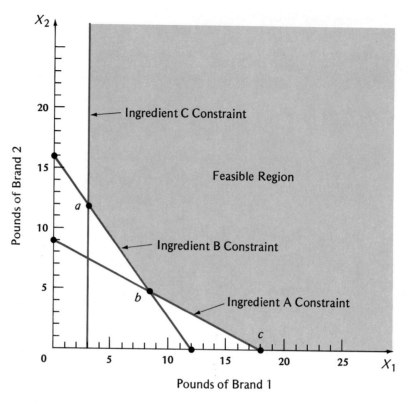

FIGURE 10.10
Feasible Region for the Holiday Meal Turkey Ranch Problem

solving for corner points algebraically

In this case, there are three corner points: a, b, and c. For point a, we find the coordinates at the intersection of the ingredient C and B constraints, that is, where the line $X_1 = 3$ crosses the line $4X_1 + 3X_2 = 48$. If we substitute $X_1 = 3$ into the B constraint equation, then the following sequence of computations may be performed:

$$4X_1 + 3X_2 = 48$$

or

$$4(3) + 3X_2 = 48$$

or

$$12 + 3X_2 = 48$$

or

$$3X_2 = 36$$
$$X_2 = 12$$

Thus, point a has the coordinates ($X_1 = 3$, $X_2 = 12$) and a corresponding cost of:

$$\text{Cost at point } a = 2X_1 + 3X_2$$
$$= 2(3) + 3(12)$$
$$= 42¢$$

To find the values of point b algebraically we solve the equations $4X_1 + 3X_2 = 48$ and $5X_1 + 10X_2 = 90$ simultaneously. This can be done by (1) multiplying the first equation (representing the ingredient B constraint) by -5, then (2) multiplying the second equation (the ingredient A constraint line) by 4, and finally (3) adding the two new equations together.

1. $-5(4X_1 + 3X_2 = 48)$		$-20X_1 - 15X_2 = -240$
2. $4(5X_1 + 10X_2 = 90)$		$\underline{20X_1 + 40X_2 = 360}$
3.		$+25X_2 = 120$
		$X_2 = 4.8$

The reason for this procedure was to eliminate one of the variables (X_1) from the equations, so that we could solve for the other (X_2). Now that we have a value for X_2, we may substitute $X_2 = 4.8$ into either of the two original equations to solve for X_1. Using the first equation:

$$4X_1 + 3(4.8) = 48$$

or

$$4X_1 + 14.4 = 48$$

or

$$4X_1 = 33.6$$

or

$$X_1 = 8.4$$

The cost at point b is now:

$$\text{Cost at point } b = 2X_1 + 3X_2$$
$$= 2(8.4) + 3(4.8)$$
$$= 31.2¢$$

Finally, the cost at point c must be computed. This is much easier, as it is evident that c has the coordinates ($X_1 = 18$, $X_2 = 0$):

$$\text{Cost at point } c = 2X_1 + 3X_2$$
$$= 2(18) + 3(0)$$
$$= 36¢$$

Hence, the minimum cost solution is to purchase 8.4 pounds of brand 1 feed and 4.8 pounds of brand 2 feed per turkey per month. This will yield a cost of 31.2¢ per turkey.

Iso-Cost Line Approach

As mentioned before, the *iso-cost line* approach may also be used to solve LP minimization problems such as that of the Holiday Meal Turkey Ranch.

iso-cost line

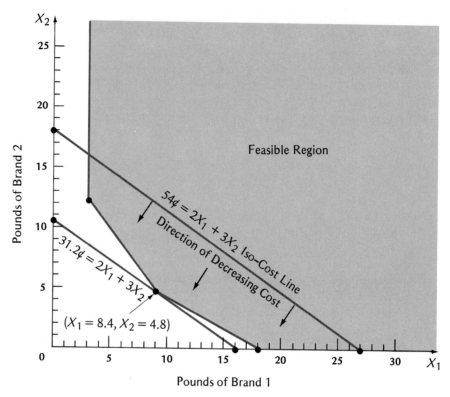

FIGURE 10.11
Graphical Solution to the Holiday Meal Turkey Ranch
Problem Using the Iso-Cost Line

As with iso-profit lines, we need not compute the cost at each corner point, but instead draw a series of parallel cost lines. The lowest cost line (that is, the one closest in toward the origin) to touch the feasible region provides us with the optimal solution corner.

For example, we start in Figure 10.11 by drawing a 54¢ cost line, namely, $54 = 2X_1 + 3X_2$. Obviously, there are many points in the feasible region that would yield a lower total cost. We proceed to move our iso-cost line toward the lower left, in a plane parallel to the 54¢ solution line. The last point we touch while still in contact with the feasible region is the same as corner point b of Figure 10.10. It has the coordinates ($X_1 = 8.4$, $X_2 = 4.8$) and an associated cost of 31.2¢.

10.6
SUMMARY OF THE GRAPHICAL SOLUTION METHOD

As you saw in the cases of the Flair Furniture Company and the Holiday Meal Turkey Ranch, the graphical method of solving linear programming problems involves several steps. Let's review them briefly before moving on.

1. Formulate the problem in terms of a series of mathematical constraints and an objective function.

2. Graph each of the constraint equations.

3. Identify the feasible solution region, that is, the area that satisfies all of the constraints simultaneously.

4. Select one of the two following graphical solution techniques and proceed to solve.

Corner Point Method	*Iso-Profit or Iso-Cost Method*
5. Identify each of the corner, or extreme, points of the feasible region by either visual inspection or the method of simultaneous equations.	5. Select a specific profit or cost line and graph it to reveal its slope or angle.
6. Compute the profit or cost at each corner point by substituting that point's coordinates into the objective function.	6. If you are dealing with a maximization problem, maintain the same slope, through a series of parallel lines, and move the line up and to the right until it touches the feasible region at only one point. If you have a minimization problem, move down and to the left until it touches only one point in the feasible region.
7. Identify the optimal solution as that corner point with the highest profit, in a maximization problem, or lowest cost, in a minimization problem.	7. Identify the optimal solution as the coordinates of that point on the feasible region touched by the highest possible iso-profit line or lowest possible iso-cost line.
	8. Read the optimal (X_1, X_2) coordinates from the graph, or compute their values by using the simultaneous equation method.
	9. Compute the profit or cost.

10.7
A FEW SPECIAL ISSUES IN LINEAR PROGRAMMING

Four special cases and difficulties arise at times when using the graphical approach to solving linear programming problems. They are called: (1) infeasibility, (2) unboundedness, (3) redundancy, and (4) alternate optimal solutions.

Infeasibility

Infeasibility is a condition that arises when there is no solution to a linear programming problem that satisfies all of the constraints given. Graphically, it means that no feasible solution region exists—a situation that might occur if the problem was formulated with conflicting constraints. This, by the way, is a frequent occurrence in real-life, large-scale LP problems that involve hundreds of constraints. For example, if one constraint is supplied by the marketing manager who states that at least 300 tables must be produced (namely, $X_1 \geq 300$) to meet sales demand, and a second restriction is supplied by the production manager who insists that no more than 220 tables be produced (namely, $X_1 \leq 220$) because of a lumber shortage, then an infeasible solution region results. Once the operations research analyst coordinating the LP problem points out this conflict, one manager or the other must revise his or her inputs. Perhaps more raw materials could be procured from a new source, or perhaps sales demand could be lowered by substituting a different model table to customers.

As a further graphic illustration of infeasibility, let us consider the following three constraints:

$$X_1 + 2X_2 \leq 6$$
$$2X_1 + X_2 \leq 8$$
$$X_1 \qquad \geq 7$$

As seen in Figure 10.12, there is no feasible solution region for this LP problem because of the presence of conflicting constraints.

Unboundedness

Sometimes a linear program will not have a finite solution. This means that in a maximization problem, for example, one or more solution variables,

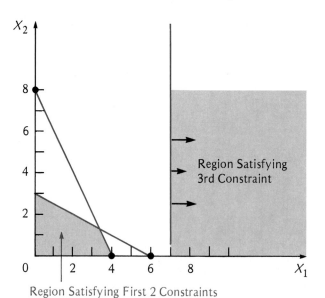

FIGURE 10.12
Problem with No Feasible Solution

and the profit, can be made infinitely large without violating any constraints. If we try to solve such a problem graphically, we will note that the feasible region is open-ended.

Let us consider a simple example to illustrate the situation. A firm has formulated the following LP problem:

$$\text{Maximize profit} = \$3X_1 + \$5X_2$$

$$\text{Subject to:} \quad X_1 \qquad \geq 5$$
$$X_2 \leq 10$$
$$X_1 + 2X_2 \geq 10$$
$$X_1, \quad X_2 \geq 0$$

As you see in Figure 10.13, since this is a maximization problem and the feasible region extends infinitely to the right, there is an unbounded solution. This implies that the problem has been improperly formulated. It would indeed be wonderful for the company to be able to produce an infinite number of units of X_1 (at a profit of $3 each!), but obviously no firm has infinite resources available or infinite product demand.

Redundancy

The presence of redundant constraints is another common situation that occurs in large linear programming formulations. Redundancy causes no major difficulties in solving LP problems graphically, but you should be able to identify its occurrence. A redundant constraint is simply one that does not affect the feasible solution region. In other words, one constraint may be more binding or restrictive than another and thereby negate its need to be considered.

redundant constraints

Let's look at the following example of an LP problem with three constraints:

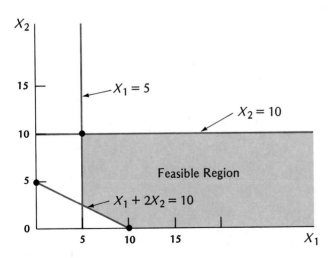

FIGURE 10.13
Solution Region That Is Unbounded to the Right

$$\text{Maximize profit} = \$1X_1 + \$2X_2$$

$$\text{Subject to:} \quad X_1 + X_2 \leq 20$$
$$2X_1 + X_2 \leq 30$$
$$X_1 \leq 25$$
$$X_1, \; X_2 \geq 0$$

The third constraint, $X_1 \leq 25$, is redundant and unnecessary in the formulation and solution of the problem because it has no effect on the feasible region set from the first two more restrictive constraints. See Figure 10.14.

Alternate Optimal Solutions

multiple optimal solutions

A linear programming problem may, on occasion, have two or more optimal solutions. Graphically, this is the case when the objective function's iso-profit or iso-cost line runs perfectly parallel to one of the problem's constraints—in other words, they have the same slope.

Management of a firm noticed the presence of more than one optimal solution when they formulated this simple LP problem:

$$\text{Maximize profit} = \$3X_1 + \$2X_2$$

$$\text{Subject to:} \quad 6X_1 + 4X_2 \leq 24$$
$$X_1 \leq 3$$
$$X_1, \; X_2 \geq 0$$

As we see in Figure 10.15, our first iso-profit line of $8 runs parallel to the constraint equation. At a profit level of $12, the iso-profit line will rest

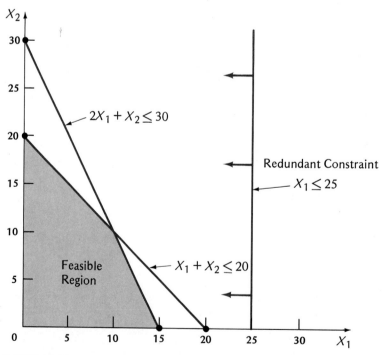

FIGURE 10.14
Problem with a Redundant Constraint

APPLICATIONS OF QA

Production Scheduling with LP at Owens-Corning

Owens-Corning Fiberglass was a worldwide pioneer in the development of many glass fiber products. One of its large manufacturing plants is in Anderson, South Carolina. This location produces a number of different fiberglass products, which makes production planning and scheduling difficult and complex.

An example of one of its products is fiberglass mat, which is sold in rolls of various widths and weights. The mat can be trimmed on either one or both of the edges or not at all. At the Anderson facility, fiberglass mat is produced using two parallel processors—mat line one and mat line two. Each line has a different capacity and different abilities in the production of fiberglass mat. It has been estimated that these processor lines can contribute over $1,000 per hour of profit per machine.

One of the most difficult problems facing

Source: Michael Oliff and Earl Burch, "Multi-product Production Scheduling at Owens-Corning Fiberglass," *Interfaces* Vol. 15, No. 5, September–October 1985, pp. 25–34.

Owens-Corning Fiberglass is developing an effective scheduling system. The scheduling system needs to specify an aggregate plan that takes into account relevant costs for the work force, overtime, and inventory levels. In addition, it must look at production run quantities and what types of mats are assigned which line and which process. Finally, the system must specify when and how both standard and special order products are to be handled and scheduled.

The overall objective in solving the scheduling of this problem was to minimize total cost. The constraints dealt with overall production balance, inventory capacity, processor capacity, and change over from one process to another. Linear programming was able to determine inventory lot sizes, various assignments for the mat lines, and inventory levels. Then, an efficient heuristic method was used for final job sequencing. As a result of the use of these quantitative analysis techniques, a savings of over $100,000 during the first two years of operation was realized.

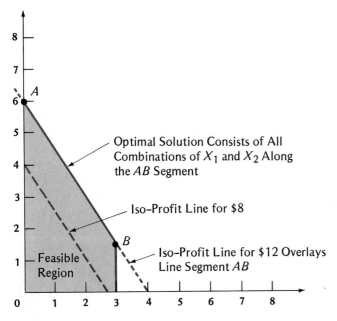

FIGURE 10.15
Example of Alternate Optimal Solutions

directly on top of the segment of the first constraint line. This means that any point along the line between *A* and *B* provides an optimal X_1 and X_2 combination. Far from causing problems, the existence of more than one optimal solution allows management great flexibility in deciding which combination to select. The profit remains the same at each alternate solution.

The graphical solution approaches of this chapter provide a conceptual basis for tackling larger, more complex problems. To solve real-life linear programming problems with numerous variables and constraints, we need a solution procedure such as the simplex algorithm, the subject of our next chapter.

GLOSSARY

Linear Programming (LP). A mathematical technique to help management decide how to make the most effective use of an organization's resources.

Mathematical Programming. The general category of mathematical modeling and solution techniques used to allocate resources while optimizing a measurable goal. LP is one type of programming model.

Objective Function. A mathematical statement of the goal of an organization, stated as an intent to maximize or to minimize some important quantity such as profits or costs.

Constraint. A restriction on the resources available to a firm (stated in the form of an inequality or an equation).

Inequality. A mathematical expression containing a greater-than-or-equal-to relation ($\geq$) or a less-than-or-equal-to relation ($\leq$) used to indicate that the total consumption of a resource must be $\geq$ or $\leq$ some limiting value.

Product Mix Problem. A common LP problem involving a decision as to which products a firm should produce, given that it faces limited resources.

Nonnegativity Constraints. A set of constraints that require each decision variable to be nonnegative; that is, each X_i must be greater than or equal to 0.

Feasible Region. The area satisfying all of the problem's resource restrictions; that is, the region where all constraints overlap. All possible solutions to the problem lie in the feasible region.

Feasible Solution. A point lying in the feasible region. Basically, it is any point that satisfies all of the problem's constraints.

Infeasible Solution. Any point lying outside the feasible region. It violates one or more of the stated constraints.

Iso-Profit Line. A straight line representing all nonnegative combinations of X_1 and X_2 for a particular profit level.

Corner Point or Extreme Point. A point that lies on one of the corners of the feasible region. This means that it falls at the intersection of two constraint lines.

Corner Point Method. The method of finding the optimal solution to a linear programming problem by testing the profit or cost level at each corner point of the feasible region. The theory of LP states that the optimal solution must lie at one of the corner points.

Simultaneous Equation Method. The algebraic means of solving for the intersection point of two or more linear constraint equations.

Iso-Cost Line. A straight line representing all combinations of X_1 and X_2 for a particular cost level.

Infeasibility. A condition that arises when there is no solution to an LP problem that satisfies all of the constraints.

Unboundedness. A condition that exists when a solution variable and the profit can be made infinitely large without violating any of the problem's constraints.

Redundancy. The presence of one or more constraints that do not bound the feasible solution region.

Alternate Optimal Solution. A situation when more than one optimal solution is possible. It arises when the angle or slope of the objective function is the same as the slope of a constraint.

SOLVED PROBLEMS

Solved Problem 10-1

Personal Mini Warehouses is planning to expand its successful Orlando business into Tampa. In doing so, the company must determine how many storage rooms of each size to build. Its objective and constraints follow:

Maximize monthly earnings $= 50X_1 + 20X_2$

Subject to:
$$2X_1 + 4X_2 \leq 400 \quad \textit{(Advertising budget available)}$$
$$100X_1 + 50X_2 \leq 8,000 \quad \textit{(square footage required)}$$
$$X_1 \qquad \leq 60 \quad \textit{(rental limit expected)}$$
$$X_1, \quad X_2 \geq 0$$

where

X_1 = number of large spaces developed, and

X_2 = number of small spaces developed.

Solution

An evaluation of the five corner points of the accompanying graph indicates that corner point *C* produces the greatest earnings. Refer to the graph and table.

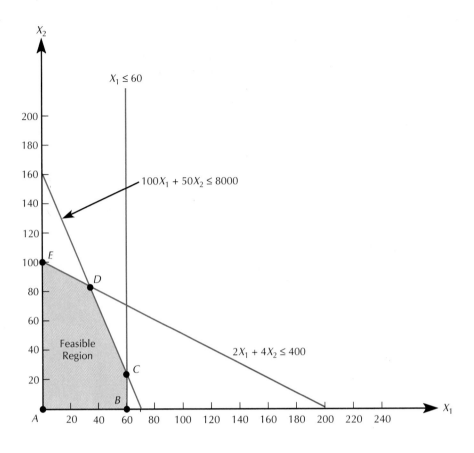

CORNER POINT	VALUES OF X_1, X_2	OBJECTIVE FUNCTION VALUE ($)
A	(0, 0)	0
B	(60, 0)	3,000
C	(60, 80)	3,800
D	(40, 80)	3,600
E	(0, 100)	2,000

Solved Problem 10-2

Solve the following LP formulation graphically, using the iso-cost line approach:

$$\text{Minimize costs} = 24X_1 + 28X_2$$

$$\begin{aligned} \text{Subject to:} \quad 5X_1 + 4X_2 &\le 2{,}000 \\ X_1 &\ge 80 \\ X_1 + X_2 &\ge 300 \\ X_2 &\ge 100 \\ X_1, \quad X_2 &\ge 0 \end{aligned}$$

Solution

A graph of the four constraints is shown below. The arrows indicate the direction of feasibility for each constraint. The next graph illustrates the feasible solution

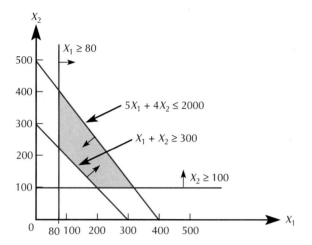

region and plots of two possible objective function cost lines. The first, $10,000, was selected arbitrarily as a starting point. To find the optimal corner point, we need to move the cost line in the direction of lower cost, that is, down and to the left. The last point where a cost line touches the feasible region as it moves toward the origin is corner point D. Thus D, which represents $X_1 = 200$, $X_2 = 100$, and a cost of $7,600, is optimal.

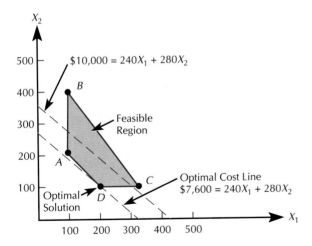

Solved Problem 10-3

Solve the following problems given these constraints and objective function:

$$\text{Maximize profit} = 30X_1 + 40X_2$$

$$
\begin{array}{lrcr}
\text{Subject to:} & 4X_1 + & 2X_2 & \leq 16 \\
& 2X_1 - & X_2 & \geq 2 \\
& & X_2 & \leq 2 \\
& X_1, & X_2 & \geq 0 \\
\end{array}
$$

(a) Graph the feasible region.
(b) Evaluate the objective function at each corner point.
(c) Identify the optimal solution.

Solution

(a) The graph appears as follows, with the feasible region shaded.

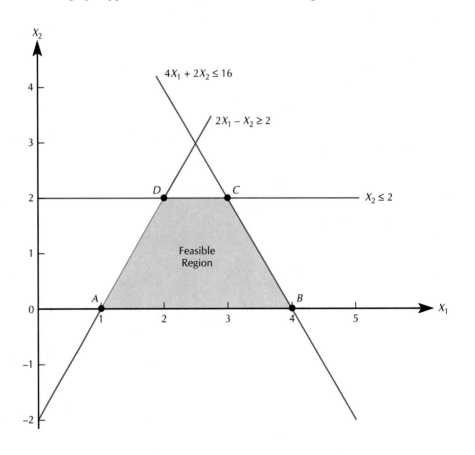

(b)

CORNER POINT	COORDINATES	PROFIT ($)
A	$X_1 = 1, X_2 = 0$	30
B	$X_1 = 4, X_2 = 0$	120
C	$X_1 = 3, X_2 = 2$	170
D	$X_1 = 2, X_2 = 2$	140

(c) The optimal profit of $170 is at corner point C.

DISCUSSION QUESTIONS AND PROBLEMS

Discussion Questions

10-1 Discuss the similarities and differences between minimization and maximization problems using the graphical solution approaches of linear programming.

10-2 It is important to understand the assumptions underlying the use of any quantitative analysis model. What are the assumptions and requirements for a linear programming model to be formulated and used?

10-3 It has been said that each linear programming problem that has a feasible region has an infinite number of solutions. Explain.

10-4 You have just formulated a maximization linear programming problem and are preparing to solve it graphically. What criteria should you consider in deciding whether it would be easier to solve the problem by the corner point method versus the iso-profit line approach?

10-5 Under what condition is it possible for an LP problem to have more than one optimal solution?

10-6 Develop your own individual set of constraint equations and inequalities and use them to illustrate graphically each of the following conditions:
(a) An unbounded problem.
(b) An infeasible problem.
(c) A problem containing redundant constraints.

10-7 The production manager of a large Cincinnati manufacturing firm once made the statement, "I would like to use linear programming, but it's a technique that operates under conditions of certainty. My plant doesn't have that certainty; it's a world of uncertainty. So LP can't be used here." Do you think this statement has any merit? Explain why the manager may have said it.

10-8 The mathematical relationships that follow were formulated by an operations research analyst at the Smith-Lawton Chemical Company. Which ones are invalid for use in a linear programming problem, and why?

$$\text{Maximize profit} = 4X_1 + 3X_1X_2 + 8X_2 + 5X_3$$

$$\begin{aligned}
\text{Subject to:} \quad 2X_1 + X_2 + 2X_3 &\leq 50 \\
8X_1 - 4X_2 &\geq 6 \\
1.5X_1 + 6X_2 + 3X_3 &\geq 21 \\
19X_2 - \tfrac{1}{3}X_3 &= 17 \\
5X_1 + 4X_2 + 3\sqrt{X_3} &\leq 80 \\
-X_1 - X_2 + X_3 &= 5
\end{aligned}$$

Problems

10-9 The Electrocomp Corporation manufactures two electrical products: air conditioners and large fans. The assembly process for each is similar in that both require a certain amount of wiring and drilling. Each air conditioner takes 3 hours of wiring and 2 hours of drilling. Each fan must go through

2 hours of wiring and 1 hour of drilling. During the next production period, 240 hours of wiring time are available and up to 140 hours of drilling time may be used. Each air conditioner sold yields a profit of $25. Each fan assembled may be sold for a $15 profit. Formulate and solve this LP production mix situation to find the best combination of air conditioners and fans that yields the highest profit. Use the corner point graphical approach.

· **10-10** Electrocomp's management realizes that it forgot to include two critical constraints (see Problem 10-9). In particular, management decides that, to ensure an adequate supply of air conditioners for a contract, at least 20 air conditioners should be manufactured. Since Electrocomp incurred an oversupply of fans the previous period, management also insists that no more than 80 fans be produced during this production period. Resolve this product mix problem to find the new optimal solution.

· **10-11** The Marriott Tub Company manufactures two lines of bathtubs, called model A and model B. Every tub requires blending a certain amount of steel and zinc; the company has available a total of 25,000 pounds of steel and 6,000 pounds of zinc. Each model A bathtub requires a mixture of 125 pounds of steel and 20 pounds of zinc, and each yields a profit to the firm of $90. Each model B tub produced can be sold for a profit of $70; it in turn requires 100 pounds of steel and 30 pounds of zinc. Find by graphical linear programming the best production mix of bathtubs.

· **10-12** The Outdoor Furniture Corporation manufactures two products, benches and picnic tables, for use in yards and parks. The firm has two main resources: its carpenters (labor force) and a supply of redwood for use in the furniture. During the next production cycle, 1,200 hours of manpower are available under a union agreement. The firm also has a stock of 3,500 feet of quality redwood. Each bench that Outdoor Furniture produces requires four labor hours and 10 feet of redwood; each picnic table takes six labor hours and 35 feet of redwood. Completed benches will yield a profit of $9 each, and tables will result in a profit of $20 each. How many benches and tables should Outdoor Furniture produce in order to obtain the largest possible profit? Use the graphical linear programming approach.

· **10-13** The dean of the Western College of Business must plan the school's course offerings for the fall semester. Student demands make it necessary to offer at least 30 undergraduate and 20 graduate courses in the term. Faculty contracts also dictate that at least 60 courses be offered in total. Each undergraduate course taught costs the college an average of $2,500 in faculty wages, while each graduate course costs $3,000. How many undergraduate and graduate courses should be taught in the fall so that total faculty salaries are kept to a minimum?

: **10-14** MSA Computer Corporation manufactures two models of minicomputers, the Alpha 4 and the Beta 5. The firm employs five technicians, working 160 hours each per month, on its assembly line. Management insists that full employment (that is, *all* 160 hours of time) be maintained for each worker during next month's operations. It requires 20 labor hours to assemble each Alpha 4 computer and 25 labor hours to assemble each Beta 5 model. MSA wants to see at least 10 Alpha 4s and at least 15 Beta 5s produced during the production period. Alpha 4s generate a $1,200 profit per unit, and Beta 5s yield $1,800 each. Determine the most profitable number of each model of minicomputer to produce during the coming month.

: **10-15** The Sweet Smell Fertilizer Company markets bags of manure labeled "not less than 60 pounds dry weight." The manure packaged is a combination of compost and sewage wastes. To provide a quality fertilizer, each bag should contain at least 30 pounds of compost, but no more than 40 pounds of sewage. Each pound of compost costs Sweet Smell 5¢ and each pound of sewage costs 4¢. Use a graphical linear programming method to determine the least cost blend of compost and sewage in each bag.

· **10-16** The National Credit Union has $250,000 available to invest in a 12-month commitment. The money can be placed in treasury notes yielding an 8% return or in municipal bonds at an average rate of return of 9%. Credit union regulations require diversification to the extent that at least 50% of the investment be placed in treasury notes. Because of defaults in such municipalities as Cleveland and New York, it is decided that no more than 40% of the investment be placed in bonds. How much should the National Credit Union invest in each security so as to maximize its return on investment?

: **10-17** Solve the following linear programming problem using the corner point graphical method:

$$\text{Maximize profit} = 4X_1 + 4X_2$$

$$\text{Subject to:} \quad 3X_1 + 5X_2 \le 150$$
$$X_1 - 2X_2 \le 10$$
$$5X_1 + 3X_2 \le 150$$
$$X_1, X_2 \ge 0$$

: **10-18** Consider this linear programming formulation:

$$\text{Minimize cost} = \$1X_1 + \$2X_2$$

$$\text{Subject to:} \quad X_1 + 3X_2 \ge 90$$
$$8X_1 + 2X_2 \ge 160$$
$$3X_1 + 2X_2 \ge 120$$
$$X_2 \le 70$$

Graphically illustrate the feasible region and apply the iso-cost line procedure to indicate which corner point produces the optimal solution. What is the cost of this solution?

: **10-19** The stock brokerage firm of Blank, Leibowitz, and Weinberger has analyzed and recommended two stocks to an investors' club of college professors. The professors were interested in factors such as short-term growth, intermediate growth, and dividend rates. These data on each stock are as follows:

	STOCK	
FACTORS	LOUISIANA GAS AND POWER	TRIMEX INSULATION COMPANY
Short-term growth potential, per dollar invested	$ .36	$ .24
Intermediate growth potential (over next three years), per dollar invested	$1.67	$1.50
Dividend rate potential	4%	8%

Each member of the club has an investment goal of: (1) an appreciation of no less than $720 in the short term, (2) an appreciation of at least $5,000 in the next three years, and (3) a dividend income of at least $200 per year. What is the smallest investment that a professor can make in order to meet these three goals?

: **10-20** The advertising agency promoting the new Breem dishwashing detergent wants to get the best exposure possible for the product within the $100,000 advertising budget ceiling placed upon it. To do so, the agency needs to decide how much of the budget to spend on each of its two most effective media: (1) television spots during the afternoon hours and (2) large ads in the city's Sunday newspaper. Each television spot costs $3,000; each Sunday newspaper ad costs $1,250. The expected exposure, based on industry ratings, is 35,000 viewers for each TV commercial and 20,000 readers for each newspaper advertisement. The agency director, Mavis Early, knows from experience that it is important to use both media in order to reach the broadest spectrum of potential Breem customers. She decides that at least 5 but no more than 25 television spots should be ordered; and that at least 10 newspaper ads should be contracted. How many times should each of the two media be used to obtain maximum exposure while staying within the budget? Use the graphical method to solve.

: **10-21** The seasonal yield of olives in a Pireaus, Greece, vineyard is greatly influenced by a process of branch pruning. If olive trees are pruned every two weeks, output is increased. The pruning process, however, requires considerably more labor than permitting the olives to grow on their own and results in a smaller size olive. It also, though, permits olive trees to be spaced closer together. The yield of one barrel of olives by pruning requires 5 hours of labor and 1 acre of land. The production of a barrel of olives by the normal process requires only 2 labor hours, but takes 2 acres of land. An olive grower has 250 hours of labor available and a total of 150 acres for growing. Because of the olive size difference, a barrel of olives produced on pruned trees sells for $20, whereas a barrel of regular olives has a market price of $30. The grower has determined that because of uncertain demand, no more than 40 barrels of pruned olives should be produced. Use graphical linear programming to find:

(a) The maximum possible profit.
(b) The best combination of barrels of pruned and regular olives.
(c) The number of acres that the olive grower should devote to each growing process.

: **10-22** Consider the following four LP formulations. Using a graphical approach, determine:

(a) Which formulation has more than one optimal solution.
(b) Which formulation is unbounded.
(c) Which formulation is infeasible.
(d) Which formulation is correct as is.

Formulation 1	*Formulation 3*
Maximize: $10X_1 + 10X_2$	Maximize: $3X_1 + 2X_2$
Subject to: $2X_1 \leq 10$	Subject to: $X_1 + X_2 \geq 5$
$2X_1 + 4X_2 \leq 16$	$X_1 \geq 2$
$4X_2 \leq 8$	$2X_2 \geq 8$
$X_1 \geq 6$	

Formulation 2   *Formulation 4*

Maximize: $X_1 + 2X_2$ Maximize: $3X_1 + 3X_2$

Subject to: $X_1 \leq 1$ Subject to: $4X_1 + 6X_2 \leq 48$

$2X_2 \leq 2$ $4X_1 + 2X_2 \leq 12$

$X_1 + 2X_2 \leq 2$ $3X_2 \geq 3$

$2X_1 \geq 2$

: **10-23 Serendipity***

The three princes of Serendip
Went on a little trip.
They could not carry too much weight;
More than 300 pounds made them hesitate.
They planned to the ounce. When they returned to Ceylon
They discovered that their supplies were just about gone
When, what to their joy, Prince William found
A pile of coconuts on the ground.
"Each will bring 60 rupees," said Prince Richard with a grin
As he almost tripped over a lion skin.
"Look out!" cried Prince Robert with glee
As he spied some more lion skins under a tree.
"These are worth even more—300 rupees each
If we can just carry them all down to the beach."
Each skin weighed fifteen pounds and each coconut, five,
But they carried them all and made it alive.
The boat back to the island was very small
15 cubic feet baggage capacity—that was all.
Each lion skin took up one cubic foot
While eight coconuts the same space took.
With everything stowed they headed to sea
And on the way calculated what their new wealth might be.
"Eureka!" cried Prince Robert, "Our worth is so great
That there's no other way we could return in this state.
Any other skins or nut which we might have brought
Would now have us poorer. And now I know what—
I'll write my friend Horace in England, for surely
Only he can appreciate our serendipity."

Formulate and *solve* Serendipity by graphical linear programming in order to calculate "what their new wealth might be."

Problems 10.24 and 10.25 test your ability to formulate linear programming problems that have more than two variables. They cannot be solved graphically, but will give you a chance to set up a larger problem.

: **10-24** The Feed 'N Ship Ranch fattens cattle for local farmers and ships them to meat markets in Kansas City and Omaha. The owners of the ranch seek to determine the amounts of cattle feed to buy so that minimum nutritional standards are satisfied, and at the same time total feed costs are minimized.

The feed mix used can be made up of three grains that contain the following ingredients per pound of feed:

---

* The word *serendipity* was coined by the English writer Horace Walpole after a fairy tale entitled *The Three Princes of Serendip*. Source of problem is unknown.

INGREDIENT	FEED (OZ.)		
	STOCK X	STOCK Y	STOCK Z
A	3	2	4
B	2	3	1
C	1	0	2
D	6	8	4

The cost per pound of grains X, Y, and Z are $.02, $.04, and $.025, respectively. The minimum requirement per cow per month is 4 lbs. of ingredient A, 5 lbs. of ingredient B, 1 lb. of ingredient C, and 8 lbs. of ingredient D.

The ranch faces one additional restriction: it can only obtain 500 lbs. of stock Z per month from the feed supplier regardless of its need. Since there are usually 100 cows at the Feed 'N Ship Ranch at any given time, this means that no more than 5 lbs. of stock Z can be counted on for use in the feed of each cow per month.

Formulate this as a linear programming problem, but do not solve.

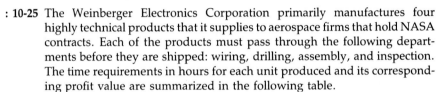

: **10-25** The Weinberger Electronics Corporation primarily manufactures four highly technical products that it supplies to aerospace firms that hold NASA contracts. Each of the products must pass through the following departments before they are shipped: wiring, drilling, assembly, and inspection. The time requirements in hours for each unit produced and its corresponding profit value are summarized in the following table.

PRODUCT	DEPARTMENT				UNIT PROFIT ($)
	WIRING	DRILLING	ASSEMBLY	INSPECTION	
XJ201	.5	3	2	.5	9
XM897	1.5	1	4	1	12
TR29	1.5	2	1	.5	15
BR788	1	3	2	.5	11

The production available in each department each month, and the minimum monthly production requirement to fulfill contracts, are as follows:

DEPARTMENT	CAPACITY IN HOURS	PRODUCT	MINIMUM PRODUCTION LEVEL
Wiring	15,000	XJ201	150
Drilling	17,000	XM897	100
Assembly	26,000	TR29	300
Inspection	12,000	BR788	400

The production manager has the responsibility of specifying production levels for each product for the coming month. Help him by formulating (that is, setting up the constraints and objective function) Weinberger's problem using linear programming.

: **10-26** Androgynous Bicycle Company (ABC) has the hottest new product on the upscale toy market—boy's and girl's bikes in bright fashion colors, with oversized hubs and axles, shell design safety tires, a strong padded frame, chrome-plated chains, brackets and valves, and a nonslip handlebar. Due to the seller's market for high-quality toys for the newest baby boomers, ABC can sell all the bicycles it manufactures at the following prices: boy's bikes—$220, girl's bikes—$175. This is the price payable to ABC at its Orlando plant.

The firm's accountant has determined that direct labor costs will be 45% of the price ABC receives for the boy's model and 40% of the price received for the girl's model. Production costs other than labor, but excluding painting and packaging, are $44 per boy's bicycle and $30 per girl's bicycle. Painting and packaging are $20 per bike, regardless of model.

The Orlando plant's overall production capacity is 390 bicycles per day. Each boy's bike requires 2.5 labor hours while each girl's model takes 2.4 hours to complete. ABC currently employs 120 workers, who each put in an 8-hour day. The firm has no desire to hire or fire to affect labor availability for it believes its stable work force is one of its biggest assets.

Using a graphical approach, determine the best product mix for ABC.

: **10-27** Capitol Hill Construction Company (CHCC) must complete its current office building renovation as quickly as possible. The first portion of the project consists of six activities, some of which must be finished before others are started. The activities, their precedences, and their estimated times are shown in this table:

ACTIVITY		PRECEDENCE	TIME (IN DAYS)
Prepare financing options	(A)	—	2
Prepare preliminary sketches	(B)	—	3
Outline specifications	(C)	—	1
Prepare drawings	(D)	A	4
Write specifications	(E)	C and D	5
Run off prints	(F)	B	1

This network of tasks can be drawn as follows:

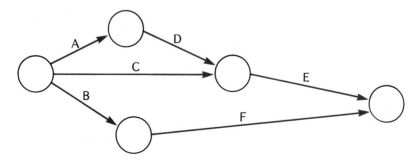

Let X_i represent the earliest completion of an activity where i = A, B, C, D, E, F. Formulate (only) CHCC's problem as a linear program.

: **10-28** Amalgamated Products has just received a contract to construct steel body frames for automobiles that are to be produced at the new Japanese factory in Tennessee. The Japanese auto manufacturer has strict quality control standards for all of its component subcontractors and has informed Amalgamated that each frame must have the following steel content:

MATERIAL IN STEEL	MINIMUM PERCENT	MAXIMUM PERCENT
Manganese	2.1	2.3
Silicon	4.3	4.6
Carbon	5.05	5.35

Amalgamated mixes batches of eight different available materials to produce one ton of steel used in the body frames. The table that follows details these materials:

MATERIAL AVAILABLE	MANGANESE (%)	SILICON (%)	CARBON (%)	POUNDS AVAILABLE	COST PER POUND
Alloy 1	70.0	15.0	3.0	No limit	$.12
Alloy 2	55.0	30.0	1.0	300	$.13
Alloy 3	12.0	26.0	0	No limit	$.15
Iron 1	1.0	10.0	3.0	No limit	$.09
Iron 2	5.0	2.5	0	No limit	$.07
Carbide 1	0	24.0	18.0	50	$.10
Carbide 2	0	25.0	20.0	200	$.12
Carbide 3	0	23.0	25.0	100	$.09

Formulate (only) the linear programming model that will indicate how much each of the eight materials should be blended into a one-ton load of steel so that Amalgamated meets its requirements while minimizing costs.

: **10-29** Modem Corporation of America (MCA) is the world's largest producer of modem communication devices for microcomputers. Recognized by his computer peers as a brilliant entrepreneur, Hilliard Blank successfully carved out a small niche in the huge microcomputer industry by concentrating on only two devices: the MCA 300 Baud Modem and the MCA 1200 Baud Intelligent Modem. Both devices work on the same principle of modulation–demodulation, converting digital impulses to audio impulses and audio to digital. This process permits computers, which operate in digital signals, to "talk" to other computers via telephone lines, which use audio impulses. The MCA 1200 Baud Intelligent Modem is a high-speed device that has a microprocessor built into it to dial phone numbers automatically. The MCA 300 Baud Modem is slower (300 bits of data per second) and does not have its own microprocessor.

MCA sold 9,000 of the 300 Baud model and 10,400 of the 1200 Baud model this September. Its income statement for the month is shown on the next page. Costs presented are typical of prior months and are expected to remain at the same levels in the near future.

The firm is facing several constraints as it prepares its November production plan. First, it has experienced a tremendous demand and has been unable to keep any significant inventory in stock. This situation is not expected to change. Second, the firm is located in a small Iowa town from which additional labor is not readily available. Workers can be shifted from production of one modem to another, however. To produce the 9,000 of the 300 Baud Modems in September required 5,000 direct labor hours. The 10,400 of the 1200 Baud Intelligent Modems absorbed 10,400 direct labor hours. Third, MCA is experiencing a problem affecting the Intelligent Modems model. Its component supplier is able to guarantee only 8,000 mi-

	MCA INCOME STATEMENT MONTH ENDED SEPTEMBER 30	
	REGULAR MODEMS	SMART MODEMS
Sales	$450,000	$640,000
Less: Discounts	10,000	15,000
Returns	12,000	9,500
Warranty replacements	4,000	2,500
Net Sales	$424,000	$613,000
Sales Costs		
Direct labor	60,000	76,800
Indirect labor	9,000	11,520
Materials cost	90,000	128,000
Depreciation	40,000	50,800
Cost of sales	$199,000	$267,120
Gross Profit	$225,000	$345,880
Selling and General Expenses		
General expenses—variable	30,000	35,000
General expenses—fixed	36,000	40,000
Advertising	28,000	25,000
Sales commissions	31,000	60,000
Total operating cost	$125,000	$160,000
Pre-tax income	$100,000	$185,880
Income taxes (25%)	25,000	46,470
Net income	$ 75,000	$139,410

croprocessors for November delivery. Each Intelligent Modem requires one of these specially made microprocessors. Alternative suppliers are not available on short notice.

Hilliard Blank wants to plan the optimal mix of the two modem models to produce in November to maximize profits for MCA.

(a) Formulate, using September's data, MCA's problem as a linear program.
(b) Solve the problem graphically.
(c) Discuss the implications of your recommended solution.

Golding Landscaping and Plants, Inc.

Kenneth and Patricia Golding spent a career as a husband and wife real estate investment partnership in Washington, D.C. When they finally retired to a 25-acre farm in northern Virginia's Fairfax County, they became ardent amateur gardeners. Kenneth Golding planted shrubs and fruit trees, while Patricia spent her hours potting all sizes of plants. When the volume of shrubs and plants reached the point where the Goldings began to think of their hobby in a serious vein, they built a greenhouse adjacent to their home and installed heating and watering systems in it.

Shortly thereafter, whenever a family member, friend, or neighbor of the Goldings was about to celebrate a birthday, anniversary, or seasonal holiday, it was quite likely that a plant or small decorative shrub would arrive as a gift. The Goldings' green thumbs even began to generate some demand for plants and shrubs that friends and neighbors were more than happy to pay for. By 1984, the Goldings realized their retirement from real estate had really only led to a second career—in the plant and shrub business—and they filed for a Virginia business license. Within a matter of months, they asked their attorney to file incorporation documents and formed the firm Golding Landscaping and Plants, Inc.

In addition to marketing potted plants to supermarkets and other retail stores, the Goldings received a series of small landscaping contracts. They designed and planted shrubs at banks, small shopping centers, gasoline stations, and a few apartment complexes.

Early in the new business's existence, Kenneth Golding recognized the need for a high-quality commercial fertilizer that he could blend himself, both for sale and for his own nursery. His goal was to keep his costs to a minimum while producing a top-notch product that was especially suited to the northern Virginia climate.

Working with chemists at Virginia Tech and George Mason Universities, Golding blended "Golding-Grow." It consists of four chemical compounds, C-30, C-92, D-21, and E-11. The cost per pound for each compound is indicated below.

CHEMICAL COMPOUND	COST PER POUND
C-30	$.12
C-92	.09
D-21	.11
E-11	.04

The specifications for Golding-Grow are established as:

a. Chemical E-11 must comprise at least 15% of the blend.

b. C-92 and C-30 must together constitute at least 45% of the blend.

c. D-21 and C-92 can together constitute no more than 30% of the blend.

d. Golding-Grow is packaged and sold in 50-pound bags.

Discussion Questions:

1. Formulate an LP problem to determine what blend of the four chemicals will allow Golding to minimize the cost of a 50-pound bag of the fertilizer.

2. Solve by computer to find the best solution. (LP Computer Software is documented in Ch. 12)

BIBLIOGRAPHY

Balbirer, Sheldon D., and Shaw, David. "An Application of Linear Programming to Bank Financial Planning." *Interfaces* Vol. 11, No. 5, October 1981, pp. 77–82.

Beare, G. C. "Linear Programming in Air Defence Modelling." *Journal of the Operational Research Society* Vol. 38, 1987, pp. 899–905.

Brosch, Lee C., Buck, Richard J., Sparrow, William H., and

White, James R. "Boxcars, Linear Programming, and the Sleeping Kitten." *Interfaces* Vol. 10, No. 6, December 1980, pp. 53–61.

Cabraal, R. Anil. "Production Planning in a Sri Lanka Coconut Mill Using Parametric Linear Programming." *Interfaces* Vol. 11, No. 3, June 1981, pp. 16–21.

Erenguc, S. S., and others. "A Non-Dual Approach to Sensitivity Analysis—The Righthand Side Case." *Decision Sciences* Vol. 16, Spring 1985, pp. 223–229.

Evren, R. "Interactive Compromise Programming." *Journal of Operational Research Society* Vol. 38, February 1987, pp. 163–172.

Ferris, M. C., and Philpott, A. B. "On the Performance of Karmarkar's Algorithm." *Journal of Operational Research Society* Vol. 39, March 1988, pp. 257–270.

Glen, J. J. "A Linear Programming Model for an Integrated Crop and Intensive Beef Production Enterprise." *Journal of Operational Research Society* Vol. 37, May 1986, pp. 487–494.

Gosselin, Karl, and Truchon, Michel. "Allocation of Classrooms by Linear Programming." *Journal of the Operational Research Society* Vol. 37, 1986, pp. 561–569.

Hilal, Said S., and Erikson, Warren. "Matching Supplies to Save Lives: Linear Programming the Production of Heart Valves." *Interfaces* Vol. 11, No. 6, December 1981, pp. 48–56.

Hollorann, Thomas, and Byrn, Judson. "United Airlines Stationed Manpower Planning System." *Interfaces* Vol. 16, No. 1, January–February 1986, pp. 39–50.

Jackson, Bruce L., and Brown, John M. "Using LP for Crude Oil Sales at Elk Hills." *Interfaces* Vol. 10, No. 3, June 1980, pp. 65–70.

Lanzenauer, Christoph Haehling von. "RRSP Flood: LP to the Rescue." *Interfaces* Vol. 17, No. 4, July–August 1987, pp. 27–33.

Leff, H. Stephen, Dada, Maqbool, and Graves, Stephen C. "An LP Planning Model for a Mental Health Community Support System." *Management Science* Vol. 32, No. 2, February 1986, pp. 139–155.

Marsten, Roy E., and Muller, Michael R. "A Mixed Integer Programming Approach to Air Cargo Fleet Planning." *Management Science* Vol. 26, No. 11, November 1980, pp. 1096–1107.

McKay, A. C. "Linear Programming Applications on Microcomputers." *Journal of Operational Research Society* Vol. 36, July 1985, pp. 633–635.

Nauss, Robert M., and Keeler, B. R. "Minimizing Net Interest Cost in Municipal Bond Bidding." *Management Science* Vol. 27, No. 4, April 1981, pp. 365–376.

Oliff, Michael, and Burch, Earl. "Multiproduct Production Scheduling at Owens-Corning Fiberglass." *Interfaces* Vol. 15, No. 5, September–October 1985, pp. 25–34.

Roy, Asim, Defalomir, Emma E., and Lasdon, Leon. "An Optimization-Based Decision Support System for a Product Mix Problem." *Interfaces* Vol. 12, No. 2, April 1982, pp. 26–33.

Sullivan, Robert, and Secrest, Steven. "A Simple Optimization DSS for Production Planning at Dairyman's Cooperative Creamery." *Interfaces* Vol. 15, No. 5, September–October, 1985.

Wild, W. G., Jr. "The Startling Discovery Bell Labs Kept in the Shadows." *Business Week* September 21, 1987, p. 69+.

11

Linear Programming: The Simplex Method

11.1
INTRODUCTION

In Chapter 10 we looked at examples of linear programming problems that contained two decision variables. With only two variables it was possible to use a graphical approach. We plotted the feasible region and then searched for the optimal corner point and corresponding profit or cost. This approach provided a good way to understand the basic concepts of linear programming. Most real-life LP problems, however, have more than two variables and are thus too large for the simple graphical solution procedure. Problems faced in business and government can have dozens, hundreds, or even a thousand variables. We need a more powerful method than graphing—so in this chapter we turn to a procedure called the *simplex method*.

How does the simplex method work? The concept is simple, and similar to graphical LP in one important respect. In graphical linear programming we examined each of the corner points; LP theory told us that the optimal solution lies at one of them. In LP problems containing *several* variables, we may not be able to graph the feasible region, but the optimal solution will *still* lie at a corner point of the many-sided, many-dimensional figure (called an *n*-dimensional polyhedron) that represents the area of feasible

simplex as an iterative method

solutions. The simplex method examines the corner points in a systematic fashion, using basic algebraic concepts. It does so in an *iterative* manner, that is, repeating the same set of procedures time after time until an optimal solution is reached. Each iteration brings a higher value for the objective function so that we are always moving closer to the optimal solution.

importance of simplex

Why should we study the simplex method? It is important to understand the ideas used to produce solutions. The simplex approach yields not only the optimal solution to the X_i variables and the maximum profit (or minimum cost), but valuable economic information as well.[1] To be able to use computers successfully and to interpret LP computer printouts, we need to know what the simplex method is doing and why.

In this chapter, we begin by solving a maximization problem using the simplex method. We then tackle a minimization problem and look at a few technical issues that are faced when employing the simplex procedure.

11.2
HOW TO SET UP THE INITIAL SIMPLEX SOLUTION

Let us consider again the case of the Flair Furniture Company from Chapter 10. Instead of the graphical solution we used in that chapter, we now demonstrate the simplex method. You may recall that we let

$$X_1 = \text{Number of tables produced}$$

$$X_2 = \text{Number of chairs produced}$$

---

[1] The simplex method also applies for problems requiring integer solutions, as we see in Chapter 15.

and that the problem was formulated as:

Maximize profit = $\$7X_1 + \$5X_2$ (*objective function*)

Subject to: $2X_1 + 1X_2 \leqslant 100$ (*painting hours constraint*)

$4X_1 + 3X_2 \leqslant 240$ (*carpentry hours constraint*)

$X_1, \quad X_2 \geqslant 0$ (*nonnegativity constraints*)

Converting the Constraints to Equations

The first step of the simplex method requires that we convert each inequality constraint in an LP formulation into an equation.[2] Less-than-or-equal-to constraints ($\leqslant$) such as in the Flair problem are converted to equations by adding a *slack variable* to each constraint. Slack variables represent unused resources; these may be in the form of time on a machine, labor hours, money, warehouse space, or any number of such resources in various business problems.

In our case at hand, we can let

S_1 = Slack variable representing unused hours in the painting department

S_2 = Slack variable representing unused hours in the carpentry department

slack variables

KEY IDEA

The constraints to the problem may now be written as:

$$2X_1 + 1X_2 + S_1 = 100$$

and

$$4X_1 + 3X_2 + S_2 = 240$$

Thus, if the production of tables (X_1) and chairs (X_2) uses less than 100 hours of painting time available, the unused time is the value of the slack variable, S_1. For example, if $X_1 = 0$ and $X_2 = 0$, in other words, nothing is produced, we have $S_1 = 100$ hours of slack time in the painting department. If Flair produces $X_1 = 40$ tables and $X_2 = 10$ chairs, then,

$$2X_1 + 1X_2 + S_1 = 100$$
$$2(40) + 1(10) + S_1 = 100$$
$$S_1 = 10$$

and there will be 10 hours of slack, or unused, painting time available.

To include all variables in each equation, which is a requirement of the next simplex step, slack variables not appearing in an equation are added with a coefficient of 0. This means, in effect, that they have no influence on the equations in which they are inserted; but it does allow us to keep tabs on all variables at all times. The equations now appear as:

$$2X_1 + 1X_2 + 1S_1 + 0S_2 = 100$$
$$4X_1 + 3X_2 + 0S_1 + 1S_2 = 240$$
$$X_1, X_2, S_1, S_2 \geqslant 0$$

---

[2] This is because the simplex is a matrix algebra method that requires all mathematical relationships to be equations, with each equation containing all of the variables.

Since slack variables yield no profit, they are added to the original objective function with 0 profit coefficients. The objective function becomes:

$$\text{Maximize profit} = \$7X_1 + \$5X_2 + \$0S_1 + \$0S_2$$

Finding an Initial Solution Algebraically

Let's take another look at the new constraint equations. We see that there are two equations and four variables. Think back to your last algebra course. When you have the same number of unknown variables as you have equations, it is possible to solve for unique values of the variables. But when there are four unknowns (X_1, X_2, S_1, and S_2, in this case) and only two equations, you can let two of the variables equal 0 and then solve for the other two. For example, if $X_1 = X_2 = 0$, then $S_1 = 100$, and $S_2 = 240$.

The simplex method begins with an initial feasible solution in which all real variables (such as X_1 and X_2) are set equal to 0. This trivial solution always produces a profit of $0, as well as slack variables equal to the constant (right-hand side) terms in the constraint equations. It's not a very exciting solution in terms of economic returns, but it is one of the original corner point solutions (see Figure 11.1). As mentioned, the simplex method will start at this corner point (*A*), then move up or over to the corner point that yields the most improved profit (*B* or *D*). Finally, the technique will move

simplex considers only corner points

to corner point *C*, which happens to be the optimal solution to the Flair Furniture problem. The simplex method considers only feasible solutions

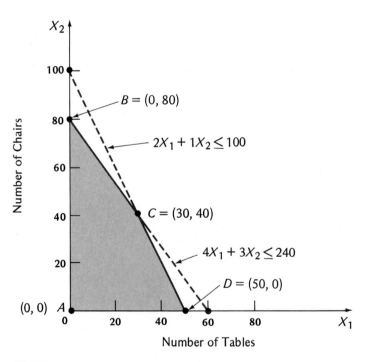

FIGURE 11.1
Corner Points of the Flair Furniture Company Problem

and hence will touch no possible combinations other than the corner points of the shaded region in Figure 11.1.

The First Simplex Tableau

To simplify handling the equations and objective function in an LP problem, we place all of the coefficients into a tabular form. The first *simplex tableau* is shown in Table 11.1. An explanation of its parts and how the tableau is derived follows.

Constraint Equations. We see that Flair Furniture's two constraint equations can be expressed as:

SOLUTION MIX	X_1	X_2	S_1	S_2	QUANTITY (RIGHT HAND SIDE)
S_1	2	1	1	0	100
S_2	4	3	0	1	240

constraints in tabular form

The numbers (2, 1, 1, 0) in the first row represent the coefficients of the first equation, namely, $2X_1 + 1X_2 + 1S_1 + 0S_2$. The numbers (4, 3, 0, 1) in the second row are the algebraic equivalent of the constraint $4X_1 + 3X_2 + 0S_1 + 1S_2$.

As suggested earlier, we begin the initial solution procedure at the origin, where $X_1 = 0$ and $X_2 = 0$. The values of the two other variables must then

TABLE 11.1 Flair Furniture's Initial Simplex Tableau

		Profit per Unit Column	Production Mix Column	Real Variables Columns		Slack Variables Columns		Constant Column
$C_j \rightarrow$		$7	$5	$0	$0		Profit per unit row
	Solution Mix	X_1	X_2	S_1	S_2	Quantity	
$0	S_1	2	1	1	0	100	Constraint
$0	S_2	4	3	0	1	240	equation rows
	Z_j	$0	$0	$0	$0	$0	Gross profit row
	$C_j - Z_j$	$7	$5	$0	$0	$0	Net profit row

initial solution mix

be nonzero, so $S_1 = 100$ and $S_2 = 240$. These two slack variables comprise the *initial solution mix;* their values are found in the *quantity* (or right hand side—RHS) *column.* Since X_1 and X_2 are not in the solution mix, their initial values are automatically equal to 0.

This initial solution is termed a *basic feasible solution* and is described in vector, or column, form as:

basic feasible solution

$$\begin{bmatrix} X_1 \\ X_2 \\ S_1 \\ S_2 \end{bmatrix} = \begin{bmatrix} 0 \\ 0 \\ 100 \\ 240 \end{bmatrix}$$

basic and nonbasic variables

Variables in the solution mix, which is called the *basis* in LP terminology, are referred to as *basic variables.* In this example, the basic variables are S_1 and S_2. Variables not in the solution mix or basis (X_1 and X_2 in this case) are called *nonbasic variables.* Of course, if the optimal solution to this linear programming problem turned out to be $X_1 = 30$, $X_2 = 40$, $S_1 = 0$, and $S_2 = 0$, or

$$\begin{bmatrix} X_1 \\ X_2 \\ S_1 \\ S_2 \end{bmatrix} = \begin{bmatrix} 30 \\ 40 \\ 0 \\ 0 \end{bmatrix} \qquad \text{in vector form,}$$

then X_1 and X_2 would be the final basic variables, while S_1 and S_2 would be the nonbasic variables.

Substitution Rates. Many students are unsure as to the actual meaning of the numbers in the columns under each variable. We know that the entries are the coefficients for that variable. Under X_1 are the coefficients $\begin{pmatrix} 2 \\ 4 \end{pmatrix}$, under X_2 are $\begin{pmatrix} 1 \\ 3 \end{pmatrix}$, under S_1 are $\begin{pmatrix} 1 \\ 0 \end{pmatrix}$, and under S_2 are $\begin{pmatrix} 0 \\ 1 \end{pmatrix}$. But what is

substitution rates

KEY IDEA

their interpretation? The numbers in the body of the simplex tableau (see Table 11.1) may be thought of as *substitution rates.* For example, suppose we now wish to make X_1 larger than 0, that is, produce some tables. For every unit of the X_1 product introduced into the current solution, 2 units of S_1 and 4 units of S_2 must be removed from the solution. This is so because each table requires 2 hours of the currently unused painting department slack time, S_1. It also takes 4 hours of carpentry time; hence 4 units of variable S_2 must be removed from the solution for every unit of X_1 that enters. Likewise, the substitution rates for each unit of X_2 that enters the current solution are 1 unit of S_1 and 3 units of S_2.

Another point that you are reminded of throughout this chapter is that for any variable ever to appear in the solution mix column, it must have a number 1 someplace in its column and 0s in every other place in that column. We see that column S_1 contains $\begin{pmatrix} 1 \\ 0 \end{pmatrix}$, so variable S_1 is in the solution.

Likewise, the S_2 column is $\begin{pmatrix} 0 \\ 1 \end{pmatrix}$, so S_2 is also in the solution.[3]

Adding the Objective Function. We now continue to the next step in establishing the first simplex tableau. We add a row to reflect the objective function values for each variable. These contribution rates, called C_j, appear just above each respective variable as seen below:

$C_j \longrightarrow$ $\downarrow$	SOLUTION MIX	$7 X_1$	$5 X_2$	$0 S_1$	$0 S_2$	QUANTITY
$0	S_1	2	1	1	0	100
$0	S_2	4	3	0	1	240

The unit profit rates are not just found in the top C_j row: in the left-most column, C_j indicates the unit profit for each variable *currently* in the solution mix. If S_1 were removed from the solution and replaced, for example, by X_2, then $5 would appear in the C_j column just to the left of the term X_2.

The Z_j and $C_j - Z_j$ Rows. We may complete the initial Flair Furniture simplex tableau by adding two final rows. These last two rows provide us with important economic information, including the total profit and the answer as to whether the current solution is optimal.

We compute the Z_j value for each column of the initial solution in Table 11.1 by multiplying the 0 contribution value of each number in the C_j column by each number in that row and the jth column, and summing. The Z_j value for the quantity column provides the total contribution (gross profit in this case) of the given solution.

adding the Z and $C - Z$ rows

$$Z_j \text{ (For gross profit)} = (\text{Profit per unit of } S_1) \times (\text{Number of units of } S_1)$$
$$+ (\text{Profit per unit of } S_2) \times (\text{Number of units of } S_2)$$
$$= \$0 \times 100 \text{ units} + \$0 \times 240 \text{ units}$$
$$= \$0 \text{ profit}$$

The Z_j values for the other columns (under the variables X_1, X_2, S_1, and S_2) represent the gross profit *given up* by adding one unit of this variable into the current solution. Their calculations are as follows:

$$Z_j(\text{For column } X_1) = (\$0)(2) + (\$0)(4) = \$0$$
$$Z_j(\text{For column } X_2) = (\$0)(1) + (\$0)(3) = \$0$$

---

[3] If there had been *three* less-than-or-equal-to constraints in the Flair Furniture problem, then there would be three slack variables, S_1, S_2 and S_3. The 1s and 0s would appear like this:

SOLUTION MIX	S_1	S_2	S_3
S_1	1	0	0
S_2	0	1	0
S_3	0	0	1

$$Z_j(\text{For column } S_1) = (\$0)(1) + (\$0)(0) = \$0$$

$$Z_j(\text{For column } S_2) = (\$0)(0) + (\$0)(1) = \$0$$

We see that there is no profit *lost* by adding one unit of either X_1 (tables), X_2 (chairs), S_1, or S_2.

$C_j - Z_j$ is the net profit row

The $C_j - Z_j$ number in each column represents the net profit, that is, the profit gained minus the profit given up, that will result from introducing 1 unit of each product or variable into the solution. It is not calculated for the quantity column. To compute these numbers, simply subtract the Z_j total for each column from the C_j value at the very top of that variable's column. The calculations for the net profit per unit (the $C_j - Z_j$ row) in this example are:

	COLUMN			
	X_1	X_2	S_1	S_2
C_j for column	$7	$5	$0	$0
Z_j for column	$0	$0	$0	$0
$C_j - Z_j$ for column	$7	$5	$0	$0

reaching an optimal solution

It was obvious to us when we computed a profit of $0 that the initial solution was not optimal. By examining the numbers in the $C_j - Z_j$ row of Table 11.1, we see that total profit can be increased by $7 for each unit of X_1 (tables) and by $5 for each unit of X_2 (chairs) added to the solution mix. A negative number in the $C_j - Z_j$ row would tell us that profits would *decrease* if the corresponding variable were added to the solution mix. An optimal solution is reached in the simplex method when the $C_j - Z_j$ row contains no positive numbers. Such is not the case in our initial tableau.

11.3
SIMPLEX SOLUTION PROCEDURES

Once an initial tableau has been completed, we proceed through a series of five steps to compute all the numbers needed in the next tableau. The calculations are not difficult, but they are complex enough that the smallest arithmetic error can produce a very wrong answer.

five simplex steps

We first list the five steps and then carefully explain and apply them in completing the second and third tableaus for the Flair Furniture Company data.

variable entering

Step 1. Determine which variable to enter into the solution mix next. One way of doing this is by identifying the column, and hence, the variable, with the largest positive number in the $C_j - Z_j$ row of the previous tableau. This means that we will now be producing some of the product contributing the greatest additional profit per unit. The column identified in this step is called the *pivot column*.

variable leaving

Step 2. Determine which variable to replace. Since we have just chosen a new variable to enter the solution mix, we must decide which basic variable currently in the solution will have to leave to make room for it. Step 2 is accomplished by dividing each amount in the *quantity* column by the corresponding number in the column selected in step 1. The row with the *smallest nonnegative number* calculated in this fashion will be replaced in the next tableau. (This smallest number, by the way, gives the maximum number of units of the variable which may be placed in the solution.) This row is often referred to as the *pivot row*. The number at the intersection of the pivot row and pivot column is referred to as the *pivot number*.

Step 3. Compute new values for the pivot row. To do this, we simply divide every number in the row by the pivot number.   **new pivot row**

Step 4. Compute new values for each remaining row. (In our Flair Furniture problem there are only two rows in the LP tableau, but most larger problems have many more rows.) All remaining row(s) are calculated as follows: **other new rows**

$$\text{(New row numbers)} = \text{(Numbers in old row)} -$$

$$\left[\left(\begin{array}{l} \text{Number above or below} \\ \text{pivot number} \end{array} \right) \times \left(\begin{array}{l} \text{Corresponding number in} \\ \text{the new row, that is, the} \\ \text{row replaced in step 3} \end{array} \right) \right] \quad \text{(11-1)}$$

Step 5. Compute the Z_j and $C_j - Z_j$ rows, as previously demonstrated in the initial tableau. If all numbers in the $C_j - Z_j$ row are 0 or negative, an optimal solution has been reached. If this is not the case, return to step 1.   **Z_j and $C_j - Z_j$ rows**

11.4
THE SECOND SIMPLEX TABLEAU

Now that we have listed the five steps needed to move from an initial solution to an improved solution, we apply them to the Flair Furniture problem. Our goal is to add a new variable to the solution mix, or basis, in order to raise the profit from its current tableau value of $0.   **applying the five steps**

Step 1. To decide which of the variables will enter the solution next (it must be either X_1 or X_2, since they are the only two nonbasic variables at this point), we select the one with the largest positive $C_j - Z_j$ value. Variable X_1, tables, has a $C_j - Z_j$ value of $7, implying that each unit of X_1 added into the solution mix will contribute $7 to the overall profit. Variable X_2, chairs, has a $C_j - Z_j$ value of only $5. The other two variables, S_1 and S_2, have 0 values, and can add nothing more to profit. Hence, we select X_1 as the variable to enter the solution mix, and identify its column (with an arrow) as the pivot column. This is shown in Table 11.2.   **X_1 (tables) enters the solution mix**

Step 2. Since X_1 is about to enter the solution mix, we must decide which variable is to be replaced. There can only be as many basic variables as there are constraints in any LP problem, so either S_1 or S_2 will have to leave to make room for the introduction of tables, X_1, into the basis. To identify

TABLE 11.2 Pivot Column Identified in the Initial Simplex Tableau

$C_j \longrightarrow$		$7	$5	$0	$0	
$\downarrow$	SOLUTION MIX	X_1	X_2	S_1	S_2	QUANTITY (RHS)
$0	S_1	2	1	1	0	100
$0	S_2	4	3	0	1	240
	Z_j	$0	$0	$0	$0	$0
	$C_j - Z_j$	$7	$5	$0	$0	(total profit)
		Pivot column				

the pivot row, each number in the quantity column is divided by the corresponding number in the X_1 column.

For the S_1 row:

$$\frac{100 \text{ (hours of painting time available)}}{2 \text{ (hours required per table)}} = 50 \text{ tables}$$

For the S_2 row:

$$\frac{240 \text{ (hours of carpentry time available)}}{4 \text{ (hours required per table)}} = 60 \text{ tables}$$

S_1 leaves the solution mix

The smaller of these two ratios, 50, indicates the maximum number of units of X_1 that can be produced without violating either of the original constraints. It also points out that the pivot row will be the first row. This means that S_1 will be the variable to be replaced at this iteration of the simplex method. The pivot row and the pivot number (the number at the intersection of the pivot row and pivot column) are identified in Table 11.3.

Step 3. Now that we have decided which variable is to enter the solution mix (X_1) and which is to leave (S_1), we begin to develop the second, improved simplex tableau. Step 3 involves computing a replacement for the pivot row. This is done by dividing every number in the pivot row by the pivot number:

the new pivot row

$$\frac{2}{2} = 1 \qquad \frac{1}{2} = \frac{1}{2} \qquad \frac{1}{2} = \frac{1}{2} \qquad \frac{0}{2} = 0 \qquad \frac{100}{2} = 50$$

TABLE 11.3 Pivot Row and Pivot Number Identified in the Initial Simplex Tableau

$C_j \rightarrow$		$7	$5	$0	$0	
$\downarrow$	Solution Mix	X_1	X_2	S_1	S_2	Quantity
$0	S_1	②	1	1	0	100 ← Pivot row
$0	S_2	4	3	0	1	240
			Pivot number			
	Z_j	$0	$0	$0	$0	$0
	$C_j - Z_j$	$7	$5	$0	$0	
		Pivot column				

The new version of the entire pivot row appears in the accompanying table. Note that X_1 is now in the solution mix and that 50 units of X_1 are being produced. The C_j value is listed as a $7 contribution per unit of X_1 in the solution. This will definitely provide Flair Furniture with a more profitable solution than the $0 generated in the initial tableau.

C_j	SOLUTION MIX	X_1	X_2	S_1	S_2	QUANTITY
$7	X_1	1	$\frac{1}{2}$	$\frac{1}{2}$	0	50

Step 4. This step is intended to help us compute new values for the other row in the body of the tableau, that is, the S_2 row. It is slightly more complex than replacing the pivot row and uses the formula (Equation 11-1) shown earlier. The expression on the right side of the following equation is used to calculate the left side.

recomputing the S_2 row

$\begin{pmatrix} \text{NUMBER IN} \\ \text{NEW } S_2 \text{ ROW} \end{pmatrix}$	=	$\begin{pmatrix} \text{NUMBER IN} \\ \text{OLD } S_2 \text{ ROW} \end{pmatrix}$	−	$\left[\begin{pmatrix} \text{NUMBER BELOW} \\ \text{PIVOT NUMBER} \end{pmatrix} \right.$	×	$\left. \begin{pmatrix} \text{CORRESPONDING NUMBER} \\ \text{IN THE NEW } X_1 \text{ ROW} \end{pmatrix} \right]$
0	=	4	−	(4)	×	(1)
1	=	3	−	(4)	×	($\frac{1}{2}$)
−2	=	0	−	(4)	×	($\frac{1}{2}$)
1	=	1	−	(4)	×	(0)
40	=	240	−	(4)	×	(50)

This new S_2 row will appear in the second tableau in the following format:

C_j	SOLUTION MIX	X_1	X_2	S_1	S_2	QUANTITY
$7	X_1	1	$\frac{1}{2}$	$\frac{1}{2}$	0	50
$0	S_2	0	1	−2	1	40

Now that X_1 and S_2 are in the solution mix, take a look at the values of the coefficients in their respective columns. The X_1 column contains $\begin{pmatrix} 1 \\ 0 \end{pmatrix}$, a condition necessary for that variable to be in the solution. Likewise the S_2 column has $\begin{pmatrix} 0 \\ 1 \end{pmatrix}$, that is, it contains a 1 and a 0. Basically, the algebraic

KEY IDEA

manipulations we just went through in steps 3 and 4 were simply directed at producing 0s and 1s in the appropriate positions. In step 3 we divided every number in the pivot row by the pivot number; this guaranteed that there would be a 1 in the X_1 column's top row. To derive the new second row, we multiplied the first row (each row is really an equation) by a constant (the number 4 here), and subtracted it from the second equation. The result was the new S_2 row with a 0 in the X_1 column.

Step 5. The final step of the second iteration is to introduce the effect of the objective function. This involves computing the Z_j and $C_j - Z_j$ rows.

finding the new profit

Recall that the Z_j entry for the quantity column gives us the gross profit for the current solution. The other Z_j values represent the gross profit given up by adding one unit of each variable into this new solution. The Z_j values are calculated as follows:

$$Z_j \text{(for } X_1 \text{ column)} = (\$7)(1) + (\$0)(0) = \$7$$

$$Z_j \text{(for } X_2 \text{ column)} = (\$7)(\tfrac{1}{2}) + (\$0)(1) = \$\tfrac{7}{2}$$

$$Z_j \text{(for } S_1 \text{ column)} = (\$7)(\tfrac{1}{2}) + (\$0)(-2) = \$\tfrac{7}{2}$$

$$Z_j \text{(for } S_2 \text{ column)} = (\$7)(0) + (\$0)(1) = \$0$$

$$Z_j \text{(for total profit)} = (\$7)(50) + (\$0)(40) = \$350$$

Note that the current profit is $350.

The $C_j - Z_j$ numbers represent the net profit that will result, given our present production mix, if we add one unit of each variable into the solution.

	COLUMN			
	X_1	X_2	S_1	S_2
C_j for column	$7	$5	$0	$0
Z_j for column	$7	$\tfrac{7}{2}$	$\tfrac{7}{2}$	$0
$C_j - Z_j$ for column	$0	$\tfrac{3}{2}$	$-\tfrac{7}{2}$	$0

The Z_j and $C_j - Z_j$ rows are inserted into the complete second tableau as shown in Table 11.4.

TABLE 11.4 Completed Second Simplex Tableau for Flair Furniture

$C_j \longrightarrow$		$7	$5	$0	$0	
$\downarrow$	SOLUTION MIX	X_1	X_2	S_1	S_2	QUANTITY
$7	X_1	1	$\tfrac{1}{2}$	$\tfrac{1}{2}$	0	50
$0	S_2	0	1	-2	1	40
	Z_j	$7	$\tfrac{7}{2}$	$\tfrac{7}{2}$	$0	$350
	$C_j - Z_j$	$0	$\tfrac{3}{2}$	$-\$\tfrac{7}{2}$	$0	

Interpreting the Second Tableau

Table 11.4 summarizes all of the information for the Flair Furniture Company's production mix decision as of the second iteration of the simplex method. Let's briefly look over a few important items.

current solution as corner point in graphical method

Current Solution. At this point, the solution point of 50 tables and 0 chairs ($X_1 = 50$, $X_2 = 0$) generates a profit of $350. X_1 is a basic variable; X_2 is a nonbasic variable. Using a graphical LP approach, this corresponds to corner point D, as shown in Figure 11.2.

Resource Information. We also see in Table 11.4 that slack variable S_2, representing the amount of unused time in the carpentry department, is

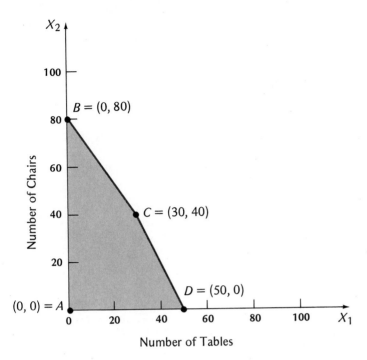

FIGURE 11.2
Flair Furniture Company's Feasible Region and Corner Points

in the basis. It has a value of 40, implying that 40 hours of carpentry time remain available. Slack variable S_1 is nonbasic, and has a value of 0 hours. There is no slack time in the painting department.

Substitution Rates. We mentioned earlier that the substitution rates are the coefficients in the heart of the tableau. Look at the X_2 column. If 1 unit of X_2 (1 chair) is added to the current solution, $\frac{1}{2}$ unit of X_1 and 1 unit of S_2 must be given up. This is because the solution $X_1 = 50$ tables uses up all 100 hours of time in the painting department. (The original constraint, you may recall, was $2X_1 + 1X_2 + S_1 = 100$.) To capture the 1 painting hour needed to make 1 chair, $\frac{1}{2}$ of a table *less* must be produced. This frees up 1 hour to be used in making 1 chair.

meaning of substitution rates

But why must 1 unit of S_2 (namely, 1 hour of carpentry time) be given up in order to produce 1 chair? The original constraint was $4X_1 + 3X_2 + S_2 = 240$ hours of carpentry time. Doesn't this indicate that 3 hours of carpentry time are required to produce 1 unit of X_2? The answer is that we are looking at *marginal* rates of substitution. Adding 1 chair replaced $\frac{1}{2}$ table. Since $\frac{1}{2}$ table required ($\frac{1}{2} \times 4$ hours per table) $= 2$ hours of carpentry time, 2 units of S_2 are freed. Thus only 1 *more* unit of S_2 is needed to produce 1 chair.

Just to be sure you have this concept down pat, let's look at one more column, S_1, as well. The coefficients are $\begin{pmatrix} \frac{1}{2} \\ -2 \end{pmatrix}$. These substitution rate values mean that if 1 hour of slack painting time is added to the current solution, $\frac{1}{2}$ of a table (X_1) *less* will be produced. However, note that if 1 unit of S_1 is added into the solution, 2 hours of carpentry time (S_2) will no longer be used. These will be *added* to the current 40 slack hours of carpentry time. Hence, a *negative* substitution rate means that if 1 unit of a column variable is added to the solution, the value of the corresponding solution (or row) variable will be increased. A *positive* substitution rate tells us that if 1 unit of the column variable is added to the solution, the row variable will decrease by the rate.

Can you interpret the rates in the X_1 and S_2 columns now?

is solution optimal?

Net Profit Row. The $C_j - Z_j$ row is important to us for two reasons. First, it indicates whether or not the current solution is optimal. When there are no positive numbers in the bottom row, an optimum solution to an LP maximization problem has been reached. In the case of Table 11.4, we see that values for X_1, S_1, and S_2 are 0 or negative. The value for X_2 ($\frac{3}{2}$) means that the net profit can be increased by $1.50 ($=\frac{3}{2}$) for each chair added into the current solution.

Because the $C_j - Z_j$ value for X_1 is 0, for every unit of X_1 added the total profit will remain unchanged, because we are already producing as many tables as possible. A negative number, such as the $-\frac{7}{2}$ in the S_1 column, implies that total profit will *decrease* by $3.50 if 1 unit of S_1 is added to the solution. In other words, making one slack hour available in the painting department ($S_1 = 0$ currently) means we would have to produce one half table less. Since each table results in a $7 contribution, we will be losing $\frac{1}{2} \times \$7 = \$\frac{7}{2}$, for a net loss of $3.50.

shadow prices

In Chapter 12, we introduce the subject of *shadow prices*. These relate to $C_j - Z_j$ values in the slack variable columns. Shadow prices are simply another way of interpreting negative $C_j - Z_j$ values; they may be viewed as the potential *increase* in profit if one more hour of the scarce resource (such as painting or carpentry time) could be made *available*.

We mentioned previously that there are two reasons to consider carefully the $C_j - Z_j$ row. The second reason, of course, is that we use the row to determine which variable will enter the solution next. Since an optimal solution has not been reached yet, let's proceed to the third simplex tableau.

11.5
DEVELOPING THE THIRD TABLEAU

Since not all numbers in the $C_j - Z_j$ row of the latest tableau are 0 or negative, the previous solution is not optimal, and we must repeat the five simplex steps.

X_2 (chairs) will be the next new variable

Step 1. Variable X_2 will enter the solution next by virtue of the fact that its $C_j - Z_j$ value of $\frac{3}{2}$ is the largest (and only) positive number in the row. This means that for every unit of X_2 (chairs) we start to produce, the objective function will increase in value by $\$\frac{3}{2}$, or $1.50. The X_2 column is the new pivot column.

replacing a variable, S_2, in this case

Step 2. The next step involves identifying the pivot row. The question is which variable currently in the solution (X_1 or S_2) will have to leave to make room for X_2 to enter? Again, each number in the quantity column is divided by its corresponding number in the X_2 column.

$$\text{For the } X_1 \text{ row: } \frac{50}{\frac{1}{2}} = 100 \text{ chairs}$$

$$\text{For the } S_2 \text{ row: } \frac{40}{1} = 40 \text{ chairs}$$

The S_2 row has the smallest ratio, meaning that variable S_2 will leave the basis and be replaced by X_2. The new pivot row, pivot column, and pivot number are all shown in Table 11.5.

Step 3. The pivot row is replaced by dividing every number in it by the (circled) pivot number. Since every number is divided by 1, there is no change.

pivot row for the third tableau

$$\frac{0}{1} = 0 \quad \frac{1}{1} = 1 \quad \frac{-2}{1} = -2 \quad \frac{1}{1} = 1 \quad \frac{40}{1} = 40$$

The entire new X_2 row looks like this:

C_j	SOLUTION MIX	X_1	X_2	S_1	S_2	QUANTITY
\$5	X_2	0	1	-2	1	40

It will be placed in the new simplex tableau in the same row position that S_2 was in before (see Table 11.6).

TABLE 11.5 Pivot Row, Pivot Column, and Pivot Number Identified in the Second Simplex Tableau

$C_j \rightarrow$ $\downarrow$	Solution Mix	\$7 X_1	\$5 X_2	\$0 S_1	\$0 S_2	Quantity
\$7	X_1	1	$\frac{1}{2}$	$\frac{1}{2}$	0	50
\$0	S_2	0	① *Pivot number*	-2	1	40 ← *Pivot row*
	Z_j	\$7	$\$\frac{7}{2}$	$\$\frac{7}{2}$	\$0	\$350 (Total profit)
	$C_j - Z_j$	\$0	$\$\frac{3}{2}$	$-\$\frac{7}{2}$	\$0	

Pivot column

Step 4. The new values for the X_1 row may now be computed.

the new X_1 row

$$\begin{pmatrix} \text{Number} \\ \text{in new} \\ X_1 \text{ row} \end{pmatrix} = \begin{pmatrix} \text{Number} \\ \text{in old} \\ X_1 \text{ row} \end{pmatrix} - \left[\begin{pmatrix} \text{Number} \\ \text{above} \\ \text{pivot} \\ \text{number} \end{pmatrix} \times \begin{pmatrix} \text{Corresponding} \\ \text{no. in new} \\ X_2 \text{ row} \end{pmatrix} \right]$$

1	=	1	−	$(\frac{1}{2})$	×	(0)
0	=	$\frac{1}{2}$	−	$(\frac{1}{2})$	×	(1)
$\frac{3}{2}$	=	$\frac{1}{2}$	−	$(\frac{1}{2})$	×	(-2)
$-\frac{1}{2}$	=	0	−	$(\frac{1}{2})$	×	(1)
30	=	50	−	$(\frac{1}{2})$	×	(40)

Hence, the new X_1 row will appear in the third tableau in the following position:

C_j	SOLUTION MIX	X_1	X_2	S_1	S_2	QUANTITY
$7	X_1	1	0	$\frac{3}{2}$	$-\frac{1}{2}$	30
$5	X_2	0	1	-2	1	40

Step 5. Finally, the Z_j and $C_j - Z_j$ rows for third tableau are calculated:

final step

$$Z_j(\text{for } X_1 \text{ column}) = (\$7)(1) + (\$5)(0) = \$7$$
$$Z_j(\text{for } X_2 \text{ column}) = (\$7)(0) + (\$5)(1) = \$5$$
$$Z_j(\text{for } S_1 \text{ column}) = (\$7)(\tfrac{3}{2}) + (\$5)(-2) = \$\tfrac{1}{2}$$
$$Z_j(\text{for } S_2 \text{ column}) = (\$7)(-\tfrac{1}{2}) + (\$5)(1) = \$\tfrac{3}{2}$$
$$Z_j(\text{for total profit}) = (\$7)(30) + (\$5)(40) = \$410$$

The net profit per unit row appears as follows:

	COLUMN			
	X_1	X_2	S_1	S_2
C_j for column	$7	$5	$0	$0
Z_j for column	$7	$5	$\frac{1}{2}$	$\frac{3}{2}$
$C_j - Z_j$ for column	$0	$0	$-$\frac{1}{2}$	$-$\frac{3}{2}$

optimal solution reached

All results for the third iteration of the simplex method are summarized in Table 11.6. Note that since every number in the tableau's $C_j - Z_j$ row is 0 or negative, an optimal solution has been reached.

final solution

That solution is:

$$X_1 = 30 \text{ tables} \qquad X_2 = 40 \text{ chairs}$$
$$S_1 = 0 \text{ slack hours in the painting department}$$
$$S_2 = 0 \text{ slack hours in the carpentry department}$$
$$\text{Profit} = \$410 \text{ for the optimal solution}$$

X_1 and X_2 are the final basic variables, while S_1 and S_2 are nonbasic (and thus automatically equal to 0). This solution corresponds to corner point C in Figure 11.2.

TABLE 11.6 Final Simplex Tableau for the Flair Furniture Problem

$C_j \longrightarrow$	SOLUTION MIX $\downarrow$	$7	$5	$0	$0	
		X_1	X_2	S_1	S_2	QUANTITY
$7	X_1	1	0	$\frac{3}{2}$	$-\frac{1}{2}$	30
$5	X_2	0	1	-2	1	40
	Z_j	$7	$5	$\frac{1}{2}$	$\frac{3}{2}$	$410
	$C_j - Z_j$	$0	$0	$-$\frac{1}{2}$	$-$\frac{3}{2}$	

Since it's always possible to make an arithmetic error when you are going through the numerous simplex steps and iterations, it is a good idea to verify your final solution. This can be done in part by looking at the original Flair Furniture Company constraints and objective function.

verifying the solution

First constraint: $2X_1 + 1X_2 \leq 100$ painting department hours
$$2(30) + 1(40) \leq 100$$
$$100 \leq 100 \checkmark$$

Second constraint: $4X_1 + 3X_2 \leq 240$ carpentry department hours
$$4(30 + 3(40) \leq 240$$
$$240 \leq 240 \checkmark$$

Objective function: Profit $= \$7X_1 + \$5X_2$
$$= \$7(30) + \$5(40)$$
$$= \$410$$

11.6
REVIEW OF PROCEDURES FOR SOLVING LP MAXIMIZATION PROBLEMS

Before moving on to other issues concerning the simplex method, we briefly review what we've learned so far for LP maximization problems.

I. Formulate the LP problem's objective function and constraints.

simplex steps reviewed

II. Add slack variables to each less-then-or-equal-to constraint and to the problem's objective function.

III. Develop an initial simplex tableau with slack variables in the basis and their variables (the X_1's) set equal to 0. Compute the Z_j and $C_j - Z_j$ values for this tableau.

IV. Follow these five steps until an optimal solution has been reached:

    A. Choose the variable with the greatest positive $C_j - Z_j$ to enter the solution. This is the pivot column.

    B. Determine the row to be replaced by selecting the one with the smallest (nonnegative) quantity-to-pivot column ratio. This is the pivot row.

    C. Calculate the new values for the pivot row.

    D. Calculate the new values for the other row(s).

    E. Calculate the Z_j and $C_j - Z_j$ values for this tableau. If there are any $C_j - Z_j$ numbers greater than 0, return to step A. If there are no $C_j - Z_j$ numbers that are greater than 0, an optimal solution has been reached.

11.7
SURPLUS AND ARTIFICIAL VARIABLES

Up to this point in the chapter, all of the linear programming constraints you have seen were of the less-than-or-equal-to ($\leq$) variety. Just as common

KEY IDEA

in real-life problems—especially in LP minimization problems—are greater-than-or-equal-to ($\geq$) constraints and equalities. To use the simplex method, each of these must be converted to a special form also. If they are not, the simplex technique is unable to set up an initial feasible solution in the first tableau.

Before moving on to the next section of this chapter which deals with solving LP minimization problems with the simplex method, we take a look at how to convert a few typical constraints.

$$\text{Constraint 1: } 5X_1 + 10X_2 + 8X_3 \geq 210$$

$$\text{Constraint 2: } 25X_1 + 30X_2 = 900$$

Surplus Variables

subtracting surplus variables to form equalities

Greater-than-or-equal-to ($\geq$) constraints, such as constraint 1 as just described, require a different approach than do the less-than-or-equal-to ($\leq$) constraints we saw in the Flair Furniture problem. They involve the subtraction of a *surplus variable*, rather than the addition of a slack variable. The surplus variable tells us how much the solution exceeds the constraint resource. Because of its analogy to a slack variable, surplus is sometimes simply called *negative slack*. To convert the first constraint, we begin by subtracting a surplus variable, S_1, to create an equality.

$$\text{Constraint 1 rewritten: } 5X_1 + 10X_2 + 8X_3 - S_1 = 210$$

If, for example, a solution to an LP problem involving this constraint is $X_1 = 20$, $X_2 = 8$, $X_3 = 5$, then the amount of surplus, or unused resource, could be computed as follows:

$$5X_1 + 10X_2 + 8X_3 - S_1 = 210$$

$$5(20) + 10(8) + 8(5) - S_1 = 210$$

$$100 + 80 + 40 - S_1 = 210$$

$$-S_1 = 210 - 220$$

$$S_1 = 10 \text{ Surplus units of first resource}$$

There is one more step, however, in preparing a $\geq$ constraint for the simplex method.

Artificial Variables

There is one small problem in trying to use the first constraint (as it has just been rewritten) in setting up an initial simplex solution. Since all "real" variables such as X_1, X_2, and X_3 are set to 0 in the initial tableau, S_1 takes on a negative value.

$$5(0) + 10(0) + 8(0) - S_1 = 210$$

$$0 - S_1 = 210$$

$$S_1 = -210$$

All variables in LP problems, be they real, slack, or surplus, *must* be non-negative at all times. If $S_1 = -210$, this important condition is violated.

To resolve the situation, we introduce one last kind of variable, called an *artificial variable*. We simply add the artificial variable, A_1, to the constraint as follows:

Constraint 1 completed: $5X_1 + 10X_2 + 8X_3 - S_1 + A_1 = 210$

Now, not only the X_1, X_2, and X_3 variables may be set to 0 in the initial simplex solution, but the S_1 surplus variable as well. This leaves us with $A_1 = 210$.

Let's turn our attention to constraint 2 for a moment. This constraint is already an equality, so why worry about it? To be included in the initial simplex solution, it turns out, even an equality must have an artificial variable added to it.

Constraint 2 rewritten: $25X_1 + 30X_2 + A_2 = 900$

The reason for inserting an artificial variable into an equality constraint deals with the usual problem of finding an initial LP solution. In a simple constraint such as number 2, it's easy to guess that $X_1 = 0$, $X_2 = 30$ would yield an initial feasible solution. But what if our problem had ten equality constraints, each containing seven variables? It would be *extremely* difficult to sit down and "eyeball" a set of initial solutions. By adding artificial variables, such as A_2, we can provide an automatic initial solution. In this case, when X_1 and X_2 are set equal to 0, $A_2 = 900$.

Artificial variables have no meaning in a physical sense, and are nothing more than computational tools for generating initial LP solutions. Before the final simplex solution has been reached, all artificial variables must be gone from the solution mix. This matter is handled through the problem's objective function.

Surplus and Artificial Variables in the Objective Function

Whenever an artificial or surplus variable is added to one of the constraints, it must also be included in the other equations and in the problem's objective function, just as was done for slack variables. Since artificial variables must be forced out of the solution, we can assign a very high C_j cost to each. In minimization problems, variables with *low* costs are the most desirable ones and the first to enter the solution. Variables with *high* costs leave the solution quickly, or never enter it at all. Rather than set an actual dollar figure of $10,000 or $1 million for each artificial variable, however, we simply use the letter $\$M$ to represent a very large number.[4]

KEY IDEA

Surplus variables, like slack variables, carry a 0 cost.

If a problem we were about to solve had an objective function that read

Minimize cost $= \$5X_1 + \$9X_2 + \$7X_3$

and constraints such as the two mentioned previously, then the completed objective function and constraints would appear as follows:

Minimize cost $= \$5X_1 + \$9X_2 + \$7X_3 + \$0S_1 + \$MA_1 + \$MA_2$
Subject to: $\quad\quad 5X_1 + 10X_2 + 8X_3 - 1S_1 + 1A_1 + 0A_2 = 210$
$\quad\quad\quad\quad\quad 25X_1 + 30X_2 + 0X_3 + 0S_1 + 0A_1 + 1A_2 = 900$

---

[4] A technical point: If an artificial variable is ever used in a *maximization* problem (an occasional event), it is assigned an objective function value of $-\$M$ to force it from the basis.

APPLICATIONS OF QA

RRSP Flood: LP to the Rescue

The Financial Services Group, a division of Canada Systems Group Incorporated (CSG), consists of three major but separate strategic business units: Banking and Trust Services, Shared Processing, and the Financial Services Division. The latter includes brokerage services, insurance services, and investment fund services (IFS). IFS provides a variety of processing activities on behalf of its clients. From the time of its start-up, IFS was the only firm in the transaction processing business large enough to handle registered retirement savings plans (RRSP) contributions. (Canada's RRSP is similar to the IRA in the United States.)

The IFS division has had its difficulties—primarily because of the highly seasonal nature of some of its business. The RRSP season (late January to early March) in particular created overload and staffing problems that reached a boiling point in the spring of 1984. The volume of transactions had unexpectedly grown by more than 100%, a condition the IFS division had neither anticipated nor prepared for. With no plan in place, management had to cope in an ad hoc manner. Such a reactive approach led to errors and thus necessary rework, lengthy delays, and significant overtime as well as underutilization of staff and high personnel turnover. These conditions translated into substantial labor-related costs. All in all, additional costs of almost $500,000 were incurred for managing the short RRSP season from the beginning of February to the middle of March. Perhaps even worse, IFS's reputation within Canada's investment industry had deteriorated to the point that some of the major clients did not intend to renew contracts, which were to be renegotiated in mid-1985.

Dramatic changes were called for. A new manager for operations and two staff members with business school training were hired to plan for a successful 1985 RRSP season. It soon became clear that the task of planning the personnel requirements for the short RRSP season could be accomplished by modeling the problem. The two staff

members who had formal training in management science helped significantly.

The transaction processing of the IFS division involved essentially two major sequential tasks: data preparation and data entry. Data preparation encompassed sorting and coding of forms, checking for errors and making corrections, and grouping the forms into categories for specific funds. These forms were then passed to the data entry people who entered the relevant data into IFS's computer system, which in turn stored and reconciled the data. Clearly, the data entry people were dependent on the output of the data preparation department.

After realizing that a more formal planning process was needed, it became clear that the personnel problem could be formulated as a linear programming problem. The linear programming model was used for the purpose of planning the incremental staffing requirements during the six-week period beginning February 1, 1985. The initial concern centered around two issues: (1) what are the sources from which additional temporary personnel could be obtained?, and (2) how can the decision variables be appropriately defined?

Since overtime by IFS regular staff was ruled out because of economic considerations and the fear of burn-out, temporary people were hired by the CSG personnel office for managing the RRSP surge. Furthermore, clerks could also be hired from a service bureau called Manpower Temporary Services. These sources of labor were constrained by the number of computer terminals available in each shift and period. Office space limitations and a maximum number of people who could be recruited from both sources for respective periods, shifts, and tasks, added further restrictions.

The incremental cost of managing the short RRSP season in 1985 amounted to $170,000. The corresponding figure for 1984 was just shy of $500,000. Thus, in spite of somewhat higher wage rates and a 25% larger volume, net savings of over $320,000 were realized over the six-week period through the application of LP. In addition, the reputation of IFS as a reliable transaction processor was restored.

Source: C. Haehling von Lanzenauer, and others, *Interfaces* Vol. 17, No. 4, July–August 1987, pp. 27–33.

SOLVING MINIMIZATION PROBLEMS

Now that we have learned how to deal with objective functions and constraints associated with minimization problems, let's see how to use the simplex method to solve a typical problem.

The Muddy River Chemical Corporation must produce exactly 1,000 pounds of a special mixture of phosphate and potassium for a customer. Phosphate costs $5 per pound and potassium costs $6 per pound. No more than 300 pounds of phosphate can be used, and at least 150 pounds of potassium must be used. The problem is to determine the least-cost blend of the two ingredients.

This problem may be restated mathematically as:

$$\text{Minimize cost} = \$5X_1 + \$6X_2$$

Subject to:
$$X_1 + X_2 = 1{,}000 \text{ lbs.}$$
$$X_1 \leq 300 \text{ lbs.}$$
$$X_2 \geq 150 \text{ lbs.}$$
$$X_1, \quad X_2 \geq 0$$

mathematical formulation of minimization problem

where

X_1 = number of pounds of phosphate, and

X_2 = number of pounds of potassium.

Note that there are three constraints, not counting the nonnegativity constraints: the first is an equality, the second a less-than-or-equal-to, and the third a greater-than-or-equal-to constraint.

Graphical Analysis

To have a better understanding of the problem, a brief graphical analysis may prove useful. There are only two decision variables, X_1 and X_2, so we are able to plot the constraints and feasible region. Since the first constraint, $X_1 + X_2 = 1{,}000$, is an equality, the solution must lie somewhere on the line ABC (see Figure 11.3). It must also lie between points A and B because of the constraint $X_1 \leq 300$. The third constraint, $X_2 \geq 150$, is actually redundant (or nonbinding) since X_2 will automatically be greater than 150 pounds if the first two constraints are observed. Hence, the feasible region consists of all points on the line segment AB. As you recall from Chapter 10, however, an optimal solution will always lie at a corner point of the feasible region (even if the region is only a straight line). The solution must therefore be either at point A or point B. A quick analysis reveals that the least-cost solution lies at corner B, namely $X_1 = 300$ pounds of phosphate, $X_2 = 700$ pounds of potassium. The total cost is $5,700.

looking at a graphical solution first

You don't need the simplex method to solve the Muddy River Chemical problem, of course. But we can guarantee you that few problems will be this simple. In general, you can expect to see several variables and many constraints. The purpose of this section is to illustrate the straightforward application of the simplex method to minimization problems.

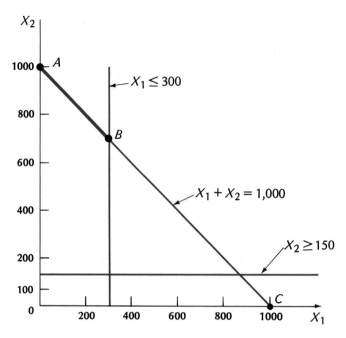

FIGURE 11.3
Muddy River Chemical Corporation's Feasible Region Graph

Converting the Constraints and Objective Function

insert slack, surplus, and artificial variables

The first step is to apply what we learned in the preceding section in order to convert the constraints and objective function into the proper form for the simplex method.

The equality constraint, $X_1 + X_2 = 1,000$, just involves adding an artificial variable, A_1.

$$X_1 + X_2 + A_1 = 1,000$$

The second constraint, $X_1 \leq 300$, requires the insertion of a slack variable—let's call it S_1.

$$X_1 + S_1 = 300$$

The last constraint is $X_2 \geq 150$, which is converted to an equality by subtracting a surplus variable, S_2, and adding an artificial variable, A_2.

$$X_2 - S_2 + A_2 = 150$$

Finally, the objective function, cost $= \$5X_1 + \$6X_2$, is rewritten as:

$$\text{Minimize cost} = \$5X_1 + \$6X_2 + \$0S_1 + \$0S_2 + \$MA_1 + \$MA_2$$

The complete set of constraints can now be expressed as follows:

$$1X_1 + 1X_2 + 0S_1 + 0S_2 + 1A_1 + 0A_2 = 1000$$
$$1X_1 + 0X_2 + 1S_1 + 0S_2 + 0A_1 + 0A_2 = 300$$
$$0X_1 + 1X_2 + 0S_1 - 1S_2 + 0A_1 + 1A_2 = 150$$
$$X_1, X_2, S_1, S_2, A_1, A_2 \geq 0$$

Rules of the Simplex Method for Minimization Problems

Minimization problems are quite similar to the maximization problems tackled earlier in this chapter. The significant difference involves the $C_j - Z_j$ row. Since our objective is now to minimize costs, the new variable to enter the solution in each tableau (the pivot column) will be the one with the *largest negative* number in the $C_j - Z_j$ row. Thus, we choose the variable that decreases costs the most. In minimization problems, an optimal solution is reached when all numbers in the $C_j - Z_j$ row are 0 or *positive*—just the opposite from the maximization case.[5] All other simplex steps, as seen in the following, remain the same.

minimization rules are slightly different

1. Choose the variable with the largest negative $C_j - Z_j$ to enter the solution. This is the pivot column.

2. Determine the row to be replaced by selecting the one with the smallest (nonnegative) quantity-to-pivot column ratio. This is the pivot row.

3. Calculate new values for the pivot row.

4. Calculate new values for the other rows.

5. Calculate the Z_j and $C_j - Z_j$ values for this tableau. If there are any $C_j - Z_j$ numbers less than 0, return to step 1.

First Simplex Tableau for the Muddy River Problem

Now we solve Muddy River Chemical Corporation's linear programming formulation using the simplex method. The initial tableau is set up just as in the earlier maximization example. Its first three rows are shown in the

[5] We should note that there is a *second* way to solve minimization problems with the simplex method: it involves a simple mathematical trick. It happens that *minimizing* the cost objective is the same as *maximizing* the negative of the cost objective function. This means that instead of writing the Muddy River objective function as

$$\text{Minimize cost} = 5X_1 + 6X_2$$

we can instead write

$$\text{Maximize } (-\text{cost}) = -5X_1 - 6X_2$$

The solution that maximizes ($-$cost) also minimizes cost. It also means that the same simplex procedure shown earlier for maximization problems can be used if this trick is employed. The only change is that the objective function must be multiplied by (-1).

accompanying table. We note the presence of the $\$M$ costs associated with artificial variables A_1 and A_2, but we treat them as if they were any large number. As noted earlier, they have the effect of forcing the artificial variables out of the solution quickly because of their large costs.

C_1	SOLUTION MIX	X_1	X_2	S_1	S_2	A_1	A_2	QUANTITY
$\$M$	A_1	1	1	0	0	1	0	1,000
$\$0$	S_1	1	0	1	0	0	0	300
$\$M$	A_2	0	1	0	-1	0	1	150

The numbers in the Z_j row are computed by multiplying the C_j column on the far left of the tableau times the corresponding numbers in each other column. They are then entered into Table 11.7.

$$Z_j \text{ (for } X_1 \text{ column)} = \$M(1) \quad + \$0(1) \quad + \$M(0) \quad = \$M$$
$$Z_j \text{ (for } X_2 \text{ column)} = \$M(1) \quad + \$0(0) \quad + \$M(1) \quad = \$2M$$
$$Z_j \text{ (for } S_1 \text{ column)} = \$M(0) \quad + \$0(1) \quad + \$M(0) \quad = \$0$$
$$Z_j \text{ (for } S_2 \text{ column)} = \$M(0) \quad + \$0(0) \quad + \$M(-1) = \$-M$$
$$Z_j \text{ (for } A_1 \text{ column)} = \$M(1) \quad + \$0(0) \quad + \$M(0) \quad = \$M$$
$$Z_j \text{ (for } A_2 \text{ column)} = \$M(0) \quad + \$0(0) \quad + \$M(1) \quad = \$M$$
$$Z_j \text{ (for total cost)} \quad = \$M(1,000) + \$0(300) + \$M(150) = \$1,150M$$

The $C_j - Z_j$ entries are determined as follows:

	COLUMN					
	X_1	X_2	S_1	S_2	A_1	A_2
C_j for column	$\$5$	$\$6$	$\$0$	$\$0$	$\$M$	$\$M$
Z_j for column	$\$M$	$\$2M$	$\$0$	$-\$M$	$\$M$	$\$M$
$C_j - Z_j$ for column	$-\$M + \$5$	$-\$2M + \$6$	$\$0$	$\$M$	$\$0$	$\$0$

TABLE 11.7 Initial Simplex Tableau for the Muddy River Chemical Problem

$C_j \rightarrow$	Solution Mix	$\$5$	$\$6$	$\$0$	$\$0$	$\$M$	$\$M$	
		X_1	X_2	S_1	S_2	A_1	A_2	Quantity
$\$M$	A_1	1	1	0	0	1	0	1000
$\$0$	S_1	1	0	1	0	0	0	300
$\$M$	A_2	0	①	0	-1	0	1	150 ← Pivot row
			Pivot number					
	Z_j	$\$M$	$\$2M$	0	$\$-M$	$\$M$	$\$M$	$\$1,150M$ (Total cost)
	$C_j - Z_j$	$-\$M + 5$	$-\$2M + 6$	$\$0$	$\$M$	$\$0$	$\$0$	
			Pivot column					

initial simplex solution

This initial solution was obtained by letting each of the variables X_1, X_2, and S_2 assume a value of 0. The current basic variables are $A_1 = 1,000$,

$S_1 = 300$, and $A_2 = 150$. This complete solution could be expressed in vector, or column, form as

$$\begin{bmatrix} X_1 \\ X_2 \\ S_1 \\ S_2 \\ A_1 \\ A_2 \end{bmatrix} = \begin{bmatrix} 0 \\ 0 \\ 300 \\ 0 \\ 1{,}000 \\ 150 \end{bmatrix}$$

An extremely high cost, $\$1{,}150M$, is associated with the above answer. We know this can be reduced significantly and now move on to the solution procedures.

Developing a Second Tableau

In the $C_j - Z_j$ row of Table 11.7, we see that there are two entries with negative values, X_1 and X_2. In the simplex rules for minimization problems, this means that an optimal solution does not yet exist. The pivot column is the one with the *largest negative* entry in the $C_j - Z_j$ row—indicated in Table 11.7 to be the X_2 column, meaning that X_2 will enter the solution next.

is current solution optimal?

Which variable will leave the solution to make room for the new variable, X_2? To find out, we divide the elements of the quantity column by the respective pivot column values.

For the A_1 row $= \dfrac{1{,}000}{1} = 1{,}000$

A_2 is pivot row

For the S_1 row $= \dfrac{300}{0}$ *(This is an undefined ratio, so we ignore it.)*

For the A_2 row $= \dfrac{150}{1} = 150$ *Smallest quotient, indicating pivot row*

Hence, the pivot row is the A_2 row, and the pivot number (circled) is at the intersection of the X_2 column and the A_2 row.

The entering row for the next simplex tableau is found by dividing each element in the pivot row by the pivot number, 1. This leaves the old pivot row unchanged, except that it now represents the solution variable X_2. The other two rows are altered one at a time by again applying the formula shown earlier in step 4.

(New row numbers) = (Numbers in old row)

$$- \left[\left(\frac{\text{Number above or below}}{\text{pivot number}} \right) \times \left(\begin{array}{c} \text{Corresponding number} \\ \text{in newly replaced row} \end{array} \right) \right]$$

A_1 Row	S_1 Row
$1 = \quad 1 - (1)(0)$	$1 = \quad 1 - (0)(0)$
$0 = \quad 1 - (1)(1)$	$0 = \quad 0 - (0)(1)$
$0 = \quad 0 - (1)(0)$	$1 = \quad 1 - (0)(0)$
$1 = \quad 0 - (1)(-1)$	$0 = \quad 0 - (0)(-1)$
$1 = \quad 1 - (1)(0)$	$0 = \quad 0 - (0)(0)$
$-1 = \quad 0 - (1)(1)$	$0 = \quad 0 - (0)(1)$
$850 = 1{,}000 - (1)(150)$	$300 = 300 - (0)(150)$

The Z_j and $C_j - Z_j$ rows are computed next.

$$
\begin{aligned}
Z_j(\text{for } X_1) &= \$M(1) + \$0(1) + \$6(0) = \$M \\
Z_j(\text{for } X_2) &= \$M(0) + \$0(0) + \$6(1) = \$6 \\
Z_j(\text{for } S_1) &= \$M(0) + \$0(1) + \$6(0) = \$0 \\
Z_j(\text{for } S_2) &= \$M(1) + \$0(0) + \$6(-1) = \$M - 6 \\
Z_j(\text{for } A_1) &= \$M(1) + \$0(0) + \$6(0) = \$M \\
Z_j(\text{for } A_2) &= \$M(-1) + \$0(0) + \$6(1) = -\$M + 6 \\
Z_j(\text{for total cost}) &= \$M(850) + \$0(300) + \$6(150) = \$850M + 900
\end{aligned}
$$

	COLUMN					
	X_1	X_2	S_1	S_2	A_1	A_2
C_j for column	\$5	\$6	\$0	\$0	\$M	\$M
Z_j for column	\$M	\$6	\$0	\$M - 6	\$M	-\$M + 6
$C_j - Z_j$ for column	-\$M + 5	\$0	\$0	-\$M + 6	\$0	\$2M - 6

All of these computational results are presented in Table 11.8.

solution after second tableau

The solution at the end of the second tableau is $A_1 = 850$, $S_1 = 300$, $X_2 = 150$. X_1, S_2, and A_2 are currently the nonbasic variables and have 0 value. The cost at this point is still quite high, $\$850M + \$900$. This answer is not optimal because not every number in the $C_j - Z_j$ row is 0 or positive.

Developing a Third Tableau

The new pivot column is the X_1 column. To determine which variable will leave the basis to make room for X_1, we check the quantity column-to-pivot column ratios again.

third tableau developed

$$\text{For the } A_1 \text{ row} = \frac{850}{1} = 850$$

$$\text{For the } S_1 \text{ row} = \frac{300}{1} = 300 \quad \textit{Smallest ratio}$$

$$\text{For the } X_2 \text{ row} = \frac{150}{0} = \text{Undefined}$$

TABLE 11.8 Second Simplex Tableau for the Muddy River Chemical Problem

$C_j \rightarrow$	Solution Mix	\$5 X_1	\$6 X_2	\$0 S_1	\$0 S_2	\$M A_1	\$M A_2	Quantity
\$M	A_1	1	0	0	1	1	-1	850
\$0	S_1	①	0	1	0	0	0	300 ← Pivot row
		Pivot number						
\$6	X_2	0	1	0	-1	0	1	150
	Z_j	\$M	\$6	\$0	\$M - 6	\$M	-\$M + 6	\$850M + \$900
	$C_j - Z_j$	-\$M + 5	\$0	\$0	-\$M + 6	\$0	\$2M - 6	
		Pivot column						

TABLE 11.9 Third Simplex Tableau for the Muddy River Chemical Problem

$C_j \rightarrow$	Solution Mix	$5	$6	$0	$0	$M	$M	
$\downarrow$		X_1	X_2	S_1	S_2	A_1	A_2	Quantity
$M	A_1	0	0	-1	(1)	1	-1	550 ← Pivot row
					Pivot number			
$5	X_1	1	0	1	0	0	0	300
$6	X_2	0	1	0	-1	0	1	150
	Z_j	$5	$6	$-$M$ + 5$	$$M$ - 6$	$$M$	$-$M$ + 6$	$550M +2400$
	$C_j - Z_j$	$0	$0	$$M$ - 5$	$-$M$ + 6$	$0	$2M$ - 6$	
				Pivot column				

Hence, variable S_1 will be replaced by X_1.[6] The pivot number, row, and column are labeled in Table 11.8.

To replace the pivot row, we divide each number in the S_1 row by 1 (the circled pivot number), leaving the row unchanged. The new X_1 row is shown in Table 11.9. The other computations for this third simplex tableau are as follows:

A_1 Row	X_2 Row
$0 = 1 - (1)(1)$	$0 = 0 - (0)(1)$
$0 = 0 - (1)(0)$	$1 = 1 - (0)(0)$
$-1 = 0 - (1)(1)$	$0 = 0 - (0)(1)$
$1 = 1 - (1)(0)$	$-1 = -1 - (0)(0)$
$1 = 1 - (1)(0)$	$0 = 0 - (0)(0)$
$-1 = -1 - (1)(0)$	$1 = 1 - (0)(0)$
$550 = 850 - (1)(300)$	$150 = 150 - (0)(300)$

$$Z_j(\text{for } X_1) = \$M(0) + \$5(1) + \$6(0) = \$5$$
$$Z_j(\text{for } X_2) = \$M(0) + \$5(0) + \$6(1) = \$6$$
$$Z_j(\text{for } S_1) = \$M(-1) + \$5(1) + \$6(0) = -\$M + 5$$
$$Z_j(\text{for } S_2) = \$M(1) + \$5(0) + \$6(-1) = \$M - 6$$
$$Z_j(\text{for } A_1) = \$M(1) + \$5(0) + \$6(0) = \$M$$
$$Z_j(\text{for } A_2) = \$M(-1) + \$5(0) + \$6(1) = -\$M + 6$$
$$Z_j(\text{for total cost}) = \$M(550) + \$5(300) + \$6(150) = \$550M + \$2,400$$

	COLUMN					
	X_1	X_2	S_1	S_2	A_1	A_2
C_j for column	$5	$6	$0	$0	$M	$M
Z_j for column	$5	$6	$-$M$ + 5$	$$M$ - 6$	$$M	$-$M$ + 6$
$C_j - Z_j$ for column	$0	$0	$$M$ - 5$	$-$M$ + 6$	$0	$2M$ - 6$

[6] At this point, it might appear to be more cost-effective to replace the A_1 row instead of the S_1 row. This would remove the last artificial variable, and its large $M cost, from the basis. The simplex method, however, does not always pick the most direct route to reaching the final solution. You may be assured, though, that it *will* lead us to the correct answer.

third solution still not optimal

The solution at the end of the three iterations is still not optimal because the S_2 column contains a $C_j - Z_j$ value that is negative. Note that the current total cost is nonetheless lower than at the end of the second tableau, which in turn is lower than the initial solution cost. We are headed in the right direction but have one more tableau to go!

Fourth Tableau for the Muddy River Chemical Problem

The pivot column is now the S_2 column. The ratios that determine the row and variable to be replaced are computed as follows:

$$\text{For the } A_1 \text{ row: } \frac{550}{1} = 550 \quad \textit{Row to be replaced}$$

$$\text{For the } X_1 \text{ row: } \frac{300}{0} \quad \textit{(Undefined)}$$

computing fourth solution

$$\text{For the } X_2 \text{ row: } \frac{150}{-1} \quad \textit{Not considered because it is negative}$$

Each number in the pivot row is divided by the pivot number (again 1, by coincidence). The other two rows are computed as follows and are shown in Table 11.10.

X_1 Row	X_2 Row
$1 = 1 - (0)(0)$	$0 = 0 - (-1)(0)$
$0 = 0 - (0)(0)$	$1 = 1 - (-1)(0)$
$1 = 1 - (0)(-1)$	$-1 = 0 - (-1)(-1)$
$0 = 0 - (0)(1)$	$0 = -1 - (-1)(1)$
$0 = 0 - (0)(1)$	$1 = 0 - (-1)(1)$
$0 = 0 - (0)(-1)$	$0 = 1 - (-1)(-1)$
$300 = 300 - (0)(550)$	$700 = 150 - (-1)(550)$

$$
\begin{aligned}
Z_j(\text{for } X_1) &= \$0(0) + \$5(1) + \$6(0) = \$5 \\
Z_j(\text{for } X_2) &= \$0(0) + \$5(0) + \$6(1) = \$6 \\
Z_j(\text{for } S_1) &= \$0(-1) + \$5(1) + \$6(-1) = -\$1 \\
Z_j(\text{for } S_2) &= \$0(1) + \$5(0) + \$6(0) = \$0 \\
Z_j(\text{for } A_1) &= \$0(1) + \$5(0) + \$6(1) = \$6 \\
Z_j(\text{for } A_2) &= \$0(-1) + \$5(0) + \$6(0) = \$0 \\
Z_j(\text{for total cost}) &= \$0(550) + \$5(300) + \$6(700) = \$5,700
\end{aligned}
$$

	COLUMN					
	X_1	X_2	S_1	S_2	A_1	A_2
C_j for column	$\$5$	$\$6$	$\$\ 0$	$\$0$	$\$M$	$\$M$
Z_j for column	$\$5$	$\$6$	$\$-1$	$\$0$	$\$6$	$\$0$
$C_j - Z_j$ for column	$\$0$	$\$0$	$\$1$	$\$0$	$\$M - 6$	$\$M$

optimal solution

On examining the $C_j - Z_j$ row in Table 11.10, only positive or 0 values are found. The fourth tableau therefore contains the optimum solution. That

TABLE 11.10 Fourth and Optimal Solution to the Muddy River Chemical Problem

$C_j \longrightarrow$	SOLUTION MIX	$5	$6	$0	$0	$M	$M	
$\downarrow$		X_1	X_2	S_1	S_2	A_1	A_2	QUANTITY
$0	S_2	0	0	-1	1	1	-1	550
$5	X_1	1	0	1	0	0	0	300
$6	X_2	0	1	-1	0	1	0	700
	Z_j	$5	$6	$$-1$	$0	$6	$0	$5,700
	$C_j - Z_j$	$0	$0	$1	$0	$M - 6$	$M	

solution is $X_1 = 300$, $X_2 = 700$, $S_2 = 550$. The artificial variables are both equal to 0, as is S_1. Translated into management terms, the chemical company's decision should be to blend 300 pounds of phosphate (X_1) with 700 pounds of potassium (X_2). This provides a surplus (S_2) of 550 pounds of potassium more than required by the constraint $X_2 \geqslant 150$. The cost of this solution is $5,700. If you look back to Figure 11.3, you can see that this is identical to the answer found by the graphical approach.

Although small problems such as this can be solved graphically, more realistic product blending problems demand use of the simplex method, usually in computerized form. We discuss the role of computers in linear programming in Chapter 12.

11.9
SPECIAL CASES IN USING THE SIMPLEX METHOD

In the last chapter we addressed some special cases that may arise when solving LP problems graphically (see Section 7 of Chapter 10). Here we again describe these cases, this time as they refer to the simplex method.

Infeasibility

Infeasibility, you may recall, comes about when there is no solution that satisfies all of the problem's constraints. In the simplex method, an infeasible solution is indicated by looking at the final tableau. In it, all $C_j - Z_j$ row entries will be of the proper sign to imply optimality, but an artificial variable (A_1) will still be in the solution mix.

no feasible solution exists

Table 11.11 illustrates the final simplex tableau for a hypothetical minimization type of linear programming problem. The table provides an example of an improperly formulated problem, probably containing conflicting constraints. No feasible solution is possible because an artificial variable, A_2, remains in the solution mix, even though all $C_j - Z_j$ are positive or 0 (the criterion for an optimal solution in a minimization case).

TABLE 11.11 An Illustration of Infeasibility

$C_j \longrightarrow$		$5	$8	$0	$0	$M	$M	
$\downarrow$	SOLUTION MIX	X_1	X_2	S_1	S_2	A_1	A_2	QUANTITY
$5	X_1	1	0	-2	3	-1	0	200
$8	X_2	0	1	1	2	-2	0	100
$M	A_2	0	0	0	-1	-1	1	20
	Z_j	5	8	-2	$31 - M$	$-21 - M$	M	$1,800 + 20M$
	$C_j - Z_j$	$0	$0	$2	$M - 31$	$2M + 21$	$0	

Unbounded Solutions

Unboundedness describes linear programs that do not have finite solutions. It occurs in maximization problems, for example, when a solution variable **no finite solution exists** can be made infinitely large without violating a constraint (refer back to Figure 10.13). In the simplex method, the condition of unboundedness will be discovered prior to reaching the final tableau. We will note the problem when trying to decide which variable to remove from the solution mix. The procedure, as seen earlier in this chapter, is to divide each quantity column number by the corresponding pivot column number. The row with the smallest positive ratio is replaced. But if all the ratios turn out to be negative or undefined, it indicates that the problem is unbounded.

Table 11.12 illustrates the second tableau calculated for a particular LP maximization problem by the simplex method. It also points to the condition of unboundedness. The solution is not optimal because not all $C_j - Z_j$ entries are 0 or negative, as required in a maximization problem. The next variable to enter the solution should be X_1. To determine which variable will leave the solution, we examine the ratios of the quantity column numbers to their corresponding numbers in the X_1, or pivot, column.

$$\text{Ratio for the } X_2 \text{ row: } \frac{30}{-1}$$

Negative ratios unacceptable

$$\text{Ratio for the } S_2 \text{ row: } \frac{10}{-2}$$

Since both pivot column numbers are negative, an unbounded solution is indicated.

TABLE 11.12 A Problem with an Unbounded Solution

$C_j \longrightarrow$		$6	$9	$0	$0	
$\downarrow$	SOLUTION MIX	X_1	X_2	S_1	S_2	QUANTITY
$9	X_2	-1	1	2	0	30
$0	S_2	-2	0	-1	1	10
	Z_j	-9	$9	$18	$0	$270
	$C_j - Z_j$	$15	$0	$-$18	$0	

Pivot column

Degeneracy

Degeneracy is another situation that can occur when solving an LP problem using the simplex method. It may develop when a problem contains a redundant constraint; that is, one or more of the constraints in the formulation makes another unnecessary. For example, if a problem has the three constraints $X_1 \leq 10$, $X_2 \leq 10$, and $X_1 + X_2 \leq 20$, the latter is unnecessary because the first two constraints make it redundant. Degeneracy arises when the ratio calculations are made. If there is a *tie* for the smallest ratio, this is a signal that degeneracy exists.

tied ratios

Table 11.13 provides an example of a degenerate problem. At this iteration of the given maximization LP problem, the next variable to enter the solution will be X_1, since it has the only positive $C_j - Z_j$ number.

The ratios are computed as follows:

$$\text{For the } X_2 \text{ row: } \frac{10}{1/4} = 40$$

$$\text{For the } S_2 \text{ row: } \frac{20}{4} = 5$$

Tie for the smallest ratio indicates degeneracy

$$\text{For the } S_3 \text{ row: } \frac{10}{2} = 5$$

Theoretically, degeneracy could lead to a situation known as *cycling*, in which the simplex algorithm alternates back and forth between the same nonoptimal solutions; that is, it puts a new variable in, then takes it out in the next tableau, puts it back in, and so on. One simple way of dealing with the issue is to select either row (S_2 or S_3 in this case) arbitrarily. If we are unlucky, and cycling does occur, we simply go back and select the other row.

cycling

More Than One Optimal Solution

Multiple, or alternate, optimal solutions are spotted when the simplex method is being used by looking at the final tableau. If the $C_j - Z_j$ value is equal to 0 for a variable that is *not* in the solution mix, more than one optimal solution exists.

alternate optimal solution

TABLE 11.13 A Problem Illustrating Degeneracy

$C_j \longrightarrow$	SOLUTION MIX ↓	$\$5$ X_1	$\$8$ X_2	$\$2$ X_3	$\$0$ S_1	$\$0$ S_2	$\$0$ S_3	QUANTITY
$\$8$	X_2	$1/4$	1	1	-2	0	0	10
$\$0$	S_2	4	0	$1/3$	-1	1	0	20
$\$0$	S_3	2	0	2	$2/5$	0	1	10
	Z_j	$\$2$	$\$8$	$\$8$	$\$16$	$\$0$	$\$0$	$\$80$
	$C_j - Z_j$	$\$3$	$\$0$	$-\$6$	$-\$16$	$\$0$	$\$0$	

Pivot column

TABLE 11.14 A Problem with Alternate Optimal Solutions

$C_j \longrightarrow$	SOLUTION MIX	$3	$2	$0	$0	
$\downarrow$		X_1	X_2	S_1	S_2	QUANTITY
$2	X_2	$\frac{3}{2}$	1	1	0	6
$0	S_2	1	0	$\frac{1}{2}$	1	3
	Z_j	$3	$2	$2	$0	$12
	$C_j - Z_j$	$0	$0	$-$2	$0	

Let's take Table 11.14 as an example. Here is the last tableau of a maximization problem; each entry in the $C_j - Z_j$ row is 0 or negative, indicating that an optimal solution has been reached. That solution is read as $X_2 = 6$, $S_2 = 3$, profit = \$12. Note, however, that variable X_1 can be brought into the solution mix without increasing or decreasing profit. The new solution, with X_1 in the basis, would become $X_1 = 3$, $X_2 = \frac{3}{2}$, with profit still at \$12. Can you modify Table 11.14 to prove this? You might note, by the way, that this example of alternate optimal solution corresponds to the graphical solution shown in Figure 10.15.

11.10
KARMARKAR'S ALGORITHM

The biggest change to take place in the field of linear programming solution techniques in four decades has been the 1984 arrival of an alternative to the simplex algorithm. Developed by Narendra Karmarkar, the new method, called Karmarkar's algorithm, often takes significantly less computer time to solve very large scale LP problems.[7]

As we saw, the simplex algorithm finds a solution by moving from one adjacent corner point to the next, following the outside edges of the feasible region. In contrast, Karmarkar's method follows a path of points on the *inside* of the feasible region. Karmarkar's method is also unique in its ability to handle an *extremely* large number of constraints and variables, thereby giving LP users the capability to solve previously unsolvable problems.

Although it is likely that the simplex method will continue to be used for many LP problems, a new generation of LP software built around Karmarkar's algorithm is already becoming popular. Delta Air Lines became the first commercial airline to use the Karmarkar program called KORBX, which was developed and is sold by AT&T. Delta found that the program streamlined the monthly scheduling of 7,000 pilots who fly more than 400 airplanes to 166 cities worldwide. With increased efficiency in allocating limited resources, Delta thinks it will save millions of dollars in crew time and related costs.

[7] For details, see Narendra Karmarkar, "A New Polynomial Time Algorithm for Linear Programming," *Combinatorica* Vol. 4, No. 4, 1984, pp. 373–395, or J. N. Hooker, "Karmarkar's Linear Programming Algorithm," *Interfaces* Vol. 16, No. 4, July–August 1986, pp. 75–90.

Finding Fast Algorithms Means Better Airline Service

Thomas Cook is Director of Operations at American Airlines. Linear-programming techniques have a direct impact on the efficiency and profitability of major airlines, and Cook shares his ideas on why optimal solutions are essential to his business:

Finding an optimal solution means finding the best solution. Let's say you are trying to minimize a cost function of some kind. For example, we may want to minimize the excess costs related to scheduling crews, hotels, and other costs that are not associated with flight time. So we try to minimize that excess cost, subject to a lot of constraints, such as the amount of time a pilot can fly, how much rest time is needed, and so forth.

An optimal solution, then, is either a minimum-cost solution or a maximizing solution. For example, we might want to maximize the profit associated with assigning aircrafts to the schedule; so we assign large aircraft to high-need segments and small aircraft to low-load segments. Whether it's a minimum or maximum solution depends on what function we are trying to optimize.

Finding fast solutions to linear-programming problems is also essential. If we can get an algorithm that's 50 to 100 times faster, we could do a lot of things that we can't do today. For example, some applications could be real-time applications, as opposed to batch applications. So instead of running a job overnight and getting an answer the next morning, we could actually key in the data or access the data base, generate the matrix, and come up with a solution that could be implemented a few minutes after keying in the data.

A good example of this kind of application is what we call a major weather disruption. If we get a major weather disruption at one of the hubs, such as Dallas or Chicago, then a lot of flights may get cancelled, which means we have a lot of crews and airplanes in the wrong places. What we need is a way to put that whole operation back together again, so that the crews and airplanes are in the right places. That way, we minimize the cost of the disruption and minimize the passenger inconvenience.

The simplex method, which was developed some 40 years ago by George Dantzig, has been very useful at American Airlines and, indeed, at a lot of large businesses. The difference between his solution and Karmarkar's is that if we can get an algorithm that comes up with basically the same optimal answer 50 to 100 times faster, then we can apply that technology to new problems, and even to problems that we wouldn't have tried using the simplex method. I think that's the primary reason for the excitement.

Source: Introduction to Contemporary Mathematics New York: W. H. Freeman and Company, 1988, pp. 82–83.

11.11
SUMMARY

In Chapter 10, we examined the use of graphical methods to solve linear programming problems that contained only two decision variables. This chapter moved us one giant step further by introducing the simplex method. The simplex method is an iterative procedure for reaching the optimal solution to LP problems of any dimension. It consists of a series of rules that, in effect, algebraically examine corner points in a systematic way. Each step moves us closer to the optimum solution by increasing profit or decreasing cost, while at the same time maintaining feasibility.

simplex systematically improves solution

We saw the procedure for converting less-than-or-equal-to, greater-than-or-equal-to, and equality constraints into the simplex format. These conversions employed the inclusion of slack, surplus, and artificial variables.

An initial simplex tableau was developed that portrayed the problem's original data formulations. It also contained a row providing profit or cost information and a net evaluation row. The latter, identified as the $C_j - Z_j$ row, was examined in determining whether an optimal solution had yet been reached. It also pointed out which variable would next enter the solution mix, or basis, if the current solution was nonoptimal.

The simplex method consists of five steps: (1) identifying the pivot column, (2) identifying the pivot row and number, (3) replacing the pivot row, (4) computing new values for each remaining row, and (5) computing the Z_j and $C_j - Z_j$ rows and examining for optimality. Each tableau of this iterative procedure was displayed and explained for a sample maximization and minimization problem.

Finally, a few special issues in linear programming that arise in using the simplex method were discussed. Examples of infeasibility, unbounded solutions, degeneracy, and multiple optimal solutions were presented.

Although large LP problems are seldom if ever solved by hand, the purpose of this chapter was to help you gain an understanding of how the simplex method works. Understanding the underlying principles will be of great help in interpreting and analyzing computerized linear programming solutions, one of the topics in Chapter 12. It will also provide a foundation for another issue in the next chapter: answering questions about the problem after an optimal solution has been found, which is called postoptimality, or sensitivity, analysis.

GLOSSARY

Simplex Method. A matrix algebra method for solving linear programming problems.

Iterative Procedure. A process (algorithm) that repeats the same steps over and over.

Slack Variable. A variable added to less-than-or-equal-to constraints in order to create an equality for a simplex method. It represents a quantity of unused resource.

Simplex Tableau. A table for keeping track of calculations at each iteration of the simplex method.

Solution Mix. A column in the simplex tableau that contains all the variables in the solution.

Quantity Column. A column in the simplex tableau that gives the numeric value of each variable in the solution mix column.

Basic Feasible Solution. A solution to an LP problem that corresponds to a corner point of the feasible region.

Basis. The set of variables that are in the solution, that is, have positive, nonzero values, and are listed in the solution mix column. They are also called basic variables.

Nonbasic Variables. Variables not in the solution mix or basis. Nonbasic variables are equal to 0.

Substitution Rates. The coefficients in the central body of each simplex table. They indicate the number of units of each basic variable that must be removed from the solution if a new variable (as represented at any column head) is entered.

Z$_j$ Row. The row containing the figures for gross profit or loss given up by adding one unit of a variable into the solution.

C$_j$ − Z$_j$ Row. The row containing the net profit or loss that will result from introducing one unit of the variable indicated in that column into the solution.

Pivot Column. The column with the largest positive number in the $C_j - Z_j$ row of a maximization problem, or the largest negative $C_j - Z_j$ value in a minimization problem. It indicates which variable will enter the solution next.

Pivot Row. The row corresponding to the variable that will leave the basis in order to make room for the variable entering (as indicated by the new pivot column). This is the smallest positive ratio found by dividing the quantity column values by the pivot column values for each row.

Pivot Number. The element at the intersection of the pivot row and pivot column.

Current Solution. The basic feasible solution that is the set of variables presently in the solution. It corresponds to a corner point of the feasible region.

Surplus Variable. A variable inserted in a greater-than-or-equal-to constraint to create an equality. It represents the amount of resource usage above the minimum required usage.

Artificial Variable. A variable that has no meaning in a physical sense but acts as a tool to help generate an initial LP solution.

Infeasibility. The situation in which there is no solution that satisfies all of a problem's constraints.

Unboundedness. A condition describing LP maximization problems having solutions that can become infinitely large without violating any stated constraints.

Degeneracy. A condition that arises when there is a tie in the values used to determine which variable will enter the solution next. It can lead to cycling back and forth between two nonoptimal solutions.

KEY EQUATION

(11-1) New row numbers = (Numbers in old row)

$$- \left[\left(\frac{\text{Number above or below}}{\text{pivot number}} \right) \times \left(\begin{array}{c} \text{Corresponding number} \\ \text{in new row, that is, new} \\ \text{values for pivot row} \end{array} \right) \right]$$

Formula for computing new values for nonpivot rows in the simplex tableau (step 4 of the simplex procedure).

SOLVED PROBLEMS

Solved Problem 11.1

Convert the following constraints and objective function into the proper form for use in the simplex method.

$$\text{Minimize cost} = 4X_1 + 1X_2$$
$$\text{Subject to:} \quad 3X_1 + X_2 = 3$$
$$4X_1 + 3X_2 \geq 6$$
$$X_1 + 2X_2 \leq 3$$

Solution

$$\text{Minimize cost} = 4X_1 + 1X_2 + 0S_1 + 0S_2 + MA_1 + MA_2$$

$$
\begin{aligned}
\text{Subject to:} \quad & 3X_1 + 1X_2 && + 1A_1 && = 3 \\
& 4X_1 + 3X_2 - 1S_1 && + 1A_2 && = 6 \\
& 1X_1 + 2X_2 && + 1S_2 && = 3
\end{aligned}
$$

Solved Problem 11.2

Solve the following LP problem.

$$\text{Maximize profit} = \$9X_1 + \$7X_2$$

$$
\begin{aligned}
\text{Subject to:} \quad & 2X_1 + 1X_2 \leq 40 \\
& X_1 + 3X_2 \leq 30
\end{aligned}
$$

Solution

We begin by adding slack variables and converting inequalities into equalities.

$$\text{Maximize profit} = 9X_1 + 7X_2 + 0S_1 + 0S_2$$

$$
\begin{aligned}
\text{Subject to:} \quad & 2X_1 + 1X_2 + 1S_1 + 0S_2 = 40 \\
& 1X_1 + 3X_2 + 0S_1 + 1S_2 = 30
\end{aligned}
$$

The initial tableau is then:

$C_j \rightarrow$		$\$9$	$\$7$	$\$0$	$\$0$	
$\downarrow$	SOLUTION MIX	X_1	X_2	S_1	S_2	QUANTITY
0	S_1	(2)	1	1	0	40
0	S_2	1	3	0	1	30
	Z_j	0	0	0	0	0
	$C_j - Z_j$	9	7	0	0	

The correct second tableau and third tableau and some of their calculations appear below. The optimal solutions, given in the third tableau, are: $X_1 = 18$, $X_2 = 4$, $S_1 = 0$, $S_2 = 0$, and profit = $\$190$.

Steps 1 and 2. To go from the first to the second tableau, we note that the pivot column (in the first tableau) is X_1, which has the highest $C_j - Z_j$ value, $\$9$. The pivot row is S_1 since 40/2 is less than 30/1, and the pivot number is 2.

Step 3. The new X_1 row is found by dividing each number in the old S_1 row by the pivot number, namely, 2/2 = 1, 1/2 = 1/2, 1/2 = 1/2, 0/2 = 0, and 40/2 = 20.

Step 4. The new values for the S_2 row are computed as follows:

$$
\begin{pmatrix} \text{Number in} \\ \text{new } S_2 \text{ row} \end{pmatrix} = \begin{pmatrix} \text{Number in} \\ \text{old } S_2 \text{ row} \end{pmatrix} - \left[\begin{pmatrix} \text{Number} \\ \text{below pivot} \\ \text{number} \end{pmatrix} \times \begin{pmatrix} \text{Corresponding} \\ \text{number in} \\ \text{new } X_1 \text{ row} \end{pmatrix} \right]
$$

$$
\begin{aligned}
0 &= 1 - [(1) \times (1)] \\
5/2 &= 3 - [(1) \times (1/2)]
\end{aligned}
$$

$-1/2$	$=$	0	$-$	$[(1)$	$\times$	$(1/2)]$
1	$=$	1	$-$	$[(1)$	$\times$	$(0)]$
10	$=$	30	$-$	$[(1)$	$\times$	$(20)]$

Step 5. The following new Z_j and $C_j - Z_j$ rows are formed:

Z_j (for X_1) $= \$9(1) + 0(0) = \$9$ $C_j - Z_j = \$9 - \$9 = 0$

Z_j (for X_2) $= \$9(1/2) + 0(5/2) = \$9/2$ $C_j - Z_j = \$7 - 9/2 = \$5/2$

Z_j (for S_1) $= \$9(1/2) + 0(-1/2) = \$9/2$ $C_j - Z_j = 0 - 9/2 = -\$9/2$

Z_j (for S_2) $= \$9(0) + 0(1) = \$0$ $C_j - Z_j = 0 - 0 = 0$

Z_j (profit) $= \$9(20) + 0(10) = \$180$

$C_j \rightarrow$	SOLUTION MIX	$\$9$ X_1	$\$7$ X_2	$\$0$ S_1	$\$0$ S_2	QUANTITY	
$\$9$	X_1	1	1/2	1/2	0	20	
0	S_2	0	(5/2)	$-1/2$	1	10	← pivot row
	Z_j	$\$9$	$\$9/2$	$\$9/2$	0	$\$180$	
	$C_j - Z_j$	0	$\$5/2$	$-\$9/2$	0		

↑
pivot column

The above solution is not optimal and you must perform steps 1–5 again. The new pivot column is X_2, the new pivot row is S_2, and 5/2 (circled in the second tableau) is the new pivot number.

$C_j \rightarrow$	SOLUTION MIX	$\$9$ X_1	$\$7$ X_2	$\$0$ S_1	$\$0$ S_2	QUANTITY
$\$9$	X_1	1	0	3/5	$-1/5$	18
$\$7$	X_2	0	1	$-1/5$	2/5	4
	Z_j	$\$9$	$\$7$	$\$4$	$\$1$	$\$190$
	$C_j - Z_j$	0	0	$-\$4$	$-\$1$	

The final solution is $X_1 = 18$, $X_2 = 4$, profit $= \$190$.

DISCUSSION QUESTIONS AND PROBLEMS

Discussion Questions

11-1 Explain the purpose and procedures of the simplex method.

11-2 How do the graphical and simplex methods of solving linear programming problems differ? In what ways are they the same? Under what circumstances would you prefer to use the graphical approach?

11-3 What are slack, surplus, and artificial variables? When is each used, and why? What value does each carry in the objective function?

11-4 You have just formulated an LP problem with 12 decision variables and 8 constraints. How many basic variables will there always be? What is the difference between a basic and a nonbasic variable?

11-5 What are the simplex rules for selecting the pivot column? The pivot row? The pivot number?

11-6 How do maximization and minimization problems differ when applying the simplex method?

11-7 What is the reason behind the use of the minimum ratio test in selecting the pivot row? What might happen without it?

11-8 A particular linear programming problem has the following objective function:

$$\text{Maximize profit} = \$8X_1 + \$6X_2 + \$12X_3 - \$2X_4$$

Which variable should enter at the second simplex tableau? If the objective function was

$$\text{Minimize cost} = \$2.5X_1 + \$2.9X_2 + \$4.0X_3 + \$7.9X_4$$

which variable would be the best candidate to enter the second tableau?

11-9 What happens if an artificial variable is in the final optimal solution? What should the manager who formulated the LP problem do?

11-10 The great Romanian operations researcher, Dr. Ima Student, proposes that instead of selecting the variable with the largest positive $C_j - Z_j$ value (in a maximization LP problem) to enter the solution mix next, a different approach be used. She suggests that any variable with a positive $C_j - Z_j$ can be chosen, even if it isn't the largest. What will happen if we adopt this new rule for the simplex procedure? Will an optimal solution still be reached?

Problems

· **11-11** The Dreskin Development Company is building two apartment complexes. It must decide how many units to construct in each complex subject to labor and material constraints. The profit generated for each apartment in the first complex is estimated at $900, for each apartment in the second complex, $1,500. A partial initial simplex tableau for Dreskin is given in the accompanying table.

$C_j \rightarrow$		$900	$1,500	$0	$0	
$\downarrow$	SOLUTION MIX	X_1	X_2	S_1	S_2	QUANTITY
		14	4	1	0	3,360
		10	12	0	1	9,600
	Z_j					
	$C_j - Z_j$					

(a) Complete the initial tableau.
(b) Reconstruct the problem's original constraints (excluding slack variables).

(c) Write the problem's original objective function.

(d) What is the basis for the initial solution?

(e) Which variable should enter the solution at the next iteration?

(f) Which variable will leave the solution at the next iteration?

(g) How many units of the variable entering the solution next will be in the basis in the second tableau?

· **11-12** Consider the following linear programming problem:

$$\text{Maximize earnings} = \$.80X_1 + \$.40X_2 + \$1.20X_3 - \$.10X_4$$

Subject to:
$$X_1 + 2X_2 + X_3 + 5X_4 \leq 150$$
$$X_2 - 4X_3 + 8X_4 = 70$$
$$6X_1 + 7X_2 + 2X_3 - X_4 \geq 120$$
$$X_1, X_2, X_3, X_4 \geq 0$$

(a) Convert these constraints to equalities by adding the appropriate slack, surplus, or artificial variables. Also, add the new variables into the problem's objective function.

(b) Set up the complete initial simplex tableau for this problem. Do not attempt to solve.

· **11-13** Solve the following linear programming problem graphically. Then set up a simplex tableau and solve the problem using the simplex method. Indicate the corner points generated at each iteration by the simplex method on your graph.

$$\text{Maximize profit} = \$3X_1 + \$5X_2$$

Subject to:
$$X_2 \leq 6$$
$$3X_1 + 2X_2 \leq 18$$
$$X_1, X_2 \geq 0$$

· **11-14** Convert the following LP problem into the proper simplex form and solve by applying the simplex algorithm.

$$\text{Maximize profit} = 20X_1 + 10X_2$$

Subject to:
$$5X_1 + 4X_2 \leq 250$$
$$2X_1 + 5X_2 \leq 150$$
$$X_1, X_2 \geq 0$$

Also solve the problem graphically and compare your answers.

· **11-15** Solve the following linear programming problem first graphically and then by the simplex algorithm.

$$\text{Minimize cost} = 4X_1 + 5X_2$$

Subject to:
$$X_1 + 2X_2 \geq 80$$
$$3X_1 + X_2 \geq 75$$
$$X_1, X_2 \geq 0$$

What are the values of the basic variables at each iteration? Which are the nonbasic variables at each iteration?

· **11-16** The final simplex tableau for an LP maximization problem is shown in the accompanying table.

$C_j \longrightarrow$		3	5	0	0	$-M$	
$\downarrow$	SOLUTION MIX	X_1	X_2	S_1	S_2	A_1	QUANTITY
5	X_2	1	1	2	0	0	6
$-M$	A_1	-1	0	-2	-1	1	2
	Z_j	$5 + M$	5	$10 + 2M$	$+M$	$-M$	$30 - 2M$
	$C_j - Z_j$	$-2 - M$	0	$-10 - 2M$	$-M$	0	

Describe the situation encountered here.

· **11-17** Solve the following problem by the simplex method. What condition exists that prevents you from reaching an optimal solution?

$$\text{Maximize profit} = 6X_1 + 3X_2$$

$$\text{Subject to:} \quad 2X_1 - 2X_2 \leqslant 2$$
$$-X_1 + X_2 \leqslant 1$$
$$X_1, X_2 \geqslant 0$$

: **11-18** Consider the following financial problem:

$$\text{Maximize return on investment} = \$2X_1 + \$3X_2$$

$$\text{Subject to:} \quad 6X_1 + 9X_2 \leqslant 18$$
$$9X_1 + 3X_2 \geqslant 9$$
$$X_1, X_2 \geqslant 0$$

(a) Find the optimal solution using the simplex method.
(b) What evidence indicates that an alternate optimal solution exists?
(c) Find the alternate optimal solution.
(d) Solve this problem graphically as well, and illustrate the alternate optimal corner points.

: **11-19** At the third iteration of a particular linear programming maximization problem, the following tableau is established.

$C_j \rightarrow$		\$6	\$3	\$5	0	0	0	
$\downarrow$	SOLUTION MIX	X_1	X_2	X_3	S_1	S_2	S_3	QUANTITY
\$5	X_3	0	1	1	1	0	3	5
\$6	X_1	1	-3	0	0	0	1	12
\$0	S_2	0	2	0	1	1	-1	10
	Z_j	\$6	$-\$13$	\$5	\$5	\$0	\$21	\$97
	$C_j - Z_j$	\$0	\$16	\$0	$-\$5$	\$0	$-\$21$	

What special condition exists as you improve the profit and move to the next iteration? Proceed to solve the problem for the optimal solution.

: **11-20** A pharmaceutical firm is about to begin production of three new drugs. An objective function designed to minimize ingredient costs, and three production constraints, are shown below.

$$\text{Minimize cost} = 50X_1 + 10X_2 + 75X_3$$

$$\begin{aligned}
\text{Subject to:} \quad X_1 \quad - X_2 \quad &= 1{,}000 \\
2X_2 + \quad 2X_3 &= 2{,}000 \\
X_1 \quad\quad\quad &\leq 1{,}500 \\
X_1,\, X_2,\, X_3 &\geq 0
\end{aligned}$$

(a) Convert these constraints and objective function to the proper form for use in the simplex tableau.

(b) Solve the problem by the simplex method. What is the optimal solution and cost?

: **11-21** The S. Gillespie Corporation faces a blending decision in developing a new cat food called Yum-Mix. Two basic ingredients have been combined and tested, and the firm has determined that to each can of Yum-Mix at least 30 units of protein and at least 80 units of riboflavin must be added. These two nutrients are available in two competing brands of animal food supplements. The cost per kilogram of the brand A supplement is $9, while the cost per kilogram of brand B supplement is $15. A kilogram of brand A added to each production batch of Yum-Mix provides a supplement of 1 unit of protein and 1 unit of riboflavin to each can. A kilogram of brand B provides 2 units of protein and 4 units of riboflavin in each can. Gillespie must satisfy these minimum nutrient standards while keeping costs of supplements to a minimum.

(a) Formulate this problem to find the best combination of the two supplements to meet the minimum requirements at the least cost.

(b) Solve for the optimal solution by the simplex method.

· **11-22** The Roniger Company produces two products: bed mattresses and box springs. A prior contract requires that the firm produce at least 30 mattresses or box springs, in any combination. In addition, union labor agreements demand that stitching machines be kept running at least 40 hours per week, which is one production period. Each box spring takes two hours of stitching time, while each mattress takes one hour on the machine. Each mattress produced costs $20, each box spring costs $24.

(a) Formulate this problem so as to minimize total production costs.

(b) Solve using the simplex method.

· **11-23** Each coffee table produced by Meising Designers nets the firm a profit of $9. Each bookcase yields a $12 profit. Meising's firm is small, and its resources limited. During any given production period of one week, 10 gallons of varnish and 12 lengths of high-quality redwood are available. Each coffee table requires approximately 1 gallon of varnish and 1 length of redwood. Each bookcase takes 1 gallon of varnish and 2 lengths of wood. Formulate Meising's production mix decision as a linear programming problem, and solve using the simplex method. How many tables and bookcases should be produced each week? What will the maximum profit be?

· **11-24** Bagwell Distributors packages and distributes industrial supplies. A standard shipment can be packaged in a class A container, a class K container, or a class T container. A single class A container yields a profit of $8; a class K container, a profit of $6; and a class T container, a profit of $14. Each shipment prepared requires a certain amount of packing material and a certain amount of time, as seen in the following table.

	RESOURCES NEEDED PER STANDARD SHIPMENT	
CLASS OF CONTAINER	PACKING MATERIAL (POUNDS)	PACKING TIME (HOURS)
A	2	2
K	1	6
T	3	4
Total amount of resource available each week	120 pounds	240 hours

Bill Bagwell, head of the firm, must decide the optimal number of each class of container to pack each week. He is bound by the previously mentioned resource restrictions, but he also decides that he must keep his six full-time packers employed all 240 hours (6 workers × 40 hours) each week. Formulate and solve this problem using the simplex method.

 : **11-25** The Foggy Bottom Development Corporation has just purchased a small hotel for conversion to condominium apartments. The building, in a popular area of Washington, D.C., near the U.S. State Department, will be highly marketable, and each condominium sale is expected to yield a good profit. The conversion process, however, includes several options. Basically, four types of condominiums can be designed out of the former hotel rooms. They are: deluxe one-bedroom apartments, regular one-bedroom apartments, deluxe studios, and efficiency apartments. Each will yield a different profit, but each type also requires a different level of investment in carpeting, painting, appliances, and carpentry work. Bank loans dictate a limited budget that may be allocated to each of these needs. Profit and cost data, and cost of conversion requirements for each apartment are shown in the accompanying table.

	TYPE OF APARTMENT				
RENOVATION REQUIREMENT	DELUXE 1-BEDROOM ($)	REGULAR 1-BEDROOM ($)	DELUXE STUDIO ($)	EFFICIENCY ($)	TOTAL BUDGETED ($)
New carpeting	1,100	1,000	600	500	35,000
Painting	700	600	400	300	28,000
New appliances	2,000	1,600	1,200	900	45,000
Carpentry work	1,000	400	900	200	19,000
Profit per unit	8,000	6,000	5,000	3,500	

Thus, we see that the cost of carpeting a deluxe one-bedroom unit will be $1,100, the cost of carpeting a regular one-bedroom unit is $1,000, and so on. A total of $35,000 is budgeted for all new carpeting in the building.

Zoning regulations dictate that the building contain no more than 50 condominiums when the conversion is completed—and no less than 25 units. The development company also decides that to have a good blend of owners, at least 40% but no more than 70% of the units should be one-bedroom apartments. Not all money budgeted in each category need be spent, although profit is not affected by cost savings. But since the money represents a bank loan, under no circumstances may it be exceeded or even shifted from one area, such as carpeting, to another, such as painting.

(a) Formulate Foggy Bottom Development Corporation's decision as a linear program to maximize profits.

(b) Convert your objective function and constraints to a form containing the appropriate slack, surplus, and artificial variables. Do not attempt to solve the problem.

: **11-26** The accompanying initial simplex tableau was developed by Tommy Gibbs, vice president of a large cotton spinning mill. Gibbs unfortunately quit before completing this important linear programming application. Stephanie Robbins, the newly hired replacement, was immediately given this task of using LP to determine what different kinds of yarn the mill should use to minimize costs. Her first need was to be certain that Gibbs correctly formulated the objective function and constraints. Since she could find no statement of the problem in the files, she decided to reconstruct the problem from the initial tableau.

(a) What is the correct formulation, using real decision variables (that is, X_is) only?

(b) Which variable will enter this current solution mix in the second tableau? Which basic variable will leave?

$C_j \rightarrow$		$12	$18	$10	$20	$7	$8	$0	$0	$0	$0	$0	M	M	M	M	
↓	SOLUTION MIX	X_1	X_2	X_3	X_4	X_5	X_6	S_1	S_2	S_3	S_4	S_5	A_1	A_2	A_3	A_4	QUANTITY
M	A_1	1	0	−3	0	0	0	0	0	0	0	0	1	0	0	0	100
0	S_1	0	25	1	2	8	0	1	0	0	0	0	0	0	0	0	900
M	A_2	2	1	0	4	0	1	0	−1	0	0	0	0	1	0	0	250
M	A_3	18	−15	−2	−1	15	0	0	0	−1	0	0	0	0	1	0	150
0	S_4	0	0	0	0	0	25	0	0	0	1	0	0	0	0	0	300
M	A_4	0	0	0	2	6	0	0	0	0	0	−1	0	0	0	1	70
	Z_j	21M	−14M	−5M	5M	21M	M	0	0	−M	0	−M	M	M	M	M	570M
	$C_j - Z_j$	12 − 21M	18 + 14M	10 + 5M	20 − 5M	7 − 21M	8 − M	0	0	M	0	M	0	0	0	0	

Coastal States Chemicals and Fertilizers

In December 1985, Bill Stock, general manager for the Louisiana Division of Coastal States Chemicals and Fertilizers, received a letter from Fred McNair of Cajan Pipeline Company which notified Coastal States that priorities had been established for the allocation of natural gas. The letter stated that Cajan Pipeline, the primary supplier of natural gas to Coastal States, might be instructed to curtail natural gas supplies to its industrial and commercial customers by as much as 40% during the ensuing winter months. Moreover, Cajan Pipeline had the approval of the Federal Power Commission (FPC) to curtail such supplies.

Possible curtailment was attributed to the priorities established for the use of natural gas:

First priority: Residential and commercial heating

Second priority: Commercial and industrial users whereby natural gas is used as a source of raw material

Third priority: Commercial and industrial users whereby natural gas is used as boiler fuel

Almost all of Coastal State's uses of natural gas were in the second and third priorities. Hence, its plants were certainly subject to brown-outs, or natural gas curtailments. The occurrence and severity of the brown-outs depended on a number of complex factors. First of all, Cajan Pipeline was part of an interstate transmission network that delivered natural gas to residential and commercial buildings on the Atlantic Coast and in northeastern regions of the United States. Hence, the severity of the forthcoming winter in these regions would have a direct impact on the use of natural gas.

Secondly, the demand for natural gas was soaring because it was the cleanest and most efficient fuel. There were almost no environmental problems in burning natural gas. Moreover, maintenance problems due to fuel-fouling in fireboxes and boilers were negligible with natural gas systems. Also, burners were much easier to operate with natural gas as compared to the use of oil or the stoking operation when coal was used as fuel.

Finally, the supply of natural gas was dwindling. The traditionally depressed price of natural gas had discouraged new exploration for gas wells; hence, shortages appeared imminent.

Stock and his staff at Coastal States had been aware of the possibility of shortages of natural gas and had been investigating ways of converting to fuel oil or coal as a substitute for natural gas. Their plans, however, were still in the developmental stages. Coastal States required an immediate contingency plan to minimize the effect of a natural gas curtailment on its multiplant operations. The obvious question was, what operations should be curtailed and to what extent to minimize the adverse effect upon profits? Coastal States had the approval from the FPC and Cajan Pipeline to specify which of its plants would bear the burden of the curtailment if such cutbacks were necessary. McNair, of Cajan Pipeline, replied, "It's your 'pie': we don't care how you divide it if we make it smaller."

The Model

Six plants of Coastal States Louisiana Division were to share in the "pie." They were all located in the massive Baton Rouge-Geismar-Gramercy industrial complex along the Mississippi River between Baton Rouge and New Orleans. Products produced at those plants which required significant amounts of natural gas were phosphoric acid, urea, ammonium phosphate, ammonium nitrate, chlorine, caustic soda, vinyl chloride monomer, and hydroflouric acid.

Stock called a meeting of members of his technical staff to discuss a contingency plan for allocation of natural gas among the products if a curtailment developed. The objective was to minimize the impact on profits. After detailed discussion, the meeting was adjourned. Two weeks later, the meeting reconvened. At this session, the data in the accompanying table were presented.

Coastal State's contract with Cajan Pipeline specified a maximum natural gas consumption of 36,000 cu ft $\times$ 10^3 per day for all of the six member plants. With these data, the technical staff proceeded to develop a model that would specify changes in production rates in response to a natural gas curtailment. (Curtailments are based on contracted consumption and not current consumption.)

Contribution to Profit and Overhead

PRODUCT	$ PER TON	CAPACITY (TONS PER DAY)	MAXIMUM PRODUCTION RATE (PERCENT OF CAPACITY)	NATURAL GAS CONSUMPTION (1,000 CU FT PER TON)
Phosphoric acid	60	400	80	5.5
Urea	80	250	80	7.0
Ammonium phosphate	90	300	90	8.0
Ammonium nitrate	100	300	100	10.0
Chlorine	50	800	60	15.0
Caustic soda	50	1,000	60	16.0
Vinyl chloride monomer	65	500	60	12.0
Hydroflouric acid	70	400	80	11.0

1. Develop a contingency model and specify the production rates for each product for:
   (a) a 20% natural gas curtailment and
   (b) a 40% natural gas curtailment.

2. Explain which of the products in the table should require the most emphasis with regard to energy conservation.

3. What problems do you foresee if production rates are not reduced in a planned and orderly manner?

4. What impact will the natural gas shortage have on company profits?

   Source: Jerry Kinard (Francis Marion College) and Joe C. Iverstine (deceased). Used by permission.

BIBLIOGRAPHY
See References at end of Chapter 10.

12

Linear Programming: Sensitivity Analysis, Duality, and Computer Use

CHAPTER OUTLINE

12.1
INTRODUCTION

sensitivity analysis

In Chapters 10 and 11, we studied how to formulate linear programming problems and how to find optimal solutions by using the graphical and simplex methods. As important as these subjects were, they do not complete our analysis of LP. We have saved for this chapter three of the most valuable aspects of linear programming from a managerial perspective. The first, *sensitivity analysis,* recognizes that management operates in a dynamic environment. This means that costs and prices change, resources diminish or become more readily available, and technological advances affecting production occur. And it means that a company using LP must explore the sensitivity of an optimal LP solution to changes in the data used to build the model.

duality

The second topic addressed in this chapter is the concept of the *dual,* or duality. It turns out that all linear programming problems exist in pairs. For every problem you have formulated so far in studying LP, a sister dual problem could also have been designed. Its use in providing economic information and in helping to reach a solution more quickly will be discussed.

Finally, any treatment of linear programming would not be complete without a discussion of the use of computers to solve problems. The problems that we formulate can, with some long and careful computations, be solved by hand, following the steps of the simplex method. Indeed, it is important to understand how that algorithm works. Unfortunately, the only good way to do that is to solve several problems by hand. Once you comprehend the mechanics of the simplex technique, however, it should not be necessary to struggle with the manual method again. *Computerized LP programs* are widely available. In closing this chapter, we present both sample data inputs and sample computer printouts and discuss their meaning.

12.2
SENSITIVITY ANALYSIS

Optimal solutions to linear programming problems have thus far been found under what are called *deterministic assumptions.* This means that we assume complete certainty in the data and relationships of a problem—namely, prices are fixed, resources known, time needed to produce a unit exactly set. But in the real world, conditions are dynamic and changing. How can we handle this apparent discrepancy?

One way we can do so is by continuing to treat each particular LP problem as a deterministic situation. However, when an optimal solution is found, we recognize the importance of seeing just how *sensitive* that solution is to model assumptions and data. For example, if a firm realizes that profit per unit is not $5 as estimated, but instead closer to $5.50, how will the final solution mix and total profit change? If additional resources, such as ten labor hours or three hours of machine time, should become available, will

how sensitive is optimal solution?

this change the problem's answer? Such analyses are used to examine the effects of changes in three areas: (1) contribution rates (C_j's) for each variable, (2) technological coefficients (the numbers in the constraint equations), and (3) available resources (the right-hand-side quantities in each constraint). This task is alternately called *sensitivity analysis, postoptimality analysis, parametric programming,* or *optimality analysis.*

The use of sensitivity analysis by management is also often centered about the asking of a series of what-if questions. What if the profit on product 1 increases by 10%? What if less money is available in the advertising budget constraint? What if workers each stay one hour longer every day at $1\frac{1}{2}$-time pay to provide increased production capacity? What if new technology will allow a product to be wired in one-third the time it used to take? So we see that sensitivity analysis can be used to deal not only with errors in estimating input parameters to the LP model, but also with management's experiments with possible future changes in the firm that may affect profits.

There are two approaches to determining just how sensitive an optimal solution is to changes. The first is simply a trial-and-error approach. This approach usually involves resolving the entire problem, preferably by computer, each time one input data item or parameter is changed. It can take a long time to test a series of possible changes in this way.

The approach we prefer is the analytic postoptimality method. After an LP problem has been solved, we attempt to determine a range of changes in problem parameters that will not affect the optimal solution or change the variables in the basis. This is done without resolving the whole problem.

Let's investigate sensitivity analysis by developing a small production mix problem similar to those in earlier chapters. Our goal will be to demonstrate graphically and through the simplex tableau how sensitivity analysis can be used to make linear programming concepts more realistic and insightful.

The High Note Sound Company

The High Note Sound Company manufactures quality stereo record players and stereo receivers. Each of these products requires a certain amount of skilled craftsmanship, of which there is a limited weekly supply. The firm formulates the following linear programming problem in order to determine the best production mix of record players (X_1) and receivers (X_2):

Maximize profit = $\$50X_1 + \$120X_2$

Subject to:

$2X_1 + 4X_2 \leq 80$ (*Hours of available electricians' time*)

$3X_1 + 1X_2 \leq 60$ (*Hours of audio technicians' time available*)

$X_1, \quad X_2 \geq 0$

The solution to this problem is illustrated graphically in Figure 12.1. Given this information and deterministic assumptions, the firm should produce only stereo receivers (20 of them) for a weekly profit of $2,400.

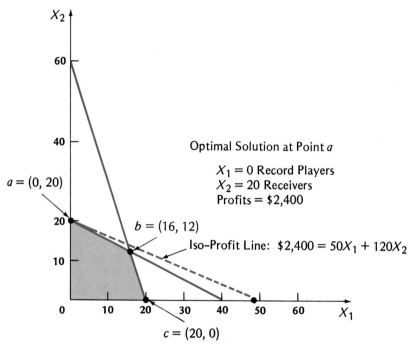

FIGURE 12.1
High Note Sound Company Graphical Solution

Changes in the Objective Function Coefficient

changes in contribution rates

In real-life problems, contribution rates (usually profit or cost) in the objective functions fluctuate periodically, as do most of a firm's expenses. Graphically, this means that although the feasible solution region remains exactly the same, the slope of the iso-profit or iso-cost line will change. It is easy to see in Figure 12.2 that the High Note Sound Company's profit line is optimal to point a. But what if a technical breakthrough just occurred that raised the profit per stereo receiver (X_2) from \$120 to \$150? Is the solution still optimal? The answer is definitely *yes*, for in this case the slope of the profit line accentuates the profitability at point a. The new profit is \$3,000 = 0(\$50) + 20(\$150).

On the other hand, if X_2's profit coefficient was overestimated and should only have been \$80, the slope of the profit line changes enough to cause a new corner point (b) to become optimal. Here the profit is \$1,760 = 16(\$50) + 12(\$80).

A second way of illustrating the sensitivity analysis of objective function coefficients is to consider the problem's final simplex tableau. For the High Note Sound Company, this tableau is shown in Table 12.1. The optimal solution is seen to be:

$X_2 = 20$ stereo receivers   } *Basic*
$S_2 = 40$ hours of slack time of audio technicians   } *variables*

$X_1 = 0$ record players   } *Nonbasic*
$S_1 = 0$ hours of slack time of electricians   } *variables*

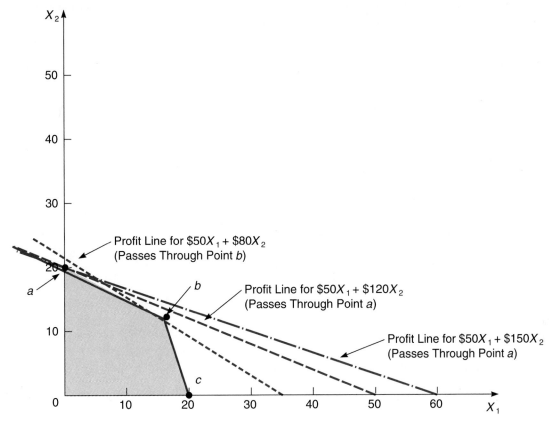

FIGURE 12.2
Changes in the Receiver Contribution Coefficients

Basic variables (those in the solution mix) and *nonbasic variables* (those set equal to 0) must be handled differently using sensitivity analysis. Let us first consider the case of a nonbasic variable.

Nonbasic Objective Function Coefficient. Our goal here is to find out how sensitive the problem's optimal solution is to changes in the contribution rates of variables not currently in the basis (X_1 and S_1). Just how much would the objective function coefficients have to change before X_1 or S_1 would enter the solution mix and replace one of the basic variables?

nonbasic variables

TABLE 12.1 Optimal Solution by the Simplex Method

$C_j \longrightarrow$	SOLUTION MIX	$50	$120	$0	$0	
$\downarrow$		X_1	X_2	S_1	S_2	QUANTITY
$120	X_2	$\frac{1}{2}$	1	$\frac{1}{4}$	0	20
$0	S_2	$\frac{5}{2}$	0	$-\frac{1}{4}$	1	40
	Z_j	60	120	30	0	$2,400
	$C_j - Z_j$	-10	0	-30	0	

solution optimal as long as all $C_j - Z_j \leq 0$

The answer lies in the $C_j - Z_j$ row of the final simplex tableau (as in Table 12.1). Since this is a maximization problem, the basis will not change unless the $C_j - Z_j$ value of one of the nonbasic variables becomes positive. That is, the current solution will be optimal as long as all numbers in the bottom row are less than or equal to 0. It will not be optimal if X_1's $C_j - Z_j$ value is positive, or if S_1's $C_j - Z_j$ value is greater than 0. Therefore, the values of C_j for X_1 and S_1 that do not bring about any change in the optimal solution are given by:

$$C_j - Z_j \leq 0$$

This is the same as writing:

$$C_j \leq Z_j$$

Since X_1's C_j value is $50 and its Z_j value is $60, the current solution is optimal as long as the profit per record player does not exceed $60, or correspondingly, does not increase by more than $10. Likewise, the contribution rate per unit of S_1 (or per hour of electricians' time) may increase from $0 up to $30 without changing the current solution mix.

range over which C_j rates remain valid

In both cases, when you are maximizing an objective function, you may increase the value of C_j up to the value of Z_j. You may also *decrease* the value of C_j for a nonbasic variable to negative infinity ($-\infty$) without affecting the solution. This range of C_j values is called the *range of insignificance* for nonbasic variables.

$$-\infty \leq C_j \text{ (for } X_1) \leq \$60$$

$$-\infty \leq C_j \text{ (for } S_1) \leq \$30$$

testing basic variables involves reworking final simplex tableau

Basic Objective Function Coefficient. Sensitivity analysis on objective function coefficients of variables that are in the basis or solution mix is slightly more complex. We saw that a change in the objective function coefficient for a nonbasic variable affects only the $C_j - Z_j$ value for that variable. But a change in the profit or cost of a basic variable can affect the $C_j - Z_j$ values of *all* nonbasic variables.

Let us consider changing the profit contribution of stereo receivers in the High Note Sound Company problem. Currently, the objective function coefficient is $120. The change in this value can be denoted by the Greek letter Δ. We rework the final simplex tableau (first shown in Table 12.1) and see our results in Table 12.2.

TABLE 12.2 A Change in the Profit Contribution of Stereo Receivers

$C_j \longrightarrow$	SOLUTION MIX	$50 X_1	$120 + \Delta$ X_2	$0 S_1	$0 S_2	QUANTITY
$120 + \Delta$	X_2	$\frac{1}{2}$	1	$\frac{1}{4}$	0	20
$0	S_2	$\frac{5}{2}$	0	$-\frac{1}{4}$	1	40
	Z_j	$60 + \frac{1}{2}\Delta$	$120 + \Delta$	$30 + \frac{1}{4}\Delta$	0	$2,400 + 20\Delta$
	$C_j - Z_j$	$-10 - \frac{1}{2}\Delta$	0	$-30 - \frac{1}{4}\Delta$	0	

Notice the new $C_j - Z_j$ values for nonbasic variables X_1 and S_1. These were determined in exactly the same way as done in Chapter 11. But wherever the C_j value for X_2 of $120 was seen in Table 12.1, a new value of $120 + \Delta$ is used in Table 12.2.

Once again, we recognize that the current optimal solution will change only if one or more of the $C_j - Z_j$ row values becomes greater than 0. The question is, how may the value of Δ vary so that all $C_j - Z_j$ entries remain positive? To find out, we solve for Δ in each column.

From the X_1 column:

$$-10 - \tfrac{1}{2}\Delta \leq 0$$
$$-10 \leq \tfrac{1}{2}\Delta$$
$$-20 \leq \Delta \quad \text{or} \quad \Delta \geq -20$$

This inequality means that the optimal solution will not change unless X_2's profit coefficient decreases by at least $20, which is a change of $\Delta = \$-20$. Hence, variable X_1 will not enter the basis unless the profit per stereo receiver drops from $120 to $100 or less. This, interestingly, is exactly what we noticed graphically in Figure 12.2. When the profit per stereo dropped to $80, the optimal solution changed from corner point a to corner point b.

Now we examine the S_1 column:

$$-30 - \tfrac{1}{4}\Delta \leq 0$$
$$-30 \leq \tfrac{1}{4}\Delta$$
$$-120 \leq \Delta \quad \text{or} \quad \Delta \geq -120$$

This inequality implies that S_1 is less sensitive to change than X_1. S_1 will not enter the basis unless the profit per unit of X_2 drops from $120 all the way down to $0.

Since the first inequality is more binding, we can say that the *range of optimality* for X_2's profit coefficient is:

$$\$100 \leq C_j \text{ (for } X_2) \leq \infty$$

As long as the profit per stereo receiver is greater than or equal to $100, the current production mix of $X_2 = 20$ receivers and $X_1 = 0$ record players will be optimal.

In analyzing larger problems, we would use this procedure to test for the range of optimality of every real decision variable in the final solution mix. The procedure helps us avoid the time-consuming process of reformulating and resolving the entire linear programming problem each time a small change occurs. Within the bounds set, changes in profit coefficients would not force a firm to alter its product mix decision or change the number of units produced. Overall profits, of course, will change if a profit coefficient increases or decreases, but such computations are quick and easy to perform.

range of optimality

Changes in the Technological Coefficients

Changes in what are called the *technological coefficients* often reflect changes in the state of technology. If fewer or more resources are needed to produce

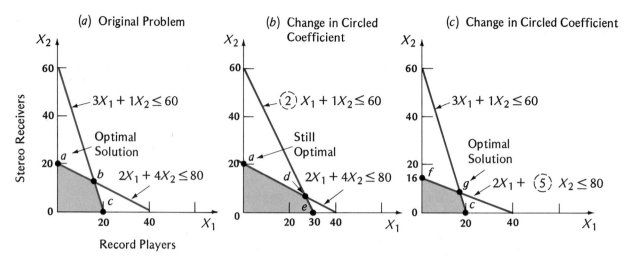

FIGURE 12.3
**Changes in the Technological Coefficients for the
High Note Sound Company**

**changes in technological
coefficients affect feasible
solution region**

a product such as a record player or stereo receiver, coefficients in the constraint equations will change. These changes will have no effect on the objective function of an LP problem, but they can produce a significant change in the shape of the feasible solution region, and hence in the optimal profit or cost. Sensitivity analysis of technological coefficients by the simplex method can become very detailed and is beyond the scope of this text. But a graphical demonstration should suit your needs at this time.

Figure 12.3 illustrates the original High Note Sound Company graphical solution as well as two separate changes in technological coefficients. In Figure 12.3a, we see that the optimal solution lies at point a, which represents $X_1 = 0$, $X_2 = 20$. You should be able to prove to yourself that point a remains optimal in Figure 12.3b despite a constraint change from $3X_1 + 1X_2 \leq 60$ to $2X_1 + 1X_2 \leq 60$. Such a change might take place when the firm discovers that it no longer demands three hours of audio technicians' time to produce a record player, but now only two hours.

In Figure 12.3c, however, a change in the other constraint changes the shape of the feasible region enough to cause a new corner point (g) to become optimal. Before moving on, see if you reach an objective function value of $1,954 profit at point g (versus a profit of $1,920 at point f).[1]

Changes in the Resources or Right-Hand-Side Values

The values on the right-hand-side of linear programming constraints can be considered to represent the resources available to the firm. These re-

---

[1] Note that the values for X_1 and X_2 at point g are fractions. Although High Note Sound Company cannot produce $\frac{2}{3}$, $\frac{3}{4}$, or $\frac{9}{10}$ of a record player or stereo, we can assume the firm can *begin* a unit one week and complete it the next. As long as the production process is fairly stable from week to week, this raises no major problems. If solutions *must* be whole numbers each period, refer to Chapter 15's discussion of integer programming to handle the situation.

sources may be labor hours or machine time available, or perhaps money or production materials available. In the High Note Sound Company example, the two resources are hours of available electricians' time and hours of audio technicians' time. Knowledge of how sensitive the optimal solution is to changes in resources such as these is important because of dynamic marketplace conditions.

Changes in the right-hand-side values result in changes in the feasible region and often in the optimal solution. Figure 12.4 illustrates two resource changes dealing with the number of hours of available electricians' time for each week's production process. An iso-profit line or corner point approach indicates in both Figure 12.4a and 12.4b that corner point a is optimal. However, in Figure 12.4a, the new resource of 100 electricians' hours (as

resource changes affect feasible region

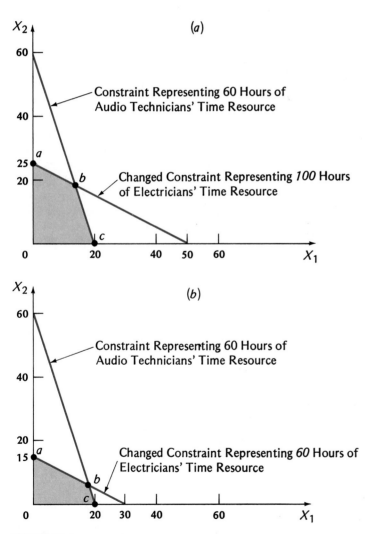

FIGURE 12.4
Changes in the Electricians' Time Resource for the
High Note Sound Company

compared to 80 in the original problem) yields a solution of $X_1 = 0$ record players, $X_2 = 25$ receivers, and profit = \$3,000. Reducing the available resource to only 60 hours, in Figure 12.4*b*, alters the feasible region again. This time the optimal solution is to produce $X_1 = 0$ record players and $X_2 = 15$ receivers, at a profit of \$1,800.

Shadow Prices. This graphical example leads us to the important subject of *shadow prices*. Exactly how much should a firm be willing to pay to make additional resources available? Is one more hour of machine time worth \$1 or \$5 or \$20? Is it worthwhile to pay workers an overtime rate to stay one extra hour each night in order to increase production output? Valuable management information could be provided if the worth of additional resources was known.

value of additional resources

Fortunately, this information is available to us by looking at the final simplex tableau of an LP problem. An important property of the $C_j - Z_j$ row is that the negatives of the numbers in its slack variable (S_i) columns provide us with what we call shadow prices. A *shadow price* is the change in value of the objective function from an increase of one unit of a scarce resource (e.g., by making one more hour of machine time or labor time or other resource available).

The final simplex tableau for the High Note Sound Company problem is repeated as Table 12.3 (it was first shown as Table 12.1) The tableau indicates that the optimal solution is $X_1 = 0$, $X_2 = 20$, $S_1 = 0$, $S_2 = 40$, profit = \$2,400. Recall that S_1 represents slack availability of the electricians' resource and S_2 the unused time in the audio technicians' department.

The firm is considering hiring an extra electrician on a part-time basis. Let's say it will cost \$22 per hour in wages and benefits to bring the part-timer on board. Should the firm do this? The answer is *yes:* the shadow price of the electrician time resource is \$30. Thus, the firm will *net* \$8 (= \$30 − \$22) for every hour the new worker helps in the production process.

Should High Note also hire a part-time audio technician at a rate of \$14 per hour? The answer is *no:* the shadow price is \$0, implying no increase in the objective function by making more of this second resource available. Why? Because not all of the resource is currently being used—40 hours are still available. It would hardly pay to buy more of the resource.

Right-Hand-Side Ranging. Obviously we can't add an unlimited number of units of resources without eventually violating one of the problem's constraints. Once we understand and compute the shadow price for an additional hour of electricians' time (\$30), we will want to determine how many hours we can actually use to increase profits. Should the new resource be added 1 hour per week, 2 hours, or 200 hours? In linear programming terms, this process involves finding the range over which shadow prices will stay valid. *Right-hand-side* (RHS) *ranging* tells us the number of hours High Note can add or remove from the electrician department and still have a shadow price of \$30.

range over which shadow prices remain valid

Ranging is simple in that it resembles the simplex process we used in Chapter 11 to find the minimum ratio for a new variable. The S_1 column and quantity column from Table 12.3 are repeated below; the ratios, both positive and negative, are also shown.

QUANTITY	S_1	RATIO		
20	$\frac{1}{4}$	$20/(\frac{1}{4})$	$=$	80
40	$-\frac{1}{4}$	$40/(-\frac{1}{4})$	$=$	-160

The smallest positive ratio (80 in this example) tells us by how many hours the electricians' time resource can be *reduced* without altering the current solution mix. Hence, we may decrease the right-hand-side resource by as much as 80 hours—basically from the current 80 hours all the way to 0 hours—without causing a basic variable to be pivoted out of the solution.

how to do RHS ranging

The smallest negative ratio (-160) tells us the number of hours that can be added to the resource before the solution mix changes. In this case, we may increase electricians' time by 160 hours, up to 240 ($= 80$ currently $+$ 160 may be added) hours. We have now established the range of electricians' time over which the shadow price of $30 is valid. That range is from 0 to 240 hours.

The audio technician resource is slightly different in that all 60 hours of time originally available have not been used. (Note that $S_2 = 40$ hours in Table 12.3.) If we apply the ratio test, we see that we can reduce the number of audio technician hours by only 40 before a shortage occurs. But since we are not using all the hours currently available, we can increase them indefinitely without altering the problem's solution. Hence, the valid range for *this* shadow price would be from 20($= 60 - 40$) hours to an unbounded upper limit.

Virtually all of the LP computer programs used in corporate and university settings have right-hand-side ranging analyses as standard or optional outputs.

TABLE 12.3 Final Tableau for the High Note Sound Company

$C_j \longrightarrow$	SOLUTION MIX	$50	$120	$0	$0	
$\downarrow$		X_1	X_2	S_1	S_2	QUANTITY
$120	X_2	$\frac{1}{2}$	1	$\frac{1}{4}$	0	20
$0	S_2	$\frac{5}{2}$	0	$-\frac{1}{4}$	1	40
	Z_j	60	120	30	0	$2,400
	$C_j - Z_j$	-10	0	-30	0	

Objective function increases by $30 if 1 additional hour of electricians' time is made available.

12.3
THE DUAL IN LINEAR PROGRAMMING

KEY IDEA

every LP primal has a dual

Every linear programming problem has another LP problem associated with it, which is called its *dual*. The first way of stating a linear program is called the *primal* of the problem: we can view all of the problems formulated thus far as primals. The second way of stating the same problem is called the dual. The optimal solutions for the primal and the dual are equivalent, but they are derived through alternative procedures.

dual provides useful information

The dual contains economic information useful to management, and it may also be easier to solve, in terms of less computation, than the primal problem. Generally, if the LP primal involves maximizing a profit function subject to less-than-or-equal-to resource constraints, the dual will involve minimizing total opportunity costs subject to greater-than-or-equal-to product profit constraints. Formulating the dual problem from a given primal is not terribly complex, and once it is formulated, the solution procedure is exactly the same as for any LP problem.

Let's illustrate the *primal-dual relationship* with the High Note Sound Company data. As you recall, the primal problem is to determine the best production mix of record players (X_1) and stereo receivers (X_2) in order to maximize profit.

$$\text{Maximize profit} = \$50X_1 + \$120X_2$$

Subject to:	$2X_1 +$	$4X_2 \leq 80$	(*Hours of available electrician time*)
	$3X_1 +$	$1X_2 \leq 60$	(*Hours of audio technician time available*)

dual variables are potential value of resources

The dual of this problem has the objective of minimizing the opportunity cost of not using the resources in an optimal manner. Let's call the variables that it will attempt to solve for U_1 and U_2. U_1 represents the potential hourly contribution or worth of electrician time, in other words the dual value of one hour of the electrician's resource. U_2 stands for the imputed worth of the audio technician's time, or the dual technician resource.

The right-hand-side quantities of the primal *constraints* become the dual's *objective function* coefficients. The total opportunity cost that is to be minimized will be represented by the function $80U_1 + 60U_2$, namely,

$$\text{Minimize opportunity cost} = 80U_1 + 60U_2$$

formulating the dual

The corresponding dual constraints are formed from the transpose[2] of the primal constraints coefficients. Note that if the primal constraints are $\leq$, the dual constraints are $\geq$.

---

[2] For example, the transpose of the set of numbers $\begin{pmatrix} a & b \\ c & d \end{pmatrix}$ is $\begin{pmatrix} a & c \\ b & d \end{pmatrix}$. In the case of the transpose of the primal coefficients $\begin{pmatrix} 2 & 4 \\ 3 & 1 \end{pmatrix}$, the result is $\begin{pmatrix} 2 & 3 \\ 4 & 1 \end{pmatrix}$. Refer to Module A, dealing with matrices and determinants, for a review of the transpose concept.

Linear Programming at Dairyman's Cooperative

In many cases, decision makers and managers need an interactive decision support system (DSS) to assist in analyzing data instead of an automated system that will replace traditional decision making.

The Dairyman's Cooperative Creamery Association (DCCA) needed a decision support system to help in its daily production planning. This cooperative, like other milk processing cooperatives, was concerned with the most efficient way of getting milk products through the processing plants. The DCCA is one of the largest single milk processing plants whose facilities are at one location in the United States. Approximately 5 million pounds of raw milk per day is received and stored in silos. The raw milk is then transferred to various stations for processing. From the raw milk, there are about 50 products that are produced.

Daily production planning, inventory control, and forecasting are made difficult by all of the interactions between the various milk products. For any of the 50 products, a number of by-products

Source: Robert Sullivan and Steven Secrest, "A Simple Optimization DSS for Production Planning at Dairyman's Cooperative Creamery," *Interfaces* Vol. 15, No. 5, September–October 1985.

are automatically produced. Many of these products can then be used as raw materials for other products. In the cheese processing plant, for example, there are a number of by-products, including whey, scrap cheese, fines, and salty whey.

To help solve the problem, an interactive milk flow analysis program (MFAP) was developed. This program includes a preprocessor module and the actual solution module that uses a linear programming approach. The preprocessor asks the decision maker to enter various capacities, current inventory levels, supply and demand, and other related information. This information is then used by the second module, which is a linear programming module. The LP module automatically develops 36 linear programming constraints, including production conversion constraints, product flow and balancing constraints, and equipment and inventory capacity limitation constraints. These constraints are saved on a disk and can be used and modified. The objective function is to maximize the expected profit for the DCCA. Hardware and software cost amounted to only $15,000. It is estimated that the program will increase daily throughput at the plant, which should increase net profits by approximately $100,000 per year.

$$2\ U_1 + 3\ U_2 \geq 50 \longrightarrow \textit{Primal profit coefficients}$$
$$4\ U_1 + 1\ U_2 \geq 120$$

Coefficients from the second primal constraint

Coefficients from the first primal constraint

Let's look at the meaning of these dual constraints. In the first inequality, the right-hand-side constant ($50) is the income from one record player. The coefficients of U_1 and U_2 are the amounts of each scarce resource (electrician time and audio technician time) that are required to produce a record player. That is, two hours of electricians' time and three hours of audio technicians' time are used up in making one record player. Each record player produced yields $50 of revenue to High Note Sound Company. This inequality states that the total imputed value or potential worth of the scarce resources needed to produce a record player must be at least equal to the profit derived from the product. The second constraint makes an analogous statement for the stereo receiver product.

Dual Formulation Procedures

The mechanics of formulating a dual from the primal problem may be summarized as follows:

rules for formulating dual

1. If the primal is maximization, the dual is a minimization, and vice versa.

2. The right-hand-side values of the primal constraints become the dual's objective function coefficients.

3. The primal objective function coefficients become the right-hand-side values of the dual constraints.

4. The transpose of the primal constraint coefficients become the dual constraint coefficients.

5. Constraint inequality signs are reversed.[3]

Solving the Dual of the High Note Sound Company Problem

The simplex algorithm, as we learned it in Chapter 11, is applied to solve the preceding dual problem. With appropriate surplus and artificial variables, it may be restated as:

Minimize opportunity cost $= 80U_1 + 60U_2 + 0S_1 + 0S_2 + MA_1 + MA_2$

Subject to:
$$2U_1 + 3U_2 - 1S_1 + 1A_1 \qquad\qquad = 50$$
$$4U_1 + 1U_2 \qquad - 1S_2 + 1A_2 = 120$$

The first and second tableaus are shown in Table 12.4. The third tableau, containing the optimal solution of $U_1 = 30$, $U_2 = 0$, $S_1 = 10$, $S_2 = 0$, opportunity cost $= \$2,400$, appears in Figure 12.5 along with the final tableau of the primal problem.

We mentioned earlier that the primal and dual lead to the same solution even though they are formulated differently. How can this be?

KEY IDEA

It turns out that in the final simplex tableau of a primal problem, the absolute values of the numbers in the $C_j - Z_j$ row under the slack variables represent the solutions to the dual problem, that is, the optimal U_i's. (See Figure 12.5.) In the preceding section on sensitivity analysis we termed these numbers in the columns of the slack variables *shadow prices*. Thus, the solution to the dual problem presents the marginal profits of each additional unit of resource.

dual solution yields shadow prices

It also happens that the absolute value of the $C_j - Z_j$ values of the slack variables in the optimal *dual* solution represent the optimal values of the

---

[3] If the *j*th primal constraint should be an equality, then the *i*th dual variable is unrestricted in sign. This technical issue is discussed on page 170 of *Methods and Applications of Linear Programming*, by L. Cooper and D. Steinberg, Saunders Co., 1974.

APPLICATIONS OF QA

Optimizing Wood Procurement in Cabinet Manufacturing

The Wellborn Cabinet Company is a cabinet manufacturing facility located in Alabama. It consists of a sawmill, four dry kilns, and a wood cabinet assembly plant that includes a rough mill for producing blanks (that is, cabinet components). The cabinet industry in the United States has been growing steadily and has been relatively profitable for the past 20 years because of an expanding new housing market and an active replacement market. Manufacturers experience constant pressure to market quality products at competitive prices.

Maintaining consistency in product quality is a major concern in cabinet making because the production process is basically an assembly operation in which parts are made from different materials acquired from different sources. A rational raw material procurement policy is necessary to control the quality and costs of raw materials. An optimum wood procurement policy for cabinet manufacturing was determined during an Auburn University technical assistance program. The project applied linear programming (LP) to determine the optimum (least-cost) policy for procuring wood raw material. Unlike previous LP applications, however, the Auburn project was the first to consider the purchasing options of a cabinet manufacturing company that has an integrated sawmill and cabinet manufacturing system. Both log processing at Wellborn's sawmill and lumber processing into blanks at its cabinet manufacturing site were considered.

To produce blanks, Wellborn has been purchasing number 1 and number 2 grade hardwood logs as well as number 1 and number 2 common grade lumber (dry or green). Common grades of lumber are suitable for construction and general utility purposes; better quality is indicated by lower grade number. About 65% of Wellborn's total volume of input logs is grade number 1; the rest is number 2. On an annual basis, about 73% of the needed supply comes from logs that are processed at the company's sawmill, and the rest is purchased from outside sources. All green lumber, whether from the sawmill or from outside suppliers, is first dried at the kilns to an average moisture content of 7% before being planed and converted into blanks at the rough mill.

Management is primarily concerned with the high cost of wood raw materials, which make up about 45% of the total material cost of producing cabinets. Managers had no way of knowing what the least-cost combination of raw materials should be for processing blanks into cabinets and whether or not the sawmill and drying operations were cost-effective. An LP model of the blank production system was developed; it was structured to minimize the total cost of producing blanks. Several data inputs were required for the model; they included the diameter and length measurements of randomly selected logs, a tally of the grades and sizes, the maximum weekly throughput, the delivered cost of logs and lumber, the costs of conversion and drying, and the weekly requirements of blanks.

Results from the initial computer run with the LP model indicate that Wellborn can minimize the total cost of producing blanks by purchasing only number 2 grade logs, which should have a small-end diameter of 9 to 15 inches, and number 2 common green lumber. By volume, about 88% of the dry lumber input requirements of the rough mill should come from number 2 grade logs and the rest should come from purchased number 2 common green lumber. By pursuing such a policy, the company can expect to save about $412,000 in raw material costs annually, that is, approximately 32% of the total costs of raw material purchases in 1985–86.

These results have several implications for management. The most direct is an improved profit due to reduced material costs. Another benefit resulting from the cost differential between number 1 grade logs and number 2 grade logs and between number 1 common green lumber and number 2 common green lumber is that the market area for raw material purchases is greatly expanded. The company's management can use lowered costs to lower prices. Aggressive marketing with better pricing can increase sales and profits.

The LP model will be useful to Wellborn's management in trying to simulate mill operations under expected or assumed conditions so that what-if questions can be answered quickly and inexpensively. It can provide the information needed to resolve many important questions.

Source: Honorio F. Carino and Clinton H. LeNoir, Jr., *Interfaces* Volume 18, No. 2, March–April 1988, pp. 10–19.

TABLE 12.4 First and Second Tableaus of the High Note Dual Problem

$C_j \rightarrow$ ↓	SOLUTION MIX	80 U_1	60 U_2	0 S_1	0 S_2	M A_1	M A_2	QUANTITY
M	A_1	2	3	−1	0	1	0	50
M	A_2	4	1	0	−1	0	1	120
	Z_j	6M	4M	−M	−M	M	M	170M
	$C_j - Z_j$	80 − 6M	60 − 4M	M	M	0	0	

$C_j \rightarrow$ ↓	SOLUTION MIX	80 U_1	60 U_2	0 S_1	0 S_2	M A_1	M A_2	QUANTITY
80	U_1	1	$\frac{3}{2}$	$-\frac{1}{2}$	0	$\frac{1}{2}$	0	25
M	A_2	0	−5	2	−1	−2	1	20
	Z_j	80	120 − 5M	−40 + 2M	−M	40 − 2M	M	2000 + 20M
	$C_j - Z_j$	0	5M − 60	−2M + 40	M	3M − 40	0	

primal X_1 and X_2 variables. The minimum opportunity cost derived in the dual must always equal the maximum profit derived in the primal.

Also note the other relationships between the primal and the dual that are indicated in Figure 12.5 by arrows. The columns A_1 and A_2 in the optimal dual tableau may be ignored because, as you recall, artificial variables have no physical meaning.

Computational Advantage of the Dual

solving the dual versus the primal

It was mentioned briefly at the beginning of this section on duality that sometimes it is computationally easier to solve the dual than the primal. Let's close the section with a quick example of how this can occur.

The following primal problem could take seven or more simplex tableaus to reach an optimal solution:

$$\text{Maximize profit} = \$3X_1 + \$4X_2 + \$2X_3$$

$$
\begin{aligned}
\text{Subject to:} \quad X_1 + X_2 & \leqslant 8 \\
X_2 + X_3 & \leqslant 15 \\
8X_1 - 2X_2 & \leqslant 2 \\
X_1 + X_2 - X_3 & \leqslant 12 \\
2X_1 + 2X_2 + X_3 & \leqslant 22 \\
4X_1 + 3X_2 & \leqslant 21 \\
X_3 & \leqslant 3 \\
X_1, X_2, X_3 & \geqslant 0
\end{aligned}
$$

The dual will yield an equivalent solution. But because it contains only three constraints, it can reach an optimal solution in the fourth tableau,

Primal's Optimal Solution

$C_j \longrightarrow$	Solution Mix	Quantity	$50	$120	$0	$0
$\downarrow$			X_1	X_2	S_1	S_2
$120	X_2	20	$\frac{1}{2}$	1	$\frac{1}{4}$	0
$0	S_2	40	$\frac{5}{2}$	0	$-\frac{1}{4}$	1
	Z_j	$2,400	60	120	30	0
	$C_j - Z_j$		−10	0	−30	0

Dual's Optimal Solution

$C_j \longrightarrow$	Solution Mix	Quantity	80	60	0	0	M	M
$\downarrow$			U_1	U_2	S_1	S_2	A_1	A_2
80	U_1	30	1	$\frac{1}{4}$	0	$-\frac{1}{4}$	0	$\frac{1}{2}$
0	S_1	10	0	$-\frac{5}{2}$	1	$-\frac{1}{2}$	−1	$\frac{1}{2}$
	z_j	$2,400	80	20	0	−20	0	40
	$C_j - Z_j$		0	40	0	20	M	M − 40

FIGURE 12.5
Comparison of the Primal and Dual Optimal Tableaus

and hence save a great deal of computer time or time spent with a calculator by hand.[4]

Minimize cost $= 8U_1 + 15U_2 + 2U_3 + 12U_4 + 22U_5 + 21U_6 + 3U_7$

Subject to:

$$1U_1 + \qquad\qquad 8U_3 + 1U_4 + 2U_5 + 4U_6 \qquad\qquad \geqslant 3$$
$$1U_1 + 1U_2 - 2U_3 + 1U_4 + 2U_5 + 3U_6 \qquad\qquad \geqslant 4$$
$$1U_2 \quad - \quad 1U_4 + 1U_5 + \qquad\qquad 1U_7 \geqslant 2$$

12.4
SOLVING LP PROBLEMS BY COMPUTER

Almost every university, business, and government organization has access to computer programs that are capable of solving enormous linear pro-

[4] For a more comprehensive analysis of duality, see Jay E. Strum, *Introduction to Linear Programming* (San Francisco: Holden-Day, 1972).

gramming problems. For example, organizations using General Electric Company computers may use a program called LINPRO. IBM mainframe users have Mathematical Program Systems (MPSX). Control Data's package is called Optima. Honeywell's is Advanced Linear Programming System (ALPS), and Grumman Data Systems has programs called LINPROG and SIMPLEX. In addition, universities provide students with variations of these and other LP programs with such names as LINDO, STORM, or MicroManager.

Although each computer program is slightly different, the approach each takes toward handling LP problems is basically the same. The format of the input data and the level of detail provided in output results may differ from program to program and computer to computer, but once you are experienced in dealing with computerized LP algorithms, you can easily adjust to minor changes.

In this section we demonstrate our own microcomputer software, AB:QM, as well as two other popular commercial packages for microcomputers. As you can see in Programs 12.1, 12.2, and 12.3, all are easy to run and provide several useful pieces of output such as dual values and sensitivity analysis. To provide a side-by-side comparison of formats and features, and to help you review the section on sensitivity analysis, all three programs use the High Note Sound Company data discussed earlier in this chapter. Much larger problems can, of course, be solved with each program.

PROGRAM 12.1 Sample Linear Programming Computer Run Using AB:QM Microcomputer Software

```
Linear Programming

Problem Title :  HIGH NOTE SOUND
Type of Problem  (Max=1/Min=2)      1        Tableau (All=1/Final=2/No=3) 1
Number of Constraints               2        Number of Variables          2


              X1          X2 T        Rhs
   Obj        50         120 x xxxxxxxxxx
   C1          2           4 <         80
   C2          3           1 <         60


   Help   New   Load   Save   Edit   Run   Print   Install   Directory   Esc
```

Program: Linear Programming

Problem Title : HIGH NOTE SOUND

***** Input Data *****

Max. Z = 50x1 + 120x2

Subject to

C1   2x1 + 4x2 <= 80
C2   3x1 + 1x2 <= 60

***** Program Output *****

Simplex Tableau :   0

| \Cj | | | 50.000 | 120.000 | 0.000 | 0.000 |
Cb \	Basis	Bi	x 1	x 2	s 1	s 2
0.000	s 1	80.000	2.000	4.000	1.000	0.000
0.000	s 2	60.000	3.000	1.000	0.000	1.000
	Zj	0.000	0.000	0.000	0.000	0.000
	Cj − Zj		50.000	120.000	0.000	0.000

Simplex Tableau :   1

| \Cj | | | 50.000 | 120.000 | 0.000 | 0.000 |
Cb \	Basis	Bi	x 1	x 2	s 1	s 2
120.000	x 2	20.000	0.500	1.000	0.250	0.000
0.000	s 2	40.000	2.500	0.000	− 0.250	1.000
	Zj	2400.000	60.000	120.000	30.000	0.000
	Cj − Zj		− 10.000	0.000	− 30.000	0.000

Final Optimal Solution

Z =   2400.000

Variable	Value	Reduced Cost
x 1	0.000	10.000
x 2	20.000	0.000

Constraint	Slack/Surplus	Shadow Price
C 1	0.000	30.000
C 2	40.000	0.000

PROGRAM 12.1   Sample Linear Programming Computer Run Using AB:QM Microcomputer Software Continued

Objective Coefficient Ranges

Variables	Lower Limit	Current Values	Upper Limit	Allowable Increase	Allowable Decrease
x 1	No limit	50.000	60.000	10.000	No limit
x 2	100.000	120.000	No limit	No limit	20.000

Right Hand Side Ranges

Constraints	Lower Limit	Current Values	Upper Limit	Allowable Increase	Allowable Decrease
C 1	0.000	80.000	240.000	160.000	80.000
C 2	20.000	60.000	No limit	No limit	40.000

***** End of Output*****

PROGRAM 12.2 High Note Sound Company Data Solved by STORM

```
————————— STORM EDITOR : Linear & Integer Programming Module —————————
Title : HIGH NOTE SOUND
Number of variables       :        2
Number of constraints     :        2
Starting solution given   :       NO
Objective type (MAX/MIN)  :      MAX
```

R4 : C2	VAR 1	VAR 2	CONST TYPE	R H S	RANGE
OBJ COEFF	50.	120.	XXXX	XXXX	XXXX
CONSTR 1	2.	4.	<=	80.	.
CONSTR 2	3.	1.	<=	60.	.
VARBL TYPE	POS	POS	XXXX	XXXX	XXXX
LOWR BOUND	.	.	XXXX	XXXX	XXXX
UPPR BOUND	.	.	XXXX	XXXX	XXXX
INIT SOLN	0.	0.	XXXX	XXXX	XXXX

F1 Block F2 GoTo F3 InsR F4 DelR F5 InsC F6 DelC F7 Done F8 Help KB:C

                         HIGH NOTE SOUND
           OPTIMAL SOLUTION — SUMMARY REPORT (NONZERO VARIABLES)
                   Variable   Value   Cost

              2   VAR   2   20.0000   120.0000

              Slack Variables
              4   CONSTR 2   40.0000   0.0000

           Objective Function Value = 2400

PROGRAM 12.2 High Note Sound Company Data Solved by STORM
Continued

HIGH NOTE SOUND
SENSITIVITY ANALYSIS OF COST COEFFICIENTS

	Variable		Current Coeff.	Allowable Minimum	Allowable Maximum
1	VAR	1	50.0000	−Infinity	60.0000
2	VAR	2	120.0000	100.0000	Infinity

HIGH NOTE SOUND
SENSITIVITY ANALYSIS OF RIGHT-HAND SIDE VALUES

	Constraint		Type	Current Value	Allowable Minimum	Allowable Maximum
1	CONSTR	1	<=	80.0000	0.0000	240.0000
2	CONSTR	2	<=	60.0000	20.0000	Infinity

PROGRAM 12.3 High Note Sound Company Data Solved by LINDO

```
LINDO/PC  (UC 21 AUG 84)

COPYRIGHT © 1984 LINDO SYSTEMS, INC.

?
: MAX 50X1 + 120X2
? ST
? 2X1+4X2<80
? 3X1+1X2<60
?
: LOOK
ROW:
ALL


MAX    50 X1 + 120 X2
SUBJECT TO
    2)  2 X1 + 4 X2 <= 80
    3)  3 X1 + X2 <= 60
END

: GO
LP OPTIMUM FOUND AT STEP 1
```

PROGRAM 12.3 High Note Sound Company Data Solved by LINDO Continued

```
                    OBJECTIVE FUNCTION VALUE


     1)         2400.00000

     VARIABLE           VALUE          REDUCED COST
          X1           .000000          10.000000
          X2         20.000000           .000000


         ROW      SLACK OR SURPLUS     DUAL PRICES
          2)           .000000         30.000000
          3)         40.000000          .000000

     NO. ITERATIONS = 1

     DO RANGE (SENSITIVITY) ANALYSIS?
     ? YES



     RANGES IN WHICH THE BASIS IS UNCHANGED:

                                  OBJ COEFFICIENT RANGES
     VARIABLE        CURRENT         ALLOWABLE      ALLOWABLE
                      COEF           INCREASE       DECREASE
          X1        50.000000       10.000000       INFINITY
          X2       120.000000        INFINITY      20.000000

                                  RIGHTHAND SIDE RANGES
        ROW          CURRENT         ALLOWABLE      ALLOWABLE
                       RHS           INCREASE       DECREASE
         2          80.000000      160.000000      80.000000
         3          60.000000        INFINITY      40.000000
```

12.5
SUMMARY

In this chapter we presented the important concept of sensitivity analysis. Sometimes referred to as postoptimality analysis, sensitivity analysis is used by management to answer a series of what-if questions about LP model parameters. It also tests just how sensitive the optimal solution is to changes in profit or cost coefficients, technological coefficients, and right-hand-side resources. The value of additional resources was also analyzed through a discussion of shadow prices.

The relationship between a primal LP problem and its dual was explored. We illustrated how to derive the dual from a primal and how the solution to the dual variables is actually the shadow prices.

We concluded Chapter 12 with examples of three of the many LP computer programs available. Computer programs have proven to be extremely cost-effective means of tackling large problems.

GLOSSARY

Sensitivity Analysis. The study of how sensitive an optimal solution is to model assumptions and to data changes. It is often referred to as postoptimality analysis.

Range of Insignificance. The range of values over which a nonbasic variable's coefficient can vary without causing a change in the optimal solution mix.

Range of Optimality. The range of values over which a basic variable's coefficient can change without causing a change in the optimal solution mix.

Technological Coefficients. Coefficients of the variables in the constraint equations. The coefficients represent the amount of resources needed to produce one unit of the variable.

Shadow price. The coefficients of slack variables in the $C_j - Z_j$ row. They represent the value of one additional unit of a resource.

Right-Hand-Side Ranging. A method used to find the range over which shadow prices remain valid.

Primal-Dual Relationship. Alternative ways of stating a linear programming problem.

SOLVED PROBLEM

Solved Problem 12-1

Solve the following LP problem using LINDO and answer the questions regarding a firm that manufactures both lawn mowers and snowblowers.

Maximize profit = $30 Mower + $80 Blower

Subject to: 2 Mower +   4 Blower ≤ 1,000 labor hours available
              6 Mower +   2 Blower ≤ 1,200 lbs. of steel available
                          1 Blower ≤ 200 snowblower engines available

(a) What is the best product mix? What is the optimal profit?
(b) What are the shadow prices? When the optimal solution has been reached, which resource has the highest marginal value?
(c) Over what range in each of the RHS values are these shadows valid?
(d) What are the ranges over which the objective function coefficients can vary for each of the two decision variables?
(e) State the dual to this problem. What is its solution?

Solution

PROGRAM 12.4 LINDO Printout for Solved Problem 12-1

```
LOOK ALL
MAX      30 MOWER  +  80 BLOWER
SUBJECT TO
        2)     2 MOWER  +  4 BLOWER  <=    1000
        3)     6 MOWER  +  2 BLOWER  <=    1200
        4)     BLOWER  <=    200

END

: GO
LP OPTIMUM Found  AT STEP     2

            OBJECTIVE FUNCTION VALUE

1)        19000.0000

VARIABLE          VALUE          REDUCED COST
   MOWER      100.000000            .000000
   BLOWER     200.000000            .000000

     ROW    SLACK OR SURPLUS    DUAL PRICES
     2)          .000000        15.000000
     3)        200.000000         .000000
     4)          .000000        20.000000

NO. ITERATIONS=        2

DO RANGE(SENSITIVITY) ANALYSIS?
? YES



RANGES IN WHICH THE BASIS IS UNCHANGED:

                        OBJ COEFFICIENT RANGES
VARIABLE        CURRENT        ALLOWABLE        ALLOWABLE
                COEF           INCREASE         DECREASE
   MOWER        30.000000       10.000000        30.000000
   BLOWER       80.000000       INFINITY         20.000000

                     RIGHTHAND SIDE RANGES
   ROW          CURRENT        ALLOWABLE        ALLOWABLE
                RHS            INCREASE         DECREASE
     2        1000.000000      66.666660       200.000000
     3        1200.000000      INFINITY        200.000000
     4         200.000000      50.000000        20.000000


: TABL
```

PROGRAM 12.4 Continued

```
THE TABLEAU
    ROW   (BASIS)      MOWER     BLOWER      SLK2       SLK3       SLK4
     1  ART            .000       .000     15.000      .000     20.000  19000.000
     2     MOWER      1.000       .000       .500      .000     -2.000    100.000
     3  SLK    3       .000       .000     -3.000     1.000     10.000    200.000
     4     BLOWER      .000      1.000       .000      .000      1.000    200.000
```

(a) The best product mix is 100 lawn mowers and 200 snowblowers, yielding a profit (in row 1 of the output) of $19,000.

(b) The shadow prices are the "dual prices" in LINDO's printout. Each constraint (labeled rows 2, 3, and 4 for the three constraints) has one shadow price associated with it. For labor, the value of one additional hour over the existing 1,000 is $15. There is zero value to an additional pound of steel since the row 3 slack variable currently has a value of 200 pounds. In other words, with 200 unused pounds of steel, there is no point in paying for additional steel. Finally, there is a value of $20 for each additional snowblower engine made available. So snowblower engines have the highest marginal value at the optimal solution.

(c) The shadow price for labor hours is valid from 800 hours to 1,066.66 hours; that is, it can increase by $66\frac{2}{3}$ (or 67) hours or decrease by as much as 200 hours. The shadow price for pounds of steel is valid from 1,000 pounds up to an infinite number of pounds. The shadow price for snowblower engines ranges from 180 engines up to 250 engines.

(d) Without changing the current solution mix, the profit coefficient for the mowers can range from $0 to $40, while the coefficient for the blowers can range from $60 to infinity.

(e) The dual can be written as:

$$\text{Minimize } 1,000 \quad U_1 + 1,200\ U_2 + 200\ U_3$$
$$\text{Subject to:} \quad 2U_1 + \quad 6U_2 + \quad 0U_3 \geqslant 30$$
$$4U_1 + \quad 2U_2 + \quad 1U_3 \geqslant 80$$

The solution to the dual will be the shadow prices in the primal. So, $U_1 = 15$, $U_2 = 0$, $U_3 = 20$. The dual solution provides the marginal profits of each additional unit of resource.

DISCUSSION QUESTIONS AND PROBLEMS

Discussion Questions

12-1 Discuss the role of sensitivity analysis in linear programming. Under what circumstances is it needed and under what conditions do you think it is not necessary?

12-2 Is sensitivity analysis a concept applied to linear programming only, or should it also be used when analyzing other techniques? Provide examples to prove your point.

12-3 What is a shadow price? How does the concept relate to the dual of an LP problem? How does it relate to the primal?

12-4 Develop your own original linear programming problem with two constraints and two real variables.

   (a) Explain the meaning of the numbers on the right-hand side of each of your constraints.
   (b) Explain the significance of the technological coefficients.
   (c) Solve your problem graphically to find the optimal solution.
   (d) Illustrate graphically the effect of increasing the contribution rate of your first variable (X_1) by 50% over the value you first assigned it. Does this change the optimal solution?

12-5 Explain how a change in a technological coefficient can affect a problem's optimal solution. How can a change in resource availability affect a solution?

12-6 If a primal problem has 12 constraints and 8 variables, how many constraints and variables will its corresponding dual have?

12-7 Explain the relationship between each number in a primal and corresponding numbers in the dual.

12-8 Create your own original LP maximization problem with two variables and three less-than-or-equal-to constraints. Now form the dual for this primal problem.

12-9 What is the value of the computer in solving linear programming problems today?

Problems

· **12-10** Graph the following LP problem and indicate the optimal solution point.

$$\text{Maximize profit} = \$3X_1 + \$2X_2$$
$$\text{Subject to:} \quad 2X_1 + 1X_2 \le 150$$
$$2X_1 + 3X_2 \le 300$$

   (a) Does the optimal solution change if the profit per unit of X_1 changes to \$4.50?
   (b) What happens if the profit function should have been $\$3X_1 + \$3X_2$?

· **12-11** Graphically analyze the following problem:

$$\text{Maximize profit} = \$4X_1 + \$6X_2$$
$$\text{Subject to:} \quad 1X_1 + 2X_2 \le 8$$
$$6X_1 + 4X_2 \le 24$$

   (a) What is the optimal solution?
   (b) If the first constraint is altered to $1X_1 + 3X_2 \le 8$, do the feasible region or optimal solution change?

· **12-12** Consider the following linear programming problem:

$$\text{Maximize profit} = \$1X_1 + \$1X_2$$
$$\text{Subject to:} \quad 2X_1 + 1X_2 \leqslant 100$$
$$1X_1 + 2X_2 \leqslant 100$$

(a) What is the optimal solution to this problem? Solve it graphically.
(b) If a technical breakthrough occurred that raised the profit per unit of X_1 to $3, would this affect the optimal solution?
(c) Instead of an increase in the profit coefficient of X_1 to $3, suppose profit was overestimated and should only have been $1.25. Does this change the optimal solution?

· **12-13** Consider the LP formulation given in Problem 12-12. If the second constraint is changed from $1X_1 + 2X_2 \leqslant 100$ to $1X_1 + 4X_2 \leqslant 100$, what effect will this have on the optimal solution? (Use the same objective function, Profit = $1X_1 + 1X_2$.)

· **12-14** Examine the LP formulation in Problem 12-11. The problem's second constraint reads:

$$6X_1 + 4X_2 \leqslant 24 \text{ hours} \quad \text{(time available on machine 2)}$$

If the firm decides that 36 hours of time can be made available on machine 2 (namely, an additional 12 hours) at an additional cost of $10, should they add the hours?

: **12-15** Consider the following optimal tableau where S_1 and S_2 are slack variables added to the original problem.

$C_j \longrightarrow$	SOLUTION MIX	$10	$30	$0	$0	
$\downarrow$		X_1	X_2	S_1	S_2	QUANTITY
$10	X_1	1	4	2	0	160
$0	S_2	0	6	-7	1	200
	Z_j	10	40	$+20$	0	$1,600
	$C_j - Z_j$	0	-10	-20	0	

(a) What is the range of optimality for the contribution rate of the variable X_1?
(b) What is the range of insignificance of the contribution rate of the variable X_2?
(c) How much would you be willing to pay for one more unit of the first resource, which is represented by slack variable S_1?
(d) What is the value of one more unit of the second resource? Why?

· **12-16** The following is the final simplex tableau of an LP problem that has three constraints and four variables.

$C_j \longrightarrow$		$4	$6	$3	$1	$0	$0	$0	
$\downarrow$	SOLUTION MIX	X_1	X_2	X_3	X_4	S_1	S_2	S_3	QUANTITY
3	X_3	$1/20$	0	1	$1/2$	$3/10$	0	$-1/5$	125
0	S_2	$39/12$	0	0	$-1/2$	$-1/2$	1	0	425
6	X_2	$39/60$	1	0	$1/2$	$-1/10$	0	$3/5$	25
	Z_j	$81/20$	6	3	$9/2$	$3/10$	0	3	$525
	$C_j - Z_j$	$-1/20$	0	0	$-7/2$	$-3/10$	0	-3	

What are the values of each of the shadow prices? What meaning does a 0 shadow price have and how can it occur?

· **12-17** Clapper Electronics produces two models of telephone-answering devices, Model 102 (X_1) and Model H23 (X_2). Jim Clapper, vice president for production, formulates their constraints as:

$$2X_1 + 1X_2 \leqslant 40 \quad \text{(Hours of time available on soldering machine)}$$

$$1X_1 + 3X_2 \leqslant 30 \quad \text{(Hours of time available in inspection department)}$$

Clapper's objective function is:

$$\text{Maximize profit} = \$9X_1 + \$7X_2$$

Solving this problem using the simplex method, he produces the following final tableau.

$C_j \longrightarrow$		$9	$7	$0	$0	
$\downarrow$	SOLUTION MIX	X_1	X_2	S_1	S_2	QUANTITY
$9	X_1	1	0	$3/5$	$-1/5$	18
$7	X_2	0	1	$-1/5$	$2/5$	4
	Z_j	$9	$7	$4	$1	$190
	$C_j - Z_j$	$0	$0	$-4	$-1	

(a) What is the optimal mix of Models 102 and H23 to produce?
(b) What do variables S_1 and S_2 represent?
(c) Clapper is considering renting a second soldering machine at a cost to the firm of $2.50 per hour. Should he do so?
(d) Clapper computes that he can hire a part-time inspector for only $1.75 per hour. Should he do so?

: **12-18** Refer to Table 11.6 in the previous chapter, which is the optimal tableau for the Flair Furniture Company problem.

(a) What are the values of the shadow prices?
(b) Interpret the physical meaning of each shadow price in the context of the furniture problem.
(c) What is the range over which the profit per table can vary without changing the optimal basis (solution mix)?
(d) What is the range of optimality for X_2 (number of chairs produced)?
(e) How many hours can Flair Furniture add to or remove from the first resource (painting department time) without changing the basis?
(f) Conduct right-hand-side ranging on the carpentry department resource to determine the range over which the shadow price remains valid.

: **12-19** Consider the optimal solution to the Muddy River Chemical Company problem in Table 11.10 of Chapter 11.

   (a) For each of the two chemical ingredients, phosphate and potassium, determine the range over which their cost may vary without affecting the basis.

   (b) If the original constraint that "no more than 300 pounds of phosphate can be used" ($X_1 \leq 300$) were changed to $X_1 \leq 400$, would the basis change? Would the values of X_1, X_2, and S_2 change?

· **12-20** Formulate the dual of this LP problem.

$$\text{Maximize profit} = 80X_1 + 75X_2$$
$$1X_1 + 3X_2 \leq 4$$
$$2X_1 + 5X_2 \leq 8$$

Find the dual of the problem's dual.

· **12-21** What is the dual of the following LP problem?

$$\text{Primal: Minimize cost} = 120X_1 + 250X_2$$
$$\text{Subject to:} \quad 12X_1 + 20X_2 \geq 50$$
$$1X_1 + 3X_2 \geq 4$$

· **12-22** The third, and final, simplex tableau for the LP problem stated here follows:

$$\text{Maximize profit} = 200X_1 + 200X_2$$
$$\text{Subject to:} \quad 2X_1 + X_2 \leq 8$$
$$X_1 + 3X_2 \leq 9$$

What are the solutions to the dual variables, U_1 and U_2? What is the optimal dual cost?

$C_i \longrightarrow$		$200	$200	$0	$0	
$\downarrow$	SOLUTION MIX	X_1	X_2	S_1	S_2	QUANTITY
$200	X_1	1	0	$3/5$	$-1/5$	3
$200	X_2	0	1	$-1/5$	$2/5$	2
	Z_j	200	200	80	40	$1,000
	$C_j - Z_j$	$0	$0	$-80	$-40	

· **12-23** The accompanying tableau provides the optimal solution to this dual:

$$\text{Minimize cost} = 120U_1 + 240U_2$$
$$\text{Subject to:} \quad 2U_1 + 2U_2 \geq .5$$
$$U_1 + 3U_2 \geq .4$$

$C_i \longrightarrow$		120	240	0	0	M	M	
$\downarrow$	SOLUTION MIX	U_1	U_2	S_1	S_2	A_1	A_2	QUANTITY
120	U_1	1	0	$-3/4$	$1/2$	$3/4$	$-1/2$	.175
240	U_2	0	1	$1/4$	$-1/2$	$-1/4$	$1/2$	.075
	Z_j	120	240	-30	-60	30	60	$39
	$C_j - Z_j$	0	0	30	60	$M - 30$	$M - 60$	

What does the corresponding primal problem look like, and what is its optimal solution?

: **12-24** Given the following dual formulation, reconstruct the original primal problem.

$$\text{Minimize cost} = 28U_1 + 53U_2 + 70U_3 + 18U_4$$

Subject to:
$$U_1 \qquad\qquad + \quad U_4 \geqslant 10$$
$$U_1 + 2U_2 + \quad U_3 \qquad\qquad \geqslant 5$$
$$-2U_2 \qquad + \quad 5U_4 \geqslant 31$$
$$5U_3 \qquad\qquad \geqslant 28$$
$$12U_1 \qquad + \quad 2U_3 - \quad U_4 \geqslant 17$$
$$U_1, U_2\, U_3,\, U_4 \geqslant 0$$

· **12-25** A firm that makes three products, and has three machines available as resources, constructs the following LP problem.

$$\text{Maximize profit} = 4X_1 + 4X_2 + 7X_3$$

Subject to:
$$1X_1 + 7X_2 + 4X_3 \leqslant 100 \ \textit{(hours on machine 1)}$$
$$2X_1 + 1X_2 + 7X_3 \leqslant 110 \ \textit{(hours on machine 2)}$$
$$8X_1 + 4X_2 + 1X_3 \leqslant 100 \ \textit{(hours on machine 3)}$$

Solve this problem by computer and answer these questions:

(a) Before the third iteration of the simplex method, which machine still has unused time available?

(b) When the final solution is reached, is there any unused time available on any of the three machines?

(c) What would it be worth to the firm to make an additional hour of time available on the third machine?

(d) How much would the firm's profit increase if an extra 10 hours of time were made available on the second machine at no extra cost?

: **12-26** Management analysts at a Fresno laboratory have developed the following LP primal problem:

$$\text{Minimize cost} = 23X_1 + 18X_2$$

Subject to:
$$8X_1 + 4X_2 \geqslant 120$$
$$4X_1 + 6X_2 \geqslant 115$$
$$9X_1 + 4X_2 \geqslant 116$$

This model represents a decision concerning number of hours of time spent by biochemists on certain laboratory experiments (X_1) and number of hours spent by biophysicists on the same series of experiments (X_2). A biochemist costs \$23 per hour while a biophysicist's salary averages \$18 per hour. Both types of scientists can be used on three needed laboratory operations: test 1, test 2, and test 3. The experiments and their times are:

LAB EXPERIMENT	SCIENTIST TYPE		MINIMUM TEST TIME NEEDED PER DAY
	BIOPHYSICIST	BIOCHEMIST	
Test 1	8	4	120
Test 2	4	6	115
Test 3	9	4	116

This means that a biophysicist can complete 8, 4, and 9 of tests 1, 2, and 3 per hour. Likewise, a biochemist can perform 4 of test 1, 6 of test 2, and 4 of test 3 per hour. The optimal solution to the lab's primal problem is:

$$X_1 = 8.12 \text{ hours and } X_2 = 13.75 \text{ hours}$$

$$\text{Total cost} = \$434.37 \text{ per day}$$

The optimal solution to the dual problem is:

$$U_1 = 2.07, \ U_2 = 1.63, \ U_3 = 0$$

(a) What is the dual of the above primal LP problem?

(b) Interpret the meaning of the dual and its solution.

: **12-27** The Flair Furniture Company first decribed in Chapter 10 manufactures inexpensive tables (X_1) and chairs (X_2). The firm's daily LP formulation was given earlier as:

$$\text{Maximize profits} = \$7X_1 + \$5X_2$$

Subject to:
$$4X_1 + 3X_2 \leq 240 \text{ hours of carpentry time available}$$
$$2X_1 + 1X_2 \leq 100 \text{ hours of painting time available}$$

In addition, Flair finds that three more constraints are in order. First, each table and chair must be inspected and many need rework. The constraint describing the time required on the average for each is as follows:

$$\tfrac{1}{2}X_1 + \tfrac{3}{5}X_2 \leq 36 \text{ hours of inspection/ rework time available}$$

Second, Flair faces a resource constraint relating to the lumber needed for each table or chair and the amount available each day:

$$32X_1 + 10X_2 \leq 1,248 \text{ linear feet of lumber available for production}$$

Finally, the demand for tables is found to be a maximum of 40 daily. There are no similar constraints regarding chairs.

$$X_1 \leq 40 \text{ maximum table production daily}$$

These data have been entered in the LP software program that is available with this book. The inputs and results are shown in the accompanying printout. Refer to the computer output in answering these questions.

(a) How many tables and chairs should Flair Furniture produce daily? What is the profit generated by this solution?

(b) Will Flair use all of its resources to their limits each day? Be specific in explaining your answer.

(c) Explain the physical meaning of each shadow price.

(d) Should Flair purchase more lumber if it is available at $.07 per linear foot? Should it hire more carpenters at $12.75 per hour?

(e) Flair's owner has been approached by a friend whose company would like to use several hours in the painting facility every day. Should Flair sell time to the other firm? If so, how much? Explain.

(f) What is the range within which the carpentry hours, painting hours, and inspection/rework hours can fluctuate before the optimal solution changes?

(g) Within what range for the current solution can the profit contribution of tables and chairs change?

PROGRAM 12.5 Computer Printout for Problem 12-27

Program: Linear Programming

Problem Title : REVISED FLAIR FURNITURE FOR PROBLEM 12.27

***** Input Data *****

Max.   Z =   7x1 + 5x2

Subject to

C1   4x1 + 3x2 <= 240
C2   2x1 + 1x2 <= 100
C3   .5x1 + .6x2 <= 36
C4   32x1 + 10x2 <= 1248
C5   1x1 <= 40

***** Program Output *****

Simplex Tableau :   2

\Cj Cb \	Basis	Bi	7.000 x 1	5.000 x 2	0.000 s 1	0.000 s 2
0.000	s 1	18.930	0.000	0.000	1.000	0.000
0.000	s 2	8.056	0.000	0.000	0.000	1.000
5.000	x 2	37.183	0.000	1.000	0.000	0.000
7.000	x 1	27.380	1.000	0.000	0.000	0.000
0.000	s 5	12.620	0.000	0.000	0.000	0.000
Zj		377.577	7.000	5.000	0.000	0.000
Cj − Zj			0.000	0.000	0.000	0.000

\Cj Cb \	Basis	Bi	0.000 s 3	0.000 s 4	0.000 s 5
0.000	s 1	18.930	−3.944	−0.063	0.000
0.000	s 2	8.056	−0.845	−0.049	0.000
5.000	x 2	37.183	2.254	−0.035	0.000
7.000	x 1	27.380	−0.704	0.042	0.000
0.000	s 5	12.620	0.704	−0.042	1.000
Zj		377.577	6.338	0.120	0.000
Cj − Zj			−6.338	−0.120	0.000

PROGRAM 12.5 Computer Printout for Problem 12-27 Continued

```
Final Optimal Solution

Z =      377.577
```

Variable	Value	Reduced Cost
x 1	27.380	0.000
x 2	37.183	0.000

Constraint	Slack/Surplus	Shadow Price
C 1	18.930	0.000
C 2	8.056	0.000
C 3	0.000	6.338
C 4	0.000	0.120
C 5	12.620	0.000

Objective Coefficient Ranges

Variables	Lower Limit	Current Values	Upper Limit	Allowable Increase	Allowable Decrease
x 1	4.167	7.000	16.000	9.000	2.833
x 2	2.188	5.000	8.400	3.400	2.813

Right Hand Side Ranges

Constraints	Lower Limit	Current Values	Upper Limit	Allowable Increase	Allowable Decrease
C 1	221.070	240.000	No limit	No limit	18.930
C 2	91.944	100.000	No limit	No limit	8.056
C 3	19.500	36.000	40.800	4.800	16.500
C 4	600.000	1248.000	1411.429	163.429	648.000
C 5	27.380	40.000	No limit	No limit	12.620

```
***** End of Output*****
```

Data Set Problem

 12-28 A Chicago manufacturer of office equipment is desperately attempting to control its profit and loss statement. The company currently manufactures 15 different products, each coded with a one-letter and three-digit designation.

PRODUCT	STEEL ALLOY REQUIRED (LBS.)	PLASTIC REQUIRED (SQ. FT.)	WOOD REQUIRED (BD. FT.)	ALUMINUM REQUIRED (LBS.)	FORMICA REQUIRED (BD. FT.)	LABOR REQUIRED (HOURS)	MINIMUM MONTHLY DEMAND (UNITS)	CONTRIBUTION TO PROFIT
A158	—	.4	.7	5.8	10.9	3.1	—	$18.79
B179	4	.5	1.8	10.3	2.0	1.0	20	6.31
C023	6	—	1.5	1.1	2.3	1.2	10	8.19
D045	10	.4	2.0	—	—	4.8	10	45.88
E388	12	1.2	1.2	8.1	4.9	5.5	—	63.00
F422	—	1.4	1.5	7.1	10.0	.8	20	4.10
G366	10	1.4	7.0	6.2	11.1	9.1	10	81.15
H600	5	1.0	5.0	7.3	12.4	4.8	20	50.06
I701	1	.4	—	10.0	5.2	1.9	50	12.79
J802	1	.3	—	11.0	6.1	1.4	20	15.88
K900	—	.2	—	12.5	7.7	1.0	20	17.91
L901	2	1.8	1.5	13.1	5.0	5.1	10	49.99
M050	—	2.7	5.0	—	2.1	3.1	20	24.00
N150	10	1.1	5.8	—	—	7.7	10	88.88
P259	10	—	6.2	15.0	1.0	6.6	10	77.01
Availability per month	980	400	600	2,500	1,800	1,000		

(a) How many of each of the 15 products should be produced each month?

(b) Clearly explain the meaning of each shadow price.

(c) A number of workers interested in saving money for the holidays have offered to work overtime next month at a rate of $12.50 per hour. What should the response of management be?

(d) Two tons of steel alloy are available from an overstocked supplier at a total cost of $8,000. Should the steel be purchased? All or part of the supply?

(e) The accountants have just discovered that an error was made in the contribution to profit for product N150. The correct value is actually $8.88. What are the implications of this error?

(f) Management is considering the abandonment of five product lines (those beginning with the letters A through E). If no minimum monthly demand is established, what are the implications? Note that there already is no minimum for two of these products. Use the corrected value for N150.

Red Brand Canners

On Monday, September 13, 1990, Mr. Mitchell Gordon, vice president of operations, asked the controller, the sales manager, and the production manager to meet with him to discuss the amount of tomato products to pack that season. The tomato crop, which had been purchased at planting, was beginning to arrive at the cannery, and packing operations would have to be started by the following Monday. Red Brand Canners is a medium-sized company that cans and distributes a variety of fruit and vegetable products under private brands in the western states.

William Cooper, the controller, and Charles Myers, the sales manager, were the first to arrive in Gordon's office. Dan Tucker, the production manager, came in a few minutes later and said that he had picked up Produce Inspection's latest estimate of the quality of the incoming tomatoes. According to the report, about 20% of the crop was grade A quality and the remaining portion of the 3-million pound crop was grade B.

Gordon asked Myers about the demand for tomato products for the coming year. Myers replied that they could sell all of the whole canned tomatoes they could produce. The expected demand for tomato juice and tomato paste, on the other hand, was limited. The sales manager then passed around the latest demand forecast, which is shown in Table 1. He reminded the group that the selling prices had been set in light of the long-term marketing strategy of the company and that the potential sales had been forecast at these prices.

Bill Cooper, after looking at Myers' estimates of demand, said that it looked like the company "should do quite well [on the tomato crop] this year." With the new accounting system that had been set up, he had been able to compute the contribution for each product, and according to his analysis the incremental profit on whole tomatoes was greater than the incremental profit on any other tomato product. In May, after Red Brand had signed contracts agreeing to purchase the grower's production at an average delivered price of 6 cents per pound, Cooper had computed the tomato products' contributions (see Table 2).

Dan Tucker brought to Cooper's attention that although there was ample production capacity, it was impossible to produce all whole tomatoes since too small a portion of the tomato crop was "grade A" quality. Red Brand used a numerical scale to record the quality of both raw produce and prepared products. This scale ran from 0 to 10—the higher number representing better quality. According to this scale, grade A tomatoes averaged nine points per pound and grade B tomatoes averaged five points per pound. Tucker noted that the minimum average input quality was eight points per pound for canned whole tomatoes and six points per pound for juice. Paste could be made entirely from grade B tomatoes. This meant that whole tomato production was limited to 800,000 pounds.

Gordon stated that this was not a real limitation. He had been recently solicited to purchase 80,000 pounds of grade A tomatoes at $8\frac{1}{2}$ cents per pound and at that time had turned down the offer. He felt, however, that the tomatoes were still available.

Myers, who had been doing some calculations, said that although he agreed that the company "should do quite well this year," it would not be by canning whole tomatoes. It seemed to him that the tomato cost should be allocated on the basis of

TABLE 1 Demand Forecasts

PRODUCT	SELLING PRICE PER CASE ($)	DEMAND FORECAST (CASES)
24—2½ whole tomatoes	4.00	800,000
24—2½ choice peach halves	5.40	10,000
24—2½ peach nectar	4.60	5,000
24—2½ tomato juice	4.50	50,000
24—2½ cooking apples	4.90	15,000
24—2½ tomato paste	3.80	80,000

TABLE 2 Product Item Profitability

PRODUCT	24—2½ WHOLE TOMATOES	24—2½ CHOICE PEACH HALVES	24—2½ PEACH NECTAR	24—2½ TOMATO JUICE	24—2½ COOKING APPLES	24—2½ TOMATO PASTE
Selling price	$4.00	$5.40	$4.60	$4.50	$4.90	$3.80
Variable costs:						
Direct labor	1.18	1.40	1.27	1.32	.70	.54
Variable overhead	.24	.32	.23	.36	.22	.26
Variable selling	.40	.30	.40	.85	.28	.38
Packaging material	.70	.56	.60	.65	.70	.77
Fruit*	1.08	1.80	1.70	1.20	.90	1.50
Total variable costs	$3.60	$4.38	$4.20	$4.38	$2.80	$3.45
Contribution	.40	1.02	.40	.12	1.10	.35
Less allocated overhead	.28	.70	.52	.21	.75	.23
Net profit	$ .12	$ .32	($ .12)	($ .09)	$ .35	$ .12

* Product usage is as given below:

Product	Pounds per Case
Whole tomatoes	18
Peach halves	18
Peach nectar	17
Tomato juice	20
Cooking apples	27
Tomato paste	25

quality and quantity rather than by quantity only, as Cooper had done. Therefore, he had recomputed the marginal profit on this basis (see Table 3), and from his results had concluded that Red Brand should use 2 million pounds of the grade B tomatoes for paste, and the remaining 400,000 pounds of grade B tomatoes and all of the grade A tomatoes for juice. If the demand expectations were realized, a contribution of $48,000 would be made on this year's tomato crop.

TABLE 3 Marginal Analysis of Tomato Products

Z = Cost per pound of grade A tomatoes in cents.

Y = Cost per pound of grade B tomatoes in cents.

$$(600,000 \text{ lb.} \times Z) + (2,400,000 \text{ lb.} \times Y) = (3,000,000 \text{ lb.} \times 6) \quad (1)$$

$$\frac{Z}{9} = \frac{Y}{5} \quad (2)$$

Z = 9.32 cents per pound

Y = 5.18 cents per pound

PRODUCT	CANNED WHOLE TOMATOES	TOMATO JUICE	TOMATO PASTE
Selling price	$4.00	$4.50	$3.80
Variable cost			
(excluding tomato cost)	2.52	3.18	1.95
	$1.48	$1.32	$1.85
Tomato cost	1.49	1.24	1.30
Marginal profit	($ .01)	$ .08	$ .55

Discussion Questions

1. Structure this problem verbally, including a written description of the constraints and objective. What are the decision variables?

2. Develop a *mathematical* formulation for Red Brand's objective function and constraints.

3. Solve the problem and discuss the results.

The Oakton River Bridge

The Oakton River had long been considered an impediment to the development of a certain medium-sized metropolitan area in the southeast. Lying to the east of the city, the river made it difficult for people living on its eastern bank to commute to jobs in and around the city and to take advantage of the shopping and cultural attractions that the city had to offer. Similarly, the river inhibited those on its western bank from access to the ocean resorts lying one hour to the east. The bridge over the Oakton River had been built prior to World War II and was grossly inadequate to handle the existing traffic, much less the increased traffic that would accompany the forecasted growth in the area. A congressional delegation from the state prevailed upon the federal government to fund a major portion of a new toll bridge over the Oakton River and the state legislature appropriated the rest of the needed monies for the project.

Progress in construction of the bridge has been in accordance with what was anticipated at the start of construction. The state highway commission, which will have operational jurisdiction over the bridge, has concluded that opening of the bridge for traffic is likely to take place at the beginning of the next summer, as scheduled. A personnel task force has been established to recruit, train, and schedule the workers needed to operate the toll facility.

The personnel task force is well aware of the budgetary problems facing the state. They have taken as part of their mandate the requirement that personnel costs be kept as low as possible. One particular area of concern is the number of toll collectors that will be needed. The bridge is scheduling three shifts of collectors: shift A from midnight to 8 A.M., shift B from 8 A.M. to 4 P.M., and shift C from 4 P.M. to midnight. Recently, the state employees union negotiated a contract with the state which requires that all toll collectors be permanent, full-time employees. In addition, all collectors must work a five-on, two-off schedule on the same shift. Thus, for example, a worker could be assigned to work Tuesday, Wednesday, Thursday, Friday, and Saturday on shift A, followed by Sunday and Monday off. An employee could not be scheduled to work, say, Tuesday on shift A followed by Wednesday, Thursday, Friday, and Saturday on shift B or on any other mixture of shifts during a five-day block. The employees would choose their assignments in order of their seniority.

The task force has received projections of traffic flow on the bridge by day and hour. These projections are based on extrapolations of existing traffic patterns—the pattern of commuting, shopping, and beach traffic currently experienced with growth projections factored in. Standards data from other state-operated toll facilities have allowed the task force to convert these traffic flows into toll collector requirements, that is, the minimum number of collectors required per shift, per day, to handle the anticipated traffic load. These toll collector requirements are summarized in the accompanying table.

Minimum Number of Toll Collectors Required per Shift

SHIFT	SUN.	MON.	TUE.	WED.	THU.	FRI.	SAT.
A	8	13	12	12	13	13	15
B	10	10	10	10	10	13	15
C	15	13	13	12	12	13	8

The numbers in the table include one or two extra collectors per shift to fill in for collectors who call in sick and to provide relief for collectors on their scheduled breaks. Note that each of the eight collectors needed for shift A on Sunday, for example, could have come from any of the A shifts scheduled to begin on Wednesday, Thursday, Friday, Saturday, or Sunday.

Discussion Questions

1. Determine the minimum number of toll collectors that would have to be hired to meet the requirements expressed in the table.

2. The union had indicated that it might lift its opposition to the mixing of shifts in a five-day block in exchange for additional compensation and benefits. By how much could the numbers of toll collectors required be reduced if this is done?

Source: Adopted from B. Render, R. Stair, and I. Greenberg, *Cases and Readings,* 2nd ed., Boston: Allyn and Bacon, 1990.

BIBLIOGRAPHY

See references at end of Chapter 10.

13

Linear Programming Applications

13.1
INTRODUCTION

The linear programming topics discussed in Chapters 10, 11, and 12 are useful for deciding when LP is an appropriate decision-making tool and for interpreting the results and significance of a linear programming solution. The purpose of this chapter is to go one step further and show how a large number of real-life problems can be tackled using linear programming. We do this by presenting examples of applications in the areas of production mix, labor scheduling, job assignment, production scheduling, marketing research, media selection, shipping and transportation, ingredient mix, and financial portfolio selection.

Although some of these problems are relatively small numerically, the principles developed here are definitely applicable to larger problems. Moreover, this practice in "paraphrasing" LP model formulations should help develop your skills in applying the technique to other, less common applications.

13.2
MARKETING APPLICATIONS

Media Selection

Linear programming models have been used in the advertising field as a decision aid in selecting an effective media mix. Sometimes the technique is employed in allocating a fixed or limited budget across various media, which might include radio or television commercials, newspaper ads, direct mailings, magazine ads, and so on. In other applications, the objective is taken to be the maximization of audience exposure. Restrictions on the allowable media mix might arise through contract requirements, limited media availability, or company policy. An example follows.

uses of media selection

The Win Big Gambling Club promotes gambling junkets from a large midwestern city to casinos in the Bahamas. The club has budgeted up to $8,000 per week for local advertising; the money is to be allocated among four promotional media: TV spots, newspaper ads, and two types of radio advertisements. Win Big's goal is to reach the largest possible high-potential audience through the various media. The following table presents the number of potential gamblers reached by making use of an advertisement in each of the four media. It also provides figures regarding the cost per advertisement placed and the maximum number of ads that can be purchased per week.

MEDIUM	AUDIENCE REACHED PER AD	COST PER AD ($)	MAXIMUM ADS PER WEEK
TV spot (1 minute)	5,000	800	12
Daily newspaper (full-page ad)	8,500	925	5
Radio spot (½ minute, prime time)	2,400	290	25
Radio spot (1 minute, afternoon)	2,800	380	20

Win Big's contractual arrangements require that at least 5 radio spots be placed each week. To ensure a broad-scoped promotional campaign, management also insists that no more than $1,800 be spent on all radio advertising every week.

The problem can now be stated mathematically as follows. Let

X_1 = number of one-minute TV spots taken each week

X_2 = number of full-page daily newspaper ads
taken each week

X_3 = number of 30-second prime-time radio
spots taken each week

X_4 = number of one-minute afternoon radio spots
taken each week

Objective:

Maximize audience coverage = $5,000X_1 + 8,500X_2 + 2,400X_3 + 2,800X_4$

Subject to: $X_1 \leq 12$ (*maximum TV spots/week*)
$X_2 \leq 5$ (*maximum newspaper ads/week*)
$X_3 \leq 25$ (*maximum 30-second radio spots/week*)
$X_4 \leq 20$ (*maximum one-minute radio spots/week*)

$800X_1 + 925X_2 + 290X_3 + 380X_4 \leq \$8,000$ (*weekly advertising budget*)
$X_3 + X_4 \geq 5$ (*minimum radio spots contracted*)
$290X_3 + 380X_4 \leq \$1,800$ (*maximum \$ spent on radio*)

The solution to this LP formulation, using our microcomputer software package, was found to be:

$X_1 = 1.9$ *TV spots*

$X_2 = 5$ *newspaper ads*

$X_3 = 6.2$ *30-second radio spots*

$X_4 = 0$ *one-minute radio spots*

This produces an audience exposure of 67,240 contacts. Since X_1 and X_3 are fractional, Win Big would probably round them to 2 and 6, respectively. Problems that demand all-integer solutions are discussed in detail in Chapter 15.

Marketing Research

Linear programming has also been applied to marketing research problems and the area of consumer research. The next example illustrates how statistical pollsters can reach strategy decisions with LP.

Management Sciences Associates (MSA) based in Washington, D.C., is a marketing and computer research firm that handles consumer surveys for several clients. One client is a national press service that periodically conducts political polls on issues of widespread interest. In order to draw statistically valid conclusions on the sensitive issue of new U.S. immigration laws, in a survey for the press service, MSA determines that it must fulfill several requirements:

marketing research applications

1. Survey at least 2,300 U.S. households in total.
2. Survey at least 1,000 households whose heads are 30 years of age or younger.
3. Survey at least 600 households whose heads are between 31 and 50 years of age.
4. Ensure that at least 15% of those surveyed live in a state that borders on Mexico.
5. Ensure that no more than 20% of those surveyed who are 51 or over live in states that border on Mexico.

MSA decides that all surveys should be conducted in person. It estimates that the costs of reaching people in each age and region category are as follows:

	COST PER PERSON SURVEYED ($)		
REGION	AGE ⩽ 30 YEARS	AGE 31–50	AGE ⩾ 51
State bordering Mexico	7.50	6.80	5.50
State not bordering Mexico	6.90	7.25	6.10

MSA's goal is to meet the five sampling requirements at the least possible cost.

We let

X_1 = number surveyed who are 30 or younger and live in a border state

X_2 = number surveyed who are 31–50 and live in a border state

X_3 = number surveyed who are 51 or older and live in a border state

X_4 = number surveyed who are 30 or younger and do not live in a border state

X_5 = number surveyed who are 31–50 and do not live in a border state

X_6 = number surveyed who are 51 or older and do not live in a border state

Objective function:

$$\text{Minimize total interview costs} = \$7.50X_1 + \$6.80X_2 + \$5.50X_3 + \$6.90X_4 + \$7.25X_5 + \$6.10X_6$$

Constraints:

$$X_1 + X_2 + X_3 + X_4 + X_5 + X_6 \geq 2{,}300 \ (\textit{total households})$$
$$X_1 \qquad\quad + X_4 \qquad\qquad \geq 1{,}000 \ (\textit{households 30 or younger})$$
$$X_2 \qquad\quad + X_5 \qquad \geq \ 600 \ (\textit{households 31–50 in age})$$
$$(X_1 + X_2 + X_3) \geq .15(X_1 + X_2 + X_3 + X_4 + X_5 + X_6)(\textit{border states})$$
$$X_3 \leq .2(X_3 + X_6) \ \ (\textit{limit on age group 51+ who can live in border state})$$
$$X_1, X_2, X_3, X_4, X_5, X_6 \geq 0$$

The solution to MSA's problem costs $15,166 and is presented on the top of next page.

REGION	AGE ≤ 30 YEARS	AGE 31–50	AGE ≥ 51
State bordering Mexico	0	600	140
Nonborder state	1,000	0	560

13.3
MANUFACTURING APPLICATIONS

Production Mix

A fertile field for the use of LP is in planning for the optimal mix of products to manufacture. A company must meet a myriad of constraints, ranging from financial to sales demand to material contracts to union labor demands. Its primary goal is to generate the largest profit possible.

Fifth Avenue Industries, a nationally known manufacturer of menswear, produces four varieties of ties. One is an expensive, all-silk tie, one is an all-polyester tie, and two are blends of polyester and cotton. The following table illustrates the cost and availability (per monthly production planning period) of the three materials used in the production process.

MATERIAL	COST PER YARD ($)	MATERIAL AVAILABLE PER MONTH (YARDS)
Silk	21	800
Polyester	6	3,000
Cotton	9	1,600

The firm has fixed contracts with several major department store chains to supply ties. The contracts require that Fifth Avenue Industries supply a minimum quantity of each tie, but allow for a larger demand if Fifth Avenue chooses to meet that demand. (Most of the ties are not shipped with the name Fifth Avenue on their label, incidentally, but with "private stock" labels supplied by the stores). Table 13.1 summarizes the contract

TABLE 13.1 Data for Fifth Avenue Industries

VARIETY OF TIE	SELLING PRICE PER TIE ($)	MONTHLY CONTRACT MINIMUM	MONTHLY DEMAND	MATERIAL REQUIRED PER TIE (YARDS)	MATERIAL REQUIREMENTS
All Silk	6.70	6,000	7,000	.125	100% silk
All Polyester	3.55	10,000	14,000	.08	100% polyester
Poly-Cotton Blend #1	4.31	13,000	16,000	.10	50% polyester 50% cotton
Poly-Cotton Blend #2	4.81	6,000	8,500	.10	30% polyester 70% cotton

demands for each of the four styles of ties, the selling price per tie, and the fabric requirements of each variety.

Fifth Avenue's goal is to maximize its monthly profit. It must decide upon a policy for product mix. Let

X_1 = number of all-silk ties produced per month

X_2 = number of polyester ties

X_3 = number of blend #1 poly-cotton ties

X_4 = number of blend #2 poly-cotton ties

But first the firm must establish the profit per tie.

1. For all-silk ties (X_1), each requires .125 yards of silk, at a cost of $21 per yard. Therefore, the cost per tie is $2.62. The selling price per silk tie is $6.70, leaving a net profit of ($6.70 − $2.62 =) $4.08 per unit of X_1.

2. For all-polyester ties (X_2), each requires .08 yards of polyester at a cost of $6 per yard. The cost per tie is, therefore, $.48. The net profit per unit of X_2 is ($3.55 − $.48 =) $3.07.

3. For poly-cotton blend #1 (X_3), each tie requires .05 yards of polyester at $6 per yard and .05 yards of cotton at $9 per yard, for a cost of $.30 + $.45 = $.75 per tie. The profit is $3.56.

4. Try to compute the net profit for blend #2, yourself. You should reach a cost of $.81 per tie and a net profit of $4.

The objective function may now be stated as:

Maximize profit = $4.08X_1 + $3.07X_2 + $3.56X_3 + $4.00X_4

Subject to constraints:

$$.125X_1 \leq 800 \ (yards\ of\ silk)$$
$$.08X_2 + .05X_3 + .03X_4 \leq 3,000 \ (yards\ of\ polyester)$$
$$.05X_3 + .07X_4 \leq 1,600 \ (yards\ of\ cotton)$$
$$X_1 \geq 6,000 \ (contract\ minimum\ for\ all\ silk)$$
$$X_1 \leq 7,000 \ (contract\ maximum)$$
$$X_2 \geq 10,000 \ (contract\ minimum\ for\ all\ polyester)$$
$$X_2 \leq 14,000 \ (contract\ maximum)$$
$$X_3 \geq 13,000 \ (contract\ minimum\ for\ blend\ \#1)$$
$$X_3 \leq 16,000 \ (contract\ maximum)$$
$$X_4 \geq 6,000 \ (contract\ minimum\ for\ blend\ \#2)$$
$$X_4 \leq 8,500 \ (contract\ maximum)$$
$$X_1, X_2, X_3, X_4 \geq 0$$

The computer-generated solution is to produce 6,400 all-silk ties each month; 14,000 all-polyester ties; 16,000 blend #1 poly-cotton ties; and 8,500 blend #2 poly-cotton ties. This produces a profit of $160,052 per production period.

Production Scheduling

Setting a low-cost production schedule over a period of weeks or months is a difficult and important management problem in most plants. The production manager has to consider many factors: labor capacity, inventory and storage costs, space limitations, product demand, labor relations. Since most companies produce more than one product, the scheduling process is often quite complex.

Basically, the problem resembles the product mix model for each period in the future. The objective is either to maximize profit or to minimize the total cost (production plus inventory) of carrying out the task.

Production scheduling is amenable to solution by LP because it is a problem that must be solved on a regular basis. Once the objective function and constraints for a firm are established, the inputs can easily be changed each month to provide an updated schedule.

Greenberg Motors, Inc., manufactures two different electrical motors for sale under contract to Drexel Corp., a well-known producer of small kitchen appliances. Its model GM3A is found in many Drexel food processors and its model GM3B is used in the assembly of blenders.

an example of production scheduling: Greenberg Motors

Three times each year, the procurement officer at Drexel contacts Irwin Greenberg, the founder of Greenberg Motors, to place a monthly order for each of the coming four months. Drexel's demand for motors varies each month based on its own sales forecasts, production capacity, and financial position. Greenberg has just received the January–April order and must begin his own four-month production plan. The demand for motors is shown in Table 13.2.

Production planning at Greenberg Motors must consider four factors:

1. The desirability of producing the same number of each motor each month. This simplifies planning and the scheduling of workers and machines.

2. The necessity to keep down inventory carrying, or holding, costs. This suggests producing in each month only what is needed in that month.

3. Warehouse limitations that cannot be exceeded without great additional storage costs.

4. The company's no-layoff policy, which has been effective in preventing a unionization of the shop. This suggests a minimum production capacity that should be used each month.

TABLE 13.2 Four-Month Order Schedule for Electrical Motors

MODEL	JANUARY	FEBRUARY	MARCH	APRIL
GM3A	800	700	1,000	1,100
GM3B	1,000	1,200	1,400	1,400

Although these four factors are often conflicting, Greenberg has found that linear programming is an effective tool in setting up a production schedule that will minimize his total costs of per unit production and monthly holding.

using double-subscripted variables

Double-subscripted variables can be used here to develop the LP model. We let

$$X_{A,i} = \text{number of model GM3A motors produced in month } i$$
$$(i = 1, 2, 3, 4 \text{ for January–April})$$
$$X_{B,i} = \text{number of model GM3B motors produced in month } i$$

Production costs are currently $10 per GM3A motor produced and $6 per GM3B unit. A labor agreement going into effect on March 1 will raise each figure by 10%, however. We can write the part of the objective function that deals with production cost as:

$$\text{Cost of production} = \$10X_{A1} + \$10X_{A2} + \$11X_{A3} + \$11X_{A4} + \$6X_{B1}$$
$$+ \$6X_{B2} + \$6.60X_{B3} + \$6.60X_{B4}$$

To include the inventory carrying costs in the model, we can introduce a second variable. Let

$$I_{A,i} = \text{level of on-hand inventory for GM3A motors at end of month } i$$
$$(i = 1, 2, 3, 4)$$
$$I_{B,i} = \text{level of on-hand inventory for GM3B motors at end of month } i$$

Each GM3A motor held in stock costs $.18 per month, while each GM3B has a carrying cost of $.13 per motor per month. Greenberg's accountants allow monthly ending inventories as an acceptable approximation to the average inventory levels during the month. So the carrying cost part of the LP objective function is:

$$\text{Cost of carrying inventory} = \$.18I_{A1} + .18I_{A2} + .18I_{A3} + .18I_{A4}$$
$$+ .13I_{B1} + .13I_{B2} + .13I_{B3} + .13I_{B4}$$

The total objective function becomes:

$$\text{Minimize total costs} = 10X_{A1} + 10X_{A2} + 11X_{A3} + 11X_{A4} + 6X_{B1} + 6X_{B2}$$
$$+ 6.6X_{B3} + 6.6X_{B4} + .18I_{A1} + .18I_{A2} + .18I_{A3} + .18I_{A4} + .13I_{B1} + .13I_{B2}$$
$$+ .13I_{B3} + .13I_{B4}$$

inventory constraints

In setting up the constraints, we must recognize the relationship between last month's ending inventory, the current month's production, and the sales to Drexel this month. The inventory at the end of a month is:

$$\begin{pmatrix} \text{Inventory} \\ \text{at the} \\ \text{end of} \\ \text{this month} \end{pmatrix} = \begin{pmatrix} \text{Inventory} \\ \text{at the} \\ \text{end of} \\ \text{last month} \end{pmatrix} + \begin{pmatrix} \text{Current} \\ \text{month's} \\ \text{production} \end{pmatrix} - \begin{pmatrix} \text{Sales} \\ \text{to} \\ \text{Drexel} \\ \text{this month} \end{pmatrix}$$

Suppose Greenberg is starting the new four-month production cycle with a change in design specifications that left no old motors in stock on January 1. Then, recalling that January's demand for GM3As is 800 and for GM3Bs is 1,000, we can write:

$$I_{A1} = 0 + X_{A1} - 800$$
$$I_{B1} = 0 + X_{B1} - 1,000$$

Transposing all unknown variables to the left of the equal sign and multiplying all terms by a minus 1, these January constraints can be re-written as:

$$X_{A1} - I_{A1} = 800$$

$$X_{B1} - I_{B1} = 1,000$$

The constraints on demand in February, March, and April follow:

$$X_{A2} + I_{A1} - I_{A2} = \quad 700 \qquad \textit{February GM3A demand}$$
$$X_{B2} + I_{B1} - I_{B2} = 1,200 \qquad \textit{February GM3B demand}$$

$$X_{A3} + I_{A2} - I_{A3} = 1,000 \qquad \textit{March GM3A demand}$$
$$X_{B3} + I_{B2} - I_{B3} = 1,400 \qquad \textit{March GM3B demand}$$

$$X_{A4} + I_{A3} - I_{A4} = 1,100 \qquad \textit{April GM3A demand}$$
$$X_{B4} + I_{B3} - I_{B4} = 1,400 \qquad \textit{April GM3B demand}$$

If Greenberg wants to also have on hand an additional 450 GM3As and 300 GM3Bs at the end of April, then we add the constraints:

$$I_{A4} = 450$$

$$I_{B4} = 300$$

The constraints discussed address demand; they do not, however, consider warehouse space or labor requirements. First, we note that Greenberg Motor's storage area can hold a maximum of 3,300 motors of either type (they are similar in size) at any one time. Then

$$I_{A1} + I_{B1} \leq 3,300$$

$$I_{A2} + I_{B2} \leq 3,300$$

$$I_{A3} + I_{B3} \leq 3,300$$

$$I_{A4} + I_{B4} \leq 3,300$$

warehouse constraints

Second, we return to the issue of employment. So that no worker is ever laid off, Greenberg has a base employment level of 2,240 labor hours per month. In a busy period, though, the company can bring two skilled former employees on board (they are now retired) to increase capacity to 2,560 hours per month. Each GM3A motor produced requires 1.3 hours of labor, while each GM3B takes a worker .9 hours to assemble.

$$1.3X_{A1} + .9X_{B1} \geq 2,240 \qquad \textit{(January minimum worker hours/month)}$$
$$1.3X_{A1} + .9X_{B1} \leq 2,560 \qquad \textit{(January maximum labor available/month)}$$

$$1.3X_{A2} + .9X_{B2} \geq 2,240 \qquad \textit{(February labor minimum)}$$
$$1.3X_{A2} + .9X_{B2} \leq 2,560 \qquad \textit{(February labor maximum)}$$

employment constraints

$$1.3X_{A3} + .9X_{B3} \geq 2,240 \qquad \textit{(March labor minimum)}$$
$$1.3X_{A3} + .9X_{B3} \leq 2,560 \qquad \textit{(March labor maximum)}$$

$$1.3X_{A4} + .9X_{B4} \geq 2,240 \qquad \textit{(April labor minimum)}$$
$$1.3X_{A4} + .9X_{B4} \leq 2,560 \qquad \textit{(April labor maximum)}$$

The solution to the Greenberg Motor problem is shown in Table 13.3. The four-month total cost is $76,301.61.

This example illustrates a relatively simple production planning problem in that there were only two products being considered. The 16 variables

TABLE 13.3 Solution to Greenberg Motor Problem

PRODUCTION SCHEDULE	JANUARY	FEBRUARY	MARCH	APRIL
Units of GM3A produced	1,277	1,138	842	792
Units of GM3B produced	1,000	1,200	1,400	1,700
Inventory of GM3A carried	477	915	758	450
Inventory of GM3B carried	0	0	0	300
Labor hours required	2,560	2,560	2,355	2,560

and 22 constraints may not seem trivial, but the technique can also be successfully applied with dozens of products and hundreds of constraints.

13.4
EMPLOYEE SCHEDULING APPLICATIONS

Assignment Problems

assigning people to jobs using LP

Assignment problems involve determining the most efficient assignment of people to jobs, machines to tasks, police cars to city sectors, salespeople to territories, and so on. The objective might be to minimize travel times or costs or to maximize assignment effectiveness. Assignments can be handled with their own special solution procedures (see Chapter 14). Assignment problems are unique because they not only have a coefficient of 1 associated with each variable in the LP constraints, but because the right-hand side of each constraint is always equal to 1 also. The use of LP in solving this type of problem yields solutions of either 0 or 1 for each variable in the formulation. The following is an example situation.

The law firm of Ivan and Ivan maintains a large staff of young attorneys who hold the title of junior partner. Ivan, concerned with the effective utilization of his personnel resources, seeks some objective means of making lawyer-to-client assignments.

On March 1, four new clients seeking legal assistance come to Ivan. While the current staff is overloaded, Ivan would like to accommodate the new clients. He reviews current case loads and identifies four junior partners who, although busy, could possibly be assigned to the cases. Each young lawyer can handle at most one new client. Furthermore, each lawyer differs in skills and specialty interests.

Seeking to maximize the overall effectiveness of the new client assignments, Ivan draws up the following table in which he rates the estimated effectiveness (on a 1-to-9 scale) of each lawyer on each new case.

	IVAN'S EFFECTIVENESS RATINGS			
	CLIENT'S CASE			
LAWYER	DIVORCE	CORPORATE MERGER	EMBEZZLEMENT	EXHIBITIONISM
Adams	6	2	8	5
Brooks	9	3	5	8
Carter	4	8	3	4
Darwin	6	7	6	4

To solve using LP, we again employ double-scripted variables. Let

$$X_{ij} = \begin{cases} 1 & \text{if attorney } i \text{ is assigned to case } j \\ 0 & \text{otherwise} \end{cases}$$

where

$i = 1, 2, 3, 4$ stands for Adams, Brooks, Carter, and Darwin, respectively, and

$j = 1, 2, 3, 4$ stands for divorce, merger, embezzlement, and exhibitionism, respectively.

The LP formulation follows:

$$\text{Maximize effectiveness} = 6X_{11} + 2X_{12} + 8X_{13} + 5X_{14}$$
$$+ 9X_{21} + 3X_{22} + 5X_{23} + 8X_{24}$$
$$+ 4X_{31} + 8X_{32} + 3X_{33} + 4X_{34}$$
$$+ 6X_{41} + 7X_{42} + 6X_{43} + 4X_{44}$$

Subject to:
$$\begin{array}{ll} X_{11} + X_{21} + X_{31} + X_{41} = 1 & \textit{(divorce case)} \\ X_{12} + X_{22} + X_{32} + X_{42} = 1 & \textit{(merger)} \\ X_{13} + X_{23} + X_{33} + X_{43} = 1 & \textit{(embezzlement)} \\ X_{14} + X_{24} + X_{34} + X_{44} = 1 & \textit{(exhibitionism)} \\ X_{11} + X_{12} + X_{13} + X_{14} = 1 & \textit{(Adams)} \\ X_{21} + X_{22} + X_{23} + X_{24} = 1 & \textit{(Brooks)} \\ X_{31} + X_{32} + X_{33} + X_{34} = 1 & \textit{(Carter)} \\ X_{41} + X_{42} + X_{43} + X_{44} = 1 & \textit{(Darwin)} \end{array}$$

The law firm's problem is solved with a total effectiveness rating of 30 by letting $X_{13} = 1$, $X_{24} = 1$, $X_{32} = 1$, and $X_{41} = 1$. All other variables are therefore equal to 0.

Labor Planning

Labor planning problems address staffing needs over a specific time period. They are especially useful when managers have some flexibility in assigning workers to jobs that require overlapping or interchangeable talents. Large banks frequently use LP to tackle their labor scheduling.

Arlington Bank of Commerce and Industry is a busy bank that has requirements for between 10 and 18 tellers depending on the time of day. The lunch time, from noon to 2 P.M., is usually heaviest. Table 13.4 indicates the workers needed at various hours that the bank is open.

TABLE 13.4 Arlington Bank of Commerce and Industry

TIME PERIOD	NUMBER OF TELLERS REQUIRED
9 A.M.–10 A.M.	10
10 A.M.–11 A.M.	12
11 A.M.–Noon	14
Noon–1 P.M.	16
1 P.M.–2 P.M.	18
2 P.M.–3 P.M.	17
3 P.M.–4 P.M.	15
4 P.M.–5 P.M.	10

The bank now employs 12 full-time tellers, but many people are on its roster of available part-time employees. A part-time employee must put in exactly four hours per day, but can start anytime between 9 A.M. and 1 P.M. Part-timers are a fairly inexpensive labor pool, since no retirement or lunch benefits are provided them. Full-timers, on the other hand, work from 9 A.M.–5 P.M., but are allowed one hour for lunch. (Half of the full-timers eat at 11 A.M., the other half at noon.) Full-timers thus provide 35 hours per week of productive labor time.

By corporate policy, the bank limits part-time hours to a maximum of 50% of the day's total requirement.

Part-timers earn $4 per hour (or $16 per day) on the average, while full-timers earn $50 per day in salary and benefits, on the average. The bank would like to set a schedule that would minimize its total personnel costs. It will release one or more of its full-time tellers if it is profitable to do so.

We can let

$$F = \text{full-time tellers}$$

$$P_1 = \text{part-timers starting at 9 A.M. (leaving at 1 P.M.)}$$

$$P_2 = \text{part-timers starting at 10 A.M. (leaving at 2 P.M.)}$$

$$P_3 = \text{part-timers starting at 11 A.M. (leaving at 3 P.M.)}$$

$$P_4 = \text{part-timers starting at noon (leaving at 4 P.M.)}$$

$$P_5 = \text{part-timers starting at 1 P.M. (leaving at 5 P.M.)}$$

Objective function:

Minimize total daily personnel cost

$$= \$50F + \$16(P_1 + P_2 + P_3 + P_4 + P_5)$$

Constraints:

For each hour, the available labor hours be at least equal to the required labor hours.

$$F + P_1 \geq 10 \text{ (9 A.M.–10 A.M. needs)}$$

$$F + P_1 + P_2 \geq 12 \text{ (10 A.M.–11 A.M. needs)}$$

$$\tfrac{1}{2}F + P_1 + P_2 + P_3 \geq 14 \text{ (11 A.M.–noon needs)}$$

$$\tfrac{1}{2}F + P_1 + P_2 + P_3 + P_4 \geq 16 \text{ (noon–1 P.M. needs)}$$

$$F + P_2 + P_3 + P_4 + P_5 \geq 18 \text{ (1 P.M.–2 P.M. needs)}$$

$$F + P_3 + P_4 + P_5 \geq 17 \text{ (2 P.M.–3 P.M. needs)}$$

labor constraints

$$F + P_4 + P_5 \geq 15 \text{ (3 P.M.–4 P.M. needs)}$$

$$F + P_5 \geq 10 \text{ (4 P.M.–5 P.M. needs)}$$

Only 12 full-time tellers are available so,

$$F \leq 12$$

Part-time worker hours cannot exceed 50% of total hours required each day, which is the sum of the tellers needed each hour.

$$4(P_1 + P_2 + P_3 + P_4 + P_5)$$

$$\leq .50(10 + 12 + 14 + 16 + 18 + 17 + 15 + 10)$$

APPLICATIONS OF QA

Optimizing Flight Crew Schedules

Because of restrictive work rules and interacting cost components, building flight crew schedules is a complex process. However, quantitative analysis techniques, though complex, have been successful in reducing crew costs. At American Airlines, a linear programming approach is now used instead of the previously used enumeration methods.

Clearly, every airline flight needs a full crew of pilots and flight attendants, but developing schedules that maintain a high level of crew utilization is a challenging logistics problem. Since crew members are people and not machines, scheduling their deployment is considerably more complicated than scheduling the use of aircraft, gates, or other equipment. The Federal Aviation Administration has established a complex set of limitations designed to ensure that crew members can fulfill their duties without significant risk of degradation of performance due to fatigue.

In addition, financial issues affect scheduling practices. At most major airlines, union contracts specify that flight crews will be guaranteed pay for some number of hours each day or each trip. Because of this, airline planners must try to build crew schedules that meet or exceed the crews' pay guarantees to the maximum extent possible. A trip containing one or more days with small amounts of flying time might be very expensive, because the crews would receive extra pay over and above the assigned flying time.

Pressure to deliver viable schedules in the face of these problems is all the more intense because of the high cost of flight crews. Captain salaries of $140,000 per year are typical; average pilot pay and benefits is about $80,000 per pilot for major U.S. and European carriers. Crew costs are the second highest component of direct operating costs (fuel costs are first); poor crew scheduling can easily

Source: I. Gershkoff, *Interfaces*, Vol. 19, No. 4, July–August 1989, pp. 29–43.

inflict serious damage to an airline's bottom line.

The good news is that the rigid rules that make crew planning difficult also present opportunities. Since average costs are high, relatively small improvements in efficiency leverage into large cost savings. Fortunately, the crew optimization problem fits nicely into a classical integer linear programming (ILP) formulation. However, solving the ILP is the easy part: the biggest problem is accommodating all of the pay guarantees and work rule limitations into the matrix before the ILP is solved.

The crew scheduling process is a subset of a broader crew allocation problem. Allocations are normally built on a fleet-by-fleet basis because pilots are qualified to fly only one type of aircraft. (A fleet is a group of flights confined to a specific aircraft type.) An allocation consists of a number of pairings, which are sequences of flight segments that begin at a base station, fly around the system, and return to the original base station. All pairings in the allocation must conform to the limitations imposed by the Federal Aviation Regulations and the carrier's specific work rules.

Except for the smallest fleets, it is not possible to obtain a globally optimal solution—the problem is too large. Problems begin to explode with more than 100 segments and become unmanageable for 200 or more. It is therefore necessary to work in subproblems small enough that a reasonably sized matrix can be built and solved optimally. To a large extent, it is desirable to solve as large a subproblem as computer resources will allow; the limit on size will depend on the software design or on constraints of available storage or processor power.

Although there can be practical problems involved with implementation of optimal solutions, the potential benefits make exploring further solutions worthwhile. A reasonable estimate of the savings directly attributable to innovations in the crew pairing optimization program would be about $18 million per year for American Airlines.

---

or

$$4P_1 + 4P_2 + 4P_3 + 4P_4 + 4P_5 \leq .50(112)$$
$$F, P_1, P_2, P_3, P_4, P_5 \geq 0$$

There are two alternative optimal schedules that Arlington Bank can follow. The first is to employ only 10 full-time tellers ($F = 10$) and to start two part-timers at 10 A.M. ($P_2 = 2$), 7 part-timers at 11 A.M. ($P_3 = 7$) and 5 part-timers at noon ($P_4 = 5$). No part-timers would begin at 9 A.M. or 1 P.M.

alternate optimal solutions

The second solution also employs 10 full-time tellers, but starts 6 part-timers at 9 A.M. ($P_1 = 6$), 1 part-timer at 10 A.M. ($P_2 = 1$), 2 part-timers at 11 A.M. and noon ($P_3 = 2$ and $P_4 = 2$), and 3 part-timers at 1 P.M. ($P_5 = 3$). The cost of either of these two policies is $724 per day.

13.5
FINANCIAL APPLICATIONS

Portfolio Selection

maximizing return on investment

A problem frequently encountered by managers of banks, mutual funds, investment services, and insurance companies is the selection of specific investments from among a wide variety of alternatives. The manager's overall objective is usually to maximize expected return on investment, given a set of legal, policy, or risk restraints.

For example, the International City Trust (ICT) invests in short-term trade credits, corporate bonds, gold stocks, and construction loans. The board of directors has placed limits on the amount that can be committed to any one type of investment in order to encourage a diversified portfolio. ICT has $5 million available for immediate investment and wishes to do two things: (1) maximize the interest earned on the investments made over the next six months, and (2) satisfy the diversification requirements as set by the board of directors.

The specifics of the investment possibilities are:

INVESTMENT	INTEREST EARNED (%)	MAXIMUM INVESTMENT ($ MILLION)
Trade credit	7	1.0
Corporate bonds	11	2.5
Gold stocks	19	1.5
Construction loans	15	1.8

In addition, the board specifies that at least 55% of the funds invested must be in gold stocks and construction loans, and that no less than 15% be invested in trade credit.

To formulate ICT's investment decision as a linear programming problem, we let

$$X_1 = \$ \text{ invested in trade credit}$$

$$X_2 = \$ \text{ invested in corporate bonds}$$

$$X_3 = \$ \text{ invested in gold stocks}$$

$$X_4 = \$ \text{ invested in construction loans}$$

Objective:

Maximize dollars of interest earned $= .07X_1 + .11X_2 + .19X_3 + .15X_4$

$$
\begin{aligned}
\text{Subject to:} \quad X_1 &\leq 1,000,000 \\
X_2 &\leq 2,500,000 \\
X_3 &\leq 1,500,000 \\
X_4 &\leq 1,800,000 \\
X_3 + X_4 &\geq .55(X_1 + X_2 + X_3 + X_4) \\
X_1 &\geq .15(X_1 + X_2 + X_3 + X_4) \\
X_1 + X_2 + X_3 + X_4 &\leq 5,000,000
\end{aligned}
$$

ICT maximizes its interest earned by making the following investment: $X_1 = \$750,000$, $X_2 = \$950,000$, $X_3 = \$1,500,000$, and $X_4 = \$1,800,000$.

13.6
TRANSPORTATION APPLICATIONS

The Shipping Problem

The transportation or shipping problem involves determining the amount of goods or items to be transported from a number of origins to a number of destinations. The objective usually is to minimize total shipping costs or distances. Constraints in this type of problem deal with capacities at each origin and requirements at each destination. The transportation problem is a very specific case of linear programming and, in fact, a special algorithm has been developed to solve it. That solution procedure is one of the topics of Chapter 14.

transporting goods from several origins to several destinations efficiently

The Top Speed Bicycle Co. manufactures and markets a line of ten-speed bicycles nationwide. The firm has final assembly plants in two cities in which labor costs are low, New Orleans and Omaha. Its three major warehouses are located near the large market areas of New York, Chicago, and Los Angeles.

The sales requirements for the next year at the New York warehouse are 10,000 bicycles, at the Chicago warehouse 8,000 bicycles, and at the Los Angeles warehouse 15,000 bicycles. The factory capacity at each location is limited. New Orleans can assemble and ship 20,000 bicycles, while the Omaha plant can produce 15,000 bicycles per year.

The cost of shipping one bicycle from each factory to each warehouse differs, and these unit shipping costs are:

FROM \ TO	NEW YORK	CHICAGO	LOS ANGELES
NEW ORLEANS	$2	$3	$5
OMAHA	$3	$1	$4

The company wishes to determine a shipping schedule that will minimize its total annual transportation costs.

double-subscripted variables

To formulate this problem using LP, we again employ the concept of double-subscripted variables.

$$X_{11} = \text{number of bicycles shipped from New Orleans to New York}$$

We let the first subscript represent the origin (factory) and the second subscript the destination (warehouse). Thus, in general, X_{ij} refers to the number of bicycles shipped from origin i to destination j. We could instead denote X_6 as the variable for origin 2 to destination 3, but we think you will find the double subscripts more descriptive and easier to use. So let

$$X_{12} = \text{number of bicycles shipped from New Orleans to Chicago}$$
$$X_{13} = \text{number of bicycles shipped from New Orleans to Los Angeles}$$
$$X_{21} = \text{number of bicycles shipped from Omaha to New York}$$
$$X_{22} = \text{number of bicycles shipped from Omaha to Chicago}$$
$$X_{23} = \text{number of bicycles shipped from Omaha to Los Angeles}$$

Minimize total shipping costs

$$= 2X_{11} + 3X_{12} + 5X_{13} + 3X_{21} + 1X_{22} + 4X_{23}$$

demand and supply constraints

Subject to:
$$X_{11} + X_{21} = 10{,}000 \ (\textit{New York demand})$$
$$X_{12} + X_{22} = 8{,}000 \ (\textit{Chicago demand})$$
$$X_{13} + X_{23} = 15{,}000 \ (\textit{Los Angeles demand})$$
$$X_{11} + X_{12} + X_{13} \leq 20{,}000 \ (\textit{New Orleans factory supply})$$
$$X_{21} + X_{22} + X_{23} \leq 15{,}000 \ (\textit{Omaha factory supply})$$

Why are transportation problems a special class of linear programming problems? The answer is that every coefficient in front of a variable in the constraint equations is always equal to 1. This special trait is also seen in another special category of LP problems, the assignment problem discussed earlier.

The computer-generated solution to Top Speed's problem is shown below. The total shipping cost is $96,000.

	TO		
FROM	NEW YORK	CHICAGO	LOS ANGELES
New Orleans	10,000	0	8,000
Omaha	0	8,000	7,000

13.7
INGREDIENT BLENDING APPLICATIONS

Diet Problems

The diet problem, one of the earliest applications of linear programming, was originally used by hospitals to determine the most economical diet for patients. Known in agricultural applications as the feed mix problem, the diet problem involves specifying a food or feed ingredient combination that satisfies stated nutritional requirements at a minimum cost level.

The Whole Food Nutrition Center uses three bulk grains to blend a natural cereal that it sells by the pound. The store advertises that each two-ounce serving of the cereal, when taken with 1/2 cup of whole milk, meets an average adult's minimum daily requirement for protein, riboflavin, phosphorus, and magnesium. The cost of each bulk grain and the protein, riboflavin, phosphorus, and magnesium units per pound of each are shown in Table 13.5.

blending different grains to make a brand of cereal

TABLE 13.5 Whole Food's Natural Cereal Requirements

GRAIN	COST PER POUND (¢)	PROTEIN (UNITS/LB.)	RIBOFLAVIN (UNITS/LB.)	PHOSPHORUS (UNITS/LB.)	MAGNESIUM (UNITS/LB.)
A	33	22	16	8	5
B	47	28	14	7	0
C	38	21	25	9	6

The minimum adult daily requirement (called the U.S. Recommended Daily Allowance, or USRDA) for protein is 3 units; for riboflavin, 2 units; for phosphorus, 1 unit; and for magnesium, .425 units. Whole Food wants to select the blend of grains that will meet the USRDA at a minimum cost.

We let

$$X_A = \text{pounds of grain A in one 2-ounce serving of cereal}$$

$$X_B = \text{pounds of grain B in one 2-ounce serving of cereal}$$

$$X_C = \text{pounds of grain C in one 2-ounce serving of cereal}$$

Objective function:

$$\text{Minimize total cost of mixing a 2-ounce serving}$$
$$= \$.33X_A + \$.47X_B + \$.38X_C$$

Constraints:

$$22X_A + 28X_B + 21X_C \geq 3 \quad \textit{(protein units)}$$

$$16X_A + 14X_B + 25X_C \geq 2 \quad \textit{(riboflavin units)}$$

$$8X_A + 7X_B + 9X_C \geq 1 \quad \textit{(phosphorus units)}$$

$$5X_A + 0X_B + 6X_C \geq .425 \quad \textit{(magnesium units)}$$

$$X_A + X_B + X_C = 1/8 \quad \textit{(total mix is 2 ounces or 1/8 pound)}$$

$$X_A, X_B, X_C \geq 0$$

The solution to this problem requires mixing together .025 lbs. of grain A, .050 lbs. of grain B, and .050 lbs. of grain C. Another way of stating the solution is in terms of the proportion of the 2-ounce serving of each grain, namely, 2/5 ounce of grain A, 4/5 ounce of grain B, and 4/5 ounce of grain C in each serving. The cost per serving is $.05075, a little over $.05 per serving.

Ingredient Mix and Blending Problems

Diet and feed mix problems are actually special cases of a more general class of linear programming problems known as *ingredient* or *blending problems*. Blending problems arise when a decision must be made regarding the blending of two or more resources in order to produce one or more products. Resources, in this case, contain one or more essential ingredients that must be blended so that each final product contains specific percentages of each ingredient. The following example deals with an application frequently seen in the petroleum industry, the blending of crude oils to produce refinable gasoline.

blending crude oils to produce gasoline grades

The Low Knock Oil Company produces two grades of cut-rate gasoline for industrial distribution. The grades, regular and economy, are produced by refining a blend of two types of crude oil, Type X100 and Type X220. Each crude oil differs not only in cost per barrel, but in composition as well. The accompanying table indicates the percentage of crucial ingredients found in each of the crude oils and the cost per barrel for each.

CRUDE OIL TYPE	INGREDIENT A (%)	INGREDIENT B (%)	COST/ BARREL ($)
X100	35	55	30.00
X220	60	25	34.80

Weekly demand for the regular grade of Low Knock gasoline is at least 25,000 barrels, while demand for the economy is at least 32,000 barrels per week. *At least* 45% of each barrel of regular must be ingredient A. *At most* 50% of each barrel of economy should contain ingredient B.

The Low Knock management must decide how many barrels of each type of crude oil to buy each week for blending in order to satisfy demand at minimum cost. To solve this as an LP problem, the firm lets

X_1 = barrels of crude X100 blended to produce the refined regular

X_2 = barrels of crude X100 blended to produce the refined economy

X_3 = barrels of crude X220 blended to produce the refined regular

X_4 = barrels of crude X220 blended to produce the refined economy

Objective:

$$\text{Minimize cost} = \$30X_1 + \$30X_2 + \$34.80X_3 + \$34.80X_4$$
$$X_1 + X_3 \geq 25,000 \qquad \textit{(demand for regular)}$$
$$X_2 + X_4 \geq 32,000 \qquad \textit{(demand for economy)}$$

At least 45% of each barrel of regular must be ingredient A.

$$(X_1 + X_3) = \text{total amount of crude blended to produce the refined regular gasoline demand}$$

Thus

$$.45(X_1 + X_3) = \text{minimum amount of ingredient A required}$$

But

$.35X_1 + .60X_3 =$ amount of ingredient A in refined regular gas

So

$$.35X_1 + .60X_3 \geqslant .45X_1 + .45X_3$$

or

$-.10X_1 + .15X_3 \geqslant 0$ *(ingredient A in regular constraint)*

Likewise, at most 50% of each barrel of economy should be ingredient B.

$(X_2 + X_4) =$ total amount of crude blended to produce
the refined economy gasoline demanded

Thus

$.50(X_2 + X_4) =$ maximum amount of ingredient B allowed

But

$.55X_2 + .25X_4 =$ amount of ingredient B in refined economy gas

So

$$.55X_2 + .25X_4 \leqslant .50X_2 + .50X_4$$

or

$.05X_2 - .25X_4 \leqslant 0$ *(ingredient B in economy constraint)*

Here is the entire LP formulation:

$$\text{Minimize cost} = 30X_1 + 30X_2 + 34.80X_3 + 34.80X_4$$

$$
\begin{aligned}
\text{Subject to:} \quad & X_1 + X_3 \geqslant 25{,}000 \\
& X_2 + X_4 \geqslant 32{,}000 \\
& -.10X_1 + .15X_3 \geqslant 0 \\
& .05X_2 - .25X_4 \leqslant 0
\end{aligned}
$$

The solution to Low Knock Oil's formulation was found to be:

$X_1 = 15{,}000$ barrels of X100 into regular

$X_2 = 26{,}666\frac{2}{3}$ barrels of X100 into economy

$X_3 = 10{,}000$ barrels of X220 into regular

$X_4 = 5{,}333\frac{1}{3}$ barrels of X220 into economy

The cost of this mix is \$1,783,600.

PROBLEMS

 · **13-1** Winkler Furniture manufactures two different types of china cabinets, a French Provincial model and a Danish Modern model. Each cabinet produced must go through three departments: carpentry, painting, and finishing. The **production problem** accompanying table contains all relevant information concerning production times per cabinet produced and production capacities for each operation per day, along with net revenue per unit produced. The firm has a contract with an Indiana distributor to produce a minimum of 300 of each cabinet per week (or 60 cabinets per day). Owner Bob Winkler would like to determine a product mix to maximize his daily revenue.

(a) Formulate as a linear programming problem.
(b) Solve using a microcomputer LP software program.

CABINET STYLE	CARPENTRY (HRS./CABINET)	PAINTING (HRS./CABINET)	FINISHING (HRS./CABINET)	NET REVENUE/ CABINET ($)
French Provincial	3	$1\frac{1}{2}$	$\frac{3}{4}$	28
Danish Modern	2	1	$\frac{3}{4}$	25
Department capacity (hrs.)	360	200	125	

investment decision problem

13-2 The Heinlein and Krampf Brokerage firm has just been instructed by one of its clients to invest $250,000 for her—money recently obtained through the sale of land holdings in Ohio. The client has a good deal of trust in the investment house, but she also has her own ideas about the distribution of the funds being invested. In particular, she requests that the firm select whatever stocks and bonds they believe are well rated, but within the following guidelines:

1. Municipal bonds should comprise at least 20% of the investment.
2. At least 40% of the funds should be placed in a combination of electronics firms, aerospace firms, and drug manufacturers.
3. No more than 50% of the amount invested in municipal bonds should be placed in a high-risk, high-yield nursing home stock.

Subject to these restraints, the client's goal is to maximize projected return on investments. The analysts at Heinlein and Krampf, aware of these guidelines, prepare a list of quality stocks and bonds and their corresponding rates of return.

INVESTMENT	PROJECTED RATE OF RETURN (%)
Los Angeles Municipal Bonds	5.3
Thompson Electronics, Inc.	6.8
United Aerospace Corp.	4.9
Palmer Drugs	8.4
Happy Days Nursing Homes	11.8

(a) Formulate this portfolio selection problem using linear programming.
(b) Solve this problem.

restaurant work scheduling problem

13-3 The famous Y. S. Chang Restaurant is open 24 hours a day. Waiters and busboys report for duty at 3 A.M., 7 A.M., 11 A.M., 3 P.M., 7 P.M., or 11 P.M., and each works an eight-hour shift. The following table shows the minimum number of workers needed during the six periods into which the day is divided. Chang's scheduling problem is to determine how many waiters and busboys should report for work at the start of each time period in order to minimize the total staff required for one day's operation. (*Hint:* Let X_i

PERIOD	TIME	NUMBER OF WAITERS AND BUSBOYS REQUIRED
1	3 A.M.– 7 A.M.	3
2	7 A.M.–11 A.M.	12
3	11 A.M.– 3 P.M.	16
4	3 P.M.– 7 P.M.	9
5	7 P.M.–11 P.M.	11
6	11 P.M.– 3 A.M.	4

equal the number of waiters and busboys beginning work in time period i, where $i = 1, 2, 3, 4, 5, 6$.)

: **13-4** The Battery Park Stable feeds and houses the horses used to pull tourist-filled carriages through the streets of Charleston's historic waterfront area. The stable owner, an ex-race horse trainer, recognizes the need to set a nutritional diet for the horses in his care. At the same time, he would like to keep the overall daily cost of feed to a minimum.

animal feed mix problem

The feed mixes available for the horses' diet are an oat product, a highly enriched grain, and a mineral product. Each of these mixes contains a certain amount of five ingredients needed daily to keep the average horse healthy. The accompanying table shows these minimum requirements, units of each ingredient per pound of feed mix, and costs for the three mixes.

	FEED MIX			
DIET REQUIREMENT (INGREDIENTS)	OAT PRODUCT (UNITS/LB.)	ENRICHED GRAIN (UNITS/LB.)	MINERAL PRODUCT (UNITS/LB.)	MINIMUM DAILY REQUIREMENT (IN UNITS)
A	2	3	1	6
B	$\frac{1}{2}$	1	$\frac{1}{2}$	2
C	3	5	6	9
D	1	$1\frac{1}{2}$	2	8
E	$\frac{1}{2}$	$\frac{1}{2}$	$1\frac{1}{2}$	5
Cost/lb.	$.09	$.14	$.17	

In addition, the stable owner is aware that an overfed horse is a sluggish worker. Consequently, he determines that six pounds of feed per day is the most any horse needs in order to function properly. Formulate this problem and solve for the optimal daily mix of the three feeds.

: **13-5** The Dubuque Sackers, a class D baseball team, face a tough four-game road trip against league rivals in Des Moines, Davenport, Omaha, and Peoria. Manager "Red" Revelle faces the task of scheduling his four starting pitchers for appropriate games. Since the games are to be played back to back in less than one week, Revelle cannot count on any pitcher to start in more than one game.

ballplayer selection problem

Revelle knows the strengths and weaknesses not only of his pitchers, but also of his opponents, and he is able to estimate the probability of winning of each of the four games with each of the four starting pitchers. Those probabilities are listed in the following table.

STARTING PITCHER	OPPONENT			
	DES MOINES	DAVENPORT	OMAHA	PEORIA
"Dead-Arm" Jones	.60	.80	.50	.40
"Spitball" Baker	.70	.40	.80	.30
"Ace" Parker	.90	.80	.70	.80
"Gutter" Wilson	.50	.30	.40	.20

What pitching rotation should manager Revelle set so as to provide the highest winning probability (that is, the sum of the probabilities of winning each game) for the Sackers?

(a) Formulate this problem using linear programming.

(b) Solve the problem.

media selection problem

13-6 The advertising director for Diversey Paint and Supply, a chain of four retail stores on Chicago's North Side, is considering two media possibilities. One plan is for a series of half-page ads in the Sunday *Chicago Tribune* newspaper, and the other is for advertising time on Chicago TV. The stores are expanding their lines of do-it-yourself tools, and the advertising director is interested in an exposure level of at least 40% within the city's neighborhoods and 60% in northwest suburban areas.

The TV viewing time under consideration has an exposure rating per spot of 5% in city homes and 3% in the northwest suburbs. The Sunday newspaper has corresponding exposure rates of 4% and 3% per ad. The cost of a half-page *Tribune* advertisement is $925; a television spot costs $2,000.

Diversey Paint would like to select the least costly advertising strategy that would meet desired exposure levels.

(a) Formulate using LP.

(b) Solve the problem.

hospital expansion problem

13-7 New Orlean's Mt. Sinai Hospital is a large, private, 600-bed facility complete with laboratories, operating rooms, and x-ray equipment. In seeking to increase revenues, Mt. Sinai's administration has decided to make a 90-bed addition on a portion of adjacent land currently used for staff parking. The administrators feel that the labs, operating rooms, and x-ray department are not being fully utilized at present and do not need to be expanded to handle additional patients. The addition of 90 beds, however, involves deciding how many beds should be allocated to the medical staff for medical patients and how many to the surgical staff for surgical patients.

The hospital's accounting and medical records departments have provided the following pertinent information. The average hospital stay for a medical patient is eight days and the average medical patient generates $2,280 in revenues. The average surgical patient is in the hospital five days and receives a $1,515 bill. The laboratory is capable of handling 15,000 tests per year more than it was handling. The average medical patient requires 3.1 lab tests and the average surgical patient takes 2.6 lab tests. Furthermore, the average medical patient uses one x-ray, while the average surgical patient requires two x-rays. If the hospital were expanded by 90 beds, the x-ray department could handle up to 7,000 x-rays without significant additional cost. Finally, the administration estimates that up to 2,800 additional operations could be performed in existing operating room facilities. Medical patients, of course, require no surgery, while each surgical patient generally has one surgery performed.

Formulate this problem so as to determine how many medical beds and how many surgical beds should be added in order to maximize revenues. Assume that the hospital is open 365 days a year. Then solve the problem.

: **13-8** The Arden County, Maryland, superintendent of education is responsible for assigning students to the *three* high schools in his county. He recognizes the need to bus a certain number of students, for several sectors of the county are beyond walking distance to a school. The superintendent partitions the county into *five* geographic sectors as he attempts to establish a plan that will minimize the total number of student miles traveled by bus. He also recognizes that if a student happens to live in a certain sector and is assigned to the high school in that sector, there is no need to bus him since he can walk from home to school. The three schools are located in sectors B, C, and E.

high school busing problem

The accompanying table reflects the number of high-school-age students living in each sector and the distance in miles from each sector to each school.

| | DISTANCE TO SCHOOL | | | |
SECTOR	SCHOOL IN SECTOR B	SCHOOL IN SECTOR C	SCHOOL IN SECTOR E	NO. OF STUDENTS
A	5	8	6	700
B	0	4	12	500
C	4	0	7	100
D	7	2	5	800
E	12	7	0	400
			Total	2,500

Each high school has a capacity of 900 students. Set up the objective function and constraints of this problem using linear programming so that the total number of student miles traveled by bus is minimized. Note the resemblance to the transportation problem illustrated earlier in this chapter. Then solve the problem.

: **13-9** Bob Bell's fortieth birthday party promised to be the social event of the year in Cookeville. To prepare, Bob stocked up on the following liquors.

ingredient mix problem

LIQUOR	AMOUNT ON HAND (OZ.)
Bourbon	52
Brandy	38
Vodka	64
Dry vermouth	24
Sweet vermouth	36

Bob decides to mix four drinks for the party: Chaunceys, Sweet Italians, bourbon on the rocks, and Russian martinis. A Chauncey consists of $\frac{1}{4}$ bourbon, $\frac{1}{4}$ vodka, $\frac{1}{4}$ brandy, and $\frac{1}{4}$ sweet vermouth. A Sweet Italian contains $\frac{1}{4}$ brandy, $\frac{1}{2}$ sweet vermouth, and $\frac{1}{4}$ vermouth. Bourbon on the rocks contains only bourbon. Finally, a Russian martini consists of $\frac{1}{3}$ dry vermouth and $\frac{2}{3}$ vodka. Each drink contains 4 fluid ounces.

Bob's objective is to mix these ingredients in such a way as to make the largest possible number of drinks in advance.

(a) Formulate using linear programming.
(b) Solve using LP software.

pricing and marketing strategy problem

: **13-10** The I. Kruger Paint and Wallpaper Store is a large retail distributor of the Supertrex brand of vinyl wallcoverings. Kruger will enhance its citywide image in Miami if it can outsell other local stores in total number of rolls of Supertrex next year. It is able to estimate the demand function as follows:

Number of rolls of Supertrex sold = 20 × Dollars spent on advertising + 6.8 × Dollars spent on in-store displays + 12 × Dollars invested in on-hand wallpaper inventory − 65,000 × Percentage markup taken above wholesale cost of a roll

The store budgets a total of $17,000 for advertising, in-store displays, and on-hand inventory of Supertrex for next year. It decides it must spend at least $3,000 on advertising; in addition, at least 5% of the amount invested in on-hand inventory should be devoted to displays. Markups on Supertrex seen at other local stores range from 20% to 45%. Kruger decides that its markup had best be in this range as well.

(a) Formulate as an LP problem.
(b) Solve the problem.
(c) What is the difficulty with the answer?
(d) What constraint would you add?

college meal selection problem

: **13-11** Kathy Roniger, campus dietician for a small Idaho college, is responsible for formulating a nutritious meal plan for students. For an evening meal, she feels that the following five meal content requirements should be met: (1) between 900 and 1,500 calories; (2) at least 4 milligrams of iron; (3) no more than 50 grams of fat; (4) at least 26 grams of protein; and (5) no more than 50 grams of carbohydrates. On a particular day, Roniger's food stock includes seven items that can be prepared and served for supper to meet these requirements. The cost per pound for each food item and its contribution to each of the five nutritional requirements are given in the accompanying table. What combination and amounts of food items will provide the nutrition Roniger requires at the least total food cost?

TABLE OF FOOD VALUES* AND COSTS

FOOD ITEM	CALORIES/ POUND	IRON (MG/LB.)	FAT (GMS./LBS.)	PROTEIN (GMS./LBS.)	CARBOHY-DRATES (GMS./LBS.)	COST/ POUND ($)
Milk	295	.2	16	16	22	.60
Ground meat	1216	.2	96	81	0	2.35
Chicken	394	4.3	9	74	0	1.15
Fish	358	3.2	.5	83	0	2.25
Beans	128	3.2	.8	7	28	.58
Spinach	118	14.1	1.4	14	19	1.17
Potatoes	279	2.2	.5	8	63	.33

*Source: Bowes and Church, *Food Values of Portions Commonly Used,* 12th ed. (Philadelphia: Lippincott, 1975).

(a) Formulate as an LP problem.
(b) What is the cost per meal?
(c) Is this a well-balanced diet?

 : **13-12** Quitmeyer Electronics Incorporated manufactures the following six micro-computer peripheral devices: internal modems, external modems, graphics circuit boards, floppy disk drives, winchester disk drives, and memory expansion boards. Each of these technical products requires time, in minutes, on three types of electronic testing equipment as shown below:

high tech production problem

	DEVICE					
	INTER-NAL MODEM	EXTER-NAL MODEM	CIRCUIT BOARD	FLOPPY DISKS	WINCHESTER DISKS	MEMORY BOARDS
Test device #1	7	3	12	6	18	17
Test device #2	2	5	3	2	15	17
Test device #3	5	1	3	2	9	2

The first two test devices are available 120 hours per week. The third (device #3) requires more preventive maintenance and may be used only 100 hours each week. The market for all six computer components is vast and Quitmeyer Electronics believes it can sell as many units of each product as it can manufacture. The table that follows summarizes the revenues and material costs for each product.

DEVICE	REVENUE PER UNIT SOLD ($)	MATERIAL COST PER UNIT ($)
Internal modem	200	35
External modem	120	25
Graphics circuit board	180	40
Floppy disk drive	130	45
Winchester disk drive	430	170
Memory expansion board	260	60

In addition, variable labor costs are $15 per hour for test device #1, $12 per hour for test device #2, and $18 per hour for test device #3. Quitmeyer Electronics wants to maximize its profits.

(a) Formulate this problem as a linear programming model.
(b) Solve the problem by computer. What is the best product mix?
(c) What is the value of an additional hour of time per week on test device #1? Test device #2? Test device #3? Should Quitmeyer Electronics add more test device time? If so, on which equipment?

: **13-13** South Central Utilities has just announced the August 1 opening of its second nuclear generator at its Baton Rouge, Louisiana, nuclear power plant. Its personnel department has been directed to determine how many nuclear technicians need to be hired and trained over the remainder of the year.

nuclear plant staffing problem

The plant currently employs 350 fully trained technicians and projects the following personnel needs:

MONTH	PERSONNEL NEEDED (HOURS)
August	40,000
September	45,000
October	35,000
November	50,000
December	45,000

By Louisiana law, a reactor employee can actually work no more than 130 hours per month. (Slightly over one hour per day is used for check-in and check-out, record keeping, and for daily radiation health scans.) Policy at South Central Utilities also dictates that layoffs are not acceptable in those months when the nuclear plant is overstaffed. So, if more trained employees are available than are needed in any month, each worker is still fully paid, even though he or she is not required to work the 130 hours.

Training new employees is an important and costly procedure. It takes one month of one-on-one classroom instruction before a new technician is permitted to work alone in the reactor facility. Therefore, South Central must hire trainees one month before they are actually needed. Each trainee teams up with a skilled nuclear technician and requires 90 hours of that employee's time, meaning that 90 hours less of the technician's time are available that month for actual reactor work.

Personnel department records indicate a turnover rate of trained technicians at 5% per month. In other words, about 5% of the skilled employees at the start of any month resign by the end of that month.

A trained technician earns an average monthly salary of $2,000 (regardless of the number of hours worked, as noted earlier). Trainees are paid $900 during their one month of instruction.

(a) Formulate this staffing problem using LP.
(b) Solve the problem. How many trainees must begin each month?

agricultural production planning problem

: 13-14 Margaret Young's family owns five panels of farmland broken into a southeast sector, north sector, northwest sector, west sector, and southwest sector. Young is primarily involved in growing wheat, alfalfa, and barley crops and is currently preparing her production plan for next year. The Pennsylvania Water Authority has just announced its yearly water allotment, with the Young farm receiving 7,400 acre-feet. Each parcel can only tolerate a specified amount of irrigation per growing season, as specified below:

PARCEL	AREA (IN ACRES)	WATER IRRIGATION LIMIT (ACRE-FEET)
Southeast	2,000	3,200
North	2,300	3,400
Northwest	600	800
West	1,100	500
Southwest	500	600

Each of Young's crops needs a minimum amount of water per acre and there is a projected limit on sales of each crop. Crop data follow:

CROP	MAXIMUM SALES	WATER NEEDED PER ACRE (ACRE-FEET)
Wheat	110,000 bushels	1.6
Alfalfa	1,800 tons	2.9
Barley	2,200 tons	3.5

Young's best estimate is that she can sell wheat at a net profit of $2 per bushel, alfalfa at $40 per ton and barley at $50 per ton. One acre of land yields an average of 1.5 tons of alfalfa and 2.2 tons of barley. The wheat yield is approximately 50 bushels per acre.

(a) Formulate Young's production plan.
(b) What should the crop plan be and what profit will it yield?
(c) The Water Authority informs Young that for a special fee of $6,000 this year, her farm will qualify for an additional allotment of 600 acre-feet of water. How should she respond?

Chase Manhattan Bank

The work load in many areas of bank operations has the characteristics of a nonuniform distribution with respect to time of day. For example, at Chase Manhattan Bank in New York, the number of domestic money transfer requests received from customers, if plotted against time of day, would appear to have the shape of an inverted U curve with the peak around 1 P.M. For efficient use of resources, the personnel available should, therefore, vary correspondingly. The accompanying illustration shows a typical work load curve and corresponding personnel requirements at different hours of the day.

3. Part-timers work for at least four hours per day but less than eight hours and are not allowed a lunch break.

4. Fifty percent of the full-timers go to lunch between 11 A.M. and noon and the remaining 50% between noon and 1 P.M.

5. The shift starts at 9 A.M. and ends at 7 P.M. (that is, overtime is limited to two hours). Any work left over at 7 P.M. is considered holdover for the next day.

6. A full-time employee is not allowed to work more than five hours overtime per week. He or

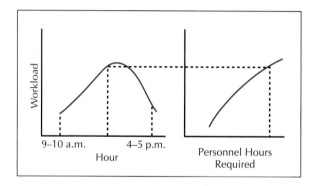

Work Load Curve

A variable capacity can be achieved effectively by employing part-time personnel. Since part-timers are not entitled to all the fringe benefits, they are often more economical than full-time employees. Other considerations, however, may limit the extent to which part-time people can be hired in a given department. The problem is to find an optimum work force schedule that would meet personnel requirements at any given time and also be economical.

Some of the factors affecting personnel assignment are listed here:

1. By corporate policy, part-time personnel hours are limited to a maximum of 40% of the day's total requirement.

2. Full-time employees work for eight hours (one hour for lunch included) per day. Thus, a full-timer's productive time is 35 hours per week.

she is paid at the normal rate for overtime hours—*not* at one-and-a-half times the normal rate applicable to hours in excess of 40 per week. Fringe benefits are not applied to overtime hours.

In addition, the following costs are pertinent:

1. The average cost per full-time personnel hour (fringe benefits included) is $10.11.

2. The average cost per overtime personnel hour for full-timers (straight rate excluding fringe benefits) is $8.08.

3. The average cost per part-time personnel hour is $7.82.

The personnel hours required, by hour of day, are given in the table.

The bank's goal is to achieve the minimum possible personnel cost subject to meeting or exceeding

Work Force Requirements

TIME PERIOD	NUMBER OF PERSONNEL REQUIRED
9–10 A.M.	14
10–11	25
11–12	26
12–1 P.M.	38
1–2	55
2–3	60
3–4	51
4–5	29
5–6	14
6–7	9

Source: Adopted by Barry Render from Shyam L. Moondra, "An L.P. Model for Work Force Scheduling for Banks," *Journal of Bank Research,* Winter 1976.

the hourly work force requirements as well as the constraints on the workers listed earlier.

Discussion Questions

1. What is the minimum-cost schedule for the bank?

2. What are the limitations of the model used to answer the above question?

3. Costs might be reduced by relaxing the constraint that no more than 40% of the day's requirement be met by part-timers. Would changing the 40% to a higher value significantly reduce costs?

BIBLIOGRAPHY

See references at end of Chapter 10.

14

Transportation and Assignment Problems

14.1
INTRODUCTION

In this chapter, we explore two special linear programming models. Because of their structure, these models—called the transportation and assignment models—can be solved using more efficient computational procedures than the simplex method.

Both transportation and assignment problems are members of a category of linear programming techniques called *network flow problems*. Networks, described in detail in Chapter 18, consist of nodes (or points) and arcs (or lines) that join the modes together. Roadways, telephone systems, and citywide water systems are all examples of networks.

Transportation Model

The first model we will examine, the *transportation problem*, deals with the distribution of goods from several points of supply (sources) to a number of points of demand (destinations). Usually, we have a given capacity of goods at each source and a given requirement for the goods at each destination. An example of this is shown in Figure 14.1. The objective of such a problem is to schedule shipments from sources to destinations so that total transportation and production costs are minimized.

Transportation models can also be used when a firm is trying to decide where to locate a new facility. Before opening a new warehouse, factory, or sales office, it is good practice to consider a number of alternative sites. Good financial decisions concerning facility location also attempt to minimize total transportation and production costs for the entire system.

Assignment Model

The assignment problem refers to the class of linear programming problems that involve determining the most efficient assignment of people to projects, salespeople to territories, contracts to bidders, jobs to machines, and so

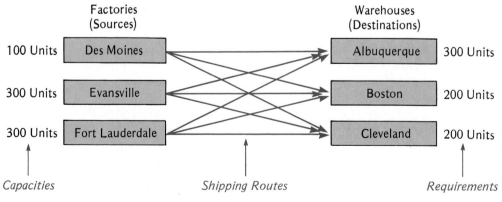

FIGURE 14.1
Example of a Transportation Problem

TABLE 14.1 Transportation Costs per Desk for Executive Furniture Corp.

FROM \ TO	ALBUQUERQUE	BOSTON	CLEVELAND
Des Moines	$5	$4	$3
Evansville	$8	$4	$3
Fort Lauderdale	$9	$7	$5

tation problem may now be described as *how to select the shipping routes to be used and the number of desks shipped on each route so as to minimize total transportation cost.* This, of course, must be done while observing the restrictions regarding factory capacities and warehouse requirements.

minimizing total transportation cost

The first step at this point is setting up a *transportation table;* its purpose is to summarize conveniently and concisely all relevant data and to keep track of algorithm computations. (In this respect, it serves the same role as the simplex tableau did for linear programming problems.) Using the information for the Executive Furniture Corporation displayed in Figure 14.1 and Table 14.1, we proceed to construct a transportation table and to label its various components in Table 14.2.

transportation table

We see in Table 14.2 that the total factory supply available is exactly equal to the total warehouse demand. When this situation of equal demand

TABLE 14.2 Transportation Table for Executive Furniture Corp.

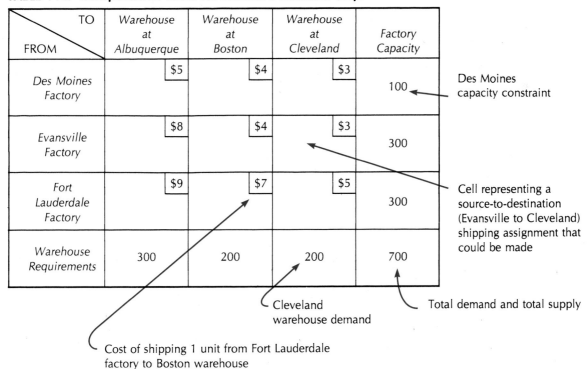

FROM \ TO	Warehouse at Albuquerque	Warehouse at Boston	Warehouse at Cleveland	Factory Capacity
Des Moines Factory	$5	$4	$3	100
Evansville Factory	$8	$4	$3	300
Fort Lauderdale Factory	$9	$7	$5	300
Warehouse Requirements	300	200	200	700

Des Moines capacity constraint

Cell representing a source-to-destination (Evansville to Cleveland) shipping assignment that could be made

Cleveland warehouse demand

Total demand and total supply

Cost of shipping 1 unit from Fort Lauderdale factory to Boston warehouse

balanced supply and demand

and supply occurs (something that is rather unusual in real life) a *balanced problem* is said to exist. Later in this chapter, we take a look at how to deal with unbalanced problems, namely, those where destination requirements may be greater than or less than origin capacities.

14.3
DEVELOPING AN INITIAL SOLUTION: NORTHWEST CORNER RULE

Once the data have been arranged in tabular form, we must establish an initial feasible solution to the problem. One systematic procedure, known as the *northwest corner rule*, requires that we start in the upper left-hand cell (or northwest corner) of the table and allocate units to shipping routes as follows:

1. Exhaust the supply (factory capacity) at each row before moving down to the next row.

2. Exhaust the (warehouse) requirements of each column before moving to the right to the next column.

3. Check that all supply and demands are met.

We can now use the northwest corner rule to find an initial feasible solution to the Executive Furniture Corporation problem shown in Table 14.2.

It takes five steps in this example to make the initial shipping assignments (see Table 14.3):

explanation of steps

1. Beginning in the upper left-hand corner, we assign 100 units from Des Moines to Albuquerque. This exhausts the capacity or supply at the Des Moines factory. But it still leaves the warehouse at Albuquerque 200 desks short. Move down to the second row in the same column.

2. Assign 200 units from Evansville to Albuquerque. This meets Albuquerque's demand for a total of 300 desks. Since the Evansville factory has 100 units remaining, we move to the right to the next column of the second row.

3. Assign 100 units from Evansville to Boston. The Evansville supply has now been exhausted, but Boston's warehouse is still short by 100 desks. At this point, we move down vertically in the Boston column to the next row.

4. Assign 100 units from Fort Lauderdale to Boston. This shipment will fulfill Boston's demand for a total of 200 units. We note, though, that the Fort Lauderdale factory still has 200 units available that have not been shipped.

TABLE 14.3 Initial Solution to Executive Furniture Problem Using the Northwest Corner Method

FROM \ TO	Albuquerque (A)	Boston (B)	Cleveland (C)	Factory Capacity
Des Moines (D)	$5 — 100	$4	$3	100
Evansville (E)	$8 — 200	$4 — 100	$3	300
Fort Lauderdale (F)	$9	$7 — (100)	$5 — 200	300
Warehouse Requirements	300	200	200	700

Means that the firm is shipping 100 units along the Fort Lauderdale to Boston route

5. Assign 200 units from Fort Lauderdale to Cleveland. This final move exhausts Cleveland's demand *and* Fort Lauderdale's supply. This always happens with a balanced problem. The initial shipment schedule is now complete.

We can easily compute the cost of this shipping assignment.

TOTAL COST OF INITIAL SOLUTION

ROUTE FROM	TO	UNITS SHIPPED	× PER UNIT COST ($)	= TOTAL COST ($)
D	A	100	5	500
E	A	200	8	1,600
E	B	100	4	400
F	B	100	7	700
F	C	200	5	1,000
			Total	4,200

This solution is feasible since demand and supply constraints are all satisfied. It was also very quick and easy to reach. However, we would be very lucky if this solution yielded the optimal transportation cost for the problem, because this route-loading method totally ignored the costs of shipping over each of the routes.

feasible solution

14.4
STEPPING-STONE METHOD: FINDING A LEAST-COST SOLUTION

The *stepping-stone method* is an iterative technique for moving from an initial feasible solution to an optimal feasible solution. In order for the stepping-stone method to be applied to a transportation problem, one rule about the number of shipping routes being used must first be observed. The rule is this: *the number of occupied routes (or squares) must always be equal to one less than the sum of the number of rows plus the number of columns.* In the Executive Furniture problem, this means that the initial solution must have $3 + 3 - 1 = 5$ squares used. Thus,

$$\text{Occupied shipping routes (squares)} = \text{Number of rows} + \text{Number of columns} - 1$$
$$5 = 3 + 3 - 1$$

When the number of occupied routes is less than this, the solution is called *degenerate*. Later in this chapter, we talk about what to do if the number of used squares is less than the number of rows plus the number of columns minus 1.

Testing the Solution for Possible Improvement

testing each unused route

How does the stepping-stone method work? Its approach is to evaluate the cost-effectiveness of shipping goods via transportation routes *not* currently in the solution. Each unused shipping route (or square) in the transportation table is tested by asking the following question: "What would happen to total shipping costs if *one* unit of our product (in our example, one desk) were tentatively shipped on an unused route?"

This testing of each unused square is conducted by the following five steps:

1. Select an unused square to be evaluated.

2. Beginning at this square, trace a closed path back to the original square via squares that are currently being used and moving with only horizontal and vertical moves.

3. Beginning with a plus (+) sign at the unused square, place alternate minus (−) signs and plus signs on each corner square of the closed path just traced.

4. Calculate an *improvement index* by adding together the unit cost figures found in each square containing a plus sign and then subtracting the unit costs in each square containing a minus sign.

5. Repeat steps 1–4 until an improvement index has been calculated for all unused squares. If all indices computed are greater than or equal to 0, an optimal solution has been reached. If not, it is possible to improve the current solution and decrease total shipping costs.

To see how the stepping-stone method works, let us apply these steps to the Executive Furniture Corporation data in Table 14.3 to evaluate unused shipping routes. The four currently unassigned routes are: Des Moines to Boston, Des Moines to Cleveland, Evansville to Cleveland, and Fort Lauderdale to Albuquerque.

Steps 1 and 2. Beginning with the Des Moines–Boston route, we first trace a closed path using only currently occupied squares (see Table 14.4), and then place alternate plus signs and minus signs in the corners of this path. To indicate more clearly the meaning of a *closed path,* we see that only squares currently used for shipping can be used in turning the corners of the route being traced. Hence, the path Des Moines–Boston to Des Moines–Albuquerque to Fort Lauderdale–Albuquerque to Fort Lauderdale–Boston to Des Moines–Boston would not be acceptable since the Fort Lauderdale–Albuquerque square is currently empty. It turns out that *only one* closed route is possible for each square we wish to test.

closed paths

Step 3. How do we decide which squares are given plus signs and which minus signs? The answer is simple. Since we are testing the cost-effectiveness of the Des Moines-to-Boston shipping route, we pretend as if we are shipping one desk from Des Moines to Boston. This is one more unit than we *were* sending between the two cities, so we place a plus sign in the box. But, if we ship one *more* unit than before from Des Moines to Boston, we end up sending 101 desks out of the Des Moines factory.

how to assign + and − signs

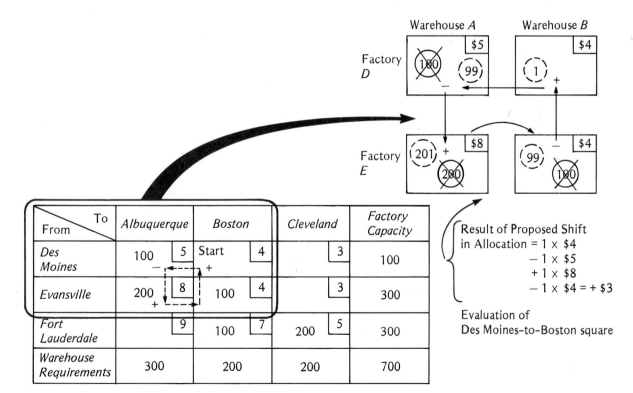

TABLE 14.4 Evaluating the Unused Des Moines–Boston Shipping Route

That factory's capacity is only 100 units, hence we must ship one desk *less* from Des Moines to Albuquerque—this change is made to avoid violating the factory capacity constraint. To indicate that the Des Moines-to-Albuquerque shipment has been reduced, we place a minus sign in its box. Continuing along the closed path, we notice that we are no longer meeting the Albuquerque warehouse requirement for 300 units. In fact, if the Des Moines-to-Albuquerque shipment is reduced to 99 units, the Evansville-to-Albuquerque load has to be increased by 1 unit, to 201 desks. Therefore, we place a plus sign in that box to indicate the increase. Finally, we note that if the Evansville-to-Albuquerque route is assigned 201 desks, then the Evansville-to-Boston route must be reduced by 1 unit, to 99 desks, in order to maintain the Evansville factory capacity constraint of 300 units. Thus, a minus sign is placed in the Evansville-to-Boston box. We observe in Table 14.4 that all four routes on the closed path are hereby balanced in terms of demand-and-supply limitations.

Step 4. An improvement index for the Des Moines–Boston route is now computed by adding unit costs in squares with plus signs and subtracting costs in squares with minus signs. Hence,

**improvement index
computation**

Des Moines–Boston index = $+ \$4$ $\$5 + \$8 - \$4 = +\$3$

This means that for every desk shipped via the Des Moines–Boston route, total transportation costs will *increase* by $3 over their current level.

Step 5. Let us now examine the Des Moines–Cleveland unused route, which is slightly more difficult to trace with a closed path. Again, you will notice that we turn each corner along the path only at squares that represent existing routes. The path can go *through* the Evansville–Cleveland box, but cannot turn a corner or place a + or − sign there. Only an occupied square may be used as a stepping stone (Table 14.5).

TABLE 14.5 Evaluating the Des Moines–Cleveland (D–C) Shipping Route

FROM \ TO	A	B	C	FACTORY CAPACITY
D	$5 — 100	$4	$3 start +	100
E	$8 + 200	$4 — 100	$3	300
F	$9	$7 + 100	$5 — 200	300
WAREHOUSE REQUIREMENTS	300	200	200	700

The closed path we use is $+ DC - DA + EA - EB + FB - FC$.

Des Moines–Cleveland improvement index
$$= + \$3 - \$5 + \$8 - \$4 + \$7 - \$5 = +\$4$$

Thus, opening this route will also not lower our total shipping costs.

The other two routes may be evaluated in a similar fashion:

Evansville–Cleveland index $= +\$3 - \$4 + \$7 - \$5 = +\$1$

(Closed path is $+ EC - EB + FB - FC$.)

Fort Lauderdale–Albuquerque index $= +\$9 - \$7 + \$4 - \$8$
$$= -\$2$$

(Closed path is $+ FA - FB + EB - EA$.)

Because this last improvement index is negative, a cost savings may be attained by making use of the (currently unused) Fort Lauderdale–Albuquerque route.

Obtaining an Improved Solution

Each negative index computed by the stepping-stone method represents the amount by which total transportation costs could be decreased if 1 unit or product were shipped on that route. We found only one negative index in the Executive Furniture problem, that being $-\$2$ on the Fort Lauderdale-factory-to-Albuquerque-warehouse route. If, however, there were more than one negative improvement index, our strategy would be to choose the route (unused square) with the *largest* negative index.

selecting route with largest negative index

The next step, then, is to ship the maximum allowable number of units (or desks, in our case) on the new route (Fort Lauderdale to Albuquerque). What is the maximum quantity that can be shipped on the money-saving route? That quantity is found by referring to the closed path of plus signs and minus signs drawn for the route and selecting the *smallest number* found in those squares containing *minus signs*.

To obtain a new solution, that number is added to all squares on the closed path with plus signs, and subtracted from all squares on the path assigned minus signs.

changing the shipping route

Let us see how this process can help improve Executive Furniture's solution. We repeat the transportation table (Table 14.6) for the problem. Note that the stepping-stone route for Fort Lauderdale to Albuquerque (F to A) is drawn in.

The maximum quantity that can be shipped on the newly opened route (F–A) is the smallest number found in squares containing minus signs— in this case, 100 units. Why 100 units? Since the total cost decreases by $2 per unit shipped, we know we would like to ship the maximum possible number of units. Table 14.6 indicates that each unit shipped over the F–A route results in an increase of 1 unit shipped from E to B and a decrease of 1 unit in both the amounts shipped from F to B (now 100 units) and from E to A (now 200 units). Hence, the maximum we can ship over the F–A route is 100. This results in 0 units being shipped from F to B.

We add 100 units to the 0 now being shipped on route F–A; then proceed to subtract 100 from route F–B, leaving 0 in that square (but still balancing

TABLE 14.6 Stepping-Stone Path Used to Evaluate Route F–A

FROM \ TO	A	B	C	FACTORY
D	$5 100	$4	$3	100
E	$8 – 200	$4 + 100	$3	300
F	$9 +	$7 – 100	$5 200	300
WAREHOUSE	300	200	200	700

the row total for F); then add 100 to route E–B, yielding 200; and finally, subtract 100 from route E–A, leaving 100 units shipped. Note that the new numbers still produce the correct row and column totals as required.

The new solution is shown in Table 14.7.

TABLE 14.7 Second Solution to the Executive Furniture Problem

FROM \ TO	A	B	C	FACTORY
D	$5 100	$4	$3	100
E	$8 100	$4 200	$3	300
F	$9 100	$7	$5 200	300
WAREHOUSE	300	200	200	700

Total shipping cost has been reduced by (100 units) × ($2 saved per unit) = $200, and is now $4,000. This cost figure can, of course, also be derived by multiplying each unit shipping cost times the number of units transported on its route, namely, (100 × $5) + (100 × $8) + (200 × $4) + (100 × $9) + (200 × $5) = $4,000.

The solution shown in Table 14.7 may or may not be optimal. To determine whether further improvement is possible, we return to the first five steps given earlier to test each square that is *now* unused. The four improvement indices—each representing an available shipping route—are as follows:

improvement indices

$$D \text{ to } B = +\$4 - \$5 + \$8 - \$4 = +\$3$$
$$(\text{closed path: } + DB - DA + EA - EB)$$
$$D \text{ to } C = +\$3 - \$5 + \$9 - \$5 = +\$2$$
$$(\text{closed path: } + DC - DA + FA - FC)$$
$$E \text{ to } C = +\$3 - \$8 + \$9 - \$5 = -\$1$$
$$(\text{closed path: } + EC - EA + FA - FC)$$
$$F \text{ to } B = +\$7 - \$4 + \$8 - \$9 = +\$2$$
$$(\text{closed path: } + FB - EB + EA - FA)$$

Hence, an improvement can be made by shipping the maximum allowable number of units from E to C. Only the squares E–A and F–C have minus signs in the closed path; since the smallest number in these two squares is 100, we add 100 units to E–C and F–A and subtract 100 units from E–A and F–C. The new cost for this third solution of $3,900 is computed below.

TOTAL COST OF THIRD SOLUTION

ROUTE FROM	TO	DESKS SHIPPED	×	PER UNIT COST ($)	=	TOTAL COST ($)
D	A	100		5		500
E	B	200		4		800
E	C	100		3		300
F	A	200		9		1,800
F	C	100		5		500
					Total	3,900

Table 14.9 contains the optimal shipping assignments because each improvement index that can be computed at this point is greater than or equal to zero as shown in the following equations. Improvement indices for the table are:

KEY IDEA

$$D \text{ to } B = + \$4 - \$5 + \$9 - \$5 + \$3 - \$4$$
$$= +\$2 \quad (\text{path: } + DB - DA + FA - FC + EC - EB)$$
$$D \text{ to } C = + \$3 - \$5 + \$9 - \$5 = +\$2 \quad (\text{path: } + DC - DA + FA - FC)$$
$$E \text{ to } A = + \$8 - \$9 + \$5 - \$3 = +\$1 \quad (\text{path: } + EA - FA + FC - EC)$$
$$F \text{ to } B = + \$7 - \$5 + \$3 - \$4 = +\$1 \quad (\text{path: } + FB - FC + EC - EB)$$

TABLE 14.8 Path to Evaluate the E–C Route

FROM \ TO	A	B	C	FACTORY
D	100 $5	$4	$3	100
E	100 $8 —	200 $4	Start + $3	300
F	100 $9 +	$7	200 $5 —	300
WAREHOUSE	300	200	200	700

The hardest part in solving problems like this is identifying every stepping-stone path so that we may compute the improvement indices. An easier way to find the optimal solution to transportation problems, especially larger ones with more sources and destinations, is called the MODI method.

TABLE 14.9 Third and Optimal Solution

FROM \ TO	A	B	C	FACTORY
D	100 $5	$4	$3	100
E	$8	200 $4	100 $3	300
F	200 $9	$7	100 $5	300
WAREHOUSE	300	200	200	700

Transportation Problem for Irish Pharmaceutical Distributor

The Cahill May Roberts company (CMR), one of Ireland's largest wholesale distributors of pharmaceuticals, faced a major *transportation problem*. The firm had its head office and three warehouses in the Dublin area, with five more warehouses scattered about Ireland. CMR supplied 400 customers (mainly retail druggists) in the Dublin area and over 800 customers in 300 outlying towns and villages. Customers were supplied by a fleet of delivery vans, with a drop-off frequency varying from twice per day to once per week.

Prior to the transportation problem analysis, no coherent distribution plan for the whole company had been formulated. It was even common for cus-

Source: H. Harrison, "A Planning System for Facilities and Resources in Distribution Networks," *Interfaces*, Vol. 9, No. 2, February 1979, pp. 6–22.

tomers to receive their supplies from more than one warehouse. The illogical transportation system meant that delivery patterns were not very efficient in satisfying druggists' demands.

According to Mr. Higgins, the director of finance, the transportation planning model yielded the following results:

1. A 27% reduction in delivery and transportation costs.

2. A $765,000 savings in overhead.

3. A reduction of $125,000 in capital investments, with more savings anticipated.

4. A 60% increase in customer service leading to a sales increase of $2,457,000.

14.5
MODI METHOD

The MODI (*modified distribution*) *method* allows us to compute improvement indices quickly for each unused square without drawing all of the closed paths. Because of this, it can often provide considerable time savings over the stepping-stone method for solving transportation problems.

MODI versus stepping-stone method

MODI provides a new means of finding the unused route with the largest negative improvement index. Once the largest index is identified, we are required to trace only one closed path. Just as with the stepping-stone approach, this path helps determine the maximum number of units that can be shipped via the best unused route.

How to Use the MODI Approach

In applying the MODI method, we begin with an initial solution obtained by using the northwest corner rule.[2] But now, we must compute a value for each row (call the values R_1, R_2, R_3 if there are three rows) and for each column (K_1, K_2, K_3) in the transportation table. In general, we let

R_i = value assigned to row i

K_j = value assigned to column j

C_{ij} = cost in square ij (cost of shipping from source i to destination j)

[2] Note that any initial feasible solution will do: northwest corner rule, Vogel's approximation method solution, or any arbitrary assignment.

MODI steps

The MODI method then requires five steps.

1. To compute the values for each row and column, set

$$R_i + K_j = C_{ij} \qquad \qquad (14\text{-}1)$$

but *only for those squares that are currently used or occupied.* For example, if the square at the intersection of row 2 and column 1 is occupied, we set $R_2 + K_1 = C_{21}$.

2. After all equations have been written, set $R_1 = 0$.

3. Solve the system of equations for all R and K values.

4. Compute the improvement index for each unused square by the formula:

$$\text{Improvement index} = C_{ij} - R_i - K_j \qquad \qquad (14\text{-}2)$$

5. Select the largest negative index and proceed to solve the problem as you did using the stepping-stone method.

Solving the Executive Furniture Problem with MODI

Let us try out these rules on the Executive Furniture Corporation problem. The initial northwest corner solution is repeated in Table 14.10. MODI will be used to compute an improvement index for each unused square. Note that the only change in the transportation table is the border labeling the R_is (rows) and K_js (columns).

TABLE 14.10 Initial Solution to Executive Furniture Problem in the MODI Format

K_j		K_1	K_2	K_3	
R_i	TO / FROM	ALBUQUERQUE	BOSTON	CLEVELAND	FACTORY CAPACITY
R_1	DES MOINES	5 / 100	4	3	100
R_2	EVANSVILLE	8 / 200	4 / 100	3	300
R_3	FORT LAUDERDALE	9	7 / 100	5 / 200	300
	WAREHOUSE REQUIREMENTS	300	200	200	700

We first set up an equation for each occupied square:

(1) $R_1 + K_1 = 5$

(2) $R_2 + K_1 = 8$

(3) $R_2 + K_2 = 4$

(4) $R_3 + K_2 = 7$

(5) $R_3 + K_3 = 5$

solving for R and K values

Letting $R_1 = 0$, we can easily solve, step by step, for $K_1, R_2, K_2, R_3,$ and K_3.

(1) $R_1 + K_1 = 5$

   $0 + K_1 = 5$ $K_1 = 5$

(2) $R_2 + K_1 = 8$

   $R_2 + 5 = 8$ $R_2 = 3$

(3) $R_2 + K_2 = 4$

   $3 + K_2 = 4$ $K_2 = 1$

(4) $R_3 + K_2 = 7$

   $R_3 + 1 = 7$ $R_3 = 6$

(5) $R_3 + K_3 = 5$

   $6 + K_3 = 5$ $K_3 = -1$

You can observe that these R and K values will not always be positive; it is common for 0 and negative values to occur as well. We also think that after solving for the Rs and Ks in a few practice problems, you may become so proficient that the calculations can be done in your head instead of by writing the equations out.

The next step is to compute the improvement index for each unused cell. That formula, again, is: Improvement index $= C_{ij} - R_i - K_j$.

Des Moines–Boston index	$= C_{12} - R_1 - K_2 = 4 - 0 - 1$
	$= +\$3$
Des Moines–Cleveland index	$= C_{13} - R_1 - K_3 = 3 - 0 - (-1)$
	$= +\$4$
Evansville–Cleveland index	$= C_{23} - R_2 - K_3 = 3 - 3 - (-1)$
	$= +\$1$
Fort Lauderdale–Albuquerque index	$= C_{31} - R_3 - K_1 = 9 - 6 - 5$
	$= -\$2$

Note that these indices are exactly the same as the ones calculated when we used the stepping-stone approach (see Tables 14.4 and 14.5). Since one of the indices is negative, the current solution is not optimal. But now it is necessary to trace only the one closed path, for Fort Lauderdale–Albuquerque, in order to proceed with the solution procedures as used in the stepping-stone method.

KEY IDEA

For your convenience, the steps we follow to develop an improved solution after the improvement indices have been computed are briefly outlined:

improving the solution

1. Beginning at the square with the best improvement index (Fort Lauderdale–Albuquerque), trace a closed path back to the original square via squares that are currently being used.

2. Beginning with a plus ($+$) sign at the unused square, place alternate minus ($-$) signs and plus signs on each corner square of the closed path just traced.

3. Select the smallest quantity found in those squares containing minus signs. *Add* that number to all squares on the closed path with plus signs; *subtract* the number from all squares assigned minus signs.

4. Compute new improvement indices for this new solution using the MODI method.

Following this procedure, the second and third solutions to the Executive Furniture Corporation problem can be found. In tabular form, the result of your MODI computations will look identical to Tables 14.7 (second solution using stepping-stone) and 14.9 (optimal solution). With each new MODI solution, we must recalculate the R and K values. These values then are used to compute new improvement indices in order to determine whether further shipping cost reduction is possible.

14.6
VOGEL'S APPROXIMATION METHOD: ANOTHER WAY TO FIND AN INITIAL SOLUTION

In addition to the northwest corner method of setting an initial solution to transportation problems, we talk about one other important technique— *Vogel's approximation method* (VAM). VAM is not quite as simple as the northwest corner approach, but it facilitates a very good initial solution— as a matter of fact, one that is often the *optimal* solution.

Vogel's approximation method tackles the problem of finding a good initial solution by taking into account the costs associated with each route alternative. This is something that the northwest corner rule did not do. To apply the VAM, we first compute for each row and column the penalty faced if we should ship over the *second best* route instead of the *least-cost* route.

The six steps involved in determining an initial VAM solution are illustrated on our now familiar Executive Furniture Corporation data. (We begin with the same layout originally shown in Table 14.2.)

steps of VAM

VAM Step 1. For each row and column of the transportation table, find the difference between the two lowest unit shipping costs. These numbers represent the difference between the distribution cost on the *best* route in the row or column and the *second best* route in the row or column. (This is the *opportunity cost* of not using the best route.)

Step 1 has been done in Table 14.11. The numbers at the heads of the columns and to the right of the rows represent these differences.

For example, in row E the three transportation costs are $8, $4, and $3. Since the two lowest costs are $4 and $3, their difference is $1.

VAM Step 2. Identify the row or column with the greatest opportunity cost, or difference. In case of Table 14.11, the row or column selected is column *A*, with a difference of 3.

VAM Step 3. Assign as many units as possible to the lowest-cost square in the row or column selected.

assignment based on penalty costs

Step 3 has been done in Table 14.12. Under column *A*, the lowest cost route is *D–A* (with a cost of $5) and 100 units have been assigned to that square. No more were placed in the square because doing so would exceed *D*'s availability.

VAM Step 4. Eliminate any row or column that has just been completely satisfied by the assignment just made. This can be done by placing X's in each appropriate square.

Step 4 has been done in Table 14.12's *D* row. No future assignments will be made to the *D–B* or *D–C* routes.

VAM Step 5. Recompute the cost differences for the transportation table, omitting rows or columns crossed out in the preceding step.

This is also shown in Table 14.12. *A*'s, *B*'s, and *C*'s differences each change. *D*'s row is eliminated, and *E*'s and *F*'s differences remain the same as in Table 14.11.

VAM Step 6. Return to step 2 and repeat the steps until an initial feasible solution has been obtained.

In our case, column *B* now has the greatest difference, which is 3. We assign 200 units to the lowest-cost square in column *B* that has not been crossed out. This is seen to be *E–B*. Since *B*'s requirements have now been met, we place an X in the *F–B* square to eliminate it. Differences are once again recomputed. This process is summarized in Table 14.13.

TABLE 14.11 Transportation Table with VAM Row and Column Differences Shown

		3		0		0			
FROM \ TO	ALBUQUERQUE A		BOSTON B		CLEVELAND C		TOTAL AVAILABLE	
DES MOINES D		5		4		3	100	1
EVANSVILLE E		8		4		3	300	1
FORT LAUDERDALE F		9		7		5	300	2
TOTAL REQUIRED	300		200		200		700	

TABLE 14.12 VAM Assignment with D's Requirements Satisfied

FROM \ TO	A (X̶ 1)	B (Ø 3)	C (Ø 2)	TOTAL AVAILABLE	
D	5 — 100	4 — X	3 — X	100	X̶
E	8	4	3	300	1
F	9	7	5	300	2
TOTAL REQUIRED	300	200	200	700	

The greatest difference is now in row E. Hence, we shall assign as many units as possible to the lowest-cost square in row E, that is, E–C with a cost of \$3. The maximum assignment of 100 units depletes the remaining availability at E. The square E–A may therefore be crossed out. This is illustrated in Table 14.14.

The final two allocations, at F–A and F–C, may be made by inspecting

TABLE 14.13 Second VAM Assignment with B's Requirements Satisfied

FROM \ TO	A (X̶ 1)	B (Ø X̶ X̶)	C (Ø 2)	TOTAL AVAILABLE	
D	5 — 100	4 — X	3 — X	100	X̶
E	8	4 — 200	3	300	X̶ 5
F	9	7 — X	5	300	X̶ 4
TOTAL REQUIRED	300	200	200	700	

TABLE 14.14 Third VAM Assignment with C's Requirements Satisfied

FROM \ TO	A	B	C	TOTAL AVAILABLE
D	5 100	4 X	3 X	100
E	8 X	4 200	3 100	300
F	9 X	7	5	300
TOTAL REQUIRED	300	200	200	700

supply restrictions (in the rows) and demand requirements (in the columns). We see that an assignment of 200 units to *F–A* and 100 units to *F–C* completes the table (see Table 14.15).

The cost of this VAM assignment is = (100 units × \$5) + (200 units × \$4) + (100 units × \$3) + (200 units × \$9) + (100 units × \$5) = \$3,900.

It is worth noting that the use of Vogel's approximation method on the

TABLE 14.15 Final Assignments to Balance Column and Row Requirements

FROM \ TO	A	B	C	TOTAL AVAILABLE
D	5 100	4 X	3 X	100
E	8 X	4 200	3 100	300
F	9 200	7 X	5 100	300
TOTAL REQUIRED	300	200	200	700

APPLICATIONS OF QA

Assigning and Transporting Naval Recruits to Bases in Thailand

When a man is called into the Thai Navy, he first reports to a drafting center in his home locality. Then he is transported by land vehicle to a naval base. If the draftee is from a northern province, he is taken to the main naval base in Satahep, near Bangkok. If the draftee is from a southern province, he is first brought overland to a branch naval base and then transported by ship to the main base. There are 36 drafting centers and 4 branch bases in the southern provinces. A major problem is deciding how many men from each drafting center should be assigned and transported to each branch base.

The data available to solve this problem are: (1) the number of men to be transported from each drafting center, (2) the capacity (in number of men) of each branch base, and (3) the cost per man for transportation between each drafting center and each branch base. The number of men to be transported between each drafting center and each base was determined using a standard *transportation model*. The results of the transportation analysis also provide the number of men assigned to each branch base.

According to Captain C. Israngkul, Royal Thai naval attaché, the results from the transportation model are superior to results obtained through the manual procedures currently employed. The manual procedure is to just send each man to the nearest base. Sometimes this procedure works; however, in other instances, it has resulted in violations of base capacities, making it necessary to transport men from oversubscribed bases to undersubscribed bases. By using the optimization model, the cost and time delays of these extra trips can be avoided.

Source: P. Choypeng, P. Puakpong, and R. E. Rosenthal, "Optimal Ship Routing and Personnel Assignment for Naval Recruitment in Thailand," *Interfaces*, Vol. 16, No. 4, July–August 1986, pp. 47–52.

VAM may yield optimal solution

Executive Furniture Corporation data produces the optimal solution to this problem. Even though VAM takes many more calculations to find an initial solution than does the northwest corner rule, it almost always produces a much better initial solution. Hence, VAM tends to minimize the total number of computations needed to reach an optimal solution.

14.7
UNBALANCED TRANSPORTATION PROBLEMS

> KEY IDEA

dummy sources or destinations

A situation occurring quite frequently in real-life problems is the case where total demand is not equal to total supply. These *unbalanced problems* can be handled easily by the preceding solution procedures if we first introduce *dummy sources* or *dummy destinations*. In the event that total supply is greater than total demand, a dummy destination (warehouse), with demand exactly equal to the surplus, is created. If total demand is greater than total supply, we introduce a dummy source (factory) with a supply equal to the excess of demand over supply. In either case, shipping cost coefficients of zero are assigned to each dummy location or route because no shipments will actually be made from a dummy factory or to a dummy warehouse.

Demand Less Than Supply

Considering the original Executive Furniture Corporation problem, suppose that the Des Moines factory increases its rate of production to 250 desks. (That factory's capacity used to be 100 desks per production period.)

The firm is now able to supply a total of 850 desks each period. Warehouse requirements, however, remain the same (at 700 desks), so the row and column totals do not balance.

To balance this type of problem, we simply add a dummy column which will represent a fake warehouse requiring 150 desks. This is somewhat analogous to adding a slack variable in solving a linear programming problem. And just as slack variables were assigned a value of 0 dollars in the LP objective function, the shipping costs to this dummy warehouse are all set equal to 0.

The northwest corner rule is used once again, in Table 14.16, to find an initial solution to this modified Executive Furniture problem. As you can see, expanding capacity at Des Moines has decreased total cost. If you wanted to complete this task and find an optimal solution, either stepping-stone or MODI methods would now be employed.

Note that the 150 units from Fort Lauderdale to the dummy warehouse represent 150 units that are *not* shipped from Fort Lauderdale.

Demand Greater Than Supply

The second type of unbalanced condition occurs when total demand is greater than total supply. This means that customers or warehouses require

TABLE 14.16 Initial Solution to an Unbalanced Problem Where Demand Is Less Than Supply

FROM \ TO	ALBUQUER-QUE A	BOSTON B	CLEVELAND C	DUMMY WAREHOUSE	FACTORY CAPACITY
DES MOINES D	5 / 250	4	3	0	250 (← New Des Moines capacity)
EVANSVILLE E	8 / 50	4 / 200	3 / 50	0	300
FORT LAUDERDALE F	9	7	5 / 150	0 / 150	300
WAREHOUSE REQUIRE-MENTS	300	200	200	150	850

Total cost = 250($5) + 50($8) + 200($4) + 50($3) + 150($5) + 150($0) = $3,350

more of a product than the firm's factories can provide. In this case, we need to add a dummy row representing a fake factory. The new factory will have a supply exactly equal to the difference between total demand and total real supply. The shipping costs from the dummy factory to each destination will be 0.

Let us set up such an unbalanced problem for the Happy Sound Stereo Company. Happy Sound assembles high-fidelity stereophonic systems at three plants and distributes through three regional warehouses. The production capacities at each plant, demand at each warehouse, and unit shipping costs are presented in Table 14.17.

As can be seen in Table 14.18, a dummy plant adds an extra row, balances the problem, and allows us to apply the northwest corner rule to find the initial solution shown. This initial solution shows 50 units being shipped from the dummy plant to warehouse C. This means that warehouse C will be 50 units short of its requirements. In general, any units shipped from a dummy source represent unmet demand at the respective destination.

14.8
DEGENERACY IN TRANSPORTATION PROBLEMS

We briefly mentioned the subject of *degeneracy* earlier in this chapter. Degeneracy occurs when the number of occupied squares or routes in a transportation table solution is less than the number of rows plus the number of columns minus 1. Such a situation may arise in the initial solution or in

TABLE 14.17 Unbalanced Transportation Table for Happy Sound Stereo Company

FROM \ TO	WAREHOUSE A	WAREHOUSE B	WAREHOUSE C	PLANT SUPPLY
PLANT W	$6	$4	$9	200
PLANT X	$10	$5	$8	175
PLANT Y	$12	$7	$6	75
WAREHOUSE DEMAND	250	100	150	500 / 450

Totals do not balance

APPLICATIONS OF QA

Moving Sand with the Transportation Approach

Most large construction and civil engineering projects require the transportation of gravel, rock, sand, and other materials from one location to another. The modification of the Brisbane International Airport in Australia posed such a problem. Sand from nearby bay areas was to be moved to various parts of the airport site and used as a fill. This became a classic transportation problem involving the shipment of sand, in this case, from various sources to various destinations.

The estimated quantity of sand to be moved in total was approximately 1.8 million cubic meters.

Source: Mervyn Lawrence and Chad Perry, "Earthmoving On Construction Projects: A Postscript," *Interfaces*, Vol. 14, No. 2, March–April 1984, pp. 84–86.

There were about 26 sources or sites and about 35 final fill destinations that were identified. In addition to cost and distance factors, there was also a time factor. Sand could not be removed from the initial reclaimed areas or sites until one year after it was placed at the sites. Final dates for sand removal were also set by the construction program and the construction schedule. As a result of some of these time constraints, an approach called the out-of-kilter algorithm (OKA) was used to solve this transportation problem. It was estimated that using this algorithm and this transportation approach saved approximately $802,044, which represented about 27% of the total hauling component for the project.

TABLE 14.18 Initial Solution to an Unbalanced Problem Where Demand Is Greater Than Supply

FROM \ TO	WAREHOUSE A	WAREHOUSE B	WAREHOUSE C	PLANT SUPPLY
PLANT W	6 200	4	9	200
PLANT X	10 50	5 100	8 25	175
PLANT Y	12	7	6 75	75
DUMMY	0	0	0 50	50
WAREHOUSE DEMAND	250	100	150	500

Total cost of initial solution = 200($6) + 50($10) + 100($5) + 25($8) + 75($6) + 50($0)
= $2,850

any subsequent solution. Degeneracy requires a special procedure in order to correct the problem. Without enough occupied squares to trace a closed path for each unused route, it would be impossible to apply the stepping-stone method or to calculate the R and K values needed for the MODI technique. You might recall that no problem discussed in Chapter 14 thus far has been degenerate.

KEY IDEA

To handle degenerate problems, we create an artificially occupied cell—that is, we place a 0 (representing a fake shipment) in one of the unused squares and then treat that square as if it were occupied. The square chosen must be in such a position as to allow *all* stepping-stone paths to be closed, although there is usually a good deal of flexibility in selecting the unused square that will receive the 0.

Degeneracy in an Initial Solution

Degeneracy can occur in our application of the northwest corner rule to find an initial solution, as we see in the case of the Martin Shipping Company. Martin has three warehouses from which to supply its three major retail customers in San Jose. Martin's shipping costs, warehouse supplies, and customer demands are presented in Table 14.19. Note that origins in this problem are warehouses and destinations are retail stores. Initial shipping assignments are made in the table by application of the northwest corner rule.

This initial solution is degenerate because it violates the rule that the number of used squares must be equal to the number of rows plus the

TABLE 14.19 Initial Solution of a Degenerate Problem

FROM \ TO	CUSTOMER 1	CUSTOMER 2	CUSTOMER 3	WAREHOUSE SUPPLY
WAREHOUSE 1	8 — 100	2	6	100
WAREHOUSE 2	10	9 — 100	9 — 20	120
WAREHOUSE 3	7	10	7 — 80	80
CUSTOMER DEMAND	100	100	100	300

number of columns minus 1 (namely, $3 + 3 - 1 = 5$ is greater than the number of occupied boxes). In this particular problem, degeneracy arose because both a column and a row requirement (that being column 1 and row 1) were satisfied simultaneously. This broke the stair-step pattern we usually see with northwest corner solutions.

To correct the problem, we may place a 0 in an unused square. In this case, those squares representing either the shipping route from warehouse 1 to customer 2 or from warehouse 2 to customer 1 will do. If you treat the new 0 square just like any other occupied square, any of the regular solution methods can be used.

Degeneracy During Later Solution Stages

A transportation problem can become degenerate *after* the initial solution stage if adding an unused square results in the elimination of two previously occupied routes, instead of eliminating the usual *one*. Such a problem occurs when two squares assigned minus signs on a closed path both have the same quantity.

After one iteration of the stepping-stone method, cost analysts at Bagwell Paint produced the following transportation table (see Table 14.20). We observe that the solution in Table 14.20 is not degenerate, but it is also not optimal.

TABLE 14.20 Bagwell Paint Transportation Table

FROM \ TO	WAREHOUSE 1	WAREHOUSE 2	WAREHOUSE 3	FACTORY CAPACITY
FACTORY A	8 70	5	16	70
FACTORY B	15 50	10 80	7	130
FACTORY C	3 30	9	10 50	80
WAREHOUSE REQUIREMENT	150	80	50	280

Total shipping cost = $2,700

TABLE 14.21 Tracing a Closed Path for the Factory B–Warehouse 3 Route

FROM \ TO	WAREHOUSE 1	WAREHOUSE 3
FACTORY B	15 50 − ← − − − +	7
FACTORY C	3 30 + − − − → − 50	10

The improvement indices for the four currently unused squares are:

Factory A – Warehouse 2 index = + 2
Factory A – Warehouse 3 index = + 1
Factory B – Warehouse 3 index = − 15 ← *Only route with a negative index*
Factory C – Warehouse 2 index = +11

Hence, an improved solution may be obtained by opening the route from factory B to warehouse 3. Let us go through the stepping-stone procedure for finding the next solution to Bagwell Paint's problem. We begin by drawing a closed path for the unused square representing factory B–warehouse 3. This is shown in Table 14.21, which is an abbreviated version of Table 14.20 and contains only the factories and warehouses necessary to close the path.

Since the smallest quantity in a square containing a minus sign is 50, we assign 50 units to the factory B–warehouse 3 and factory C–warehouse 1 routes, and subtract 50 units from the two squares containing minus signs. However, this act causes both formerly occupied squares to drop to 0. It also means that there are not enough occupied squares in the new solution and that it will be degenerate. We will have to place an artificial 0 in one of the squares (generally, the one with the lowest shipping cost) in order to handle the degeneracy problem.

14.9
MORE THAN ONE OPTIMAL SOLUTION

KEY IDEA

Just as with linear programming problems, it is possible for a transportation problem to have multiple optimal solutions. Such a situation is indicated when one or more of the improvement indices that we calculate for each unused square is 0 in the optimal solution. This means that it is possible to design alternate shipping routings with the same total shipping cost. The alternate optimal solution can be found by shipping the most to this unused square. Practically speaking, multiple optimal solutions provide management with greater flexibility in selecting and using resources.

14.10
COMPUTER SOLUTIONS TO THE TRANSPORTATION PROBLEM

Computer programs exist to solve not only linear programming problems, but the less complicated transportation problems as well. In this section, we illustrate how both our AB:QM microcomputer software program (see Program 14.1) and STORM (see Program 14.2) handle transportation problems. Note that the problem need not be balanced before the data are entered. The computer programs are demonstrated on a small problem involving allocation of shipments from three factories to three warehouses. All appropriate costs and shipment data are summarized in Table 14.22 (on p. 542).

PROGRAM 14.1 Sample Transportation Model Computer Run Using AB:QM

```
Transportation

 Problem Title :  SAMPLE TRANSPORTATION RUN, TABLE 14.22
 Type of Problem  (Max=1/Min=2)  2      Initial  (NW=1/MC=2/VAM=3)   1
 Number of Sources              3       Number of Destinations       3


           D1        D2        D3     Sources
 S1        200       600       300        8
 S2        400       200       700       11
 S3        500       800       300       12
 Des.       10        12         9       31







 Help  New  Load  Save  Edit  Run  Print  Install  Directory  Esc
```

PROGRAM 14.1 (Continued)

```
Program: Transportation

Problem Title : SAMPLE TRANSPORTATION RUN, TABLE 14.22

***** Input Data *****

Minimization Problem:

           |         1          2          3|    Supply
---------------------------------------------------------
   1       |     200.0      600.0      300.0|      8.0
   2       |     400.0      200.0      700.0|     11.0
   3       |     500.0      800.0      300.0|     12.0
---------------------------------------------------------
Demand|        10.0       12.0        9.0|     31.0


***** Program Output *****


Initial Solution by Northwest Corner Method
           |         1          2          3|    Supply
---------------------------------------------------------
   1       |       8.0        0.0        0.0|      8.0
   2       |       2.0        9.0        0.0|     11.0
   3       |       0.0        3.0        9.0|     12.0
---------------------------------------------------------
Demand|        10.0       12.0        9.0|     31.0

Initial Solution    :        9300.0


Optimal Solution by MODI
           |         1          2          3|    Supply
---------------------------------------------------------
   1       |       8.0        0.0        0.0|      8.0
   2       |       0.0       11.0        0.0|     11.0
   3       |       2.0        1.0        9.0|     12.0
---------------------------------------------------------
Demand|        10.0       12.0        9.0|     31.0

Optimal Solution    :        8300.0


***** End of Output *****
```

PROGRAM 14.2 STORM Program Output on Table 14.22

```
─────────── STORM EDITOR : Transportation Module ───────────

Title : SAMPLE RUN OF STORM ON TABLE 14.22 DATA

Capacitated (CAP/UNCP)      :    UNCP   Number of rows          :      3
Number of columns           :      3    Objective type (MAX/MIN) :    MIN
Bounds(ROW/COL/BOTH/NONE)   :    NONE
─────────────────────────────────────────────────────────────

R2  : C1    COLUMN   1 COLUMN   2 COLUMN   3    DUMMY    SUPPLY
ROW    1        200.      600.      300.         ¦         8
ROW    2        400.      200.      700.         ¦        11
ROW    3        500.      800.      300.         ¦        12
DUMMY          ----      ----      ----         ----      ----
DEMAND           10        12         9          ¦        XXXX


F1 Block  F2 GoTo  F3 InsR  F4 DelR  F5 InsC  F6 DelC  F7 Done  F8 Help KB:C
```

                SAMPLE RUN OF STORM ON TABLE 14.22 DATA
          TRANSPORTATION - OPTIMAL SOLUTION - TABLEAU OUTPUT

```
              COLUMN 1   COLUMN 2   COLUMN 3   U(I)\SUPPLY
            +--------+---------+--------+
    ROW 1   |200.000 |600.000  |300.000 |0.000
            |      8 | 100.000 | 300.000 |      8
            +--------+---------+--------+
    ROW 2   |400.000 |200.000  |700.000 |-300.000
            | 500.000|        11|1000.000|     11
            +--------+---------+--------+
    ROW 3   |500.000 |800.000  |300.000 |300.000
            |      2 |       1 |       9 |    12
            +--------+---------+--------+
    V(J)    200.000   500.000   0.000
    DEMAND     10        12        9
```

                    Total Cost = 8300.0000

                SAMPLE RUN OF STORM ON TABLE 14.22 DATA
          TRANSPORTATION - OPTIMAL SOLUTION - SUMMARY REPORT

------- Cell ------			Unit	Cell
Row	Column	Amount	Cost	Cost
ROW 1	COLUMN 1	8	200.0000	1600.0000
ROW 1 Subtotal = 1600.0000				
ROW 2	COLUMN 2	11	200.0000	2200.0000
ROW 2 Subtotal = 2200.0000				
ROW 3	COLUMN 1	2	500.0000	1000.0000
ROW 3	COLUMN 2	1	800.0000	800.0000
ROW 3	COLUMN 3	9	300.0000	2700.0000
ROW 3 Subtotal = 4500.0000				

Total Cost = 8300.0000
Number of iterations = 1

TABLE 14.22 Sample Data for Computer Program

FROM \ TO	WAREHOUSE 1	WAREHOUSE 2	WAREHOUSE 3	AMOUNT AVAILABLE
FACTORY 1	200	600	300	8
FACTORY 2	400	200	700	11
FACTORY 3	500	800	300	12
AMOUNT NEEDED	10	12	9	31

14.11
FACILITY LOCATION ANALYSIS

locating a new facility

The transportation method has proved to be especially useful in helping a firm decide where to locate a new factory or warehouse. Since a new location is an issue of major financial importance to a company, several alternative locations must ordinarily be considered and evaluated. Even though a wide variety of subjective factors are considered, including quality of labor supply, presence of labor unions, community attitude and appearance, utilities, and recreational and educational facilities for employees, a final decision also involves minimizing total shipping and production costs. This means that each alternative facility location should be analyzed within the framework of one *overall* distribution system. The new location that will yield the *minimum cost* for the *entire system* will be the one recommended. Let us consider the case of the Hardgrave Machine Company.

Locating a New Factory for Hardgrave Machine Company

The Hardgrave Machine Company produces computer components at its plants in Cincinnati, Salt Lake City, and Pittsburgh. These plants have not been able to keep up with demand for orders at Hardgrave's four warehouses in Detroit, Dallas, New York, and Los Angeles. As a result, the firm has decided to build a new plant to expand its productive capacity.

TABLE 14.23 Hardgrave's Demand and Supply Data

WAREHOUSE	MONTHLY DEMAND (UNITS)	PRODUCTION PLANT	MONTHLY SUPPLY	COST TO PRODUCE ONE UNIT ($)
Detroit	10,000	Cincinnati	15,000	48
Dallas	12,000	Salt Lake	6,000	50
New York	15,000	Pittsburgh	14,000	52
Los Angeles	9,000		35,000	
	46,000			

Supply needed from new plant = 46,000 − 35,000 = 11,000 units per month

ESTIMATED PRODUCTION COST PER UNIT AT PROPOSED PLANTS	
Seattle	$53
Birmingham	$49

The two sites being considered are Seattle and Birmingham, Alabama; both cities are attractive in terms of labor supply, municipal services, and ease of factory financing.

Table 14.23 presents the production costs and output requirements for each of the three existing plants, demand at each of the four warehouses, and estimated production costs of the new proposed plants.

Transportation costs from each plant to each warehouse are summarized in Table 14.24.

TABLE 14.24 Hardgrave's Shipping Costs

FROM \ TO	DETROIT	DALLAS	NEW YORK	LOS ANGELES
CINCINNATI	$25	$55	$40	$60
SALT LAKE	35	30	50	40
PITTSBURGH	36	45	26	66
SEATTLE	60	38	65	27
BIRMINGHAM	35	30	41	50

TABLE 14.25 Birmingham Plant Optimal Solution: Total Hardgrave Cost Is $3,741,000

TO FROM	DETROIT	DALLAS	NEW YORK	LOS ANGELES	MONTHLY SUPPLY
CINCINNATI	73 10,000	103	88 1,000	108 4,000	15,000
SALT LAKE	85	80 1,000	100	90 5,000	6,000
PITTSBURGH	88	97	78 14,000	118	14,000
BIRMINGHAM	84	79 11,000	90	99	11,000
MONTHLY DEMAND	10,000	12,000	15,000	9,000	46,000

**new plant with lowest
system cost**

The important question that Hardgrave now faces is "which of the new locations will yield the lowest cost for the firm in combination with the existing plants and warehouses?" Note that the cost of each individual plant-to-warehouse route is found by adding the shipping costs (in the body of Table 14.24) to the respective unit production costs (from Table 14.23). Thus, the total production plus shipping cost of one computer component from Cincinnati to Detroit is $73 ($25 for shipping plus $48 for production).

To determine which new plant (Seattle or Birmingham) shows the lowest total systemwide cost of distribution and production, we solve two transportation problems—one for each of the two possible combinations. Tables 14.25 and 14.26 show the resulting two optimum solutions with the total cost for each. (We used the computer program to solve each problem.) It appears that Seattle should be selected as the new plant site: its total cost of $3,704,000 is less than the $3,741,000 cost at Birmingham.

14.12
APPROACH OF THE ASSIGNMENT MODEL

The second special purpose LP algorithm to be discussed in this chapter is the assignment method. Each assignment problem has a table, or matrix,

TABLE 14.26 Seattle Plant Optimal Solution: Total Hardgrave Cost Is $3,704,000

FROM \ TO	DETROIT	DALLAS	NEW YORK	LOS ANGELES	MONTHLY SUPPLY
CINCINNATI	73 10,000	103 4,000	88 1,000	108	15,000
SALT LAKE	85	80 6,000	100	90	6,000
PITTSBURGH	88	97	78 14,000	118	14,000
SEATTLE	113	91 2,000	118	80 9,000	11,000
MONTHLY DEMAND	10,000	12,000	15,000	9,000	46,000

associated with it. Generally, the rows contain the objects or people we wish to assign, and the columns comprise the tasks or things we want them assigned to. The numbers in the table are the costs associated with each particular assignment.

assignment table

As an illustration of the assignment method, let us consider the case of the Fix-It Shop, which has just received three new rush projects to repair: (1) a radio, (2) a toaster oven, and (3) a broken coffee table. Three repairmen, each with different talents and abilities, are available to do the jobs. The Fix-It Shop owner estimates what it will cost in wages to assign each of the workers to each of the three projects. The costs, which are shown in Table 14.27, differ because the owner believes each worker will differ in speed and skill on these quite varied jobs.

TABLE 14.27 Estimated Project Repair Costs for the Fix-It Shop Assignment Problem

PERSON	PROJECT 1	PROJECT 2	PROJECT 3
Adams	$11	$14	$ 6
Brown	8	10	11
Cooper	9	12	7

TABLE 14.28 Summary of Fix-It Shop Assignment Alternatives and Costs

PROJECT ASSIGNMENTS			LABOR COSTS ($)	TOTAL COSTS $
1	2	3		
Adams	Brown	Cooper	11 + 10 + 7	28
Adams	Cooper	Brown	11 + 12 + 11	34
Brown	Adams	Cooper	8 + 14 + 7	29
Brown	Cooper	Adams	8 + 12 + 6	26
Cooper	Adams	Brown	9 + 14 + 11	34
Cooper	Brown	Adams	9 + 10 + 6	25

enumeration of solutions

The owner's objective is to assign the three projects to the workers in a way that will result in the lowest total cost to the shop. Note that the assignment of people to projects must be on a one-to-one basis; each project will be assigned exclusively to one worker only. Hence, the number of rows must always equal the number of columns in an assignment problem's cost table.

Since the Fix-It Shop problem only consists of three workers and three projects, one easy way to find the best solution is to list all possible assignments and their respective costs. For example, if Adams is assigned to project 1, Brown to project 2, and Cooper to project 3, the total cost will be $11 + $10 + $7 = $28. Table 14.28 summarizes all six assignment options.

The table also shows that the least-cost solution would be to assign Cooper to project 1, Brown to project 2, and Adams to project 3, at a total cost of $25.

Obtaining solutions by enumeration works well for small problems, but quickly becomes inefficient as assignment problems become larger. For example, a problem involving the assignment of four workers to four projects requires that we consider 4! (= 4 × 3 × 2 × 1) or 24 alternatives. A problem with eight workers and eight tasks, which actually is not that large in a realistic situation, yields 8! (= 8 × 7 × 6 × 5 × 4 × 3 × 2 × 1) or 362,880 possible solutions! Since it would clearly be impractical to compare so many alternatives, a more efficient solution method is needed.

The Hungarian Method (Flood's Technique)

opportunity costs

The Hungarian method of assignment provides us with an efficient means of finding the optimal solution without having to make a direct comparison of every option. It operates on a principle of *matrix reduction,* which means that by subtracting and adding appropriate numbers in the cost table or matrix, we can reduce the problem to a matrix of *opportunity costs.* Opportunity costs show the relative penalties associated with assigning *any* person to a project as opposed to making the *best* or least-cost assignment. If we can reduce the matrix to the point where there is one 0 element in each row and column, it will then be possible to make optimal assignments, that is, assignments in which all of the opportunity costs are 0.

There are basically three steps in the assignment method.[3]

1. *Find the opportunity cost table* by
   (a) Subtracting the smallest number in each row of the original cost table or matrix from every number in that row, and
   (b) Then subtracting the smallest number in each column of the table obtained in part a from every number in that column.

2. *Test the table resulting from step 1 to see whether an optimal assignment can be made.* The procedure is to draw the minimum number of vertical and horizontal straight lines necessary to cover all zeros in the table. If the number of lines equals either the number of rows or columns in the table, then an optimal assignment can be made. If the number of lines is less than the number of rows or columns, we proceed to step 3.

3. *Revise the present opportunity cost table.* This is done by subtracting the smallest number not covered by a line from every other uncovered number. This same smallest number is also added to any number(s) lying at the intersection of horizontal and vertical lines. We then return to step 2 and continue the cycle until an optimal assignment is possible.

steps of assignment method

This assignment "algorithm" is not nearly as difficult to apply as the linear programming algorithm we discussed in Chapters 10–13, or even as complex as the transportation procedures we saw earlier in this chapter. All it requires is some careful addition and subtraction and close attention to the three preceding steps. These steps are charted for your convenience in Figure 14.3. Let us now apply them.

assignment method easier than LP

Step 1: Find the Opportunity Cost Table. As we mentioned earlier, the opportunity cost of any decision we make in life consists of the opportunities that are sacrificed in making that decision. For example, the opportunity cost of the unpaid time a person spends starting a new business is the salary that person would earn for those hours he or she could have worked on another job. This important concept in the assignment method is best illustrated by applying it to a problem. For your convenience, the original cost table for the Fix-It Shop problem is repeated in Table 14.29 (on p. 549).

Suppose we decide to assign Cooper to project 2. The table shows that the cost of this assignment is $12. Based on the concept of opportunity costs, this is not the best decision, since Cooper could perform project 3 for only $7. The assignment of Cooper to project 2 then involves an opportunity cost of $5 (= $12 − $7), the amount we are sacrificing by making this assignment instead of the least-cost one. Similarly, an assignment of Cooper to project 1 represents an opportunity cost of $9 − $7 = $2. Finally, since the assignment of Cooper to project 3 is the best assignment, we can say that the opportunity cost of this assignment is 0 ($7 − $7). The results

row opportunity costs

[3] The steps apply if we can assume the matrix is balanced, that is, the number of rows in the matrix equals the number of columns. In Section 14.13 we discuss how to handle unbalanced problems.

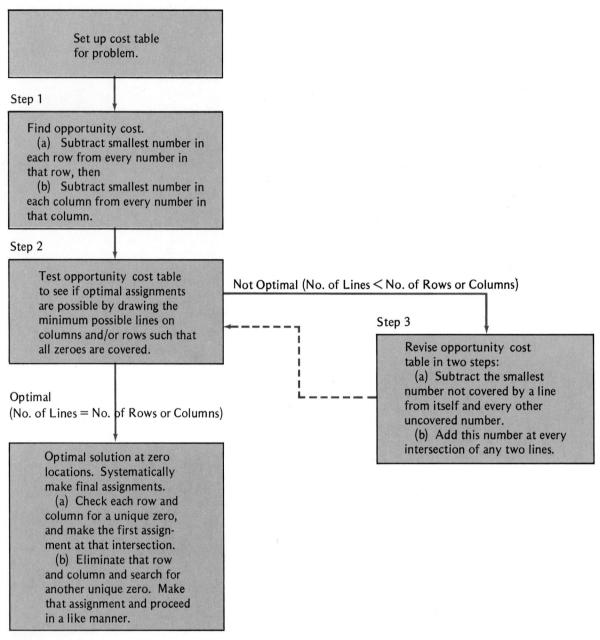

FIGURE 14.3
Steps in the Assignment Method

of this operation for each of the rows in Table 14.29 are called the *row opportunity costs* and are shown in Table 14.30.

We note at this point that, although the assignment of Cooper to project 3 is the cheapest way to make use of Cooper, it is not necessarily the least-expensive approach to completing project 3. Adams can perform the same task for only $6. In other words, if we look at this assignment problem

column opportunity costs

TABLE 14.29 Cost of Each Person-Project Assignment for the Fix-It Shop Problem

PERSON	PROJECT		
	1	2	3
Adams	$11	$14	$ 6
Brown	8	10	11
Cooper	9	12	7

total opportunity costs

from a project angle, instead of a people angle, the *column* opportunity costs may be completely different.

What we need to complete step 1 of the assignment method is a *total* opportunity cost table, that is, one that reflects both row and column opportunity costs. This involves following part b of step 1 to derive column opportunity costs.[4] We simply take the costs in Table 14.30 and subtract the smallest number in each column from each number in that column. The resulting total opportunity costs are given in Table 14.31.

You might note that the numbers in columns 1 and 3 are the same as those in Table 14.30, since the smallest column entry in each case was 0. Thus, it may turn out that the assignment of Cooper to project 3 is part of the optimal solution because of the relative nature of opportunity costs. What we are trying to measure are the relative efficiencies for the entire cost table and to find what assignments are best for the overall solution.

TABLE 14.30 Row Opportunity Cost Table for the Fix-It Shop Step 1, Part a

PERSON	PROJECT		
	1	2	3
Adams	5	8	0
Brown	0	2	3
Cooper	2	5	0

TABLE 14.31 Total Opportunity Cost Table for the Fix-It Shop Step 1, Part b

PERSON	PROJECT		
	1	2	3
Adams	5	6	0
Brown	0	0	3
Cooper	2	3	0

[4] Can you think of a situation in which part b of step 1 would not be required? See if you can design a cost table in which an optimal solution is possible after part a of step 1 is completed.

Step 2: Test for an Optimal Assignment. The objective of the Fix-It Shop owner is to assign the three workers to the repair projects in such a way that total labor costs are kept at a minimum. When translated to making assignments using our total opportunity cost table, this means that we would like to have a total assigned opportunity cost of 0. In other words, an optimal solution has 0 opportunity costs for all of the assignments.

Looking at Table 14.31, we see that there are four possible 0 opportunity cost assignments. We could assign Adams to project 3 and Brown to either project 1 or project 2. But this leaves Cooper without a 0 opportunity cost assignment. Recall that two workers cannot be given the same task; each must do one and only one repair project, and each project must be assigned to only one person. Hence, even though four 0s appear in this cost table, it is not yet possible to make an assignment yielding a total opportunity cost of 0.

A simple test has been designed to help us determine whether an optimal assignment can be made. The method consists of finding the *minimum* number of straight lines (vertical and horizontal) necessary to cover all 0s in the cost table. (Each line is drawn so that it covers as many 0s as possible at one time.) If the number of lines equals the number of rows or columns in the table, then an optimal assignment can be made. If, on the other hand, the number of lines is less than the number of rows or columns, an optimal assignment cannot be made. In this latter case, we must proceed to step 3 and develop a new total opportunity cost table.

Table 14.32 illustrates that it is possible to cover all four 0 entries in Table 14.31 with only two lines. Because there are three rows, an optimal assignment may not yet be made.

Step 3: Revise the Opportunity-Cost Table. An optimal solution is seldom obtained from the initial opportunity cost table. Often, we need to revise the table in order to shift one (or more) of the 0 costs from its present location (covered by lines) to a new uncovered location in the table. Intuitively, we would want this uncovered location to emerge with a new 0 opportunity cost.

This is accomplished by *subtracting* the smallest number not covered by a line from all numbers not covered by a straight line. This same smallest number is then added to every number (including 0s) lying at the intersection of any two lines.

The smallest uncovered number in Table 14.32 is 2, so this value is

TABLE 14.32 Test for Optimal Solution to Fix-It Shop Problem

	PROJECT		
PERSON	1	2	3
Adams	5	6	0
Brown	0	0	0 → Covering line 1
Cooper	2	3	0

Covering line 2

optimal solution at 0 opportunity costs

line test to see if solution is optimal

TABLE 14.33 Revised Opportunity Cost Table for the Fix-It Shop Problem

	PROJECT		
PERSON	1	2	3
Adams	3	4	0
Brown	0	0	5
Cooper	0	1	0

TABLE 14.34 Optimality Test on the Revised Fix-It Shop Opportunity Cost Table

	PROJECT			
PERSON	1	2	3	
Adams	3	4	0	
Brown	0	0	5	→ Covering line 2
Cooper	0	1	0	
	Covering line 1		Covering line 3	

subtracted from each of the four uncovered numbers. A 2 is also added to the number that is covered by the intersecting horizontal and vertical lines. The results of step 3 are shown in Table 14.33.

To test now for an optimal assignment, we return to step 2 and find the minimum number of lines necessary to cover all 0s in the revised opportunity cost table. Since it requires three lines to cover the zeroes (see Table 14.34), an optimal assignment can be made.

Making the Final Assignment

It is apparent that the Fix-It Shop problem's optimal assignment is Adams to project 3, Brown to project 2, and Cooper to project 1. In solving larger problems, however, it is best to rely on a more systematic approach to making valid assignments. One such way is to first select a row or column that contains only one 0 cell. Such a situation is found in the first row, Adams's row, in which the only 0 is in the project 3 column. An assignment can be made to that cell, and then lines drawn through its row and column

making an optimal assignment

TABLE 14.35 Making the Final Fix-It Shop Assignments

(A) FIRST ASSIGNMENT				(B) SECOND ASSIGNMENT				(C) THIRD ASSIGNMENT			
	1	2	3		1	2	3		1	2	3
Adams	3	4	[0]	Adams	3	4	[0]	Adams	3	4	[0]
Brown	0	0	5	Brown	0	0	5	Brown	0	[0]	5
Cooper	0	1	0	Cooper	[0]	1	0	Cooper	[0]	1	0

(see Table 14.35). From the uncovered rows and columns, we again choose a row or column in which there is only one 0 cell. We make that assignment and continue the procedure until each person is assigned to one task.

The total labor costs of this assignment are computed from the original cost table (see Table 14.29). They are as follows:

ASSIGNMENT	COST ($)
Adams to project 3	6
Brown to project 2	10
Cooper to project 1	9
Total cost	25

14.13
DUMMY ROWS AND DUMMY COLUMNS

The solution procedure to assignment problems just discussed requires that the number of rows in the table equal the number of columns. Often, however, the number of people or objects to be assigned does not equal the number of tasks or clients or machines listed in the columns. When this occurs and we have more rows than columns, we simply add a *dummy column* or task (similar to how we handled unbalanced transportation problems earlier in this chapter). If the number of tasks that need to be done exceeds the number of people available, we add a *dummy row*. This creates a table of equal dimensions and allows us to solve the problem as before. Since the dummy task or person is really nonexistent, it is reasonable to enter zeroes in its row or column as the cost or time estimate.

Suppose the owner of the Fix-It Shop realizes that a fourth worker, Davis, is also available to work on one of the three rush jobs that just came in. Davis can do the first project for $10, the second for $13, and the third project for $8. The shop's owner still faces the same basic problem, that is, which worker to assign to which project in order to minimize total labor costs. Since we do not have a fourth project, however, we simply add a dummy column or dummy project. The initial cost table is shown in Table 14.36. One of the four workers, you should realize, will be assigned to the dummy project; in other words, the worker will not really be assigned any

TABLE 14.36 Estimated Project Repair Costs for Fix-It Shop with Davis Included

PERSON	PROJECT			
	1	2	3	DUMMY
Adams	$11	$14	$ 6	$0
Brown	8	10	11	0
Cooper	9	12	7	0
Davis	10	13	8	0

Scheduling American League Umpires with the Assignment Model

Scheduling umpires in professional baseball is a complex problem that must include a number of criteria. The American Baseball League, like most professional, collegiate, and high school athletic organizations has a supervisor of officials whose major responsibilities include selecting, training, and evaluating officials as well as assigning them to games. In assigning officials to games, one objective typically is to minimize total travel cost while satisfying a set of frequency-oriented constraints such as limiting the number of times an official or crew is exposed to each team, balancing home and away game exposures, balancing exposures to teams over the course of a season, and so on. These constraints complicate the problem to such an extent that, except for the most trivial cases, the use of a computer-based system is essential.

The American League is composed of 14 professional baseball teams organized into Western and Eastern divisions. The Western Division is

comprised of Seattle, Oakland, California, Texas, Kansas City, Minnesota, and Chicago. The Eastern Division is comprised of Milwaukee, Detroit, Cleveland, Toronto, Baltimore, New York, and Boston. The game schedule, constructed each winter prior to the start of the baseball season, is a difficult scheduling problem in itself. Consideration must be given to such factors as the number of games played against other teams both within and outside a division, the split between home games and road trips, travel time, and possible conflicts in cities that have teams in the National League.

The objective of balancing crew assignments relatively evenly and minimizing travel costs are by nature conflicting. Attempting to balance crew assignments necessitates considerable airline travel and equipment moves, and hence increased travel costs.

Using an assignment model as part of a microcomputer-based decision support system, the American League was able to reduce travel mileage by about 4% during the first year of use. This not only saved the league $30,000 but improved the crew exposure balance.

Source: James R. Evans, "Scheduling American League Umpires: A Microcomputer-Based DSS," *Proceedings of the Annual Meeting of the Decision Sciences Institute,* Honolulu, 1986, pp. 914–16.

of the tasks. Problem 14-32 at the end of this chapter asks you to find the optimal solution for the data in Table 14.36.

14.14
MAXIMIZATION ASSIGNMENT PROBLEMS

Some assignment problems are phrased in terms of maximizing the payoff, profit, or effectiveness of an assignment instead of minimizing costs. It is easy to obtain an equivalent minimization problem by converting all numbers in the table to opportunity costs. This is brought about by subtracting every number in the original payoff table from the largest single number in that table. The transformed entries represent opportunity costs; it turns out that minimizing opportunity costs produces the same assignment as the original maximization problem. Once the optimal assignment for this transformed problem has been computed, the total payoff or profit is found by adding the original payoffs of those cells that are in the optimal assignment.

KEY IDEA

Let us consider the following example. The British navy wishes to assign four ships to patrol four sectors of the North Sea. Since in some areas ships are to be on the outlook for illegal fishing boats, and in other sectors to watch for enemy submarines, the commander rates each ship in terms of its probable efficiency in each of the sectors. These relative efficiencies are illustrated in Table 14.37. On the basis of the ratings shown, the commander wants to determine the patrol assignments producing the greatest overall efficiencies.

TABLE 14.37 Efficiencies of British Ships in Patrol Sectors

SHIP	SECTOR			
---	A	B	C	D
1	20	60	50	55
2	60	30	80	75
3	80	100	90	80
4	65	80	75	70

subtract each rating from largest in table

Step by step, the solution procedure is as follows. We first convert the maximizing efficiency table into a minimizing opportunity cost table. This is done by subtracting each rating from 100, the largest rating in the whole table. The resulting opportunity costs are given in Table 14.38.

TABLE 14.38 Opportunity Costs of British Ships

SHIP	SECTOR			
---	A	B	C	D
1	80	40	50	45
2	40	70	20	25
3	20	0	10	20
4	35	20	25	30

We now follow steps 1 and 2 of the assignment algorithm. The smallest number in each row is subtracted from every number in that row (see Table 14.39); and then the smallest number in each column is subtracted from every number in that column (as shown in Table 14.40).

TABLE 14.39 Row Opportunity Costs for the British Navy Problem

row subtractions

SHIP	SECTOR			
---	A	B	C	D
1	40	0	10	5
2	20	50	0	5
3	20	0	10	20
4	15	0	5	10

TABLE 14.40 Total Opportunity Costs for the British Navy Problem

SHIP	SECTOR			
	A	B	C	D
1	25	0	10	0
2	5	50	0	0
3	5	0	10	15
4	0	0	5	5

The minimum number of straight lines needed to cover all 0s in this total opportunity cost table is four. Hence, an optimal assignment can be made already. You should be able by now to spot the best solution, namely, ship 1 to sector D, ship 2 to sector C, ship 3 to sector B, and ship 4 to sector A.

The overall efficiency, computed from the original efficiency data in Table 14.37, can now be shown:

ASSIGNMENT	EFFICIENCY
Ship 1 to sector D	55
Ship 2 to sector C	80
Ship 3 to sector B	100
Ship 4 to sector A	65
Total efficiency	300

14.15
USING THE COMPUTER TO SOLVE ASSIGNMENT PROBLEMS

Computer programs designed to solve the standard assignment problem are as commonly available as are computerized linear programming and transportation problem programs. They are quick and efficient, especially for large assignments. Printouts illustrating both the microcomputer software that accompanies this text (AB:QM) and STORM are provided in Programs 14.3 and 14.4.

computer program for assignment problems

These programs are very flexible and capable of handling unbalanced as well as balanced problems. They can also solve both maximization and minimization problems.

Let us consider the following problem for a computerized assignment. The Carhart Machine Tool Company has three drilling jobs that can each be completed on any of three available drilling machines. The cost of each assignment differs according to job specifications and the age of each machine. Costs are estimated in Table 14.41.

See Program 14.3 for the AB:QM sample run and Program 14.4 for the STORM package output.

TABLE 14.41 Cost Data for Carhart Machine Tool Company

JOB	DRILLING MACHINE		
	1	2	3
1	$100	$60	$80
2	124	80	76
3	140	96	68

PROGRAM 14.3 Computer Solution to the Carhart Machine Tool Problem Using AB:QM

```
Assignment

Problem Title :  CARHART MACHINE TOOL
Type of Problem  (Max=1/Min=2)  2
Number of Rows                  3          Number of Columns      3


            C1          C2          C3
R1         100         60          80
R2         124         80          76
R3         140         96          68




Help  New  Load  Save  Edit  Run  Print  Install  Directory  Esc


Program: Assignment

Problem Title : CARHART MACHINE TOOL

***** Input Data *****

Minimization Problem :

     |    1      2      3
-----------------------------
  1 |  100.0   60.0   80.0
  2 |  124.0   80.0   76.0
  3 |  140.0   96.0   68.0
-----------------------------
```

PROGRAM 14.3 (Continued)

```
***** Program Output *****

Final Revised Cost Table
     !        1        2        3
-----------------------------
  1 !      0.0      0.0     24.0
  2 !      4.0      0.0      0.0
  3 !     28.0     24.0      0.0
-----------------------------


Optimum Solution :       248.0
     !  1  2  3
----------------
  1 !  1  0  0
  2 !  0  1  0
  3 !  0  0  1
----------------


***** End of Output *****
```

PROGRAM 14.4 STORM Solution to Carhart Machine Tool Problem

```
─────────── STORM EDITOR : Assignment Module ───────────

   Title : CARHART MACHINE TOOL COMPANY
   Number of rows          :       3
   Number of columns       :       3
   Objective type (MAX/MIN) :     MIN


   R1  : C3    COLUMN   1 COLUMN   2 COLUMN   3
   ROW   1              100        60        80
   ROW   2              124        80        76
   ROW   3              140        96        68



F1 Block   F2 GoTo   F3 InsR   F4 DelR   F5 InsC   F6 DelC   F7 Done   F8 Help KB:C
```

```
                     REDUCED COST MATRIX

                 COLUMN   1 COLUMN   2 COLUMN   3
                +----------+----------+----------+
          ROW  1 !ASSIGNMENT!        0 !       24 !
                +----------+----------+----------+
          ROW  2 !        4 !ASSIGNMENT!        0 !
                +----------+----------+----------+
          ROW  3 !       28 !       24 !ASSIGNMENT !
                +----------+----------+----------+
```

557

PROGRAM 14.4 (Continued)

```
              CARHART MACHINE TOOL COMPANY
                    OPTIMAL SOLUTION
       Row                  Column           Cost

       ROW   1      COLUMN   1               100
       ROW   2      COLUMN   2                80
       ROW   3      COLUMN   3                68

       Total Cost = 248
       Number of Iterations = 2
```

GLOSSARY

Transportation Problem. A specific case of linear programming concerned with scheduling shipments from sources to destinations so that total transportation costs are minimized.

Source. An origin or supply location in a transportation problem.

Destination. A demand location in a transportation problem.

Transportation Table. A table summarizing all transportation data to help keep track of all algorithm computations. It stores information on demands, supplies, shipping costs, units shipped, origins, and destinations.

Northwest Corner Rule. A systematic procedure for establishing an initial feasible solution to the transportation problem.

Stepping-Stone Method. An iterative technique for moving from an initial feasible solution to an optimal solution in transportation problems.

Improvement Index. The net cost of shipping one unit on a route not used in the current transportation problem solution.

Modified Distribution (MODI) Method. Another algorithm for finding the optimal solution to a transportation problem. It can be used in place of the stepping-stone method.

Vogel's Approximation Method (VAM). An algorithm used to find a relatively efficient initial feasible solution to a transportation problem. This initial solution is often the optimal solution.

Balanced Problem. The condition under which total demand (at all destinations) is equal to total supply (at all sources).

Unbalanced Problem. A situation in which total demand is not equal to total supply.

Dummy Source. An artificial source added when total demand is greater than total supply. The supply at the dummy source is set so that total demand and supply are equal. The transportation cost for dummy source cells is zero.

Dummy Destination. An artificial destination added when total supply is greater than total demand. The demand at the dummy destination is set so that total supply and demand are equal. The transportation cost for dummy destination cells is zero.

Degeneracy. A condition that occurs when the number of occupied squares in any solution is less than the number of rows plus the number of columns minus 1 in a transportation table.

Facility Location Analysis. An application of the transportation method to help a firm decide where to locate a new factory or warehouse.

Matrix Reduction. The approach of the assignment method which reduces the original assignment costs to a table of opportunity costs.

Opportunity Costs. The costs associated with a sacrificed opportunity in order to make a particular decision.

Dummy Rows or Columns. Extra rows or columns added in order to "balance" an assignment problem so that the number of rows equals the number of columns.

KEY EQUATIONS

(14-1) $R_i + K_j = C_{ij}$
An equation used to compute the MODI cost values (R_i, K_j) for each column and row intersection for squares in the solution.

(14-2) Improvement index $= C_{ij} - R_i - K_j$
The equation used to compute the improvement index for each unused square by the MODI method. If all improvement indices are greater than or equal to 0, an optimal solution has been reached.

SOLVED PROBLEMS

Solved Problem 14.1

Don Yale, president of Hardrock Concrete Company, has plants in three locations and is currently working on three major construction projects, located at different sites. The shipping cost per truckload of concrete, plant capacities, and project requirements are provided in the accompanying table.

(a) Formulate an initial feasible solution to Hardrock's transportation problem using the northwest corner rule.

(b) Then evaluate each unused shipping route (each empty cell) by applying the stepping-stone method and computing all improvement indices. Remember to:

1. Check that supply and demand are equal.
2. Load the table via the northwest corner method.
3. Check that there are the proper number of occupied cells for a "normal" solution, namely, number of rows + number of columns − 1 = number of occupied cells.
4. Find a closed path to empty cell.
5. Determine the improvement index for each unused cell.
6. Move as many units as possible to the cell that provides the most improvement (if there is one).
7. Repeat steps 3 through 6 until no further improvement can be found.

TO FROM	PROJECT A	PROJECT B	PROJECT C	PLANT CAPACITY
PLANT 1	$10	$ 4	$11	70
PLANT 2	$12	$ 5	$ 8	50
PLANT 3	$ 9	$ 7	$ 6	30
PROJECT REQUIRE-MENTS	40	50	60	150

Solution

(a) Northwest Corner Solution

$$\text{Initial cost} = 40(\$10) + 30(\$4) + 20(\$5) + 30(\$8) + 30(\$6) = \$1,040$$

To From	Project A	Project B	Project C	Plant capacities
Plant 1	$10 40	$4 30	$11	70
Plant 2	$12	$5 20	$8 30	50
Plant 3	$9	$7	$6 30	30
Project requirements	40	50	60	150

(b) Using the stepping-stone method, the following improvement indices are computed:

$$\text{Path: Plant 1 to project } C = \$11 - \$4 + \$5 - \$8 = +\$4$$
$$(\text{Closed path} = 1C \text{ to } 1B \text{ to } 2B \text{ to } 2C)$$

To From	Project A	Project B	Project C	Plant capacities	
Plant 1	10	4	11	70	Path: plant 1 to project C
Plant 2	12	5	8	50	
Plant 3	9	7	6	30	
Project requirements	40	50	60	150	

Path: Plant 2 to project $A = \$12 - \$5 + \$4 - \$10 = +\$1$
(Closed path = $2A$ to $2B$ to $1B$ to $1A$)

From \ To	Project A	Project B	Project C	Plant capacities
Plant 1	10	4	11	70
Plant 2	12	5	8	50
Plant 3	9	7	6	30
Project requirements	40	50	60	150

Path: plant 2 to project A

Path: Plant 3 to project $A = \$9 - \$6 + \$8 - \$5 + \$4 - \$10 = \$0$
(Closed path = $3A$ to $3C$ to $2C$ to $2B$ to $1B$ to $1A$)

From \ To	Project A	Project B	Project C	Plant capacity
Plant 1	10	4	11	70
Plant 2	12	5	8	50
Plant 3	9	7	6	30
Project requirements	40	50	60	150

Path: plant 3 to project A

Path: Plant 3 to project $B = \$7 - \$6 + \$8 - \$5 = +\$4$
(Closed path = $3B$ to $3C$ to $2C$ to $2B$)

From \ To	Project A	Project B	Project C	Plant capacity
Plant 1	10	4	11	70
Plant 2	12	5	8	50
Plant 3	9	7	6	30
Project requirements	40	50	60	150

Path: plant 3 to project B

Since all indices are greater than or equal to zero (all are positive or 0), this initial solution provides the optimal transportation schedule, namely, 40 units from 1 to A, 30 units from 1 to B, 20 units from 2 to B, 30 units from 2 to C, and 30 units from 3 to C.

Had we found a path that allowed improvement, we would move all units possible to that cell and then check every empty cell again.

Solved Problem 14.2

Use a software package such as LINDO to solve the Hardgrave Machine Company facility location problem seen in Table 14.26 with a linear programming formulation.

Solution

First we shall formulate this transportation problem as an LP model by introducing double-subscripted decision variables. We let X_{11} denote the number of units shipped from origin 1 (Cincinnati) to destination 1 (Detroit), X_{12} denote shipments from origin 1 (Cincinnati) to destination 2 (Dallas), and so on. In general, the decision variables for a transportation problem having m origins and n destinations are written as:

$$X_{ij} = \text{number of units shipped from origin } i \text{ to destination } j$$

where $i = 1, 2, \ldots , m$ and $j = 1, 2, \ldots , n$

Since the objective of the transportation model is to minimize total transportation costs, we develop the following cost expression:

$$
\begin{aligned}
\text{Minimize} = \ & 73X_{11} + 103X_{12} + 88X_{13} + 108X_{14} \\
& + 85X_{21} + 80X_{22} + 100X_{23} + 90X_{24} \\
& + 88X_{31} + 97X_{32} + 78X_{33} + 118X_{34} \\
& + 113X_{41} + 91X_{42} + 118X_{43} + 80X_{44}
\end{aligned}
$$

Now we establish supply constraints for each of the four plants:

$$
\begin{aligned}
X_{11} + X_{12} + X_{13} + X_{14} &\leq 15,000 \ (\textit{Cincinnati supply}) \\
X_{21} + X_{22} + X_{23} + X_{24} &\leq \ \ 6,000 \ (\textit{Salt Lake supply}) \\
X_{31} + X_{32} + X_{33} + X_{34} &\leq 14,000 \ (\textit{Pittsburgh supply}) \\
X_{41} + X_{42} + X_{43} + X_{44} &\leq 11,000 \ (\textit{Seattle supply})
\end{aligned}
$$

With four warehouses as the destinations, we need the following four demand constraints:

$$
\begin{aligned}
X_{11} + X_{21} + X_{31} + X_{41} &= 10,000 \ (\textit{Detroit demand}) \\
X_{12} + X_{22} + X_{32} + X_{42} &= 12,000 \ (\textit{Dallas demand}) \\
X_{13} + X_{23} + X_{33} + X_{43} &= 15,000 \ (\textit{New York demand}) \\
X_{14} + X_{24} + X_{34} + X_{44} &= \ \ 9,000 \ (\textit{Los Angeles demand})
\end{aligned}
$$

In Chapter 12, we saw how LINDO can be used to solve LP problems. We now see that the same program can handle transportation problems as well.

The computer solution in the accompanying program confirms that total shipping costs will be \$3,704,000. With $X_{11} = 10,000$ we see that 10,000 units should be

PROGRAM 14.5 LINDO LP Solution to a Facility Location Problem

```
: LOOK ALL

MIN      73 X11 + 103 X12 + 88 X13 + 108 X14 + 85 X21 + 80 X22 + 100 X23
      + 90 X24 + 88 X31 + 97 X32 + 78 X33 + 118 X34 + 113 X41 + 91 X42
      + 118 X43 + 80 X44
SUBJECT TO
      2)   X11 + X12 + X13 + X14 <=    15000
      3)   X21 + X22 + X23 + X24 <=    6000
      4)   X31 + X32 + X33 + X34 <=    14000
      5)   X42 + X41 + X43 + X44 <=    11000
      6)   X11 + X21 + X31 + X41 =     10000
      7)   X12 + X22 + X32 + X42 =     12000
      8)   X13 + X23 + X33 + X43 =     15000
      9)   X14 + X24 + X34 + X44 =     9000


: GO
LP OPTIMUM FOUND   AT STEP     10

            OBJECTIVE FUNCTION VALUE

  1)          3704000.00

  VARIABLE        VALUE          REDUCED COST
      X11      10000.000000         .000000
      X12       4000.000000         .000000
      X13       1000.000000         .000000
      X14          .000000        16.000000
      X21          .000000        35.000000
      X22       6000.000000         .000000
      X23          .000000        35.000000
      X24          .000000        21.000000
      X31          .000000        25.000000
      X32          .000000         4.000000
      X33      14000.000000         .000000
      X42       2000.000000         .000000
      X34          .000000        36.000000
      X41          .000000        52.000000
      X43          .000000        42.000000
      X44       9000.000000         .000000


      ROW    SLACK OR SURPLUS    DUAL PRICES
--More--
      2)          .000000            .000000
      3)          .000000          23.000000
      4)          .000000          10.000000
      5)          .000000          12.000000
      6)          .000000         -73.000000
      7)          .000000        -103.000000
      8)          .000000         -88.000000
      9)          .000000         -92.000000

NO. ITERATIONS =      10
```

shipped from Cincinnati to Detroit. With $X_{44} = 9,000$, we also see that 9,000 units should be sent from Seattle to Los Angeles. Other answers likewise match with findings in Table 14.26.

Although linear programming codes such as LINDO can indeed be used on transportation problems, the special codes of AB:QM and STORM, illustrated earlier in Programs 14.1 and 14.2, tend to be easier to input, run, and interpret.

Solved Problem 14.3

Allyn and Bacon, Inc., a publisher headquartered in Boston, wants to assign three recently hired college graduates, Jones, Smith, and Wilson to regional sales districts in Omaha, Dallas, and Miami. But the firm also has an opening in New York and would send one of the three there if it were more economical than a move to Omaha, Dallas, or Miami. It will cost $1,000 to relocate Jones to New York, $800 to relocate Smith there, and $1,500 to move Wilson. What is the optimal assignment of personnel to offices?

HIREE \ OFFICE	OMAHA	MIAMI	DALLAS
JONES	$800	$1,100	$1,200
SMITH	$500	$1,600	$1,300
WILSON	$500	$1,000	$2,300

Solution

(a) The cost table has a fourth column to represent New York. To balance the problem, we add a dummy row (person) with a zero relocation cost to each city.

HIREE \ OFFICE	OMAHA	MIAMI	DALLAS	NEW YORK
JONES	$800	$1,100	$1,200	$1,000
SMITH	$500	$1,600	$1,300	$ 800
WILSON	$500	$1,000	$2,300	$1,500
DUMMY	0	0	0	0

(b) Subtract smallest number in each row and cover zeros (column subtraction will give the same numbers and therefore is not necessary).

HIREE \ OFFICE	OMAHA	MIAMI	DALLAS	NEW YORK
JONES	0	300	400	200
SMITH	0	1,100	800	300
WILSON	0	500	1,800	1,000
DUMMY	0	0	0	0

(c) Subtract smallest uncovered number (200), add it to each square where two lines intersect, and cover all zeros.

HIREE \ OFFICE	OMAHA	MIAMI	DALLAS	NEW YORK
JONES	0	100	200	0
SMITH	0	900	600	100
WILSON	0	300	1,600	800
DUMMY	200	0	0	0

(d) Subtract smallest uncovered number (100), add it to each square where two lines intersect, and cover all zeros.

HIREE \ OFFICE	OMAHA	MIAMI	DALLAS	NEW YORK
JONES	0	0	100	0
SMITH	0	800	500	100
WILSON	0	200	1,500	800
DUMMY	300	0	0	100

(e) Subtract smallest uncovered number (100), add it to squares where two lines intersect, and cover all zeros.

HIREE \ OFFICE	OMAHA	MIAMI	DALLAS	NEW YORK
JONES	~~100~~	0	~~100~~	~~0~~
SMITH	~~0~~	700	400	~~0~~
WILSON	~~0~~	100	1,400	~~700~~
DUMMY	400	0	0	~~100~~

(f) Since it takes four lines to cover all zeros, an optimal assignment can be made at zero squares. We assign:

> Dummy (no one) to Dallas
> Wilson to Omaha
> Smith to New York
> Jones to Miami

> Cost = $0 + $500 + $800 + $1,100
> = $2,400

DISCUSSION QUESTIONS AND PROBLEMS

Discussion Questions

14-1 Is the transportation model an example of decision making under certainty or decision making under uncertainty? Why?

14-2 Why does Vogel's approximation method provide a good initial feasible solution? Could the northwest corner rule ever provide an initial solution with as low a cost?

14-3 What is a *balanced* transportation problem? Describe the approach you would use to solve an *unbalanced* problem.

14-4 How do the MODI and stepping-stone methods differ?

14-5 Develop a *northeast* corner rule and explain how it would work. Set up an initial solution to the Executive Furniture Corporation problem shown in Table 14.2 using your new approach. What comment might you make about this initial solution?

14-6 Explain what happens when the solution to a transportation problem does not have $m + n - 1$ occupied squares (where m = number of rows in the table and n = number of columns in the table).

14-7 What is the enumeration approach to solving assignment problems? Is it a practical way to solve a 5 row × 5 column problem? A 7 × 7 problem? Why?

14-8 Think back to the transportation problem in the beginning of this chapter. How could an assignment problem be solved using the transportation approach? Set up the Fix-It Shop problem (shown in Table 14.27) using the transportation approach. What condition will make the solution of this problem difficult?

14-9 You are the plant supervisor and are responsible for scheduling workers to jobs on hand. After estimating the cost of assigning each of five available workers in your plant to five projects that must be completed immediately, you solve the problem using the Hungarian method. The following solution is reached and you post these job assignments:

> Jones to project A
> Smith to project B
> Thomas to project C
> Gibbs to project D
> Heldman to project E

The optimal cost was found to be $492 for these assignments.

The plant general manager inspects your original cost estimates and informs you that increased employee benefits mean that each of the 25 numbers in your cost table is too low by $5. He suggests that you immediately rework the problem and post the new assignments.

Is this necessary? Why? What will the new optimal cost be?

14-10 Sue Simmons's marketing research firm has local representatives in all but five states. She decides to expand to cover the whole United States by transferring five experienced volunteers from their current locations to new offices in each of the five states. Simmons's goal is to relocate the five representatives at the least total cost. Consequently, she sets up a 5 × 5 relocation cost table and prepares to solve it for the best assignment by use of the Hungarian method. At the last moment, Simmons recalls that, although the first four volunteers did not pose any objections to being placed in any of the five new cities, the fifth volunteer *did* make one restriction. That person absolutely refused to be assigned to the new office in Tallahassee, Florida—fear of Southern roaches, the representative claimed! How should Sue Simmons alter the cost matrix to assure that this assignment is not included in the optimal solution?

Problems

· **14-11** The management of the Executive Furniture Corporation decided to expand the production capacity at its Des Moines factory and to cut back production at its other factories. It also recognizes a shifting market for its desks and revises the requirements at its three warehouses.

NEW WAREHOUSE REQUIREMENTS		NEW FACTORY CAPACITIES	
Albuquerque (A)	200 desks	Des Moines (D)	300 desks
Boston (B)	200 desks	Evansville (E)	150 desks
Cleveland (C)	300 desks	Fort Lauderdale (F)	250 desks

(a) Use the northwest corner rule to establish an initial feasible shipping schedule and calculate its cost.

(b) Use the stepping-stone method to test whether an improved solution is possible.

TO FROM	ALBUQUERQUE	BOSTON	CLEVELAND
DES MOINES	5	4	3
EVANSVILLE	8	4	3
FORT LAUDERDALE	9	7	5

(c) Explain the meaning and implications of an improvement index that is equal to 0. What decisions might management make with this information? Exactly how is the final solution affected?

: **14-12** The Hardrock Concrete Company has plants in three locations and is currently working on three major construction projects, each located at a different site. The shipping cost per truckload of concrete, daily plant capacities, and daily project requirements are provided in the accompanying table.

TO FROM	PROJECT A	PROJECT B	PROJECT C	PLANT CAPACITY
PLANT 1	$10	$ 4	$11	70
PLANT 2	12	5	8	50
PLANT 3	9	7	6	30
PROJECT REQUIREMENTS	40	50	60	150

(a) Formulate an initial feasible solution to Hardrock's transportation problem using the northwest corner rule. Then evaluate each unused shipping route by computing all improvement indices. Is this solution optimal? Why?

(b) Is there more than one optimal solution to this problem? Why?

: **14-13** Hardrock Concrete's owner has decided to increase the capacity at his smallest plant (see Problem 14.12). Instead of producing 30 loads of concrete per day at plant 3, that plant's capacity is doubled to 60 loads.

Find the new optimal solution using the northwest corner rule and stepping-stone method. How has changing the third plant's capacity altered the optimal shipping assignment? Discuss the concepts of degeneracy and multiple optimal solutions with regard to this problem.

· **14-14** The Saussy Lumber Company ships pine flooring to three building supply houses from its mills in Pineville, Oak Ridge, and Mapletown. Determine the best transportation schedule for the data given in the accompanying table. Use the northwest corner rule and the stepping-stone method.

FROM \ TO	SUPPLY HOUSE 1	SUPPLY HOUSE 2	SUPPLY HOUSE 3	MILL CAPACITY (TONS)
PINEVILLE	$3	$3	$2	25
OAK RIDGE	4	2	3	40
MAPLETOWN	3	2	3	30
SUPPLY HOUSE DEMAND (TONS)	30	30	35	95

· **14-15** Using the same Saussy Lumber Company data and the same initial solution you found with the northwest corner rule, resolve Problem 14-14 using the MODI method.

 : **14-16** The Krampf Lines Railway Company specializes in coal handling. On Friday, April 13, Krampf had empty cars at the following towns in the quantities indicated.

TOWN	SUPPLY OF CARS
Morgantown	35
Youngstown	60
Pittsburgh	25

By Monday, April 16, the following towns will need coal cars as follows:

TOWN	DEMAND FOR CARS
Coal Valley	30
Coaltown	45
Coal Junction	25
Coalsburg	20

Using a railway city-to-city distance chart, the dispatcher constructs a mileage table for the preceding towns. The result is:

	TO			
FROM	COAL VALLEY	COALTOWN	COAL JUNCTION	COALSBURG
Morgantown	50	30	60	70
Youngstown	20	80	10	90
Pittsburgh	100	40	80	30

Minimizing total miles over which cars are moved to new locations, compute the best shipment of coal cars. Use the northwest corner rule and the MODI method.

: **14-17** The Jessie Cohen Clothing Group owns factories in three towns (W, Y, and Z) which distribute to three Cohen retail dress shops (in A, B, and C). Factory availabilities, projected store demands, and unit shipping costs are summarized in the table that follows.

FROM \ TO	A	B	C	FACTORY AVAILABILITY
W	4	3	3	35
X	6	7	6	50
Y	8	2	5	50
STORE DEMAND	30	65	40	135

Use Vogel's approximation method to find an initial feasible solution to this transportation problem. Is your VAM solution optimal?

: **14-18** The state of Missouri has three major power-generating companies (A, B, and C). During the months of peak demand, the Missouri Power Authority authorizes these companies to pool their excess supply and to distribute it to smaller independent power companies that do not have generators large enough to handle the demand.

Excess supply is distributed on the basis of cost per kilowatt-hour transmitted. The accompanying table shows the demand and supply in millions of kilowatt-hours and the costs per kilowatt-hour of transmitting electric power to four small companies in cities W, X, Y, and Z.

FROM \ TO	W	X	Y	Z	EXCESS SUPPLY
A	12¢	4¢	9¢	5¢	55
B	8¢	1¢	6¢	6¢	45
C	1¢	12¢	4¢	7¢	30
UNFILLED POWER DEMAND	40	20	50	20	

Use Vogel's approximation method to find an initial transmission assignment of the excess power supply. Then apply the MODI technique to find the least cost distribution system.

· **14-19** Consider the following transportation problem.

TO FROM	DESTINATION A	DESTINATION B	DESTINATION C	SUPPLY
SOURCE 1	8	9	4	72
SOURCE 2	5	6	8	38
SOURCE 3	7	9	6	46
SOURCE 4	5	3	7	19
DEMAND	110	34	31	175

Find an initial solution using the northwest corner rule. What special condition exists? Explain how you will proceed to solve the problem.

 : **14-20** The three blood banks in Franklin County are coordinated through a central office which facilitates blood delivery to four hospitals in the region. The cost to ship a standard container of blood from each bank to each hospital is shown in the next table. Also given are the biweekly number of containers available at each bank and the biweekly number of containers of blood needed at each hospital.

How many shipments should be made biweekly from each blood bank to each hospital so that total shipment costs are minimized?

TO FROM	HOSPITAL 1	HOSPITAL 2	HOSPITAL 3	HOSPITAL 4	SUPPLY
BANK 1	8	9	11	16	50
BANK 2	12	7	5	8	80
BANK 3	14	10	6	7	120
DEMAND	90	70	40	50	250

: **14-21** The B. Hall Real Estate Investment Corporation has identified four small apartment buildings in which it would like to invest. Mrs. Hall has approached three savings and loan companies regarding financing. Because Hall has been a good client in the past and has maintained a high credit rating in the community, each savings and loan company is willing to consider providing all or part of the mortgage loan needed on each property. Each loan officer has set differing interest rates on each property (rates are affected by the neighborhood of the apartment building, condition of the property, and desire by the individual savings and loan to finance various size buildings), *and* each loan company has placed a maximum credit ceiling on how much it will lend Hall in total. This information is summarized in the accompanying table.

SAVINGS AND LOAN COMPANY	PROPERTY (INTEREST RATES) (%)				MAXIMUM CREDIT LINE ($)
	HILL ST.	BANKS ST.	PARK AVE.	DRURY LANE	
First Homestead	8	8	10	11	80,000
Commonwealth	9	10	12	10	100,000
Washington Federal	9	11	10	9	120,000
Loan Required to Purchase Building	$60,000	$40,000	$130,000	$70,000	

Each apartment building is equally attractive as an investment to Hall, so she has decided to purchase all buildings possible at the lowest total payment of interest. From which savings and loan companies should she borrow to purchase which buildings? More than one savings and loan can finance the same property.

: **14-22** The J. Mehta Company's production manager is planning for a series of one-month production periods for stainless steel sinks. The demand for the next four months is as follows:

MONTH	DEMAND FOR STAINLESS STEEL SINKS
1	120
2	160
3	240
4	100

The Mehta firm can normally produce 100 stainless steel sinks in a month. This is done during regular production hours at a cost of $100 per sink. If demand in any one month cannot be satisfied by regular production, the production manager has three other choices: (1) he can produce up to 50 more sinks per month in overtime, but at a cost of $130 per sink; (2) he can purchase a limited number of sinks from a friendly competitor for resale (the maximum number of outside purchases over the four-month period is 450 sinks, at a cost of $150 each); or (3) he can fill the demand from his on-hand inventory. The inventory carrying cost is $10 per sink per month. Back orders are not permitted.

Inventory on hand at the beginning of month 1 is 40 sinks.

Set up this "production smoothing" problem as a transportation problem to minimize cost. Use the northwest corner rule to find an initial level for production and outside purchases over the four-month period.

: **14-23** Ashley's Auto Top Carriers currently maintains plants in Atlanta and Tulsa which supply major distribution centers in Los Angeles and New York. Because of an expanding demand, Ashley has decided to open a third plant and has narrowed the choice to one of two cities—New Orleans or Houston. The pertinent production and distribution costs, as well as the plant capacities and distribution demands, are shown in the accompanying table.

TO DISTRIBUTION CENTERS FROM PLANTS	LOS ANGELES	NEW YORK	NORMAL PRODUCTION	UNIT PRODUCTION COST ($)	
ATLANTA	$8	$5	600	6	
TULSA	$4	$7	900	5	
NEW ORLEANS	$5	$6	500	4	(anticipated)
HOUSTON	$4	$6	500	3	(anticipated)
FORECAST DEMAND	800	1,200	2,000		

Existing plants → ATLANTA, TULSA
Proposed locations → NEW ORLEANS, HOUSTON

(Indicates distribution cost (shipping, handling, storage) will be $6 per carrier if sent from Houston to New York)

Which of the new possible plants should be opened?

· **14-24** In a job shop operation, four jobs may be performed on any of four machines. The hours required for each job on each machine are presented in the accompanying table. The plant supervisor would like to assign jobs so that total time is minimized. Use the assignment method to find the best solution.

	MACHINE			
JOB	W	X	Y	Z
A12	10	14	16	13
A15	12	13	15	12
B 2	9	12	12	11
B 9	14	16	18	16

· **14-25** The personnel director of Dollar Finance Corp. must assign three recently hired college graduates to three regional offices. The three new loan officers are equally well qualified, so the decision will be based on the costs of relocating the graduates' families. Cost data are presented in the accompanying table.

OFFICE OFFICER	OMAHA	MIAMI	DALLAS
Jones	$800	$1,100	$1,200
Smith	$500	$1,600	$1,300
Wilson	$500	$1,000	$2,300

Use the assignment algorithm to solve this problem.

· **14-26** The Orange Top Cab Company has a taxi waiting at each of four cab stands in Evanston, Illinois. Four customers have called and requested service. The distances, in miles, from the waiting taxis to the customers are given in the accompanying table. Find the optimal assignment of taxis to customers so as to minimize total driving distances to the customers.

	CUSTOMER			
CAB SITE	A	B	C	D
Stand 1	7	3	4	8
Stand 2	5	4	6	5
Stand 3	6	7	9	6
Stand 4	8	6	7	4

· **14-27** The Burlington Police Department has five detective squads available for assignment to five open crime cases. The chief of detectives wishes to assign the squads so that the total time to conclude the cases is minimized. The average number of days, based on past performance, for each squad to complete each case is as follows:

	CASE				
SQUAD	A	B	C	D	E
1	14	7	3	7	27
2	20	7	12	6	30
3	10	3	4	5	21
4	8	12	7	12	21
5	13	25	24	26	8

Each squad is composed of different types of specialists and, as noted, whereas one squad may be very effective in certain types of cases, they may be almost useless in others. Solve the problem by using the assignment method.

: **14-28** Roscoe Davis, chairman of a college's business department, has decided to apply the Hungarian method in assigning professors to courses next semester. As a criterion for judging who should teach each course, Professor Davis reviews the past two years' teaching evaluations (which were filled out by students). Since each of the four professors taught each of the four courses at one time or another during the two-year period, Davis is able to record a course rating for each instructor. These ratings are shown in the accompanying table. Find the best assignment of professors to courses to maximize the overall teaching rating.

	COURSE			
PROFESSOR	STATISTICS	MANAGEMENT	FINANCE	ECONOMICS
Anderson	90	65	95	40
Sweeney	70	60	80	75
Williams	85	40	80	60
McKinney	55	80	65	55

: **14-29** The hospital administrator at St. Charles General must appoint head nurses to four newly established departments: urology, cardiology, orthopedics, and obstetrics. In anticipation of this staffing problem, she had hired four nurses: Hawkins, Condriac, Bardot, and Hoolihan. Believing in the quantitative analysis approach to problem solving, the administrator has interviewed each nurse, considered her background, personality, and talents, and developed a cost scale ranging from 0 to 100 to be used in the assignment. A 0 for Nurse Bardot being assigned to the cardiology unit implies that she would be perfectly suited to that task. A value close to 100, on the other hand, would imply that she is not at all suited to head that unit. The accompanying table gives the complete set of cost figures that the hospital administrator felt represented all possible assignments. Which nurse should be assigned to which unit?

	DEPARTMENT			
NURSE	Urology	Cardiology	Orthopedics	Obstetrics
Hawkins	28	18	15	75
Condriac	32	48	23	38
Bardot	51	36	24	36
Hoolihan	25	38	55	12

: **14-30** The Gleaming Company has just developed a new dishwashing liquid and is preparing for a national television promotional campaign. The firm has decided to schedule a series of one-minute commercials during the peak homemaker audience viewing hours of 1–5 P.M. To reach the widest possible audience, Gleaming wants to schedule one commercial on each of four networks and to have one commercial appear during each of the four one-hour time blocks. The exposure ratings for each hour, which represent the number of viewers per $1,000 spent, are presented in the accompanying table. Which network should be scheduled each hour in order to provide the maximum audience exposure?

	NETWORKS			
VIEWING HOURS	A	B	C	Independent
1–2 P.M.	27.1	18.1	11.3	9.5
2–3 P.M.	18.9	15.5	17.1	10.6
3–4 P.M.	19.2	18.5	9.9	7.7
4–5 P.M.	11.5	21.4	16.8	12.8

: **14-31** The G. Saussy Manufacturing Company is putting out four new electronic components. Each of Saussy's four plants has the capacity to add one more product to its current line of electronic parts. The unit manufacturing costs for producing the different parts at the four plants are shown in the accompanying table. How should Saussy assign the new products to the plants in order to minimize manufacturing costs?

ELECTRONIC COMPONENTS	PLANTS			
	1	2	3	4
C53	$.10	$.12	$.13	$.11
C81	.05	.06	.04	.08
D5	.32	.40	.31	.30
D44	.17	.14	.19	.15

: **14-32** As mentioned in Section 14.12 of this chapter, the Fix-It Shop has added a fourth repairman, Davis. Solve the accompanying cost table for the new optimal assignment of workers to projects. Why did this solution occur?

WORKER	PROJECT			
	1	2	3	DUMMY
Adams	$11	$14	$ 6	$ 0
Brown	8	10	11	0
Cooper	9	12	7	0
Davis	10	13	8	0

: **14-33** The Patricia Garcia Company is producing seven new medical products. Each of Garcia's eight plants can add one more product to its current line of medical devices. The unit manufacturing costs for producing the different parts at the eight plants are shown below. How should Garcia assign the new products to the plants in order to minimize manufacturing costs?

ELECTRONIC COMPONENTS	PLANTS							
	1	2	3	4	5	6	7	8
C53	$.10	$.12	$.13	$.11	$.10	$.06	$.16	$.12
C81	.05	.06	.04	.08	.04	.09	.06	.06
D5	.32	.40	.31	.30	.42	.35	.36	.49
D44	.17	.14	.19	.15	.10	.16	.19	.12
E2	.06	.07	.10	.05	.08	.10	.11	.05
E35	.08	.10	.12	.08	.09	.10	.09	.06
G99	.55	.62	.61	.70	.62	.63	.65	.59

Data Set Problem

14-34 Haifa Instruments, an Israeli producer of portable kidney dialysis units and other medical products, develops an eight-month aggregate plan. Demand and capacity (in units) are forecast as follows:

CAPACITY SOURCE	JAN.	FEB.	MAR.	APR.	MAY	JUNE	JULY	AUG.
Labor								
Regular Time	235	255	290	300	300	290	300	290
Overtime	20	24	26	24	30	28	30	30
Subcontract	12	15	15	17	17	19	19	20
Demand	255	294	321	301	330	320	345	340

The cost of producing each dialysis unit is $1,000 on regular time, $1,300 on overtime, and $1,500 on a subcontract. Inventory carrying cost is $100 per unit per month. There is no beginning or ending inventory in stock.

(a) Set up a production plan, using the transportation model, that minimizes cost. What is this plan's cost?

(b) Through better planning, regular time production can be set at exactly the same value, 275, per month. Does this alter the solution?

(c) If overtime costs rise from $1,300 to $1,400, does this change your answer to part a? What if they fall to $1,200?

Data Set Problem

 14-35 NASA's astronaut crew currently includes 10 mission specialists who hold a Ph.D. in either astrophysics or astromedicine. One of these specialists will be assigned to each of the 10 flights scheduled for the upcoming nine months. Mission specialists are responsible for carrying out scientific and medical experiments in space or for launching, retrieving, or repairing satellites. The chief of astronaut personnel, himself a former crew member with three missions under his belt, must decide who should be assigned and trained for each of the very different missions. Clearly, astronauts with medical educations are more suited to missions involving biological or medical experiments, while those with engineering- or physics-oriented degrees best suited to other types of missions. The chief assigns each astronaut a rating on a scale of 1 to 10 for each possible mission, with a 10 being a perfect match for the task at hand and a 1 being a mismatch. Only one specialist is assigned to each flight, and none is reassigned until all others have flown at least once.

	MISSION									
ASTRONAUT	JAN. 12	JAN. 27	FEB. 5	FEB. 26	MAR. 26	APR. 12	MAY 1	JUN. 9	AUG. 20	SEP. 19
Vincze	9	7	2	1	10	9	8	9	2	6
Veit	8	8	3	4	7	9	7	7	4	4
Anderson	2	1	10	10	1	4	7	6	6	7
Herbert	4	4	10	9	9	9	1	2	3	4
Schatz	10	10	9	9	8	9	1	1	1	1
Plane	1	3	5	7	9	7	10	10	9	2
Certo	9	9	8	8	9	1	1	2	2	9
Moses	3	2	7	6	4	3	9	7	7	9
Brandon	5	4	5	9	10	10	5	4	9	8
Drtina	10	10	9	7	6	7	5	4	8	8

(a) Who should be assigned to which flight?

(b) We have just been notified that Anderson is getting married in February and has been granted a highly sought publicity tour in Europe that month. (He intends to take his wife and let the trip double as a honeymoon.) How does this change the final schedule?

(c) Certo has complained that he was misrated on his January mission. Both ratings should be 10s, he claims to the chief, who agrees and recomputes the schedule. Do any changes occur over the schedule set in part b?

(d) What are the strengths and weaknesses of this approach to scheduling?

Custom Vans, Inc.

Custom Vans, Inc. specializes in converting standard vans into campers. Depending on the amount of work and customizing to be done, the customizing could cost less than $1,000 to over $5,000. In less than four years, Tony Rizzo was able to expand his small operation in Gary, Indiana, to other major outlets in Chicago, Milwaukee, Minneapolis, and Detroit.

Innovation was the major factor in Tony's success in converting a small van shop into one of the largest and most profitable custom van operations in the Midwest. Tony seemed to have a special ability to design and develop unique features and devices that were always in high demand by van owners. An example was Shower-Rific, which was developed by Tony only six months after Custom Vans, Inc. was started. These small showers were completely self-contained, and they could be placed in almost any type of van and in a number of different locations within a van. Shower-Rific was made of fiberglass, and contained towel racks, built-in soap and shampoo holders, and a unique plastic door. Each Shower-Rific took 2 gallons of fiberglass and 3 hours of labor to manufacture.

Most of the Shower-Rifics were manufactured in Gary in the same warehouse where Custom Vans, Inc. was founded. The manufacturing plant in Gary could produce 300 Shower-Rifics in a month, but this capacity never seemed to be enough. Custom Van shops in all locations were complaining about not getting enough Shower-Rifics, and because Minneapolis was farther away from Gary than the other locations, Tony was always inclined to ship Shower-Rifics to the other locations before Minneapolis. This infuriated the manager of Custom Vans at Minneapolis, and after many heated discussions, Tony decided to start another manufacturing plant for Shower-Rifics at Fort Wayne, Indiana. The manufacturing plant at Fort Wayne could produce 150 Shower-Rifics per month.

The manufacturing plant at Fort Wayne was still not able to meet current demand for Shower-Rifics, and Tony knew that the demand for his unique camper shower would grow rapidly in the next year. After consulting with his lawyer and banker, Tony concluded that he should open two new manufacturing plants as soon as possible. Each plant would have the same capacity as the Fort Wayne

manufacturing plant. An initial investigation into possible manufacturing locations was made, and Tony decided that the two new plants should be located in Detroit, Michigan; Rockford, Illinois; or Madison, Wisconsin. Tony knew that selecting the best location for the two new manufacturing plants would be difficult. Transportation costs and demands for the various locations should be important considerations.

The Chicago shop was managed by Bill Burch. This Custom Van shop was one of the first established by Tony, and it continued to outperform the other locations. The manufacturing plant at Gary was supplying 200 Shower-Rifics each month, although Bill knew that the demand for the showers in Chicago was 300 units. The transportation cost per unit from Gary was $10, and although the transportation cost from Fort Wayne was double that amount, Bill was always pleading with Tony to get an additional 50 units from the Fort Wayne manufacturer. The two additional manufacturing plants would certainly be able to supply Bill with the additional 100 showers he needed. The transportation costs would, of course, vary, depending on which two locations Tony picked. The transportation cost per shower would be $30 from Detroit, $5 from Rockford, and $10 from Madison.

Wilma Jackson, manager of the Custom Van shop in Milwaukee, was the most upset about not getting an adequate supply of showers. She had a demand for 100 units, and at the present time, she was only getting half of this demand from the Fort Wayne manufacturing plant. She could not understand why Tony didn't ship her all 100 units from Gary. The transportation cost per unit from Gary was only $20, while the transportation cost from Fort Wayne was $30. Wilma was hoping that Tony would select Madison for one of the manufacturing locations. She would be able to get all of the showers needed, and the transportation cost per unit would only be $5. If not Madison, a new plant in Rockford would be able to supply her total needs, but the transportation cost per unit would be twice as much as it would be from Madison. Because the transportation cost per unit from Detroit would be $40, Wilma speculated that even if Detroit became one of the new plants, she would not be getting any units from Detroit.

Custom Vans, Inc. of Minneapolis was managed

by Tom Poanski. He was getting 100 showers from the Gary plant. Demand was 150 units. Tom faced the highest transportation costs of all locations. The transportation cost from Gary was $40 per unit. It would cost $10 more if showers were sent from the Fort Wayne location. Tom was hoping that Detroit would not be one of the new plants, as the transportation cost would be $60 per unit. Rockford and Madison would have a cost of $30 and $25, respectively, to ship one shower to Minneapolis.

The Detroit shop's position was similar to Milwaukee's—only getting half of the demand each month. The 100 units that Detroit did receive came directly from the Fort Wayne plant. The transportation cost was only $15 per unit from Fort Wayne, while it was $25 from Gary. Dick Lopez, manager of Custom Vans, Inc. of Detroit, placed the probability of having one of the new plants in Detroit fairly high. The factory would be located across town, and the transportation cost would be only $2 per unit. He could get 150 showers from the new plant in Detroit and the other 50 showers from Fort Wayne. Even if Detroit was not selected, the other two locations were not intolerable. Rockford had a transportation cost per unit of $35, and Madison had a transportation cost of $40.

Tony pondered the dilemma of locating the two new plants for several weeks before deciding to call a meeting of all the managers of the van shops. The decision was complicated, but the objective was clear—to minimize total costs. The meeting was held in Gary, and everyone was present except Wilma.

Tony: Thank you for coming. As you know, I have decided to open up two new plants at Rockford, Madison, or Detroit. The two locations, of course, will change our shipping practices, and I sincerely hope that they will supply you with the Shower-Rifics that you have been wanting. I know you could have sold more units, and I want you to know that I am sorry for this situation.

Dick: Tony, I have given this situation a lot of consideration, and I feel strongly that at least one of the new plants should be located in Detroit. As you know, I am now only getting half of the showers that I need. My brother, Leon, is very interested in running the plant, and I know he would do a good job.

Tom: Dick, I am sure that Leon could do a good job, and I know how difficult it has been since the recent layoffs by the auto industry. Nevertheless, we should be considering total costs and not personalities. I believe that the new plants should be located in Madison and Rockford. I am further away from the other plants than any other shop, and these locations would significantly reduce transportation costs.

Dick: That may be true, but there are other factors. Detroit has one of the largest suppliers of fiberglass, and I have checked prices. A new plant in Detroit would be able to purchase fiberglass for $2 less than any of the other existing or proposed plants.

Tom: At Madison, we have an excellent labor force. This is primarily due to the large number of students attending the University of Madison. These students are hard workers, and they will work for $1 less per hour than the other locations that we are considering.

Bill: Calm down, you two. It is obvious that we will not be able to satisfy everyone in locating the new plants. Therefore I would like to suggest that we vote on the two best locations.

Tony: I don't think that voting would be a good idea. Wilma was not able to attend, and we should be looking at all of these factors together in some type of logical fashion.

Where would you locate the two new plants?

Old Oregon Wood Store

In 1975, George Brown started the Old Oregon Wood Store to manufacture Old Oregon tables. Each table is carefully constructed by hand using the highest quality oak. Old Oregon tables can support over 500 pounds, and since the start of the Old Oregon Wood Store, not one table has been returned because of faulty workmanship or structural problems. In addition to being rugged, each table is beautifully finished using a urethane varnish that George developed over 20 years of working with wood-finishing materials.

The manufacturing process consists of four steps: preparation, assembly, finishing, and packaging. Each step is performed by one person. In addition to overseeing the entire operation, George does all of the finishing. Tom Surowski performs the preparation step, which involves cutting and forming the basic components of the tables. Leon Davis is in charge of the assembly, and Cathy Stark performs the packaging.

While each person is responsible for only one step in the manufacturing process, everyone can perform any one of the steps. It is George's policy that occasionally everyone should complete several tables on his or her own without any help or assistance. A small competition is used to see who can complete an entire table in the least amount of time. George maintains average total and intermediate completion times. The data are shown in Figure 1.

It takes Cathy longer than the other employees to construct an Old Oregon table. In addition to being slower than the other employees, Cathy is also unhappy about her current responsibility of packaging, which leaves her idle most of the day. Her first preference is finishing, and her second preference is preparation.

In addition to quality, George is concerned with costs and efficiency. When one of the employees misses a day, it causes major scheduling problems. In some cases, George assigns another employee overtime to complete the necessary work. At other times, George simply waits until the employee returns to work to complete his or her step in the manufacturing process. Both solutions cause problems. Overtime is expensive, and waiting causes

FIGURE 1
Manufacturing Time in Minutes

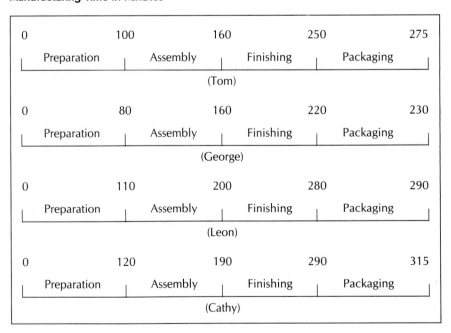

delays and sometimes stops the entire manufacturing process.

To overcome some of these problems, Randy Lane was hired. Randy's major duties are to perform miscellaneous jobs and to help out if one of the employees is absent. George has given Randy training in all phases of the manufacturing process, and he is pleased with the speed at which Randy has been able to learn how to completely assemble Old Oregon tables. Total and intermediate completion times for Randy are given in Figure 2.

Discussion Questions

1. What is the fastest way to manufacture Old Oregon tables using the original crew? How many could be made per day?

2. Would production rates and quantities change significantly if George would allow Randy to perform one of the four functions and make one of the original crew the backup person?

3. What is the fastest time to manufacture a table with the original crew if Cathy is moved to either preparation or finishing?

4. Whoever performs the packaging function is severely underutilized. Can you find a better way of utilizing the four- or five-person crew than either giving each a single job or allowing each to manufacture an entire table? How many tables could be manufactured per day with this scheme?

FIGURE 2
Manufacturing Times in Minutes for Randy Lane

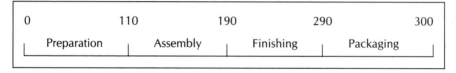

CASE STUDY

Northwest General Hospital

Northwest General, a large hospital in Providence, Rhode Island, has initiated a new procedure to ensure that patients receive their meals while the food is still as hot as possible. The hospital will continue to prepare the food in its kitchen, but will now deliver it in bulk (not individual servings) to one of three new serving stations in the building. From there, the food will be reheated, meals will be placed on individual trays, loaded onto a cart, and distributed to the various floors and wings of the hospital.

The three new serving stations are as efficiently located as possible to reach the various hallways in the hospital. The number of trays that each station can serve are shown below:

LOCATION	CAPACITY (MEALS)
Station 5A	200
Station 3G	225
Station 1S	275

There are six wings to Northwest General that must be served. The number of patients in each follows:

WING	PATIENTS
1	80
2	120
3	150
4	210
5	60
6	80

The purpose of the new procedure is to increase the temperature of the hot meals that the patient receives. Therefore, the amount of time needed to deliver a tray from a serving station will determine the proper distribution of food from serving station to wing. The table below summarizes the time associated with each possible distribution channel.

What is your recommendation for handling the distribution of trays from the three serving stations?

DISTRIBUTION TIME (minutes)						
TO FROM	WING 1	WING 2	WING 3	WING 4	WING 5	WING 6
Station 5A	12	11	8	9	6	6
Station 3G	6	12	7	7	5	8
Station 1S	8	9	6	6	7	9

BIBLIOGRAPHY

Aarvik, O., and Randolph, P. "The Application of Linear Programming to the Determination of Transmission Fees in an Electrical Power Network." *Interfaces* Vol. 6, Nov. 1975.

Bowman, E. "Production Scheduling by the Transportation Method of Linear Programming," *Operations Research* Vol. 4, 1956.

Breslaw, J. A. "A Linear Programming Solution to the Faculty Assignment Problem." *Socio-Economic Planning Sciences* Vol. 10, No. 6, 1976.

Choypeng, P., Puakpong, P., and Rosenthal, Richard E. "Optimal Ship Routing and Personnel Assignment for Naval Recruitment in Thailand," *Interfaces* Vol. 16, No. 4, July–Aug. 1986, pp. 49–52.

Evans, James R., Hebert, John E., and Deckro, Richard F. "Play Ball! The Scheduling of Sports Officials," *Perspectives in Computing* Vol. 4, No. 1, Spring 1984, pp. 18–29.

Glassey, C. Roger, and Mizrach, Michael. "A Decision Support System for Assigning Classes to Rooms" *Interfaces* Vol. 16, No. 5, September–October 1986, pp. 92–100.

Harrison, H. "A Planning System for Facilities and Resources in Distribution Networks." *Interfaces* Vol. 9, No. 2, Part 2, February 1979.

Holladay, J. "Some Transportation Problems and Techniques for Solving Them." *Naval Research Logistics Quarterly* Vol. 11, 1974.

McKeown, P., and Workman, B. "A Study in Using Linear Programming to Assign Students to Schools." *Interfaces* Vol. 6, No. 4, August 1976.

Render, B., Stair, R. M., and Greenberg, I. *Cases and Readings in Management Science,* 2nd ed. Boston: Allyn and Bacon, Inc., 1990.

Ross, G. T., and Soland, R. M. "Modeling Facility Location Problems as Generalized Assignment Problems." *Management Science* Vol. 24, No. 3, 1977.

15

Integer Programming, Goal Programming, and the Branch and Bound Method

15.1
INTRODUCTION

We have just seen two special types of linear programming models—the transportation and assignment models—that were handled by making certain modifications to the general LP approach. This chapter presents a series of other important mathematical programming models that arise when some of the basic assumptions of LP are made more or less restrictive.

For example, one assumption of linear programming is that decision variables can take on fractional values such as $X_1 = .33$, $X_2 = 1.57$, or $X_3 = 109.4$. Yet a large number of business problems can be solved only if variables have *integer* values. When an airline decides how many Boeing 757s or Boeing 767s to purchase, it can't place an order for 5.38 aircraft; it must order 4, 5, 6, 7 or some other integer amount. In Section 15.2, we present the subject of *integer programming*. We show you how to solve integer programming problems both graphically and by use of an algorithm called the *branch and bound method*.

integer programming

A major limitation of linear programming is that it forces the decision maker to state one objective only. But what if a business has several objectives? Management may indeed want to maximize profit, but also maximize market share, maintain full employment, and minimize costs. Many of these goals can be conflicting and difficult to quantify. South States Power and Light, for example, wants to build a nuclear power plant in Taft, Louisiana. Its objectives are to maximize power generated, reliability and safety, and to minimize cost of operating the system and the environmental effects on the community. *Goal programming* is an extension to linear programming that can permit multiple objectives such as these.

goal programming

Linear programming can, of course, be applied only to cases in which the constraints and objective function are linear. Yet in many situations this is not the case. The price of various products, for example, may be a function of the number of units produced. As more are made, the price per unit decreases. Hence, an objective function may read:

nonlinear programming

$$\text{Maximize profit} = 25X_1 - .4X_1^2 + 30X_2 - .5X_2^2$$

Because of the squared terms, this is a nonlinear programming problem.

Let's examine each of these extensions of LP—integer, goal, and nonlinear programming—one at a time.

15.2
INTEGER PROGRAMMING

An integer programming model is a model that has constraints and an objective function identical to that formulated by linear programming. The only difference is that one or more of the decision variables has to take on an integer value in the final solution. Let's look at a simple example of an integer programming problem and see how to solve it.

solution values must be whole numbers

584

The Harrison Electric Company Example of Integer Programming

The Harrison Electric Company, located in Chicago's Old Town area, produces two products popular with home renovators: old-fashioned chandeliers and ceiling fans. Both the chandeliers and fans require a two-step production process involving wiring and assembly. It takes about 2 hours to wire each chandelier, and 3 hours to wire a ceiling fan. Final assembly of the chandeliers and fans require 6 and 5 hours, respectively. The production capability is such that only 12 hours of wiring time and 30 hours of assembly time are available. If each chandelier produced nets the firm $7 and each fan $6, Harrison's production mix decision can be formulated using linear programming as follows:

$$\text{Maximize profit} = \$7X_1 + \$6X_2$$

$$\begin{array}{lll} \text{Subject to:} & 2X_1 + 3X_2 \le 12 & \textit{(wiring hours)} \\ & 6X_1 + 5X_2 \le 30 & \textit{(assembly hours)} \\ & X_1, \ X_2 \ge 0 \end{array}$$

where

X_1 = number of chandeliers produced, and

X_2 = number of ceiling fans produced.

With only two variables and two constraints, Harrison's production planner, Wes Wellace, employed the graphical linear programming approach (see Figure 15.1) to generate the optimal solution of X_1 = 3.75 chandeliers and X_2 = 1.5 ceiling fans during the production cycle. Recognizing that the company could not produce and sell a fraction of a product, Wes decided that he was dealing with an integer programming problem.

It seemed to Wes that the simplest approach was to round off the optimal fractional solutions for X_1 and X_2 to integer values of X_1 = 4 chandeliers and X_2 = 2 ceiling fans. Unfortunately, rounding can produce two problems. First, the new integer solution may not be in the feasible region and thus is not a practical answer. This is the case if we round to X_1 = 4, X_2 = 2. Second, even if we round off to a feasible solution, such as X_1 = 4, X_2 = 1, it may not be the *optimal* feasible integer solution. Table 15.1 lists the entire set of integer-valued solutions to the Harrison Electric problem. By inspecting the right-hand column, we see that the optimal *integer* solution is:

rounding off

$$X_1 = 5 \text{ chandeliers, } X_2 = 0 \text{ ceiling fans with a profit} = \$35$$

Note that this integer restriction results in a lower profit level than the original optimal linear programming solution. As a matter of fact, an integer programming solution can *never* produce a greater profit than the LP solution to the same problem; *usually* it means a lesser value.

The Cutting Plane Method

Although it is possible to solve simple integer programming problems like Harrison Electric's by inspection or enumeration, several more complicated

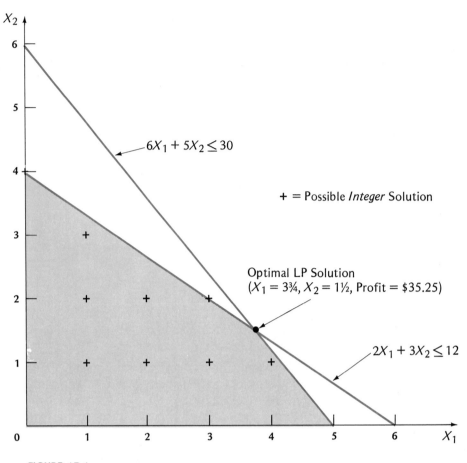

FIGURE 15.1
Harrison Electric Problem

method for solving integer programs

methods are available to handle larger, more complex problems. Gomory's *cutting plane method* is one such integer programming algorithm.

In applying the cutting plane algorithm, integer requirements are first ignored, and the linear programming problem is solved in the usual way, usually with the simplex method. If the solution has all integer values, then the current answer is also the integer programming answer and no further steps are needed. But if the solution does *not* have integer values,

adding Gomory cuts

we must add one or more new constraints to the problem. These new constraints, called *Gomory cuts*, construct a new, smaller area covering all integer values of the feasible region. They exclude the original optimal *noninteger* solution and allow us to converge on the integer solution.

Figure 15.2 illustrates the addition of a first cut, the constraint $X_1 + X_2 \leq 5$. This equation was selected as a first cut by observation.[1] It goes

---

[1] An algorithm also exists for the simplex method to do the cuts.

TABLE 15.1 Integer Solutions to the Harrison Electric Company Problem

CHANDELIERS (X_1)	CEILING FANS (X_2)	PROFIT ($\$7X_1 + \$6X_2$)	
0	0	$ 0	
1	0	7	
2	0	14	
3	0	21	
4	0	28	
5	0	35	⟵ Optimal solution to integer
0	1	6	programming problem
1	1	13	
2	1	20	
3	1	27	
4	1	34	⟵ Solution if rounding off is used
0	2	12	
1	2	19	
2	2	26	
3	2	33	
0	3	18	
1	3	25	
0	4	24	

through a series of integer points without excluding any that were in the original feasible region. If you look carefully, you will also see it is the *only* constraint that could be added to cut the size of the feasible region without excluding any integer points.

The cut creates a new feasible region *ABCD*. Once the cut is made, the revised problem can be solved by the simplex method, or graphically. If an integer solution is reached now, we are done. If not, we continue to add Gomory cuts, one at a time. Sooner or later, the optimal integer solution will be found.

Types of Integer Programming Problems

The Harrison Electric production decision is an example of one of the three types of integer programming problems:

1. *Pure integer programming* problems, such as Harrison Electric's, are cases in which *all* decision variables must have integer solutions.

2. *Mixed-integer programming* problems are cases in which *some*, but not all, of the decision variables are required to have integer values.

3. *Zero-one integer programming* problems are special cases in which all decision variables must have integer solution values of 0 or 1.

We now look at application examples of the latter two problems.

pure integer programming, mixed-integer programming, zero-one integer programming

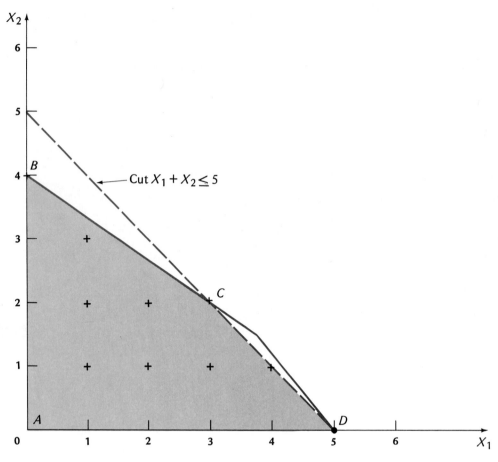

FIGURE 15.2
Harrison Electric Problem with Cut $X_1 + X_2 \leq 5$
Added

A Mixed-Integer Programming Problem Example

Bagwell Chemical Company, in Jackson, Mississippi, produces two industrial chemicals. The first product, xyline, must be produced in 50-pound bags; the second, hexall, is sold by the pound in dry bulk and hence can be produced in any quantity. Both xyline and hexall are composed of three ingredients, A, B, and C, as follows:

AMOUNT PER 50-POUND BAG OF XYLINE (lbs.)	AMOUNT PER POUND OF HEXALL (lbs.)	AMOUNT OF INGREDIENTS AVAILABLE
30	0.5	2,000 lbs.—ingredient A
18	0.4	800 lbs.—ingredient B
2	0.1	200 lbs.—ingredient C

APPLICATIONS OF QA

Applying Integer Linear Programming to the Fleet Assignment Problem

American Airlines, as most commercial carriers, has a problem assigning its fleet to meet its schedules with limited resources. American has over 2,300 flights per day to over 150 different cities and utilizes more than 500 jet aircraft. In situations with numerous variables and constraints, it is important to use a computer model to minimize calculation time and allow for quicker management responses. Several benefits can be achieved with integer linear programming.

The computerized integer linear programming model used by American tackles a variety of problems and has three objectives: maximizing profit, minimizing costs, and finding the optimal utilization of a particular fleet type. The goal of the fleet assignment process is to assign as many flight segments as possible in a schedule pattern to 1 or more aircraft types (American currently operates 10 fleet types) while optimizing one of the three objectives. Given a schedule (with departure and arrival times indicated), the model determines which flights should be assigned to which aircraft types. Constraints within the problem are flight coverage, continuity of equipment, schedule balance, aircraft count, and all other user-specified rules.

Significant improvements have been achieved as a result of this application of linear programming. Operating costs have been reduced by 0.5%. In addition, revenues gained were approximately 1%, or in excess of $75 million.

Even for medium-sized schedules, problem sizes can get very large. For example, a 400-flight schedule with 60 stations and 3 aircraft types would involve approximately 6,300 columns and 1,800 rows in the ensuing LP matrix. The size of the problem is compounded by the fact that the decision variables must be integers—requiring that an integer linear programming algorithm be invoked. Computer runs on an IBM 3081 mainframe can take over one hour when 4 aircraft types are involved.

Several departments at American Airlines use the integer linear programming model described in their planning and development. It will become 1 of 10 key decision modules for the next generation scheduling system, which is currently being developed by American Airlines Decision Technologies.

Source: J. Abara, *Interfaces*, Vol. 19, No. 4, July–August 1989, pp. 20–28.

Bagwell sells 50-pound bags of xyline for $85 and hexall in any weight for $1.50 per pound.

If we let X_1 = number of 50-pound bags of xyline produced and X_2 = number of pounds of hexall (in dry bulk) mixed, Bagwell's problem can be described with mixed integer programming:

$$\text{Maximize profit} = \$85X_1 + \$1.50X_2$$

$$\begin{aligned}
\text{Subject to:} \quad 30X_1 + 0.5X_2 &\leq 2{,}000 \\
18X_1 + 0.4X_2 &\leq 800 \\
2X_1 + 0.1X_2 &\leq 200
\end{aligned}$$

with $X_1, X_2 \geq 0$ and X_1 integer.

Note that X_2 represents bulk weight of hexall and is not required to be integer valued.

LINDO, the linear programming package first demonstrated in Chapter 12, is also capable of handling mixed-integer programming problems such

PROGRAM 15.1 LINDO Analysis of Bagwell's Mixed-Integer Program

```
    LINDO/PC  (UC   21   AUG  84)

:  MAX 85X1+ 1.50X2
?  ST
?  30X1 + .5X2<2000
?  18X1+.4X2<800
?  2X1+.1X2<200
?  END
:  INTEGER 1
:  GO


NEW  INTEGER  SOLUTION OF    3017.50      AT BRANCH      0 PIVOT      2

          OBJECTIVE FUNCTION VALUE

   1)         3017.50000

   VARIABLE           VALUE        REDUCED COST
        X1          1.000000       -17.500000
        X2       1955.000000          .000000


      ROW     SLACK OR SURPLUS     DUAL PRICES
       2)         992.500000          .000000
       3)           .000000         3.750000
       4)          2.500000          .000000
```

as the Bagwell case. Program 15.1 illustrates the input data and solution computed by LINDO. The optimal value of $3,017.50 is obtained when one bag of xyline and 1,955 pounds of hexall are produced. The INTEGER 1 command (which could also have been entered as INTEGER X1) indicates that only the first variable must appear as a whole number in the final solution.

Zero-One Integer Programming Problem Example

stock portfolio analysis with zero-one programming

The Houston-based investment firm of Simkin, Simkin, and Steinberg specializes in recommending oil stock portfolios for wealthy clients. One such client has made the following specifications: (1) at least two Texas oil firms must be in the portfolio, (2) no more than one investment can be made in foreign oil companies, (3) one of the two California oil stocks must be purchased. The client has up to $3 million available for investments and insists on purchasing exactly 10,000 shares of each company that he invests in. Table 15.2 describes various stocks that Simkin considers. The objective is to maximize annual return on investment subject to the constraints.

APPLICATIONS OF QA

Using Integer Programming to Place a Lockheed Warehouse

The cost of storing and distributing products can be substantial, and one objective of any company is to reduce these costs. This was the case with Lockheed Missiles and Space Company's operation in Sunnyvale, California. This location employs approximately 24,000 people. The complex consists of a main area of several buildings and satellite facilities or buildings spread over an area with a radius of about 15 miles. Stationery inventory, including computer paper and other paper products, was located about 10 miles from each of the main areas or regions that used the product. Furthermore, transportation costs for transporting the stationery, computer paper, and other paper products to various locations had gone up substantially. As a result, a number of alternatives were investigated. These included: (1) keeping the stationery stores at their present location, (2) upgrading the facilities and equipment of the stationery stores at the present location, (3) relocating the stores in the main area or complex, or (4) keeping the present mode of operation and relocating the stationery stores while upgrading the system to a more efficient and effective mode of operation.

One of the first steps was to collect data to be analyzed. This was a difficult and tedious process.

It involved visual inspection, a number of on-site observations, a large number of physical measurements, a close examination of records, and a number of discussions and interviews with personnel who dealt with material and distribution within the organization. Once collected, the data were placed into a number of cost and data subcategories. These included facility costs, operation costs, and transportation costs. The facility costs included utilities, insurance, taxes, depreciation, and maintenance. Operation costs included handling and storage of equipment, fuel cost, and administrative and personnel cost. The transportation costs included trucks and associated equipment depreciation, maintenance, various mileage costs, and insurance.

In order to solve the problem and to determine the best way to store and distribute stationery goods, a mixed integer programming model was formulated. Like other mathematical programming models, this one was solved on a computer. After comparing the optimal solution from the mathematical programming model with the existing situation, it was estimated that the present value of the savings over a 10-year period would be $665,000.

Source: Spyros Economides and Edwin Fok, "Warehouse Relocation Or Modernization: Modeling the Managerial Dilemma," *Interfaces,* Vol. 14, No. 3, May–June 1984, pp. 63–67.

To formulate this as a 0-1 integer programming problem, Simkin lets X_i be a 0-1 integer variable, where $X_i = 1$ if stock i is purchased and $X_i = 0$ if stock i is not purchased.

TABLE 15.2 Oil Investment Opportunities

STOCK	COMPANY NAME	EXPECTED ANNUAL RETURN (in $1,000's)	COST FOR BLOCK OF 10,000 SHARES (in $1,000's)
1	Trans-Texas Oil	50	480
2	British Petroleum	80	540
3	Dutch Shell	90	680
4	Houston Drilling	120	1,000
5	Texas Petroleum	110	700
6	San Diego Oil	40	510
7	California Petro	75	900

$$\text{Maximize return} = 50X_1 + 80X_2 + 90X_3 + 120X_4 + 110X_5 + 40X_6 + 75X_7$$

$$\begin{aligned}
\text{Subject to:} \quad & X_1 + X_4 + X_5 && \geq 2 && \textit{(Texas constraint)} \\
& X_2 + X_3 && \leq 1 && \textit{(foreign oil constraint)} \\
& X_6 + X_7 && = 1 && \textit{(California constraint)} \\
& 480X_1 + 540X_2 + 680X_3 + 1{,}000X_4 + 700X_5 \\
& \quad + 510X_6 + 900X_7 \leq \$3{,}000 \;\textit{(\$3 million limit)}
\end{aligned}$$

All variables must be 0 or 1 in value.

To solve this problem by computer, you may run the software with this text (AB:QM), LINDO, or STORM. Program 15.2 illustrates the AB:QM input and output, while Program 15.3 shows the LINDO approach.

PROGRAM 15.2 AB:QM Solution to Simkins 0-1 Programming Problem

```
Program: Zero One Programming

Problem Title : SIMKIN INVESTMENT

***** Input Data *****

Max.  Z =  50x1 + 80x2 + 90x3 + 120x4 + 110x5 + 40x6 + 75x7

Subject to

C1    1x1 + 1x4 + 1x5 >= 2
C2    1x2 + 1x3 <= 1
C3    1x6 + 1x7 = 1
C4    480x1 + 540x2 + 680x3 + 1000x4 + 700x5 + 510x6 + 900x7 <= 3000

***** Program Output *****


Final Optimal Solution

Z =   360.000

----------------------
Variable        Value
----------------------
   x 1            0
   x 2            0
   x 3            1
   x 4            1
   x 5            1
   x 6            1
   x 7            0
----------------------

***** End of Output *****
```

PROGRAM 15.3 Use of LINDO to Solve the 0-1 Integer Programming Problem for Simkin

```
:  MAX  50X1 + 80X2 + 90X3 + 120X4 + 110X5 + 40X6 + 75X7
?  ST
?  X1 + X4 + X5>2
?  X2 + X3<1
?  X6 + X7 = 1
?  480X1 + 540X2 + 680X3 + 1000X4 + 700X5 + 510X6 + 900X7<3000
?  END
:  INTEGER  X1
:  INTEGER  X2
:  INTEGER  X3
:  INTEGER  X4
:  INTEGER  X5
:  INTEGER  X6
:  INTEGER  X7
:  GO
LP OPTIMUM FOUND   AT STEP      10

            OBJECTIVE FUNCTION VALUE

  1)        376.041700


VARIABLE         VALUE           REDUCED COST
      X1          .520833              .000000
      X2         1.000000            -4.583328
      X3          .000000              .000000
      X4         1.000000           -15.833340
      X5         1.000000           -37.083340
      X6         1.000000            -5.625000
      X7          .000000              .000000


     ROW   SLACK OR SURPLUS      DUAL PRICES
      2)          .520833              .000000
      3)          .000000            19.166670
      4)          .000000           -18.750000
      5)          .000000              .104167


NO. ITERATIONS =       10
BRANCHES =     0 DETERM = -4.800E  2
SET       X1 TO  0 AT    1 BND =   372.43590 TWIN =   372.40000
SET       X7 TO  0 AT    2 BND =   360.00000 TWIN =   372.43590



NEW INTEGER SOLUTION OF    360.000     AT BRANCH    2 PIVOT    16

            OBJECTIVE FUNCTION VALUE

  1)        360.000000
```

PROGRAM 15.3 (Continued)

VARIABLE	VALUE	REDUCED COST
X1	.000000	−50.000000
X2	.000000	10.000000
X3	1.000000	.000000
X4	1.000000	−120.000000
X5	1.000000	−110.000000
X6	1.000000	.000000
X7	.000000	−35.000000

ROW	SLACK OR SURPLUS	DUAL PRICES
2)	.000000	.000000
3)	.000000	90.000000
4)	.000000	40.000000
5)	110.000000	.000000

LINDO first solves the general LP problem, then applies a technique called the branch and bound method (our next topic in this chapter) to find the best integer answer. As we see in the printout, X_3, X_4, X_5, and X_6 are all equal to 1 in the all-integer solution, while X_1, X_2, and X_7 are 0. This means Simkin should invest in Dutch Shell, Houston Drilling, Texas Petroleum, and San Diego Oil, and not in the other three oil firms. The expected return is $360,000.

You might also recall that assignment problems solved by linear programming, in Chapter 13, are also actually 0-1 integer programs. All assignments of people to jobs, for example, are presented by either a 1 (person gets job) or a 0 (person not assigned to particular job).

15.3
THE BRANCH AND BOUND METHOD

The *branch and bound method* is an algorithm that can be used to solve all-integer and mixed-integer linear programs. It searches for an optimal solution by examining only a small part of the total number of possible solutions. This is especially useful when enumeration becomes economically impractical or impossible because there are a large number of feasible solutions.

subproblems   Branch and bound works by breaking the area of feasible solutions into smaller and smaller parts (subproblems) until the optimal solution is reached. It introduces the concept of feasible and infeasible bounds. Each subproblem that we examine with a total cost or profit worse than the current feasible bound will be discarded, and we will only examine the

---

APPLICATIONS OF QA

A Decision Support System for Assigning Classes to Rooms

The University of California at Berkeley enrolls about 30,000 students who are distributed among 80 academic departments. Responsibility for assigning 4,000 classes to about 250 classrooms falls on a scheduling office. In 1983, this office consisted of three schedulers (one for each academic quarter) plus a supervisor. The manual assignment strategy they used was "don't rock the boat"; that is, they began with the schedule for the corresponding quarter of the previous year and made the minimum necessary modifications to accommodate changes in departmental requests.

In the Fall of 1983, Berkeley converted from a quarter to a semester calendar. The list of courses offered in Fall semester 1983 was so unlike the previous Fall quarter that the old schedule was not a particularly useful starting point. The change to semesters forced the university to take a fresh look at the room assignment process and presented an opportunity to develop a decision support system. The problem of assigning classes to rooms is part of a larger scheduling problem, often referred to as the timetabling problem, in which the time each class is offered and the professor are also decision variables. A large *zero-one integer program* is solved as part of a decision support system for assigning classes to rooms.

From the professor's point of view, a room close to the office is more desirable than one on the other side of the campus. A room with fewer seats than students is, of course, undesirable, as is one that is too large. Some courses require special equipment such as TV monitors, slide projectors, and so forth. Students prefer consecutive classes close together, but that is an objective difficult to address directly. However, if professorial travel is minimized, then at least students who take consecutive classes in the same department will not have far to travel. For each section of each course, departments provide an estimated enrollment, a requested meeting time, and the special requirements of the class. Furthermore, certain time blocks are defined as prime time; at Berkeley, it was decided that departments should not request that more than 60% of their courses be offered during prime time.

A rough calculation indicates how large this program for Berkeley would be. Since an activity is defined for each feasible assignment of a class to a room, about half a million variables are needed, assuming that on average half the rooms are feasible for a randomly selected class. There are at least 26,500 constraints. There is only a limited opportunity to reduce the size of the problem by grouping rooms of similar size (as was done), because rooms in different buildings must be kept separate if distance is to be an objective.

The decision support system at Berkeley is used as follows. Six months before the start of the semester, departments return room-request forms that list all the classes scheduled for the semester. Within a few weeks, a preliminary schedule is issued, showing those classes that could not be assigned to rooms. Departments then submit revised requests and negotiate with the scheduling office about possible preassignments. The algorithm is then run again; certain standard classes which had been assigned to rooms are flagged as preassigned. The resulting set of assignments is then published in time for preenrollment. With the aid of this algorithm, the scheduling office is able to accomplish its part of the cycle several weeks faster than it was with the entirely manual method.

The system is considered a success because it is still being used. The success is attributed to several factors. Probably the most important factor was the adoption of the decision support approach instead of the prescriptive model approach. Although an optimization model is used, its behavior can be altered easily to explore different trade-off strategies. Furthermore, the algorithm is designed to accept partial solutions in the form of easily generated preassignments and then to do its best with the rest of the problem. Hence, special needs not anticipated when the model was designed can be accommodated, and schedulers can evaluate their own heuristics. Finally, minimal disruption of the rest of the decision process resulted from replacing the manual procedure with this computer-assisted procedure.

Source: C. Glassey and M. Mizrach, *Interfaces*, Vol. 16, No. 5, September–October 1986, pp. 92–100.

remaining subproblems. At the point where no more subproblems can be created, we will find an optimal solution.

An Assignment Problem Example

In the previous chapter, we faced the problem of trying to make the best assignment of three workers to three projects. Table 15.3 shows the costs associated with assigning each employee in the Fix-It Shop to a project. For example, it costs the firm $14 for Adams to complete project number 2. The firm's objective is to minimize the total cost of doing all three jobs. We demonstrate the use of the branch and bound method to solve this problem in three steps.

Step 1: First, the lowest possible total-cost bound is found. This is the assignment which yields the lowest cost; it does *not* have to be a feasible solution. This means we are allowed to assign more than one worker to the same project. We are "bounding" total cost on the low side, saying that no possible assignment of people to projects can cost less.

lower bound on total cost

The easiest way to set the lower bound is to select the smallest cost from each row. We assign Adams to project 3 (A3), Brown to 1 (B1) and Cooper to 3 (C3) for a total cost of $6 + $8 + $7 = $21.

LOWER BOUND ASSIGNMENT	COST ($)
A3	6
B1	8
C3	7
Total	21

Because two people were assigned the same project (both A and C are assigned to 3), this solution is infeasible. If it had been feasible, incidentally, it would also be the optimal solution and we would be done. Since it was not, we begin with this *lower bound* and proceed to find the lowest-cost feasible solution.

Step 2: We now do our first branching and divide the problem to search for solutions. We can change any one assignment in the current infeasible solution of A3, B1, C3 and create three new problems. Suppose we con-secutively assign A, B, and C to project 2 and observe each of the outcomes.

creating new subproblems

TABLE 15.3 Cost of Each Person-Project Assignment

PERSON	PROJECT		
	1	2	3
Adams (A)	$11	$14	$ 6
Brown (B)	8	10	11
Cooper (C)	9	12	7

First *A* is assigned to project 2; the other original assignments of *B*1 and *C*3 remain unchanged. This solution is feasible with a cost of $29:

ASSIGNMENT	COST ($)
*A*2	14
*B*1	8
*C*3	7
Total	29

A assigned to project 2

Second, *B* is assigned to project 2; *A*'s and *C*'s original assignments of *A*3 and *C*3 are kept. This solution is *infeasible,* with a cost of $23:

ASSIGNMENT	COST ($)
*A*3	6
*B*2	10
*C*3	7
Total	23

B assigned to project 2

Finally, *C* is assigned to project 2; the original assignment of *A*3 and *B*1 are kept. This solution is also feasible and has a $26 cost:

ASSIGNMENT	COST ($)
*A*3	6
*B*1	8
*C*2	12
Total	26

C assigned to project 2

As we can see in Figure 15.3, the original problem has now been partitioned into three new problems. The *best* solution, which is still infeasible, is now $23; this becomes the *new lower bound* and replaces the previous problem's lower bound of $21. Why is $23 best? Because it's the smallest of the three new costs. Notice that the new lower bound is closer to the feasible region than the previous one. Of the two feasible solutions, the one with the lowest value, $26, is the best one. It is set as an *upper feasible bound.* The optimal solution to this assignment problem must lie between the upper bound of $26 and the lower bound of $23. Solution branch *A*2 is dropped from further consideration because it is above the upper bound.

We can see at this point that branch and bound method evaluates only a portion of the possible solutions, while not eliminating any possible optimal solutions.

Step 3: In the second branching, we start from *B*2 because this is currently the best solution that is infeasible. Even though the $23 cost of *B*2 is not feasible, other higher-cost solutions on this branch *may* be feasible.

This time there are only *two* possible branches from *A*3, *B*2, and *C*3 because *B*2 is already set and we can only change one assignment. Either *A*3 can become *A*1, or *C*3 can become *C*1. Branches *A*1 and *C*1 are shown in Figure 15.4.

Branch *A*1 is dropped because its cost of assigning *A*1, *B*2, and *C*3 is

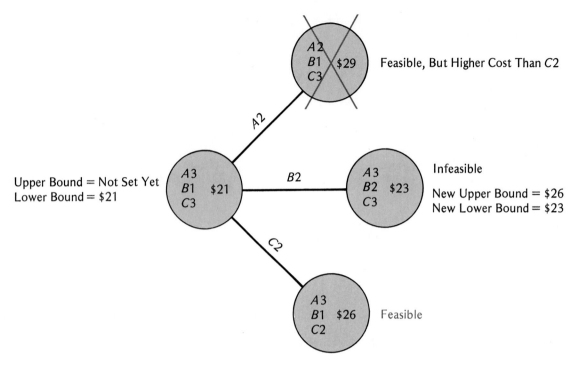

FIGURE 15.3
First Branching: Steps 1 and 2 of Branch and Bound Method

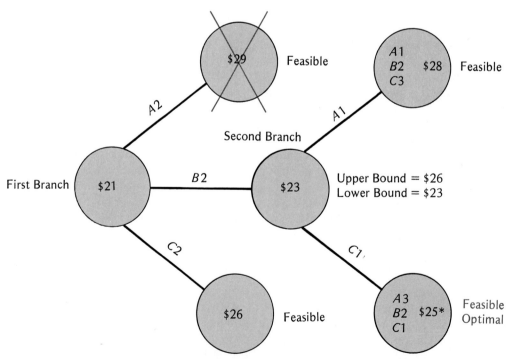

FIGURE 15.4
Second Branching: Steps 1, 2, and 3 of Branch and Bound Method

($11 + 10 + 7 =) $28, which is greater than the current upper bound of $26. Because both alternatives in step 3 are feasible, and feasible solutions are not partitioned, we see that branch C1 provides the optimal solution of $25. The assignment is:

OPTIMAL ASSIGNMENT	COST ($)
A to 3	6
B to 2	10
C to 1	9
Total	25

The branch and bound procedure we followed is very flexible in that we could have looked at the problem from a perspective of column assignment instead of row assignment. This means that we could have selected the smallest number in each column at step 1 and still reached the same answer.

Branch and bound can also be used in maximization problems, of course. We need only rephrase the three steps slightly.

maximization problems

Step 1: Find the maximum possible profit assignment, row by row, disregarding the infeasibility of the assignment. (If the solution is feasible, it means we have found the optimal solution.)

Step 2: Change any one assignment in this newly established infeasible solution. This partitions the problem into a series of new subproblems— three if there are three people or machines, four if there are four people, and so on. The *new upper bound* is the infeasible solution closer to the lower feasible area value than the previous upper bound was. Of the proposed feasible solutions, the one with the highest value is chosen as the best, and labeled the *new lower (feasible) bound.*

Step 3: We continue branching, if necessary, from the current best feasible solution until no further branches are possible.

Solving an Integer Programming Problem with Branch and Bound

Let us now turn to the familiar Harrison Electric Company integer programming problem again, using the branch and bound method to solve it this time. The approach entails six steps when dealing with a maximization problem[2]:

Step 1: Solve the original problem using LP. If the answer satisfies the integer constraints, we are done. If not, this value provides an initial upper bound.

Step 2: Find any feasible solution that meets the integer constraints for use as a lower bound. Usually rounding down each variable will accomplish this.

Step 3: Branch on one variable from step 1 that does not have an integer value. Split the problem into two subproblems based on integer values that

[2] Minimization problems involve reversing the roles of the upper and lower bounds.

are immediately above and below the noninteger value. For example, if $X_2 = 3.75$ was in the final LP solution, introduce the constraint $X_2 \geq 4$ in the first subproblem and $X_2 \leq 3$ in the second subproblem.

Step 4: Create nodes at the top of these new branches by solving the new problems.

Step 5: a. If a branch yields a solution to the LP problem that is *not feasible*, terminate the branch.
  b. If a branch yields a solution to the LP problem that is feasible, but not an integer solution, go to step 6.
  c. If the branch yields a *feasible integer* solution, examine the value of the objective function. If this value equals the upper bound, an optimal solution has been reached. If it is not equal to the upper bound, but exceeds the lower bound, set it as the new lower bound and go to step 6. Finally, if it is less than the lower bound, terminate this branch.

Step 6: Examine both branches again and set the upper bound equal to the maximum value of the objective function at all final nodes. If the upper bound equals the lower bound, stop. If not, go back to step 3.

Harrison Electric Company Revisited

We recall from earlier in this chapter that the Harrison Electric Company's integer programming formulation was:

$$\text{Maximize profit} = \$7X_1 + \$6X_2$$

$$\text{Subject to:} \qquad 2X_1 + 3X_2 \leq 12$$
$$6X_1 + 5X_2 \leq 30$$

and both X_1 and X_2 must be nonnegative integers,

where

$$X_1 = \text{number of chandeliers produced, and}$$

$$X_2 = \text{number of ceiling fans produced.}$$

Figure 15.1 illustrated graphically that the optimal, noninteger solution is:

$$X_1 = 3.75 \text{ chandeliers}$$

$$X_2 = 1.5 \text{ ceiling fans}$$

$$\text{Profit} = \$35.25$$

Since X_1 and X_2 are not integers, this solution is not valid. The profit value of \$35.25 will serve as an initial *upper bound*. We note that rounding down gives $X_1 = 3$, $X_2 = 1$, profit $= \$27$, which is feasible and can be used as a *lower bound*.

subproblems *A* and *B*   The problem is now divided into two subproblems, A and B. We can consider branching on either variable that does not have an integer solution; let us pick X_1 this time.

Subproblem A	Subproblem B
Maximize profit $= \$7X_1 + \$6X_2$	Maximize profit $= \$7X_1 + \$6X_2$
Subject to:	Subject to:
$2X_1 + 3X_2 \leq 12$	$2X_1 + 3X_2 \leq 12$
$6X_1 + 5X_2 \leq 30$	$6X_1 + 5X_2 \leq 30$
$X_1 \geq 4$	$X_1 \leq 3$

If you solve both subproblems graphically, you will observe the solutions:

Subproblem A's optimal solution $= [X_1 = 4, X_2 = 1.2,$ Profit $= \$35.20]$

Subproblem B's optimal solution $= [X_1 = 3, X_2 = 2,$ Profit $= \$33.00]$

This information is presented in branch form in Figure 15.5. We have completed steps 1–4 of the branch and bound method.

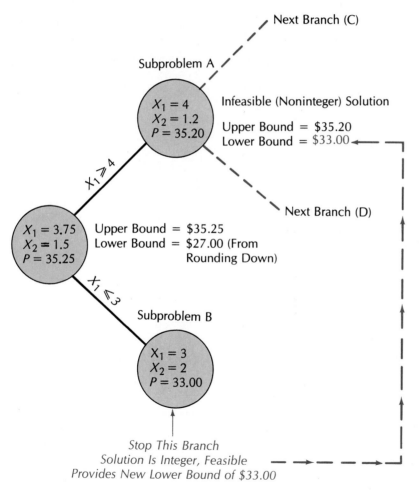

FIGURE 15.5

Harrison Electric's First Branching: Subproblems A and B

We may stop the search of the subproblem B branch since it has an all-integer feasible solution (see step 5c). The profit value of $33 becomes the new *lower bound*. Subproblem A's branch is searched further since it has a noninteger solution. The second *upper bound* takes on the value $35.20, replacing $35.25 from the first node.

subproblems *C* and *D*

Subproblem A is now branched into two new subproblems: C and D. Subproblem C has the additional constraint of $X_2 \geq 2$. Subproblem D adds the constraint $X_2 \leq 1$. The logic for developing these subproblems is that, since subproblem A's optimal solution of $X_2 = 1.2$ is not feasible, the integer feasible answer must lie either in the region $X_2 \geq 2$ or in the region $X_2 \leq 1$.

Subproblem C	Subproblem D
Maximize profit = $7X_1 + \$6X_2$	Maximize profit = $7X_1 + \$6X_2$
Subject to:	Subject to:
$2X_1 + 3X_2 \leq 12$	$2X_1 + 3X_2 \leq 12$
$6X_1 + 5X_2 \leq 30$	$6X_1 + 5X_2 \leq 30$
$X_1 \geq 4$	$X_1 \geq 4$
$X_2 \geq 2$	$X_2 \leq 1$

Subproblem C has no feasible solution whatsoever because the first two constraints are violated if the $X_1 \geq 4$ and $X_2 \geq 2$ constraints are observed. We terminate this branch and do not consider its solution.

Subproblem D's optimal solution = $[X_1 = 4\frac{1}{6}, X_2 = 1, \text{Profit} = \$35.16]$. This noninteger solution yields a *new upper bound* of $35.16, replacing $35.20. Subproblems C and D, as well as the final branches for the problem, are shown in Figure 15.6.

Finally, we create subproblems E and F and solve for X_1 and X_2 with the added constraints $X_1 \leq 4$ and $X_1 \geq 5$. The subproblems and their solutions are:

Subproblem E	Subproblem F
Maximize profit = $7X_1 + \$6X_2$	Maximize profit = $7X_1 + \$6X_2$
Subject to:	Subject to:
$2X_1 + 3X_2 \leq 12$	$2X_1 + 3X_2 \leq 12$
$6X_1 + 5X_2 \leq 30$	$6X_1 + 5X_2 \leq 30$
$X_1 \geq 4$	$X_1 \geq 4$
$X_1 \leq 4$	$X_1 \geq 5$
$X_2 \leq 1$	$X_2 \leq 1$
Optimal solution to E:	Optimal solution to F:
$X_1 = 4, X_2 = 1, \text{Profit} = \$34$	$X_1 = 5, X_2 = 0, \text{Profit} = \$35$

The stopping rule for the branching process is that we continue until the new upper bound is less than or equal to the lower bound *or* no further branching is possible. The latter is the case here since both branches yielded feasible integer solutions. The optimal solution is at subproblem F's node: $X_1 = 5, X_2 = 0, \text{Profit} = \$35$. You can, of course, confirm this by looking back to Table 15.1.

The branch and bound method has been computerized and does a good job of solving problems with a small to medium number of integer variables.

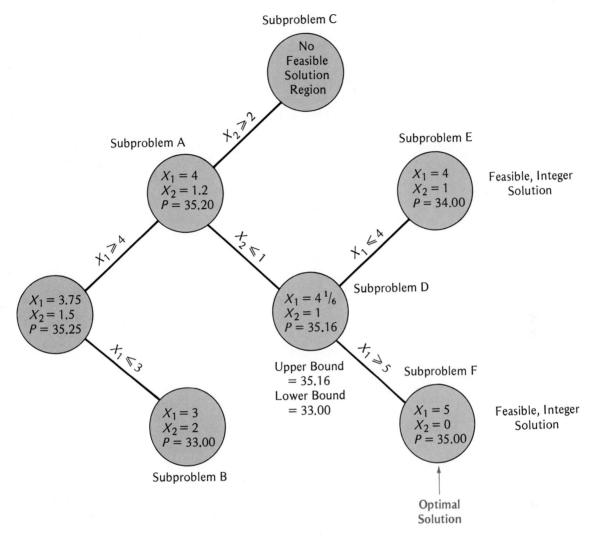

FIGURE 15.6
Harrison Electric's Full Branch and Bound Solution

On especially large problems, the analyst must sometimes settle for a near-optimal answer. Much research has been conducted on this subject and new algorithms that increase the computer's efficiency are constantly under study.

15.4
GOAL PROGRAMMING

In today's business environment, profit maximization or cost minimization are not always the only objectives that a firm sets forth. Often maximizing total profit is just one of several goals, including such contradictory objectives as maximizing market share, maintaining full employment, providing

firms usually have more than one goal

APPLICATIONS OF QA

Branch and Bound Technique for Establishing Insurance Sales Territories

Breaking up any territory or geographical area into distinct sales territories is an important decision for an organization since good sales territory decisions can result in substantial savings. This type of decision can be complex when obstacles such as mountains, rivers, and/or roads must be taken into account.

The Variable Annuity Life Insurance Company (VALIC), located in Houston, faced just this problem. VALIC offers annuity and insurance products to employees of nonprofit organizations and var-

Source: Betsy Gelb and Basheer Khumawala, "Reconfiguration of an Insurance Company's Sales Regions," *Interfaces* Vol. 14, No. 6, November–December 1984.

ious governmental agencies and organizations. With approximately 346 employees and 16 distinct regions, VALIC had to determine various sales territories.

This problem was tackled by the branch and bound technique, which involves splitting a decision into branches and then binding these decisions or eliminating ones that are not feasible or don't need to be considered further. The problem involved minimizing both variable costs and fixed costs of potential alternatives. As a result of the branch and bound technique, VALIC was able to obtain a cost savings of $8,833,000.

quality ecological management, minimizing noise level in the neighborhood, and meeting numerous other noneconomic goals.

Mathematical programming techniques such as linear and integer programming have the shortcoming that their objective function is measured in one dimension only. It's not possible for linear programming to have *multiple goals* unless they are all measured in the same units (such as dollars), a highly unusual situation. An important technique that has been developed to supplement linear programming is called *goal programming*.

goal programming permits multiple goals

Goal programming is capable of handling decision problems involving multiple goals. A relatively new concept, it began with the work of Charnes and Cooper in 1961 and has been refined and extended by Lee in the 1970s (see Bibliography).

In typical decision-making situations, the goals set by management can be achieved only at the expense of other goals. It is necessary to establish a hierarchy of importance among these goals so that lower-priority goals are tackled only after higher-priority ones are satisfied. Since it is not always possible to achieve every goal to the extent the decision maker desires, goal programming attempts to reach a satisfactory level of multiple objectives. This, of course, differs from linear programming which tries to find the best possible outcome for a *single* objective. Nobel laureate Herbert A. Simon, of Carnegie-Mellon University, states that modern managers may not be able to optimize, but may instead have to "*satisfice*" or "come as close as possible" to reaching goals. This is the case with models such as goal programming.

goal programming "satisfices"

KEY IDEA →

How, specifically, does goal programming differ from linear programming? The objective function is the main difference. Instead of trying to maximize or minimize the objective function directly, with goal programming we try to minimize *deviations* between set goals and what we can actually achieve within the given constraints. In the LP simplex approach, such deviations are called *slack variables* and they are used only as dummy variables. In goal programming, these slack terms are either positive or negative, and not only are they real variables, but they are also the only terms in the objective function. The objective is to minimize these *deviational variables*.

deviational variables

Once the goal programming model is formulated, the computational algorithm is almost the same as a minimization problem solved by the simplex method.

An Example of Goal Programming: Harrison Electric Revisited

To illustrate the formulation of a goal programming problem, let's look back at the Harrison Electric Company case, presented earlier in this chapter as an integer programming problem. That problem's LP formulation, you recall, was:

$$\text{Maximize profit} = \$7X_1 + \$6X_2$$

$$\begin{array}{lll} \text{Subject to:} & 2X_1 + 3X_2 \leq 12 & \text{(\textit{wiring hours})} \\ & 6X_1 + 5X_2 \leq 30 & \text{(\textit{assembly hours})} \\ & X_1, X_2 \geq 0 & \end{array}$$

where

$$X_1 = \text{number of chandeliers produced, and}$$

$$X_2 = \text{number of ceiling fans produced.}$$

We saw that if Harrison's management had a single goal, say profit, linear programming could be used to find the optimal solution. But let's assume that the firm is moving to a new location during a particular production period and feels that maximizing profit is not a realistic goal. Management sets a profit level, which would be satisfactory during the adjustment period, of $30. We now have a goal programming problem in which we want to find the production mix that achieves this goal as closely as possible, given the production time constraints. This simple case will provide a good starting point for tackling more complicated goal programs.

We first define two deviational variables:

$$d_1^- = \text{the underachievement of the profit target}$$

$$d_1^+ = \text{the overachievement of the profit target}$$

Now we can state the Harrison Electric problem as a *single-goal* programming model.

$$\text{Minimize under- or overachievement of profit target} = d_1^- + d_1^+$$

$$\begin{array}{lll} \text{Subject to: } \$7X_1 + \$6X_2 + d_1^- - d_1^+ = \$30 & \text{(\textit{profit goal constraint})} \\ \qquad\qquad 2X_1 + 3X_2 \leq 12 & \text{(\textit{wiring hours constraint})} \\ \qquad\qquad 6X_1 + 5X_2 \leq 30 & \text{(\textit{assembly hours constraint})} \\ \qquad X_1, X_2, d_1^-, d_1^+ \geq 0 & \end{array}$$

Note that the first constraint states that the profit made, $7X_1 + \$6X_2$, plus any underachievement of profit minus any overachievement of profit has to equal the target of \$30. For example, if $X_1 = 3$ chandeliers and $X_2 = 2$ ceiling fans, then \$33 profit has been made. This exceeds \$30 by \$3, so d_1^+ must be equal to 3. Since the profit goal constraint was *overachieved*, Harrison did not underachieve and d_1^- will clearly be equal to 0. This problem is now ready for solution by a goal programming algorithm.

If the target profit of \$30 is exactly achieved, we see that both d_1^+ and d_1^- are equal to 0. The objective function will also be minimized at 0. If Harrison's management was only concerned with *underachievement* of the target goal, how would the objective function change? It would be: minimize underachievement = d_1^-. This is also a reasonable goal since the firm would probably not be upset with an overachievement of its target.

In general, once all goals and constraints are identified in a problem, management should analyze each goal to see if underachievement or overachievement of that goal is an acceptable situation. If overachievement is acceptable, the appropriate d^+ variable can be eliminated from the objective function. If underachievement is okay, the d^- variable should be dropped. If management seeks to attain a goal exactly, both d^- and d^+ must appear in the objective function.

An Extension to Equally Important Multiple Goals

Let's now look at the situation in which Harrison's management wants to achieve several goals, each equal in priority.

Goal 1: To produce as much profit above \$30 as possible during the production period.

Goal 2: To fully utilize the available wiring department hours.

Goal 3: To avoid overtime in the assembly department.

Goal 4: To meet a contract requirement to produce at least seven ceiling fans.

The deviational variables can be defined as follows:

d_1^- = underachievement of the profit target

d_1^+ = overachievement of the profit target

d_2^- = idle time in the wiring department (underutilization)

d_2^+ = overtime in the wiring department (overutilization)

d_3^- = idle time in the assembly department (underutilization)

d_3^+ = overtime in the assembly department (overutilization)

d_4^- = underachievement of the ceiling fan goal

d_4^+ = overachievement of the ceiling fan goal

Management is unconcerned about whether there is overachievement of the profit goal, overtime in the wiring department, idle time in the assembly department, or whether more than seven ceiling fans are produced: hence, d_1^+, d_2^+, d_3^-, and d_4^+ may be omitted from the objective function. The new objective function and constraints are:

$$\text{Minimize total deviation} = d_1^- + d_2^- + d_3^+ + d_4^-$$

$$
\begin{array}{ll}
\text{Subject to:} & 7X_1 + 6X_2 + d_1^- - d_1^+ = 30 \quad \textit{(profit constraint)} \\
& 2X_1 + 3X_2 + d_2^- - d_2^+ = 12 \quad \textit{(wiring hours constraint)} \\
& 6X_1 + 5X_2 + d_3^- - d_3^+ = 30 \quad \textit{(assembly constraint)} \\
& \qquad\quad X_2 + d_4^- - d_4^+ = 7 \quad \textit{(ceiling fan constraint)}
\end{array}
$$

All X_i, d_i variables ≥ 0.

Ranking Goals

In most goal programming problems, one goal will be more important than another, which in turn will be more important than a third. The idea is that goals can be ranked with respect to their importance in management's eyes. Lower-order goals are considered only after higher-order goals are met. Priorities (P_i's) are assigned to each deviational variable—with the ranking that P_1 is the most important goal, P_2 the next most important, then P_3 and so on.

KEY IDEA

assigning priorities

Let's say Harrison Electric sets the priorities shown in the accompanying table.

GOAL	PRIORITY
Reach a profit as much above $30 as possible	P_1
Fully use wiring department hours available	P_2
Avoid assembly department overtime	P_3
Produce at least seven ceiling fans	P_4

This means, in effect, that the priority of meeting the profit goal (P_1) is infinitely more important than the wiring goal (P_2), which is, in turn, infinitely more important than the assembly goal (P_3), which is infinitely more important than producing at least seven ceiling fans (P_4).

With ranking of goals considered, the new objective function becomes:

$$\text{Minimize total deviation} = P_1 d_1^- + P_2 d_2^- + P_3 d_3^+ + P_4 d_4^-$$

The constraints remain identical to the previous ones.

Solving Goal Programming Problems Graphically

Just as we solved linear programming problems graphically in Chapter 10, we can analyze goal programming problems graphically. First, we must be aware of three characteristics of goal programming problems: (1) goal programming models are all minimization problems; (2) there is no single objective, but multiple goals to be attained; and (3) the deviation from a high-priority goal must be minimized to the greatest extent possible before the next-highest-priority goal is considered.

Let us use the Harrison Electric Company goal programming problem as an example. The model was formulated as:

$$\text{Minimize total deviation} = P_1 d_1^- + P_2 d_2^- + P_3 d_3^+ + P_4 d_4^-$$

$$
\begin{aligned}
\text{Subject to:} \quad & 7X_1 + 6X_2 + d_1^- - d_1^+ = 30 \quad (\textit{profit}) \\
& 2X_1 + 3X_2 + d_2^- - d_2^+ = 12 \quad (\textit{wiring}) \\
& 6X_1 + 5X_2 + d_3^- - d_3^+ = 30 \quad (\textit{assembly}) \\
& X_2 + d_4^- - d_4^+ = 7 \quad (\textit{ceiling fans}) \\
& X_1, X_2, d_i^-, d_i^+ \geq 0 \quad (\textit{nonnegativity})
\end{aligned}
$$

where

$$X_1 = \text{number of chandeliers produced, and}$$

$$X_2 = \text{number of ceiling fans produced.}$$

graphical constraints

To solve this problem, we graph one constraint at a time, starting with the one that has the highest-priority deviational variables. This is the profit constraint, since d_1^- has priority P_1 in the objective function. Figure 15.7 shows the profit constraint line. Note that in graphing the line, the deviational variables d_1^- and d_1^+ are ignored. To minimize d_1^- (the underachieve-

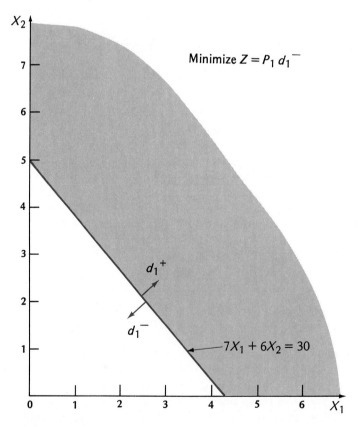

FIGURE 15.7
Analysis of First Goal

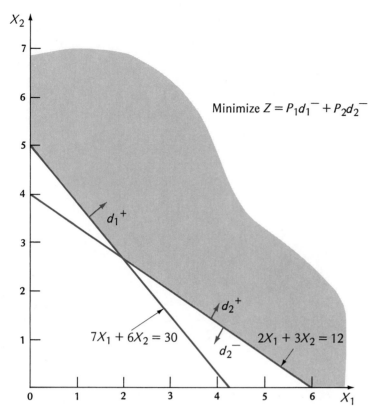

FIGURE 15.8
Analysis of First and Second Goals

ment of \$30 profit), the feasible area is the shaded region. Any point in the shaded region satisfies the first goal because profit exceeds \$30.

Figure 15.8 includes the second priority goal of minimizing d_2^-. The region below the constraint line $2X_1 + 3X_2 = 12$ represents the values for d_2^-, while the region above the line stands for d_2^+. To avoid underutilizing wiring department hours, the area below the line is eliminated. But this goal must be attained within the feasible area already defined by satisfying the first goal.

The third goal is to avoid overtime in the assembly department, which means we want d_3^+ to be as close to 0 as possible. As we can see in Figure 15.9, this goal can also be fully attained. The area that contains solution points that will satisfy the first three priority goals is bounded by the points A, B, C, D. Inside this narrow strip, any solution will meet the three most critical goals.

The fourth goal is to produce at least seven ceiling fans, and hence to minimize d_4^-. To achieve this final goal, the area below the constraint line $X_2 = 7$ must be eliminated. But we cannot do this without violating one of the higher-priority goals. We want, then, to find a solution point that still satisfies the first three goals, and also comes as close as possible to achieving the fourth goal. Do you see which point this would be?

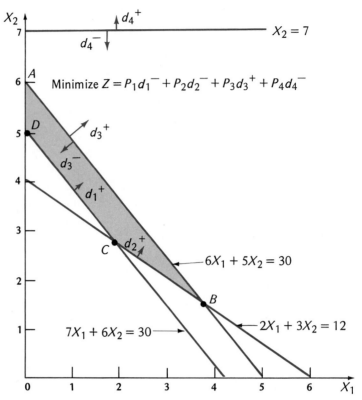

FIGURE 15.9
Analysis of All Four Priority Goals

solution

Corner point A appears to be the optimal solution. We easily see that its coordinates are $X_1 = 0$ chandeliers and $X_2 = 6$ ceiling fans. Substituting these values into the goal constraints, we find the other variables are:

$$d_1^- = \$0, \ d_1^+ = \$6, \ d_2^- = 0 \text{ hours}, \ d_2^+ = 6 \text{ hours},$$

$$d_3^- = 0 \text{ hours}, \ d_3^+ = 0 \text{ hours}, \ d_4^- = 1 \text{ ceiling fan},$$

$$d_4^+ = 0 \text{ ceiling fans}$$

Thus, the profit goal was met and exceeded by $6 (a $36 profit was attained), the wiring department was fully utilized as six hours of overtime were used there, the assembly department had no idle time (or overtime), and the ceiling fan goal was underachieved by only one fan. This was the most satisfactory solution to the problem.

The graphical approach to goal programming has the same drawbacks as it did to linear programming, namely, it can only handle problems with two real variables. By modifying the simplex method of LP, a more general solution to goal programming problems can be found.

A Modified Simplex Method for Goal Programming

To demonstrate how the modified simplex method can be used to solve a goal programming problem, we again turn to the Harrison Electric Company example.

$$\text{Minimize} = P_1 d_1^- + P_2 d_2^- + P_3 d_3^+ + P_4 d_4^-$$

$$\text{Subject to:} \quad 7X_1 + 6X_2 + d_1^- - d_1^+ = 30$$
$$2X_1 + 3X_2 + d_2^- - d_2^+ = 12$$
$$6X_1 + 5X_2 + d_3^- - d_3^+ = 30$$
$$X_2 + d_4^- - d_4^+ = 7$$
$$X_1, X_2, d_i^-, d_i^+ \geq 0$$

Table 15.4 presents the initial simplex tableau for this problem. We should point out four features of this tableau that differ from the simplex tableaus we saw in Chapter 11:

1. The variables in the problem are listed at the top, with the decision variables (X_1 and X_2) first, then the negative deviational variables, and finally the positive deviational variables. The priority level of each variable is assigned on the very top row.

differences between LP simplex tableau and GP tableau

2. The negative deviational variables for each constraint provide the initial basic feasible solution. This is analogous to the LP simplex tableau in which slack variables provide the initial solution. (Thus, we see that $d_1^- = 30$, $d_2^- = 12$, $d_3^- = 30$, and $d_4^- = 7$.) The priority level of each variable in the current solution mix is entered in the C_j column on the far left. Note that the coefficients in the body of the tableau are set up exactly as they were in the regular simplex approach.

3. There is a separate Z_j and $C_j - Z_j$ row for each of the P_i priorities. Since profit goals, department hour goals, and production goals are each measured in different units, the four separate priority rows are needed. In goal programming, the bottom row of the simplex tableau contains the highest ranked (P_1) goal, the next row up has the P_2 goal,

TABLE 15.4 Initial Goal Programming Tableau

$C_j \rightarrow$	SOLUTION	0	0	P_1	P_2	0	P_4	0	0	P_3	0	
$\downarrow$	MIX	X_1	X_2	d_1^-	d_2^-	d_3^-	d_4^-	d_1^+	d_2^+	d_3^+	d_4^+	QUANTITY
P_1	d_1^-	7	6	1	0	0	0	−1	0	0	0	30
P_2	d_2^-	2	3	0	1	0	0	0	−1	0	0	12
0	d_3^-	6	5	0	0	1	0	0	0	−1	0	30
P_4	d_4^-	0	1	0	0	0	1	0	0	0	−1	7
P_4	Z_j	0	1	0	0	0	1	0	0	0	−1	7
	$C_j - Z_j$	0	−1	0	0	0	0	0	0	0	+1	
P_3	Z_j	0	0	0	0	0	0	0	0	0	0	0
	$C_j - Z_j$	0	0	0	0	0	0	0	0	1	0	
P_2	Z_j	2	3	0	1	0	0	0	−1	0	0	12
	$C_j - Z_j$	−2	−3	0	0	0	0	0	1	0	0	
P_1	Z_j	7	6	1	0	0	0	−1	0	0	0	30
	$C_j - Z_j$	−7	−6	0	0	0	0	1	0	0	0	

$\uparrow$
Pivot
column

and so on. The rows are computed exactly as in the regular simplex method, but they are done for each priority level. In Table 15.4, the $C_j - Z_j$ value for column X_1, for example, is read as $-7P_1 - 2P_2 - 0P_3 - 0P_4$.

4. In selecting the variable to enter the solution mix, we start with the highest-priority row, P_1, and select the most negative $C_j - Z_j$ value in it. (The pivot column is X_1 in Table 15.4.) If there was no negative number in the $C_j - Z_j$ row for P_1, we would move up to priority P_2's $C_j - Z_j$ row and select the largest negative number there. A negative $C_j - Z_j$ that has a positive number in a P row underneath it, however, is ignored. This means that deviations from a more important goal (one in a lower row) would be *increased* if that variable were brought into the solution.

After we set up the initial modified simplex tableau, we move toward the optimal solution just as with the regular minimization simplex procedures described in detail in Chapter 11. Keeping in mind the four features just listed, the next step in moving from Table 15.4 to Table 15.5 is to find the pivot row. We do this by dividing the quantity values by their corresponding pivot column (X_1) values and picking the one with the smallest positive ratio. Thus d_1^- leaves the basis in the second tableau and is replaced by X_1.

The new rows of the tableau are computed exactly as they are in the regular simplex method. You may recall that this means first computing a new pivot row, then using the formula in Section 3 of Chapter 11 to find the other new rows.

We see in the new $C_j - Z_j$ row for priority P_1, in Table 15.5, that there

TABLE 15.5 Second Goal Programming Tableau

$C_j \rightarrow$ ↓	SOLUTION MIX	0 X_1	0 X_2	P_1 d_1^-	P_2 d_2^-	0 d_3^-	P_4 d_4^-	0 d_1^+	0 d_2^+	P_3 d_3^+	0 d_4^+	QUANTITY
0	X_1	1	$6/7$	$1/7$	0	0	0	$-1/7$	0	0	0	$30/7$
P_2	d_2^-	0	$9/7$	$-2/7$	1	0	0	$2/7$	-1	0	0	$24/7$
0	d_3^-	0	$-1/7$	$-6/7$	0	1	0	$6/7$	0	-1	0	$30/7$
P_4	d_4^-	0	1	0	0	0	1	0	0	0	-1	7
P_4	Z_j	0	1	0	0	0	1	0	0	0	-1	7
	$C_j - Z_j$	0	-1	0	0	0	0	0	0	0	$+1$	
P_3	Z_j	0	0	0	0	0	0	0	0	0	0	0
	$C_j - Z_j$	0	0	0	0	0	0	0	0	1	0	
P_2	Z_j	0	$9/7$	$-2/7$	1	0	0	$2/7$	-1	0	0	$24/7$
	$C_j - Z_j$	0	$-9/7$	$+2/7$	0	0	0	$-2/7$	$+1$	0	0	
P_1	Z_j	0	0	0	0	0	0	0	0	0	0	0
	$C_j - Z_j$	0	0	1	0	0	0	1	0	0	0	

↑
Pivot
column

are no negative values. Thus, the first priority's goal has been reached. Priority 2 is the next objective, and we find two negative entries in its $C_j - Z_j$ row. Again, the largest one is selected as the pivot column and X_2 will become the next variable to enter the solution mix.

Let us skip two tableaus and go directly to Table 15.6, which contains the most satisfactory solution to the problem. (One of the homework problems gives you the chance to work through to this final tableau.)

Notice in the final solution that the first, second, and third goals have been totally achieved: there are no negative $C_j - Z_j$ entries in their rows. A negative value appears (in the d_3^+ column) in the priority 4 row, however, indicating that it has not been fully attained. Indeed, d_4^- is equal to 1, meaning we have underachieved the ceiling fan goal by one fan. But there is a positive number (see the shaded "1") in the d_3^+ column at the P_3 priority level, and thus at a higher-priority level. If we try to force d_3^+ into the solution mix to attain the P_4 goal, it will be at the expense of a more important goal (P_3) which has already been satisfied. We do not want to sacrifice the P_3 goal, so this will be the best possible goal programming solution. The answer is:

$$X_1 = 0 \text{ chandeliers produced}$$

$$X_2 = 6 \text{ ceiling fans produced}$$

$$d_1^+ = \$6 \text{ over the profit goal}$$

$$d_2^+ = 6 \text{ wiring hours over the minimum set}$$

$$d_4^- = 1 \text{ fan less than desired}$$

Our microcomputer software program, AB:QM, has a goal programming module which is illustrated in Program 15.4. The input screen appears first, followed by the final tableau, which is identical in content to Table 15.6. Program 15.4 also provides analyses of deviations and goal achievement and has a final section on goal conflicts.

TABLE 15.6 Final Solution to Harrison Electrical's Goal Program

$C_j \rightarrow$ / ↓	SOLUTION MIX	0 X_1	0 X_2	P_1 d_1^-	P_2 d_2^-	0 d_3^-	P_4 d_4^-	0 d_1^+	0 d_2^+	P_3 d_3^+	0 d_4^+	QUANTITY
0	d_2^+	$8/5$	0	0	-1	$3/5$	0	0	1	$-3/5$	0	6
0	X_2	$6/5$	1	0	0	$1/5$	0	0	0	$-1/5$	0	6
0	d_1^+	$1/5$	0	-1	0	$6/5$	0	1	0	$-6/5$	0	6
P_4	d_4^-	$-6/5$	0	0	0	$-1/5$	1	0	0	$1/5$	-1	1
P_4	Z_j	$-6/5$	0	0	0	$-1/5$	1	0	0	$1/5$	-1	1
	$C_j - Z_j$	$6/5$	0	0	0	$1/5$	0	0	0	$-1/5$	$+1$	
P_3	Z_j	0	0	0	0	0	0	0	0	0	0	0
	$C_j - Z_j$	0	0	0	0	0	0	0	0	1	0	
P_2	Z_j	0	0	0	0	0	0	0	0	0	0	0
	$C_j - Z_j$	0	0	0	1	0	0	0	0	0	0	
P_1	Z_j	0	0	0	0	0	0	0	0	0	0	0
	$C_j - Z_j$	0	0	1	0	0	0	0	0	0	0	

PROGRAM 15.4 Harrison Electric's Goal Programming Analysis Using AB:QM

```
Goal Programming
─────────────────────────────────────────────────────────────────────
Problem Title :  HARRISON ELECTRIC CO.
Tableau (Yes=1/No=2)              1
Number of Constraints             4          Number of Variables        2
─────────────────────────────────────────────────────────────────────

      W(d+)  P(d+)  W(d-)  P(d-)        X1          X2 T         RHS
C1                   1      1            7           6  =          30
C2                   1      2            2           3  =          12
C3      1      3                         6           5  =          30
C4                   1      4                        1  =           7
```
```
─────────────────────────────────────────────────────────────────────
─────────────────────────────────────────────────────────────────────
Help   New   Load   Save   Edit   Run   Print   Install   Directory   Esc
─────────────────────────────────────────────────────────────────────


Program: Goal Programming

Problem Title : HARRISON ELECTRIC CO.

*****  Input Data *****

Min Z =       1P1d-1 +      1P2d-2 +      1P3d+3 +      1P4d-4
Subject to

C1    7X1 + 6X2 + d-1 - d+1 = 30
C2    2X1 + 3X2 + d-2 - d+2 = 12
C3    6X1 + 5X2 + d-3 - d+3 = 30
C4    1X2 + d-4 - d+4 = 7

***** Program Output *****
```

PROGRAM 15.4 (Continued)

```
Final Solution Tableau at Iteration   4
```

Cb\	\Cj Basis	Bi	0 x1	0 x2	1P1 d-1	1P2 d-2
0	d+2	6.000	1.600	0.000	0.000	-1.000
0	x2	6.000	1.200	1.000	0.000	0.000
0	d+1	6.000	0.200	0.000	-1.000	0.000
1P4	d-4	1.000	-1.200	0.000	0.000	0.000
Zj-Cj	1P4	1.000	-1.200	0.000	0.000	0.000
	1P3	0.000	0.000	0.000	0.000	0.000
	1P2	0.000	0.000	0.000	0.000	-1.000
	1P1	0.000	0.000	0.000	-1.000	0.000

Cb\	\Cj Basis	Bi	0 d-3	1p4 d-4	0 d+1	0 d+2
0	d+2	6.000	0.600	0.000	0.000	1.000
0	x2	6.000	0.200	0.000	0.000	0.000
0	d+1	6.000	1.200	0.000	1.000	0.000
1P4	d-4	1.000	-0.200	1.000	0.000	0.000
Zj-Cj	1P4	1.000	-0.200	0.000	0.000	0.000
	1P3	0.000	0.000	0.000	0.000	0.000
	1P2	0.000	0.000	0.000	0.000	0.000
	1P1	0.000	0.000	0.000	0.000	0.000

Cb\	\Cj Basis	Bi	1P3 d+3	0 d+4
0	d+2	6.000	-0.600	0.000
0	x2	6.000	-0.200	0.000
0	d+1	6.000	-1.200	0.000
1P4	d-4	1.000	0.200	-1.000
Zj-Cj	1P4	1.000	0.200	-1.000
	1P3	0.000	-1.000	0.000
	1P2	0.000	0.000	0.000
	1P1	0.000	0.000	0.000

```
Analysis of deviations
```

Constraint	RHS Value	d+	d-
C1	30.000	6.000	0.000
C2	12.000	6.000	0.000
C3	30.000	0.000	0.000
C4	7.000	0.000	1.000

PROGRAM 15.4 (Continued)

```
Analysis of decision variables
------------------------------
Variable      Solution Value
------------------------------
   X1                0.000
   X2                6.000
------------------------------

Analysis of the objective function
----------------------------------
Priority          Nonachievement
----------------------------------
   P1                    0.000
   P2                    0.000
   P3                    0.000
   P4                    1.000
----------------------------------

Analysis of Goal Conflicts
-------------------------------------------------------------------------------
                                                                    Marginal
Goal          Relevant     Relevant    Allowable    Allowable    Substitution
Conflict      Variable     Column      Increase     Decrease        Rate
-------------------------------------------------------------------------------
Priority4      (d-4)                      1.00                        0.20
Priority3      (d+3)       (d+3)                       5.00           1.00
-------------------------------------------------------------------------------

***** End of Output *****
```

15.5
NONLINEAR PROGRAMMING

Linear, integer, and goal programming all assume that a problem's objective function and constraints are linear. That means that they contain no nonlinear terms such as X_1^3, $1/X_2$, $\log X_3$, or $5X_1X_2$. Yet in many mathematical programming problems, the objective function and/or one or more of the constraints are nonlinear.

A Nonlinear Objective Function

nonlinear objective function

The Great Western Appliance Company sells two models of toaster ovens, the Microtoaster (X_1) and the Self-Clean Toaster Oven (X_2). The firm earns a profit of $28 for each Microtoaster regardless of the number sold. Profits for the Self-Clean model, however, increase as more units are sold because of fixed overhead. Profit on this model may be expressed as $21X_2 + .25X_2^2$.

Hence, the firm's objective function is nonlinear:

$$\text{Maximum profit} = 28X_1 + 21X_2 + .25X_2^2$$

APPLICATIONS OF QA

An Integer Goal Programming Model for Determining Capital Expenditures for Correctional Facilities

The selection of capital expenditure projects for the construction of state correctional facilities is often complicated by the existence of multiple and conflicting objectives on the part of the various interest groups involved in the decision-making process. Some groups view the limited availability of state funds to construct such facilities as the paramount consideration. Others, however, consider adequate capacity to house prisoners in a satisfactory manner or the effect of prison overcrowding on prisoner sentencing as the primary factors in the decision to construct new facilities. It is imperative, therefore, that the limited funds available for constructing correctional facilities be allocated in the most efficient and satisfactory manner possible.

This example demonstrates the applicability of goal programming to the capital allocation problem faced by the department of corrections of a southeastern state. As is the case in most states, correctional institutions are overcrowded and there is need for immediate expansion of prison capacity and replacement or renovation of obsolete facilities.

The expenditure items considered by the corrections department in this state include new and renovated maximum, medium, and minimum security facilities; community diversion programs; and personnel increases. The integer goal programming technique forces all prison projects to be completely accepted or rejected. Personnel increases are considered in integer increments only.

The goal programming model encompasses two types of model variables. The variables define the

construction, renovation, or establishment of a particular type of correctional facility for a specific location or purpose. The variables also indicate the number of personnel required by the facilities and programs determined in the model. The goal constraints in this model fall into five categories: additional inmate capacity created by new and renovated correctional facilities; operating and personnel costs associated with each expenditure item; the impact of facility construction and renovation on imprisonment, sentence length, and early releases and parole; the mix of different facility types required by the system; and the personnel requirements resulting from the various capital expenditures for correctional facilities.

Both the determination of goal levels and priority (that is, the ranking of the importance of goals) for capital allocation in a correctional system would typically be determined by a variety of groups and individuals such as system officials, government officials, legislators, and citizens via pressure groups and the press. As such, the formulation of goals is a dynamic process, and there is a tendency for the final goals to be generalities due to the variety of inputs involved.

For this particular state, the solution results are as follows: one new maximum security facility for drug, alcohol, and psychiatric treatment activities; one new minimum security facility for youthful offenders; two new regular minimum security facilities; one new community diversion program in urban area 1; one new community diversion program in urban area 2; one renovation of an existing medium security facility; one renovation of an existing minimum security facility; 250 new correctional officers; four new administrators; 46 new treatment specialist/counselors; and six new medical personnel.

Source: R. Russell, B. Taylor III, and A. Keown, *Computer Environmental Urban Systems*, Vol. 11, No. 4, 1986, pp. 135–146.

Great Western's profit is subject to two linear constraints on production capacity and sales time available.

$$X_1 + X_2 \leq 1,000 \qquad \textit{(units of production capacity)}$$

$$.5X_1 + .4X_2 \leq 500 \qquad \textit{(hours of sales time available)}$$

$$X_1, X_2 \geq 0$$

quadratic programming

When an objective function contains squared terms (such as $.25X_2^2$) and the problem's constraints are linear, it is called a *quadratic programming* problem. A number of useful problems in the field of portfolio selection fall into this category. Quadratic programs can be solved by a modified method of the simplex method. Such work is outside the scope of this text but can be found in sources listed in the Bibliography.

Other Nonlinear Problems

Two more types of *nonlinear programming* problems are possible. Case 1 is a situation with nonlinear constraints, but a linear objective function, and case 2 has both a nonlinear objective and constraints.

nonlinear constraints

Case 1:　　Minimize cost $= 5X_1 + 7X_2$

Subject to:
$$3X_1 + .25X_1^2 + 4X_2 + .3X_2^2 \geq 125$$
$$13X_1 + X_1^3 \geq 80$$
$$.7X_1 + X_2 \geq 17$$

objective and constraints both nonlinear

Case 2:　　Maximize revenue $= 13X_1 + 6X_1X_2 + 5X_2 + 1/X_2$

Subject to:
$$2X_1^2 + 4X_2 \leq 90$$
$$X_1 + X_2^3 \leq 75$$
$$8X_1 - 2X_2 \leq 61$$

Unlike linear programming methods, computational procedures to solve many nonlinear problems do not always yield an optimal solution in a finite number of steps. In addition, there is no general method for solving all nonlinear problems. *Classical optimization* techniques, based on calculus, can handle some special cases, usually simpler types of problems. The **gradient method**

gradient method, sometimes called the *steepest ascent method*, is an iterative procedure that moves from one feasible solution to the next in improving the value of the objective function. It has been computerized and can handle problems with both nonlinear constraints and objectives. But perhaps the best way to deal with nonlinear problems is to try to reduce them into a **separable programming** form that is linear or almost linear. *Separable programming* deals with a class of problems in which the objective and constraints are approximated by linear functions. In this way, the powerful simplex algorithm may again be applied. In general, work in the area of nonlinear programming is the least charted and most difficult of all the quantitative analysis models.

GLOSSARY

Integer Programming. A mathematical programming technique that produces integer solutions to linear programming problems.

Cutting Plane Method. A means of adding one or more constraints to linear programming problems to help produce an optimum integer solution.

Zero-One Integer Programming. Problems in which all decision variables must have integer values of 0 or 1.

Branch and Bound Method. An algorithm for solving all-integer and mixed-integer linear programs. It divides the set of feasible solutions into subsets that are systematically examined.

Goal Programming. A mathematical programming technique that permits decision makers to set and prioritize multiple objective functions.

Satisficing. The process of coming as close as possible to reaching your set of objectives.

Deviational Variables. Terms that are minimized in a goal programming problem.

Nonlinear Programming. A category of mathematical programming techniques that allow the objective function and/or constraints to be nonlinear.

SOLVED PROBLEMS

Solved Problem 15.1

Consider the 0–1 integer programming problem that follows:

Maximize	$50X_1 + 45X_2 + 48X_3$
Subject to:	$19X_1 + 27X_2 + 34X_3 \leq 80$
	$22X_1 + 13X_2 + 12X_3 \leq 40$
	X_2, X_2, X_3 must be either 0 or 1

Now reformulate this problem with additional constraints so that no more than two of the three variables can take on a value equal to 1 in the solution. Further, make sure that if $X_1 = 1$, then $X_2 = 1$ also. Then solve the new problem using LINDO's IP coding.

Solution

The LINDO program can handle all-integer, mixed-integer, and 0–1 integer problems. Program 15.5 shows two new constraints to handle the reformulated problem. It also illustrates the Integer n command in LINDO which specifies that the first n variables in the problem must be 0–1. The optimal solution is $X_1 = 1$, $X_2 = 1$, $X_3 = 0$, with an objective function value of 95.

Solved Problem 15.2

Recall the Harrison Electrical Company goal programming problem seen in Section 15.4 of this chapter. Its LP formulation was:

Maximize profit =	$\$7X_1 + \$6X_2$
Subject to:	$2X_1 + 3X_2 \leq 12$ *(wiring hours)*
	$6X_1 + 5X_2 \leq 30$ *(assembly hours)*
	$X_1, X_2 \geq 0$

where X_1 = number of chandeliers produced, and
   X_2 = number of ceiling fans produced.

Reformulate Harrison Electrical as a goal programming model with the following goals:

Priority 1: Produce at least 4 chandeliers and 3 ceiling fans.
Priority 2: Maximize profit.

PROGRAM 15.5 LINDO Output for Solved Problem 15.1

```
:  MAX  50X1 + 45X2 + 48X3
?  ST
?  19X1 + 27X2 + 34X3 < 80
?  22X1 + 13X2 + 12X3 < 40
?  X1 + X2 + X3 < 2
?  X1 − X2 = 0

?  END

:  INTEGER 3
:  GO
```

OBJECTIVE FUNCTION VALUE

1)   95.0000000

VARIABLE	VALUE	REDUCED COST
X1	1.000000	−50.000000
X2	1.000000	−45.000000
X3	.000000	−48.000000
INTEGER	.000000	.000000

ROW	SLACK OR SURPLUS	DUAL PRICES
2)	34.000000	.000000
3)	5.000000	.000000
4)	.000000	.000000
5)	.000000	.000000
6)	.000000	.000000

Priority 3: Limit overtime in the assembly department to 10 hours and in the wiring department to 6 hours.

Solution

$$\text{Minimize} = P_1(d_1^- + d_2^-) + P_2 d_3^- + P_3(d_4^+ + d_5^+)$$

$$\text{Subject to:} \quad X_1 + d_1^- - d_1^+ = 4 \qquad \Big\} \quad \textit{Priority 1}$$
$$X_2 + d_2^- - d_2^+ = 3$$
$$7X_1 + 6X_2 + d_3^- - d_3^+ = 99{,}999 \quad \Big\} \quad \textit{Priority 2}$$
$$2X_1 + 3X_2 + d_4^- - d_4^+ = 18 \qquad \Big\}$$
$$6X_1 + 5X_2 + d_5^- - d_5^+ = 40 \qquad \Big\} \quad \textit{Priority 3}$$

In the priority 2 goal constraint, the 99,999 represents an unrealistically high profit. It is just a mathematical trick to use as a target so we can get as close as possible to the maximum profit.

DISCUSSION QUESTIONS AND PROBLEMS

Discussion Questions

15-1 Compare the similarities and differences between linear and goal programming.

15-2 Provide your own examples of five applications of integer programming.

15-3 List the advantages and disadvantages of solving integer programming problems by (a) rounding off, (b) enumeration, (c) the cutting plane method, and (d) the branch and bound method.

15-4 Explain in your own words how the cutting plane method works.

15-5 What is the difference between the three types of integer programming problems? Which do you think is most common and why?

15-6 What is the meaning and role of the lower bound and upper bound in the branch and bound method?

15-7 What is meant by "satisficing," and why is the term often used in conjunction with goal programming?

15-8 What are deviational variables? How do they differ from decision variables in traditional linear programming problems?

15-9 If you were the president of the college you are attending and were employing goal programming to assist in decision making, what might your goals be? What kinds of constraints would you include in your model?

15-10 What does it mean to rank goals in goal programming? How does this affect the problem's solution?

15-11 How does the solution of goal programming problems with the modified simplex method differ from the use of the regular simplex approach for LP problems?

15-12 Which of the following are nonlinear programming problems, and why?

(a) Maximize profit $= 3X_1 + 5X_2 + 99X_3$

Subject to:
$$X_1 \geqslant 10$$
$$X_2 \leqslant 5$$
$$X_3 \geqslant 18$$

(b) Minimize cost $= 25X_1 + 30\ X_2 + 8X_1X_2$

Subject to:
$$X_1 \geqslant 8$$
$$X_1 + X_2 \geqslant 12$$
$$.0005X_1 - X_2 = 11$$

(c) Minimize $Z = P_1d_1^- + P_2d_2^+ + P_3d_3^+$

Subject to:
$$X_1 + X_2 + d_1^- - d_1^+ = 300$$
$$X_2 + d_2^- - d_2^+ = 200$$
$$X_1 + d_3^- - d_3^+ = 100$$

(d) Maximize profit $= 3X_1 + 4X_2$

Subject to:
$$X_1^2 - 5X_2 \geqslant 8$$
$$3X_1 + 4X_2 \geqslant 12$$

(e) Minimize cost $= 18X_1 + 5X_2 + X_2^2$

Subject to: $4X_1 - 3X_2 \geq 8$

$X_1 + X_2 \geq 18$

Are any of these quadratic programming problems?

Problems

· **15-13** Use the cutting plane method to solve the following pure-integer programming problem.

Maximize profit $=$ $8X_1 + 6X_2$

Subject to: $4X_1 + 6X_2 \leq 16$

$15X_1 + 3X_2 \leq 27$

X_1, X_2 integers ≥ 0

: **15-14** Student Enterprises sells two sizes of wall posters, a large 3-by-4-foot poster and a smaller 2-by-3-foot poster. The profit earned from the sale of each large poster is $3; each smaller poster earns $2. The firm, although profitable, is not large; it consists of one art student, Jan Meising, at the University of Kentucky. Because of her classroom schedule, Jan has the following weekly constraints: (1) up to three large posters can be sold, (2) up to five smaller posters can be sold, (3) up to 10 hours can be spent on posters during the week, with each large poster requiring 2 hours of work, and each small one taking 1 hour. With the semester almost over, Jan plans on taking a three-month summer vacation to England and doesn't want to leave any unfinished posters behind. Find the integer solution that will maximize her profit.

· **15-15** An airline owns an aging fleet of Boeing 727 jet airplanes. It is considering a major purchase of up to 17 new Boeing model 757 and 767 jets. The decision must take into account numerous cost and capability factors, including the following: (1) the airline can finance up to $400 million in purchases; (2) each Boeing 757 will cost $35 million, while each Boeing 767 will cost $22 million; (3) at least one-third of the planes purchased should be the longer-ranged 757; (4) the annual maintenance budget is to be no more than $8 million; (5) the annual maintenance cost per 757 is estimated to be $800,000, it is $500,000 for each 767 purchased; and finally (6), each 757 can carry 125,000 passengers per year, while each 767 can fly 81,000 passengers annually. Formulate this as an integer programming problem to maximize the annual passenger-carrying capability. What category of integer programming problem is this?

: **15-16** Solve Problem 15-15 by the cutting plane method.

· **15-17** Innis Construction Company specializes in building moderately priced homes in Cincinnati, Ohio. Tom Innis has identified eight potential locations to construct new single family dwellings, but he cannot put up homes on all of the sites because he has only $300,000 to invest in all projects. The accompanying table shows the cost of constructing homes in each area, and the expected profit to be made from the sale of each home. Note that the home-building costs differ considerably due to lot costs, site preparation, and differences in the models to be built. Note also that a fraction of a home cannot be built.

PROBLEMS

LOCATION	COST OF BUILDING AT THIS SITE ($)	EXPECTED PROFIT ($)
1. Clifton	60,000	5,000
2. Mt. Auburn	50,000	6,000
3. Mt. Adams	82,000	10,000
4. Amberly	103,000	12,000
5. Norwood	50,000	8,000
6. Covington	41,000	3,000
7. Roselawn	80,000	9,000
8. Eden Park	69,000	10,000

Formulate Innis's problem using 0–1 integer programming.

: **15-18** Stockbroker Anna Lundberg has made the following recommendations to her client:

TYPE OF INVESTMENT	COST ($)	EXPECTED RETURN ($)
Hanover Municipal bonds	500	50
Hamilton City bonds	1,000	100
S.E. Power & Light Co.	350	30
Nebraska Electric Service	490	45
Southern Gas and Electric	700	65
Samuels Products Co.	270	20
Nation Builder Paint Co.	800	90
Hammer Head Hotels Co.	400	35

The client agrees to this list, but provides several conditions: (1) no more than $3,000 can be invested, (2) the money is to be spread among at least five investments, (3) no more than one type of bond can be purchased, (4) at least two utility stocks and at least two regular stocks must be purchased. Formulate this as a 0–1 integer programming problem for Ms. Lundberg to maximize expected return.

: **15-19** Solve Problem 15-13 using the branch and bound method.

: **15-20** Solve Problem 15-15 using the branch and bound method.

: **15-21** Four incoming jobs at Golding Manufacturing must be assigned to any of four available machines. The cost of doing each job on each machine is shown below:

JOBS	MACHINES			
	#1	#2	#3	#4
A	$85	$70	$60	$10
B	6	15	90	76
C	50	80	5	75
D	75	84	82	25

Use the branch and bound method to generate the least-total-cost assignment of performing the four jobs.

: **15-22** Solve the following integer programming problem using the branch and bound approach.

$$\text{Maximize profit} = \$2X_1 + \$3X_2$$

Subject to:
$$X_1 + 3X_2 \leq 9$$
$$3X_1 + X_2 \leq 7$$
$$X_1 - X_2 \leq 1$$

where both X_1 and X_2 must be nonnegative integer values.

: **15-23** Geraldine Shawhan is president of Shawhan File Works, a firm that manufactures two types of metal file cabinets. The demand for her two-drawer model is up to 600 cabinets per week; demand for a three-drawer cabinet is limited to 400 per week. Shawhan File Works has a weekly operating capacity of 1,300 hours, with the two-drawer cabinet taking one hour to produce and the three-drawer cabinet requiring two hours. Each two-drawer model sold yields a $10 profit, while the profit for the large model is $15. Shawhan has listed the following goals in order of importance:

1. Attain a profit as close to $11,000 as possible each week.
2. Avoid underutilization of the firm's production capacity.
3. Sell as many two-drawer and three-drawer cabinets as the demand indicates.

Set this up as a goal programming problem.

: **15-24** Solve Problem 15-23 graphically. Are any goals unachieved in this solution? Explain.

: **15-25** Harris Segal, marketing director for North-Central Power and Light, is about to begin an advertising campaign promoting energy conservation. In trying to budget between television and newspaper advertisements, he sets the following goals in order of importance:

1. The total advertising budget of $120,000 should not be exceeded.
2. There should be a mix of TV and newspaper ads, with at least 10 TV spots (costing $5,000 each) and at least 20 newspaper ads (costing $2,000 each).
3. The total number of people to read or hear the advertisements should be at least 9 million.

Each television spot reaches approximately 300,000 people. A newspaper advertisement is read by about 150,000 persons. Formulate Segal's goal programming problem to find out how many of each type of ad to place.

: **15-26** Solve Problem 15-25 graphically. How many people, in total, will read or hear the advertisements?

: **15-27** Hilliard Electronics produces specially coded computer memory chips in 64K, 256K, and 512K sizes. (1K means the chip holds 1,024 bits of information—thus a 64K chip contains 65,536 bits.) To produce a 64K chip requires 8 hours of labor, a 256K chip takes 13 hours, and a 512K chip requires 16 hours. Hilliard's monthly production capacity is 1,200 hours. Mr. Blank, the firm's sales manager, estimates that the maximum monthly sales of the 64K, 256K, and 512K chips are 40, 50, and 60 respectively. The company has the following goals (ranked in order from most important to least important):

1. Fill an order from the best customer for thirty 64K chips and thirty-five 256K chips.
2. Provide sufficient chips to at least equal the sales estimates set by Mr. Blank.
3. Avoid underutilization of the production capacity.

Formulate this problem using goal programming.

: **15-28** The modified simplex method was presented for the Harrison Electrical Company example in Tables 15.4, 15.5, and 15.6 in this chapter. Two iterations of the method were skipped between the second tableau in Table 15.5 and the final tableau in Table 15.6. Apply the method to provide the missing third and fourth tableaus. Which corner points (A, B, C, or D) in Figure 15.9 does each of these tableaus correspond to?

: **15-29** An Oklahoma manufacturer produces two products: speaker telephones (X_1) and push-button telephones (X_2). The following goal programming model has been formulated to find the number of each to produce each day to meet the firm's goals.

$$\text{Minimize} \quad P_1 d_1^- + P_2 d_2^- + P_3 d_3^+ + P_4 d_1^+$$

$$\begin{array}{lrll}
\text{Subject to:} & 2X_1 + 4X_2 + d_1^- - d_1^+ = & 80 \\
& 8X_1 + 10X_2 + d_2^- - d_2^+ = & 320 \\
& 8X_1 + 6X_2 + d_3^- - d_3^+ = & 240 \\
& \text{All} \qquad\qquad X_i, d_i \geqslant 0
\end{array}$$

(a) Set up the complete initial goal programming tableau for this problem.
(b) Find the optimal solution using the modified simplex method.

: **15-30** Major Bill Bligh, director of the Army War College's new six-month attaché training program, is concerned about how the 20 officers taking the course spend their precious time while in his charge. Major Bligh recognizes that there are 168 hours per week and thinks his students have been using them rather inefficiently. Bligh lets

X_1 = number of hours of sleep needed per week

X_2 = number of personal hours (eating, personal hygiene, handling laundry, and so on)

X_3 = number of hours of class and studying

X_4 = number of hours of social time off base (dating, sports, family visits, and so on)

He thinks that 30 hours per week should be enough study/class time for students to absorb the material, and that this is his most important goal. Bligh feels that students need at most 7 hours sleep per night on average and that this goal is number 2. He believes that goal number 3 is to provide at least 20 hours per week of social time. Formulate this as a goal programming problem. Solve, using AB:QM, for the best possible answer.

: **15-31** Hinkel Rotary Engine, Ltd., produces four- and six-cylinder models of automobile engines. The firm's profit for each four-cylinder engine sold during its quarterly production cycle is $1,800 - $50X_1$, where X_1 is the number sold. Hinkel makes $2,400 - $70X_2$ for each of the larger engines sold, with X_2 equal to the number of six-cylinder engines sold. There are 5,000 hours of production time available during each production cycle. A four-cylinder engine requires 100 hours of production time, whereas six-cylinder engines take 130 hours to manufacture. Formulate but do not solve this production planning problem for Hinkel.

Data Set Problem

: **15-32** The following integer programming problem has been developed to help First National Bank decide where, out of 10 possible sites, to locate four new branch offices:

Maximize expected returns =
$$120X_1 + 100X_2 + 110X_3 + 140X_4 + 155X_5 + 128X_6$$
$$+ 145X_7 + 190X_8 + 170X_9 + 150X_{10}$$

such that

$$20X_1 + 30X_2 + 20X_3 + 25X_4 + 30X_5 + 30X_6 + 25X_7$$
$$+ 20X_8 + 25X_9 + 30X_{10} \leq 110$$
$$15X_1 + 5X_2 + 20X_3 + 20X_4 + 5X_5 + 5X_6$$
$$+ 10X_7 + 20X_8 + 5X_9 + 20X_{10} \leq 50$$
$$X_2 + X_6 + X_7 + X_9 + X_{10} \leq 3$$
$$X_2 + X_3 + X_5 + X_8 + X_9 \geq 2$$
$$X_1 + X_3 + X_{10} \geq 1$$
$$\Sigma X_i \leq 4$$
$$\text{All } X_i = 0 \text{ or } 1$$

where X_i = Winter Park, Maitland, Osceola, Downtown, South Orlando, Airport, Winter Garden, Apopka, Lake Mary, Cocoa Beach for i equals 1 to 10 respectively.

(a) Where should the four new sites be located and what will be the expected return?

(b) If at least one new branch *must* be opened in Maitland or Osceola, will this change the answers? Add the new constraint and rerun.

(c) The expected return at Apopka was overestimated. The correct value is $160,000 per year (that is, 160). Does your answer to part a change?

CASE STUDY

Schank Marketing Research

Schank Marketing Research has just signed contracts to conduct studies for four clients. At present, three project managers are free for assignment to the tasks. Although all are capable of handling each assignment, the times and costs to complete the studies depend on the experience and knowledge of each manager. Using his judgment, John Schank, the president, has been able to establish a cost for each possible assignment. These costs, which are really the salaries each manager would draw on each task, are summarized below.

	CLIENT			
PROJECT MANAGER	Hines Corp.	NASA	General Foundry	CBT Television
Gardener	$3,200	$3,000	$2,800	$2,900
Ruth	2,700	3,200	3,000	3,100
Hardgraves	1,900	2,100	3,300	2,100

Schank is very hesitant about neglecting NASA, which has been an important customer in the past. (NASA has employed the firm to study the public's attitude toward the Space Shuttle and proposed Space Station.) In addition, Schank has promised to try to provide Ruth a salary of at least $3,000 on his next assignment. From previous contracts, Schank also knows that Gardener does not get along well with the management at CBT Television so he hopes to avoid assigning her to CBT. Finally, as Hines Corporation is also an old and valued client, Schank feels it is twice as important to immediately assign a project manager to Hines's task as it is to provide one to General Foundry, a brand-new client. Schank wants to minimize the total costs of all projects while considering each of these goals. He feels that all of these goals are important, but if he had to rank them, he would put his concern about NASA first, his worry about Gardener

Schank Marketing Research

second, his need to keep Hines Corporation happy third, his promise to Ruth fourth, and his concern about minimizing all costs last.

Each project manager can handle, at most, one new client.

1. If Schank were not concerned about noncost goals, how would he formulate this problem so that it could be solved quantitatively?
2. Develop a formulation that will incorporate all five objectives.

BIBLIOGRAPHY

Anderson, A. M., and Earle, M. D. "Diet Planning in the Third World by Linear and Goal Programming." *Journal of Operations Research Society* Vol. 34, 1983, pp. 9–16.

Bean, James C., Noon, Charles E., Ryan, Sarah M., and Salton, Gary J. "Selecting Tenants in a Shopping Mall." *Interfaces* Vol. 18, No. 2, March–April 1988, pp. 1–9.

Boot, J. C. G. *Quadratic Programming*. Chicago: Rand McNally, 1964.

Bres, E. S., Burns, D., Charnes, A., and Cooper, W. W. "A Goal Programming Model for Planning Officer Accessions." *Management Science* Vol. 26, No. 8, August 1980, pp. 773–781.

Buffa, Frank P., and Jackson, Wade M. "A Goal Programming Model for Purchasing Planning." *Journal of Purchasing and Material Management* Fall 1983, pp. 27–34.

DeKluyver, Cornelis A., and Moskowitz, Herbert. "Assessing Scenario Probabilities Via Interactive Goal Programming." *Management Science* Vol. 30, No. 3, March 1984, pp. 273–278.

Gass, S. I. "A Process for Determining Priorities and Weights for Large-Scale Linear Goal Programs." *Journal of Operational Research Society* Vol. 37, August 1986, pp. 779–785.

Ignizio, J. P. *Goal Programming and Extensions*. Lexington, Mass.: D. C. Heath and Co., 1976.

Jones, Lawrence, and Kwak, N. K. "A Goal Programming Model for Allocating Human Resources for the Good Laboratory Practice Regulations." *Decision Sciences* Vol. 13, No. 1, 1982, pp. 156–166.

Lee, S. M. *Goal Programming for Decision Analysis*. Philadelphia: Auerbach Publishers, Inc., 1972.

Lee, Sang M., and Schniederjans, Marc J. "A Multicriterial Assignment Problem: A Goal Programming Approach." *Interfaces* Vol. 13, No. 4, August 1983, pp. 75–79.

Nauss, Robert M., and Markland, Robert E. "Theory and Application of an Optimizing Procedure for Lock Box Location Analysis." *Management Science* Vol. 27, No. 8, August 1981, pp. 855–865.

Russell, Roberta S., Taylor, Bernard W. III, and Keown, Art J. "An Integer Goal Programming Model for Determining Capital Expenditures for Correctional Facilities." *Computer Environment Urban Systems* Vol. 11, No. 4, 1986, pp. 135–146.

Ruth, R. Jean. "A Mixed Integer Programming Model for Regional Planning of a Hospital Inpatient Service." *Management Science* Vol. 27, No. 5, May 1981, pp. 521–533.

Schniederjans, Marc J., Kwak, N. K., and Helmer, Mark C. "An Application of Goal Programming to Resolve a Site Location Problem." *Interfaces* Vol. 12, No. 3, June 1982, pp. 65–72.

Schniederjans, Marc J., and Kim, Gyu Chan. "A Goal Programming Model to Optimize Departmental Preference in Course Assignments." *Computer Operations Research* Vol. 14, No. 2, 1987, pp. 87–96.

Stafford, E. F. "On the Development of a Mixed-Integer Linear Programming Model for the Flowshop Sequencing Problem." *Journal of Operational Research Society* Vol. 39, December 1988, pp. 1163–1174.

Stowe, J. D. "An Integer Programming Solution for the Optimal Credit Investigation/Credit Granting Sequence." *Financial Management* Vol. 14, Summer 1985, pp. 66–76.

Taylor, B. W., and others. "An Integer Nonlinear Goal Programming Model for the Deployment of State Highway Patrol Units." *Management Science* Vol. 31, No. 11, November 1985, pp. 1335–1347.

Tingley, Kim M., and Liebmen, Judith S. "A Goal Programming Example in Public Health Resource Allocation." *Management Science* Vol. 30, No. 3, March 1984, pp. 279–289.

Zangwill, W. I. *Nonlinear Programming: A Unified Approach*. Englewood Cliffs, N.J.: Prentice Hall, 1969.

16

Waiting Lines: Queuing Theory

16.1
INTRODUCTION

The study of *waiting lines*, called *queuing theory*, is one of the oldest and most widely used quantitative analysis techniques. Waiting lines are an everyday occurrence, affecting people shopping for groceries, buying gasoline, making a bank deposit, or waiting on the telephone for the first available airline reservationist to answer. Queues,[1] another term for waiting lines, may also take the form of machines waiting to be repaired, trucks in line to be unloaded, or airplanes lined up on a runway waiting for permission to take off. The three basic components of a queuing process are arrivals, service facilities, and the actual waiting line.

In this chapter we discuss how analytical models of waiting lines can help managers evaluate the cost and effectiveness of service systems. We begin with a look at waiting line costs, then describe the characteristics of waiting lines and the underlying mathematical assumptions used to develop queuing models. We also provide the equations needed to compute the operating characteristics of a service system and show examples of how they are used. Later in the chapter, you will see how to save computational time by applying queuing tables and by running waiting line computer programs.

16.2
WAITING LINE COSTS

Most waiting line problems are centered about the question of finding the ideal level of services that a firm should provide. Supermarkets must decide how many cash register checkout positions should be opened. Gasoline stations must decide how many pumps should be opened and how many attendants should be on duty. Manufacturing plants must determine the optimal number of mechanics to have on duty each shift to repair machines that break down. Banks must decide how many teller windows to keep open to serve customers during various hours of the day. In most cases, this level of service is an option over which management has control. An extra teller, for example, can be borrowed from another chore or can be quickly hired and trained if demand warrants it. This may not always be the case, though. A plant may not be able to locate or hire skilled mechanics to repair sophisticated electronic machinery. And a gas station owner with 10 pumps may have a gasoline allotment large enough to open only 5 or 6 pumps.

finding the best level of service

When an organization *does* have control, its objective is usually to find a happy medium between two extremes. On the one hand, a firm can retain a large staff and provide *many* service facilities. This may result in excellent customer service, with seldom more than one or two customers in a queue. Customers are kept happy with the quick response and appreciate the convenience. This, however, can become expensive.

---

[1] The word queue is pronounced like the letter *Q*, that is, "kew."

630

HISTORY

How Queuing Models Began

Queuing theory had its beginning in the research work of a Danish engineer named A. K. Erlang. In 1909 Erlang experimented with fluctuating demand in telephone traffic. Eight years later he published a report addressing the delays in automatic dialing equipment. At the end of World War II, Erlang's early work was extended to more general problems and to business applications of waiting lines.

The other extreme is to have the *minimum* possible number of checkout lines, gas pumps, or teller windows open. This keeps the *service cost* down, but may result in customer dissatisfaction. How many times would you return to a large discount department store that had only one cash register open during the day you shop? As the average length of the queue increases and poor service results, customers and goodwill may be lost.

Most managers recognize the trade-off that must take place between the cost of providing good service and the cost of customer waiting time. They want queues that are short enough so that customers don't become unhappy and either storm out without buying or buy but never return. But they are willing to allow some waiting in line if it is balanced by a significant savings in service costs.

 KEY IDEA

One means of evaluating a service facility is thus to look at *total expected cost*, a concept illustrated in Figure 16.1. Total expected cost is the sum of expected *service costs* plus expected *waiting costs*.

total expected cost

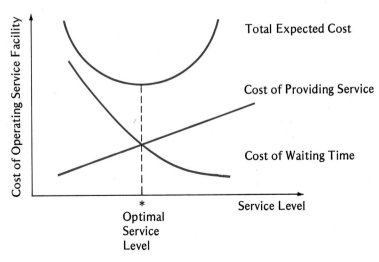

FIGURE 16.1
Queuing Costs and Service Levels

Service costs are seen to increase as a firm attempts to raise its level of service. For example, if three teams of stevedores, instead of two, are employed to unload a cargo ship, service costs are increased by the additional price of wages. As service improves in speed, however, the cost of time spent waiting in lines decreases. This waiting cost may reflect lost productivity of workers while their tools or machines are awaiting repairs, or may simply be an estimate of the cost of customers lost because of poor service and long queues.

As an illustration, let's look at the case of the Three Rivers Shipping Company. Three Rivers runs a huge docking facility located on the Ohio River near Pittsburgh. Approximately five ships arrive to unload their cargoes of steel and ore during every 12-hour work shift. Each hour that a ship sits idle in line waiting to be unloaded costs the firm a great deal of money, about $1,000 per hour. From experience, management estimates that if one team of stevedores is on duty to handle the unloading work, each ship will wait an average of 7 hours to be unloaded. If two teams are working, the average waiting time drops to 4 hours; for three teams, it's 3 hours; and for four teams of stevedores, only 2 hours. But each additional team of stevedores is also an expensive proposition, due to union contracts.

minimum total expected cost

Three River's superintendent would like to determine the optimal number of teams of stevedores to have on duty each shift. The objective is to minimize total expected costs. This analysis is summarized in Table 16.1.

In order to minimize the sum of service costs and waiting costs, the firm makes the decision to employ two teams of stevedores each shift.

TABLE 16.1 Three Rivers Shipping Company Waiting Line Cost Analysis

	NUMBER OF TEAMS OF STEVEDORES WORKING			
	1	2	3	4
(a) Average number of ships arriving per shift	5	5	5	5
(b) Average time each ship waits to be unloaded (hours)	7	4	3	2
(c) Total ship hours lost per shift (a × b)	35	20	15	10
(d) Estimated cost per hour of idle ship time	$ 1,000	$ 1,000	$ 1,000	$ 1,000
(e) Value of ship's lost time or waiting cost (c × d)	$35,000	$20,000	$15,000	$10,000
(f) Stevedore team salary,* or service cost	$ 6,000	$12,000	$18,000	$24,000
(g) Total expected cost (e + f)	$41,000	($32,000)	$33,000	$34,000
		⤷Optimal cost		

* Stevedore team salaries are computed as the number of people in a typical team (assumed to be 50), times the number of hours each person works per day (12 hours), times an hourly salary of $10 per hour. If two teams are employed the rate is just doubled.

milk, frozen food, or meats, simply abandon the shopping cart before checking out because the line was too long? This expensive occurrence for the store makes managers acutely aware of the importance of service level decisions.

Waiting Line Characteristics

The waiting line itself is the second component of a queuing system. The length of a line can be either *limited* or *unlimited*. A queue is limited when it cannot, by law or physical restrictions, increase to an infinite length. This may be the case in a small restaurant that has only 10 tables and can serve no more than 50 diners an evening. Analytic queuing models are treated in this chapter under an assumption of *unlimited* queue length. A queue is unlimited when its size is unrestricted, as in the case of the toll booth serving arriving automobiles.

limited and unlimited lines

A second waiting line characteristic deals with *queue discipline*. This refers to the rule by which customers in the line are to receive service. Most systems use a queue discipline known as the *first-in, first-out rule* (FIFO). In a hospital emergency room or an express checkout line at a supermarket, however, various assigned priorities may preempt FIFO. Patients who are critically injured will move ahead in treatment priority over patients with broken fingers or noses. Shoppers with fewer than 10 items may be allowed to enter the express checkout queue but are *then* treated as first come, first served. Computer programming runs are another example of queuing systems that operate under priority scheduling. In most large companies, when computer-produced paychecks are due out on a specific date, the payroll program has highest priority over other runs.[2]

first-in, first-out rule

Service Facility Characteristics

The third part of any queuing system is the service facility. It is important to examine two basic properties: (1) the configuration of the service system and (2) the pattern of service times.

Basic Queuing System Configurations. Service systems are usually classified in terms of their number of channels, or number of servers, and number of phases, or number of service stops, that must be made. A *single-channel system*, with one server, is typified by the drive-in bank that has only one open teller, or by the type of drive-through fast-food restaurant that has become increasingly popular in the United States. If, on the other hand, the bank had several tellers on duty, and each customer waited in one common line for the first available teller, then we would have a *multiple-channel system* at work. Many banks today are multichannel service systems, as are most large barber shops and many airline ticket counters.

number of service channels

A *single-phase system* is one in which the customer receives service from only one station and then exits the system. A fast-food restaurant in which

single-phase versus multiphase systems

[2] The term *FIFS* (first in first served) is often used in place of FIFO. Another discipline, LIFS (Last in, first served), is common when material is stacked or piled and the items on top are used first.

Queuing Theory at Eastman Kodak

In some cases, inventory control is so complex that traditional inventory control models are not appropriate. This was the case with Eastman Kodak, a multi-item manufacturer. In many situations at Eastman, a particular job would spend only 10% to 15% of its time in actual processing. The other time was wasted waiting in line or in queues at particular processing centers before processing actually began. When this occurred, both the lead time, or waiting time, before processing and the size of batches that are to be processed were of concern. In order to analyze the lot-sizing and lead-time performance, the firm employed simulation and queuing techniques.

Source: Uday Karmarkar, Sham Kekre, Sunder Kekre, Susan Freeman, "Lot-Sizing and Lead-Time Performance in a Manufacturing Cell." *Interfaces,* Vol. 15, No. 2, March–April 1985, pp. 1–9.

Using queuing theory, a formula was developed to determine the time spent in the system by a given batch. Time was a function of the total work to be done, the processing rate or service rate, the batch size, and the setup time per batch. Furthermore, the queuing theory approach was used to help validate the simulation models that were used. It was shown that the queuing and simulation approaches were close, but that the queuing theory had a 20% advantage in terms of cost. As a result of the analysis, John C. Barnes, the manager of planning at the US Apparatus Division of the Eastman Kodak Company stated: "We are now planning to establish lot sizes using the analytical model instead of the traditional EOQ approach. The confidence gained has allowed us to commit the manufacturing operation to accomplish a very substantial reduction in planned lead time and, therefore, inventory level."

the person who takes your order also brings you the food and takes your money is a single-phase system. So is a driver's license agency in which the person taking your application also grades your test and collects the license fee. But if the restaurant requires you to place your order at one station, pay at a second, and pick up the food at a third service stop, it becomes a *multiphase system*. Likewise, if the driver's license agency is large or busy, you will probably have to wait in a line to complete the application (the first service stop), then queue again to have the test graded (the second service stop), and finally go to a third service counter to pay the fee. To help you relate the concepts of channels and phases, Figure 16.3 presents four possible configurations.

Service Time Distribution. Service patterns are like arrival patterns in that they may be either constant or random. If service time is constant, it takes the same amount of time to take care of each customer. This is the case in a machine-performed service operation such as an automatic car wash. More often, service times are randomly distributed. In many cases, it can be assumed that random service times are described by the *negative exponential probability distribution*. This is a mathematically convenient assumption if arrival rates are Poisson distributed.

> service times often follow negative exponential distribution

Figure 16.4 illustrates that if service times follow an exponential distribution, the probability of any very long service time is low. For example, when an average service time is 20 minutes, seldom if ever will a customer require more than 90 minutes in the service facility. If the mean service

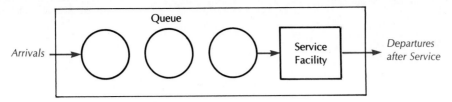

Single-Channel, Single-Phase System

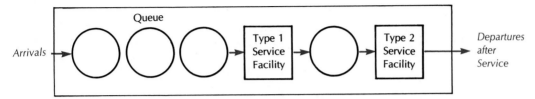

Single-Channel, Multiphase System

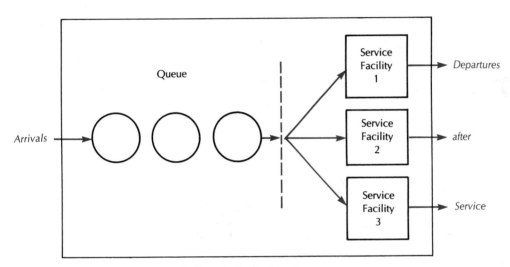

Multichannel, Single-Phase System

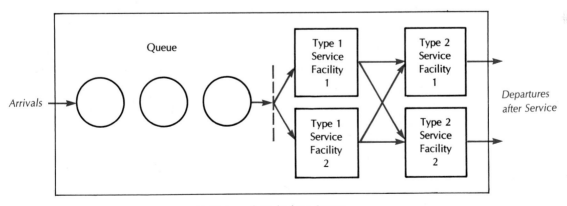

Multichannel, Multiphase System

FIGURE 16.3
Four Basic Queuing System Configurations

637

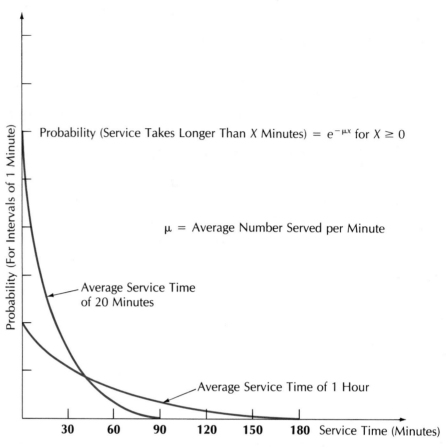

FIGURE 16.4
**Two Examples of the Exponential Distribution
for Service Times**

time is one hour, the probability of spending more than 180 minutes in service is virtually zero.

The exponential distribution is important to the process of building mathematical queuing models since many of the models' theoretical underpinnings are based on the assumption of Poisson arrivals and exponential services. Before they are applied, however, the quantitative analyst can and should observe, collect, and plot service time data to determine if they fit the exponential distribution.

KEY IDEA

16.4
SINGLE-CHANNEL QUEUING MODEL WITH POISSON ARRIVALS AND EXPONENTIAL SERVICE TIMES[3]

In this section, we present an analytical approach to determine important measures of performance in a typical service system. Once these numeric

[3] In the technical terminology of the operations research world, this model is also referred to as the M/M/1 queuing model.

measures have been computed, it will be possible to add in cost data and begin to make decisions that balance desirable service levels with waiting line service costs.

Assumptions of the Model

The single-channel, single-phase model considered here is one of the most widely used and simplest queuing models. It assumes that seven conditions exist:

KEY IDEA

1. Arrivals are served on a first-in, first-out (FIFO) basis.

2. Every arrival waits to be served regardless of the length of the line; that is, there is no balking or reneging.

3. Arrivals are independent of preceding arrivals, but the average number of arrivals (the arrival rate) does not change over time.

4. Arrivals are described by a Poisson probability distribution and come from an infinite or very large population.

5. Service times also vary from one customer to the next and are independent of one another, but their average rate is known.

6. Service times occur according to the negative exponential probability distribution.

7. The average service rate is greater than the average arrival rate.

When these seven conditions are met, we can develop a series of equations that define the queue's *operating characteristics*. The mathematics used to derive each equation is rather complex and outside the scope of this text, so we will just present the resulting formulas here.

Queuing Equations

We let

λ = mean number of arrivals per time period (for example, per hour)

μ = mean number of people or items served per time period

The queuing equations follow.

1. The average number of customers or units in the system, L; that is, the number in line plus the number being served:

queuing equations for the single-channel, single-phase model

$$L = \frac{\lambda}{\mu - \lambda} \tag{16-2}$$

2. The average time a customer spends in the system, W; that is, the time spent in line plus the time spent being served:

$$W = \frac{1}{\mu - \lambda} \tag{16-3}$$

---

3. The average number of customers in the queue, L_q:

$$L_q = \frac{\lambda^2}{\mu(\mu - \lambda)} \tag{16-4}$$

4. The average time a customer spends waiting in the queue, W_q:

$$W_q = \frac{\lambda}{\mu(\mu - \lambda)} \tag{16-5}$$

5. The utilization factor for the system, ρ; that is, the probability that the service facility is being used:

$$\rho = \frac{\lambda}{\mu} \qquad (\rho \text{ is the Greek letter rho}) \tag{16-6}$$

6. The percent idle time, P_0; that is, the probability that no one is in the system:

$$P_0 = 1 - \frac{\lambda}{\mu} \tag{16-7}$$

7. The probability that the number of customers in the system is greater than k, $P_{n>k}$:

$$P_{n>k} = \left(\frac{\lambda}{\mu}\right)^{k+1} \tag{16-8}$$

Arnold's Muffler Shop Case

We now apply these formulas to the case of Arnold's Muffler Shop in New Orleans. Arnold's mechanic, Reid Blank, is able to install new mufflers at an average rate of 3 per hour, or about 1 every 20 minutes. Customers needing this service arrive at the shop on the average of 2 per hour. Larry

Arnold, the shop owner, studied queuing models in an MBA program and feels that all seven of the conditions for a single-channel model are met. He proceeds to calculate the numerical values of the preceding operating characteristics.

λ = 2 cars arriving per hour

μ = 3 cars serviced per hour

$$L = \frac{\lambda}{\mu - \lambda} = \frac{2}{3 - 2} = \frac{2}{1} = 2 \text{ cars in the system on the average}$$

$$W = \frac{1}{\mu - \lambda} = \frac{1}{3 - 2} = 1 \text{ hour that an average car spends in the system}$$

$$L_q = \frac{\lambda^2}{\mu(\mu - \lambda)} = \frac{2^2}{3(3 - 2)} = \frac{4}{3(1)} = \frac{4}{3} = 1.33 \text{ cars waiting in line on the average}$$

$$W_q = \frac{\lambda}{\mu(\mu - \lambda)} = \frac{2}{3(3 - 2)} = \frac{2}{3} \text{ hour} = 40 \text{ minutes} = \text{Average waiting time per car}$$

$$\rho = \frac{\lambda}{\mu} = \frac{2}{3} = .67 = \text{Percent of time mechanic is busy, or the probability that the server is busy}$$

$$P_0 = 1 - \frac{\lambda}{\mu} = 1 - \frac{2}{3} = .33 = \text{Probability there are 0 cars in the system}$$

Probability of More than _k_ Cars in the System

k	$P_{n>k} = (2/3)^{k+1}$	
0	(.667)	⟵ _Note that this is equal to 1 − P_0 = 1 − 0.33 = 0.667._
1	.444	
2	.296	
3	(.198)	⟵ _Implies that there is a 19.8% chance that more than 3 cars are in the system._
4	.132	
5	.088	
6	.058	
7	.039	

Program 16.1 illustrates the ease of use of AB:QM in dealing with queuing problems. The only required inputs to this program were a title, the average arrival rate (2 cars per hour), and the service rate (3 cars per hour).

Now that the characteristics of the queuing system have been computed, Arnold decides to do an economic analysis of their impact. The waiting line model was valuable in predicting potential waiting times, queue lengths, idle times, and so on. But it did not identify optimal decisions or consider cost factors. As stated earlier, the solution to a queuing problem may require management to make a trade-off between the increased cost of providing better service and the decreased waiting costs derived from providing that service.

conducting an economic analysis

Arnold estimates that the cost of customer waiting time, in terms of customer dissatisfaction and lost goodwill, is $10 per hour of time spent _waiting_ in line. (Once customers' cars are actually being serviced on the

PROGRAM 16.1 Sample Computer Run Using AB:QM

```
Program: Queuing Theory / M/M/1

Problem Title : ARNOLD MUFFLER SINGLE CHANNEL MODEL

***** Input Data *****

Mean Arrival Rate                          :     2.000
Mean Service Rate                          :     3.000


***** Program Output *****

Mean Number of Units in the System         :     2.000
Mean Number of Units in the Queue          :     1.333
Mean Time in the System                    :     1.000
Mean Time In the Queue                     :     0.667
Service Facility Utilization Factor        :     0.667
Probability of No Units in System          :     0.333

***** End of Output *****
```

customer waiting time

rack, they don't seem to mind waiting.) Since on the average a car has a $\frac{2}{3}$ hour wait and there are approximately 16 cars serviced per day (2 per hour times 8 working hours per day), the total number of hours that customers spend waiting for mufflers to be installed each day is $\frac{2}{3} \times 16 = \frac{32}{3}$, or $10\frac{2}{3}$ hours. Hence, in this case,

$$\text{Customer waiting cost} = (\$10/\text{hour}) \times (10\frac{2}{3} \text{ hours/day}) = \$106 \text{ per day}$$

service cost and total cost

The only other major cost that Larry Arnold can identify in the queuing situation is the salary of Reid Blank, the mechanic. Blank is paid $7 per hour, or $56 per day. Total anticipated costs, then, are $106 + $56 = $162 per day.

Now comes a decision. Arnold finds out through the muffler business grapevine that The Rusty Muffler, a crosstown competitor, employs a mechanic named Jimmy Smith who can efficiently install new mufflers at the rate of 4 per hour. Larry Arnold contacts Smith and inquires as to his interest in switching employers. Smith says he would consider leaving The Rusty Muffler, but only if he were paid a $9 per hour salary. Arnold, being a crafty businessman, decides that it may be worthwhile to fire Blank and replace him with the speedier but more expensive Smith.

He first recomputes all the operating characteristics using a new service rate of 4 mufflers per hour.

$\lambda = 2$ cars arriving per hour

$\mu = 4$ cars serviced per hour

$L = \dfrac{\lambda}{\mu - \lambda} = \dfrac{2}{4 - 2} = 1$ car in the system on the average

$W = \dfrac{1}{\mu - \lambda} = \dfrac{1}{4 - 2} = \dfrac{1}{2}$ hour in the system on the average

$L_q = \dfrac{\lambda^2}{\mu(\mu - \lambda)} = \dfrac{2^2}{4(4 - 2)} = \dfrac{4}{8} = \dfrac{1}{2}$ car waiting in line on the average

$W_q = \dfrac{\lambda}{\mu(\mu - \lambda)} = \dfrac{2}{4(4 - 2)} = \dfrac{2}{8} = \dfrac{1}{4}$ hour = 15 minutes average waiting time per car in the queue

$\rho = \dfrac{\lambda}{\mu} = \dfrac{2}{4} = .5 =$ Percent of time mechanic is busy

$P_0 = 1 - \dfrac{\lambda}{\mu} = 1 - .5 = .5 =$ Probability that there are 0 cars in the system

Probability of More than k Cars in the System

k	$P_{n>k} = (\frac{2}{4})^{k+1}$
0	.5
1	.25
2	.125
3	.062
4	.031
5	.016
6	.008
7	.004

It is quite evident that Smith's speed will result in considerably shorter queues and waiting times. For example, a customer would now spend an average of $\frac{1}{2}$ hour in the system and $\frac{1}{4}$ hour waiting in the queue, as opposed to one hour in the system and $\frac{2}{3}$ hour in the queue with Blank as mechanic. Total hours customers spend *waiting* if Smith is on duty = (16 cars/day) × ($\frac{1}{4}$ hour/car) = 4 hours.

recompute total cost and decide

Customer waiting cost = \$10/hour × 4 hours = \$40 per day

Service cost of Smith = 8 hours/day × \$9/hour = \$72 per day

Total expected cost = Waiting cost + Service cost = \$40 + \$72

= \$112 per day

Since the total daily expected cost with Blank as mechanic was \$162, Arnold may very well decide to hire Smith and reduce costs by \$162 − \$112 = \$50 per day.

16.5
MULTIPLE-CHANNEL QUEUING MODEL WITH POISSON ARRIVALS AND EXPONENTIAL SERVICE TIMES[4]

The next logical step is to look at a multiple-channel queuing system, in which two or more servers or channels are available to handle arriving customers. Let us still assume that customers awaiting service form one single line and then proceed to the first available server. An example of such a multichannel, single-phase waiting line is found in many banks today. A common line is formed and the customer at the head of the line proceeds to the first free teller. (Refer back to Figure 16.3 for a typical multichannel configuration.)

assumptions of the model

The multiple channel system presented here again assumes that arrivals follow a Poisson probability distribution and that service times are exponentially distributed. Service is first come, first served, and all servers are assumed to perform at the same rate. Other assumptions listed earlier for the single-channel model apply as well.

Equations for the Multichannel Queuing Model

If we let M equal the number of channels open, then the following formulas may be used in the waiting line analysis.

$$\lambda = \text{average arrival rate}$$

$$\mu = \text{average service rate at each channel}$$

queuing equations

The probability that there are 0 customers or units in the system:

$$P_0 = \frac{1}{\left[\sum_{n=0}^{n=M-1} \frac{1}{n!}\left(\frac{\lambda}{\mu}\right)^n\right] + \frac{1}{M!}\left(\frac{\lambda}{\mu}\right)^M \frac{M\mu}{M\mu - \lambda}} \qquad \text{for } M\mu > \lambda \quad (16\text{-}9)$$

The average number of customers or units in the system:

$$L = \frac{\lambda\mu(\lambda/\mu)^M}{(M-1)!(M\mu - \lambda)^2}P_0 + \frac{\lambda}{\mu} \qquad (16\text{-}10)$$

The average time a unit spends in the waiting line or being serviced (namely, in the system):

$$W = \frac{\mu(\lambda/\mu)^M}{(M-1)!(M\mu - \lambda)^2}P_0 + \frac{1}{\mu} = \frac{L}{\lambda} \qquad (16\text{-}11)$$

The average number of customers or units in line waiting for service:

$$L_q = L - \frac{\lambda}{\mu} \qquad (16\text{-}12)$$

---

[4] This model is also known by the technical name of the M/M/m model.

The average time a customer or unit spends in the queue waiting for service:

$$W_q = W - \frac{1}{\mu} = \frac{L_q}{\lambda} \qquad (16\text{-}13)$$

Utilization rate:

$$\rho = \frac{\lambda}{M\mu} \qquad (16\text{-}14)$$

These equations are obviously more complex than the ones used in the single-channel model, yet they are used in exactly the same fashion and provide the same type of information as did the simpler model.

Arnold's Muffler Shop Revisited

For an application of the multichannel queuing model, let's return to the case of Arnold's Muffler Shop. Larry Arnold previously examined two options. He could retain his current mechanic, Reid Blank, at a total expected cost of $162 per day. Or he could fire Blank and hire a slightly more expensive but faster worker named Jimmy Smith. With Smith on board, service system costs could be reduced to $112 per day.

A third option is now explored. Arnold finds that at minimal after-tax cost he can open a *second* garage bay in which mufflers can be installed. Instead of firing his first mechanic, Blank, he would hire a second worker. The new mechanic would be expected to install mufflers at the same rate as Blank—about $\mu = 3$ per hour. Customers, who would still arrive at the rate of $\lambda = 2$ per hour, would wait in a single line until one of the two mechanics is free. To find out how this option compares to the old single-channel waiting line system, Arnold computes several operating characteristics for the $M = 2$ channel system.

opening a second muffler service channel

$$P_0 = \cfrac{1}{\left[\sum_{n=0}^{1} \frac{1}{n!}\left(\frac{2}{3}\right)^n\right] + \frac{1}{2!}\left(\frac{2}{3}\right)^2 \left(\frac{2(3)}{2(3) - 2}\right)}$$

$$= \cfrac{1}{1 + \frac{2}{3} + \frac{1}{2}\left(\frac{4}{9}\right)\left(\frac{6}{6 - 2}\right)} = \cfrac{1}{1 + \frac{2}{3} + \frac{1}{3}} = \frac{1}{2} = .5$$

= Probability of 0 cars in the system

$$L = \left(\frac{(2)(3)(2/3)^2}{1![2(3) - 2]^2}\right)\left(\frac{1}{2}\right) + \frac{2}{3} = \frac{8/13}{16}\left(\frac{1}{2}\right) + \frac{2}{3} = \frac{3}{4} = .75$$

= Average number of cars in the system

$$W = \frac{L}{\lambda} = \frac{3/4}{2} = \frac{3}{8} \text{ hours} = 22\tfrac{1}{2} \text{ minutes}$$

= Average time a car spends in the system

$$L_q = L - \frac{\lambda}{\mu} = \frac{3}{4} - \frac{2}{3} = \frac{1}{12} = .083 = \text{Average number of cars in the queue}$$

$$W_q = \frac{L_q}{\lambda} = \frac{.83}{2} = .0415 \text{ hours} = 2\tfrac{1}{2} \text{ minutes}$$

= Average time a car spends in the queue

PROGRAM 16.2 AB:QM Output for Arnold's Muffler Shop with Two Servers

```
Program: Queuing Theory / M/M/m

Problem Title : ARNOLD

***** Input Data *****

Mean Arrival Rate                          :      2.000
Mean Service Rate                          :      3.000
Number of Servers                          :      2.000


***** Program Output *****

Mean Number of Units in the System         :      0.750
Mean Number of Units in the Queue          :      0.083
Mean Time In the System                    :      0.375
Mean Time In the Queue                     :      0.042
Service Facility Utilization Factor        :      0.333
Probability of No Units in System          :      0.500

***** End of Output *****
```

Program 16.2 confirms these computations. The only difference between this run and that of Program 16.1 is that the number of servers has been entered as 2.

These data are compared to earlier operating characteristics in Table 16.2. The increased service from opening a second channel has a dramatic effect on almost all characteristics. In particular, time spent waiting in line drops from 40 minutes with one mechanic (Blank) or 15 minutes with Smith down to only 2½ minutes! Likewise, the average number of cars in the queue falls to .083 (about $\frac{1}{12}$ of a car).[5] But does this mean that a second bay should be opened?

lower waiting time results from second bay

To complete his economic analysis, Arnold assumes that the second mechanic would be paid the same as the current one, Blank, namely, $7 per hour. Total time customers will now spend waiting will be = (16 cars per day) × (0.0415 hours per car) = .664 hours.

cost analysis

Customer waiting cost = $10/hour × .664 hours = $6.64 per day

Service cost of 2 mechanics = 2 × 8 hours each/day × $7/hour = $112 per day

Total expected cost = Waiting cost + Service cost
= $6.64 + $112.00 = $118.64 per day

[5] You might note that adding a second mechanic does not cut queue waiting time and length just in half, but makes it even smaller. This is because of the *random* arrival and service processes. When there is only one mechanic and two customers arrive within a minute of each other, the second will have a long wait. The fact that the mechanic may have been idle for 30 to 40 minutes before they both arrive does not change this average waiting time. Thus, single-channel models often have high wait times relative to multichannel models.

TABLE 16.2 Effect of Service Level on Arnold's Operating Characteristics

OPERATING CHARACTERISTIC	LEVEL OF SERVICE		
	ONE MECHANIC (REID BLANK) $\mu = 3$	TWO MECHANICS $\mu = 3$ FOR EACH	ONE FAST MECHANIC (JIMMY SMITH) $\mu = 4$
Probability the system is empty (P_o)	.33	.50	.50
Average number of cars in the system (L)	2 cars	.75 cars	1 car
Average time spent in the system (W)	60 min.	22.5 min.	30 min.
Average number of cars in the queue (L_q)	1.33 cars	.083 cars	.50 cars
Average time spent in the queue (W_q)	40 min.	2.5 min.	15 min.

As you recall, total cost with just Blank as mechanic was found to be $162 per day. Cost with just Smith was just $112. Although opening a second channel would be likely to have a positive effect on customer goodwill and hence lower the cost of waiting time, it means an increase in the cost of providing service. Look back to Figure 16.1 and you will see that such trade-offs are the basis of queuing theory. Arnold's decision is to replace his present worker with the speedier Smith, and *not* to open a second service bay.

Use of Waiting Line Tables

Imagine the work a manager would face in dealing with $M = 3$, 4, or 5 channel waiting line models if he or she did not have a computer readily available. The arithmetic becomes increasingly troublesome. Fortunately, much of the burden of manually examining multiple channel queues can be avoided by turning to tables such as Table 16.3. This table, the result of hundreds of computations, represents the relationship between three things: (1) service facility utilization factor, ρ (which is simple to find—it's just λ/μ), (2) number of service channels open, and (3) the average number of customers in the queue, L_q (which is what we'd like to find). For any combination of utilization rate (ρ) and $M = 1$, 2, 3, 4, or 5 open service channels, you can quickly look in the body of the table to read off the appropriate value for L_q.

waiting line tables simplify computations

Let's say, for example, that a bank is trying to decide how many drive-in teller windows to open on a busy Saturday. It estimates that customers arrive at a rate of about $\lambda = 18$ per hour, and that each teller can service about $\mu = 20$ customers per hour. Then the utilization rate is $\rho = \lambda/\mu = {}^{18}\!/_{20} = .90$. Turning to Table 16.3, under $\rho = .90$, we see that if only $M = 1$ service window is open, the average number of customers in line will be 8.1. If two windows are open, L_q drops to .2285 customers, to .03 for $M = 3$ tellers, and to .0041 for $M = 4$ tellers. Adding more open windows at this point will result in an average queue length of 0.

It is also a simple matter to compute the average waiting time in the queue, W_q, since $W_q = L_q/\lambda$. When one channel is open, $W_q = 8.1$ customers/ (18 customers per hour) = .45 hours = 27 minutes waiting time; when

TABLE 16.3 Values of L_q for $M = 1$–5 Service Channels and Various Values of $\rho = \lambda/\mu$*

	POISSON ARRIVALS, EXPONENTIAL SERVICE TIMES				
	NUMBER OF SERVICE CHANNELS, M				
ρ	1	2	3	4	5
.10	.0111				
.15	.0264	.0008			
.20	.0500	.0020			
.25	.0833	.0039			
.30	.1285	.0069			
.35	.1884	.0110			
.40	.2666	.0166			
.45	.3681	.0239	.0019		
.50	.5000	.0333	.0030		
.55	.6722	.0449	.0043		
.60	.9000	.0593	.0061		
.65	1.2071	.0767	.0084		
.70	1.6333	.0976	.0112		
.75	2.2500	.1227	.0147		
.80	3.2000	.1523	.0189		
.85	4.8166	.1873	.0239	.0031	
.90	8.1000	.2285	.0300	.0041	
.95	18.0500	.2767	.0371	.0053	
1.0		.3333	.0454	.0067	
1.2		.6748	.0904	.0158	
1.4		1.3449	.1778	.0324	.0059
1.6		2.8444	.3128	.0604	.0121
1.8		7.6734	.5320	.1051	.0227
2.0			.8888	.1739	.0398
2.2			1.4907	.2770	.0659
2.4			2.1261	.4305	.1047
2.6			4.9322	.6581	.1609
2.8			12.2724	1.0000	.2411
3.0				1.5282	.3541
3.2				2.3856	.5128
3.4				3.9060	.7365
3.6				7.0893	1.0550
3.8				16.9366	1.5184
4.0					2.2164
4.2					3.3269
4.4					5.2675
4.6					9.2885
4.8					21.6384

* Reprinted by permission of John Wiley & Sons, Inc., from Elwood S. Buffa, *Modern Production Management: Managing the Operations Function,* 5th edition, 1977.

two tellers are open, $W_q = .2285$ customers/(18 customers per hour) $=$ .0126 hours $= \frac{3}{4}$ minute; and so on. Perhaps you might check Larry Arnold's computations against tabled values just to practice their use. Don't forget to interpolate if your exact ρ value is not found in the first column.

Other common operating characteristics besides L_q have been published in table form and are often found in production management books and manuals.

16.6
CONSTANT SERVICE TIME MODEL[6]

Some service systems have constant service times instead of exponentially distributed times. When customers or equipment are processed according to a fixed cycle, as in the case an automatic car wash or an amusement park ride, constant service rates are appropriate. Because constant rates are certain, the values for L_q, W_q, L, and W are always less than they would be in the models we have just discussed, which have variable service times. As a matter of fact, both the average queue length and the average waiting time in the queue are halved with the constant service rate model.

constant service rates speed the process

Equations for the Constant Service Time Model

Constant service model formulas follow:

1. Average length of the queue: $L_q = \dfrac{\lambda^2}{2\mu(\mu - \lambda)}$ (16–15)

2. Average waiting time in the queue: $W_q = \dfrac{\lambda}{2\mu(\mu - \lambda)}$ (16–16)

3. Average number of customers in the system: $L = L_q + \dfrac{\lambda}{\mu}$ (16–17)

4. Average waiting time in the system: $W = W_q + \dfrac{1}{\mu}$ (16–18)

Garcia-Golding Recycling Inc.

Garcia-Golding Recycling, Inc. collects and compacts aluminum cans and glass bottles in New York City. Their truck drivers who arrive to unload these materials for recycling currently wait an average of 15 minutes before emptying their loads. The cost of the driver and truck time wasted while in queue is valued at $60 per hour. A new automated compactor can be purchased that will process truck loads at a constant rate of 12 trucks per hour (that is, 5 minutes per truck). Trucks arrive according to a Poisson distribution at an average rate of 8 per hour. If the new compactor is put in use, its cost will be amortized at a rate of $3 per truck unloaded. A

---

[6] In the operations research literature, this is also referred to as the M/D/1 model.

PROGRAM 16.3 Computer Run Using AB:QM for Garcia-Golding's Constant Service Time Problem

```
Program: Queuing Theory / M/D/1

Problem Title : GARCIA-GOLDING RECYCLING INC.

***** Input Data *****

Mean Arrival Rate                          :      8.000
Constant Service Rate                      :     12.000


***** Program Output *****

Mean Number of Units in the System         :      1.333
Mean Number of Units in the Queue          :      0.667
Mean Time in the System                    :      0.167
Mean Time in the Queue                     :      0.083
Service Facility Utilization Factor        :      0.667
Probability of No Units in System          :      0.333

***** End of Output *****
```

summer intern from a local college did the following analysis to evaluate the costs versus benefits of the purchase.

Current waiting cost/trip = ($\frac{1}{4}$ hr. waiting now)($60/hr. cost) = $15/trip

New system: λ = 8 trucks/hr. arriving μ = 12 trucks/hr. served

Average waiting time in queue = $W_q = \dfrac{\lambda}{2\mu(\mu - \lambda)} = \dfrac{8}{2(12)(12 - 8)} = \dfrac{1}{12}$ hr.

Waiting cost/trip with new compactor = ($\frac{1}{12}$ hr. wait)($60/hr. cost) = $5/trip

Savings with new equipment = $15 (current system) − $5 (new system) = $10/trip

Cost of new equipment amortized = $3/trip

Net savings = $7/trip

    The complete analysis for this problem using AB:QM is seen in Program 16.3. (Note that $\frac{1}{12}$ of an hour = .083 hour average/mean waiting time in queue.)

16.7
MORE COMPLEX QUEUING MODELS AND THE USE OF SIMULATION

Many practical waiting line problems that occur in production and operations service systems have characteristics like those of Arnold's Muffler Shop or Garcia-Golding Recycling Inc. This is true when the situation calls for single- or multiple-channel waiting lines, with Poisson arrivals and exponential or constant service times, an infinite calling population, and first-in, first-out service.

Often, however, *variations* of this specific case are present in an analysis. Service times in an automobile repair shop, for example, tend to follow the normal probability distribution instead of the exponential. A 20-bed hospital ward with one or two nurses serving the patients is a queuing problem with a finite population instead of an infinite population.[7] A college registration system in which seniors have first choice of courses and hours over all other students is an example of a first-come, first-served model with a preemptive priority queue discipline. A physical examination for military recruits is an example of a multiphase system—one that differs from the single-phase models discussed in this chapter. A recruit first lines up to have blood drawn at one station, then waits to take an eye exam at the next station, talks to a psychiatrist at the third, and is examined by a doctor for medical problems at the fourth. At each phase, the recruit must enter another queue and wait his or her turn.

models exist to handle variations of basic assumptions

Models to handle these cases have been developed by operations researchers. The computations for the resulting mathematical formulations are somewhat more complex than the ones covered in this chapter.[8] And many real-world queuing applications are too complex to be modeled analytically at all. When this happens, quantitative analysts usually turn to *computer simulation.*

simulation defined

Simulation, the topic of Chapter 17, is a technique in which random numbers are used to draw inferences about probability distributions (such as arrivals and services). Using this approach, many hours, days, or months of data can be developed by a computer in a few seconds. This allows analysis of controllable factors, such as adding another service channel, without actually doing so physically. Basically, whenever a standard analytical queuing model provides only a poor approximation of the actual service system, it is wise to develop a simulation model instead.

16.8
SUMMARY

Waiting lines and service systems are important parts of the business world. In this chapter, we described several common queuing situations and presented mathematical models for analyzing waiting lines following certain assumptions. Those assumptions were that: (1) arrivals come from an infinite, or very large, population; (2) arrivals are Poisson distributed; (3)

assumptions recalled

---

[7] As a matter of fact, finite queuing tables are available to handle calling populations of up to 250. Although there is no definite number that we can use to divide finite from infinite populations, the general rule of thumb is this: if the number in the queue is a significant proportion of the calling population, use a finite queuing model. *Finite Queuing Tables,* by Peck and Hazelwood (John Wiley & Sons, 1958), eliminates much of the mathematics involved in computing the operating characteristics for such a model.

[8] Often the *qualitative* results of queuing models are as useful as the quantitative results. Results show that it is inherently more efficient to pool resources, use central dispatching, and provide single multiple-server systems rather than multiple single-server systems.

arrivals are treated on a first-in, first-out basis and do not balk or renege; (4) service times follow the negative exponential distribution or are constant; and (5) the average service rate is faster than the average arrival rate.

The models illustrated in this chapter were for single-channel, single-phase and multiple-channel, single-phase problems. After a series of operating characteristics were computed, total expected costs were studied. As shown graphically in Figure 16.1, total cost is the sum of the cost of providing service plus the cost of waiting time.

key system characteristics

Key operating characteristics for a system were shown to be: (1) utilization rate, (2) percent idle time, (3) average time spent waiting in the system and in the queue, (4) average number of customers in the system and in the queue, and (5) probabilities of various numbers of customers in the system.

It was emphasized that a variety of queuing models exist that do not meet all of the assumptions of the traditional models. In these cases, we use more complex mathematical models or turn to a technique called computer simulation. The application of simulation to problems of queuing systems, inventory control, machine breakdown, and other quantitative analysis situations is our next topic as you will see in Chapter 17.

GLOSSARY

Waiting Line. One or more customers or objects waiting to be served.

Queuing Theory. The mathematical study of waiting lines or queues.

Service Cost. The cost of providing a particular level of service.

Waiting Cost. The cost to the firm of having customers or objects waiting in line to be serviced.

Calling Population. The population of items from which arrivals at the queuing system come.

Unlimited or Infinite Population. A calling population that is very large relative to the number of customers currently in the system.

Limited or Finite Population. A case in which the number of customers in the system is a significant proportion of the calling population.

Poisson Distribution. A probability distribution that is often used to describe random arrivals in a queue.

Balking. The case in which arriving customers refuse to join the waiting line.

Reneging. The case in which customers enter a queue but then leave before being serviced.

Limited Queue Length. A waiting line that cannot increase beyond a specific size.

Unlimited Queue Length. A queue that can increase to an infinite size.

Queue Discipline. The rule by which customers in line receive service.

FIFO. A queue discipline (meaning first-in, first-out) in which the customers are served in the strict order of arrival.

Operating Characteristics. Descriptive characteristics of a queuing system, including the average number of customers in a line and in the system, the average waiting times in a line and in the system, and percent idle time.

Single-Channel Queuing System. A system with one service facility fed by one queue.

Multiple-Channel Queuing System. A system that has more than one service facility, all fed by the same single queue.

Single-Phase System. A queuing system in which service is received at only one station.

Multiphase System. A system in which service is received from more than one station, one after the other.

Negative Exponential Distribution. A probability distribution that is often used to describe random service times in a service system.

M/M/1. Another name for the single-channel model with Poisson arrivals and exponential service times.

Utilization Factor (ρ). The proportion of the time service facilities are in use.

M/M/m. A technical name for the multichannel queuing model (with m servers) and Poisson arrivals and exponential service times.

M/D/1. A technical name for the constant service time model.

Waiting Line Tables. Tabled values that help in determining the operating characteristics of large or complex queuing systems.

Simulation. A technique for representing queuing models that are complex and difficult to model analytically.

KEY EQUATIONS

λ = Mean number of arrivals per time period

μ = Mean number of people or items served per time period

(16-1) $P(X) = \dfrac{e^{-\lambda}\lambda^X}{X!}$

Poisson probability distribution used in describing arrivals.

Equations 16-2 through 16-8 describe operating characteristics in the single-channel model that has Poisson arrival and exponential service rates.

(16-2) L = Average number of units (customers) in the system

$= \dfrac{\lambda}{\mu - \lambda}$

(16-3) W = Average time a unit spends in the system (Waiting time + Service time) $= \dfrac{1}{\mu - \lambda}$

(16-4) L_q = Average number of units in the queue $= \dfrac{\lambda^2}{\mu(\mu - \lambda)}$

(16-5) W_q = Average time a unit spends waiting in the queue $= \dfrac{\lambda}{\mu(\mu - \lambda)}$

(16-6) ρ = Utilization factor for the system $= \dfrac{\lambda}{\mu}$

(16-7) P_o = Probability of 0 units in the system (that is, the service unit is idle)

$$= 1 - \frac{\lambda}{\mu}$$

(16-8) $P_{n>k}$ = Probability of more than k units in the system = $\left(\dfrac{\lambda}{\mu}\right)^{k+1}$

Equations 16-9 through 16-14 describe operating characteristics in multiple-channel models that have Poisson arrival and exponential service rates, where M = the number of open channels.

(16-9) $P_o = \dfrac{1}{\left[\displaystyle\sum_{n=0}^{n=M-1} \dfrac{1}{n!}\left(\dfrac{\lambda}{\mu}\right)^{n}\right] + \dfrac{1}{M!}\left(\dfrac{\lambda}{\mu}\right)^{M} \dfrac{M\mu}{M\mu - \lambda}}$ for $M\mu > \lambda$

The probability that there are 0 people or units in the system.

(16-10) $L = \dfrac{\lambda\mu(\lambda/\mu)^{M}}{(M-1)!(M\mu-\lambda)^2} P_o + \dfrac{\lambda}{\mu}$

The average number of people or units in the system.

(16-11) $W = \dfrac{\mu(\lambda/\mu)^{M}}{(M-1)!(M\mu-\lambda)^2} P_o + \dfrac{1}{\mu} = \dfrac{L}{\lambda}$

The average time a unit spends in the waiting line or being serviced (namely, in the system).

(16-12) $L_q = L - \dfrac{\lambda}{\mu}$

The average number of people or units in line waiting for service.

(16-13) $W_q = W - \dfrac{1}{\mu} = \dfrac{L_q}{\lambda}$

The average time a person or unit spends in the queue waiting for service.

(16-14) $\rho = \dfrac{\lambda}{M\mu}$

Utilization rate.

Equations 16-15 through 16-18 describe operating characteristics in single-channel models that have Poisson arrivals and constant service rates.

(16-15) $L_q = \dfrac{\lambda^2}{2\mu(\mu-\lambda)}$

The average length of the queue.

(16-16) $W_q = \dfrac{\lambda}{2\mu(\mu-\lambda)}$

The average waiting time in the queue.

(16-17) $L = L_q + \dfrac{\lambda}{\mu}$

The average number of customers in the system.

(16-18) $W = W_q + \dfrac{1}{\mu}$

The average waiting time in the system.

SOLVED PROBLEMS

Solved Problem 16-1

The Maitland Furniture store gets an average of 50 customers per shift. The manager of Maitland wants to calculate whether she should hire 1, 2, 3, or 4 salespeople. She has determined that average waiting times will be 7 minutes with one salesperson, 4 minutes with two salespeople, 3 minutes with three salespeople, and 2 minutes with four salespeople. She has estimated the cost per minute that customers wait at $1. The cost per salesperson per shift (including fringe benefits) is $70.

How many salespeople should be hired?

Solution

The manager's calculations are as follows:

	NUMBER OF SALESPEOPLE			
	1	2	3	4
(a) Average number of customers per shift	50	50	50	50
(b) Average waiting time per customer (minutes)	7	4	3	2
(c) Total waiting time per shift (a × b) (minutes)	350	200	150	100
(d) Cost per minute of waiting time (estimated)	$1.00	$1.00	$1.00	$1.00
(e) Value of lost time (c × d) per shift	$350	$200	$150	$100
(f) Salary cost per shift	$ 70	$140	$210	$280
(g) Total cost per shift	$420	$340	$360	$380

Since the minimum total cost per shift relates to two salespeople, the manager's optimum strategy is to hire two salespeople.

Solved Problem 16-2

Marty Schatz owns and manages a chili dog and soft drink store near the campus. While Marty can service 30 customers per hour on the average (μ), he only gets 20 customers per hour (λ). Since Marty could wait on 50% more customers than actually visit his store, it doesn't make sense to him that he should have any waiting lines.

Marty hires you to examine the situation and to determine some characteristics of his queue. After looking into the problem, you make the seven assumptions listed in Section 16.4. What are your findings?

Solution

$$L = \frac{\lambda}{\mu - \lambda} = \frac{20}{30 - 20} = 2 \text{ customers in the system on the average}$$

$$W = \frac{1}{\mu - \lambda} = \frac{1}{30 - 20} = .1 \text{ hours (6 minutes) that the average}$$
$$\text{customer spends in the total system}$$

$$L_q = \frac{\lambda^2}{\mu(\mu - \lambda)} = \frac{20^2}{30\,(30 - 20)} = 1.33 \text{ customers waiting for}$$
$$\text{service in line on the average}$$

$$W_q = \frac{\lambda}{\mu(\mu - \lambda)} = \frac{20}{30\,(30 - 20)} = 1/15 \text{ hour} = (4 \text{ minutes}) = \text{Average}$$
$$\text{waiting time of a customer}$$
$$\text{in the queue awaiting service}$$

$$\rho = \frac{\lambda}{\mu} = \frac{20}{30} = .67 = \text{Percent of the time Marty is busy waiting on customers}$$

$$P_0 = 1 - \frac{\lambda}{\mu} = 1 - \rho = .33 = \text{Probability that there are no customers}$$
$$\text{in the system (being waited on or}$$
$$\text{waiting in queue) at any given time}$$

Probability of k or More Customers Waiting in Line and/or Being Waited On:

k	$P_{(n>k)} = \left(\dfrac{\lambda}{\mu}\right)^{k+1}$
0	.667
1	.444
2	.296
3	.198

Solved Problem 16-3

Refer to the preceding solved problem. Marty agreed that these figures seemed to represent his approximate business situation. You are quite surprised at the length of the lines and elicit from him an estimated value of the customer's waiting time (in the queue, not being waited on) at 10¢ per minute. During the 12 hours that he is open he gets $(12 \times 20) = 240$ customers. The average customer is in a queue 4 minutes, so the total customer waiting time is $(240 \times 4 \text{ minutes}) = 960$ minutes. The value of 960 minutes is $(\$.10)\,(960 \text{ minutes}) = \$96$. You tell Marty that not only is 10¢ per minute quite conservative, but he could probably save most of that \$96 of customer ill-will if he hired another salesclerk. After much haggling, Marty agrees to provide you with all the chili dogs you can eat during a week-long period in exchange for your analysis of the results of having two clerks wait on the customers.

Assuming that Marty hires one additional salesclerk whose service rate equals Marty's rate, complete the analysis.

Solution

With two cash registers open, the system becomes two-channel, or $M = 2$. The computations yield:

$$L = \left[\frac{(20)\,(30)\,(20/30)^2}{(2-1)!\,[(2)\,(30)-20]^2}\right].5 + \frac{20}{30} = .75 \text{ customers in the system}$$
on the average

$$W = \frac{L}{\lambda} = \frac{3/4}{20} = \frac{3}{80} \text{ hours} = 2.25 \text{ minutes that the average}$$
customer spends in the total system

$$L_q = L - \frac{\lambda}{\mu} = \frac{3}{4} - \frac{20}{30} = \frac{1}{12} = .083 \text{ customers waiting for service}$$
in line on the average

$$W_q = \frac{L_q}{\lambda} = \frac{1/12}{20} = \frac{1}{240} \text{ hour} = \frac{1}{4} \text{ minute} = \text{Average waiting time}$$
of a customer in the queue
itself (not being serviced)

$$\rho = \frac{\lambda}{M\mu} = \frac{20}{2\,(30)} = \frac{1}{3} = .33 = \text{Utilization rate}$$

$$P_0 = \frac{1}{\left[\sum_{n=0}^{n=M-1}\frac{1}{n!}\left[\frac{20}{30}\right]^n\right] + \frac{1}{2!}\left[\frac{20}{30}\right]^2\left[\frac{2(30)}{(2)\,(30)-20}\right]}$$

$$= \frac{1}{(1)\,(2/3)^0 + (1)\,(2/3)^1 + (1/2)\,(4/9)\,(6/4)} = .5$$

= Probability of no customers in the system

You now have (240 customers) × (1/240 hours) = 1 hour total customer waiting time per day.

Total cost of 60 minutes of customer waiting time is (60 minutes) ($.10 per minute) = $6.

Now you are ready to point out to Marty that the hiring of one additional clerk will save $96 − $6 = $90 of customer ill will per 12-hour shift. Marty responds that the hiring should also reduce the number of people who look at the line and leave as well as those who get tired of waiting in line and leave. You tell Marty that you are ready for two chili dogs, extra hot.

DISCUSSION QUESTIONS AND PROBLEMS

Discussion Questions

16-1 What is the waiting line problem? What are the components in a waiting line system?

16-2 What are the assumptions underlying common queuing models?

16-3 Describe the important operating characteristics of a queuing system.

16-4 Why must the service rate be greater than the arrival rate in a single-channel queuing system?

16-5 Briefly describe three situations in which the first-in, first-out (FIFO) discipline rule is not applicable in queuing analysis.

16-6 Provide examples of four situations in which there is a limited, or finite, waiting line.

16-7 What are the components of the following systems? Draw and explain the configuration of each.

(a) Barber shop.

(b) Car wash.

(c) Laundromat.

(d) Small grocery store.

16-8 Do doctor's offices generally have random arrival rates for patients? Are service times random? Under what circumstances might service times be constant?

16-9 Do you think the Poisson distribution, which assumes independent arrivals, is a good estimation of arrival rates in the following queuing systems? Defend your position in each case.

(a) Cafeteria in your school.

(b) Barbershop.

(c) Hardware store.

(d) Dentist's office.

(e) College class.

(f) Movie theatre.

Problems

: 16-10 The Golding Discount Department Store has approximately 300 customers shopping in its store between 9 A.M. and 5 P.M. on Saturdays. In deciding how many cash registers to keep open each Saturday, Golding's manager considers two factors: customer waiting time (and the associated waiting cost) and the service costs of employing additional checkout clerks. Checkout clerks are paid an average of $4 per hour. When only one is on duty, the waiting time per customer is about 10 minutes (or $\frac{1}{6}$ of an hour); when two clerks are on duty, the average checkout time is 6 minutes per person; 4 minutes when three clerks are working; and 3 minutes when four clerks are on duty.

Golding's management has conducted customer satisfaction surveys and has been able to estimate that the store suffers approximately $5 in lost sales and goodwill for every *hour* of customer time spent waiting in checkout lines. Using the information provided, determine the optimal number of clerks to have on duty each Saturday in order to minimize the store's total expected cost.

· 16-11 The Rockwell Electronics Corporation retains a service crew to repair machine breakdowns that occur on an average of $\lambda = 3$ per day (approximately Poisson in nature). The crew can service an average of $\mu = 8$ machines per day, with a repair time distribution that resembles the exponential distribution.

(a) What is the utilization rate of this service system?

(b) What is the average downtime for a machine that is broken?

(c) How many machines are waiting to be serviced at any given time?

(d) What is the probability that more than one machine is in the system? Probability that more than two are broken and waiting to be repaired or being serviced? More than three? More than four?

· 16-12 Harry's Car Wash is open six days a week, but its heaviest day of business is always on Saturday. From historical data, Harry estimates that dirty cars arrive at the rate of 20 per hour all day Saturday. With a full crew working the wash line, he figures that cars can be cleaned at the rate of one every two minutes. One car at a time is cleaned in this example of a single-channel waiting line.

Assuming Poisson arrivals and exponential service times, find the

(a) Average number of cars in line.
(b) Average time a car waits before it is washed.
(c) Average time a car spends in the service system.
(d) Utilization rate of the car wash.
(e) Probability no cars are in the system.

· **16-13** Mike Dreskin manages a large Los Angeles movie theatre complex called Cinema I, II, III, and IV. Each of the four auditoriums plays a different film; the schedule is set so that starting times are staggered to avoid the large crowds that would occur if all four movies started at the same time. The theatre has a single ticket booth and a cashier who can maintain an average service rate of 280 movie patrons per hour. Service times are assumed to follow an exponential distribution. Arrivals on a normally active day are Poisson distributed and average 210 per hour.

In order to determine the efficiency of the current ticket operation, Mike wishes to examine several queue operating characteristics.

(a) Find the average number of moviegoers waiting in line to purchase a ticket.
(b) What percentage of the time is the cashier busy?
(c) What is the average time a customer spends in the system?
(d) What is the average time spent waiting in line to get to the ticket window?
(e) What is the probability that there are more than two people in the system? More than three people? More than four?

: **16-14** A university cafeteria line in the student center is a self-serve facility in which students select the food items they want, then form a single line to pay the cashier. Students arrive at a rate of about four per minute according to a Poisson distribution. The single cashier ringing up sales takes about 12 seconds per customer, following an exponential distribution.

(a) What is the probability there are more than two students in the system? More than three students? More than four?
(b) What is the probability that the system is empty?
(c) How long will the average student have to wait before reaching the cashier?
(d) What is the expected number of students in the queue?
(e) What is the average number in the system?
(f) If a second cashier is added (who works at the same pace), how will the operating characteristics computed in (b), (c), (d), and (e) change? Assume customers wait in a single line and go to the first available cashier.

: **16-15** The wheat harvesting season in the American Midwest is short, and most farmers deliver their truckloads of wheat to a giant central storage bin within a two-week span. Because of this, wheat-filled trucks waiting to unload and return to the fields have been known to back up for a block at the receiving bin. The central bin is owned cooperatively, and it is to every farmer's benefit to make the unloading/storage process as efficient as possible. The cost of grain deterioration caused by unloading delays and the cost of truck rental and idle driver time are significant concerns to the cooperative members. Although farmers have difficulty quantifying crop damage, it is easy to assign a waiting and unloading cost for truck and driver of $18 per hour. The storage bin is open and operated 16 hours per day and 7 days per week during the harvest season and is capable of unloading 35 trucks per hour according to an exponential distribution. Full trucks arrive all day long (during the hours the bin is open) at a rate of about 30 per hour, following a Poisson pattern.

To help the cooperative get a handle on the problem of lost time while trucks are waiting in line or unloading at the bin, find the

(a) Average number of trucks in the unloading system.

(b) Average time per truck in the system.

(c) Utilization rate for the bin area.

(d) Probability that there are more than three trucks in the system at any given time.

(e) Total daily cost to the farmers of having their trucks tied up in the unloading process.

(f) The cooperative, as mentioned, uses the storage bin only two weeks per year. Farmers estimate that enlarging the bin would cut unloading costs by 50% next year. It will cost $9,000 to do so during the off-season. Would it be worth the cooperative's while to enlarge the storage area?

: 16-16 Ashley's Department Store in Kansas City maintains a successful catalogue sales department in which a clerk takes orders by telephone. If the clerk is occupied on one line, incoming phone calls to the catalogue department are answered automatically by a recording machine and asked to wait. As soon as the clerk is free, the party that has waited the longest is transferred and answered first. Calls come in at a rate of about 12 per hour. The clerk is capable of taking an order in an average of four minutes. Calls tend to follow a Poisson distribution, and service times tend to be exponential.

The clerk is paid $5 per hour, but because of lost goodwill and sales, Ashley's loses about $25 per hour of customer time spent waiting for the clerk to take an order.

(a) What is the average time that catalogue customers must wait before their calls are transferred to the order clerk?

(b) What is the average number of callers waiting to place an order?

(c) Ashley is considering adding a second clerk to take calls. The store would pay that person the same $5 per hour. Should it hire another clerk? Explain.

: 16-17 Sal's International Barber Shop is a popular haircutting and styling salon near the campus of the University of New Orleans. Four barbers work full-time and spend an average of 15 minutes on each customer. Customers arrive all day long at an average rate of 12 per hour. When they enter, they take a number to wait for the first available barber. Arrivals tend to follow the Poisson distribution, while service times are exponentially distributed.

(a) What is the probability that the shop is empty?

(b) What is the average number of customers in the barber shop?

(c) What is the average time spent in the shop?

(d) What is the average time that a customer spends waiting to be called to the barber chair?

(e) What is the average number waiting to be served?

(f) What is the shop's utilization factor?

(g) Sal's is thinking of adding a fifth barber. How will this affect the utilization rate?

⌨ : **16-18** The medical director of a large emergency clinic faces a problem of providing treatment for patients who arrive at different rates during the day. There are four doctors available to treat patients when needed. If not needed, they can be assigned to other responsibilities (for example, lab tests, reports, x-ray diagnoses) or else rescheduled to work at other hours.

It is important to provide quick and responsive treatment, and the medical director feels that, on the average, patients should not have to sit in the waiting area for more than five minutes before being seen by a doctor. Patients are treated on a first-come, first-served basis and see the first available doctor after waiting in the queue. The arrival pattern for a typical day is:

TIME	ARRIVAL RATE
9 A.M.–3 P.M.	6 patients/hour
3 P.M.–8 P.M.	4 patients/hour
8 P.M.–Midnight	12 patients/hour

These arrivals follow a Poisson distribution, and treatment times, 12 minutes on the average, follow the exponential pattern.

How many doctors should be on duty during each period in order to maintain the level of patient care expected?

⌨ · **16-19** Juhn and Sons Wholesale Fruit Distributors employ one worker whose job it is to load fruit on outgoing company trucks. Trucks arrive at the loading gate at an average of 24 per day, or 3 per hour, according to a Poisson distribution. The worker loads them at a rate of 4 per hour, following approximately the exponential distribution in service times.

Determine the operating characteristics of this loading gate problem. What is the probability that there will be more than three trucks either being loaded or waiting? Discuss the result of your queuing model computation.

⌨ : **16-20** Juhn believes that adding a second fruit loader will substantially improve the firm's efficiency. He estimates that a two-person crew, still acting like a single-server system, at the loading gate will double the loading rate from 4 trucks per hour to 8 trucks per hour. Analyze the effect on the queue of such a change and compare the results to those found in Problem 16-19.

⌨ · **16-21** Truck drivers working for Juhn and Sons (see Problems 16-19, 16-20) are paid a salary of $10 per hour on the average. Fruit loaders receive about $6 per hour. Truck drivers waiting in the queue or at the loading gate are drawing a salary, but are productively idle and unable to generate revenue during that time. What would be the *hourly* cost savings to the firm associated with employing two loaders instead of one?

⌨ : **16-22** Juhn and Sons Wholesale Fruit Distributors (of Problem 16-19) are considering building a second platform or gate to speed the process of loading their fruit trucks. This, they think, will be even more efficient than simply hiring another loader to help out on the first platform (as in Problem 16-20).

Assume that workers at each platform will be able to load 4 trucks per hour each and that trucks will continue to arrive at the rate of 3 per hour. Then apply the preceding equations to find the waiting line's new operating conditions. Is this new approach indeed speedier than the other two considered?

· **16-23** Customers arrive at an automated coffee vending machine at a rate of four per minute, following a Poisson distribution. The coffee machine dispenses a cup of coffee at a constant rate of 10 seconds.

(a) What is the average number of people waiting in line?

(b) What is the average number in the system?

(c) How long does the average person wait in line before receiving service?

⋮ **16-24** The average number of customers in the system in the single-channel, single-phase model described in Section 16.4 is:

$$L = \frac{\lambda}{\mu - \lambda}$$

Show that for $M = 1$ server, the multichannel queuing model in Section 16.5, shown as follows,

$$L = \frac{\lambda\mu \left(\frac{\lambda}{\mu}\right)^M}{(M - 1)!(M\mu - \lambda)^2} P_0 + \frac{\lambda}{\mu}$$

is identical to the single-channel system. Note that the formula for P_0 (Equation 16-9) must be utilized in this highly algebraic exercise.

The Metropolis Subway System

The sophisticated new subway system in Metropolis maximizes the use of computerized turnstiles to collect fares. The system works as follows: passengers buy up to $5 worth of riding credits from automated vending machines at the entrance to each subway station. Each ride card has a magnetic coded strip on its back that records the value of the card. Passengers then proceed to entrance turnstiles that provide access to the subway trains. They insert fare cards into the turnstile machines, which record the time of day and location and then return the cards. Riding down on escalators to the train level, passengers await and board the subway for the ride to their destinations. Upon leaving the destination station, they insert their cards into computerized turnstiles once again. This time, the turnstiles deduct the correct fare from the value of the card. (For example, if a ride costs 50¢ and the passenger had purchased a $5 fare card, the exit turnstile would make the subtraction and print $4.50 as remaining value on the fare card. If the card contains 60¢ worth of fare credit and the ride costs exactly 60¢, the turnstile opens but keeps the card.)

The typical subway station has six turnstiles, each of which can be controlled by the station manager to be used for either entrance or exit control—but never for both. Hence, the manager must decide at different times of the day just how many turnstiles to use for entering passengers and how many to be set up to allow exiting passengers. If five turnstiles are set to accept entering riders, and only one for exiting riders, entering passengers will probably experience virtually no delays. Exiting passengers, however, may be caught in a lengthy queue and experience annoying delays in leaving the station.

At the Washington College Station, passengers enter the station at a rate of about 84 per minute between the hours of 7 and 9 A.M. Passengers exiting trains at the stop reach the exit turnstile area at a rate of about 48 per minute during the same morning rush hours. Each turnstile can allow an average of 30 passengers per minute to enter or exit. Arrival and service times have been thought to follow Poisson and exponential distributions, respectively. Assume riders form a common queue at both entry and exit turnstile areas and proceed to the first empty turnstile.

The Washington College Station manager does not want the average passenger at his station to have to wait in a turnstile line for more than six seconds and does not want more than eight people in any queue at any average time.

Discussion Questions

1. How many turnstiles should be opened in each direction every morning?

2. Discuss the assumptions underlying the solution of this problem using queuing theory.

New England Castings

For over 75 years, New England Castings, Inc. has manufactured wood stoves for home use. In recent years, with increasing energy prices, George Mathison, president of New England Castings, has seen sales triple. This dramatic increase in sales has made it even more difficult for George to maintain quality in all of the wood stoves and related products.

Unlike other companies manufacturing wood stoves, New England Castings is *only* in the business of making stoves and stove-related products. Their major products are the Warmglo I, the Warmglo II, the Warmglo III, and the Warmglo IV. The Warmglo I is the smallest wood stove, with a heat output of 30,000 BTUs, while the Warmglo IV is the largest, with a heat output of 60,000 BTUs. In addition, New England Castings, Inc. produces a large array of products that have been designed to be used with one of their four stoves. These products include warming shelves, surface thermometers, stovepipes, adaptors, stove gloves, trivets, mitten racks, andirons, chimneys, and heat shields. New England Castings also publishes a

newsletter and several paperback books on stove installation, stove operation, stove maintenance, and wood sources. It is George's belief that their wide assortment of products was a major contributor to the sales increases.

The Warmglo III outsells all of the other stoves by a wide margin. The heat output and available accessories are ideal for the typical home. The Warmglo III also has a number of outstanding features that make it one of the most attractive and heat efficient stoves on the market. Each Warmglo III has a thermostatically controlled primary air intake valve that allows the stove to adjust itself automatically to produce the correct heat output for varying weather conditions. A secondary air opening is used to increase the heat output in case of very cold weather. The internal stove parts produce a horizontal flame path for more efficient burning, and the output gases are forced to take an S-shaped path through the stove. The S-shaped path allows more complete combustion of the gases and better heat transfer from the fire and gases through the cast iron to the area to be heated. These features,

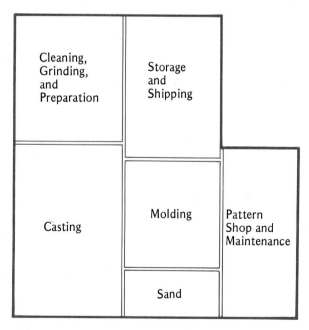

FIGURE 1
Overview of Factory

along with the accessories, resulted in expanding sales and prompted George to build a new factory to manufacture Warmglo III stoves. An overview diagram of the factory is shown in Figure 1.

The new foundry uses the latest equipment, including a new Disamatic that helps in manufacturing stove parts. Regardless of new equipment or procedures, casting operations have remained basically unchanged for hundreds of years. To begin with, a wooden pattern is made for every cast iron piece in the stove. The wooden pattern is an exact duplication of the cast iron piece that is to be manufactured. New England Castings has all of its patterns made by Precision Patterns, Inc., and these patterns are stored in the pattern shop and maintenance room. Then, a specially formulated sand is molded around the wooden pattern. There can be two or more sand molds for each pattern. Mixing the sand and making the molds are done in the molding room. When the wooden pattern is removed, the resulting sand molds form a negative image of the desired casting. Next, the molds are transported to the casting room, where molten iron is poured into the molds and allowed to cool. When the iron has solidified, the molds are moved into the cleaning, grinding, and preparation room.

The molds are dumped into large vibrators that shake most of the sand from the casting. The rough castings are then subjected to both sandblasting to remove the rest of the sand and grinding to finish some of the surfaces of the castings. The castings are then painted with a special heat-resistant paint, assembled into workable stoves, and inspected for manufacturing defects that may have gone undetected thus far. Finally, the finished stoves are moved to storage and shipping, where they are packaged and shipped to the appropriate locations.

At present, the pattern shop and the maintenance department are located in the same room. One large counter is used by both maintenance personnel to get tools and parts and by sand molders that need various patterns for the molding operation. Pete Nawler and Bob Bryan, who work behind the counter, are able to service a total of 10 people per hour (or about 5 per hour each). On the average, 4 people from maintenance and 3 people from the molding department arrive at the counter per hour. People from the molding department and from maintenance arrive randomly, and to be served they form a single line. Pete and Bob have always had a policy of first come, first served. Because of the location of the pattern shop

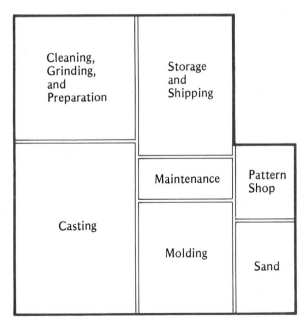

FIGURE 2
Overview of Factory after Changes

and maintenance department, it takes about three minutes for an individual from the maintenance department to walk to the pattern and maintenance room, and it takes about one minute for an individual to walk from the molding department to the pattern and maintenance room.

After observing the operation of the pattern shop and maintenance room for several weeks, George decided to make some changes to the layout of the factory. An overview of these changes appears in Figure 2.

Separating the maintenance shop from the pattern shop had a number of advantages. It would take people from the maintenance department only one minute instead of three to get to the new maintenance department. Using time and motion stud-

ies, George was also able to determine that improving the layout of the maintenance department would allow Bob to serve 6 people from the maintenance department per hour, and improving the layout of the pattern department would allow Pete to serve 7 people from the molding shop per hour.

Discussion Questions

1. How much time would the new layout save?

2. If maintenance personnel were paid $9.50 per hour and molding personnel were paid $11.75 per hour, how much could be saved per hour with the new factory layout?

BIBLIOGRAPHY

Albin, Susan L. "Delays for Customers from Different Arrival Streams to a Queue." *Management Science* Vol. 32, No. 3, March 1986, pp. 329–340.

Byrd, J. "The Value of Queuing Theory." *Interfaces* Vol. 8, No. 3, May 1978, pp. 22–26.

Corkindale, D. R. "Queuing Theory in the Solution of a Transport Evaluation Problem." *Operational Research Quarterly* Vol. 26, No. 2, p. 259.

Cooper, R. B. *Introduction to Queuing Theory*, 2nd Edition. New York: Elsevier-North Holland, 1980.

Cox, D. R., and Smith W. L. *Queues.* New York: John Wiley & Sons, 1965.

Edmond, E. D., and Maggs, R. P. "How Useful Are Queue Models in Port Investment Decisions for Container Berths." *Journal of the Operations Research Society* Vol. 29, No. 8.

Erikson, W. "Management Science and the Gas Shortage." *Interfaces* Vol. 4, No. 4, August 1974, pp. 47–51.

Eschcoli, A. Z., and Adiri, I. "Single-Lane Budget Serving Two-Lane Traffic." *Naval Research Logistics Quarterly* Vol. 24, No. 1, March 1977, pp. 113–25.

Foote, B. L. "Queuing Case Study of Drive-In Banking." *Interfaces* Vol. 6, No. 4, August 1976.

Gostl, J., and Greenberg, I. "An Application of Queuing Theory to the Design of a Message-Switching Computer System." *Communications of the ACM* Vol. 28, No. 5, May 1985, pp. 500–505.

Graff, G. "Simple Queuing Theory Saves Unnecessary Equipment." *Industrial Engineering* Vol. 3, February 1971, pp. 15–18.

Grassmann, Winfried K. "Finding the Right Number of Servers in Real-World Queueing Systems." *Interfaces* Vol. 18, No. 2, March–April 1988, pp. 94–104.

Green, L., and Kolesar, P. "The Feasibility of One-Officer Patrol in New York City." *Management Science* Vol. 30, No. 8, August 1974, pp. 964–981.

Kaplan, Edward H. "A Public Housing Queue with Reneging and Task-Specific Servers." *Decision Sciences* Vol. 19, 1988, pp. 383–391.

Larson, Richard C. "Travel-Time Analysis of New York City Police Patrol Cars." *Interfaces* Vol. 17, No. 2, March–April 1987, pp. 15–20.

Lawless, Michael W. "Institutionalization of a Management Science Innovation in Police Departments." *Management Science* Vol. 33, No. 2, February 1987, pp. 244–252.

Morse, Philip M., *Queues, Inventories and Maintenance.* New York: John Wiley & Sons, 1958.

Panico, J. A., *Queuing Theory: A Study of Waiting Lines for Business, Economics and Sciences.* Englewood Cliffs, N.J.: Prentice-Hall, 1969.

Paul, R. J., and Stevens, R. E. "Staffing Service Activities with Waiting Line Models." *Decision Sciences* Vol. 2, April 1971, pp. 206–218.

Sze, D. "A Queuing Model for Telephone Operator Staffing." *Operations Research* Vol. 32, No. 2, March–April, 1984, pp. 229–249.

Worthington, D. J. "Queuing Models for Hospital Waiting Lists." *Journal of the Operational Research Society* Vol. 38, No. 5, pp. 413–422.

17

Simulation

CHAPTER OUTLINE

17.1
INTRODUCTION

We are all aware to some extent of the importance of simulation models in our world. The Boeing, McDonnell Douglas, and Lockheed companies, for example, commonly build simulation models of their proposed jet aircraft and then test the aerodynamic properties of the models. Your local civil defense organization may carry out rescue and evacuation practices as it simulates the natural disaster conditions of a hurricane or tornado. The U.S. Army simulates enemy attacks and defense strategies in war games played on a computer. Business students take courses that use management games to simulate realistic competitive business situations. And thousands of business, government, and service organizations develop simulation models to assist in making decisions concerning inventory control, maintenance scheduling, plant layout, investments, and sales forecasting.

As a matter of fact, simulation is one of the most widely used quantitative analysis tools. Various surveys of the largest U.S. corporations revealed that 25% to 30% use simulation in corporate planning.

Simulation sounds like it may be the solution to all management problems. This is, unfortunately, by no means true. Yet we think you may find it one of the most flexible and fascinating of the quantitative techniques in your studies. Let's begin our discussion of simulation with a simple definition.

To *simulate* is to try to duplicate the features, appearance, and characteristics of a real system. In this chapter, we show how to simulate a business or management system by building a *mathematical model* that comes as close as possible to representing the reality of the system. We won't build any *physical* models, as might be used in airplane wind tunnel simulation tests. But just as physical model airplanes are tested and modified under experimental conditions, so our mathematical models are experimented with to estimate the effects of various actions. The idea behind simulation is to imitate a real-world situation mathematically, then to study its properties and operating characteristics, and finally to draw conclusions and make action decisions based on the results of the simulation. In this way, the real-life system is not touched until the advantages and disadvantages of what may be a major policy decision are first measured on the system's model.

KEY IDEA

steps of simulation

Using simulation, a manager should: (1) define a problem; (2) introduce the variables associated with the problem; (3) construct a numerical model; (4) set up possible courses of action for testing; (5) run the experiment; (6) consider the results (possibly deciding to modify the model or change data inputs); and (7) decide what course of action to take. These steps are illustrated in Figure 17.1.

The problems tackled by simulation may range from very simple to extremely complex, from bank teller lines to an analysis of the U.S. economy. Although very small simulations may be conducted by hand, effective use of this technique requires some automated means of calculation,

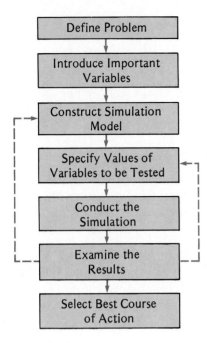

FIGURE 17.1
Process of Simulation

namely, a computer. Even large-scale models, simulating perhaps years of
business decisions, can be handled in a reasonable amount of time by
computer. Though simulation is one of the oldest quantitative analysis
tools (see the "History" box), it was not until the introduction of computers
in the mid-1940s and early 1950s that it became a practical means of solving
management and military problems.

    We begin this chapter with a presentation of the advantages and dis-
advantages of simulation. An explanation of the Monte Carlo method of
simulation follows. Three sample simulations, in the areas of inventory
control, queuing, and maintenance planning, are presented. Other simulation models besides the Monte Carlo approach are also briefly discussed.
And finally, the important role of computers in simulation is illustrated.

computers and simulation

17.2
ADVANTAGES AND DISADVANTAGES OF SIMULATION

Simulation is a tool that has become widely accepted by managers for several
reasons.

1. It is relatively straightforward and flexible.

2. It can be used to analyze large and complex real-world situations that
   can't be solved by conventional quantitative analysis models. For
   example, it may not be possible to build and solve a mathematical

advantages of simulation

model of a city government system that incorporates important economic, social, environmental, and political factors. Simulation has been successfully used to model urban systems, hospitals, educational systems, national and state economies, and even world food systems.

3. Sometimes simulation is the only method available. When the National Aeronautics and Space Administration (NASA) is unable to observe the actual environment on the planet Saturn, a simulation may be needed.

4. Simulation models are built for management problems and require management input. The quantitative analyst must interface extensively with the manager. This means that the user is usually involved in the modeling process, has a stake in its success, and is not afraid to use it.

5. Simulation allows what-if types of questions. Managers like to know in advance what options are attractive. With a computer, a manager can try out several policy decisions within a matter of minutes.

6. Simulations do not interfere with the real-world system. It may be too disruptive, for example, to actually experiment with new policies or ideas in a hospital, school, or manufacturing plant. With simulation, experiments are done with the model, not on the system itself.

7. Simulation allows us to study the interactive effect of individual components or variables in order to determine which ones are important.

8. "Time compression" is possible with simulation. The effect of ordering, advertising, or other policies over many months or years can be obtained by computer simulation in a short time.

9. Simulation allows for the inclusion of real-world complications that most quantitative analysis models cannot permit. For example, some queuing models require exponential or Poisson distributions; some inventory and network models require normality. But simulation can use *any* probability distribution that the user defines; it does not require standard distributions.

The main disadvantages of simulation are:

disadvantages of simulation

1. Good simulation models can be very expensive. It is often a long, complicated process to develop a model. A corporate planning model, for example, may take years to develop.

2. Simulation does not generate optimal solutions to problems as do other quantitative analysis techniques such as EOQ, linear programming, or PERT. It is a trial and error approach that may produce different solutions in repeated runs.

3. Managers must generate all of the conditions and constraints for solutions that they want to examine. The simulation model doesn't produce answers by itself.

Simulation

The history of simulation goes back 5,000 years to Chinese war games, called *weich'i*, and continues through 1780, when the Prussians used the games to help train their army. Since then, all major military powers have used war games to test out military strategies under simulated environments.

From military or operational gaming, a new concept, *Monte Carlo simulation*, was developed as a quantitative technique by the great mathematician John Von Neumann during World War II. Working with neutrons at the Los Alamos Scientific Laboratory, Von Neumann used simulation to solve physics problems that were too complex or expensive to analyze by hand or by physical model. The random nature of the neutrons suggested the use of a roulette wheel in dealing with probabilities. Because of the gaming nature, Von Neumann called it the Monte Carlo model of studying laws of chance.

With the advent and common use of business computers in the 1950s, simulation grew as a management tool. Specialized computer languages were developed in the 1960s (GPSS and SIMSCRIPT) to handle large-scale problems more effectively. In the 1980s, prewritten simulation programs to handle situations ranging from queuing to inventory were developed. They have such names as Xcell, SLAM, Witness, and MAP/1.

4. Each simulation model is unique. Its solutions and inferences are not usually transferable to other problems.

17.3
MONTE CARLO SIMULATION

When a system contains elements that exhibit chance in their behavior, the *Monte Carlo method* of simulation may be applied. The basis of Monte Carlo simulation is experimentation on the chance (or *probabilistic*) elements through random sampling.

The technique breaks down into five simple steps:

1. Setting up a probability distribution for important variables.

2. Building a cumulative probability distribution for each variable in step 1.

3. Establishing an interval of random numbers for each variable.

4. Generating random numbers.

5. Actually simulating a series of trials.

This section examines each of these steps in turn.

Step 1: Establishing Probability Distributions. The basic idea in Monte Carlo simulation is to generate values for the variables making up the model being studied. There are a lot of variables in real-world systems that are probabilistic in nature and that we might want to simulate. A few of these variables are:

variables we may want to simulate

1. Inventory demand on a daily or weekly basis.

2. Lead time for inventory orders to arrive.

3. Times between machine breakdowns.

4. Times between arrivals at a service facility.

5. Service times.

6. Times to complete project activities.

7. Number of employees absent from work each day.

One common way to establish a *probability distribution* for a given variable is to examine historical outcomes. The probability, or relative frequency, for each possible outcome of a variable is found by dividing the frequency of observation by the total number of observations.

establish a probability distribution for tires

The daily demand for radial tires, for example, at Harry's Auto Tire over the past 200 days is shown in Table 17.1. We can convert these data to a probability distribution, if we assume that past arrival rates will hold in the future, by dividing each demand frequency by the total demand, 200. This is illustrated in Table 17.2.

Probability distributions, we should note, need not be based solely on historical observations. Often, managerial estimates based on judgment

TABLE 17.1 Historical Daily Demand for Radial Tires at Harry's Auto Tire

DEMAND FOR TIRES	FREQUENCY (DAYS)
0	10
1	20
2	40
3	60
4	40
5	30
	200

TABLE 17.2 Probability of Demand for Radial Tires

DEMAND VARIABLE	PROBABILITY OF OCCURRENCE	
0	$10/200 =$	.05
1	$20/200 =$	.10
2	$40/200 =$	.20
3	$60/200 =$	.30
4	$40/200 =$	.20
5	$30/200 =$	.15
	$200/200 =$	1.00

and experience are used to create a distribution. Sometimes, a sample of sales, machine breakdowns, or service rates is used to create probabilities for those variables. And the distributions themselves can be either empirical, as in Table 17.1, or based on the commonly known normal, binomial, Poisson, or exponential patterns.

Step 2: Building a Cumulative Probability Distribution for Each Variable. The conversion from a regular probability distribution, such as in the right-hand column of Table 17.2, to a *cumulative distribution* is an easy job. In Table 17.3, we see that the cumulative probability for each level of demand is the sum of the number in the probability column (middle column)

cumulative probabilities

TABLE 17.3 Cumulative Probabilities for Radial Tires

DAILY DEMAND	PROBABILITY	CUMULATIVE PROBABILITY
0	.05	.05
1	.10	.15
2	.20	.35
3	.30	.65
4	.20	.85
5	.15	1.00

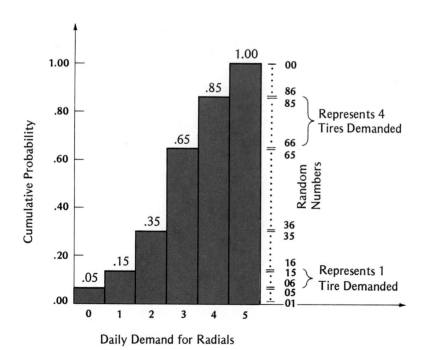

FIGURE 17.2
Graphical Representation of the Cumulative Probability Distribution for Radial Tires

added to the previous cumulative probability (right-most column). The cumulative probability, graphed in Figure 17.2, is used in step 3 to help assign random numbers.

Step 3: Setting Random Number Intervals. Once we have established a cumulative probability distribution for each variable included in the simulation, we must assign a set of numbers to represent each possible value or outcome. These are referred to as *random number intervals*. Random numbers are discussed in detail in step 4. Basically, a *random number* is a series of digits (say two digits from 01, 02, . . . , 98, 99, 00) that have been selected by a totally random process.

assigning random numbers

If there is a 5% chance that demand for a product (such as Harry's radial tires) is 0 units per day, then we want 5% of the random numbers available to correspond to a demand of 0 units. If a total of 100 two-digit numbers is used in the simulation (think of them as being numbered chips in a bowl), we could assign a demand of 0 units to the first 5 random numbers: 01, 02, 03, 04, and 05.[1] Then a simulated demand for 0 units would be created every time one of the numbers 01 to 05 was drawn. If there is also a 10% chance that demand for the same product is one unit per day, we could let the next 10 random numbers (06, 07, 08, 09, 10, 11, 12, 13, 14, and 15) represent that demand—and so on for other demand levels.

In general, using the cumulative probability distribution computed and graphed in step 2, we can set the interval of random numbers for each level of demand in a very simple fashion. You will note in Table 17.4 that the interval selected to represent each possible daily demand is very closely related to the cumulative probability on its left. The top end of each interval is always equal to the cumulative probability percentage.

relation between intervals and cumulative probability

Similarly, we can see in Figure 17.2 and in Table 17.4 that the length of each interval on the right corresponds to the probability of one of each of the possible daily demands. Hence, in assigning random numbers to the daily demand for three radial tires, the range of the random number interval (36 to 65) corresponds *exactly* to the probability (or proportion) of that

TABLE 17.4 Assignment of Random Number Intervals for Harry's Auto Tire

DAILY DEMAND	PROBABILITY	CUMULATIVE PROBABILITY	INTERVAL OF RANDOM NUMBERS
0	.05	.05	01 to 05
1	.10	.15	06 to 15
2	.20	.35	16 to 35
3	.30	.65	36 to 65
4	.20	.85	66 to 85
5	.15	1.00	86 to 00

[1] Alternatively, we could have assigned the random numbers 00, 01, 02, 03, 04 to represent a demand of 0 units. The two digits 00 can be thought of as either 0 or 100. As long as 5 numbers out of 100 are assigned to the 0 demand, it doesn't make any difference which 5 they are.

TABLE 17.5 Table of Random Numbers

52	06	50	88	53	30	10	47	99	37	66	91	35	32	00	84	57	07
37	63	28	02	74	35	24	03	29	60	74	85	90	73	59	55	17	60
82	57	68	28	05	94	03	11	27	79	90	87	92	41	09	25	36	77
69	02	36	49	71	99	32	10	75	21	95	90	94	38	97	71	72	49
98	94	90	36	06	78	23	67	89	85	29	21	25	73	69	34	85	76
96	52	62	87	49	56	59	23	78	71	72	90	57	01	98	57	31	95
33	69	27	21	11	60	95	89	68	48	17	89	34	09	93	50	44	51
50	33	50	95	13	44	34	62	64	39	55	29	30	64	49	44	30	16
88	32	18	50	62	57	34	56	62	31	15	40	90	34	51	95	26	14
90	30	36	24	69	82	51	74	30	35	36	85	01	55	92	64	09	85
50	48	61	18	85	23	08	54	17	12	80	69	24	84	92	16	49	59
27	88	21	62	69	64	48	31	12	73	02	68	00	16	16	46	13	85
45	14	46	32	13	49	66	62	74	41	86	98	92	98	84	54	33	40
81	02	01	78	82	74	97	37	45	31	94	99	42	49	27	64	89	42
66	83	14	74	27	76	03	33	11	97	59	81	72	00	64	61	13	52
74	05	81	82	93	09	96	33	52	78	13	06	28	30	94	23	37	39
30	34	87	01	74	11	46	82	59	94	25	34	32	23	17	01	58	73
59	55	72	33	62	13	74	68	22	44	42	09	32	46	71	79	45	89
67	09	80	98	99	25	77	50	03	32	36	63	65	75	94	19	95	88
60	77	46	63	71	69	44	22	03	85	14	48	69	13	30	50	33	24
60	08	19	29	36	72	30	27	50	64	85	72	75	29	87	05	75	01
80	45	86	99	02	34	87	08	86	84	49	76	24	08	01	86	29	11
53	84	49	63	26	65	72	84	85	63	26	02	75	26	92	62	40	67
69	84	12	94	51	36	17	02	15	29	16	52	56	43	26	22	08	62
37	77	13	10	02	18	31	19	32	85	31	94	81	43	31	58	33	51

Source: Excerpted from *A Million Random Digits with 100,000 Normal Deviates,* The Free Press, 1955, p. 7, with permission of the Rand Corporation.

outcome. A daily demand for three radial tires occurs 30% of the time. Any of the 30 random numbers greater than 35 up to and including 65 are assigned to that event.

Step 4: Generating Random Numbers. Random numbers may be generated for simulation problems in several ways. If the problem is very large and the process being studied involves thousands of simulation trials, computer programs are available to generate the random numbers needed.

If the simulation is being done by hand, as in this book, the numbers may be selected by the spin of a roulette wheel that has 100 slots, by blindly grabbing numbered chips out of an urn, or by any method that allows you to make a random selection.[2] The most commonly used means is to choose numbers from a table of random digits such as Table 17.5.

several ways to pick random numbers

---

[2] One more method of generating random numbers is called the Von Neumann midsquare method, developed in the 1940s. Here's how it works: (1) select any arbitrary number with n digits (for example, $n = 4$ digits), (2) square the number, (3) extract the middle n digits as the next random number. As an example of a 4-digit arbitrary number, use 3,614. The square of 3,614 is 13,060,996. The middle four digits of this new number are 0609. Thus 0609 is the next random number and steps 2 and 3 are repeated. The midsquare method is simple and easily programmed, but sometimes the numbers repeat quickly and are *not* random. For example, try using the method starting with 6,100 as your first arbitrary number!

Table 17.5 was itself generated by a computer program. It has the characteristic that every digit or number in it has an equal chance of occurring. In a very large random number table, 10% of all digits would be 1s, 10 percent 2s, 10 percent 3s, and so on. Because *everything* is random, we can select numbers from anywhere in the table to use in our simulation procedure in step 5.

Step 5: Simulating the Experiment. We may simulate outcomes of an experiment by simply selecting random numbers from Table 17.5. Beginning anywhere in the table, we note the interval in Table 17.4 or Figure 17.2 into which each number falls. For example, if the random number chosen is 81 and the interval 65 to 85 represents a daily demand for four tires, then we select a demand of four tires.

sample simulation

We now illustrate the concept further by simulating 10 days of demand for radial tires at Harry's Auto Tire (see Table 17.6). We select the random numbers needed from Table 17.5, starting in the upper left-hand corner and continuing down the first column.

simulated versus analytical results

It is interesting to note that the average demand of 3.9 tires in this 10-day simulation differs significantly from the *expected* daily demand, which we may compute from the data in Table 17.2.

$$\text{Expected daily demand} = \sum_{i=0}^{5} (\text{Probability of } i \text{ tires}) \times (\text{Demand of } i \text{ tires})$$

$$= (.05)(0) + (.10)(1) + (.20)(2) + (.30)(3)$$
$$+ (.20)(4) + (.15)(5)$$
$$= 2.95 \text{ tires}$$

 KEY IDEA

If this simulation were repeated hundreds or thousands of times, it is much more likely that the average *simulated* demand would be nearly the same as the *expected* demand.

Naturally, it would be risky to draw any hard and fast conclusions regarding the operation of a firm from only a short simulation. It is also unlikely that anyone would actually want to go to the effort of simulating

TABLE 17.6 Ten-Day Simulation of Demand for Radial Tires

DAY NUMBER	RANDOM NUMBER	SIMULATED DAILY DEMAND
1	52	3
2	37	3
3	82	4
4	69	4
5	98	5
6	96	5
7	33	2
8	50	3
9	88	5
10	90	5

39   Total 10-day demand

3.9 = Average daily demand for tires

such a simple model containing only one variable. Simulating by hand does, however, demonstrate the important principles involved and *may* be useful in small-scale studies. As you might expect, the computer can be a very helpful tool in carrying out the tedious work in larger simulation undertakings.

Program 17.1 is a Monte Carlo simulation using our accompanying software package, AB:QM. It reveals that after 250 runs the average daily demand is 2.968 tires. If even more repetitions occurred, we would clearly come closer to the expected value of 2.95 tires.

17.4
SIMULATION AND INVENTORY ANALYSIS

In Chapter 8 we introduced the subject of deterministic inventory models. These commonly used models are based on the assumption that both product demand and reorder lead time are known, constant values. In many real-world inventory situations, though, demand and lead time are variables, and accurate analysis becomes extremely difficult to handle by any means other than simulation.

In this section we present an inventory problem with two decision variables and two probabilistic components. The owner of the hardware store we are about to describe would like to establish *order quantity* and *reorder point* decisions for a particular product that has probabilistic (uncertain) daily demand and reorder lead time. He wants to make a series of simulation runs, trying out various order quantities and reorder points, in order to minimize his total inventory cost for the item. Inventory costs in this case include an ordering, holding, and stockout cost.

simulation useful when demand and lead time are probabilistic

Simkin's Hardware Store

Simkin's Hardware sells the Ace model electric drill. Daily demand for the drill is relatively low but subject to some variability. Over the past 300 days, Simkin has observed the sales shown in column 2 of Table 17.7. He converts this historical frequency data into a probability distribution for

TABLE 17.7 Probabilities and Random Number Intervals for Daily Ace Drill Demand

(1) DEMAND FOR ACE DRILL	(2) FREQUENCY (DAYS)	(3) PROBABILITY	(4) CUMULATIVE PROBABILITY	(5) INTERVAL OF RANDOM NUMBERS
0	15	.05	.05	01 to 05
1	30	.10	.15	06 to 15
2	60	.20	.35	16 to 35
3	120	.40	.75	36 to 75
4	45	.15	.90	76 to 90
5	30	.10	1.00	91 to 00
	300	1.00		

PROGRAM 17.1 Monte Carlo Computer Simulation Using AB:QM

```
Simulation / Monte Carlo Simulation
_____

Problem Title :  HARRY'S AUTO TIRE
Number of Runs Desired        250
Number of Categories          6
_____


            Value  Probability
Category 1       0          .05
Category 2       1          .10
Category 3       2          .20
Category 4       3          .30
Category 5       4          .20
Category 6       5          .15




_____
_____

Help  New  Load  Save  Edit  Run  Print  Install  Directory  Esc
_____




        Program: Simulation / Monte Carlo Simulation

        Problem Title : HARRY'S AUTO TIRE

        ***** Program Output *****


        ------------------------------------

                                  Cumulative
                       Value      Probability
        ------------------------------------
        Category 1     0.000        0.050
        Category 2     1.000        0.150
        Category 3     2.000        0.350
        Category 4     3.000        0.650
        Category 5     4.000        0.850
        Category 6     5.000        1.000
        ------------------------------------

        Number of Runs            250
        Average Value           2.968

        ***** End of Output *****
```

the variable daily demand (column 3). A cumulative probability distribution is formed in column 4. Finally, Simkin establishes an interval of random numbers to represent each possible daily demand (column 5).

When Simkin places an order to replenish his inventory of Ace electric drills, there is a delivery lag of from one to three days. This means that lead time may also be considered a probabilistic variable. The number of days it took to receive the past 50 orders is presented in Table 17.8. In a fashion similar to that for the demand variable, Simkin establishes a probability distribution for the lead time variable (column 3 of Table 17.8), computes the cumulative distribution (column 4), and assigns random number intervals for each possible time (column 5).

TABLE 17.8 Probabilities and Random Number Intervals for Reorder Lead Time

(1) LEAD TIME (DAYS)	(2) FREQUENCY (ORDERS)	(3) PROBABILITY	(4) CUMULATIVE PROBABILITY	(5) RANDOM NUMBER INTERVAL
1	10	.20	.20	01 to 20
2	25	.50	.70	21 to 70
3	15	.30	1.00	71 to 00
	50	1.00		

The first inventory policy that Simkin's Hardware wants to simulate is an order quantity of 10 with a reorder point of 5. That is, every time the on-hand inventory level at the end of the day is 5 or less, Simkin will call his supplier and place an order for 10 more drills. If the lead time is one day, by the way, the order will not arrive the next morning, but rather at the beginning of the following working day.

The logic of the simulation process is presented in Figure 17.3. Such a *flow diagram* or *flowchart* is useful in the logical coding procedures for programming this simulation process.

The entire process is simulated for a 10-day period in Table 17.9. We can assume that beginning inventory is 10 units on day 1. (Actually, it makes little difference in a long simulation what the initial inventory level is. Since we would tend in real life to simulate hundreds or thousands of days, the beginning values will tend to be averaged out.) Random numbers for Simkin's inventory problem are selected from the second column of Table 17.5.

Table 17.9 is filled in by proceeding one day (or line) at a time, working from left to right. It is a four-step process:

1. Begin each simulated day by checking whether any ordered inventory has just arrived (column 2). If it has, increase the current inventory (in column 3) by the quantity ordered (10 units, in this case).

2. Generate a daily demand from the demand probability distribution in Table 17.7 by selecting a random number. This random number is recorded in column 4. The demand simulated is recorded in column 5.

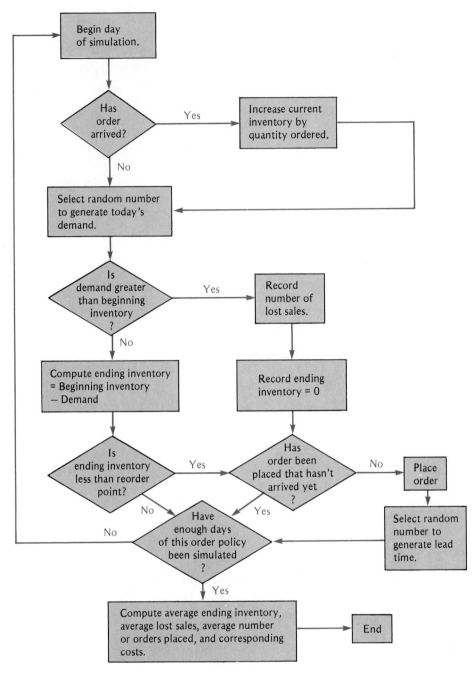

FIGURE 17.3
Flow Diagram for Simkin's Inventory Example

3. Compute the ending inventory every day and record it in column 6. Ending inventory equals beginning inventory minus demand. If on-hand inventory is insufficient to meet the day's demand, satisfy as much as possible and note the number of lost sales (in column 7).

TABLE 17.9 Simkin Hardware's First Inventory Simulation

		ORDER QUANTITY = 10 UNITS			REORDER POINT = 5 UNITS				
(1)	(2)	(3)	(4)	(5)	(6)	(7)	(8)	(9)	(10)
DAY	UNITS RECEIVED	BEGINNING INVENTORY	RANDOM NUMBER	DEMAND	ENDING INVENTORY	LOST SALES	ORDER?	RANDOM NUMBER	LEAD TIME
1	...	10	06	1	9	0	No		
2	0	9	63	3	6	0	No		
3	0	6	57	3	③ [1]	0	Yes	⑩ [2]	1
4	0	3	㊙ [3]	5	0	2	No [4]		
5	⑩ [5]	10	52	3	7	0	No		
6	0	7	69	3	4	0	Yes	33	2
7	0	4	32	2	2	0	No		
8	0	2	30	2	0	0	No		
9	⑩ [6]	10	48	3	7	0	No		
10	0	7	88	4	3	0	Yes	14	1
				Totals	41	2			

[1] This is the first time inventory dropped to the reorder point of 5 drills. Since no prior order was outstanding, an order is placed.
[2] The random number 02 is generated to represent the first lead time. It was drawn from column 2 of Table 17.5 as the next number in the list being used. A separate column could have been used to draw lead time random numbers from if we had wanted to do so, but in this example we did not do so.
[3] Again, notice that the random digits 02 were used for lead time (see footnote 2). So the next number in the column is 94.
[4] No order is placed on day 4 because there is one outstanding from the previous day that has not yet arrived.
[5] The lead time for the first order placed is one day, but as noted in the text, an order does not arrive the next morning, but rather the beginning of the following day. Thus, the first order arrives at the start of day 5.
[6] This is the arrival of the order placed at the close of business on day 6. Fortunately for Simkin, no lost sales occurred during the two-day lead time until the order arrived.

4. Determine whether the day's ending inventory has reached the re-order point (5 units). If it has, and if there are no outstanding orders, place an order (column 8). Lead time for a new order is simulated by first choosing a random number from Table 17.5 and recording it in column 9. (We may continue down the same string of the random number table that we were using to generate numbers for the demand variable.) Finally, we convert this random number into a lead time by using the distribution set in Table 17.8.

Analyzing Simkin's Inventory Costs

Simkin's first inventory simulation yields some interesting results. The average daily ending inventory is:

$$\text{Average ending inventory} = \frac{41 \text{ total units}}{10 \text{ days}} = 4.1 \text{ units per day}$$

We also note the average lost sales and number of orders placed per day:

$$\text{Average lost sales} = \frac{2 \text{ sales lost}}{10 \text{ days}} = .2 \text{ units per day}$$

$$\text{Average number of orders placed} = \frac{3 \text{ orders}}{10 \text{ days}} = .3 \text{ orders per day}$$

These data are useful in studying the inventory costs of the policy being simulated.

Simkin's store is open for business 200 days per year. He estimates that the cost of placing each order for Ace drills is $10. The cost of holding a drill in stock is $6 per drill per year, which can also be viewed as 3¢ per drill per day (over a 200-day year). Finally, Simkin estimates that the cost of each shortage, or lost sale, is $8. What is Simkin's total daily inventory cost for the ordering policy of order quantity, $Q = 10$ and reorder point, ROP $= 5$?

Let us examine the three cost components:

$$\text{Daily order cost} = (\text{Cost of placing one order}) \times (\text{Number of orders placed per day})$$
$$= \$10 \text{ per order} \times .3 \text{ orders per day} = \$3$$

$$\text{Daily holding cost} = (\text{Cost of holding one unit for one day}) \times (\text{Average ending inventory})$$
$$= \$.03 \text{ per unit per day} \times 4.1 \text{ units per day}$$
$$= \$0.12$$

$$\text{Daily stockout cost} = (\text{Cost per lost sale}) \times (\text{Average number of lost sales per day})$$
$$= \$8 \text{ per lost sale} \times .2 \text{ lost sales per day}$$
$$= \$1.60$$

$$\text{Total daily inventory cost} = \text{Daily order cost} + \text{Daily holding cost} + \text{Daily stockout cost} = \$4.72$$

Thus, the total daily inventory cost for this simulation is $4.72. Annualizing this daily figure to a 200-day working year suggests that this inventory policy's cost is approximately $1,330.

> **KEY IDEA**

Now once again we want to emphasize something very important. This simulation should be extended many more days before we draw any conclusions as to the cost of the inventory policy being tested. If a hand simulation is being conducted, 100 days would provide a better representation. If a computer is doing the calculations, 1,000 days would be helpful in reaching accurate cost estimates.

Let's say that Simkin *does* complete a 1,000-day simulation of the policy that order quantity $= 10$ drills, reorder point $= 5$ drills. Does this complete his analysis? The answer is *no*—this is just the beginning! Simkin must now compare *this* potential strategy to other possibilities. For example, what about $Q = 10$, ROP $= 4$; or $Q = 12$, ROP $= 6$; or $Q = 14$, ROP $= 5$? Perhaps every combination of values of Q from 6 to 20 drills and ROP from 3 to 10 should be simulated. After simulating all reasonable combinations of order quantities and reorder points, Simkin would likely select the pair yielding the lowest total inventory cost.

A Computer Simulation to Help Simkin

AB:QM, the software package that accompanies this text, contains an inventory simulation module in addition to the Monte Carlo module illustrated in Program 17.1. This inventory simulation, shown in Program 17.2, examines a range of Q and ROP values of our choosing. It conducts a

PROGRAM 17.2 Computer Inventory Simulation Using AB:QM

```
Program: Simulation / Inventory Simulation

Problem Title : SIMKIN'S HARDWARE

***** Input Data *****

Ordering cost          ($/order)        10.00
Holding cost           ($/units)         6.00
Shortage cost          ($/units)         8.00
Business days          (/year)         200.00
Min order quantity     (units)           9.00
Max order quantity     (units)          11.00
Min reorder point      (units)           4.00
Max reorder point      (units)           6.00
Initial inventory      (units)          10.00
```

Demand	Probability	Cumulative Probability	Lead Time	Probability	Cumulative Probability
0.00	0.050	0.050	1.00	0.200	0.200
1.00	0.100	0.150	2.00	0.500	0.700
2.00	0.200	0.350	3.00	0.300	1.000
3.00	0.400	0.750			
4.00	0.150	0.900			
5.00	0.100	1.000			

```
***** Program Output *****

Annual Inventory cost after 25 simulation runs
```

Order Quantity	Reorder Quantity	Ordering Cost	Holding Cost	Shortage Cost	Total Cost
9	4	480.000	3936.000	832.000	5248.000
	5	560.000	912.000	8064.000	9536.000
	6	640.000	2928.000	1152.000	4720.000
10	4	480.000	3648.000	960.000	5088.000
	5	480.000	4032.000	640.000	5152.000
	6	560.000	1728.000	1920.000	4208.000
11	4	480.000	3600.000	896.000	4976.000
	5	480.000	5712.000	128.000	6320.000
	6	480.000	3840.000	512.000	4832.000

PROGRAM 17.2 (Continued)

```
Annual total inventory cost for various Q and R combinations

---------------------------------------------------------------
(Q\R)        4          5          6
---------------------------------------------------------------
   9      5248.000   9536.000   4720.000
  10      5088.000   5152.000   4208.000
  11      4976.000   6320.000   4832.000
---------------------------------------------------------------


Minimum Annual Total Inventory Cost  :    4208.000
Minimum Order Quantity               :          10
Minimum Reorder Point                :           6

***** End of Output *****
```

number of simulations on each combination of Q and ROP and then shows the costs for ordering, holding, shortage, and the total. In Program 17.2, for example, we selected Qs ranging from a minimum order quantity of 9 to a maximum order quantity of 11 and ROPs ranging from a minimum reorder point of 4 to a maximum reorder point of 6. After entering the appropriate demand and lead time distributions and responding to cost data requests, we receive a printout analyzing all 9 combinations of Q and ROP. After 25 simulation runs, this particular printout indicates we should order $Q = 10$ drills per order with a ROP $= 6$ drills as the reorder point. Even with 25 runs, we should note, however, that randomness exists. Simulating 100, 200, or 1,000 runs can lead to different conclusions.

Computer simulation may not provide an exact conclusion, but it does permit some interesting sensitivity analyses. For example, we can quickly rerun the program with a shortage cost of $10 or with a holding cost of $7 to inspect the impact of small (or large) changes on the conclusions.

17.5
SIMULATION OF A QUEUING PROBLEM

An important area of simulation application has been in the analysis of waiting line problems. As mentioned earlier, the assumptions required for solving queuing problems analytically are quite restrictive. For most realistic queuing systems, simulation may actually be the only approach available.

This section illustrates the simulation at a large unloading dock and its associated queue. Arrivals of barges at the dock are not Poisson distributed, and unloading rates (service times) are not exponential or constant. As such, the mathematical waiting line models of Chapter 16 cannot be used.

Port of New Orleans

Fully loaded barges arrive at night in New Orleans following their long trips down the Mississippi River from industrial midwestern cities. The number of barges docking on any given night ranges from 0 to 5. The probability of 0, 1, 2, 3, 4, or 5 arrivals is displayed in Table 17.10. In the same table, we establish cumulative probabilities and corresponding random number intervals for each possible value.

barge arrivals are probabilistic

A study by the dock superintendent reveals that because of the nature of their cargo, the number of barges unloaded also tends to vary from day to day. The superintendent provides information from which we can create a probability distribution for the variable *daily unloading rate* (see Table 17.11). As we just did for the arrival variable, we can set up an interval of random numbers for the unloading rates.

unloading rates vary

Barges are unloaded on a first-in, first-out basis. Any barges that are not unloaded the day of arrival must wait until the following day. Tying up a barge in dock is an expensive proposition, and the superintendent cannot ignore the angry phone calls from barge line owners reminding him that "time is money!" He decides that, before going to the Port of New Orleans's controller to request additional unloading crews, a simulation study of arrivals, unloadings, and delays should be conducted. A 100-day simulation would be ideal, but for purposes of illustration, the superintendent begins with a shorter 15-day analysis. Random numbers are drawn from the top row of Table 17.5 to generate daily arrival rates. They are drawn from the

TABLE 17.10 Overnight Barge Arrival Rates and Random Number Intervals

NUMBER OF ARRIVALS	PROBABILITY	CUMULATIVE PROBABILITY	RANDOM NUMBER INTERVAL
0	.13	.13	01 to 13
1	.17	.30	14 to 30
2	.15	.45	31 to 45
3	.25	.70	46 to 70
4	.20	.90	71 to 90
5	.10	1.00	91 to 00

TABLE 17.11 Unloading Rates and Random Number Intervals

DAILY UNLOADING RATE	PROBABILITY	CUMULATIVE PROBABILITY	RANDOM NUMBER INTERVAL
1	.05	.05	01 to 05
2	.15	.20	06 to 20
3	.50	.70	21 to 70
4	.20	.90	71 to 90
5	.10	1.00	91 to 00
	1.00		

second row of Table 17.5 to create daily unloading rates. Table 17.12 shows the day-by-day port simulation.

The superintendent will likely be interested in at least three useful and important pieces of information:

simulation results

Average number of barges delayed to the next day

$$= \frac{20 \text{ delays}}{15 \text{ days}} = 1.33 \text{ barges delayed per day}$$

$$\text{Average number of nightly arrivals} = \frac{41 \text{ arrivals}}{15 \text{ days}} = 2.73 \text{ arrivals}$$

$$\text{Average number of barges unloaded each day} = \frac{39 \text{ unloadings}}{15 \text{ days}}$$
$$= 2.60 \text{ unloadings}$$

When these data are analyzed in the context of delay costs, idle labor costs, and the cost of hiring extra unloading crews, it will be possible for the dock superintendent and port controller to make a better staffing decision. They may even elect to resimulate the process assuming different unloading rates that would correspond to increased crew sizes. Although simulation is a tool that cannot guarantee an optimal solution to problems such as this, it can be helpful in recreating a process and identifying good decision alternatives.

TABLE 17.12 Queuing Simulation of Port of New Orleans Barge Unloadings

(1) DAY	(2) NUMBER DELAYED FROM PREVIOUS DAY	(3) RANDOM NUMBER	(4) NUMBER NIGHTLY ARRIVALS	(5) TOTAL TO BE UNLOADED	(6) RANDOM NUMBER	(7) NUMBER UNLOADED
1	—[1]	52	3	3	37	3
2	0	06	0	0	63	0[2]
3	0	50	3	3	28	3
4	0	88	4	4	02	1
5	3	53	3	6	74	4
6	2	30	1	3	35	3
7	0	10	0	0	24	0[3]
8	0	47	3	3	03	1
9	2	99	5	7	29	3
10	4	37	2	6	60	3
11	3	66	3	6	74	4
12	2	91	5	7	85	4
13	3	35	2	5	90	4
14	1	32	2	3	73	3[4]
15	0	00	5	5	59	3
	20		41			39
	Total delays		Total arrivals			Total unloadings

[1] We can begin with no delays from the previous day. In a long simulation, even if we started with 5 overnight delays, that initial condition would be averaged out.
[2] Three barges *could* have been unloaded on day 2. But because there were no arrivals and no backlog existed, zero unloadings took place.
[3] The same situation as noted in footnote 2 takes place.
[4] This time 4 barges could have been unloaded, but since only 3 were in queue, the number unloaded is recorded as 3.

maintenance problems

17.6
SIMULATION MODEL FOR A MAINTENANCE POLICY

Simulation is a valuable technique for analyzing various maintenance policies before actually implementing them. A firm can decide whether to add additional maintenance staff based on machine downtime costs and costs of additional labor. It can simulate replacing parts that have not yet failed in exploring ways to prevent future breakdowns. Many companies use computerized simulation models to decide if and when to shut down a whole plant for maintenance activities. This section provides an example of the value of simulation in setting maintenance policy.

maintenance problems

Three Hills Power Company

The Three Hills Power Company provides electricity to a large metropolitan area through a series of almost 200 hydroelectric generators. Management recognizes that even a well-maintained generator will have periodic failures or breakdowns. Energy demands over the past three years have been consistently high, and the company is concerned over downtime of generators. It currently employs four highly skilled and highly paid ($30 per hour) repairpersons. Each works every fourth 8-hour shift. In this way there is a repairperson on duty 24 hours a day, seven days a week.

generator breakdowns

As expensive as the maintenance staff salaries are, breakdown expenses are even more costly. For each hour that one of its generators is down, Three Hills loses approximately $75. This amount is the charge for reserve power that Three Hills must "borrow" from the neighboring utility company.

Stephanie Robbins has been assigned to conduct a management analysis of the breakdown problem. She determines that simulation is a viable tool because of the probabilistic nature of two important maintenance system components.

First, the time between successive generator breakdowns varies historically from as little as one-half hour to as much as three hours. For the past 100 breakdowns Robbins tabulates the frequency of various times between machine failures (see Table 17.13). She also creates a probability distribution and assigns random number intervals to each expected time range.

Robbins then notes that the people who do repairs log their maintenance time in one-hour time blocks. Because of the time it takes to reach a broken generator, repair times are generally rounded to one, two, or three hours. In Table 17.14 she performs a statistical analysis of past repair times, similar to that conducted for breakdown times.

Robbins's objective is to determine: (1) the service maintenance cost, (2) the simulated machine breakdown cost, and (3) the total simulated maintenance cost of the current system. She does this by selecting a series of random numbers to generate simulated times between generator breakdowns and a second series to simulate repair times required. A simulation

TABLE 17.13 Time between Generator Breakdowns at Three Hills Power

TIME BETWEEN RECORDED MACHINE FAILURES (hours)	NUMBER OF TIMES OBSERVED	PROBABILITY	CUMULATIVE PROBABILITY	RANDOM NUMBER INTERVAL
$\frac{1}{2}$	5	.05	.05	01 to 05
1	6	.06	.11	06 to 11
$1\frac{1}{2}$	16	.16	.27	12 to 27
2	33	.33	.60	28 to 60
$2\frac{1}{2}$	21	.21	.81	61 to 81
3	19	.19	1.00	82 to 00
	100	1.00		

TABLE 17.14 Generator Repair Times Required

REPAIR TIME REQUIRED (hours)	NUMBER OF TIMES OBSERVED	PROBABILITY	CUMULATIVE PROBABILITY	RANDOM NUMBER INTERVAL
1	28	.28	.28	01 to 28
2	52	.52	.80	29 to 80
3	20	.20	1.00	81 to 00
	100	1.00		

of 15 machine failures is presented in Table 17.15. We now examine the elements in that table, one column at a time.

Column 1, Breakdown Number. This is just the count of breakdowns as they occur, going from 1 to 15.

Column 2, Random Number for Breakdowns. This is a number used to simulate time between breakdowns. The numbers in this column have been selected from Table 17.5, from the second column from the right.

Column 3, Time between Breakdowns. This number is generated from column 2 random numbers and the random number intervals defined in Table 17.13. The first random number, 57, falls in the interval 28 to 60, implying a time of 2 hours since the prior breakdown.

Column 4, Time of Breakdown. This converts the data in column 3 into an actual time of day for each breakdown. This simulation assumes that the first day begins at midnight (00:00 hours). Since the time between zero breakdowns and the first breakdown is 2 hours, the first recorded machine failure is at 02:00 on the clock. The second breakdown, you note, occurs $1\frac{1}{2}$ hours later, at a calculated clock time of 03:30 (or 3:30 A.M.).

Column 5, Time Repairperson Is Free to Begin Repair. This is 02:00 hours for the first breakdown if we assume that the repairperson began work at 00:00 hours and was not tied up from a previous generator failure. Before

---

APPLICATIONS OF QA

Simulating Canadian National Railways Line Capacity

The Canadian National Railway is one of the largest and oldest companies owned by the federal government of Canada. Geographically, the Canadian National Railway operates in areas that range all the way from Thunder Bay, Ontario, to Prince Rupert, in British Columbia. Included in this stretch are the beautiful Rocky Mountains that go through such areas as Jasper and Blue River. The railway originally started in 1923 from a collection of Canadian railways that were near bankruptcy. Since then, many changes have been made. In the 1970s, estimates were made that traffic and volume over Canada's National Railway would double. Any significant increase in traffic requires a lot of planning and a large investment in new equipment, tracks, and so forth.

In order to handle this new traffic, very large amounts of capital were needed to improve railway service, equipment, and manpower. These costs

Source: Norma Welch and James Gusso, "Expansion of Canadian National Railways Line Capacity," *Interfaces* Vol. 16, No. 1, January–February 1986, pp. 51–64.

were projected to be approximately 3.5 billion Canadian dollars between 1985 and 1989. This represented a projected increase of traffic ranging from 60 to 75 million gross tons by 1990, up from 40 to 50 million gross tons in 1980.

In order to plan for this expansion, a number of simulation models were developed and used. The Signal Wake model was used to determine the minimum train headway that should be established for a given fleet or number of trains that are following each other. Another simulation model, the Route Capacity Model, investigated such important variables as train delay and overall efficiency as a function of specified track maintenance activities.

Using simulation, a number of initial studies and investigations were made and were subsequently refined. The overall result was a proposal for future capacity expansion. Using computer simulation, Canadian National Railway was able to defer spending approximately 350 million Canadian dollars.

TABLE 17.15 Simulation of Generator Breakdowns and Repairs

(1) BREAKDOWN NUMBER	(2) RANDOM NUMBER FOR BREAKDOWNS	(3) TIME BETWEEN BREAKDOWNS	(4) TIME OF BREAKDOWN	(5) TIME REPAIRPERSON IS FREE TO BEGIN THIS REPAIR	(6) RANDOM NUMBER FOR REPAIR TIME	(7) REPAIR TIME REQUIRED	(8) TIME REPAIR ENDS	(9) NUMBER OF HOURS MACHINE DOWN
1	57	2	02:00	02:00	07	1	03:00	1
2	17	1½	03:30	03:30	60	2	05:30	2
3	36	2	05:30	05:30	77	2	07:30	2
4	72	2½	08:00	08:00	49	2	10:00	2
5	85	3	11:00	11:00	76	2	13:00	2
6	31	2	13:00	13:00	95	3	16:00	3
7	44	2	15:00	16:00	51	2	18:00	3
8	30	2	17:00	18:00	16	1	19:00	2
9	26	1½	18:30	19:00	14	1	20:00	1½
10	09	1	19:30	20:00	85	3	23:00	3½
11	49	2	21:30	23:00	59	2	01:00	3½
12	13	1½	23:00	01:00	85	3	04:00	5
13	33	2	01:00	04:00	40	2	06:00	5
14	89	3	04:00	06:00	42	2	08:00	4
15	13	1½	05:30	08:00	52	2	10:00	4½
							Total	44

recording this time on the second and all subsequent lines, however, we must check column 8 to see what time the repairperson finishes the previous job. Look, for example, at the seventh breakdown. The breakdown occurs at 15:00 hours (or 3:00 P.M.). But the repairperson does not complete the previous job, the sixth breakdown, until 16:00 hours. Hence the entry in column 5 is 16:00 hours.

One further assumption is made in order to handle the fact that each repairperson works only an 8-hour shift. It is that when each person is replaced by the next shift, he or she simply hands the tools over to the new worker. The new repairperson continues working on the same broken generator until the job is completed. There is no lost time and no overlap of workers. Hence, labor costs for each 24-hour day are exactly 24 hours × $30 per hour = $720.

Column 6, Random Number for Repair Time. This is a number selected from the right-most column of Table 17.5. It helps simulate repair times.

Column 7, Repair Time Required. This is generated from column 6's random numbers and Table 17.14's repair time distribution. The first random number, 07, represents a repair time of 1 hour since it falls in the random number interval 01 to 28.

Column 8, Time Repair Ends. This is the sum of the entry in column 5 (time repairperson is free to begin) plus the required repair time from column 7. Since the first repair begins at 02:00 and takes one hour to complete, the time repair ends is recorded in column 8 as 03:00.

Column 9, Number of Hours the Machine Is Down. This is the difference between column 4 (time of breakdown) and column 8 (time repair ends). In the case of the first breakdown, that difference is 1 hour (03:00 minus 02:00). In the case of the tenth breakdown, the difference is 23:00 hours minus 19:30 hours, or $3\frac{1}{2}$ hours.

Cost Analysis of the Simulation

The simulation of 15 generator breakdowns in Table 17.15 spans a time of 34 hours of operation. The clock began at 00:00 hours of day 1 and ran until the final repair at 10:00 hours of day 2.

The critical factor that interests Robbins is the total number of hours that generators are out of service (from column 9). This is computed to be 44 hours. She also notes that toward the end of the simulation period, a backlog is beginning to appear. The thirteenth breakdown occurred at 01:00 hours, but could not be worked on until 04:00 hours. The fourteenth and fifteenth breakdowns experienced similar delays. Robbins is determined to write a computer program to carry out a few hundred more simulated breakdowns, but first wants to analyze the data she has collected thus far.

She measures her objectives as follows:

$$\text{Service maintenance cost} = 34 \text{ hours of worker service time}$$
$$\times \, \$30 \text{ per hour}$$
$$= \$1,020$$

APPLICATIONS OF QA

Planning Academic Microcomputer Laboratory Resources: A Simulation Approach

The introduction of microcomputers into academic computing has revolutionized the entire range of the academic curriculum. The use of the microcomputer in industry has become commonplace; consequently, it is imperative for academic institutions to train their graduates in its use.

A primary objective of today's college graduate is to know how to access information and use it to solve problems. An important part of providing the necessary computer training is to plan and maintain adequate academic computing resources. Microcomputer laboratories must have an optimal mix of hardware and software resources so that adequate equipment is available for teachers in the classroom.

Resource planning for a microcomputer laboratory can be a complex problem. The simulation model that is presented for this problem incorporates the resource decision criteria for a micro lab into a SIMSCRIPT program. This program offers insights by performing what-if analysis, which can then be used for resource planning and scheduling for the micro lab.

The lab resource planning problem can be analyzed in terms of the demand pattern, the resources currently available in the lab, and the resource decision trade-offs that are possible. Since the structure of the lab resource planning problem does not lend itself to mathematical modeling or analytical solution, simulation seemed an appropriate tool for the decisions involved.

The three modules of this simulation model are: (1) a parameter estimation module, (2) a scheduling decision module, and (3) a simulation and printing

Source: P. Dileepan and L. Johnson, Jr., *Journal of Education for Business* February 1988, pp. 210–214.

module. The statistics collected in the simulation are hardware utilization, software utilization, queue statistics for the hardware queue, and queue statistics for the software queue.

For one sample run in a typical college, the utilization statistics reveal that the available resources are equally used. However, the queue statistics indicate a need for additional hardware and software resources. About 11% of the arrivals are being lost because of long waiting lines. The percentage of arrivals who have to wait for resources seems to be rather high, and the maximum waiting time is long. Although the average waiting time may not seem long, on the average 22,161 arrivals wait for 8 minutes, giving a total of about 3,000 hours of waiting time. Therefore, a strong case can be made for increasing the resources of the lab.

Within the structure studied in this simulation model, added workstations lower both the arrivals lost and hardware and software waiting times. An increase to 30 hardware units gives acceptable waiting times, and availability of 10 copies of each software program substantially lowers the number of arrivals lost.

The simulation model presented in this article allows a clear understanding of relationships between possible acquisition decisions and the ability of the lab to effectively serve the needs of faculty and students. In such an environment, decisions concerning the annual equipment budget, the schedule of operations, and the amount of class lab assignments given, can be discussed and negotiated in a rational manner. Thus, output from the simulation model provides valuable information to support the optimum level of operation for the academic microcomputer laboratory.

Simulated machine breakdown cost = 44 total hours of breakdown
$$\times \ \$75 \text{ lost per hour of downtime}$$
$$= \$3,300$$

Total simulated maintenance
cost of the current system = Service cost + Breakdown cost
$$= \$1,020 + \$3,300$$
$$= \$4,320$$

A total cost of $4,320 is reasonable only when compared to other more attractive or less attractive maintenance options. Should, for example, the

Three Hills Power Company add a second full-time repairperson to each shift? Should it add just one more worker, and let him or her come on duty every fourth shift to help catch up on any backlogs? These are two alternatives that Robbins may choose to consider through simulation. You may help by solving Problem 17-19 at the end of this chapter.

preventive maintenance

As mentioned at the outset of this section, simulation can also be used in other maintenance problems, including the analysis of *preventive maintenance*. Perhaps the Three Hills Power Company should consider strategies for replacing generator motors, valves, wiring, switches, and other miscellaneous parts that typically fail. It could: (1) replace all parts of a certain type when one fails on any generator, or (2) repair or replace all parts after a certain length of service based on an estimated average service life. This would again be done by setting probability distributions for failure rates, selecting random numbers, and simulating past failures and their associated costs.

17.7
TWO OTHER TYPES OF SIMULATION MODELS

Simulation models are often broken into three categories. The first, the Monte Carlo method just discussed, uses the concepts of probability distribution and random numbers to evaluate system responses to various policies. The two other categories are called operational gaming and systems simulation. Although in theory the three methods are distinctly different, the growth of computerized simulation has tended to create a common basis in procedures and blur these differences.[3]

Operational Gaming

Operational gaming refers to simulation involving two or more competing players. The best examples are military games and business games. Both allow participants to match their management and decision-making skills in hypothetical situations of conflict.

military games

Military games are used worldwide to train a nation's top military officers, to test offensive and defensive strategies, and to examine the effectiveness of equipment and armies.

business games

Business games, first developed by the firm Booz, Allen and Hamilton in the 1950s, are popular with both executives and business students. They provide an opportunity to test business skills and decision-making ability in a competitive environment. The person or team that performs best in the simulated environment is rewarded by knowing that his or her company has been most successful in earning the largest profit, grabbing a high market share, or perhaps increasing the firm's trading value on the stock exchange.

A sample output of a management game is shown in Program 17.3.

---

[3] Theoretically, random numbers are used only in Monte Carlo simulation. However, in some complex gaming or systems simulation problems in which all relationships cannot be defined exactly, it may be necessary to use the probability concepts of the Monte Carlo method.

PROGRAM 17.3 Sample Computer Output from a Management Game

```
                        EXECUTIVE GAME
MODEL 1 PERIOD  1 JAS PRICE INDEX 100.2 FORECAST,ANNUAL CHANGE  3.0 0/0
SEAS.INDEX   95 NEXT QTR.  115  ECON.INDEX  101 FORECAST,NEXT QTR.  106
```

	INFORMATION		ON	COMPETITORS	
	PRICE	DIVIDEND	SALES VOLUME		NET PROFIT
FIRM 1	$ 6.25	$ 25000	474560	$	58506
FIRM 2	$ 6.35	$ 50000	456553	$	152309
FIRM 3	$ 6.10	$ 0	492000	$	107327
FIRM 4	$ 6.39	$ 15000	260613	$	-124109
FIRM 5	$ 6.40	$ 75000	429588	$	114134
FIRM 6	$ 6.00	$ 50000	669576	$	278956
FIRM 7	$ 6.20	$ 0	651000	$	38517
FIRM 8	$ 6.33	$ 50000	402960	$	17794
FIRM 9	$ 6.40	$ 50000	551000	$	27593

```
                        FIRM 1 1
                  OPERATING STATEMENTS
MARKET POTENTIAL                        474560
SALES VOLUME                            474560
PERCENT SHARE OF INDUSTRY SALES            11
PRODUCTION,THIS QUARTER                 480000
INVENTORY,FINISHED GOODS                 56440
PLANT CAPACITY,NEXT QUARTER             429317
                   INCOME STATEMENT
RECEIPTS,SALES REVENUE                           $    2966001
EXPENSES,MARKETING               $    275000
  RESEARCH AND DEVELOPMENT             250000
  ADMINISTRATION                       332800
  MAINTENANCE                           85000
  LABOR(COST/UNIT EX.OVERTIME $ 1.42)  730288
  MATERIALS CONSUMED(COST/UNIT  1.55)  744427
  REDUCTION,FINISHED GOODS INV.        -16320
  DEPRECIATION(2.500 0/0)              207500
  FINISHED GOODS CARRYING COSTS         28220
  RAW MATERIALS CARRYING COSTS          60000
  ORDERING COSTS                        50000
  SHIFTS CHANGE COSTS                       0
  PLANT INVESTMENT EXPENSES             25000
  FINANCING CHARGES AND PENALTIES           0
  SUNDRIES                              84700       2856615
PROFIT BEFORE INCOME TAX                            109386
INCOME TAX(IN.TX.CR.   0 0/0,SURTAX    0 0/0)        50880
NET PROFIT AFTER INCOME TAX                          58506
DIVIDENDS PAID                                       25000
ADDITION TO OWNERS EQUITY                            33506
                       CASH FLOW
RECEIPTS,SALES REVENUE                           $    2966001
DISBURSEMENTS,CASH EXPENSE        $   1921008
  INCOME TAX                            50880
  DIVIDENDS PAID                        25000
  PLANT INVESTMENT                     500000
  MATERIALS PURCHASED                 1000000       3496888
ADDITION TO CASH ASSETS                            -530887
                  FINANCIAL STATEMENT
NET ASSETS,CASH                                  $    516113
  INV. VALUE,FINISHED GOODS                           169320
  INVENTORY VALUE,MATERIALS                          1455573
  PLANT BOOK VALUE(REPLACE.VAL.$   8693381)          8592500
OWNERS EQUITY(ECONOMIC EQUITY   10834386)          10733506
```

During each period of competition, be it a week, month, or quarter, teams respond to market conditions by coding their latest management decisions with respect to inventory, production, financing, investment, marketing, and research. The competitive business environment is simulated by computer, and a new printout summarizing current market conditions is presented to players. This allows teams to simulate years of operating conditions in a matter of days, weeks, or a semester.

computer outputs for a business game

Systems Simulation

Systems simulation is similar to business gaming in that it allows users to test various managerial policies and decisions to evaluate their effect on the operating environment. This variation of simulation models the dynamics of large *systems*. Such systems include corporate operations,[4] the national economy, a hospital, or a city government system.

corporate operating systems

In a *corporate operating system,* sales, production levels, marketing policies, investments, union contracts, utility rates, financing, and other factors are all related in a series of mathematical equations that are examined by simulation. In a simulation of an *urban government,* systems simulation may be employed to evaluate the impact of tax increases, capital expenditures for roads and buildings, housing availability, new garbage routes, in-migration and out-migration, locations of new schools or senior citizen centers, birth and death rates, and many more vital issues. Simulations of *economic systems,* often called econometric models, are used by government agencies, bankers, and large organizations to predict inflation rates, domestic and foreign money supplies, and unemployment levels. Inputs and outputs of a typical economic system simulation are illustrated in Figure 17.4.

economic systems

allows what-if questions

The value of systems simulation lies in its allowance of what-if questions to test the effects of various policies. A corporate planning group, for example, can change the value of any input, such as an advertising budget, and examine the impact on sales, market share, or short-term costs. Simulation can also be used to evaluate different research and development projects or to determine long-range planning horizons.

17.8
ROLE OF COMPUTERS IN SIMULATION

KEY IDEA

We have used the AB:QM software twice in this chapter to conduct simulations of small problems. We also recognize that computers are critical in simulating complex tasks. They can generate random numbers, simulate thousands of time periods in a matter of seconds or minutes, and provide management with reports that make decision making easier. As a matter

---

[4] This is sometimes referred to as *industrial dynamics,* a term coined by Jay Forrester. Forrester's goal was to find a way "to show how policies, decisions, structure, and delays are interrelated to influence growth and stability" in industrial systems. See J. W. Forrester, *Industrial Dynamics* (Cambridge, Mass.: The M.I.T. Press, 1961).

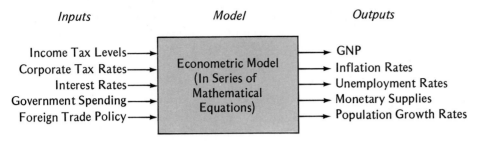

FIGURE 17.4
Inputs and Outputs of a Typical Economic System Simulation

of fact, a computer approach is almost a necessity in order for us to draw valid conclusions from a simulation. Since we require a very large number of simulations, it would be a real burden to rely on pencil and paper alone.

Two types of computer programming languages are available to help the simulation process. The first type, *general purpose languages*, includes FORTRAN, BASIC, COBOL, PL/1, Pascal, and Ada. If you have taken an introductory computer course you undoubtedly have been exposed to one or more of these.

general purpose programming languages

Let's look at the second type of programming languages available: *special purpose simulation languages*. These languages have been specially developed to handle simulation problems and have three advantages: (1) they require less programming time for large simulations, (2) they are usually more efficient and easier to check for errors, and (3) they have random number generators already built in as subroutines. The major special purpose languages are: GPSS (*General Purpose System Simulator*, developed by IBM), SIMSCRIPT (created by the Rand Corporation), DYNAMO (developed at MIT) and GASP (*General Activity Simulation Package*, also by IBM). A detailed discussion of the logic and technique of these languages is beyond the scope of this book, but you might wish to read the reference manuals that exist for each.

special simulation languages

A sample of a microcomputer-based GPSS program is provided in Program 17.4. It represents a queuing simulation in which customers arrive at a bank according to a known arrival pattern. If a teller is free, the deposit is made; if the teller is busy, the customer enters a queue. When the transaction is completed, the customer "gives up" the teller, takes a taxi home, and departs the simulation. Quite similar GPSS programs can be written to handle such diverse queuing analyses as waiting at a barbershop, buying a ticket at a theater, or receiving service at a repair facility.

sample GPSS queuing simulation

Simulation has proven so popular that commercial, easy-to-use pre-written simulation programs are also available. Some are generalized to handle a wide variety of situations ranging from queuing to inventory. The names of a few such programs are: Witness (by Istel Incorporated, Chicago), Xcell, MAP/1, and Slam (by Pritsker and Associates, Inc., West Lafayette, Indiana). Program 17.5 indicates the ease of data input in MAP/1.

PROGRAM 17.4 GPSS Language Sample Simulation for a Bank
(*Source:* Minuteman Software, P.O. Box 171, Stowe, MA
01775)

```
 ;    GPSS/PC Program file TEST24.GPS              02-11-1984    10:03:34
 7 MOTORPOOL STORAGE        3                    ;
 9 LINETABLE TABLE          Q$TELLER,2,2,10      ;
10 ***********************************************************************
12 *                                                                    *
14 *                    Bank Simulation                                 *
16 *                                                                    *
18 ***********************************************************************
20            GENERATE      300,100,,,300         ;Create next customer.
30            QUEUE         TELLER                ;Begin queue time.
40            SEIZE         TELLER                ;Own or wait for teller.
50            DEPART        TELLER                ;End queue time.
60            ADVANCE       400,200               ;Bank deposit takes a few minutes.
65            TABULATE      LINETABLE             ;Record waiting line in histogram.
70            RELEASE       TELLER                ;Deposit done. Give up the teller.
71            ASSIGN        LINESIZE,Q$TELLER     ;Remember the size of the queue.
72            SAVEVALUE     CLOCKSAVE,C1          ;Save the clock
73            LOGIC S       SWITCH1               ;Set the switch.
75            JOIN          DEPOSITS,1995         ;Record the deposit.
76            JOIN          CUSTOMERS             ;Join the group of customers
77            LINK          TAXILINE,FIFO,EXITDOOR    ;
79 EXITDOOR   ENTER         MOTORPOOL             ;Get a taxi.
86            ADVANCE       2000                  ;Go home.
88            UNLINK        TAXILINE,EXITDOOR,1,BACK    ;Leave the taxi queue
89            LEAVE         MOTORPOOL             ;Give up the taxi.
90            SPLIT         1,DESTINATION         ;Create a new transaction.
95            BUFFER
100           TERMINATE     1                     ;Customer leaves the simulation.
102   DESTINATION PRIORITY   200
103           ASSIGN        COLOR,BLUE            ;Initialize a parameter.
104           BUFFER                              ;Let parent terminate.
105           TERMINATE
112           REPORT        TEST24                ;Bank Simulation
115           START         50,,,1                ;
```

PROGRAM 17.5 Data Input for a Simulation Using MAP/1
(*Source:* Pritsker and Associates, Inc., West Lafayette, IN 47806)

```
MAP/1 INPUT SYSTEM

MAIN MENU

B) BUILD A MODEL

R) REPORT A MODEL

U) UTILITIES

H) HELP

E) EXIT MAP/1 INPUT SYSTEM

ENTER THE LETTER OF THE DESIRED FUNCTION
```

```
PART TYPE NAME: GEAR

ENTER PART TYPE NAME.

POSSIBLE VALUES-ANY ALPHANUMERIC LABEL.

_____MODEL NAME: YES  _____DOWN_____PAGE 1 OF 3_____

PART TYPE NAME: GEAR      PART TYPE PRIORITY:  0

PART TYPE INTERARRIVAL: 2,4

FIRST PART ARRIVAL 0.000000000E_00

ARRIVING LOT SIZE: 2

EXPECTED FLOWTIME: 0.000000000E_00
```

```
STATION NAME: MILL2

ENTER STATION NAME.

POSSIBLE VALUES-ANY ALPHANUMERIC LABEL.

_____MODEL NAME: YES  _____DOWN_____PAGE 1 OF 1_____

STATION NAME: MILL2        STATION SIZE: 1

PREPROCESS INVENTORY STORAGE SPACE: 1

POSTPROCESS INVENTORY STORAGE SPACE: 1

MATERIAL HANDLING CLASS: REGULAR

MATERIAL HANDLING EQUIPMENT NAME: CART   TRANSPORTATION LOT SIZE: 1

EXCESS RULE: BLOCK

SHIFT SCHEDULE IDENTIFIER: 1 END OF SHIFT RULE: START

MAXIMUM OVERTIME: 0.100000000E_10

OPERATION MODE: REGULAR
```

APPLICATIONS OF QA

The Integration of Simulation and other Models for Netherlands Water Planning

For many applications, one quantitative analysis technique such as *mathematical programming* or *decision theory* is all that is needed to make more effective decisions. In other cases, the problem can be complex, requiring a number of quantitative approaches. These multiple models need to be coordinated and used together in an efficient way in making decisions and developing policy. Such was the case in planning the Netherlands water resources.

Because of a severe drought, the Netherlands had approximately $2.5 billion in agricultural losses. This represented about 4 percent of the gross domestic product. To state the problem simply, during this period, the Dutch faced a problem of too little fresh water and too much pollution in existing water systems.

One of the main water systems for the Netherlands is the Rhine River, which enters the Netherlands from Germany. It is a major water source for agricultural purposes, and also a major river for shipping and general transportation. Unfortunately, the Rhine River is also used as a dumping ground for many power plants and other industrial operations located along the river. This is why some people have referred to the Rhine River as the "Sewer of Europe."

In order to clean up the water pollution and to supply a higher quality and more abundant source of fresh water, the PAWN project was initiated. The PAWN project, standing for "Policy Analysis for the Water Management of the Netherlands," was conducted by the Netherlands and the Rand Corporation. The overall objective was to assess the consequences of water management policies, generate alternative water management policies that could be implemented, develop the capability for the Dutch to perform further analysis, and to provide recommendations for overall water management.

Source: Bruce Goeller and the PAWN Team, "Planning the Netherlands Water Resources," *Interfaces* Vol. 15, No. 1, January–February 1985, pp. 3–33.

There are a number of different policies concerning water management that can be implemented and used. For example, building additional canals or waterways is one approach. Placing taxes on particular usages is another approach. The tactics considered by the PAWN project included additions and modifications to the current water distribution system, changes in managerial structure and policies, the use of taxes and other charges on water use, discharge, pollution, and various regulations and legal restrictions on the use of water or the discharge of materials into the water system.

In order to develop an effective decision-making approach, PAWN produced 50 integrated models. These included environmental models, power plant models, shipping and locks models, industrial and agricultural models, and various water uses and distribution models. The water uses and distribution models included lakes, external water supplies, ground water storage, and a water distribution system. The models included 12 computer simulations of water distribution; six mathematical programming models; and two heuristic, or "rule of thumb," optimization models. The mathematical programming models included nonlinear models.

It was estimated that the new national water management policy developed from these models saved hundreds of millions of dollars in investment expenditures and resulted in the reduction of agriculturally related problems. It was estimated that the agricultural damage was reduced by approximately $15 million per year. The Minister of the Netherlands Ministry of Transport and Public Works, Mrs. N. Smit-Kroes stated: "The new national water management policy for the Netherlands is based largely on the PAWN Project. Without the PAWN methodology and analysis, or something equivalent, to assess the cost and benefits of alternative policy actions in a credible way, many of the changes to the previous policy would not have been made."

17.9
SUMMARY

The purpose of this chapter was to discuss the concept and approach of simulation as a problem-solving tool. Simulation involves building a mathematical model that attempts to describe a real-world situation. The model's goal is to incorporate important variables and their interrelationships in such a way that we can study the impact of managerial changes upon the total system. The approach has many advantages over other quantitative analysis techniques and is especially useful when a problem is too complex or difficult to solve by other means.

The Monte Carlo method of simulation is developed through the use of probability distributions and random numbers. Random number intervals are established to represent possible outcomes for each probabilistic variable in the model. Random numbers are then either selected from a random number table or generated by computer to simulate variable outcomes. The simulation procedure is conducted for many time periods in order to evaluate the long-term impact of each policy value being studied. Monte Carlo simulation was illustrated by hand on problems of inventory control, queuing, and machine maintenance.

Operational gaming and systems simulation, two other categories of simulation, were also presented in this chapter. We concluded with a discussion of the important role of the computer in the simulation process.

GLOSSARY

Simulation. A quantitative analysis technique that involves building a mathematical model that represents a real-world situation. The model is then experimented with to estimate the effects of various actions and decisions.

Monte Carlo Simulation. Simulations that experiment with probabilistic elements of a system by generating random numbers to create values for those elements.

Random Number. A number whose digits are selected completely at random.

Random Number Interval. A range of random numbers assigned to represent a possible simulation outcome.

Flow Diagram or Flowchart. A graphical means of presenting the logic of a simulation model. It is a tool that helps in writing a simulation computer program.

Operational Gaming. The use of simulation in competitive situations such as military games and business or management games.

Systems Simulation. Simulation models dealing with the dynamics of large organizational or governmental systems.

General Purpose Languages. Computer programming languages, such as FORTRAN, BASIC, or COBOL, that are used to simulate a problem.

Special Purpose Simulation Languages. Programming languages especially designed to be efficient in handling simulation problems. The category includes GPSS, SIMSCRIPT, GASP, DYNAMO, Xcell, MAP/1, and SLAM.

SOLVED PROBLEMS

Solved Problem 17.1

Higgins Plumbing and Heating maintains a stock of 30-gallon hot water heaters that it sells to homeowners and installs for them. Owner Jerry Higgins likes the idea of having a large supply on hand to meet customer demand, but he also recognizes that it is expensive to do so. He examines hot water heater sales over the past 50 weeks and notes the following:

HOT WATER HEATER SALES PER WEEK	NUMBER OF WEEKS THIS NUMBER WAS SOLD
4	6
5	5
6	9
7	12
8	8
9	7
10	3
	50

(a) If Higgins maintains a constant supply of 8 hot water heaters in any given week, how many times will he be out of stock during a 20-week simulation? We use random numbers from the seventh column of Table 17.5, beginning with the random digits 10.

(b) What is the average number of sales per week (including stockouts) over the 20-week period?

(c) Using an analytic nonsimulation technique, what is the expected number of sales per week? How does this compare to the answer in b?

Solution

HEATER SALES	PROBABILITY	RANDOM NUMBER INTERVALS
4	.12	01 to 12
5	.10	13 to 22
6	.18	23 to 40
7	.24	41 to 64
8	.16	65 to 80
9	.14	81 to 94
10	.06	95 to 00
	1.00	

(a)

WEEK	RANDOM NUMBER	SIMULATED SALES	WEEK	RANDOM NUMBER	SIMULATED SALES
1	10	4	11	08	4
2	24	6	12	48	7
3	03	4	13	66	8
4	32	6	14	97	10
5	23	6	15	03	4

WEEK	RANDOM NUMBER	SIMULATED SALES	WEEK	RANDOM NUMBER	SIMULATED SALES
6	59	7	16	96	10
7	95	10	17	46	7
8	34	6	18	74	8
9	34	6	19	77	8
10	51	7	20	44	7

With a supply of 8 heaters, Higgins will be out of stock three times during the 20-week period (in weeks 7, 14, and 16).

(b) Average sales by simulation = total sales/20 weeks = $\dfrac{135}{20}$ = 6.75 per week.

(c) Using expected values,

$$E(\text{sales}) = .12 \ (4 \text{ heaters}) + .10 \ (5)$$
$$+ \ .18 \ (6) + .24 \ (7) + .16 \ (8)$$
$$+ \ .14 \ (9) + .06 \ (10) = 6.88 \text{ heaters}$$

With a longer simulation, these two approaches will lead to even closer values.

Solved Problem 17.2

The manager of Denton Savings and Loan is attempting to determine how many tellers are needed at the drive-in window during peak times. As a general policy, the manager wishes to offer service such that average customer waiting time does not exceed 2 minutes. Given the existing service level, as shown in the data below, does the drive-in window meet this criteria?

DATA FOR CUSTOMER ARRIVALS

TIME BETWEEN SUCCESSIVE CUSTOMER ARRIVALS	PROBABILITY (FREQUENCY)	CUMULATIVE PROBABILITY	RANDOM NUMBER INTERVAL
0	.10	.10	01 to 10
1.0	.35	.45	11 to 45
2.0	.25	.70	46 to 70
3.0	.15	.85	71 to 85
4.0	.10	.95	86 to 95
5.0	.05	1.00	96 to 00

DATA FOR SERVICE TIME

SERVICE TIME (MINUTES)	PROBABILITY (FREQUENCY)	CUMULATIVE PROBABILITY	RANDOM NUMBER INTERVAL
0	.00	.00	(impossible)
1.0	.25	.25	01 to 25
2.0	.20	.45	26 to 45
3.0	.40	.85	46 to 85
4.0	.15	1.00	86 to 00

Solution

(1) CUSTOMER NUMBER	(2) RANDOM NUMBER	(3) INTERVAL TO ARRIVAL	(4) TIME OF ARRIVAL	(5) RANDOM NUMBER	(6) SERVICE TIME	(7) START SERVICE	(8) END SERVICE	(9) WAIT TIME	(10) IDLE TIME
1	50	2	9:02	52	3	9:02	9:05	0	2
2	28	1	9:03	37	2	9:05	9:08	2	0
3	68	2	9:05	82	3	9:08	9:11	3	0
4	36	1	9:06	69	3	9:11	9:14	5	0
5	90	4	9:10	98	4	9:14	9:18	4	0
6	62	2	9:12	96	4	9:18	9:22	6	0
7	27	1	9:13	33	2	9:22	9:24	9	0
8	50	2	9:15	50	3	9:24	9:27	9	0
9	18	1	9:16	88	4	9:27	9:31	11	0
10	36	1	9:17	90	4	9:31	9:35	14	0
11	61	2	9:19	50	3	9:35	9:38	16	0
12	21	1	9:20	27	2	9:38	9:40	18	0
13	46	2	9:22	45	2	9:40	9:42	18	0
14	01	0	9:22	81	3	9:42	9:45	20	0
15	14	1	9:23	66	3	9:45	9:48	22	0

Read the data as in the following example for the first row:

Column 1: Number of customer.
Column 2: From third column of random number Table 17.5.
Column 3: Time interval corresponding to random number (random number of 50 implies a 2-minute interval).
Column 4: Starting at 9 A.M. the first arrival is at 9:02.
Column 5: From the first column of the random number Table 17.5.
Column 6: Teller time corresponding to random number 52 is 3 minutes.
Column 7: Teller is available and can start at 9:02.
Column 8: Teller completes work at 9:05 (9:02 + :03).
Column 9: Wait time for customer is 0 as the teller was available.
Column 10: Idle time for the teller was 2 minutes (9:00 to 9:02).

The drive-in window clearly does not meet the manager's criteria for an average wait time of 2 minutes. As a matter of fact, we can observe an increasing queue buildup after only a few customer simulations. This observation can be confirmed by expected value calculations on both arrival and service rates.

DISCUSSION QUESTIONS AND PROBLEMS

Discussion Questions

17-1 What are the advantages and limitations of simulation models?

17-2 Why might a manager be forced to use simulation instead of an analytical model in dealing with a problem of:
   (a) Inventory ordering policy.
   (b) Ships docking in a port to unload.
   (c) Bank teller service windows.
   (d) The U.S. economy.

17-3 What types of management problems can be solved more easily by quantitative analysis techniques other than simulation?

17-4 What are the major steps in the simulation process?

17-5 What is Monte Carlo simulation? What principles underlie its use, and what steps are followed in applying it?

17-6 List three ways in which random numbers may be generated for use in a simulation.

17-7 In the simulation of an order policy for drills at Simkin's Hardware, would the results (Table 17.9) change significantly if a longer period were simulated? Why is the 10-day simulation valid or invalid?

17-8 Why is a computer necessary in conducting a real-world simulation?

17-9 What is operational gaming? What is systems simulation? Give examples of how each may be applied.

17-10 Do you think the application of simulation will increase strongly in the next 10 years? Why or why not?

17-11 Why would an analyst ever prefer a general purpose language such as FORTRAN or BASIC in a simulation when there are advantages to using special purpose languages such as GPSS or SIMSCRIPT?

Problems

The problems that follow involve simulations that are to be done by hand. You are aware that in order to obtain accurate and meaningful results, long periods must be simulated. This is usually handled by computer. If you are able to program some of the problems in a language you are familiar with, we suggest you try to do so. If not, the hand simulations will still help you in understanding the simulation process.

 · **17-12** Clark Property Management is responsible for the maintenance, rental, and day-to-day operation of a large apartment complex on the east side of New Orleans. George Clark is especially concerned about the cost projections for replacing air conditioner compressors. He would like to simulate the number of compressor failures each year over the next 20 years. Using data from a similar apartment building he manages in a New Orleans suburb, Clark establishes a table of relative frequency of failures during a year as follows:

NUMBER OF A.C. COMPRESSOR FAILURES	PROBABILITY (RELATIVE FREQUENCY)
0	.06
1	.13
2	.25
3	.28
4	.20
5	.07
6	.01

He decides to simulate the 20-year period by selecting two-digit random numbers from the third column of Table 17.5, starting with the random number 50.

Conduct the simulation for Clark. Is it common to have three or more consecutive years of operation with two or less compressor failures per year?

· **17-13** The number of cars arriving at Lundberg's Car Wash during the past 200 hours of operation is observed to be the following:

NUMBER OF CARS ARRIVING	FREQUENCY
3 or less	0
4	20
5	30
6	50
7	60
8	40
9 or more	0
	200

(a) Set up a probability and cumulative probability distribution for the variable of car arrivals.
(b) Establish random number intervals for the variable.
(c) Simulate 15 hours of car arrivals and compute the average number of arrivals per hour. Select the random numbers needed from the first column, Table 17.5, beginning with the digits 52.

· **17-14** Refer to the data in Solved Problem 17.1, which deals with Higgins Plumbing and Heating. Higgins has now collected 100 weeks of data and finds the following distribution for sales.

HOT WATER HEATER SALES PER WEEK	NUMBER OF WEEKS THIS NUMBER WAS SOLD
3	2
4	9
5	10
6	15
7	25
8	12
9	12
10	10
11	5

(a) Resimulate the number of stockouts incurred over a 20-week period (assuming Higgins maintains a constant supply of 8 heaters).
(b) Conduct this 20-week simulation two more times and compare your answers with those in part a. Did they change significantly? Why or why not?
(c) What is the new expected number of sales per week?

· **17-15** An increase in the size of the barge unloading crew at the Port of New Orleans (see Section 5) has resulted in a new probability distribution for daily unloading rates. In particular, Table 17.11 may be revised as shown here.

DAILY UNLOADING RATE	PROBABILITY
1	.03
2	.12
3	.40
4	.28
5	.12
6	.05

(a) Resimulate 15 days of barge unloadings and compute the average number of barges delayed, average number of nightly arrivals, and average number of barges unloaded each day. Draw random numbers from the bottom row of Table 17.5 to generate daily arrivals and from the second-from-the-bottom row to generate daily unloading rates.

(b) How do these simulated results compare to those in the chapter?

· **17-16** Simkin's Hardware Store simulated an inventory ordering policy for Ace electric drills that involved an order quantity of 10 drills with a reorder point of 5. This first attempt to develop a cost-effective ordering strategy was illustrated in Table 17.9 of Section 4. The brief simulation resulted in a total daily inventory cost of $4.72.

Simkin would now like to compare this strategy to one in which he orders 12 drills, with a reorder point of 6. Conduct a 10-day simulation for him and discuss the cost implications.

: **17-17** Draw a flow diagram to represent the logic and steps of simulating barge arrivals and unloadings at the Port of New Orleans (see Section 5). For a refresher in flowcharts see Figure 17.3.

: **17-18** Draw a flow diagram for the simulation of generator maintenance by the Three Hills Power Company (Section 6 of this chapter).

: **17-19** Stephanie Robbins is the Three Hills Power Company management analyst assigned to simulate maintenance costs. Section 6 described the simulation of 15 generator breakdowns and the repair times required when one repairperson is on duty per shift. The total simulated maintenance cost of the current system was $4,320.

Robbins would now like to examine the relative cost-effectiveness of adding one more worker per shift. The new repairperson would be paid $30 per hour, the same rate as the first is paid. The cost per breakdown hour is still $75. Robbins makes one vital assumption as she begins—that repair times with two workers will be exactly one-half the times required with only one repairperson on duty per shift. Table 17.14 can then be restated as:

REPAIR TIME REQUIRED (HOURS)	PROBABILITY
$\frac{1}{2}$	.28
1	.52
$1\frac{1}{2}$	.20
	1.00

(a) Simulate this proposed maintenance system change over a 15-generator breakdown period. Select the random numbers needed for time between breakdowns from the second-from-the-bottom row of Table 17.5 (beginning with the digits 69). Select random numbers for generator repair times from the last row of the table (beginning with 37).

(b) Should Three Hills add a second repairperson each shift?

· **17-20** Vincent Maruggi, an MBA student at Northern Massachusetts University, has been having problems balancing his checkbook. His monthly income is derived from a graduate research assistantship; however, he also makes extra money in most months by tutoring undergraduates in their quantitative analysis course. His chances of various income levels are shown here.

MONTHLY INCOME* ($)	PROBABILITY
350	.40
400	.20
450	.30
500	.10

* Assume this income is received at the beginning of each month.

Maruggi's expenditures also vary from month to month, and he estimates that they will follow this distribution:

MONTHLY EXPENSES ($)	PROBABILITY
300	.10
400	.45
500	.30
600	.15

He begins his final year with $600 in his checking account. Simulate the entire year (12 months) and discuss Maruggi's financial picture.

: **17-21** The Brennan Aircraft Division of TLN Enterprises operates a large number of computerized plotting machines. For the most part, the plotting devices are used to create line drawings of complex wing airfoils and fuselage part dimensions. The engineers operating the automated plotters are called loft lines engineers.

The computerized plotters consist of a minicomputer system connected to a 4-by-5-foot flat table with a series of ink pens suspended above it. When a sheet of clear plastic or paper is properly placed on the table, the computer directs a series of horizontal and vertical pen movements until the desired figure is drawn.

The plotting machines are highly reliable, with the exception of the four sophisticated ink pens that are built in. The pens constantly clog and jam in a raised or lowered position. When this occurs, the plotter is unusable.

Currently, Brennan Aircraft replaces each pen as it fails. The service manager has, however, proposed replacing all four pens every time one fails. This should cut down the frequency of plotter failures. At present, it takes one hour to replace one pen. All four pens could be replaced in two hours. The total cost of a plotter being unusable is $50 per hour. Each pen costs $8.

If only one pen is replaced each time a clog or jam occurs, the following breakdown data are thought to be valid:

HOURS BETWEEN PLOTTER FAILURES IF ONE PEN IS REPLACED DURING A REPAIR	PROBABILITY
10	.05
20	.15
30	.15
40	.20
50	.20
60	.15
70	.10

Based on the service manager's estimates, if all four pens are replaced each time one pen fails, the probability distribution between failures is:

HOURS BETWEEN PLOTTER FAILURES IF ALL FOUR PENS ARE REPLACED DURING A REPAIR	PROBABILITY
100	.15
110	.25
120	.35
130	.20
140	.05

(a) Simulate Brennan Aircraft's problem and determine the best policy. Should the firm replace one pen or all four pens on a plotter each time a failure occurs?

(b) Develop a second approach to solving this problem, this time without simulation. Compare the results. How does it affect Brennan's policy decision using simulation?

17-22 Dr. Mark Greenberg practices dentistry in Topeka, Kansas. Greenberg tries hard to schedule appointments so that patients do not have to wait beyond their appointment time. His October 20 schedule is shown in the accompanying table.

SCHEDULED APPOINTMENT AND TIME		EXPECTED TIME NEEDED
Adams	9:30 A.M.	15
Brown	9:45 A.M.	20
Crawford	10:15 A.M.	15
Dannon	10:30 A.M.	10
Erving	10:45 A.M.	30
Fink	11:15 A.M.	15
Graham	11:30 A.M.	20
Hinkel	11:45 A.M.	15

Unfortunately, not every patient arrives exactly on schedule, and expected times to examine patients are just that, *expected*. Some examinations take longer than expected, while some take less time.

Greenberg's experience dictates the following:

(a) 20% of the patients will be 20 minutes early.
(b) 10% of the patients will be 10 minutes early.
(c) 40% of the patients will be on time.
(d) 25% of the patients will be 10 minutes late.
(e) 5% of the patients will be 20 minutes late.

He further estimates that:

(a) 15% of the time he will finish in 20% less time than expected.
(b) 50% of the time he will finish in the expected time.
(c) 25% of the time he will finish in 20% more time than expected.
(d) 10% of the time he will finish in 40% more time than expected.

Dr. Greenberg has to leave at 12:15 P.M. on October 20 in order to catch a flight to a dental convention in New York. Assuming he is ready to start his workday at 9:30 A.M., and that patients are treated in order of their scheduled exam (even if one late patient arrives after an early one), will he be able to make the flight? Comment on this simulation.

: 17-23 The Pelnor Corporation is the nation's largest manufacturer of industrial-size washing machines. A main ingredient in the production process is 8-by-10 foot sheets of stainless steel. The steel is used for both interior washer drums and outer casings.

Steel is purchased weekly on a contractual basis from the Smith-Layton Foundry which, because of limited availability and lot sizing, can ship either 8,000 or 11,000 square feet of stainless steel each week. When Pelnor's weekly order is placed, there is a 45% chance that 8,000 square feet will arrive and a 55% chance of receiving the larger size order.

Pelnor uses the stainless steel on a stochastic (nonconstant) basis. The probabilities of demand each week are:

STEEL NEEDED PER WEEK (SQ. FT.)	PROBABILITY
6,000	.05
7,000	.15
8,000	.20
9,000	.30
10,000	.20
11,000	.10

Pelnor has a capacity to store no more than 25,000 square feet of steel at any time. Because of the contract, orders *must* be placed each week regardless of the on-hand supply.

(a) Simulate stainless steel order arrivals and use for 20 weeks. (Begin the first week with a starting inventory of 0 stainless steel.) If an end-of-week inventory is ever negative, assume that back orders are permitted and fill the demand from the next arriving order.

(b) Should Pelnor add more storage area? If so, how much? If not, comment on the system.

: 17-24 Milwaukee's General Hospital has an emergency room that is divided into six departments: (1) the initial exam station to treat minor problems or make diagnoses; (2) an X-ray department; (3) an operating room; (4) a cast-fitting room; (5) an observation room for recovery and general observation before final diagnoses or release; and (6) an out-processing department where clerks check patients out and arrange for payment or insurance forms.

The probabilities that a patient will go from one department to another are presented in the accompanying table.

FROM	TO	PROBABILITY
Initial exam at emergency room entrance	X-ray department	.45
	Operating room	.15
	Observation room	.10
	Out-processing clerk	.30
X-ray department	Operating room	.10
	Cast-fitting room	.25
	Observation room	.35
	Out-processing clerk	.30
Operating room	Cast-fitting room	.25
	Observation room	.70
	Out-processing clerk	.05
Cast-fitting room	Observation room	.55
	X-ray department	.05
	Out-processing clerk	.40
Observation room	Operating room	.15
	X-ray department	.15
	Out-processing clerk	.70

(a) Simulate the trail followed by 10 emergency room patients. Proceed one patient at a time from each one's entry at the initial exam station until he or she leaves through out-processing. You should be aware that a patient can enter the same department more than once.

(b) Using your simulation data, what are the chances that a patient enters the X-ray department twice?

17-25 Management of the First Syracuse Bank is concerned over a loss of customers at its main office downtown. One solution that has been proposed is to add one or more drive-through teller stations to make it easier for customers in cars to obtain quick service without parking. Chris Carlson, the bank president, thinks the bank should only risk the cost of installing one drive-through. He is informed by his staff that the cost (amortized over a 20-year period) of building a drive-through is $12,000 per year. It also costs $16,000 per year in wages and benefits to staff each new teller window.

The director of management analysis, Anita Greenberg, believes that the following two factors encourage the immediate construction of two drive-through stations, however. According to a recent article in *Banking Research* magazine, customers who wait in long lines for drive-through teller service will cost banks an average of $1 per minute in loss of goodwill. Also, adding a second drive-through will cost an additional $16,000 in staffing, but amortized construction costs can be cut to a total of $20,000 per year if two drive-throughs are installed together, instead of one at a time. To complete her analysis, Greenberg collected one month's arrival and service rates at a competing downtown bank's drive-through stations. These data are shown as Observation Analysis 1 and 2 on the following page.

(a) Simulate a one-hour time period, from 1 to 2 P.M., for a single-teller drive-through.

(b) Simulate a one-hour time period, from 1 to 2 P.M., for a two-teller system.

(c) Conduct a cost analysis of the two options. Assume the bank is open 7 hours per day and 200 days per year.

OBSERVATION ANALYSIS 1—INTERARRIVAL TIMES
FOR 1,000 OBSERVATIONS

TIME BETWEEN ARRIVALS (MINUTES)	NUMBER OF OCCURRENCES
1	200
2	250
3	300
4	150
5	100

OBSERVATION ANALYSIS 2—CUSTOMER
SERVICE TIME FOR 1,000 CUSTOMERS

SERVICE TIME (MINUTES)	NUMBER OF OCCURRENCES
1	100
2	150
3	350
4	150
5	150
6	100

: **17-26** The Alfredo Fragrance Company produces only one product, a perfume called Hint of Elegance. Hint of Elegance consists of two secret ingredients blended into an exclusive fragrance which is marketed in Zurich. An economic expression referred to as the Cobb-Douglas function describes the production of Hint of Elegance, as follows:

$$X = \sqrt{(\text{Ingredient 1})(\text{Ingredient 2})}$$

where X is the amount of perfume produced.

The company operates at a level where ingredient 1 is set daily at 25 units and ingredient 2 at 36 units. Although the price Alfredo pays for ingredient 1 is fixed at $50 per unit, the cost of ingredient 2 and the selling price for the final perfume are both probabilistic. The sales price for Hint of Elegance follows this distribution:

SALES PRICE ($)	PROBABILITY
300	.2
350	.5
400	.3

The cost for ingredient 2 is:

INGREDIENT 2 COST ($)	PROBABILITY
35	.1
40	.6
45	.3

(a) What is the profit equation for Alfredo Fragrance Company?
(b) What is the expected profit to the firm?
(c) Simulate the firm's profit for a period of nine days, using these random numbers from Table 17.5: 52, 06, 50, 88, 53, 30, 10, 47, 99, 37, 66, 91, 35, 32, 00, 84, 57, 07.
(d) What is the expected daily profit as simulated in part c?

: **17-27** Julia Walters owns and operates one of the largest Mercedes-Benz auto dealerships in Washington, D.C. In the past 36 months her sales of this luxury car have ranged from a low of 6 new cars to a high of 12 new cars, as reflected in the following table:

SALES OF NEW CARS PER MONTH	FREQUENCY
6	3
7	4
8	6
9	12
10	9
11	1
12	1
	36 months

Walters believes that sales will continue during the next 24 months at about the same historical rates and that delivery times will also continue to follow this pace (stated in probability form):

DELIVERY TIME (MONTHS)	PROBABILITY
1	.44
2	.33
3	.16
4	.07
	1.00

Walters's current policy is to order 14 cars at a time (two full truckloads, with 7 autos on each truck) and to place a new order whenever the stock on hand reaches 12 autos. What are the results of this policy when simulated over the next two years?

· **17-28** Referring to problem 17-27, Julia Walters establishes the following relevant costs: (1) the carrying cost per Mercedes per month is $600; (2) the cost of a lost sale averages $4,350; and (3) the cost of placing an order is $570. What is the total inventory cost of the policy simulated ($Q = 14$, ROP = 12) in problem 17-27?

: **17-29** Julia Walters (see problems 17-27 and 17-28) wishes to try a new simulated policy, ordering 21 cars per order, with a reorder point of 10 autos. Which policy is better, this one or the one formulated in problems 17-27 and 17-28?

Synergistic Systems Corporation

Norman Jenkins, manager of office equipment at Synergistic Systems Corporation, one of the top seven government contractors, was reasoning with George Wilson, manager of the contract typing pool. "George, I can't approve your request for a third copying machine just because you say you see typists waiting in line practically every time you're near your two machines. Back in 1986, I could have approved it without question, but this is 1990. You know that we aren't doing as well these days due to the government cutbacks in aerospace spending. The word has come down from upstairs that we have to cut expenses wherever possible.

"As a matter of fact, we have been running a survey on usage of the machines in the building, hoping to reduce costs by eliminating unnecessary machines. Let me show you our results for your machines, George. This first table shows that you average 16.17 pages per contract. This second table shows that the average time between users arriving at the machines is 16.48 minutes.

"Previous surveys have shown that it takes one minute to make the required 20 copies of each contract page. Therefore, the average user should be on a machine 16.17 minutes. Since secretaries arrive to use the machine an average of 16.48 minutes apart, but only use the machine an average of 16.17 minutes, one machine should be adequate for your copying needs. Each machine costs us $220 per month or $10 per working day. How can I approve your request for a third machine with these facts in front of me? In fact, I was thinking of taking away one of your machines."

Wilson puzzled over the tables a bit and then asked, "Why are all the times even numbers? Don't the users arrive three minutes apart, or five minutes apart?"

"Yes, but we found that it was convenient and accurate enough to record the information to the nearest two minutes. Anything up to one minute was recorded a 0, anything from one to three minutes was recorded as 2, etc. By the way, here's the form we used to record the results," he added, showing Wilson the form shown on the next page. "We just used two of the machine columns in your case since you only had two machines, and we recorded 20 all the time in the number of copies column. We fitted a smooth curve to what we recorded on both the pages and time between arrivals."

"Well, I don't really care how you recorded that data," said Wilson. "The important point is that secretaries are waiting in line and that's costing us money.

"You're familiar with our system of assigning each typist to only one contract at a time and having the typist make his or her own copies when finished with the typing. The worst drawback of our present system is that the time anyone spends waiting to use a machine is wasted time, and those who type with the speed and accuracy that we need don't work for peanuts. The 15 secretaries who work for me cost us about $10 an hour each, including variable overhead, and that's $80 per working day. That's why I worry when I see them waiting in line at the machine."

Jenkins asked, "Why don't you hire someone

PAGES PER CONTRACT

PAGES	PERCENTAGE OF CONTRACTS	PAGES	PERCENTAGE OF CONTRACTS	PAGES	PERCENTAGE OF CONTRACTS
6	1	13	6	20	7
7	1	14	8	21	5
8	2	15	9	22	3
9	2	16	11	23	2
10	2	17	12	24	1
11	3	18	11	25	1
12	4	19	9		

TIME BETWEEN ARRIVALS

TIME SINCE LAST ARRIVAL	PERCENTAGE OF ARRIVALS	TIME SINCE LAST ARRIVAL	PERCENTAGE OF ARRIVALS	TIME SINCE LAST ARRIVAL	PERCENTAGE OF ARRIVALS
0	17	20	3	40	2
2	8	22	3	42	1
4	7	24	3	44	1
6	6	26	2	46	1
8	6	28	2	48	1
10	5	30	2	50	1
12	5	32	2	52	1
14	4	34	2	54	1
16	4	36	2	56	1
18	3	38	2	58	1
				60	1

just to make copies? You ought to be able to get someone to do that for only $4 an hour. You would save the time your typists spend making copies, and eliminate all waiting time, and still get by with only one machine.''

"I fought that battle last year with Bob Johnson in Security. He agreed that we could save money by hiring someone just to run the copying machines, but he won't allow it. Most of the contracts are classified secret or top secret, and he's scared stiff of what the government security inspectors will say about any procedure where extra personnel handle the documents,'' Wilson replied. "Now the problem is worse. With the aerospace spending cuts, we've got a hiring freeze. We wouldn't be allowed to hire a copying operator, even if we thought it was desirable.''

"George, I understand your concerns, but I just

DATA SHEET

TIME OF ARRIVAL	NUMBER OF PAGES	NUMBER OF COPIES	MACHINE 1		MACHINE 2		MACHINE 3	
			TIME ON	TIME OFF	TIME ON	TIME OFF	TIME ON	TIME OFF

can't help you when the numbers show that I should take a machine away from you rather than give you another one. Take this copy of our survey with you. If you can show me that I'm wrong, you'll get your machine."

Wilson folded the copy of the survey, put it in his shirt pocket and walked out dejectedly.

1. Using the data as collected, determine if another machine can be economically justified by simulating one day for each machine configuration. Use the random numbers in Table 17.5, within this chapter.

2. What are the simulated costs for two machines and three machines?

CASE STUDY

Gardner Trucking Company operates a fleet of seven specially constructed semitrailers and cabs for commercial long distance hauling of radioactive waste materials. Each truck averages one completed load per week, picking up the radioactive containers from chemical companies and other manufacturers in the southeastern United States. The loads are carefully driven to a federally directed dump site in Nevada. Currently, pickups are made in eight states: Florida, South Carolina, North Carolina, Georgia, Alabama, Mississippi, Louisiana, and Tennessee.

Gardner maintains an office in the capital of each state that it serves. Staffing not only includes a manager and a secretary at each state office, but a part-time lobbyist/attorney to assist in the many political and legal issues that arise in the nuclear waste disposal industry.

Ella Gardner, owner of the firm, is seriously considering dropping the state of North Carolina as a source of business. Last year, only 25 truckloads of wastes were handled there. Since furniture and textile manufacturers in North Carolina are the primary source of trucking for Gardner, the size and revenues from their shipments will determine if it is profitable to retain an office and do business in that state.

To analyze whether it is financially attractive to continue serving the North Carolina market, Gardner gathers data on last year's shipments and revenues. Each of the 25 trucks that were loaded in North Carolina last year carried between 26 and 50 barrels of waste. The income generated per barrel differed significantly (ranging from $50 to $80)

based on the type of radioactive material being loaded and the weight of the barrels to be shipped. (See the accompanying table for details.)

Gardner decided that if she were to simulate 25 truckloads out of North Carolina she could determine if it would be profitable to continue to operate there next year. She estimates that each shipment to the Nevada dump site costs $900, including driver, gasoline, and truck expenses; other cargo loading and unloading costs average $120 per shipment. In addition, it costs $41,000 per year to operate the North Carolina office. This includes salaries and indirect overhead costs that are allocated from the home office in Atlanta.

GARDNER'S NORTH CAROLINA DATA

NUMBER OF 55-GALLON BARRELS OF WASTE LOADED	NUMBER OF TIMES TRUCK CARRIED THIS SIZE LOAD LAST YEAR	REVENUE PER BARREL ($)	NUMBER OF TRIPS AT THIS REVENUE
26–30	3	50	5
31–35	4	60	11
36–40	6	70	7
41–45	9	80	2
46–50	3		
	25		25

Will the shipments in North Carolina next year generate enough revenues to cover Gardner's costs there?

BIBLIOGRAPHY

Dileepan, Parthasarati, and Johnson, Louis M., Jr. "Planning Academic Microcomputer Laboratory Resources: A Simulation Approach." *Journal of Education for Business* February 1988, pp. 210–214.

Easa, Said M. "Assessing Future Management Strategies in the Port of Thunder Bay." *Transportation Research* Vol. 20A, No. 3, 1986, pp. 185–195.

Eyrl, A. D. "Modelling the Emergency Service in North Eastern Gas." *Journal of the Operational Research Society* Vol. 37, No. 8, 1986, pp. 769–778.

Ginter, P. M., and Ricks, A. C. "Strategic Models and Simulations: An Emerging Decision-Making Aid." *Journal of Systems Management* Vol. 35, June 1984, pp. 12–16.

Gordon, G. *System Simulation*. Englewood Cliffs, N.J.: Prentice-Hall, 1969.

Hamzawi, Salah G. "Management and Planning of Airport Gate Capacity: A Microcomputer-Based Gate Assignment Simulation Model." *Transportation Planning and Technology* Vol. 11, 1986, pp. 189–202.

Hannan, Edward L., and Gimbrone, Christopher J. "Predicting the Impact of Instituting a Priority Readmission Policy in Nursing Homes." *Computers and Operations Research* Vol. 14, No. 6, 1987, pp. 493–505.

Harris, Carl M., Hoffman, Karla L., and Saunders, Patsy B. "Modeling the IRS Telephone Taxpayer Information System." *Operations Research* Vol. 35, No. 4, July–August 1987, pp. 504–522.

Kaplan, A., and Frazza, S. "Empirical Inventory Simulation: A Case Study." *Decision Sciences* Vol. 14, January 1983, pp. 62–75.

Keating, Barry. "Simulations: Put the Real World in Your Computer." *Creative Computing* Vol. 11, November 1985, pp. 56–62.

Lambo, E. "The Use of Simulation Models to Improve Health Institutions in Nigeria." *Interfaces* Vol. 13, June 1983, p. 29.

Lev, Benjamin, and Kwatny, Eugene. "Simulation of a Regional Scheduling Problem." *Interfaces* Vol. 18, No. 2, March–April 1988, pp. 28–37.

Main, Linda. "Computer Simulation and Library Management." *Journal of Information Science* Vol. 13, 1987, pp. 285–296.

Parkan, Celik. "Simulation of a Fast-Food Operation Where Dissatisfied Customers Renege." *Journal of Operational Research Society* Vol. 38, No. 2, 1987, pp. 137–148.

Riccio, Lucius J. and Litke, Ann. "Making a Clean Sweep: Simulating the Effects of Illegally Parked Cars on New York City's Mechanical Street-Cleaning Efforts." *Operations Research* Vol. 34, No. 5, September–October 1986, pp. 661–666.

Romanin-Jacur, Giorgio, and Faccin, Paola. "Optimal Planning of a Pediatric Semi-Intensive Care Unit via Simulation." *European Journal of Operational Research* Vol. 29, 1987, pp. 192–198.

Russell, Robert A., and Hickle, Regina. "Simulation of a CD Portfolio." *Interfaces* Vol. 16, No. 3, May–June 1986, pp. 49–54.

Solomon, S. L. *Simulation of Waiting Lines*. Englewood Cliffs, N.J.: Prentice-Hall, 1983.

Stein, K. J. "Simulation Techniques Converging to Meet Military, Commercial Needs." *Aviation Week & Space Technology* March 18, 1985, p. 239.

Watson, H. J. *Computer Simulation in Business*. New York: John Wiley & Sons, 1981.

Welch, Norma, and Gussow, James. "Expansion of Canadian National Railway's Line Capacity." *Interfaces* Vol. 16, No. 1, January–February 1986, pp. 51–64.

Wright, M. B. "The Application of a Surgical Bed Simulation Model." *European Journal of Operational Research* Vol. 32, 1987, pp. 26–32.

18

Network Models

INTRODUCTION

Most realistic projects that organizations undertake are large and complex. A builder putting up an office building, for example, must complete thousands of activities costing millions of dollars. NASA must inspect countless components before it launches a rocket. Avondale Shipyards in New Orleans requires tens of thousands of steps in constructing an ocean-going tugboat. Almost every industry worries about how to manage similar large-scale, complicated projects effectively.

managing complex projects

It is a difficult problem, and the stakes are high. Millions of dollars in cost overruns have been wasted due to poor planning of projects. Unnecessary delays have occurred due to poor scheduling. How can such problems be solved?

Program Evaluation and Review Technique (PERT) and the *Critical Path Method* (CPM) are two popular quantitative analysis techniques that help managers plan, schedule, monitor, and control large and complex projects. They were developed because there was a critical need for a better way to manage (see the "History" box).

Framework of PERT and CPM

There are six steps common to both PERT and CPM. The procedure is as follows:

1. Define the project and *all* of its significant activities or tasks.

2. Develop the relationships among the activities. Decide which activities must precede and follow others.

3. Draw the network connecting all of the activities.

4. Assign time and/or cost estimates to each activity.

5. Compute the longest time path through the network; this is called the *critical path*.

6. Use the network to help plan, schedule, monitor, and control the project.

critical path

▶ KEY IDEA

Finding the critical path is a major part of controlling a project. The activities on the critical path represent tasks that will delay the entire project if they are delayed. Managers derive flexibility by identifying noncritical activities and replanning, rescheduling, and reallocating resources such as personnel and finances.

PERT versus CPM

Although PERT and CPM are similar in their basic approach, they do differ in the way activity times are estimated. For every PERT activity, three time estimates are combined to determine the expected activity completion time and its variance. Thus, PERT is a *probabilistic* technique: it allows us to find the probability the entire project will be completed by any given date. CPM, on the other hand, is called a *deterministic* approach. It uses

---

How PERT and CPM Started

Managers have been planning, scheduling, monitoring, and controlling large-scale projects for hundreds of years, but it has only been in the last 50 years that QA techniques have been applied to major projects. One of the earliest techniques was the *Gantt chart*. This type of chart shows the start and finish time of one or more activities as seen in the accompanying figure.

In 1958, the Special Projects Office of the U.S. Navy developed Program Evaluation and Review Technique (PERT) to plan and control the Polaris missile program. This project involved the coordination of thousands of contractors. Today PERT is still used to monitor numerous government contract schedules. At about the same time (1957), Critical Path Method (CPM) was developed by J. E. Kelly of Remington Rand and M. R. Walker of du Pont. Originally, CPM was used to assist in the building and maintenance of chemical plants at du Pont.

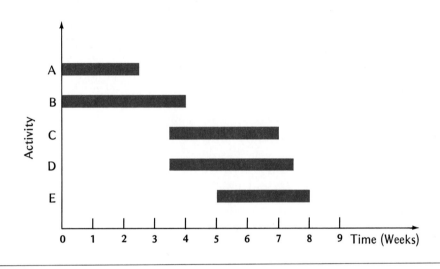

---

two time estimates, the *normal time* and the *crash time* for each activity. The normal completion time is the time we estimate it will take under normal conditions to complete the activity. The crash completion time is the shortest time it would take to finish an activity if additional funds and resources were allocated to the task.

In this chapter we investigate not only PERT and CPM, but also a technique called PERT/Cost that combines the benefits of both PERT and CPM.

Other Network Techniques

In addition to PERT and CPM, several other network techniques will be covered in this chapter. The *minimal-spanning tree technique* determines the path through the network that connects all the points while minimizing total distance. When the points represent houses in a subdivision, the minimal-spanning tree technique can be used to determine the best way to connect all of the houses to electrical power, water systems, and so on, in a way that minimizes the total distance or length of power lines or water pipes. The *maximal-flow technique* finds the maximum flow of any quantity or substance through a network. This technique can determine, for example, the maximum number of vehicles (cars, trucks, and so forth), that can go through a network of roads from one location to another. Finally, the *shortest-route technique* can find the shortest path through a network. For example, this technique can find the shortest route from one city to another through a network of roads.

All of the examples used to describe the various network techniques in this chapter are small and simple compared to real problems. This is done to make it easier for you to understand the techniques. In many cases, these smaller network problems can be solved by inspection or intuition. For larger problems, however, finding a solution can be very difficult and it becomes necessary to use these powerful network techniques. Larger problems may require hundreds, or even thousands, of iterations. In order to computerize these techniques, the systematic approach we present is needed.

18.2
PERT

Almost any large project can be subdivided into a series of smaller activities or tasks that can be analyzed with PERT. When you recognize that projects can have thousands of specific activities, you see why it is important to be able to answer such questions as:

1. When will the entire project be completed?

2. What are the *critical* activities or tasks in the project, that is, the ones that will delay the entire project if they are late?

3. Which are the *noncritical* activities, that is, the ones that can run late without delaying the whole project's completion?

4. What is the probability that the project will be completed by a specific date?

5. At any particular date, is the project on schedule, behind schedule, or ahead of schedule?

6. On any given date, is the money spent equal to, less than, or greater than the budgeted amount?

7. Are there enough resources available to finish the project on time?

8. If the project is to be finished in a shorter amount of time, what is the best way to accomplish this at the least cost?

PERT (or PERT/Cost) can help answer each of these questions.

General Foundry Example of PERT

General Foundry, Inc., a metalworks plant in Milwaukee, has long been trying to avoid the expense of installing air pollution control equipment. The local environmental protection group has recently given the foundry

16 weeks to install a complex air filter system on its main smokestack. General Foundry was warned that it will be forced to close unless the device is installed in the allotted period. Lester Harky, the managing partner, wants to make sure the installation of the filtering system progresses smoothly and on time.

When the project begins, the building of the internal components for the device (activity A) and the modifications that are necessary for the floor and roof (activity B) can be started. The construction of the collection stack (activity C) can begin once the internal components are completed, and the pouring of the new concrete floor and installation of the frame (activity D) can be completed as soon as the roof and floor have been modified. Once the collection stack has been constructed, the high-temperature burner can be built (activity E), and the installation of the pollution control system (activity F) can begin. The air pollution device can be installed (activity G) after the high-temperature burner has been built, the concrete floor has been poured, and the frame has been installed. Finally, after the control system and pollution device have been installed, the system can be inspected and tested (activity H).

All of these activities seem rather confusing and complex until they are placed in a network. First, all of the activities must be listed. This information is shown in Table 18.1.

We see in the table that before the collection stack can be constructed (activity C), the internal components must be built (activity A). Thus, activity A is the immediate predecessor to activity C. Likewise, both activities D and E must be performed just prior to installation of the air pollution device (activity G).

project activities

predecessors

Drawing the PERT Network

Once the activities have all been specified (step 1 of the PERT procedure) and management has decided which activities must precede and follow others (step 2), the network can be drawn (step 3).

An *activity* carries the arrow symbol, →. This represents a task or subproject that uses time or resources. The only other piece needed to create a network is called an *event*. An event marks the start or completion of a

activities and events

TABLE 18.1 Activities and Immediate Predecessors for General Foundry, Inc.

ACTIVITY	DESCRIPTION	IMMEDIATE PREDECESSORS
A	Build internal components	
B	Modify roof and floor	
C	Construct collection stack	A
D	Pour concrete and install frame	B
E	Build high-temperature burner	C
F	Install control system	C
G	Install air pollution device	D,E
H	Inspection and testing	F,G

particular activity. It is denoted by the symbol ◯, which contains a number that helps identify its location. For example, activity A can be drawn as follows:

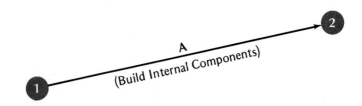

It begins with event 1 and ends with event 2. Activity C's only *immediate predecessor* is activity A, so it can be drawn like this:

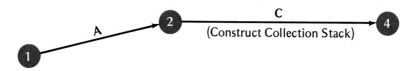

The number inside the event is used to identify the beginning or ending of an activity more easily.

Now we are ready to draw the whole *network* for General Foundry. This is shown in Figure 18.1.

You should note that drawing a PERT network takes some time and experience. You start with the beginning node, node 1. You then draw the activities from this node that do not have any immediate predecessor activities (in this case, A and B). Successive nodes and activities are drawn, making sure that the appropriate relationships between activities and nodes are maintained. You must take care that all immediate predecessor activities

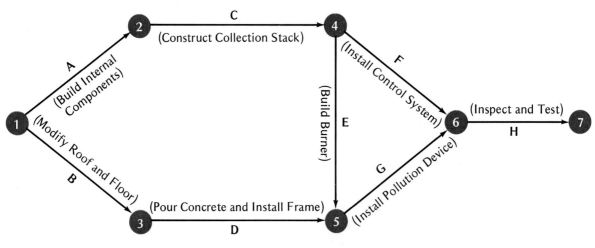

FIGURE 18.1
Network for General Foundry, Inc.

are appropriately reflected in the network. When you first draw the network, it is usually impossible to draw all the activities as straight lines. It is good to first get a rough draft version of the network, making sure that all of the appropriate relationships are intact. Then, you can redraw the network to make all of the activity lines straight.

Activity Times

The next step in the PERT procedure is to assign estimates of the time required to complete each activity. Time is usually given in units of weeks.

For one-of-a-kind projects or for new jobs, providing *activity time estimates* is not always an easy task. Without solid historical data, managers are often uncertain as to activity times. For this reason, the developers of PERT employed a probability distribution based on three time estimates for each activity.

The three estimates are:

Optimistic time (a) = Time an activity will take if everything goes as well as possible. There should be only a small probability (say, $\frac{1}{100}$) of this occurring.

Most likely time (m) = Most realistic time estimate to complete the activity.

Pessimistic time (b) = Time an activity would take assuming very unfavorable conditions. There should also be only a small probability the activity will really take this long.

PERT often assumes time estimates follow the *beta probability distribution* (see Figure 18.2). This continuous distribution has been found to be appropriate, in many cases, for determining an expected value and variance for activity completion times.

beta probability distribution

To find the expected time (*t*) for an activity, the beta distribution weights the estimates as follows:

KEY IDEA

$$t = \frac{a + 4m + b}{6} \tag{18-1}$$

To compute the dispersion or variance of this expected time estimate, we use the formula[1]:

$$\text{Variance} = \left(\frac{b - a}{6}\right)^2 \tag{18-2}$$

Table 18.2 shows General Foundry's optimistic, most likely, and pessimistic time estimates for each activity. It also reveals the expected time (*t*) and variance for each of the activities, as computed with Equations 18-1 and 18-2.

---

[1] This formula (18-2) is based on the statistical concept that from one end of the beta distribution to the other is 6 standard deviations ($\pm$ 3 standard deviations from the mean). Since $b - a$ is 6 standard deviations, one standard deviation is $(b - a)/6$. Thus, the variance is $[(b - a)/6]^2$.

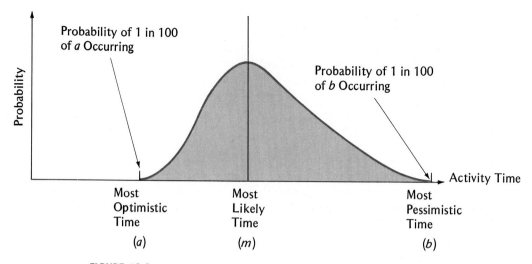

FIGURE 18.2
Beta Probability Distribution with Three Time Estimates

TABLE 18.2 Time Estimates (in weeks) for General Foundry, Inc.

ACTIVITY	OPTIMISTIC a	MOST PROBABLE m	PESSIMISTIC b	EXPECTED TIME $t = [(a + 4m + b)/6]$	VARIANCE $[(b-a)/6]^2$
A	1	2	3	2	$\left(\dfrac{3-1}{6}\right)^2 = \dfrac{4}{36}$
B	2	3	4	3	$\left(\dfrac{4-2}{6}\right)^2 = \dfrac{4}{36}$
C	1	2	3	2	$\left(\dfrac{3-1}{6}\right)^2 = \dfrac{4}{36}$
D	2	4	6	4	$\left(\dfrac{6-2}{6}\right)^2 = \dfrac{16}{36}$
E	1	4	7	4	$\left(\dfrac{7-1}{6}\right)^2 = \dfrac{36}{36}$
F	1	2	9	3	$\left(\dfrac{9-1}{6}\right)^2 = \dfrac{64}{36}$
G	3	4	11	5	$\left(\dfrac{11-3}{6}\right)^2 = \dfrac{64}{36}$
H	1	2	3	2	$\left(\dfrac{3-1}{6}\right)^2 = \dfrac{4}{36}$
				Total 25	

Every Moment Counts in Airline Scheduling at Eastern

When people think of airline scheduling, the first thing that comes to mind is how quickly a particular plane can safely reach its destination. But using ground time efficiently is just as important to an airline's timetable as the time spent in flight. Bill Rodenhizer is the manager of control operations for Eastern Airlines in Boston. He is considered to be an expert on airplane turnaround time, the process by which an airplane is prepared for almost immediate take-off once it has landed. He tells us how this well-orchestrated effort works:

Scheduling, to the airline, is just about the whole ballgame. Everything is scheduled right to the minute. The whole fleet operates on a strict schedule. Each of the departments responsible for turning around an aircraft has an allotted period of time in which to perform its function. Manpower is geared to the amount of ground time scheduled for that aircraft. This would be adjusted during off-weather or bad-weather days or during heavy air-traffic delays.

Most of our aircraft in Boston are scheduled for a 42- to 65-minute ground time. Boston is the end of the line, so it is a "terminating and originating station." In plain talk, that means almost every aircraft that comes in must be fully unloaded, refueled, serviced, and dispatched within roughly an hour's time.

Source: Introduction to Contemporary Mathematics, New York: W. H. Freeman and Co., 1988, p. 38.

This is how the process works: In the larger aircraft, it takes passengers roughly 20 minutes to load and 20 minutes to unload. During this period, we will have completely cleaned the aircraft and unloaded the cargo, and the caterers will have taken care of the food. The ramp service may take 20 to 30 minutes to unload the baggage, mail, and cargo from underneath the plane, and it will take the same amount of time to load it up again. We double-crew those aircraft with heavier weights so that the work load will fit the time it takes passengers to load and unload upstairs.

While this has been going on, the fueler has fueled the aircraft. As to repairs, most major maintenance is done during the midnight shift, when all but 20 of Eastern's several hundred aircraft are inactive.

We all work under a very strict time frame. There are four functional departments. If any of the four cannot fit its work into its time frame, then it advises us at the control center, and we adjust the departure time or whatever, so that the other departments can coordinate their activities accordingly.

Eastern, and other airlines, use PERT and quantitative analysis not only in dealing with this problem of allocating scarce resources, but in a whole variety of other areas, ranging from crew scheduling, to purchasing jet fuel, to refurbishing old airplanes.

How to Find the Critical Path

Once the expected completion time for each activity has been determined, we accept it as the actual time of that task. Variability in times will be considered later.

Although Table 18.2 indicates that the total expected time for all eight of General Foundry's activities is 25 weeks, it is obvious in Figure 18.3 that several of the tasks can be taking place simultaneously. To find out just how long the project will take, we perform the critical path analysis for the network.

The *critical path* is the longest time path route through the network. If Lester Harky wants to reduce the total project time for General Foundry, he will have to reduce the length of some activity on the critical path.

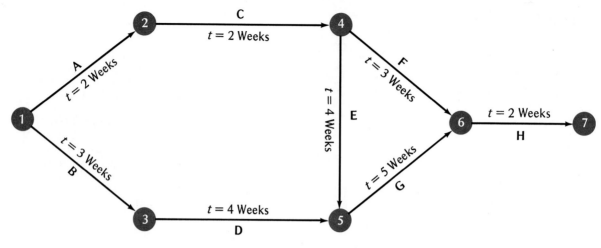

FIGURE 18.3
General Foundry's Network with Expected Activity Times

Conversely, any delay of an activity on the critical path will delay completion of the entire project.

To find the critical path we need to determine the following quantities for each activity in the network.

1. *Earliest start time* (ES). This is the earliest time an activity can begin without violation of immediate predecessor requirements.

2. *Earliest finish time* (EF). This is the earliest time at which an activity can end.

3. *Latest start time* (LS). This is the latest time an activity can begin without delaying the entire project.

4. *Latest finish time* (LF). This is the latest time an activity can end without delaying the entire project.

computing earliest start and finish

We begin at the network's origin, event 1, to compute the earliest start time (ES) and earliest finish time (EF) for each activity. For the first event, the starting time is always set equal to 0. Since activity A has an expected time of 2 weeks, its earliest finish time is 2, as seen here.

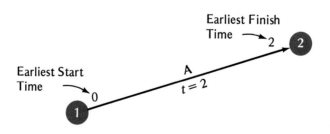

The earliest finish time can be computed by:

$$\text{Earliest finish time} = \text{Earliest start time} + \text{Expected activity time}$$
$$EF = ES + t \qquad \text{(18-3)}$$

Earliest Start Time Rule. There is one basic rule to follow as you find ES and EF for all activities in the network. Before any activity can be started, *all* of its predecessor activities must be completed. In other words, we search for the *longest* path to an activity in determining ES. For example, we see that ES for activity C is 2 weeks. Its only predecessor activity is A which has an EF of 2 weeks.

all predecessor activities must be completed

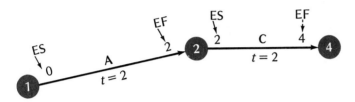

Earliest start time for activity G, however, is 8 weeks. It has 2 predecessor activities, D and E. Since activity D has an EF of 7 weeks and activity E's EF is 8 weeks, the earliest time that activity G can begin is at the 8-week mark.

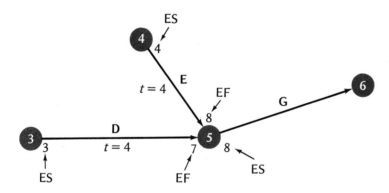

To complete the ES and EF times for all activities, we make what is called a *forward pass* through the network. Figure 18.4 illustrates the results. At each step, we see that EF = ES + t. Note that the earliest the *entire project can be finished is 15 weeks.* This is because activity H cannot be started until 13 weeks (ES = 13) and its expected time is 2 weeks; hence, EF = 13 + 2 = 15 weeks. So the best Lester Harky can expect to do is have the air pollution control device installed and tested in 15 weeks.

forward pass through the network

Latest Finish Time Rule. The next step in finding the critical path is to compute the latest start time (LS) and latest finish time (LF) for each activity. We do this by making a *backward pass* through the network, that is, starting at the last activity and working backward to the first activities. This means assigning a latest finish time of 15 weeks to activity H.

backward pass through the network

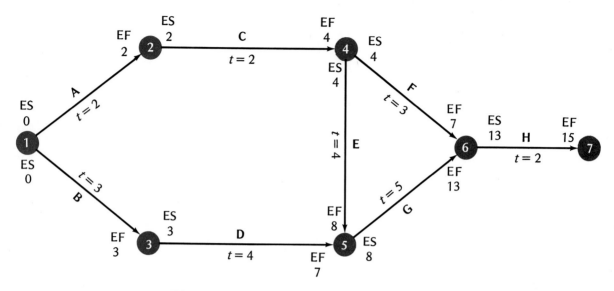

FIGURE 18.4
General Foundry's Earliest Start (ES) and Earliest Finish (EF) Times

Recall that latest finish time is the latest an activity can end without delaying the project. To compute the latest *start* time, we apply the following formula:

computing latest start time

$$\text{Latest start time} = \text{Latest finish time} - \text{Expected activity time}$$
$$LS = LF - t \tag{18-4}$$

For example, with LF = 15 for activity H, the latest start time for the activity is:

$$LS = 15 - 2 = 13 \text{ weeks}$$

In general, the rule we apply is that the latest finish time for an activity equals the *smallest* latest starting time for all activities leaving that same event. Thus, LF for activity C is 4 weeks, which is the smaller of the LS times for the two activities leaving event 4 (see accompanying figure).

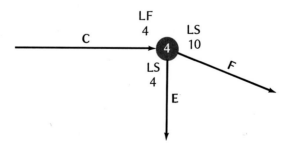

LS and LF times for all activities in the General Foundry case are shown in Figure 18.5.

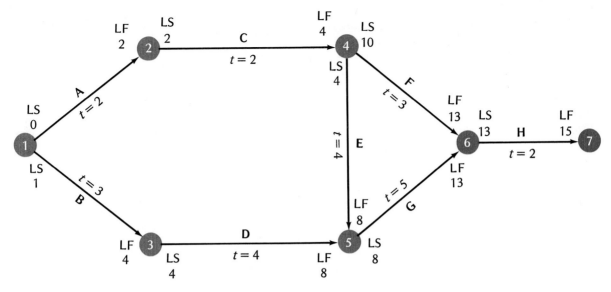

FIGURE 18.5
General Foundry's Latest Start (LS) and Latest Finish
(LF) Times

Concept of Slack in Critical Path Computations. Once ES, LS, EF, and LF have been determined, it is a simple matter to find the amount of *slack time*, or free time, each activity has. Slack is the length of time an activity can be delayed without delaying the whole project. Mathematically,

slack time

KEY IDEA

$$\text{Slack} = \text{LS} - \text{ES} \quad \text{or} \quad \text{Slack} = \text{LF} - \text{EF} \qquad \textbf{(18-5)}$$

Table 18.3 summarizes the ES, EF, LS, LF, and slack times for all of General Foundry's activities. Activity B, for example, has 1 week of slack time since $\text{LS} - \text{ES} = 1 - 0 = 1$ (or likewise, $\text{LF} - \text{EF} = 4 - 3 = 1$). This means it can be delayed up to 1 week without causing the project to run any longer than expected.

On the other hand, activities A, C, E, G, and H have *no* slack time: this means that none of them can be delayed without delaying the entire project.

TABLE 18.3 General Foundry's Schedule and Slack Times

ACTIVITY	EARLIEST START (ES)	EARLIEST FINISH (EF)	LATEST START (LS)	LATEST FINISH (LF)	SLACK (LS − ES)	ON CRITICAL PATH?
A	0	2	0	2	0	Yes
B	0	3	1	4	1	No
C	2	4	2	4	0	Yes
D	3	7	4	8	1	No
E	4	8	4	8	0	Yes
F	4	7	10	13	6	No
G	8	13	8	13	0	Yes
H	13	15	13	15	0	Yes

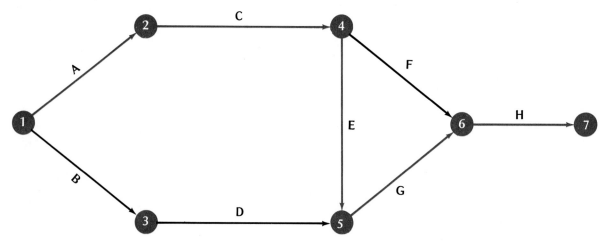

FIGURE 18.6
General Foundry's Critical Path (A–C–E–G–H)

Because of this, they are called *critical* activities and are said to be on the *critical path*. Lester Harky's critical path is shown in network form in Figure 18.6. The total project completion time, 15 weeks, is seen as the largest number in the EF or LF columns of Table 18.3. Industrial managers call this a boundry time table.

Probability of Project Completion

The *critical path analysis* helped us determine that the foundry's expected project completion time is 15 weeks. Harky knows, however, that if the project is not completed in 16 weeks, General Foundry will be forced to close by environmental controllers. He is also aware that there is significant variation in the time estimates for several activities. Variation in activities that are on the critical path can impact on overall project completion—possibly delaying it. This is one occurrence that worries Harky considerably.

PERT uses the variance of critical path activities to help determine the variance of the overall project. Project variance is computed by summing variances of critical activities:

$$\text{Project variance} = \Sigma \text{ Variances of activities on critical path} \quad (18\text{-}6)$$

From Table 18.2, we know that:

CRITICAL ACTIVITY	VARIANCE
A	$4/36$
C	$4/36$
E	$36/36$
G	$64/36$
H	$4/36$

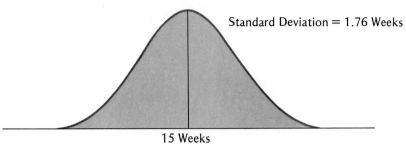

FIGURE 18.7
Probability Distribution for Project Completion Times

Hence the project variance is:

$$\text{Project variance} = \tfrac{4}{36} + \tfrac{4}{36} + \tfrac{36}{36} + \tfrac{64}{36} + \tfrac{4}{36} = \tfrac{112}{36} = 3.111$$

We know that the standard deviation is just the square root of the variance, so:

$$\text{Project standard deviation} = \sigma_T = \sqrt{\text{Project variance}}$$
$$= \sqrt{3.11} = 1.76 \text{ weeks}$$

How can this information be used to help answer questions regarding the probability of finishing the project on time? PERT makes two more assumptions: (1) total project completion times follow a normal probability distribution; and (2) activity times are statistically independent. With these assumptions, the bell-shaped curve shown in Figure 18.7 can be used to represent project completion dates. It also means that there is a 50% chance that the entire project will be completed in less than the expected 15 weeks and a 50% chance that it will exceed 15 weeks.[2]

In order for Harky to find the probability that his project will be finished on or before the 16-week deadline, he needs to determine the appropriate area under the normal curve. The standard normal equation can be applied as follows:

PERT assumptions

$$Z = \frac{\text{Due date} - \text{Expected date of completion}}{\sigma_T} \qquad (18\text{-}7)$$

using the normal distribution

$$Z = \frac{16 \text{ weeks} - 15 \text{ weeks}}{1.76 \text{ weeks}} = .57$$

where

Z = number of standard deviations the due date or target date lies from the mean or expected date.

[2] You should be aware that noncritical activities also have variability (as seen in Table 18.2). This means it is possible for a noncritical path to have a higher probability of completion in a shorter time than the probability of completion along the critical path. In fact, a different critical path can evolve because of the probabilistic situation.

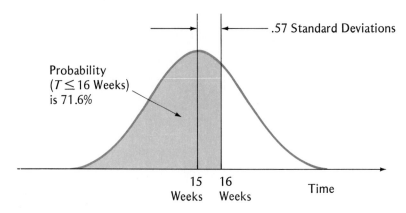

FIGURE 18.8
**Probability of General Foundry's Meeting the
16-Week Deadline**

Referring to the normal table in Appendix A, we find a probability of .71567. Thus, there is a 71.6% chance that the pollution control equipment can be put in place in 16 weeks or less. This is shown in Figure 18.8.

What PERT Was Able to Provide

PERT has thus far been able to provide Lester Harky with several valuable pieces of management information.

information provided by PERT

1. The project's expected completion date is 15 weeks.

2. There is a 71.6% chance that the equipment will be in place within the 16-week deadline. And PERT can easily find the probability of finishing by date Harky is interested in.

3. Five activities (A, C, E, G, H) are on the critical path. If any one of them is delayed for any reason, the whole project will be delayed.

4. Three activities (B, D, F) are not critical, but have some slack time built in. This means Harky can borrow from their resources, if needed, possibly to speed up the whole project.

5. A detailed schedule of activity starting and ending dates has been made available (Table 18.3).

Dummy Activities in PERT

role of dummy activities

Before leaving the basics of PERT, we should point out that it is sometimes necessary to use dummy activities to draw a network. A *dummy activity* is an imaginary activity that consumes no time: it is inserted for the sole purpose of preserving the precedence logic of the network.

This can be illustrated by assuming that General Foundry has one more restriction in installing its air pollution control equipment. Recall that activity D (pour concrete/install frame) had only one activity preceding it (B)

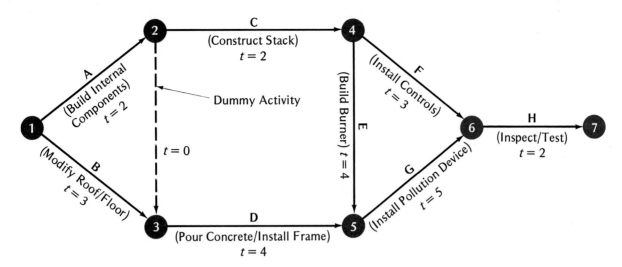

FIGURE 18.9
Illustration of a Dummy Activity in General Foundry's PERT Network.

in the original network. What would happen if activity A also had to be completed before D could begin? A beginning student might try to draw an arrow for activity A from node 1 to node 3 where activity D starts. This would result in two arrows (or two activities) being drawn from node 1 to node 3. This would make drawing the rest of the network extremely difficult, and it would make solving the network a nightmare. Another mistake that some beginning students make is to do nothing and leave the network the way it is. The solution will most likely be wrong. If activity A took 6 weeks instead of 2 weeks, what would happen if you did not change the network? The solution to the network, shown in Table 18.3, reveals that activity D can be started after week 3 (ES = 3 for activity D). But because activity A takes 6 weeks and it must be completed before activity D can be started, the entire solution is incorrect. One of the best solutions to these problems is to use a dummy activity. A dummy activity will allow you to draw and solve the network correctly. Here is how it is done.

In this case a dummy activity, shown in Figure 18.9 as a dashed line, must be inserted between events 2 and 3 to make the diagram reflect the actual situation. Although the dummy activity has a time of 0 weeks, it is possible for it to impact on the critical path analysis. Check for yourself to see if this occurs in the example. Is the path A-C-E-G-H still critical, or has it changed because of the dummy activity in Figure 18.9?

adding a dummy activity to the network

18.3
PERT/Cost

Although PERT is an excellent method of monitoring and controlling project length, it does not consider another very important factor, project *cost*. *PERT/Cost* is a modification of PERT that allows a manager to plan, schedule, monitor, and control cost as well as time.

using PERT/Cost to plan, schedule, monitor, and control project cost

---

Using PERT at British Airways

Developing a new image can be a huge undertaking for a medium- or large-sized company. This was certainly the case for British Airways when it decided to enhance its image and to transform the components that go into how the public views the corporation. For any airline company, developing a new image could include remodeling and reconfiguring aircraft, modifying tickets, changing the layout of lounges and shops, redoing ground vehicles, and producing a vast array of printed material with a new logo. Printed timetables, airline tickets, company stationery, and baggage claim tickets could be revamped. Even the uniforms worn by pilots and other employees of the airline could be redone.

In order to help with the process, British Airways used one of its internal consulting branches. The Market Place Performance Department do-

nated Joe Garratt, a senior internal management consultant, to assist.

Garratt had previous experience with critical path analysis and decided to use it in planning the new image. With a group of staff members and a network analysis program, Garratt planned aircraft turnarounds in a short time span and the introduction of new aircraft over a longer period of time. Garratt used PERT to analyze the potential of refurbishing different types of airlines for the new image as well as all the aspects that go into changing how the public views a major corporation. The PERTMASTER computer program found the critical path and performed basic critical path analysis. This program was instrumental in determining which aircraft should be used for the campaign as well as in establishing a workable schedule for determining when new uniforms could be issued.

Source: Excerpted from *Industrial Management and Data Systems,* March–April 1986, pp. 6–7.

We begin this section by investigating how costs can be planned and scheduled. Then we see how costs can be monitored and controlled.

Planning and Scheduling Project Costs: The Budgeting Process

The overall approach in the budgeting process of a project is to determine how much is to be spent every week or month. This is accomplished by following four steps:

budgeting process

1. Identify all costs associated with each of the activities. Then add these costs together to get one estimated cost or budget for each activity.

2. If you are dealing with a large project, several activities may be combined into larger work packages. A *work package* is simply a logical collection of activities. Since the General Foundry project we have been discussing is small, one activity will be a work package.

3. Convert the budgeted cost per activity into a cost per time period. To do this, we assume the cost of completing any activity is spent at a uniform rate over time. Thus, if the budgeted cost for a given activity is $48,000, and the activity's expected time is four weeks, the budgeted cost per week is $12,000 (= $48,000/4 weeks).

4. Using the earliest and latest start times, find out how much money should be spent during each week or month in order to finish the project at the desired date.

Let us apply this budgeting process to the General Foundry problem. Lester Harky has carefully computed the costs associated with each of his eight activities. He has also divided the total budget for each activity by the activity's expected completion time to determine the weekly budget for the activity. The budget for activity A, for example, is $22,000 (see Table 18.4). Since its expected time (t) is 2 weeks, $11,000 is spent each week to complete the activity. Table 18.4 also provides two pieces of data we found earlier using PERT, namely, the earliest start time (ES) and latest start time (LS) for each activity.

Looking at the total of the budgeted activity costs, we see that the entire project will cost $308,000. Finding the weekly budget will help Harky determine how the project is progressing on a week-to-week basis.

The weekly budget for the project is developed from the data in Table 18.4. The earliest start time for activity A, for example, is 0. Because A takes 2 weeks to complete, its weekly budget of $11,000 should be spent in weeks 1 and 2. For activity B, the earliest start time is 0, the expected completion time is 3 weeks, and the budgeted cost per week is $10,000. Thus, $10,000 should be spent for activity B in each of weeks 1, 2, and 3. Using the earliest start time, we can find the exact weeks during which the budget for each activity should be spent. These weekly amounts can be summed for all activities to arrive at the weekly budget for the entire project. This is shown in Table 18.5.

Do you see how the weekly budget for the project (total per week) is determined in Table 18.5? The only two activities that can be performed during the first week are activities A and B because their earliest start times are 0. Thus, during the first week, a total of $21,000 should be spent. Since activities A and B are still being performed in the second week, a total of $21,000 should also be spent during that period. The earliest start time for activity C is at the end of week 2 (ES = 2 for activity C). Thus, $13,000 is spent on activity C in both weeks 3 and 4. Because activity B is also being performed during week 3, the total budget in week 3 is $23,000. Similar

developing a weekly budget

computing a budget using ES

TABLE 18.4 Activity Cost for General Foundry, Inc.

ACTIVITY	EARLIEST START TIME (ES)	LATEST START TIME (LS)	EXPECTED TIME (t)	TOTAL BUDGETED COST ($)	BUDGETED COST PER WEEK ($)
A	0	0	2	22,000	11,000
B	0	1	3	30,000	10,000
C	2	2	2	26,000	13,000
D	3	4	4	48,000	12,000
E	4	4	4	56,000	14,000
F	4	10	3	30,000	10,000
G	8	8	5	80,000	16,000
H	13	13	2	16,000	8,000
			Total	308,000	

TABLE 18.5 Budgeted Cost for General Foundry, Inc., Using Earliest Start Times (Costs are in thousands of dollars.)

	WEEK															
ACTIVITY	1	2	3	4	5	6	7	8	9	10	11	12	13	14	15	TOTALS
A	11	11														22
B	10	10	10													30
C			13	13												26
D				12	12	12	12									48
E					14	14	14	14								56
F					10	10	10									30
G									16	16	16	16	16			80
H														8	8	16
																308
Total per week	21	21	23	25	36	36	36	14	16	16	16	16	16	8	8	
Total to date	21	42	65	90	126	162	198	212	228	244	260	276	292	300	308	

computations are done for all activities to determine the total budget for the entire project for each week. Then, these weekly totals can be added to determine the total amount that should be spent to date (total to date). This information is displayed in the bottom row of the table.

budget with latest start times

Those activities along the critical path must spend their budgets at the times shown in Table 18.5. The activities that are *not* on the critical path, however, can be started at a later date. This concept is embodied in the latest starting time, LS, for each activity. Thus, if *latest starting times* are used, another budget can be obtained. This budget will delay the expenditure of funds until the last possible moment. The procedures for computing the budget when LS is used are the same as when ES is used. The results of the new computations are shown in Table 18.6.

TABLE 18.6 Budgeted Cost for General Foundry, Inc., Using Latest Start Times (Costs are in thousands of dollars.)

ACTIVITY	1	2	3	4	5	6	7	8	9	10	11	12	13	14	15	TOTALS
A	11	11														22
B		10	10	10												30
C			13	13												26
D					12	12	12	12								48
E					14	14	14	14								56
F											10	10	10			30
G									16	16	16	16	16			80
H														8	8	16
																308
Total per week	11	21	23	23	26	26	26	26	16	16	26	26	26	8	8	
Total to date	11	32	55	78	104	130	156	182	198	214	240	266	292	300	308	

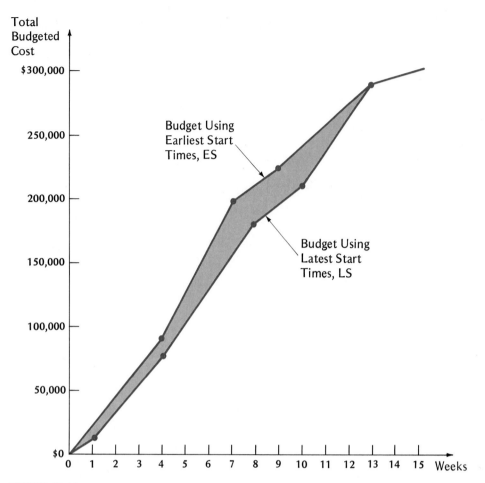

FIGURE 18.10
Budget Ranges for General Foundry

Compare the budgets given in Tables 18.5 and 18.6. The amount that should be spent to date (total to date) for the budget in Table 18.6 uses less financial resources in the first few weeks. This is due to the fact that this budget is prepared using the latest start times. Thus, the budget in Table 18.6 shows the *latest* possible time that funds can be expended and still finish the project on time. The budget in Table 18.5 reveals the *earliest* possible time that funds can be expended. Therefore, a manager can choose any budget that falls between the budgets presented in these two tables. These two tables form feasible budget ranges. This concept is illustrated in Figure 18.10.

The budget ranges for General Foundry were established by plotting the total-to-date budgets for ES and LS. Lester Harky can use any budget between these feasible ranges and still complete the air pollution project on time. Budgets like the ones shown in Figure 18.10 are normally developed before the project is started. Then, as the project is being completed, funds expended should be monitored and controlled.

Monitoring and Controlling Project Costs

**is the project on
schedule?**

The purpose of monitoring and controlling project costs is to ensure that the project is progressing on schedule and that cost overruns are kept to a minimum. The status of the entire project should be checked periodically.

Lester Harky wants to know how his air pollution project is going. It is now the sixth week of the 15-week project. Activities A, B, and C have been completely finished. These activities incurred costs of $20,000, $36,000, and $26,000, respectively. Activity D is only 10% completed and so far the cost expended has been $6,000. Activity E is 20% completed with an incurred cost of $20,000, and activity F is 20% completed with an incurred cost of $4,000. Activities G and H have not been started. Is the air pollution project on schedule? What is the value of work completed? Are there any cost overruns?

The value of work completed, or the cost to date for any activity, can be computed as follows:

value of work completed

$$\text{Value of work completed} = (\text{Percent of work completed}) \quad \textbf{(18-8)}$$
$$\times (\text{Total activity budget})$$

The activity difference is also of interest.

$$\text{Activity difference} = \text{Actual cost} - \text{Value of work completed} \quad \textbf{(18-9)}$$

If an activity difference is negative, there is a cost underrun, but if the number is positive, there has been a cost overrun.

Table 18.7 provides this information for General Foundry. The second column contains the total budgeted cost (from Table 18.5), while the third column contains the percent of completion. With these data and the actual cost expended for each activity, we can compute the value of work completed and the overruns or underruns for every activity.

TABLE 18.7 Monitoring and Controlling Budgeted Cost

ACTIVITY	TOTAL BUDGETED COST ($)	PERCENT OF COMPLETION	VALUE OF WORK COMPLETED ($)	ACTUAL COST ($)	ACTIVITY DIFFERENCE ($)
A	22,000	100	22,000	20,000	−2,000
B	30,000	100	30,000	36,000	6,000
C	26,000	100	26,000	26,000	0
D	48,000	10	4,800	6,000	1,200
E	56,000	20	11,200	20,000	8,800
F	30,000	20	6,000	4,000	−2,000
G	80,000	0	0	0	0
H	16,000	0	0	0	0
Totals			100,000	112,000	12,000 Overrun

**computing the value of
work completed**

One way to measure the value of the work completed is to multiply the total budgeted cost times the percent of completion for every activity.[3]

---

[3] The percent of completion for each activity can be measured in other ways as well. For example, one might examine the ratio of labor hours expended to total labor hours estimated.

Activity D, for example, has a value of work completed for $4,800 (= $48,000 times 10%). To determine the amount of overrun or underrun for any activity, the value of work completed is subtracted from the actual cost. These differences can be added to determine the overrun or underrun for the project. As you see, at week 6 there is a $12,000 cost overrun. Furthermore, the value of work completed is only $100,000, and the actual cost of the project to date is $112,000. How do these costs compare to the budgeted costs for week 6? If Harky had decided to use the budget for earliest start times (see Table 18.5) we can see that $162,000 should have been spent. Thus, the project is behind schedule and there are cost overruns. Harky needs to move faster on this project to finish on time, and he must carefully control future costs to try to eliminate the current cost overrun of $12,000. To monitor and control costs, the budgeted amount, the value of work completed, and the actual costs should be computed periodically.

In the next section, we see how a project can be shortened by spending additional money. The technique is called the *critical path method* (CPM).

18.4
CRITICAL PATH METHOD

As mentioned earlier, CPM is a *deterministic* network model. This means it assumes that both the time to complete each activity and the cost of doing so are known with certainty. Unlike PERT, it does not employ probability concepts. CPM instead uses two sets of time and cost estimates for activities: a normal time and cost and a crash time and cost. The *normal time* estimate is like PERT's expected time. The *normal cost* is an estimate of how much money it will take to complete an activity in its normal time. The *crash time* is the shortest possible activity time. *Crash cost* is the price of completing the activity on a crash or deadline basis. The critical path calculations for a CPM network follow the same steps as used in PERT: you just find the early start times (ES), late start times (LS), early finish (EF), late finish (LF), and slack as shown earlier.

CPM is deterministic

Project Crashing with CPM. Suppose General Foundry had been given 12 weeks instead of 16 weeks to install the new pollution control equipment or face a court-ordered shutdown. As you recall, the length of Lester Harky's critical path was 15 weeks. What can he do? We see that Harky cannot possibly meet the deadline unless he is able to shorten some of the activity times. This process of shortening a project is called *crashing* and is usually achieved by adding extra resources (such as equipment or people) to an activity. Naturally, crashing costs more money, and managers are usually interested in speeding up a project at the *least additional cost*.

Project crashing with CPM involves four steps:

1. Find the normal critical path and identify the critical activities.

2. Compute the crash cost per week (or other time period) for all activities in the network. This process uses the following formula[4]:

steps of project crashing

---

[4] This formula assumes that crash costs are linear. If they are not, the approach will not work.

$$\text{Crash cost/Time period} = \frac{\text{Crash cost} - \text{Normal cost}}{\text{Normal time} - \text{Crash time}} \quad \text{(18-10)}$$

3. Select the activity on the critical path with the smallest crash cost per week. Crash this activity to the maximum extent possible or to the point at which your desired deadline has been reached.

4. Check to be sure the critical path you were crashing is still critical. Often a reduction in activity time along the critical path causes a noncritical path or paths to become critical. If the critical path is still the longest path through the network, return to step 3. If not, find the new critical path and then return to step 3.

General Foundry's normal and crash times and normal and crash costs are shown in Table 18.8. Note, for example, that activity B's normal time is 3 weeks (this estimate was also used for PERT) and its crash time is 1 week. This means that the activity can be shortened by 2 weeks if extra resources are provided. The normal cost is $30,000, while the crash cost is $34,000. This implies that crashing activity B will cost General Foundry an additional $4,000. CPM assumes that crashing costs are linear. As seen in Figure 18.11, activity B's crash cost per week is $2,000. Crash costs for all other activities can be computed in a similar fashion. Then steps 3 and 4 may be applied to reduce the project's completion time.

Activities A, C, and E are on the critical path and have minimum crash cost per week—$1,000. Harky can crash A by 1 week and E by 2 weeks for an additional cost of $3,000.

For small networks, such as General Foundry's, it is possible to use the four-step procedure to find the least cost of reducing the project completion dates. For larger networks, however, this approach is difficult and impractical, and more sophisticated techniques, such as linear programming, must be employed.

Project Crashing with Linear Programming

Linear programming is another approach to finding the best project-crashing schedule. We illustrate its use on General Foundry's network. The data needed are derived from Table 18.8 and Figure 18.12 (on p. 744).

TABLE 18.8 Normal and Crash Data for General Foundry

ACTIVITY	TIME (WEEKS) NORMAL	CRASH	COST ($) NORMAL	CRASH	CRASH COST PER WEEK ($)	CRITICAL PATH?
A	2	1	22,000	23,000	1,000	Yes
B	3	1	30,000	34,000	2,000	No
C	2	1	26,000	27,000	1,000	Yes
D	4	3	48,000	49,000	1,000	No
E	4	2	56,000	58,000	1,000	Yes
F	3	2	30,000	30,500	500	No
G	5	2	80,000	86,000	2,000	Yes
H	2	1	16,000	19,000	3,000	Yes

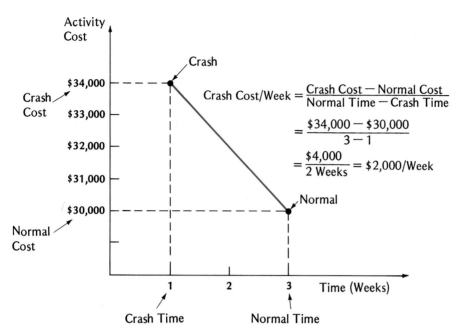

FIGURE 18.11
Crash and Normal Times and Costs for Activity B

We begin by defining the decision variables. If X is the time an event will occur, measured since the beginning of the project, then:

$$X_1 = \text{time event 1 will occur}$$ **decision variables for LP**
$$X_2 = \text{time event 2 will occur}$$
$$X_3 = \text{time event 3 will occur}$$
$$X_4 = \text{time event 4 will occur}$$
$$X_5 = \text{time event 5 will occur}$$
$$X_6 = \text{time event 6 will occur}$$
$$X_7 = \text{time event 7 will occur}$$

Y is defined as the number of weeks that each activity is crashed. Y_A is the number of weeks we decide to crash activity A, Y_B the amount of crash time used for activity B, and so on, up to Y_H.

Objective Function. Since the objective is to minimize the cost of crashing the total project, our LP objective function is:

$$\text{Minimize crash cost} = 1{,}000\,Y_A + 2{,}000\,Y_B + 1{,}000\,Y_C + 1{,}000\,Y_D$$ **objective function**
$$+ 1{,}000\,Y_E + 500\,Y_F + 2{,}000\,Y_G + 3{,}000\,Y_H$$

(These cost coefficients were drawn from the sixth column of Table 18.8.)

Crash Time Constraints. Constraints are required to ensure each activity is not crashed more than its maximum allowable crash time. The maximum

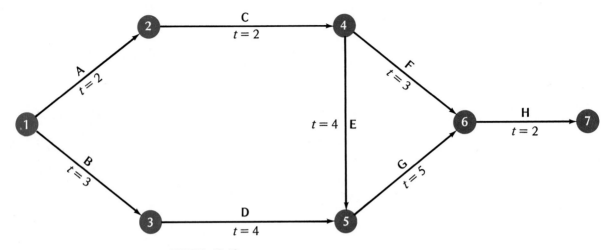

FIGURE 18.12
General Foundry's Network with Activity Times

for each Y variable is the difference between the normal time and the crash time (from Table 18.8):

crash constraints

$$Y_A \leq 1$$
$$Y_B \leq 2$$
$$Y_C \leq 1$$
$$Y_D \leq 1$$
$$Y_E \leq 2$$
$$Y_F \leq 1$$
$$Y_G \leq 3$$
$$Y_H \leq 1$$

Project Completion Constraint. This constraint specifies that the last event must take place before the project deadline date. If Harky's project must be crashed down to 12 weeks, then:

$$X_7 \leq 12$$

Constraints Describing the Network. The final set of constraints describes the structure of the network. There will be one or more constraints for each event. We begin by setting the event-occurrence time for event 1 to be $X_1 = 0$.
For event 2,

event constraints

X_2	$\geq$ Normal time for A	$-$	Y_A	$+$	0
Occurrence time for event 2	*2 weeks it takes for activity A*		*Number of weeks A is crashed*		*Start time for activity A* $(X_1 = 0)$

$$X_2 \geq 2 - Y_A$$

or

$$X_2 + Y_A \geqslant 2$$

For event 3,

$$X_3 \geqslant 3 - Y_B + 0$$

or

$$X_3 + Y_B \geqslant 3$$

For event 4, we note that activity C begins with event 2, X_2, not 0.

$$X_4 \geqslant 2 - Y_C + X_2$$

or

$$X_4 - X_2 + Y_C \geqslant 2$$

For event 5, we need two constraints. The first represents the path from activity D.

$$X_5 \geqslant 4 - Y_D + X_3$$

or

$$X_5 - X_3 + Y_D \geqslant 4$$

The second constraint is the path along activity E.

$$X_5 \geqslant 4 - Y_E + X_4$$

or

$$X_5 - X_4 + Y_E \geqslant 4$$

For event 6, again two constraints are needed.

$$X_6 \geqslant 3 - Y_F + X_4$$

or

$$X_6 - X_4 + Y_F \geqslant 3$$

The second constraint is:

$$X_6 \geqslant 5 - Y_G + X_5$$

or

$$X_6 - X_5 + Y_G \geqslant 5$$

For event 7,

$$X_7 \geqslant 2 - Y_H + X_6$$

or

$$X_7 - X_6 + Y_H \geqslant 2$$

After adding nonnegativity constraints, this linear programming problem can be solved for the optimal Y values. This can be done with AB:QM, LINDO, STORM, or with one of the many other LP computer programs available.

18.5
MINIMAL-SPANNING TREE TECHNIQUE

The *minimal-spanning tree technique* seeks to connect all the points of a network together while minimizing the distance between them. It has been applied, for example, by telephone companies to connect a number of phones together while minimizing the total length of telephone cable.

Let us consider the Lauderdale Construction Company, which is currently developing a luxurious housing project on Panama City Beach. Melvin Lauderdale, owner and president of Lauderdale Construction, must determine the least-expensive way to provide water and power to each house. The network of houses is shown in Figure 18.13.

As seen in Figure 18.13, there are eight houses on the gulf. The distance between each house in hundreds of feet is shown on the network. For example, the distance between houses 1 and 2 is 300 feet. (See the number 3 between nodes 1 and 2.) Now, the minimal-spanning tree technique will be used to determine the minimum distance that can be used to connect all of the nodes. The approach is outlined below:

steps for minimal spanning tree problem

1. Select any node in the network.

2. Connect this node to the nearest node that minimizes the total distance.

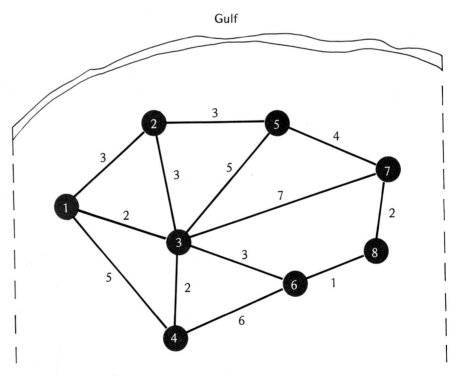

FIGURE 18.13
Network for Lauderdale Construction

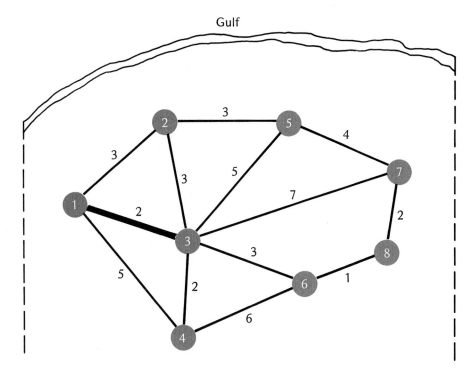

FIGURE 18.14
First Iteration for Lauderdale Construction

3. Considering all of the nodes that are now connected, find and connect the nearest node that is not connected.

4. Repeat the third step until all nodes are connected.

5. If there is a tie in the third step and two or more nodes that are not connected are equally near, arbitrarily select one and continue. A tie suggests that there might be more than one optimal solution.

Now, we solve the network in Figure 18.13 for Melvin Lauderdale. We start by arbitrarily selecting node 1. Since the nearest node is the third node at a distance of 2 (200 feet), we connect node 1 to node 3. This is shown in Figure 18.14.

Considering nodes 1 and 3, we look for the next nearest node. This is node 4, which is the closest to node 3. The distance is 2 (200 feet). Again, we connect these nodes. See Figure 18.15a.

We continue, looking for the nearest unconnected node to nodes 1, 3, and 4. This is node 2 or node 6, both at a distance of 3 from node 3. We will pick node 2. Thus, we connect these two nodes. See Figure 18.15b.

We continue the process. There is another tie for the next iteration with a minimum distance of 3 (node 2–node 5 and node 3–node 6). You should note that we do not consider node 1–node 2 with a distance of 3 because both nodes 1 and 2 are already connected. We arbitrarily select node 5 and connect it to node 2. See Figure 18.16a. The next nearest node is node 6, and we connect it to node 3. See Figure 18.16b.

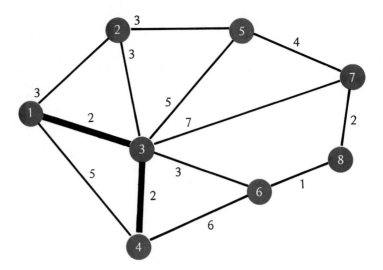

(a) Second Iteration

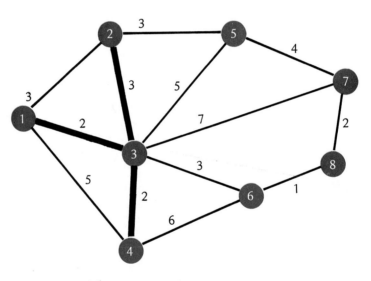

(b) Third Iteration

FIGURE 18.15
Second and Third Iterations

At this stage, we only have two nodes to go. Node 8 is the nearest to node 6 with a distance of 1 and we connect it. See Figure 18.17a (on p. 750). Then the remaining node 7 is connected to node 8. See Figure 18.17b (on p. 750).

The final solution can be seen from the seventh and final iteration. Nodes 1, 2, 4, and 6 are all connected to node 3. Node 2 is connected to node 5. Node 6 is connected to node 8, and node 8 is connected to node 7. All of the nodes are connected.

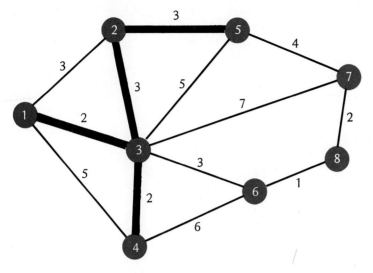

(a) Fourth Iteration

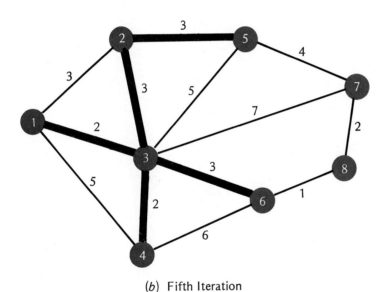

(b) Fifth Iteration

FIGURE 18.16
Fourth and Fifth Iterations

18.6
MAXIMAL-FLOW TECHNIQUE

The *maximal-flow technique* allows us to determine the maximum amount of a material that can flow through a network. It has been used, for example, to find the maximum number of automobiles that can flow through a state highway system.

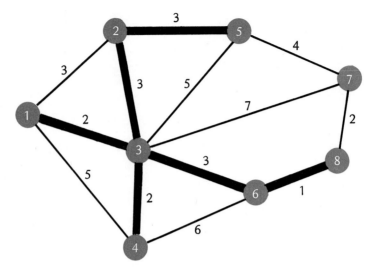

(a) Sixth Iteration

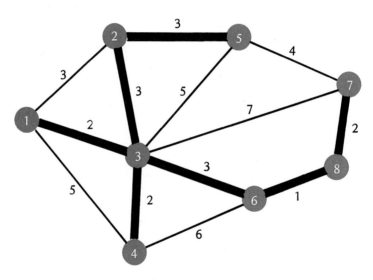

(b) Seventh Iteration

FIGURE 18.17
Sixth and Final Iterations

Waukesha, a small town in Wisconsin, is in the process of developing a road system for the downtown area. Bill Blackstone, one of the city planners, would like to determine the maximum number of cars that can flow through the town from west to east. The road network is shown in Figure 18.18.

The streets are indicated by their respective nodes. Look at street 1–2, the street between node 1 and node 2. The numbers by the nodes indicate

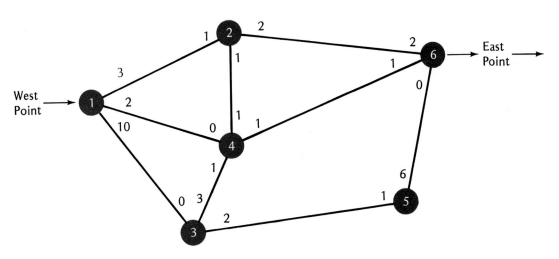

FIGURE 18.18
Road Network for Waukesha

the maximum number of cars (in hundreds of cars per hour) that can flow *from* the various nodes. The number 3 by node 1 indicates that 300 cars per hour can flow from node 1 to node 2. Look at the numbers 1, 1, and 2 by node 2. These numbers indicate the maximum flow *from* node 2 to nodes 1, 4, and 6, respectively. As you can see, the maximum flow from node 2 back to node 1 is 100 cars per hour (1). One hundred cars per hour (1) can flow from node 2 to node 4, and 200 cars (2) can flow to node 6. Note that traffic can flow in both directions down a street. A zero (0) means no flow or a one-way street.

The maximal-flow technique is not too difficult. It involves the following steps.

maximal-flow technique steps

1. Pick any path (streets from west to east) with some flow.

2. Increase the flow (number of cars) as much as possible.

3. Adjust the flow capacity numbers on the path (streets).

4. Repeat the above steps until an increase in flow is no longer possible.

We start by arbitrarily picking the path 1–2–6, which is at the top of the network. What is the maximum flow from west to east? It is 2 because only 2 units (200 cars) can flow from node 2 to node 6. Now we adjust the flow capacities. Refer to Figure 18.19. As you can see in the figure, we subtracted the maximum flow of 2 along the path 1–2–6 in the direction of the flow (west to east) and added 2 to the path in the direction against the flow (east to west). The result is the new path in Figure 18.19.

arbitrarily picking a path and adjusting the flow

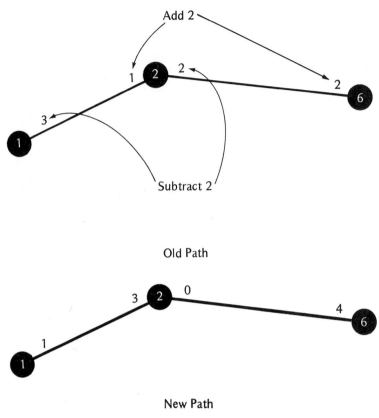

FIGURE 18.19
Capacity Adjustment for Path 1–2–6 Iteration 1

It is important to note that the new path in Figure 18.19 reflects the new relative capacity at this stage. The flow number by any node represents two factors. One factor is the flow that can come *from* that node. The second factor is flow that can be *reduced* coming *into* the node. First, consider the flow from west to east. Look at the path that goes from node 1 to node 2. The number 1 by node 1 tells us that 100 cars can flow *from* node 1 to node 2. Looking at the path from node 2 to node 6, we can see that the number 0 by node 2 tells us that 0 cars can flow *from* node 2 to node 6. Now, consider the flow from east to west shown in the new path in Figure 18.19. First, consider the path from node 6 to node 2. The number 4 by node 6 tells us that we can reduce the flow *into* node 6 by 2 (or 200 cars) and that there is a capacity of 2 (or 200 cars) that can come *from* node 6. These two factors total 4. Looking at the path from node 2 to node 1, we see the number 3 by node 2. This tells us that we can reduce the flow *into* node 2 by 2 (or 200 cars) and that we have a capacity of 1 (or 100 cars) *from* node 2 to node 1. At this stage, we have a flow of 200 cars through the network from node 1 to node 2 to node 6. We have also reflected the new relative capacity as seen in the new path in Figure 18.19.

Now we repeat the process by picking another path with existing ca-

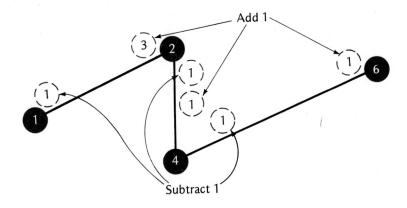

Old Path

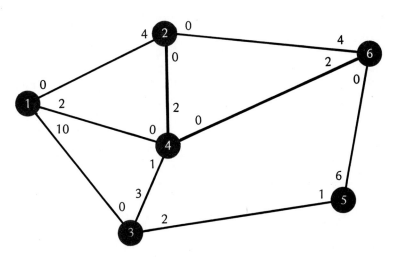

New Network

FIGURE 18.20
Second Iteration

pacity. We will arbitrarily pick path 1–2–4–6. The maximum capacity along this path is 1. In fact, the capacity at every node along this path (1–2–4–6) going from west to east is 1. Remember, the capacity of branch 1–2 is now 1 because 2 units (200 cars per hour) are now flowing through the network. Thus, we increase the flow along path 1–2–4–6 by 1 and adjust the capacity flow. See Figure 18.20.

repeating the process

Now we have a flow of 3 units (300 cars): 200 cars per hour along path 1–2–6 plus 100 cars per hour along path 1–2–4–6. Can we still increase the flow? Yes, along path 1–3–5–6. This is the bottom path. The maximum flow is 2 because this is the maximum from node 3 to node 5. The increased flow along this path is shown in Figure 18.21.

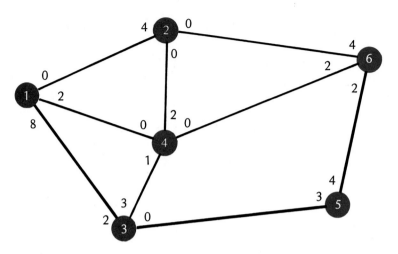

FIGURE 18.21
Third Iteration

**no more paths with
unused capacity**

Again we repeat the process, trying to find a path with any unused capacity through the network. If you carefully check the last iteration in Figure 18.21, you will see that there are no more paths from node 1 to node 6 with unused capacity, even though several other branches in the network do have unused capacity. The maximum flow of 500 cars per hour is summarized below:

PATH	FLOW (CARS PER HOUR)
1–2–6	200
1–2–4–6	100
1–3–5–6	200
Total	500

You can also compare the original network to the final network to see the flow between any of the nodes.

18.7
SHORTEST-ROUTE TECHNIQUE

The *shortest-route technique* finds how a person or item can travel from one location to another while minimizing the total distance traveled. In other words, it finds the shortest route to a series of destinations.

Every day, Ray Design, Inc. must transport beds, chairs, and other furniture items from the factory to the warehouse. This involves going through several cities. Ray would like to find the route with the shortest distance. The road network is shown in Figure 18.22.

The shortest-route technique can be used to minimize total distance from any starting node to a final node. The technique is summarized in the following steps.

1. Find the nearest node to the origin (plant). Put the distance in a box by the node.

2. Find the next nearest node to the origin (plant), and put the distance in a box by the node. In some cases, several paths will have to be checked to find the nearest node.

3. Repeat this process until you have gone through the entire network. The last distance at the ending node will be the distance of the shortest route. You should note that the distances placed in the boxes by each node are the shortest route to this node. These distances are used as intermediate results in finding the next nearest node.

shortest-route technique steps

Looking at Figure 18.22, we can see that the nearest node to the plant is node 2, with a distance of 100 miles. Thus, we will connect these two nodes. This first iteration is shown in Figure 18.23.

Now we look for the next nearest node to the origin. We check nodes 3, 4, and 5. Node 3 is the nearest, but there are two possible paths. Path

looking for the nearest node to the origin

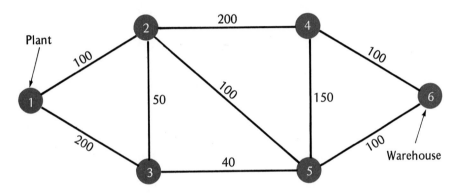

FIGURE 18.22
Roads from Ray's Plant to Warehouse

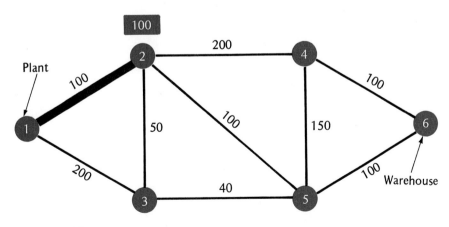

FIGURE 18.23
First Iteration

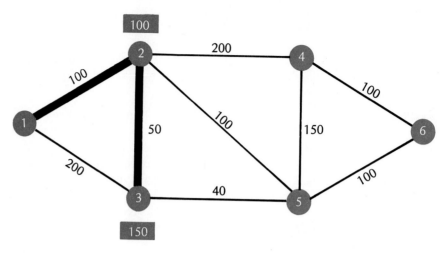

FIGURE 18.24
Second Iteration

1–2–3 is nearest to the origin with a total distance of 150 miles. See Figure 18.24.

repeating the process

We repeat the process. The next nearest node is either node 4 or node 5. Node 4 is 200 miles from node 2, and node 2 is 100 miles from node 1. Thus, node 4 is 300 miles from the origin. There are two paths for node 5, 2–5 and 3–5, to the origin. Note that we don't have to go all the way back to the origin because we already know the shortest route from node 2 and node 3 to the origin. The minimum distances are placed in boxes by these nodes. Path 2–5 is 100 miles, and node 2 is 100 miles from the origin. Thus, the total distance is 200 miles. In a similar fashion, we can determine that the path from node 5 to the origin through node 3 is 190 (40 miles between node 5 and 3 plus 150 miles from node 3 to the origin). Thus, we pick node 5 going through node 3 to the origin. See Figure 18.25.

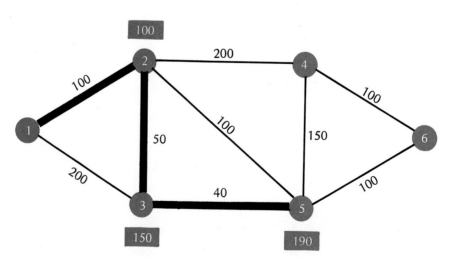

FIGURE 18.25
Third Iteration

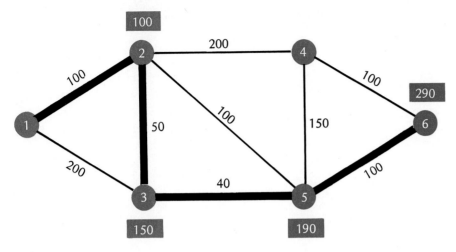

FIGURE 18.26
Fourth and Final Iteration

The next nearest node will be either node 4 or node 6, the last remaining nodes. Node 4 is 300 miles from the origin (300 = 200 from node 4 to node 2 plus 100 from node 2 to the origin). Node 6 is 290 miles from the origin (290 = 100 + 190). Node 6 has the minimum distance, and because it is the ending node, we are done. Refer to Figure 18.26. The shortest route is path 1–2–3–5–6 with a minimum distance of 290 miles.

finding the minimum distance

18.8
USING THE COMPUTER TO SOLVE NETWORK PROBLEMS

AB:QM and STORM can be used to solve network-related problems. Both packages can assist in solving PERT and CPM problems along with other network problems—minimal-spanning tree, maximal flow, and shortest route. We will begin with the AB:QM package.

Using AB:QM to Solve PERT, CPM, and Other Network-Related Problems

In this section, we will investigate the use of AB:QM to solve a number of network problems discussed in this chapter. For all of the network models, it is necessary to enter the starting node number and the ending node number for the network. On the input screen, SN is used to represent the starting node number, while EN is used to represent the ending node number.

The PERT/CPM submenu contains three programs: PERT, CPM, and CPM with crashing. The first program we will look at is PERT, which can have a maximum of 50 activities. All nodes must be numbered using a positive integer less than 101. The program uses optimistic, most likely, and pessimistic time estimates for each activity. Output includes the mean, standard deviation, and variance for each activity; expected completion

using PERT

PROGRAM 18.1 Using AB:QM's PERT Program on General Foundry Data

```
CPM/PERT / PERT

Problem Title :   General Foundry

Number of Activities            8


                  SN  EN  Optimistic  Most Likely  Pessimistic
Activity  1    1   2           1            2            3
Activity  2    1   3           2            3            4
Activity  3    2   4           1            2            3
Activity  4    3   5           2            4            6
Activity  5    4   5           1            4            7
Activity  6    4   6           1            2            9
Activity  7    5   6           3            4           11
Activity  8    6   7           1            2            3




PERT
***** Program Output *****


------------------------------------------------------------
Activity    Activity Nodes     Mean       S.D.     Variance
------------------------------------------------------------
   1 *          1 --> 2       2.000      0.333      0.111
   2            1 --> 3       3.000      0.333      0.111
   3 *          2 --> 4       2.000      0.333      0.111
   4            3 --> 5       4.000      0.667      0.444
   5 *          4 --> 5       4.000      1.000      1.000
   6            4 --> 6       3.000      1.333      1.778
   7 *          5 --> 6       5.000      1.333      1.778
   8 *          6 --> 7       2.000      0.333      0.111
------------------------------------------------------------
(* : Critical Path Activities)

Expected Completion Time :       15.000

***** End of Output *****
```

time is also given. The input data screen and the program output for the General Foundry problem are shown in Program 18.1.

The CPM program is similar to PERT, but three time estimates are *not* needed for each activity. Unlike the PERT program, however, the CPM program does compute early times, late times, and slack values for all activities. Since the input and output from this program are so similar to PERT, we do not provide a sample printout for CPM.

using CPM

The third program under the submenu is CPM with crashing. For this application, you enter the normal time, the crash time, the normal cost, and the crash cost for your particular network. The computer then determines the maximum crash time along with the total crash cost. This program allows you to specify how many days, weeks, or time periods you want the network to be crashed. This is called the expected project time.

using CPM with crashing

The program computes the crash cost, the activity time, and the activity cost for all activities. The normal completion time and expected crash completion time are also given. The input screen and the program output are shown in Program 18.2.

Using AB:QM to Solve Other Network Models

The shortest-route, minimum-spanning tree, and maximal-flow problems can also be solved using AB:QM. The first problem we will illustrate is the minimum-spanning tree case illustrated by the Lauderdale Construction problem we saw earlier in this chapter. The program determines the best way to connect all points in a network while minimizing the distance between them. It can handle between 3 and 50 nodes and 3 and 50 branches. The input screen and program output for the Lauderdale Construction problem are given in Program 18.3.

minimum-spanning tree problem

The maximum-flow program can be used to determine the maximum number of cars or vehicles going through a road system given the flows on each road or branch. It can handle between 3 and 50 nodes and between 3 and 50 branches. The input screen and output are shown in Program 18.4. You should note that "Value" is used to enter the flow in one direction along the network, while "Inv.Value" is used to show the flow in the opposite direction. (Inv.Value stands for *inverse value* or capacity on the branch.)

maximal-flow technique

The final network program, the shortest-route technique, determines the shortest route through a network from one point to the other. Like the other two network models, this one can handle between 3 and 50 branches and between 3 and 50 nodes. The input data resemble that for the minimum spanning tree program, so they are not illustrated here.

shortest-route technique

Using STORM for Project Management

STORM provides a project management module, which can be initiated by choosing selection 6 from the main STORM menu shown in Chapter 1. This begins the PERT/CPM module; the module will be used to solve the General Foundry problem discussed in this chapter. The results are shown in Program 18.5.

PROGRAM 18.2 AB:QM's Program for CPM with Crashing

```
CPM/PERT / CPM With Crashing

Problem Title :  General Foundry
Expected Project Time        7
Number of Activities         8


             SN EN  Normal Time  Crashed Time  Normal Cost  Crashed Cost
Activity  1   1  2         2            1          22000        23000
Activity  2   1  3         3            1          30000        34000
Activity  3   2  4         2            1          26000        27000
Activity  4   3  5         4            3          48000        49000
Activity  5   4  5         4            2          56000        58000
Activity  6   4  6         3            2          30000        30500
Activity  7   5  6         5            2          80000        86000
Activity  8   6  7         2            1          16000        19000


Help   New   Load   Save   Edit   Run   Print   Install   Directory   Esc
```

CPM With Crashing

***** Program Output *****

```
-------------------------------------------------------------------
                                   Crashing  Activity Activity
Activity    Activity Nodes Crash by   Cost      Time     Cost
-------------------------------------------------------------------
   1 *        1 --> 2     1.000   1000.000    1.000  23000.000
   2 *        1 --> 3     2.000   4000.000    1.000  34000.000
   3 *        2 --> 4     1.000   1000.000    1.000  27000.000
   4 *        3 --> 5     1.000   1000.000    3.000  49000.000
   5 *        4 --> 5     2.000   2000.000    2.000  58000.000
   6          4 --> 6     0.000      0.000    3.000  30000.000
   7 *        5 --> 6     3.000   6000.000    2.000  86000.000
   8 *        6 --> 7     1.000   3000.000    1.000  19000.000
-------------------------------------------------------------------
(* : Critical Path Activities)      18000.00          326000.000

Expected Normal Completion Time  :   15.000
Expected Crashed Completion Time :    7.000

***** End of Output *****
```

PROGRAM 18.3 AB:QM's Minimum-Spanning Tree Program on Lauderdale Construction Company Data

```
Network Models / Minimum Spanning Tree

 Problem Title :  Lauderdale Construction
 Number of Nodes              8
 Number of Branches          13


            SN     EN      Value
 Branch   1    1      2          3
 Branch   2    1      3          2
 Branch   3    1      4          5
 Branch   4    2      3          3
 Branch   5    2      5          3
 Branch   6    3      4          2
 Branch   7    3      5          5
 Branch   8    3      6          3
 Branch   9    3      7          7
 Branch  10    4      6          6
 Branch  11    5      7          4
 Branch  12    6      8          1
 Branch  13    7      8          2


 Help   New   Load   Save   Edit   Run   Print   Install   Directory   Esc


 Program: Network Models / Minimum Spanning Tree

 ***** Program Output *****


 ---------------------------
   SN      EN        Value
 ---------------------------
   1 <--->  2         3.00
   1 <--->  3         2.00
   2 <--->  5         3.00
   3 <--->  6         3.00
   3 <--->  4         2.00
   6 <--->  8         1.00
   7 <--->  8         2.00
 ---------------------------

 Total Minimum Spanning Tree Lengths  :      16.00

 ***** End of Output *****
```

PROGRAM 18.4 AB:QM's Maximum-Flow Program on Waukesha Data

```
Network Models / Maximum Flow

Problem Title :  Waukesha
Number of Nodes                        6
Number of Branches                     9


               SN    EN        Value      Inv.Value
Branch   1     1     2            3             1
Branch   2     1     3           10             0
Branch   3     1     4            2             0
Branch   4     2     4            1             1
Branch   5     2     6            2             2
Branch   6     3     4            3             1
Branch   7     3     5            2             1
Branch   8     4     6            1             1
Branch   9     5     6            6             0




Program: Network Models / Maximum Flow

***** Program Output *****


----------------------------
 SN        EN           Flow
----------------------------

  1 ----> 2            2.00
  1 ----> 3            2.00
  1 ----> 4            1.00
  2 ----> 6            2.00
  3 ----> 5            2.00
  4 ----> 6            1.00
  5 ----> 6            2.00
----------------------------


Total Maximum Flow    :      5.00

***** End of Output *****
```

project management

As with other STORM modules, the opening module (Program 18.5a) for the project management program allows the user to read an existing data file or to create a new data set. We select option 2 to create a new data set. Next, we are given a beginning data screen **(b)**. Here, we enter the problem title, the number of activities, whether or not the activity times are probabilistic or deterministic, whether the activity representation is *arc* or *node*, and the number of predecessor columns. As you can see, for the General Foundry problem there are eight activities. We will use probabilistic time estimates and *arc* notation. Arc representation was used throughout this chapter. We do not require predecessor columns because we are not

PROGRAM 18.5 STORM's Project Management Program on General
Foundry Data

(a)

PROJECT MANAGEMENT (PERT/CPM) : INPUT

```
1)   Read an existing data file
2)   Create a new data set
```

Select option   2

(b)

──── STORM EDITOR : Project Management Module ────

```
Title :  GENERAL FOUNDRY
Number of activities                               8
Activity time option (DET/PROB)                 PROB
Activity representation option (ARC/NODE)        ARC
Number of predecessor columns (NODE only)          0
```

(c)

R8 : C6		SYMBOL	OPTIMISTIC	LIKELY	PESSIMISTIC	START NODE	END MODE
ACT	1	A	1.	2.	3.	1	2
ACT	2	B	2.	3.	4.	1	3
ACT	3	C	1.	2.	3.	2	4
ACT	4	D	2.	4.	6.	3	5
ACT	5	E	1.	4.	7.	4	5
ACT	6	F	1.	2.	9.	4	6
ACT	7	G	3.	4.	11.	5	6
ACT	8	H	1.	2.	3.	6	7

(d)

PROJECT MANAGEMENT : PROCESS

```
1)   Edit the current data set
2)   Save the current data set
3)   Print the current data set
4)   Execute the module with the current data set
```

Select option   4

(e)

GENERAL FOUNDRY
ACTIVITIES IN THE ORDER AS ENTERED

Activity Name		Symb	Mean Time /Std Dev	Earliest Start/Fin	Latest Start/Fin	Slack
ACT	1	A	2.0000	0.0000	0.0000	0.0000 c
			0.3333	2.0000	2.0000	
ACT	2	B	3.0000	0.0000	1.0000	1.0000
			0.3333	3.0000	4.0000	
ACT	3	C	2.0000	2.0000	2.0000	0.0000 c
			0.3333	4.0000	4.0000	
ACT	4	D	4.0000	3.0000	4.0000	1.0000
			0.6667	7.0000	8.0000	
ACT	5	E	4.0000	4.0000	4.0000	0.0000 c
			1.0000	8.0000	8.0000	
ACT	6	F	3.0000	4.0000	10.0000	6.0000
			1.3333	7.0000	13.0000	
ACT	7	G	5.0000	8.0000	8.0000	0.0000 c
			1.3333	13.0000	13.0000	
ACT	8	H	2.0000	13.0000	13.0000	0.0000 c
			0.3333	15.0000	15.0000	

PROGRAM 18.5 Continued

(f)

GENERAL FOUNDRY
ACTIVITIES IN THE ORDER AS ENTERED

Activity Name	Symb	Mean Time /Std Dev	Earliest Start/Fin	Latest Start/Fin	Slack

The computations were based on 8 activities
Expected project completion time = 15.0000

Activity std dev = (pessimistic − optimistic) / 6.0
Std dev of project completion time = 1.7638

(g)

GENERAL FOUNDRY
BAR CHART: NONCRITICAL ACTIVITIES SORTED BY SLACK

```
        0                                                    15
    ----+-----+-----+-----+-----+-----+-----+-----+-----+-----+
    A   ¦ccccccccc                                            ¦
    C   ¦           ccccccccc                                 ¦
    E   ¦               cccccccccccccccc                      ¦
    G   ¦                           ccccccccccccccccccccc     ¦
    H   ¦                                            ccccccccc
    B   ¦xxxxxxxxxxxx....                                     ¦
    D   ¦          xxxxxxxxxxxxxxxx....                       ¦
    F   ¦          xxxxxxxxxxxxx......................... ..  ¦
    ----+-----+-----+-----+-----+-----+-----+-----+-----+-----+
```

(h)

```
95% ¦ PROBABILITY OF PROJECT COMPLETION                    *  ¦ 95%
90% ¦ Expected project completion time   = 15.0000       *    ¦ 90%
85% ¦ Std dev of project completion time = 1.7638      *      ¦ 85%
    ¦                                                         ¦
75% ¦                                               *         ¦ 75%
    ¦                                                         ¦
65% ¦                                          *              ¦ 65%
    ¦                                                         ¦
    ¦                                                         ¦
50% ¦                                   *                     ¦ 50%
    ¦                                                         ¦
    ¦                                                         ¦
35% ¦                             *                           ¦ 35%
    ¦                                                         ¦
25% ¦                       *                                 ¦ 25%
    ¦                                                         ¦
15% ¦                 *                                       ¦ 15%
10% ¦          *                                              ¦ 10%
 5% ¦    *                                                    ¦  5%
    ¦ 12.10      13.17      14.32      15.68      16.38      17.90 ¦
    +---+-----+-----+-----+-----+-----+-----+-----+-----+------+---+
        12.74      13.81      15.00      16.19      17.26      Time
    Enter target time for project completion:
```

using the *node* representation. Once we enter this beginning data, STORM provides us another screen to enter the appropriate data **(c).** In this screen, we enter the likely, optimistic, and pessimistic time estimates for all eight of the activities. We also indicate the starting node numbers and ending node numbers as well. Once these data have been entered, STORM gives us a processing menu **(d),** which is the same processing menu shown with other applications. As before, the processing menu allows us to edit the current data set, save the current data set, print the current data set, or execute the existing module. We select option 4, which executes the module.

The first output screen **(e)** gives the average, or mean, times and the standard deviations for all activities. In addition, the earliest and latest start and finished times are given. Slack times for all activities are also presented. Note that the letter c beside an activity represents an activity that is on the critical path. The next screen **(f)** summarizes the calculations by giving the average (mean) completion time and the standard deviation of project completion time.

Once this basic information is presented, other outputs can also be displayed. STORM allows us to obtain bar charts **(g)** for completion times for the various activities. The bar chart shows us which activities are critical and which are not. The c in the charts again indicates critical activities. We are also given a graph of the probability of project completion **(h).** This shows us the probability of completing the project in a range of time from about 12 periods to 18 periods.

Using STORM's Distance Network Module

shortest-route technique

STORM has two different subprograms, or modules, that are used to handle the other network techniques discussed in this chapter. Distance networks, which is selection 4 from the STORM main menu, allows us to perform the shortest-route technique and the maximal-flow technique. The flow networks module, which is selection 5 from the main menu, allows us to perform the minimal-spanning tree technique. We illustrate STORM's features by looking at applications for the distance network module.

Shortest-route problems can be solved using the distance networks module. First we are given a screen (Program 18.6**a**) that allows us to read an existing data file or to create a new data set. We will create a new data set. Next, STORM allows us to enter the appropriate data, including the problem title, the number of nodes, and the network type **(b).**

As you can see, we have entered the title Ray Design. The number of nodes is 6 and this will be an asymmetrical matrix. Next, we are given a screen **(c)** showing the various network algorithms. Selection 1 is the shortest-path alternative, and thus we will select this alternative to solve the Ray Design problem. Now we are allowed to enter data and to make various selections **(d).** Once this is done, the shortest path from node 1 is determined and displayed by the computer **(e).**

Commercial Software for Project Management

There are several good commercial software packages available that perform PERT analysis. An example is Harvard Total Project Manager (HTPM). This

PROGRAM 18.6 STORM's Shortest-Route Program on Ray Design Data

(a)

DISTANCE NETWORKS (PATHS, TOURS, TREES) : INPUT

```
1)   Read an existing data file
2)   Create a new data set
        Select option    2
```

(b)

─────── STORM EDITOR : Distance Networks Module ───────

```
Title : RAY DESIGN
Number of nodes                    :        6
Distance matrix type (SYM/ASYM)    :      ASYM
```

	C1	NODE 1	NODE 2	NODE 3	NODE 4	NODE 5	NODE 6
DIST	1	.	100.	200.	.	.	.
DIST	2	.	.	50.	200.	100.	.
DIST	3	.	.	.	.	40.	.
DIST	4	.	.	.	.	150.	100.
DIST	5	.	.	.	.	.	100.
DIST	6	.	.	.	.	.	.

(c)

NETWORK ALGORITHMS

```
1)      Shortest paths
2)      Longest paths
3)      Traveling salesperson's tour
4)      Minimal spanning tree
5)      Maximal spanning tree
         Select option    1
```

(d)

SELECTION OF DESTINATION NODES   CANDIDATES

Select destination nodes to which paths   * NODE 2
    from NODE 1 are to be computed   * NODE 3
                                                  * NODE 4
Note : * marks nodes of interest   * NODE 5
                                                  * NODE 6

(e)

RAY DESIGN
SHORTEST PATHS FROM NODE 1

Destination	Distance	Path
NODE 2	100.0000	NODE 2
NODE 3	150.0000	NODE 2--NODE 3
NODE 4	300.0000	NODE 2--NODE 4
NODE 5	190.0000	NODE 2--NODE 3--NODE 5
NODE 6	290.0000	NODE 2--NODE 3--NODE 5--NODE 6

PROGRAM 18.7 Sample PERT Chart Using Harvard Total Project Manager Software

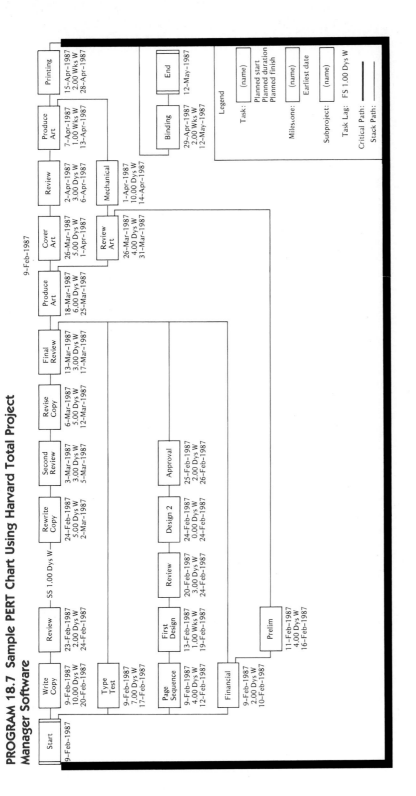

767

package allows you to enter a network and modify the network as a project is being completed. A number of useful reports are available that help managers control and monitor the progress of the project. These reports include PERT diagrams, specific start and finish dates, cost graphs, and resource loading charts. Program 18.7 illustrates one such output from the HTPM package.

18.9
SUMMARY

The fundamentals of PERT and CPM have been presented in this chapter. Both of these techniques are excellent for controlling large and complex projects.

PERT is probabilistic and allows three time estimates for each activity. These estimates are used to compute the project's expected completion time, variance, and the probability that the project will be completed by a given date. PERT/Cost, an extension of standard PERT, can be used to plan, schedule, monitor, and control project costs. Using PERT/Cost, it is possible to determine if there are cost overruns or underruns at any point in time. It is also possible to determine whether or not the project is on schedule.

CPM, although similar to PERT, has the ability to crash projects by reducing their completion time through additional resource expenditures. Finally, we saw that linear programming can also be used to crash a network by a desired amount at a minimum cost.

In addition to PERT and CPM, three other network techniques are useful. The minimal-spanning tree technique determines the path through the network that connects all of the nodes while minimizing total distance. The maximal-flow technique finds the maximum flow of any quantity or substance that can go through a network. Finally, the shortest-route technique can find the shortest path through a network.

GLOSSARY

PERT. Program evaluation and review technique. A network technique that allows three time estimates for each activity in a project.

Activity. A time-consuming job or task that is a key subpart of the total project.

Event. A point in time that marks the beginning or ending of an activity.

Immediate Predecessor. An activity that must be completed before another activity can be started.

Network. A graphical display of a project that contains both activities and events.

Activity Time Estimates. Three time estimates that are used in determining the expected completion time and variance for an activity in a PERT network.

Optimistic Time (a). The shortest amount of time that could be required to complete the activity.

Pessimistic Time (b). The greatest amount of time that could be required to complete the activity.

Most Likely Time (m). The amount of time that you would expect it would take to complete the activity.

Beta Distribution. A probability distribution that is often used in computing the expected activity completion times and variances in networks.

Earliest Start Time (*ES*). The earliest time that an activity can start without violation of precedence requirements.

Latest Start Time (*LS*). The latest time that an activity can be started without delaying the entire project.

Earliest Finish Time (*EF*). The earliest time that an activity can be finished without violation of precedence requirements.

Latest Finish Time (*LF*). The latest time that an activity can be finished without delaying the entire project.

Forward Pass. A procedure that moves from the beginning of a network to the end of the network. It is used in determining earliest activity start times and earliest finish times.

Backward Pass. A procedure that moves from the end of the network to the beginning of the network. It is used in determining the latest finish and start times.

Slack. The amount of time that an activity can be delayed without delaying the entire project. Slack is equal to the latest start time minus the earliest start time, or the latest finish time minus the earliest finish time.

Critical Path. The series of activities that have a zero slack. It is the longest time path through the network. A delay for any activity that is on the critical path will delay the completion of the entire project.

Critical Path Analysis. An analysis that determines the total project completion time, the critical path for the project, slack, ES, EF, LS, and LF for every activity.

Expected Activity Time. The average time that it should take to complete an activity. $t = (a + 4m + b)/6$.

Variance of Activity Completion Time. A measure of dispersion of the activity completion time. Variance $= [(b - a)/6]^2$.

Dummy Activity. A fictitious activity that consumes no time and is inserted into a network to make the network display the proper predecessor relationships between activities.

PERT/Cost. A technique that allows a decision maker to plan, schedule, monitor, and control project *cost* as well as project time.

CPM. Critical path method. A deterministic network technique that is similar to PERT, but allows for project crashing.

Crashing. The process of reducing the total time that it takes to complete a project by expending additional funds.

Minimal-Spanning Tree Technique. Determines the path through the network that connects all of the nodes while minimizing total distance.

Maximal-Flow Technique. Finds the maximum flow of any quantity or substance through a network.

Shortest-Route Technique. Determines the shortest path through a network.

KEY EQUATIONS

(18-1) $$t = \frac{a + 4m + b}{6}$$

Expected activity completion time.

(18-2) Variance $= \left(\dfrac{b - a}{6}\right)^2$
Activity variance.

(18-3) EF = ES + t
Earliest finish time.

(18-4) LS = LF − t
Latest start time.

(18-5) Slack = LS − ES or Slack = LF − EF
Slack time in an activity.

(18-6) Project variance = Σ Variances of activities on critical path

(18-7) $Z = \dfrac{\text{Due date} - \text{Expected date of completion}}{\sigma_T}$
Number of standard deviations the target date lies from the expected date, using the normal distribution.

(18-8) Value of work completed = (Percent of work completed) × (Total activity budget)

(18-9) Activity difference = Actual cost − Value of work completed

(18-10) Crash cost/time period $= \dfrac{\text{Crash cost} - \text{Normal cost}}{\text{Normal time} - \text{Crash time}}$
The cost in CPM of reducing an activity's length per time period.

SOLVED PROBLEMS

Solved Problem 18-1

In order to complete the wing assembly for an experimental aircraft, Scott DeWitte has laid out the major steps and seven activities involved. These activities have been labeled A through G in the following table, which also shows their estimated completion times and immediate predecessors. Determine the expected time and variance for each activity.

ACTIVITY	a	m	b	IMMEDIATE PREDECESSORS
A	1	2	2	—
B	2	3	3	—
C	4	5	6	A
D	8	9	11	B
E	2	5	5	C, D
F	3	5	6	B
G	1	2	3	E

Solution

Although not required for this problem, a diagram showing all of the activities can be useful. A PERT diagram for the wing assembly follows:

Expected times and variances can be computed using the formulas presented in the chapter. The results are summarized in the accompanying table.

PERT Diagram for Scott DeWitte (Solved Problem 18.1)

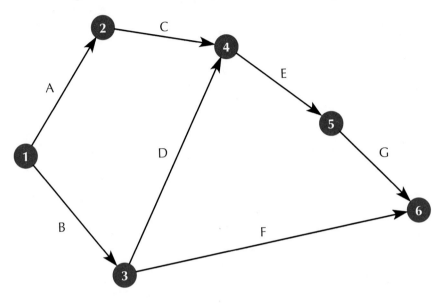

ACTIVITY	NODES	EXPECTED TIME	EXPECTED VARIANCE
A	1 → 2	1.83	0.028
B	1 → 3	2.83	0.028
C	2 → 4	5.00	0.111
D	3 → 4	9.17	0.250
E	4 → 5	4.50	0.250
F	3 → 6	4.83	0.250
G	5 → 6	2.00	0.111

Solved Problem 18-2

Now Scott would like to determine the critical path for the entire wing assembly project as well as expected completion time for the total project. In addition, he would like to determine the earliest and latest start and finish times for all activities.

Solution

The critical path, earliest start times, earliest finish times, latest start times, and latest finish times can be determined using the procedures outlined in the chapter. The results are summarized in the following table.

ACTIVITY	NODES	ACTIVITY TIMES				SLACK
		ES	EF	LS	LF	
A	1 → 2	0.00	1.83	5.17	7.00	5.17
B	1 → 3	0.00	2.83	0.00	2.83	0.00
C	2 → 4	1.83	6.83	7.00	12.00	5.17
D	3 → 4	2.83	12.00	2.83	12.00	0.00
E	4 → 5	12.00	16.50	12.00	16.50	0.00
F	3 → 6	2.83	7.67	13.67	18.50	10.83
G	5 → 6	16.50	18.50	16.50	18.50	0.00

Expected project length = 18.5

Variance of the critical path = .6388

Standard deviation of the critical path = .7993

The activities along the critical path are B, D, E, and G. These activities have 0 slack, as seen in the table. The expected project completion time is 18.5. The earliest and latest start and finish times are shown in the table.

DISCUSSION QUESTIONS AND PROBLEMS

Discussion Questions

18-1 What are some of the questions that can be answered with PERT and CPM?

18-2 What are the major differences between PERT and CPM?

18-3 What is an activity? What is an event? What is an immediate predecessor?

18-4 Describe how expected activity times and variances can be computed in a PERT network.

18-5 Briefly discuss what is meant by critical path analysis. What are critical path activities and why are they important?

18-6 What are the earliest activity start time and latest activity start time? How are they computed?

18-7 Describe the meaning of slack and discuss how it can be determined.

18-8 How can we determine the probability that a project will be completed by a certain date? What assumptions are made in this computation?

18-9 Briefly describe PERT/Cost and how it is used.

18-10 What is crashing and how is it done by hand?

18-11 Why is linear programming useful in CPM crashing?

Problems

· **18-12** Sid Davidson is the personnel director of Babson and Willcount, a company that specializes in consulting and research. One of the training programs that Sid is considering for the middle-level managers of Babson and Willcount is leadership training. Sid has listed a number of activities that must be completed before a training program of this nature could be conducted. The activities and immediate predecessors appear in the accompanying table.

ACTIVITY	IMMEDIATE PREDECESSOR
A	
B	
C	
D	B
E	A, D
F	C
G	E, F

Develop a network for this problem.

: **18-13** Sid Davidson was able to determine the activity times for the leadership training program. He would like to determine the total project completion time and the critical path. The activity times appear in the accompanying table. (See Problem 18-12.)

ACTIVITY	TIME (DAYS)
A	2
B	5
C	1
D	10
E	3
F	6
G	8
Total	35

· **18-14** Monohan Machinery specializes in developing weed-harvesting equipment that is used to clear small lakes of weeds. George Monohan, president of Monohan Machinery, is convinced that harvesting weeds is far better than using chemicals to kill weeds. Chemicals cause pollution, and the weeds seem to grow faster after chemicals have been used. George is contemplating the construction of a machine that could harvest weeds on narrow rivers and waterways. The activities that are necessary to build one of these experimental weed-harvesting machines are listed in the accompanying table. Construct a network for these activities.

ACTIVITIES	IMMEDIATE PREDECESSORS
A	
B	
C	A
D	A
E	B
F	B
G	C, E
H	D, F

: **18-15** After consulting with Butch Radner, George Monohan was able to determine the activity times for constructing the weed-harvesting machine to be used on narrow rivers. George would like to determine ES, EF, LS, LF, and slack for each activity. The total project completion time and the critical path should also be determined. See Problem 18-14 for details. Here are the activity times.

ACTIVITY	TIME (WEEKS)
A	6
B	5
C	3
D	2
E	4
F	6
G	10
H	7

: **18-16** Zuckerman Wiring and Electric is a company that installs wiring and electrical fixtures in residential construction. John Zuckerman has been concerned with the amount of time that it takes to complete wiring jobs. Some of his workers are very unreliable. A list of activities and their optimistic, the pessimistic, and the most likely completion times (in days) are given in the accompanying table.

ACTIVITY	a	m	b	IMMEDIATE PREDECESSORS
A	3	6	8	
B	2	4	4	
C	1	2	3	
D	6	7	8	C
E	2	4	6	B, D
F	6	10	14	A, E
G	1	2	4	A, E
H	3	6	9	F
I	10	11	12	G
J	14	16	20	C
K	2	8	10	H, I

Determine the expected completion time and variance for each activity.

· **18-17** John Zuckerman would like to determine the total project completion time and the critical path for installing electrical wiring and equipment in residential houses. See Problem 18-16 for details. In addition, determine ES, EF, LS, LF, and slack for each activity.

· **18-18** What is the probability that Zuckerman will finish the project described in Problems 18-16 and 18-17 in 40 days or less?

: **18-19** Tom Schriber, director of personnel of Management Resources, Inc., is in the process of designing a program that their customers can use in the job-finding process. Some of the activities include preparing resumes, writing letters, making appointments to see prospective employers, researching companies and industries, and so on. Some of the information on the activities appears in the accompanying table.

ACTIVITY	a	(DAYS) m	b	IMMEDIATE PREDECESSORS
A	8	10	12	
B	6	7	9	
C	3	3	4	
D	10	20	30	A
E	6	7	8	C
F	9	10	11	B, D, E
G	6	7	10	B, D, E
H	14	15	16	F
I	10	11	13	F
J	6	7	8	G, H
K	4	7	8	I, J
L	1	2	4	G, H

(a) Construct a network for this problem.
(b) Determine the expected times and variances for each activity.
(c) Determine ES, EF, LS, LF, and slack for each activity.
(d) Determine the critical path and project completion time.
(e) Determine the probability that the project will be finished in 70 days.
(f) Determine the probability that the project will be finished in 80 days.
(g) Determine the probability that the project will be finished in 90 days.

· **18-20** Using PERT, Ed Rose was able to determine that the expected project completion time for the construction of a pleasure yacht is 21 months, and the project variance is 4 months.

(a) What is the probability that the project will be completed in 17 months?
(b) What is the probability that the project will be completed in 20 months?
(c) What is the probability that the project will be completed in 23 months?
(d) What is the probability that the project will be completed in 25 months?

: **18-21** The air pollution project discussed in the chapter has progressed over the last several weeks and it is now week 8. Lester Harky would like to know the value of the work completed, the amount of any cost overruns or underruns for the project, and the extent to which the project is ahead of schedule or behind schedule by developing a table like Table 18.7. The revised cost figures appear in the accompanying table.

ACTIVITY	PERCENT OF COMPLETION	ACTUAL COST ($)
A	100	20,000
B	100	36,000
C	100	26,000
D	100	44,000
E	50	25,000
F	60	15,000
G	10	5,000
H	10	1,000

: **18-22** Fred Ridgeway has been given the responsibility of managing a training and development program. He knows the earliest start time, the latest start time, and the total costs for each activity. This information is given in the accompanying table.

ACTIVITY	ES	LS	t	TOTAL COST ($1,000's)
A	0	0	6	10
B	1	4	2	14
C	3	3	7	5
D	4	9	3	6
E	6	6	10	14
F	14	15	11	13
G	12	18	2	4
H	14	14	11	6
I	18	21	6	18
J	18	19	4	12
K	22	22	14	10
L	22	23	8	16
M	18	24	6	18

(a) Using earliest start times, determine Fred's total monthly budget.
(b) Using latest start times, determine Fred's total monthly budget.

: **18-23** General Foundry's project crashing data were shown in Table 18.8. Crash this project to 13 weeks using CPM. What are the final times for each activity after crashing?

: **18-24** Bowman Builders manufactures steel storage sheds for commercial use. Joe Bowman, president of Bowman Builders, is contemplating producing sheds for home use. The activities necessary to build an experimental model and related data are given in the accompanying table.

ACTIVITY	NORMAL TIME	CRASH TIME	NORMAL COST ($)	CRASH COST ($)	IMMEDIATE PREDECESSORS
A	3	2	1,000	1,600	
B	2	1	2,000	2,700	
C	1	0	300	600	
D	7	3	1,300	1,600	A
E	6	3	850	1,000	B
F	2	1	4,000	5,000	C
G	4	2	1,500	2,000	D, E

(a) What is the project completion date?
(b) Formulate a linear programming problem to crash this project to 10 weeks.

: **18-25** Bechtold Construction is in the process of installing power lines to a large housing development. Steve Bechtold wants to minimize the total length of wire used, which will minimize his costs. The housing development is shown as a network in the following illustration. Each house has been numbered, and the distances between houses is given in hundreds of feet. What do you recommend?

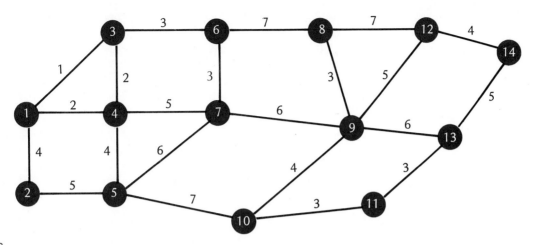

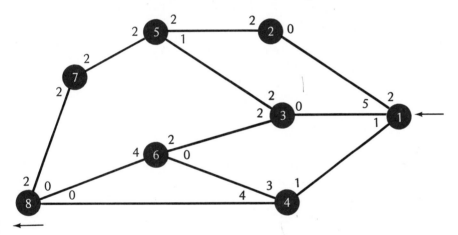

: **18-26** The City of New Berlin is considering making several of its streets one way. What is the maximum number of cars per hour that can travel from east to west? The network is shown in the following illustration.

: **18-27** Transworld Moving has been hired to move the office furniture and equipment of Cohen Properties to their new headquarters. What route do you recommend? The network of roads is shown in the next diagram.

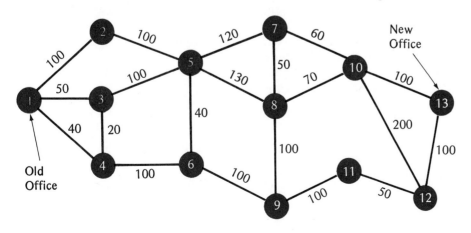

: **18-28** Software Development Specialists (SDS) is involved with developing software for customers in the banking industry. SDS breaks a large programming project into teams that perform the necessary steps. Team A is responsible for going from general systems design all the way through to actual systems testing. This involves 18 separate activities. Team B is then responsible for the final installation.

In order to determine cost and time factors, optimistic, most likely, and pessimistic time estimates have been made for all of the 18 activities involved for team A. The first step that this team performs is general systems design. The optimistic, most likely, and pessimistic times are 3 weeks, 4 weeks, and 5 weeks. Following this, a number of activities can begin. Activity 2 is involved with procedures design. Optimistic, most likely, and pessimistic times for completing this activity are 4, 5, and 7 weeks. Activity 3 is developing detailed report designs. Optimistic, most likely, and pessimistic time estimates are 6, 8, and 9 weeks. Activity 4, detailed forms design, has optimistic, most likely, and pessimistic time estimates of 2, 3, and 5 weeks.

The fifth and sixth activities involve writing detailed program specifications and developing file specifications. The three time estimates for activity 5 are 6, 7, and 9 weeks, and the 3 time estimates for activity 6 are 3, 4, and 5 weeks. Activity 7 is to specify system test data. Before this is done, activity 6 involving file specifications must be completed. The time estimates for activity 7 are 2, 4, and 5 weeks. Activity 8 involves reviewing forms. Before activity 8 can be conducted, detailed forms design must be completed first. The time estimates for activity 8 are 3, 4, and 6 weeks. The next activity, activity 9, is reviewing the detailed report design. This requires that the detailed report design, activity 3, be completed first. The time estimates for activity 9 are 1, 2, and 4 weeks, respectively.

Activity 10 involves reviewing procedures design. Time estimates are 1, 3, and 4 weeks. Of course, procedures design must be done before activity 10 can be started. Activity 11 involves the system design check-point review. A number of activities must be completed before this is done. These activities include reviewing the forms, reviewing the detailed report design, reviewing the procedures design, writing detailed program specs, and specifying system test data. The optimistic, most likely, and pessimistic time estimates for activity 11 are 3, 4, and 6 weeks. Performing program logic design is activity 12. This can only be started after the system design check-point review is completed. The time estimates for activity 12 are 4, 6, and 7 weeks.

Activity 13, coding the programs, is done only after the program logic design is completed. The time estimates for this activity are 6, 8, and 10 weeks. Activity 14 is involved in developing test programs. Activity 13 is the immediate predecessor. Time estimates for activity 14 are 3, 4, and 6 weeks. Developing a system test plan is activity 15. A number of activities must be completed before activity 15 can be started. These activities include specifying system test data, writing detailed program specifications, and reviewing procedure designs, the detailed report design, and forms.

The time estimates for activity 15 are 3, 4, and 5 weeks. Activity 16, creating system test data, has time estimates of 2, 4, and 6 weeks. Activity 15 must be done before activity 16 can be started. Activity 17 is reviewing program test results. The immediate predecessor to activity 17 is to test the programs (activity 14). The three time estimates for activity 17 are 2, 3, and 4 weeks. The final activity is conducting systems tests. This is activity 18. Before activity 18 can be started, activities 16 and 17 must be complete. The three time estimates for conducting these system tests are 3, 5, and 6 weeks.

How long will it take for team A to complete their programming assignment? What would happen if activity 5, writing detailed program specifications, had larger time estimates. Assume these time estimates are 12, 14, and 15.

: **18-29** The Bender Construction Co. is involved in constructing municipal buildings and other structures that are used primarily by city and state municipalities. This requires developing legal documents, drafting feasibility studies, obtaining bond ratings, and so forth. Recently, Bender was given a request to submit a proposal for the construction of a municipal building. The first step is to develop legal documents and to perform all necessary steps before the construction contract is signed. This requires approximately 20 separate activities that must be completed. These activities, their immediate predecessors, and time requirements are given in the following table.

ACTIVITY	a	TIME REQUIRED (WEEKS) m	b	DESCRIPTION OF ACTIVITY	IMMEDIATE PREDECESSOR(S)
1	1	4	5	Drafting legal documents	—
2	2	3	4	Preparation of financial statements	—
3	3	4	5	Draft of history	—
4	7	8	9	Draft demand portion of feasibility study	—
5	4	4	5	Review and approval of legal documents	1
6	1	2	4	Review and approval of history	3
7	4	5	6	Review feasibility study	4
8	1	2	4	Draft final financial portion of feasibility study	7
9	3	4	4	Draft facts relevant to the bond transaction	5
10	1	1	2	Review and approval of financial statements	2
11	18	20	26	Firm price received of project	—
12	1	2	3	Review and completion of financial portion of feasibility study	8
13	1	1	2	Draft statement completed	6, 9, 10, 11, 12
14	.10	.14	.16	All material sent to bond rating services	13
15	.2	.3	.4	Statement printed and distributed to all interested parties	14
16	1	1	2	Presentation to bond rating services	14
17	1	2	3	Bond rating received	16
18	3	5	7	Marketing of bonds	15, 17
19	.1	.1	.2	Purchase contract executed	18
20	.1	.14	.16	Final statement authorized and completed	19
21	2	3	6	Purchase contract	19
22	.1	.1	.2	Bond proceeds available	20
23	.0	.2	.2	Sign construction contract	21, 22

As you can see, optimistic (*a*), most likely (*m*), and pessimistic (*b*) time estimates have been given for all of the activities described in the table. Using the data, determine the total project completion time for this preliminary step, the critical path, and slack time for all activities involved.

18-30 Getting a degree from a college or university can be a long and difficult task. Certain courses must be completed before other courses may be taken. Develop a network diagram, where every activity is a particular course that must be taken for a given degree program. The immediate predecessors will be course prerequisites. Don't forget to include all university, college, and departmental course requirements. Then try to group these courses into semesters or quarters for your particular school. How long do you think it will take you to graduate? Which courses, if not taken in the proper sequence, could delay your graduation?

Data Set Problem

18-31 Sager Products has been in the business of manufacturing and marketing toys for toddlers for the past two decades. Jim Sager, president of the firm, is considering the development of a new manufacturing line to allow it to produce high-quality plastic toys at reasonable prices. The development process is long and complex. Jim estimates that there are five phases involved and multiple activities for each phase.

Phase 1 of the development process involves the completion of four activities. These activities have no immediate predecessors. Activity A has an optimistic completion time of 2 weeks, a probable completion time of 3 weeks, and a pessimistic completion time of 4 weeks. Activity B has estimated completion times of 5, 6, and 8 weeks; these represent optimistic, probable, and pessimistic time estimates. Similarly, activity C has estimated completion times of 1 week, 1 week, and 2 weeks; and activity D has expected completion times of 8 weeks, 9 weeks, and 11 weeks.

Phase 2 involves six separate activities. Activity E has activity A as an immediate predecessor. Time estimates are 1 week, 1 week, and 4 weeks. Activity F and activity G both have activity B as their immediate predecessor. For activity F, the time estimates are 3 weeks, 3 weeks, and 4 weeks. For activity G, the time estimates are 1 week, 2 weeks, and 2 weeks. The only immediate predecessor for activity H is activity C. Time estimates for activity H are 5 weeks, 5 weeks, and 6 weeks. Activity D must be performed before activity I and activity J can be started. Activity I has estimated completion times of 9 weeks, 10 weeks, and 11 weeks. Activity J has estimated completion times of 1 week, 2 weeks, and 2 weeks.

Phase 3 is the most difficult and complex of the entire development project. It also consists of six separate activities. Activity K has three time estimates of 2 weeks, 2 weeks, and 3 weeks. The immediate predecessor for this activity is activity E. The immediate predecessor for activity L is activity F. The time estimates for activity L are 3 weeks, 4 weeks, and 6 weeks. Activity M has 2 weeks, 2 weeks, and 4 weeks for the estimates of the optimistic, probable, and pessimistic time estimates. The immediate predecessor for activity M is activity G. Activities N and O both have activity I as their immediate predecessor. Activity M has 8 weeks, 9 weeks, and 11 weeks for its three time estimates. Activity O has 1 week, 1 week, and 3 weeks as its time estimates. Finally, activity P has time estimates of 4 weeks, 4 weeks, and 8 weeks. Activity J is its only immediate predecessor.

Phase 4 involves five activities. Activity Q requires activity K to be completed before it can be started. The three time estimates for activity Q are 6 weeks, 6 weeks, and 7 weeks. Activity R requires that both activity L and activity M be completed first. The three time estimates for activity R are 1, 2, and 4 weeks. Activity S requires activity N to be completed first. Its time estimates are 6 weeks, 6 weeks, and 7 weeks. Activity T requires that activity O be completed. The time estimates for activity T are 3 weeks, 3 weeks, and 4 weeks. The final activity for phase 4 is activity U. The time estimates for this activity are 1 week, 2 weeks, and 3 weeks. Activity P must be completed before activity U can be started.

Phase 5 is the final phase of the development project. It consists of only two activities. Activity V requires that activity Q and activity R be completed before it can be started. Time estimates for this activity are 9 weeks, 10 weeks, and 11 weeks. Activity W is the final activity of the process. It requires three activities to be completed before it can be started. These are activities S, T, and U. The estimated completion times for activity W are 2 weeks, 4 weeks, and 5 weeks.

(a) Given this information, determine the expected completion time for the entire process. Also determine those activities along the critical path. Jim hopes that the total project will take less than 40 weeks. Is this likely to occur?

(b) Jim has just determined that activity D has already been completed and no additional work is required. What is the impact of this change on the activities along the critical path?

(c) What is the impact on the critical path and total project completion time if both activity D and activity I have been completed?

(d) What would happen if the immediate predecessor activity changed? For example, activity F may have an immediate predecessor of activity A instead of activity B. Is it possible to handle this type of change with AB:QM?

CASE STUDY

Haygood Brothers Construction Company

George and Harry Haygood are building contractors who specialize in the construction of private home dwellings, storage warehouses, and small businesses (less than 20,000 sq. ft. of floor space). Both George and Harry entered a carpenter union's apprenticeship program in the early 1980s and, upon completion of the apprenticeship, became skilled craftsmen in 1986. Before going into business for themselves, they worked for several local building contractors in the Detroit area.

Typically, the Haygood Brothers submit competitive bids for the construction of proposed dwellings. Whenever their bids are accepted, various aspects of the construction (electrical wiring, plumbing, brick laying, painting, and so forth) are subcontracted. George and Harry, however, perform all carpentry work. In addition, they plan and schedule all construction operations, frequently arrange interim financing, and supervise all construction activities.

The philosophy under which the Haygood Brothers have always operated can be simply stated—"Time is money." Delays in construction increase the costs of interim financing and postpone the initiation of their building projects. Consequently, they deal with all bottlenecks promptly and avoid all delays whenever possible. To minimize the time consumed in a construction project, the Haygood Brothers use PERT.

First, all construction activities and events are itemized and properly arranged (in parallel and sequential combinations) in a network. Then, time estimates for each activity are made; the expected time for completing each activity is determined; and the critical (longest) path is calculated. Finally, earliest times, latest times, and slack values are computed. Having made these calculations, George and Harry can place their resources in the critical areas in order to minimize the time of completing the project.

The following are the activities that constitute an upcoming project (home dwelling) of the Haygood Brothers:

1. Arrange financing (AB).

2. Let subcontracts (BC).

3. Set and pour foundations (CD).

4. Plumbing (CE)

5. Framing (DF).

6. Roofing (FG).

7. Electrical wiring (FH).

8. Installation of windows and doors (FI).

9. Duct work and insulation (including heating and cooling units) (FJ).

10. Sheet rock, paneling, and paper hanging (JK).

11. Installation of cabinets (KL).

12. Bricking (KM).

13. Outside trim (MN).

14. Inside trim (including fixtures) (LO).

15. Painting (OP).

16. Flooring (PQ).

The PERT diagram, together with the optimistic (a), most likely (m), and pessimistic (b) time estimates, are as follows:

ACTIVITY	a	m	b
AB	4	5	6
BC	2	5	8
CD	5	7	9
CE	4	5	6
DF	2	4	6
FG	3	5	9
FH	4	5	6
FI	3	4	7
FJ	5	7	9
JK	10	11	12
KL	4	6	8
KM	7	8	9
MN	4	5	10
LO	5	7	9
OP	5	6	7
PQ	2	3	4

1. What is the time length of the critical path? What is the significance of the critical path?

2. Compute the amount of time that the completion of each event can be delayed without affecting the overall project.

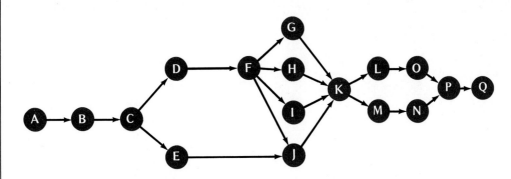

Source: Jerry Kinard (Francis Marion College) and Joe C. Iverstine (deceased). Used with permission of author.

3. The project was begun August 1. What is the probability that this project can be completed by September 30? (*Note:* Scheduled completion time = 60 days.)

CASE STUDY

Bay Community Hospital

The staff of the Bay Community Hospital had committed itself to introduce a new diagnostic procedure in the clinic. This procedure required the acquisition, installation, and introduction of a new medical instrument. Dr. Ed Windsor was assigned the responsibility for assuring that the introduction be performed as quickly and smoothly as possible.

Dr. Windsor created a list of activities that would have to be completed before the new service could begin. Initially, three individual steps had to be taken: (1) write instructions and procedures, (2) select techniques to operate the equipment, and (3) procure the equipment. The instructions and selection of the operators had to be completed before the training could commence. Dr. Windsor also believed it was necessary to choose the operators and evaluate their qualifications before formally announcing the new service to the local medical community. Upon arrival and installation of the equipment and completion of the operators' training, Dr. Windsor wanted to spend a period checking the procedures, operators, and equipment before declaring the project was successfully completed. The activities and times are listed in the accompanying table.

Source: W. E. Sasser, R. P. Olsen, and D. D. Wyckoff, *Management Service Operations,* Boston: Allyn and Bacon, 1978, pp. 97–98.

Jack Worth, a member of the Bay Community Hospital staff, reported that it would be possible to save time on the project by paying some premiums to complete certain activities faster than the normal schedule listed in the table. Specifically, if the equipment were shipped by express truck, 1 week could be saved. Air freight would save 2 weeks. However, a premium of $200 would be paid for the express truck shipment and $750 would be paid for air shipment. The operator training period could also be reduced by 1 week if the trainees worked overtime. However, this would cost the hospital an additional $600. The time required to complete the instructions could be reduced by 1 week with the additional expenditure of $400. However, $300 could be saved if this activity was allowed to take 3 weeks.

Discussion Questions

1. What is the shortest time period in which the project can be completed using the expected times listed in the table?

2. What is the shortest time in which the project can be completed?

3. What is the lowest-cost schedule for this shortest time?

ACTIVITY	DURATION (WEEKS)	IMMEDIATELY PRECEDING ACTIVITIES	IMMEDIATELY FOLLOWING ACTIVITIES
A: Write instructions	2	Start	C
B: Select operators	4	Start	C, D
C: Train operators	3	A, B	F
D: Announce new service	4	B	End
E: Purchase, ship, and receive equipment	8	Start	F
F: Test new operators on equipment	2	C, E	End

BIBLIOGRAPHY

Ameiss, A. P., and Thompson, W. A. "PERT for Monthly Financial Closing." *Management Advisor* January–February 1974.

Badiru, A. B. "Towards the Standardization of Performance Measures for Project Scheduling Heuristics." *IEEE Transactions on Engineering Management* Vol. 35, May 1988, pp. 82–89.

Bennington, G. E. "Applying Network Analysis." *Industrial Engineering* Vol. 6, January 1974, pp. 17–25.

Berman, O., and Jewkes, B. "Optimal M/G/I Server Location on a Network Having a Fixed Facility." *Journal of Operational Research Society* Vol. 39, December 1988, pp. 1137–1146.

Chan, K. H. "Decision Support Systems for Human Resource Management." *Journal of Systems Management* April 1984, pp. 17–25.

Clayton, E. R., and Moore, L. J. "PERT vs. GERT." *Journal of Systems Management* Vol. 23, February 1972, pp. 11–19.

Current, J. "The Minimum-Covering / Shortest Path Problem." *Decision Sciences* Vol. 19, Summer 1988, pp. 490–503.

Dodin, Bajis M., and Elmaghraby, Salah E. "Approximating the Critical Indices of the Activities in PERT Network." *Management Science* Vol. 31, No. 2, February 1985, pp. 207–223.

Dusenbury, W. "CPM for New Product Introductions." *Harvard Business Review* July–August 1967.

Golenko, Ginzburg D. "On the Distribution of Activity Time in PERT." *Journal of Operational Research Society* Vol. 39, August 1988, pp. 767–771.

Hanson, R. S. "Moving the Hospital to a New Location." *Industrial Engineering* Vol. 4, 1972.

Jain, A., and Mamer, J. W. "Approximations for the Random Minimal Spanning Tree with Application to Network Provisioning." *Operations Research* Vol. 36, July–August 1988, pp. 575–584.

Kefalas, A. G. "PERT Applied to Environmental Impact Statements." *Industrial Engineering* Vol. 8, No. 10, October 1976, pp. 38–42.

Krakowski, M. "PERT and Parkinson's Law." *Interfaces* Vol. 5, No. 1, November 1974.

Krogstad, J. L., Grudnitski, G., and Bryand, D. W. "PERT and PERT/Cost for Audit Planning and Control." *Journal of Accountancy* November 1977.

Levy, F., Thompson, A., and Wiest, S. "The ABC's of Critical Path Method." *Harvard Business Review* Vol. 41, September–October 1963, pp. 98–108.

Martin, J. R. "Computer Time Sharing Applications in Management Accounting." *Management Accounting* July 1978.

Phillips, Cecil R., and Davis, Edward W. *Project Management with CPM, PERT, and Precedence Diagramming,* 3rd ed. New York: Van Nostrand Reinhold, 1983.

Render, B., and Stair, R. M. *Cases and Readings in Management Science,* 2nd ed. Boston: Allyn and Bacon, 1990.

Rooks, Dana C. *PERT: Programming Evaluation and Review Technique: An Annotated Bibliography,* Monticello, IL.: Council of Planning Librarians, 1976.

Russell, A. H. "Cash Flows in Networks." *Management Science* Vol. 16, 1970, pp. 357–372.

Ryan, W. G. "Management Practice and Research—Poles Apart." *Business Horizons* June 1977.

Sancho, N. G. F. "On the Maximum Expected Flow in a Network." *Journal of Operational Research Society,* Vol. 39, May 1988, pp. 481–485.

Shelmerdine, E. K. "Planning for Project Management." *Journal of Systems Management* Vol. 40, January 1989, pp. 16–20.

Steinmetz, L. L. "PERT Personnel Practices." *Personnel Journal* Vol. 44, 1965, pp. 419–424.

Vemuganti, R. R., and others. "Network Models for Fleet Management." *Decision Sciences* Vol. 20, Winter 1989, pp. 182–197.

Wiest, J. D., and Levy, Ferdinand K. *A Management Guide to PERT, CPM, with Gert, PDM, DCPM, and Other Networks.* Englewood Cliffs, N.J.: Prentice-Hall, 1977.

19

Markov Analysis

19.1
INTRODUCTION

use of Markov analysis

Markov analysis is a technique that deals with the probabilities of future occurrences by analyzing presently known probabilities.[1] The technique has numerous applications in business, including market share analysis, bad debt prediction, university enrollment predictions, and determining whether a machine will break down in the future.

Markov analysis makes the assumption that the system starts in an initial state or condition. For example, two competing manufacturers might have 40% and 60% of the market sales, respectively, as initial states. Perhaps in two months the market shares for the two companies will change to 45% and 55% of the market, respectively. Predicting these future states involves knowing the system's likelihood or probability of changing from one state to another. For a particular problem, these probabilities can be collected and placed in a matrix or table. This *matrix of transition probabilities* reveals the likelihood that the system will change from one time period to the next. This is the Markov process, and it enables us to predict future states or conditions.

matrix of transition probabilities

Like many other quantitative techniques, Markov analysis can be studied at any level of depth and sophistication. Fortunately, the major mathematical requirements are just that you know how to perform basic matrix manipulations and solve several equations with several unknowns. If you are not familiar with these techniques, you may wish to review Module A, which covers matrices and other useful mathematical tools, before you begin this chapter.

Since the level of this course prohibits a detailed study of Markov mathematics, we limit our discussion to Markov processes that follow four assumptions:

assumptions of Markov analysis

1. There is a limited or finite number of possible states.

2. The probability of changing states remains the same over time.

3. We can predict any future state from the previous state and the matrix of transition probabilities.

4. The size and makeup of the system (for example, the total number of manufacturers and customers) do not change during the analysis.

━━━
19.2
STATES AND STATE PROBABILITIES:
A GROCERY STORE EXAMPLE

States are used to identify all possible conditions of a process or a system. For example, a machine can be in one of two states at any point in time.

---

[1] The founder of the concept was A. A. Markov, whose 1905 studies of the sequence of experiments connected in a chain were used to describe the principle of Brownian motion.

It can be either functioning correctly or not functioning correctly. We can call the proper operation of the machine the first state, and we can call the incorrect functioning the second state. Indeed, it is possible to identify specific states for many processes or systems. If there are only three grocery stores in a small town, a resident can be a customer of any one of the three at any point in time. Therefore, there are three states corresponding to the three grocery stores. If students can take one of three specialties in the management area (let's say management science, management information systems, or general management), then each of these areas can be considered a state.

examples of states

In Markov analysis, we also assume that the states are both *collectively exhaustive* and *mutually exclusive*. Collectively exhaustive means that we can list all of the possible states of a system or process. Our discussion of Markov analysis assumes that there is a finite number of states for any system. Mutually exclusive means that a system can be in only one state at any point in time. A student can be in only one of the three management specialty areas and *not* in two or more areas at the same time. It also means that a person can only be a customer of *one* of the three grocery stores at any point in time.

collectively exhaustive and mutually exclusive states

Once the states have been identified, the next step is to determine the probability that the system is in this state. Such information is then placed into a *vector of state probabilities*.

$$\pi(i) = \text{vector of state probabilities for period } i$$

$$\pi(i) = (\pi_1, \pi_2, \pi_3, \ldots, \pi_n) \qquad (19\text{-}1)$$

where

$$n = \text{the number of states, and}$$

$$\pi_1, \pi_2, \ldots, \pi_n = \text{probability of being in state 1, state 2, } \ldots, \text{ state } n.$$

In some cases, where we are only dealing with one item, such as one machine, it is possible to know with complete certainty what state this item is in. For example, if we are investigating only one machine, we may know that at this point in time the machine is functioning correctly. Then, the vector of states can be represented as follows:

states of a machine

$$\pi(1) = (1, 0)$$

where

$$\pi(1) = \text{vector of states for the machine in period 1,}$$

$$\pi_1 = 1 = \text{probability of being in the first state, and}$$

$$\pi_2 = 0 = \text{probability of being in the second state.}$$

This shows that the probability the machine is functioning correctly, state 1, is 1, and the probability that the machine is functioning incorrectly, state 2, is 0 for the first period. In most cases, however, we are dealing with more than one item.

Let's look at the vector of states for people in the small town with the three grocery stores. There could be a total of 100,000 people that shop at the three grocery stores during any given month. Forty thousand people may be shopping at American Food Store, which will be called state 1.

Thirty thousand people may be shopping at Food Mart, which will be called state 2, and 30,000 people may be shopping at Atlas Foods, which will be called state 3. The probability that a person will be shopping at one of these three grocery stores is as follows:

State 1—American Food Store: 40,000/100,000 = .40 = 40%

State 2—Food Mart   : 30,000/100,000 = .30 = 30%

State 3—Atlas Foods   : 30,000/100,000 = .30 = 30%

These probabilities can be placed in the vector of state probabilities shown below:

$$\pi(1) = (.4, .3, .3)$$

where

$\pi(1) = $ vector of state probabilities for the three grocery stores for period 1,

$\pi_1 = .4 = $ probability that a person will shop at American Food, state 1,

$\pi_2 = .3 = $ probability that a person will shop at Food Mart, state 2, and

$\pi_3 = .3 = $ probability that a person will shop at Atlas Foods, state 3.

using market shares   You should also notice that the probabilities in the vector of states for the three grocery stores represent the *market shares* for these three stores for the first period. Thus, American Food has 40% of the market, Food Mart has 30%, and Atlas Foods has 30% of the market in period 1. When we are dealing with market shares, the market shares can be used in place of probability values.

Once the initial states and state probabilities have been determined, the next step is to find the matrix of transition probabilities. This matrix is used along with the state probabilities in predicting the future.

19.3
MATRIX OF TRANSITION PROBABILITIES

The concept that allows us to get from a current state, such as market shares, to a future state is the *matrix of transition probabilities.* This is a matrix of conditional probabilities of being in a future state given a current state. The following definition is helpful:

Let $P_{ij} = $ conditional probability of being in state j in the future given the current state of i

For example, P_{12} is the probability of being in state 2 in the future given the event was in state 1 in the period before.

Let $P = $ matrix of transition probabilities

$$P = \begin{bmatrix} P_{11} & P_{12} & P_{13} \cdots & P_{1n} \\ P_{21} & P_{22} & P_{23} \cdots & P_{2n} \\ \vdots & & & \\ P_{m1} & & \cdots & P_{mn} \end{bmatrix} \qquad \textbf{(19-2)}$$

Individual P_{ij} values are usually determined empirically. For example, if we have observed over time that 10% of the people currently shopping at store 1 (or state 1) will be shopping at store 2 (state 2) next period, then we know that $P_{12} = .1$ or 10%.

Transition Probabilities for the Three Grocery Stores

Let's say we can determine the matrix of transition probabilities for the three grocery stores by using historical data. The results of our analysis appear in the following matrix:

$$P = \begin{bmatrix} .8 & .1 & .1 \\ .1 & .7 & .2 \\ .2 & .2 & .6 \end{bmatrix}$$

Recall that American Food represents state 1, Food Mart is state 2, and Atlas Foods is state 3. The meaning of these probabilities can be expressed in terms of the various states, as follows.

Row 1

$.8 = P_{11} =$ Probability of being in state 1 after being in state 1 the previous period

$.1 = P_{12} =$ Probability of being in state 2 after being in state 1 the previous period

$.1 = P_{13} =$ Probability of being in state 3 after being in state 1 the previous period

Row 2

$.1 = P_{21} =$ Probability of being in state 1 after being in state 2 the previous period

$.7 = P_{22} =$ Probability of being in state 2 after being in state 2 the previous period

$.2 = P_{23} =$ Probability of being in state 3 after being in state 2 the previous period

Row 3

$.2 = P_{31} =$ Probability of being in state 1 after being in state 3 the previous period

$.2 = P_{32} =$ Probability of being in state 2 after being in state 3 the previous period

$.6 = P_{33} =$ Probability of being in state 3 after being in state 3 the previous period

Note that the three probabilities in the top row sum to 1. The probabilities for any row in a matrix of transition probabilities will also sum to 1.

KEY IDEA

Once the state probabilities have been determined along with the matrix of transition probabilities, it is possible to predict future state probabilities.

19.4
PREDICTING FUTURE MARKET SHARES

One of the purposes of Markov analysis is to predict the future. Given the vector of state probabilities and the matrix of transition probabilities, it is not very difficult to determine the state probabilities at a future date. With this type of analysis, we are able to compute the probability that a person will be shopping at one of the grocery stores in the future. Because this probability is equivalent to market share, it is possible to determine future market shares for American Food, Food Mart, and Atlas Foods. When the current period is 1, calculating the state probabilities for the next period (period 2) can be accomplished as follows:

$$\pi(2) = \pi(1)P \tag{19-3}$$

Furthermore, if we are in any period n, we can compute the state probabilities for period $n + 1$ as follows:

$$\pi(n + 1) = \pi(n)P \tag{19-4}$$

future state

Equation 19-3 can be used to answer the question of next period's market shares for the grocery stores. The computations are:

$$\pi(2) = \pi(1)P$$

$$\pi(2) = (.4, .3, .3) \begin{bmatrix} .8 & .1 & .1 \\ .1 & .7 & .2 \\ .2 & .2 & .6 \end{bmatrix}$$

$$\pi(2) = [(.4)(.8) + (.3)(.1) + (.3)(.2), (.4)(.1) + (.3)(.7) \\ + (.3)(.2), (.4)(.1) + (.3)(.2) + (.3)(.6)]$$

$$\pi(2) = (.41, .31, .28)$$

As you can see, the market share for American Food and Food Mart has increased, while the market share for Atlas Foods has decreased. Will this trend continue in the future? Will Atlas eventually lose all of its market share? Or will a stable condition be reached for all three grocery stores? Questions such as these can be answered with a discussion of equilibrium conditions. To help introduce the concept of equilibrium, we present a second application of Markov analysis—machine breakdowns.

19.5
MARKOV ANALYSIS OF MACHINE OPERATIONS

machine matrix of transition probabilities

Paul Tolsky, owner of Tolsky Works, has recorded the operation of his milling machine for several years. Over the past two years, 80% of the time the milling machine functioned correctly during the current month if it had functioned correctly in the previous month. This also means that only 20% of the time did the machine not function correctly for a given month when it was functioning correctly during the previous month. In addition, it has been observed that 90% of the time the machine remained incorrectly adjusted for any given month if it was incorrectly adjusted the previous month. Only 10% of the time did the machine operate correctly in a given month when it did *not* operate correctly during the last month. In other words, this machine *can* correct itself when it has not been functioning correctly in the past, and this happens 10% of the time. These values can now be used to construct the matrix of transition probabilities. Again, state 1 is a situation where the machine is functioning correctly, and state 2 is

---

APPLICATIONS OF QA

Using Markov Analysis in Pavement Management Systems

The poor condition of U.S. road surfaces has received much attention both statewide and nationally. Some of the road systems, built 50 to 100 years ago, are simply falling apart. Estimates of the costs to refurbish major road systems are staggering. Thus, an effective approach to making good decisions about paving roads is essential.

A key element in effective road-paving decisions is how rapidly roads and transportation systems deteriorate over time. To achieve a better understanding of this important change process, a Markov model was developed for the Arizona Pavement Management System (PMS). The model was used to predict the timing and extent of changes in road systems. Based on probability assessments, the Markov model was able to accommodate flexible pavement decisions, to identify actions and approaches that should be taken immediately, to compare expected and actual road conditions, and to assist in developing significant cost savings over older approaches.

Source: Abbas Butt, Mohamed Shahin, Kieran Feighan, and Samuel Carpenter, "Pavement Performance Prediction Model Using the Markov Process," *Transportation Research Record* November 1986, pp. 12–19.

The overall approach in the utilization of Markov analysis was to develop a pavement condition index (PCI) based on a numerical index that ranged from 0 to 100, where 100 represented excellent road conditions. Then, a database, called PAVER, was developed to store data about road conditions. The PCI/and the PAVER database were used in the modeling approach.

Next, Markov analysis was done using the following steps:

1. Retrieving pavement-related data.

2. Filtering and scanning for data errors.

3. Identifying outlying or unusual data points.

4. Developing the Markov model.

The Markov approach allows systematic study of the changing conditions of today's road systems. Used in conjunction with other quantitative analysis techniques (for example, dynamic programming), good, and in some cases optimal, road strategies can be developed. In addition, Markov analysis can be used as a planning tool by predicting future road conditions for various time periods.

---

a situation where the machine is not functioning correctly. The matrix of transition probabilities for this machine is:

$$P = \begin{bmatrix} .8 & .2 \\ .1 & .9 \end{bmatrix}$$

where

$P_{11} = .8 =$ Probability that the machine will be *correctly* functioning this month given it was *correctly* functioning last month.

$P_{12} = .2 =$ Probability that the machine will *not* be correctly functioning this month given it was *correctly* functioning last month.

$P_{21} = .1 =$ Probability that the machine will be functioning *correctly* this month given it was *not* correctly functioning last month, and

$P_{22} = .9 =$ Probability that the machine will *not* be correctly functioning this month given that it was *not* correctly functioning last month.

Look at this matrix for the machine. The two probabilities in the top row are the probabilities of functioning correctly and not functioning correctly, given that the machine was functioning correctly in the last period. Because these are mutually exclusive and collectively exhaustive, the row probabilities again sum to 1.

What is the probability that Tolsky's machine will be functioning correctly one month from now? What is the probability that the machine will be functioning correctly in two months? To answer these questions, we again apply Equation 19-3:

$$\pi(2) = \pi(1)P$$

$$\pi(2) = (1, 0) \begin{bmatrix} .8 & .2 \\ .1 & .9 \end{bmatrix}$$

$$\pi(2) = [(1)(.8) + (0)(.1), (1)(.2) + (0)(.9)]$$

$$\pi(2) = (.8, .2)$$

Therefore, the probability that the machine will be functioning correctly one month from now, given that it is now functioning correctly, is .80. The probability that it will *not* be functioning correctly in one month is .20. Now we can use these results to determine the probability that the machine will be functioning correctly two months from now. The analysis is exactly the same:

$$\pi(3) = \pi(2)P$$

$$\pi(3) = (.8, .2) \begin{bmatrix} .8 & .2 \\ .1 & .9 \end{bmatrix}$$

$$\pi(3) = [(.8)(.8) + (.2)(.1), (.8)(.2) + (.2)(.9)]$$

$$\pi(3) = (.66, .34)$$

This means that in the third period, or month, there is a probability of .66 that the machine will still be functioning correctly. The probability that the machine will not be functioning correctly is .34. Of course, we could continue this analysis as many times as we want in computing state probabilities for future months.

19.6
EQUILIBRIUM CONDITIONS

Looking at the Tolsky machine example, it is easy to think that eventually all market shares or state probabilities will be either 0 or 1. This is usually not the case. *Equilibrium share* of the market values or probabilities are normally encountered.

One way to compute the equilibrium share of the market, or equilibrium state probabilities, is to use Markov analysis for a large number of periods. It is possible to see if the future values are approaching a stable value. For example, it is possible to repeat Markov analysis for 15 periods for Tolsky's machine. This is not too difficult to do by hand. The results for this computation appear in Table 19.1.

computing equilibrium share of market

The machine starts off functioning correctly (in state 1) in the first period. In period 5, there is only a .4934 probability that the machine is still functioning correctly, and by period 10, this probability is only .360235. In period

**TABLE 19.1 State Probabilities for the Machine
Example for 15 Periods**

PERIOD	STATE 1	STATE 2
1	1.0	.0
2	.8	.2
3	.66	.34
4	.562	.438
5	.4934	.5066
6	.44538	.55462
7	.411766	.588234
8	.388236	.611763
9	.371765	.628234
10	.360235	.639754
11	.352165	.647834
12	.346515	.653484
13	.342560	.657439
14	.339792	.660207
15	.337854	.662145

15, the probability that the machine is still functioning correctly is about .34. The probability that the machine will be functioning correctly at a future period is decreasing—but is it decreasing at a decreasing rate. What would you expect in the long run? If we made these calculations for 100 periods, what would happen? Would there be an equilibrium in this case? If the answer is *yes*, what would it be? Looking at Table 19.1, it appears that there will be an equilibrium at .333333 or $\frac{1}{3}$. But how can we be sure?

determining equilibrium conditions

By definition, an *equilibrium condition* exists if the state probabilities or market shares do not change after a large number of periods. Thus, at equilibrium, the state probabilities for a future period must be the same as the state probabilities for the current period. This fact is the key to solving for the equilibrium state probabilities. This relationship can be expressed as follows:

KEY IDEA

At equilibrium,

$$\pi(\text{next period}) = \pi(\text{this period})P$$

or

$$\pi = \pi P \qquad \qquad (19\text{-}5)$$

Equation 19-5 states that, at equilibrium, the state probabilities for the *next* period are the same as the state probabilities for the *current* period. For Tolsky's machine, this can be expressed as follows:

$$\pi = \pi P$$

$$(\pi_1, \pi_2) = (\pi_1, \pi_2) \begin{bmatrix} .8 & .2 \\ .1 & .9 \end{bmatrix}$$

Using matrix multiplication we get:

equilibrium computations

$$(\pi_1, \pi_2) = [(\pi_1)(.8) + (\pi_2)(.1), (\pi_1)(.2) + (\pi_2)(.9)]$$

The *first term* on the left-hand side, π_1, is equal to the *first term* on the right-hand side, $(\pi_1)(.8) + (\pi_2)(.1)$. In addition, the *second term* on the left-hand side, π_2, is equal to the *second term* on the right-hand side, $(\pi_1)(.2) + (\pi_2)(.9)$. This gives us the following:

$$\pi_1 = .8\pi_1 + .1\pi_2 \tag{19-6}$$

$$\pi_2 = .2\pi_1 + .9\pi_2 \tag{19-7}$$

We also know that the state probabilities, π_1 and π_2 in this case, must sum to 1. (Looking at Table 19.1, you note that π_1 and π_2 sum to 1 for all 15 periods.) We can express this property as follows:

$$\pi_1 + \pi_2 + \cdots + \pi_n = 1 \tag{19-8}$$

For Tolsky's machine, we have:

$$\pi_1 + \pi_2 = 1 \tag{19-9}$$

dropping one equation

Now, we have three equations for the machine (19-6, 19-7, and 19-9). We know that Equation 19-9 must hold. Thus, we can drop either Equation 19-6 or 19-7 and solve the remaining two equations for π_1 and π_2. It is necessary to drop one of the equations so that we end up with two unknowns and two equations. If we were solving for equilibrium conditions that involved three states, we would end up with four equations. Again, it would be necessary to drop one of the equations so that we end up with three equations and three unknowns. In general, when solving for equilibrium conditions, it will always be necessary to drop one of the equations such that the total number of equations is the same as the total number of variables that we are solving for. The reason that we can drop one of the equations is that they are mathematically interrelated. In other words, one of the equations is redundant in specifying the relationships between the various equilibrium equations.

Let us arbitrarily drop Equation 19-6. Thus, we will be solving the following two equations:

$$\pi_2 = .2\pi_1 + .9\pi_2$$

$$\pi_1 + \pi_2 = 1$$

Rearranging the first equation, we get:

$$.1\pi_2 = .2\pi_1$$

or

$$\pi_2 = 2\pi_1$$

Substituting this into Equation 19-9, we have:

$$\pi_1 + \pi_2 = 1$$

or

$$\frac{\pi_1}{20} + 2\pi_1 = 1$$

or

$$3\pi_1 = 1$$

$$\pi_1 = \frac{1}{3} = .33333333$$

Thus,

$$\pi_2 = \frac{2}{3} = .66666667$$

Compare these results with Table 19.1. As you can see, the equilibrium state probability for state 1 is .33333333, and the equilibrium state probability for state 2 is .66666667. These values are what you would expect by looking at the tabled results. This analysis indicates that it is only necessary to know the matrix of transition in determining the equilibrium market shares. The initial values for the state probabilities or the market shares do not influence the equilibrium state probabilities. The analysis for determining equilibrium state probabilities or market shares is the same when there are more states. If there are three states (as in the grocery store example), we have to solve three equations for the three equilibrium states; if there are four states, we have to solve four simultaneous equations for the four unknown equilibrium values, and so on.

matrix of transition

You may wish to prove to yourself that the equilibrium states we have just computed are, in fact, equilibrium states. This can be done by multiplying the equilibrium states times the original matrix of transition. The result will be the same equilibrium states. Performing this analysis is also an excellent way to check your answers to end-of-chapter problems or examination questions.

19.7
ABSORBING STATES AND THE FUNDAMENTAL MATRIX: AN ACCOUNTS RECEIVABLE APPLICATION

In the examples discussed thus far, we assumed that it is possible for the process or system to go from one state to any other state between any two periods. In some cases, however, if you are in a state, you cannot go to another state in the future. In other words, once you are in a given state, you are "absorbed" by it, and you will remain in that state. Any state that has this property is called an *absorbing state*. An example of this is the accounts receivable application.

absorbing states

An accounts receivable system normally places debts or receivables from its customers into one of several categories or states depending on how overdue the oldest unpaid bill is. Of course, the exact categories or states depend on the policy set by each company. Four typical states or categories for an accounts receivable application are shown below.

State 1 (π_1): Paid, all bills.

State 2 (π_2): Bad debt, overdue more than three months.

State 3 (π_3): Overdue less than one month.

State 4 (π_4): Overdue between one and three months.

At any given period, in this case one month, a customer can be in one of these four states.[2] For this example, it will be assumed that if the oldest unpaid bill is over three months due, it is automatically placed in the bad debt category. Therefore, a customer can be paid in full (state 1), have the oldest unpaid bill overdue less than one month (state 3), have the oldest unpaid bill overdue between one and three months inclusive (state 4), or have the oldest unpaid bill overdue more than three months, which is a bad debt (state 2).

matrix of transition probabilities

Like any other Markov process, we can set up a matrix of transition probabilities for these four states. This matrix will reflect the propensity of customers to move among the four accounts receivable categories from one month to the next. The probability of being in the paid category for any item or bill in a future month, given that a customer is in the paid category for a purchased item this month, is 100% or 1.0. It is impossible for a customer to completely pay for a product one month and to owe money on it in a future month. Another absorbing state is the bad debts state. If a bill is not paid in three months, we are assuming that the company will completely write it off and not try to collect it in the future. Thus, once a person is in the bad debt category, that person will remain in that category forever. For any absorbing state, the probability that a customer will be in this state in the future is 1, and the probability that a customer will be in any other state is 0.

probabilities for absorbing states

probabilities of being in various states

These values will be placed in the matrix of transition probabilities. But before we construct this matrix, we need to know the probabilities for the other two states—a debt of less than one month and a debt that is between one and three months old. For a person in the less than one month category, there is a .60 probability of being in the paid category, a 0 probability of being in the bad debt category, a .20 probability of remaining in the less than one month category, and a probability of .20 of being in the one to three month category in the next month. Note that there is a 0 probability of being in the bad debt category the next month because it is impossible to get from state 3, less than one month, to state 2, more than three months overdue, in just one month. For a person in the one to three month category, there is a .40 probability of being in the paid category, a .10 probability of being in the bad debt category, a .30 probability of being in the less than one month category, and a .20 probability of remaining in the one to three month category in the next month.

How can we get a probability of .30 of being in the one to three month category for one month, and in the one month or less category in the next month? Because these categories are determined by the oldest unpaid bill,

---

[2] You should also be aware that the four states can be placed in any order you choose. For example, it might seem more natural to order this problem with the states:

1. Paid.

2. Overdue less than one month.

3. Overdue one to three months.

4. Overdue more than three months; bad debt.

This is perfectly legitimate and the only reason this ordering is not used is to facilitate some matrix manipulations you will see shortly.

it is possible to pay one bill which is one to three months old and still have another bill that is one month or less old. In other words, any customer may have more than one outstanding bill at any point in time. With this information, it is possible to construct the matrix of transition probabilities of the problem.

| | | THE NEXT MONTH | | |
THIS MONTH	PAID	BAD DEBT	< 1 MONTH	1 TO 3 MONTHS
Paid	1	0	0	0
Bad debt	0	1	0	0
Less than 1 month	.6	0	.2	.2
1 to 3 months	.4	.1	.3	.2

Thus,

$$P = \begin{bmatrix} 1 & 0 & 0 & 0 \\ 0 & 1 & 0 & 0 \\ .6 & 0 & .2 & .2 \\ .4 & .1 & .3 & .2 \end{bmatrix}$$

If we know the fraction of the people in each of the four categories or states for any given period, we can determine the fraction of the people in these four states or categories for any future period. These fractions are placed in a vector of state probabilities and multiplied times the matrix of transition probabilities. This procedure was described in Section 4 of this chapter.

Even more interesting are the equilibrium conditions. Of course, in the long run, everyone will be either in the paid or bad debt category. This is because the categories are absorbing states. But how many people, or how much money, will be in each of these categories? Knowing the total amount of money that will be in either the paid or bad debt category will help a company manage its bad debts and cash flow. This analysis requires the use of the *fundamental matrix.*

determining equilibrium conditions

In order to obtain the fundamental matrix, it is necessary to *partition* the matrix of transition, P. This can be done as follows:

fundamental matrix

$$P = \begin{bmatrix} \overset{I}{\downarrow} & & \overset{0}{\downarrow} & \\ 1 & 0 & 0 & 0 \\ 0 & 1 & 0 & 0 \\ .6 & 0 & .2 & .2 \\ .4 & .1 & .3 & .2 \\ & \underset{A}{\uparrow} & & \underset{B}{\uparrow} \end{bmatrix}$$

(19-10)

$$I = \begin{bmatrix} 1 & 0 \\ 0 & 1 \end{bmatrix} \qquad 0 = \begin{bmatrix} 0 & 0 \\ 0 & 0 \end{bmatrix}$$

$$A = \begin{bmatrix} .6 & 0 \\ .4 & .1 \end{bmatrix} \qquad B = \begin{bmatrix} .2 & .2 \\ .3 & .2 \end{bmatrix}$$

where

> I = an identity matrix (that is, a matrix with 1s on the diagonal and 0s everyplace else), and
>
> 0 = a matrix with all zeros.

The fundamental matrix can be computed as follows:

$$F = (I - B)^{-1} \qquad \text{(19-11)}$$

In Equation 19-11, $(I - B)$ means that we subtract matrix B from matrix I. The superscript -1 means that we take the inverse of the result of $(I - B)$. Here is how we can compute the fundamental matrix for the accounts receivable application:

$$F = (I - B)^{-1}$$

or

$$F = \left(\begin{bmatrix} 1 & 0 \\ 0 & 1 \end{bmatrix} - \begin{bmatrix} .2 & .2 \\ .3 & .2 \end{bmatrix} \right)^{-1}$$

Subtracting B from I, we get

$$F = \begin{bmatrix} .8 & -.2 \\ -.3 & .8 \end{bmatrix}^{-1}$$

Taking the inverse, -1, involves several steps, described in Module A. The results of these steps are:

$$F = \begin{bmatrix} 1.38 & .34 \\ .52 & 1.38 \end{bmatrix}$$

Now we are in a position to use the fundamental matrix in computing the amount of bad debts that we could expect in the long run. First we need to multiply the fundamental matrix, F, times the matrix A. This is accomplished as follows:

$$FA = \begin{bmatrix} 1.38 & .34 \\ .52 & 1.38 \end{bmatrix} \cdot \begin{bmatrix} .6 & 0 \\ .4 & .1 \end{bmatrix}$$

or

$$FA = \begin{bmatrix} .97 & .03 \\ .86 & .14 \end{bmatrix}$$

meaning of the *FA* matrix

The new FA matrix has an important meaning. It indicates the probability that an amount in one of the nonabsorbing states will end up in one of the absorbing states. The top row of this matrix indicates the probabilities that an amount in the less than one month category will end up in the paid and the bad debt category. The probability that an amount that is less than one month overdue will be paid is .97, and the probability that an amount that is less than one month overdue will end up as a bad debt is .03. The second row has a similar interpretation for the other nonabsorbing state, which is the one to three month category. Therefore, .86 is the probability that an amount that is one to three months overdue will eventually be paid, and .14 is the probability that an amount that is one to three months overdue will never be paid, but will become a bad debt.

| **APPLICATIONS OF QA** |

Using Markov Analysis to Forecast Long-Term Care

Long-term care of elderly patients has become more important and more expensive in the past several years. Programs on television and in-depth articles in newspapers and magazines have described how dramatic increases in life expectancy have been realized. Unfortunately, the quality of life and general health of the aged has not followed suit. Many individuals who are living longer need expensive long-term care.

In order to forecast long-term care in British Columbia, Canada, a Markov model was used. This model investigated changes in traditional modes of health care and analyzed the nature and extent of required services. More than 9,000 clients, members of British Columbia's long-term care (LTC) program, were studied through data collected between 1978 and 1983. The Markov approach was able to trace movement between the following levels of health care treatment:

Source: Health Services Researcher, Vol. 22, December 1987, pp. 671–707.

1. Personal care at home or at facility.

2. Intermediate care 1 at home or at facility.

3. Intermediate care 2 at home or at facility.

4. Intermediate care 3 at home or at facility.

5. Extended care at home or at facility.

In addition to these five levels, two absorbing or inactive states were considered—one that represented a patient being discharged and one that represented a dead patient. Aggregated client data were studied.

One of the most important measures of success of health care treatment programs is adequate patient care. A key aspect of long-term health for elderly patients is forecasting health-related needs. A good forecasting procedure can be the heart of long-term planning and effective delivery of needed health care. In British Columbia's LTC program, Markov analysis was used to determine important projections of future health care needs. It is expected that this type of forecasting will provide superior health care at a reasonable cost.

This matrix can be used in a number of ways. If we know the amount of the less than one month category and the one to three month category, we can determine the amount of money that will be paid and the amount of money that will become bad debts. We let the matrix M represent the amount of money that is in each of the nonabsorbing states as follows:

matrix M

$$M = (M_1, M_2, M_3, \ldots, M_n)$$

where

n = number of nonabsorbing states,

M_1 = amount in the first state or category,

M_2 = amount in the second state or category, and

M_n = amount in the nth state or category.

Assume that there is \$2,000 in the less than one month category and \$5,000 in the one to three month category. Then M would be represented as follows:

$$M = (2000, 5000)$$

The amount of money that will end up as being paid and the amount that will end up as bad debts can be computed by multiplying the matrix

determining amount paid and bad debts

M times the FA matrix that was computed previously. Here are the computations:

Amount paid and amount in bad debts $= MFA$

$$= (2000, 5000) \begin{bmatrix} .97 & .03 \\ .86 & .14 \end{bmatrix}$$

$$= (6240, 760)$$

Thus, out of the total of $7,000 ($2,000 in the less than one month category and $5,000 in the one to three month category), $6,240 will be eventually paid, and $760 will end up as bad debts.

19.8
SOLVING MARKOV ANALYSIS PROBLEMS BY COMPUTER

AB:QM's Markov analysis program allows for a maximum of 200 periods and 20 states. In this chapter, we discussed a problem involving three food stores. The input screen and the computer output for the problem are shown in Program 19.1.

19.9
SUMMARY

With the assumptions discussed in this chapter, it was possible to use Markov analysis to predict future states and to determine equilibrium conditions. We also explored a special case of Markov analysis where there were one or more absorbing states. This involved using the fundamental matrix to determine equilibrium conditions.

In this chapter only three applications of Markov analysis were explored. We investigated Tolsky's machine, the market shares for three grocery stores, and an accounts receivable system. The applications of the method, as seen in the Bibliography, are far reaching, and any dynamic system that meets the model's assumptions can be analyzed by the Markov approach.

GLOSSARY

Markov Analysis. A type of analysis that allows us to predict the future by using the state probabilities and the matrix of transition probabilities.

State Probability. The probability of an event occurring at a point in time. Examples include the probability that a person will be shopping at a given grocery store during a given month.

Vector of State Probabilities. A collection or vector of all state probabilities for a given system or process. The vector of state probabilities could be the initial state or future state.

Market Share. The fraction of the population that shops at a particular store or market. When expressed as a fraction, market shares can be used in place of state probabilities.

PROGRAM 19.1   Using AB:QM's Markov Analysis Program

```
Markov Analysis

Problem Title :  Market Share
Number of Periods                     5
Number of ''From'' States (Row) 3          Number of ''To'' States (Col) 3


         Initial Value    State 1    State 2    State 3
State 1           .4           .8         .1         .1
State 2           .3           .1         .7         .2
State 3           .3           .2         .2         .6
```

```
Help  New  Load  Save  Edit  Run  Print  Install  Directory  Esc

***** Program Output *****

≪Transition Matrix for Each Period≫

<Initial Matrix>
-----------------------------------------------------
From\To      Value     State 1    State 2    State 3
-----------------------------------------------------
State 1       0.40     0.80000    0.10000    0.10000
State 2       0.30     0.10000    0.70000    0.20000
State 3       0.30     0.20000    0.20000    0.60000
-----------------------------------------------------


< Period  1 >
-----------------------------------------------------
From\To      Value     State 1    State 2    State 3
-----------------------------------------------------
State 1       0.41     0.80000    0.10000    0.10000
State 2       0.31     0.10000    0.70000    0.20000
State 3       0.28     0.20000    0.20000    0.60000
-----------------------------------------------------


< Period  2 >
-----------------------------------------------------
From\To      Value     State 1    State 2    State 3
-----------------------------------------------------
State 1       0.41     0.67000    0.17000    0.16000
State 2       0.31     0.19000    0.54000    0.27000
State 3       0.27     0.30000    0.28000    0.42000
-----------------------------------------------------
```

PROGRAM 19.1   continued

```
< Period  3 >
------------------------------------------------
From\To      Value    State 1    State 2    State 3
------------------------------------------------
State 1      0.42     0.58500    0.21800    0.19700
State 2      0.32     0.26000    0.45100    0.28900
State 3      0.27     0.35200    0.31000    0.33800
------------------------------------------------


< Period  4 >
------------------------------------------------
From\To      Value    State 1    State 2    State 3
------------------------------------------------
State 1      0.42     0.52920    0.25050    0.22030
State 2      0.32     0.31090    0.39950    0.28960
State 3      0.26     0.38020    0.31980    0.30000
------------------------------------------------


<<Transition Matrix for Final Period>>

< Period  5 >
------------------------------------------------
From\To      Value    State 1    State 2    State 3
------------------------------------------------
State 1      0.42     0.49247    0.27233    0.23520
State 2      0.32     0.34659    0.36866    0.28475
State 3      0.26     0.39614    0.32188    0.28198
------------------------------------------------


<<Steady State>>

    --------------------------------------------
States          Probability          Value
    --------------------------------------------
     1             0.42105            0.42
     2             0.31579            0.32
     3             0.26316            0.26
    --------------------------------------------


***** End of Output *****
```

Transition Probability. The conditional probability that we will be in a future state given a current or existing state.

Matrix of Transition Probabilities. A matrix containing all transition probabilities for a certain process or system.

Equilibrium Condition. A condition that exists when the state probabilities for a future period are the same as the state probabilities for a previous period.

Absorbing State. A state that, once entered, cannot be left. The probability of going from an absorbing state to any other state is 0.

Fundamental Matrix. A matrix that is the inverse of the I minus B matrix. It is needed to compute equilibrium conditions when absorbing states are involved.

KEY EQUATIONS

(19-1) $\pi(i) = (\pi_1, \pi_2, \pi_3, \ldots, \pi_n)$

The vector of state probabilities for period i.

(19-2) $P = \begin{bmatrix} P_{11} & P_{12} & P_{13} & \cdots & P_{1n} \\ P_{21} & P_{22} & P_{23} & \cdots & P_{2n} \\ \cdot & & & & \cdot \\ \cdot & & & & \cdot \\ \cdot & & & & \cdot \\ P_{m1} & P_{m2} & P_{m3} & & P_{mn} \end{bmatrix}$

The matrix of transition probabilities, that is, the probability of going from one state into another.

(19-3) $\pi(2) = \pi(1)P$

Formula for calculating the state 2 probabilities, given state 1 data.

(19-4) $\pi(n + 1) = \pi(n)P$

Formula for calculating the state probabilities for the period $n + 1$ if we are in period n.

(19-5) $\pi = \pi P$ at equilibrium

The equilibrium state equation used to derive equilibrium probabilities.

(19-10) $P = \left[\dfrac{I}{A} + \dfrac{0}{B} \right]$

The partition of the matrix of transition for absorbing state analysis.

(19-11) $F = (I - B)^{-1}$

The fundamental matrix, used in computing probabilities of ending up in an absorbing state.

SOLVED PROBLEMS

Solved Problem 19-1

George Walls, president of Bradley School, is concerned about declining enrollments. Bradley School is a technical college that specializes in training computer programmers and computer operators. Over the years, there has been a lot of competition among Bradley School, International Technology, and Career Academy. The three schools compete in providing education in the areas of programming, computer operations, and basic secretarial skills.

In order to gain a better understanding of which of these schools is emerging as a leader, George decided to conduct a survey. His survey looked at the number of students who transferred from one school to the other during their academic careers. On the average, Bradley School was able to retain 65% of those students it originally enrolled. Twenty percent of the students originally enrolled transferred to International Technology and 15% transferred to Career Academy. Career Academy had the highest retention rate: 90% of its students remained at Career Academy for their full academic program. George estimated that about half the students who left Career Academy went to Bradley School, while the other half went to International Technology. International Technology was able to retain 80% of its students, once they enrolled. Ten percent of the originally enrolled students transferred to Career Academy and the other 10% percent enrolled in Bradley School.

Currently, Bradley School has 40% of the market. Career Academy, a much newer school, has 35% of the market. The remaining market share—25%—consists of students attending International Technology. George would like to determine the market share for Bradley for the next year. What are the equilibrium market shares for Bradley School, International Technology, and Career Academy?

Solution

The data for this problem are summarized below:

$$\text{State 1 initial share} = .40\text{—Bradley School}$$
$$\text{State 2 initial share} = .35\text{—Career Academy}$$
$$\text{State 3 initial share} = .25\text{—International Technology}$$

The transition matrix values are:

	TO		
FROM	1 BRADLEY	2 CAREER	3 INTERNATIONAL
1 Bradley	.65	.20	.15
2 Career	.05	.90	.05
3 International	.10	.10	.80

In order for George to determine market share for Bradley School for next year, he has to multiply the current market shares times the matrix of transition probability. Here is the overall structure of these calculations:

$$(.40 \quad .35 \quad .25) \begin{bmatrix} .65 & .20 & .15 \\ .05 & .90 & .05 \\ .10 & .10 & .80 \end{bmatrix}$$

Thus, the market shares for Bradley School, International Technology, and Career Academy can be computed by multiplying the current market shares times the matrix of transition probabilities as shown. The result will be a new matrix with three numbers, each representing the market share for one of the schools. The detailed matrix computations follow:

$$\text{Market share for Bradley School} = (.40)(.65) + (.35)(.05) + (.25)(.10)$$
$$= .303$$

$$\text{Market share for Career Academy} = (.40)(.20) + (.35)(.90) + (.25)(.10)$$
$$= .420$$

$$\text{Market share for International Technology} = (.40)(.15) + (.35)(.05) + (.25)(.80)$$
$$= .278$$

Now George would like to compute the equilibrium market shares for the three schools. At equilibrium conditions, the future market share is equal to the existing or current market share times the matrix of transition probabilities. By letting the variable X represent various market shares for these three schools, it is possible to develop a general relationship that will allow us to compute equilibrium market shares:

$$\text{Let } X_1 = \text{Market share for Bradley School}$$
$$X_2 = \text{Market share for Career Academy}$$
$$X_3 = \text{Market share for International Technology}$$

At equilibrium,

$$(X_1, X_2, X_3) = (X_1, \quad X_2, \quad X_3) \begin{bmatrix} .65 & .20 & .15 \\ .05 & .90 & .05 \\ .10 & .10 & .80 \end{bmatrix}$$

The next step is to make the appropriate multiplications on the right-hand side of the equation. Doing this will allow us to obtain three equations with the three unknown X values. In addition, we also know that the sum of the market shares for any particular period must equal 1. Thus, we are able to generate four equations, which are now summarized:

$$X_1 = .65X_1 + .05X_2 + .10X_3$$
$$X_2 = .20X_1 + .90X_2 + .10X_3$$
$$X_3 = .15X_1 + .05X_2 + .80X_3$$
$$1 = X_1 + X_2 + X_3$$

Since we have four equations and only three unknowns, we are able to delete one of the top three equations, which will give us three equations and three unknowns. These equations can then be solved using standard algebraic procedures to obtain the equilibrium market share values for Bradley School, International Technology, and Career Academy. The results of these calculations are shown in the following table:

SCHOOL	MARKET SHARE
X_1 (Bradley)	.158
X_2 (Career)	.579
X_3 (International)	.263

Solved Problem 19-2

Central State University administers computer competency examinations every year. These exams allow students to "test out" of the introductory computer class held at the university. Results of the exams can be placed in one of the following four states:

State 1 = Pass all of the computer exams and be exempt from the course

State 2 = Do not pass all of the computer exams on the third attempt and be required to take the course

State 3 = Fail the computer exams on the first attempt

State 4 = Fail the computer exams on the second attempt

The course coordinator for the exams has noticed the following matrix of transition probabilities:

$$\begin{bmatrix} 1 & 0 & 0 & 0 \\ 0 & 1 & 0 & 0 \\ .8 & 0 & .1 & .1 \\ .2 & .2 & .4 & .2 \end{bmatrix}$$

Currently, there are 200 students who did not pass all of the exams on the first attempt. In addition, there are 50 students who did not pass on the second attempt. In the long run, how many students will be exempted from the course by passing the exams? How many of the 250 students will be required to take the computer course?

Solution

The transition matrix values are summarized below:

	TO			
FROM	1	2	3	4
1	1.00	.00	.00	.00
2	.00	1.00	.00	.00
3	.80	.00	.10	.10
4	.20	.20	.40	.20

The first step in determining how many students will be required to take the course and how many will be exempt from it is to partition the transition matrix into four matrices. These are the I, 0, A, and B matrices:

$$I = \begin{bmatrix} 1 & 0 \\ 0 & 1 \end{bmatrix}$$

$$0 = \begin{bmatrix} 0 & 0 \\ 0 & 0 \end{bmatrix}$$

$$A = \begin{bmatrix} .8 & 0 \\ .2 & .2 \end{bmatrix}$$

$$B = \begin{bmatrix} .1 & .1 \\ .4 & .2 \end{bmatrix}$$

The next step is to compute the fundamental matrix, which is represented by the letter F. This matrix is determined by subtracting the B matrix from the I matrix and taking the inverse of the result:

$$F = (I - B)^{-1}$$

$$F = \begin{bmatrix} 1.176 & 0.147 \\ .588 & 1.324 \end{bmatrix}$$

Now multiply the F matrix by the A matrix. This step is needed to determine how many students will be exempt from the course and how many will be required to take it. Multiplying the F matrix times the A matrix is fairly straightforward:

$$FA = \begin{bmatrix} 1.176 & .147 \\ .588 & 1.324 \end{bmatrix} \begin{bmatrix} .8 & 0 \\ .2 & .2 \end{bmatrix}$$

$$FA = \begin{bmatrix} .971 & .029 \\ .735 & .265 \end{bmatrix}$$

The final step is to multiply the results from the FA matrix by the M matrix, as shown below:

$$MFA = (200 \quad 50) \begin{bmatrix} .971 & .029 \\ .735 & .265 \end{bmatrix}$$

$$= (231 \quad 19)$$

As you can see, the MFA matrix consists of two numbers. The number of students who will be exempt from the course is 231. The number of students who will eventually have to take the course is 19.

DISCUSSION QUESTIONS AND PROBLEMS

Discussion Questions

19-1 List the assumptions that are made in Markov analysis.

19-2 What are the vector of state probabilities and the matrix of transition probabilities and how can they be determined?

19-3 Describe how we can use Markov analysis to make future predictions.

19-4 What is an equilibrium condition? How do we know that we have an equilibrium condition, and how can we compute equilibrium conditions given the matrix of transition probabilities?

19-5 What is an absorbing state? Give several examples of absorbing states.

19-6 What is the fundamental matrix, and how is it used in determining equilibrium conditions?

Problems

19-7 Ray Cahnman is the proud owner of a 1955 sports car. On any given day, Ray never knows whether or not his car will start. Ninety percent of the time it will start if it started the previous morning, and 70% of the time it will not start if it did not start the previous morning.

(a) Construct the matrix of transition probabilities.

(b) What is the probability that it will start tomorrow if it started today?

(c) What is the probability that it will start tomorrow if it did *not* start today?

: **19-8** Alan Resnik, a friend of Ray Cahnman, bet Ray five dollars that Ray's car would not start five days from now. (See Problem 19-7.)

(a) What is the probability that it will not start five days from now if it started today?

(b) What is the probability that it will not start five days from now if it did not start today?

(c) What is the probability that it will start in the long run if the matrix of transition probabilities does not change?

: **19-9** Over any given month, Dress-Rite loses 10% of its customers to Fashion, Inc. and 20% of its market to Luxury Living. But Fashion, Inc. loses 5% of its market to Dress-Rite and 10% of its market to Luxury Living each month; and Luxury Living loses 5% of its market to Fashion, Inc. and 5% of its market to Dress-Rite. At the present time, each of these clothing stores has an equal share of the market. What do you think the market shares will be next month? What will they be in three months?

: **19-10** Goodeating Dog Chow Company produces a variety of brands of dog chow. One of their best values is the 50-pound bag of Goodeating Dog Chow. George Hamilton, president of Goodeating, uses a very old machine to automatically load 50 pounds of Goodeating Chow into each bag. Unfortunately, because the machine is old, it occasionally over or under fills the bags. When the machine is *correctly* placing 50 pounds of dog chow into each bag, there is a .10 probability that the machine will only put 49 pounds in each bag the following day, and there is a .20 probability that 51 pounds will be placed in each bag the next day. If the machine is currently placing 49 pounds of dog chow in each bag, there is a .30 probability that it will put 50 pounds in each bag tomorrow and a .20 probability that it will put 51 pounds in each bag tomorrow. In addition, if the machine is placing 51 pounds in each bag today, there is a .40 probability it will place 50 pounds in each bag tomorrow and a .10 probability it will place 49 pounds in each bag tomorrow.

(a) If the machine is loading 50 pounds in each bag today, what is the probability that it will be placing 50 pounds in each bag tomorrow?

(b) Resolve part **a** when the machine is only placing 49 pounds in each bag today.

(c) Resolve part **a** when the machine is placing 51 pounds in each bag today.

: **19-11** The University of South Wisconsin has had steady enrollments over the past five years. The school has its own bookstore, called University Book Store, but there are also three private bookstores in town: Bill's Book Store, College Book Store, and Battle's Book Store. The university is concerned about the large number of students who are switching to one of the private stores. As a result, South Wisconsin's president, Andy Lange, has decided to give a student three hours of university credit to look into the problem. The following matrix of transition probabilities was obtained.

	UNIVERSITY	BILL's	COLLEGE	BATTLE's
University	.6	.2	.1	.1
Bill's	0	.7	.2	.1
College	.1	.1	.8	0
Battle's	.05	.05	.1	.8

At the present time, each of the four book stores has an equal share of the market. What will the market shares be for the next period?

: **19-12** Resolve Problem 19-10 (Goodeating Dog Chow) for five periods.

: **19-13** Andy Lange, president of the University of South Wisconsin, is concerned with the declining business at the University Book Store. (See Problem 19-11 for details.) The students tell him that the prices are simply too high. Andy, however, has decided not to lower the prices. If the same conditions exist, what long-run market shares can Andy expect for the four book stores?

: **19-14** During the day, the traffic on North Monroe Street in Quincy is fairly steady, but the traffic conditions can vary considerably from one hour to the next due to slow drivers and traffic accidents. As one driver said, "The traffic conditions on Monroe can be either fair, tolerable, or miserable." If the traffic conditions are fair in one hour, there is a 20% chance that they will be tolerable in the next hour and a 10% chance that they will be miserable. If the traffic conditions are tolerable, there is a 20% chance that they will be fair in the next hour and a 5% chance that they will be miserable. In addition, if the traffic conditions are miserable, there is a 60% chance that they will remain that way and a 30% chance that they will be fair in the next hour. If the traffic conditions are miserable at this time, what is the probability that they will be fair in two hours? What is the probability that they will be tolerable in two hours?

: **19-15** Greg Cracker, mayor of Quincy, is alarmed about the traffic conditions on Monroe Street. (See Problem 19-14.) In the long run, what percent of the time will traffic conditions be fair, tolerable, and miserable on Monroe Street?

: **19-16** The tiger minnow, which can be found in Lake Jackson and in Lake Bradford, is a small meat-eating fish. At the present time, there are 900 tiger minnows in Lake Jackson and 100 tiger minnows in Lake Bradford, but a new 10-foot-wide canal between these two lakes will soon change these numbers. Since tiger minnows eat other fish and themselves, the total population remains about the same. Bob Brite, an Eagle Scout from Troop B, has done nothing but watch the tiger minnows going through the canal. During the past month Bob has observed 90 tiger minnows go from Lake Jackson to Lake Bradford, and he has observed 5 tiger minnows go from Lake Bradford to Lake Jackson. Assuming that these migration patterns will remain the same, how many tiger minnows will be in each lake in the long run?

: **19-17** The residents of Lake Bradford are angry about the canal between Lake Bradford and Lake Jackson. This canal has allowed too many tiger minnows into Lake Bradford, and, as a result, the value of the lake property on Lake

Bradford has gone down considerably. One solution would be to place a one-way dam in the canal. This would only reduce the fraction of the tiger minnows migrating from Lake Jackson to Lake Bradford. (See Problem 19-16 for details.) In other words, the dam would have the effect of reducing the probability of a tiger minnow migrating from Lake Jackson to Lake Bradford. What would this probability have to be to restore the original number of tiger minnows in each lake?

⋮ **19-18** In Section 7 of this chapter, we investigated an accounts receivable problem. How would the paid category and the bad debt category change with the following matrix of transition probabilities?

$$P = \begin{bmatrix} 1 & 0 & 0 & 0 \\ 0 & 1 & 0 & 0 \\ .7 & 0 & .2 & .1 \\ .4 & .2 & .2 & .2 \end{bmatrix}$$

⋮ **19-19** Professor Green gives two-month computer programming courses during the summer term. Students must pass a number of exams to pass the course, and each student is given three chances to take the exams. The following states describe the possible situations that could occur.

1. State 1: Pass all of the exams and pass the course.
2. State 2: Do not pass all of the exams by the third attempt and flunk the course.
3. State 3: Fail an exam in the first attempt.
4. State 4: Fail an exam in the second attempt.

After observing several classes, Professor Green was able to obtain the following matrix of transition probabilities:

$$P = \begin{bmatrix} 1 & 0 & 0 & 0 \\ 0 & 1 & 0 & 0 \\ .6 & 0 & .1 & .3 \\ .3 & .3 & .2 & .2 \end{bmatrix}$$

At the present time there are 50 students who did not pass all exams on the first attempt, and there are 30 students who did not pass all remaining exams on the second attempt. How many students in these two groups will pass the course and how many will fail the course?

⋮ **19-20** Hicourt Industries is a commercial printing outfit in a medium-sized town in Central Florida. Its only competitors are the Printing House and Gandy Printers. Last month, Hicourt Industries had approximately 30% of the market for the printing business in the area. The Printing House had 50% of the market, and Gandy Printers had 20% of the market. The association of printers, a locally run association, had recently determined how these three printers and smaller printing operations not involved in the commercial market were able to retain their customer base. Hicourt was the most successful in keeping its customers. Eighty percent of its customers for any one month remained customers for the next month. The Printing House, on the other hand, had only a 70% retention rate. Gandy Printers was in the worst condition. Only 60% of the customers for any one month remained with the firm. In one month, the market share had significantly changed. This was very exciting to George Hicourt, president of Hicourt Industries. This month Hicourt Industries was able to obtain a 38% market share. The Printing House, on the other hand, lost market share. This month, it only had 42% of the market share. Gandy Printers remained the same; it kept its 20% of the market. Just looking at market share, George concluded that he was able to take 8% per month away from the Printing House. George estimated that in a few short months, he could basically run the Printing House out of business. His hope was to capture 80% of the total market, representing his original 30% along with the 50% share that the Printing House started off with. Will George be able to reach his goal? What market share can George expect next month? What do you think the long-term market shares will be for these three commercial printing operations? Will Hicourt Industries be able to completely run the Printing House out of business?

19-21 John Jones of Bayside Laundry has been providing cleaning and linen service for rental condominiums on the gulf coast for over 10 years. Currently, John is servicing 26 condominium developments. John's two major competitors are Cleanco, which currently services 15 condominium developments, and Beach Services, which performs laundry and cleaning services for 11 condominium developments.

Recently, John contacted Bay Bank about a loan to expand his business operations. In order to justify the loan, John has kept detailed records of his customers and the customers that he received from his two major competitors. During the last year, he was able to keep 18 of his original 26 customers. During the same period, he was able to get 1 new customer from Cleanco and 2 new customers from Beach Services. Unfortunately, John lost 6 of his original customers to Cleanco and 2 of his original customers to Beach Services during the same year. John has also learned that Cleanco has kept 80% of its current customers. He also knows that Beach Services will keep at least 50% of its customers. In order for John to get the loan from Bay Bank, he needs to show the loan officer that he will maintain an adequate share of the market. The officers of Bay Bank are concerned about the recent trends for market share, and they have decided not to give John a loan unless he will keep at least 35% of the market share in the long run. What types of equilibrium market shares can John expect? If you were an officer of Bay Bank, would you give John a loan?

Data Set Problem

19-22 Sandy Sprunger is part-owner in one of the largest quick oil change operations for a medium-sized city in the Midwest. Currently, the firm has 60% of the market. There are a total of 10 quick lubrication shops in the area. After performing some basic marketing research, Sandy has been able to capture the initial probabilities, or market shares, along with the matrix of transition, which represents probabilities that customers will switch from one quick lubrication shop to another. These values are shown in the following table:

FROM	TO									
	1	2	3	4	5	6	7	8	9	10
1	.60	.10	.10	.10	.05	.01	.01	.01	.01	.01
2	.01	.80	.01	.01	.01	.10	.01	.01	.01	.03
3	.01	.01	.70	.01	.01	.10	.01	.05	.05	.05
4	.01	.01	.01	.90	.01	.01	.01	.01	.01	.02
5	.01	.01	.01	.10	.80	.01	.03	.01	.01	.01
6	.01	.01	.01	.01	.01	.91	.01	.01	.01	.01
7	.01	.01	.01	.01	.01	.10	.70	.01	.10	.04
8	.01	.01	.01	.01	.01	.10	.03	.80	.01	.01
9	.01	.01	.01	.01	.01	.10	.01	.10	.70	.04
10	.01	.01	.01	.01	.01	.10	.10	.05	.00	.70

Initial probabilities, or market share, for shops 1 through 10 are .6, .1, .1, .1, .05, .01, .01, .01, .01 and .01.

(a) Given these data, determine market shares for the next period for each of the 10 shops.

(b) What are the equilibrium market shares?

(c) Sandy believes that the original estimates for market share were wrong. She believes that shop 1 has 40% of the market, while shop 2 has 30%. All other values are the same. If this is the case, what is the impact on market shares for next-period and equilibrium shares?

(d) A marketing consultant believes that shop 1 has tremendous appeal. She believes that this shop will retain 99% of its current market share; 1% may switch to shop 2. If the consultant is correct, will shop 1 have 90% of the market in the long run?

Sure-Sweet Sugar Mill

Sure-Sweet Sugar's latest mill is located in Livonia, Louisiana, a small town approximately 25 miles west of Baton Rouge in the heart of the sugar cane belt. In April 1985, initial plans were formulated to modernize the mill as a result of the enormous profits the sugar industry enjoyed in 1984. By November, specific details were being worked out by Pierre LeBlanc, manager of the Livonia mill, and by representatives of North American Foods, the parent corporation.

A large percentage of sugar profits was directly attributable to soaring sugar prices in 1984. Although sugar prices declined during the first half of 1985, they remained substantially higher than in the pre-1984 period. Certain factors supported the higher prices. First, the possible lifting of trade embargoes with Cuba was not expected to have a significant influence on price. Cuba had established alternative markets for her sugar during the embargo, and a removal of the embargo was not expected to substantially affect the supply of sugar in the United States.

A second reason for the higher price was the failure of consumers to endorse artificial sweeteners as a sugar substitute. The unfavorable publicity surrounding the alleged carcinogenic properties of cyclamates tended to cause certain consumers to doubt the safety of all artificial sweeteners. Consequently, consumers were willing to pay higher prices to retailers who were passing along higher costs.

The increased profits had a profound effect on sugar cane growers and sugar processors alike. The sugar cane growers of south Louisiana were planning to cultivate and plant sugar cane on farmland that had been dormant for decades. Sugar processors were discovering financial incentives for the modernization of old mills to gain additional processing capacities and efficiencies.

The incentive to modernize mills was particularly strong for Sure-Sweet Sugar because the parent company, North American Foods, needed a reliable supplier of sugar, which was a basic raw material used by many of its food processing subsidiaries. In fact, approximately 40% of Sure-Sweet Sugar's output was captive (sold to the parent corporation). As North American expected to enjoy substantial growth in the years ahead, its own demand for sugar would grow at a commensurate rate.

The Livonia Mill

Because it was the largest supplier of sugar to the parent corporation, there was particular interest in modernizing the Livonia mill. A prominent local sugar cane plantation owner built the mill in 1921. In 1957, Sure-Sweet Sugar purchased it. Over the years, capital improvements to the mill were negligible. In fact, a few pieces of the original equipment were still being used in the process. As a result, the Livonia mill's maintenance department had to manufacture many spare parts for the old equipment because vendors had stopped supplying parts for the old, somewhat obsolete machines.

A thorough modernization of the mill was planned, however. Antiquated equipment was to be replaced, and the mill's capacity was to be increased by 50%. The representatives from North American Foods stated clearly to Pierre LeBlanc and other representatives from Sure-Sweet Sugar that policies of efficiency and process reliability should guide the modernization program.

One segment of the mill that was to be modernized was the bagging operation. The existing operation consisted of an old single-line bagging system. The single-line bagging system comprised a hopper that fed a single, stationary weight-feeder that deposited the appropriate weight of sugar into a bag. The loaded bag was then dumped onto a V-belt conveyor that carried the bag through a sealing machine and finally to a packing station. At the packing station, the bags were palletized (100-pound bags) or placed into cardboard cases (less than 100-pound bags) for shipment.

The single-line system was to be replaced by a carrousel bagging system. The proposed system consisted of a carrousel weight-feeder that loads eight bags as the carrousel completes a revolution. The carrousel bagging machine would also seal the bag and deposit it on one of several V-belt conveyors for distribution in the warehouses.

Two vendors, Mechanized Transit and Amalgamated Container Co., submitted bids to supply the carrousel bagging machine. The machines from

CASE STUDY (continued)

Sure-Sweet Sugar Mill

each of these companies were almost identical in loading rates, price, and installment cost. Pierre LeBlanc and sugar engineers from Livonia mill visited plants (arranged by the vendors) and observed the operation of each bagging machine. They decided that the factor that determined selection would be process reliability, because the reliability of the bagging system was critical to the entire operation of the mill. The hoppers that fed the bagging system had a normal inventory capacity to store mill output for 12 hours if the bagging system was not in operation. Because of the planned increases in mill capacity, this inventory time had been reduced to 8 hours. (The bagging machine for both the old and the planned system had excess capacity; therefore, the inventory of sugar in the feed hoppers would be reduced quickly to create the normal inventory space of 12 and 8 hours respectively.) If the bagging system was down for more than 8 hours, the mill would have to sharply reduce rates of production or shut down. This caused severe process upsets and costly inefficiencies. Because of the problems encountered in storing large volumes of sugar in hoppers, the mill engineers decided not to expand the size of the feed hopper.

Mechanized Transit indicated that its bagging

machine had a demonstrated stream factor* of .92. Amalgamated Container Co. stated that the stream factor for its bagging machine was .88, but due to local service engineers and a spare parts distribution center located in Baton Rouge (25 miles away), the probability that its machine would be in operation within 8 hours following a major breakdown was .80. In contrast, the closest service center for Mechanized Transit was in Atlanta, Georgia. Hence, Mechanized Transit could commit only to a .30 probability that its machine would be in operation within 8 hours following a major breakdown. The duration of very unusual breakdowns (those that would halt operations of both machines for periods in excess of 8 hours) was determined to be equal for both machines. LeBlanc pondered his purchasing decision.

1. Considering the process reliability as a major objective, which machine would you recommend?

2. What problems are encountered in most operations when there is either a sharp curtailment in production rates or a shutdown?

3. What additional information would be of value to LeBlanc in his purchasing decision?

Source: Jerry Kinard (Francis Marion College) and Joe C. Iverstine (deceased). Used with permission of author.

* Stream factor is the percentage of time that a given piece of equipment is operable.

Burgers Galore

Born and raised in New Orleans, Rick Lamothe has seen a lot for his age. The French Quarter, the Garden District, the Lake area, and many other areas of New Orleans each have a distinct flavor and characteristic. After graduating from the University of New Orleans, Rick had many outstanding job offers. Unfortunately, all of them were out of the city of New Orleans. As a result, Rick decided to take a low-level management job with a new company in the fast-foods industry. The small and new company Rick worked for was called New Orleans Fried Chicken. Both a mild and spicy version of the fried chicken were available. This was very similar to another local fried chicken operation, named Domino's after a famous musician.

The owners of New Orleans Fried Chicken, however, had their eyes on large profits and a national franchise. Within a matter of years, New Orleans Fried Chicken franchises could be seen throughout the United States and in select locations throughout the world. During this time, Rick quickly advanced within the company and learned the ins and outs of the fast-food industry.

It was during these two years that Rick decided to venture out on his own and to apply the same success formula used by New Orleans Fried Chicken. Because Rick signed a noncompetitive contract when employed by New Orleans Fried Chicken, he would have to look for another type of fast food. He decided on the fast-food hamburger industry.

The two major competitors for hamburgers in the New Orleans area were McDaniels and Burger Zing. In under a year and a half, Rick had started his new company, Burgers Galore, and had made some progress in the hamburger market. Rick estimated that he had approximately 6% of the market. McDaniels had approximately 80% of the market and Burger Zing had approximately 14% of the market.

Rick's plan was to establish several Burgers Galore restaurants in New Orleans, and if successful, try to franchise Burgers Galore at a national level. To distinguish Burgers Galore from McDaniels and Burger Zing, Rick decided to go after a more adult hamburger market. Instead of advertising cookies for kids or toys and trinkets, Rick decided to give away tickets to movies and small gift certificates at local department stores. He even established an advertising campaign that showed a James Bond-like figure encountering all types of danger above water and below to obtain a burger and fries from Burgers Galore.

Rick's promotional campaign and advertising pieces were so successful that he started to gain market share. To help plan for future expansion, Rick decided to conduct a marketing survey to help him predict future market share for Burgers Galore as well as McDaniels and Burger Zing. The survey would canvass 10,000 people and analyze their propensity to change from one burger establishment to another.

As expected, the sample of 10,000 people closely reflected the current market share. McDaniels had a total of 8,000 customers, Burger Zing had 1,400 customers, and Burgers Galore had only 600 customers. An analysis of customers for each of the three burger establishments was very interesting. Of the 8,000 McDaniels customers, it was estimated that only 5,200 would remain with McDaniels. The survey indicated that 2,000 customers would switch to Burgers Galore, while 800 would switch to Burger Zing. Burger Zing, which started with 1,400 customers, would retain 910 customers, according to the survey; 140 customers would switch to McDaniels, and 350 customers would switch to Burgers Galore. Finally, the analysis revealed that of the 600 Burgers Galore customers, 510 would remain loyal to Burgers Galore. Only 30 would switch to McDaniels, while 60 would switch to Burger Zing.

To Rick, the results of the survey were confusing. It was obvious that a lot of switching from one burger establishment to another was going on. Furthermore, these switches were expected to take place within a month. What would happen in the next few months, and what would happen over the years? These were important questions that needed answers.

1. If the survey accurately reveals how customers will switch from one burger establishment to another, what can Rick expect in terms of his market share in one month?

2. What will Rick's market share be in three months, assuming that the results of the survey,

CASE STUDY (continued)

Burgers Galore

revealing customer propensity to change, remain the same?

3. If the market conditions for burger establishments and the propensity of customers to

change remain the same, what will the market share for McDaniels, Burger Zing, and Burgers Galore be in the long run? Could Burgers Galore end up with more than 50% of the market in New Orleans?

BIBLIOGRAPHY

Blumental, R. *Markov Process and Potential Theory.* New York: Academic Press, Inc. 1968.

Bowein, O. T. "The Refunding Decision." *Journal of Finance* March 1966.

Chung, K. H. "A Markov Chain Model of Human Needs: An Extension of Maslow's Need Theory." *Academy of Management Journal* Vol. 12, No. 2, June 1969, p. 223.

Butt, Abbas A., Shahin, Mohamed Y., Feighan, Kieran J., and Carpenter, Samuel H. "Pavement Performance Prediction Model Using the Markov Process." *Transportation Research Record* 1123, November 1986, pp. 12–19.

Derman, C. *Finite State Markov Decision Process.* New York: Academic Press, Inc., 1970.

Derman, C. "Optimal Replacement and Maintenance under Markov Deterioration with Probability Bounds on Failure." *Management Science* Vol. 9, January 1963.

Ehrenberg, A. "An Appraisal of Markov Brand-Switching Models." *Journal of Marketing Research* Vol. 2, November 1965, pp. 347–62.

Eppen, G., and Fama, E. "Solutions for Cash Balance and Simple Dynamic Portfolio Problems." *Journal of Business* Vol. 41, January 1968.

Freedman, D. *Markov Chains.* San Francisco: Holden-Day, Inc., 1971.

Goldenberg, D. H. "Trading Frictions and Futures Price Movements." *Journal of Financial and Quantitative Analysis* Vol. 23, December 1988, pp. 465–481.

Hannan, Edward L. "A Markov Sensitivity Model for Examining the Impact of Cost Allocation in Hospitals." *Journal of the Operational Research Society* Vol. 35, No. 2, February 1984, pp. 117–129.

Hipp, S. K., and Holzbaur, U. D. "Decision Processes with Monotone Hysteretic Policies." *Operations Research* Vol. 36, July–August 1988, pp. 585–588.

Howard, R. A. *Dynamic Programming and Markov Processes.* New York: John Wiley & Sons, 1960.

Judge, G. G., and Zellner, A. *Estimating the Parameters of the Markov Probability Model From Aggregate Time Series Data.* 2nd ed. Amsterdam, N.Y.: North Holland, 1977.

Kallberg, J. G., and Saunders, A. "Markov Chain Approaches to the Analysis of Payment Behavior of Retail Credit Customers." *Financial Management* Vol. 12, No. 2, 1983, pp. 5–14.

Lal, R., and Bhat, U. N. "Reduced Systems Algorithms for Markov Chain" *Management Science* Vol. 34, October 1988, pp. 1202–1220.

Liebman, L. H. "A Markov Decision Model for Selecting Optimal Credit Card Control Policies." *Management Science* Vol. 28, June 1972.

Martin, J. *Bayesian Decision Problems and Markov Chains.* New York: John Wiley & Sons, Inc., 1967.

Meliha, D. "Markov Processes and Credit Collection Policy." *Decision Sciences* Vol. 3, April 1972.

Monahan, George E. "Optimal Advertising with Stochastic Demand." *Management Science* Vol. 29, No. 1, January 1983, pp. 106–117.

Monahan, George E. "A Survey of Partially Observable Markov Decision Process: Theory, Models, and Algorithms." *Management Science* Vol. 28, No. 1, January 1982, pp. 1–16.

Render, B., Stair, R. M. and Greenberg, Irwin. *Cases and Readings in Quantitative Analysis* Second Edition. Boston: Allyn and Bacon, Inc., 1990.

Shanthikumar, J. G., and Tien, C. C. "An Algorithm Solution to Two-Stage Transfer Lines with the Possible Scrapping of Units." *Management Science* Vol. 29, No. 9, September 1983, pp. 1069–1086.

Swersey, Arthur J. "A Markovian Decision Model for Deciding How Many Fire Companies to Dispatch." *Management Science* Vol. 28, No. 4, April 1982, pp. 352–365.

Szpankowski, W. "Stability Conditions for Multidimensional Queueing Systems with Computer Applications." *Operations Research* Vol. 36, November–December 1988, pp. 944–957.

White, Douglas John. *Finite Dynamic Programming: An Approach to Finite Markov Decision Processes.* New York: John Wiley, 1978.

White, Douglas John. "Real Applications to Markov Decision Processes." *Interfaces* Vol. 15, November–December 1985, pp. 73–83.

Wort, Donald H., and Zumwalt, J. Kenton. "The Trade Discount Decision: A Markov Chain Approach." *Decision Sciences* Vol. 16, No. 1, Winter 1985, pp. 43–56.

Modules

Mathematical Tools: Determinants and Matrices

A.1
INTRODUCTION

Two new mathematical concepts, determinants and matrices, are introduced in this module. These tools are especially useful in Chapter 19 and Module B, which deal with Markov analysis and game theory, but they are also handy computational aids for many other quantitative analysis problems, including linear programming, the topic of Chapters 10, 11, 12, and 13.

A.2
DETERMINANTS

A *determinant* is simply a square array of numbers arranged in rows and columns. Every determinant has a unique numerical value for which we can solve. As a mathematical tool, determinants are of value in helping to solve a series of simultaneous equations.

determinants help solve simultaneous equations

A 2-row-by-2-column (2 × 2) determinant will have the following form, where *a, b, c,* and *d* are numbers.

$$\begin{vmatrix} a & b \\ c & d \end{vmatrix}$$

Similarly, a 3 × 3 determinant has 9 entries.

$$\begin{vmatrix} a & b & c \\ d & e & f \\ g & h & i \end{vmatrix}$$

primary and secondary diagonals

One common procedure for finding the numerical value of a 2 × 2 or 3 × 3 determinant is to draw its primary and secondary diagonals. In the case of a 2 × 2 determinant, the value is found by multiplying the numbers on the primary diagonal and subtracting from that product the product of the numbers on the secondary diagonal:

$$\text{Value} = (a)(d) - (c)(b)$$

Primary diagonal ⟶ $\begin{vmatrix} a & b \\ c & d \end{vmatrix}$ ⟵ *Secondary diagonal*

For a 3 × 3 determinant, we redraw the first two columns to help visualize all diagonals and follow a similar procedure.

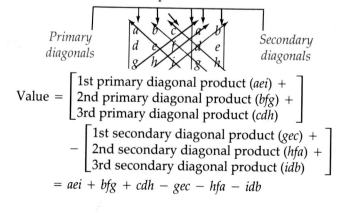

Primary diagonals / *Secondary diagonals*

$$\text{Value} = \begin{bmatrix} \text{1st primary diagonal product } (aei) + \\ \text{2nd primary diagonal product } (bfg) + \\ \text{3rd primary diagonal product } (cdh) \end{bmatrix}$$

$$- \begin{bmatrix} \text{1st secondary diagonal product } (gec) + \\ \text{2nd secondary diagonal product } (hfa) + \\ \text{3rd secondary diagonal product } (idb) \end{bmatrix}$$

$$= aei + bfg + cdh - gec - hfa - idb$$

Let's use this approach to find the numerical values of the following 2×2 and 3×3 determinants:

(a) $\begin{vmatrix} 2 & 5 \\ 1 & 8 \end{vmatrix}$

(b) $\begin{vmatrix} 3 & 1 & 2 \\ 2 & 5 & 1 \\ 4 & -2 & -1 \end{vmatrix}$

(a) $\begin{vmatrix} 2 & 5 \\ 1 & 8 \end{vmatrix}$ Value $= (2)(8) - (1)(5) = 11$

(b) $\begin{vmatrix} 3 & 1 & 2 & 3 & 1 \\ 2 & 5 & 1 & 2 & 5 \\ 4 & -2 & -1 & 4 & -2 \end{vmatrix}$

Value $= (3)(5)(-1) + (1)(1)(4) + (2)(2)(-2) - (4)(5)(2) - (-2)(1)(3)$
$\qquad - (-1)(2)(1)$
$\qquad = -15 + 4 - 8 - 40 + 6 + 2 = -51$

A set of *simultaneous equations* may be solved through the use of determinants by setting up a ratio of two special determinants for each unknown variable. This fairly easy procedure is best illustrated with an example.

Given the three simultaneous equations

$$2X + 3Y + 1Z = 10$$
$$4X - 1Y - 2Z = 8$$
$$5X + 2Y - 3Z = 6$$

simultaneous equations

we may structure determinants to help solve for unknown quantities X, Y, and Z.

Coefficients for right-hand side
Coefficients for Y
Coefficients for Z

$$X = \frac{\begin{vmatrix} 10 & 3 & 1 \\ 8 & -1 & -2 \\ 6 & 2 & -3 \end{vmatrix}}{\begin{vmatrix} 2 & 3 & 1 \\ 4 & -1 & -2 \\ 5 & 2 & -3 \end{vmatrix}}$$

Numerator determinant, in which column with Xs is replaced by column of numbers to the right-hand side of the equal sign

Denominator determinant, in which coefficients of all unknown variables are listed (all columns to the left of the equal sign)

Coefficients for Z
Coefficients for Y
Coefficients for X

$$Y = \frac{\begin{vmatrix} 2 & 10 & 1 \\ 4 & 8 & -2 \\ 5 & 6 & -3 \end{vmatrix}}{\begin{vmatrix} 2 & 3 & 1 \\ 4 & -1 & -2 \\ 5 & 2 & -3 \end{vmatrix}}$$

Numerator determinant, in which column with Ys is replaced by right-hand side numbers

Denominator determinant stays the same regardless of which variable we are solving for

$$Z = \frac{\begin{vmatrix} 2 & 3 & 10 \\ 4 & -1 & 8 \\ 5 & 2 & 6 \end{vmatrix}}{\begin{vmatrix} 2 & 3 & 1 \\ 4 & -1 & -2 \\ 5 & 2 & -3 \end{vmatrix}}$$

Numerator determinant, in which column with Zs is replaced by right-hand side numbers

Denominator determinant, again the same as when solving for X and Y

Determining the values of X, Y, and Z now involves finding the numerical values of the four separate determinants using the method shown earlier in this module.

$$X = \frac{\text{Numerical value of numerator determinant}}{\text{Numerical value of denominator determinant}} = \frac{128}{33} = 3.88$$

$$Y = \frac{-20}{33} = -.61$$

$$Z = \frac{134}{33} = 4.06$$

verifying the solution

To verify that $X = 3.88$, $Y = -.61$, and $Z = 4.06$, we may choose any one of the original three simultaneous equations and insert these numbers. For example,

$$2X + 3Y + 1Z = 10$$
$$2(3.88) + 3(-.61) + 1(4.06) = 7.76 - 1.83 + 4.06 = 10$$

A.3
MATRICES

A *matrix*, like a determinant, can also be defined as an array of numbers arranged in rows and columns. Matrices, which are usually enclosed in parentheses or brackets, have no numerical value as do determinants, but are used as an effective means of presenting or summarizing business data.

matrices help summarize data

The following 2-row-by-3-column (2 × 3) matrix, for example, might be used by television station executives to describe the channel switching behavior of their 5 o'clock TV news audience.

AUDIENCE SWITCHING PROBABILITIES, NEXT MONTH'S ACTIVITY				
CURRENT STATION	CHANNEL 6	CHANNEL 8	STOP VIEWING	2 × 3 matrix
Channel 6	.80	.15	.05	
Channel 8	.20	.70	.10	

The number in the first row and first column indicates that there is a .80 probability that someone currently watching the Channel 6 news will continue to do so next month. Likewise, 15% of Channel 6's viewers are expected to switch to Channel 8 next month (row 1, column 2), 5% will not be watching the 5 o'clock news at all (row 1, column 3), and so on for the second row.

The remainder of this module deals with the numerous mathematical operations that can be performed on matrices. These include matrix addition, subtraction and multiplication, transposing a matrix, finding its cofactors and adjoint, and matrix inversion.

Matrix Addition and Subtraction

Matrix addition and *subtraction* are the easiest operations. Matrices of the same dimensions, that is, the same number of rows and columns, can be added or subtracted by adding or subtracting the numbers in the same row and column of each matrix. Here are two small matrices:

$$\text{matrix } A = \begin{pmatrix} 5 & 7 \\ 2 & 1 \end{pmatrix}$$

$$\text{matrix } B = \begin{pmatrix} 3 & 6 \\ 3 & 8 \end{pmatrix}$$

To find the sum of these 2×2 matrices, we add corresponding elements to create a new matrix.

$$\text{matrix } C = \text{matrix } A + \text{matrix } B = \begin{pmatrix} 5 & 7 \\ 2 & 1 \end{pmatrix} + \begin{pmatrix} 3 & 6 \\ 3 & 8 \end{pmatrix} = \begin{pmatrix} 8 & 13 \\ 5 & 9 \end{pmatrix}$$

adding matrices

To subtract matrix B from matrix A, we simply subtract the corresponding elements in each position.

$$\text{matrix } C = \text{matrix } A - \text{matrix } B = \begin{pmatrix} 5 & 7 \\ 2 & 1 \end{pmatrix} - \begin{pmatrix} 3 & 6 \\ 3 & 8 \end{pmatrix} = \begin{pmatrix} 2 & 1 \\ -1 & -7 \end{pmatrix}$$

subtracting matrices

Matrix Multiplication

Matrix multiplication is an operation that may take place *only* if the number of columns in the first matrix equals the number of rows in the second matrix. Thus, matrices of the dimensions in the table below may be multiplied.

MATRIX A SIZE	MATRIX B SIZE	SIZE OF A × B RESULTING
3 × 3	3 × 3	3 × 3
3 × 1	1 × 3	3 × 3
3 × 1	1 × 1	3 × 1
2 × 4	4 × 3	2 × 3
6 × 9	9 × 2	6 × 2
8 × 3	3 × 6	8 × 6

matrix dimensions

We also note, in the far right column in the table, that the outer two numbers in the matrix sizes determine the dimensions of the new matrix. That is, if an 8-row-by-3-column matrix is multiplied by a 3-row-by-6-column matrix, the resultant product will be an 8-row-by-6-column matrix.

Matrices of the dimensions in the following table may *not* be multiplied.

MATRIX A SIZE	MATRIX B SIZE
3 × 4	3 × 3
1 × 2	1 × 2
6 × 9	8 × 9
2 × 2	3 × 3

To actually perform the multiplication process, we take each row of the first matrix and multiply its elements times the numbers in each column of the second matrix. Hence, the number in the first row and first column

multiplying two matrices

of the new matrix is derived from the product of the first row of the first matrix times the first column of the second matrix. Likewise, the number in the first row and second column of the new matrix is the product of the first row of the first matrix times the second column of the second matrix. This concept is not nearly as confusing as it may sound.

Let us begin by computing the value of matrix C, which is the product of matrix A times matrix B.

$$\text{matrix } A = \begin{pmatrix} 5 \\ 2 \\ 3 \end{pmatrix} \qquad \text{matrix } B = (4 \quad 6)$$

This is a legitimate task since matrix A is 3 × 1 and matrix B is 1 × 2. The product, matrix C, will have 3 rows and 2 columns (3 × 2).

Symbolically, the operation is matrix A × matrix B = matrix C

$$\begin{pmatrix} a \\ b \\ c \end{pmatrix} \times (d \quad e) = \begin{pmatrix} ad & ae \\ bd & be \\ cd & ce \end{pmatrix} \tag{A-1}$$

Using the actual numbers, we have

$$\begin{pmatrix} 5 \\ 2 \\ 3 \end{pmatrix} \times (4 \quad 6) = \begin{pmatrix} 20 & 30 \\ 8 & 12 \\ 12 & 18 \end{pmatrix} = \text{matrix } C$$

As a second example, let matrix R be (6 2 5) and matrix S be

$$\begin{pmatrix} 3 \\ 1 \\ 2 \end{pmatrix}$$

Then the product, matrix T = matrix R × matrix S, will be of dimension 1 × 1 since we are multiplying a 1 × 3 matrix by a 3 × 1 matrix.

$$\begin{array}{ccc} \text{matrix } R \times & \text{matrix } S = & \text{matrix } T \\ (1 \times 3) & (3 \times 1) & (1 \times 1) \end{array}$$

$$(a \quad b \quad c) \times \begin{pmatrix} d \\ e \\ f \end{pmatrix} = \quad (ad + be + cf)$$

$$(6 \quad 2 \quad 5 \ ) \times \begin{pmatrix} 3 \\ 1 \\ 2 \end{pmatrix} = \quad ((6)(3) + (2)(1) + (5)(2)) = (30)$$

To multiply any larger-sized matrices, we combine the approaches of the preceding examples.

$$\text{matrix } U = \begin{pmatrix} 6 & 2 \\ 7 & 1 \end{pmatrix} \qquad \text{matrix } V = \begin{pmatrix} 3 & 4 \\ 5 & 8 \end{pmatrix}$$

$$\begin{array}{ccc} \text{matrix } U \times \text{matrix } V = & & \text{matrix } Y \\ (2 \times 2) \quad (2 \times 2) & & (2 \times 2) \end{array}$$

$$\begin{pmatrix} a & b \\ c & d \end{pmatrix} \times \begin{pmatrix} e & f \\ g & h \end{pmatrix} = \begin{pmatrix} ae + bg & af + bh \\ ce + dg & cf + dh \end{pmatrix} \tag{A-2}$$

$$\begin{pmatrix} 6 & 2 \\ 7 & 1 \end{pmatrix} \times \begin{pmatrix} 3 & 4 \\ 5 & 8 \end{pmatrix} = \begin{pmatrix} 18 + 10 & 24 + 16 \\ 21 + 5 & 28 + 8 \end{pmatrix} = \begin{pmatrix} 28 & 40 \\ 26 & 36 \end{pmatrix}$$

To introduce a special type of matrix, called the *identity matrix*, let's try **identity matrix** a final multiplication example.

$$\text{matrix } H = \begin{pmatrix} 4 & 7 \\ 2 & 3 \end{pmatrix} \qquad \text{matrix } I = \begin{pmatrix} 1 & 0 \\ 0 & 1 \end{pmatrix}$$

$$\text{matrix } H \times \text{matrix } I = \text{matrix } J$$

$$\begin{pmatrix} 4 & 7 \\ 2 & 3 \end{pmatrix} \times \begin{pmatrix} 1 & 0 \\ 0 & 1 \end{pmatrix} = \begin{pmatrix} 4 + 0 & 0 + 7 \\ 2 + 0 & 0 + 3 \end{pmatrix} = \begin{pmatrix} 4 & 7 \\ 2 & 3 \end{pmatrix}$$

Matrix I is called an identity matrix. An identity matrix has 1s on its diagonal and 0s in all other positions. When multiplied by any matrix of the same square dimensions, it yields the original matrix. So in this case, matrix J = matrix H.

Matrix multiplication can also be useful in performing business computations.

Blank Plumbing and Heating is about to bid on three contract jobs—to install plumbing fixtures in a new university dormitory, an office building, and an apartment complex.

The number of toilets, sinks, and bathtubs needed at each project is summarized in matrix notation as follows. The cost per plumbing fixture is also given. Matrix multiplication may be used to provide an estimate of total cost of fixtures at each job.

PROJECT	DEMAND				COST/UNIT	
	Toilets	Sinks	Bathtubs			
Dormitory	5	10	2	Toilet	$40	
Office	20	20	0	Sink	$25	
Apartments	15	30	15	Bathtub	$50	

Job demand matrix × Fixture cost matrix = Job cost matrix
    (3 × 3)   (3 × 1)   (3 × 1)

$$\begin{pmatrix} 5 & 10 & 2 \\ 20 & 20 & 0 \\ 15 & 30 & 15 \end{pmatrix} \times \begin{pmatrix} \$40 \\ \$25 \\ \$50 \end{pmatrix} = \begin{pmatrix} \$200 + 250 + 100 \\ \$800 + 500 + 0 \\ \$600 + 750 + 750 \end{pmatrix} = \begin{pmatrix} \$ 550 \\ \$1{,}300 \\ \$2{,}100 \end{pmatrix}$$

Hence, Blank Plumbing can expect to spend $550 on fixtures at the dormitory project, $1,300 at the office building, and $2,100 at the apartment complex.

Matrix Transpose

The *transpose* of a matrix is a means of presenting data in a different form. To create the transpose of a given matrix, we simply interchange the rows with the columns. Hence, the first row of a matrix becomes its first column, the second row becomes the second column, and so on.

Two matrices are transposed here:

$$\text{matrix } A = \begin{pmatrix} 5 & 2 & 6 \\ 3 & 0 & 9 \\ 1 & 4 & 8 \end{pmatrix}$$

$$\text{Transpose of matrix } A = \begin{pmatrix} 5 & 3 & 1 \\ 2 & 0 & 4 \\ 6 & 9 & 8 \end{pmatrix}$$

transposing matrices

$$\text{matrix } B = \begin{pmatrix} 2 & 7 & 0 & 3 \\ 8 & 5 & 6 & 4 \end{pmatrix}$$

$$\text{Transpose of matrix } B = \begin{pmatrix} 2 & 8 \\ 7 & 5 \\ 0 & 6 \\ 3 & 4 \end{pmatrix}$$

Matrix of Cofactors and Adjoint

Two more useful concepts in the mathematics of matrices are the *matrix of cofactors* and the *adjoint* of a matrix. A *cofactor* is defined as the set of numbers that remains after a given row and column have been taken out of a matrix. An *adjoint* is simply the transpose of the matrix of cofactors. The real value of the two concepts lies in their usefulness in forming the inverse of a matrix—something that we investigate in the next section.

In order to compute the matrix of cofactors for a particular matrix, we proceed as follows.

computing a cofactor

1. Select an element in the original matrix.

2. Draw a line through the row and column of the element selected. The numbers uncovered represent the cofactor for that element.

3. Calculate the value of the determinant of the cofactor.

4. Add together the location numbers of the row and column crossed out in step 2. If the sum is even, the sign of the determinant's value (from step 3) does not change. If the sum is an odd number, change the sign of the determinant's value.

5. The number just computed becomes an entry in the matrix of cofactors; it is located in the same position as the element selected in step 1.

6. Return to step 1 and continue until all elements in the original matrix have been replaced by their cofactor values.

Let's compute the matrix of cofactors, and then the adjoint, for the following matrix.

$$\begin{pmatrix} 3 & 7 & 5 \\ 2 & 0 & 3 \\ 4 & 1 & 8 \end{pmatrix}$$

$$\text{Matrix of cofactors} = \begin{pmatrix} -3 & -4 & 2 \\ -51 & 4 & 25 \\ 21 & 1 & -14 \end{pmatrix} \qquad \text{(from Table A.1)}$$

$$\text{Adjoint of the matrix} = \begin{pmatrix} -3 & -51 & 21 \\ -4 & 4 & 1 \\ 2 & 25 & -14 \end{pmatrix}$$

TABLE A.1 Matrix of Cofactor Calculations

ELEMENT REMOVED	COFACTORS	DETERMINANT OF COFACTORS	VALUE OF COFACTOR
Row 1, Column 1	$\begin{pmatrix} 0 & 3 \\ 1 & 8 \end{pmatrix}$	$\begin{vmatrix} 0 & 3 \\ 1 & 8 \end{vmatrix} = -3$	−3 (sign not changed)
Row 1, Column 2	$\begin{pmatrix} 2 & 3 \\ 4 & 8 \end{pmatrix}$	$\begin{vmatrix} 2 & 3 \\ 4 & 8 \end{vmatrix} = 4$	−4 (sign changed)
Row 1, Column 3	$\begin{pmatrix} 2 & 0 \\ 4 & 1 \end{pmatrix}$	$\begin{vmatrix} 2 & 0 \\ 4 & 1 \end{vmatrix} = 2$	2 (sign not changed)
Row 2, Column 1	$\begin{pmatrix} 7 & 5 \\ 1 & 8 \end{pmatrix}$	$\begin{vmatrix} 7 & 5 \\ 1 & 8 \end{vmatrix} = 51$	−51 (sign changed)
Row 2, Column 2	$\begin{pmatrix} 3 & 5 \\ 4 & 8 \end{pmatrix}$	$\begin{vmatrix} 3 & 5 \\ 4 & 8 \end{vmatrix} = 4$	4 (sign not changed)
Row 2, Column 3	$\begin{pmatrix} 3 & 7 \\ 4 & 1 \end{pmatrix}$	$\begin{vmatrix} 3 & 7 \\ 4 & 1 \end{vmatrix} = -25$	25 (sign changed)
Row 3, Column 1	$\begin{pmatrix} 7 & 5 \\ 0 & 3 \end{pmatrix}$	$\begin{vmatrix} 7 & 5 \\ 0 & 3 \end{vmatrix} = 21$	21 (sign not changed)
Row 3, Column 2	$\begin{pmatrix} 3 & 5 \\ 2 & 3 \end{pmatrix}$	$\begin{vmatrix} 3 & 5 \\ 2 & 3 \end{vmatrix} = -1$	1 (sign changed)
Row 3, Column 3	$\begin{pmatrix} 3 & 7 \\ 2 & 0 \end{pmatrix}$	$\begin{vmatrix} 3 & 7 \\ 2 & 0 \end{vmatrix} = -14$	−14 (sign not changed)

Finding the Inverse of a Matrix

The *inverse* of a matrix is a unique matrix of the same dimensions which, when multiplied by the original matrix, produces a *unit* or *identity* matrix. For example, if A is any 2×2 matrix, and its inverse is denoted A^{-1}, then

$$A \times A^{-1} = \begin{pmatrix} 1 & 0 \\ 0 & 1 \end{pmatrix} = \text{Identity matrix} \qquad \text{(A-3)}$$

The adjoint of a matrix is extremely helpful in forming the inverse of the original matrix. We simply compute the value of the determinant of the original matrix and divide each term of the adjoint by this value.   **using the adjoint to compute the inverse**

To find the inverse of the matrix just presented, we need to know the adjoint (already computed) and the value of the determinant of the original matrix.

$$\begin{pmatrix} 3 & 7 & 5 \\ 2 & 0 & 3 \\ 4 & 1 & 8 \end{pmatrix} = \text{Original matrix}$$

Value of determinant

$$\begin{vmatrix} 3 & 7 & 5 & 3 & 7 \\ 2 & 0 & 3 & 2 & 0 \\ 4 & 1 & 8 & 4 & 1 \end{vmatrix}$$

Value $= 0 + 84 + 10 - 0 - 9 - 112 = -27$

The inverse is found by dividing each element in the adjoint by -27.

$$\text{Inverse} = \begin{pmatrix} -3/-27 & -51/-27 & 21/-27 \\ -4/-27 & 4/-27 & 1/-27 \\ 2/-27 & 25/-27 & -14/-27 \end{pmatrix} = \begin{pmatrix} 3/27 & 51/27 & -21/27 \\ 4/27 & -4/27 & -1/27 \\ -2/27 & -25/27 & 14/27 \end{pmatrix}$$

We may verify that this is indeed the correct inverse of the original matrix by multiplying the original matrix times the inverse.

Original matrix ×   Inverse   = Identity matrix

verifying the results

$$\begin{pmatrix} 3 & 7 & 5 \\ 2 & 0 & 3 \\ 4 & 1 & 8 \end{pmatrix} \times \begin{pmatrix} 3/27 & 51/27 & -21/27 \\ 4/27 & -4/27 & -1/27 \\ -2/27 & -25/27 & 14/27 \end{pmatrix} = \begin{pmatrix} 1 & 0 & 0 \\ 0 & 1 & 0 \\ 0 & 0 & 1 \end{pmatrix}$$

A.4
SUMMARY

This module contained a brief presentation of determinants and matrices, two mathematical tools often used in quantitative analysis. Determinants are useful in solving a series of simultaneous equations. Matrices are the basis for the simplex method of linear programming. The module's discussion included matrix addition, subtraction, multiplication, transposition, cofactors, adjoints, and inverses.

GLOSSARY

Determinant. A square array of numbers arranged in rows and columns. Every determinant has a unique numerical value.

Simultaneous Equations. A series of equations that must be solved at the same time.

Matrix. An array of numbers that can be used to present or summarize business data.

Identity Matrix. A square matrix with 1s on its diagonal and 0s in all other positions.

Transpose. The interchange of rows and columns in a matrix.

Matrix of cofactors. The determinants of the numbers remaining in a matrix after a given row and column have been removed.

Adjoint. The transpose of a matrix of cofactors.

Inverse. A unique matrix that may be multiplied by the original matrix to create an identity matrix.

Problems

A-1 Find the numerical values of the following determinants.

(a) $\begin{vmatrix} 6 & 3 \\ -5 & 2 \end{vmatrix}$ (b) $\begin{vmatrix} 3 & 7 & -6 \\ 1 & -1 & 2 \\ 4 & 3 & -2 \end{vmatrix}$

A-2 Use determinants to solve the following set of simultaneous equations.

$$5X + 2Y + 3Z = 4$$
$$2X + 3Y + 1Z = 2$$
$$3X + 1Y + 2Z = 3$$

A-3 Perform the following operations.

  (a) Add matrix A to matrix B.
  (b) Subtract matrix A from matrix B.
  (c) Add matrix C to matrix D.
  (d) Add matrix C to matrix A.

$$\text{matrix } A = \begin{pmatrix} 2 & 4 & 1 \\ 3 & 8 & 7 \end{pmatrix} \qquad \text{matrix } C = \begin{pmatrix} 3 & 6 & 9 \\ 7 & 8 & 1 \\ 9 & 2 & 4 \end{pmatrix}$$

$$\text{matrix } B = \begin{pmatrix} 7 & 6 & 5 \\ 0 & 1 & 2 \end{pmatrix} \qquad \text{matrix } D = \begin{pmatrix} 5 & 1 & 6 \\ 4 & 0 & 6 \\ 3 & 1 & 5 \end{pmatrix}$$

A-4 Perform the following matrix multiplications.

  (a) matrix C = matrix A × matrix B
  (b) matrix G = matrix E × matrix F
  (c) matrix T = matrix R × matrix S
  (d) matrix Z = matrix W × matrix Y

$$\text{matrix } A = \begin{pmatrix} 2 \\ 1 \end{pmatrix} \qquad\qquad \text{matrix } B = (3 \quad 4 \quad 5)$$

$$\text{matrix } E = (5 \quad 2 \quad 6 \quad 1) \qquad \text{matrix } F = \begin{pmatrix} 4 \\ 3 \\ 2 \\ 0 \end{pmatrix}$$

$$\text{matrix } R = \begin{pmatrix} 2 & 3 \\ 1 & 4 \end{pmatrix} \qquad \text{matrix } S = \begin{pmatrix} 1 & 0 \\ 0 & 1 \end{pmatrix}$$

$$\text{matrix } W = \begin{pmatrix} 3 & 5 \\ 2 & 1 \\ 4 & 4 \end{pmatrix} \qquad \text{matrix } Y = \begin{pmatrix} 1 & 4 & 5 & 1 \\ 2 & 3 & 6 & 5 \end{pmatrix}$$

A-5 RLB Electrical Contracting, Inc. bids on the same three jobs as Blank Plumbing (Section 3 of this module). RLB must supply wiring, conduits, electrical wall fixtures, and lighting fixtures. The following are needed supplies and their costs per unit.

	DEMAND			
PROJECT	WIRING (ROLLS)	CONDUITS	WALL FIXTURES	LIGHTING FIXTURES
Dormitory	50	100	10	20
Office	70	80	20	30
Apartments	20	50	30	10

ITEM	COST/UNIT ($)
Wiring	1.00
Conduits	2.00
Wall fixtures	3.00
Lighting fixtures	5.00

Use matrix multiplication to compute the cost of materials at each job site.

A-6 Transpose matrices R and S.

$$\text{matrix } R = \begin{pmatrix} 6 & 8 & 2 & 2 \\ 1 & 0 & 5 & 7 \\ 6 & 4 & 3 & 1 \\ 3 & 1 & 2 & 7 \end{pmatrix}$$

$$\text{matrix } S = \begin{pmatrix} 3 & 1 \\ 2 & 2 \\ 5 & 4 \end{pmatrix}$$

A-7 Find the matrix of cofactors and adjoint of this matrix.

$$\begin{pmatrix} 1 & 4 & 7 \\ 2 & 0 & 8 \\ 3 & 6 & 9 \end{pmatrix}$$

A-8 Find the inverse of original matrix of Problem A-7 and verify its correctness.

BIBLIOGRAPHY

Childress, R. L. *Sets, Matrices, and Linear Programming*. Englewood Cliffs, N.J.: Prentice-Hall, Inc., 1974.

Reiner, I. *Introduction to Matrix Theory and Linear Algebra*. New York: Holt, Rinehart and Winston, Inc., 1971.

B

Game Theory

B.1
INTRODUCTION

This module deals with the fascinating subject of game theory. A *game* is a contest involving two or more decision makers, each of whom wants to win. *Game theory* is the study of how optimal strategies are formulated in conflict.

The subject dates back to 1944, the year in which John Von Neumann and Oscar Morgenstern published their classic book *Theory of Games and Economic Behavior*. Since then, game theory has been used by army generals to plan war strategies, by union negotiators and managers in collective bargaining sessions, and by poker and chess players trying to win their games. Game models are classified by the *number of players*, the *sum of all payoffs* and the *number of strategies* employed. Owing to the mathematical complexity of game theory, we limit the analysis in this module to games that are two person and zero sum. A *two-person game* is one where only two parties can play—as in the case of a union and a company in a bargaining session. For simplicity, X and Y represent the two game players. *Zero sum* means that the sum of losses for one player must equal the sum of gains for the other player. Thus, if X wins 20 points or dollars, Y loses 20 points or dollars. With any zero sum game, the sum of the gains for one player is always equal to the sum of the losses for the other player. When you sum the gains and losses for both players, the result is zero. This is why these games are called zero sum games.

B.2
LANGUAGE OF GAMES

To introduce you to the notation used in game theory, let us consider a simple game. Suppose there are only two lighting fixture stores, X and Y, in Urbana, Illinois (this is called a duopoly). The respective market shares have been stable up until now, but the situation may change. The daughter of the owner of store X has just completed her MBA and has developed two distinct advertising strategies, one using radio spots and the other newspaper ads. Upon hearing this, the owner of store Y also proceeds to prepare radio and newspaper ads.

TABLE B.1 Store *X*'s Payoff Matrix

		GAME PLAYER Y'S STRATEGIES	
		Y_1 (Use radio)	Y_2 (Use newspaper)
GAME PLAYER X'S	X_1 (Use radio)	2	7
STRATEGIES	X_2 (Use newspaper)	6	−4

The 2 × 2 payoff matrix in Table B.1 shows what will happen to current market shares if both stores begin advertising. By convention, payoffs are shown only for the first game player, X, in this case. Y's payoffs will just be the negative of each number. For this game, there are only two strategies being used by each player. If store Y had a third strategy, a situation illustrated in Section 7 of this module, we would be dealing with a 2 × 3 payoff matrix.

A positive number in Table B.1 means that X wins and Y loses.

A negative number means that Y wins and X loses.

Look at Table B.1. It is obvious that the game favors competitor X, since all values are positive except one. If the game had favored player Y, the values in the table would have been negative. In other words, the game in Table B.1 is biased against Y. However, since Y must play the game, he or she will play to minimize total losses.

Game Outcomes

STORE X'S STRATEGY	STORE Y'S STRATEGY	OUTCOME (IN % CHANGE IN MARKET SHARE)
X_1 (use radio)	Y_1 (use radio)	X wins 2, and Y loses 2
X_1 (use radio)	Y_2 (use newspaper)	X wins 7, and Y loses 7
X_2 (use newspaper)	Y_1 (use radio)	X wins 6, and Y loses 6
X_2 (use newspaper)	Y_2 (use newspaper)	X loses 4, and Y wins 4

B.3
PURE STRATEGY GAMES

In some games, the strategies each player follows will always be the same regardless of the other player's strategy. This is called a *pure strategy*. A *saddle point* is a situation where both players are facing pure strategies. Strategies for *saddle point games* can be determined without performing any calculations.

Consider the following game. Does it have a saddle point?   **saddle point**

		SECOND PLAYER'S (Y) STRATEGIES	
		Y_1	Y_2
FIRST PLAYER'S	X_1	3	5
(X) STRATEGIES	X_2	1	−2

determining strategies for X and Y

The answer is *yes*. Here is how we can determine the strategies for X and Y.

1. X will always play strategy X_1. The worst outcome for X playing strategy X_1 is $+3$ points. The best outcome for X playing X_2 is $+1$.

2. Knowing that X will always play strategy X_1, Y will always play strategy Y_1. Y will lose three points by playing Y_1. If Y_2 is played, Y will lose five points.

3. Both players have a dominant or pure strategy, and therefore the game has a saddle point. The numerical value of the saddle point is the game outcome. For this example, the saddle point is 3.

	Y'S PURE STRATEGY	
	Y_1	Y_2
X_1	③	5
X_2	1	-2

SADDLE POINT → ③

X'S PURE STRATEGY → X_1

Why do we have a saddle point for this situation? Looking at the payoffs, we can see that X will always play strategy X_1. The lowest, or worst, outcome for playing this strategy is better than the best outcome for playing the other strategy, X_2. Thus, player X will always play strategy X_1. Knowing this, Y will always play strategy Y_1 to minimize losses. The loss for playing strategy Y_1 is 3, while the loss for playing Y_2 is 5.

In reality, players X and Y may not see the saddle point at first. After the game is played for some time, however, each player will realize that there is only one strategy that should be played. From then on, these players will play only one strategy, which corresponds to the saddle point.

value of the game

The *value of the game* is the average or expected game outcome if the game is played an infinite number of times. The value of the game for this example is 3. If a game has a saddle point, the value of the game is equal to its numerical value.

You will note that the saddle point in this example, 3, is the largest number in its column and the smallest number in its row. This is true of all saddle points. There is a convenient way of determining whether or not a game has a saddle point. A saddle point exists if both of the following conditions exist for a number in the table: if it is the largest number in its column, and if it is the smallest number in its row.

B.4
MINIMAX CRITERION

In Chapter 5 it was shown that a pessimistic decision maker would want to maximize his or her minimum gains. This is called the *maximin decision criteria*. Minimizing one's maximum losses is identical to maximizing one's minimum gains. In game theory, this is the so-called *minimax criterion*. This criterion is one approach to selecting strategies that will minimize losses for each player.

TABLE B.2 Example of the Minimax Criterion

		PLAYER Y'S STRATEGIES		Minimum row number ↓
		Y_1	Y_2	
PLAYER X'S STRATEGIES	X_1	10	6	⑥ *Lower value*
	X_2	−12	2	−12
Maximum column number →		10	⑥	

Upper value

The minimax procedure is accomplished as follows. Find the smallest number in each row. Pick the largest of these numbers. This number is called the *lower value* of the game, and the row is X's maximin strategy. Next, find the largest number in each column. Pick the smallest of these numbers. This number is called the *higher value* of the game, and the column is Y's minimax strategy.

minimax procedure

If the upper value and lower value of the game are the same, there is a saddle point which is equal to the upper or lower value. This is an alternate method of determining whether or not a saddle point exists. Table B.2 illustrates how we can determine if there is a saddle point using the minimax criterion. Since the upper value equals the lower value of the game, the saddle point is 6. X's strategy is to play X_1, and Y's strategy is to play Y_2.

B.5
MIXED STRATEGY GAMES

When there is no saddle point, then players will play each strategy for a certain percentage of the time. This is called a *mixed strategy game*, and the rest of this module investigates ways to determine the percentage of the time each strategy will be played.

For 2 × 2 games (where both players have only two possible strategies), an algebraic approach can be used to solve for the percentage of the time each strategy is played. The following diagram can be helpful:

algebraic approach

	P	$1 - P$
Q		
$1 - Q$		

where

$Q, 1 - Q$ = fraction of the time X plays strategies X_1 and X_2, respectively, and

$P, 1 - P$ = fraction of the time Y plays strategies Y_1 and Y_2, respectively.

The overall objective of each player is to determine the fraction of the time each strategy is to be played to maximize winnings. Each player desires a strategy that will result in the most winnings no matter what the other player's strategy happens to be.

KEY IDEA → The solution to the mixed strategy 2×2 game may be found by equating a player's expected winnings for one of the opponent's strategies with his expected winnings for the opponent's other strategy. With this approach, X wants to divide its plays between the two rows in such a way that the expected winnings from playing the first row will be exactly equal to the expected winnings from playing the second row despite what Y does. In other words, X wants to determine the best possible strategy that is independent of the strategy that player Y will adopt. Thus, it is necessary to equate the expected winnings of strategy X_1, which is row 1, and strategy X_2, which is row 2.

The same approach used to determine X's strategy can be used to determine Y's strategy. Y will want to divide its time between the columns in such a way that no matter what X does, Y will minimize its losses or maximize its winnings.

1. To find X's best strategy, multiply Q and $1 - Q$ times the appropriate game outcome numbers and solve for Q and $1 - Q$ by setting column 1 equal to column 2 in the game.

2. To find Y's best strategy, multiply P and $1 - P$ times the appropriate game outcome numbers and solve for P and $1 - P$ by setting row 1 equal to row 2 in the game.

Here is how you would determine the optimal strategies for X and Y in the following game.

	Y'S STRATEGIES	
	Y_1	Y_2
X_1	4	2
X_2	1	10

X'S STRATEGIES

Step 1:

	P	$1 - P$
Q	4	2
$1 - Q$	1	10

determining X's strategy

Step 2: X's optimal strategy:
  (a) Column 1 is $4Q + 1(1 - Q)$.
  (b) Column 2 is $2Q + 10(1 - Q)$.
  (c) Equating column 1 and column 2 gives: $4Q + 1(1 - Q) = 2Q + 10(1 - Q)$.

(d) Solving for Q and $1 - Q$ yields the following: $4Q - Q - 2Q + 10Q = -1 + 10$. $Q = \frac{9}{11}$, and thus $1 - Q = 1 - \frac{9}{11} = \frac{2}{11}$.

(e) $\frac{9}{11}$ and $\frac{2}{11}$ represent the fraction of the time X should play X_1 and X_2, respectively.

Step 3: Y's optimal strategy:

(a) Row 1 is $4(P) + 2(1 - P)$.

(b) Row 2 is $1(P) + 10(1 - P)$.

(c) Equating row 1 and row 2 gives: $4(P) + 2(1 - P) = 1(P) + 10(1 - P)$.

(d) Solving for P and $1 - P$ yields the following: $4P - 2P - P + 10P = -2 + 10$. $P = \frac{8}{11}$; $1 - P = \frac{3}{11}$.

(e) $\frac{8}{11}$ and $\frac{3}{11}$ represent the fraction of the time Y should play Y_1 and Y_2, respectively.

Once this procedure is understood, it is possible to write the appropriate equations directly from the game. This is shown in the following example game:

writing equations directly

	Y_1	Y_2
X_1	-6	-1
X_2	-2	-8

Step 1:

	P	$1 - P$
Q	-6	-1
$1 - Q$	-2	-8

Step 2: The equation for X's strategy is:

$-6Q - 2(1 - Q) = -1Q - 8(1 - Q)$

$-6Q + 2Q + Q - 8Q = 2 - 8$

$Q = \frac{6}{11}$; $1 - Q = \frac{5}{11}$

Step 3: The equation for Y's strategy is:

$-6P - 1(1 - P) = -2P - 8(1 - P)$

$-6P + P + 2P - 8P = +1 - 8$

$P = \frac{7}{11}$; $1 - P = \frac{4}{11}$

Once player strategies have been determined, the value of the game can be calculated. The value of the game is the average or expected game outcome after a large number of plays. It can be computed by multiplying each game outcome times the P and Q factors of respective strategies. The results are then added up to obtain the value of the game. The following example shows how the exact calculations are performed:

value of the game

	Y_1	Y_2
X_1	4	2
X_2	1	10

$$Q = \tfrac{9}{11}$$
$$1 - Q = \tfrac{2}{11}$$
$$P = \tfrac{8}{11}$$
$$1 - P = \tfrac{3}{11}$$

The next diagram is usually helpful:

	$P = \tfrac{8}{11}$	$1 - P = \tfrac{3}{11}$
$Q = \tfrac{9}{11}$	4	2
$1 - Q = \tfrac{2}{11}$	1	10

computing value of the game

To get a game outcome of 4, strategies X_1 and Y_1 must be played. The P and Q factors are $\tfrac{9}{11}$ and $\tfrac{8}{11}$. Therefore, we multiply 4 times $\tfrac{9}{11}$ times $\tfrac{8}{11}$. We do the same for all game outcomes and add the results. The calculations are displayed in the accompanying table.

GAME OUTCOME		P FACTOR		Q FACTOR	
4	$\times$	$\tfrac{9}{11}$	$\times$	$\tfrac{8}{11}$	$= 2.38$
2	$\times$	$\tfrac{9}{11}$	$\times$	$\tfrac{3}{11}$	$= .45$
1	$\times$	$\tfrac{2}{11}$	$\times$	$\tfrac{8}{11}$	$= .13$
10	$\times$	$\tfrac{2}{11}$	$\times$	$\tfrac{3}{11}$	$= \underline{.50}$
			Value of the game		$= 3.46$

Thus, on the average, X will win 3.46 points and Y will lose 3.46 points per game if the game is played many times.

second way to compute game value

Although this procedure will give the expected value of the game, a shortcut method does exist. Since optimal strategies are obtained by equating expected gains of both strategies for each player, the value of the game may be computed by multiplying game outcomes times their probabilities of occurrence for any row or column. The following illustration reveals the computational procedures.

		COLUMN 1 $P = \tfrac{8}{11}$	COLUMN 2 $1 - P = \tfrac{3}{11}$
ROW 1	$Q = \tfrac{9}{11}$	4	2
ROW 2	$1 - Q = \tfrac{2}{11}$	1	10

Row 1: Value of the game $=$
$$(4)(\tfrac{8}{11}) + (2)(\tfrac{3}{11}) = \tfrac{38}{11}$$

Row 2: Value of the game $=$
$$(1)(\tfrac{8}{11}) + (10)(\tfrac{3}{11}) = \tfrac{38}{11}$$

Column 1: Value of the game $=$
$$(4)(^9/_{11}) + (1)(^2/_{11}) = {^{38}/_{11}}$$
Column 2: Value of the game $=$
$$(2)(^9/_{11}) + (10)(^2/_{11}) = {^{38}/_{11}}$$

Thus, the value of the game can be computed using any row or column. The value of this game, which was computed to be 3.46, is $^{38}/_{11}$.

B.6
DOMINANCE

The principle of *dominance* can be used to reduce the size of games by eliminating strategies that would never be played. A strategy for a player can be eliminated if the player can always do as well or better playing another strategy. In other words, a strategy can be eliminated if all its game's outcomes are the same or worse than the corresponding game outcomes of another strategy.

Using the principle of dominance, we reduce the size of the following game:

	Y_1	Y_2
X_1	4	3
X_2	2	20
X_3	1	1

In this game, X_3 will never be played because X can always do better by playing X_1 or X_2. The new game is:

	Y_1	Y_2
X_1	4	3
X_2	2	20

Here is another example:

	Y_1	Y_2	Y_3	Y_4
X_1	-5	4	6	-3
X_2	-2	6	2	-20

In this game, Y would never play Y_2 and Y_3 because Y could *always* do better playing Y_1 or Y_4. The new game is:

	Y_1	Y_4
X_1	-5	-3
X_2	-2	-20

B.7
GAMES LARGER THAN 2 × 2

It is not always possible to reduce a large game to a 2 × 2 game. There are several techniques, including solution by *subgames* and the graphical approach that may be used to solve 2 × *m* and *m* × 2 games where *m* is a number larger than 2. The procedure used to solve 2 × 2 games can also be expanded to solve larger games. One final technique is discussed, however, that is appropriate for any game. This approach is linear programming. Figure B.1 shows when linear programming should be used. There are several advantages in using linear programming:

linear programming

1. It is appropriate for 2 × 2 or larger games.

2. Linear programming computer programs are usually available, making the process of solution much easier.

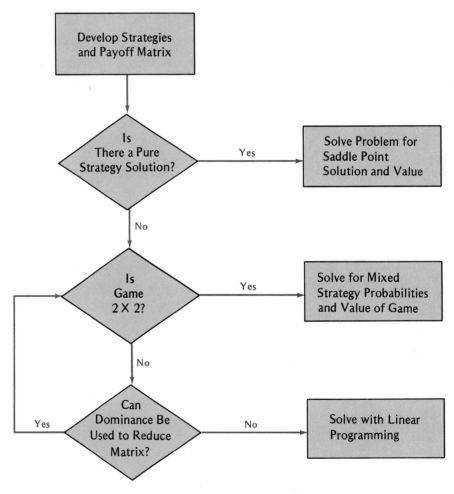

FIGURE B.1
Procedure for Solving Two-Person, Zero Sum Games

3. Most linear programming computer programs have postoptimality techniques that allow the decision maker to analyze what effect changes in the game will have on optimal strategies.

Before we begin, several terms should be defined. Let

$$V = \text{Optimal value of the game}$$

$$\hat{X}_i = \text{Fraction of time } X \text{ plays strategy } X_i$$

$$\hat{Y}_i = \text{Fraction of time } Y \text{ plays strategy } Y_i$$

To illustrate the use of linear programming, consider the following game.

		Y'S STRATEGIES		
		Y_1	Y_2	Y_3
X'S STRATEGIES	X_1	3	2	1
	X_2	1	4	6

Since this is not a pure strategy game, each strategy will be played a certain fraction of the time. It will be our objective to find V and every $\hat{X}_i$ and $\hat{Y}_i$.

X wants to maximize the value of the game, but if X plays only one strategy, the value of the game will be less than or equal to the optimal value of the game, V. For example, if X plays only X_1, then the value of this game, which is $3\hat{Y}_1 + 2\hat{Y}_2 + 1\hat{Y}_3$, will be less than or equal to the optimal value of the game, which is V. Stating this algebraically we get:

$$3\hat{Y}_1 + 2\hat{Y}_2 + 1\hat{Y}_3 \leq V$$

Using the same reasoning for X_2, we get:

$$1\hat{Y}_1 + 4\hat{Y}_2 + 6\hat{Y}_3 \leq V$$

These inequalities become linear programming constraints.

We also know that all of Y's fractions must add up to 1.

$$\hat{Y}_1 + \hat{Y}_2 + \hat{Y}_3 = 1$$

This equation is used to construct the objective function. Now, to obtain our linear programming formulation, we divide each of these equations by V, and note that Y wants to minimize V, or maximize $1/V$. **objective function**

$$\frac{\hat{Y}_1}{V} + \frac{\hat{Y}_2}{V} + \frac{\hat{Y}_3}{V} = \frac{1}{V} \qquad Y \text{ will want to maximize } \frac{1}{V}$$

$$\frac{3\hat{Y}_1}{V} + \frac{2\hat{Y}_2}{V} + \frac{1\hat{Y}_3}{V} \leq 1 \qquad \text{subject to these constraints}$$

$$\frac{1\hat{Y}_1}{V} + \frac{4\hat{Y}_2}{V} + \frac{6\hat{Y}_3}{V} \leq 1$$

If we define $\overline{Y}_i = \dfrac{\hat{Y}_i}{V}$ the linear programming formulation is:

$$\text{Maximize:} \quad \overline{Y}_1 + \overline{Y}_2 + \overline{Y}_3$$
$$\text{Subject to:} \quad 3\overline{Y}_1 + 2\overline{Y}_2 + 1\overline{Y}_3 \leq 1$$
$$1\overline{Y}_1 + 4\overline{Y}_2 + 6\overline{Y}_3 \leq 1$$

With experience, a linear programming formulation for Y's strategies and the value of the game can be made directly from a game. Here is an example.

direct formulation

	Y_1	Y_2	Y_3
X_1	3	2	3
X_2	1	4	4
X_3	5	6	1

The solution is:

$$\text{Maximize:} \quad \overline{Y}_1 + \overline{Y}_2 + \overline{Y}_3$$
$$\text{Subject to:} \quad 3\overline{Y}_1 + 2\overline{Y}_2 + 3\overline{Y}_3 \leq 1$$
$$1\overline{Y}_1 + 4\overline{Y}_2 + 4\overline{Y}_3 \leq 1$$
$$5\overline{Y}_1 + 6\overline{Y}_2 + 1\overline{Y}_3 \leq 1$$

B.8
USING THE COMPUTER TO SOLVE GAME THEORY PROBLEMS

The game theory program for AB:QM can accommodate up to 50 strategies for each of the two players. In this module, we discussed a 2 × 2 game theory problem. That problem's input screen and output are shown in Program B.1 (on p. 845).

B.9
SUMMARY

Game thory is the study of how optimal strategies are formulated in conflict. Because of the mathematical complexities of game theory, this module was limited to two-person and zero sum games. A two-person game allows only two individuals or groups to be involved in the game. Zero sum means that the sum of the losses for one player must equal the sum of the gains for the other player. The overall sum of the losses and gains for both players, in other words, must be zero.

Depending on the actual payoffs in the game and the size of the game, a number of solution techniques can be used. In a pure strategy game, strategies for the players can be obtained without making any calculations. When there is *not* a pure strategy, also called a saddle point, for both players, it is necessary to use other techniques, such as the mixed strategy approach, dominance, and linear programming for games larger than 2 × 2.

PROGRAM B.1 AB:QM's Game Theory Program

```
Game Theory

Problem Title :  Game1

No. of A's Strategies (Row)    2    No. of B's Strategies (Col)  2


              Strategy  1 Strategy  2
Strategy  1              4            2
Strategy  2              1            10




Help   New   Load   Save   Edit   Run   Print   Install   Directory   Esc


Game Theory

***** Program Output *****

--------------
Mixed Strategy
--------------

For Player A:

Probability of Strategy   1        0.818
Probability of Strategy   2        0.182

For Player B:

Probability of Strategy   1        0.727
Probability of Strategy   2        0.273

Value for this game is        3.45

***** End of Output *****
```

GLOSSARY

Two-Person Game. A game that only has two players.

Zero Sum Game. A game where the losses for one player equal the gains for the other player.

Pure Strategy. A game where both players will always play just one strategy.

Saddle Point Game. A game that has a pure strategy.

Value of the Game. The expected winnings of the game if the game is played a large number of times.

Minimax Criterion. A criterion that minimizes one's maximum losses. This is another way of solving a pure strategy game.

Mixed Strategy Game. A game where the optimal strategy for both players involves playing more than one strategy over time. Each strategy is played a given percentage of the time.

Dominance. A procedure that is used to reduce the size of the game.

Games Larger than 2 × 2. A game that involves more than two strategies for one or both players. One way of solving this type of game is to use linear programming.

DISCUSSION QUESTIONS AND PROBLEMS

Discussion Questions

B-1 What is a two-person, zero sum game?

B-2 How do you compute the value of the game?

B-3 What is a pure strategy and how is dominance used?

B-4 What is a mixed game, and how is it solved?

B-5 How is linear programming used to solve games that are larger than 2 × 2?

Problems

B-6 Determine the strategies for X and Y given the following game. What is the value of the game?

	Y_1	Y_2
X_1	2	−4
X_2	6	10

B-7 What is the value of the following game and the strategies for A and B?

	B_1	B_2
A_1	19	20
A_2	5	−4

: **B-8** Determine each player's strategy and the value of the game given the following table.

	Y_1	Y_2
X_1	86	42
X_2	36	106

: **B-9** What is the value of the following game?

	S_1	S_2
R_1	21	116
R_2	89	3

: **B-10** Player A has a one-dollar bill and a twenty-dollar bill, while player B has a five-dollar bill and a ten-dollar bill. Each player will select a bill from the other player without knowing what bill the other player selected. If the total of the bills selected is odd, player A gets both bills, but if the total is even, player B gets both bills.

(a) Develop a payoff table for this game.
(b) What are the best strategies for each player?
(c) What is the value of the game? Which player would you like to be?

: **B-11** Resolve Problem B-10. If the total of the bills is even, player A gets both bills, but if the total is odd, player B gets both bills.

: **B-12** Solve the following game.

	Y_1	Y_2
X_1	-5	-10
X_2	12	8
X_3	4	12
X_4	-40	-5

: **B-13** Shoe Town and Fancy Foot are both vying for more share of the market. If Shoe Town does no advertising, it will not lose any share of the market if Fancy Foot does nothing. It will lose 2% of the market if Fancy Foot invests $10,000 in advertising, and it will lose 5% of the market if Fancy Foot invests $20,000 in advertising. On the other hand, if Shoe Town invests $15,000 in advertising, it will gain 3% of the market if Fancy Foot does nothing; it will gain 1% of the market if Fancy Foot invests $10,000 in advertising; and it will lose 1% if Fancy Foot invests $20,000 in advertising.

(a) Develop a payoff table for this problem.
(b) How would you determine the various strategies using linear programming?
(c) How would you determine the value of the game?

: **B-14** Assume that a 1% increase in the market means a profit of $1,000. Resolve Problem B-13 using monetary value instead of market share.

BIBLIOGRAPHY

Bowen, Kenneth Credson, with contributions by Harris, Janet I. *Research Games: An Approach to the Study of Decision Processes.* New York: Halstead Press, 1978.

Davis, M. *Game Theory: A Nontechnical Introduction.* New York: Basic Books, Inc., 1970.

Fowler, A. "Impact! A Business Simulation." *Personnel Management* Vol. 20, June 1988, p. 69.

Fryer, Michael John. *An Introduction to Linear Programming and Matrix Game Theory.* London: Edward Arnold, 1978.

Ichiishi, Tatsuro. *Game Theory for Economic Analysis.* New York: Academic Press, 1983.

Kadane, Joseph B., and Larkey, Patrick D. "Subjective Probability and the Theory of Games." *Management Science* Vol. 28, No. 2, February 1982, pp. 113–119.

Karnani, Aneel. "The Value of Market Share and the Product Life Cycle—A Game Theoretic Model." *Management Science* Vol. 30, No. 6, June 1984, pp. 696–712.

Klein, J. H. "The Level of Interpretation of Games." *Journal of Operational Research Society* Vol. 39, June 1988, pp. 527–535.

Lucas, W. "An Overview of the Mathematical Theory of Games." *Management Science* Vol. 8, No. 5, Part II, January 1972, pp. 3–19.

Luce, R. D., and Raiffa, H. *Games and Decisions.* New York: John Wiley and Sons, 1957.

Matthews, S. A. "Veto Threats: Rhetoric in a Bargaining Game." *Quarterly Journal of Economics* Vol. 104, May 1989, pp. 347–369.

Rapoport, A. *Two Person Game Theory.* Ann Arbor, Michigan: The University of Michigan Press, 1966.

Shubik, M. *The Uses and Methods of Game Theory.* New York: American Elsevier, 1957.

Sterman, J. D. "Modeling Managerial Behavior: Misperceptions of Feedback in a Dynamic Decision Making Experiment." *Management Science* Vol. 35, March 1989, pp. 321–339.

Troutt, M. D. "A Purchase Timing Model for Life Insurance Decision Support Systems." *Journal of Risk and Insurance* Vol. 55, December 1988, pp. 628–643.

Von Neumann, J., and Morgenstern, O. *Theory of Games and Economic Behavior.* Princeton, N.J.: Princeton University Press, 1944.

Williams, J. D. *The Compleat Strategyst.* Revised Edition. New York: McGraw-Hill Book Company, 1966.

C

Dynamic Programming

MODULE OUTLINE

INTRODUCTION

Dynamic programming is a quantitative analysis technique that has been widely applied to large, complex problems that have a sequence of decisions to be made. Dynamic programming divides problems into a number of *decision stages*, where the outcome of a decision at one stage affects the decision at each of the next stages. The technique is useful in a large number of multiperiod business problems, such as smoothing production employment, allocating capital funds, allocating salespeople to marketing areas, and evaluating investment opportunities.

Dynamic programming differs from linear programming in two ways. First, there is no algorithm (like the simplex method) that can be programmed to solve all problems. Dynamic programming is instead a technique that allows us to break up difficult problems into a sequence of easier subproblems, which are then evaluated by stages. Second, linear programming is a method that gives *single-stage* (one time period) solutions. Dynamic programming has the power to determine the optimal solution over a one-year time horizon by breaking the problem into 12 smaller one-month time horizon problems and to solve each of these optimally. Hence, it uses a *multistage* approach.

Solving problems with dynamic programming involves four steps.

1. Divide the original problem into subproblems called stages.

2. Solve the last stage of the problem for all possible conditions or states.

3. Working backwards from the last stage, solve each intermediate stage. This is done by determining optimal policies from that stage to the end of the problem (last stage).

4. Obtain the optimal solution for the original problem by solving all stages sequentially.

In this brief module, we show how to solve one typical dynamic programming problem as an illustration of the approach. The problem is commonly referred to as a shortest-route problem.

C.2

A SHORTEST-ROUTE PROBLEM SOLVED BY DYNAMIC PROGRAMMING

George Yates is about to make a trip from Rice, Georgia (1) to Dixieville, Georgia (7). George would like to find the shortest route. Unfortunately, there are a number of small towns between Rice and Dixieville. His road map is shown in Figure C.1.

The circles on the map, called *nodes*, represent cities such as Rice, Dixieville, Brown, and so on. The arrows, called *arcs*, represent highways between the cities. Distances in miles are indicated along each arc.

Dynamic Programming at Weyerhaeuser

Weyerhaeuser is a very large company involved with forest products located primarily in the northwest. Its annual revenues are in the billions of dollars. Weyerhaeuser uses a number of mills and other production facilities to produce plywood, paper products, lumber, and even wood fuel from logs and other tree-related products. The firm processes a staggering volume of over one billion cubic feet of lumber products every year.

One of the most difficult and critical decisions is to find the most effective and profitable use of its raw materials, logs and other wood products. Depending on how the logs are cut and subsequently used to produce final products, Weyerhaeuser can have a profound impact on its own profits. But with logs of different sizes and shapes and a large variety of end products, how is it pos-

Source: Mark Lembersky and Uli Chi, "Weyerhaeuser Decision Simulator Improves Timber Products," *Interfaces* Vol. 16, No. 1, January–February, 1986.

sible to determine the best use of a particular log or a set of logs to produce the best results? To assist Weyerhaeuser's managers in making important raw material decisions, a decision simulator called VISION was developed.

One of the main purposes of the VISION decision simulator is to help determine the best overall use of raw materials coming into Weyerhaeuser's plants. First designed in 1984, VISION uses dynamic programming to allocate resources to various production operations which produce the final products. In the past several years, this program has gone through several changes resulting in a number of improvements.

What has been the impact of the decision simulator? It has been estimated that benefits so far have increased by approximately $1 million. Using dynamic programming and the VISION decision simulator, Weyerhaeuser has been able to significantly improve the use of its major raw material, incoming logs, to produce the most profitable mix of finished products.

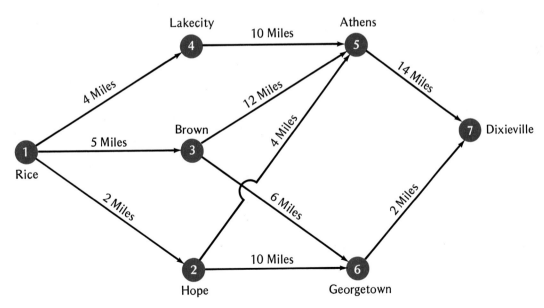

FIGURE C.1
Highway Map Between Rice and Dixieville

Using Dynamic Programming in Sports

Although most quantitative analysis techniques are used to solve government or business problems, many techniques can be used in other areas. In this applications box, the use of dynamic programming in tennis is explored.

At a minimum, most tennis players have both a fast serve and a slow serve. While the fast serve is harder to return, there is less likelihood that a fast serve will land in bounds. Thus, a tennis player

must decide when, where, and how to use a fast serve rather than a slow one.

Dynamic programming is one approach that can be used to solve the problem. On the first serve, the possibilities are to serve in bounds and win the point, serve in bounds and lose the point, or serve out of bounds and take a second serve. On the second serve, the possibilities are to win or lose the point. With dynamic programming and 36 distinct states, a systematic approach can be used to determine the best serving policy. Although such an approach probably would not be appropriate for decisions *during* the game, it can be used for good game planning before an important match.

Source: J. M. Norman, "Dynamic Programming in Tennis—When to Use a Fast Serve," *Journal of the Operations Research Society,* Vol. 36, No. 1, 1985, pp. 75–77.

This problem can, of course, be solved by inspection. But seeing how dynamic programming can be used on this simple problem will teach you how to solve larger and more complex problems.

Step 1: The first step is to divide the problem into subproblems or stages. Figure C.2 reveals the stages of this problem. In dynamic programming, we usually start with the last part of the problem, stage 1, and work backwards to the beginning of the problem or network, which is stage 3 in this problem. Table C.1 summarizes the arcs and arc distances for each stage.

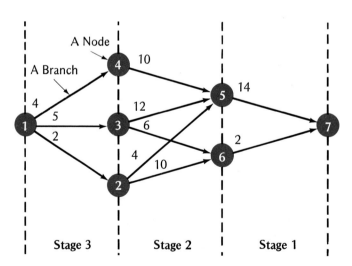

FIGURE C.2
Three Stages to George Yates's Problem

TABLE C.1 Distance Along Each Arc

STAGE	ARC	ARC DISTANCE
1	5–7	14
	6–7	2
2	4–5	10
	3–5	12
	3–6	6
	2–5	4
	2–6	10
3	1–4	4
	1–3	5
	1–2	2

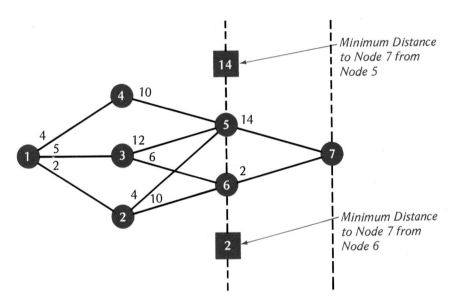

FIGURE C.3
Solution for the One-Stage Problem

Step 2: We next solve stage 1, the last part of the network. Usually this is trivial. We find the shortest path to the end of the network, node 7 in this problem. At stage 1, the shortest paths from node 5 and node 6 to node 7 are the *only* paths. You may also note in Figure C.3 that the minimum distances are enclosed in boxes by the entering nodes to stage 1, node 5 and node 6. The objective is to find the shortest distance to node 7. The following table summarizes this procedure for stage 1. As previously mentioned, the shortest distance is the only distance at stage 1.

| | STAGE 1 | |
BEGINNING NODE	SHORTEST DISTANCE TO NODE 7	ARCS ALONG THIS PATH
5	14	5–7
6	2	6–7

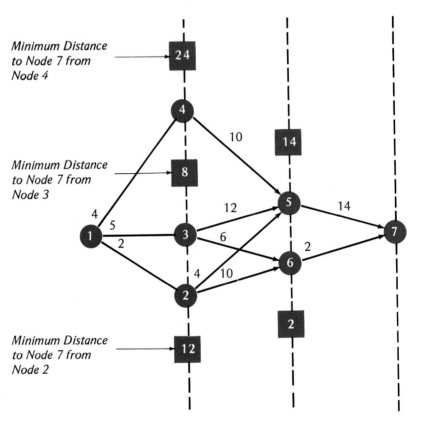

Minimum Distance to Node 7 from Node 4

Minimum Distance to Node 7 from Node 3

Minimum Distance to Node 7 from Node 2

FIGURE C.4
Solution for the Two-Stage Problem

Step 3: Moving backwards, we now solve for stages 2 and 3. At stage 2 we will use Figure C.4.

If we are at node 4, the shortest and *only* route to node 7 is arcs 4–5 and 5–7. At node 3, the shortest route is arcs 3–6 and 6–7 with a total minimum distance of 8 miles. If we are at node 2, the shortest route is arcs 2–6 and 6–7 with a minimum total distance of 12 miles. This information is summarized in the stage 2 table on the next page.

| | STAGE 2 | |
BEGINNING NODE	SHORTEST DISTANCE TO NODE 7	ARCS ALONG THIS PATH
4	24	4–5 5–7
3	8	3–6 6–7
2	12	2–6 6–7

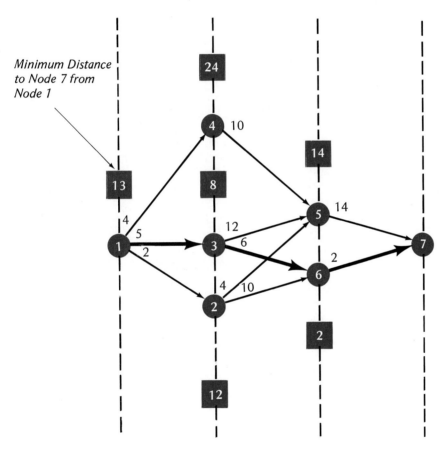

Minimum Distance to Node 7 from Node 1

FIGURE C.5
Solution for the Three-Stage Problem

The solution to stage 3 can be completed using the accompanying table and the network in Figure C.5.

	STAGE 3	
BEGINNING NODE	SHORTEST DISTANCE TO NODE 7	ARCS ALONG THIS PATH
1	13	1–3
		3–6
		6–7

To obtain the optimal solution at any stage, all we consider are the arcs to the next stage and the optimal solution at the next stage. For stage 3, we only have to consider the three arcs to stage 2 (1–2, 1–3, and 1–4) and the optimal policies at stage 2, given in a previous table. This is how we arrived at the preceding solution. Once the procedure is understood, we can perform all the calculations on one network. You may want to study the relationship between the networks and the tables because more complex problems are usually solved by using tables only.

C.3
DYNAMIC PROGRAMMING TERMINOLOGY

Regardless of the type or size of a dynamic programming problem, there are some important terms and concepts that are inherent in every problem. Some of the more important ones are:

1. *Stage:* A period or a logical subproblem.

2. *State Variables:* Possible beginning situations or conditions of a stage. These have also been called the input variables.

3. *Decision Variables:* Alternatives or possible decisions that exist at each stage.

4. *Decision Criterion:* A statement concerning the objective of the problem.

5. *Optimal Policy:* A set of decision rules, developed as a result of the decision criteria, that gives optimal decisions for any entering condition at any stage.

6. *Transformation:* Normally an algebraic statement that reveals the relationship between stages.

In the shortest-route problem, the following transformation can be given:

$$
\begin{matrix}
\text{Distance from the} \\
\text{beginning of a} \\
\text{given stage to} \\
\text{the last node}
\end{matrix}
=
\begin{matrix}
\text{Distance from the beginning} \\
\text{of the } \textit{previous } \text{stage} \\
\text{to the last node}
\end{matrix}
+
\begin{matrix}
\text{Distance from the} \\
\text{given stage to} \\
\text{the previous} \\
\text{stage}
\end{matrix}
$$

This relationship shows how we were able to go from one stage to the next in solving for the optimal solution to the shortest-route problem. In

---

APPLICATIONS OF QA

Using Dynamic Programming to Solve a Seasonal Staffing Problem

It is common for firms in the hospitality industry to experience seasonal business swings. Depending on the location of the firm and the type of business, revenues and profits can vary considerably from one season to the next. Thus, staffing decisions and policies are difficult to set. On one hand, new employees are not as productive as experienced employees, so there is a tendency to maintain a permanent staff through all seasons of the year. On the other hand, maintaining a large permanent staff can be expensive during the off season.

Dynamic programming can help solve the seasonal staffing problem. It allows a series of interrelated decisions to be made in an optimal fashion. Several features allow the staffing problem to be formulated in a dynamic programming environment:

1. The problem can be divided into stages or seasons.

Source: Manuel Jose and Michael Olsen, "A Dynamic Programming Approach to the Seasonal Staffing Problem," *International Journal of Hospitality Management*, Vol. 4, No. 1, 1985, pp. 9–13.

2. Each stage or season has a number of possible states or alternatives.

3. The impact of a decision at any stage can be related to decisions at other stages.

4. Given any current condition or state, an optimal solution or policy for remaining stages can be obtained.

5. The solution procedure begins by finding an optimal policy for the last stage.

6. A recursive relationship can be developed that identifies optimal policies for each stage.

7. By using a recursive relationship, the solution procedure moves backwards, stage by stage, until the optimal policy for the complete solution can be found.

One of the advantages of using dynamic programming for staffing in the hospitality industry is flexibility. The approach can be applied to a wide variety of problems. Dynamic programming can be a successful approach for developing staffing policies where staffing requirements vary from one season to the next.

---

more complex problems, we can use symbols to show the relationship between stages.

State variables, decision variables, the decision criterion, and the optimal policy can be determined for any stage of a dynamic programming problem. This is done here for stage 2 of the George Yates shortest-route problem.

1. State variables for stage 2 are the entering nodes, which are:
   (a) Node 2.
   (b) Node 3.
   (c) Node 4.

2. Decision variables for stage 2 are the following arcs or routes:
   (a) 4–5
   (b) 3–5
   (c) 3–6
   (d) 2–5
   (e) 2–6

   decision variables

3. The decision criterion is the minimization of the total distance traveled.

4. The optimal policy for any beginning condition is:

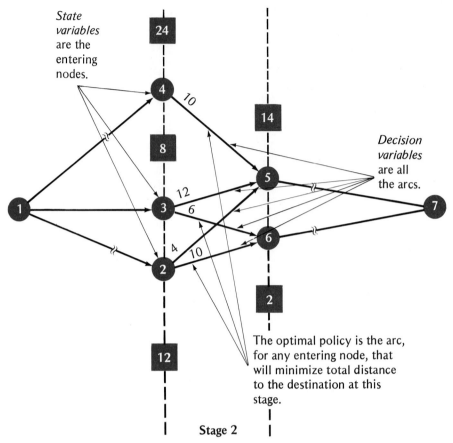

FIGURE C.6
Stage 2 from the Shortest-Route Problem

GIVEN THIS ENTERING CONDITION	THIS ARC WILL MINIMIZE TOTAL DISTANCE TO NODE 7
2	2–6
3	3–6
4	4–5

Figure C.6 may also be helpful in understanding some of these terms.

C.4
USING THE COMPUTER TO SOLVE DYNAMIC PROGRAMMING PROBLEMS

The dynamic programming module included with AB:QM can handle up to 10 stages and 10 decisions, or branches, at each node. The maximum number of nodes that can be handled by the program is 75. In this text module, we used dynamic programming to solve the shortest-route problem. The input screen and output for this problem are shown in Program C.1.

PROGRAM C.1 AB:QM's Dynamic Programming Software

```
Dynamic Programming / Network

Problem Title : Dynamic
```

	Starting Node	Ending Node	Return Value
Stage 3	1	2	2
	1	3	5
	1	4	4
Stage 2	2	5	4
	2	6	10
	3	5	12
	3	6	6
	4	5	10
Stage 1	5	7	14
	6	7	2

```
Help   New   Load   Save   Edit   Run   Print   Install   Directory   Esc
```

***** Program Output *****

Stage 1

S(1)	D(1)	R(1)	S(0)	f(0)	f(1)
6	6 -> 7	2.000	7	0.000	2.000
5	5 -> 7	14.000	7	0.000	14.000

Stage 2

S(2)	D(2)	R(2)	S(1)	f(1)	f(2)
4	4 -> 5	10.000	5	14.000	24.000
3	3 -> 6	6.000	6	2.000	8.000
	3 -> 5	12.000	5	14.000	26.000
2	2 -> 6	10.000	6	2.000	12.000
	2 -> 5	4.000	5	14.000	18.000

Stage 3

1	1 -> 4	4.000	4	24.000	28.000
	1 -> 3	5.000	3	8.000	13.000
	1 -> 2	2.000	2	12.000	14.000

PROGRAM C.1 (Continued)

```
Final Solution
------------------------------------------------
Stage      Optimal Decision      Optimal Return
------------------------------------------------
  3             1 --> 3               5.000
  2             3 --> 6               6.000
  1             6 --> 7               2.000
------------------------------------------------
Total                                13.000

***** End of Output *****
```

GLOSSARY

Dynamic Programming. A quantitative technique that works backwards from the end of the problem to the beginning of the problem in determining the best decision for a number of interrelated decisions.

Stage. A logical subproblem in a dynamic programming problem.

State Variable. A term used in dynamic programming to describe the possible beginning situations or conditions of a stage.

Decision Variable. The alternatives or possible decisions that exist at each stage of a dynamic programming problem.

Decision Criterion. A statement concerning the objective of a dynamic programming problem.

Optimal Policy. A set of decision rules, developed as a result of the decision criterion, that gives optimal decisions at any stage of a dynamic programming problem.

Transformation. An algebraic statement that shows the relationship between stages in a dynamic programming problem.

DISCUSSION QUESTIONS AND PROBLEMS

Discussion Questions

C-1 What is a stage in dynamic programming?

C-2 What is the difference between a state variable and a decision variable?

C-3 Describe the meaning and use of a decision criterion.

C-4 Do all dynamic programming problems require an optimal policy?

C-5 Why is transformation important for dynamic programming problems?

Problems

 : **C-6** Refer to Figure C.1. What is the shortest route between Rice and Dixieville if the road between Hope and Georgetown is improved and the distance is reduced to 4 miles?

: **C-7** Due to road construction between Georgetown and Dixieville, a detour must be taken through country roads. See Figure C.1. Unfortunately, this detour has increased the distance from Georgetown to Dixieville to 14 miles. What should George do? Should he take a different route?

: **C-8** The Rice Brothers have a gold mine between Rice and Brown. In their zeal to find gold, they have blown up the road between Rice and Brown. The road will not be in service for five months. What should George do? Refer to Figure C.1.

: **C-9** Solve the following shortest route problem.

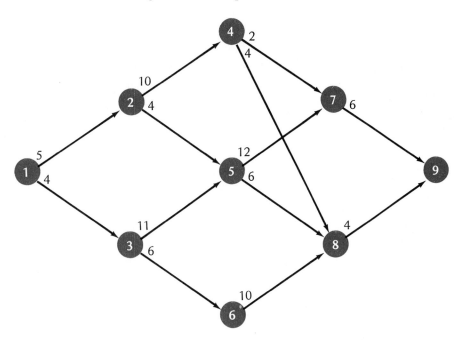

C-10 Identify the state variables, decision variables, the decision criterion, and the optimal policy for the third state of Problem C-9.

BIBLIOGRAPHY

Bellman, R. E. *Dynamic Programming*. Princeton, N.J.: Princeton University Press, 1957.

Blog, B., Vander hoek, G., Rinnooy Kan, A. H. G., and Timmer, G. T. "The Optimal Selection of Small Portfolios." *Management Science* Vol. 29, No. 7, July 1983, pp. 792–798.

Carraway, R. L. "A Dynamic Programming Approach to Stochastic Assembly Line Balancing." *Management Science* Vol. 35, April 1989, pp. 459–471.

Cooper, Leon. *Introduction to Dynamic Programming*. Oxford and New York: Pergamon Press, 1981.

Denardo, Eric V. *Dynamic Programming: Models and Applications*. Englewood Cliffs, N.J.: Prentice-Hall, Inc., 1982.

Glazebrook, K. D. "Methods for the Evaluation of a Permutation as Strategies in Stochastic Scheduling Problems." *Management Science* Vol. 29, No. 10, October 1983, pp. 1142–1155.

Gotz, Glenn A., and McCall, John J. "Sequential Analysis of the Stay/Leave Decision: U.S. Air Force Officers." *Management Science* Vol. 29, No. 3, March 1983, pp. 335–351.

Goyal, S. K. "Optimal Decision Rules for Producing Greeting Cards." *Operational Research Quarterly* Vol. 1, No. 24, pp. 391–401.

Howard, R. A. *Dynamic Programming*. Cambridge, Mass.: MIT Press, 1960.

Kreimer, J. "Allocation of Control Points in Stochastic Dynamic Programming Models." *Journal of Operational Research Society* Vol. 39, September 1988, pp. 847–853.

Lee, S. B., and Zipkin, P. H. "A Dynamic Lot-Size Model with Make-or-Buy Decisions." *Management Science* Vol. 35, April 1989, pp. 447–458.

Mjelde, J. W. "Valuing Forecasting Characteristics in a Dynamic Agricultural Production System." *American*

Journal of Agricultural Economics Vol. 70, August 1988, pp. 674–684.

Moores, B. "Dynamic Programming in Transformer Design." *Journal of Operational Research Society* Vol. 37, October 1986, pp. 967–969.

Norman, J. M. "Dynamic Programming in Tennis—When to Use a Fast Serve." *Journal of Operational Research Society* Vol. 36, No. 1, 1985, pp. 75–77.

Potts, C. N., and Wassenhove, L. N. V. "Algorithm for Scheduling a Single Machine to Minimize the Weighted Number of Late Jobs." *Management Science* Vol. 34, July 1988, pp. 843–858.

Rodriguez, A., and Taylor, R. G. "Stochastic Modeling of Short-Term Cattle Operations." *American Journal of Agricultural Economics* Vol. 70, February 1988, pp. 121–132.

Roman, R. J. "Mine-Mill Production Scheduling by Dynamic Programming." *Operational Research Quarterly* Vol. 22, pp. 319–328.

Ross, Sheldon M. *Introduction to Stochastic Dynamic Programming.* New York: Academic Press, 1983.

Sarker, B. R. "An Optimum Solution for One-Dimensional Slitting Problems: A Dynamic Programming Approach." *Journal of Operational Research Society* Vol. 39, August 1988, pp. 749–755.

Starbird, S. A. "Optimal Loading Sequence for Fresh-Apple Storage Facilities." *Journal of Operational Research Society* Vol. 39, October 1988, pp. 911–917.

Stensland, G., and Tjosteim, D. "Optimal Investments Using Empirical Dynamic Programming with Application to Natural Resources." *Journal of Business* Vol. 62, January 1989, pp. 99–120.

Williams, Jack F. "A Hybrid Algorithm for Simultaneous Scheduling of Production and Distribution in Multiechelon Structures." *Management Science* Vol. 29, No. 1, January 1983, pp. 72–92.

Appendixes

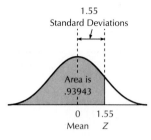

1.55
Standard Deviations

Area is
.93943

0   1.55
Mean   Z

APPENDIX A. AREAS UNDER THE STANDARD NORMAL TABLE

Example: To find the area under the normal curve, you must know how many standard deviations that point is to the right of the mean. Then, the area under the normal curve can be read directly from the normal table. For example, the total area under the normal curve for a point that is 1.55 standard deviations to the right of the mean is .93943.

	00	.01	.02	.03	.04	.05	.06	.07	.08	.09
0.0	.50000	.50399	.50798	.51197	.51595	.51994	.52392	.52790	.53188	.53586
0.1	.53983	.54380	.54776	.55172	.55567	.55962	.56356	.56749	.57142	.57535
0.2	.57926	.58317	.58706	.59095	.59483	.59871	.60257	.60642	.61026	.61409
0.3	.61791	.62172	.62552	.62930	.63307	.63683	.64058	.64431	.64803	.65173
0.4	.65542	.65910	.66276	.66640	.67003	.67364	.67724	.68082	.68439	.68793
0.5	.69146	.69497	.69847	.70194	.70540	.70884	.71226	.71566	.71904	.72240
0.6	.72575	.72907	.73237	.73536	.73891	.74215	.74537	.74857	.75175	.75490
0.7	.75804	.76115	.76424	.76730	.77035	.77337	.77637	.77935	.78230	.78524
0.8	.78814	.79103	.79389	.79673	.79955	.80234	.80511	.80785	.81057	.81327
0.9	.81594	.81859	.82121	.82381	.82639	.82894	.83147	.83398	.83646	.83891
1.0	.84134	.84375	.84614	.84849	.85083	.85314	.85543	.85769	.85993	.86214
1.1	.86433	.86650	.86864	.87076	.87286	.87493	.87698	.87900	.88100	.88298
1.2	.88493	.88686	.88877	.89065	.89251	.89435	.89617	.89796	.89973	.90147
1.3	.90320	.90490	.90658	.90824	.90988	.91149	.91309	.91466	.91621	.91774
1.4	.91924	.92073	.92220	.92364	.92507	.92647	.92785	.92922	.93056	.93189
1.5	.93319	.93448	.93574	.93699	.93822	.93943	.94062	.94179	.94295	.94408
1.6	.94520	.94630	.94738	.94845	.94950	.95053	.95154	.95254	.95352	.95449
1.7	.95543	.95637	.95728	.95818	.95907	.95994	.96080	.96164	.96246	.96327
1.8	.96407	.96485	.96562	.96638	.96712	.96784	.96856	.96926	.96995	.97062
1.9	.97128	.97193	.97257	.97320	.97381	.97441	.97500	.97558	.97615	.97670
2.0	.97725	.97784	.97831	.97882	.97932	.97982	.98030	.98077	.98124	.98169
2.1	.98214	.98257	.98300	.98341	.98382	.98422	.98461	.98500	.98537	.98574
2.2	.98610	.98645	.98679	.98713	.98745	.98778	.98809	.98840	.98870	.98899
2.3	.98928	.98956	.98983	.99010	.99036	.99061	.99086	.99111	.99134	.99158
2.4	.99180	.99202	.99224	.99245	.99266	.99286	.99305	.99324	.99343	.99361
2.5	.99379	.99396	.99413	.99430	.99446	.99461	.99477	.99492	.99506	.99520
2.6	.99534	.99547	.99560	.99573	.99585	.99598	.99609	.99621	.99632	.99643
2.7	.99653	.99664	.99674	.99683	.99693	.99702	.99711	.99720	.99728	.99736
2.8	.99744	.99752	.99760	.99767	.99774	.99781	.99788	.99795	.99801	.99807
2.9	.99813	.99819	.99825	.99831	.99836	.99841	.99846	.99851	.99856	.99861
3.0	.99865	.99869	.99874	.99878	.99882	.99886	.99899	.99893	.99896	.99900
3.1	.99903	.99906	.99910	.99913	.99916	.99918	.99921	.99924	.99926	.99929
3.2	.99931	.99934	.99936	.99938	.99940	.99942	.99944	.99946	.99948	.99950
3.3	.99952	.99953	.99955	.99957	.99958	.99960	.99961	.99962	.99964	.99965
3.4	.99966	.99968	.99969	.99970	.99971	.99972	.99973	.99974	.99975	.99976
3.5	.99977	.99978	.99978	.99979	.99980	.99981	.99981	.99982	.99983	.99983
3.6	.99984	.99985	.99985	.99986	.99986	.99987	.99987	.99988	.99988	.99989
3.7	.99989	.99990	.99990	.99990	.99991	.99991	.99992	.99992	.99992	.99992
3.8	.99993	.99993	.99993	.99994	.99994	.99994	.99994	.99995	.99995	.99995
3.9	.99995	.99995	.99996	.99996	.99996	.99996	.99996	.99996	.99997	.99997

Source: Reprinted from Robert O. Schlaifer, *Introduction to Statistics for Business Decisions,* published by McGraw-Hill Book Company, 1961, by permission of the copyright holder, the President and Fellows of Harvard College.

APPENDIX B. UNIT NORMAL LOSS INTEGRAL

D	.00	.01	.02	.03	.04	.05	.06	.07	.08	.09
.0	.3989	.3940	.3890	.3841	.3793	.3744	.3697	.3649	.3602	.3556
.1	.3509	.3464	.3418	.3373	.3328	.3284	.3240	.3197	.3154	.3111
.2	.3069	.3027	.2986	.2944	.2904	.2863	.2824	.2784	.2745	.2706
.3	.2668	.2630	.2592	.2555	.2518	.2481	.2445	.2409	.2374	.2339
.4	.2304	.2270	.2236	.2203	.2169	.2137	.2104	.2072	.2040	.2009
.5	.1978	.1947	.1917	.1887	.1857	.1828	.1799	.1771	.1742	.1714
.6	.1687	.1659	.1633	.1606	.1580	.1554	.1528	.1503	.1478	.1453
.7	.1429	.1405	.1381	.1358	.1334	.1312	.1289	.1267	.1245	.1223
.8	.1202	.1181	.1160	.1140	.1120	.1100	.1080	.1061	.1042	.1023
.9	.1004	.09860	.09680	.09503	.09328	.09156	.08986	.08819	.08654	.08491
1.0	.08332	.08174	.08019	.07866	.07716	.07568	.07422	.07279	.07138	.06999
1.1	.06862	.06727	.06595	.06465	.06336	.06210	.06086	.05964	.05844	.05726
1.2	.05610	.05496	.05384	.05274	.05165	.05059	.04954	.04851	.04750	.04650
1.3	.04553	.04457	.04363	.04270	.04179	.04090	.04002	.03916	.03831	.03748
1.4	.03667	.03587	.03508	.03431	.03356	.03281	.03208	.03137	.03067	.02998
1.5	.02931	.02865	.02800	.02736	.02674	.02612	.02552	.02494	.02436	.02380
1.6	.02324	.02270	.02217	.02165	.02114	.02064	.02015	.01967	.01920	.01874
1.7	.01829	.01785	.01742	.01699	.01658	.01617	.01578	.01539	.01501	.01464
1.8	.01428	.01392	.01357	.01323	.01290	.01257	.01226	.01195	.01164	.01134
1.9	.01105	.01077	.01049	.01022	$.0^2 9957$	$.0^2 9698$	$.0^2 9445$	$.0^2 9198$	$.0^2 8957$	$.0^2 8721$
2.0	$.0^2 8491$	$.0^2 8266$	$.0^2 8046$	$.0^2 7832$	$.0^2 7623$	$.0^2 7418$	$.0^2 7219$	$.0^2 7024$	$.0^2 6835$	$.0^2 6649$
2.1	$.0^2 6468$	$.0^2 6292$	$.0^2 6120$	$.0^2 5952$	$.0^2 5788$	$.0^2 5628$	$.0^2 5472$	$.0^2 5320$	$.0^2 5172$	$.0^2 5028$
2.2	$.0^2 4887$	$.0^2 4750$	$.0^2 4616$	$.0^2 4486$	$.0^2 4358$	$.0^2 4235$	$.0^2 4114$	$.0^2 3996$	$.0^2 3882$	$.0^2 3770$
2.3	$.0^2 3662$	$.0^2 3556$	$.0^2 3453$	$.0^2 3352$	$.0^2 3255$	$.0^2 3159$	$.0^2 3067$	$.0^2 2977$	$.0^2 2889$	$.0^2 2804$
2.4	$.0^2 2720$	$.0^2 2640$	$.0^2 2561$	$.0^2 2484$	$.0^2 2410$	$.0^2 2337$	$.0^2 2267$	$.0^2 2199$	$.0^2 2132$	$.0^2 2067$
2.5	$.0^2 2004$	$.0^2 1943$	$.0^2 1883$	$.0^2 1826$	$.0^2 1769$	$.0^2 1715$	$.0^2 1662$	$.0^2 1610$	$.0^2 1560$	$.0^2 1511$
2.6	$.0^2 1464$	$.0^2 1418$	$.0^2 1373$	$.0^2 1330$	$.0^2 1288$	$.0^2 1247$	$.0^2 1207$	$.0^2 1169$	$.0^2 1132$	$.0^2 1095$
2.7	$.0^2 1060$	$.0^2 1026$	$.0^3 9928$	$.0^3 9607$	$.0^3 9295$	$.0^3 8992$	$.0^3 8699$	$.0^3 8414$	$.0^3 8138$	$.0^3 7870$
2.8	$.0^3 7611$	$.0^3 7359$	$.0^3 7115$	$.0^3 6879$	$.0^3 6650$	$.0^3 6428$	$.0^3 6213$	$.0^3 6004$	$.0^3 5802$	$.0^3 5606$
2.9	$.0^3 5417$	$.0^3 5233$	$.0^3 5055$	$.0^3 4883$	$.0^3 4716$	$.0^3 4555$	$.0^3 4398$	$.0^3 4247$	$.0^3 4101$	$.0^3 3959$
3.0	$.0^3 3822$	$.0^3 3689$	$.0^3 3560$	$.0^3 3436$	$.0^3 3316$	$.0^3 3199$	$.0^3 3087$	$.0^3 2978$	$.0^3 2873$	$.0^3 2771$
3.1	$.0^3 2673$	$.0^3 2577$	$.0^3 2485$	$.0^3 2396$	$.0^3 2311$	$.0^3 2227$	$.0^3 2147$	$.0^3 2070$	$.0^3 1995$	$.0^3 1922$
3.2	$.0^3 1852$	$.0^3 1785$	$.0^3 1720$	$.0^3 1657$	$.0^3 1596$	$.0^3 1537$	$.0^3 1480$	$.0^3 1426$	$.0^3 1373$	$.0^3 1322$
3.3	$.0^3 1273$	$.0^3 1225$	$.0^3 1179$	$.0^3 1135$	$.0^3 1093$	$.0^3 1051$	$.0^3 1012$	$.0^4 9734$	$.0^4 9365$	$.0^4 9009$
3.4	$.0^4 8666$	$.0^4 8335$	$.0^4 8016$	$.0^4 7709$	$.0^4 7413$	$.0^4 7127$	$.0^4 6852$	$.0^4 6587$	$.0^4 6331$	$.0^4 6085$
3.5	$.0^4 5848$	$.0^4 5620$	$.0^4 5400$	$.0^4 5188$	$.0^4 4984$	$.0^4 4788$	$.0^4 4599$	$.0^4 4417$	$.0^4 4242$	$.0^4 4073$
3.6	$.0^4 3911$	$.0^4 3755$	$.0^4 3605$	$.0^4 3460$	$.0^4 3321$	$.0^4 3188$	$.0^4 3059$	$.0^4 2935$	$.0^4 2816$	$.0^4 2702$
3.7	$.0^4 2592$	$.0^4 2486$	$.0^4 2385$	$.0^4 2287$	$.0^4 2193$	$.0^4 2103$	$.0^4 2016$	$.0^4 1933$	$.0^4 1853$	$.0^4 1776$
3.8	$.0^4 1702$	$.0^4 1632$	$.0^4 1563$	$.0^4 1498$	$.0^4 1435$	$.0^4 1375$	$.0^4 1317$	$.0^4 1262$	$.0^4 1208$	$.0^4 1157$
3.9	$.0^4 1108$	$.0^4 1061$	$.0^4 1016$	$.0^5 9723$	$.0^5 9307$	$.0^5 8908$	$.0^5 8525$	$.0^5 8158$	$.0^5 7806$	$.0^5 7469$
4.0	$.0^5 7145$	$.0^5 6835$	$.0^5 6538$	$.0^5 6253$	$.0^5 5980$	$.0^5 5718$	$.0^5 5468$	$.0^5 5227$	$.0^5 4997$	$.0^5 4777$
4.1	$.0^5 4566$	$.0^5 4364$	$.0^5 4170$	$.0^5 3985$	$.0^5 3807$	$.0^5 3637$	$.0^5 3475$	$.0^5 3319$	$.0^5 3170$	$.0^5 3027$
4.2	$.0^5 2891$	$.0^5 2760$	$.0^5 2635$	$.0^5 2516$	$.0^5 2402$	$.0^5 2292$	$.0^5 2188$	$.0^5 2088$	$.0^5 1992$	$.0^5 1901$
4.3	$.0^5 1814$	$.0^5 1730$	$.0^5 1650$	$.0^5 1574$	$.0^5 1501$	$.0^5 1431$	$.0^5 1365$	$.0^5 1301$	$.0^5 1241$	$.0^5 1183$
4.4	$.0^5 1127$	$.0^5 1074$	$.0^5 1024$	$.0^6 9756$	$.0^6 9296$	$.0^6 8857$	$.0^6 8437$	$.0^6 8037$	$.0^6 7655$	$.0^6 7290$
4.5	$.0^6 6942$	$.0^6 6610$	$.0^6 6294$	$.0^6 5992$	$.0^6 5704$	$.0^6 5429$	$.0^6 5167$	$.0^6 4917$	$.0^6 4679$	$.0^6 4452$
4.6	$.0^6 4236$	$.0^6 4029$	$.0^6 3833$	$.0^6 3645$	$.0^6 3467$	$.0^6 3297$	$.0^6 3135$	$.0^6 2981$	$.0^6 2834$	$.0^6 2694$
4.7	$.0^6 2560$	$.0^6 2433$	$.0^6 2313$	$.0^6 2197$	$.0^6 2088$	$.0^6 1984$	$.0^6 1884$	$.0^6 1790$	$.0^6 1700$	$.0^6 1615$
4.8	$.0^6 1533$	$.0^6 1456$	$.0^6 1382$	$.0^6 1312$	$.0^6 1246$	$.0^6 1182$	$.0^6 1122$	$.0^6 1065$	$.0^6 1011$	$.0^7 9588$
4.9	$.0^7 9096$	$.0^7 8629$	$.0^7 8185$	$.0^7 7763$	$.0^7 7362$	$.0^7 6982$	$.0^7 6620$	$.0^7 6276$	$.0^7 5950$	$.0^7 5640$

Example of table notation: $.0^4 5848$ = .00005848.

Source: Reproduced from Robert O. Schlaifer, *Introduction to Statistics for Business Decisions,* published by McGraw-Hill Book Company, 1961, by permission of the copyright holder, the President and Fellows of Harvard College.

APPENDIX C. CUMULATIVE BINOMIAL DISTRIBUTION

n = 1

P / R	01	02	03	04	05	06	07	08	09	10
1	0100	0200	0300	0400	0500	0600	0700	0800	0900	1000

P / R	11	12	13	14	15	16	17	18	19	20
1	1100	1200	1300	1400	1500	1600	1700	1800	1900	2000

P / R	21	22	23	24	25	26	27	28	29	30
1	2100	2200	2300	2400	2500	2600	2700	2800	2900	3000

P / R	31	32	33	34	35	36	37	38	39	40
1	3100	3200	3300	3400	3500	3600	3700	3800	3900	4000

P / R	41	42	43	44	45	46	47	48	49	50
1	4100	4200	4300	4400	4500	4600	4700	4800	4900	5000

n = 2

P / R	01	02	03	04	05	06	07	08	09	10
1	0199	0396	0591	0784	0975	1164	1351	1536	1719	1900
2	0001	0004	0009	0016	0025	0036	0049	0064	0081	0100

P / R	11	12	13	14	15	16	17	18	19	20
1	2079	2256	2431	2604	2775	2944	3111	3276	3439	3600
2	0121	0144	0169	0196	0225	0256	0289	0324	0361	0400

P / R	21	22	23	24	25	26	27	28	29	30
1	3759	3916	4071	4224	4375	4524	4671	4816	4959	5100
2	0441	0484	0529	0576	0625	0676	0729	0784	0841	0900

P / R	31	32	33	34	35	36	37	38	39	40
1	5239	5376	5511	5644	5775	5904	6031	6156	6279	6400
2	0961	1024	1089	1156	1225	1296	1369	1444	1521	1600

P / R	41	42	43	44	45	46	47	48	49	50
1	6519	6636	6751	6864	6975	7084	7191	7296	7399	7500
2	1681	1764	1849	1936	2025	2116	2209	2304	2401	2500

n = 3

P / R	01	02	03	04	05	06	07	08	09	10
1	0297	0588	0873	1153	1426	1694	1956	2213	2464	2710
2	0003	0012	0026	0047	0073	0104	0140	0182	0228	0280
3				0001	0001	0002	0003	0005	0007	0010

P / R	11	12	13	14	15	16	17	18	19	20
1	2950	3185	3415	3639	3859	4073	4282	4486	4686	4880
2	0336	0397	0463	0533	0608	0686	0769	0855	0946	1040
3	0013	0017	0022	0027	0034	0041	0049	0058	0069	0080

Source: Reprinted from Robert O. Schlaifer, *Introduction to Statistics for Business Decisions,* published by McGraw-Hill Book Company, 1961, by permission of the copyright holder, the President and Fellows of Harvard College.

APPENDIX C *(CONTINUED)*

P	21	22	23	24	25	26	27	28	29	30
R										
1	5070	5254	5435	5610	5781	5948	6110	6268	6421	6570
2	1138	1239	1344	1452	1563	1676	1793	1913	2035	2160
3	0093	0106	0122	0138	0156	0176	0197	0220	0244	0270

P	31	32	33	34	35	36	37	38	39	40
R										
1	6715	6856	6992	7125	7254	7379	7500	7617	7730	7840
2	2287	2417	2548	2682	2818	2955	3094	3235	3377	3520
3	0298	0328	0359	0393	0429	0467	0507	0549	0593	0640

P	41	42	43	44	45	46	47	48	49	50
R										
1	7946	8049	8148	8244	8336	8425	8511	8594	8673	8750
2	3665	3810	3957	4104	4253	4401	4551	4700	4850	5000
3	0689	0741	0795	0852	0911	0973	1038	1106	1176	1250

$n = 4$

P	01	02	03	04	05	06	07	08	09	10
R										
1	0394	0776	1147	1507	1855	2193	2519	2836	3143	3439
2	0006	0023	0052	0091	0140	0199	0267	0344	0430	0523
3			0001	0002	0005	0008	0013	0019	0027	0037
4									0001	0001

P	11	12	13	14	15	16	17	18	19	20
R										
1	3726	4003	4271	4530	4780	5021	5254	5479	5695	5904
2	0624	0732	0847	0968	1095	1228	1366	1509	1656	1808
3	0049	0063	0079	0098	0120	0144	0171	0202	0235	0272
4	0001	0002	0003	0004	0005	0007	0008	0010	0013	0016

P	21	22	23	24	25	26	27	28	29	30
R										
1	6105	6298	6485	6664	6836	7001	7160	7313	7459	7599
2	1963	2122	2285	2450	2617	2787	2959	3132	3307	3483
3	0312	0356	0403	0453	0508	0566	0628	0694	0763	0837
4	0019	0023	0028	0033	0039	0046	0053	0061	0071	0081

P	31	32	33	34	35	36	37	38	39	40
R										
1	7733	7862	7985	8103	8215	8322	8425	8522	8615	8704
2	3660	3837	4015	4193	4370	4547	4724	4900	5075	5248
3	0915	0996	1082	1171	1265	1362	1464	1569	1679	1792
4	0092	0105	0119	0134	0150	0168	0187	0209	0231	0256

P	41	42	43	44	45	46	47	48	49	50
R										
1	8788	8868	8944	9017	9085	9150	9211	9269	9323	9375
2	5420	5590	5759	5926	6090	6252	6412	6569	6724	6875
3	1909	2030	2155	2283	2415	2550	2689	2831	2977	3125
4	0283	0311	0342	0375	0410	0448	0488	0531	0576	0625

$n = 5$

P	01	02	03	04	05	06	07	08	09	10
R										
1	0490	0961	1413	1846	2262	2661	3043	3409	3760	4095
2	0010	0038	0085	0148	0226	0319	0425	0544	0674	0815
3		0001	0003	0006	0012	0020	0031	0045	0063	0086
4						0001	0001	0002	0003	0005

P	11	12	13	14	15	16	17	18	19	20
R										
1	4416	4723	5016	5296	5563	5818	6061	6293	6513	6723
2	0965	1125	1292	1467	1648	1835	2027	2224	2424	2627
3	0112	0143	0179	0220	0266	0318	0375	0437	0505	0579
4	0007	0009	0013	0017	0022	0029	0036	0045	0055	0067
5				0001	0001	0001	0001	0002	0002	0003

continued

APPENDIX C (CONTINUED)

P R	21	22	23	24	25	26	27	28	29	30
1	6923	7113	7293	7464	7627	7781	7927	8065	8196	8319
2	2833	3041	3251	3461	3672	3883	4093	4303	4511	4718
3	0659	0744	0836	0933	1035	1143	1257	1376	1501	1631
4	0081	0097	0114	0134	0156	0181	0208	0238	0272	0308
5	0004	0005	0006	0008	0010	0012	0014	0017	0021	0024

P R	31	32	33	34	35	36	37	38	39	40
1	8436	8546	8650	8748	8840	8926	9008	9084	9155	9222
2	4923	5125	5325	5522	5716	5906	6093	6276	6455	6630
3	1766	1905	2050	2199	2352	2509	2670	2835	3003	3174
4	0347	0390	0436	0486	0540	0598	0660	0726	0796	0870
5	0029	0034	0039	0045	0053	0060	0069	0079	0090	0102

P R	41	42	43	44	45	46	47	48	49	50
1	9285	9344	9398	9449	9497	9541	9582	9620	9655	9688
2	6801	6967	7129	7286	7438	7585	7728	7865	7998	8125
3	3349	3525	3705	3886	4069	4253	4439	4625	4813	5000
4	0949	1033	1121	1214	1312	1415	1522	1635	1753	1875
5	0116	0131	0147	0165	0185	0206	0229	0255	0282	0313

$n = 6$

P R	01	02	03	04	05	06	07	08	09	10
1	0585	1142	1670	2172	2649	3101	3530	3936	4321	4686
2	0015	0057	0125	0216	0328	0459	0608	0773	0952	1143
3		0002	0005	0012	0022	0038	0058	0085	0118	0159
4					0001	0002	0003	0005	0008	0013
5										0001

P R	11	12	13	14	15	16	17	18	19	20
1	5030	5356	5664	5954	6229	6487	6731	6960	7176	7379
2	1345	1556	1776	2003	2235	2472	2713	2956	3201	3446
3	0206	0261	0324	0395	0473	0560	0655	0759	0870	0989
4	0018	0025	0034	0045	0059	0075	0094	0116	0141	0170
5	0001	0001	0002	0003	0004	0005	0007	0010	0013	0016
6										0001

P R	21	22	23	24	25	26	27	28	29	30
1	7569	7748	7916	8073	8220	8358	8487	8607	8719	8824
2	3692	3937	4180	4422	4661	4896	5128	5356	5580	5798
3	1115	1250	1391	1539	1694	1856	2023	2196	2374	2557
4	0202	0239	0280	0326	0376	0431	0492	0557	0628	0705
5	0020	0025	0031	0038	0046	0056	0067	0079	0093	0109
6	0001	0001	0001	0002	0002	0003	0004	0005	0006	0007

P R	31	32	33	34	35	36	37	38	39	40
1	8921	9011	9095	9173	9246	9313	9375	9432	9485	9533
2	6012	6220	6422	6619	6809	6994	7172	7343	7508	7667
3	2744	2936	3130	3328	3529	3732	3937	4143	4350	4557
4	0787	0875	0969	1069	1174	1286	1404	1527	1657	1792
5	0127	0148	0170	0195	0223	0254	0288	0325	0365	0410
6	0009	0011	0013	0015	0018	0022	0026	0030	0035	0041

P R	41	42	43	44	45	46	47	48	49	50
1	9578	9619	9657	9692	9723	9752	9778	9802	9824	9844
2	7819	7965	8105	8238	8364	8485	8599	8707	8810	8906
3	4764	4971	5177	5382	5585	5786	5985	6180	6373	6563
4	1933	2080	2232	2390	2553	2721	2893	3070	3252	3438
5	0458	0510	0566	0627	0692	0762	0837	0917	1003	1094
6	0048	0055	0063	0073	0083	0095	0108	0122	0138	0156

APPENDIX C *(CONTINUED)*

n = 7

P	01	02	03	04	05	06	07	08	09	10
R										
1	0679	1319	1920	2486	3017	3515	3983	4422	4832	5217
2	0020	0079	0171	0294	0444	0618	0813	1026	1255	1497
3		0003	0009	0020	0038	0063	0097	0140	0193	0257
4				0001	0002	0004	0007	0012	0018	0027
5								0001	0001	0002

P	11	12	13	14	15	16	17	18	19	20
R										
1	5577	5913	6227	6521	6794	7049	7286	7507	7712	7903
2	1750	2012	2281	2556	2834	3115	3396	3677	3956	4233
3	0331	0416	0513	0620	0738	0866	1005	1154	1313	1480
4	0039	0054	0072	0094	0121	0153	0189	0231	0279	0333
5	0003	0004	0006	0009	0012	0017	0022	0029	0037	0047
6					0001	0001	0001	0002	0003	0004

P	21	22	23	24	25	26	27	28	29	30
R										
1	8080	8243	8395	8535	8665	8785	8895	8997	9090	9176
2	4506	4775	5040	5298	5551	5796	6035	6266	6490	6706
3	1657	1841	2033	2231	2436	2646	2861	3081	3304	3529
4	0394	0461	0536	0617	0706	0802	0905	1016	1134	1260
5	0058	0072	0088	0107	0129	0153	0181	0213	0248	0288
6	0005	0006	0008	0011	0013	0017	0021	0026	0031	0038
7					0001	0001	0001	0001	0002	0002

P	31	32	33	34	35	36	37	38	39	40
R										
1	9255	9328	9394	9454	9510	9560	9606	9648	9686	9720
2	6914	7113	7304	7487	7662	7828	7987	8137	8279	8414
3	3757	3987	4217	4447	4677	4906	5134	5359	5581	5801
4	1394	1534	1682	1837	1998	2167	2341	2521	2707	2898
5	0332	0380	0434	0492	0556	0625	0701	0782	0869	0963
6	0046	0055	0065	0077	0090	0105	0123	0142	0164	0188
7	0003	0003	0004	0005	0006	0008	0009	0011	0014	0016

P	41	42	43	44	45	46	47	48	49	50
R										
1	9751	9779	9805	9827	9848	9866	9883	9897	9910	9922
2	8541	8660	8772	8877	8976	9068	9153	9233	9307	9375
3	6017	6229	6436	6638	6836	7027	7213	7393	7567	7734
4	3094	3294	3498	3706	3917	4131	4346	4563	4781	5000
5	1063	1169	1282	1402	1529	1663	1803	1951	2105	2266
6	0216	0246	0279	0316	0357	0402	0451	0504	0562	0625
7	0019	0023	0027	0032	0037	0044	0051	0059	0068	0078

n = 8

P	01	02	03	04	05	06	07	08	09	10
R										
1	0773	1492	2163	2786	3366	3904	4404	4868	5297	5695
2	0027	0103	0223	0381	0572	0792	1035	1298	1577	1869
3	0001	0004	0013	0031	0058	0096	0147	0211	0289	0381
4			0001	0002	0004	0007	0013	0022	0034	0050
5							0001	0001	0003	0004

P	11	12	13	14	15	16	17	18	19	20
R										
1	6063	6404	6718	7008	7275	7521	7748	7956	8147	8322
2	2171	2480	2794	3111	3428	3744	4057	4366	4670	4967
3	0487	0608	0743	0891	1052	1226	1412	1608	1815	2031
4	0071	0097	0129	0168	0214	0267	0328	0397	0476	0563
5	0007	0010	0015	0021	0029	0038	0050	0065	0083	0104
6		0001	0001	0002	0002	0003	0005	0007	0009	0012
7									0001	0001

continued

APPENDIX C (CONTINUED)

P R	21	22	23	24	25	26	27	28	29	30
1	8483	8630	8764	8887	8999	9101	9194	9278	9354	9424
2	5257	5538	5811	6075	6329	6573	6807	7031	7244	7447
3	2255	2486	2724	2967	3215	3465	3718	3973	4228	4482
4	0659	0765	0880	1004	1138	1281	1433	1594	1763	1941
5	0129	0158	0191	0230	0273	0322	0377	0438	0505	0580
6	0016	0021	0027	0034	0042	0052	0064	0078	0094	0113
7	0001	0002	0002	0003	0004	0005	0006	0008	0010	0013
8									0001	0001

P R	31	32	33	34	35	36	37	38	39	40
1	9486	9543	9594	9640	9681	9719	9752	9782	9808	9832
2	7640	7822	7994	8156	8309	8452	8586	8711	8828	8936
3	4736	4987	5236	5481	5722	5958	6189	6415	6634	6846
4	2126	2319	2519	2724	2936	3153	3374	3599	3828	4059
5	0661	0750	0846	0949	1061	1180	1307	1443	1586	1737
6	0134	0159	0187	0218	0253	0293	0336	0385	0439	0498
7	0016	0020	0024	0030	0036	0043	0051	0061	0072	0085
8	0001	0001	0001	0002	0002	0003	0004	0004	0005	0007

P R	41	42	43	44	45	46	47	48	49	50
1	9853	9872	9889	9903	9916	9928	9938	9947	9954	9961
2	9037	9130	9216	9295	9368	9435	9496	9552	9602	9648
3	7052	7250	7440	7624	7799	7966	8125	8276	8419	8555
4	4292	4527	4762	4996	5230	5463	5694	5922	6146	6367
5	1895	2062	2235	2416	2604	2798	2999	3205	3416	3633
6	0563	0634	0711	0794	0885	0982	1086	1198	1318	1445
7	0100	0117	0136	0157	0181	0208	0239	0272	0310	0352
8	0008	0010	0012	0014	0017	0020	0024	0028	0033	0039

$n = 9$

P R	01	02	03	04	05	06	07	08	09	10
1	0865	1663	2398	3075	3698	4270	4796	5278	5721	6126
2	0034	0131	0282	0478	0712	0978	1271	1583	1912	2252
3	0001	0006	0020	0045	0084	0138	0209	0298	0405	0530
4			0001	0003	0006	0013	0023	0037	0057	0083
5					0001	0002	0003	0005	0009
6										0001

P R	11	12	13	14	15	16	17	18	19	20
1	6496	6835	7145	7427	7684	7918	8131	8324	8499	8658
2	2599	2951	3304	3657	4005	4348	4685	5012	5330	5638
3	0672	0833	1009	1202	1409	1629	1861	2105	2357	2618
4	0117	0158	0209	0269	0339	0420	0512	0615	0730	0856
5	0014	0021	0030	0041	0056	0075	0098	0125	0158	0196
6	0001	0002	0003	0004	0006	0009	0013	0017	0023	0031
7						0001	0001	0002	0002	0003

P R	21	22	23	24	25	26	27	28	29	30
1	8801	8931	9048	9154	9249	9335	9411	9480	9542	9596
2	5934	6218	6491	6750	6997	7230	7452	7660	7856	8040
3	2885	3158	3434	3713	3993	4273	4552	4829	5102	5372
5	0994	1144	1304	1475	1657	1849	2050	2260	2478	2703
5	0240	0291	0350	0416	0489	0571	0662	0762	0870	0988
6	0040	0051	0065	0081	0100	0122	0149	0179	0213	0253
7	0004	0006	0008	0010	0013	0017	0022	0028	0035	0043
8			0001	0001	0001	0001	0002	0003	0003	0004

APPENDIX C *(CONTINUED)*

P	31	32	33	34	35	36	37	38	39	40
R										
1	9645	9689	9728	9762	9793	9820	9844	9865	9883	9899
2	8212	8372	8522	8661	8789	8908	9017	9118	9210	9295
3	5636	5894	6146	6390	6627	6856	7076	7287	7489	7682
4	2935	3173	3415	3662	3911	4163	4416	4669	4922	5174
5	1115	1252	1398	1553	1717	1890	2072	2262	2460	2666
6	0298	0348	0404	0467	0536	0612	0696	0787	0886	0994
7	0053	0064	0078	0094	0112	0133	0157	0184	0215	0250
8	0006	0007	0009	0011	0014	0017	0021	0026	0031	0038
9				0001	0001	0001	0001	0002	0002	0003

P	41	42	43	44	45	46	47	48	49	50
R										
1	9913	9926	9936	9946	9954	9961	9967	9972	9977	9980
2	9372	9442	9505	9563	9615	9662	9704	9741	9775	9805
3	7866	8039	8204	8359	8505	8642	8769	8889	8999	9102
4	5424	5670	5913	6152	6386	6614	6836	7052	7260	7461
5	2878	3097	3322	3551	3786	4024	4265	4509	4754	5000
6	1109	1233	1366	1508	1658	1817	1985	2161	2346	2539
7	0290	0334	0383	0437	0498	0564	0637	0717	0804	0898
8	0046	0055	0065	0077	0091	0107	0125	0145	0169	0195
9	0003	0004	0005	0006	0008	0009	0011	0014	0016	0020

$n = 10$

P	01	02	03	04	05	06	07	08	09	10
R										
1	0956	1829	2626	3352	4013	4614	5160	5656	6106	6513
2	0043	0162	0345	0582	0861	1176	1517	1879	2254	2639
3	0001	0009	0028	0062	0115	0188	0283	0401	0540	0702
4			0001	0004	0010	0020	0036	0058	0088	0128
5					0001	0002	0003	0006	0010	0016
6									0001	0001

P	11	12	13	14	15	16	17	18	19	20
R										
1	6882	7215	7516	7787	8031	8251	8448	8626	8784	8926
2	3028	3417	3804	4184	4557	4920	5270	5608	5932	6242
3	0884	1087	1308	1545	1798	2064	2341	2628	2922	3222
4	0178	0239	0313	0400	0500	0614	0741	0883	1039	1209
5	0025	0037	0053	0073	0099	0130	0168	0213	0266	0328
6	0003	0004	0006	0010	0014	0020	0027	0037	0049	0064
7			0001	0001	0001	0002	0003	0004	0006	0009
8									0001	0001

P	21	22	23	24	25	26	27	28	29	30
R										
1	9053	9166	9267	9357	9437	9508	9570	9626	9674	9718
2	6536	6815	7079	7327	7560	7778	7981	8170	8345	8507
3	3526	3831	4137	4442	4744	5042	5335	5622	5901	6172
4	1391	1587	1794	2012	2241	2479	2726	2979	3239	3504
5	0399	0479	0569	0670	0781	0904	1037	1181	1337	1503
6	0082	0104	0130	0161	0197	0239	0287	0342	0404	0473
7	0012	0016	0021	0027	0035	0045	0056	0070	0087	0106
8	0001	0002	0002	0003	0004	0006	0007	0010	0012	0016
9							0001	0001	0001	0001

P	31	32	33	34	35	36	37	38	39	40
R										
1	9755	9789	9818	9843	9865	9885	9902	9916	9929	9940
2	8656	8794	8920	9035	9140	9236	9323	9402	9473	9536
3	6434	6687	6930	7162	7384	7595	7794	7983	8160	8327
4	3772	4044	4316	4589	4862	5132	5400	5664	5923	6177
5	1679	1867	2064	2270	2485	2708	2939	3177	3420	3669
6	0551	0637	0732	0836	0949	1072	1205	1348	1500	1662
7	0129	0155	0185	0220	0260	0305	0356	0413	0477	0548
8	0020	0025	0032	0039	0048	0059	0071	0086	0103	0123
9	0002	0003	0003	0004	0005	0007	0009	0011	0014	0017
10									0001	0001	0001

continued

APPENDIX C *(CONTINUED)*

P R	41	42	43	44	45	46	47	48	49	50
1	9949	9957	9964	9970	9975	9979	9983	9986	9988	9990
2	9594	9645	9691	9731	9767	9799	9827	9852	9874	9893
3	8483	8628	8764	8889	9004	9111	9209	9298	9379	9453
4	6425	6665	6898	7123	7340	7547	7745	7933	8112	8281
5	3922	4178	4436	4696	4956	5216	5474	5730	5982	6230
6	1834	2016	2207	2407	2616	2832	3057	3288	3526	3770
7	0626	0712	0806	0908	1020	1141	1271	1410	1560	1719
8	0146	0172	0202	0236	0274	0317	0366	0420	0480	0547
9	0021	0025	0031	0037	0045	0054	0065	0077	0091	0107
10	0001	0002	0002	0003	0003	0004	0005	0006	0008	0010

n = 11

P R	01	02	03	04	05	06	07	08	09	10
1	1047	1993	2847	3618	4312	4937	5499	6004	6456	6862
2	0052	0195	0413	0692	1019	1382	1772	2181	2601	3026
3	0002	0012	0037	0083	0152	0248	0370	0519	0695	0896
4			0002	0007	0016	0030	0053	0085	0129	0185
5					0001	0003	0005	0010	0017	0028
6								0001	0002	0003

P R	11	12	13	14	15	16	17	18	19	20
1	7225	7549	7839	8097	8327	8531	8712	8873	9015	9141
2	3452	3873	4286	4689	5078	5453	5811	6151	6474	6779
3	1120	1366	1632	1915	2212	2521	2839	3164	3494	3826
4	0256	0341	0442	0560	0694	0846	1013	1197	1397	1611
5	0042	0061	0087	0119	0159	0207	0266	0334	0413	0504
6	0005	0008	0012	0018	0027	0037	0051	0068	0090	0117
7		0001	0001	0002	0003	0005	0007	0010	0014	0020
8							0001	0001	0002	0002

P R	21	22	23	24	25	26	27	28	29	30
1	9252	9350	9436	9511	9578	9636	9686	9730	9769	9802
2	7065	7333	7582	7814	8029	8227	8410	8577	8730	8870
3	4158	4488	4814	5134	5448	5753	6049	6335	6610	6873
4	1840	2081	2333	2596	2867	3146	3430	3719	4011	4304
5	0607	0723	0851	0992	1146	1313	1493	1685	1888	2103
6	0148	0186	0231	0283	0343	0412	0490	0577	0674	0782
7	0027	0035	0046	0059	0076	0095	0119	0146	0179	0216
8	0003	0005	0007	0009	0012	0016	0021	0027	0034	0043
9			0001	0001	0001	0002	0002	0003	0004	0006

P R	31	32	33	34	35	36	37	38	39	40
1	9831	9856	9878	9896	9912	9926	9938	9948	9956	9964
2	8997	9112	9216	9310	9394	9470	9537	9597	9650	9698
3	7123	7361	7587	7799	7999	8186	8360	8522	8672	8811
4	4598	4890	5179	5464	5744	6019	6286	6545	6796	7037
5	2328	2563	2807	3059	3317	3581	3850	4122	4397	4672
6	0901	1031	1171	1324	1487	1661	1847	2043	2249	2465
7	0260	0309	0366	0430	0501	0581	0670	0768	0876	0994
8	0054	0067	0082	0101	0122	0148	0177	0210	0249	0293
9	0008	0010	0013	0016	0020	0026	0032	0039	0048	0059
10	0001	0001	0001	0002	0002	0003	0004	0005	0006	0007

P R	41	42	43	44	45	46	47	48	49	50
1	9970	9975	9979	9983	9986	9989	9991	9992	9994	9995
2	9739	9776	9808	9836	9861	9882	9900	9916	9930	9941
3	8938	9055	9162	9260	9348	9428	9499	9564	9622	9673
4	7269	7490	7700	7900	8089	8266	8433	8588	8733	8867
5	4948	5223	5495	5764	6029	6288	6541	6787	7026	7256
6	2690	2924	3166	3414	3669	3929	4193	4460	4729	5000
7	1121	1260	1408	1568	1738	1919	2110	2312	2523	2744
8	0343	0399	0461	0532	0610	0696	0791	0895	1009	1133
9	0072	0087	0104	0125	0148	0175	0206	0241	0282	0327
10	0009	0012	0014	0018	0022	0027	0033	0040	0049	0059
11	0001	0001	0001	0001	0002	0002	0002	0003	0004	0005

APPENDIX C *(CONTINUED)*

n = 12

P R	01	02	03	04	05	06	07	08	09	10
1	1136	2153	3062	3873	4596	5241	5814	6323	6775	7176
2	0062	0231	0486	0809	1184	1595	2033	2487	2948	3410
3	0002	0015	0048	0107	0196	0316	0468	0652	0866	1109
4		0001	0003	0010	0022	0043	0075	0120	0180	0256
5				0001	0002	0004	0009	0016	0027	0043
6							0001	0002	0003	0005
7										0001

P R	11	12	13	14	15	16	17	18	19	20
1	7530	7843	8120	8363	8578	8766	8931	9076	9202	9313
2	3867	4314	4748	5166	5565	5945	6304	6641	6957	7251
3	1377	1667	1977	2303	2642	2990	3344	3702	4060	4417
4	0351	0464	0597	0750	0922	1114	1324	1552	1795	2054
5	0065	0095	0133	0181	0239	0310	0393	0489	0600	0726
6	0009	0014	0022	0033	0046	0065	0088	0116	0151	0194
7	0001	0002	0003	0004	0007	0010	0015	0021	0029	0039
8					0001	0001	0002	0003	0004	0006
9										0001

P R	21	22	23	24	25	26	27	28	29	30
1	9409	9493	9566	9629	9683	9730	9771	9806	9836	9862
2	7524	7776	8009	8222	8416	8594	8755	8900	9032	9150
3	4768	5114	5450	5778	6093	6397	6687	6963	7225	7472
4	2326	2610	2904	3205	3512	3824	4137	4452	4765	5075
5	0866	1021	1192	1377	1576	1790	2016	2254	2504	2763
6	0245	0304	0374	0453	0544	0646	0760	0887	1026	1178
7	0052	0068	0089	0113	0143	0178	0219	0267	0322	0386
8	0008	0011	0016	0021	0028	0036	0047	0060	0076	0095
9	0001	0001	0002	0003	0004	0005	0007	0010	0013	0017
10						0001	0001	0001	0002	0002

P R	31	32	33	34	35	36	37	38	39	40
1	9884	9902	9918	9932	9943	9953	9961	9968	9973	9978
2	9256	9350	9435	9509	9576	9634	9685	9730	9770	9804
3	7704	7922	8124	8313	8487	8648	8795	8931	9054	9166
4	5381	5681	5973	6258	6533	6799	7053	7296	7528	7747
5	3032	3308	3590	3876	4167	4459	4751	5043	5332	5618
6	1343	1521	1711	1913	2127	2352	2588	2833	3087	3348
7	0458	0540	0632	0734	0846	0970	1106	1253	1411	1582
8	0118	0144	0176	0213	0255	0304	0359	0422	0493	0573
9	0022	0028	0036	0045	0056	0070	0086	0104	0127	0153
10	0003	0004	0005	0007	0008	0011	0014	0018	0022	0028
11					0001	0001	0001	0001	0002	0002	0003

P R	41	42	43	44	45	46	47	48	49	50
1	9982	9986	9988	9990	9992	9994	9995	9996	9997	9998
2	9834	9860	9882	9901	9917	9931	9943	9953	9961	9968
3	9267	9358	9440	9513	9579	9637	9688	9733	9773	9807
4	7953	8147	8329	8498	8655	8801	8934	9057	9168	9270
5	5899	6175	6443	6704	6956	7198	7430	7652	7862	8062
6	3616	3889	4167	4448	4731	5014	5297	5577	5855	6128
7	1765	1959	2164	2380	2607	2843	3089	3343	3604	3872
8	0662	0760	0869	0988	1117	1258	1411	1575	1751	1938
9	0183	0218	0258	0304	0356	0415	0481	0555	0638	0730
10	0035	0043	0053	0065	0079	0095	0114	0137	0163	0193
11	0004	0005	0007	0009	0011	0014	0017	0021	0026	0032
12				0001	0001	0001	0001	0001	0002	0002

continued

APPENDIX C *(CONTINUED)*

						$n = 13$				
P R	01	02	03	04	05	06	07	08	09	10
1	1225	2310	3270	4118	4867	5526	6107	6617	7065	7458
2	0072	0270	0564	0932	1354	1814	2298	2794	3293	3787
3	0003	0020	0062	0135	0245	0392	0578	0799	1054	1339
4		0001	0005	0014	0031	0060	0103	0163	0242	0342
5				0001	0003	0007	0013	0024	0041	0065
6						0001	0001	0003	0005	0009
7									0001	0001

P R	11	12	13	14	15	16	17	18	19	20
1	7802	8102	8364	8592	8791	8963	9113	9242	9354	9450
2	4270	4738	5186	5614	6017	6396	6751	7080	7384	7664
3	1651	1985	2337	2704	3080	3463	3848	4231	4611	4983
4	0464	0609	0776	0967	1180	1414	1667	1939	2226	2527
5	0097	0139	0193	0260	0342	0438	0551	0681	0827	0991
6	0015	0024	0036	0053	0075	0104	0139	0183	0237	0300
7	0002	0003	0005	0008	0013	0019	0027	0038	0052	0070
8			0001	0001	0002	0003	0004	0006	0009	0012
9								0001	0001	0002

P R	21	22	23	24	25	26	27	28	29	30
1	9533	9604	9666	9718	9762	9800	9833	9860	9883	9903
2	7920	8154	8367	8559	8733	8889	9029	9154	9265	9363
3	5347	5699	6039	6364	6674	6968	7245	7505	7749	7975
4	2839	3161	3489	3822	4157	4493	4826	5155	5478	5794
5	1173	1371	1585	1816	2060	2319	2589	2870	3160	3457
6	0375	0462	0562	0675	0802	0944	1099	1270	1455	1654
7	0093	0120	0154	0195	0243	0299	0365	0440	0527	0624
8	0017	0024	0032	0043	0056	0073	0093	0118	0147	0182
9	0002	0004	0005	0007	0010	0013	0018	0024	0031	0040
10			0001	0001	0001	0002	0003	0004	0005	0007
11									0001	0001

P R	31	32	33	34	35	36	37	38	39	40
1	9920	9934	9945	9955	9963	9970	9975	9980	9984	9987
2	9450	9527	9594	9653	9704	9749	9787	9821	9849	9874
3	8185	8379	8557	8720	8868	9003	9125	9235	9333	9421
4	6101	6398	6683	6957	7217	7464	7698	7917	8123	8314
5	3760	4067	4376	4686	4995	5301	5603	5899	6188	6470
6	1867	2093	2331	2581	2841	3111	3388	3673	3962	4256
7	0733	0854	0988	1135	1295	1468	1654	1853	2065	2288
8	0223	0271	0326	0390	0462	0544	0635	0738	0851	0977
9	0052	0065	0082	0102	0126	0154	0187	0225	0270	0321
10	0009	0012	0015	0020	0025	0032	0040	0051	0063	0078
11	0001	0001	0002	0003	0003	0005	0006	0008	0010	0013
12							0001	0001	0001	0001

P R	41	42	43	44	45	46	47	48	49	50
1	9990	9992	9993	9995	9996	9997	9997	9998	9998	9999
2	9895	9912	9928	9940	9951	9960	9967	9974	9979	9983
3	9499	9569	9630	9684	9731	9772	9808	9838	9865	9888
4	8492	8656	8807	8945	9071	9185	9288	9381	9464	9539
5	6742	7003	7254	7493	7721	7935	8137	8326	8502	8666
6	4552	4849	5146	5441	5732	6019	6299	6573	6838	7095
7	2524	2770	3025	3290	3563	3842	4127	4415	4707	5000
8	1114	1264	1426	1600	1788	1988	2200	2424	2659	2905
9	0379	0446	0520	0605	0698	0803	0918	1045	1183	1334
10	0096	0117	0141	0170	0203	0242	0287	0338	0396	0461
11	0017	0021	0027	0033	0041	0051	0063	0077	0093	0112
12	0002	0002	0003	0004	0005	0007	0009	0011	0014	0017
13							0001	0001	0001	0001

APPENDIX C *(CONTINUED)*

					n = 14					
P	01	02	03	04	05	06	07	08	09	10
R										
1	1313	2464	3472	4353	5123	5795	6380	6888	7330	7712
2	0084	0310	0645	1059	1530	2037	2564	3100	3632	4154
3	0003	0025	0077	0167	0301	0478	0698	0958	1255	1584
4		0001	0006	0019	0042	0080	0136	0214	0315	0441
5				0002	0004	0010	0020	0035	0059	0092
6						0001	0002	0004	0008	0015
7									0001	0002

P	11	12	13	14	15	16	17	18	19	20
R										
1	8044	8330	8577	8789	8972	9129	9264	9379	9477	9560
2	4658	5141	5599	6031	6433	6807	7152	7469	7758	8021
3	1939	2315	2708	3111	3521	3932	4341	4744	5138	5519
4	0594	0774	0979	1210	1465	1742	2038	2351	2679	3018
5	0137	0196	0269	0359	0467	0594	0741	0907	1093	1298
6	0024	0038	0057	0082	0115	0157	0209	0273	0349	0439
7	0003	0006	0009	0015	0022	0032	0046	0064	0087	0116
8		0001	0001	0002	0003	0005	0008	0012	0017	0024
9						0001	0001	0002	0003	0004

P	21	22	23	24	25	26	27	28	29	30
R										
1	9631	9691	9742	9786	9822	9852	9878	9899	9917	9932
2	8259	8473	8665	8837	8990	9126	9246	9352	9444	9525
3	5887	6239	6574	6891	7189	7467	7727	7967	8188	8392
4	3366	3719	4076	4432	4787	5136	5479	5813	6137	6448
5	1523	1765	2023	2297	2585	2884	3193	3509	3832	4158
6	0543	0662	0797	0949	1117	1301	1502	1718	1949	2195
7	0152	0196	0248	0310	0383	0467	0563	0673	0796	0933
8	0033	0045	0060	0079	0103	0132	0167	0208	0257	0315
9	0006	0008	0011	0016	0022	0029	0038	0050	0065	0083
10	0001	0001	0002	0002	0003	0005	0007	0009	0012	0017
11						0001	0001	0001	0002	0002

P	31	32	33	34	35	36	37	38	39	40
R										
1	9945	9955	9963	9970	9976	9981	9984	9988	9990	9992
2	9596	9657	9710	9756	9795	9828	9857	9881	9902	9919
3	8577	8746	8899	9037	9161	9271	9370	9457	9534	9602
4	6747	7032	7301	7556	7795	8018	8226	8418	8595	8757
5	4486	4813	5138	5458	5773	6080	6378	6666	6943	7207
6	2454	2724	3006	3297	3595	3899	4208	4519	4831	5141
7	1084	1250	1431	1626	1836	2059	2296	2545	2805	3075
8	0381	0458	0545	0643	0753	0876	1012	1162	1325	1501
9	0105	0131	0163	0200	0243	0294	0353	0420	0497	0583
10	0022	0029	0037	0048	0060	0076	0095	0117	0144	0175
11	0003	0005	0006	0008	0011	0014	0019	0024	0031	0039
12		0001	0001	0001	0001	0002	0003	0003	0005	0006
13										0001

P	41	42	43	44	45	46	47	48	49	50
R										
1	9994	9995	9996	9997	9998	9998	9999	9999	9999	9999
2	9934	9946	9956	9964	9971	9977	9981	9985	9988	9991
3	9661	9713	9758	9797	9830	9858	9883	9903	9921	9935
4	8905	9039	9161	9270	9368	9455	9532	9601	9661	9713
5	7459	7697	7922	8132	8328	8510	8678	8833	8974	9102
6	5450	5754	6052	6344	6627	6900	7163	7415	7654	7880
7	3355	3643	3937	4236	4539	4843	5148	5451	5751	6047
8	1692	1896	2113	2344	2586	2840	3105	3380	3663	3953
9	0680	0789	0910	1043	1189	1348	1520	1707	1906	2120
10	0212	0255	0304	0361	0426	0500	0583	0677	0782	0898
11	0049	0061	0076	0093	0114	0139	0168	0202	0241	0287
12	0008	0010	0013	0017	0022	0027	0034	0042	0053	0065
13	0001	0001	0001	0002	0003	0003	0004	0006	0007	0009
14										0001

continued

APPENDIX C *(CONTINUED)*

						$n = 15$				
P **R**	01	02	03	04	05	06	07	08	09	10
1	1399	2614	3667	4579	5367	6047	6633	7137	7570	7941
2	0096	0353	0730	1191	1710	2262	2832	3403	3965	4510
3	0004	0030	0094	0203	0362	0571	0829	1130	1469	1841
4		0002	0008	0024	0055	0104	0175	0273	0399	0556
5			0001	0002	0006	0014	0028	0050	0082	0127
6					0001	0001	0003	0007	0013	0022
7								0001	0002	0003

P **R**	11	12	13	14	15	16	17	18	19	20
1	8259	8530	8762	8959	9126	9269	9389	9490	9576	9648
2	5031	5524	5987	6417	6814	7179	7511	7813	8085	8329
3	2238	2654	3084	3520	3958	4392	4819	5234	5635	6020
4	0742	0959	1204	1476	1773	2092	2429	2782	3146	3518
5	0187	0265	0361	0478	0617	0778	0961	1167	1394	1642
6	0037	0057	0084	0121	0168	0227	0300	0387	0490	0611
7	0006	0010	0015	0024	0036	0052	0074	0102	0137	0181
8	0001	0001	0002	0004	0006	0010	0014	0021	0030	0042
9					0001	0001	0002	0003	0005	0008
10									0001	0001

P **R**	21	22	23	24	25	26	27	28	29	30
1	9709	9759	9802	9837	9866	9891	9911	9928	9941	9953
2	8547	8741	8913	9065	9198	9315	9417	9505	9581	9647
3	6385	6731	7055	7358	7639	7899	8137	8355	8553	8732
4	3895	4274	4650	5022	5387	5742	6086	6416	6732	7031
5	1910	2195	2495	2810	3135	3469	3810	4154	4500	4845
6	0748	0905	1079	1272	1484	1713	1958	2220	2495	2784
7	0234	0298	0374	0463	0566	0684	0817	0965	1130	1311
8	0058	0078	0104	0135	0173	0219	0274	0338	0413	0500
9	0011	0016	0023	0031	0042	0056	0073	0094	0121	0152
10	0002	0003	0004	0006	0008	0011	0015	0021	0028	0037
11			0001	0001	0001	0002	0002	0003	0005	0007
12									0001	0001

P **R**	31	32	33	34	35	36	37	38	39	40
1	9962	9969	9975	9980	9984	9988	9990	9992	9994	9995
2	9704	9752	9794	9829	9858	9883	9904	9922	9936	9948
3	8893	9038	9167	9281	9383	9472	9550	9618	9678	9729
4	7314	7580	7829	8060	8273	8469	8649	8813	8961	9095
5	5187	5523	5852	6171	6481	6778	7062	7332	7587	7827
6	3084	3393	3709	4032	4357	4684	5011	5335	5654	5968
7	1509	1722	1951	2194	2452	2722	3003	3295	3595	3902
8	0599	0711	0837	0977	1132	1302	1487	1687	1902	2131
9	0190	0236	0289	0351	0422	0504	0597	0702	0820	0950
10	0048	0062	0079	0099	0124	0154	0190	0232	0281	0338
11	0009	0012	0016	0022	0028	0037	0047	0059	0075	0093
12	0001	0002	0003	0004	0005	0006	0009	0011	0015	0019
13					0001	0001	0001	0002	0002	0003

P **R**	41	42	43	44	45	46	47	48	49	50
1	9996	9997	9998	9998	9999	9999	9999	9999	10000	10000
2	9958	9966	9973	9979	9983	9987	9990	9992	9994	9995
3	9773	9811	9843	9870	9893	9913	9929	9943	9954	9963
4	9215	9322	9417	9502	9576	9641	9697	9746	9788	9824
5	8052	8261	8454	8633	8796	8945	9080	9201	9310	9408
6	6274	6570	6856	7131	7392	7641	7875	8095	8301	8491
7	4214	4530	4847	5164	5478	5789	6095	6394	6684	6964
8	2374	2630	2898	3176	3465	3762	4065	4374	4686	5000
9	1095	1254	1427	1615	1818	2034	2265	2510	2767	3036
10	0404	0479	0565	0661	0769	0890	1024	1171	1333	1509
11	0116	0143	0174	0211	0255	0305	0363	0430	0506	0592
12	0025	0032	0040	0051	0063	0079	0097	0119	0145	0176
13	0004	0005	0007	0009	0011	0014	0018	0023	0029	0037
14			0001	0001	0001	0002	0002	0003	0004	0005

APPENDIX C *(CONTINUED)*

					n = 16					
P	01	02	03	04	05	06	07	08	09	10
R										
1	1485	2762	3857	4796	5599	6284	6869	7366	7789	8147
2	0109	0399	0818	1327	1892	2489	3098	3701	4289	4853
3	0005	0037	0113	0242	0429	0673	0969	1311	1694	2108
4		0002	0011	0032	0070	0132	0221	0342	0496	0684
5			0001	0003	0009	0019	0038	0068	0111	0170
6					0001	0002	0005	0010	0019	0033
7							0001	0001	0003	0005
8										0001

P	11	12	13	14	15	16	17	18	19	20
R										
1	8450	8707	8923	9105	9257	9386	9493	9582	9657	9719
2	5386	5885	6347	6773	7161	7513	7830	8115	8368	8593
3	2545	2999	3461	3926	4386	4838	5277	5698	6101	6482
4	0907	1162	1448	1763	2101	2460	2836	3223	3619	4019
5	0248	0348	0471	0618	0791	0988	1211	1458	1727	2018
6	0053	0082	0120	0171	0235	0315	0412	0527	0662	0817
7	0009	0015	0024	0038	0056	0080	0112	0153	0204	0267
8	0001	0002	0004	0007	0011	0016	0024	0036	0051	0070
9			0001	0001	0002	0003	0004	0007	0010	0015
10							0001	0001	0002	0002

APPENDIX D. VALUES OF $e^{-\lambda}$ FOR USE IN THE POISSON DISTRIBUTION

VALUES OF $e^{-\lambda}$

λ	$e^{-\lambda}$	λ	$e^{-\lambda}$
0.0	1.0000	3.1	0.0450
0.1	0.9048	3.2	0.0408
0.2	0.8187	3.3	0.0369
0.3	0.7408	3.4	0.0334
0.4	0.6703	3.5	0.0302
0.5	0.6065	3.6	0.0273
0.6	0.5488	3.7	0.0247
0.7	0.4966	3.8	0.0224
0.8	0.4493	3.9	0.0202
0.9	0.4066	4.0	0.0183
1.0	0.3679	4.1	0.0166
1.1	0.3329	4.2	0.0150
1.2	0.3012	4.3	0.0136
1.3	0.2725	4.4	0.0123
1.4	0.2466	4.5	0.0111
1.5	0.2231	4.6	0.0101
1.6	0.2019	4.7	0.0091
1.7	0.1827	4.8	0.0082
1.8	0.1653	4.9	0.0074
1.9	0.1496	5.0	0.0067
2.0	0.1353	5.1	0.0061
2.1	0.1225	5.2	0.0055
2.2	0.1108	5.3	0.0050
2.3	0.1003	5.4	0.0045
2.4	0.0907	5.5	0.0041
2.5	0.0821	5.6	0.0037
2.6	0.0743	5.7	0.0033
2.7	0.0672	5.8	0.0030
2.8	0.0608	5.9	0.0027
2.9	0.0550	6.0	0.0025
3.0	0.0498		

Solutions to Selected Problems

Chapter 2

2-8 .30
2-10 **(a)** .10   **(b)** .04   **(c)** .25
          (d) .40
2-12 **(a)** .20   **(b)** .09   **(c)** .31
          (d) dependent
2-13 .54
2-15 into Abu Ilan .384; into El Kamin .616
2-17 .947
2-20 **(a)** .995   **(b)** .885   **(c)** assumed
          events are independent
2-22 .78

Chapter 3

3-10 2.85
3-11 $E(X) = 5.45$; variance $= 4.047$
3-12 probability ranked no. 1 $= .05086$;
          probability win all four games $= .0039$
3-15 $P(11.5 - 12.5 \text{ oz.}) = .25$; $P(12 \text{ oz.}) = 0$
3-16 .8849
3-18 .3413
3-20 $P(\text{oven causes defect}) = .1587$; $P(460°–470°) = .1327$
3-22 **(a)** 1.0, .80   **(b)** 1.0, .80
          (c) equivalent results

3-24 **(a)** .2778   **(b)** .0555   **(c)** 11.4
3-26 .0668
3-27 1829.27
3-28 **(b)** .6125
3-29 .7365

Chapter 4

4-10 **(a)** 337   **(b)** 380   **(c)** 423
4-12 3 month MAD $= 6.703$; 4 month MAD $= 7.78$
4-13 weighted M.A. slightly more accurate
4-15 MAD for 2 year M.A. $= 2.22$, which is lowest
4-17 1985: 410.0; 1986: 422.0; 1987: 443.9; 1988: 466.1; 1989: 495.2; 1990: 521.8
4-19 MAD for $\alpha = .3$ is 74.56; MAD for $\alpha = .6$ is 51.8; MAD for $\alpha = .9$ is 38.1
4-21 $Y = 522 + 33.6X$; 1990 sales $= 622.8$
4-23 **(b)** $Y = 1.0 + 1.0X$ **(c)** 10
4-31 **(a)** $Y = 1 + 1X$; $r = .845$
4-32 **(b)** $Y = 5.06 + 1.593X$ **(c)** 209,900
          people
4-36 $130,000, $108,000, $98,000, $184,000
4-38 $Y = .972 + .0035X$, $r^2 = .479$
          $Y = 2.197$, $Y = 3.77$

Chapter 5

5-9 maximin criterion: best alternative is Texan
5-11 best decision: deposit $10,000 in bank
5-14 **(a)** $200 **(b)** yes $80
5-15 **(b)** large wing **(c)** no
5-17 **(b)** medium sized facility
5-20 **(b)** back roads **(c)** $3\frac{1}{3}$ minutes
5-21 produce 300 cases and stock them

Chapter 6

6-12 construct clinic
6-13 the survey should be taken; EVSI = $11,140
6-15 if the survey is favorable, build large shop. Otherwise, do not build.
6-17 P(successful shop|unfavorable study) = .25
6-18 do not gather information but build quadplex
6-21 **(b)** use supplier A **(c)** $60 less than supplier A
6-24 do not conduct survey and do not construct clinic. They are risk avoiders.
6-27 yes. He would not conduct the study but he would build the large plant.
6-28 **(a)** Broad street—27.5 minutes
     (b) expressway
     (c) Lynn is a risk avoider
6-30 Jack should accept his kids' bet
6-32 **(b)** stock 1,500 gallons **(c)** EVPI = $1,500
6-33 do not conduct survey. Build medium sized facility; EMV = $670,000

Chapter 7

7-8 **(a)** 20,000 books **(b)** $320,000
7-10 **(a)** 3.571 **(b)** .20045
      (c) $18,000 **(d)** $2,399.71
7-12 EMV = $264,000; No effect
7-15 **(a)** Go ahead with new process; EMV = $283,000 **(b)** Increase selling price; new EMV = $296,000
7-16 $999.60
7-17 produce 12 cases
7-19 Harry should stock 62 bottles.
7-20 breakeven point is 4,955 pumps.
7-22 Linda should stock 385 cases.
7-25 Paul should produce 3,016 reports each week.

Chapter 8

8-12 $Y = \sqrt{(DC_h)/2C_o}$
8-15 $Q^* = 20,000$ screws
8-16 ROP = 4,000 screws
8-19 $D = 8$ million loads of plywood
8-23 yes; total cost = $41,416
8-24 expand to 10,000 cu. ft. to hold 100 motors; expansion worth $250 per year
8-26 $1,920 on a yearly basis

Chapter 9

9-8 $Q_p^* = 2,697$ scissors
9-9 1,217 wheel bearings
9-10 take the discount; cost = **$49,912.50**
9-12 30 units of safety stock
9-14 item 33CP needs strict control; no strict control for the others
9-17 maintain a safety stock of 400
9-20 order quantity = 852; total cost = $176
9-23 order quantity = 51; total cost = $1,901.22
9-25 order 300 units; total cost = $9,066.83
9-27 safety stock level is 150 units; total cost is $1,848.66

Chapter 10

10-9 40 air conditioners, 60 fans, profit = $1,900
10-11 200 Model A tubs, 0 Model B tubs, $18,000 profit
10-13 40 undergraduate, 20 graduate, $160,000
10-14 10 Alpha 4's, 24 Beta 5's, $55,200
10-17 $X_1 = 18\frac{3}{4}$, $X_2 = 18\frac{3}{4}$, Profit = $150
10-18 $X_1 = 25.71$, $X_2 = 21.43$, Cost = $68.57
10-20 5 TV spots, 68 ads, exposure of 1,535,000
10-23 24 coconuts, 12 skins, Profit = 5,040 rupees

Chapter 11

11-11 **(b)** $14X_1 + 4X_2 \leq 3,360$; $10X_1 + 12X_2 \leq 9,600$ **(d)** $S_1 = 3,360$, $S_2 = 9,600$
       (e) X_2 **(f)** S_2 **(g)** 800 units of X_2
11-13 $X_1 = 2$, $X_2 = 6$, $S_1 = 0$, $S_2 = 0$, $P = $36
11-14 $X_1 = 50$, $X_2 = 0$, $P = $1,000
11-15 $X_1 = 14$, $X_2 = 33$, $C = $221
11-19 degeneracy; $X_1 = 27$, $X_2 = 5$, $X_3 = 0$, $P = $177
11-21 **(a)** Min $C = 9X_1 + 15X_2$
$$X_1 + 2X_2 \geq 30$$
$$X_1 + 4X_2 \geq 80$$
       (b) $X_1 = 0$, $X_2 = 20$, $C = $300
11-22 **(a)** Min $C = 20X_1 + 24X_2$
$$X_1 + X_2 \geq 30$$
$$X_1 + 2X_2 \geq 40$$
       (b) $X_1 = 20$, $X_2 = 10$, $C = $640

11-24 $X_1 = 0$, $X_2 = 17.14$, $X_3 = 34.29$, $P = \$582.86$

11-26   **(b)** X_5 will enter; A_3 will leave

Chapter 12

12-10   **(a)**   yes   **(b)**   doesn't change

12-11   **(b)** $X_1 = 2$, $X_2 = 3$ **(b)**   yes

12-12   **(b)** $X_1 = 33.33$, $X_2 = 33.33$ **(b)**   yes
   (c)   no

12-15   **(a)** $\$7\frac{1}{2}$ to infinity   **(b)**   negative infinity
to $\$40$ **(c)** $\$20$ **(d)** $\$0$

12-16   30¢, 0, $\$3.00$

12-19   **(a)**   negative infinity to $\$6$ for phosphate; $\$5$
to infinity for potassium   **(b)**   basis won't
change; but X_1, X_2, and S_2 will change.

12-21   max $P = 50U_1 + 4U_2$
$$12U_1 + 1U_2 \le 120$$
$$20U_1 + 3U_2 \le 250$$

Chapter 13

13-1   max $R = 28X_1 + 25X_2$
$$3X_1 + 2X_2 \le 360$$
$$1\tfrac{1}{2}X_1 + 1X_2 \le 200$$
$$\tfrac{3}{4}X_1 + \tfrac{3}{4}X_2 \le 125$$
$$X_1 \ge 60$$
$$X_2 \ge 60$$
$$X_1 = 60, X_2 = 90, P = \$3,930$$

13-6   min $C = 925X_1 + 2,000X_2$
$$.04X_1 + .05X_2 \ge .40$$
$$.03X_1 + .03X_2 \ge .60$$
$$X_1 = 20, X_2 = 0, C = \$18,500$$

13-9 $X_1 = 26$, $X_2 = 5$, $X_3 = 6.5$, $X_4 = 14.25$,
51.75 drinks

13-10   min rolls $= 20X_1 + 6.8X_2 + 12X_3 -$
$$65,000X_4$$
$$X_1 + X_2 + X_3 \le 17,000$$
$$X_1 \ge 3,000$$
$$X_2 - .05X_3 \ge 0$$
$$X_4 \ge .20$$
$$X_4 \le .45 \quad \text{sell } 327,000 \text{ rolls}$$

13-11 $X_1 = 0$, $X_2 = .499$, $X_3 = .173$, $X_4 = 0$, $X_5 =$
0, $X_6 = .105$, $X_7 = .762$, $C = \$1.75$

13-12 $X_1 = 497$, $X_2 = 1241$, $P = \$195,505$

13-14   1250 wheat in N parcel, 500 wheat in NW,
312.5 wheat in W, 137.5 wheat in SW, 131
alfalfa in SW, 600 barley in SE, 400 barley in
N, profit $= \$337,862.10$

Chapter 14

14-14   Oak Ridge to House 2 $= 30$; Oak Ridge to
House 3 $= 10$; Pineville to House 3 $= 25$;
Mapletown to House 1 $= 30$; cost $= \$230$

14-16   Morgantown to Coaltown $= 35$; Youngstown
to Coal Valley $= 30$; Youngstown to
Coaltown $= 5$; Pittsburgh to Coaltown $= 5$;
Pittsburgh to Coalsburg $= 20$; cost $= 3,100$
miles

14-19   degeneracy; need to place a zero in an empty
cell (such as 2-C)

14-23   New Orleans' systems cost $= \$20,000$;
Houston's is $\$19,500$, so Houston should be
selected

14-24 $A12$ to W, $A15$ to Z, $B2$ to Y, $B9$ to X, 50
hours

14-26   post 1 to C, post 2 to B, post 3 to A, post 4 to
D, 18 miles

14-28   total rating $= 335$

14-29   total "cost" $= 86$

14-30   overall rating $= 75.5$

14-31 $C53$ at plant 1, $C81$ at plant 3, $D5$ at plant 4,
$D44$ at plant 2, 58¢

14-33   total cost $= \$1.18$

Chapter 15

15-13 $X_1 = 1$, $X_2 = 2$, $P = \$20$

15-14 $X_1 = 3$, $X_2 = 4$, $P = \$17$

15-16 $X_1 = 5$, $X_2 = 8$, $Z = 1,273,000$ passengers

15-21 $A4$, $B1$, $C3$, $D2$ or $A4$, $B2$, $C3$, $D1$; both cost
$\$105$

15-22 $X_1 = 0$, $X_2 = 3$, $P = \$9$

15-24 $X_1 = 500$, $X_2 = 400$, $d_3^- = 100$

15-26 $X_1 = 10$ TV spots, $X_2 = 35$ ads, exposure $=$
8,250,000

Chapter 16

16-11   **(a)**   .375   **(b)**   .2 days or 1.6 hours
   (c)   .225   **(d)**   .141, .053, .020, .007

16-12   **(a)**   1.33   **(b)**   4 min.   **(c)**   6 min.
   (d)   .667   **(e)**   .333

16-15   **(a)**   6   **(b)**   12 min.   **(c)**   .857
   (d)   .54   **(e)** $\$1,728$/day   **(f)**   yes

16-18   3, 2, 4

16-21 $\$36$ with 1 loader, $\$18$ with 2 loaders; saving
$\$18$ with 2 loaders

16-22   no

Chapter 17

17-12 no

17-14 **(a)** 3 times   **(b)** 6.95/week
(c) 7.16 heaters

17-19 **(a)** from the 15 breakdown simulation, there are $14\frac{1}{2}$ hours of machine down time $\times$ $75/hour = $1,087.50. Cost of labor is $29\frac{1}{2}$ hours $\times$ $60/hour = $1,770. Total cost = $2,857.50
(b) hire second worker; one repairman costs $4,320

17-21 **(a)** cost/hour is generally more expensive replacing 1 pen each time
(b) expected cost/hour with 1 pen policy = $1.38 (or $58/breakdown); expected cost/hour with 4 pen policy = $1.12 (or $132/breakdown)

Chapter 18

18-13 completion time is 26 days; critical path is 1–2–3–5–6

18-15 completion time is 19 weeks; critical paths are A–C–G and B–E–G

18-17 critical path is C–D–E–F–H–K; completion time is 36.33 days

18-18 P(finishing in less than 40 days) = .9463

18-21 value of work completed = $181,600; actual cost = $172,000; cost underrun = $9,600; project is behind schedule

18-22 total budget/month using ES = $146,000; total budget/month using LS = $146,000

18-26 500 cars/hour

18-27 take route 1–3–5–7–10–13; distance is 430 miles

18-28 expected project length is 44 weeks; variance = 2.166; after changing activity 5, new expected project length = 47.8 weeks; new variance = 1.92 weeks

Chapter 19

19-7 **(b)** 90%   **(c)** 30%
19-8 **(a)** 23.056%   **(b)** 30.832%
(c) 75%
19-10 **(a)** 70%   **(b)** 30%   **(c)** 40%

19-11 25% for Battles; 18.75% for University; 26.25% for Bill's; 30% for College

19-14 41% that conditions will be fair; 19.5% that conditions will be tolerable

19-16 333 in Lake Jackson and 667 in Lake Bradford

19-18 new MFA = (5645.16, 1354.84)

19-19 61 will pass and 19 will fail

Module A

A-1 **(a)** 27   **(b)** 16

A-2 $X = -\frac{3}{2},\ Y = \frac{1}{2},\ Z = \frac{7}{2}$

A-5 $380, $440, $260

A-7
$$\begin{pmatrix} -48 & 6 & 12 \\ 6 & -12 & 6 \\ 32 & 6 & -8 \end{pmatrix} = \text{Matrix of cofactors}$$

$$\begin{pmatrix} -48 & 6 & 32 \\ 6 & -12 & 6 \\ 12 & 6 & -8 \end{pmatrix} = \text{Adjoint of matrix}$$

A-8
$$\begin{pmatrix} -\frac{48}{60} & \frac{6}{60} & \frac{32}{60} \\ \frac{6}{60} & -\frac{12}{60} & \frac{6}{60} \\ \frac{12}{60} & \frac{6}{60} & -\frac{8}{60} \end{pmatrix}$$

Module B

B-6 strategy for $X\colon X_2$; strategy for $Y\colon Y_2$; value of the game = 6

B-8 $X_1 = \frac{35}{57};\ X_2 = \frac{22}{57};\ Y_1 = \frac{32}{57};\ Y_2 = \frac{25}{57}$; value of game = 66.70

B-11 $A_1 = \frac{41}{72};\ A_2 = \frac{31}{72};\ B_1 = \frac{55}{72};\ B_2 = \frac{17}{72}$; value of game = -1.32; would rather be B.

B-13 maximize $\overline{Y}_1 + \overline{Y}_2 + \overline{Y}_3$; subject to: $-2\overline{Y}_2 - 5\overline{Y}_3 \leq 1;\ 3\overline{Y}_1 + \overline{Y}_2 - \overline{Y}_3 \leq 1$; value of the game $= \dfrac{1}{(\overline{Y}_1 + \overline{Y}_2 + \overline{Y}_3)}$.

Module C

C-6 shortest route is 1–2–6–7; total distance is 10 miles

C-7 shortest route is 1–2–5–7; total distance is 20 miles

C-8 shortest route is 1–2–5–7; total distance is 14 miles

C-9 shortest route is 1–2–5–8–9; total distance is 19 miles

Index